KV-191-244

Manifesto for Beer Drinkers

Not since the founding of the Campaign for Real Ale in the early 1970s has beer drinkers' choice been under such sustained attack. Following the sale of the Bass and Whitbread brewing operations to Interbrew of Belgium, more than 60 per cent of all the beer brewed in Britain is now controlled by two giants, Interbrew and Scottish Courage. With Carlsberg-Tetley's share added, the proportion of beer in the hands of the multinationals rises to more than 80 per cent.

Crucially, only a tiny amount of that production is natural, living, cask-conditioned real ale. The giants are interested solely in maximising profits from the certainties of dead, pressurised keg lager and nitro-keg ale. For them, cask beer is a marginal product, an irritant with a short shelf life.

This edition of the Good Beer Guide is a call to arms to British beer lovers to save real ale, to restore choice, to halt the loss of rural pubs, to encourage the development of organic beers that will appeal to the new, 'green' generation, to make it possible for new breweries to enter the beer market, and to stop mergers and takeovers that further threaten choice and diversity. We urge readers who support these demands to make their voices heard to brewers, pub groups, MPs, MEPs, members of the Scottish Parliament, the Welsh Assembly, and central and local government.

● The Department of Trade and Industry needs a blueprint for the brewing industry that lays down a policy for protecting beer drinkers' interests. There must be a rigorous investigation of any further mergers that threaten choice and the closure of brewing plants, with the loss of local brands.

● The government must, as a matter of urgency, bring pub groups within the provisions of the Beer Orders to enable licensees to offer guest beers from regional and micro breweries to their customers.

● The Ministry of Agriculture must encourage farmers, with the aid of grants where necessary, to grow far greater amounts of organic barley and hops. The ministry and brewers must give beer drinkers a categorical assurance that they will never use any genetically modified ingredients in British beer.

● The Chancellor of the Exchequer must introduce a staged reduction in excise duty on beer to bring duty down to the EU average within a decade. This would reduce cheap imports from France, encourage drinkers to return to British pubs, increase beer production and jobs at home, and would not lead to a loss of revenue to the government.

● Country pubs must be given rate relief in line with the provisions in place for rural post offices and other key rural services. See page 19 for CAMRA's full policy on helping country pubs.

● The Home Office must speed up proposals for licensing reform. Publicans need greater flexibility to enable them to stay open later. Flexibility in opening hours would help tackle the problems connected with rigid 11pm closing, a view shared by the police.

These manifesto demands have two aims: to save real ale and pubs. If you support these aims, join CAMRA, and show brewers and government that we have strength in numbers.

Beer
goes global

The loss of Bass and Whitbread to a Belgian giant is a devastating blow but offers fresh opportunities for dedicated real ale brewers, **Roger Protz** *argues*

A page has turned in the history of beer with the sale of Bass and Whitbread to Interbrew of Belgium. British brewing is being sucked into the global economy. And that means lager, for 93 per cent of all the beer produced in the world is based on the cold-fermented style fashioned in Pilsen in the 1840s.

It may well be that Interbrew will pump new life into the handful of ale brands bequeathed it by Bass and Whitbread. But the main thrust of Interbrew's activities will be to maximise the sales of its lager brands. It owns Stella Artois, the leading premium lager in Britain. It will take on the sales of the draught version of another premium beer, Grolsch. And in Carling Black Label it controls a massive brand that enjoys a lucrative connection with the top echelon of English football.

Interbrew is not the only interloper. Tetley was once the ale of God's Own Country, but its fortunes today are dictated not in Leeds but in Copenhagen by its Danish owner,

Down the hatch? Hugo Powell, boss of Interbrew UK, celebrates buying Bass and Whitbread with a pint of Draught Bass. But will cask beer survive as Interbrew pushes its lager brands?

Carlsberg. Scottish Courage may be the last national brewing group based in Britain, but it has formed a partnership with Danone of France that includes an option to buy Danone's subsidiary, Brasseries Kronenbourg, during the next three years. This would hand ScotCo ownership of France's biggest beer brand plus Alken Maes of Belgium, and a substantial share in Peroni of Italy.

None of this means that ale is about to fall into the abyss. ScotCo is aware that cask beer's fortunes are starting to revive after three or four years of calamitous decline at the hands of nitro-keg. It plans to promote the naturally-conditioned version of its main ale brand by inserting the word 'cask' between John Smith's and Bitter. The autumn of 2000 saw the national launch of a new Theakston beer called Cool Cask, served at a lower temperature than the conventional 11-13 degrees. While beer lovers will neither forgive nor forget the years of neglect for cask beer and the brutal closure of the Courage Bristol brewery, ScotCo's initiatives are nonetheless welcome. But they cannot detract from the depressing fact that, for the beer giants, cask ale is at best just a niche market product.

The decline and fall of Bass and Whitbread serve as a paradigm for what happens to great companies when they lose their focus. Not only did they play pivotal roles in the development of brewing – Whitbread the first major commercial brewer of the 18th century with porter, Bass a century later leading the charge with a revolutionary new style known as pale ale -- but they were rooted also in a philosophy that saw brewing as more than just a crude means of amassing wealth. They believed they also had duties and responsibilities to their communities, best expressed by providing good beer at reasonable prices in decent pubs for working people. It is an attitude still alive among the dwindling band of family brewers in Britain, but it disappeared once Bass and Whitbread became public companies with the majority of their shares owned by institutions. The likes of banks and pension funds have no interest in beer. Bass and Whitbread might have produced baked beans for all they cared. They are interested solely in maximising profits. If Bass and

...and not a penguin to be seen. Scottish Courage at long last is promoting the real version of John Smith's Bitter after years of pushing the 'smooth' nitro-keg version.

Whitbread could make more money from their hotels, pubs and leisure centres, then the message from the City was a simple one: Get out of brewing.

It would be wrong, however, to paint a picture of the national brewers as hapless playthings of the City of London. They have played a major role in their own downfall. Encouraged by accountants and marketing departments, with their 'pile 'em high' attitude to making and selling beer, the two national brewers retreated into the laager. When Sir Ian Prosser of Bass said, as he tasted Caffrey's nitro-keg and Hooch alcopop in the mid-1990s, that he 'had seen the future of brewing', he was signing Bass's death warrant as a quality producer. Draught Bass, once worth a million barrels a year, was allowed to wither on the bine, unpromoted, unloved and now reduced to level-pegging in sales with Marston's Pedigree. In the 1990s Whitbread, fleetingly, seemed to revive an interest in cask beer. It developed the Hogshead chain devoted to real ale, and for a while produced a series of seasonal and occasional ales of some distinction: a chocolate mild and a cask version of Murphy's Stout made with oysters were especially memorable. But the euphoria was short lived. The accountants irritably clicked the company abacus, and Stella Artois became the icon. Even Boddingtons, that once sublime nectar of Manchester, joined the ranks of ice-cold, bland nitro-kegs.

Now Bass and Whitbread have shuffled off the brewing coil to run Holiday Inns, Marriott Hotels and Pizza Hut, leaving Interbrew with a 32 per cent share of the British beer market. This may prompt a government referral to the competition authorities, but the Belgians will point to the fact that, as they do not own pubs, there is no danger of 'vertical integration' (owning breweries and a retail estate), while other European brewers enjoy even bigger slices of their domestic markets.

Ironically, despite its size, Interbrew remains a family-owned company, and has not lost its appetite for brewing. Hugo Powell, chief executive of Interbrew UK, describes beer as a 'local business' and says the emphasis will be on local brands. Only time will tell whether this is PR persiflage or whether cask ales will flourish. What cannot be disputed is that the emergence of three multinational brewing giants will place the free trade – which accounts for the overwhelming majority of pubs – in an even tighter straitjacket, offering deep discounts that regional and craft brewers will be unable to match. Fortunately, Nomura and Punch may be large companies, but they don't control the country's entire stock of 60,000 pubs, and, as the listings in the Guide show, regional brewers' beers pop up a long way from their points of production.

It is a time of both alarm and optimism for independent brewers. Stuart Neame of Shepherd Neame of Kent said, in the wake of the Interbrew takeovers, 'Foreign owners will almost certainly concentrate on a few global lager brands, and this will mean less choice for the British drinker.' But Simon Loftus of Adnams and Stuart Bateman of Bateman's glimpsed a few lifebelts bobbing on the crest of the lager tidal wave. Loftus commented that the arrival of Interbrew 'will accelerate the process where strong independent brands survive and prosper while the weaker ones find the going more and more difficult.' Bateman said his company will concentrate on developing its premium cask ale, XXXB. 'There will be casualties,' he added, 'but those who have positioned themselves with a good core brand will prosper. Independent brewers will have to become much more focused. We can't afford to have the big spread of operations that was common in the past.

Chill out...a new Theakston's ale will be served at a cool temperature in a bid to win younger drinkers.

We will have to learn to do a few things well.'

That should not be taken as a call to return to the days when regional brewers were content to brew a drop of mild, some cooking bitter and a strong 'un for winter. Some small brewers may over-indulge where occasional and seasonal brews are concerned, but a whole new beer market has been fashioned in recent years, one that must not be lightly abandoned. Regional and smaller craft brewers have brought fun back to brewing – and drinkers back to pubs – as a result of fashioning a dynamic new range of beers. When journalists on the City pages of the national press write the epitaph for cask beer, they ignore the enormous range now available, and the passion and commitment that has gone into developing it. Summer beers tangy with hops and citrus fruits; autumn beers made with the first malts and hops of the harvest; winter ales booming with nutty, fruity and hoppy aromas and flavours; single varietal beers brewed to allow one variety of hop to express its character to the full; spiced ales where the likes of coriander, cinnamon and ginger vie with the peppery nature of English hops; fruit beers with elderberry, gooseberry and grapefruit adding rich new flavours;

Cask Marque

The Good Beer Guide is delighted to welcome Cask Marque as its new sponsor. For the first time since CAMRA was launched in the early 1970s, consumers now have dedicated support on the other side of the bar. Backed by brewers and pub groups, Cask Marque is dedicated to quality real ale that is looked after with care and commitment in the cellar and at the bar. The Cask Marque plaque in a pub indicates that the publican has passed a series of intensive tests that prove he can guarantee real ale of the finest quality pint after pint. Like all good friends, CAMRA and Cask Marque may occasionally disagree over some points, such as the ideal temperature at which beer should be served. But such debates are healthy, and can only strengthen the appreciation of real ale. It is important to stress that the Good Beer Guide maintains its total independence in the selection of pubs, which are chosen by CAMRA members and branches alone. Cask Marque supplies us with a list of all its accredited pubs and those chosen for the Guide have the appropriate symbol added during editing.

porters, stouts and India Pale Ales based on original 18th and 19th-century recipes; a growing number of organic beers – all bringing new dimensions and pleasures to beer drinking.

Perhaps the most revealing event of 2000 (and one that should give pause to those commentators who argue that lager alone chimes with the Cool Britannia times) is that Adnams of Southwold had to delay the launch of a new pale, summery beer called Trinity as a result of the clamour for another new brand called Fisherman. It is made from pale malt, rye crystal malt, chocolate malt and pinhead oats, and hopped with Goldings. Dark, complex, fruity, chocolatey and bitter, it shouldn't exist in the age of Intergalactic Breweries' Krapmeister Pils.

But drinkers queued to get Fisherman. Don't write real ale's epitaph just yet.

Independents: exits and entrances

The year 2000 saw further casualties among the ranks of regional brewers. Morland, bought by Greene King, closed in January, and both its own brands and Ruddles' beers were transferred to Bury St Edmunds. Wolverhampton & Dudley has yet to close either of its two new acquisitions, Marston's and Mansfield, but the storm clouds are gathering.

In the spring of 2000, Wolves' managing director David Thompson warned that a review of brewing activities was being undertaken. The words had scarcely left his lips when it was announced he was stepping down to become part-time chairman. He was replaced by his finance director, Ralph Findlay, who ominously comes from the City of London.

With disappointing half-year profits in June 2000, Wolves is in the firing line. Thompson is 'family', a member of the dynasty that built Banks of Wolverhampton into a powerful regional force. But Findlay has no such ties. Wolverhampton is safe as the flagship brewery, and it would be madness to move Marston's Pedigree from its Burton brewery with the unique 'union room' method of fermentation. But Marston's is substantially under capacity and could comfortably assimilate the Mansfield brands.

Wolves' northern outpost, Cameron's of Hartlepool, is working close to capacity thanks to some lucrative lager contracts, principally for Kronenbourg. But if ScotCo buys Brasseries Kronenbourg from Danone of France (see main article) it could move the brewing of the British version of Kronenbourg elsewhere, leaving Cameron's dangerously exposed. An unhappy Heineken, sidelined and marginalised by arch rival Interbrew, could be taking a close look at Cameron's unless it buys the former Bass plant at Samlesbury in Lancashire.

The closure of King & Barnes of Horsham, Sussex, was a tragi-comedy. Shepherd Neame offered a takeover on the grounds that its Faversham brewery is working at full capacity and it cannot expand on the site. It promised to keep K&B open and to continue to brew the Horsham beers for its 57 pubs. King & Barnes first said it would fight the takeover tooth and nail, but somewhere along the line managing director Bill King panicked, rang all his chums in the beerage and urged anyone – but anyone – to buy him to keep out Shepherd Neame, for whom Mr King seemed to have a well-nurtured dislike.

The result was that Hall & Woodhouse of Dorset agreed to buy K&B but on the terms that it would close the brewery. It is hard to see how this was a better deal for King & Barnes' workforce, licensees and loyal customers, but the deal was done, Horsham closed, and some of the beers were transferred to Blandford Forum. Only two of K&B's bottle-conditioned ales have survived. One glimmer of good news from this debacle is that Worthington White Shield has returned to its natal town of Burton-on-Trent, where it is now brewed by the Musuem Brewing Company, part of the Bass/Interbrew complex.

The fall of the house of Usher was a mighty one. Usher of Trowbridge was a West Country giant, with a large brewery and a substantial tied estate close to 1,000 outlets. It emerged, thanks to a management buyout, from the corpse of Grand Metropolitan in 1991, and enjoyed growth and success. But the writing was on the wall in 1999 when

Ushers merged with the Alehouse pub group of Southampton. The key Ushers' managers were pushed out while, ominously, the Alchemy Group, famous for its ruthless, stripped-down approach to business, emerged as the power behind Alehouse.

Valley parade...Simon Buckley (foreground) with colleagues from the Tomos Watkin Brewery celebrating their move from Llandeilo to a bigger plant in Swansea.

Alchemy made no attempt to disguise its distaste for low-profit brewing and announced the closure of Ushers in order to concentrate on pub retailing. While 'Ushers' beers, brewed by Thomas Hardy, will appear in Ushers' pubs, Alchemy made it clear it will take discounted national brands as well. It may not be long before Ushers beers disappear completely, leaving West Country drinkers to peer disconsolately into their pints of Tetley.

Meanwhile the genuine and dedicated independent breweries continue to perform well. Fuller's and Young's in London had record years, with sales and profits increased. George Gale of Horndean, Hampshire, increased turnover by 8 per cent in 1999 and recorded record profits of £30 million. In Cumbria, Jennings Brothers of Cockermouth increased profits by a staggering 73 per cent. In 1999 Timothy Taylor of Keighley, Yorkshire, brewed more beer than at any time in its history and in July 2000 installed new fermenters to cope with the demand for its beers. In Wales, the Tomos Watkin Brewery moved from micro to small regional status when it transferred production from Llandeilo to an industrial park in Swansea.

There's life in the old cask yet.

THE GREEN BEER REPORT
Too little, too late?

*Brewers are slow to respond to consumer demand for organic beer, says **Roger Protz***

The head brewer of a famous regional brewery in the Midlands, a man revered among his peers, raised his eyes to the heavens when I mentioned organic beer. 'You should see the rubbish I get sent,' he said and moved swiftly on to another issue.

By 'rubbish' he meant organic barley malt and hops. His response was not merely depressing, but underscored the deep-seated conservatism of an industry faced by falling beer consumption and brewery closures.

You would expect brewers to be busily, even frantically, seeking out new niches in the beer market. Organic beer should be high on their list as consumers reject food and drink produced with the aid of chemicals, and supermarkets can scarcely keep up with the demand for organic produce.

The situation improved a little in 2000, with several brewers adding new brands to go alongside Golden Promise from Edinburgh's Caledonian Brewery, for years the only regularly-brewed organic beer in cask-conditioned form. Golden Promise is named after a variety of malting barley, but the brewery now uses a different type called Chariot. Ironically, all its other beers use Golden Promise but the price of the organic version proved prohibitive. Caledonian is working with a whisky distiller and a farmers' co-operative in an attempt to grow a regular crop of organic Golden Promise. Where hops are concerned, Caledonian buys almost the entire crop of Target grown by Peter Hall in Marden in Kent, currently the only commercial grower of organic hops, though a breakthrough could be on the way (see following article).

Sam Smith, which has won several prizes in the annual Organic Food and Drink Awards sponsored by the Soil Association, uses English Chariot organic malt but has to import Hallertauer hops from New Zealand. Hallertauer is a Bavarian hop variety that has transferred and flourished in New Zealand, where it is grown without chemical sprays. Smith's Best Organic Ale and Organic Lager are available only in filtered bottled form.

It's an expensive business importing hops all the way from Australasia. The tiny Pitfield Brewery in Hoxton, North

Organic cask ales

Batemans
Yella Belly (Nov-Dec)

Brakspear
Ted and Ben (March-April)

Caledonian
Golden Promise

Fuller's
Organic Honey Dew (spring)

Organic Brewery
Lizard Point

Pitfield
Bitter; East Kent Goldings;
Eco Warrior; Hoxton Heavy;
Black Eagle; Shoreditch
1850 Porter

St Peter's
Organic Ale

What's in a name...Caledonian Brewery in Edinburgh is the best-known brewer of organic beer with its Golden Promise ale. But it can no longer get sufficient quantities of organic Golden Promise barley and has to use a variety called Chariot instead.

London, also uses New Zealand Hallertauer. Since Pitfield's Eco Warrior organic ale was given media coverage, owner Martin Kemp has struggled to keep up with demand. But in 2000 he took the brave step of converting his entire range of beers to organic. At one stage he was thinking of going to mainland Europe for organic malt, but he can now get sufficient supplies in England: the former Guinness maltings at Warminster have started to produce organic malt, along with Muntons and Simpsons.

A similar problem of sourcing organic materials faces the owners of the Northumberland Brewery in Bedlington. The solar-powered brewery is part of the Earth Balance eco-community at the 220-acre West Sleekburn Farm. But plans to brew only organic beers have been frustrated by the shortage and cost of ingredients. Northumberland Brewery plans to grow organic barley but West Sleekburn is too far north for hops to flourish. In the deepest South-west of England, the new Organic Brewery on the Lizard Peninsular wears its heart on its sleeve and produces one cask ale made with 'green' ingredients. It will add to the range if more organic material becomes available.

Big brewers may scorn the efforts of minnows such as Organic and Pitfield, but Caledonian and Sam Smith, recently joined by Batemans, Brakspear and Fuller's, aren't exactly bucket-and-shed producers. They are

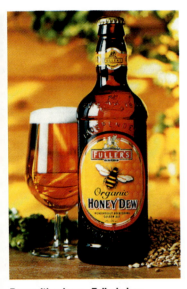

Beer with a buzz...Fuller's has converted its Honey Dew to organic ingredients

not, however, being trampled in the rush as competitors attempt to grab a share of the organic beer market.

Conventional farmers and seed merchants concentrate on developing new hybrid barley varieties that, with the help of chemical fertilisers, are 'high yielding', which means they produce more per acre than older varieties, grow tall yet don't fall over in high winds. As a result, England's finest malting barley, Maris Otter, preferred by many brewers for its juicy and biscuity character, has been de-listed and has to be contract grown at a much higher price.

Moves towards hops grown with less reliance on fertilisers and pesticides received a setback when the ADAS Rosemaund research farm at Preston Wynne in Herefordshire closed. The Ministry of Agriculture withdrew funding from the farm and told researchers at Preston Wynne to carry out their work on conventional hop farms.

Preston Wynne had made great strides in recent years in developing hops where ladybirds, hoverfly larvae and parasitic wasps were allowed to thrive and kill the pests, such as aphids and red spider mite, that attack hops. Conventional hop growers' sprays destroy the natural habitat where predators live, seemingly impervious to the argument that nature can do the work for them. However, important scientific research into resistance to hop disease and pest attack continues at Horticultural Research International at Wye College in Kent.

At Marden in Kent, Peter Hall's list of the chemicals used by conventional hop growers makes depressing reading: nitrates, organo-phosphorous compounds, weed killers and fungicides. In the place of chemicals, Hall ploughs in legumes

High five...the Pitfield Brewery in London has converted all its beers – cask and bottle conditioned – to organic production. But it has to import organic hops all the way from New Zealand.

Germans trial a 'GM' lager

The threat of 'Frankenstein beer' drew nearer with the news in 2000 that German researchers are working on a genetically modified lager with a long-lasting head. The frothy head is obtained by using a GM yeast culture.

The work is being carried out by Dr Ulf Stahl and a team of scientists at the Technical University in Berlin. They have developed a brewer's yeast that is enhanced with a gene called LTP1.

'The basis of foaming in beer is the LTP1 gene,' Dr Stahl said. The protein made by the gene forms bubbles of carbon dioxide during fermentation. More LTP1 produces more proteins, which in turn create a more stable froth.

Levels of natural LTP1 vary in barley crops: more of the gene is produced in barley during dry summers than in wet ones. The genetically modified yeast secretes so much of the froth-making protein that the beer will have the same amount of foam regardless of the quality of the barley.

Dr John Hammond of Brewing Research International in Surrey, which ran its own experiments with GM yeast in the early 1990s, said the work in Berlin was interesting but he doubted whether it would ever be used commercially in Britain.

'There's no knock-on effect from GM yeast,' he said. 'It's not like pollen that can affect other cereals and plants. Raw materials in beer, principally barley, are changing and brewers are keen to have a stable beer. GM yeast could help smooth out any difference in proteins from one batch to another. But I'm surprised this research is being carried out in Germany as there's so much opposition to GM food, as there is in Britain.'

Dr Hammond added that he thought it unlikely GM yeast would ever be used by craft brewers in Britain who are mindful of the key role yeast strains play in the flavour of beer. His views were endorsed by Dr Stahl in Berlin, who said German brewers had expressed interest in his work but they did not think there was a market for GM beer due to public opposition.

But there could a backdoor use for GM yeast among the large number of 'own label' brewers in mainland Europe, who concentrate on producing iden-tikit cheap lagers for supermarkets. The biggest brewery in the Netherlands almost exclusively makes own label beers and such manufacturers are not concerned with quality or flavour, and would welcome any ingredients that ensure consistency of blandness and a frothy head.

that provide natural nitrogen to the soil and eventually turn into green manure. The legumes also conserve nutrients in the soil.

Later in the season, Hall sows white mustard seed around and between the trellises where the hop bines grow. The seed produces more green manure and provides a habitat for lacewings and ladybirds that attack the damson aphid, a major hop pest. He also sprays the tops of the bines with a solution of soapy water that kills the aphids.

Hall tackles mildew, which can turn hops black, by 'rogueing' – digging out infected bines -- and spraying with copper oxychloride, the only approved fungicide permitted by the Soil Association. Every February he ploughs in 'shoddy' – waste from the clothing industry that is rich in nitrogen, feeds the roots of the bines and conditions the soil.

Peter Hall says his Target hops taste better than conventional ones because they are free from chemicals. His hops are more expensive as they are labour-intensive but they account for only a fraction of the cost of a pint of beer.

Brewers will only produce more organic beers if there is consumer pressure. In the 1970s, CAMRA, backed by millions of beer lovers, forced brewers to rethink their addiction to keg beer and return to cask produc-tion. Now, in the green 21st century, we must urge them once again to clean up their act and Go Organic.

THE GREEN BEER REPORT

Organic floodgates may open

With one major supermarket chain, Waitrose, estimating that within a few years 10 per cent of its beer brands will be accounted for by organic versions, brewers, maltsters and hop farmers will have to throw off conservative habits and hurry to meet the demand.

Bigger brewers dominated by accountants will only switch to organic beer if they can source ingredients in Britain. They will jib at buying malt from France, and laugh at the suggestion they should have to import hops all the way from New Zealand.

But now such leading British maltsters as Crisps, Muntons, Simpsons and Warminster are supplying organic grain. Tuckers of Newton Abbot is working at full capacity producing conventional malt, but will be happy to introduce organic malt when space permits.

The news on the hop front is dramatic. Horticultural Research International at Wye College in Kent, with funding from the Ministry of Agriculture, combats hop diseases and pest attacks, and develops new hop varieties that are resistant to these problems. HRI has developed 'dwarf hops', so called because they grow to half the height of conventional hops, 2.4 metres or eight feet, compared to 4.8 metres or 16 feet. HRI is leading the world in both dwarf hop development and combating aphids, which attack 95 per cent of global hop production.

The dwarf First Gold variety, introduced commercially in the mid-1990s, has been a great success. Dwarf or 'low trellis' hops are easier and cheaper to pick, and are more resistant to aphid attack and powdery mildew than conventional varieties, though they are still open to attack from downy mildew and red spider.

The reason dwarf varieties are more resistant to disease and pests is because they are the result of research into all the problems affecting hops, including verticillium wilt, downy and powdery mildews, aphids and red spider mite. Peter Darby, who is Head of Research at HRI at

Why beer needs aroma therapy

The cone of the hop contains a yellow powder called lupulin that contains the oils and bittering compounds needed by the brewer. The compounds include alpha acids that give bitterness to beer.

Hops divide into two main varieties: bittering hops and aroma hops. Craft brewers will often blend both varieties – such as Fuggles and Goldings – in their beers, but big global brewers are more and more switching to 'high alpha' hops for bitterness. 'Cream flow' nitro-keg ales are served so cold and covered in gas that aroma hops would have no impact.

The battle is on to save aroma hops. High alphas are so important globally that they are bought and sold on the world commodity markets, but aroma hops are being marginalised. In Britain there is currently a glut of aroma hops mainly as a result of brewery closures.

Aroma hops, which give delightful spicy, peppery, and fruity characteristics to ale, will disappear unless Britain's regional brewers can be saved from oblivion.

Wye, says that 13 years ago his team of scientists found a strong source of genetic resistance to the hop aphid, and have learnt how to pass that resistance on to future generations of hops. They take the good genes from current varieties to develop new varieties. This is known as 'good parental breeding' and has nothing to do with genetic modification, which, for example, may involve taking a gene from a potato and implanting it into a tomato. Dwarf hops are a product of 'good parental breeding'.

Every year the National Hop Association of England and HRI sponsor the Beauty of Hops competition to encourage British brewers to use hops imaginatively and create greater consumer awareness of the importance of hops to beer appreciation. The 2000 competition included categories for India Pale Ale, single varietal beers that use just one hop variety, and the Ultimate Fish and Chip Beer.

As a result of the research and breeding progamme, HRI at Wye has now developed a new 'low alpha' hop variety – that's a variety that offers good aroma but moderate bitterness – that is resistant to all diseases and pests. As it needs no spraying it could be designated an organic hop when it becomes commercially available in about two years' time. Peter Darby says he considers it an important challenge to develop organic hops, and believes the work of low trellis dwarf varieties will help that development enormously.

This scientific breakthrough could open the flood gates for organic beer in Britain, giving brewers a bigger home-grown source of organic hops. The initiative will only be seized, however, if regional and craft breweries survive in the age of global brands.

Closing time...an all-too-familiar image of the countryside. Six country pubs are closing every week and urgent action is needed to stop the cull.

Crisis
in the countryside

Rural pubs are closing at a rate of knots and need urgent help, says **Ted Bruning**

Every day, somewhere in Britain, a country pub closes for good. It seems hard to believe, doesn't it? Rationally, we know that the economy and demography of the countryside have changed profoundly since the war. We know about the mechanisation of agriculture, the migration of rural workers to towns and cities, the ageing population, the gentrification of farmworkers' cottages. It's all been in the papers, over and over again.

But surely, we think, chocolate-box pubs with roses round the door are immune? Surely the village inn with its cool, hoppy ale, its hearty meals of fresh-baked bread and farm-made ham and cheese, its equally hearty landlord, its jolly fellowship of lusty yokels and bluff squires, has such potent appeal that customers are queuing down the street? Yet one by one they close, remorsely and irresistibly. How can this be? I doubt that country pubs, taken as a whole, make less money than they used to. In fact the opposite is probably true.

The farmworkers who used to be their mainstay were appallingly badly paid: they could make a pint of mild last all night and were renowned for cadging drinks off gullible travellers. The rural population today is far wealthier than it was 50 or even 30 years ago; it is also far readier to part with its cash. High-margin wines, spirits and minerals make up a much bigger part of the country pub's wet trade than in the 1960s, when beer sales dominated.

Then there's food. Eating out in country pubs, almost unknown in the 1960s, is now commonplace. Most country pubs are also happy to cater for families with children, although the law is still ambivalent on the subject. Food is a comparatively new source of income for country pubs, and although most country landlords 30 years ago would have turned up their noses at the idea of cooking three-course meals, few could now survive without it.

(Incidentally, I also question the orthodoxy that drink-drive laws have crucified country pubs. The breathalyser came in 33 years ago; surely its impact has been absorbed by now? And how much did the country pub of 1968 depend on car-borne trade anyway? There

Dun Drinkin...it was a pub once but the owners made more money selling it as a private house.

were far fewer cars on the road then than now, and having been left outside innumerable country pubs with orangeade and crisps as a child in the 1960s, my impression is that pub car-parks are fuller now than they were then).

So it's not simply that business is bad. There are plenty of country pubs which seem to be empty most of the time; but then there always were. No, it's that country pubs today are expected to yield a far greater return than they did traditionally, or than they can sensibly manage.

● Pub rents are proportionately much higher than they were.
● Business rates for pubs are calculated according to a unique and unfair formula. Pubs pay far higher rates than other businesses.
● Landlords are expected to make the pub their sole livelihood. It used to be common for the landlord to have another job, while the landlady would open up during the day. Today breweries frown on tenants having day jobs; and with the ever-increasing burden of paperwork necessary to comply with VAT, health regulations, PAYE and so on, few landlords have the time anyway.
● The average wholesale price of beer has gone down in the last 10 years, but not for small tenants. They have to pay full list price for their beer to subsidise investment in the town-centre circuit pubs, which – to add injury to injury – actually lure away much of their vital Friday and Saturday night custom.
● The basic level of provision – bare benches, an outdoor gents' open to the stars, and no ladies' loo at all (women customers were usually shown upstairs to the landlord's bathroom when necessary) – once considered adequate is no longer acceptable. Today's country pub requires huge capital outlay compared to its predecessor, with maintenance costs to match.

Compounding all this over the last 20 years has been house-price inflation. Most country pubs, especially pretty ones, are worth 50 or even 100 per cent more as private houses than as going concerns. The

Beer to go...the Bell in Hertfordshire, near London Colney, was handy for the M25 and proved a tempting bait for McDonald's. Now it's a drive-through burger bar and another pub has been lost to the global fast food business.

temptation to give up the struggle and cash in is overwhelming.

At the current rate of closure, there will be no country pubs at all in 20 years. Of course, that won't happen. The trend will bottom out in time – but when? France has lost over half of its rural bars in 30 years: can Britain stop the slide before it goes that far?

Part of the answer lies with publicans. They have to ask themselves honestly what customers expect of country pubs. Only a handful can survive as traditional village beerhouses: the rest must attract drinkers and diners in from a wide area – which they won't do by offering lack-lustre mass-produced ales indifferently kept, and unimaginative food indifferently cooked.

What people expect are country-brewed ales in top condition, not national brands from Leeds or Manchester. Sausages, hams, bacon, and pies from the village butcher, not from some distant factory. Seasonal fruit and veg from local growers, not year-round mange-tout from Guatemala. Maybe some traditional regional dishes on the menu. In short, a distinctive rural identity that repays the customer in full.

Many country publicans who have asked themselves hard questions and come up with intelligent answers are doing a roaring trade. But publicans alone, however enterprising, cannot overcome all the problems that face country pubs. Action both from the Government and from brewers and pub companies is urgently needed.

● Licensing reform promises to allow longer opening hours. Midnight closing on Fridays and Saturdays, in particular, would increase the competitiveness of country pubs. This reform needs to be introduced quickly.
● A review of the rating system is promised, but will take five years. Pubs urgently need to be rated on the same basis as other businesses.
● Tenants, especially of pub companies, need more freedom in the ales they can stock, and at better prices. Buying national brands cheap and charging tenants top dollar for them may make short-term sense for shareholders, but in the longer term it's disastrous.
● Pub rents are too high. Statutory rent tribunals need to be introduced

Clarion call to save rural pubs

CAMRA is committed to defending and promoting the rich diversity of Britain's beer heritage. Country pubs are a vital and beautiful part of that heritage – and country landlords remain great champions of real ale.

Among our key campaigning initiatives are:

● The **National Inventory of Historic Pub Interiors**. Many pubs, both urban and rural, are listed by the government as buildings of historical and architectural importance. By seeking to extend the protection of statutory listing to unspoilt pub interiors, CAMRA and its caseworker – jointly funded with English Heritage – are ensuring that many of the country's most interesting old pubs remain in use as pubs.

● The **Public House Viability Test**. Many owners of country pubs seek planning permission to convert them into private houses on the grounds that they are no longer viable as businesses. In the past, planning authorities have had to decide the question of viability on the basis of adversarial evidence presented by surveyors acting for opposing parties. Our Public House Viability Test seeks to eliminate this adversarial element by offering planning authorities a clear and objective checklist of relevant factors on which they can make up their own minds without having to decide between conflicting arguments.

● **Loss of amenity policies**. CAMRA has had great success in persuading local authorities to include a presumption against loss of village amenities in their District Plans.

● **Mandatory rate relief**. Shops and Post Offices in small settlements are at present entitled to up to 100 per cent relief from business rates. For pubs, this relief is at the discretion of the local council. CAMRA is lobbying for country pubs to share the same right to mandatory relief enjoyed by shops and Post Offices.

● **Statutory consultation**. More and more local CAMRA branches are demanding and winning a place on local authorities' lists of statutory consultees on planning matters. This not only means that the council will automatically seek CAMRA's views on any proposal to close a pub; it also means that CAMRA branches are among the first to know when a pub is threatened with change of use and can play an important role in the early mobilisation of local opposition.

● **Guest ales**. Many country pubs are owned by non-brewing pub companies which do not have to allow their tenants to choose what beers they can stock. CAMRA is in the forefront of the campaign to win pub tenants the right to satisfy the wishes of their own customers by stocking guest ales.

to replace the industry's own inadequate system of arbitration.

● City-centre circuit pubs, with all their attendant problems of drink-related nuisance, need to be curbed by stricter planning and licensing controls and tougher enforcement.

● The burden of compliance, especially in food safety, desperately needs to be simplified and reduced.

But there's one thing that landlords, brewers, and Government can't do, and only you can.

TV, I suspect, has been the country pub's biggest enemy. Too many people seem content to sit at home watching programmes they don't actually enjoy and then grumbling about them at work next day.

Don't! Instead, register your protest by switching the telly off.

Then go to the pub.

Ted Bruning edits CAMRA's newspaper What's Brewing, *and is the author of* Historic Inns of England, *Prion, £14.99, available from CAMRA.*

WHAT IS THE CASK MARQUE TRUST?

A non-profit-making organisation.

An independent accreditation scheme to recognise excellence in the service of cask ale.

Awarded to the licensee and not the pub, as it is his skills that produce the 'perfect pint'.

Jointly funded by brewers and retailers.

HOW DOES THE SCHEME WORK IN PRACTICE?

Once a licensee has agreed to join the Cask Marque scheme, an Assessor will, unannounced, visit his outlet twice in a three month period:

The Assessor will check the temperature, appearance, aroma and taste of all his cask ales.

Once accredited, the licensee will receive:

A plaque
To fix to the outside of his premises.

A certificate
To display inside the pub which is issued annually.

Adverising material
Telling the customer about the award.

Further inspections are made twice a year
And the Trust reserves the right to make additional random inspections as it sees fit.

THE CHALLENGE

The quality of beer in cask is better than it ever has been, but all too often that quality is less than satisfactory at the point of dispense.

Our concerns were underlined by an independent survey of over 1,000 pubs and amongst its findings the survey shows that one in five pints sold is of poor quality and that temperature at the point of dispense is a very important factor.

The consumer demands refreshing consistent quality. That challenge must be met.

That is why we formed the Cask Marque Trust.

WHAT DO WE WANT TO ACHIEVE?

Highlight and reward licensees who serve excellent cask beer.

To raise quality standards to meet the demands and expectation of today's consumer.

To reassure the consumer when he sees the Cask Marque logo.

To allow and encourage the consumer to give feedback to our organisation.

We have produced 17 free regional guides and we would be happy to send you a guide for your area.

You can learn more about Cask Marque and details of the pubs where Cask Marque licensees reside by visiting our Website on **www.cask-marque.co.uk**

Write to us at: **The Cask Marque Trust, Seedbed Centre, Severalls Park, Colchester, Essex CO4 4HT.**
E-mail us on **cask-marque@mcno.com**

'...and a half for the good lady?'

*Should women take up rugby to get noticed by brewers and ad men, **Lynne Pearce** asks*

If beer had a gender, would it be a boy or a girl? According to the vast majority of those who earn their livelihood by promoting the sales of beer, anything sold in a pint glass is about as macho as you can get, barring a rugby scrum or stag night.

And while the statistics show that increasing numbers of women enjoy a trip to the pub, in the mythical world of advertising the local is still perceived as a predominantly male domain, where the female of the species is tolerated only if she's pulling your pint, looks like Denise Van Outen, and has a brain the size of a walnut.

But for us ordinary mortals who quaff the stuff and occasionally write about it, beer is a drink and a pub is a place where we go to consume it. It's as simple as that. So why all the machismo? And does anyone benefit from it?

For Paul Nunny of beer quality guardians Cask Marque, clinging to stale stereotypes does no one any favours, least of all brewers, as it works against increasing sales. 'Real ale is living with its history, rather than focusing on new target groups,' he believes. 'It's marketing history, rather than marketing the values of today's society. One of the real issues is to get the perception of beer right and the industry needs to target a wider profile.'

It's an opinion shared by pub chain Wetherspoon's, which has taken a radical approach to selling real ale in its 400-plus outlets. 'We wanted to make our point-of-sale advertising of real beer very contemporary, trendy in design and attractive to men and women,' explained marketing manager Nathan Wall. 'We were trying to create as much distance as possible away from the image of sandals, holey jumpers and beards. I've never believed that beer was the preserve of men over the age of 35. Indeed, my experience of CAMRA beer festivals is that a huge proportion of women as well as men attend and lots of them are young.'

And he's right. Increasing numbers of women are both joining CAMRA and attending beer festivals up and down the country. A quarter of the Campaign's members are female and many more than that attend its flagship event, the Great British Beer Festival, every year.

Reflecting this egalitarian view, Wetherspoon's devised a groundbreaking poster campaign, based upon a series of photographs featuring young, attractive men and women. One of a well-toned, semi-naked man advertising that most prestigious of beers, Hook Norton, proved so popular that stocks ran out as posters disappeared from pub walls.

Nicht verboten...the young women opposite are used in advertisements for Schneider Weisse wheat beer in Bavaria. But in Britain women are rarely shown enjoying the pleasures of beer.

Clearly the company has swapped an emphasis on tradition and heritage for a more specific appeal to the youth market, the theory being that if you can convert youngsters to ale, whether male or female, they are less likely to change their tipple as they grow older. 'It's a two-pronged attack based on giving beer a contemporary image and serving it properly, ensuring that the quality is consistently good,' said Wall. And for Wetherspoon's, the results have already paid dividends, as sales of real ale are rising.

Another company that has deliberately tried to ditch the old-fashioned image of beer in its advertising is London brewery Fuller's. Before launching a new campaign to promote London Pride, the company commissioned some research that examined the semiotics associated with marketing cask-conditioned beer. The results made fascinating reading, revealing what many of us have suspected for a long time – real ale is suffering from an identity crisis. While advertising for some brands of lager has been able to take the imaginative high ground – for those in any doubt, have another glance at the creativity of Budweiser – real ale

The Good Beer Guide 2001

Figment of the imagination...she's young, she's a woman and she's drinking beer at CAMRA's Great British Beer Festival. But for British brewers she doesn't exist as only lads enjoy beer.

has become the Cinderella of the brewing world, only ever talked about in terms of its heritage and contents.

'And the last thing that consumers want to know is that it's been brewed in a bucket for 200 years,' said Fuller's brands manager, David Spencer.

In response to what it discovered and rather than seeking to out-lad the worst of the lager ads, the company opted for a much more subtle approach for its spring 2000 television advert. It's based on four male friends having a relaxed chat over a quiet pint in the pub. 'We wanted characters, not four John Wayne types,' explained Spencer. 'They are enjoying each other's company and are discerning in the company they keep and what they drink. They're not macho men but confident and sophisticated. All the conversations that they have are intimate, show that they have known each other for a long time and reveal their vulnerability. For example, although they talk about women, one of them has been dumped and we purposely picked the handsome one for that role.'

It's a far cry from the Men Behaving Badly school of marketing, yet women are still noticeably absent. Spencer agrees, but counters that the last thing he wants to do is include women in an ill-thought-out way, when it becomes a token effort or patronising. And he argues that while the advert for London Pride is an 'attack on masculine territory', it was created to appeal to women, too. 'Women are just as ad literate as men, so why be less subtle? I'd like to think that in time, when we are successful in claiming back the real ale market, then we can start to be more experimental'. Does that mean ads with women? 'Why not?' said Spencer.

But perhaps a more apt question is: When? Although no one seems to collate figures on how many women drink beer, there's plenty of evidence to suggest that women and families are still the pub's flourishing consumer groups. The dirty, smoky bar full of men drinking their own weight in beer has all but disappeared.

Today's pubgoers are as likely to be female as male. Expectations include a smoke-free area, a choice of good food, a welcome for their children – and a decent pint to boot. It must be in brewers' interests to begin to woo the female pound. As a result, women may have the last laugh after all – but this time it won't be at our expense.

Lynne Pearce writes a monthly column My Pint of View for CAMRA's newspaper What's Brewing. It won her a pewter tankard award from the British Guild of Beer Writers in 1999.

A little of what you fancy...

According to the medical bible, the Lancet, a moderate consumption of beer can protect us against heart disease. A press release that accompanied the issue of the Lancet in April 2000 carried the indisputable heading 'Beer Is Good For You'.

The journal of the medical profession reported on research carried out by Henk Hendriks and colleagues from the TNO Nutrition and Food Research Institute in the Netherlands. They found that beer contains vitamin B6, which prevents the accumulation of homocysteine, an amino acid that can help cause CVD – cardiovascular disease.

The researchers studied 11 healthy men who drank, in a random order, beer, red wine, spirits and water for three months with their meals. The men were aged 44 to 59 years, healthy non-smokers with a moderate intake of alcohol. They drank four glasses of red wine, beer, gin or sparkling water with dinner. The drinks were switched every three weeks. The water was a control and played no role in the actual research.

Homocysteine concentrations were raised after three weeks' consumption of red wine and spirits, while no increase was recorded following beer drinking. Beer drinkers had a 30 per cent increase of vitamin B6 in blood plasma, compared to 17 per cent in red wine and 15 per cent in gin.

The benefits of beer have been known for a millennia or two. In the Old World of Egypt, Babylonia and Mesopotamia, the people gave up their nomadic lifestyle to settle down and grown grain in

Swigging Sixties...Fuller's had no inhibitions 40 years ago promoting the healthy attributes of beer

order to make beer. A Sumerian poet wrote around 3000 BC: 'I feel wonderful, drinking beer in a blissful mood, with joy in my heart and a happy liver'.

In Britain, once the tribes had learnt the skill of brewing, beer became an equally vital part of the daily diet. While the recent research in the Netherlands has shown that vitamin B6 can help prevent heart disease, the same vitamin has for centuries kept scrofulous hair and skin diseases at bay.

In modern times, one of the most famous advertising slogans said, simply, 'Guinness is good for you'. Doctors advised nursing mothers to drink a bottle of Guinness a day, a stout rich in yeast, vitamin B and iron. Then along came the health fanatics in both the United States and Britain and we could no longer be told that Guinness was good for us.

Now, thanks to the Dutch research, we have official confirmation that beer is good for us. It is rich in essential vitamins. Taken in moderation, it will keep you fit, with a healthy ticker.

Growing old
with dignity

*Laying down bottle-conditioned ales can produce
some stunning results, **Jeff Evans** reports*

One reason why I prefer to drink real ale – bottled or cask – is because it tastes fresher. It hasn't been blasted with heat to pasteurise it. It hasn't had its life-giving yeast ripped out. It is living and fresh. Because of this, most bottled real ales benefit from being drunk as young as possible. There's a best before date on the label and you should generally observe this to enjoy the beer at its best. But bottled real ale can also last extremely well. It can be set aside like a good wine and, providing it is kept cool and in the dark, to prevent heat and light spoiling it, it can be enjoyed many years after it was brewed.

Not all beers treated in this way will prove rewarding, but there have been many stories about mediocre brews that have been miraculously transformed with age into pure nectar. Good Beer Guide editor Roger Protz and I sat down to see if there was any truth in these tales and put the ageing theory to the test. We chose our beers carefully and didn't consider brews at the weaker end of the spectrum. For a beer to mature in the bottle it needs plenty of body, a good malt base on which fermentation can continue for a while, and strong flavours that can be rounded out by ageing.

Setting aside a beer of under 4 per cent, for instance, is unlikely to prove successful. At this strength, ales just don't have the body to develop: they become dry,

He nose, you know...Jeff Evans finds some remarkable aromas in a glass of bottle-conditioned ale

thin and gassy, as the yeast eats away at the sugars and creates carbon dioxide. To begin, we blew the dust off a nine-year old bottle of Worthington White Shield. As a control, we also cracked open a bottle of the same beer bought that day from a supermarket. In fairness, White Shield is a tricky ale to evaluate in this way, as the ex-Bass beer has been brewed in numerous breweries in recent years.

Our young sample was produced at King & Barnes and even as we drank it we knew that its fate was once again in the air with the imminent closure of the Sussex brewery. This new beer was pleasant but a touch disappointing, thanks to a very dry, almost astringent, finish. Then we turned to the sample bottled in 1991. The brewers at Bass in days gone by knew all about White Shield and how it aged. They reckoned that after good early drinking the beer would fall into a 'sickness period' after around six months, during which it tasted less good, eventually recovering to mature beautifully from about three months later.

As we anxiously ran the beer into the glass, it appeared much darker and poured with more than a hint of sediment haze, unlike the crystal clear new version. However, from the first sniff it was a revelation. The slightly toffeeish, fruity nose of today's beer was replaced by rich, sherry notes and a distinct, but not unpleasant, whiff of

Nipps inside...there were remarkable variations in aroma and flavour between two vintages of Norfolk Nips

Marmite. The taste was remarkable. This 5.5 per cent beer had developed into a mellow, full ale that seemed nearer to 8 per cent alcohol, although it is unlikely to have gained that much strength in the bottle. The full, smooth, toffee apple flavour was a treat and there was still just the right amount of carbonation to lift the beer.

Continuing our journey up the alcohol ladder, we arrived at the 8 per cent King & Barnes Christmas Ale, tasting samples from 1996 and 1998. The same basic flavours were evident in both – loads of fruit, marzipan and spice – but here the benefits of maturity really began to stand out.

The young sample seemed to struggle for balance. To quote Roger, 'there were bits poking out all over the place'. But the 1996 beer was heavenly, all elements in proportion and a perfect way, we agreed, to round off a Christmas lunch.

The contrast in the samples of our next beer was even more dramatic. We opened 1997 and 1998 versions of Woodforde's Norfolk Nips, a dark ruby ale. The newer beer was deeply disappointing, with a thick yeast nose and a strange 'cough candy' taste. We wondered if this ugly duckling would ever turn out to be a swan, but all doubts were cast aside when we poured out the year-older bottle. The aroma was amazing, like leaning over a barrel of Granny Smith apples. Apple flavour is not always a good thing in brewing, as it can indicate fermentation problems, but this was just delightful. At 8.2 per cent it was surprisingly refreshing, with rich dark malt flavours combining with the fruit to leave a pleasant 'apple pie' finish.

Just when we thought we had reached the apex of our tasting pyramid, we stumbled on to the 10 per cent Imperial Russian Stout. This world classic has its roots in Britain's trade with the Baltic in pre-Napoleonic times. It has not been brewed by Scottish Courage since 1993 but it is only when you relax into a glass that you really get angry that the brewery should allow this amazing beer to die. We tried a 1993 and a 1992. The younger beer was typically complex and had a distinct woody character. It was fairly acidic and, although a pleasure in itself, was quickly outshone by the mighty 1992. Roger and I sat back and

Eye, eye...Roger Protz looks ruminatively at the clarity of a bottled brew

smiled. Life ground to a halt for a few satisfying minutes. We both agreed that it came close to being the finest beer we had ever tasted – rich, perfectly balanced, creamy and fruity, steeped in flavours like liquorice and molasses.

We were loathe to move on, but we still had one last beer to sample. Thomas Hardy's Ale was introduced by Eldridge Pope in 1968, to commemorate the 40th anniversary of the writer's death. Regrettably, no one is selling the beer any longer and orders – like its fermenters – have dried up. Hardy, at a formidable 12 per cent, is one of those beers with which you can have great fun. All bottles are marked with the year of production, so you can enjoy vintage taste-offs. We began with a tired-looking bottle whose torn, faded label read 1983. Inside was a beautifully clear, 17 year-old ruby ale with an aroma so heady that inhaling was as good as drinking. The taste was immensely fruity, with a fine rhubarb tartness. We then opted for a 1996 bottle, which could easily have been a different beer altogether. It tasted raw, as if it had not yet come together. Could this be, like White Shield's, a kind of sickness period? It's possible, as our final bottle was the most recent (1999) brew of Hardy and that

turned out to be quite magnificent, with a stunning creamy, peachy fruitiness that made you wonder how much better it could possibly get in years to come.

Roger and I are old hands at tasting bottled real ales but we were both astonished at the results of our tasting. The experiment had proved yet again that bottle-conditioned beer has everything going for it, from the freshness of youth to the maturity of old age. Is it too unrealistic to think that, given properly labelled 'vintages', we might soon be able to request a bottle of Prize Old Ale '94, or a Special London Ale '99 in our local beer shop?

Literary debuts...Thomas Hardy's Ale, first brewed in 1968, offers dramatic differences in character from one year to the next.

Photos by Cressida Feiler

Jeff Evans is the author of the Good Bottled Beer Guide, CAMRA Books, £8.99.

Since the tasting, it has been announced that Worthington White Shield will be brewed by the Museum Brewing Co in Burton-on-Trent. An American craft brewery, Phoenix, is negotiating to buy the rights to brew Thomas Hardy's Ale.

Beers of the Year

The beers listed below are the CAMRA Beers of the Year. They were short-listed for the Champion Beer of Britain competition in August 2000, and the Champion Winter Beer of Britain competition in Manchester in January 2000. Each beer was found by panels of trained CAMRA judges to be consistently outstanding in its category and they all receive a 'full tankard' symbol in the Breweries Section.

DARK AND LIGHT MILDS
Batemans Dark Mild
Belhaven 60/-
Brains Dark
Elgood's Black Dog Mild
Moorhouses Black Cat
Riverhead Sparth Mild
Tripple fff Pressed Rat & Warthog

BITTERS
Adnams Bitter
Big Lamp Bitter
Blackawton Bitter
Brakspear Bitter
Bridgewater Navigator
Caledonian Deuchars IPA
Fuller's Chiswick Bitter
Glentworth Light Year
Harviestoun Brooker's Bitter & Twisted
Kelham Island Bitter
Oakham JHB
Smiles Golden
Tripple fff After Glow
Woodfordes Wherry Best Bitter

BEST BITTERS
Batham Best Bitter
Beartown Kodiak Gold
Butts Barbus Barbus
Concertina Bengal Tiger
Cotleigh Barn Owl
Fuller's London Pride
Harvey's Sussex Best Bitter
Hogs Back TEA
Houston St Peter's Well
Mighty Oak Burntwood Bitter
RCH Pitchfork
Reepham Rapier Pale Ale
Taylor Landlord
York Yorkshire Terrier Bitter

STRONG BITTERS
Branscombe Vale Summa That
Cropton Monkmans Slaughter
Fuller's ESB
Gale's HSB
Hop Back Summer Lightning
Plassey Cwrw Tudno
Wolf Granny Wouldn't Like It

OLD ALES AND STRONG MILDS
Gale's Festival Mild
Harvey's Sussex XXXX Old Ale
Sarah Hughes Dark Ruby
Theakstons Old Peculier
Young's Winter Warmer

PORTERS AND STOUTS
Burton Bridge Porter
Flannery's Oatmeal Stout
Hambleton Nightmare
High Force Cauldron Stout
RCH Old Slug Porter
Wye Valley Dorothy Goodbody
Wholesome Stout

BARLEY WINES
Burton Bridge Old Expensive
Exmoor Beast
Hoskins & Oldfield Old Navigation Ale
Lees Moonraker
Orkney Skullsplitter
Robinson's Old Tom
Woodfordes Headcracker

SPECIALITY BEERS
Heather Fraoch Heather
Harviestoun Schiehallion
Heather Fraoch Heather Ale
Isle of Skye Hebridean Gold
O'Hanlon's Wheat
Oakham White Dwarf Wheat Beer
Nethergate Umbel Ale
Young's Waggle Dance

BOTTLE-CONDITIONED BEERS/REAL ALES IN BOTTLE
King & Barnes Worthington White Shield
Hampshire Pride of Romsey
Fuller's 1845
Young's Special London Ale
King & Barnes Festive
Gale's Prize Old Ale
Hop Back Summer Lightning
B&T Dragon Slayer
Batham Best Bitter

CHAMPION WINTER BEER OF BRITAIN
Robinson's Old Tom

CHAMPION BEER OF BRITAIN
Moorhouses Black Cat

2 In the malt store, grain is weighed and kept until needed. The malt drops down a floor to the mills, which grind it into a coarse powder suitable for brewing. From the mills, the ground malt or grist is poured into the mash tuns along with heated liquor. During the mashing period, natural enzymes in the malt convert starches into fermentable malt sugars.

3 On the same floor as the conditioning tanks are the coppers, where after mashing, the wort is boiled with hops, which add aroma, flavour and bitterness.

4 At the end of the boil, the hopped wort is clarified in a vessel called the hop back on the ground floor. The clarified wort is pumped back to the malt store level where it is passed through a heat exchange unit. See 5.

How beer is brewed

Beer – real beer – is made by taking raw ingredients from the fields, the finest malting barley and tangy English hops, along with pure water from natural springs or the public supply, and carefully cultivated strains of brewers' yeast. In this exploded drawing by Trevor Hatchett of a classic British ale brewery, it is possible to follow the process that begins with raw grain and finishes with natural, living cask beer.

1 On the top floor, in the roof, are the tanks where pure water – called liquor by brewers – is stored. Soft water is not suited to ale brewing, and brewers will add such salts as gypsum and magnesium to replicate the hard, flinty waters of Burton-on-Trent, home of pale ale.

5 The heat exchange unit cools the hopped wort prior to fermentation.

6 The fermenters are on the same floor as the mash tuns. The house yeast is blended or pitched with the wort. Yeast converts the malt sugars in the wort into alcohol and carbon dioxide. Excess yeast is skimmed off by funnels called parachutes.

7 Fermentation lasts for a week and the 'green' beer is then stored for a few days in conditioning tanks.

8 Finally, the fresh beer is run into casks on the ground floor, where additional hops for aroma and sugar to encourage a secondary fermentation may be added. The casks then leave for pubs, where the beer reaches maturity in the cellars.

Home and away

These latest guides from CAMRA Books allow you to enjoy good beer in a bottle, good food in the pub, and a pleasant place to stay when the evening's enjoyment is over.

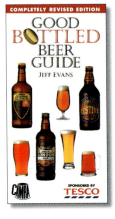

The CAMRA Good Bottled Beer Guide

sponsored by Tesco is written and researched by Jeff Evans, former editor of the Good Beer Guide, and one of the most respected British beer writers. It lists all the growing number of real bottled beers with information about ingredients and tasting notes. Price £8.99

Good Pub Food

The fifth edition of Susan Nowak's seminal guide that has transformed the quality of pub food. You no longer have to put up with soggy sandwiches, plastic ploughman's or microwaved pap but can eat well and affordably in the country's pubs with dishes that range from steak and kidney pie to authentic curries, Thai dishes and even French cuisine. £9.99

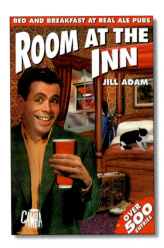

Room At The Inn

The second edition of Jill Adam's popular guide to pubs offering top-notch bed and breakfast accommodation throughout the British Isles. As well as detailing accommodation, the book is fully mapped and each pub entry lists the beers available as well as opening times and meal times. £8.99

The books are available from good bookshops or direct from CAMRA (post free), 230 Hatfield Road, St Albans AL1 4LW; cheques or postal made out to 'CAMRA'. To order by Access or Visa, phone 01727 867201 between 9am and 5pm, Monday to Friday (answerphone outside office hours). Allow 28 days for delivery.

A unique guide

We start with the quality of the beer: if a landlord can serve good pints, everything else in the pub should be in good order, too

IT'S CALLED the Good *Beer* Guide because it's more than just another pub guide. It's owned and controlled by Britain's most influential consumer movement, the Campaign for Real Ale, and it's CAMRA that sets the tone of the Guide. It's our belief that beer comes first in a good pub: not the food, the wine or the welcome, but the pints of cool, refreshing cask-conditioned ale. If the beer is good then everything else in the pub should fall into place. A landlord who spends time and devotion ripening each cask in the cellar is likely also to ensure that everything else in the pub is in first-class condition.

The Good Beer Guide is not just a guide to thatched and weather-boarded rural idylls. CAMRA cares passionately about country pubs and campaigns to ensure that every village and hamlet has one as our special feature in this edition shows. But there are good pubs in towns and cities, and they get due recognition in these pages. The pubs in every town and city feature in abundance in the Good Beer Guide.

It is the democracy of CAMRA that is the strength of the Guide. We employ no paid inspectors who make one lightning visit to a pub each year. 57,000 dedicated CAMRA members regularly visit all the pubs in their areas to evaluate the quality of the beer. CAMRA branches draw up recommended lists of pubs for the Guide and in many cases hold a vote or a ballot on which pubs to choose.

The focus of the Guide is beer quality. We list only those pubs that serve beer that has undergone a natural second fermentation in its cask and which is unaided by applied gas pressure. But as CAMRA is a consumer protection body, it also rejects pubs that rob drinkers by consistently serving short-measure pints. Pubs that attempt to fool drinkers by serving keg ales or ciders through fake handpumps will also get short shrift from CAMRA members.

Even dedicated CAMRA members may occasionally miss a good pub. This is why we welcome recommendations from our readers. Such pubs will not automatically go into the Guide but will be evaluated by the relevant branch of the Campaign.

Pubs in the Guide are listed in areas that follow the county or local authority system. In some cases, where local authorities are small, they have been amalgamated into larger regions. The Key Map on the inside back cover shows the sub-divisions used. English pubs are listed first, county by county, followed by pubs in Wales, Scotland, Northern Ireland and the offshore islands. Greater London and Greater Manchester are listed under L and M respectively. In Wales and Scotland, where counties and regions have been largely abolished in recent years, details of the precise local authority areas covered by each section are given on the first page. Each county or area has a location map pinpointing where the pubs are located and also locating independent breweries and brew pubs.

BEDFORDSHIRE

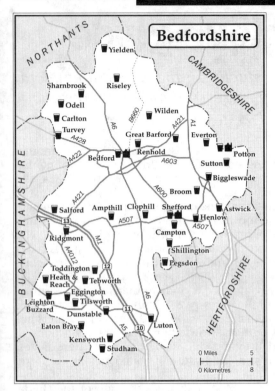

Bedfordshire

10.30-11; 12-10.30 Sun

Wells Eagle; guest beer (occasional) H
One-bar, town-centre pub
hosting live music Fri eve
and Sun afternoons.
Sometimes noisy at other
times and often crowded at
weekends, parking is diffult
during the working day. In
every edition of this *Guide*.
No food Sun. ◖

Wellington Arms

40-42 Wellington Street (left
off A6 Southbound at N end
of one-way system)
☎ (01234) 308033
12-11; 12-10.30 Sun
**Adnams Bitter; B&T Shefford Bitter;
guest beers** H
Warm, welcoming, street-
corner local refurbished by
B&T but operating as a real
ale free house, offering an
ever-changing range of guest
ales plus Belgian bottled
beers. Music jam sessions
held Tue and Thu eves.
🏵 ♣ ▱

BIGGLESWADE

Brown Bear

29 Hitchin Street
☎ (01767) 316161
12-3.30, 6-11; 12-11 Thu-Sat; 12-3, 7-
10.30 Sun
Beer range varies H
Notable for its ever-changing
range of eight ales from
micros: 1700 in its first three
years, this pub sells no nitro-
keg! Different beers are often
available from the cellar at
weekends with unusual and
rare beers the order of the
day. Several mini beer
festivals are held each year.
Limited, but good value
menu served.
🚶 🏵 ◖ ▶ ≠ ⊞ ✂ ▯

Wheatsheaf

5 Lawrence Road (near
library)
☎ (01767) 222220
11-3.30, 7-11 (11-11 Sat); 12-10.30
Sun
Greene King XX Mild, IPA H
Not many examples of this
type of pub remain: a small
unpretentious local; no food,
no frills, but good beer and
men's talk. Do you remember
trips to the races, crib leagues
and meat raffles? Well they're
still here! Mild always on. A
little gem.
🏵 ≠ ♣

BROOM

Cock ☆

23 High Street (off the village
green)
☎ (01767) 314411
11-3 (4 Sat), 6-11; 12-4, 7-10.30 Sun
Greene King IPA, Triumph, Abbot G
A pub with a diffrence: how a

AMPTHILL

Engine & Tender

11 Dunstable Street
☎ (01525) 403319
11-3, 5-11; 12-4, 7-10.30 Sun
**Greene King IPA; Ruddles Best
Bitter, County** H
Friendly, one-bar local
frequented by the local rugby
club. There is a large patio for
summer drinking. Bar snacks
served 12-2 weekdays.
🚶 🏵 ♣

Try also: **Wheatsheaf**, High
St, Flitwick (Wells)

ASTWICK

Tudor Oaks

1 Taylors Road
☎ (01462) 834133
11-11; 12-3.30, 7-10.30 Sun
**B&T Weleks Wallop; Mauldons White
Adder; guest beers** H
A *Guide* regular where seven
handpumps serve an ever-
changing range of ales from
micros; the landlord refuses
to have smooth flow beers in
the place. Exceptional food is
based on fresh ingredients.
This Tudor building boasts
seven open fireplaces and lots
of beams.
🚶 🏵 ⌑ ◖ ▷ ⌣ P ▯

BEDFORD

De Parys Hotel

45 De Parys Avenue
(continue N from High St,
A6)
☎ (01234) 352121
11-11; (midnight supper licence); 12-
10.30 Sun
Wells Eagle; guest beers H
Nicely-appointed hotel near
the town centre. The
extensive gardens are used
for barbecues and occasional
beer festivals are held in the
conservatory. A spacious
restaurant and children's
certificate complete the
picture.
⌣ 🏵 ⌑ ◖ ▶ P

Devonshire Arms

32 Dudley Street (between
Castle Rd & Russell Park)
☎ (01234) 359329
5.30 (4 Fri, 12 Sat)-11; 12-3, 7-10.30
Sun
**Wells Eagle, Bombardier; seasonal
beers** H
A mass of bright blossoms at
all times of the year
pinpoints 'The Devvy' which
has been refurbished and
revitalised by landladies Val
and Joy. Themed eves are
popular, when food is
available. A wide range of
wines is sold by the jug.
🚶 🏵 ⌑ ♣ ⊞

Fleur de Lis

12 Mill Street (off A6, High
St)
☎ (01234) 211004

34

pub used to be before the fashionable concept of the bar. Barrels on gravity dispense are kept in the step-down cellar. The front and back parlour are warmed by wood fires in the winter. The skittles room and dining room are cosy too, in this listed interior.
🏚️🏮◑▶🜂♣ P

CAMPTON
White Hart
Mill Lane
☎ (01462) 812657
12-3 (not Mon & Tue), 6.30-11; 12-11 Sat; 12-3, 7.10.30 Sun
Adnams Best Bitter; Courage Directors; Hook Norton Best Bitter; Ruddles Best Bitter, County; Theakston Best Bitter; guest beers Ⓗ
300-year-old, Grade II listed brick and beam pub featuring quarry-tiled floors and inglenooks. It hosts live music Wed; pétanque played and good play equipment in the garden.
🏚️🏮♣ P

CARLTON
Royal Oak
23 Bridgend (N of A428 at Turvey) OS955558
☎ (01234) 720441
12-3, 7-11; 12-11 Fri & Sat; 12-10.30 Sun
Wells Eagle, Bombardier; guest beer Ⓗ
This village local offers games, and a family function room, plus a courtyard and garden. Close to Harrold-Odell Country Park. Homely pub food served; sandwiches only Sun.
🏚️🍽️🏮◑🜂♣ P

CLOPHILL
Stone Jug
10 Back Street (off A6)
☎ (01525) 860526
11-3, 6-11; 11-11 Sat; 12-10.30 Sun
B&T Shefford Bitter; John Smith's Bitter; guest beers Ⓗ
A back-street gem and a *Guide* regular. Popular with locals, it is convenient for the Greensand Ridge walk. Check before arriving with children. No food Sun. Parking can be difficult.
Q 🍽️🏮◑♣ P 🏠

DUNSTABLE
Victoria
69 West Street
☎ (01582) 662682
11-11; 12-10.30 Sun
Tetley Bitter; guest beers Ⓗ
Friendly, one-bar, town-centre local, strong on pub games and TV sports. It has a house beer from Tring,

alongside three ever-changing guests (well over 1000 to date); regular beer festivals held. A frequent South Beds CAMRA *Pub of the Year*. Good value lunches.
🏮◑♣

EATON BRAY
Hope & Anchor
63 Bower Lane
☎ (01525) 220386
11.30-2 (3 Thu-Sat), 6-11; 12-10.30 Sun
Courage Best Bitter; Theakston Best Bitter; Vale Wychert Ale; guest beer Ⓗ
Old, low-beamed village inn, combining an urban-style main bar and a restaurant (supper licence until 1am); popular with locals. The enclosed garden has a children's play area.
🏮◑▶🜂♣ P

EGGINGTON
Horseshoes
High Street
☎ (01525) 210282
11-2.30 (not Mon), 6-11; 12-10.30 Sun
Theakston Best Bitter; Wadworth 6X; guest beer Ⓗ
Picture-postcard village pub at the village centre, featuring a bar with scrubbed wooden tables, much used for dominoes and cards, a restaurant and a large garden. Superb food (not served Mon).
🏚️Q🏮◑▶♣ P

EVERTON
Thornton Arms
Potton Road
☎ (01767) 681149
12-3, 6-11; 11-11 Sat; 12-10.30 Sun
Wells Eagle; guest beers Ⓗ
Formidable building at the village centre, but always a warm welcome inside from friendly staff and customers. A good range of home-cooked food is served at this well-used community pub.
🏚️🏮◑▶🍺🜂♣ P

GREAT BARFORD
Golden Cross
2-4 Bedford Road (A421 crossroads)
☎ (01234) 870439
12-2.30, 5-11; 12-11 Sat; 12-10.30 Sun
Greene King IPA; guest beers Ⓗ
'Olde English' pub with a Chinese restaurant attached (take-aways available). It hosts live music or karaoke Fri eve. Up to four guest beers usually on tap.
🏮◑▶🍺♣ P

Try also: Anchor Inn, High St (Wells)

HEATH & REACH
Dukes Head
7-9 Leighton Road
☎ (01525) 237285
11-11; 12-10.30 Sun
Courage Directors; Wells Eagle; guest beers Ⓗ
Friendly local comprised of three converted 17th-century thatched cottages; the L-shaped bar has three distinct areas. Beer festivals held Easter and summer Bank Holiday weekends.
🏮◑▵♣ P

HENLOW
Engineers Arms
66 High Street
☎ (01462) 812284
12-11; 12-10.30 Sun
Everards Tiger; Taylor Landlord; guest beers Ⓗ
Welcoming two-bar village free house with six handpumps serving a wide range of ales including many from micros. It hosts the annual village beer festival in Oct, plus regular and varied live music. Lots of breweriana and sporting memorabilia on display. Occasional ciders stocked.
🏚️🏮🍺🠔

Try also: Red Cow, Langford High St. (Greene King)

KENSWORTH
Farmers Boy
216 Common Road
☎ (01582) 872207
11-11; 12-10.30 Sun
Fuller's London Pride, ESB, seasonal beers Ⓗ
Friendly village pub with a small public bar, a comfortable lounge and a dining area serving excellent food. The children's certificate covers the lounge and dining area; the garden features a children's play area.
🏚️◑▶♣ P

LEIGHTON BUZZARD
Hunt Hotel
19 Church Road
☎ (01525) 374692
11-2.30, 5.30-11; 11-11 Sat; 12-3, 7-10.30 Sun
Draught Bass; Fuller's London Pride; Tetley Bitter; guest beers Ⓗ
Comfortable, family-owned hotel and restaurant offering two ever-changing guest beers (usually strong). Children welcome in the daytime. Wheelchair access is from the rear. No food Sun.
Q 🍽️🏮🛏️◑▶🜂🍴 P

Stag
1 Heath Road

☎ (01525) 372710
12-2.30, 6-11; 12-3, 7-10.30 Sun

Fuller's Chiswick, London Pride, ESB, seasonal beer H

Triangular pub on a road junction appealing to drinkers of all ages; one comfortable bar serving good food (not Sun).

◖◗ ♣ P ⊞

LUTON

Bricklayers Arms

14-16 Hightown Road (100 yds N of station)
☎ (01582) 611017
12-2.30, 5-11; (12-11 Fri & Sat); 12-10.30 Sun

Bateman Mild; Everards Beacon, Tiger; guest beers H

Friendly, unpretentious town pub. The basic furnishings include old casks scattered about. Two ever-changing guest beers stocked.

❀ ≈ ♣ P

Mother Redcap

80 Latimer Road
☎ (01582) 730913
11-3, 5-11; 11-11 Fri & Sat; 12-3, 7-10.30 Sun

Greene King Martha Greene, IPA, Abbot H

Wood-panelled, one-bar pub with a games area separated from the lounge by a chimney breast. Sky Sports TV. No food Sun.

◖◗ ♣ P

Two Brewers

43 Dumfries Street
☎ (01582) 616008
12-11; 12-10.30 Sun

B&T Shefford Bitter, Edwin Taylor's Extra Stout; guest beers H

Basic, street-corner local away from the town centre; welcoming to all, including visiting football fans. Food may be available on request – if there's anything in the fridge! An unspoilt traditional boozer.

▟ ❀ ♣

Wheelwrights Arms

34 Guildford Street
☎ (01582) 759321
10.30-11; 12-10.30 Sun

Flowers IPA; Fuller's London Pride, ESB; guest beer H

One-roomed free house, close to the town centre; the only outlet for real cider for miles. Opens for breakfast at 7am.

▟ ◖◗ ≈ ♣ ☺

Windmill

93 Windmill Road
☎ (01582) 721062
10.30-11; 12-10.30 Sun

Bateman XB; Fuller's London Pride; Tetley Bitter H

Smart, friendly pub close to the Vauxhall works. Children welcome most times (special menu available on request).

The L-shaped bar has Sky sports at one end and features regular live music. Good value food. Q ◖◗
≈ (Airport Parkway) ♣ P

ODELL

Bell

Horsefair Lane OS965577
☎ (01234) 720254
11-3, 6-11; 12-3, 7-10.30 Sun

Greene King IPA, Triumph, Abbot, seasonal beers H

Popular, thatched, multi-roomed village pub with good food. The large riverside garden is home to an aviary of unusual birds. A path leads to the Harrold-Odell Country Park. No food Sun eve in winter.

▟ ❀ ◖◗ P

PEGSDON

Live & Let Live

Pegsdon Way
☎ (01582) 881739
12-2.30, 5-11; 12-11 Sun; 12-10.30 Sun

B&T Shefford Bitter; Greene King IPA; guest beer H

Ex-Greene King country pub, recently re-opened after a period of closure. Three rooms have quarry-tiled floors; bar billiards and skittles played. All-day opening is likely in summer. Popular with walkers. Live music Thu eve; no food Sun eve.

▟ ◖◗ ♣ P

POTTON

Rose & Crown Hotel

12 Market Square
☎ (01767) 260221
12-3, 5.30-11; 12-11 Sun; 12-10.30 Sun

Adnams Bitter; Potton Shambles; guest beers H

Old coaching inn rebuilt after the great fire of Potton in 1783. It has a dining area in the bar, plus a restaurant offering an adventurous menu. The management is keen on real ales and likes to try different beers.

▟ Q ❀ ▱ ◖◗ P ⊞

RENHOLD

Three Horseshoes

42 Top End (1 mile N of A421) OS095528
☎ (01234) 870218
11-3, 6-11; 11-11 Sat; 12-10.30 Sun

Greene King XX Mild, IPA; guest beer (occasional) H

Friendly, traditional, country pub with a real fire in the lounge bar, games in the public. Good value home-cooked food includes fresh fish in beer batter (no food Sun, or Tue eve). Children's

play area in the garden.
▟ Q ❀ ◖◗ ▱ ♣ P

RIDGMONT

Rose & Crown

89 High Street
☎ (01525) 280245
10.30-2.30 (12-3 Sat), 6-11; 12-3.30, 7-10.30 Sun

Adnams Broadside; Wells Eagle, Bombardier, seasonal beers H

Welcoming pub, popular with drinkers and diners alike, offering an extensive menu. The grounds offer camping and caravanning facilities. In every edition of this *Guide*.

❀ ◖◗ ▲ P ⊞

RISELEY

Fox & Hounds

High Street
☎ (01234) 708240
11.30-2.30, 6.30-11; 12-3, 7-10.30 Sun

Wells Eagle, Bombardier, guest beers H

Busy village pub where a warm welcome is assured. It enjoys a reputation for good food – the charcoal-grilled steaks are sold by weight.

Q ❀ ◖◗ P

SALFORD

Red Lion Country Inn Hotel

Wavendon road (off M1 Jct 13) OS934392
☎ (01908) 583117
11-3, 6-11; 12-2.30, 7-10.30 Sun

Wells Eagle, Bombardier; guest beer (occasional) H

Attractive country pub and restaurant featuring a good range of home-cooked meals, also served in the bar. The garden has a children's play area.

▟ Q ❀ ▱ ◖◗ ♣ P

SHARNBROOK

Swan With Two Nicks

High Street
☎ (01234) 781585
11-3, 5-11; 11-11 Sat; 12-10.30 Sun

Wells Eagle, Bombardier; guest beers H

Friendly village local with a courtyard garden. Good value home-cooked meals include daily specials and a vegetarian choice.

▟ ❀ ◖◗ ▱ ♣ P

SHEFFORD

Brewery Tap

14 North Bridge Street
☎ (01462) 628448
11-11; 12-10.30 Sun

B&T Shefford Mild, Bitter; guest beers H

Basic, popular local selling six B&T beers at low prices, plus

an additional guest. Decorated with breweriana and bottled beers, it hosts live music most Fri eves.
❀ ♣ P

SHILLINGTON
Musgrave Arms
16 Apsley End Road
☎ (01462) 711286
12-3, 5-11; 12-11 Sat; 12-10.30 Sun
Greene King XX Mild, Ⓗ IPA, Abbot; guest beers Ⓖ
Friendly, smart, one-bar country pub; the raised 'public' end has scrubbed wooden tables, popular with domino players. The large garden features pétanque and a children's play area. Good reputation for food, served in a no-smoking dining room.
🏠 Q ❀ ◐ ♣ P

STUDHAM
Red Lion at Studham
Church Road
☎ (01582) 872530
11.30-3, 5.30-11; 11-11 Sat; 12-10.30 Sun
Adnams Bitter; Greene King IPA, Abbot; guest beer Ⓗ
Well-furnished, comfortable, inn facing the village common, comprising a lounge bar, dining room and a snug. Popular with walkers, it is convenient for Whipsnade Zoo. A house beer is supplied by Vale Brewery. No eve meals Sun or Mon.
🏠 Q ❀ ◐ ♣ P

SUTTON
John O'Gaunt Inn
30 High Street
☎ (01767) 260377
12-3, 7-11; 12-3, 7-10.30 Sun
Greene King IPA, Abbot; guest beer Ⓗ
Thirteen consecutive years in this *Guide*, this characterful village pub dates back to the 18th-century; note the village quilt in the lounge bar. Various teams play here; live folk music last Sat of the month. No meals Sun eve.
🏠 Q ❀ ◐ 🍴 ♣ P

Try also: **Chequers**, Wrestlingworth (Greene King)

TEBWORTH
Queens Head
The Lane
☎ (01525) 874101
11-3, (3.30 Sat), 6 (7 Sat)-11; 12-3, 10.30 Sun
Adnams Broadside; Ⓖ Wells Eagle; Ⓗ guest beer Ⓖ
Welcoming village local with two small bars offering good value food (not served Sun).

Choosing Pubs
Pubs in the Good Beer Guide are chosen by CAMRA members and branches. There is no payment for entry, and pubs are inspected on a regular basis by personal visits, not sent a questionnaire once a year, as is the case with some pub guides. CAMRA branches monitor all the pubs in their areas, and the choice of pubs for the Guide is often the result of voting at branch meetings. However, recommendations from readers are warmly welcomed and will be passed on to the relevant CAMRA branch: please use the form at the back of the Guide.

Quiz night Thu; live music Fri.
🏠 ◐ 🍴 ♣ P

Try also: **Plough**, Tebworth Rd, Wingfield (Fuller's)

TILSWORTH
Anchor
1 Dunstable Road
☎ (01525) 210289
11-11; 12-10.30 Sun
Greene King IPA; guest beers Ⓗ
Lively, welcoming, village local; the L-shaped bar has games at one end. Families welcome at all times; the large garden has children's play equipment.
🏠 ❀ ◐ ♿ ♣ P ⊞

TODDINGTON
Oddfellows Arms
2 Conger Lane
☎ (01525) 872021
12-3 (not Wed), 5.30-11; 12-10.30 Sun
Draught Bass; Caledonian Deuchars IPA; Courage Best Bitter, Directors; guest beer Ⓗ
Attractive 15th-century pub on the village green. One of the two bars has a small gallery area. A range of Belgian beers is available, also good value food (not Sun eve). A sheltered patio allows for *al fresco* summer drinking.
🏠 ❀ ◐ ♣ ⊞

Sow & Pigs
19 Church Square
☎ (01525) 873089
11-11; 12-10.30 Sun
Greene King IPA, Abbot, seasonal beers Ⓗ
19th-century commercial inn with one long, narrow bar, extensively redecorated after a fire in 1999. New facilities include B&B and a function room. Rolls are made to order. In every edition of this *Guide*.
🏠 Q ❀ 🍴 ♣ P ⊞

TURVEY
Three Cranes

High Street (off A428)
☎ (01234) 881305
11-2.30, 6-11; 12-3, 7-10.30 Sun
Adnams Best Bitter; Courage Best Bitter, Directors; Fuller's London Pride; Hook Norton Best Bitter Ⓗ
17th-century coaching inn serving an excellent range of food in both the bar and restaurant; vegetarian choice available.
🏠 Q ❀ 🍴 ◐ P

WILDEN
Victoria Arms
23 High Street
☎ (01234) 772146
11-2.30, 6.30-11; 12-11 Sun; 12-3.30, 7-11 Sun
Greene King XX Mild, IPA, Abbot Ⓗ
Lively village pub with a single bar and a restaurant, serving good, home-cooked food with weekday specials (no food Sun eve).
🏠 ❀ ◐ ♿ ♣ P

YIELDEN
Chequers
High Street
☎ (01933) 356383
12-2.30 (not Mon), 5.30-11; 12-11 Sat; 12-10.30 Sun
Fuller's London Pride; Greene King Abbot; Thwaites Best Bitter; guest beers Ⓗ
Village pub with a family skittles room and restaurant plus a large garden with children's play equipment. Good value bar food is available (meals served Wed-Sun). The village is on the Three Shires Way walkers' route and boasts impressive earthworks of a Norman castle.
🏠 🛏 ❀ ◐ ♣ ⌂ P

INDEPENDENT BREWERIES

B&T: Shefford

Potton: Potton

Wells: Bedford

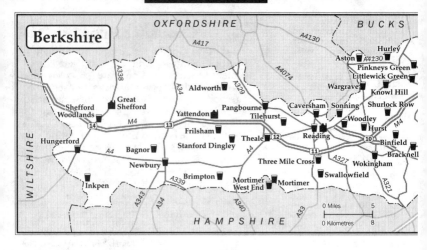

ALDWORTH

Bell Inn ☆
OS556797
☎ (01635) 578272
11-3, 6-11 (closed Mon); 12-3, 7-10.30
Sun

Arkell's 3B, Kingsdown; Crouch Vale Best Bitter; West Berkshire Old Tyler, Magg's Magnificent Mild Ⓗ
Unspoilt village gem, run by the same family for over 200 years. An ideal stop for walkers on the nearby Ridgeway Path, it has two bars and a large garden next to the cricket ground.
🏚Q🍴🕮◑▶♣P

ASCOT

Duke of Edinburgh
Woodside Road, Woodside
(200 yds W of A332)
OS927708
☎ (01344) 882736
11-3, 5-11; 12-10.30 Sun

Arkell's 2B, 3B, Kingsdown Ⓗ
Comfortable pub set out in semi-open style, a rare outlet for Arkell's in this area. It also has a restaurant (closed Sun eve). Handy for the racecourse. 🏚◑▶♣P

ASTON

Flower Pot
Ferry Lane (off A4130, 1 mile from Henley)
☎ (01491) 574721
11-3, 6-11; 12-3, 7-10.30 Sun

Brakspear Mild, Bitter, Old, Special Ⓗ
Delightful little hotel in a rural setting with its own jetty on the Thames. The characterful public bar is complemented by a comfortable restaurant extension. Note the large collection of stuffed fish. Free range chickens roam outside.
🏚Q🍴🚲◑▶⊟P⊟

BAGNOR

Blackbird
☎ (01635) 40638
11.30-3, 6-11; 12-3, 7-10.30 Sun

Brakspear Bitter; Butts Barbus Barbus; Ushers Best Bitter Ⓗ
Picturesque village pub at the confluence of the Winterbourne and Lambourn rivers. The long single bar with partitioned restaurant offers a good choice of beers and wines and a sophisticated menu. The famous Watermill Theatre stands nearby.
🏚Q🕮◑▶🍽P

BINFIELD

Victoria Arms
Terrace Road North (B3018)
☎ (01344) 483856
11.30-3, 6 (6.30 Sat)-11; 12-10.30 Sun

Fuller's Chiswick, London Pride, ESB, seasonal beers Ⓗ
Lively village pub popular with all, displaying an extensive bottle collection in the rafters. No food Sun eves. The large garden hosts occasional barbecues.
🏚🕮◑▶♣P

BRACKNELL

Old Manor
High Street
☎ (01344) 304490
11-11; 12-10.30 Sun

Boddingtons Bitter; Courage Directors; Theakston Best Bitter; guest beer Ⓗ
Usual Wetherspoon's format, but this one is housed in a beautiful old manor house boasting nooks and crannies galore; look out for priest holes in the Monk's Room. Children welcome in the no-smoking area if eating.
Q🕮◑▶🚲♿🚭⊟P⊬

BRIMPTON

Three Horseshoes
Brimpton Lane (1½ miles off A4, E of Thatcham)
OS559648
☎ (0118) 971 2183
11-2.30 (3 Sat), 6-11; 12-3, 7-10.30
Sun

Adnams Bitter or Wadworth 6X; Fuller's London Pride, ESB, seasonal beers Ⓗ
Cosy, two-bar, traditional village pub: a large public bar with darts, pool and TV – and a smaller, quiet, wood-panelled lounge bar. Lunches served Mon-Sat.
Q🕮◑▶♣P

CAVERSHAM

Prince of Wales
76 Prospect Street
☎ (0118) 947 2267
11-3, 6-11; 11-11 Sat; 12-10.30 Sun

Brakspear Bitter, Special, seasonal beers; Coniston Bluebird Ⓗ
Lively, one-bar pub with a pool table hosting occasional live music. Children welcome for Sun lunch.
◑♣P

Try also: Baron Cadogan,
Prospect St (Wetherspoons);
Clifton Arms, Gosbrook Rd
(Brakspear)

COLNBROOK

Olde George
146 High Street
☎ (01753) 682010
11-3, 5-11; 12-3, 7-11 Sat; 12-3, 7-
10.30 Sun

Courage Best Bitter; Ushers Best Bitter, Founders Ⓗ
Historic coaching inn that retains much of its traditional charm, enhanced by original Tudor beams. Before becoming Queen, Elizabeth I once stayed here

whilst a prisoner of her half
sister Queen Mary.
Q 🍽 ⛺ ◖❚ P

Ostrich
High Street
☎ (01753) 682628
11-3, 5.30-11; 12-10.30 Sun
**Courage Best Bitter, Directors;
Fuller's London Pride** H
One of England's oldest inns,
dating in part back to 1106.
In a grisly past, hotel guests
were murdered and
dispatched by trapdoor from
their beds to a boiling
cauldron. Nowadays the
extensive menu includes
ostrich instead of customers.
🏨 Q 🛏 🍽 ◖❚ P

Try also: Red Lion, High St
(Ushers)

COOKHAM
Old Swan Uppers
The Pound (B4447, N of
Maidenhead)
☎ (01628) 521324
11-11; 12-10.30 Sun
Greene King IPA, Abbot H
150-year-old village pub with
a beamed ceiling and
flagstone floor. The
restaurant offers an *à la carte*
menu (no food Sun eve).
🍽 🛏 ◖❚ ⇌ P

DATCHET
Royal Stag
The Green
☎ (01753) 548218
11-11; 12-10.30 Sun
**Ind Coope Burton Ale; Marston's
Pedigree; Tetley Bitter; guest
beer** H
Traditional, 16th-century
local, popular with darts
players. The main bar retains
many original features – look
out for the ghostly child's
handprint on the window

overlooking the churchyard.
🏨 ◖❚ ⛺ ⇌ ♣ P

ETON
New College
55 High Street
☎ (01753) 865516
12-11; 12-10.30 Sun
**Badger IPA, Dorset Best,
Tanglefoot** H
Much improved since Badger
took it over in 1998, the
single bar is split up by
wooden partitions. Children
welcome until early eve.
🍽 ◖❚ ⇌ (Windsor & Eton
Riverside) ⌐

Watermans Arms
Brocas Street
☎ (01753) 861001
11-2.30, 6-11 (may vary); 12-3, 7-
10.30 Sun
**Brakspear Bitter; Courage Best
Bitter, Directors; John Smith's
Bitter; guest beers** H
500-year-old local between
the High Street and
the Thames; boating
memorablia abounds. An
extensive menu is served
both in the bar and
restaurant (no meals Sun
eve). Parking difficult.
🏨 🍽 ◖❚ ⇌ (Windsor & Eton
Riverside) ♣ ⌐

FRILSHAM
Pot Kiln ☆
On Yattendon-Bucklebury
road (ignore signs to
Frilsham) OS553732
☎ (01635) 201366
12-2.30 (not Tue), 6.30-11; 12-3, 7-
10.30 Sun
**Arkell's 3B; Morland Original, Old
Speckled Hen; West Berkshire
Goldstar** H
This 200-year-old country
pub with its excellent small
bars is a welcome stop for
locals, walkers and ale-lovers.
West Berkshire Brick Kiln is
brewed exclusively for the
pub.
🏨 Q 🛏 🍽 ◖❚ ⛺ ♣ P ⌐

HUNGERFORD
Hungerford Club
3 The Croft (off Church St)
☎ (01488) 682357
12-3 (not Mon-Fri), 7-11; 12-3, 7-10.30
Sun
**Greene King IPA; Morland Original;
guest beers** H
CAMRA National *Club of the
Year* runner-up 1999, a
bowls, tennis and social
club in a delightfully
secluded but central part of
town. One or two guest beers
are chosen freely from
independents. Show this
Guide or CAMRA
membership to be signed in.
🍽 ⇌ ♣ P

HURLEY
Dew Drop Inn
Honey Lane, Batts Green (off
A423 near Grasslands
Research Inst.) OS824815
☎ (01628) 824327
12-3, 6-11; 12-3, 7-10.30 Sun
**Brakspear Bitter, Special, seasonal
beers** H
300-year-old cottagey pub in
Ashley Woods, popular with
walkers and horse riders,
offering a good choice of
home-cooked food. This
hidden gem is well worth
finding.
🏨 Q 🍽 ◖❚ ♿ P ⌐

HURST
Green Man
Hinton Road (off A321,
Twyford-Wokingham road)
☎ (0118) 934 2599
11.30-2.30, 6-11; 12-3, 7-10.30
(longer in summer) Sun
**Brakspear Bitter, Special, seasonal
beers** H
The pub's child-friendly
garden boasts wonderful
hanging basket displays,
while the interior features
oak beams. The food is great,
but there's space for drinkers
too; food specials change
regularly.
🏨 Q 🍽 ◖❚ ♿ P ⌐

INKPEN
Crown & Garter
Great Common (follow signs
from A4 to Kintbury and
Inkpen Common) OS378638
☎ (01488) 668325
12-3.30 (not Mon & Tue); 6.30-11; 12-
3.30, 7-10.30 Sun
**Archers Village, West Berkshire
Good Old Boy; guest beers**
(seasonal) H
Thriving rural pub in
beautiful walking country,
now with B&B
accommodation. A wide
choice of interesting home-
cooked food, local ales and a
pleasant garden with a
climbing frame for children
complete the attractions.
🏨 Q 🍽 🛏 ◖❚ ♿ ♣ P

Swan Inn
Lower Green (from
Hungerford take Inkpen road
across common) OS359643
☎ (01488) 668326
12 (11 Sat)-3, 7-11; 12-3, 7-10.30 Sun
**Butts Bitter; Hook Norton Mild,
Bitter; guest beers** H
Large, 16th-century inn near
the famous Combe Gibbet
and Wayfarers' Walk.
Recently extended by new
owners, the premises now
include a games room, an
organic farm shop, an oak-
beamed restaurant and

accommodation. The mild and local cider are now permanent fixtures.

🏾 ⊛ 🛏 🕽 & ♣ ⌂ P ✗

KNOWL HILL

Old Devil Inn
Bath Road (W end of village, on S side of A4)
☎ (01628) 822764
11-11; 12-10.30 Sun
Badger Dorset Best, Tanglefoot, Golden Champion Ale ⊞
Long-established roadside inn comprising several distinct areas; a rare local outlet for Badger beers. The patio and garden (with play area for children) give a pleasantly rural outlook.
⊛ 🛏 🕽 P ✗

LANGLEY

Red Lion
St Marys Road
☎ (01753) 582235
11-11; 12-10.30 Sun
Courage Best Bitter; Greene King IPA, Abbot; Ruddles County; guest beer ⊞
Centuries-old pub, near Langley church, that once doubled as a mortuary. A community local, its busy lunchtime food trade makes table reservation advisable on weekdays. Accompanied children are welcome in the restaurant area where seafood is a speciality.
⊛ 🕽 P ✗

LITTLEWICK GREEN

Cricketers
Coronation Road
☎ (01628) 822888
11-11; 12-10.30 Sun
Brakspear Bitter; Fuller's London Pride; guest beers ⊞
Overlooking the green and cricket ground the pub features a predictable decorative theme. Note the factory clock in the main bar. Good value food.
🏾 ⊛ 🛏 🕽 ♣ P

MAIDENHEAD

Hand & Flowers
15 Queen Street
☎ (01628) 623800
11.30-11; 6-10.30 Sun
Brakspear Bitter, Special, seasonal beers ⊞
Since its last *Guide* entry (1998) this small town-centre pub has had a refurbishment that has happily retained its style and atmosphere (to which the landlady's parrot contributes).
🕽 ⇌

Vine
20 Market Place

☎ (01628) 782112
11-11; 12-10.30 Sun
Brakspear Bitter, Special, seasonal beers ⊞
Small, popular, town-centre local, notable for its historic exterior.
⊛ 🕽 ▶ ⇌

MORTIMER

Fox & Horn
The Street, Stratfield
☎ (0118) 933 2428
11-2.30, 5.30-11; 12-3, 7-10.30 Sun
Fuller's London Pride; Hook Norton Best Bitter; King & Barnes Sussex; Wadworth 6X; guest beers ⊞
The new owner has recreated the ambience of a country hotel where you will feel comfortably at home. The restaurant is no-smoking, but the menu is available in the bar for weed-lovers.
🏾 Q ⊛ 🛏 🕽 ⇌ P

MORTIMER WEST END

Turners Arms
West End Road
☎ (0118) 933 2961
11.30-2.30, 5-11; 11.30-3, 6-11 Sat; 12-3, 7-10.30 Sun
Brakspear Bitter, Special, seasonal beers ⊞
L-shaped pub and restaurant, offering a changing menu of interesting bar snacks, and regular speciality food eves.
🏾 Q ⊛ 🕽 ♣ P

NEWBURY

Lion
West Street (off Northbrook St)
☎ (01635) 528468
12-3, 5-11; 12-11 Sat; 12-10.30 Sun
Badger Tanglefoot; Wadworth IPA, 6X; guest beers ⊞
Town-centre pub off the main shopping street: a single drinking area surrounds an island bar; over 18s only. Eve meals finish early.
⊛ 🕽 & ⇌

Monument (Tap & Spile)
57 Northbrook Street (near clock tower)
☎ (01635) 41964
11-11; 12-10.30 Sun
Butts Butts, Barbus Barbus; Gale's HSB; Tap & Spile Premium; Theakston Old Peculier; guest beers ⊞
Lively town boozer, often noisily busy, this 16th-century building has a bar split into three cubicles – two with TV and one with table football. Live blues/folk Wed eve; the games night Tue eve includes everything from Backgammon to Game Boy.
⊛ 🕽 ⇌ ♣ ♣ ⌂

Try also: Lock, Stock & Barrel, Northbrook St (Fuller's); **Old London Apprentice**, Hambridge Rd (Inntrepreneur)

PANGBOURNE

Copper Inn
Church Road (A340)
☎ (0118) 984 2244
11-3, 5-11; 11-11 (Fri & Sat); 12-10.30 Sun
Brakspear Bitter; Morland Original; ⊞ **West Berkshire Mr Chubb's** ⊞/G
Up-market hotel lounge bar near the old church at the centre of this Thames-side village. The restaurant is high class.
🏾 Q ⊛ 🛏 🕽 ⇌ P ⊟

PINKNEYS GREEN

Stag & Hounds
1 Lee Lane (1/2 mile along Pinkneys Drive from A308 jct)
☎ (01628) 630268
12-3, 5-11; 12-3, 7-10.30 Sun
Arkell's 3B; Brakspear Bitter; Fuller's London Pride; Theakston Old Peculier; guest beers ⊞
Attractive little pub set in rural surroundings with a large garden but limited parking. It offers an extensive menu (no food Sun eve). The function room houses a skittle alley.
⊛ 🕽 ♣ P

READING

Butler
89-91 Chatham Street (W of inner ring road)
☎ (0118) 939 1635
11-11; 12-3, 7-10.30 Sun
Fuller's Chiswick, London Pride, ESB, seasonal beers ⊞
Well-established pub close to the town centre, drawing a strong local following. Named after the wine merchants who formerly occupied the premises, Guinness was once bottled on the site.
🏾 ⊛ 🕽 P

Dove
119 Orts Road
☎ (0118) 935 2556
12-2.30 (3 Sat), 6-11; 12-4, 7-10.30 Sun
Brakspear Bitter, Special ⊞
Bustling, active, community pub; it hosts regular live music (jazz, blues, folk, etc) and plenty of other events. Weekday lunches served.
⊛ 🕽 ♣ P

Hobgoblin
2 Broad Street
☎ (0118) 950 8119
11-11; 12-10.30 Sun

Wychwood Special, Hobgoblin, **seasonal beers; guest beers** Ⓗ
Friendly, no-frills town-centre local where the accent is firmly on excellent beer: three Wychwood ales are supplemented by five ever-changing guest beers, frequently including a mild or porter, plus Inch's Stonehouse cider.
≈ ⌂

Hop Leaf
163-165 Southampton Street (A33, one-way system towards the centre)
☎ (0118) 931 4700
4 (12 Fri & Sat)-11; 12-2, 4-11 Wed & Thu; 12-10.30 Sun
Hop Back GFB, Best Bitter, Summer Lightning, seasonal beers Ⓗ
Excellent local, voted Reading CAMRA *Pub of the Year* 1999. Recently refurbished, it includes a small brewing plant, producing Reading Lion beers for the pub.
🌫 ♣ ⌿

Retreat
8 St. John's Street (off Queens Rd)
☎ (0118) 957 1593
11-11; 12-10.30 Sun
Brakspear Bitter; guest beers Ⓗ
Reading's last remaining terraced pub with a small front bar, plus a larger rear bar where pool and darts are played. Folk music is performed most Thu eves. Up to three guest beers on tap, mainly from independent breweries.
♣

SHEFFORD WOODLANDS
Pheasant Inn
Baydon Road (B4000, 1/2 mile N of M4 jct 14)
☎ (01488) 648284
11-3, 5.15-11; 12-3, 7-10.30 Sun
Brakspear Bitter; Butts Barbus Barbus; Fuller's London Pride; Wadworth 6X; guest beer Ⓗ
Small, friendly two-bar inn, once known as 'the Boarden House' from its wood cladding; before that 'the Paraffin House' when it doubled as a local store. Popular with rugby fans travelling between Twickenham and Wales or the West Country.
🏨 Q 🌸 ◑ ▶ ⌻ ♣ P

SHURLOCK ROW
White Hart
The Street (100 yds from B3018)
☎ (0118) 934 3301
12-2.30, 7-11; 12-3, 7-10.30 Sun
Brakspear bitter; guest beers Ⓗ

Traditional pub run by the same licensees for 25 years; a friendly, welcoming atmosphere in comfortable surroundings. A large real fire separates two distinct drinking areas. The garden, away from the road, has children's play equipment.
🏨 🌸 ◑ ▶ P

SLOUGH
Moon & Spoon
86 High Street (opp. library)
☎ (01753) 531650
10.30-11; 12-10.30 Sun
Boddingtons Bitter; Courage Directors; Shepherd Neame Spitfire; Theakston Best Bitter; guest beer Ⓗ
Large Wetherspoon's pub dating from 1995 attracting a good mix of clientele, often very crowded weekend eves.
Q ◑ ▶ ♿ ≈ ⌂ ⌿ ⊞

Rose & Crown
312 High Street (E end)
☎ (01753) 521114
11-11; 12-10.30 Sun
Beer range varies Ⓗ
Superb two-bar local, built circa 1690, but first licensed in 1820. Three handpumps serve constantly changing guest ales. Sun lunch served.
🌸 ▶ ≈

Wheatsheaf
15 Albert Street
☎ (01753) 522019
11-11; 12-10.30 Sun
Fuller's Chiswick, London Pride, ESB, seasonal beers Ⓗ
Single bar pub away from the town centre. The covered garden is heated in winter. Note the red phone box in the bar. Pies cooked with beer are a speciality. 🌸 ◑

Try also: **Queen of England**, Park St (Free)

SONNING
Bull
High Street (off B478, opp. church)
☎ (0118) 969 3901
11-3, 5.30-11 (11-11 summer Sat); 12-2.30, 7-10.30 Sun
Gales Butser, GB, HSB Ⓗ
Outstanding inn of considerable historic merit, parts of which date from the 14th century. Many tables are laid for diners to enjoy the high quality, imaginative menu, but the locals' bar is a haven for the drinker. Beware the low beams. Excellent, but pricey accommodation.
🏨 Q 🌸 🛏 ◑ ▶ ⌻ P ⊞

STANFORD DINGLEY
Bull

200 yds S of church OS576716
☎ (0118) 974 4409
12-3 (not Mon) 7-11; 12-3, 7-10.30 Sun
Brakspear Bitter; West Berkshire Skiff; Good Old Boy, Goldstar Ⓗ
Local CAMRA *Pub of the Year*, this 14th-century rural gem offers two bars, a superb menu and beers from the local brewery. Ring the Bull is played at quieter periods. Children welcome in the saloon until 8.30 (not Sat).
🏨 Q 🌸 ◑ ▶ ♣ P

Try also: **Old Boot** (free)

SUNNINGHILL
Dukes Head
Upper Village Road (near B3020)
☎ (01344) 626949
11-11; 12-10.30 Sun
Greene King IPA, Abbot, seasonal beers; guest beers Ⓗ
Friendly pub in a village back street, offering Thai food Mon-Sat eves and an English menu Sun eve. Children allowed in the no-smoking area. Prices match the area.
🌸 ◑ ▶ P ⌿

SWALLOWFIELD
Crown
The Street
☎ (01118) 988 3260
11-3, 6-11, 12-3, 7-10.30 Sun
Greene King Abbot; Morland Original; Ruddles Best Bitter Ⓗ
The village local: two bars, lots of chat and a good atmosphere. It hosts occasional live music.
🏨 🌸 ◑ ▶ 🛏 ♣ P

THEALE
Falcon
31 High Street (old A4, near M4 jct 12)
☎ (0118) 930 2523
10.30-11; 12-10.30 Sun
Archers Best Bitter; Courage Best Bitter; guest beers Ⓗ
Historic, 16th-century coaching inn where access to the car park is through two arches.
🏨 Q 🌸 ◑ 🛏 ≈ ♣ P

Fox & Hounds
Station Road, Sunnyside (past station, over canal)
☎ (0118) 930 2295
11-3; 5 (6 Sat)-11; 12-4, 7-10.30 Sun
Adnams Bitter; Badger Tanglefoot; Draught Bass; Wadworth IPA, 6X, seasonal beers; guest beers Ⓗ
Large country pub near the Kennet and Avon Canal, that attracts a good mix of customers. Popular for good value food and the beer range (usually eight ales). Live jazz

on Tue; other music nights on occasion. Families welcome.

🏚 ⛺ ⊛ ◖ ▶ ⓰ ⇌ ♣ P

Lamb

22 Church Street (old A4, near M4 jct 12)
☎ (0118) 930 2216
12-3, 6-11; 12-3, 7-10.30 Sun
Beer range varies Ⓗ
Enjoying a relaxing atmosphere during the day, the Lamb livens up at night, featuring regular live bands. Meals served Mon-Sat.

🏚 Q ⛺ ⊛ ◖ ▶ ⓰ ⇌ ♣ P

THREE-MILE CROSS

Swan

Basingstoke Road (old A33, S of M4 jct 11)
☎ (0118) 988 3674
11-11; 12-3, 7-11 Sat; 12-3, 7-10.30 Sun
Brakspear Bitter; Courage Best Bitter; Fuller's London Pride; Gale's HSB; Wadworth IPA, 6X Ⓗ
Old oak-beamed building at the centre of this bypassed village. Two bars, one is used as a restaurant at times, the other has an inglenook and a room for families. Well known for home-made food, try the steak and kidney pie or fresh cod.

🏚 Q ⛺ ⊛ ◖ ▶ P

TILEHURST

Butchers Arms

9 Lower Armour Road
☎ (0118) 942 4313
11-3, 6-11; 12-3, 7-10.30 Sun
Archers Best Bitter; Flowers IPA Ⓗ
Surrounded by houses, but off the beaten track, this two-bar pub thrives due to its friendly welcome and no-frills approach.

⊛ ⓰ ♣ P

Fox & Hounds

116 City Road (off School Rd)
☎ (0118) 942 2982
11.30-3.30, 5.30-11; 11-11 Fri & Sat; 12-10.30 Sun
Courage Best Bitter; guest beers Ⓗ
Cottage-style pub, lost in suburbia, but with a loyal local following. Worth seeking out for its two imaginative guest beers. TV for sport. No meals Sat eve or Sun; eve meals served 5.30-7.

◖ ▶ ♣ P

WARGRAVE

Bull

High Street (A321)
☎ (0118) 940 3120
11-3, 6-11; 12-4, 7-10.30 Sun
Brakspear Bitter, Special, seasonal beers Ⓗ
Fine, unspoilt 15th-century coaching inn; rambling, cosy and very well run. Diners

---

enjoying the extensive, high quality food menu can sometimes dominate the pub but a small central area is reserved for drinkers.

🏚 Q ⊛ ⛺ ◖ ▶ ⇌

WINDSOR

Queen

382 Dedworth Road (B3024)
☎ (01753) 675248
11-3, 5-11; 11-11 Fri & Sat; 12-10.30 Sun
Morlands Original; Ruddles Best Bitter; guest beer Ⓗ
Comfortable, single bar pub in Windsor's western suburbs. It hosts occasional quizzes and 'easy listening' live music.

⛺ ◖ ▶ ♣ P ✂ ⊞

Swan

9 Mill Lane, Clewer Village (off A308, near A332 jct)
☎ (01753) 862069
12-2 (not Mon-Fri), 6-11; 12-3, 7-10.30 Sun
Flowers IPA, Original; Fuller's London Pride Ⓗ
Small, 16th-century pub near the racecourse. The function room once served as a court house and the kitchen as a mortuary. Good spirit trade!

⊛ ⛺ ♣ P

Vansittart Arms

105 Vansittart Road
☎ (01753) 865988
11-11; 12-10.30 Sun
Fuller's London Pride, ESB, seasonal beers Ⓗ
Back-street pub, popular with both diners and drinkers, so often crowded. A chip-free zone. No meals Sun eve.

🏚 ⊛ ◖ ▶ P

Try also: Criterion, Peasecod St (Free); **Mitre**, Oxford Rd (Free)

WOKINGHAM

Broad Street Tavern

29 Broad Street
☎ (0118) 977 3706
11-11, 12-10.30 Sun
Wadworth IPA, 6X; seasonal beers Ⓗ
Former wine-bar that looks as if it has been a pub for many years. As well as selling the

---

full range of Wadworth beers, it holds occasional beer festivals. Large garden.

⊛ ◖ ⇌ ✂

Crooked Billet

Honey Hill (1½ miles SE of town, 1 mile N of B3430)
OS826667
☎ (0118) 978 0438
11-11; 12-10.30 Sun
Brakspear Bitter, Special, seasonal beers Ⓗ
Worth finding, this attractive building boasts an unspoilt bar, a snug area and a small restaurant.

🏚 Q ⊛ ◖ ▶ ⓰ ♣ P

Duke's Head

56 Denmark Street (A321, 500 yds from station)
☎ (0118) 978 0316
11.30-3, 5.30 (5 Fri, 6 Sat)-11; 12-3, 7-10.30 Sun
Brakspear Bitter, Special, seasonal beers Ⓗ
Plush town pub of three distinct drinking areas; one displays a portrait of Churchill. Weekday lunches served, when a no-smoking area is available.

Q ⊛ ◖ ⇌ P ✂

Hope & Anchor

Station Road
☎ (0118) 978 0918
11-2.30, 5-11; 11-11 Fri & Sat; 12-10.30 Sun
Brakspear Bitter, Special, seasonal beers Ⓗ
This pub has had a chequered history but is now back on track as part of David Bruce's stable with Brakspear's Honeypot Inns.

⛺ ⊛ ◖ ⇌ ♣

Try also: Red Lion, Market Place (Brakspear); **Ship**, Peach St (Fuller's)

WOODLEY

Inn on the Park

Woodford Park, Haddon Drive
☎ (0118) 962 8655
11-3, 6-11; 11-11 Fri & Sat; 12-10.30 Sun
Brakspear Bitter, Special, guest beers Ⓗ
Owned by Woodley town council, as part of its sports centre, its outside patio is next to the paddling pool, bowling and putting green. Ideal for families.

⊛ ⓰ ♣ P

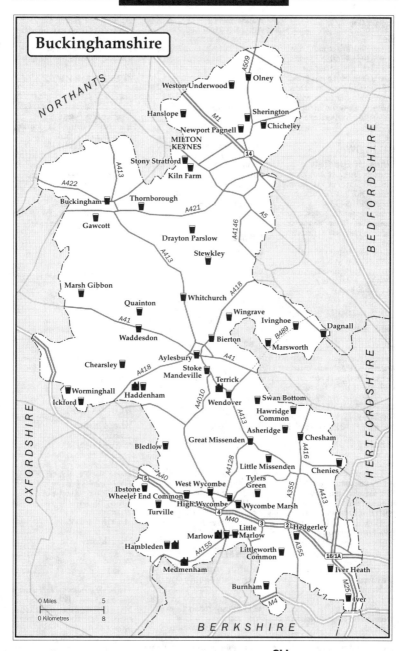

Buckinghamshire

(map showing towns and locations including Olney, Weston Underwood, Hanslope, Sherington, Chicheley, Newport Pagnell, MILTON KEYNES, Stony Stratford, Kiln Farm, Buckingham, Thornborough, Gawcott, Drayton Parslow, Stewkley, Marsh Gibbon, Quainton, Waddesdon, Whitchurch, Wingrave, Ivinghoe, Dagnall, Bierton, Marsworth, Chearsley, Aylesbury, Stoke Mandeville, Terrick, Swan Bottom, Worminghall, Haddenham, Wendover, Hawridge Common, Ickford, Asheridge, Chesham, Bledlow, Great Missenden, Little Missenden, Chenies, Ibstone, West Wycombe, Tylers Green, Wheeler End Common, High Wycombe, Wycombe Marsh, Turville, Little Marlow, Hedgerley, Marlow, Hambleden, Littleworth Common, Medmenham, Iver Heath, Burnham, Iver)

NORTHANTS · BEDFORDSHIRE · HERTFORDSHIRE · OXFORDSHIRE · BERKSHIRE

0 Miles 5
0 Kilometres 8

ASHERIDGE

Blue Ball
1½ miles NW of Chesham
☎ (01494) 758263
12-2.30, 5.30-11; 12-11 Fri & Sat; 12-10.30 Sun
Beer range varies H
Set in beautiful countryside, this family-run pub is a true free house with four beers on tap. No food Sun eve.
🛏 ❀ ◖ ▶ ⚲ P

AYLESBURY

Queen's Head
1 Temple Square
☎ (01296) 415484
11.30-3, 5.30-11; 11.30-11 Fri; 11.30-5, 7-11 Sat; 12-5, 7-10.30 Sun
Adnams Bitter; Courage Directors; Greene King IPA; guest beer H
17th-century village pub at the heart of Aylesbury: two bars plus a new dining area.
🛏 ❀ ⌂ ◖ ⇌

Ship
59 Walton Street
☎ (01296) 421888
11.30-2.30, 5.30-11; 11.30-11 Fri & Sat; 12-3. 7-10.30 Sun
Greene King Abbot; Marston's Pedigree; guest beer H
Warm, friendly, family-run pub by a canal basin on the Grand Union Canal, with an outdoor drinking area.
❀ ◖ ⅊ ⇌ ♣ P

Try also: Hogshead, off Market Sq (Whitbread)

43

BIERTON

Bell

191 Aylesbury Road
☎ (01296) 436055
11-3, 6-11; 12-3, 7-10.30 Sun
Fuller's Chiswick, London Pride, ESB, seasonal beers; guest beer Ⓗ
Small, two-bar local with a thriving food trade. Opens all day in the football season.
✿ ◖▶ ♣ P

BLEDLOW

Lions of Bledlow

Church End (off B4009, Chinnor-Princes Risborough Road) OS776020
☎ (01844) 343345
11.30-3, 6-11; 12-3, 7-10.30 Sun
Courage Best Bitter; Marston's Pedigree; Wadworth 6X; guest beer Ⓗ
Rambling, unspoilt 16th-century pub in a picturesque setting. The guest beer is always a local brew.
⚌ Q ✿ ◖▶ ♣ P

BUCKINGHAM

New Inn

18 Bridge Street
☎ (01280) 815713
10-11; 12-3, 7-10.30 Sun
Greene King IPA, Abbot, Morland Old Speckled Hen; guest beer Ⓗ
Old-style public house where meals are usualy available all day – Sri Lankan cuisine is a speciality. Live jazz Fri and Wed eves. ⚌ ⛵ ✿ ◖▶ ♣ ⌀

Whale

14 Market Hill
☎ (01280) 815537
11-11; 12-10.30 Sun
Fuller's Chiswick, London Pride, ESB, seasonal beers Ⓗ
Traditional, town-centre pub with a split-level bar and original gas lights; a friendly, welcoming place. No food Sun eve. ⚌ ✿ ⇔ ◖▶ ♣ P⊞

BURNHAM

George

20 High Street
☎ (01628) 605047
11-11; 12-10.30 Sun
Courage Best Bitter, Directors; Vale Notley Ale Ⓗ
One-bar pub run by a long-established publican. Directors is known here as Alice. ⚌ ✿ ♣ P

Try also: Bee, High St (Brakspear)

CHEARSLEY

Bell

The Green
☎ (01844) 208077
12-2.30 (not Mon), 6-11; 12-3, 7-10.30 Sun
Fuller's Chiswick, London Pride,

seasonal beers Ⓗ
Attractive thatched, one-bar local by the village green serving an excellent range of food (eve meals Tue-Sat).
⚌ Q ✿ ◖ Ⓐ P⊞

CHENIES

Red Lion

Off A404
☎ (01923) 282722
11-2, 5.30-11; 12-3, 7-10.30 Sun
Benskins BB; Vale Notley Ale; Wadworth 6X Ⓗ
Popular free house in small village, with a tiny snug bar. A thoughtful choice of food is provided. Lion Pride is brewed by Rebellion.
Q ✿ ◖▶ P

CHESHAM

Queen's Head

116 Church Street, Old Chesham ☎ (01494) 783773
11-2.30 (3 Sat), 5-11; 12-3, 7-10.30 Sun
Brakspear Bitter, Special; Fuller's London Pride; guest beer Ⓗ
Traditional old town pub with two bars. Thai food is served Mon-Sat.
⚌ Q ✿ ◖▶ ⊡ ⊖ ♣ P

Try also: Last Post, Broadway (Wetherspoon's)

CHICHELEY

Chester Arms

Bedford Road (2 miles NE of Newport Pagnell)
☎ (01234) 391214
11-3, 6 (7 Sat)-11; 12-3, 7-10.30 Sun
Greene King IPA, Abbot Ⓗ
Old, whitewashed roadside pub, with a pleasant interior: divided drinking areas with a split-level room. Good value home-made food served, except Sun eve.
⚌ Q ✿ ◖▶ ♣ P⌀

DAGNALL

Golden Rule

Main Road, South Dagnall (A4146) ☎ (01442) 843227
11.30-3, 5.30-11; 12-3, 7-10.30 Sun
Adnams Bitter; Fuller's London Pride, ESB; guest beer Ⓗ
Cosy roadside free house, close to Whipsnade Zoo and Dunstable Downs. Excellent food and seven real ales always available.
✿ ◖▶ ♣ P

DRAYTON PARSLOW

Three Horseshoes

10 Main Road (3 miles SW of Bletchley)
☎ (01296) 720296
11-11; 12-3, 7-10.30 Sun
Courage Best Bitter; Everards Tiger; Fuller's London Pride, ESB; John Smith's Bitter; guest beers Ⓗ

Popular old village pub, which has been extended without changing its character. No food Sun eve; always a good range of ales on tap.
⚌ ⛵ ✿ ◖▶ P ⌀

GAWCOTT

Cuckoo's Nest

Back Street (off A421, 1 mile W of Buckingham)
☎ (01280) 812092
11-2.30 (3 Sat), 6-11; 11-3, 7-10.30 Sun
Vale Notley Ale, seasonal beers, guest beers Ⓗ
Owned by Vale Brewery the pub has a friendly atmosphere enhanced by the real fire in the inglenook. Hoegaarden White Beer is available on draught.
⚌ Q ✿ ◖▶ ⊡ ♣ P

GREAT MISSENDEN

Cross Keys

40 High Street
☎ (01494) 865373
11-3, 5-11; 12-3, 10.30 Sun
Fuller's Chiswick, London Pride, ESB, seasonal beers Ⓗ
Congenial 400-year-old pub featuring original beams and high-backed settles, plus an Italian restaurant.
Q ✿ ◖▶ ⇌ P

HADDENHAM

Kings Head

52 High Street
☎ (01844) 291391
12-2.30, 5-11; 12-11 Fri & Sat; 12-3.30, 7-10.30 Sun
Greene King IPA, Ⓗ **Abbot;** Ⓖ **Fuller's London Pride** Ⓗ
Traditional village pub, dating back to the 16th century.
⚌ Q ✿ ◖▶ ⊡ ♣ P

Red Lion

2 Church End
☎ (01844) 291606
11.30-3, 5.30-11; 11-11 Sat; 12-10.30 Sun
Ansells Mild; Flowers IPA; Marston's Pedigree; Young's Bitter Ⓗ
Straightforward two-bar local overlooking the village green and duckpond.
⚌ Q ✿ ⇔ ◖▶ ♣ P

Rising Sun

9 Thame Road
☎ (01844) 291744
11-3, 5.30-11; 11-11 Fri & Sat; 12-10.30 Sun
Wells Eagle; guest beers Ⓗ
Small, friendly, one-bar village local. Real cider is sold in summer. No food Sun.
✿ ◖▶ ⇌ ♣ ⌂

HAMBLEDEN

Stag & Huntsman

1 mile N of A4155
☎ (01491) 571227
11-2.30 (3 Sat), 6-11; 12-3, 7-10.30 Sun
Brakspear Bitter; Wadworth 6X; guest beers Ⓗ
Unspoilt, three-bar pub in a picturesque brick and flint NT village. An extensive range of meals is available at all times (except winter Sun eve). ♨ ⊛ 🍴 ◖▶ 🖛 ♣ ᗡ

HANSLOPE
Globe
50 Hartwell Road, Long Street
☎ (01908) 510336
12-2.30 (not Tue, 3.30 Sat), 6-11; 12-3, 7-10.30 Sun
Banks's Bitter, seasonal beers; guest beers Ⓗ/Ⓟ
Local CAMRA *Pub of the Year* 1999 and winner of Banks's *Best Cellar* award, this classic country pub is friendly and community-minded. A games-room, public and lounge bars and excellent restaurant complete the amenities inside; the pleasant garden has a climbing frame. ♨Q ⊛ ◖▶ 🖛 ♣ P ᗡ

HAWRIDGE COMMON
Full Moon
Cholesbury Lane OS936069
☎ (01494) 758959
12-3, 5.30-11; 11-11 Sat; 12-4, 7-10.30 (12-10.30 summer) Sun
Draught Bass; Boddingtons Bitter; Fuller's London Pride; guest beers Ⓗ
Fine old country pub and restaurant in the heart of the Chilterns, popular with cyclists, walkers, diners and casual visitors. Three interesting guest beers are stocked. No meals Sun eve.
🐕 ⊛ ◖▶ ⅃ Å

HEDGERLEY
White Horse
Village Lane OS969874
☎ (01753) 643225
11-2.30, 5-11; 11-11 Sat; 12-10.30 Sun
Greene King IPA; guest beers Ⓖ
Local CAMRA *Pub of the Year* 2000; a free house in an idyllic village. The small stone-floored public bar and more spacious lounge, both boast real fires. Six ever-changing guest ales on tap.
♨Q ⊛ ◖▶ ♣ ᗡ

HIGH WYCOMBE
Rose & Crown
Desborough Road
☎ (01494) 527982
12-3, 5-11; 12-11 Fri & Sat; 12-10.30 Sun
Draught Bass; Courage Best Bitter; Greene King IPA; Smiles Best Bitter; Wells Bombardier Ⓗ

Wycombe's continuing mini-beer festival always includes a Rebellion beer. Busy with lunchtime office trade and with sports fans eves. No food weekends. ♨ ◖ ☭ ♣

Wycombe Wines
20 Crendon Street (near station) ☎ (01494) 437228
10-10; 12-2, 7-10. Sun
Adnams Broadside; Brakspear Special or Old; Fuller's ESB; guest beers Ⓖ
Small, busy, friendly off-licence, stocking five or six draught beers and a range of bottled beers including Belgian. ☭ ᗡ

IBSTONE
Fox
The Common (off M40 jct 5) OS752939
☎ (01491) 638289
11-3, 6-11; 12-3, 7-10.30 Sun
Brakspear Bitter; Fuller's London Pride; guest beer Ⓗ
Popular pub offering high quality accommodation and food at all times. The Fox has a large garden set in superb countryside. Guest beers are sourced locally.
♨Q ⊛ 🖛 ◖▶ ♣ P

ICKFORD
Rising Sun
36 Worminghall Road
☎ (01844) 339238
12-3 (not Mon), 5-11; 12-11 Sat; 12-10.30 Sun
Hancock's HB; Marston's Pedigree; Wadworth 6X; guest beer Ⓗ
Attractive, atmospheric 15th-century timber-framed thatched coaching inn, enjoying a thriving local trade. No eve meals Tue or Sun. ♨ ⊛ ◖▶ ♣ P

IVER
Bull Inn
7 High Street (B470)
☎ (01753) 651115
11-3, 5-11; 11-11 Sat; 12-3, 7-10.30 Sun
Ind Coope Burton Ale; Young's Bitter Ⓗ
Traditional High Street local: a small public bar where the emphasis is on games, and a larger, comfortable saloon.
🖛 ◖▶ ⅃ P

IVER HEATH
Black Horse
95 Slough Road (A4007)
☎ (01753) 653044
11-11; 12-10.30 Sun
Badger IPA, Dorset Best, Tanglefoot Ⓗ
Large single bar with a conservatory at the rear; a rare local outlet for Badger beers. ⊛ ◖ P

Stag & Hounds
Church Road (A412)
☎ (01753) 655144
11-11; 12-10.30 Sun
Courage Best Bitter; Fuller's London Pride; Morland Old Speckled Hen Ⓗ
Friendly local with an L-shaped bar, it is reputedly the original pub of this name. Q ⊛ ◖ P ⊞

IVINGHOE
Rose & Crown
Vicarage Lane
☎ (01296) 668472
12-2.30 (3 Sat), 6-11; 12-3, 7-10.30 Sun
Adnams Bitter; Bateman Mild; Greene King IPA; guest beer Ⓗ
Hard-to-find, street-corner two-bar local; high quality food and lively atmosphere add to its appeal.
♨ ⊛ ◖▶ Å ♣ ⅄

LITTLE MARLOW
King's Head
Church Road (A4155)
☎ (01628) 484407
11-3, 5-11; 11-11 Sat; 12-10.30 Sun
Brakspear Bitter; Fuller's London Pride; Taylor Landlord; guest beers Ⓗ
Characterful village pub where varied, home-cooked meals are always available, plus six ales. Families welcome. Wheelchair WC.
♨ ⊛ ◖▶ & P ⅄

LITTLE MISSENDEN
Crown
Off A413 ☎ (01494) 862571
11-2.30, 6-11; 12-3, 7-10.30 Sun
Adnams Bitter; Bateman Valiant; Marston's Pedigree; guest beer Ⓗ
Superb traditional pub, very much a focal point in the village, it gives a warm welcome to visitors.
♨Q ⊛ ♣ P

LITTLEWORTH COMMON
Jolly Woodman
Littleworth Road OS 935866
☎ (01753) 644350
11-11; 12-10.30 Sun
Brakspear Bitter; Flowers Original; guest beers Ⓗ
Long, single bar on the edge of Burnham Beeches. A rowing boat hanging from a central beam, plus agricultural and woodcutting tools provide an unusual decor. No eve meals winter Sun. ♨Q ⊛ ◖▶ ♣ P ⅄

MARLOW
Carpenters Arms
15 Spittal Street
☎ (01628) 473649
11-11; 12-10.30 Sun
Morrells Bitter, Varsity Ⓗ

Thriving workingman's local of considerable character.

🏠 🍺 ⇌ ♣

Crown & Anchor
45 Oxford Road
☎ (01628) 891161
11.30-2.30, 5.30-11; 11-11 Sat; 12-10.30 Sun
Trueman's Best, seasonal beers; guest beers Ⓗ
This 18th-century town pub was acquired in 1999 by Sam Trueman's Brewery. Sympathetically refurbished, it is now the sole outlet for their beers. It specialises in music (jam sessons), crib and quiz eves. Meals not always available.

🏠 🌸 🍴 ▶ ⇌ ♣ ◔ 🍺

Hogshead
80-82 High Street
☎ (01628) 478737
11-11; 12-10.30 Sun
Adnams Bitter; Brakspear Special; Fuller's London Pride; Rebellion IPA; Wadworth 6X; Ⓗ **guest beers** Ⓗ/Ⓖ
Spacious, modern pub on the old Wethered's site displaying the defunct brewery's memorabilia. Always at least ten ales plus one cider. Wheelchair WC.

🌸 ◖ ▶ ♿ ⇌ ◔ ✂

Try also: **Duke of Cambridge**, Queens Rd (Whitbread)

MARSH GIBBON
Greyhound
West Edge
☎ (01869) 277365
12-3.30, 6-11 (closed Mon); 12-4, 7-10.30 Sun
Fuller's London Pride; Greene King IPA, Abbot; Ⓗ
Listed building, probably of Tudor origin, rebuilt after a fire in 1740. Specialising in Thai cuisine, it is also popular for steaks and quick business lunches. 🏠 Q 🌸 ◖ ▶ P 🍺

MARSWORTH
Red Lion
90 Vicarage Road (off B489, near canal bridge 130)
OS919147
☎ (01296) 668366
11-3, 6-11; 12-3, 7-10.30 Sun
Fuller's London Pride; Vale Notley Ale; guest beers Ⓗ
Idyllic, three-bar pub by the Grand Union Canal. Skittles played regularly in winter. Eve meals served Tue-Sat.

🏠 Q 🌸 🍴 ◖ ▶ 🍽 ♣ ◔ P

MILTON KEYNES: KILN FARM
Kiln Farm Club
Kellers Close, Tilers Road (400 yds from A422, Monks Way/Watling St jct)

☎ (01908) 567043
12-2.30 (not Mon-Thu), 5.30-11; 12-11 Sat; 12-10.30 Sun
Draught Bass; Fuller's London Pride; guest beers Ⓗ
Local CAMRA *Club of the Year* 1999, with two bars, based in a former farm. The ales change on a regular basis. CAMRA members welcome. Weekday meals.
Q 🍽 🌸 ◖ ▶ ♣ P

STONY STRATFORD
Bull Hotel & Vaults Bar
64 High Street
☎ (01908) 567104
12-11; 12-10.30 Sun
Adnams Bitter; Draught Bass; Courage Best Bitter; Fuller's London Pride; Wadworth 6X; guest beers Ⓗ
The Bull has three bars, Vaults Bar, a lounge and Las Cuadras tapas bar. The lounge has a warm, welcoming, 17th-century feel, with wooden floors and five handpumps, while the Vaults boasts a stone floor and seven handpumps. Folk music jam sessions happen Sun lunch in the Vaults.
🏠 Q 🌸 🍴 ◖ ▶ ♣ P

Fox & Hounds
87 High Street
☎ (01908) 563307
12-11; 12-10.30 Sun
Arkell's 3B; Castle Eden Ale; guest beers Ⓗ
One of the best live music venues around, a friendly town pub and local CAMRA *Pub of the Year* 1998. A wide range of games includes Northant's skittles.
Q 🌸 ◖ ♣ P

NEWPORT PAGNELL
Cannon
50 High Street
☎ (01908) 211495
11-11; 12-10.30 Sun
Draught Bass; M&B Brew XI; guest beers Ⓗ
Listed free house in the town centre. Bass Museum's range of historic beers are well worth sampling. This is a drinking man's pub, and can get crowded. 🏠 A ♣ P

Try also: **Bull**, Tickford St (Free)

OLNEY
Swan Inn & Bistro
12 High Street
☎ (01234) 711111
11-11; 12-4, 7-10.30 Sun
Fuller's London Pride; Hook Norton Best Bitter; Jennings Bitter; Morrells Bitter; RCH Old Slug Porter; guest beers Ⓗ
1700s stone inn retaining ceilings, original beams and wood fires. A warm welcome

and excellent value food await you (no food Sun eve).
🏠 Q 🌸 🍴 ◖ ▶ ♿ A P

QUAINTON
White Hart
4 The Strand
☎ (01296) 655234
12-2 (not Thu; 3 Sat), 7 (5.30 Mon)-11; 12-3, 7-10.30 Sun
Adnams Bitter; Benskins BB; Young's Bitter Ⓗ
1930s two-bar pub that has remained substantially unaltered. It stands on North Bucks long distance path and near the Railway Centre.
🏠 🌸 🍴 ◖ ▶ P

SHERINGTON
White Hart
1 Gun Lane OS891468
☎ (01908) 611953
12-3, 6 (5 Fri)-11; 12-3, 7-10.30 Sun
Fuller's London Pride; Hook Norton Best Bitter; Vale Wychert, seasonal beers; guest beers Ⓗ
This characterful village inn has two bars and a restaurant with oak beams; a real local (no food Sun eve).
🏠 Q 🌸 ◖ ▶ ♣ P

STEWKLEY
Swan
High Street North
☎ (01525) 240285
12-3 (not winter Tue), 5.30-11; 12-4, 7-10.30 (12-10.30 summer) Sun
Courage Best Bitter, Directors; Greene King Abbot Ⓗ
Fine Georgian village pub, enjoying a good atmosphere in its old beamed bar and dining area (no food Sun eve). Live music alternate Sat.
🌸 ◖ ▶ ♣ P

STOKE MANDEVILLE
Bull
5 Risborough Road
☎ (01296) 613632
11.30-3, 5.30-11; 11.30-11 Sat; 12-10.30 Sun
Draught Bass; Fuller's London Pride; Greene King Abbot; Tetley Bitter Ⓗ
Friendly, two-bar local where the 'sports' bar contrasts with a quieter lounge. A good choice of cooked lunches is served Mon-Sat.
Q 🌸 🍴 ⇌ ♣ P

SWAN BOTTOM
Old Swan
Kingswood, The Lee
OS902055
☎ (01494) 837239
12-3, 6-11; 12-11 Sat; closed Mon; 12-10.30 Sun
Adnams Bitter; Brakspear Bitter; guest beer Ⓗ
Old country pub in the Chilterns. An additional guest beer is stocked in

summer. Large garden. Good home-made food requires booking at weekends.
🏠 Q 🕷 P

THORNBOROUGH
Lone Tree
Bletchley Road (A421)
☎ (01280) 812334
11.30-3, 6-11; 12-3, 6.30-10.30 Sun
Beer range varies Ⓗ
Isolated 17th-century free house combines superb food (book) with a permanent festival of beers (including a mild) from micro-brewers. Add a real ale, traditional games and a pleasant outdoor area and you almost have perfection.
🏠 🕷 ◖▶ ♣ ⌂ P ⅍ 🖫

TURVILLE
Bull & Butcher
Off M40 jct 5, through Ibstone OS768911
☎ (01491) 638283
11-3, 6 (6.30 Sat)-11; 12-5, 7-10.30 (not winter eve) Sun
Brakspear Mild, Bitter, Old, Special, seasonal beers; Coniston Bluebird Ⓗ
Unspoilt pub set in attractive countryside, first licensed in 1617. The extensive menu includes vegetarian dishes (no food Sun eve or winter Mon). 🏠 Q 🕷 ◖▶ 🍽 ⌂ P

TYLERS GREEN
Horse & Jockey
Church Road
☎ (01494) 815963
12-3, 5.30-11; 12-3.30, 7-10.30 Sun
Brakspear Bitter; Greene King Abbot; Ind Coope Burton Ale; Tetley Bitter; guest beer Ⓗ
Tucked away near the church and historic Penn village. Meals always available.
🏠 🕷 ◖▶ ♣ P

WADDESDON
Lion
High Street
☎ (01296) 651227
12-2.30, 5.30 (6 Sat)-11; 12-3, 7-10.30 Sun
Adnams Bitter; Draught Bass; Fuller's ESB Ⓗ
Free house specialising in quality meals, served at a leisurely pace. Ample portions and plenty of elbow room at the large wooden tables add to its appeal. No meals winter Sun eve.
🏠 Q 🕷 ◖▶ P ⅍

WENDOVER
End of the World
Aylesbury Road, Worlds End (1 mile NW of village)
☎ (01296) 622299
12-2.30, 6-11; (12-11 summer); closed

Mon; 12-10.30 Sun
Brakspear Bitter; Greene King IPA; guest beers Ⓗ
18th-century coaching inn with a comfortable bar and restaurant serving freshly prepared food.
🕷 ◖▶ ♿ P 🖫

Try also: Shoulder of Mutton, Pound St (Greenalls)

WEST WYCOMBE
George & Dragon
High Street
☎ (01494) 464414
11-2.30 (3 Sat), 5.30-11; 12-3, 7-10.30 Sun
Courage Best Bitter; Fuller's London Pride; guest beers Ⓗ
18th-century coaching inn offering a good selection of bar food. The main bar boasts a heavily beamed ceiling. The small back bar is for non-smokers. Nice garden with children's play area.
🏠 Q 🛏 🕷 🚃 ◖▶ P ⅍

WESTON UNDERWOOD
Cowpers Oak
High Street
☎ (01234) 711382
12-3, 5.30-11 (12-11 summer Sat); 12-3, 5.30-10.30 (12-11 summer) Sun
Ash Vine Challenger; Courage Directors; Greene King Abbot; Marston's Pedigree; Ruddles Best Bitter; guest beers Ⓗ
Traditional pub set in a beautiful village with two bars. The games area features Northants skittles. Cider is available most of the time. Eve meals Tue-Sat.
🏠 Q 🕷 ◖▶ ♣ ⌂ P

Beer site
Keep in touch with CAMRA:
www.camra.org.uk

WHEELEREND COMMON
Brickmakers Arms
1 mile off B482, between Stokenchurch and Lane End OS802931
☎ (01494) 881526
12-3, 5.30-11; 12-11 Sat; 12.30-10.30 Sun
Adnams Broadside; Brakspear Bitter; Fuller's London Pride; Morrells Varsity; guest beers Ⓗ
Large, friendly 17th-century pub, overlooking the common. A wide range of food is always available.

🏠 Q 🛏 🕷 ◖▶ ♣ P

WHITCHURCH
White Swan
10 High Street
☎ (01296) 641228
11-11; 12-3, 7-10.30 Sun
Fuller's Chiswick, London Pride, ESB, seasonal beers Ⓗ
Attractive, part-thatched 16th-century pub with a large mature garden. It boasts distinctive wood panelling in the lounge bar. No meals Sun eve. 🏠 Q 🕷 ◖▶ 🏠 ♣ P

WINGRAVE
Rose & Crown
The Green
☎ (01296) 681257
11.30-3, 5.30-11; 11.30-11 Sat; 12-10.30 Sun
Adnams Bitter; Fuller's London Pride; Greene King IPA; guest beer Ⓗ
Early 17th-century, three-bar local: a stone-flagged public bar, a small snug, a lounge, a spacious family room plus a dining area.
🏠 Q 🛏 🕷 ◖▶ 🏠 ♣ P ⅍

WORMINGHALL
Clifden Arms
75 Clifden Road OS640083
☎ (01844) 339273
12-2.30, 6-11; 12-11 Sat; 12-4 Sun
Adnams Broadside; Brakspear Bitter; Hook Norton Best Bitter; guest beer Ⓗ
Picturesque village local; off the beaten track, it offers good food. The large garden has Aunt Sally. Bar billiards is played indoors. The guest ale often comes from a micro.
🏠 🕷 ◖▶ ♣ P

WYCOMBE MARSH
General Havelock
114 Kingsmead Road OS889915
☎ (01494) 520391
12-2.30, 5.30-11; 12-11 Fri & Sat; 12-10.30 Sun
Fuller's Chiswick, London Pride, ESB, seasonal beers Ⓗ
Smart, traditional, family pub, set away from the busy A40. Eve meals served Fri and Sat. 🏠 🕷 ◖▶ ♣ P

INDEPENDENT BREWERIES

Chiltern: Terrick

Old Luxters: Hambleden

Rebellion: Marlow

Trueman's: Medmenham

Vale: Haddenham

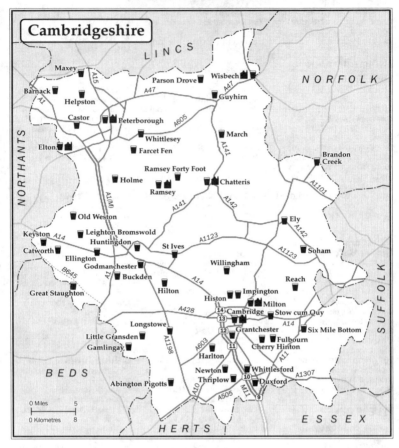

Cambridgeshire

LINCS

NORFOLK

NORTHANTS

SUFFOLK

Maxey
Barnack
Helpston
Castor
Elton
Peterborough
Whittlesey
Farcet Fen
Parson Drove
Wisbech
Guyhirn
March
Brandon Creek
Ramsey Forty Foot
Holme
Ramsey
Chatteris
Old Weston
Keyston
Leighton Bromswold
Huntingdon
Catworth
Ellington
Godmanchester
Buckden
Great Staughton
Hilton
St Ives
Willingham
Ely
Soham
Reach
Impington
Histon
Milton
Cambridge
Stow cum Quy
Longstowe
Grantchester
Six Mile Bottom
Little Gransden
Gamlingay
Fulbourn
Cherry Hinton
Harlton
Newton
Thriplow
Abington Pigotts
Whittlesford
Duxford

BEDS

HERTS

ESSEX

0 Miles 5
0 Kilometres 8

ABINGTON PIGOTTS

Pig & Abbot
High Street (off A505 towards Litlington) OS306444
☎ (01763) 853515
12-2 (3 Sat), 7-11 (6.30 Fri); 12-3, 7-10.30 Sun
Adnams Bitter; City of Cambridge True Blue; guest beers H
Busy, welcoming, village pub, saved by a village buyout in 1997. Always an imaginative range of guest beers on offer, plus eve meals Wed-Sun and weekend lunches.
🚶 Q ✿ ◑ ▶ ♣ 🖙 P

BARNACK

Millstone
Millstone Lane (small back street between Hills and Hollows and Main St)
☎ (01780) 740296
11.30-2.30, 5.30 (6 Sat)-11; 12-4, 7-10.30 Sun
Adnams Bitter; Everards Tiger, Old Original; guest beer H
Stone-built, Everard's pub comprising four rooms, a regular *Guide* entry. The patio/courtyard is a suntrap. The Millstone combines

passing dining trade with a friendly local atmosphere. Good food served (no meals Sun eve). Wheelchair WC.
Q ✿ ◑ ▶ ♿ P ✗

BRANDON CREEK

Ship
On A10, Littleport-Southery road
☎ (01353) 676228
Hours vary
Beer range varies H
Welcoming, one-bar riverside inn and restaurant. The beer range is always changing, and a cider is stocked in summer. Hours can vary dramatically; ring before travelling.
🚶 ✿ 🛏 ◑ ▶ 🖙 P

BUCKDEN

Vine
35 High Street (off A1)
☎ (01480) 810367
12-2.30 (3 Sat), 5 (7 Sat)-11; 12-3, 7-10.30 Sun
Draught Bass; Wadworth 6X; guest beer H
Comfortable pub with a large lounge. The constantly

changing guest beer comes from regional independents. No food Sun eve.
✿ ◑ ▶ ♣ P

CAMBRIDGE

Alma
26 Russel Court
☎ (01223) 364965
11-11; 10-11 Sat; 10-10.30 Sun
Ridleys IPA, ESX, Rumpus, seasonal beers H
Spacious, modern pub creating a traditional, friendly atmosphere. A music venue, specialising in rock and indie, it draws an interesting mix of music fans and locals. Note: the piranhas in the 'phone box are fed Wed and Sat.
◑ ▶ ≋ ♣

Cambridge Blue
85-87 Gwydir Street (off Mill Road)
☎ (01223) 361382
12-2.30 (3 Sat), 6-11; 12-3, 7-10.30 Sun
Beer range varies H
No-smoking pub with a large garden and a children's certificate. The beers mostly

come from East Anglian breweries, the cider is from Cassels.

🏚 Q ☎ ❀ ◖▶ ♣ ⌣ ✼

Castle
38 Castle Street
☎ (01223) 353194
11.30-3, 5-(6 Sat)-11; 12-3, 6.30-10.30 Sun
Adnams Bitter, Broadside, seasonal beers; Marston's Pedigree; guest beers H
Adnams' western flagship is a superb example of sensitive renovation: five drinking areas on the ground floor and more upstairs, plus a suntrap patio.
🏚 ☎ ☎ ◖▶ ♣ ✼ ⊞

Champion of the Thames
68 King Street
☎ (01223) 352043
11-11; 12-10.30 Sun
Greene King IPA, H **Abbot;** G **Ruddles County; guest beer** H
Unspoilt pub with two small bars, close to the centre. Note the etched windows showing the 'Champ'.
🏚 Q ♣

Elm Tree
Elm Street (from the Grafton Centre, Fitzroy St. then Eden Street)
☎ (01223) 363905
12-2.30, 4-11; 12-11 Sat; 1-10.30 Sun
Adnams Broadside; Wells Eagle, Bombardier; guest beer H
Small, back-street Regency-style pub with a relaxed 'living-room' atmosphere. Live jazz is important here, and is performed three nights a week; Sky TV for football.
❀ ♣

Empress
72 Thoday Street (off Mill Rd)
☎ (01223) 247236
11-2.30, 6.30-11; 12-2.30, 7-10.30 Sun
Castle Eden Ale; Flowers Original; Marston's Pedigree; guest beers H
Thriving back-street pub; surprisingly large, it has three distinct drinking areas plus a space for games. Cassels and Crones cider sold.
❀ ♣ ⌣

Live & Let Live
40 Mawson Road (off Mill Road)
☎ (01223) 460261
11.30-2.30; 5.30-11; 12-2.30, 7-10.30 Sun
Adnams Bitter; B&T Edwin Taylor's Extra Stout; Bateman Mild; Everards Tiger; Nethergate Umbel Ale; guest beers H
Friendly, popular pub with a snug bar and real gas lighting. Bar skittles played. Local CAMRA *Pub of the Year* 1999.
🏚 Q ◖▶ ≈ ♣ ⌣ ✼ ⊞

NCI Sports & Social Club
Holland Street (from Mitchams corner, second left off Victoria Rd)
☎ (01223) 352342
11-2.30, 6.30-11; 12-3, 7-10.30 Sun
Greene King IPA; guest beers H
Large, friendly club which hosts family and social eves. Pool, snooker, billiards, darts, skittles, carpet bowls and table tennis all played. CAMRA card-carriers can ask to be signed in. Four guest beers on tap. ♣

Portland Arms
129 Chesterton Road
☎ (01223) 357268
11-2.30 (3.30 Sat), 6-11; 12-3.30, 7-10.30 Sun
Greene King XX Mild, IPA, Triumph, Abbot, seasonal beers; guest beers H
Virtually unaltered example of a Greene King inter-war 'improved public house'; the panelled lounge is especially fine. The back room hosts live music most eves. Good value food (eve meals Wed-Sat).
🏚 Q ❀ ◖▶ ⊟ ♣

St. Radegund
129 King Street
☎ (01223) 311794
4.30 (12 Sat)-11; 6-10.30 Sun; hours may vary
Adnams Bitter; Fuller's London Pride; Shepherd Neame Spitfire; guest beer H
Small, but perfectly formed, free house.

University Sports & Social Club
Mill Lane (off Trumpington Street)
☎ (01223) 566397
12-2.30, 5-11; closed at weekends
Adnams Bitter; guest beers H
University staff bar, recently refurbished, serving good value meals at lunchtimes, especially Dave's chilli. CAMRA card-carriers can ask to be signed in. ◖▶ ♣

Wrestlers
337 Newmarket Road
☎ (01223) 566554
12-3, 5-11; closed Sun
Adnams Broadside; Wells Eagle, Bombardier; guest beers H
Lively, cosy pub with an area for pool. Live music staged Thu, Fri and Sat when it becomes very busy. Excellent Thai food is cooked to order.
🏚 ◖▶ ♿ ⌣

Zebra
80 Maids Causeway
☎ (01223) 464116
12-3, 6-11; 12-3, 7-10.30 Sun
Greene King IPA, Triumph, Abbot, seasonal beers; guest beer H
Although basically open-

plan, this friendly 1930s pub has several drinking areas. Food is good, cheap, plentiful and served until 10.30pm (not available Sun eve).
◖▶ ♣

Try also: Six Bells, Covent Garden (Greene King)

CASTOR
Royal Oak
24 Peterborough Road (off A47, W of Peterborough)
☎ (01733) 380217
12-3, 5-11; 12-11 Sat; 12-10.30 Sun
Ind Coope Burton Ale; Tetley Bitter; guest beers H
This 17th-century thatched, three-roomed pub is noted not only for its beer, but also for its front patio garden. Children welcome. Snacks available Tue-Sat lunch.
🏚 Q ❀ ⊟ ♣ P

CATWORTH
Racehorse
43 High Street (B660, off A14)
☎ (01832) 710262
11-2.30, 6-11; 11-11 Sat; 12-10.30 Sun
Marston's Pedigree; Theakston Best Bitter; Wadworth 6X; guest beer H
Smart village pub with a restaurant serving unusual and traditional food. Chess and bridge nights held, and skittles played.
🏚 Q ☎ ❀ ◖▶ ⊟ Å ♣ P

CHATTERIS
Walk the Dog
34 Bridge Street
☎ (01354) 695693
12-2.30 (not Tue), 6.30-11; 12-2.30, 7-10.30 Sun
Adnams Bitter; Fuller's London Pride; guest beers H
Traditional market town local enjoying a warm, friendly atmosphere. A good variety of ales on the guest pump, and traditional and modern games always available – ask if anyone wants to play. Lunchtime snacks.
🏚 Q ❀ ♣ P ⊟

CHERRY HINTON
Red Lion
Millend Road
☎ (01223) 248826
11-11; 12-10.30 Sun
Draught Bass; Greene King Martha Greene, IPA, Abbot H
This 16th-century village pub features original oak beams and an interesting decor, including a large collection of bank notes and postcards. Wide range of food served.
🏚 ❀ ◖▶ ♣

DUXFORD

Plough
57 St Peters Street
☎ (01223) 833170
11-3, 5.30-11; 11-11 Sat; 12-3, 6.30-10.30 Sun

Adnams Bitter; Everards Tiger, Old Original; guest beers Ⓗ
Lively, traditional local, handy for the Air Museum. Children always welcome. No food Sun or Mon eves.
🚪 🏵 ◖ ▶ P

ELLINGTON

Mermaid
High Street (off A14)
☎ (01480) 891450
12-3.30, 7-11; 12-3, 7-10.30 Sun

Draught Bass; Greene King IPA Ⓗ
Unspoilt, single room village pub offering a friendly welcome. Pétanque played.
🚪 Q 🐾 🏵 🛏 ◖ ♣

ELTON

Black Horse
14 Overend (old A605)
☎ (01832) 280240
11-2.30, 6-11; 12-3, 7-11 Sun

Adnams Bitter; Draught Bass; Marston's Pedigree; Taylor Landlord Ⓗ **guest beers** Ⓗ/Ⓖ
Stone building dating back to 1650 comprising four rooms. At peak periods it may be difficult for non-diners to sit at a table; food is expensive but popular. Wheelchair entrance is via the back door.
🚪 Q 🏵 ◖ ▶ 🚻 P ⊟

ELY

Fountain
1 Silver Street
☎ (01353) 663122
5-11; 12-2, 6-11 Sat; 12-2, 7-10.30 Sun

Adnams Bitter, Regatta (summer), **Broadside** (winter)**; Fuller's London Pride; guest beer** Ⓗ
Very welcoming drinkers' pub, handy for the Cathedral. Interesting pictures and stuffed animals adorn the bar. Once settled, you don't want to leave!
🚪 🏵 ≠

Prince Albert
62 Silver Street
☎ (01353) 663494
11-3 (3.30 Fri-Sat), 6.30-11; 12-3.30, 7-10.30 Sun

Greene King XX Mild, IPA, Triumph, Abbot, seasonal or guest beer Ⓗ
Classic town local boasting a beautiful back garden where your own food may be eaten as long as you buy a drink. Books for sale. Do not miss this classic pub – a rare regular mild outlet.
Q ◖ ≠

FARCET FEN

Plough
Milk and Water Drove, Ramsey Road (2 miles from A605 at Horsey toll turn)
☎ (01733) 844307
11.30-3 (not Mon-Fri), 5.30 (6 Sat)-11; 12-10.30 Sun

Home Mild; John Smith's Bitter; Oakham JHB; guest beers Ⓗ
1740 alehouse and restaurant at the heart of fenland; a CAMRA *Gold Award* winner. Book for meals (Sun meals served 2-8).
🚪 Q 🏵 ◖ ▶ 🍴 🛏 🔥 ▲ ♣ P ⊟

FULBOURN

Six Bells
5 High Street
☎ (01223) 880244
11.30-3, 6-11; 12-11 Sat; 12-10.30 Sun

Flowers IPA; Ind Coope Burton Ale; Tolly Cobbold Mild; guest beer Ⓗ
Parts of this village pub date back to the 15th century; this was discovered during repairs after a fire in 1999. A good local, it also welcomes visitors. Excellent food (eve meals Tue-Sat).
🚪 Q 🏵 ◖ ▶ ▲ ♣ P

Try also: Bakers Arms, Hinton Rd (Greene King)

GAMLINGAY

Cock
25 Church Street
☎ (01767) 650255
11.30-3, 5.30-11; 11.30-11 Sat; 12-4, 7-10.30 Sun

Greene King IPA, Abbot; guest beer Ⓗ
Old timber-framed pub which boasts much wood panelling and a large inglenook. It is popular for good value food (eve meals Tue-Sat).
🚪 🐾 🏵 ◖ ▶ 🍴 ♣ P

GODMANCHESTER

Exhibition
London Road
☎ (01480) 459134
11.30-3, 5.30-11; 11.30-11 Fri & Sat; 12-10.30 Sun

Greene King IPA; Morland Old Speckled Hen; guest beer Ⓗ
Large, busy and lively town pub with bistro dining in the spacious restaurant area. Note the unusual mock-up Victorian shop fronts in the lounge bar. Good garden and facilities.
🏵 ◖ ▶ P

GRANTCHESTER

Blue Ball Inn
57 Broadway
☎ (01223) 840679
11.30-3, 5.30-11; 12-3, 7-10.30 Sun

GREAT STAUGHTON

White Hart
56 The Highway (B645)
☎ (01480) 860345
12-2 (3 Sat), 5 (7 Sat)-11; 12-3, 7-11 Sun

Bateman XB, seasonal beers Ⓗ
Village local, styled as a coaching inn with a large games room.
🚪 Q 🏵 ◖ ▶ ♣ P

GUYHIRN

Oliver Twist
High Road (on riverbank, just off A47)
☎ (01945) 450523
11.30-2.30, 6-11; 12-2.30, 7-10.30 Sun

Beer range varies Ⓗ
Rural free house where the emphasis is on food and real ale; the licensee is an award-winning cellarman. This level of quality comes at a price. Mild is always available.
🚪 Q ◖ ▶ P ⊞

HARLTON

Hare & Hounds
60 High Street
☎ (01223) 262672
11.30-3 (not Mon), 5-11; 12-4, 7-10.30 Sun

Wells Eagle, Bombardier; guest beer Ⓗ
Friendly, olde-worlde single bar free house. Play crazy golf and skittles in the large garden, home to traction engines. No meals Sun eve or Mon.
🚪 Q 🏵 ◖ ▶ ♣ P

HELPSTON

Bluebell
10 Woodgate (off B1443)
☎ (01733) 252394
11-2 (3 Sat), 5 (6 Sat)-11; 12-3, 7-10.30 Sun

Bateman XB; John Smith's Bitter; guest beers Ⓗ
Traditional, two-roomed village pub that hosts a beer festival in June. The cosy wood-panelled lounge is decorated with teapots and Toby jugs. CAMRA *Gold Award* winner 1999. Sun lunch served.
🚪 Q 🏵 🛏 ♣ 🍴 P ⊟

HILTON

Prince of Wales
Potton Road
☎ (01480) 830257

Greene King IPA, Abbot Ⓗ
Small, unspoilt local which commemorates a hot air balloon. Off the tourist track, it serves an excellent chip-free menu (no food Sun eve or Mon). Live music Tue.
🚪 Q 🏵 🛏 ◖ ▶ ♣

11 (12 winter)-2.30 (3 Sat; not Mon), 6 (7 winter Sat)-11; 12-3, 7-10.30 Sun
Adnams Bitter; Elgood's Black Dog Mild; guest beer (occasional) H
Village local providing good facilities and a friendly welcome; popular for its accommodation. No food Mon or winter Sun eve.
🏨 🏷 🛏 ◑ ▶ 🍴 ♣ P

HISTON
Red Lion
27 High Street
☎ (01223) 564437
11.30-3, 5-11; 11.30-11 Sat; 12-5, 7-10.30
Bateman Mild; Everards Beacon, Tiger; Nethergate Augustinian; guest beers H
Friendly, two-bar pub: a lively revamped public bar and a quiet comfy lounge, old photos and brewery paraphernalia feature throughout. No food Sun.
🏨 Q 🏷 ◑ ♣ P

HOLME
Admiral Wells
41 Station Road (B660, off A1 S next to level crossing)
☎ (01487) 831214
5.30 (4 Fri, 12 Sat)-11; closed Mon; 12-10.30 Sun
Draught Bass; Elgood's Black Dog Mild; Oakham JHB; guest beers H
Victorian, yellow brick purpose-built pub with a half-acre fenced garden. It hosts a beer and jazz festival in July. CAMRA *Gold Award* winner 1999, with five guest beers on tap.
🏨 Q 🏷 🍴 ♣ P ✆

HUNTINGDON
Old Bridge Hotel
1 High Street
☎ (01480) 452681
11-11; 12-10.30 Sun
Adnams Bitter; City of Cambridge Hobson's Choice; guest beer H
Attractive, relaxing wood-panelled lounge bar in an attractive 18th-century riverside building, formerly a bank. It offers excellent food and a comprehensive wine list.
🏨 Q 🏷 🛏 ◑ ▶ 🍽 P

IMPINGTON
Railway Vue
163 Station Road
☎ (01223) 232426
11.30-11; 12-3.30, 7-11 Sat; 12-3.30, 7-10.30 Sun
Flowers IPA, Original; Marston's Pedigree; guest beer H
Two-bar pub, near the former railway station, where children are welcome until 7pm. A pool table, cricket team, pub cats, meat raffle and occasional live music

add interest. Eve meals served 5-7.
Q 🏷 ◑ ▶ 🍴 ♣ P ✆

KEYSTON
Pheasant
Village loop road (off A14)
☎ (01832) 710241
12-3, 6-11; 12-3, 7-10.30 Sun
Adnams Bitter; guest beers H
Characterful, multi-roomed conversion of a series of village cottages. A constantly changing range of beers is drawn from independents and local micro-breweries. An outstanding quality seasonal menu includes blackboard specials.
🏨 Q 🍃 🏷 ◑ ▶ P ✆

LEIGHTON BROMSWOLD
Green Man
37 The Avenue (off A14, W of Huntingdon)
☎ (01480) 890238
12-3 (not Mon-Thu), 7-11 (not Mon); 12-3, 7-10.30 Sun
Nethergate IPA; G guest beers H
Welcoming, relaxing village local with a varying range of real ales and bottled Belgian beers; also popular for food (no eve meals Sun). Northants skittles and bar billiards played.
🍃 🏷 ◑ ▶ ♣ P

LITTLE GRANSDEN
Chequers
71 Main Road
☎ (01767) 677348
12-2.30, 5-11; 11-11 Sat; 12-3, 7-10.30 Sun
Adnams Bitter; guest beesr H
Friendly, welcoming, rural pub, full of character; an interesting and well-documented history adorns the walls. An ever-changing range of guest beers comes from independent breweries.
🏨 🍃 🏷 🍴 ♣ P

LONGSTOWE
Red House
34 Old North Road
☎ (01954) 718480
12-3 (not Mon), 5.30-11; 12-3, 7-10.30 Sun
Fuller's London Pride; Greene King IPA; guest beers H
Situated on the main road south of the village, this enterprising free house offers a choice of drinking and eating areas, along with a warm welcome. Ask about the suitcase over the bar.
🏨 🍃 🏷 ◑ ▶ ♣ P

MARCH
Rose & Crown
41 St Peters Road (B1099)
☎ (01354) 652879

12-2.30 (3 Sat, not Wed), 7-11; 12-3, 7-10.30 Sun
Shepherd Neame Master Brew Bitter; guest beers H
Olde-worlde suburban local, boasting a collection of 106 whiskies. Over 800 different real ales served to date – one of the five guests is usually a mild. CAMRA *Gold Award* winner. Lunch served Thu-Sat. Q ◑ ▶ 👌 P ✆

MAXEY
Bluebell
37-39 High Street (village signed off A15 and A16)
☎ (01778) 348182
5.30-11; 12-5, 7-11 Sat; 12-5, 7-10.30 Sun
Everards Beacon, Tiger; Fuller's London Pride; guest beers H
Stone-built, 16th-century former grain store run by a beer-loving landlord. On entering, look out for the double hinged door used for delivering large beer barrels 150 years ago.
🏨 Q 🏷 🛏 Å ♣ 👌 P ✆ 🍽

MILTON
Waggon & Horses
39 High Street
☎ (01223) 860313
12-2.30 (4 Sat), 5 (6 Sat)-11; 12-3, 7-10.30 Sun
Elgood's Black Dog Mild, Cambridge, Golden Newt, Greyhound Strong; guest beers H
Elgood's first acquisition for 55 years, an imposing mock Tudor, one-roomed pub displaying a large collection of hats. The sizeable child-safe garden houses chickens; pétanque played. Cassels cider served. Meals represent good choice and value.
🏨 🏷 ◑ ▶ 👌 P ✆

Try also: **Lion & Lamb**, High St (Whitbread)

NEWTON
Queens Head
Fowlmere Road
☎ (01223) 8704346
11.30-2.30, 6-11; 12-2.30, 7-10.30 Sun
Adnams Bitter, Broadside, seasonal beers G
Idyllic village inn that has appeared in all editions of this *Guide*. The stuffed goose used to patrol the car park! Soup-in-a-basket is a lunchtime speciality.
🏨 Q 🏷 ◑ ♣ 👌 P

OLD WESTON
Swan
Main Street (B660, off A14)
☎ (01832) 293400
6.30-11; 12-3, 7-11 Sat; 12-3, 7-10.30 Sun

Adnams Bitter; Greene King Abbot; Taylor Landlord; guest beers Ⓗ
Characterful, welcoming village pub where the impressive beer range often includes a mild. Hood skittles played. Good value food Wed-Sat eves and Sun lunch.
🏨 Q ☆ ▶ ▲ ♣ P

PARSON DROVE
Swan
Main Road
☎ (01945) 700291
7 (11 Fri & Sat)-11; 12-10.30 Sun
Elgood's Cambridge; guest beer Ⓗ
Traditional 16th-century village inn offering accommodation and an à la carte restaurant. Black Dog Mild also available with use of cask breather. Weekday hours may be extended in summer.
🏨 Q ⟿ ⇔ ▶ ⌸ P ⚥

PETERBOROUGH
Blue Bell
Welland Road, Dogsthorpe (1 mile off A47 and A15)
☎ (01733) 554890
11-2.30 (11.30-3 Sat), 6-11; 12-3, 7-10.30 Sun
Eelgood's Black Dog Mild, Cambridge, Greyhound Strong, seasonal beers; guest beers Ⓗ
One of the oldest pubs in Peterborough, converted from a farmhouse in 1665. Two large rooms: the lounge has a separate oak-panelled snug. Four ales are always available. The garden has a large pub and a children's play area. Weekday meals.
🏨 Q ☆ ⌸ ♣ P ⊞

Bogart's
17 North Street (opp Westgate House car park)
☎ (01733) 703599
11-11; 12-10.30 Sun
Fuller's London Pride; Iceni Fine Soft Day; Oakham JHB; guest beers Ⓗ
Lively, exciting city-centre, one-room pub with six ales always on tap. Pub-wide conversations usually relate to sporting events shown on the pub's TV. There is a small suntrap patio. A varied lunchtime menu is served. Ten years in the Guide.
⟐ ⇌

Brewery Tap
80 Westgate (NW corner of Queensgate shopping centre)
☎ (01733) 358500
11-11 (1.30am Fri & Sat); 12-10.30 Sun
Draught Bass; Fuller's London Pride; Oakham JHB, White Dwarf, Bishops Farewell, seasonal beers; guest beers Ⓗ
Largest brew-pub in Europe: a glass wall looks over Oakham Ales Brewery. Nine ales

available and excellent Thai food served in the mezzanine restaurant area or the bar. This building was formerly a government benefits office. Admission fee after 11pm.
⟐ ▶ ⇌

Charters
Town Bridge (steps down from W side of bridge on to S bank)
☎ (01733) 315700
12-11; 12-10.30 Sun
Draught Bass; Everards Tiger; Fuller's London Pride; Oakham JHB, White Dwarf, seasonal beers; guest beers Ⓗ
Dutch barge built in 1907 and moored on the south bank of the River Nene. The twelve ales on tap include the full Oakham range. A charming nautical atmosphere extends to the balcony restaurant and very large garden. Winner of many CAMRA awards.
☆ ⟐ ▶ ⇌

Coach & Horses
39-41 High Street, Old Fletton (2 miles S of centre near flyover)
☎ (01733) 343400
11.30-11; 12-10.30 Sun
Draught Bass; John Smith's Bitter; guest beers Ⓗ/Ⓖ
Two rooms: a lively public bar and a quiet 'foody' lounge. Busy at weekends, with six ales available (at least four during the week). There is a large garden with a patio. Good selection of meals.
🏨 Q ☆ ▶ ⟐ ⌸ ♣ P ⊟

College Arms
40 Broadway
☎ (01733) 319745
10-11; 12-10.30 Sun
Beer range varies Ⓖ
Spacious Wetherspoon's pub, converted from a city-centre technical college. Very busy at weekends as a meeting place before going clubbing. Six ales available and a large selection of meals served all day. Door control is in place Fri and Sat eves. Tiny car park.
Q ☆ ⟐ ▶ P ⊞

Hand & Heart
12 Highbury Street (off old A15, Lincoln road, N of centre)
☎ (01733) 707040
11-11; 12-10.30 Sun
Elgood's Black Dog Mild; John Smith's Bitter; guest beers Ⓗ
Unspoilt 1930s back-street pub. A frugally furnished but lively public bar hosts many traditional pub games; note the original Warwick's Brewery windows. The comfortable lounge snug has

a hatch service to the bar for the six ales and traditional cider. Winner of many CAMRA awards.
Q ⌸ ▲ ♣

Old Monk
29-31 Cowgate
☎ (01733) 566966
11-11; 12-10.30 Sun
Boddingtons Bitter; Courage Directors; Fuller's London Pride; Theakston Best Bitter; guest beers Ⓗ
Large, noisy city-centre pub, converted from a shop by the Old Monk chain. Continous music, alcove seating, six ales and a selection of food make it busy at weekends, and popular with clubbers.
⟐ ▶ ⇌

Palmerston Arms
82 Oundle Road, Woodston (10 mins walk S from centre)
☎ (01733) 565865
12-11; 12-10.30 Sun
Beer range varies Ⓖ
400-year-old listed building: two rooms of character with up to 14 ales, each one brought direct from the cellar cask. No food (pork pie excepted), no music and no hassle, just very good conversation. Note: entry is likely to be restricted to regulars at weekends.
Q ☆ ⟐ ♣ ⌂

Try also: Cherry Tree, Oundle Rd (Allied)

RAMSEY
Jolly Sailor
43 Great Whyte (B1040)
☎ (01487) 813388
11-3, 5.30 (6 Sat)-11; 12-3, 7-10.30 Sun
Draught Bass; Greene King IPA, Abbot; Tetley Bitter; guest beer Ⓗ
An absolute classic: good beer and conversation in a pub full of copper, brass and pewter; friendly, unspoilt and food-free with no distractions. Very popular with shoppers, local workers and boaters from nearby moorings. A regular in this Guide.
🏨 Q ☆ ♣ P

RAMSEY FORTY FOOT
George Inn
1 Ramsey Road (3 miles NE of Ramsey on B1096)
☎ (01487) 812775
12-4, 6-11; 12-4, 7-10.30 Sun
John Smith's Bitter; Courage Directors; guest beer Ⓗ
Cosy, friendly, Fen village free house with a great atmosphere. Lots of corners give the impression of several rooms. Handy for boaters and anglers on the adjacent

Forty Foot Drain. Good quality home-cooked food on a limited menu. The family room is used for pool and TV.
🏠 Q 🍴 🐕 🎼 🍺 🎵 ⚓ ♣ P

REACH

Dykes End
8 Fair Green
☎ (01638) 743816
12-3 (not Mon), 6-11;12-3, 7-10.30 Sun

Adnams Bitter; Greene King IPA; Milton Pegasus; guest beers 🅷
Rescued from closure in 1999 by a group of villagers, the pub has since gone from strength to strength. The upstairs restaurant has an excellent reputation (booking advisable); bar food also served.
🏠 🐕 🍴 🍺 P

ST IVES

Nelson's Head
7 Merryland (off Bridge St)
☎ (01480) 463342
11-11; 12-10.30 Sun

Greene King IPA, Abbot; 🅷 **guest beers** 🅷/🅶
Busy, town-centre pub, refurbished in alehouse style, with up to four guest beers changed monthly. Bar billiards played.
🍴 🍺 ♣

Royal Oak
13 Crown Street
☎ (01480) 462586
11-11; 12-10.30 Sun

Marston's Pedigree; Tetley Bitter; guest beers 🅷
Lively, Festival Alehouse in an unspoilt Grade II listed market town pub, serving a constantly changing range of at least six guest beers; sparklers happily removed on request.
🍴 🍺 ♣ P 🎲

SIX MILE BOTTOM

Green Man
London Road
☎ (01638) 570373
11.30-3, 5-11 (closed Mon); 12-5 Sun

Adnams Bitter; Greene King IPA; guest beers 🅷
Recently voted *Horse Racing Pub of the Year*, the decor of this lively free house celebrates the activities up the road in Newmarket. Candles, fresh flowers and plants decorate the tables in the bar and dining room (no food Sun eve). 🏠 🍴 🍺 ♣ P

SOHAM

Fountain
1 Churchgate Street
☎ (01353) 720374
11-2, 6-11; 11-11 Sat; 12-4, 7-10.30 Sun

Draught Bass; Courage Best Bitter; Marston's Pedigree 🅷
Historic local, partly listed due to a weighbridge at the side. Two bars separate drinking and eating (book for meals). Welcoming atmosphere; the beers may change.
🏠 🍴 🐟 🍺 P

Try also: Ship, High St (Greene King)

STOW-CUM-QUY

White Swan
11 Main Street
☎ (01223) 811821
11-3, 5.30 (6 Sat)-11; closed Mon; 12-3, 7-10.30 Sun

Adnams Bitter; Greene King IPA; Woodforde's Wherry; guest beers 🅷
Convivial meeting place for connoisseurs of interesting beers and outstanding food. The restaurant is a no-smoking zone.
Q 🍴 🍺 P 🎲

Heritage Pubs

The pubs chosen as illustrations in the Guide are taken from CAMRA's National Inventory. These are pubs with unspoilt interiors that need to be preserved for future generations. The illustrations are used as examples of pubs on the inventory and may not necessarily have been chosen for inclusion in the Guide for beer quality.

THRIPLOW

Green Man
2 Lower Street (1 mile from A505)
☎ (01763) 208855
12-2.30, 6-11; closed Tue; 12-2.30, 7-10.30 Sun

Taylor Landlord; guest beers 🅷
Expertly refurbished, early 19th-century building. It offers an ever-changing selection of guest ales (no Greene King here) and interesting dishes, home-cooked by the landlord.
🏠 Q 🍴 🍺 P ✂

WHITTLESEY

Bricklayers Arms
9 Station Road (B1093)
☎ (01733) 202593

11-4, 7-11; 12-4, 7-10.30 Sun

John Smith's Bitter; guest beer 🅷
Large, friendly bar frequented by locals of all ages, where strong language is not tolerated, also a small cosy lounge. The large garden has a children's play area and patio, plus a new floodlit pétanque terrain. Great for pub team games. Guest ale is often a mild or stout. Handy for the council boat moorings.
Q 🍴 🍺 🎼 ⚓ ≈ (Whittlesea) ♣ P 🎲

Try also: Hero of Aliwal, Church St (Free)

WHITTLESFORD

Bees in the Wall
36 North Road
☎ (01223) 834289
12-2.30 (not Mon-Fri), 6-11; 12-4, 7-10.30 Sun

City of Cambridge Hobson's Choice; Fuller's London Pride; Mansfield Bitter; Shepherd Neame Spitfire; guest beer 🅷
There really are bees in the wall of this two-bar pub on the village's northern outskirts. The public bar is the more characterful. Pleasant large garden with plenty of tables.
🏠 🍴 🍺 ♣ P

WILLINGHAM

Three Tuns
43 Church Street
☎ (01945) 260437
12-2.30, 6-11; 12-2.30, 7-10.30 Sun

Greene King XX Mild, IPA, Abbot, seasonal beers; guest beers 🅷
Unchanging epitome of the English village local. A rare mild outlet for the area. Huge garden. 🍴 🍺 ♣ P

WISBECH

Rose Tavern
53 North Brink (on river near Elgood's Brewery)
☎ (01945) 588335
12-3, 6-11; 12-3, 7-10.30 Sun

Beer range varies 🅷
Bustling free house, popular with sporting teams. Up to nine different real ales available at weekends.
Q 🍴

INDEPENDENT BREWERIES

City of Cambridge: Cambridge
Elgood's: Wisbech
Fenland: Chatteris
Milton: Milton
Oakham: Peterborough
Payn: Ramsey
Rockingham Ales: Elton

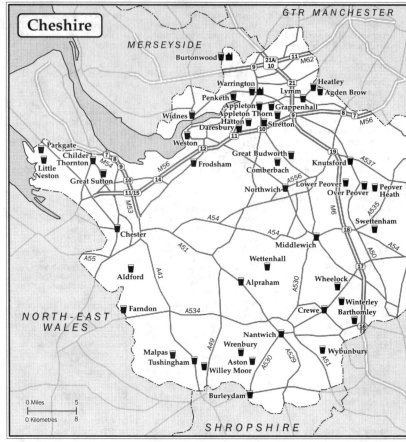

Cheshire

GTR MANCHESTER

MERSEYSIDE

Burtonwood
Warrington
Penketh
Heatley
Lymm
Agden Brow
Appleton
Grappenhall
Appleton Thorn
Widnes
Hatton
Stretton
Daresbury
Weston
Parkgate
Childer
Thornton
Little
Neston
Great Sutton
Frodsham
Great Budworth
Comberbach
Northwich
Lower Peover
Over Peover
Peover
Heath
Knutsford
Swettenham
Chester
Middlewich
Wettenhall
Aldford
Alpraham
Wheelock
Farndon
Crewe
Winterley
Barthomley
NORTH-EAST
WALES
Nantwich
Wrenbury
Wybunbury
Malpas
Tushingham
Aston
Willey Moor
Burleydam

0 Miles 5
0 Kilometres 8

SHROPSHIRE

AGDEN BROW

Jolly Thresher
Higher Lane, Broomedge,
Lymm (A56/B5159 jct)
☎ (01925) 752265
11-11; 12-10.30 Sun
**Hydes' Anvil Mild, Light, Bitter,
seasonal beer** Ⓗ
Large roadside pub: an open-
plan lounge and small bar
cater for the drinker whilst
the dining area is justifiably
popular for its good quality
and value food, including
specials and vegetarian
options. Bowling green at the
rear.
❀ ◑ ▤ P

ALDFORD

Grosvenor Arms
Chester Road (B5130)
☎ (01244) 620228
11.30-11; 12-10.30 Sun
**Boddingtons Bitter; Flowers IPA;
guest beers** Ⓗ
Spacious, open-plan, restyled
Victorian inn where bare
boards and simple, but solid,
wood furniture help create an
upmarket, but homely
atmosphere. Fine food and a

conservatory make it popular
with diners. The large garden
has seats.
🏚 Q ❀ ◑ ▤ ᕼ ♣ P

ALPRAHAM

Travellers Rest ☆
Chester Road (A51 N of
Alpraham)
☎ (01829) 260523
12-4.30 (not Mon-Fri), 6-11; 12-3,
7-10.30 Sun
**Bateman Mild; Marston's Pedigree;
Tetley Bitter** Ⓗ
Thankfully still in its 1960s
time warp – a smoky, adults'
drinking pub. A bowling
green to the rear is supported
by an active contingent.
Within walking distance of
the canal (Bunbury Lock).
🏚 Q ❀ ▤ ♣ P

APPLETON

Birchdale Hotel
Birchdale Road (off A49 at
London Bridge)
☎ (01925) 263662
6 (8.30 Fri & Sat)-11; 8.30-11 Sun
Taylor Landlord; guest beers Ⓗ
Built in mock-Tudor style, in
the early 1800s, this quiet

hotel resides down a narrow
village road. A large split-
level lounge, small games
room, large rear garden and
friendly staff provide a warm
welcome to residents and
non-residents. Eve meals
Mon-Thu 6.30-8.
Q ❀ ⇔ ◑ ♣ P ⊟

APPLETON THORN

Appleton Thorn Village
Hall
Stretton Road (B5356)
☎ (01925) 261187
8.30-11 (not Mon-Wed); 8.30-10.30
Sun
Beer range varies Ⓗ
Former school, now a
thriving village hall offering a
range of seven beers that
changes constantly and
usually includes a mild. It is
used by many village groups,
hence the restricted opening
times.
Q ❀ ᕼ P ⊟

ASTON

Bhurtpore Inn
Wrenbury Road (off A530, E
of Nantwich)

☎ (01270) 780917
12-2.30 (3 Sat), 6.30-11; 12-3, 7-10.30 Sun
Hanby Drawwell; guest beers Ⓗ
This superb 19th-century family-run pub with four drinking areas stocks at least nine guest ales, while a smoke-free dining room serves an excellent range of specials. A very friendly atmosphere and good service are keynotes. Beer festival in July.
⛰ Q ♉ ❀ ◖◗ ♿ ⇌ (Wrenbury) ♣ ⌓ P ⚟ ▯

BARTHOMLEY

White Lion ☆
Audley Road
☎ (01270) 882242
11.30 (5 Thu)-11; 12-10.30 Sun
Burtonwood Bitter, Top Hat; guest beer Ⓗ
This half-timbered black and white thatched pub dates from 1614. Set in the centre of the beautiful village of Barthomley, it offers a welcome to all. Delicious bar lunches are available.
⛰ Q ♉ ❀ ◖ ♣ P

BOLLINGTON

Poachers Inn
95 Ingersley Road
☎ (01625) 572086
12-2.30, 5.30 (7 Sat)-11; 12-4, 7-10.30 Sun
Boddingtons Bitter; Marston's Pedigree; Taylor Landlord; guest beer Ⓗ
Genuine free house offering a warm, cosy, intimate atmosphere; its popular restaurant provides excellent value. The guest beer is often from a local brewery.
⛰ ❀ ◖◗ P

BURLEYDAM

Combermere Arms
On A525, 4½ miles E of Whitchurch
☎ (01948) 871223
12-11; 12-10.30 Sun
Draught Bass; guest beers Ⓗ
Welcoming, family-run pub, once a coaching inn dating back to the 15th century. This free house stands near the famous Combermere Abbey. Guest beers are always from small, independent brewers. Note the old mounting blocks near the side entrance. There is a play room for children.
⛰ Q ♉ ❀ ◖◗ P

BURTONWOOD

Bridge Inn
Phipps Lane
☎ (01925) 225709
11.30-11; 12-10.30 Sun
Burtonwood Bitter Ⓗ
This four-roomed pub serves as a base for local sports teams. It has a bowling green and a small play area for children, who may also use the conservatory. Souvenirs of the licensee's RL playing days adorn the walls. Weekday lunches.
♉ ❀ ◖ P

CHESTER

Albion
Albion Street
☎ (01244) 340345
11.30-3, 5 (6 Sat)-11; 11.30-11 Fri; 12-2.30, 7-10.30 Sun
Cains Bitter; Greenalls Mild, Bitter; Taylor Landlord; guest beers Ⓗ
The kind of traditional pub we hope will never disappear – a must for visitors, especially those walking the adjacent city walls. Note the vast array of Great War memorabilia. Good food (no meals Mon eve).
⛰ Q ◖◗ ⊟

Centurion
1 Oldfield Drive, Vicars Cross (behind shopping square in Green Lane)
☎ (01244) 347623
11.30-11; 11-11 Sat; 12-10.30 Sun
Jennings Bitter; Tetley Bitter; guest beers Ⓗ
Suburban pub, well worth seeking out. It regularly has at least two guest beers, plus a beer festival twice a year. Children welcome lunchtime and early eve.
❀ ◖◗ ⊟ ♣ P

Duttons
10-12 Godsall Lane (access from St. Werburgh Street or Eastgate Street, Row level)
☎ (01244) 403018
11-11; 12-10.30 (may close early) Sun
Lees Bitter, seasonal beer (occasional) Ⓗ
Situated in a narrow historic lane in the heart of the city, this modern bar, with a strong emphasis on food, attracts a mixed clientele, playing music to suit. Bustling at lunchtimes, it can have a more sedate candlelit atmosphere at night.
❀ ◖◗ ♿ ⚟

Mill Hotel
Milton Street
☎ (01244) 350035
11-11; 12-10.30 Sun
Cains Bitter; Weetwood Best Bitter; guest beers Ⓗ
Local CAMRA *Pub of the Year* 2000, where 10 guest ales always include a mild and a stout/porter; a house beer is supplied by Coach House. Jazz nights Mon and a weekly beer draw Sun add to its appeal; a must when visiting the city.
Q ❀ 🛏 ◖◗ ♿ ⇌ P ⚟

Olde Custom House Inn
65-67 Watergate Street (opp. Guildhall)
☎ (01244) 324435
11-11; 12-10.30 Sun
Banks's Original, Bitter, seasonal beers; Marston's Pedigree, HBC Ⓗ
Popular, refurbished 17th-century inn of three rooms, located within the city walls, near the racecourse. Offering a varied range of good value meals, it is often busy at lunchtimes; eve meals end 8pm (no food Sun).
❀ ◖◗ ⊟ ♣ ⊞

Talbot
33 Walter Street, Newtown (near fire station)
☎ (01244) 317901
11-11; 11-5, 7-11 Sat; 12-5, 7-10.30 Sun
Burtonwood Bitter Ⓗ
Epitome of the back-street local: two rooms – one is served through a hatch from the main bar. Games include bagatelle; the pub supports one of twelve teams in the city.
⊟ ⇌ ♣

Union Vaults

44 Egerton Street
☎ (01244) 322170
11-11; 12-10.30 Sun
Greenall's Bitter; Plassey Bitter Ⓗ

Sociable street-corner local close to Mill Hotel and the canal. The quiet, raised lounge area, with its own entrance, has walls adorned with local prints. Lively conversation rules in the lower bar area which has a bagatelle table. An old BR sign marks the corner exit.
≠ ♣

CHILDER THORNTON

White Lion

New Road (off A41)
☎ (0151) 339 3402
11.30-11; 12-10.30 Sun
Thwaites Mild, Bitter Ⓗ

Unspoilt country pub on the outskirts of Ellesmere Port. A former regional CAMRA *Pub of the Year* it has recently been refurbished to create a third small room and reveal some original features. Families welcome in snug at lunchtime. No food Sun.
⚏ Q ❀ ◖ P

COMBERBACH

Spinner & Bergamot

Warrington Road (off A559, Northwich-Warrington road)
☎ (01606) 891307
11.30-3, 5.30-11; 12-3, 7-11 Sun
Greenalls Bitter; Taylor Landlord; guest beers Ⓗ

This friendly, family-run pub is very popular with locals. Bright and cosy, it offers home cooking (eve meals Tue-Sat); bowls and dominoes played. Its multiple rooms display a splendid collection of brasses. Set in a quiet village, it is handy for Marbury Park.
⚏ Q ❀ ◖ ▯ ♣ P ⌁

CONGLETON

Beartown Tap

18 Willow Street
☎ (01260) 270990
12 (4 Mon-Thu)-11; 12-10.30 Sun
Beartown Bear Ass, Kodiak, Bearskinful, Polar Eclipse, seasonal beer Ⓗ

The first Beartown-owned pub, much altered since its former guise as a wine bar, it makes a comfortable, friendly addition to the local drinking scene. Bare floorboards by the bar give way to more comfortable seating in the other rooms, including upstairs. Cider varies. Roadside parking can be difficult when busy.
⚏ Q ⌂ ⌁

Congleton Leisure Centre

Worral Street
☎ (01260) 271552
10.15-1.15 (not Mon), 7-11; 8-10.30 Sun
Beer range varies Ⓗ

Leisure centre, serving three guest beers, whose walls are adorned with brewery posters. Open to the public; sporting activities are optional.
⚏ ♿ P ⌁

Queens Head

Park Lane (opp. station)
11-11; 12-10.30 Sun
Ansells Mild; Greene King Abbot; Marston's Pedigree; Tetley Bitter; guest beer Ⓗ

Canalside pub with its own moorings, popular with locals and the canal trade. Guest beers are sometimes sourced from local breweries.
❀ ⌂ ◖ ≠ ♣ P

Wharf

121 Canal Road
☎ (01260) 272809
11-11; 12-10.30 Sun
Greenalls Mild, Bitter; Taylor Landlord Ⓗ

Smart, friendly pub on the outskirts of town offering fresh home-cooked food from a varied menu. The large garden has a children's play area. It stands near Dog Lane aqueduct.
⚏ ❀ ◖ ♣ P

White Lion

22 High Street
☎ (01260) 272702
12-11; 12-10.30 Sun
Greene King Abbot; Marston's Pedigree Ⓗ

Beamed pub built in 1670 where the single, welcoming bar serves home-cooked food; children admitted. Two Beartown beers are usually also available.
⚏ ❀ ◖ ≠ ♣

CREWE

Monkey

141 West Street (opp. Morris Motorcycles)
☎ (01270) 500079
11-11; 12-10.30 Sun
Eccleshall Slaters Bitter, Premium, Supreme; guest beers Ⓗ

Carefully refurbished street-corner pub with a strong local following, this is Slater's second house. Originally a Greenalls pub called the Wolverton Arms, its nickname was the Monkey and the name was changed on reopening in 1999. A house mild is also stocked. No meals Sun lunch.
◖ ▮ ♣ ⌂

DARESBURY

Ring O Bells

Old Chester Road (off M56, ¹/₂ mile N of jct 11)
☎ (01925) 740256
11.30-11; 12-10.30 Sun
Boddingtons Bitter; Cains Bitter; Greenalls Mild, Bitter; guest beer Ⓗ

This multi-roomed pub, dating back to the 18th century, bears many reminders of Lewis Carroll whose father was the vicar at the church opposite. This quiet pub has no-smoking rooms for diners (good food) and a large garden.
⚏ Q ❀ ◖ ▯ & ♣ P

DISLEY

Albert

75 Buxton Road (A6)
☎ (01663) 764552
12-11; 12-10.30 Sun
Camerons Strongarm; Tetley Bitter; guest beer Ⓗ

Small, but imposing red-brick pub a short distance from the village centre. Four connected but distinct areas give the interior an intimate atmosphere although the bar and lounge are taken over by the Sky sports large screen TV for major events. Eve meals end at 6.30.
⚏ ❀ ◖ ≠ ♣

FARNDON

Farndon Arms

High Street
☎ (01829) 270570
11-3, 5-11; 12-4, 7-10.30 Sun
Boddingtons Bitter; Worthington Bitter; guest beers Ⓗ

Friendly, popular, family-run village pub where restaurant and bar food is based on local produce. A short stroll from the Welsh border where the River Dee is crossed by an historic bridge.
⚏ Q ⚏ ⌂ ◖ ▲ ♣ P ⌁

FRODSHAM

Helter Skelter

31 Church Street
☎ (01928) 733361
11-11; 12-10.30 Sun
Flowers IPA; Weetwood Bitter; guest beers Ⓗ

Locally renowned for its four ever-changing independent guest beers, it is centrally located near the station. The large single bar floor is surrounded by seating areas. It offers an interesting bar menu; the upstairs restaurant opens Fri and Sat eves. The Flowers may be replaced by another Whitbread beer. No eve meals Sun.
◖ ▮ ≠ ⌂ ▯

Queens Head

92 Main Street
☎ (01928) 733289
11 (11.30 Tue & Wed)-11; 11.30-3,

6.30-11 Mon; 12-10.30 (12-2.30, 7-10.30 Jan-Mar) Sun
Greenalls Mild, Bitter; guest beer Ⓗ
Main street pub circa 16th century; it is good for games with plenty of atmosphere. Its various rooms get very busy on Thu (market day). Folk music is staged in the stables behind the pub Fri eves.
இ ◖ ≉ ♣ P

Ring O Bells
2 Bellemonte Road
☎ (01928) 732068
11.30-3, 5.30-11; 11-11 Fri; 11.30-4, 6-11 Sat; 12-3, 7-11 Sun
Greenalls Bitter; guest beers Ⓗ
Next to the church, hence the name; this 15th-century inn with its beams and low ceilings is very welcoming – tall people beware. Five small attractive rooms, an excellent cobblestone frontage and well-kept flower tubs add to its appeal. Worth finding.
ᐙ Q இ ◖ ≉ ♣ P

GAWSWORTH
Harrington Arms ☆
Church Lane (off A536)
☎ (01260) 223325
12-3, 6-11; 12-3, 7-10.30 Sun
Robinson's Hatters Mild, Best Bitter Ⓗ
Traditional alehouse that has been in the same family for over 100 years. Part of a working farm owned by Robinson's, its classic interior features scrubbed tables and wood settles. Close to Gawsworth Hall and church, it is well worth seeking out.
ᐙ Q ▲ ♣ P

GRAPPENHALL
Grappenhall Community Centre
Bellhouse Farm, Bellhouse Lane (off A50)
☎ (01925) 268633
7.30 (2 Sat)-11; 12-10.30 Sun
Ruddles Best Bitter; guest beers Ⓗ
Large private club and social centre in an old farmhouse and bar, supporting a wide range of clubs and activities. Real ale is now available in the old barn function room. A beer festival is held in April. A CAMRA membership card gains admission.
ᐅ இ ᚢ ♣ P

Parr Arms
Church Lane
☎ (01925) 267393
12-3, 5.30-11; 12-11 Sat; 12-10.30 Sun
Draught Bass; Boddingtons Bitter; Greenalls Bitter; Marston's Pedigree; guest beer Ⓗ
Standing in a cobbled street in the shadow of the parish church tower, this traditional pub with a central bar serves two lounges and a public bar, but food service dominates. The Bridgewater Canal runs through the village.
இ ◖ ▶ ⊞ ♣ P ⊬

GREAT BUDWORTH
George & Dragon
High Street (off A559 Northwich-Warrington road)
☎ (01606) 891317
11.30-3, 6-11; 11.30-11 Fri & Sat; 12-10.30 Sun
Tetley Bitter; guest beers Ⓗ
Comfortable village pub in a photogenic setting: a large public bar, a cosy front lounge and a restaurant upstairs that welcomes children. Constantly changing guest beers make regular visits worthwhile. Near Arley Estate, it is popular with locals and visitors.
Q ◖ ▶ ⊞ ♣ ⊂ P

GREAT SUTTON
White Swan
Old Chester Road (off A41)
☎ (0151) 339 9284
11.30-11; 12-10.30 Sun
Burtonwood Bitter; guest beer Ⓗ
Traditional local: an excellent public bar and a split-level lounge showing prints of old Ellesmere Port. It offers imaginative guest beers in an area where beer choice is limited. No food after 8pm or on Tue.
இ ◖ ▶ ⊞ ♣ P

HANDFORTH
Railway
Station Road
☎ (01625) 523472
12-3, 5.30-11; 12-3, 7-10.30 Sun
Robinson's Hatter Mild, Best Bitter, Old Tom Ⓗ
Multi-roomed pub facing the station; no food at weekends. Unusually Old Tom is served all year round. Q ◖ ≉ ♣ P ⟒

HATTON
Hatton Arms
Hatton Lane 1 mile from A49/B5356 jct at Stretton
☎ (01925) 730314
11.30 (11 Sat)-11; 12-10.30 Sun
Greenalls Mild, Bitter; Marston's Pedigree; Theakston Best Bitter Ⓗ
Easily accessible from M56 (junction 10), this attractive 17th-century village inn and restaurant maintains strong community links. Its low beamed interior includes a quiet lounge and small games room off an open bar area. The restaurant overlooks a large garden with picnic tables. No food Mon eve.
ᐙ இ ᐃ ◖ ▶ ♣ P

HEATLEY
Barn Owl Inn
Agden Wharf, Warrington Lane, Lymm (off A56, Altrincham-Lymm road)
OS707872
☎ (01925) 752020
11-11; 12-10.30 Sun
Banks's Original; Marston's Pedigree; guest beer Ⓗ
The open-plan, main room overlooks the canal path, with all the water-based action on full view. Children's certificate. It hosts live music Sat eve. Friendly locals provide a warm welcome.
இ ◖ ▶ ᚢ ▲ P ⊬

Railway
Mill Lane (B5159)
☎ (01925) 752742
12 (11.30 Sat)-11; 12-10.30 Sun
Boddingtons Bitter; Taylor Landlord; guest beer Ⓗ
This community pub next to the Pennine Trail is a base for many local societies and hosts a folk club Thu. Several rooms, served by a central bar, cater for all tastes. The large garden with play area is popular in summer with families. Freshly-prepared lunches (not served Sun) include specials.
ᐙ Q ᐅ இ ◖ ⊞ ♣ P

HIGHER HURDSFIELD
George & Dragon
61 Rainow Road
☎ (01625) 424300
12-3, 7-11; 12-11 Sun
Courage Directors; guest beers Ⓗ
Small, friendly pub, built of local stone, set back off the main road with a bus stop outside. Part of the pub is 400 years old. Pool played.
இ ◖ ♣ P

KNUTSFORD
Builders Arms
63 Mobberley Road
☎ (01565) 634528
11-11; 12-10.30 Sun
Banks's Original, Bitter; Marston's Pedigree Ⓗ
Wonderfully unspoilt, cosy pub on the edge of town; it is divided into two rooms by a central bar and enjoys a wonderful ambience. The garden has play equipment for children. Weekday lunches served.
Q இ ◖ ≉ ♣

LITTLE NESTON
Harp Inn
19 Quayside (from Burton Rd, turn down Marshlands Rd to marsh and turn left)
☎ (0151) 336 6980
11-11; 12-10.30 Sun

Taylor Landlord; Whitbread Trophy; guest beers [H]
Delightful, two-roomed, ex-miners' pub served by a single bar. The superb public bar has a real fire and low beams. It may be difficult to find, but well worth the trouble. Enjoy the superb view across the Dee, but beware high tides. Eve meals served 5-7.30.
🏨 Q 🍴 ◖ ▶ P

LOWER PEOVER

Crown
Crown Lane (on B5081)
☎ (01565) 722074
11.30-3, 5.30-11; 12-3, 7-10.30 (extends in summer) Sun
Boddingtons Bitter; Flowers IPA; Taylor Landlord; guest beer [H]
Homely, 17th-century village inn with an excellent cobbled frontage and hanging baskets, matched by an equally fine interior. Local breweries are supported.
🏨 🍴 ◖ ▶ ♣ P

LYMM

Spread Eagle
47 Eagle Brow
☎ (01925) 757467
11.30-11; 12-10.30 Sun
Lees GB Mild, Bitter, seasonal beer [H]
Three-roomed village local, near Lymm Cross: a basic bar, a cosy, atmospheric snug with a real fire, and a large split-level lounge. Excellent home-cooked lunches served; accommodation available Sun-Thu only.
🏨 Q 🍴 ◖ 🍺 ♣ P

MACCLESFIELD

Baths
40 Green Street (off A537, behind station)
11-4 (not Mon-Fri), 6.30-11; 12-3, 7-10.30 Sun
Banks's Original, Bitter; Boddingtons Bitter [H]
Small but thriving local, just off the Buxton road. A local bowling green inspired its original name, Bowling Green Tavern, then the now-closed public baths; the pub fortunately outlived both amenities.
🍺 🚋 ♣

British Flag
42 Coare Street
☎ (01625) 425500
5.30-11; 12-3, 7-10.30 Sun
Robinson's Hatters Mild, Best Bitter, [H] Old Tom (winter) [G]
Old-fashioned, friendly town local of four rooms. In the 1860s the pub boasted ginger beer manufacturing and had a reputation as the local Kings School brewery tap, as

it was frequented by school staff. It has large screen TV for sport, and a pool room.
🚋 ♣

George & Dragon
21-23 Sunderland Street
☎ (01625) 421898
11-4 (3 Tue & Wed), 5.30-11; 11-11 Fri; 11-5, 7-11 Sat; 12-3, 7-10.30 Sun
Robinson's Hatters Mild, Best Bitter [H]
Handy for the station, this friendly pub sells good value, home-cooked food early eve. Most pub games are catered for – skittles, pool, darts, dominoes and cards.
🍴 ▶ 🚋 ♣

Railway View
Byrons Lane (just off London road)
☎ (01625) 423657
12-2 (3 Sat; not Mon-Thu), 6-11; 12-3, 7-10.30 Sun
Bateman Mild; Boddingtons Bitter; guest beers [H]
Pleasant pub, 100 yards from the main London road. An excellent range of beers includes six guests and a house beer from Coach House. 🏨 🍴 ◖ ▶ 🚋 ♣

Ship
61-63 Beech Lane
☎ (01625) 261909
2-11; 12-3, 7-10.30 Sun
Draught Bass; Storm Ale Force; guest beers [H]
Formerly two cottages converted to a single-roomed pub in the 1960s. Food is available during the day, with occasional international cuisine eves.
🏨 Q 🍴 ◖ 🚋 ♣ ✂

Sun Inn
45 Mill Lane (Leek end of the Silk Road)
☎ (01625) 610436
12-3, 5.30-11; 12-11 Sat; 4-10.30 Sun
Burtonwood Bitter; Cains Bitter; guest beers [H]
Traditional bare-boarded alehouse with two bars, a welcoming fire in each, and an old-fashioned welcome. It offers an excellent rotation of seven guest beers. Near the canal and station, it is well worth a visit. Boules played.
🏨 Q 🍴 🚋 ♣

Waters Green Tavern
96 Waters Green
☎ (01625) 422653
11.30 (11 Sat)-3, 5.30 (7 Sat)-11
7-10.30 Sun
Beer range varies [H]
Close to the bus and rail stations, this pleasant pub was originally three storeys; the half-timbered frontage is false. Popular at lunchtime for good food, it stocks an excellent range of seven guest beers. ◖ 🚋 ♣

MALPAS

Crown Hotel
Old Hall Street
☎ (01948) 860474
11-11; 12-10.30 Sun
Beer range varies [H]
17th-century former coaching inn with a modernised, split-level interior; it stands on the Cheshire Cycleway. It always stocks at least one local brew. The games night (Mon) is popular. Watch out for the immense dog!
🏨 🍴 🛏 ◖ ▶ ⚘ ♣

MIDDLEWICH

Boars Head
26 Kinderton Street (A54)
☎ (01606) 833191
12-11; 12-10.30 Sun
Robinson's Best Bitter [H]
This multi-roomed Victorian local featuring a fine tiled floor is a popular meeting point for various clubs and societies. It has a large screen TV in the games room, plus a restaurant (no food Mon or Tue). Handy for the canal.
🏨 🍴 🛏 ◖ ▶ ⛸ ♣ P

NANTWICH

Black Lion
29 Welsh Row
☎ (01270) 628711
12-11; 12-10.30 Sun
Weetwood Best Bitter, Old Dog [H]
Small, old black and white half-timbered pub; downstairs it is all nooks and crannies. Live music is staged at weekends. Enjoy good conversation in a friendly environment. A Titanic beer is normally also on tap. Breakfast and toasties are served all day. The family room is upstairs.
🏨 Q 🐕 🍴 🛏 ♣ ○

Oddfellows Arms
97 Welsh Row (Chester road from centre)
☎ (01270) 624758
12-3 (not Mon), 6-11; 12-11 Fri & Sat; 12-4, 7-10.30 Sun
Burtonwood Bitter, Top Hat; guest beer (weekends) [H]
Lovely, small single-roomed building with beams, low ceiling and two open fires ablaze in winter. The guest beer, changed monthly, comes from Burtonwood's Cask Collection list. It hosts regular live music: bluegrass and country Wed; jazz piano and guitar Thu.
🏨 🍴 ◖ ▶ ♣

Vine
42 Hospital Street
☎ (01270) 624172
11.30-2.30 (not Mon), 5.30-11;
11.30-11 Sat; 12-2, 7-10.30 Sun

Draught Bass; Worthington Bitter; guest beer [H]
Grade II listed town-centre pub, dating from the 1640s; the comfortable interior features split levels and oak beams. Children are welcome in certain sections. Folk music is performed alternate Tue. It also sells Museum beers, brewed by the landlord. Eve meals served Wed-Sat.
◐◑♣

NORTHWICH

Freemasons Arms
43 Castle Street
☎ (01606) 79310
11-11; 12-10.30 Sun
Webster's Yorkshire Bitter; guest beers [H]
Cosy local dating from the mid-1800s; built in the typical unadorned local style.
❀ ≉ (Greenbank) ♣

OVER PEOVER

Parkgate Inn
Stocks Lane
☎ (01625) 861455
11-11; 12-4, 7-10 (12-10.30 summer) Sun
Samuel Smith OBB [H]
Attractive, multi-roomed pub hiding behind an ivy-covered exterior. Beams, settles, good food and open fires are just a few attributes of this friendly pub. Built in a row of cottages, it enjoys a good reputaton locally.
♨ ♞ ❀ ◐◑ ♣ P ⚟

PARKGATE

Red Lion
The Parade
☎ (0151) 336 1548
12-2.30, 5-11; 12-11 Fri, Sat & summer; 12-10.30 Sun
Ind Coope Burton Ale; Taylor Landlord; Tetley Bitter [H]
Wirral CAMRA *Pub of the Year* 1996, this traditional lounge and bar offer superb views of the Welsh hills across the Dee estuary and marsh (famous for birdlife). Local numbers are swelled by many summer promenaders. Nelson, the parrot, guards the bar. No food Sun.
Q ◐ ⊞ ♣

PENKETH

Ferry Tavern
Station Road (off A562, follow signs to Fiddlers Ferry yacht haven)
☎ (01925) 791117
12-3, 5.30-11; 12-11 Sat & summer; 12-10.30 Sun
Boddingtons Bitter; Courage Directors; Ruddles County; Shepherd Neame Spitfire; guest beers [H]
On a site dating back to 1160 as a ferry crossing point over the River Mersey, this 17th-century inn stocks six cask beers and nearly 250 whiskies. Fresh, home-made food is available Mon-Sat. Children allowed in the bar areas until 8.30. It has a small no-smoking restaurant upstairs (book early).
♨ Q ❀ ◐◑ P

PEOVER HEATH

Dog Inn
Well Bank Lane
☎ (01625) 861421
11.30-3, 5.30-11; 12-4.30, 7-10.30 Sun
Moorhouse's Black Cat; Flowers Original; Tetley Bitter; Weetwood Old Dog [H]
This large comfortable, rambling pub, converted from a row of 18th-century cottages has a good reputation for its food and accommodation.
♨ Q ❀ 🛏 ◐◑ ⊞ ♿ ♣ P ⚟

PRESTBURY

Admiral Rodney
New Road
☎ (01625) 829484
11-3, 5.30-11; 11-11 Fri & Sat; 12-3, 7-10.30 Sun
Robinson's Hatters Mild, Best Bitter [H]
Popular inn, situated in an attractive village terrace. A Grade II listed building, the original front door became the back door with the building of the new road through the village.
❀ ◐ ≉ P

RAINOW

Highwayman
Whaley Bridge Road (B5470)
☎ (01625) 573245
11-3, 7-11; 12-3, 7-10.30 Sun
Thwaites Bitter [H]
Remote, windswept inn, known as the Blacksmith's Arms until 1949 and locally as the Patch. Enjoy the breathtaking views from the front door and the three blazing open fires in winter.
♨ Q ◐◑ ⊞ P

STRETTON

Ring O Bells
Lower Stretton (A559, off M56 jct 10)
☎ (01925) 730556
12-3, 5.30-11; 12-3.30, 7-11 Sat; 12-3, 7-10.30 Sun
Greenalls Mild, Bitter; guest beer [H]
Once a row of cottages, this pub has one main and two side rooms; friendly and comfortable, it is a rare survivor of a country local.
♨ Q ❀ P

SWETTENHAM

Swettenham Arms
☎ (01477) 571284
11.30-3, 6-midnight; 12-4, 7-10.30 Sun
Beartown Bearskinful; Hydes' Anvil Bitter; Jennings Bitter; Tetley Bitter [H]
Large, but cosy, old pub; heavily timbered inside, it features wooden settles, heavy iron tables, a sofa and two real fires. It hosts live music Wed eve. Seats are provided in the garden and patio in summer. The award-winning food is exceptional.
♨ Q ❀ ◐◑ ♿ ⌓ P

TUSHINGHAM

Blue Bell Inn
Signed Bell 'o t'Hill from A41, 4 miles N of Whitchurch
☎ (01948) 662172
12-3, 6-11; 12-3, 7-10.30 Sun
Hanby Drawwell; guest beers [H]
Pre-Civil War inn showing original beams and artefacts, it serves good food and hosts regular theme nights. It stocks one or two guest ales and was local CAMRA *Pub of the Year* 1998. Small people beware of the big dog.
♨ Q ❀ ◐◑ ♿ ▲ ♣ P ⚟

WARRINGTON

Lower Angel
27 Buttermarket Street
☎ (01925) 633299
11-11; 12-3, 7-10.30 Sun
Ind Coope Burton Ale; Tetley Dark Mild, Bitter [H]
Traditional, two-roomed town-centre pub that still manages to retain its Walker of Warrington identity because of its windows. A house beer is brewed by Tetley at Leeds.
⊞ ≉ (Central) ♣

Wilkies Tavern
25 Church Street (A49, 500 yds from centre)
☎ (01925) 416564
12-11; 12-10.30 Sun
Beer range varies [H]
The only genuine free house in Warrington: a single room bar bearing an Irish theme. An ever-changing range of four beers is invariably sourced from smaller/micro-breweries. Occasional beer festivals are held in the rear courtyard.
≉ (Central) ♣ ⌓

WESTON

Prospect
70 Weston Road, Runcorn
☎ (01928) 561280
11-11; 12-10.30 Sun
Greenalls Mild, Bitter: Young's Special; guest beer [H]
Sympathetically refurbished

local with a vault where darts and pool are played. Note the original Greenalls etched glass window, and the collection of old local photographs. A wide range of food is available.

🏚 Q 🕸 ◖▮ & P

WETTENHALL
Little Man
Winsford Road (minor road S of Wettenhall) OS628601
☎ (01270) 528203
12-3 (not Tue), 7-11; 12-3, 7-10.30 Sun
Beer range varies Ⓗ
Friendly, rural pub much used by the farming and equestrian communities, that is welcoming to children and dogs, too. Excellent value traditional meals available, and the landlord provides an ever-changing choice of up to five real ales.

🏚 🕸 ◖▮ ♣ P 🍲

WHEELOCK
Cheshire Cheese
466 Crewe Road
☎ (01270) 760319
12-11; 12-10.30 Sun
Hydes' Anvil Dark, Bitter, seasonal beers Ⓗ
Friendly local in a recently bypassed village, taken on by Hyde's in 1999. The welcome makes it popular with canal-goers.

🏚 🕸 ◖▮ ♣

WIDNES
Horse & Jockey
18 Birchfield Road (300 yds S of station)
☎ (0151) 420 2996
11-11; 12-10.30 Sun
Greenalls Bitter; Tetley Bitter; guest beer Ⓗ
Small, friendly one-room pub, much favoured by the local community, free from juke box and fruit machines. It has a large, fully enclosed garden to the rear.

🕸 ⇌ P

Try also: **Grapes**, Widnes Rd (Greenalls)

WILLEY MOOR
Willey Moor Lock Tavern
Tarporley Road (off A49, opp. wildfowl sanctuary)
OS534452
☎ (01948) 663274
12-2.30 (3 summer), 6-11; 7-10.30 Sun
Theakston Best Bitter; guest beers Ⓗ
Next to the Llangollen Canal, it offers up to four guest ales in the summer when the fine outdoor drinking area and children's play area are very popular. Lunchtime meals

may finish early. The Sandstone Trail runs alongside the pub. Note the fine teapot collection.

🏚 Q 🕸 ◖▮ P

WILMSLOW
New Inn
Alderley Road
☎ (01625) 523123
11.30-11; 12-10.30 Sun
Hyde's Anvil Light, Bitter; Ⓟ **Jekyll's Gold** Ⓗ
Large pub where the emphasis is on lunchtime meals. Much modernised, but it retains some atmosphere enhanced by low beams.

🕸 ◖ ⇌ ♣ 🍺

Swan
Swan Street (near station)
☎ (01625) 536070
11-11; 12-10.30 Sun
Boddingtons Bitter; Taylor Landlord; guest beers Ⓗ
Well-furnished,open-plan pub at the centre of Wilmslow, stocking the best selection of guest beers in town. The pub hosts a beer festival Whit weekend.

🏚 🕸 ◖▮ ⇌ ♣ P

WINCLE
Ship
Off A54, near Danebridge
☎ (01260) 227217
12-3, 7-11; 12-3, 7-10.30) Sun
Boddingtons Bitter; Beartown Kodiak; guest beers Ⓗ
Attractive, 16th-century, village inn, set in the popular Dane Valley, next to a trout farm. It serves superb good value food and the hikers/family room is well-used by walkers.

🏚 Q 🚬 🕸 ◖▮ P 🍲 🍺

WINTERLEY
Foresters Arms
473 Crewe Road (500 yds S of the A534 Wheelock roundabout) OS748577
☎ (01270) 762642
12-11; 12-10.30 Sun
Marston's Pedigree; Tetley Dark Mild, Bitter; Weetwood Old Dog Ⓗ
This single-roomed, friendly pub enjoys strong local support. A low, beamed ceiling and interesting carved fire surrounds add to its appeal. The unusual garden houses a small dovecot and classic tractor. Home-cooked food is served at sensible prices.

🏚 🕸 ◖▮ ♣ P

WRENBURY
Cotton Arms
Cholmondeley Road (near canal)

☎ (01270) 780377
12-3, 6-11; 12-11 Sat; 12-10.30 Sun
Greenalls Bitter; guest beer Ⓗ
Comfortable, country pub with an open fire; a large raised area (no-smoking) is available for dining and drinking. One guest beer is always available, two in summer. It has an enclosed garden and a bowling green.

🏚 🕸 ◖▮ ⊞ ▲ ⇌ ♣ P 🍲

WYBUNBURY
Swan
2 Main Road (B5071, 1½ miles from A500 at Shavington)
☎ (01270) 841280
12-11; 12-10.30 Sun
Jennings Mild, Bitter, Cumberland Ale, Sneck Lifter; Marston's Pedigree; guest beers (summer) Ⓗ
Traditional, two-roomed, family-run inn, with strong local following, popular with walkers and cyclists. In a very pleasant location next to the (leaning) church tower, its beamed ceilings hint at 15th-century origins. The guest beers come from the Jennings portfolio. No-smoking area available until 9.30.

🏚 Q 🕸 ⇌ ◖▮ ⊞ ♣ P 🍲

Cask Marque
Pubs that carry the Cask Marque symbol indicate that the licensees have successfully passed a number of tests concerning beer quality, and display plaques to this effect in their outlets. However, these pubs have been chosen independently of Cask Marque by CAMRA. The Cask Marque symbol is added during the editing process and Cask Marque is not involved in the selection of pubs.

INDEPENDENT BREWERIES

Beartown: Congleton

Burtonwood: Burtonwood

Coach House: Warrington

Sarah's Hophouse: Warrington

Storm: Macclesfield

Weetwood: Tarpoley

Beery delights

These latest titles from CAMRA Books enable you to sample the beers of neighbouring European countries and to visit British pubs that offer a warm welcome to families.

Good Beer Guide to Belgium, Holland and Luxembourg

The third edition of Tim Webb's acclaimed guide pinpoints the amazing beers and styles of the Low Countries and Luxembourg, including the makers of such rare beers as lambic and gueuze, fruit beers, spiced wheat beers and Trappist ales. The guide includes the best bars in all three countries. £9.99.

Good Beer Guide to Northern France

Arthur Taylor brilliantly brings to life the great artisanal beers of Northern France, including biere de garde, styles that are at long last emerging from the giant shadow of the country's wine culture. The guide lists all the breweries of the region and recommends the best bars in which to enjoy the beers. £7.99

The Best Pubs for Families

In the third edition of this popular guide, David Perrott offers the best pubs in England, Scotland and Wales that provide good family facilities. The guide is fully mapped by the author and each pub entry gives full details of what is available for children to amuse themselves plus the beers their parents can enjoy. £8.99

The books are available from good bookshops or direct from CAMRA (post free), 230 Hatfield Road, St Albans AL1 4LW; cheques or postal made out to 'CAMRA'. To order by Access or Visa, phone 01727 867201 between 9am and 5pm, Monday to Friday (answerphone outside office hours). Allow 28 days for delivery.

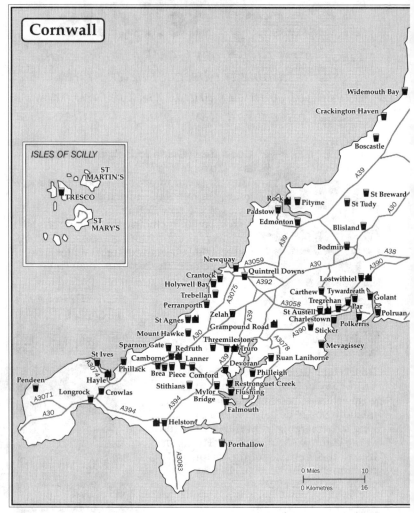

Cornwall

ISLES OF SCILLY

ST MARTIN'S

TRESCO

ST MARY'S

Widemouth Bay

Crackington Haven

Boscastle

St Breward

Rock · Pityme · St Tudy

Padstow

Edmonton

Blisland

Bodmin

A38

Newquay · A3059

Quintrell Downs

Crantock

Holywell Bay

Trebellan

Perranporth

St Agnes · Zelah

Mount Hawke

Grampound Road

Lostwithiel

Carthew · Tywardreath

Tregrehan · Golant

St Austell

Charlestown · Par · Polruan

Polkerris

Sticker

Sparnon Gate · Redruth

Threemilestone

Truro

Mevagissey

St Ives

Camborne · Lanner

Phillack · Brea · Piece · Comford

Devoran · Ruan Lanihorne

Pendeen

Hayle

Crowlas

Stithians

Philleigh

Longrock

Mylor Bridge · Restronguet Creek · Flushing

A30

A394

Helston

Falmouth

Porthallow

A3083

0 Miles 10
0 Kilometres 16

ALBASTON

Queens Head
☎ (01822) 832482
11.30-3, 6-11; 12-3, 7-10.30 Sun
**Courage Best Bitter; Morland Old
Speckled Hen; guest beers** Ⓗ
Welcoming, two-bar local,
run by the same family for
two generations. Q ❀
⇌ (Gunnislake) ♣ P

ALTARNUN

Rising Sun
1 mile N of village
(Camelford road)
☎ (01566) 86332
11-3, 6.30-11 (11-11 Sat & summer);
12-10.30 Sun
Beer range varies Ⓗ
Originally a 16th-century
farmhouse, it retains many
original features. There are
two small rooms off the main
bar area. Six real ales.
🏠 Q ❧ ❀ ⇌ ◑ ▶ ▲ ♣ P

BLISLAND

Blisland Inn
The Green ☎ (01208) 850739
11.30-11; 12-10.30 Sun
Beer range varies Ⓗ/Ⓖ
Friendly, rural pub on the
only village green in
Cornwall. Voted Cornwall
CAMRA *Pub of the Year* 1999.
Excellent food is based on
local produce. Two of the six
guest beers are Cornish.
🏠 Q ❧ ❀ ◑ ▶ ♣ ⇔ P 🍴

BODMIN

Garland Ox
65 Higher Bore Street
☎ (01208) 75372
11-11; 12-10.30 Sun
**Courage Best Bitter; Morland Old
Speckled Hen; Skinner's Spriggan
Ale** Ⓗ
100-year-old reputedly
haunted pub, the meeting
place of the Bodmin Folk

Club. This lively traditional
local has a games room.
Q ❧ ❀ ◑ ▲ ♣ ⇔ P 🍴

Hole in Wall
16 Crockwell Street
☎ (01208) 72397
12-2.30, 5-11; 12-10.30 Sun
**Draught Bass; Sharp's Doom Bar;
guest beers** Ⓗ
Warm, welcoming town pub,
with an upstairs restaurant
and outdoor seating in the
courtyard with a stream.
🏠 Q ❀ ◑ ▶ ▲ 🍴

Try also: George & Dragon,
St Nicholas St (St Austell);
Masons Arms, Hr. Bore St
(Free)

BOSCASTLE

Wellington Hotel
The Harbour
☎ (01840) 250202
11-3, 6-11, (11-11 summer);

floorboards, almost unaltered for the last 40 years. Boules played. ⚒ ☸ ♨ ♣ ○ P

BREA

Brea Inn

Higher Brea (between Four Lanes and Camborne, S of A3047) OS666404
☎ (01209) 713706
12-2.30 (not Mon), 7-11 (not Tue);
12-2.30, 7-11 Sun
Greene King Abbot; Sharp's Doom Bar or Own Ⓗ
Cosy, 18th-century inn, a former miners' alehouse. The friendly bar is on traditional lines. Tom is the resident ghost. ⚒ Q ☸ ⛵ ⛵ P

CAMBORNE

Tyacks Hotel

27 Commercial Street
☎ (01209) 612424
11-11; 12-10.30 Sun
St Austell Tinners, Daylight Robbery, HSD Ⓗ
Recently refurbished town-centre hotel: a lively, sometimes noisy public bar, a carpeted lounge, popular with lunchtime shoppers, and a good-value restaurant area. Q ☸ ⛵ ⛵ ⛵ ⮡ ≉ P ⊞

CARTHEW

Sawles Arms

On B3274, 3 miles N of St Austell ☎ (01726) 850317
11-11; 12-10.30 Sun
St Austell XXXX Mild, Tinners, seasonal beers Ⓗ
Friendly local in a small hamlet near the China Clay Museum.
⚒ ☸ ⛵ ♣ P

CHARLESTOWN

Rashleigh Arms

Off A390, S of St Austell
☎ (01726) 73635
11-11; 12-10.30 Sun
Draught Bass; Fuller's ESB; Sharp's Doom Bar, Own; Tetley Bitter; Wadworth 6X; guest beers Ⓗ
Large, friendly inn overlooking the famous port : two large bars and a no-smoking family room.
⛵ ☸ ⛵ ⛵ ⛵ ♿ ♨ ♣ P ⌿

Try also: **Pier House Hotel**, Harbour Front (Free)

COMFORD

Fox & Hounds

On A393, Redruth-Falmouth road ☎ (01209) 820251
11-3, 6-11; 12-3, 7-10.30 Sun
Draught Bass; St Austell Tinners, HSD, seasonal beer Ⓖ
Old country pub, well refurbished in recent times, but retaining the beamed ceilings. The small public bar

bears an interesting old mural. ⚒ Q ☸ ⛵ ⛵ ⛵ ♨ P

CRACKINGTON HAVEN

Coombe Barton Inn

☎ (01840) 230345
11-3, 6-11 (11-11 summer); 12-3,
7-10.30 (12-10.30 summer) Sun
St Austell Dartmoor, Daylight Robbery, HSD; Sharp's Doom Bar; guest beers Ⓗ
Spacious bar set in a 300-year-old hotel affording a splendid view out over the beach to the surf. It has a popular restaurant and a large family room.
⛵ ☸ ⛵ ⛵ ♿ ♨ ♣ P ⌿

CRANTOCK

Old Albion

Langurroc Road
☎ (01637) 830243
12-11; 12-10.30 Sun
Courage Best Bitter; John Smith's Bitter; Skinner's Betty Stogs Bitter; guest beer Ⓗ
Part-thatched village pub by the church gate, an easy walk from a safe, sandy beach and local campsites. Good value food. Cider in summer.
⚒ ⛵ ☸ ⛵ ♨ ○ P

CROWLAS

Star Inn

On A30 ☎ (01736) 740375
11-11 (11-230, 6-11 winter); 12-10.30 Sun
Beer range varies Ⓗ
Ex-Coteligh brewer has turned free house licensee and installed a microbrew plant in outbuildings here. Organic meat and veg is used in home-cooked meals and for B&B. ⚒ Q ⛵ ⛵ ⛵ P

Try also: **White Hart**, Ludgvan (Free)

DEVORAN

Old Quay Inn

St Johns Terrace (off A39)
☎ (01872) 863142
11.30-2.30, 6-11; 11.30-11 Sat & summer; 12-10.30 Sun
Draught Bass; Flowers IPA; guest beers Ⓗ
Welcoming pub, offering ever-changing guest ales and good home-cooked food. It affords fine views over quay and creek. Limited parking.
⚒ ☸ ⛵ ⛵ ♣ P

EDMONTON

Quarryman

☎ (01208) 816444
12-11; 12-10.30 Sun
Sharp's Cornish Coaster; Draught Bass; Taylor Landlord (summer); **guest beer** Ⓗ
Pleasant, relaxing pub, part of a holiday and sports

12-10.30 Sun
Flowers IPA; St Austell HSD; Wadworth 6X; guest beers Ⓗ
The long bar of this 16th-century coaching inn houses interesting artefacts. It hosts live folk music Mon eve. The 10-acre grounds offer woodland walks. Cider in summer.
⚒ ⛵ ☸ ⛵ ⛵ ♨ ♣ ○ P

Try also: **Cobweb**, The Bridge (Free)

BOTUS FLEMING

Rising Sun

1/2 mile off A388, near Saltash ☎ (01752) 842792
12-4 (not Mon-Thu), 6-11; 12-11 Sat; 12-10.30 Sun
Draught Bass; Worthington Bitter; guest beers Ⓗ
Small pub, tucked away just off the beaten track featuring low ceilings and worn

complex, close to the Camel Trail. It has a popular bistro next door. It hosts free-for-all folk music nights (Tue).
🏚 Q ❀ ⇆ ◖❳ ▲ ♣ P

FALMOUTH

Seven Stars ☆
The Moor ☎ (01326) 312111
11-3, 6-11; 12-3, 7-10.30 Sun
Draught Bass; Sharp's Own; guest beers G
Unspoilt, popular old pub with a lively tap room and a quiet snug. In the same family for five generations, the present landlord is an ordained priest. Q ❀ ⌸

FLUSHING

Royal Standard
St Peters Hill (off A393 at Penryn, also by foot ferry from Falmouth)
☎ (01326) 374250
11-2.30 (3 Fri & Sat); 6.30-11 (varies winter); 12-3, 7-10.30 (varies winter) Sun
Draught Bass; Sharp's Cornish Coaster, Doom Bar H
Friendly local, where home-made pasties and apple pies are specialities. Fine views of the Penryn River can be enjoyed from the front patio.
🏚 ❀ ◖❳ ♣

GOLANT

Fisherman's Arms
Fore Street (off B3269, up river from Fowey))
☎ (01726) 832453
12-3, 6-11 (11-11 summer); 12-10.30 Sun
Ushers Best Bitter, Founders H
Charming village pub in a lovely waterside setting, with views across the River Fowey. When parking beware of high tides. Limited parking; boules played.
🏚 Q ⏚ ❀ ⇆ ◖❳ ⬥ ♣ P

GUNNISLAKE

Rising Sun Inn
Calstock Road
☎ (01822) 832201
11-3, 5-11; 11-11 Sat; 12-2.30, 7-10.30 Sun
Draught Bass; Sharp's Cornish Coaster, Skinner's Betty Stogs Bitter; guest beers H
Friendly, 17th-century inn where a terraced garden provides views out over the Tamar valley.
🏚 Q ❀ ◖❳ ⬥ ➤ ⇌ P

Try also: **Tavistock Arms Hotel**, Fore St (Free)

HELSTON

Blue Anchor
50 Coinagehall Street
☎ (01326) 562821

11-11; 12-10.30 Sun
Blue Anchor Middle, Special, Extra Special H
A rambling, unspoilt 15th-century granite building under a thatched roof with a brewery at the rear. Good, home-made food is served.
🏚 Q ⏚ ❀ ⇆ ◖⌸

HOLYWELL BAY

St Piran's Inn
☎ (01637) 830205
11-11 (12-3; 6-11 winter); 12-10.30 Sun
Beer range varies H
Almost on the golden sands of a picturesque bay, this free house has good value meals and up to four beers.
🏚 Q ⏚ ❀ ◖❳ ⬥ ▲ P

Try also: **Treguth**, Holywell Bay (Free)

KINGSAND

Rising Sun
The Green ☎ (01752) 822840
12-11; 12-10.30 Sun
Draught Bass; Courage Best Bitter; John Smith's Bitter; guest beer H
Cosy village inn run by a welcoming landlord and landlady who source local produce for the excellent home-cooked food, including the famous half-yard of sausage, and crab dishes. The pub is frequently used by walkers from the nearby coastal footpaths. Live bands perform Fri. 🏚 Q ⇆ ♣

Try also: **Halfway House** (Free)

LANNER

Lanner Inn
The Square (A393 Redruth-Falmouth road)
☎ (01209) 215611
12-3, 4.30-11; 12-11 Fri & Sat; 12-3, 7-10.30 Sun
Sharp's Cornish Coaster, Doom Bar; guest beer H
Busy, but small community pub, whose landlord varies the guest beer regularly. Food is confined to simple pub fare (eve meals end at 7pm). An orchard doubles as the garden. Boules pitch.
🏚 Q ⏚ ❀ ⇆ ◖❳ ♣ ♠ P

LAUNCESTON

Bakers Arms
Southgate Street
☎ (01566) 772510
11-11; 12-10.30 Sun
Courage Directors; John Smith's Bitter; Skinner's Cornish Knocker; guest beers H
Popular town pub: a cosy wood-panelled lounge bar and a busy games-oriented public bar offer good value

home cooking.
🏚 Q ⇆ ⇌ ◖⌸ ♣

Try also: **White Hart Hotel**, Town Sq (Free)

LONGROCK

Mexico Inn
Gladstone Terrace (off A30 Longrock bypass)
☎ (01736) 710625
11-3, 5-11; 11-11 Sat & summer; 12-3, 5-10.30 Sun
Draught Bass; Marston's Pedigree; Skinner's Figgy's Brew; Sharp's Doom Bar, Own; guest beer H
Local, old-style free house with a single L-shaped bar and a restaurant. Close to the beach, it is especially popular in summer. The stone walls come from the mine of which the building was once part. 🏚 Q ❀ ◖❳ ⬥ P

LOSTWITHIEL

Royal Oak
Duke Street
☎ (01208) 872552
11-11; 12-10.30 Sun
Fuller's London Pride; Sharp's Doom Bar; guest beers H
Busy, friendly, 13th-century inn, very well known for its good food, comprising a traditional public bar and a comfortable lounge with a restaurant. It specializes in guest beers from small independent breweries.
🏚 Q ⏚ ❀ ⇆ ◖❳ P

Try also: **Earl of Chatham**, Grenville Rd (St Austell)

MARHAMCHURCH

Bullers Arms
☎ (01288) 361277
11-3, 6-11; 11-11 Sat & summer; 12-10.30 Sun
Sharp's Own; guest beers H
This large, popular village pub enjoys a reputation for good food. A well-appointed L-shaped bar, part of which has a slate flagstone floor.
🏚 ❀ ⇆ ◖❳ ♣ P

METHERELL

Carpenters Arms
Lower Metherell
☎ (01579) 350242
12-3, 7-11 (7-10.30 winter); 12-3, 7-10.30 Sun
Sharp's Cornish Coaster; Summerskills Best Bitter; guest beers (summer) H
Dating back in part to the 15th century, the public bar has a slate flagged floor, stone walls and dark beams, in contrast to the larger lounge and dining area. A varied menu offers local fish.
🏚 Q ❀ ⇆ ◖❳ ⌸ ♣ ✂

CORNWALL

Try also: Cross House, The Cross (Free)

MEVAGISSEY
Fountain Inn
3 Cliff Street (near harbour)
☎ (01726) 842320
11.30-11; 12-10.30 Sun
St Austell Tinners, HSD Ⓗ
Friendly, two-bar, characterful inn of slate floors, beams and old photos. It hosts piano music most weekends. The upstairs restaurant is open Mar-Oct.
🏚 Q ⇨ ◑ ▶ 🅰 ♣

Try also: Ship Inn, Fore St (St Austell)

MOUNT HAWKE
Old School Pub
W of B3277
☎ (01209) 891158
7-11 (midnight Fri & Sat); 12-3, 7-10.30 Sun
Tetley Bitter; guest beers Ⓗ
19th-century school converted into an unusual family-run inn. The large, comfortable bar is warm and friendly, and it has an active skittle alley. Quality meals are served at low prices. Live music Sat eves. 🏚 ◑ ▶ 🅰 ♣ P

MYLOR BRIDGE
Lemon Arms
Off A393 at Penryn
☎ (01326) 373666
11-3, 6-11; 12-3, 7-10.30 Sun
St Austell Tinners, Daylight Robbery, HSD Ⓗ
Friendly, one-bar village-centre pub, popular with local sports teams, offering good food. 🏚 🕸 ◑ ▶ ♣ P

NEWQUAY
Skinner's Ale House
58 East Street
☎ (01637) 876391
12-11; 12-10.30 Sun
Skinner's Spriggan Ale, Betty Stogs Bitter, Cornish Knocker, Figgy's Brew, seasonal beers; Ⓗ guest beers (summer) Ⓖ
Now owned by Skinner's Brewery this pub has been well refurbished in alehouse style, with a glass frontage. Goofy's is a house beer. Excellent food; live music Fri and Sat plus trad jazz Sun eve. ◑ ▶ ⇶

Try also: Lanherne, 32 Ulalia Rd (Free)

PADSTOW
Old Ship Hotel
Mill Square
☎ (01841) 532357
11-3, 7-11 (11-11 summer), 12-3, 7-10.30 (12-10.30 summer) Sun

Brains SA; Flowers IPA; guest beers Ⓗ/Ⓖ
Two high-ceilinged bars, just away from the busy harbour. The area in front of the hotel has sheltered seating.
🏚 🕸 ⇨ ◑ ▶ 🅰 ♣ P

Try also: Golden Lion, Lanadwell St (Greenalls)

PAR
Par Inn
Harbour Road
☎ (01726) 813961
11-11; 11-3, 5-11 Tue; 12-3, 7-10.30 Sun
St Austell XXXX Mild, Tinners, seasonal beers Ⓗ
19th-century, one-roomed, unpretentious, friendly drinkers' pub, famous for its Cornish pasties. 🅰 ⇶

Try also: Ship Inn, Polmear Hill (Free)

PENDEEN
North Inn
On B3306 ☎ (01736) 788417
11-11; 12-10.30 Sun
St Austell Bosun's Bitter, Tinners, Daylight Robbery, seasonal beer Ⓗ
Welcoming local close to the famous Geevor and Levant mines in an area of outstanding natural beauty. No food Mon.
🏚 🕸 ⇨ ◑ ▶ 🅰 ♣ P

PERRANPORTH
Watering Hole
The Beach ☎ (01872) 572888
11-11 (closed weekdays Oct-Mar); 12-10.30 Sun
Skinner's Spriggan Ale, Betty Stoggs Bitter Ⓗ
Across the sands and on the beach just above the high tide line, this is a terrific location. Enjoy stunning sunsets. Live music Fri and Sat. 🏚 🏚 🕸 ◑ ▶ 🅰 ⌣

PHILLACK
Bucket of Blood
14 Churchtown Road
☎ (01736) 752378
11-2.30 (3 Sat), 6-11; 12-4, 7-10.30 Sun
St Austell XXXX Mild, HSD, seasonal beer Ⓗ
Beware of the low beams in this friendly old pub near the dunes of Hayle Towans. Food served Easter-Oct.
🏚 🏚 🕸 ◑ ▶ 🅰 ♣ P

PHILLEIGH
Roseland Inn
Near King Harry ferry
☎ (01872) 580254
11-3, 6-11 (11-11 summer); 12-3, 7-10.30 Sun
Draught Bass; Marston's Pedigree;

Sharp's Doom Bar; guest beers Ⓗ
Picturesque, village-centre pub, accessible from the cathedral city of Truro via the King Harry ferry.
🏚 Q 🕸 ◑ ▶ P

PIECE
Countryman
On Four Lanes-Pool road
☎ (01209) 215960
11-11; 12-10.30 Sun
Courage Best Bitter, Directors; Morland Old Speckled Hen; Sharp's Own; Skinner's Spriggan Ale; Theakston Old Peculier Ⓗ
This lively country pub in former mining country, was a 'counthouse' for the nearby copper mines. Known for its live entertainment and quiz nights, the house beer from Sharp's is called No-name. Food served all day.
🏚 🏚 🕸 ◑ ▶ 🅰 ♣ P

PITYME
Pityme Inn
☎ (01208) 862228
11-2.30, 6-11 (11-11 summer); 12-3, 7-10.30 Sun
St Austell Tinners, Daylight Robbery, HSD, seasonal beer Ⓗ
One-time farmhouse where the open lounge forms part of the dining area, and the slate-flagged public bar has a games area. Good value menu. Q 🕸 ◑ ▶ ♣ P

POLKERRIS
Rashleigh Inn
Signed on St Austell-Fowey road ☎ (01726) 813991
11-4.30, 5.30-11 (11.30-3, 6.30-11 winter); 12-3, 7-10.30 Sun
Draught Bass; Ⓗ St Austell HSD; Ⓖ Sharp's Doom Bar; guest beers Ⓗ
Lovely inn on the beach with a recommended restaurant. The landlord changes his guest ales frequently. Piano singsong Fri eve. Limited parking. 🏚 Q 🕸 ◑ ▶ P

POLPERRO
Blue Peter Inn
Quay Road
☎ (01503) 272743
11-11; 12-10.30 Sun
St Austell Tinners, HSD; Sharp's Doom Bar; guest beers Ⓗ
Friendly pub by the coastal path, reached by steps from the end of the quay. No food, but you may take in your own sandwiches. Live entertainment weekend lunchtimes. 🏚 🅰 ♣ ⌣

POLRUAN
Lugger
The Quay ☎ (01726) 870007
11-11; 12-10.30 Sun
St Austell Bosun's Bitter, Tinners,

65

HSD, Daylight Robbery, seasonal beers H
Fine riverside pub with two bars, boasting nautical decor. It can be reached via foot ferry from Fowey town quay or by car ferry from Boddinick. Parking difficult.
🚶 ❀ ◑ ♣ ♠

Try also: Russell, West St (St Austell)

PORTHALLOW
Five Pilchards Inn
On minor road from St Keverne to Manaccan
☎ (01326) 280256
12-2.30, 7-11 (closed winter Mon); 12-4, 7-10.30 (not winter eve) Sun
Greene King Abbot; Sharp's Doom Bar; guest beers H
Village pub in an isolated spot on the Lizard Peninsula. The nearby beach affords good views over Falmouth Bay; good walks abound. No food winter. Q ❀ ◑ ♣ ♠

QUINTRELL DOWNS
Two Clomes
East Road (A390)
☎ (01637) 871163
12-3, 7-11 (12-11 summer); 12-3, 7-10.30 (12-10.30 summer) Sun
Sharp's Doom Bar; guest beers H
18th-century free house that takes its name from the two clome ovens either side of the open fireplace. Popular for eating out: the restaurant has a no-smoking section, up to three guest beers sold.
🚶 ❀ ◑ & ♠ 🅰 ➤ P

REDRUTH
Tricky Dickie's
Tolgus Mount (signed NW off old Redruth bypass, A3047) OS686427
☎ (01209) 219292
11-3, 6-11 (11-11 Thu-Sat summer); 12-3, 7-10.30 (12-10.30 summer) Sun
Flowers IPA; Greene King Abbot; Sharp's Own, Special; guest beer H
Converted tin mine smithy, it offers good value fresh food, good wines and exemplary service. Live jazz Tue; music Thu eve (late licence). Families welcome.
❀ ✉ ◑ & 🅰 P ✂

RESTRONGUET CREEK
Pandora Inn
End of Restronguet Hill (near A39) OS814371
☎ (01326) 372678
11-11 (12-2.30, 7-11; 12-11 Sat winter); 12-10.30 Sun
Draught Bass; St Austell Tinners, Daylight Robbery, HSD H
13th-century thatched pub at the waterside, accessible by road and water. Restaurant upstairs. 🚶 Q ❀ ◑ P

RUAN LANIHORNE
Kings Head
Off A3078 at Tregony
☎ (01872) 501263
12-2.30 (not Mon), 6-11 (closed winter Mon); 12-2.30, 7-10.30 Sun
Sharp's Doom Bar; Skinner's Cornish Knocker; guest beers H
Quiet, traditional free house, on the Roseland Peninsula overlooking the Fal estuary. Good value home-cooking. Limited parking.
🚶 Q ❀ ◑ ▷ ♠ ▷ P

ST AGNES
Driftwood Spars
Quay Road, Trevaunance Cove ☎ (01872) 552428
11-11 (midnight Fri-Sat); 12-10.30 Sun
Draught Bass; Driftwood Cuckoo Ale; St Austell HSD; Sharp's Own; guest beers H
Picturesque, 17th-century hotel with a new brewery. Welcoming and full of character, the main bar bears a nautical theme. High quality meals are available daily. Popular centre of local activities, including live theatre and music.
🚶 Q ❀ ✉ ◑ ▷ 🅰 ▷ P

ST AUSTELL
Carlyon Arms
30 Sandy Hill (1½ miles E of town on Bethel road)
☎ (01726) 72129
11-11, (11-2.30, 5-11 winter Mon-Wed); 12-10.30 Sun
St Austell Tinners, Daylight Robbery, HSD, seasonal beers H
Friendly local serving good home-cooked food (eve meals Tue-Sat). It hosts live music Wed and Sat eves.
🚶 ❀ ✉ ◑ ▷ & ♠ P

Try also: Queens Head Hotel, Fore St (Free)

ST BREWARD
Old Inn
Churchtown
☎ (01208) 850711
11-3, 6-11; 11-11 Fri & Sat; 12-10.30 Sun
Draught Bass; Sharp's Doom Bar, Special H
The highest pub in Cornwall, set on the beautiful moors, this whitewashed cob building is popular. The restaurant serves good food using local produce.
🚶 Q ▷ ❀ ◑ ▷ ♠ P ▷

ST IVES
Western Hotel
Royal Square
☎ (01736) 795277
11-11; 12-10.30 Sun
St Austell XXXX Mild, Daylight Robbery, HSD, seasonal beer H

The Kettle and Wink bar is the popular locals' venue in this friendly town-centre hotel; a second bar opens in summer. St Ives' main live music venue. 🚶 Q ✉ ◑ ▷ ➤ 🔲

Try also: Lifeboat, Wharf Rd (St Austell)

ST TUDY
Cornish Arms
☎ (01208) 850656
12-3, 6.30-11; 12-4, 7-10.30 Sun
Draught Bass; St Austell XXXX Mild; guest beers H
16th-century village pub of several rooms and a games area. Excellent food is prepared using local produce. Good disabled facilities.
Q ▷ ❀ ◑ ▷ & ♠ ▷ P ▷

SALTASH
Union Inn
Tamar Street (waterfront)
☎ (01752) 844770
11-11; 12-10.30 Sun
Courage Best Bitter; Flowers IPA; Fuller's London Pride; Wadworth 6X; guest beers G
Single bar pub on Saltash riverside, stocking a good range of guest beers. Regular live music. ➤ ♠

SPARNON GATE
Cornish Arms
On old Portreath road from Redruth ☎ (01209) 216407
12-2.30, 5 (6 Sat)-11; 12-3, 7-10.30 Sun
Sharp's Doom Bar, Own; G **guest beer** (summer) H/G
Friendly, out-of-town local where old tin and copper mine artefacts cover the walls. Excellent value pub grub is freshly prepared.
🚶 Q ❀ ◑ ▷ ◨ 🅰 ♣ P

STICKER
Hewas Inn
On old A390, St Austell road
☎ (01726) 73497
11-11; 12-10.30 Sun
St Austell Bosun's Bitter, Tinners, Daylight Robbery H
This large village inn is popular with locals and tourists; the restaurant serves excellent food.
Q ▷ ❀ ◑ 🅰 ♣ P ▣

Try also: Polgooth Inn, Polgooth (St Austell)

STITHIANS
Seven Stars
Church Road
☎ (01209) 860003
12-2, 7-11; 12-11 Sat; 12-3, 7-10.30 Sun
Sharp's Doom Bar; guest beers H
Lively village local used by a

good cross-section of the community, where euchre is enthusiastically played. No food Tue. 🏮 🏵 ◖ 🌒 ♣

Try also: Old Vicarage, Church Rd (Free)

STRATTON

King's Arms
Howells Road
☎ (01288) 352396
12-2.30, 6.30-11; 12-11 Fri & Sat; 12-10.30 Sun
Sharp's Cornish Coaster, Own; guest beers Ⓗ
Popular local in an ancient market town; a 17th-century coaching inn of two simply furnished bars with well worn slate flagstone floors. Cider in summer.
🏮 🏵 🚃 ◖ 🌒 ♣ ⌂ P

THREEMILESTONE

Victoria Inn
Chyvelah Road (off A390, 3 miles W of Truro)
☎ (01872) 278313
11-11; 12-10.30 Sun
St Austell Tinners, HSD Ⓐ
Comfortable, welcoming, two-bar inn in the village centre. Popular with locals and staff from the nearby hospital. Excellent value carvery meals.
🐦 🏵 🚃 ◖ 🌒 🔔 ♿ Ⱥ P

TREBELLAN

Smugglers Den
Off A3075 towards Cubert then first left (signed)
☎ (01637) 830209
12-2 (not Mon-Wed), 6-11 (11-11 summer); 12-10.30 Sun
Beer range varies Ⓗ/Ⓖ
Up to six regularly changing real ales are kept in this 16th-century thatched pub. The approach down steep narrow lanes is worth it for the food.
🏮 Q 🐦 🏵 ◖ 🌒 Ⱥ ⌂ P

TREGREHAN

Britannia Inn
On A390, 3 miles E of St Austell ☎ (01726) 812889
11-11; 12-10.30 Sun
Draught Bass; Fuller's London Pride; Greene King Abbot; Morland Old Speckled Hen; Sharps Own; guest beers Ⓗ
Large, 16th-century inn, serving food all day. It has a safe garden and play area.
Q 🐦 🏵 ◖ 🌒 🔔 ♿ Ⱥ ♣ P

TREMATON

Crooked Inn
Stoketon Cross (signed from A38 near Saltash)
☎ (01752) 848177
11-3, 7-11 (11-11 Fri & Sat summer); 12-3, 7-10.30 (12-10.30 summer) Sun

Draught Bass; St Austell HSD; Sharp's Doom Bar, Own; guest beer Ⓗ
A converted, 18th century farmhouse enjoying views over the Lynher Valley. A wide range of home-cooked food is available.
🏮 Q 🐦 🏵 🚃 ◖ 🌒 Ⱥ ⌂ P

TRESCO

New Inn
Townshill (5 min walk from quay at New Grimsby)
☎ (01720) 422844
11-11 (11-3, 6-11 winter); 12-10.30 (12-3; 6-10.30 winter) Sun
Skinner's Betty Stogs Bitter, Cornish Knocker; guest beers Ⓗ
This Scilly islands inn is reached by helicopter or boat. Frequented by local fishermen, visitors and islanders, it exudes a warm, friendly atmosphere; children welcome. The house beer, Tresco Tipple, is brewed by Skinner's. Good quality food and accommodation.
🏵 🚃 ◖ 🌒 Ⱥ ♣

TRURO

City Inn
Pydar Street (B3284 by rail bridge) ☎ (01872) 272623
11-11; 12-10.30 Sun
Courage Best Bitter, Directors; Sharp's Doom Bar; Skinner's Betty Stogs Bitter; guest beer Ⓗ
This busy, popular pub, just off the shopping centre, styles itself as 'Truro's real ale oasis'. Food is limited and eve meals finish early.
🏵 🚃 ◖ 🌒 🔔 ♿ ⌂

Old Ale House
7 Quay Street
☎ (01872) 271122
11-11; 12-10.30 Sun
Courage Directors; Tetley Bitter; guest beers Ⓖ/Ⓗ
Themed ale house in the city centre, boasting an array of up to eight guest beers fed by gravity; with usually a local ale. The house beer, brewed by Skinner's, is Kiddleywink. Eve meals served 6-7.30 Mon-Sat. ◖ 🌒 ≢

TYWARDREATH

New Inn
Fore Street ☎ (01726) 813901
12-3.30, 6-11; 12-3.30, 7-10.30 Sun
Draught Bass; St Austell Tinners, Daylight Robbery Ⓗ
Classic village local near the coast with a secluded garden and a games/children's room. Limited parking. It has been in this *Guide* since 1974.
🏮 Q 🏵 Ⱥ ≢ (Par) ♣ P

UPTON CROSS

Caradon Inn

On B3254 ☎ (01579) 362391
11-3.30, 5.30-11; 12-4, 7-10.30 Sun
Draught Bass; Ⓖ **Boddingtons Bitter; Flowers Original; St Austell HSD; Sharp's Doom Bar or Own** Ⓗ
Old, slate-clad pub dating from the 17th century, with a reputation for good value food. The public bar has the juke box and pool table, while the lounge is quieter.
🏮 Q 🏵 ◖ 🌒 🔔 ♿ Ⱥ ♣ ⌂ P

WEEK ST MARY

Green Inn
☎ (01288) 341450
12-3, 7-11; 12-3, 7-10.30 Sun
Flowers IPA; Ⓗ **guest beer** Ⓗ/Ⓖ
Simple village local with a collection of bottled beers. A bar is set aside for families. One Cornish beer is sold. Sun lunch served. 🐦 🏵 🚃 🌒 ⌂ P

WIDEMOUTH BAY

Bay View Inn
Marine Drive
☎ (01288) 361273
11-3, 6-11 (11-11 summer); 12-3, 6-10.30 (12-10.30 summer) Sun
Sharp's Doom Bar, Own; Skinner's Betty Stogs Bitter Ⓗ
Small, friendly pub boasting unrivalled views over a popular surfing beach. The interior is being covered by beer memorabilia. A house beer (Kitch's Classic) is from Skinner's. Cider in summer.
🐦 🏵 🚃 ◖ 🌒 🔔 ♣ ⌂ P ⌿ 🍺

ZELAH

Hawkins Arms
High Road (off A30)
☎ (01872) 540339
11-3, 6-11; 12-3, 7-10.30 Sun
Draught Bass; Tetley Bitter; guest beers Ⓗ
This village pub remains unchanged, it offers excellent meals and changing guest beers. Skinner's produce an occasional blend for the pub called Zelah Mist. Weston's Old Rosie cider is served straight from the cask.
🏮 Q 🐦 🏵 🚃 ◖ 🌒 ♿ ♣ ⌂ P 🍺

INDEPENDENT BREWERIES

Bird in Hand: Hayle

Blue Anchor: Helston

Driftwood: St. Agnes

Keltek: Lostwithiel

Redruth: Redruth

St Austell: St Austell

Sharp's: Rock

Skinner's: Truro

Ventonwyn: Grampound Road

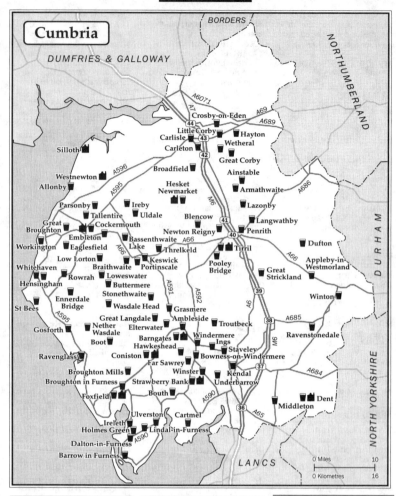

AINSTABLE

New Crown Inn
Off A6, SE of Carlisle
☎ (01768) 896273
12-3 (not Mon-Fri), 6-11; 12-3, 7-10.30
Sun

Tetley Bitter; guest beers Ⓗ
Cosy village local
with a dining room
serving good value meals.
Worth a visit.
🏚 Q ❀ 🚬 ◖ ♣ P

ALLONBY

Ship Hotel
Main Street
☎ (01900) 881017
12-3 (may vary winter), 7-11; 12-3,
7-10.30 Sun

**Yates Bitter, Premium; guest
beer** Ⓗ
Virtually Yates's
brewery tap, a peaceful
village hotel on the
pleasant Solway coast,
enjoying stunning
sunsets.
🏚 Q ❀ 🚬 ◖ ▲ ♣ P

AMBLESIDE

Golden Rule
Smithy Brow
☎ (015394) 32257
11-11; 12-10.30 Sun

**Robinson's Hatters Mild, Old
Stockport, Hartleys XB, Best Bitter,
Frederics** Ⓗ
Proper pub lacking such
'mod cons' as juke box,
muzak, pool or dining tables.
It majors on good beer and
conversation in its three
interconnecting rooms.
Snacks available. 🏚 Q ❀ ♣

Queens Hotel
Market Place
☎ (015394) 32206
11-11; 12-10.30 Sun

**Boddingtons Bitter; Jennings Bitter;
Theakston XB; guest beers** Ⓗ
Village-centre hotel with a
deserved reputation for beer
quality; guest beeers are often
from local micros. It has a
no-smoking dining room,
plus Victoria's Restaurant
Sheltered patio. 🏚 ❀ 🚬 ◖ ◗ ⊞

APPLEBY-IN-
WESTMORLAND

Golden Ball
High Wiend
☎ (017683) 51493
12-11; 12-10.30 Sun

Jennings Bitter, Cumberland Ale Ⓗ
Just off the main street, this
splendid, unpretentious town
pub has a cosy lounge and a
public bar with quiet juke
box. There is an attractive
garden courtyard.
❀ 🚬 ◳ ≉

ARMATHWAITE

Fox & Pheasant
Off A6, SE of Carlisle
☎ (016974) 72400
11-11; 12-10.30 Sun

**Jennings Mild, Cumberland Ale,
Sneck Lifter; Hesket Newmarket
Doris's 90th Birthday Ale; guest
beers** Ⓗ
17th-century coaching house
that features an oak-beamed
stable bar and lounge with a
slate-floor. Excellent food is

served in both areas. The village is on the scenic Settle-Carlisle railway line.
⛼ Q ❀ 🛏 ◑ ◗ ♿ ≠ P

BARNGATES

Drunken Duck
Off B5286 OS351013
☎ (015394) 36347
11-11; 12-3, 6-10.30 Sun
Barngates Cracker, Tag Lag, Chesters Strong & Ugly; Jennings Bitter; Theakston Old Peculier Ⓗ
One of the best-known Lakeland pubs. The legend of the name makes amusing reading. A real fire, good meals, splendid views and an expanding micro-brewery are added attractions.
⛼ Q ♘ ❀ 🛏 ◑ ◗ ♣ P ⍁ ⊞

BARROW IN FURNESS

Furness Railway
Abbey Road (A590)
☎ (01229) 820818
11-11; 12-10.30 Sun
Courage Directors; Theakston Best Bitter; Thwaites Mild; guest beer Ⓗ
Ex-department store divided into four distinct drinking areas; it can be busy lunchtimes and weekend eves.
Q ◑ ◗ ♿ ≠ ⍁ ⊞

BASSENTHWAITE LAKE

Pheasant
Signed from A66
☎ (017687) 76234
11-2.30; 5.30-10.30; 12-2.30, 6-10.30 Sun
Draught Bass; Jennings Cumberland Ale; Theakston Best Bitter Ⓗ
Georgian coaching house with an unspoilt public bar.
Q ❀ 🛏 ◑ ♿ P ⊞

BLENCOW

Crown Inn
Off B5288 W of Penrith
☎ (017684) 83369
7 (12 Sat)-11; 12-10.30 Sun
Courage Directors; Theakston Best Bitter Ⓗ
Village local on the edge of the Lake District National Park. Brasses and equine photographs abound.
⛼ 🛏 ◑ ◗ ♿ ⛺ ♣ P

BOOT

Brook House Inn
OS176008
☎ (019467) 23288
11-11; 12-10.30 Sun
Taylor Landlord; Theakston Best Bitter; guest beers Ⓗ
Bar and no-smoking lounge with a real fire. The restaurant serves food all day. Children's certificate.
⛼ Q ♘ ❀ 🛏 ◑ ◗ ⛺
≠ (Dalegarth R&ER) ♣ P ⍁

BOUTH

White Hart Inn
☎ (01229) 861229
12-2 (not Mon & Tue; 12-3 Sat), 6-11; 12-3, 6-10.30 Sun
Black Sheep Best Bitter; Jennings Cumberland Ale; Tetley Bitter; guest beers Ⓗ
Beamed country pub in a pleasant unspoilt village on the edge of the south Lakes. Old Lakeland photos and hunting memorabilia feature. A games room, pool and juke box, dining room and outside gents complete the picture.
⛼ ♘ ❀ 🛏 ◑ ◗ ⛺ ♣ P

BOWNESS-ON-WINDERMERE

Village Inn
Lake Road
☎ (015394) 43731
11-11; 12-10.30 Sun
Black Sheep Best Bitter; Boddingtons Bitter; Castle Eden Ale; Jennings Cumberland Ale; guest beers Ⓗ
Lively pub, originally the manse to the parish church opposite, catering for locals and visitors. Guest beers often come from local micros. Noted for good value meals served all day in the bar. ❀ ◑ ◗ ♿ ♣

BRAITHWAITE

Coledale Inn
Off Whinlatter road above the village
☎ (0176 87) 78272
11-11; 12-10.30 Sun
Jennings Bitter; Theakston Best Bitter, XB; Yates Bitter Ⓗ
Friendly, family-run hotel in what was the original Cumberland Pencil factory. Stunning views over the fells.
⛼ ❀ 🛏 ◑ ◗ ⛺ ♣ P

BROADFIELD

Crown Inn
4 miles S of Carlisle racecourse
☎ (0169 74) 73467
12-3 (not Tue), 6.30-11; 12-3, 7-10.30 Sun
Theakston Best Bitter; guest beers Ⓗ
Roadside community pub, serving excellent meals, where a friendly welcome is assured.
⛼ Q ❀ ◑ ◗ ♿ ⛺ ♣ P

BROUGHTON IN FURNESS

Manor Arms
The Square
☎ (01229) 716286
12-11; 12-10.30 Sun
Coniston Bluebird Bitter; Dent Aviator; Taylor Landlord; Yates Bitter; guest beers Ⓗ
18th-century village pub, on the market square, boasting an unusual basket fireplace, put to good use in colder months. Seven beers always available.
⛼ Q ❀ 🛏 ♣ P ⊟

Try also: Old Kings Head, Church St (Whitbread)

BROUGHTON MILLS

Blacksmiths Arms ☆
Off A593, 2 miles N of Broughton in Furness OS222906
☎ (01229) 716824
12-11; 12-10.30 Sun
Jennings Cumberland Ale; guest beer Ⓗ
Unspoilt character in a tiny bar with a scrubbed wooden table and real fire, plus three other pleasant farmhouse rooms. It stocks a large selection of bottled beers, plus cider in summer.
⛼ Q ❀ ◑ ◗ ♣ ⌓ P

BUTTERMERE

Bridge Hotel
On B5289 ☎ (017687) 70252
10-2.30, 6-11.30 (10-11.30 summer); 10-2.30, 6-10.30 (10-10.30 summer) Sun
Black Sheep Best Bitter; Flowers IPA; Theakston Old Peculier Ⓗ
Popular tourist hotel, between Crummock Water and Buttermere in a picturesque valley: two comfortable bars; children welcome. Q 🛏 ◑ ◗ ♿ P

CARLETON

Carrow House
On A6, off M6 juct 42
☎ (01228) 532073
11-11; 12-10.30 Sun
Banks's Bitter Ⓗ
Milestone pub and restaurant in traditional style. Meals served all day.
⛼ ❀ ◑ ◗ ♿ P ⍁ ⊟

CARLISLE

Carlisle Rugby Club
Warwick Road (A69, by Carlisle FC ground)
☎ (01228) 521300
7 (5.30 Fri; 6 Sat)-11 (12.30-11 Sat in football season); 12.30-3, 7-10.30 Sun
Tetley Bitter; Yates Bitter; guest beer Ⓗ
Welcoming club with a cosy lounge and large bar. Show this *Guide* or CAMRA membership to be signed in.
⛼ ❀ ♣ P

Gosling Bridge
Kingstown Road (A7)
☎ (01228) 515294
11-11; 12-10.30 Sun
Marston's Pedigree; guest beers Ⓗ

Comfortable suburban pub of several distinct drinking areas, serving good food at reasonable prices.
🍴 ❀ 🛏 ◖ ▮ P

Howard Arms
107 Lowther Street (next to Lane's shopping centre)
☎ (01228) 532926
11-11; 12-10.30 Sun
Theakston Best Bitter, XB; H
This busy, city-centre pub is a regular *Guide* entry; several small rooms and a superb tiled exterior. ❀ ◖ ≈

Near Boot
Whiteclosegate (B6264, 1¹/₂ miles NE of centre)
☎ (01228) 529547
11-11; 12-10.30 Sun
Taylor Landlord; Theakston Best Bitter; guest beers H
Popular, 18th-century 'village' local, due for renovation and extension. The name derives from the near-side boot when horse-riding out of Carlisle!
🍴 ❀ ◖ ▮ 🍲 ♣ P

Woodrow Wilson
49 Botchergate
☎ (01228) 819942
11-11; 12-10.30 Sun
Boddingtons Bitter; Thwaites Mild, Bitter; Theakston Best Bitter; guest beer H
Wetherspoon's pub in the former Co-op; the name is a reminder that President Wilson's mother came from Carlisle.
Q ❀ ◖ ▮ & ≈ P ⅄ H

CARTMEL

Royal Oak Inn
The Square
☎ (0153 95) 36259
12-11; 12-10.30 Sun
Castle Eden Ale; Tetley Bitter; guest beer H
Knocked-through pub that has retained its original slate floor and real fire. The extensive garden gives access to the river. It can get busy in summer and race days (the racecourse is nearby).
🍴 ❀ ◖ ♣

COCKERMOUTH

Bitter End
15 Kirkgate
☎ (01900) 828993
12-2.30 (3 Fri & Sat), 6-11; 12-3, 7-10.30 Sun
Bitter End Cockersnoot; Jennings Mild, Bitter, Cumberland Ale, Sneck Lifter, seasonal beers; Yates Bitter; guest beers H
The brewery is visible from the lounge in this friendly brew pub which was the local CAMRA branch *Pub of the Year* 1999. It stocks a range of foreign bottled beers, plus an

occasional draught cider. Children welcome at mealtimes. 🍴 ◖ ▮ ▲ 🍲

Bush Hotel
Main Street
☎ (01900) 822064
11-11; 12-10.30 Sun
Jennings Mild, Bitter, Cumberland Ale, Cocker Hoop, Sneck Lifter, seasonal beers; guest beers H
The nearest thing to a brewery tap, this friendly town pub is welcoming and comfortable. 🍴 ◖ ▲

Try also: **Fletcher Christian Tavern,** Main St (Black Sheep)

CONISTON

Black Bull Inn
Yewdale Road (A593, by the Beck) ☎ (0153 94) 41335
11-11; 12-10.30 Sun
Coniston Bluebird Bitter, Old Man Ale, seasonal beers; guest beer (occasional) H
Spacious, 16th-century coaching inn boasting a splendid slate floor. Meals are served all day; families welcome. Much Donald Campbell memorabilia includes a fragment of Bluebird. The Coniston Brewing Co is at the rear.
🍴 Q ❀ 🛏 ◖ ▮ ▲ 🍲 P

CROSBY ON EDEN

Stag Inn
Off A689, E of Carlisle)
☎ (01228) 573210
12-3, 6-11; 12-3, 6.30-10.30 Sun
Jennings Mild, Bitter, Cumberland Ale, Sneck Lifter H
Delightful village pub, featuring stone-flagged floors and low, beamed ceilings. Good food is served in the upstairs restaurant as well as the bar. ❀ ◖ ▮ ♣ P

DALTON-IN-FURNESS

Black Dog Inn
Off A590 OS233761
☎ (01229) 462561
12 (5 Mon)-11 (11-11 summer); 12-10.30 Sun
Beer range varies H
Comfortable wayside inn employing an excellent guest ale and cider policy, and offering good value food. Local CAMRA *Pub of the Year* 1998 and '99. 🍴 Q 🛏 ❀ 🛏 ◖ ▮ 🍲 ▲ ♣ 🍲 P ⅄ 🍷

Red Lion
5 Market Street (A590)
☎ (01229) 467914
12-3, 7-11 (12-11 Fri & Sat); 12-10.30 Sun
Coniston Bluebird Bitter; Theakston Best Bitter; guest beer H
Small market town pub with a country inn character enhanced by low ceilings,

black beams and a huge fireplace. A single bar serves several distinct areas plus a games room.
🍴 🛏 ◖ ▮ & ≈ ♣ P

DENT

Sun Inn
Main Street
☎ (0153 96) 25208
11-2.30, 7-11; 11-11 Sat & summer; 12-10.30 Sun
Dent Bitter, Aviator, Rambrau, Kamikaze, T'owd Tup H
Traditional village local with an L-shaped bar area and a no-smoking annexe. The games room has a pool table and juke box.
🍴 Q ❀ 🛏 ◖ ▮ ▲ ♣ P ⅄

DUFTON

Stag Inn
☎ (0176 83) 51608
12-3, 6-11; 11-11 Sat & summer; 12-5, 7-10.30 Sun
Black Sheep Best Bitter; Flowers IPA (winter)**; guest beers** (summer) H
Fine example of a village pub, overlooking the green. The main bar has a dining area and a superb kitchen range, ensuring a warm welcome in winter. The beer range is extended and includes guests in summer.
🍴 Q ❀ 🛏 ◖ ▮ ▲ ♣ P

EAGLESFIELD

Black Cock
☎ (01900) 822989
12-3 (not winter), 7-11; 12-11 Sat; 12-10.30 Sun
Jennings Bitter H
Unspoilt village local where a roaring fire, wood panelling and much brassware feature; basic facilities but worth a visit. 🍴 Q ❀

ELTERWATER

Britannia Inn
☎ (0153 94) 37210
11-11; 12-10.30 Sun
Coniston Bluebird; Dent Aviator; Jennings Bitter; guest beers H
This popular, long-standing *Guide* entry regularly needs to press the village green into use as an overflow when the front bar, entrance lobby, back room and paved patio are all full. Bar meals are also served in the no-smoking dining room.
🍴 Q ❀ 🛏 ◖ ▮ ▲

EMBLETON

Wheatsheaf
On old Cockermouth-Keswick road
☎ (0176 87) 76408
12-2, 6-11 (12-11 summer Sat); 12-10.30 Sun

Jennings Bitter, Cocker Hoop, *or* seasonal beers Ⓗ
Welcoming village pub in an old farmhouse, overlooking the Lakeland Fells, with a family/games room in a converted barn. On the X4/X5 bus route.
🚶 🚲 ✿ ◖❯ P

ENNERDALE BRIDGE
Shepherds Arms Hotel
Ennerdale Bridge
☎ (01946) 861249
11-11; 12-10.30 Sun
Courage Directors; Jennings Bitter; Theakston Best Bitter, XB; guest beer Ⓗ
On the Coast-to-Coast walk near Ennerdale Water this informal hotel has a real fire in the entrance lobby and a sitting area with easy chairs and a piano. A new garden room leads to a wild garden.
🚶 ✿ ⛁ ◖❯ ⚲ P

FAR SAWREY
Claife Crier Bar (Far Sawrey Hotel)
On B5285
☎ (0153 94) 43425
11-3, 5.30-11; 12-10.30 Sun
Black Sheep Best Bitter; Jennings Cumberland Ale; Theakston Best Bitter, Old Peculier Ⓗ
Cosy outpost,with converted stable stalls offering a secluded seating plan, while horse collars and tackle are prominent in the decor. Children's certificate until 7pm; eve meals are served in the hotel restaurant.
🚶 Q ✿ ⛁ ◖ ⚲ ♣ P

FOXFIELD
Prince of Wales
Opp. station
☎ (01229) 716238
5 (12 Fri & Sat)-11; closed Mon & Tue; 12-10.30 Sun
Beer range varies Ⓗ
Friendly atmosphere warmed by a roaring fire in a pub with its own brewery, as well as being the main outlet for Tigertops beers. The range changes weekly; also a superb bottled beer choice, and a guest cider. 🚶 Q ⚋ ♣ ◔ P ⛉

GOSFORTH
Lion & Lamb
The Square
☎ (0194 67) 25242
12-11; 12-10.30 Sun
John Smith Bitter; Ruddles Best Bitter; Theakston Best Bitter; guest beers Ⓗ
Run for real ale and sports supporters, serving good beers (often Cumbrian brewed) and food (good home cooking).
🚶 ✿ ◖❯ P

GRASMERE
Travellers Rest
On A591, $1/2$ mile N of village
☎ (0153 94) 35604
11-11; 12-10.30 Sun
Jennings Bitter, Cumberland Ale, Sneck Lifter; Marston's Pedigree Ⓗ
The cosy bar area is next to the roaring winter fire; a family/games room is up a few steps and there are two dining areas – one no-smoking. It affords fine views and is handy for the Coast-to-Coast walk.
🚶 Q 🚲 ✿ ⛁ ◖❯ ♣ P ⛉

GREAT BROUGHTON
Punchbowl
19 Main Street (off A66)
☎ (01900) 824708
11.30-4.30 (not Mon), 7-11; (11.30-11 summer); 12-5, 7-10.30 Sun
Jennings Bitter Ⓗ
Welcoming, tiny pub in a village overlooking Derwent valley. A genuine community pub. 🚶

GREAT CORBY
Corby Bridge Inn
Off A69 E of Carlisle
☎ (01228) 560221
12-11; 12-10.30 Sun
Thwaites Mild, Bitter; guest beers Ⓗ
Grade II listed building of architectural and historic interest: a single room with three distinct drinking areas and a pool table in one.
🚶 Q ✿ ⛁ ◖❯ ⚲
⇌ (Wetheral) ♣ P

GREAT LANGDALE
Old Dungeon Ghyll
☎ (0153 94) 37272
11-11; 12-10.30 Sun
Jennings Cumberland Ale; Theakston XB, Old Peculier; Yates Bitter; guest beers Ⓗ
Classic walkers' and climbers' bar with a hard floor and benches, a splendid kitchen range fire and a reputation for its informal atmosphere.
🚶 Q ✿ ⛁ ◖❯ ⚲ ♣ ◔ P ⛉

GREAT STRICKLAND
Strickland Arms
☎ (01931) 712238
12-3 (not Wed), 6-11; 12-10.30 Sun
Ind Coope Burton Ale; Jennings Bitter; Tetley Bitter; guest beers Ⓗ
Spacious, two-bar village local with a games room. Home-made meals (not served Wed); large, safe garden. 🚶 ✿ ⛁ ◖❯ ⚲ ♣ P ⛉

HAWKSHEAD
Kings Arms Hotel
The Square

☎ (0153 94) 36372
11-11; 12-10.30 Sun
Coniston Bluebird Bitter; Black Sheep Best Bitter; Tetley Bitter; guest beer Ⓗ
This traditional Lakeland inn makes an ideal base for touring the National Park. No pool, juke box or TV, but occasional live music. Real cider available in summer.
🚶 Q ✿ ⛁ ◖❯ ♣ ◔

HAYTON
Stone Inn
Off A69, E of Carlisle
☎ (01228) 670498
11-3, 5.30-11; 11-11 Sat; 12-3, 7-10.30 Sun
Thwaites Mild, Bitter; Jennings Bitter Ⓗ
Comfortable village local featuring an attractive stone bar and fireplace.
🚶 Q ♣

Try also: Lane End Inn (Jennings)

HENSINGHAM
Lowther Arms
18 Ribton Moorside (off A595) ☎ (01946) 695852
11-3, 6.30-11; 12-3, 6.30-10.30 Sun
Robinson's Hatters Mild, Hartleys XB Ⓗ
Homely, family-run local: a large open lounge and a public bar that is a must for cards and dominoes.
Q 🚲 ✿ ◖❯ ⛁ ♣ P

HESKET NEWMARKET
Old Crown
1 mile SE of Caldbeck
☎ (0169 74) 78288
12-3 (not Mon), 5.30-11; 12-11 Sat; 12-3, 7-10.30 Sun
Hesket Newmarket Great Cockup, Blencathra Bitter, Skiddaw Special, Doris's 90th Birthday Ale, Catbells Pale Ale, Old Carrock Porter Ⓗ
Superb, fellside village local, where a small, cosy drinking area serves the full range of Hesket Newmarket beers, brewed here in a converted barn. Local CAMRA *Pub of the Year* 2000.
🚶 Q ✿ ◖❯ ⚲ ♣

INGS
Watermill Inn
Just off A591
☎ (01539) 821309
12-2.30, 6-11; 12-3, 6-10.30 Sun
Black Sheep Special Bitter; Coniston Bluebird Bitter; Lees Moonraker; Theakston Best Bitter, Old Peculier; guest beers Ⓗ
Family-run pub that has won countless certificates in its ten-year history. It offers more guest beers than any other pub in Cumbria. Story-telling sessions held first Tue

eve each month.
🏧 Q 🕮 🛏 🚶 ☕ ♣ ☕ P ✂

IREBY

Lion
The Square
☎ (0169 73) 71460
5.30-11; 12-3, 6-11 Sat; 12-3, 7-10.30 Sun

Bateman XB; Marston's Pedigree; Titanic Premium; guest beer Ⓗ
Village on the edge of the Lake District's northern fells. This pub has an interesting bar (from a pub in Leeds) and wooden panelling from local chapels. Weekend lunches served. 🏧 Q 🕮 🚶 🛗 ♣

IRELETH

Bay Horse
Ireleth Brow (off A595, at top of hill)
☎ (01229) 463755
12-3 (not Mon or Tue), 7-11; 12-3, 7-10.30 Sun

Jennings Mild, Bitter, Cumberland Ale, Cocker Hoop Ⓗ
18th-century inn overlooking the Duddon estuary, this popular local offers a friendly welcome. Limited parking.
🏧 Q 🕮 🛝 ⇌ (Askam in Furness) ♣ P ✂ 🛗

KENDAL

Burgundys
19 Lowther Street
☎ (01539) 733803
11-3 (not Mon-Wed), 6.30-11 (not Mon); 7-10.30 Sun

Dent Aviator; guest beers Ⓗ
Town-centre bar with an accent on guest beers; it hosts several specialist beer festivals with sausages to match and offers an above average selection of draught and bottled continental beers.
◖ ⇌ ☕

Castle Inn
Castle Street
☎ (01539) 729983
11-11; 12-10.30 Sun

Jennings Bitter; Tetley Bitter; guest beer Ⓗ
Two-roomed, back-street pub, popular with office staff at lunchtime for its exceptional value meals, and locals eves. A raised games area with pool and a Duttons window in the bar add interest. A Dent beer is regularly stocked.
🕮 ◖ ♣ ♣

Cock & Dolphin
2 Milnthorpe Road
☎ (01539) 728268
11-11; 12-10.30 Sun

Tetley Bitter; guest beer Ⓗ
Two-roomed, edge-of-town-centre pub noted for its local atmosphere and live music (Thu eve and occasional Sun afternoons). 🕮 🛏 ◖ ♣ P

Ring o' Bells
391 Kirkland
☎ (01539) 720326
12-3 (may vary Tues), 6-11; 12-3, 7-10.30 Sun

Draught Bass; Tetley Bitter; Worthington Bitter; guest beer Ⓗ
Standing on consecrated ground this pub retains two bars with a tiny snug between them; no juke box, TV or pool. The breakfast room can be hired for meetings; good value accommodation.
🏧 🕮 🛏 ◖ 🛗 ♣ 🛗

KESWICK

Packhorse
Packhorse Yard (off Main Street)
☎ (0176 87) 71389
11-11; 12-10.30 Sun

Jennings Bitter, Cumberland Ale, Sneck Lifter, seasonal beers Ⓗ
Newly refurbished Jennings tenancy, just off the market place, hosting live music alternate Sun in winter.
🛏 ◖ 🛝 🚶 ♣ 🛗

LANGWATHBY

Shepherd Inn
Village Green (A686)
☎ (01768) 881335
12-3, 6.30-11; 12-3, 6.30-10.30 Sun

Castle Eden Ale Ⓗ
Nestling on the edge of the village green, this pub with its split-level drinking area is attractively furnished and has a friendly atmosphere.
🏧 Q 🕮 ◖ 🚶 🛝 ⇌ P

LAZONBY

Joiners Arms
Town Foot (B6413)
☎ (01768) 898728
12-3, 7 (6 summer)-11; 7-10.30 Sun

Flowers IPA; guest beers Ⓗ
Friendly village pub close to the Settle-Carlisle railway line. No food Tue.
🏧 Q 🕮 🛏 ◖ 🛝 ♣ ♣

LINDAL-IN-FURNESS

Railway Inn
6 London Road (off A590)
☎ (01229) 462889
2 (12 Sat & summer)-11; 2-10.30 Sun

Caledonian Deuchars IPA; John Smith's Bitter; guest beer (occasional) Ⓗ
Friendly village free house, close to South Lakes Wild Animal Park.
🏧 Q 🕮 ♣

LITTLE CORBY

Haywain
Off A69 ☎ (01228) 560598
7 (11 Sat)-11; 11-10.30 Sun

Robinson's Hartleys XB (occasional), **Best Bitter, Frederics** Ⓗ
Homely village pub with a

warm welcome. Good food includes traditional Sunday lunches. Live entertainment performed at weekends.
🕮 ◖ 🚶 ♣ P

LOW LORTON

Wheatsheaf Inn
On B5289, near Cockermouth
☎ (01900) 85268
11-3 (not Mon-Fri winter), 6-11; 11-3, 6-10.30 Sun

Jennings Bitter, Cumberland Ale, Sneck Lifter Ⓗ
Pleasant country pub serving excellent food in the bar and restaurant. It has a children's certificate and enclosed garden. No lunches Mon.
🏧 🕮 ◖ 🛝 ♣ P

LOWESWATER

Kirkstile Inn
Off B5289, 8 miles S of Cockermouth OS141209
☎ (01900) 85219
11-11; 12-10.30 Sun

Derwent Bill Monks; Jennings Bitter, Cumberland Ale Ⓗ
Atmospheric inn featuring beams and exposed stone in the bar. There is a games room and a dining room reached via a haunted covered corridor. Enjoy splendid views of Melbreak Fell. Good food is available all day.
🏧 Q 🕮 🛏 ◖ 🛝 ♣ P 🛗

MIDDLETON

Swan Inn
On A683 ☎ (0152 42) 76223
12-2.30 (summer only), 6-11; 12-11 Sat; 12-10.30 Sun

Black Sheep Best Bitter; guest beers Ⓗ
Built as a coaching inn, the Swan retains many original features; the dining room boasts a splendid old range. It offers good value meals (all day Sat/Sun), whilst guest beers often include a mild.
🏧 🕮 🛏 ◖ 🛝 ♣ P

NETHER WASDALE

Screes Hotel
The Screes
☎ (0194 67) 26262
12-3, 6-11 (winter hours vary); 12-3, 7-10.30 Sun

Jennings Cumberland Ale; Yates Bitter; guest beers (summer) Ⓗ
Close to the remote and lovely Wastwater, this characterful pub was once a Temperance hotel. Cumbrian beers, Belgian bottled beers, rare whiskies and interesting fruit juices are stocked. Meals served in season.
🏧 Q 🛝 🕮 🛏 ◖ 🛝 P

NEWTON REIGNY

Sun Inn
Off B5288 W of Penrith
☎ (01768) 867055
11.30-3, 6-11; 11.30-11 Sat; 12-10.30 Sun

Jennings Bitter; Theakston Best Bitter H
Comfortable, spacious village pub, but with a cosy atmosphere, serving excellent food.
🏾 🐾 ❀ 🖛 🄳 🍺 ᵬ P ⠟

PARSONBY

Horse & Jockey Inn
On B5301
☎ (0169 73) 20482
11-11; 10.30-10.30 Sun

Jennings Mild, Bitter H
Cosy rural roadside pub with a curious pig theme in evidence.
🏾 ❀ 🄳 Å ♣ P

PENRITH

Agricultural Hotel
Castlegate (near station)
☎ (017 68) 862622
11-11; 12-10.30 Sun

Jennings Mild, Bitter, Cumberland Ale, Cocker Hoop; Sneck Lifter H
Comfortable town pub; enjoy the friendly atmosphere and good home-cooked food.
🏾 ❀ 🖛 🄳 ᵬ ⥱ P ⠟

Try also: **Miners Arms**, Southend Rd (guest beers)

POOLEY BRIDGE

Sun Inn
☎ (0176 84) 86205
12-11; 12-10.30 Sun

Jennings Bitter, Cumberland Ale, Sneck Lifter, seasonal beers H
The upper bar is popular with diners and non-smokers. The lower one has Sky TV and pool (winter). Good value meals, and a good base for exploring the northern Lakes.
🏾 ❀ 🖛 🄳 🄵 ♣ P ⠟ 🎛

PORTINSCALE

Farmers Arms
Off A66, 1 mile W of Keswick
☎ (0176 87) 73442
11-3, 6-11; 12-3, 7-10.30 Sun

Jennings Bitter, Cumberland Ale; guest beers (occasional) H
Traditional country pub in an attractive Lake District village. It is convenient for fell walkers, cyclists and boating on nearby Derwentwater.
🏾 Q ❀ 🖛 🎛

RAVENGLASS

Ratty Arms
☎ (01229) 717676
11-3; 5.30-11; 11-11 Sat & summer; 12-10.30 Sun

Jennings Bitter; Ruddles Best Bitter; John Smith's Bitter; Theakston Best Bitter; guest beer H
Friendly local in old railway buildings, handy for the La'al Ratty narrow gauge railway and picturesque Eskdale.
🄳 🍺 ⥱ P

RAVENSTONEDALE

Black Swan Hotel
Off A685 ☎ (0153 96) 23204
11.30-3, 6-11; 11-11 Fri & Sat; 12-10.30 Sun

Black Sheep Best Bitter; guest beer H
Attractive Victorian hotel with an interconnecting public and comfortably furnished lounge bar. Above average meals are also served in the dining room. Extensive grounds lie across the road.
🏾 Q ❀ 🖛 🄳 🄵 ᵬ Å ♣ P

ROWRAH

Stork
Rowrah Road
☎ (01946) 861213
5.30 (12 Sat & summer)-11; 12-10.30 Sun

Jennings Bitter; guest beer (summer) H
Cosy hotel where a warm welcome is enhanced by real fires in winter and good home-cooking in summer and winter weekends. It is close to the Coast-to-Coast cycleway, and the more remote western lakes and fells. 🏾 Q 🐾 ❀ 🖛 🄳 P

ST BEES

Queens Hotel
Main Street
☎ (01946) 822287
12-3, 5.30-11; 12-3, 7-10.30 Sun

Jennings Bitter, Cumberland Ale; Yates Bitter H
Popular, friendly family-run hotel with two bars and smoking and no-smoking eating areas serving home-cooked food (no meals Tue lunch). Ideal for Coast-to-Coast walkers. Limited parking.
🏾 Q ❀ 🖛 🄳 Å ⥱ P ⠟

STAVELEY

Eagle & Child
Kendal Road
☎ (01539) 821320
11-11; 12-10.30 Sun

Jennings Bitter; guest beers H
Two-bar Victorian pub with an attractive riverside garden across the road.
🏾 ❀ 🖛 🄳 ⥱ ♣ ⌂ P 🎛

STONETHWAITE

Langstrath Country Inn
From B5289, turn up

Langstrath valley at Stonethwaite church
☎ (01767) 77239
11-11; 12-3, 6-10.30 Sun

Black Sheep Best Bitter; Jennings Bitter; guest beer H
Privately-owned inn, nestling beneath the Borrowdale fells.
🏾 Q ❀ 🖛 🄳 ᵬ Å P

STRAWBERRY BANK

Masons Arms
Off A592 OS413895
☎ (0153 95) 68486
11.30-3, 6-11 (11-11 summer); 11.30 (11 summer)-11 Fri & Sat; 12-10.30 Sun

Beer range varies H
Popular Lakeland inn, famous for its vegan cuisine and enormous range of bottled beers from around the world. Damson Beer, Barnsley beers, plus two others are usually available, and often a Kriek beer.
🏾 ❀ 🖛 🄳 Å P

TALLENTIRE

Bush Inn
Off A594, near Cockermouth
☎ (01900) 823707
12-3 (not Tue), 7-11; 12-3, 7-10.30 Sun

Theakston XB; guest beer H
Friendly country local that is also the village post office. No food Tue. The guest beer is often a Derwent brew.
🏾 Q ❀ 🄳 🍺 ♣ P

THRELKELD

Horse & Farrier Inn
Off A66 1 mile E of Keswick
☎ (0176 87) 79688
11-11; 12-10.30 Sun

Jennings Bitter, Cumberland Ale, Sneck Lifter; guest beer H
Beautifully refurbished Jennings house offering award-winning food and excellent accommodation.
🏾 ❀ 🖛 🄳 🍺 ᵬ Å ♣ P ⠟

TIRRIL

Queens Head Inn
☎ (0176 88) 63219
12-3, 6-11; 12-11 Sat ; 12-10.30 Sun

Tirril John Bewsher's Best Bitter, Thomas Slee's Academy Ale; guest beers H
The front lounge boasts a flagged floor, an award-winning fireplace and ancient beams whilst the back bar has pool and a juke box. A multi-level dining room (part no-smoking) offers above average meals.
🏾 Q ❀ 🖛 🄳 🍺 ♣ P 🎛

TROUTBECK

Mortal Man
Off A592
☎ (0153 94) 33193
11-11; 12-10.30 Sun

Jennings Cumberland Ale; Marston's

Pedigree; Theakston XB H
Comfortable bar with several
interconnecting rooms,
affording fine views of the
valley and fells. The dining
room serves an evening
menu.
🏨 Q ❀ ⇔ ◖▌ À ♣ P ⅄

ULDALE

Snooty Fox
☎ (0169 73) 71479
12-2, 6.30-11, 12-2, 6.30-10.30 Sun
Black Sheep Special; Theakston
Best Bitter H
Nestling in a peaceful village
in the northern fells this
comfortable bar provides a
warm welcome. The house
beer, Uld Ale comes from
Hesket Newmarket.
🏨 ❀ ⇔ ◖▌ ♿ ♣ P

ULVERSTON

Farmers Arms
Market Place (off A590)
☎ (01229) 584469
10-11; 11-12.30 Sun
Theakston Best Bitter; guest
beer H
Comfortable, modernised
town-centre pub with
distinct dining and lounge
areas. Only coffee/tea served
before 10.30; children
welcome until 9pm.
🏨 ❀ ◖▌ ⇌

Kings Head
14 Queen Street (off A590)
☎ (01229) 582892
10.30-11; 12-10.30 Sun
Courage Directors; Fuller's London
Pride; Theakston Best Bitter; guest
beer H
Cosy, town-centre local with
its own bowling green at the
rear. It can be hectic at times.
🏨 ❀ ⇔ ⇌ ♣

Stan Laurel Inn
31 The Ellers (off A590)
☎ (01229) 582514
12-3 (not winter), 7-11; 12-3, 7-10.30
Sun
Tetley Dark Mild, Bitter; guest
beer H
Friendly local displaying
Laurel & Hardy memorabilia
(Stan Laurel was born in
Ulverston), comprising a
lounge, bar/games room and
a dining room.
⅍ ❀ ⇔ ◖▐ ⇌ ♣ P ⊟

UNDERBARROW

Punchbowl Inn
☎ (0153 95) 68234
12-3.30 (not Tue); 6-11; 12-4, 7-10.30
Sun
Draught Bass; Jennings Cumberland
Ale; guest beer H
The small bar serves a room
full of interesting features:
ancient beams, part of a
priest hole and a spice
cupboard. Good value pub

grub – try the fresh fish on
Fri. 🏨 ❀ ◖▌ ♣ P

WASDALE HEAD

Wasdale Head Inn
OS186087
☎ (019467) 26229
11-11; 12-10.30 Sun
Beer range varies H
By England's deepest lake
and highest peak, this
historic mountaineering pub
has lots of atmosphere and
all beers are from Cumbrian
breweries.
Q ❀ ⇔ ◖▌ À P ⅄

WETHERAL

Wheatsheaf
☎ (01228) 560686
12-2.30, 5-11; 12-11 Fri & Sat;
12-10.30 Sun
Beer range varies H
Comfortable village local
with good food on offer. The
village is on the bank of the
River Eden, excellent for
walking and fishing.
🏨 ❀ ◖▌ ⇌ ♣ P

Try also: **Crown**, Station Rd
(Thwaites)

WHITEHAVEN

John Paul Jones
Duke Street`
☎ (01946) 690916
12-11 (1.30am Fri & Sat); 12-10.30 Sun
Theakston Best Bitter; guest
beers H
Close to the new marina and
the historic old port, themed
on an 18th-century sailing
ship, this pub displays John
Paul Jones memorabilia. Very
busy at weekends. Eve meals
served Mon-Thu in summer.
◖▌ ♿ ♣

Try also: **Anchor Vaults**,
Market Place (Jennings)

WINDERMERE

Elleray Hotel
Cross Street
☎ (0153 94) 43120
11-11; 12-10.30 Sun
Castle Eden Ale; Jennings
Cumberland Ale; Tetley Bitter; guest
beer H
Built when the railway
reached Windermere, this
two-bar hotel retains its
appeal to locals and visitors.
The guest beer is often from a
local micro. Good value
meals are served.
🏨 ❀ ⇔ ◖▌ ⊕ ⇌ ♣

WINSTER

Brown Horse Inn
On A5074
☎ (0153 94) 43433
11-2.30, 5.30-11; 11-11 Sat & summer;
12-10.30 Sun

Jennings Bitter, Cumberland Ale;
Thwaites Bitter; guest beer H
Popular both for good quality
meals and for giving the
drinker an equally warm
welcome. No pool or TV, just
darts and quiet background
sound.
🏨 Q ❀ ◖▌ ♣ P

WINTON

Bay Horse Inn
Off A685
☎ (0176 83) 71451
12-3 (not Tue or winter Mon), 7 (6
summer)-11; 12-3, 7-10.30 Sun
Black Sheep Best Bitter; Theakston
Best Bitter; guest beers H
Cosy local, overlooking the
village green featuring a
stone-floored bar area, a
dining room and a raised
games room with pool table
to the rear. The guest beer is
often sourced from lesser
known breweries.
🏨 Q ❀ ⇔ ◖▌ ⊕ ♣ P

WORKINGTON

George IV
Stanley Street
☎ (01900) 602266
11-11; 12-3, 7-11 Sun
Jennings Bitter H
Homely, welcoming pub in
the old harbour area of the
town.
🏨 Q ⅍ ⇌ ♣

Try also: **Commercial Inn**,
Market Place (Jennings)

INDEPENDENT
BREWERIES

Barngates: Barngates
Bitter End: Cockermouth
Coniston: Coniston
Dent: Dent
Derwent: Silloth
Foxfield: Foxfield
Hesket Newmarket:
Hesket Newmarket
Jennings: Cockermouth
Strawberry Bank:
Cartmell Fell
Tirril: Tirril
Yates: Westnewton

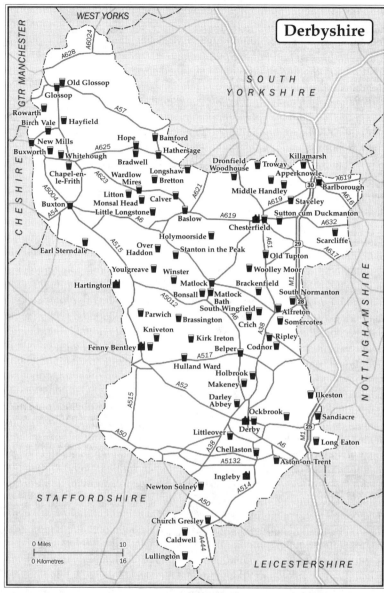

Derbyshire

(Map of Derbyshire showing towns and villages including:)

WEST YORKS
GTR MANCHESTER
SOUTH YORKSHIRE
CHESHIRE
NOTTINGHAMSHIRE
STAFFORDSHIRE
LEICESTERSHIRE

Old Glossop, Glossop, Rowarth, Birch Vale, Hayfield, New Mills, Buxworth, Whitehough, Chapel-en-le-Frith, Hope, Bamford, Hathersage, Bradwell, Wardlow Mires, Longshaw, Bretton, Dronfield Woodhouse, Troway, Killamarsh, Apperknowle, Barlborough, Litton, Monsal Head, Calver, Middle Handley, Staveley, Little Longstone, Baslow, Sutton cum Duckmanton, Buxton, Chesterfield, Earl Sterndale, Holymoorside, Scarcliffe, Over Haddon, Stanton in the Peak, Old Tupton, Youlgreave, Winster, Woolley Moor, Hartington, Matlock, Brackenfield, Bonsall, Matlock Bath, South Normanton, Parwich, South Wingfield, Alfreton, Brassington, Crich, Somercotes, Kniveton, Kirk Ireton, Ripley, Fenny Bentley, Belper, Codnor, Hulland Ward, Holbrook, Makeney, Ilkeston, Darley Abbey, Ockbrook, Sandiacre, Littleover, Derby, Long Eaton, Chellaston, Aston-on-Trent, Ingleby, Newton Solney, Church Gresley, Caldwell, Lullington

0 Miles 10
0 Kilometres 16

ALFRETON

Victoria Inn
80 Nottingham Road (off A38 via B600)
☎ (01773) 520156
1 (12 Sat)-11; 12-10.30 Sun
Beer range varies H
Busy, two-roomed local with a friendly atmosphere; extensively refurbished, it features an illuminated aquarium in the lounge and Sky TV in the public bar. Guest beers change regularly, and include local products. Parking is difficult. Long alley skittles played.
Q ❀ ⊞ ≠ ♣

APPERKNOWLE

Yellow Lion
High Street
☎ (01246) 413181
12-2, 6-11; 12-3, 7-10.30 Sun
Stones Bitter; guest beers H
Stone-built village free house comprising a large lounge and a no-smoking restaurant; in the same hands for over 30 years it offers a regularly changing range of guest beers and a beer festival (early summer). Q ❀ ⇔ ◑ ▶ P ☐

ASTON-ON-TRENT

Malt Shovel

The Green (off Derby Rd)
☎ (01332) 792256
11.30-11; 12-10.30 Sun
Draught Bass; Greene King Abbot; Marston's Pedigree; Morland Old Speckled Hen; Wells Bombardier; Young's Special H
Friendly village local: a panelled bar and comfortable lounge.
❀ ◑ ⊞ ♣ P

Try also: White Hart, Derby Road (Marston's)

BAMFORD

Angler's Rest
Taggs Knoll (A6013)

☎ (01433) 651424
12-3, 6-11; 12-11 Sat; 12-10.30 Sun
Banks's Bitter; Marston's Bitter, Pedigree; guest beer (summer) Ⓗ
Village local, renovated in open-plan style featuring high-backed pews and a no-smoking dining area. Near Ladybower and Derwent Reservoirs.
Q ✿ ⇔ ◖ ◗ ᕕ & ⇌ ♣ P

BARLBOROUGH
Rose & Crown
Near M1 jct 30
☎ (01246) 810364
12-3, 6-11; 12-3.30, 7-10.30 Sun
Hardys & Hansons Best Bitter, seasonal beers Ⓗ/Ⓟ
An historic Norman cross in front of this popular village pub sets the tone for the style of its two rooms, central bar and restaurant.
Q ✿ ◖ ◗ ⊞ ♣ P

BASLOW
Robin Hood
Chesterfield Road
(A619/B6050 jct)
☎ (01246) 583186
11.30-11; 11.30-3, 6.30-11 Mon; 12-10.30 Sun
Mansfield Mild, Riding Bitter, Bitter Ⓗ
Just outside the village, this is a popular meeting place for walkers, climbers and day visitors to the Peak District. Dogs are welcome in the hikers' den. Children's certificate. Note: Mild is served under cask breather in Jan if necessary. ♨ Q ✿ ⇔ ◖
◗ ⊞ ᕕ ♣ P ⅟ ◰ ⊞

BELPER
Queens Head
29 Chesterfield Road
☎ (01773) 825525
12-11; 12-10.30 Sun
Greene King IPA; Ind Coope Burton Ale; Tetley Bitter; guest beers Ⓗ
Lively, multi-roomed community pub whose rear terrace overlooks the town. Live music is staged in the function room most weekends.
♨ ✿ ⊞ ♣

BIRCH VALE
Vine
Hayfield Road (A6015)
☎ (01663) 741021
12-2.30, 6-11; 12-3, 7-10.30 Sun
Robinson's Hatters Mild, Best Bitter Ⓗ
Stone pub on the fringe of the Peak District, close by the Sett Valley Trail. Good value food and accommodation, and a warm welcome is assured. Limited parking.
♨ ⚲ ⇔ ◖ ◗ ♣ P

BONSALL
Barley Mow
The Dale (off the Via Gellia, A5012)
☎ (01629) 825685
6 (12 Sat)-11; 12-3, 7-10.30 Sun
Whim Hartington Bitter; guest beer Ⓗ
Friendly, 17th-century, small village local hosting live music every weekend; it is renowned for its excellent meals, cellar cave and hidden room. The landlord organises walks at weekends, and makes incredible use of small space. Hen racing in summer and boules played.
♨ ✿ ◖ ◗ ᕕ ♣ P

BRACKENFIELD
Plough Inn
Matlock Road (A615 midway between Alfreton and Matlock)
☎ (01629) 534437
12-2.30, 5.30-11; 12-3, 5.30-10.30 (12-10.30 summer) Sun
Mansfield Bitter; guest beers Ⓗ
16th-century, Grade II listed sandstone former farmhouse: a multi-roomed genuine free house where guest beers, supplied by independent breweries, regularly change. The house beer is supplied by Beer Seller. Excellent food includes themed nights.
Q ⚲ ✿ ◖ ◗ ᕕ ᕕ ♣ P

BRADWELL
Valley Lodge
Church Street (B6049)
☎ (01433) 620427
12-3 (not Mon-Fri), 7-11; 12-3, 7-10.30 Sun
Adnams Bitter; Stones Bitter; guest beers Ⓗ
Large, brick-built 1930s pub in a limestone village. The basic tap room has its own entrance; also a small foyer bar and large lounge. A wide range of guest beers is stocked.
♨ Q ✿ ⇔ ◖ ◗ ⊞ ♣ P

BRASSINGTON
Olde Gate Inn ☆
Well Street (off A5023, Ashbourne-Wirksworth road)
☎ (01629) 540448
12-2.30 (3 Fri), 6-11; 12-3, 7-10.30 Sun
Marston's Pedigree Ⓗ
Family-run, reputedly haunted, village pub built in 1616; Grade II listed, it boasts oak beams throughout. Winner of the Homefire *Real Fire Pub of the Year*. An extensive menu includes home-cooked dishes. Near Carsington Water, it is well worth a visit. Boules played.
♨ Q ✿ ◖ ◗ ᕕ & ᕕ ♣ P ⅟

BRETTON
Barrel Inn
OS201779
☎ (01433) 630856
11-3, 6-11; 11-11 Sat & summer; 12-3, 7-10.30 Sun
Marston's Pedigree; Tetley Bitter; guest beers Ⓗ
Inn dated 1597, on the 18th-century turnpike road from Sheffield to Buxton, enjoying spectacular views in all directions. The single long bar has an L-shaped extension. Irish folk music performed Wed.
♨ ☜ ✿ ⇔ ◖ ◗ P

BUXTON
Bakers Arms
26 West Road
☎ (01298) 24404
12-3, 6-11; 12-3, 7-10.30 Sun
Ind Coope Burton Ale or guest beer; Tetley Bitter Ⓗ
Small, two-roomed local displaying a large sporting trophy collection. The Burton Ale alternates with a guest beer from the Tapster's Choice range. Small car park.
Q ✿ ᕕ ⇌ P

Duke of York
123 St Johns Road, Burbage (A53)
☎ (01298) 24006
12-3, 5-11; 12-11 Sat & summer; 12-3, 7-10.30 (12-10.30 summer) Sun
Black Sheep Special; Greene King Abbot; Marston's Pedigree; Tetley Mild, Bitter; Ⓗ
Busy two-roomed local served by a now open-plan central bar; the larger room has a no-smoking area. Good home-cooked food is served all day. Walkers are welcome, with a walled seating area for use in summer. Small car park.
Q ✿ ◖ ◗ ᕕ ⇌ P ⅟

Old Sun Inn
33 High Street
☎ (01298) 23452
11-11; 12-10.30 Sun
Banks's Original, Bitter; Marston's Pedigree; guest beers Ⓗ
Eight adjoining areas surround three central bars. Restaurant quality food is served every day until 9pm; up to four guest beers, and a range of new world wines also available. There is a seating area at the front, with a small car park to the rear.
Q ✿ ◖ ◗ & ᕕ ⇌ ◰ P ⊞

Swan
41 High Street
☎ (01298) 23278
11-11; 12-10.30 Sun
Draught Bass; Tetley Bitter; guest beers Ⓗ
Very popular local of three rooms, each with its own

theme, served by a central bar. Two ever-changing guest beers and over 100 whiskies are on offer. Small car park.
Q P

BUXWORTH

Navigation
Brookside Road (off B6062 by canal basin)
(01663) 732072
11-11; 12-10.30 Sun
Marston's Pedigree; Taylor Landlord; guest beer H
Excellent, multi-roomed18th-century pub, with an extensive restaurant, worth seeking out. Partially stone-flagged bearing a canal theme, it stands alongside Britain's only remaining canal/tramway interchange. The canal basin is now restored and open again to boats. Walkers welcome. Cider in summer.
P

CALDWELL

Royal Oak
Main Street
(01283) 761486
11-11; 12-10.30 Sun
Marston's Pedigree; guest beers H
Friendly village free house with a small narrow bar and a comfortable, split-level lounge at the rear. Built as a bakery in the 17th century, it was converted to a pub in the late 1800s. Reputedly haunted; part of the garden was a burial ground for plague victims.

CALVER

Bridge Inn
Calver Bridge (A623)
(01433) 630415
11.30-3, 5.30-11; 11.30-4.30, 5.30-11 Sat; 12-4.30, 7-10.30 Sun
Hardys & Hansons Best Bitter, Classic, seasonal beers; Stones Bitter H
Cosy village local, where the smaller of its lounges houses a collection of local guide books. No food Mon eve or winter Sun eve.
Q P

CHAPEL EN LE FRITH

Roebuck
Market Place
(01298) 812274
11-11; 12-10.30 Sun
Tetley Mild, Bitter H
Thriving market place pub in a Peak District town. One bar serves the large, airy interior. This well-used and popular pub serves meals 12-6; eve meals Mon-Sat 5-8.
Q

Try also: Old Pack Horse, Town End (Robinson's)

CHELLASTON

Corner Pin
Swarkestone Road (A514)
(01332) 705715
11-11; 12-10.30 Sun
Ind Coope Burton Ale; Marston's Pedigree; guest beers H
Early 19th-century building, now incorporating a cruck-built cottage next door to serve as a pleasant parlour. The small upstairs eating area doubles as a meeting room; lively public bar. No food Mon. P

Try also: Red Lion, Derby Rd (Bass)

CHESTERFIELD

Boythorpe Inn
77 Boythorpe Road, Boythorpe (opp. Queens Park sports centre)
(01246) 235280
12-11; 12-10.30 Sun
Hardys & Hansons Best Mild, Best Bitter, Classic, seasonal beers H
This large welcoming pub, close to the sports centre has its own bowling green at the rear and a big screen TV for its many sports fans.
P

Derby Tup
387 Sheffield Road, Whittington Moor
(01246) 454316
11.30-11; 11.30-3, 5-11 Mon & Tue; 12-4, 7-10.30 Sun
Black Sheep Best Bitter; Greene King Abbot; Taylor Landlord; Theakston Old Peculier; Whim Hartington Bitter H
Traditional three-roomed local attracting customers from all walks of life, all are made welcome and feel comfortable here. It boasts one of the best beer selections in the area with four guest beers, plus excellent food; eve meals Thu-Sat 5-8. Regular live music. Q

Market
95 New Square (next to Market Hall)
(01246) 273641
11-11; 7-10.30 Sun
Greene King Abbot; Ind Coope Burton Ale; Marston's Pedigree; guest beer H
Town-centre pub sympathetically renovated; it is busy on Mon, Fri and Sat lunchtimes (market days). Five guest beers stocked.

Peacock Inn
412 Chatsworth Road, Brampton (A619)
(01246) 275115
12-3, 5-11; 11-11 Sat; 12-10.30 Sun
Draught Bass; Marston's Pedigree; Stones Bitter; guest beers H
Large two-roomed local on the road to Chatsworth and the Peak District.

Red Lion
570 Sheffield Road, Whittington Moor
(01246) 450770
11.30-4, 7-11; 11.30-11 Fri & Sat; 12-4, 7-10.30 Sun
Old Mill Mild, Nellie Dene, Bitter, Old Curiosity, Bullion, Blackjack H
Traditional, two-roomed pub built in the early 1870s, the only local outlet for Old Mill beers. It hosts regular live music, plus a summer charity barbecue and fun day.
Q P

Royal Oak
43 Chatsworth Road, Brampton (A619, opp. B&Q)
(01246) 277854
11.30-11; 12-10.30 Sun
Ruddles Best Bitter; Theakston Best Bitter, XB, Old Peculier; Townes Sunshine, Best Lockoford Bitter H
Popular, traditional pub of three wood-panelled rooms, plus a modern children's play area outside. It stages regular music nights and an 'Oakfest' beer and music festival (Aug Bank Hol).
P

Rutland
16 Stephenson Place (foot of crooked spire)
(01246) 205857
11-11; 12-10.30 Sun
Boddingtons Bitter; Marston's Pedigree; guest beer H
Popular, open-plan, town-centre Hogshead Alehouse. Meals are served all day until early eve, to complement the varying choice of up to six guest beers.

Victoria Inn
21-23 Victoria Street West, Brampton (off A619, near Safeway roundabout))
(01246) 273832
12-4 (5 Sat), 7-11; 12-5, 7-10.30 Sun
Stones Bitter; Tetley Bitter; guest beers H
Friendly, two-roomed traditional local that stages a quiz night Mon eve.
P

CHURCH GRESLEY

Rising Sun
77 Church Street
(01283) 217274
12-11; 12-10.30 Sun
Draught Bass; Marston's Pedigree; guest beers H
Built in 1889 for Bass, one of their last pubs built with

The Good Beer Guide 2001

stables. Look for the pennies on the bar. Limited parking. Sun lunch served.

🏨 🍺 🍴 ♣ P

CODNOR

Red Admiral
2 Alfreton Road (off A610)
☎ (01773) 745873
12-3, 6-11; 12-3, 7-10.30 Sun
Draught Bass; Fuller's London Pride; guest beer H
Friendly, large, open-plan, one-bar local, with a cosy sunken snug off the main bar area and a no-smoking family conservatory overlooking the garden. No food Sun.

🍺 🍴 ◖ P ⊬

CRICH

Cliff Inn
Cromford Road, Town End
☎ (01773) 852444
11.30-3, 6-11; 12-3, 7-10.30 Sun
Hardys & Hansons Best Mild, Best Bitter, Classic or seasonal beer H
Cosy, popular, two-roomed stone pub near the Tramway Museum offering a wonderful view over the Derwent Valley. Long-serving licensees have been in almost every edition of this *Guide*.

🏨 Q ◖ 🍴 ⊞ ♠ P

DARLEY ABBEY

Abbey
Darley Street (on riverside)
☎ (01332) 558297
11.30-2.30, 6-11; 12-11Sat; 12-10.30 Sun
Samuel Smith OBB H
Centre-piece of a conservation area, this inn of superb character is the only surviving out-building of the Abbey of Saint Mary de Pratis. Be sure to see both floors to fully appreciate it. A pleasant riverside park is nearby. 🏨 Q 🍴 ◖ ♣ P

DERBY

Alexandra Hotel
203 Siddals Road
☎ (01332) 293993
11-11; 12-3, 7-10.30 Sun
Draught Bass; Bateman XB; Hook Norton Best Bitter; Taylor Landlord; guest beers H
Friendly, two-roomed pub where the bar displays brewery and railway memorabilia. A large range of continental bottled beers (and five on draught), plus a good selection of malt whiskies and two traditional ciders complement the eight guest beers which always include a mild.

Q 🍴 🏨 ◖ 🍴 ⊞ 🍴 ⊨ ♣ ⊂ P ⊬

Brunswick
1 Railway Terrace

☎ (01332) 290677
11-11; 12-10.30 Sun
Brunswick Second Brew, Railway Porter, Triple Hop; Sarah Hughes Dark Ruby; Taylor Landlord H
guest beers H/G
Multi-roomed, mid-19th-century brew-pub at the apex of the preserved railway cottages. An eclectic range of 17 beers are sourced from near and far.

Q 🍺 🍴 ◖ 🍴 ⊞ ⊨ ♣ ⊂ ⊬

Drill Hall Vaults
1 Newland Street (off Curzon St, 200 yds from A616)
☎ (01332) 298073
12-3, 7-11; 12-3, 7-10.30 Sun
Marston's Pedigree H
Single-room pub with three distinctive areas – for TV, games and a quiet area, each with its own coal fire. There is an attractive garden at the back. No food Sun.

🏨 🍴 ◖ 🍴 ♣

Duke of Clarence
87 Mansfield Road (near Chester Green)
☎ (01332) 346882
12-11; 12-4, 7-10.30 Sun
Hardys & Hansons Best Mild, Best Bitter, seasonal beers H
Traditional roadside local, originally a farmhouse then a 19th-century coaching inn. A friendly community pub, it hosts singsongs around the piano most weekends. It lies near Chester Green, the site of a Roman encampment, now marked only by ancient wells and Roman street names. Lunches sometimes available.

🍴 ⊞ 🍴 ♣ P

Falstaff
74 Silverhill Road, Normanton (off Normanton Rd)
☎ (01332) 342902
12-11; 12-10.30 Sun
Greene King Abbot; guest beers H
With its richly decorated red-brick exterior and terracotta detail, this once-grand pub seems strangely out of place here. It attracts a lively crowd of regulars into its busy bow-backed bar and two side-rooms. Try the product of its new brewery served from a new five-barrel stillage in the lounge.

🏨 Q ⊞ ♣

Flower Pot
25 King Street
☎ (01332) 204955
11-11; 12-10.30 Sun
Draught Bass; G **Hook Norton Old Hooky; Marston's Pedigree; guest beers** H/G
Popular pub, near the old clock-house, where several interlinking rooms boasts different characters; live

music is staged in one. An exceptional feature is the glass cellar wall revealing row on row of stillaged firkins. Derbyshire beers and a mild are always among the dozen guests. Eve meals end at 6.45.

Q 🍴 ◖ 🍴 ⊞ 🍴 ⊂

Friargate
114 Friargate
☎ (01332) 297065
11-11; 12-3, 7-10.30 Sun
Draught Bass; Marston's Pedigree; G **Oakham JHB, Bishops Farewell, Whim Arbor Light, Hartington IPA; guest beers** H
This Victorian tavern on the site of a much older inn, stands in one of Derby's oldest streets, where a Dominican Friary also once stood. Its single room is amply proportioned. Mostly music-free, but it stages popular acoustic sessions every Wed. Dr Samuel Johnson got married just over the road.

◖ 🍴 P

Furnace
Duke Street (off old St. Mary's Bridge)
☎ (01332) 331563
11-11; 12-10.30 Sun
Hardys & Hansons Best Mild, Best Bitter, Classic, seasonal beers H
Friendly community pub close to an historic bridge chapel – one of only six left in the whole country. A former foundryman's slaker, the name commemorates the once-adjacent foundry of Andrew Handyside. A handy watering-hole for cyclists and walkers using the riverside path.

🍴 🍴 ♣

Old Dolphin
5 Queen Street (up Irongate from market place)
☎ (01332) 267711
10.30-11; 12-10.30 Sun
Draught Bass; Black Sheep Special; Caledonian Deuchars IPA; Fuller's London Pride; Greene King Abbot; Ruddles County; guest beers H
Contemporary with the cathedral tower, in whose shadow it stands, this historic four-roomed pub simply brims with character. The upstairs steak bar is licensed till midnight (opens 6pm). It stages an annual beer festival (July).

🏨 Q 🍴 ◖ 🍴 ⊞ 🍴 P

Rowditch Inn
246 Uttoxeter New Road
☎ (01332) 343123
12-2 (not Mon-Wed), 7-11; 12-2, 7-10.30 Sun
Mansfield Riding Bitter; Marston's Pedigree; guest beer H
Friendly local catering for a diverse community and

DERBYSHIRE

visiting drinkers. It stocks an excellent range of fruit wines. The restored cellar bar is open occasionally.

Ⓜ ♣ ⚜

Smithfield
Meadow Road (accessible by footpath from Alexandra, or down river from market place)
☎ (01332) 370429
11-11; 12-10.30 (12-3, 7-10.30 winter) Sun
Draught Bass; Oakham JHB, Bishop's Farwell; Whim Arbor Light, Hartington IPA; guest beers Ⓗ
High up on a willow-lined bank overlooking the chub-filled river, this bow-fronted pub has a large bar and small lounge furnished with carved benches and cluttered with curiosities. The offices of the Derby Evening Telegraph stand close by, and riverside gardens are just upriver. No food Sun.

Ⓜ ⛵ ⚜ ◖⊟ ♣ P

Station Inn
Midland Road
☎ (01332) 608014
11.30-2.30, 5 (7 Sat)-11; 11.30-11 Fri; 12-3, 7-10.30 Sun
Draught Bass; Ⓖ **Courage Directors** Ⓗ
The narrow, but ornate stone-and-stained glass frontage belies the interior of an extended front bar, huge function room and a dining area to the rear serving excellent value meals. The licensee has won many cellar awards, particularly for Draught Bass which is possibly the best in Derby.

◖⇌ ♣ ⊟

Try also: Tiger, Lock-up Yard, off Cornmarket (Bass)

DRONFIELD WOODHOUSE
Jolly Farmer
Pentland Road (off B6056)
☎ (01246) 418018
12-11; 12-10.30 Sun
Greenalls Bitter; Marston's Pedigree; Taylor Landlord; Tetley Bitter; guest beers Ⓗ
Estate pub, built by Shipstone's in 1976, later becoming a Greenalls Alehouse. Renovated in farmhouse style it is open plan with many alcoves. Note the glass-fronted cellar behind the bar. No lager/keg fonts are to be seen.

⚜ ◖▶ ⚅ ♣

EARL STERNDALE
Quiet Woman
Off B5053
☎ (01298) 83211
12-4, 7-11; 12-3, 7-10.30 Sun

Banks's Original; Everards Tiger; Marston's Bitter, Pedigree; Taylor Landlord; Whim Hartington Bitter Ⓗ
Unspoilt local by the village green, in the heart of the Peak District National Park. A warm friendly atmosphere awaits you by a real fire, along with traditional pub games; boules also played. It hosts live folk music Sun.

Ⓜ Q ⚜ ◖ ♣ P

FENNY BENTLEY
Bentley Brook Inn
On A515
☎ (01335) 350278
11-11; 12-10.30 Sun
Leatherbritches Belter, Bespoke; Mansfield Riding Bitter; Marston's Pedigree; guest beers Ⓗ
Large country pub, the home of Leatherbritches Brewery. A new terrace overlooks the extensive garden area, where regular 'Blues+Booze' festivals are held in a marquee. Informal camping facilities available. It has a skittle alley outside. Guest beers are also supplied by Leatherbritches.

Ⓜ ⚜ ⚅ ◖▶ ⚃ ♣ P

GLOSSOP
Crown Inn
142 Victoria Street
☎ (01457) 862824
11.30-3, 5-11; 11.30-11 Fri & Sat; 12-10.30 Sun
Samuel Smith OBB Ⓗ
Friendly local in the Whitfield area of town. A central curved bar serves two small, comfortable snugs (one for non-smokers) and a large games room. It sells the cheapest pint in the area.

Ⓜ Q ⚜ ⚅ ♣ ⚜

Friendship
3 Arundel Street
☎ (01457) 855277
4 (3 Fri, 12 Sat)-11; 12-3, 7-10.30 sun
Robinson's Hatters Mild, Best Bitter Ⓗ
Stone, corner local with a wood-panelled interior. The semi-circular bar is an attractive feature of the open-plan lounge. The back tap room is served by a hatch. Families welcome.

Ⓜ ⛵ ⇌ ♣

Old Gloveworks
Riverside Mill, George Street
☎ (01457) 858432
12-11; 12-10.30 Sun
Beer range varies Ⓗ
Converted mill, previously a wine bar, affording elevated views over Glossop Brook. Entertainment includes local bands, discos and Sunday cabaret from 3.30. Six ever-changing beers are available. No meals Sat.

Outdoors enjoy the riverside patio and roof terrace.

⚜ ◖⇌ P

Star Inn Ale House
2 Howard Street
☎ (01457) 853072
11-11; 12-10.30 Sun
Boddingtons Bitter; guest beers Ⓗ
Highly regarded alehouse, opposite the station, selling up to five guest beers. Bare floorboards and a tap room served by a hatch, are features of this juke box-free pub.

⚅ ⇌ ♣ P

HATHERSAGE
Scotsman's Pack
School Lane
☎ (01433) 650253
11.30-3, 6-11; 11.30-11 Sat; 12-10.30 Sun
Burtonwood Bitter, Top Hat, guest beers Ⓗ
Comfortable village pub where three lounge areas are served by a central bar. It is popular with locals, but also welcoming to visitors. Little John is reputedly buried in the nearby churchyard.

Q ⚜ ⇌ ◖▶ ⚃ ♣ P ⚜

HAYFIELD
Royal Hotel
Market Street
☎ (01663) 742721
12-3, 6-11; 12-11 Sat; 12-10.30 Sun
Marston's Pedigree; John Smith's Bitter; Theakston Best Bitter; guest beers Ⓗ
Former vicarage by the River Sett and the village cricket ground. Original oak panels and pews give a relaxing atmosphere. Regular live music includes Sun afternoon jazz. It usually holds a beer festival early Oct.

Ⓜ Q ⛵ ⚜ ⇌ ◖▶ ⚅ ▲ P ⚜

Try also: Kinder Lodge, New Mill Rd (Free)

HOLBROOK
Dead Poets Inn
Chapel Street
☎ (01332) 780301
12-2.30, 5-11; 12-11 Fri & Sat; 12-10.30 Sun
Greene King Abbot; Marston's Pedigree; Ⓖ **guest beers** Ⓗ
Popular village pub featuring candlelit tables, wooden settles and a flagged floor. The house beer 'If' is from the Brunswick Brewery. Weekday lunches served.

Ⓜ ⚜ ◖ P

Wheel Inn
14 Chapel Street
☎ (01332) 880006
11.30-3 (not Mon), 6.30-11, 11.30-11 Sat; 12-3, 7-10.30 Sun

79

Archer's Golden; G Courage Directors; Marston's Pedigree; Theakston XB; H Whim Hartington Bitter; G guest beers H/G
Friendly village local with a restaurant area and an attractive garden. A good range of home-cooked food is available (not served Sun eve or Mon).
🏚 🍺 🚲 ◑ ❨

HOLYMOORSIDE
Lamb Inn
16 Loads Road
☎ (01246) 566167
12-3 (not Mon-Thu), 7-11; 12-3, 7-10.30 Sun
Home Bitter; guest beer H
Cosy, two-roomed village pub close to the Peak District National Park. Up to four guest ales are normally available.
🏚 Q ❀ ♣ ♠ P

HOPE
Cheshire Cheese
Edale Road
☎ (01433) 620381
12-3, 6-11; 12-11 Sat; 12-4, 6-10.30 Sun
Barnsley Bitter; Mansfield Bitter; guest beer H
16th-century free house: cosy rooms in a split-level layout, set in the heart of walking country. Parking is limited.
🏚 Q ❀ 🚲 ◑ ♠ P

HULLAND WARD
Black Horse Inn
On A517, halfway between Ashbourne and Belper
☎ (01335) 370206
12-2.30, 6-11; 12-3, 7-10.30 Sun
Draught Bass; Marston's Pedigree; guest beers H
Traditional, 300-year-old inn located in the Derbyshire Dales, close to Carsington Water. Noted for its warm atmosphere, range of guest beers and home-cooked food (takeaways available). ETB commended accommodation includes four-poster beds.
Q ❀ 🚲 ◑ ❨ ♣ P ⊞

ILKESTON
Dewdrop Inn
Station Street (off A609, by railway bridge)
☎ (0115) 932 9684
11.30-3 (not Sat), 7-11; 12-5, 7-10.30 Sun
Draught Bass; Taylor Best Bitter, Ram Tam; Whim Hartington IPA; guest beers H
Welcoming, friendly, traditional, multi-roomed alehouse. TV and darts fans favour the bar; the sociable lounge has a piano and real fire (highly commended by Homefire in the 1999

competition). Local CAMRA *Pub of the Year* 1998, it offers a fine whisky selection and hosts annual beer festivals in Dec and Feb.
🏚 Q 🚬 ❀ ◑ 🍴 ♣ 🍽

Durham Ox
25 Durham Street (between Bath St and bypass)
☎ (0115) 932 4570
11-11; 12-10.30 Sun
Draught Bass; G Benskins BB; Boddingtons Bitter; H Greene King IPA; H/P guest beers H/G
Cosy back-street local that used to be the town's prison. Open plan, it offers many different drinking areas to accommodate a pool table, TV and darts. Long alley skittles is played in the adjacent public car park.
🏚 ♣ 🗄

Try also: Sir John Warren, Market Place (Hardys & Hansons)

KILLAMARSH
Angel Inn
127 Rotherham Road, Norwood End (A618)
☎ (0114) 248 5607
11-11; 12-3, 7-10.30 Sun
Beer range varies H
Formerly a farmhouse, now a smart pub with an enterprising guest beer range. Drinking straight from the bottle is forbidden here. Handy for River Valley Country Park and Chesterfield Canal.
❀ ◑ ♣ P 🍽

KIRK IRETON
Barley Mow ☆
Main Street
☎ (01335) 370306
12-2, 7-11; 12-2, 7-10.30 Sun
Hook Norton Best Bitter, Old Hooky; guest beers G
Tall Jacobean building, notable for its twin gabled frontage. The intimate interior features three interconnecting rooms with low beamed ceilings, slate tables and well-worn woodwork.
🏚 Q ❀ 🚲 🍴 ♠ ♣ 🍽 P

KNIVETON
Red Lion
Wirksworth Road
☎ (01335) 345554
12-2 (not winter Thu), 7-11; 12-3, 7-10.30 Sun
Draught Bass; Burton Bridge Bitter; guest beers H
Friendly village local with its own outdoor skittle alley in the heart of the Dales walking country and close to Carsington Water. Noted for its interesting range of

vegetarian food and good guest beer range.
🏚 ❀ ◑ ♠ ♣ P 🍽

LITTLE LONGSTONE
Packhorse Inn
Main Street
☎ (01629) 640471
11.30-3 , 5 (6 Sat)-11; 12-10.30 Sun
Marston's Bitter, Pedigree H
Unspoilt village local on the Monsal Trail; a pub since 1787. Three small rooms where ramblers are welcome; it also draws a regular local trade.
🏚 Q ❀ ◑ ♠ ♣

LITTLEOVER
White Swan
Shepherd Street (off Burton road)
☎ (01332) 766481
11-11; 12-4, 7-10.30 Sun
Ansells Bitter; Ind Coope Burton Ale; Marston's Pedigree; Tetley Bitter; guest beers H
Well-patronised community local where the big screen TV in the bar pleases sports fans. Eve meals served 5-7.
Q ❀ ◑ 🍴 ♣ P

LITTON
Red Lion
Main Street
☎ (01298) 871458
12-3, 6-1; 12-11 Sat; 12-10.30 Sun
Jennings Cumberland Ale; Tetley Bitter; guest beers H
Real gem of a village local, formerly more of a restaurant: two cosy rooms at the front, plus a larger games room at rear where children are allowed until 8pm. Good food and interesting guest beers are the norm here. No meals Sun eve.
🏚 Q ❀ ◑ ♣ P

Try also: George Hotel, Commercial Rd, Tideswell (Hardys & Hansons)

LONG EATON
Hole in the Wall
Regent Street
☎ (0115) 973 4920
10.30-3.30, 6-11; 10.30-11 Fri & Sat; 12-4.30, 7-10.30 Sun
Courage Directors; John Smith's Bitter; guest beers H
CAMRA award-winning, town-centre local stocking two regular beers and ever-changing guests. It has an outdoor skittle alley with a drinking area in the rear yard. Filled rolls available daily. ❀ 🍴 ♣ P

LONGSHAW
Grouse Inn
On A625 (formerly B6054)

OS258779
☎ (01433) 630423
12-3, 6-11; 12-11 Sat; 12-10.30 Sun
Banks's Bitter; Marston's Pedigree; guest beer Ⓗ
Isolated pub, convenient for nearby Froggatt Edge, comprising a lounge, tap room and conservatory. The guest beer is from Banks's list. An American folk group performs Wed; a bistro is open Thu-Sat (no eve meals Mon or Tue).
🏚 Q ⅋ ❀ ◖ ▮ ⊞ ♣ P ⚲

LULLINGTON

Colvile Arms
Main Street
☎ (01827) 373212
12-2 (not Mon-Fri), 7-11; 12-3, 7-10.30 Sun
Draught Bass; Marston's Pedigree; guest beers Ⓗ
Popular, 18th-century free house in a pleasant village. Amenities nclude a wood-panelled bar, a smart lounge, a second lounge/function room and a bowling green in the garden.
🏚 Q ❀ ⊞ ♣ P

MAKENEY

Holly Bush Inn
Holly Bush Lane OS352447
☎ (01332) 841729
12-3, 5-11; 12-11 Fri & Sat; 12-10.30 Sun
Brains Dark; Ⓗ **Marston's Pedigree; Ruddles County;** Ⓖ **guest beers** Ⓗ
Old pub with many rooms in a Grade II listed building. Some of the beers come from the cellar in jugs; it offers five guest beers plus an annual beer festival (Mar).
🏚 Q ❀ P

MATLOCK

Boat House
110 Dale Road (A6 between Matlock and Matlock Bath)
☎ (01629) 583776
12-11; 12-10.30 Sun
Hardys & Hansons Best Mild, Best Bitter, Classic, seasonal beers Ⓗ
Two-roomed Dales pub of character.
🏚 Q ❀ ⇌ ◖ ▮ ⅋ Å ♣ P ⚲

Crown
Derwent House, Crown Square (A6)
☎ (01629) 580991
11-11; 12-10.30 Sun
Boddingtons Bitter; Courage Directors; John Smith's Bitter; Theakston Best Bitter; guest beer Ⓗ
Wetherspoon's shop conversion on the road to Bakewell. Popular with shoppers and tourists lunchtimes, it attracts the younger set eves.
◖ ▮ ⅋ ⇌ ⌂ ⚲

MATLOCK BATH

Princess Victoria
174-176 South Parade
☎ (01629) 57462
12-11; 12-10.30 Sun
Greene King Abbot; Marston's Pedigree; Wells Bombardier; guest beer Ⓗ
Friendly, one-room pub, popular with locals and its many visitors throughout the year. Parking limited in summer.
🏚 Q ❀ ◖ ▮ ⇌ ♣

MIDDLE HANDLEY

Devonshire Arms
Westfield Lane (B6052/B6056 jct)
☎ (01246) 432189
5-11; 12-3, 7-11 Sat; 12-3, 7-10.30 Sun
Draught Bass; Stones Bitter; guest beer Ⓗ
Three-roomed, traditional pub served from a central bar; old fashioned and proud of it, it is unsurprisingly popular; a gem.
🏚 Q ❀ Å ♣ P

MONSAL HEAD

Monsal Head Hotel
On B6465
☎ (01629) 640250
11-11; 12-10.30 Sun
Courage Directors; Marston's Pedigree; Taylor Landlord; Theakston Best Bitter, Old Peculier; Whim Hartington Bitter; guest beers Ⓗ
Real ales are available in the Stable Bar at the rear of the hotel; this has the original floor and is appropriately decorated. The house beer is from Lloyds.
🏚 Q ❀ ⇌ ◖ ▮ Å ♣ P

NEW MILLS

Beehive Inn
67 Albion Road
☎ (01663) 742087
12-2.30 (not Mon; 12-3 Sat), 7.30 (5.30 Thu & Fri)-11; 12-3, 7-10.30 Sun
Boddingtons Bitter; Whim Hartington Bitter; guest beers Ⓗ
A recent first-class renovation of this once-ordinary local has produced a superb place in which to drink: comfortable and friendly, with a beer range that makes a positive addition to choice in the area. Note the interesting photos of old New Mills. An excellent restaurant is open Wed-Sun.
❀ ◖ ▮ ⇌ (Central/Newtown)

Pack Horse
Mellor Road (1 mile from centre)
☎ (01663) 742365
12-11; 12-10.30 Sun
Tetley Bitter; guest beer Ⓗ

This single-roomed country pub now offers a guest beer. Good quality meals are served until 10.30. A good outdoor drinking area affords good views across the valley towards Ollerset Moor.
🏚 ❀ ⇌ ◖ ▮ P

Try also: Masons Arms, Market St (Robinson's); **Peaks,** Market St (Whitbread)

NEWTON SOLNEY

Unicorn Inn
Repton Road (B5008)
☎ (01283) 703324
11.30-3, 5-11; 11.30-11 Sat; 12-3, 7-10.30 Sun
Draught Bass; Marston's Pedigree; guest beer Ⓗ
Busy, friendly village-centre free house, with a restaurant offering good home-cooked food (children welcome if dining; no food Sun eve. Accommodation is available in two cottages.
❀ ⇌ ◖ ▮ ♣ P

OCKBROOK

Royal Oak
Green Lane (off A52 follow Ilkeston signs)
☎ (01332) 662378
11.30-2.30, 6.30-11; 12-2.30, 7-10.30 Sun
Draught Bass; Worthington Bitter; guest beers Ⓗ
Traditional, multi-roomed pub kept by the same landlady for 47 years, a strong supporter of local micro-breweries. A regular Guide entry it is home to local societies and hosts events such as the Miniature Steam Fair (Dec 26) and Allotment Show. Hikers welcome; children's play area. Local CAMRA Pub of the Year 2000. Q ❀ ☼ ⅋ ♣ P ⚲

OLD GLOSSOP

Bulls Head
102 Church Street
☎ (01457) 853291
2 (12 Sat)-11; 12-10.30 Sun
Robinson's Old Stockport, Best Bitter Ⓗ
Listed, 16th-century roadside pub at the foot of the Pennines, renowned for its Indian/Balti cuisine. It boasts a traditional northern tap room. Sun meals served 2-10.30.
⅋ ❀ ▮ ⇌ ♣

OLD TUPTON

Royal Oak
Derby Road (A61, 3 miles S of Chesterfield)
☎ (01246) 862180
12-11; 12-10.30 Sun
Home Bitter; John Smith's Bitter;

guest beer Ⓗ
Popular pub, refurbished in
1999 but retains three
distinct drinking areas. The
beers are kept by a *Master
Cellarman*. Boules and skittles
played outside. Look out for
the Jan beer festival.
🏚 ✿ 🌢 🛦 ♣ P ☗

OVER HADDON
Lathkil Hotel
$1/2$ mile S of B5055 at Burton
Moor OS206665
☎ (01629) 812501
11.30-3 (4 Sat), 7-11 (11.30-11
summer Sat); 12-4, 7-10.30 (12-10.30
summer) Sun
**Wells Bombardier; Whim Hartington
Bitter; guest beers** Ⓗ
Free house in an idyllic
setting benefiting from views
over Lathkil Dale nature
reserve. A fine oak-panelled
bar and home-cooked food
add to its appeal; walkers
welcome. The family room is
open at lunchtime.
🏚 Q ⅋ ✿ 🌢 🛦 🛦 ♣ P ☗

PARWICH
Sycamore Inn
☎ (01335) 390212
12-2 (3 Sat), 7-11; 12-3, 7-10.30 Sun
**Robinson's Hartleys XB, Best Bitter,
Frederics, Old Tom** Ⓗ
Traditional country pub in
an unspoilt village; three
rooms with open fires giving
the pub a warm, cosy feel.
Good food is available except
Tue and Sun eves.
🏚 Q ✿ 🌢 🛦 ♣ P

RIPLEY
Rose & Crown
23 Nottingham Road
☎ (01773) 742564
12-4 (not Mon-Fri), 7-11; 12-3, 7-10.30
Sun
Bateman XB, XXXB; guest beers Ⓗ
Two-roomed local with a
friendly atmosphere; TV in
the bar and a skittle alley
outside. ✿ 🔳 ♣

Try also: **Woodman**, Maple
Ave (Hardy & Hansons)

ROWARTH
Little Mill Inn
Off Siloh Road (signed off the
back New Mills-Marple
Bridge road)
☎ (01663) 743178
11-11; 12-10.30 Sun
**Banks's Bitter; Camerons
Strongarm; Marston's Pedigree;
guest beer** Ⓗ
Spacious, characterful pub,
originally a candlewick mill
with a working waterwheel
and adventure playground
for children. Food is served
all day.
🏚 Q ⅋ ✿ 🖼 🌢 🛦 P ☗

SANDIACRE
Blue Bell
36 Church Street
☎ (0115) 939 2193
12-3 (not Mon-Fri), 6 (7 Mon & Sat)-11;
12-4, 7-10.30 Sun
**Greene King IPA; Ind Coope Burton
Ale; Mallard Waddler's Mild;
Wadworth 6X; guest beers** Ⓗ
Friendly local in a converted
300-year-old farmhouse. It
stages an annual beer festival
(Aug/Sept).
🏚 ✿ ♣ P

SCARCLIFFE
Horse & Groom
Rotherham Road
☎ (01246) 823152
12-4, 6-11; 12-3, 7-10.30 Sun
**Draught Bass; Greene King Abbot;
Mansfield Bitter; Stones Bitter;
Theakston Best Bitter; guest
beer** Ⓗ
Traditional stone inn
standing at the crossroads at
the top of the village;
friendly atmosphere.
Q 🔳 ♣ P

SOMERCOTES
Horse & Jockey
47 Leabrooks Road
☎ (01773) 602179
12-3 (not Tue-Thu), 7-11; 12-3, 7-10.30
Sun
**Home Bitter; Theakston Mild, Best
Bitter, XB; guest beers** Ⓗ
This popular, multi-roomed
local is family-run, and is a
regular *Guide* entry. Cask Ale
Classic member. Sky TV is
provided in the lounge.
🌢 ✿ 🔳 🛦 ♣

SOUTH NORMANTON
Boundary
Lea Vale, Broadmeadows
☎ (01773) 819066
12-11 (12-3, 5-11 winter Mon-Thu); 12-
10.30 Sun
**Draught Bass; Bateman seasonal
beers; Fuller's London Pride;
Morland Old Speckled Hen; guest
beers** Ⓗ
Popular, multi-roomed estate
pub where a guest beer club,
a quiz night (Thu) and live
music (Fri and Sat) are
features. Local CAMRA *Pub of
the Season*. Families are
welcome. An extensive menu
is available (eve meals end at
8pm).
🌢 ✿ 🖼 🌢 🛦 ♣ P ⅋

Clock
107 Market Street
☎ (01773) 811396
11-11; 12-10.30 Sun
**Camerons Strongarm; Castle Rock
Hemlock; Marston's Bitter,
Pedigree; Morrells Varsity; guest
beers** Ⓗ
This family-run, genuine free
house has been extensively

refurbished. Good value
home-cooked food served all
day includes daily specials. A
regular music venue: jazz
Mon, folk Tue and blues on
Fri. Driver friendly as soft
drinks are reasonably priced.
Q ✿ 🌢 🔳 🛦 P ⅋

SOUTH WINGFIELD
Old Yew Tree
51 Manor Road (through
village towards Crich)
☎ (01773) 833763
5-11; 12-3, 6.30-11 Sat; 12-10.30 Sun
**Cottage seasonal beers; Greene King
Abbot; Marston's Pedigree; guest
beers** Ⓗ
Busy, family-run free house
near Wingfield Manor,
winner of Amber Valley
Clean Air award. Meals are
available until 9pm (not
served Sun eve). Guest beers
change regularly and include
local beers. This *Guide*
entry hosts an Aug Bank
holiday beer festival. Limited
parking. 🏚 Q ✿ 🌢 🛦 🛦 ♣ P

STANTON IN THE PEAK
Flying Childers Inn
Main Road
☎ (01629) 636333
12-2 (3 Sat; not Mon-Thu); 12-3,
7-10.30 Sun
**Draught Bass; Jennings Cumberland
Ale; guest beer** Ⓗ
Typical village pub; it is
frequented by the locals all
year and enjoys walkers'
patronage in summer.
🏚 Q 🔳 ♣ P

STAVELEY
Speedwell Inn
Lowgates
☎ (01246) 472252
6 (12 Sat)-11; 12-10.30 Sun
**Townes Sunshine, Muffin Ale, Best
Lockoford Bitter, GMT, Staveleyan;
guest beer** Ⓗ
Comfortable corner house in
an ex-mining village, divided
into several distinct drinking
areas. This pub is home to
Townes' Brewery and is the
local CAMRA *Pub of the Year*
2000. ᗡ ⅋ ☗

SUTTON CUM DUCKMANTON
Arkwright Arms
Chesterfield Road (A632)
☎ (01246) 232053
11-11; 12-10.30 Sun
Marston's Pedigree; guest beer Ⓗ
Friendly, traditional, village
free house where the full
range of ales from a different
micro-brewer is offered
during the first week of every
month. A beer festival is held
every Easter. Eve meals served
Fri and Sat.
🏚 ✿ 🌢 🌢 🛦 ♣ P

CAMRA National Pub Inventory: Grapes Hotel, Eccles, Greater Manchester

TROWAY

Gate Inn

Main Road

☎ (01246) 413280

12-3, 7-11; 12-3, 7-10.30 Sun

Burtonwood Bitter, Top Hat; guest beer H

This local, with panoramic views over the Moss Valley, boasts an award-winning garden. Watch out for the marrow competition and other community events.

▥ Q ✿ ⊟ ♣ P ⬚

WARDLOW MIRES

Three Stags' Heads ☆

At A623/B6465 jct

☎ (01298) 872268

7-11 Fri; 11-11 Sat & Bank Hols; 12-10.30 Sun

Abbeydale Matins, Absolution; Broadstone Charter Ale, seasonal beers H

Carefully restored farmhouse pub of two small rooms and a stone-flagged floor. Substantial meals include game in season. It stocks no keg beers or lagers (except Guinness). Live music performed every Sat and some other times.

Note: only open weekends.

▥ Q ✿ ◖ ▷ ⚊ ♣ P

WHITEHOUGH

Old Hall

Hamlet near Chinley

☎ (01663) 750529

12-3 (not Mon), 5-11; 12-11 Fri & Sat; 12-10.30 Sun

Banks's Bitter; Marston's Bitter, Pedigree; guest beers (occasional) H

Once part of a handsome 16th-century manor house in a cosy corner of the village, its lively bars cater for all tastes.

✿ ⇔ ◖ ▷ ⇌ (Chinley) ♣ P

Try also: **Squirrels**, Chinley (Free)

WINSTER

Bowling Green

East Bank

☎ (01629) 650219

6 (12 Sat)-11; 12-10.30 Sun

Tetley Bitter; Whim Hartington Bitter; guest beer H

Derbyshire gritstone village pub, sympathetically refurbished, with a central wooden bar in the main lounge. Just off the main street, it lies in popular walking country. Boules played. Meals served Sat and Sun.

▥ Q ⛵ ✿ ◖ ▷ ⚊ ♣ P ⚡

WOOLLEY MOOR

White Horse Inn

Badger Lane (1½ miles W of A61 at Streeton) OS367614

☎ (01246) 590319

11.30-2.30, 6-11; 12-10.30 Sun

Draught Bass; guest beer H

Derbyshire Dining Pub of the Year 1998, this 17th-century village local serves four guest beers. Extensive gardens, a play area, a boules piste and idyllic rural views add to its appeal.

Q ✿ ◖ ▷ ⊟ ⚊ ⚊ ♣ P ⚡

YOULGREAVE

George Hotel

Church Street

☎ (01629) 636292

11-11; 12-10.30 Sun

John Smith's Bitter; Theakston Mild; guest beer H

Award-winning, 17th-century pub/hotel opposite the church in a popular walking area (hikers and dogs welcome). An excellent home-cooked menu specialises in game dishes.

Q ⇔ ◖ ▷ ⊟ ⚊ ♣ P

INDEPENDENT BREWERIES

Brunswick: Derby
Falstaff: Derby
Leatherbritches: Fenny Bentley
Lichfield: Ingleby
Lloyds: Ingleby
Townes: Chesterfield
Whim: Hartington

DEVON

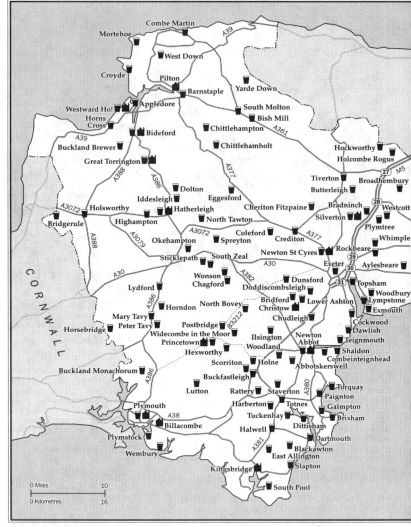

ABBOTSKERSWELL

Court Farm Inn
Wilton Way
☎ (01626) 361866
11-11; 12-10.30 Sun
Draught Bass; G Flowers IPA; Fuller's London Pride; guest beer H
Characterful 17th-century Devon longhouse in the heart of an historic village. An olde-worlde pub, it boasts old beams, brasses, open fireplaces and flagged floors. Extensive grounds include a play area. The varied menu features dishes from around the world.
⚏ ֍ ◑ ◨ ♣ ◠ P

Two Mile Oak
Totnes Road (A381, 2 miles S of Newton Abbot)
☎ (01803) 812411
11-11; 12-10.30 Sun

Draught Bass; Flowers IPA; Fuller's London Pride G
This very old coaching house has a superb public bar and stillage with all real ales on show. Good food range.
⚏ Q ֍ ◑ ◨ ◨ ▲ ♣ P

Try also: Butchers Arms, Slade Lane (Heavitree)

APPLEDORE

Beaver Inn
Irsha Street (take A386 N from Bideford)
☎ (01237) 474822
11-3.30, 6-11 (11-11 Sat); 12-10.30 Sun
Draught Bass; guest beers H
Local pub with a modern interior and riverside views. It once had connections with the Canadian fur trade.
⚏ ֍ ◑ ▲ ♣ ◠

Coach & Horses
5 Market Street (take A386 N from Bideford)
☎ (01237) 474470
12-11; 12-10.30 Sun
Exmoor Gold; guest beers H
Friendly pub set back from the main road, but worth finding for its atmosphere. A fourth guest beer is added in summer.
⚏ ֍ ◑ ▲ ♣

AXMOUTH

Ship Inn
☎ (01297) 21838
11-2.30, 6-11; 12-3, 7-10.30 Sun
Draught Bass; Otter Ale H
Cheerful village local displaying a collection of Guinness memorabilia in the public bar and costume dolls of the world in the lounge. The garden is a home to

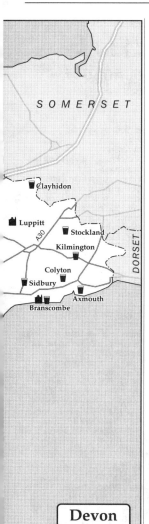

Devon

SOMERSET

Clayhidon

Luppitt

Stockland

Kilmington

Colyton

Sidbury

Axmouth

Branscombe

DORSET

convalescing owls. Skittles played.
🏠Q🍽☀🐕◖⌂♿♠♣P

AYLESBEARE

Halfway Inn
Sidmouth Road
(A3052/B1376 jct)
☎ (01395) 232273
11.30-2.30, 5.30-11; 11-3, 6-11 Sat; (11.30-11 summer Fri & Sat); 12-3, 7-10.30 (12-10.30 summer) Sun
Draught Bass; Otter Bitter; Worthington Bitter; guest beer (occasional) Ⓗ
Cob-built pub, set at a crossroads, well known for its food. It stands close to the airport (but not noisy) and Nigel Mansell's Woodbury Park Golf Club. Food is served all day in summer; well-appointed, reasonably-priced accommodation.
🏠Q🍽☀🐕◖▲P

BARNSTAPLE

Check Inn
14 Castle Street
☎ (01271) 375964
11-11; 12-10.30 Sun
Beer range varies Ⓗ
Friendly, town-centre pub, serving a wide range of beers and Thatcher's cider. It hosts live music on Sat eve and Super League darts.
🐕◖♣⌂

Corner House
108 Boutport Street
☎ (01271) 343528
11-3, 7-11; 11-11 Fri & Sat; 12-3, 7-10.30 Sun
Draught Bass; Ⓖ **guest beers** Ⓗ
Traditional, unspoilt town-centre pub where the wood-panelled, L-shaped bar stocks a good range of beers.
Q🔁♣

BIDEFORD

Joiner's Arms
Market Place
☎ (01237) 472675
12-2.30, 7-11; 12-11 Sat; 12-10.30 Sun
Draught Bass; Ⓖ **Courage Directors; Jollyboat Mainbrace; guest beer** Ⓗ
Country-style pub at the heart of the old town, hosting regular live music and a folk club. Wood-working tools and hops decorate the walls.
🐕◖

King's Arms
7 The Quay
☎ (01237) 475196
11-11; 12-10.30 Sun
Shepherd Neame Spitfire; Tetley Bitter; Wadworth 6X; guest beers Ⓗ
Popular pub, the only one remaining on the town's quay, it dates back to 1665. The dog won't leave you alone until you've thrown a beer mat for it to fetch. Chairs outside face the river in summer; the house beer is brewed by Clearwater.
🐕◖♣

BISH MILL

Mill Inn
Follow brown signs on A361, 500 yds along B3227 OS744266
☎ (01769) 550944
12 (11 summer)-3, 6.30 (6 Thu)-11 (closed winter Wed); 12-3,7-10.30 Sun
Cotleigh Tawny; guest beers Ⓖ
17th-century inn with a warm, friendly atmosphere; North Devon CAMRA *Pub of the Year* 2000 and Homefire award finalist 1999. It has a restaurant and games room. A beer festival is held early June.
🏠🐕☀🐕◖♣P

BLACKAWTON

George Inn
Main Street (1 mile off A3122)
☎ (01803) 712342
12-2.30 (not Mon or Tue summer); not Mon-Thu winter), 7-11; 12-3, 7-10.30 Sun
Princetown IPA; guest beers Ⓗ
Very pleasant traditional village local, offering a range of guest ales; regular mini-beer festivals and excellent home-made food. South Devon CAMRA *Pub of the Year 1999*.
🏠Q🐕☀🐕◖♣⌂P

BRADNINCH

Castle Inn
1 Fore Street
☎ (01392) 881378
12-3, 6-11; 11-11 Sat; 12-10.30 Sun
Cotleigh Tawny; Exe Valley Dob's Best Bitter; guest beers (occasional) Ⓗ
This late Georgian coaching inn stands in a picturesque Duchy of Cornwall town. A friendly atmosphere and good home-cooked food add to its appeal.
🏠☀◖▲♣P🍺

BRANSCOMBE

Fountain Head
Street
☎ (01297) 680359
11.30.3-2.30 (3 summer), 6.30 (6 summer)-11; 12-3, 6-11 Sun
Branscombe Vale Branoc, seasonal beers; guest beers Ⓗ
14th-century inn where the lounge was formerly a blacksmith's forge; note the original wood panelling on the walls and flagstone floors. The excellent food is good value. The landlady's husband and partner brew all the beers; annual beer fest held. Green Valley cider sold.
🏠Q🐕☀◖♿▲♣⌂P

BRIDFORD

Bridford Inn
☎ (01647) 252436
12-2.30, 6 (7 Sat)-11; 12-3, 7-10.30 Sun
Draught Bass; Scatter Rock Teign Valley Tipple; guest beer Ⓗ
This family-run village hostelry has a single, large, beamed bar with an area where children are allowed. The large fireplace features a wood-burning stove and an old bread oven. Excellent menu served; the Teign Valley Tipple is known as Shy Ted.
🏠🐕☀◖♣P

BRIDGERULE

Bridge Inn
Off A3072 by Holsworthy
golf course
☎ (01288) 381316
11-3 (not winter), 6.30-11; 12-3,
7-10.30 Sun
Flowers Original; guest beer H
The only Devon pub west of
the Tamar. A quiet village
inn full of character, with an
aviary at the rear. Small car
park.
🏰 Q 🏵 🌙 ♣ P

BRIXHAM

Blue Anchor
83 Fore Street
☎ (01803) 859373
11-11; 12-3, 7-10.30 Sun
**Dartmoor Best Bitter; Greene King
Abbot; guest beers** H
This 16th-century, ex-sail
loft, ex-chapel now
forms a small but popular
pub for tourists and locals
alike. It offers reasonably
priced food and live music
some eves.
🏰 Q 🌙

BROADHEMBURY

Drewe Arms
☎ (01404) 841267
11-3, 6-11; 12-3 (closed eve) Sun
Otter Bitter, Ale, Head G
Large, unspoilt inn in a
village of thatched, whitewashed cottages. It enjoys
a reputation for an
interesting menu, specialising
in fish.
🏰 Q 🏵 🌙 🛏 ♣ ⌂ P

BUCKFASTLEIGH

White Hart
2 Plymouth Road
☎ (01364) 642337
12 (6 Mon)-11; 12-3.30, 7-10.30 Sun
**Greene King Abbot; Teignworthy
Beachcomber; guest beers** H
Pleasant pub with a single,
open-plan bar, dining area
and restaurant. The large
sunny courtyard hosts
barbecues in summer. The
house beer is brewed by
Teignworthy, with Sam's dry
cider adding extra choice for
the drinker. Dogs allowed.
🏰 ⛺ 🏵 🛏 🌙 ♣ ⌂ ✂

BUCKLAND BREWER

Coach & Horses
Off A386 at Landcross, then
left past Hooper Water
☎ (01237) 451395
11-3, 6-11; 12-3, 7-10.30 Sun
**Flowers Original; Fuller's London
Pride; Wadworth 6X** H
Thatched inn, featuring low,
timbered ceilings, and log
fires in both bars plus a
games room at the rear.
🏰 Q 🏵 🛏 🌙 ♣ P

BUCKLAND MONACHORUM

Drake Manor Inn
☎ (01822) 853892
11.30-2.30 (3 Sat), 6.30-11; 12-3,
7-10.30 Sun
**John Smith's Bitter; Ushers Best
Bitter, Founders, seasonal beers** H
16th-century local in a
picturesque village: two bars;
the lounge is mainly used for
dining. It serves over 70
whiskies.
🏰 Q 🏵 🌙 🛏 P

BUTTERLEIGH

Butterleigh Inn
☎ (01884) 855407
12-2.30, 6 (5 Fri)-11; 12-3, 7-10.30
Sun
**Cotleigh Tawny, Barn Owl, Old
Buzzard or guest beer** H
This is what a country pub
should be: friendly and
comfortable with rustic
furniture. Different rooms
include a snug main bar with
stone-flagged floor and an
adjoining eating area.
Various guest beers replace
Old Buzzard in summer.
🏰 Q 🏵 🌙 ♿ ♣ P

CHAGFORD

Bullers Arms
7 Mill Street
☎ (01647) 432348
11-3, 6-11; 11-11 Sat & summer;
12-10.30 Sun
**St Austell Tinners; Sharp's Doom
Bar; guest beers** H
Friendly local inn, dating
back to the 17th century,
situated in a small market
town. Try the speciality
curries.
🏰 🏵 🛏 🌙 ♣

CHERITON FITZPAINE

Ring of Bells
Behind church
☎ (01363) 866374
7-11; 12-3, 7-10.30 Sun
Beer range varies H
14th-century thatched inn
where a central bar serves
several drinking areas (three
ales available). Home-cooked
food features on the menu. It
hosts an annual Anglo-Irish
folk festival (late autumn).
Boules played in the raised
garden.
🏰 🏵 🛏 🌙 ♣ P

CHITTLEHAMHOLT

Exeter Inn
Take B3226 to Crediton from
South Molton, 4 miles)
☎ (01769) 540281
11.30-2.30, 7-11 (11-11 summer);
12-3, 7-10.30 Sun
**Dartmoor Best Bitter; Greene King
Abbot** H
16th-century coaching inn

where you will find good ale,
good food and a good
atmosphere.
⛺ 🏵 🛏 🌙 ♣ A ♣ P

CHITTLEHAMPTON

Bell Inn
The Square (off B3227
between South Molton and
Umberleigh)
☎ (01769) 540368
11-3, 7-10.30; 11-10.30 Sat; 12-3,
7-10.30 Sun
Draught Bass; Fuller's London Pride;
H **guest beers** G
Village pub where a good
local atmosphere and a
friendly welcome are assured.
Ask what beers are available
as many are kept on gravity
away from the bar. Good
food; families welcome.
Thatcher's cider stocked in
summer. 🏵 🌙 ♣ ♣ ⌂

CHUDLEIGH

Bishop Lacy
Fore Street (signed from A38)
☎ (01626) 854585
11-11; 12-10.30 Sun
Branscombe Vale Bitter; H **Fuller's
London Pride; Princetown Jail Ale;
guest beers** G
Grade II listed former church
house, now a bustling village
local, offering at least three
guest ales and seasonal beer
festivals. Good food is served
in a no-smoking restaurant.
The house beer is brewed by
Branscombe Vale. South
Devon CAMRA *Pub of the
Year* 2000. 🏰 Q 🏵 🌙 🛏 ♣ P

CLAYHIDON

Half Moon Inn
☎ (01823) 680291
12-2.30 (3 Sat), 7-11 (closed Mon);
12-3 (closed eve) Sun
**Cotleigh Tawny; Juwards Bitter;
guest beers** H
Village local in the Culm
Valley, near the Somerset
border. Food and skittles are
popular here.
🏰 Q 🏵 🌙 ♣ ⌂ P

COCKWOOD

Anchor
Off A379
☎ (01626) 890203
11-11; 12-10.30 Sun
**Eldridge Pope Royal Oak; Flowers
Original; Fuller's London Pride;
Marston's Pedigree; Morland Old
Speckled Hen; Wadworth 6X** H
16th-century inn, originally a
seaman's mission, on a
beautiful inlet overlooking
the railway and harbour.
Beamed throughout, and
haunted by a friendly ghost
and dog, it was once a haven
for smugglers. Voted *Best
Food Pub* 2000 in the UK.
🏰 🏵 🌙 ♿ A ♣ ⌂ P

COLEFORD

New Inn
☎ (01363) 84242
12-3, 6-11; 12-3, 7-10.30 Sun
Badger Dorset Best; Wadworth 6X; guest beer H
Large, well-appointed, one-bar pub in a 13th-century thatched building boasting a friendly atmosphere, talkative parrot and pleasant garden by a stream. The dining area offers excellent food at restaurant prices.
🏨 Q ❀ ⇌ ◖ ♣ P

COLYTON

Gerrard Arms
Rosemary Lane
☎ (01297) 552588
11-2.30, 6-11; 12-3, 7-10.30 Sun
Draught Bass; Branscombe Vale Branoc; Otter Bitter; Ushers Best Bitter; guest beers H
Straightforward, small town pub affording comfortable surroundings and a warm welcome.
Q ➤ ❀ ◖ ♿ ▲ ⊖ ♣ ⊟

COMBEINTEIGNHEAD

Wild Goose
Between Newton Abbot and Shaldon on road S of Teign estuary
☎ (01626) 872241
11.30-3, 6.30-11; 12-3, 7-10.30 Sun
Otter Ale; guest beers H
17th-century free house in a small, quiet village. Five ever-changing ales are sourced from independent brewers. Excellent home-cooked food and trad jazz every Mon are added attractions.
🏨 Q ❀ ◖ ▲ ♣ P

COMBE MARTIN

Castle Inn
High Street
☎ (01271) 883706
12-11; 12-10.30 Sun
Draught Bass; Worthington Bitter; guest beers H
Basic working pub displaying an excellent collection of previous guest pumpclips; a beer drinkers' paradise. Cider is stocked in summer. No food Tue lunch.
❀ ⇌ ◖ ▲ ♣ ⊖ P

London Inn
Lynton Road
☎ (01271) 883409
11-4.30, 6-11; 11-11 Sat; 12-10.30 Sun
Barum Breakfast; Greene King Abbot; Marston's Pedigree; Wadworth 6X; guest beers H
Old coaching inn, bordering the Exmoor National Park, with its own large riverside garden.
🏨 Q ➤ ❀ ⇌ ◖ ♿ ▲ ♣ P

CREDITON

Crediton Inn
28a Mill Street (main Tiverton road)
☎ (01363) 772882
11-11; 12-2, 7-10.30
Draught Bass; Sharp's Doom Bar; guest beers H
Friendly, welcoming, free house just off the town centre, serving four ales in convivial surroundings. A modest menu of cooked meals and a skittle alley are additional features.
◖ ➤ ♣ P

CROYDE

Thatched Barn Inn
14 Hobbs Hill
☎ (01271) 890349
11-11; 12-10.30 Sun
Barum Original; Draught Bass; St Austell HSD; guest beers H
Spectacularly popular pub with locals and visitors alike. Despite being renowned for great food it has avoided turning into a restaurant; the bar staff are brilliantly efficient, no matter how busy.
➤ ❀ ⇌ ◖ ▲ ♣ P

DARTMOUTH

Cherub Inn
13 Higher Street
☎ (01803) 832571
11-2.30, 5.30-11 (11-11 summer); 12-10.30 Sun
Morland Old Speckled Hen; Wadworth 6X; guest beer H
This listed 700-year-old pub is Dartmouth's oldest building, originally a wool merchant's house. It only became an inn and restaurant in 1972. The name derives from a boat built for carrying wool. The house beer is brewed by Summerskills.
Q ◖ ◖ ⊖

DAWLISH

Swan
94 Old Town Street
☎ (01626) 863677
11-2.30, 5-11; 11-11 Sat; 12-4, 7-10.30 Sun
Scattor Rock Teign Valley Tipple; Teignworthy Spring Tide; guest beers H
Pub dating from circa 1642, in the old part of the town. The lounge has a wood-burning stove with an adjacent dining/family room. The bar is basic but vibrant. A house rule is that shirts should be worn.
🏨 ➤ ❀ ⇌ ◖ ◖ ⊞ ♿ ♣ P ⊬ ⊟

DITTISHAM

Red Lion Inn

The Level
☎ (01803) 722235
11-2.30, 6-11; 12-3, 7-10.30 Sun
Butcombe Bitter; guest beers H
Welcoming 18th-century local in a picturesque riverside village. Good food is served in both the restaurant and bar with its open fires. Local Pig Squeal cider is sold in summer.
🏨 ➤ ❀ ⇌ ◖ ▲ ♣ ⊖ P ⊬

DODDISCOMBESLEIGH

Nobody Inn
☎ (01647) 252394
12-2.30, 6-11; 12-3, 7-10.30 Sun
Draught Bass; Scatter Rock Teign Valley Tipple; guest beer G
Attractive village pub, famous for its food, wines and whiskies (over 260 stocked). Local cheeses are a speciality. The house beer is Branscombe Vale's own label.
🏨 Q ❀ ⇌ ◖ P

DOLTON

Royal Oak
The Square (take B3217 off B3220 between Torrington and A377)
☎ (01805) 804288
11.30-3, 6-11; 12-3, 7-10.30 Sun
Beer range varies H
Village pub where a central bar serves the main room and games area. Local beers are always available (two in winter, three summer). Good food specialises in local fish.
🏨 ➤ ❀ ⇌ ◖ ▲ ♣ ⊖ P

DUNSFORD

Royal Oak Inn
☎ (01647) 252256
12-2, 6.30 (7 Mon; 6 Fri)-11; 12-2.30, 7-10.30 Sun
Greene King IPA, Abbot; guest beers H
Popular local on the edge of Dartmoor: a single bar in a Victorian setting, with games and dining areas, offering a wide range of home-cooked food at sensible prices. There are usually two or three guest beers on tap.
🏨 ❀ ◖ ◖ ♣ ⊖ P

EAST ALLINGTON

Fortescue Arms
Left off A381 from Totnes
☎ (01548) 521215
11-2.30, 6-11 (11-11 summer); 12-3, 7-10.30 (12-10.30 summer) Sun
Palmers Best Bitter; Princetown Dartmoor IPA; guest beer (summer) H
19th-century pub and restaurant named after the local landowner. The bar has a flagstoned floor.
🏨 Q ❀ ⇌ ◖ ◖ ▲ ♣ ⊖ P

EGGESFORD

Eggesford Country Hotel
On A377, near station
☎ (01769) 580345
11-11; 12-10.30 Sun
Beer range varies Ⓗ
Fox and Hounds bar within a family-run hotel, used by locals and guests, the beer selection changes weekly. Live music or disco staged most Fris; annual beer festival Aug. Children's certificate.
🏚 🏶 🛏 ◑ 🝙 🅐 🗪 ♣ P

EXETER

Brook Green Tavern
31 Well Street
☎ (01392) 203410
12-2.30, 5-11;11-3, 6-11 Sat; 12-3, 7-10.30 Sun
Beer range varies Ⓗ
Friendly always offering a good range of beers at reasonable prices. Whitbread beers are kept under cask breathers; guest and local beers are served as nature intended. Near St James Park football ground, it has a small car park.
🗪 (St James Pk) P

Double Locks Hotel
Canal Banks, Marsh Barton (follow lane next to incinerator over canal, turn right) OS932900
☎ (01392) 256947
11-11; 12-10.30 Sun
Adnams Broadside; Everards Original; Greene King Abbot; Ⓖ Smiles Best, Heritage; Young's Special; guest beers Ⓗ
This spacious canalside pub, with outside seating, is worth finding. Food is served all day and up to 12 cask ales are available, mostly served on gravity. Live music is performed some eves.
🏚 🛏 🏶 ◑ 🝙 🅐 ◑ P 🔲

Great Western Hotel
Station Approach
☎ (01392) 274039
11-11; 12-10.30 Sun
Adnams Broadside; Draught Bass; Fuller's London Pride; guest beers Ⓗ
Friendly railway hotel/pub that places a strong emphasis on cask ales. The three regular ales are accompanied by at least four guest beers. Excellent food and atmosphere make this probably the best pub in the city. Local CAMRA *Pub of the Year* 2000.
🛏 ◑ 🝙 🗪 (St Davids) P

Jolly Porter
St David's Hill (opp station)
☎ (01392) 254848
11-11; 12-10.30 Sun
Courage Directors; John Smith's Bitter; Theakston Best Bitter; Wells Bombardier; guest beer Ⓗ
Long, narrow pub with a low-level bar and high-level seating areas. It employs a forceful guest ale policy – the landlord serves beers as the brewer recommends or as he deems suitable. It is popular with students and older people alike.
🛏 ◑ 🝙 🗪 (St Davids) ♣

Royal Oak
Fore Street, Heavitree
☎ (01392) 254121
11-3, 6 (5.30 Fri & Sat)-11; 12-3, 7-10.30 Sun
Draught Bass; Castle Eden Bitter; Flowers IPA Ⓗ
Thatched pub within the city; multi roomed, its unusual decor includes a door from Dartmoor prison. Quiz night Wed; good value food.
🏶 ◑

Welcome Inn
Canal Banks (off Haven Rd, near canal basin)
☎ (01392) 254760
11-2.30, 6.30-11; 12-3, 7-10.30 Sun
Castle Eden Ale or guest beer Ⓗ
Unspoilt pub, with flagstoned floors and gas lighting, on the canal bank. The single beer alternates between Castle Eden and a (usually local) guest.
🏶 ♣

Well House
Cathedral Yard
☎ (01392) 319953
11-11; 12-10.30 (closed Jan-Feb) Sun
Draught Bass; Gibbs Mew Bishops Tipple; guest beers Ⓗ
Well-situated pub whose picture windows overlook the Cathedral Close. An oasis for good beer in the city centre (it always stocks an Otter brew). but loud music and the big-screen TV can intrude.
◑ 🗪 (Central)

Grove
Esplanade
☎ (01395) 272101
11-11; 12-10.30 Sun
Brakspear Special; Flowers Original; Fuller's London Pride; Greene King Abbot; Wadworth 6X; guest beer (occasional) Ⓗ
Large seafront pub near a former dock, known for its food. It hosts live music Fri eve and occasional beer nights in winter. Wheelchair WC. Tiny car park.
🏶 ◑ 🝙 🅐 P

Try also: Bicton Inn, Bicton St (Free)

GALMPTON

Manor Inn
Stoke Gabriel Road (off Paignton-Brixham ring road)
☎ (01803) 842346
11-11; 12-10.30 Sun
Dartmoor Best Bitter; Greene King Abbot; Ind Coope Burton Ale; Marston's Pedigree; guest beer Ⓗ
19th-century village pub, but extensively altered to give cosy bars and a no-smoking restaurant, serving local specialities. Skittles played.
🏚 Q 🛏 🛏 ◑ 🝙 🅐 ♣ P

GREAT TORRINGTON

Black Horse Inn
High Street
☎ (01805) 622121
11-3, 6-11; 11-11 Sat; 12-4, 7-10.30 Sun
Courage Best Bitter, Directors; John Smith's Bitter; guest beer Ⓗ
Tudor inn with strong Civil War links, comprising a lively main bar and a quieter lounge. Guest ales are sourced from independent breweries around the country, whilst the food is all local. 🏚 Q 🛏 ◑ 🅐 ♣

HALWELL

Old Inn
Follow A381 from Totnes to Kingsbridge
☎ (01803) 712329
11-2.30, 6-11; 11-11 Sat; 12-3, 6-10.30 Sun
RCH East Street Cream; guest beers Ⓗ
Friendly, family-run pub with a warm village atmosphere, next to a beautiful Norman church. There has been a pub on this site since 1104. Oriental food is a speciality.
Q 🛏 🏶 🛏 ◑ 🝙 🗪 🕭 P

HARBERTON

Church House Inn
Off main Totnes-Kingsbridge road OS778586
☎ (01803) 863707
12-3, 6-11; 12-4, 7-10.30 Sun
Draught Bass; guest beers Ⓗ
Friendly, 13th-century pub boasting heavy beams and flagstoned floors in the bar, dining area and family room. Excellent food, and local cider are served.
🏚 Q 🛏 🛏 ◑ 🝙 🕭 🍽

HATHERLEIGH

Tally Ho! Country Inn & Brewery
14 Market Street
☎ (01837) 810306
11-3, 6-11; 12-3, 7-10.30 Sun
Tally Ho! Market Ale, Tarka's Tipple, Nutters; guest beer (occasional) Ⓗ
Brew-pub of character: one bar and a small restaurant, serving excellent food. The brewery is at the rear.
🏚 Q 🛏 🛏 ◑ 🝙 ♣ 🕭 P

DEVON

HEXWORTHY

Forest Inn
Off B3357, Two Bridges-
Dartmeet Road OS654728
☎ (01364) 631211
12-3, 6-11 (may extend summer); 11-11
Sat; 12-10.30 Sun
Teignworthy Reel Ale; guest beer Ⓗ
Isolated, attractive inn on
Dartmoor, a haven for
walkers, horse riders and
anglers. Extremely
comfortable, it features
chesterfield sofas in the
lounge area.
🍺 🛏 💷 ◖◗ ♣ P

HIGHAMPTON

Golden Inn
☎ (01409) 231200
12-3, 6.30-11; 12-3, 7-10.30 Sun
**Butcombe Bitter; Dartmoor Best
Bitter; Fuller's London Pride** Ⓗ
16th-century thatched inn
with a low-ceilinged bar. Its
campsite at the rear has a
children's play area.
🍺 Q 🛏 ◖◗ Å ♣ P

HOCKWORTHY

Staple Cross Inn
☎ (01398) 361374
12-3 (not Mon-Thu), 6.30-11; 12-3,
7-10.30 Sun
Cotleigh Tawny; guest beers Ⓗ
Unspoilt, 400-year-old
country pub on the Somerset
border, comprising two bars;
one with a quarry-tiled floor,
the other a carpeted lounge
area, it offers a friendly
welcome and cider in
summer.
🍺 Q 🛏 ◖◗ 🍴 ⚅ & Å ♣ 🍺 P

HOLCOMBE ROGUS

Prince of Wales
☎ (01823) 672070
12-3 (not Mon-Thu, Oct-Mar), 6.30-11;
12-3, 7-10.30 Sun
**Cotleigh Tawny; Otter Bitter; guest
beers** Ⓗ
Pleasant country pub, not far
from the Grand Western
Canal; note the unusual cash
register handpumps. It has a
pleasant lounge area, garden
and skittle alley. Cider sold in
summer.
🍺 Q 🛏 ◖◗ Å ♣ 🍺 P

HOLNE

Church House Inn
OS706696
☎ (01364) 631208
11-3, 7-11; 12-3, 7-10.30 Sun
**Badger Tanglefoot; Butcombe
Bitter, Gold; Summerskills Tamar** Ⓗ
Grade II listed, 14th-century
inn set at the centre of a
village in the Dartmoor
National Park. Two bars and
a dining area serve excellent
local fresh food; also a
restaurant (booking

essential). Children, dogs and
walkers are welcome in a
non-tourist atmosphere.
🍺 Q 🛏 💷 ◖◗ Å ♣ 🍺 🍴

HOLSWORTHY

Kings Arms ☆
Fore Street
☎ (01409) 253517
11-11; 12-3, 7-10.30 (may vary) Sun
Draught Bass; Sharp's Doom Bar Ⓗ
Town-centre pub with three
bars and a snug
separated from the public by
a snob screen. Lots of beer
and pub memorabilia are
displayed.
🍺 Q ⚅ ♣

Try also: White Hart Hotel,
Fore St (Free)

HORNDON

Elephants Nest
1½ miles E of Mary Tavy
OS517800
☎ (01822) 810273
11.30-2.30, 6.30-11; 12-2.30, 7-10.30
Sun
**Boddingtons Bitter; Palmers IPA;
St Austell HSD; guest beers** Ⓗ
Picturesque, 16th-century
moorland pub, with a relaxed
atmosphere, serving a varied
menu. The excellent garden
affords superb moorland
views.
🍺 Q 🛏 🛏 ◖◗ ♣ P

HORNS CROSS

Hoops Inn
On A39 6 miles W of
Bideford
☎ (01237) 451222
11-11; 12-10.30 Sun
Beer range varies Ⓖ
15th-century coaching inn
once used by sailors and
smugglers, close to the
coastal path. Two bars, one
resembles a grotto.
Occasional beer, jazz and
even conker festivals are
staged. It offers an
extensive fish and game
menu.
🍺 Q 🛏 🛏 💷 ◖◗ ⚅ ♣ P 🍴

HORSEBRIDGE

Royal Inn
Between Hilton Abbot
(B3362) and A388
Launceston road
☎ (01822) 870214
12-3, 7-11; 12-3, 7-10.30 Sun
**Draught Bass; Sharp's Doom Bar;
Wadworth 6X; guest beers** Ⓗ
15th-century converted
nunnery by an historic
backwater bridge over the
River Tamar which forms the
county boundary between
Devon and Cornwall. The
pub's basic amenities add to
the atmosphere.
🍺 Q 🛏 ◖◗ ♣ 🍺 P

IDDESLEIGH

Duke of York
On B3217
☎ (01837) 810253
11-11; 12-10.30 Sun
**Adnams Broadside; Cotleigh Tawny;
guest beers** Ⓖ
A welcoming 12th-century
inn with a singe bar and
rocking chairs by the fireside.
Freshly prepared food is
available all day, plus local
guest ciders.
🍺 Q 🛏 ◖◗ ♣ 🍺

ILSINGTON

Carpenters Arms
Near the school
☎ (01364) 661215
11-3, 6-11; 12-3, 7-10.30 Sun
Draught Bass; Ⓗ **Flowers IPA** Ⓖ
The single, L-shaped bar is
warmed by a lovely open fire
in winter. An old village pub,
where a friendly local
atmosphere prevails, it is
used mainly by farmers and
villagers.
🍺 Q 🛏 ◖◗ ♣

KILMINGTON

New Inn
The Hill
☎ (01297) 33376
11-2.30 (3 summer), 6-11; 12-3,
7-10.30 Sun
Palmers BB, Dorset Gold, IPA Ⓗ
Despite its name this is a
pleasantly olde-worlde pub
run by a landlord who runs
marathons. The garden
houses an aviary.
🍺 Q 🛏 ◖◗ ⚅ & Å ♣ P

Try also: Axminster Inn,
Silver St, Axminster (Palmers)

LOWER ASHTON

Manor Inn
☎ (01647) 252304
12-2.30, 6 (7 Sat)-11; closed Mon;
12-2.30, 7-10.30 Sun
Princetown Jail Ale; Ⓖ **RCH
Pitchfork; Teignworthy Reel Ale;
Theakston Best Bitter; guest
beer** Ⓗ
Small, but perfectly formed
village pub offering a friendly
atmosphere, great beer and
excellent food. Local CAMRA
Pub of the Year 1998 and a
previous regional winner.
🍺 Q 🛏 ◖◗ ⚅ Å ♣ 🍺 P

LUTTON

Mountain Inn
Old Church Lane (off
Cornwood to Sparkswell
Road) OS596594
☎ (01752) 837247
11-3, 7 (6 Fri & Sat)-11; 12-3, 7-10.30
Sun
Sutton XSB; guest beers Ⓗ
Traditional village pub, with
a large fireplace, popular with

locals and visitors. The house beer is brewed by Summerskills; cider sold in summer. Plymouth CAMRA *Pub of the Year* 1997.
♨ Q ❀ ♣ ◡ P

LYDFORD

Mucky Duck Inn
Next to White Lady Falls entrance to Lydford Gorge (NT)
☎ (01822) 820208
11-3, 6-11 (winter varies); 12-3, 7-10.30 Sun
Sharp's Cornish Coaster, Own; guest beers Ⓗ
Spacious, with a large family room, pool area and skittle alley. The bar features beams, slates and a display of ducks. Accommodation is in self-catering holiday flats.
♨ Q ♞ ❀ 🛏 ◖ ◗ ♣ P

LYMPSTONE

Redwing
Church Road
☎ (01395) 222156
11.30-3.30, 6-11; 11.30-11 Sat; 12-10.30 Sun
Draught Bass; Greene King Abbot; Ushers Best Bitter; guest beer (occasional) Ⓗ
Lively free house at the lower end of the village, well known for its excellent menu and occasional specialist food evenings. No meals Sun eve. It hosts live music Tue and Fri eves and a quiz Mon eve. It is the HQ of E Devon Hockey Club fielding four teams. Q ❀ ◖ ◗ ⊟ ≠ ♣ ◡ P

MARY TAVY

Mary Tavy Inn
Lane Head (A386, 4 miles N of Tavistock)
☎ (01822) 810326
11.45-3, 6-11; 12-3, 7-10.30 Sun
Draught Bass; St Austell HSD; guest beer Ⓗ
Cosy, friendly, two-bar pub on the edge of Dartmoor. Good value food and Sam's cider available.
♨ Q ♞ ❀ 🛏 ◖ ◗ ▲ ♣ ◡

MORTEHOE

Chichester Arms
☎ (01271) 870411
12-3, 6.30-11 (11-11 summer); 12.30-3, 7-10.30 Sun
Badger Tanglefoot; Barum Original; Shepherd Neame Bishops Finger; Ushers Best Bitter; guest beers Ⓗ
Welcoming village local, popular with visitors, too. Around 400 years old, it is still lit by gas lamps. Skittles played. Q ♞ ❀ ◗ ◖ ▲ ♣ P

NEWTON ABBOT

Golden Lion
4 Market Street
☎ (01626) 367062
11-2.30, 5-11; 11-4, 6-11 Sat; 12-3, 7-10.30 Sun
Teignworthy Reel Ale; guest beers Ⓗ
17th-century pub, named the Golden Lion since 1722; a former coaching house where the garden used to be the stables. This friendly pub boasts the best atmosphere in town; it has a games room. Usually a Scattor Rock beer replaces one of the guests.
❀ ◖ ≠ ♣

Locomotive Inn
35-37 East Street (100 yds from hospital, towards Totnes)
☎ (01626) 365249
11.30-3, 5.30-11; 11.30-11 Fri & Sat; 12-10.30 Sun
Draught Bass; guest beer Ⓗ
Cosy, friendly 17th-century pub with a games room to the rear. Friendly, displaying railway memorabilia on walls, it is popular with all ages. Note the old example of a sherry bar. No food Sun.
♨ ◖ ≠ ♣ ◡

NEWTON ST CYRES

Beer Engine
Near station, 1 mile from A377
☎ (01392) 851282
11-11; 12-10.30 Sun
Beer Engine Rail Ale; Piston Bitter; Sleeper Heavy; seasonal beers Ⓗ
1850 railway inn where the pretty garden has barbecue facilities. Excellent food is served in this friendly, popular pub. The brewery may be viewed downstairs when the downstairs bar and function room are open.
♨ Q ❀ ◖ ◗ ▲ ≠ ♣ P 🚭 ▯

NORTH BOVEY

Ring o' Bells
☎ (01647) 440375
11-3, 6-11 (11-11 summer); 12-10.30 Sun
Draught Bass; Butcombe Bitter; guest beers Ⓗ
13th-century thatched inn of two characterful bars, ideally situated for walking, hiking and cycling. It offers a good selection of food.
♨ Q ♞ ❀ 🛏 ◖ ◗ ⊟ ▲ ◡ 🚭

NORTH TAWTON

Railway Inn
Whiddon Down Road (1 mile S of village)
☎ (01837) 82789
12-2, 6-11; 12-3, 7-10.30 Sun
Teignworthy Reel Ale; guest beers Ⓗ
Still part of a working farm, and popular with locals, it stands next to the old North Tawton station. The bar decor recalls the station in past years.
♨ ❀ 🛏 ◖ ◗ ▲ ♣ P

OKEHAMPTON

Plymouth Inn
26 West Street
☎ (01837) 53633
12-3, 7-11; 12-11 Sat; 12-10.30 Sun
Beer range varies Ⓖ
Old coaching inn that brings the welcome and atmosphere of a country pub to the centre of an old market town. The landlord holds two beer festivals a year (May and Nov), with an accent on south-western beers.
♞ ❀ ◖ ◗ ♣

PAIGNTON

Devonport Arms
42 Elmbank Road (behind the zoo)
☎ (01803) 558322
11-11; 12-10.30 Sun
Courage Best Bitter; John Smith's Bitter; guest beers Ⓗ
Friendly, multi-bar 1930s-style pub, off the beaten track but worth finding. Music, general knowledge quiz nights and a skittle alley in a barn all add to its appeal. Good reasonably priced food is served, too.
♨ Q ♞ ❀ ◖ ◗ ♿ ≠ P

Isaac Merritt
54-58 Torquay Road
☎ (01803) 556066
11-11; 12-10.30 Sun
Courage Directors; Exmoor Gold; Morland Old Speckled Hen; Theakston Best Bitter; guest beers Ⓗ
Busy town alehouse on the main road, a comfortable, friendly atmosphere is enhanced by cosy seated alcoves. Excellent Wetherspoon's outlet displays a caring attitude towards the elderly and disabled.
◖ ◗ ♿ ≠ ◡ 🚭 ▣

PETER TAVY

Peter Tavy Inn
☎ (01822) 810348
12-2.30, 6-10 (12-3, 6-11 summer); 12-3, 6-10.30 Sun
Draught Bass; Princetown Jail Ale; guest beer Ⓗ
15th-century pub in a small village on Dartmoor. The original bar area still exists but is dominated by a new extension; slate and beams feature throughout.
♨ Q ♞ ❀ ◖ ◗ ▲ P 🚭

PLYMOUTH

Butchers Arms
160 Cremyll Street, Stonehouse

☎ (01752) 660510
11-11; 12-6 (10.30 summer) Sun
Courage Best Bitter; Sutton XSB [H]
Small, friendly local, opposite a Grade I listed King William Victualling Yard. Enjoy wonderful views of the River Tamar. Cider in summer.
Q ❀ ◑ ♣ ⌓ ▯

Clifton
35 Clifton Street, Greenbank
☎ (01752) 266563
5 (11 Fri & Sat)-11; 12-10.30 Sun
Draught Bass; Summerskills Indiana's Bones; Worthington Bitter; guest beers [H]
A house beer, Clifton Classic, is brewed by Summerskills for the luckiest pub in Britain, as three Lottery millionaires drink here. This warm, friendly pub fields numerous teams.
♿ ⇌ ♣ ⌓

Compton Inn
77 Priory Road, Lower Compton
☎ (01752) 266962
12-2.30, 6-11; 12-11 Sat; 12-10.30 Sun
Draught Bass; Courage Best Bitter, Directors [H]
Styled as a village inn this pub stands in a residential area. The large single bar is comfortable and enjoys a good atmosphere.
Q ❀ ◑ ♣

Dolphin
In the Barbican (opp. Dartington Glass)
☎ (01752) 660876
10-11; 12-10.30 Sun
Draught Bass [G]
The last and only unspoilt pub on Plymouth's historic Barbican opposite the old railway station. The landlord has been painted by many famous artists. Within walking distance of the National Aquarium and Plymouth Gin.
🜂 Q

Fortescue
37 Mutley Plain
☎ (01752) 660673
11-11; 12-10.30 Sun
Badger Tanglefoot; Marston's Pedigree; guest beers [H]
Carlsberg-Tetley Festival Alehouse with a friendly atmosphere, used by both locals and students. The atmospheric cellar bar is open at times.
◑ ⇌ ⊞

Hogshead
9-11 Mutley Plain
☎ (01752) 256936
11-11; 12-10.30 Sun
Boddingtons Bitter; Marston's Pedigree; Wadworth 6X; [H] **guest beers** [H]/[G]
Traditional-style, large single bar Hogshead, popular with students. A rotating range of guest beers include one on gravity dispense.
◑ ◐ ♿ ⇌ ⊘

London Inn
Church Road, Plympton St Maurice
☎ (01752) 337025
11-11; 12-10.30 Sun
Courage Best Bitter; Morland Old Speckled Hen; Ruddles County; guest beer [H]
Friendly, two-bar pub situated in an area of historic interest. Note the collection of naval memorabilia in the lounge.
🜂 Q ❀ ◑ ◐ ⊞ ♣ P

Lounge
Stopford Place, Stoke Plymouth
☎ (01752) 561330
11.30-2.30, 6-11; 12-2.30, 7.30-10.30 Sun
Draught Bass; guest beer [G]
Side-street local, decorated in red. This single room, split-level pub is popular at lunchtime for food and has a good atmosphere.
❀ ◑ ♣

Miners Arms
Hewerdon, Plympton
☎ (01752) 343252
11-2.30, 5.30-11; 12-3, 7-10.30 Sun
Draught Bass; [H]/[G] **Sutton XSB;** [H]/[P] **Ushers Best Bitter; guest beer** [H]
Unspoilt, friendly village pub on the outskirts of Plymouth where three different drinking areas include one with a genuine well. The garden has swings for children.
🜂 Q ❀ ◑ ◐ ♿ P

Prince Maurice
3 Church Hill, Eggbuckland
☎ (01752) 771515
11-3, 7 (6 Fri)-11; 11-11 Sat; 12-3, 7-10.30 Sun
Badger Tanglefoot; Draught Bass; Courage Best Bitter; Summerskill's Best Bitter, Indiana's Bones; guest beers [H]
This cosy, two-roomed pub, once served a village now swallowed by Plymouth's residential expansion. The house beer Royale is brewed by Summerskills.
❀ ⊞ ♣ P

Pym Arms
16 Pym Street, Devonport (behind council flats in Albert Rd)
☎ (01752) 561823
12-2.30, 6-11; 12-11 Thu-Sat; 12-10.30 Sun
Princetown Jail Ale; [G] **guest beers** [H]
Glorious, basic, back-street pub; a real oasis in Devonport's real ale desert. Used by students and locals with a good atmosphere, it is worth finding.
⇌ (Devonport) ♣ ⌓

Shipwright's
18 Sutton Road, Coxside
☎ (01752) 665804
11-3, 6 (5.30 Sat)-11; 12-3, 7-10.30 Sun
Courage Best Bitter, Directors [H]
Small, one-roomed local, cosy and friendly, within walking distance of the National Aquarium and Barbican.
🜂 ❀ ◑ ♿ ♣ P

Thistle Park Tavern
32 Commercial Road, Coxside
☎ (01752) 204890
11-11 (1am Sat); 12-10.30 Sun
Sutton Plymouth Pride, XSB, Comfort, Wild Blonde, Knickadroppa Glory, guest beers [H]
Popular with locals and students, this friendly pub is situated near the fish market and National Aquarium. Basic, but it offers a good range of beers from the adjacent Sutton Brewery.
❀ ◑ ◐ ♣

PLYMSTOCK

Borringdon Arms
Borringdon Terrace, Turnchapel
☎ (01752) 402053
11-11; 12-10.30 Sun
Butcombe Bitter; Oakham JHB; RCH Pitchfork; Summerskills Best Bitter; guest beers [H]
Terraced pub in a waterside village in a conservation area on the south-west coastal footpath. It holds regular beer festivals and was twice Plymouth CAMRA *Pub of the Year*. Cider sold in summer. Water taxi from Barbican available.
🜂 ❀ 🛏 ◑ ◐ ⊞ ♿ ♣ ⌓

New Inn
Borringdon Road, Turnchapel
☎ (01752) 402765
12-3 (not Mon-Thu), 6-11; 12-11 Sat; 12-10.30 Sun
Draught Bass; Princetown Jail Ale; Sharp's Doom Bar; guest beer [H]
This friendly refurbished waterside pub affords excellent views over the water to Plymouth's Barbican area. A water taxi from the Barbican is available.
🜂 Q 🛏 ◑ ◐ ♣

PLYMTREE

Blacksmiths Arms
☎ (01884) 277474
12-2.30 (not Mon), 6-11; 7-10.30 Sun
Cotleigh Tawny; Otter Bitter; Exe Valley Dob's Best Bitter [H]
Popular village pub with a reputation for freshly-cooked

food (eve meals Tue-Sat). Occasional live music, boules and skittles played. Guest beers are sourced locally.

🏚 🛏 🍴 🍺 (🄳 ♿ 🚹 ♣ ✦

POSTBRIDGE
Warren House Inn
On B3212, Postbridge-Morton Hampstead Road
☎ (01822) 880208
11-3, 6-11; 11-11 Fri, Sat & summer; 12-3, 6-10.30, (12-10.30 summer) Sun
Badger Tanglefoot; Butcombe Bitter; Lees Moonraker; Summerskills Tamar; guest beers Ⓗ
The third-highest pub in England; isolated on high Dartmoor; it is a haven for both walkers and visitors. A friendly welcome is assured at this granite building, hewn from the moor itself. A log fire has been burning continuously since 1845.

🏚 Q 🛏 🍴 (🄳 🅰 ♣ ⌂ P

PRINCETOWN
Plume of Feathers
The Square (opp. Visitors Centre)
☎ (01822) 890240
11-11; 12-10.30 Sun
Draught Bass; St Austell HSD Ⓗ
Princetown's oldest building (1785) featuring copper bars and slate floors. It is popular with locals as well as walkers and tourists – Plume Bitter is brewed by Bass.

🏚 🛏 🍴 (🄳 🄶 🅰 ♣ ⌂ P

Prince of Wales
Tavistock Road (opp. primary school)
☎ (01822) 890219
11.30-3, 6.30-11; 12-3, 7-10.30 Sun
Draught Bass; Princetown Dartmoor IPA, Jail Ale Ⓗ
Comfortable village inn, the tap for Princetown Brewery which is situated at the rear of the pub. Children's certificate.

🏚 (🄳 ♿ P

RATTERY
Church House Inn
2 miles off A38, southbound
☎ (01364) 642220
11-2.30, 6-11 (6.30-10.30 winter Mon-Thu); 12-2.30, 7-10.30 Sun
Dartmoor Best Bitter; Greene King Abbot; Marston's Pedigree Ⓗ
This Grade II listed pub was built to house monks in 1028 and now has a low-beamed single bar with two inglenooks. It enjoys an excellent reputation for food, in a pretty setting beside the church.

🏚 🍴 (🄳 P

ROCKBEARE
Jack-in-the-Green

On old A30
☎ (01404) 822240
11-3, 6-11; 12-3, 6.30-10.30 Sun
Draught Bass; Cotleigh Tawny; Otter Ale; guest beer (occasional) Ⓗ
Large popular roadside inn, near Exeter airport, well known for its food. It has a skittle alley at the rear and a new snug. The house beer Jig is from Branscombe Vale. Wheelchair WC.

🏚 Q 🛏 🍴 (🄳 ♿ 🅰 ♣ P

SCORRITON
Tradesman's Arms
On Holne road
☎ (01364) 631206
11-3, 7-11 (11-11 summer); 12-3, 7-10.30 (12-10.30 summer) Sun
Princetown IPA; guest beer Ⓗ
17th-century friendly village pub with a single bar and a family room. If requested beer will be served straight from the cask.

🏚 Q 🛏 🍴 🚌 (🄳 🅰 ♣ P ✗

SHALDON
Clifford Arms
34 Fore Street
☎ (01626) 872311
11-2.30, 5-11; 11-11 Sat; 12-10.30 Sun
Greene King Abbot; guest beers Ⓗ
Enjoy the olde-worlde atmosphere of this 18th-century pub, set in a pretty riverside village. It has been much photographed for its floral displays. Excellent food, atmosphere and company can all be enjoyed here. 🛏 🍴 (🄳

SIDBURY
Red Lion
Fore Street
☎ (01395) 597313
11.30-2.30, 5-11; 12-10.30 Sun
Ringwood Best Bitter; guest beers Ⓗ
Popular, 400-year-old coaching house in the village centre featuring beamed ceilings and brasses. It holds a beer festival every Easter; cider in summer.

Q 🍴 🚌 (🄳 ♣ ⌂

SILVERTON
Lamb Inn
Fore Street
☎ (01392) 860272
11-2.30, 6-11; 11-11 Sat; 12-10.30 Sun
Draught Bass; Ⓗ **Exe Valley Dob's Best Bitter; guest beers** Ⓖ
Well refurbished pub retaining a stone floor and stripped timber, featuring a temperature-controlled stillage behind the bar. This is a family-run pub serving a menu of good value home-made food. 🏚 (🄳 ♿ ♣

SLAPTON
Queens Arms
Signed off A379
☎ (01548) 580800
12-3, 6-11; 12-3, 7-10.30 Sun
Dartmoor Best Bitter; Princetown IPA; Shepherd Neame Spitfire; guest beers Ⓗ
14th-century inn at the village centre. The garden is a suntrap, while inside old local photos are displayed. The menu represents good quality and value; takeaways also available.

🏚 Q 🍴 (🄳 🅰 ⌂ P

SOUTH MOLTON
George Hotel
Broad Street
☎ (01769) 572514
12 (11 Thu & Sat)-2, 6-11; 12-2, 7-10.30 Sun
Draught Bass; Jollyboat Mainbrace; guest beer Ⓗ
Sympathetically refurbished 16th-century coaching inn that hosts folk, jazz and films. No food Sun lunch.

🏚 Q 🛏 🚌 (🄳 🄰 P ✗

SOUTH POOL
Millbrook Inn
Off A379 at Chillington, E of Kingsbridge
☎ (01548) 531581
12-2.30, 6.30-11; 12-2.30, 6.30-10.30 Sun
Draught Bass; Ⓖ **Ruddles Best Bitter; Wadworth 6X; guest beer** Ⓗ
Tiny, 17th-century pub with a stream at the rear overlooked by the beer garden. It gets busy at high tide when boats moor on the nearby river. Good home-made food and Heronbrook cider served.

🏚 Q 🍴 🚌 (🄳 ♣ ⌂

SOUTH ZEAL
Oxenham Arms
☎ (01837) 840244
11-2.30, 6-11; 12-2.30, 7-11 Sun
Princetown IPA; Ⓖ **guest beer** Ⓗ
12th-century inn, first licensed in 1477, described by one novelist as 'the stateliest and most ancient abode in the hamlet'. Still a fair description – though the hamlet has grown into a village. Guest beers are generally from the south-west.

🏚 Q 🛏 🍴 🚌 (🄳 🅰 ♣ P

SPREYTON
Tom Cobley Tavern
☎ (01647) 231314
12-2, 6-11 (closed Mon); 12-2, 7-10.30 Sun
Cotleigh Tawny; guest beer Ⓗ
Quiet village local reputed to be about 500 years old. The

garden gives views over to Dartmoor. Good, honest food is all home made, including the ice cream (booking essential for the restaurant). The family room houses a table tennis table.

🏚 Q ☎ 🏠 ◐ ◑ & ♣ P

STAVERTON

Sea Trout Inn
Right turn off A384 from Totnes
☎ (01803) 762274
11-3, 6-11 (11-11 Fri & Sat in summer); 12-3, 7-10.30 (12-10.30 summer) Sun
Palmers Dorset Gold, Best Bitter, 200 Ⓗ
15th-century pub, comprising two bars and a restaurant, near the River Dart and preserved steam railway.

🏚 Q ☎ 🏠 ◐ ◑ ◲ ◡ P

STICKLEPATH

Devonshire Inn
☎ (01837) 840626
11-11 (11-11, 5-11 winter); 12-3, 7-10.30 Sun
Draught Bass; St Austell Tinners, Daylight Robbery, seasonal beers Ⓖ
Unspoilt thatched local in a north Dartmoor village. Water flowing through the leat by the back wall helps to keep the stillage cool, as well as powering the water wheels in the nearby foundry museum. Eve meals can be booked.

🏚 Q ☎ ◐ ◭ ♣ P

STOCKLAND

Kings Arms
☎ (01404) 881361
12-3, 6.30-11; 12-3, 6.30-11 Sun
Courage Directors; Exmoor Ale; Otter Ale; John Smith's Bitter Ⓗ
A warm welcome awaits at this straightforward village pub, serving an excellent menu.

🏚 Q ☎ 🏠 ◐ ◑ ◲ & ♣ ◡ P

TEIGNMOUTH

Golden Lion
85 Bitton Park Road (A379)
☎ (01626) 776442
12-4, 6-11; 12-4, 7.30-10.30 Sun
Beer range varies Ⓗ
Friendly welcoming pub overlooking the docks: a cosy beamed lounge bar and a larger public bar with a pool table, it stocks three ever-changing real ales at reasonable prices.

◲ ◭ ♣ P

TIVERTON

Racehorse
Wellbrook Street
☎ (01884) 252606
11-11; 12-10.30 Sun

Draught Bass; guest beers Ⓗ
This popular local boasts a large skittle alley, whilst the garden has a children's play area and pets' corner. It stocks at least two guest beers at any time. Food is available all day. Limited parking.

🏚 ☎ ◐ ◑ & ♣ P

TOPSHAM

Bridge Inn ☆
Bridge Hill
☎ (01392) 873862
12-2, 6-10.30 (11 Fri & Sat); 12-2, 7-10.30 Sun
Adnams Broadside; Branscombe Vale Branoc, seasonal beers; Exe Valley seasonal beers; Otter Bitter Head Ⓖ
Famous 16th-century Grade II listed pub, unchanged for most of the last century, and in the present family for 103 years. The ower bar was once a brewery and maltings. Sandwiches, ploughmans, pasties and soup served both sessions.

🏚 Q ☎ ⇌ P

Try also: Lighter Inn, Topsham Quay (Badger)

TORQUAY

Crown & Sceptre
2 Petitor Rd, St Marychurch
☎ (01803) 328290
11-3 (4 Sat), 5.30 (6.30 Sat)-11; 12-3, 7-10.30 Sun
Draught Bass; Courage Best Bitter, Directors; Morland Old Speckled Hen; Ruddles County; Young's Special; Ⓗ **guest beers** Ⓗ/Ⓖ
This 200-year-old stone coaching house will not only give you a good time and a friendly atmosphere, but also a sense of belonging. A *Guide* entry for over 20 years and 1997 South Devon CAMRA *Pub of the Year*. No food Sun.

🏚 Q ☎ ◐ ◑ ◲ ♣ P

TOTNES

Kingsbridge Inn
9 Leechwell Street (off High St)
☎ (01803) 863324
11.30-3, 6-11; 12-3, 7-10.30 Sun
Draught Bass; Cotleigh Tawny; Redruth Cornish Rebellion; Theakston Old Peculier; guest beer Ⓗ
Friendly pub; a comfortable, subtly-lit bar with many alcoves and a low ceiling plus a dining area.

🏚 ☎ ◐ ◑ ⇌ ✄

TUCKENHAY

Maltsters Arms
Bow Creek (signed from A381 Totnes-Kingsbridge road)
☎ (01803) 732350
11-3, 6-11; 11-11 Sat & summer;

12-10.30 Sun
Princeton IPA; guest beers Ⓗ
Marvellous waterside pub overlooking Bow Creek, offering quality food and accommodation. Cosy rooms open off the main bar; it hosts quayside barbecues and occasional live jazz in summer. Moorings available at high tide.

🏚 Q ☎ 🏠 🏠 ◐ ◑ ♣ P

WEMBURY

Odd Wheel
Knighton Road
☎ (01752) 862289
12-3, 6.30-11; 12-11 Sat; 12-4, 7-10.30 Sun
Courage Best Bitter; Princetown Jail Ale; Sutton XSB; guest beers Ⓖ
Traditional pub in a semi-rural dormitory village on the outskirts of Plymouth, well worth seeking out; on a bus route.

☎ ◐ ◑ ♣ P

WESTCOTT

Merry Harriers
☎ (01392) 881254
11.30-2.30, 6.30-11; 12-2.30, 7-10.30 Sun
Draught Bass; Flowers IPA Ⓗ
Friendly roadside inn enjoying a well-deserved reputation for its varied range of good home-made meals.

🏚 ☎ ◐ ◑ ♣ P

WEST DOWN

Crown
The Square
☎ (01271) 862790
12-3, 7-11; 12-3, 7-10.30 Sun
Beer range varies Ⓗ
Lovely village inn, boasting one of the finest pub gardens in the area. Thatcher's cider is sold in summer.

🏚 Q ☎ ☎ ◐ ◑ ◭ ♣ ◡ P

WESTWARD HO!

Pig on the Hill
Pusehill (off A361, Bideford-Abbotsham Cross road)
☎ (01237) 425889
12-3, 6 (6.30 winter)-11; 12-3, 7-10.30 Sun
Country Life Golden Pig, Old Appledore; Ind Coope Burton Ale; guest beer (occasional) Ⓗ
A converted farm with its own brewery, visible through a large window. An intimate bar and restaurant are decorated throughout with all things porcine.

Q ☎ ☎ 🏠 ◐ ◑ & ♣ ◡ P

WHIMPLE

New Fountain Inn
Church Road
☎ (01404) 822350

CAMRA National Pub Inventory: Anchor, High Offley, Staffs

12-2.30, 6.30-11; 12-3, 7-10.30 Sun

Branscombe Vale Branoc; Ⓗ **Teignworthy Reel Ale;** Ⓖ **guest beers** Ⓗ/Ⓖ

Friendly local that welcomes strangers warmly. Look out for special events including wassailing, Morris dancing and charity quizzes.
🏚 Q 🕸 🌓 👌 ⟲ ♣ ⟳ P

WIDECOMBE IN THE MOOR

Rugglestone Inn ☆
Just S of village (signed)
OS721666
☎ (01364) 621327
11-2.30 (3 Sat), 7 (6 summer)-11;
12-3, 7 (6 summer)-10.30 Sun

Draught Bass; Butcombe Bitter Ⓖ

Unspoilt, cosy, little pub in a splendid Dartmoor setting, named after a local 'logan' stone. No children under 14 allowed inside, but across the stream is a large grassed seating area with a shelter for use in bad weather. Home-cooked food available.
🏚 Q 🕸 🌓 👌 ♣ ⟳ P ✂

WONSON

Northmore Arms
2½ miles SW of A30 jct at Whiddon Down OS674897
☎ (01647) 231428
11-11; 12-10.30 Sun

Adnams Broadside; Cotleigh Tawny; Exe Valley Dob's Best Bitter Ⓖ

Welcoming, traditional,

country local on the northern edge of Dartmoor, ideally situated for walks. It sells cider in summer.
🏚 Q 🕸 🛏 🌓 👌 Å ♣ ⟳ P

WOODBURY

White Hart
Church Stile Lane
☎ (01395) 232221
11-3, 6-11 (11-11 Sat); 12-3, 7-10.30 Sun

Draught Bass; Butcombe Bitter Ⓗ

Formerly housing for builders of the nearby church, this Grade II listed pub is at least 500 years old. Good food and a large skittle alley add to its appeal.
🏚 Q 🕸 🌓 👌 🍺 ♣ P

WOODLAND

Rising Sun
Signed off A38 southbound
☎ (01364) 652544
11-3 (not Mon Sept-Jun), 6-11 (closed Mon, Jan-Mar); 12-3, 7-10.30 Sun

Princetown Jail Ale; guest beer Ⓗ

Lovely rural free house in beautiful countryside between Torbay and Dartmoor. It specialises in home-made food, using local produce. The garden is lovely in summer.
🏚 Q 🐄 🕸 🛏 🌓 👌 Å P

YARDE DOWN

Poltimore Arms

Off A399 towards Simonsbath OS725357
☎ (01598) 710381
12-2.30 (not winter Mon-Fri), 7-11;
12-2.30, 7-10.30 Sun

Cotleigh Tawny; guest beers Ⓖ

At the edge of the Exmoor Forest, you will find this fine country pub frequented by tourists and locals enjoying a friendly atmosphere and a selection of good ales and home-cooked food.
🏚 🌓 👌 ♣ P

DORSET

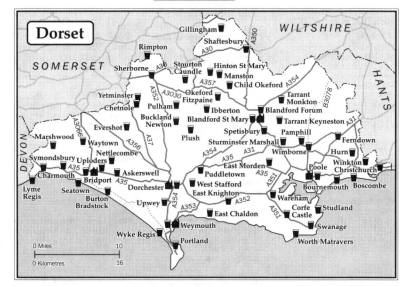

ASKERSWELL

Spyway
☎ (01308) 485250

10.30-2.30, 6-11 (closed Mon); 12-3,
7-10.30 Sun

**Adnams Bitter; Branscombe Vale
Branoc, seasonal beer** H

Rural, three-roomed pub,
served by a single bar; food
dominates at lunchtime.
Enjoy excellent views from
the garden. ⌂ Q ✿ ◖ ▶ P

BLANDFORD FORUM

Damory Oak Inn
Damory Court Street
☎ (01258) 452791

11 (10.30 Sat)-11; 12-10.30 Sun

Badger Best, Tanglefoot H

Friendly local with a two-
roomed bar, home to several
successful darts and pool
teams. Children's play area in
garden; close to the town
centre. ⌂ Q ♣ P

Dolphin
42 East Street
☎ (01258) 456813

11.30-3, 5.15-11; 11.30-11 Fri & Sat;
12-10.30 Sun

**Courage Best Bitter, Directors;
Theakston Old Peculier; Wadworth
6X; guest beers** H

Friendly, small town pub,
well laid out, whose keen crib
and quiz teams play in local
leagues. No food Sun eve.
⌂ Q ◖ ▶

BLANDFORD ST MARY

Stour Inn
5 Dorchester Road
☎ (01258) 451276

11-2.30, 6-11; 12-3, 7-10.30 Sun

Badger Best, seasonal beers H

Cosy, friendly one-bar pub,
in an attractive terrace, close

to the River Stour and Badger
Brewery. ⌂ Q ✿ ◖ ♣

BOURNEMOUTH

Goat & Tricycle
27-29 West Hill Road
☎ (01202) 314220

12-3, 5.30 (6 Sat)-11; 12-3, 7-10.30
Sun

**Wadworth IPA, 6X, Farmers Glory,
seasonal beers; guest beers** H

Split-level, cosy ale house
with at least eight ales
normally available. Close to
the town centre. The suntrap
patio is popular in summer;
the good food is excellent
value. ⌂ Q ✿ ◖ ▶ ♣

Porterhouse
113 Poole Road, Westbourne
☎ (01202) 768586

11-11; 12-10.30 Sun

**Ringwood Best Bitter, True Glory,
XXXX Porter, Fortyniner, Old
Thumper, seasonal beers; guest
beers** H

This gem has been voted
local CAMRA *Pub of the Year*
four times. A single bar caters
for drinkers – no machines or
games. Good food Mon-Sat.
Q ◖ ⇥ (Branksome) ♣ ⌣ ▣

Shoulder of Mutton
1010 Ringwood Road (400
yds from Clock Garage via
slip rd) ☎ (01202) 573344

12-2.30, 6-11; 12-4,30, 7-11 Sat;
12-3.30, 7-10.30 Sun

Flowers Original; guest beer H

Bournemouth's third oldest
pub, one of the few left with
a separate public bar; a
superb, friendly local. No
food Sun. ✿ ◖ ▣ ♣ P

BOSCOMBE

Sir Percy Florence

Shelley
673-675 Christchurch Road
☎ (01202) 300197

10.30-11; 12-10.30 Sun

**Boddingtons Bitter; Shepherd
Neame Bishops Finger; Theakston
Best Bitter; guest beers** H

Popular Wetherspoon's local,
serving a good range of ales,
at reasonable prices. Food is
available at all times, even
breakfast. Q ✿ ◖ ▷ ⌣ ✂

BRIDPORT

Hope & Anchor
13 St Michaels Lane
☎ (01308) 422160

11-11; 12-10.30 Sun

Beer range varies H

Unpretentious single bar that
offers up to three cask beers
from mainly West Country
brewers. Local CAMRA *Pub of
the Year* 1999. It offers three
ciders. ⌂ ✿ ⇥ ▷ ♣ ⌣

King Charles Tavern
114 St Andrews Road
☎ (01308) 422911

11-2.30, 6-11; 12-2.30, 7-10.30 Sun

Draught Bass; guest beer H

Friendly local on the east side
of town. Popular and
welcoming, it can get busy at
weekends with local darts
and skittles teams. ◖ ▶ ▲ ♣

BUCKLAND NEWTON

Gaggle of Geese

12-2.30, 6.30-11; 12-3, 7-10.30 Sun

**Badger Dorset Best; Ringwood Best
Bitter, Fortyniner;** H **guest beers**
(summer) H

Large, friendly village pub
comprising several
eating/drinking areas. A
goose auction is held in May
and Sept. It is popular with
ramblers. ⌂ ✿ ◖ ▶ ♣ P

95

BURTON BRADSTOCK

Anchor
High Street
☎ (01305) 897228
11-3.30, 6.30-11; 12-3, 7-10.30 Sun
Ushers Best Bitter, Founders, seasonal beers Ⓗ
Two-bar village local: a lively public bar and a quieter lounge; superb food is served.
Q ◖ ▮ ▤ ♿ ♣ ♠ ◒ P

CHARMOUTH

George
The Street ☎ (01297) 560280
11.30-3, 6.30-11; 12-3, 7-11 Sun
Otter Bitter; John Smith's Bitter Ⓗ
Busy free house, popular with walkers on the coastal path.
🏨 ❀ 🛏 ◖ ♣

Try also: **Royal Oak**, The Street (Palmers)

CHETNOLE

Chetnole Inn
1 mile E of A37
☎ (01935) 872337
11-2.30, 6.30-11; 12-2.30, 7-10.30 Sun
Branscombe Vale Branoc; guest beers Ⓗ
Excellent village pub standing opposite the church. It offers a comprehensive food menu, and hosts an Easter beer festival. Cider in summer.
🏨 Q ❀ ◖▮ ▤ ▥ ♿ ♣ ◒ P

CHILD OKEFORD

Saxon Inn
Gold Hill ☎ (01258) 860310
11.30-2.30 (3 Sat), 7-11; 12-3, 7-10.30 Sun
Draught Bass; Butcombe Bitter; guest beer Ⓗ
Friendly characterful village pub tucked behind cottages, with a pleasant, secluded garden. No eve meals Tue or Sun. 🏨 Q ❀ ❀ ◖▮ ♿ ♠ ♣ P

CHRISTCHURCH

Olde George Inn
24 Castle Street
☎ (01202) 479383
11-3, 6.30 (6 Fri & Sat)-11; 12-4, 7-10.30 Sun
Flowers Original; Hampshire Strong's Best Bitter; Ringwood Fortyniner; guest beers Ⓗ
Friendly, former Tudor coaching inn comprising two low-ceilinged rooms and a covered courtyard that admits children. It hosts jazz bands (Thu eve) and folk/rock bands (Fri). The only regular local outlet for real mild. Meals served in summer. ❀ ◖

Railway Hotel
2 Stour Road (opp. station)
☎ (01202) 484180
11-11; 12-3.30, 7-10.30 Sun
Flowers Original; Ringwood Best Bitter Ⓗ
Friendly, two-bar town pub, built in an unusual Victorian style and decorated on a railway theme.
🏨 ❀ ▤ ▬ ♣

CORFE CASTLE

Greyhound Inn
The Square
☎ (01929) 480205
11-11; 12-10.30 Sun
Flowers Original; Hampshire Strong's Best Bitter; Poole Dolphin; guest beer Ⓗ
This popular 17th-century coaching lies beneath the famous ruined castle. The food quality and choice is excellent. Handy for Swanage Steam Railway.
🏨 Q ✆ ❀ ◖▮ ▥ ♣ ✂

DORCHESTER

Blue Raddle
8 Church Street
☎ (01305) 267762
11.30-3, 7-11; 12-3, 7-10.30 Sun
Greene King Abbot; Otter Bitter; guest beers Ⓗ
Small, popular, friendly town pub with West Country guest beers. Q ◖ ♿ ♣ ◒

Tom Browns
47 High East Street
☎ (01305) 264020
11-3, 5.30-11; 11-11 Wed-Sat; 12-10.30 Sun
Goldfinch Tom Brown's, Flashman's Clout (occasional)**, Midnight Sun, Midnight Blinder** Ⓗ
The Goldfinch Brewery tap: a basic wooden-floored, single bar. ▤ ◖ ♣ ◒

EAST CHALDON

Sailors Return
1 mile S of A352 OS791834
☎ (01305) 853847
11-2.30, 6-11; 12-3, 7-10.30 Sun
Fuller's London Pride; guest beers Ⓗ
Multi-roomed, thatched pub with flagstoned floors where realy good food is served in generous portions at reasonable prices; busy in summer. Q ❀ ◖▮ ♣ ◒ P

EAST KNIGHTON

Countryman
Blacknoll Lane Just off A352 (signed) ☎ (01305) 852666
11-3, 6-11; 12-3, 7-10.30 Sun
Courage Best Bitter, Directors; Ringwood Best Bitter, Old Thumper; John Smith's Bitter; Wadworth 6X Ⓗ
Country pub, just off the main road, with a restaurant and spacious bar, with comfortable seating.
▥ ❀ ▤ ◖▮ ♿ P

EAST MORDEN

Cock & Bottle
On B3075, off A35 near Wareham ☎ (01929) 459238
11-3, 6-11; 12-3, 7-10.30 Sun
Badger Best, Tanglefoot, seasonal beers Ⓗ
Cosy, 400-year-old village pub where a sympathetic restaurant extension serves an excellent range of good value food. 🏨 ❀ ◖▮ ♿ ♣ P

EVERSHOT

Acorn
28 Fore Street
☎ (01953) 83228
11.30-2.30, 6.30-11; 12-3, 7-10.30 Sun
Fuller's London Pride; guest beers Ⓗ
17th-century coaching inn of immense character where panelled walls and stone-flagged floors lend atmosphere. Top quality food. 🏨 Q ❀ ▤ ◖▮ ♣ P

FERNDOWN

Nightjar
94 Victoria Road
☎ (01202) 855572
11-11; 12-10.30 Sun
Boddingtons Bitter; Courage Directors; Ringwood Fortyniner; Theakston Best Bitter; guest beers Ⓗ
Former supermarket, now a thriving Wetherspoon's outlet in an area not noted for real ale; good food.
Q ◖▮ ♿ ◒ P ✂ ▦

GILLINGHAM

Buffalo
Lydfords Lane, Wyke (150 yds from B3081, Wincanton road) ☎ (01747) 823759
12-2.30, 5.30 (7 Sat)-11; 12-3, 7-10.30 Sun
Badger IPA, Best Ⓗ
Single-bar country-style pub on the edge of town. Locals enjoy occasional music round the piano. No food Sun eve. 🏨 Q ❀ ◖▮ ♣ P

Phoenix
High Street
☎ (01747) 823277
10-2.30 (10.30-3 Sat), 7-11; 12-3, 7-10.30 Sun
Badger Best, seasonal beers Ⓗ
Interesting town-centre, single-bar pub, within a Georgian building, a former coaching inn. Try the house ale. No food Sun eve.
🏨 ❀ ◖▮ ▥ ▬ ♣ ▦

HINTON ST MARY

White Horse
200 yds from B3092 (signed)
☎ (01258) 472723
11.30-2.15, 6.15-11; 12-2.30, 7-10.30 Sun

DORSET

Beer range varies Ⓗ
Friendly, cheerful village free
house with a conversational
public bar and a quieter
saloon/dining room.
🏚Q🚽☪🌢❶⬛♣🍂P

HURN

Avon Causeway Hotel
Off B3073
☎ (01202) 482714
11-11; 12-10.30 Sun
Wadworth IPA; Ringwood Old
Thumper; Ⓗ guest beers/Ⓐ
Formerly Hurn railway
station with a railway
carriage still by the platform,
this large, comfortable family
pub has a children's play area
at the back. The dining room
serves good value food. It
hosts 'Murder Mystery' eves
Fri and Sat.
☪🛏❶👍P

IBBERTON

Crown Inn
Church Lane (4 miles SW of
A357) OS788077
☎ (01258) 817448
11-2.30, 7-11 (11-11 summer); 12-3,
7-10.30 (12-10.30 summer) Sun
Draught Bass; M&B Brew XI; guest
beer Ⓗ
Idyllic country pub, nestling
below Bulbarrow Hill; a
stream runs through the
attractive garden. The bar
features an original flagstone
floor, an inglenook and
photos of bygone village life.
Cider is from Burrow Hill.
🏚Q☪❶👍♣🍂P

LYME REGIS

Nags Head
Silver Street
☎ (01297) 442312
10-3, 6-11; 10-11 Tue & Sat; 12-10.30
Sun
Beer range varies Ⓗ
Old coach house, a steep
climb from the town centre;
it is the only regular outlet
for mild in west Dorset
(when available). Cider in
summer. 🏚☪❶👍♣🍂

Volunteer
31 Broad Street
☎ (01297) 442214
11-4.30, 7-11 (11-11 summer); 12-4,
7-10.30 Sun
Draught Bass; Fuller's London Pride;
Ⓗ Otter Ale; guest beer Ⓖ
Welcoming single bar at the
top of the town where the
two rooms are served by a
single L-shaped bar. The
house beer comes from
Branscombe Vale. No food
Sun eve or Mon lunch.
Q🚽❶👍🍂♣

Try also: Angel Inn, Hill St
(Palmers)

MANSTON

Plough
Shaftesbury Road (B3091)
☎ (01258) 472484
11.30-3, 6.30-11; 12-3, 7-10.30 Sun
Beer range varies Ⓗ/Ⓖ
Roadside, ex-Badger house,
now free, where a cheerful
welcome awaits. One large
bar caters for drinkers and
diners. Pétanque played.
🏚Q☪❶👍♣🍂P

MARSHWOOD

Bottle
On B3165 ☎ (01297) 678254
12-3, 6.30-11; (closed winter Mon);
12-3, 7-10.30 Sun
Caledonian Golden Promise; Otter
Bitter; Wadworth 6X Ⓗ
Classic, thatched country
pub, a favourite of locals and
walkers alike. Excellent,
mainly organic food,
includes vegetarian and
vegan choices. Organic beer
is also available.
🏚Q☪❶👍♣P🍂

NETTLECOMBE

Marquis of Lorne
Easiest approach is from
A3066 OS517956
☎ (01308) 485236
11-2.30, 6.30 (6 summer)-11; 12-3,
7-10.30 Sun
Palmers BB, Dorset Gold, IPA,
200 Ⓗ
Idyllic country pub off the
beaten track. Excellent food
and a large garden (with play
area) help make it popular.
Cider in summer.
🏚☪🛏❶👍♣🍂P🍂

OKEFORD FITZPAINE

Royal Oak
Lower Street ☎ (01258) 861561
12-3, 5.30-11; 12-11 Sat; 12-3,
7-10.30 Sun
Ringwood Best Bitter; Wadworth 6X;
guest beer Ⓗ
Friendly, thriving village
local with a comfortable
lounge and a restaurant. The
original public bar boasts a
flagstone floor and
inglenook. Other attractions
are the garden, games room,
skittle alley and good, home-
cooked food (not Sun eve).
🏚Q🚽☪❶👍♣🍂P

PAMPHILL

Vine Inn ☆
Vine Hill (off B3082)
☎ (01202) 882259
11-2.30, 7-11; 12-3, 7-10.30 Sun
Beer range varies Ⓗ
Good pub for walkers, two
small bar areas and a games
room upstairs; it has a nice
garden. Close to Kingston
Lacey House, the pub is
owned by the NT. Q☪🍂P

PLUSH

Brace of Pheasants
☎ (01300) 348357
12-2.30, 7-11; 12-3, 7-10.30 Sun
Fuller's London Pride; guest beer Ⓖ
Thatched inn, hidden in a
tiny rural hamlet. The
restaurant enjoys an
excellent reputation for food
and wine. 🏚Q🚽☪❶P🍂

POOLE

Blue Boar
29 Market Close
☎ (01202) 682247
11-3, 5-11; 12-3, 7-10.30 Sun
Cottage Southern Bitter; Courage
Best Bitter, Directors; guest
beers Ⓗ
Former merchant's house in
the old town, converted to
give a comfortable lounge
and an extensive cellar,
admitting children at lunchtime. Live bands play Wed
and Fri. No food Sun. ❶≈

Branksome Railway Hotel
429 Poole Road
☎ (01202) 769555
11-11; 12-10.30 Sun
Hampshire Strong's Best Bitter;
guest beers Ⓗ
Victorian hotel opposite the
station. The large lounge
overlooks the railway and an
area for pool and darts has
been created.
🛏🌢≈ (Branksome) ♣P

Brewhouse
68 High Street
☎ (01202) 685288
11-11, 11-5, 7-11 Sat; 12-10.30 Sun
Poole Dolphin, Bosun Ⓗ
The home of Poole Brewery,
a lively, basic local in the old
town, probably the cheapest
beer in Dorset. ≈♣

Bermuda Triangle
10 Parr Street, Lower
Parkstone ☎ (01202) 748087
12-2.30, 5.30-11; 12-11 Sat; 12-10.30
Sun
Beer range varies Ⓗ
A little gem, themed on the
Bermuda Triangle mystery.
Four ever-changing beers and
a lovely atmosphere make it
popular with locals and
visitors. ❶≈ (Parkstone) P

Queen Mary
68 West Street
☎ (01202) 661701
12-3, 6-11; 12-11 Sat; 12-10.30 Sun
Hampshire King Alfred's; Ringwood
Best Bitter, Fortyniner Ⓗ
One of Poole's old cosy pubs,
close to the quay and shops.
It stocks at least two
Ringwood beers, plus a guest.
Good quality and value
home-made food includes a
vegetarian dish.
☪❶≈P

PORTLAND

George Inn
133 Reforne, Easton
☎ (01305) 820011
11-11; 12-10.30 Sun
Castle Eden Ale; Quay Bombshell Bitter; Worthington Bitter [H]
Small, low-beamed pub of great character, opposite the cricket ground. Q ❀ ◖◗ ♣

PUDDLETOWN

Blue Vinny
12 The Moor
☎ (01305) 848228
11-2.30; 6.30-11; 12-3, 7-10.30 Sun
Flowers Original; Ringwood Fortyniner [H]
Named after the famed Dorset cheese (featured on the menu), it comprises a single bar with a comfortable lounge area. ❀ 🛏 ◗ ⛺ ♣ P

PULHAM

Halsey Arms
☎ (01258) 817344
11.30-2.30 (not Wed), 6-11; 12-2.30, 7-10.30 Sun
Courage Best Bitter; Ringwood Best Bitter; guest beers [H]
Traditional Dorset pub where a pleasant atmosphere prevails. It offers a wide range of beers and hosts a cider festival in summer.
♨ ♘ ❀ ◖◗ ♿ ⛺ ♣ ⌓ P

RIMPTON

White Post Inn
On B3148,N of Sherborne
☎ (01935) 850717
12-3, 6.30-11; 12-3, 7-10.30 Sun
Draught Bass; Butcombe Bitter; Otter; guest beers [H]
Free house straddling the Dorset/Somerset border. Excellent food.
Q ❀ ◖◗ ♿ ♣ ⌓ P 🚭

SEATOWN

Anchor
☎ (01297) 489215
Off A35 in Chideock (signed)
12-3, 6-11; (12-11 summer); 12-3, 7-10.30 Sun
Palmers BB (summer), [G] **Dorset Gold, IPA, 200** [H]
Friendly pub overlooking Lyme Bay, popular with walkers in summer. Opening times may vary.
♨ Q ❀ 🛏 ◖◗ ⛺ ♣

SHAFTESBURY

Olde Two Brewers
24 St James Street
☎ (01747) 854211
11-3, 6-11; 12-3, 7-10.30 Sun
Courage Best Bitter, Directors; Theakston XB; guest beers [H]
Popular well-run pub of many different drinking areas, plus a garden with good views and excellent, home-cooked food.
❀ ◖◗ P 🚭

Ship Inn
Bleke Street
☎ (01747) 853219
11-3, 5-11; 11-11 Thu-Sat; 11-11 Sun
Badger Best, Champion, Tanglefoot [H]
Traditional town pub, a busy friendly local, it serves wonderful home-cooked food; try the pie'n'mash.
♨ ❀ ◖◗ ⊟ ♣ ⊞

SHERBORNE

Britannia
Westbury ☎ (01935) 813300
11-2.30, 6.30-11; 12-3, 7-10.30 Sun
Wadworth 6X; guest beers [H]
Two-bar pub, near the Abbey, serving good food.
❀ 🛏 ◖◗ ≠ ♣ P

Digby Tap
Cooks Lane ☎ (01935) 813148
11-2.30, 5.30-11; 12-2.30, 7-10.30 Sun
Beer range varies [H]
Popular multi-roomed town pub, that sells over 20 different beers each week in an excellent atmosphere. No food Sun. ♨ Q ◖ ≠ ♣

Skipper's
1 Terrace View, Horsecastles
☎ (01935) 812753
11-2.30, 6.30-11; 12-3, 7-10.30 Sun
Adnams Bitter; Wadworth IPA, 6X, seasonal beers; guest beers [H]
Terraced pub on the ring road: a single bar and a restaurant serving good food.
❀ ◖◗ ≠ ♣ P

SPETISBURY

Drax Arms
High Street
☎ (01258) 452658
11.30-2.30, 7 (6.30 Sat)-11; 12-3, 7-10.30 Sun
Badger Best, Tanglefoot, seasonal beers [H]
Popular roadside inn, with two communicating bars, one has a no-smoking food area, the other darts.
❀ ◖◗ ♣ P

STOURTON CAUNDLE

Trooper
☎ (01963) 362405
12-2.30 (not Mon); 7-11; 12-2.30, 7-10.30 Sun
Cottage Champflower; Exmoor Ale; guest beer [H]
Gem of a village pub, with two small bars; a lively public, and a quieter saloon, plus a museum-cum-skittle alley. Q ♘ 🛏 ⊟ ⛺ ♣ ⌓ P

STUDLAND

Bankes Arms Hotel
Manor Road
☎ (01929) 450225
11-11; 12-10.30 Sun
Beer range varies [H]
Attractive Purbeck pub, popular with walkers. The large garden gives panoramic views of the bay. Up to eight real ales, excellent food.
♨ ❀ 🛏 ◖◗ ♣ ⌓

STURMINSTER MARSHALL

Red Lion
Church Street (1 mile E of A350) ☎ (01258) 857319
11-2.30, 7-11; 12-3, 6-10.30 Sun
Badger Best, Tanglefoot, seasonal beers [H]
Fine village inn, well known locally for its good food. The skittle alley doubles as a no-smoking family room.
♨ ♘ ❀ ◖◗ ♣ P 🚭 ⊞

SWANAGE

Red Lion
High Street
☎ (01929) 423533
11-11; 12-10.30 Sun
Fuller's London Pride; Hampshire Strong's Best Bitter; Morland Old Speckled Hen; Ringwood Best Bitter [G]
Traditional, busy, two-bar pub, near the beach and Swanage steam railway.
Q ♘ ❀ ◖◗ ⊟ ⛺ ♣ ⌓ P

SYMONDSBURY

Ilchester Arms
Off A35, W of Bridport
☎ (01308) 422600
11-3, 6-11; 12-3, 7-11 Sun
Palmers BB, IPA [H]
This low-beamed country inn enjoys a reputation for good food. A stone floor and roaring fire add atmosphere.
♨ Q ❀ ◖◗ ♿ ⛺ ♣ ⌓ P

TARRANT KEYNESTON

True Lovers Knot
On B3082 ☎ (01258) 452209
11-2.30, 7 (6.30 Sat)-11; 12-3, 7-10.30 Sun
Badger Best, seasonal beers [H]
Ivy-clad, one-bar inn in the picturesque Tarrant valley. The large garden has a children's play area. No meals Sun eve.
♨ Q ❀ ◖◗ ♿ ⛺ ♣ P

TARRANT MONKTON

Langton Arms
Off A354 ☎ (01258) 830225
11.30-11; 12-10.30 Sun
Ringwood Best Bitter; guest beers [H]
17th-century country pub that serves four ever-changing ales in its pleasant beamed lounge. The excellent restaurant with a

DORSET

conversatory is an added attraction. The no-smoking area is the family room.
🏚Q🐶🌼🍴◑▶🏠🚭🏵♣P✗

UPLODERS
Crown Inn
☎ (01308) 485356
11-3, 6-11; 12-3, 7-10.30 Sun
Palmers Dorset Gold, IPA, 200 Ⓗ
Flagstone-floored village local where a welcoming single bar serves all areas including the restaurant. 🏚Q🌼◑▶🅰♣P

UPWEY
Royal Standard
700 Dorchester Road
☎ (01305) 812558
11-3, 6-11; 12-10.30 Sun
Archers Village; guest beers Ⓗ
Unpretentious pub on the outskirts of Weymouth with a genuine public bar and lounge. Beware the fine for ringing mobile phones.
🏚Q🌼🏵⇄♣P

WAREHAM
Duke of Wellington
East Street ☎ (01929) 553015
11-11; 12-10.30 Sun
Fuller's London Pride; Ringwood Best Bitter; guest beer (summer) Ⓗ
The Duke offers a good range and standard of food, and is popular with both locals and visitors to this Saxon town. A smart dress code applies.
🏚Q🐶🌼◑▶🅰⇄♣P

Quay Inn
The Quay ☎ (01929) 552735
11-3, 7-11 (11-11 summer); 12-3, 7-10.30 Sun
Boddingtons Bitter; Greene King Abbot; Hampshire Strong's Best Bitter; Wadworth 6X Ⓗ
Lovely old pub in a market town at the river's edge, affording Purbeck and Poole harbour views. Seating outside makes it an ideal stopping point in summer for boats. 🏚🌼🍴◑▶⇄♣

WAYTOWN
Hare & Hounds
☎ (01308) 488203
11.30-3, 6.30-11; 12-3, 7-10.30 Sun
Palmers Dorset Gold, IPA Ⓖ
Superb village local where a single bar serves rooms on either side. Enjoy the magnificent views from the garden. No food Sun eve or winter Mon.
🏚Q🌼◑▶🏵🅰🏠P

WEST STAFFORD
Wise Man
☎ (01305) 263694
11-3, 6-11; 12-3, 7-10.30 Sun
Ringwood Best Bitter; guest beer Ⓗ
400-year-old thatched, ivy-

clad pub that has retained its lounge and public bars.
🏚🌼◑▶🏵♣🏠P

WEYMOUTH
Boot
High Street West (behind fire station) ☎ (01305) 770327
11-11; 12-10.30 Sun
Ringwood Best Bitter, True Glory, XXXX Porter, Fortyniner, Old Thumper Ⓗ
Weymouth's oldest inn is difficult to find (look for the fire station). A true pub where conversation rules.
🏚Q🌼◑▶⇄♣🏠

Dorothy Inn
The Esplanade
☎ (01305) 766996
11-11; 12-10.30 Sun
Draught Bass; guest beers Ⓗ
Seafront bar with a nightclub above. It stocks up to nine real ales in summer, usually from the West Country.
🌼◑▶🏵

Weatherbury
7 Carlton Road North
☎ (01305) 786040
12-11; 12-10.30 Sun
Draught Bass; Fuller's London Pride; guest beers Ⓗ
Large local in a residential area where over 200 different beers are served each year.
🌼🚌◑▶🏵⇄♣P

WIMBORNE
Cricketers Arms
Park Lane ☎ (01202) 882846
11-11; 12-10.30 Sun
Marston's Pedigree; Ringwood Best Bitter, Fortyniner; guest beer Ⓗ
Busy, but welcoming town-centre pub bearing a cricketing theme; the garden overlooks a cricket pitch. A beer festival is held in June. Cider is sold in summer.
🏚🌼♣🏠

Crown & Anchor
Walford Bridge
☎ (01202) 841405
11-2.30, 6-11; 12-3, 7-10.30 Sun
Badger Best, seasonal beers Ⓗ
Well refurbished one-room local, with a warm welcome. It is home to Wimborne Folk Club (Thu eve). A real gem, near Walford Craft Mill, its garden fronts the River Allen.
🏚Q🌼◑🅰P

WINKTON
Fisherman's Haunt
Salisbury Road
☎ (01202) 484071
10.30-2.30, 5-11; 10.30-11 Sat; 12-10.30 Sun
Draught Bass; Gale's GB, HSB; Ringwood Fortyniner Ⓗ
Spacious, multi-roomed, 17th-century pub and

restaurant overlooking the Avon Valley, popular for its good value food.
🏚🌼🚌◑▶🏵P✗🏠

Lamb Inn
Burley Road
☎ (01425) 672427
11-3, 5-11 (11-11 summer Sat); 12-10.30 Sun
Fuller's London Pride; Ringwood Best Bitter; guest beers Ⓗ
Comfortable two-roomed house, set among green fields, with a children's play area in the garden. It serves an interesting range of food.
🏚🌼◑▶🏵♣P

WORTH MATRAVERS
Square & Compass ☆
Off B3069 OS974777
☎ (01929) 439229
11-3, 6-11; 11-11 Sat; 12-3, 6-10.30 Sun
Ringwood Best Bitter, Fortyniner; guest beers Ⓖ
Run by the Newman family for nearly 100 years, this ancient stone pub boasts flagstoned floors, serving hatches and views of medieval field patterns and the sea. 🏚Q◑🅰♣🏠P

WYKE REGIS
Wyke Smugglers
76 Portland Road
☎ (01305) 760010
11-2.30, 6-11; 12-3, 7-10.30 Sun
Flowers Original; Otter Bitter; guest beers Ⓗ
Busy suburban local where pub games teams dominate. Cider is sold in summer.
🌼♣🏠P

YETMINSTER
White Hart
High Street
☎ (01935) 872338
12-2.30, 6.30 (7 Sat)-11; 12-2.30, 7-10.30 Sun
Butcombe Bitter; Ringwood Best Bitter; guest beer Ⓗ
400-year-old pub in good walking country with a convivial locals bar; a converted barn accommodates families. Imaginative food includes a vegetarian choice.
🏚Q🌼🚌◑▶🏠🏵⇄♣P

INDEPENDENT BREWERIES

Badger: Blandford St. Mary
Cranborne: Cranborne
Goldfinch: Dorchester
Hardy: Dorchester
Palmer's: Bridport
Poole: Poole
Quay: Weymouth

DURHAM

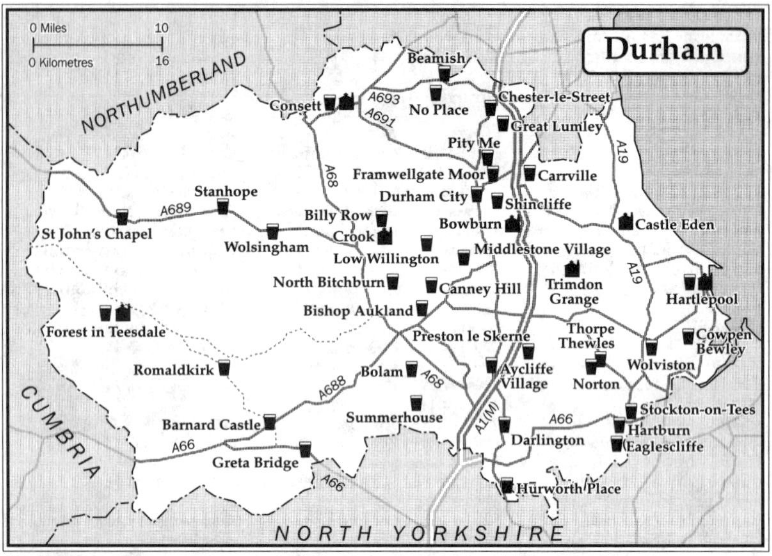

Co Durham incorporates part of the former county of Cleveland

AYCLIFFE VILLAGE

County
13 The Green (off A167)
☎ (01325) 312273
12-3. 5.30-11; 12-3, 7-10.30 Sun
John Smith's Magnet; guest beers Ⓗ
Overlooking the village green, the pub has been revamped with an emphasis on good food. The chef/landlord was Raymond Blanc's first scholarship winner – and cares for his beer with as much dedication. Advisable to book for meals, especially at weekends.
Q ❀ ◐ ◑ P

Try also: Foresters Arms, Coatham Mundeville (John Smiths)

BEAMISH MUSEUM

Sun Inn
Beamish Open Air Museum (off A1(M) Chester-le-Street)
☎ (01207) 231811
11-6 (or Museum closing time); 12-6 Sun
Theakston Best Bitter, XB; guest beers Ⓗ
Rebuilt stone by stone from its original Bishop Auckland site, this authentic reconstruction of a traditional north-eastern industrial pub, retaining original fittings and furnishings, is best experienced on a quiet day.
⌂ Q ♞ ❀ ◐ ♿ ▲ ♣

BILLY ROW

Dun Cow (Cow's Tail)
Turn left at Royal George, 1 mile along road
☎ (01388) 762714
7-11; 7-10.30 Sun
Darwin Evolution Ⓗ
This unspoilt, traditional rural pub is now in its third century of ownership by the same family. Well off the beaten track, but well worth seeking out (ring to visit during the day). Internally virtually unchanged since first licensed in 1830. Other Darwin beers may be available. ⌂ Q ❀ ⊟ P ⚡

BISHOP AUCKLAND

Newton Cap
Bank Top (near bus station)
☎ (01388) 605445
11-4 (not Tue), 7-11; 12-4, 7-10.30 Sun
John Smith's Bitter; guest beer Ⓗ
Real drinkers' pub: one of the town's unspoilt locals; a friendly, traditional bar, a pool room and a function room. Try a game of Ringo. Buses run from all parts of the region. ⌂ ♞ ⇌ ♣

Tut 'n' Shive
68 Newgate Street (near bus and rail stations)
☎ (01388) 603252
11-11; 12-10.30 Sun
Beer range varies Ⓗ
Early 20th-century pub that can be extremely busy at weekends as a 'circuit' pub. Live music Thu eve, plus jam sessions Tue eves. Under new management since 1999, it has up to four beers on tap. Handy for the shops, but limited parking. ◐ ⇌ ⌓ P

BOLAM

Countryman
Dunwell Lane (near B6275)
☎ (01388) 834577
12-2 (not Mon), 6-11; 12-2, 7-10.30 Sun
Black Sheep Best Bitter; guest beers Ⓗ
Welcoming pub with a strong belief in quality beer and food. In a tiny hillside village just off Dere Street Roman road, it comprises a long, interlinked bar, lounge and restaurant. Four guest ales mostly come from independent breweries.
⌂ ♞ ❀ ◐ ◑ P

CANNEY HILL

Sportsman
4 Canney Hill
☎ (01388) 603847
12-2.30 (not Mon), 5 (7 Mon)-11; 12-4, 7-11 Sat; 12-4, 7-10.30 Sun
Cameron's Bitter, Strongarm; guest beers Ⓗ
On the edge of Bishop Auckland, this pub has a bar, lounge and a snug. It is popular for Sun lunch and eve meals.
⌂ ❀ ◐ ◑ ⊟ ♣ P ⊓

CARRVILLE

Grange Inn
High Street (off A690, 2 miles from Durham City centre)
☎ (0191) 384 7082
11-11; 12-10.30 Sun
Castle Eden Bitter; guest beers Ⓗ
Since being acquired by Castle Eden, the Grange is building up a reputation for good food and beer. Guest ales come from Castle Eden and regional or micro-breweries. A friendly landlord and staff make this pub well worth a visit.
Q ◐ ◑ ⊟ ♿ ♣ P

CHESTER-LE-STREET

Smiths Arms
Brecon Hill, Castle Dene
☎ (0191) 385 6915
4 (12 Sat)-11; 12-5, 7-10.30 Sun
Draught Bass; Black Sheep Best Bitter; Courage Directors; guest beers Ⓗ
Traditional, 19th-century inn, offering a warm welcome to all, minutes from the A1(M) and Durham County Cricket ground. A restaurant is planned to open by time of publication.
🏠 ✿ 🍴 ♣ P 🖫

CONSETT

Grey Horse
115 Sherburn Terrace (off A692)
☎ (01207) 502585
12-11; 12-10.30 Sun
Steel Town Bitter, Target Inn Ale, Red Dust, Swordmaker, Coast to Coast; guest beers Ⓗ
Ex-coaching inn, now a brew-pub, with a traditional bar, an adjacent pool room and a cosy lounge. It offers over 100 malt and Irish whiskies, six real ales and hosts an annual beer festival. It enjoys strong community and family links. Cycling and walking groups on the Coast to Coast walk are welcome.
🏠 Q ⛵ ✿ 🍴 ♣ P

COWPEN BEWLEY

Three Horse Shoes
☎ (01642) 561541
12-2, 5.30 (6 Sat)-11; 12-10.30 Sun
Camerons Strongarm; guest beer Ⓗ
Homely village pub at one end of the green. Once owned by the Prince Bishops of Durham and used by them as a stopping-off place, there has been a pub on the site for hundreds of years.
🏠 ✿ 🍴 ▶ 🍴 & ♣ P

DARLINGTON

Binns Department Store (off-licence)
1-7 High Row
☎ (01325) 462606
9-5.30 (6 Sat); 11-5 Sun
House of Fraser department store with a growing reputation for its basement bottled beer section. Around 400 quality beers to take away, including 170 bottled-conditioned ales. A good selection of special glasses is also stocked. Sat tasting sessions frequently held. ⛵

Britannia
Archer Street (off Bondgate)
☎ (01325) 463787
11.30-3, 5.30-11; 12-3, 7-10.30 Sun
Camerons Strongarm; Tetley Bitter; guest beer Ⓗ

Fine edge-of-town-centre local in a simple early 19th-century listed building. A bastion of cask beer for 140 years, it has one small, long bar with a front parlour reserved for meetings, folk nights, etc. Guest ales from from the Tapster's Choice range.
Q ⛵ ♣ P

Glittering Star
9 Stonebridge
☎ (01325) 353191
11.30-3, 6-11 (11.30-11 Mon, Fri & Sat); 12-5, 7-10.30 Sun
Samuel Smith OBB Ⓗ
The only 'real' Sam Smith's in town: an attractive two-roomed town-centre local facing on to the 12th-century St. Cuthbert's church.
🍴 🍴 ⛵ ♣

Number Twenty-2
22 Coniscliffe Road
☎ (01325) 354590
11-11; closed Sun
Hambleton Nightmare; Ind Coope Burton Ale; Village White Boar, Bull, Old Raby; guest beers Ⓗ
Popular, award-winning, town-centre pub with a passion for cask ale.
CAMRA Regional *Pub of the Year* four times since opening in the mid-1990s: lots of glass, wood, brick – and class! It has a high turnover of guest ales on five pumps. The home pub of Village beers, commissioned from Hambleton. No food Sun.
Q 🍴 ⛵ 🖫 ▣

Quaker Coffee House (Dodger's Bar)
1-3 Mechanics' Yard, High Row (passage next to Binns' store)
☎ (01325) 468364
11-11; 7-10.30 Sun
Village White Boar; guest beers Ⓗ
Unusual, small new bar in one of Darlington's oldest buildings in the hidden town centre yards. It has the feel of a cellar bar, with a daytime restaurant upstairs. It stocks an eclectic range of five guest beers.
& ⛵ 🖫

Tap & Spile
99 Bondgate
☎ (01325) 381679
12-11 (midnight Fri & Sat); 12-10.30 Sun
Castle Eden Bitter, Nimmos XXXX; guest beers Ⓗ
Lively, town-centre pub attracting a mixed clientele. The oldest survivor from the original Tap & Spile chain, it now operates under Castle Eden Inns. Up to five guest beers. A no-smoking snug, regular live music and good bar lunches

add to its appeal.
🍴 ⛵ 🍴 ⚲

White Horse Hotel
North Road, Harrowgate Hill (A167)
☎ (01325) 382121
11.30-3, 5.30-11; 11.30-11 Sat; 12-10.30 Sun
Camerons Strongarm; Tetley Bitter; guest beer Ⓗ
Traditional pub attached to a roadside hotel. Meals are served in the bar, lounge and restaurant.
🏠 ✿ 🛏 🍴 ▶ 🍴 & ♣ P

Try also: **Old Yard Tapas Bar**, 98 Bondgate (Free)

DURHAM CITY

Dun Cow
37 Old Elvet (near Gaol)
☎ (0191) 386 9219
11-11; 12-10.30 Sun
Boddingtons Bitter; Castle Eden Ale; guest beer Ⓗ
Classic pub: a tiny bar exuding a wonderful atmosphere, popular with locals, students and visitors. It boasts the highest sales of Castle Eden Ale in the country. Outside toilets.
Q 🍴 🍴 ♣

Half Moon
New Elvet (opp. Royal County Hotel)
☎ (0191) 386 4528
11-11; 12-10.30 Sun
Draught Bass; Worthington Bitter; guest beer Ⓗ
Old classic inn with a listed interior, especially noted for its back bar. This town-centre house draws a good mixture of business people, students and locals. Guest beers come from Durham Brewery.
✿ 🍴 &

Hogshead
58 Saddler Street (between market place and Cathedral)
☎ (0191) 386 9550
11-11; 12-10.30 Sun
Boddingtons Bitter; Castle Eden Ale; Ⓗ **guest beers** Ⓗ/Ⓖ
Typical Hogshead pub sporting basic wood decor. There are usually eight beers available, including one on gravity; guest are normally from the Beer Seller's list.
🍴 & ⛵ ⚲

Old Elm Tree
12 Crossgate (off North Rd, above bus station)
☎ (0191) 386 4621
12-3, 6-11; 12-11 Sat; 12-3, 7-10.30 Sun
Tetley Bitter; Camerons Bitter; guest beers Ⓗ
Old coaching inn incorporating the original elm tree inside the bar. This open, friendly pub run by a

welcoming landlord and staff is used as a meeting place by a variety of groups, and draws a broad range of customers.

🏛 🍲 🍽 🛏 ◖ 🍴 ≈ 🌲 P

Victoria Hotel ☆

86 Hallgarth Street (between prison and Students Union)
☎ (0191) 386 5269
11-3, 6-11; 12-2, 6-10.30 Sun
Darwin Evolution; Marston's Pedigree; Theakston XB; guest beers Ⓗ
Authentic Victorian pub with a wonderful original interior – a time warp. The characterful bar boasts an open coal fire and a fine range of malts and Irish whiskies. The snug features Wm Morris wallpaper and antique fittings and furniture. A warm welcome is assured.

🏛 Q 🍲 🛏 ◖ 🍴 🚹 🌲 P

Woodman Inn

23 Claypath
☎ (0191) 386 7500
12-11; 12-10.30 Sun
Marston's Pedigree; Theakston Black Bull; guest beers Ⓗ
This busy pub, five minutes' walk from the market, and run by friendly staff, attracts a good midweek passing trade. It stocks a good range of guest beers and hosts an annual May beer festival.

◖ 🚹 🌲

EAGLESCLIFFE

Blue Bell

663 Yarm Road (A135, by Yarm bridge)
☎ (01642) 780358
11-11; 12-10.30 Sun
Courage Directors; Taylor Landlord; guest beers Ⓗ
Rebuilt in 1998, on a vast scale, from an old turnpike alehouse beside Bishop Skirlaw's bridge. The management shows unshakeable faith in real ale, usually featuring at least one beer rarely found locally.

🍲 🍽 ◖ ≈ (Allens W) 🌲 P 🍴

FOREST-IN-TEESDALE

High Force Hotel

☎ (01833) 622222
11-3, 7-11 (11-11 summer); 12-4, 7.30-10.30 (12-10.30 summer) Sun
High Force Teesdale Bitter, Forest XB, Cauldron Snout Ⓗ
Small, unpretentious old hotel – one of the highest in England, next to the spectacular falls. The public bar has two linked rooms serving beers from the hotel's own brewery, housed in a former stable.

🍽 🛏 ◖ 🍺 🌲 P

FRAMWELLGATE MOOR

Tap & Spile

27 Front Street (off A167 by-pass, 1 1/2 miles from Durham centre)
☎ (0191) 386 5451
11.30-3 , 6 (5 Fri)-11; 11-11 Sat; 12-3, 7-10.30 Sun
Hambleton Nightmare; Tap & Spile Premium; guest beers Ⓗ
Basic pub: a front bar and a rear no-smoking bar, plus a family room and a games room. Guest beers are from local micros or the Beer Seller list. Well worth a visit.

Q 🍲 ◖ 🚹 🌲 ◔ 🍴

GREAT LUMLEY

Old England

Front Street (near the Co-op)
☎ (0191) 388 5257
11-11; 12-10.30 Sun
Beer range varies Ⓗ
Busy bar, popular with younger drinkers. The lounge is more comfortable, attracting older clientele and diners preferring not to use the no-smoking dining room. Lunches served Fri-Sun; eve meals Mon-Sat. Usually three ales on tap.

Q ◖ 🍺 🌲 P

GRETA BRIDGE

Morritt Arms Hotel

Signed off A66
☎ (01833) 627232
11-11 (Sir Walter Scott bar opens 8); 12-10.30 (8-10.30 Scott bar) Sun
Black Sheep Best Bitter; Castle Eden Conciliation Ale; Taylor Landlord; Tetley Bitter Ⓗ
Fine country house hotel boasting strong connections with Dickens and Walter Scott. A comfortable, welcoming atmosphere pervades throughout. The hotel bar attracts everyone, including walkers; the detached Walter Scott bar is simpler, and is used mainly by locals, serving a reduced beer range.

🏛 Q 🍽 🛏 ◖ 🍺 🌲 P

HARTBURN

Masham Hotel

87 Hartburn Village
☎ (01642) 580414
11-11; 12-3, 7-10.30 Sun
Draught Bass; Black Sheep Special; Castle Eden Ale Ⓗ
Small, historic pub in a terrace of old houses within the village conservation area. Its layout clearly shows its domestic origins. A warm welcome is assured from the landlord and locals alike to its several drinking areas.

Q 🍽 🍺 🌲 P 🍴

HARTLEPOOL

Causeway

Vicarage Gardens, Stranton (off A689, behind church)
☎ (01429) 273954
11-11; 11-10.30 Sun
Banks's Bitter; Camerons Bitter, Strongarm; Marston's Pedigree Ⓗ
Large bar and two snugs, one dedicated to non-smokers, lie behind an impressive Victorian red brick facade. One of three Camerons' pubs around the brewery, this one is the tap. It hosts acoustic music Tue eves; folk club Sun eve. Lunches served Mon-Sat.

Q ◖ 🍺 🍴 🍴 🍺

Knights

25-27 Church Square
☎ (01429) 270274
11-3, 5-11; 11-11 Sat; 3-10.30 Sun
Castle Eden Nimmos XXXX; Black Sheep Best Bitter; guest beers Ⓗ
Opened in 1999, converted from a grocer's shop; plain but comfortable furniture and bare wood floors give a mock-Victorian ambience. Photographs of life at Castle Eden Brewery in both Nimmo's and Whitbread's days adorn the walls.

🍽 ◖ ≈

Try also: **Blacksmiths Arms**, Stranton (Camerons); **Jacksons Arms**, Tower St (Free)

HURWORTH PLACE

Station

8 Hurworth Road (off A167)
☎ (01325) 720552
11-3, 5.30-11; 11-11 Sat; 12-10.30 Sun
John Smith's Bitter, Magnet Ⓗ
Friendly local displaying an idiosyncratic collection of bric-à-brac. It comprises two linked main rooms and a small pool room. Q 🌲 P

LOW WILLINGTON

Black Horse Inn

42 Low Willington (Durham Road)
☎ (01388) 746340
12-3 (not Tue) 7-11; 12-11 Sat; 12-10.30 Sun
John Smith's Bitter; guest beers Ⓗ
Friendly pub on the edge of town, offering a warm welcome in its two bars and dining area which serves home-cooked food. Local CAMRA *Pub of the Year* 2000.

🍲 🍽 ◖ 🍺 🌲 P 🍺

MIDDLESTONE VILLAGE

Ship Inn

Low Row
☎ (01388) 810904
6-11; 12-4, 7-11 Sat; 12-4, 7-10.30 Sun

Castle Eden Nimmos XXXX; guest beers ⓗ
Closed by Vaux and re-opened after a campaign by local members, this is now a free house providing cask beers from local breweries. One of the few pubs with a large function room for hire. Booking for Sun lunch is advisable.
🏚 ☕ ◑ ♣ P

NO PLACE
Beamish Mary Inn
Front Street (600 yds from A693, 1 mile from Beamish Museum)
☎ (0191) 370 0237
12-3, 6-11; 12-11 Fri & Sat; 12-10.30 Sun
Black Sheep Best Bitter; Courage Directors; Theakston Old Peculier; guest beers ⓗ
The inn's design and furnishings must be seen to be appreciated. This pub enjoys a strong local following and it is well worth travelling to visit, especially during February, for its annual beer festival. A lively pub, it is a good live music venue and offers a good range of guest ales, plus a house beer from Big Lamp.
🏚 🍽 ⚓ ⓓ ⓗ & ♣ P 🏟

NORTH BITCHBURN
Famous Red Lion
North Bitchburn Terrace
☎ (01388) 763561
12-3, 7-11; 12-3, 7-10.30 Sun
Black Sheep Special; Greene King Abbot; Marston's Pedigree; guest beers ⓗ
Friendly, traditional village pub, popular for its excellent home-cooked meals and wide range of guest beers, including Mane Brew, brewed for the pub by Hambleton.
🏚 Q ☕ ◑ ⓓ 🛏 P 🏟

NORTON
Unicorn
147 High Street
☎ (01642) 643364
12-3, 5.30-11; 11-11 Sat; 12-4, 7-10.30 Sun
John Smith's Magnet ⓗ
Atmospheric old pub opposite the village duck pond. Warm and friendly, it features several small rooms off a central corridor. Locally known as 'Nellies' after an ex-landlady, well worth finding.
Q 🍽 ◑ ⓓ & ♣

PITY ME
Lambton Hounds
62 Front Street (off A167)
☎ (0191) 386 4742

11-11; 12-10.30 Sun
Beer range varies ⓗ
250-year-old coaching inn, recently refurbished. This ex-Vaux pub usually has three beers available, but generally these are from the national or bigger regional breweries. An area is set aside for diners.
Q 🍽 ⚓ ◑ ⓓ ⓗ & ♣ P

PRESTON-LE-SKERNE
Blacksmith's Arms
Ricknall Lane (1 mile E of A167, off Gt. Stainton road)
☎ (01325) 314873
12-3, 6.30-11 (12-11 summer); 12 (6.30 winter)-10.30 Sun
Beer range varies ⓗ
Locally known as the 'Hammers', this family-run free house offers home-cooked meals and supports local micro-breweries through its choice of four guest ales. The large garden houses a children's play area. A plant nursery and helicopter landing pad are more unusual amenities.
Q 🍽 ◑ ⓓ ⓗ ♣ P

ROMALDKIRK
Kirk Inn
The Green
☎ (01833) 650260
12-2.30 (not Mon-Wed), 6-11; 12-3, 7-10.30 Sun
Black Sheep Best Bitter; Boddingtons Bitter; Castle Eden Ale; guest beers ⓗ
Welcoming, family-run pub overlooking the handsome village green. The cosy single room doubles as the village post office before lunchtime, but it is almost impossible to detect this at other times. Fine home-cooked food appears from the labyrinthine kitchen area; lunches served Fri-Sun. Eve meals Mon and Wed-Sat.
🏚 Q ☕ ◑ ♣ P

ST. JOHNS CHAPEL
Blue Bell Inn
12 Hood Street (A689)
☎ (01388) 537256
5 (11 Sat)-11; 12-3, 6.30-10.30 Sun
Tetley Bitter ⓗ
Village local circa 1840, located in a high Pennines village, surrounded by excellent walking country, and just a few miles from Kilhope Lead Mining Centre.
▲ ⌂

SHINCLIFFE
Rose Tree
on A177, 1½ miles from Durham City centre
☎ (0191) 386 8512
11-3, 7-11; 11-11 Sat; 12-4, 7-10.30 Sun

Marston's Pedigree; Morland Old Speckled Hen; Wells Bombardier ⓗ
Friendly ex-Vaux pub beside the River Wear where an excellent menu is complemented by daily specials.
Q ☕ ◑ ⓓ ⓗ & P 🏟

Seven Stars
On A177, 1¾ miles S of Durham
☎ (0191) 384 8454
12-2.30, 6.30-11; 12-3, 7-10.30 Sun
Beer range varies ⓗ
This ex-Vaux pub has retained its olde-worlde feeling, although there is now an emphasis on food.
Q ☕ ⚓ ◑ ⓓ ⓗ &

STANHOPE
Queens Head
89 Front Street (A689)
☎ (01388) 528160
12-11 (may vary winter); 12-3.30, 7-10.30 Sun
McEwan 80/-; Theakston Best Bitter; guest beer ⓗ
Striking, three-storey, early 19th-century pub at the eastern end of this popular Dales town. Attracting locals and visitors alike, it can be very busy summer weekends. A handy base for fell walkers and cyclists, there is a bus stop on the doorstep. The beer range may be restricted in winter.
⚓ ◑ ⓓ ⓗ ▲ ♣

Try also: **Grey Bull**, West End (Free)

STOCKTON-ON-TEES
Fitzgeralds
9-10 High Street
☎ (01642) 678220
11.30-3 (3.30 Fri, 4 Sat), 6.30-11; (closed lunch) 7-10.30 Sun
Draught Bass; Taylor Landlord; guest beers ⓗ
The wonderful stone façade with its granite pillars looks too grand for a pub. Once a private club, the interior is split level and displays typical Fitzgerald & Co. touches. Regular beer festivals held, and up to three guest ales stocked.
◑ ⇌ ♣

Senators
Bishopton Road West (by Whitehouse Farm shopping centre on ring road)
☎ (01642) 672060
11-3, 6-11; 11-11 Fri & Sat; 12-10.30 Sun
Draught Bass; Marston's Pedigree; guest beers (occasional) ⓗ
Built as part of a shopping complex, the pub has a 1960s feel, but is nonetheless friendly and welcoming. The Vaux ales have sadly gone,

CAMRA National Pub Inventory: Red Lion, Snargate, Kent

but the commitment to real ale lives on (the guests come from the Tapster's Choice range). The single split-level bar has a raised dining area (no eve meals Tue or Sun; booking advised for Sun lunch). ❀ ◖ ▶ P

Sun Inn

Knowles Street
(off High St)
☎ (01642) 623921
11-11; 12-10.30 Sun
Draught Bass Ⓗ
Classic town-centre pub with an unswerving commitment to real ale, clocking up the largest sales of Bass in the UK – no surprise to those who've sampled it. A legend; if you can only visit one pub in town, make it this one. Folk club Mon.
⊟ ⇌

Thomas Sheraton

4 Bridge Road
☎ (01642) 606134
11-11; 12-10.30 Sun
Boddingtons Bitter; Courage Directors; Theakston Best Bitter; Worthington Bitter; guest beer Ⓗ
Typical Wetherspoon's treatment of a rather nice old building, in this case the former law courts. The long single bar has the usual alcoves for a little privacy or a smoke-free atmosphere. The balcony and roof garden are interesting touches. Busy at weekends.
Q ❀ ◖ ▶ & ⊁

SUMMERHOUSE

Raby Hunt

On B6279
☎ (01325) 374604
11.30-3, 6.30-11; 12-3, 7-10.30 Sun
Marston's Bitter, Pedigree; guest beer (occasional) Ⓗ
Excellent, welcoming, small stone-built free house in a pretty whitewashed hamlet, comprising a homely lounge and a cosy two-part locals' bar. Good home-cooked lunches are served (not Sun), but unusually for a country pub, no meals are served eves, just an emphasis on good beer.
🏚 Q ❀ ◖ ⊟ ♣ P

THORPE THEWLES

Hamilton Russell Arms

Bank Terrace
☎ (01740) 630757
12-11; 12-10.30 Sun;
Courage Directors; guest beers Ⓗ
Historic pub overlooking the picturesque village green. Refurbished in 1998 to provide an open-plan interior with real fires assuring a warm welcome for all. Guest beers are from north-eastern micro-breweries whenever possible. Wheelchair WC.
🏚 ❀ ◖ ▶ & ♣ P ⊁

WOLSINGHAM

Mill Race Hotel

West End (A689)
☎ (01388) 526551
11-11; 12-10.30 Sun
McEwan 80/-; guest beers Ⓗ
Friendly local on the edge of the village, enjoying a high reputation for fine food and accommodation. Conveniently located for walks of all grades, including the long distance Wear Valley Way; also good cycle routes. A recreation ground and bowling green are nearby.
🏚 Q ⭗ ❀ 🏚 ◖ ▶ ⊟ & 🅰 ♣ P

Try also: Bay Horse, Upper Town (Free)

WOLVISTON

Ship Inn

50 High Street
☎ (01740) 644420
12-3, 5-11; 12-3, 7-10.30 Sun
Black Sheep Best Bitter; guest beer Ⓗ
Smartly refurbished village inn with a strong accent on food. Built on the site of an earlier pub whose coaching stables can be seen at the rear. ❀ ◖ ▶ ♣ P ⊁

INDEPENDENT BREWERIES

Camerons: Hartlepool
Castle Eden: Castle Eden
Darwin: Crook
Derwent Rose: Consett
Durham: Bowburn
High Force: Forest-in-Teesdale
Trimdon: Trimdon Grange

Service with a spile
Jim Fox on how beer reaches your glass

After skilful work by pub cellar staff, real ale that has reached its peak of condition must be transported from the cask where it has continued to mature to the glass of the customer. There are several ways of achieving this.

Air Pressure
This version of beer dispense only applies to Scotland. Originally air pressure was produced by water engines but they have been replaced mainly by handpumps, but a few outlets use electric compressors to drive the beer to tall founts on the bar counter.

Gravity
The simplest and often easiest method to serve real ale is just to insert a tap in the cask and let the beer flow directly into the glass. Often the cask is kept on the bar counter or just behind it — the only problem here is keeping the beer at a reasonable temperature. There are still a few pubs that keep their gravity-dispensed beer in the cellar.

Handpump
Most real ale is dispensed using a beer engine that is connected to the familiar bar-top handpump or handpull. The beer engine is a simple suction pump that raises beer from cellar to bar counter via the tap connected to the cask as the pump handle is pulled. Sometimes, when the pub cellar is exceptionally deep or some distance from the bar, the beer has to travel some distance and the pump requires assistance. This is achieved either by an electric pump in the line between cellar and bar, or by the use of a pump

that is powered by cellar gasses (carbon dioxide and/or nitrogen). Although powered by it, no gas comes into contact with the beer.

Electric Pumps
Similar to handpumps but with electricity doing the work rather than the bar staff. Only a few electric pumps are found these days. Some resemble keg beer dispensers: if in doubt, ask.

METHODS NOT APPROVED BY CAMRA
Blanket and Top Pressure
A cylinder of gas — normally carbon dioxide and sometimes a mixture of carbon dioxide and nitrogen — is connected to the cask to prevent any air entering it as the beer is pulled off. This can lead to the beer not reaching its full flavour. Blanket pressure is the term used when only a light pressure of gas is used. Top pressure involving a higher pressure is used to force the beer from cellar to glass. It can result in too much carbon dioxide dissolving in the beer and giving it some of the characteristics of keg beer.

Cask Breather
A refinement of the blanket pressure system, the breather or demand valve admits a volume of gas (carbon dioxide and/or nitrogen) to replace the beer that is drawn off. It prevents oxidation and arguably some beers reaching full maturity. It does little to prevent beer losing condition and becoming flat unless used with carbon dioxide.

WHAT IS REAL ALE
Real ale is also known in the trade as cask-conditioned ale or beer. In the brewery the beer is neither filtered nor pasteurised. It still contains sufficient yeast and sugars for it to continue to ferment and mature in the cask. Once it has reached the pub cellar, it has to be laid down for maturation to continue and for the yeast to settle to the bottom of the cask. Some real ale also has extra hops added as the casks are filled — a process known as dry-hopping — giving the beer extra flavour and aroma. It is best served at cellar temperature, which is around the mid-50s Fahrenheit (12-13 C), although some stronger ales can benefit from being served a little warmer. In the pub cellar, cask beer has to be nurtured to maturity and condition. Each cask has two holes, in one of which the tap is inserted, and the other allows any extra gasses produced by secondary fermentation to be released, but cellar staff must ensure that sufficient condition is maintained so that the beer is not served flat. Condition is maintained

by using wooden pegs called spiles in the second hole to control the level of carbon dioxide in the beer. As real ale is a living product it needs care and once the cask is opened it has a limited shelf-life. It has to be consumed within a few days otherwise it will become flat, and cardboard and vinegary flavours will develop as the beer reacts with oxygen in the air.

REAL ALE IN A BOTTLE
Also known as bottle-conditioned ale, it contains sufficient yeast and sugars to allow fermentation and maturation in the bottle, unlike most bottled beers that are filtered and pasteurised. As the beer contains a sediment of yeast it has to be allowed to settle and then poured carefully to give a glass of clear beer.

Jim Fox chairs CAMRA's Technical Committee.

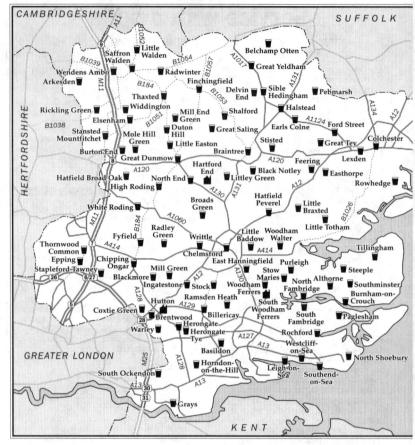

AINGERS GREEN

Royal Fusilier

Aingers Green Road (1 mile S of Gt. Bentley Green)
OS119204
☎ (01206) 250001
11-2.30 (3.30 Sat), 5.30-11; 12-4, 7-10.30 Sun
Greene King IPA; guest beers H
Rambling village local with distinct areas for games and conversation. The landlord, who has been associated with the pub for 45 years, always has a tale to tell. MG Classic Car club meets here Mon.
🏚️ 🕷️ ♣ P

ALTHORNE

Huntsman & Hounds

Green Lane (off B1018)
OS906004
☎ (01621) 740387
12-3, 5-11; 12-11 Sat; 12-10.30 Sun
Greene King IPA, Abbot; guest beer H
Cosy thatched pub with an attractive garden.
🏚️ Q 🕷️ ◑ ♿ ♣ ▲ 👜 P

ARKESDEN

Axe & Compasses

Wicken Road (opp. PO, 2 miles N of B1038) OS483344
☎ (01799) 550272
12-2.30, 6-11; 12-2.30, 7-10.30 Sun
Greene King IPA, Abbot H
Partly thatched, 17th-century local serving award-winning food. Enjoy a very friendly atmosphere in a beautiful setting. 🏚️ Q 🕷️ ◑ 🍴 ♣ P

BASILDON

Moon on the Square

1-15 Market Square (near A176/A1321)
☎ (01268) 520360
10-11; 12-10.30 Sun
Boddingtons Bitter; Courage Directors; Shepherd Neame Spitfire; Theakston Best Bitter; guest beers H
Welcoming, attractive Wetherspoon's pub which was once a bakery. Very busy at lunchtime on market days.
Q ◑ ♿ ⇌ ✂️ ▣

BELCHAMP OTTEN

Red Lion

Fowes Lane (6 miles W of Sudbury) OS798415
☎ (01787) 277537
12-3 (not winter weekdays), 7-11; 12-3, 7-10.30 Sun
Greene King IPA; guest beer H
Friendly village local, popular with walkers and hikers, free from music or machines.
🏚️ Q 🕷️ ◑ ▲ ♣ P ✂️

BILLERICAY

Coach & Horses

36 Chapel Street (near B1007)
☎ (01277) 622873
10-11; 12-3.30, 7-10.30 Sun
Greene King IPA, Abbot; Shepherd Neame Master Brew Bitter; guest beers H
Excellent friendly, one-bar Grays local, built on the Crown Brewery tap site in 1935. Look out for the elephants, beer jugs and themed paintings. No food Sun. 🕷️ ◑ ⇌ ♣ P

BLACKMORE

Leather Bottle Inn

Horse Fayre Green
☎ (01277) 821891
11-11; 12-10.30 Sun

Essex

Manningtree A120 Harwich
Little Little Oakley
Bentley Tendring
A133
Aingers Green
Wivenhoe
Brightlingsea Great Walton-on-
Clacton the-Naze
St Osyth

0 Miles 10
0 Kilometres 16

Adnams Bitter; Ridleys IPA; guest beers H
Landlord hosts regular themed mini-beer festivals and live music. A large beer garden houses children's toys and miniature animals. The pub reputedly is home to three ghosts. ❀ ◖▸♣ ⇨ P

BLACK NOTLEY
Vine Inn
105 The Street
☎ (01376) 324269
12-2, 6-11; 12-2.30, 7-11 Sat; 12-4, 7-10.30 Sun
Beer range varies H
Two-roomed village pub with a restaurant area at the far end of the long main room and a pool table in the smaller room. Good food features home-made pies and Essex Huffers as specialities. Usually four or five beers come from interesting breweries, plus a real cider in summer. ❀ ◖▸♣ ⇨ P

BRAINTREE
King William IV
114 London Road

(B1053/A120 jct)
☎ (01376) 330088
12-3, 6-11; 12-11 Sat; 12-3, 7-10.30 Sun
Ridleys IPA, ESX H
Cosy, friendly, two-room local, recently altered by the addition of an inside gents! Note the award-winning floral displays – the landlord sells hanging baskets. Lunchtime snacks available. ⚌ Q ❀ ⊞ ♣ P

BRENTWOOD
Swan (Hogshead)
123 High Street (A1023)
☎ (01277) 211848
11-11; 12-10.30 Sun
Boddingtons Bitter; Fuller's London Pride; Mighty Oak Burntwood; Wadworth 6X; Young's Special; H **guest beers** H/G
15th-century pub, that despite refurbishment, retains much of its wood panelling. It has a small garden bar patio at the rear. Up to 12 cask beers are stocked including four on gravity dispense. ⚌ Q ❀ ◖⇌

BRIGHTLINGSEA
Railway Tavern
58 Station Road (near B1029)
☎ (01206) 302581
5 (3 Fri; 12 Sat)-11; 12-10.30 Sun
Railway Tavern Crab & Winkle, Bladderwrack; guest beers H
Cracking local boozer in the centre of the community. Tendring's first micro-brewery is now brewing for beer festivals as well as the locals; the availability of the beers is irregular. A cider festival is held in May. ⚌ Q ⛵ ⊞ ▲ ♣ ⇨ P

BROADS GREEN
Walnut Tree
1 mile W of B1008 OS694125
☎ (01245) 360222
11.30-2.30, 6-11; 12-2.30, 7-10.30 Sun
Ridleys IPA G
Three-bar village pub with superb unspoilt public bar, snug and a more recent saloon. Ridleys seasonal beers are occasionally sold in this past local CAMRA *Pub of the Year*. ⚌ Q ❀ ◖▸⊞ ♣ P

BURNHAM ON CROUCH
Ship Inn
52 High Street (B1010)
☎ (01621) 785057
11-11; 12-10.30 Sun
Adnams Bitter, Broadside, seasonal beers H
Traditional local restored by Adnams at the centre of an attractive riverside town. An

excellent spot for a weekend break; yachting is popular here. The beer turnover of 420 barrels a year speaks for itself. ⚌ ◖▸ & P ⊞

BURTON END
Ash
Take airport road from M11 jct 8, then follow signs OS532237
☎ (01279) 814841
11-11; 12-10.30 Sun
Greene King IPA, Abbot, guest beer H
15th-century thatched pub with a rural atmosphere in a tiny hamlet near Stansted Airport. It has been extended to provide a large dining room. ⚌ ❀ ◖▸ P

CHELMSFORD
Cricketer's Inn
143 Moulsham Street
☎ (01245) 261157
11-11; 12-10.30 Sun
Greene King IPA, Abbot; Shepherd Neame Spitfire or guest beer H
Two-room local at the quieter end of Moulsham Street. A comfortable, quiet lounge and a noisier public bar where pool is played. The beer is competitively priced. Q ❀ ◖▸♣ ♣

Endeavour
351 Springfield Road (B1137)
☎ (01245) 257717
11-11; 12-2.30, 7-10.30 Sun
Greene King XX Mild, IPA; Shepherd Neame Masterbrew Bitter, Spitfire; guest beers H
Friendly, three-roomed local situated on an island at a road junction and featuring an unusual two-sided pub sign. It is the only regular outlet in the area for GK Mild and serves good home-cooked food (not served Sun). The charity box awaits mobile phone users. ⚌ Q ◖▸⊞ ♣ ✄

Original Plough
28 Duke Street (by station)
☎ (01245) 250145
11-11; 12-10.30 Sun
Adnams Bitter; Tetley Bitter; guest beers H
Open-plan, town-centre pub boasting lots of bare boards and beams, popular with all, from young drinkers to real ale enthusiasts. It can be noisy Fri and Sat eves, with occasional live music. Eve meals served Mon-Thu. ❀ ◖▸⇌ ♣ P

Queen's Head
30 Lower Anchor Street (near B1007)
☎ (01245) 265181

11-3, 5-11; 11-11 Fri & Sat; 12-10.30 Sun

Crouch Vale Best Bitter; guest beers H
Back-street local, recently refurbished by new owners Crouch Vale. Four guest beers always include a dark beer; cider in summer. Spot the difference between the two sides of the pub sign. Local CAMRA *Pub of the Year* 2000.
🏠Q✥🍴◖🏃♣⌒P

CHIPPING ONGAR
Cock Tavern
218 High Street
☎ (01277) 362615
11-3, 5.30-11; 11-11 Sat; 12-3.30, 7-10.30 Sun

Greene King IPA, Abbot; guest beers H
Basic, no-frills pub, popular with the locals, where the landlord is keen to exercise his options for a range of guest beers, as a Gray's tenant. 🏠◖▶⊖♣🏃 (Ongar, preserved line) P

COLCHESTER
Bricklayers
27 Bergholt Road
☎ (01206) 852008
11-3, 5.30-11; 11-11 Sat; 12-3, 7-10.30 Sun

Adnams Bitter, Broadside; Everards Tiger; Fuller's London Pride; guest beers H
Adnams flagship outlet: a large two-bar pub close to the station. Top quality food always available, it is especially popular for Sun lunches. The two guest beers are Adnams seasonal brews when available.
✥◖🍴🏃 (North) ♣P🎱

Dragoon
82 Butt Road (opp. police station, on B1026)
☎ (01206) 573464
5-11, 11.30-3, 4.45-11 Fri; 11.30-11 Sat; 12-10.30 Sun

Adnams Bitter, Broadside, seasonal beers H
Single bar pub, complete with its own ghost, comprising a lounge area at one end and public bar with large Sky TV screen at the other. A favourite with football fans, food is served on home football days only.
✥🏃 (Town)

Hospital Arms
123-125 Crouch Street (opp. hospital, near A1124)
☎ (01206) 573572
11-2.30, 5-11; 11-11 Sat; 12-3, 7-10.30 Sun

Adnams Bitter, Broadside, seasonal beers; guest beers H
Historic pub, full of hidden nooks where a very quiet, relaxed atmosphere is broken

by the background music. It livens up at weekends, when it can be hard work getting to the bar.
🏠✥◖

Kings Arms (Hogshead)
61-63 Crouch Street
☎ (01206) 572886
11-11; 12-10.30 Sun

Adnams Bitter; Boddingtons Bitter; Flowers Original; Mighty Oak Burntwood; Wadworth 6X; H **guest beers** H/G
Busy, open-plan pub offering a constantly changing range of guest beers. Popular with all ages, it hosts live music Thu eves, a quiz night Sun and fields a cricket team; Bank Hol beer festivals held. A standard Hogshead menu is supplemented by daily specials, including authentic Thai curries.
🏠✥◖🏃 (Town) P

Odd One Out
28 Mersea Road (B1025)
☎ (01206) 578140
4.30 (11.30 Fri & Sat)-11; 12-10.30 Sun

Archers Best Bitter; guest beers H
Basic, friendly, drinking pub where the beer is very reasonably priced. Up to four guest beers usually include a mild or porter; it also stocks a large selection of single malts. Local CAMRA *Pub of the Year* 1999.
🏠✥🍴🏃 (Town) ⌒🍴

Rose & Crown Hotel
51 East Street (A137, at rail crossing)
☎ (01206) 866677
10-2.30, 6-11; 12-3, 7-10.30 Sun

Adnams Broadside; Tetley Bitter H
This 17th-century bar boasts heavy beams, ironwork and a central fireplace. Popular with both locals and hotel guests, it is well respected for good food (not served Sun eve) and accommodation. A regular house beer is provided by a local brewer. Fitted sparklers are gladly removed on request.
🏠✥🛏◖▶P

Stockwell Arms
18 West Stockwell Street
☎ (01206) 575560
10.30-11; 10.30-4, 6.30-11 Sat; 12-4, 7-10.30 Sun

Courage Best Bitter, Directors; Greene King IPA; Nethergate Suffolk County; Wells Bombardier H
Over 600 years old this beamed local stands in the historic Dutch quarter area of Colchester. Excellent floral decorations have led to a *Colchester in Bloom* award. Good value snacks and light meals available.
✥◖♣

Try also: **British Grenadier**, Military Rd (Adnams); **Robin Hood**, Osborne St (Free)

COXTIE GREEN
White Horse
173 Coxtie Green Road (1 mile W of A128, between Brentwood and Ongar)
☎ (01277) 372410
11.30-11; 12-10.30 Sun

Adnams Bitter; Fuller's London Pride; Ridleys Rumpus; guest beers H
CAMRA's local *Pub of the Year* 2000, this excellent two-bar hostelry has a comfortable saloon and a more basic public. The extensive garden has children's apparatus, plus an outside bar in summer. It hosts an annual beer festival (July) and a mini-fest at Easter. No food Sun; eve meals served Thu-Sat.
Q✥◖▶🍴✥♣P

DELVIN END
Bottle Hall
Toppesfield Road (from Sible Hedingham, head for Toppesfield, 2 miles) OS756353
☎ (01787) 462405
5-11; 12-10.30 Sun

Greene King IPA; guest beers H/G
This very old, former blacksmith's gets its name from two windows which were blocked up with bottles to avoid window tax. A warm welcome is assured. Good food comes in generous portions (served all day Sun).
🏠Q✥▶♣P

DUTON HILL
Three Horseshoes
Off B184, Thaxted Road OS606268
☎ (01371) 870681
12-2.30, 6-11; 12-3, 7-10.30 Sun

Adnams Bitter; Ridleys IPA; guest beer H
Cosy village local where families are welcome. Open air theatre is staged on the terrace one weekend in July. A large wild pond is home to frogs and newts. Meals served Fri-Tue.
🏠Q✥◖🍴♣P

EARLS COLNE
Bird in Hand
Coggeshall Road (B1024 at America Road jct)
☎ (01787) 222557
12-2, 6-11; 12-2, 7-10.30 Sun

Ridleys IPA H
Friendly, two-bar country pub, near a former US air base, where wartime pictures are featured. A hallway, with a rare off-sales hatch, separates the bars. Guest

beers are supplied by Ridleys.
🏚 Q ⊛ ◖▮ 🛏 ♣ P

EAST HANNINGFIELD

Windmill Tavern
The Tye OS771012
☎ (01245) 400315
11-11; 12-10.30 Sun
Boddingtons Bitter; Crouch Vale Best Bitter; Marston's Pedigree; guest beer Ⓗ
Comfortable, popular free house facing the village green and serving reasonably priced home-made food. The guest beer usually changes three or four times weekly. The restaurant opens Thu-Sat eves and Sun lunch.
🏚 Q ⊛ ◖▮ ♣ P

EASTHORPE

House Without a Name
Easthorpe Road (1¹/₂ miles off A12)
☎ (01206) 213070
11.30-3, 6-11; 12-11 Sat; 12-10.30 Sun
Greene King IPA; guest beers Ⓗ
A warm welcome is assured at this 16th-century beamed pub which has a large open fire at its heart. Guest beers change regularly; many come from micro-breweries. Home-cooked food is lovingly prepared by qualified chefs. Family parties and business lunches are a speciality.
🏚 ⊛ ◖▮ ♣ P

ELSENHAM

Crown
High Street (B1051)
☎ (01279) 812827
11-2.30, 6-11; 12-2.30, 7-10.30 Sun
Beer range varies Ⓗ
Deservedly popular, this friendly, village pub boasts a pargetted exterior, a wealth of beams, and an inglenook. It enjoys a reputation for good food (not served Sun eve).
🏚 ⊛ ◖▮ 🛏 ♣ P

EPPING

Forest Gate
111 Bell Common (off B1393, Ivy Chimneys Road)
OS451011
☎ (01992) 572312
10-3, 5.30-11; 12-3, 7-10.30 Sun
Adnams Bitter, Ⓗ **Broadside;** Ⓖ **Ridleys IPA;** Ⓗ **Woodforde's Wherry** Ⓖ
On the edge of Epping Forest, this single-bar, traditional, 17th-century pub has been run by the same family for many years. The beers are sourced from local independents. A renowned turkey broth is sold at lunchtime.
🏚 Q ⊛ ◖ ☙ P

FEERING

Sun Inn
3 Feering Hill (B1024)
☎ (01376) 570442
11-3, 6-11; 12-3, 6-10.30 Sun
Beer range varies Ⓗ
Real thoroughbred free house, rich with 16th-century charm and carved beams. It stocks six ales, up to 20 a week and hosts beer festivals Easter and Aug Bank Holiday. It serves real food – and plenty of it. There is a lovely garden for balmy summer nights and two blazing log fires in winter.
🏚 Q ⊛ ◖▮ ≈ (Kelvedon) ♣ ☙ P

FINCHINGFIELD

Red Lion
6 Church Hill (B1053)
☎ (01371) 810400
11.30-11; 12-10.30 Sun
Ridleys IPA, seasonal beers Ⓗ
Friendly pub, in one of the most picturesque villages in Essex, attracting both locals and visitors. Food is served in the bar and the congenial restaurant.
🏚 ⊛ ◖ ☙ ▮ ♠ ♣ P

FORD STREET (ALDHAM)

Coopers Arms
Ford Street (A1124, 3 miles W of Colchester)
☎ (01206) 241177
12-3, 7-11; 12-3, 7-10.30 Sun
Adnams Bitter; Greene King IPA; Woodforde's Wherry; Ⓗ **guest beers** Ⓗ/Ⓖ
The history of this 16th-century pub is documented on its wall, and goes back to the days when it was known as the Kings Arms. Today it is a single bar pub with comfortable leather seating and a restaurant serving 'proper food' with a good vegetarian menu.
Q ⊛ ◖▮ ♣ P

FYFIELD

Queen's Head
Queen Street (off B184)
☎ (01277) 899231
11-3, 6-11; 11-11 Sat; 12-3, 7-10.30 Sun
Adnams Bitter, Broadside; Taylor Landlord; guest beers Ⓗ
Genuine free house, the focal point of the village, it is popular with all ages. Three constantly changing guest beers come from independents. The garden adjoins the infant River Roding. No food Sat eve.
🏚 ⊛ ◖▮ P

GRAYS

Grays Athletic FC

Bridge Road
☎ (01375) 377753
5 (3 Thu; 12 Fri & Sat)-11; 12-3, 7-10.30 Sun
Greene King IPA; guest beers Ⓗ
The social club of Grays Athletic Football Club admits card-carrying CAMRA members, or bearers of this *Guide*. The bar overlooks an indoor five-a-side pitch. TV sports are shown on a large screen. Uusually two guest beers on tap. Limited parking.
≈ ♣ P

Theobald Arms
141 Argent Street
☎ (01375) 372253
10.30-3, 5-11; 10.30-11 Fri & Sat; 12-10.30 Sun
Courage Best Bitter; guest beers Ⓗ
Traditional, family-run, two-bar pub near the revitalised riverside area. Note the unusual round pool table in the public bar. It usually has three guest beers which change regularly. Very good value food served weekdays.
⊛ ◖▮ ▤ ≈ ♣ P

GREAT CLACTON

Plough
1 North Road (near B1032)
☎ (01255) 429998
11-11; 12-10.30 Sun
Flowers Original; Greene King IPA, Abbot; guest beers Ⓗ
Historic two-bar pub at the centre of the village. The small public bar has changed little with time and caters for mature customers. The other bar has been expanded to make room for weekend music. The landlord is a key member of *Gt Clacton in Bloom*. 🏚 ⊛ ♣

Try also: **Queens Head**, St Johns Rd (Pubmaster)

GREAT DUNMOW

Cricketers
22 Beaumont Hill (B184, Thaxted road)
☎ (01371) 873359
11-11; 12-10.30 Sun
Ridleys IPA, seasonal beers Ⓗ
Lively Victorian pub with two bars, retaining its original baker's oven from when the pub was a bakery and ale house. Traditional pub food is served all day as well as coffee and teas. Families welcome.
⊛ ◖▮ 🛏 ♿ ♣ P

Kings Head
30 North Street
☎ (01371) 872052
12-3 (not Mon & Tue), 5.30-11; 12-11 Sat; 12-10.30 Sun
Flowers IPA; Castle Eden Ale; guest beer Ⓗ

16th-century beamed pub facing Doctors Pond where Lionel Lukin is reputed to have carried out the first experiments in self righting lifeboats. The oldest pub in Dunmow it stands next to the old maltings (listed). Eve meals served Tue-Sat.

🚶 🕭 ◐ ⊞ ♣ P

GREAT SALING
White Hart
The Street
☎ (01371) 850341
12-3, 5.30-11; 12-11 Sat; 12-10.30 Sun
Ridleys IPA, seasonal beers Ⓗ
Superb, 16th-century, beamed Tudor pub, featuring a raised timbered gallery. A speciality is the Essex 'Huffer' which the pub claims to have invented (a large roll with a choice of fillings). The restaurant is in a restored bakehouse at the rear.

🚶 Q 🕭 ◐ ⊞ P

GREAT TEY
Chequers
The Street (1¹/₂ miles N of A120)
☎ (01206) 210814
11.45-3, 6.30-11; 12-4, 7-10.30 Sun
Greene King XX Mild, IPA, Abbot; guest beers Ⓗ
16th-century pub, standing at the heart of the village, that has something for everyone: play pub games in the public bar, relax by the fire in the lounge or treat yourself to a meal in the restaurant. The garden has views of the church and features a pétanque piste. No eve meals Sun or winter Mon.

🚶 🕭 ◐ ⊞ ♣ P ⊞

GREAT YELDHAM
Waggon & Horses
High Street (A1017)
☎ (01787) 237936
11-11; 12-10.30 Sun
Greene King IPA, Abbot; guest beers Ⓗ
This village pub enjoys strong local support and offers a friendly welcome. It boasts a wider, more interesting range of food than most pubs, but at lower prices than many. Other local beers are sometimes available.

🕿 🕭 ⊨ ◐ P

White Hart
Poole Street (A1017)
☎ (01787) 237250
11-3, 6-11; 12-3, 7-10.30 Sun
Adnams Bitter; Gibbs Mew Bishops Tipple; guest beers Ⓗ
500-year-old Tudor inn with genuine olde-worlde features.

set in picturesque gardens. Restaurant and bar food served.

🚶 Q 🕭 ◐ ♣ P

HALSTEAD
Dog Inn
37 Hedingham Road (A1124)
☎ (01787) 477774
12-3, 6-11; 12-4, 7-10.30 Sun
Adnams Bitter; guest beers Ⓗ
Friendly, 17th-century local, near the town centre offering reasonably priced en-suite accommodation and bar meals.

🚶 Q 🏃 🕭 ⊨ ◐ ♣ P

HARWICH
Hanover Inn
65 Church Street
☎ (01255) 502927
10.30-2, 6.30-11; 12-3, 7-10.30 Sun
Greene King IPA; Ridleys Witchfinder; Tolly Cobbold Mild, Old Strong Ⓗ
Now Harwich's premier pub, it is situated close to the church and the oldest house in town. Much of its success is due to its flourishing pool, crib and darts teams. Conference and meeting facilities along with accommodation are now available.

🚶 ⊨ ⇌ (Town) ♣ ⇦

Try also: Haywain, West St (Free)

HATFIELD BROAD OAK
Cock
High Street (B183)
☎ (01279) 718273
12-3, 6-11; 12-3, 7-10.30 Sun
Adnams Bitter; Fuller's London Pride; guest beers Ⓗ
Simple, bare-boarded village pub where the guest beers come from independent brewers. A good varied menu is served (no meals Sun eve).

Q 🕭 ◐ ⊞ ♣ P

HATFIELD PEVEREL
Wheatsheaf
Maldon Road (B1019)
☎ (01245) 380330
11-3, 5-11; 11-11 Sat; 12-10.30 Sun
Ridleys IPA, ESX, seasonal beers Ⓗ
Interesting village local bearing a white clapboard exterior and plenty of beams inside. Home-cooked food is served in a restaurant area, warmed by a large open fire. The garden features a well-stocked aviary.

🚶 Q 🕭 ◐ ⊞ ▲ ♣ P

HERONGATE
Green Man
11 Cricketers Lane (near A128)

☎ (01277) 810292
11-3 (4 Sat), 6-11 (11-11 summer Sat); 12-4, 7-10.30 (12-10.30 summer) Sun
Adnams Bitter; Ind Coope Burton Ale; Tetley Bitter; Young's Bitter; Ⓗ guest beers Ⓖ
A comfortable main bar area has several rooms set back. Guest beers vary and there are occasional festivals in the back room. Regular quizzes are held and games are available on request. There is a children's play area in the garden. Local CAMRA *Pub of the Year* 1999.

🚶 Q 🏃 🕭 ◐ ♣ ✄

HERONGATE TYE
Old Dog Inn
Billericay Road (1 mile E of A128) OS641910
☎ (01277) 810337
11-3, 6-11; 12-3, 7-10.30 Sun
Greene King Abbot; Ridleys IPA; Ⓗ guest beers Ⓗ/Ⓖ
Friendly, low-beamed, country pub, popular for its large selection of real ales and home-cooked food. Beers from independent and micro-breweries include Mauldons and Mighty Oak, many are served straight from the cask.

Q 🕭 ◐ ♣ ⇦ P

HIGH RODING
Black Lion
3 The Street (B184)
☎ (01371) 872847
11-11; 12-10.30 Sun
Ridleys Mild, Ⓖ IPA, ESX; Ⓗ guest beers Ⓗ/Ⓖ
Former coaching inn, dating back to the 14th century. The main bar is timber-framed and the smaller bar welcomes families. Guest beers are taken from Ridleys range. A dining area is available – try the fish.

🚶 🏃 🕭 ⊨ ◐ ⊞ ▲ ♣ P

HORNDON-ON-THE-HILL
Bell Inn
High Road (near B1007)
☎ (01375) 642463
11-2.30 (3 Sat), 6 (5.30 Sat)-11; 12-4, 7-10.30 Sun
Draught Bass; Ⓖ Greene King IPA; Ⓗ guest beers Ⓗ/Ⓖ
Popular, 15th-century coaching inn with an unusual hot cross bun collection on the beams. It has a highly acclaimed restaurant and stocks up to four regularly changing guest beers.

🚶 Q 🕭 🕭 ◐ ◐ P

INGATESTONE
Star Inn
High Street (B1002)
☎ (01277) 353618

11-2.30, 5.45-11; 12-3, 6.45-10.30 Sun

Greene King IPA, Abbot G

Cosy pub where the main bar is warmed by possibly the largest fire in Essex. A small room at the rear houses video games and darts. Live country or folk music is performed Sun and Mon.

🏚 Q 🌫 🕯 ≉ ♣ P

LEIGH-ON-SEA
Broker
213-217 Leigh Road
☎ (01702) 471932
11-3, 6 (5.30 Fri & Sat)-11; 12-4, 7-10.30 Sun

Shepherd Neame Spitfire; Tolly Cobbold Original; guest beers H

Friendly, family-run, free house, serving a varied range of beers and bar or restaurant meals (no food Wed-Sun eves). Children are welcome until 7.30 in a sectioned-off, no-smoking area of the bar.

🌫 🕯 ≉ (Chalkwell)

Elms
1060 London Road (A13)
☎ (01702) 474687
10-11; 12-10.30 Sun

Boddingtons Bitter; Courage Best Bitter; Directors; Shepherd Neame Spitfire; Theakston Best Bitter; guest beers H

Busy Wetherspoon's pub.

Q 🌫 🕯 P ⊬ ⊞

LEXDEN
Crown
235 Lexden Road (A1124 jct)
☎ (01206) 572071
11.30-3, 6-11; 11.30-11 Sat; 12-3, 7-10.30 Sun

Beer range varies H

Popular, split-level pub and restaurant serving good value food. Note the WW2 shell used as a doorstop. Handy for Colchester camping park and Lexden Park – always has three beers on tap, plus a cider in summer.

Q 🌫 🕯 ♣ ⊖ P

LITTLE BADDOW
Rodney
North Hill OS778080
☎ (01245) 222385
11.30-2.30 (3 Sat), 6-11; 12-10.30 Sun

Greene King IPA; guest beers H

Two-roomed local, originally built as a farmhouse circa 1650, it offers two interesting guest beers and good home-cooked food at reasonable prices.

🏚 Q 🌫 🕯 🍴 🛆 ♣ P

LITTLE BENTLEY
Bricklayer's Arms
Rectory Road (near A120)
☎ (01206) 250405
12-3, 6.30-11; 12-3, 7-10.30 Sun

Greene King IPA; Ruddles Best Bitter H

Small, two-bar pub that serves a tiny village and a large rural community. Real ale and real food are the hallmarks of this pub which is in a superb spot for stargazing.

Q 🌫 🕯 ♣ P

LITTLE BRAXTED
Green Man
Kelvedon Road OS849130
☎ (01621) 891659
11.30-3, 6-11; 12-3, 7-10.30 Sun

Ridleys IPA, Rumpus H

Set in delightful rural surroundings, this pretty pub features hanging flower baskets and a cosy traditional lounge. Note the unusual handpumps. The interesting menu is highly recommended. A Ridleys 'beer of the month' is stocked.

🏚 Q 🌫 🕯 ♣ P

LITTLE EASTON
Stag
Duck Street (1 mile W of B184, Dunmow-Thaxted road) OS608241
☎ (01371) 870214
11.30-2.30, 6-11; 12-3, 7-10.30 Sun

Ridleys IPA, seasonal beers H

This friendly village local has a large garden and children's play area plus a nine-acre field where caravans are welcome.

🏚 🌫 🕯 🍴 🛆 ♣ P

LITTLE OAKLEY
Olde Cherry Tree
Clacton Road (B1414)
☎ (01255) 880333
11-2.30, 5-11; 12-3, 7-10.30 Sun

Adnams Bitter, Broadside; Fuller's London Pride; Wells Eagle; guest beers H

Here is a rural pub which has bucked the trend; it now sells more real ale than in the past. Recent changes have enabled a good menu to be introduced in the new no-smoking restaurant. This local CAMRA *Pub of the Year* 2000 hosts a beer fest in July.

🏚 🌫 🕯 ♣ P ⊟ ⊞

LITTLE TOTHAM
Swan
School Road (2 miles SE of B1022)
☎ (01621) 892689
11-11; 12-10.30 Sun

Greene King IPA; O'Hanlons Fire Fly; Iceni Fine Soft Day; guest beers G

Friendly, 16th-century pub near the village green with a constantly changing range of beers on gravity, including up to eight guests, plus a

cider and perry. It hosts a beer festival in June; Essex CAMRA *Pub of the Year* 2000. The food menu is limited.

🏚 🌫 🕯 🍴 🛆 🛆 ♣ ⊖ P ⊟

LITTLE WALDEN
Crown
On B1052 ☎ (01799) 522475
11-3, 6-11; 12-10.30 Sun

City of Cambridge Boathouse Bitter, Hobson's Choice; Greene King IPA; guest beer G

Characterful 18th-century beamed country pub featuring an inglenook and antique furniture and offering an extensive menu. Racked cask stillage is used for dispensing the real ales.

🏚 Q 🌫 🕯 ♣ ⊖ P

LITTLEY GREEN
Compasses
Turn off B1417 at Ridleys Brewery OS699172
☎ (01245) 362308
11.30-2.30 (3 summer), 6-11; 12-2.30 (3 summer), 7-10.30 Sun

Ridleys IPA, Mild, ESX, Rumpus, seasonal beers G

Unspoilt Victorian pub, well worth the search. The food speciality is the Huffer, a very large bap. It hosts occasional folk nights, plus Morris dancing in summer. Camping is by prior arrangement. An eve meal is served Tue.

🏚 Q 🌫 🌫 🛆 ♣ P

MANNINGTREE
Crown Hotel
51 High Street (B1352)
☎ (01206) 396333
11-11; 12-10.30 Sun

Greene King XX Mild, IPA, Abbot H

400-year-old hotel whose history has been linked to the ebb and flow of the River Stour. A warm, friendly public bar where locals gossip adjoins a dining room giving a panoramic view of the river. Two go-ahead publicans have ensured that this pub has won awards for both food and ale.

🌫 🛏 🕯 🍴 ♣ P ⊞

MILL END GREEN
Green Man
1 mile E of B184, near Dunmow OS619260
☎ (01371) 870286
12-3, 7 (6 summer)-11; 12-11 Sat; 12-10.30 Sun

Adnams Bitter; Greene King IPA; Ridleys IPA H

Very pleasant, 15th-century country pub featuring oak studwork and low beams. The excellent garden has its own tennis court. The central open fireplace is controlled by an adjustable smoke hood. Good value food.

🏚 ❀ ⊨ ◖▶ ♣ P

MILL GREEN

Viper

Mill Green Road OS641018
☎ (01277) 352010
12-2.30 (3 Sat), 6-11; 12-3, 7-10.30 Sun

Ridleys IPA or Adnams Bitter; Ⓗ **guest beers** Ⓗ/Ⓖ

Unspoilt three-roomed pub set in woodland: a wood-panelled public bar and snug and a comfortable lounge. Good pub lunches include real ale sausages. Local CAMRA *Pub of the Year* 1997-99.

🏚 Q ❀ ◖⊞ ♣ P

MOLE HILL GREEN

Three Horseshoes

Off Takeley-Elsenham road, 1 mile from Stansted Airport OS564247
☎ (01279) 870313
11-11; 12-10.30 Sun

Courage Directors; Greene King IPA, Abbot; guest beer Ⓗ

Attractive, thatched country pub boasting low beams and an inglenook. Its large outdoor areas are a valued asset to the locality. It featured in BBC's *Lovejoy*. Sun eve meals must be booked.

🏚 ❀ ◖▶ ⅙ P

NORTH END

Butcher's Arms

Dunmow Road (A130)
☎ (01245) 237481
11.30-3, 7-11; 11.30-11 Sat; 12-10.30 Sun

Ridleys Mild, IPA, seasonal beers Ⓗ

Food-centred, 500-year-old pub with an award-winning garden; camping is available on site by prior arrangement. Barbecues are held in summer.

Q ❀ ◖▶ ⊞ ⅄ ♣ P

NORTH FAMBRIDGE

Ferry Boat Inn

Ferry Road
☎ (01621) 740208
11-3, 7-11; 12-3, 7-10.30 Sun

Shepherd Neame Master Brew Bitter, Spitfire, Bishops Finger Ⓗ

Surprisingly spacious 500-year-old riverside pub, where the general drinking area retains a 'cottagey' feel. The conservatory, where children are welcome, relieves the pressure on the dining room.

🏚 🌙 ❀ ⊨ ◖▶ ♣ P

NORTH SHOEBURY

Angel Inn

Parsons Corner (A13/B1017 roundabout)

☎ (01702) 589600
11-3, 5.30-11; 12-3, 7-10.30 Sun

Greene King IPA, Abbot; guest beers Ⓗ

This gem has been well restored and made into a friendly thatched pub. It also boasts a genuine flagstone floor and carved bar depicting angels. It can be busy at weekends.

🏚 Q ❀ ◖▶ ⅙ P

PAGLESHAM

Punchbowl

Church End (from A127 follow signs to Rochford, Canewdon then Paglesham)
☎ (01702) 258376
12-3, 7-11; 12-3, 6.30-10.30 Sun

Adnams Bitter; Morland Old Speckled Hen; guest beers Ⓗ

Friendly, one bar pub fronted in white Essex board. Circa 16th century, it was originally a sailmakers, in a quiet one-street village. Low beamed ceilings, a small comfortable restaurant with an excellent menu, brassware and old pictures add to its appeal. ❀ ◖▶ P

PEBMARSH

Kings Head

The Street (1¹/₂ miles E of A131) OS851335
☎ (01787) 269306
12-3, 6-11 (closed Mon); 12-3 7-10.30 Sun

Greene King IPA; guest beers Ⓗ

Spacious, friendly, welcoming village pub and restaurant, difficult to locate but worth the effort. A large open fireplace dominates the bar which boasts a plethora of exposed beams and bricks. The games room fields pool and darts teams.

🏚 ❀ ◖♣ ♣ P

PURLEIGH

Bell

The Street (approx 2 miles from B1010)
☎ (01621) 828348
11-3, 6-11; 12-3, 7-10.30 Sun

Adnams Bitter; Benskins BB; Greene King IPA; guest beer Ⓗ

Attractive, 15th-century village pub; this friendly local has good-sized comfortable seating areas with open fires. Very good value meals are available (not Tue eve).

🏚 Q ◖▶ P

RADLEY GREEN

Cuckoo

500 yds off A414
☎ (01245) 248356
12-2, 7 (6 Sat)-11 (closed winter Tue eve); 12-2, 7-10.30 Sun

Ridleys IPA, Rumpus, seasonal beers Ⓗ

Well-hidden at the end of its own long track this one-bar pub is popular with ramblers and cyclists; caravanners welcome.

🏚 Q ❀ ◖▶ ⅄ ♣ P

RADWINTER

Plough

Sampford Road (B1053/B1054 jct)
☎ (01799) 599222
11.30-4.30, 6.30-11; 12-4, 7-10.30 Sun

Adnams Bitter; Courage Directors; Greene King IPA; guest beers Ⓗ

Atmospheric Grade II listed building on the edge of the village, serving a good selection of wholesome food. Large garden at rear.

🏚 Q ❀ ⊨ ◖▶ P

RAMSDEN HEATH

Nags Head

50 Heath Road
☎ (01268) 711875
11.30-11, 12-10.30 Sun

Ridley IPA, ESX, Rumpus Ⓗ/Ⓖ

Traditional, well-supported village pub with a recently-installed viewing area for the dispense of up to nine beers, including a range of Ridleys 'event beers' on gravity. Over 100 whiskies are on sale. It hosts a weekly quiz and fortnightly jazz.

❀ ◖▶ ♣ P

RICKLING GREEN

Cricketers Arms

¹/₂ mile W of B1383 OS511298
☎ (01799) 543210
12-11; 12-10.30 Sun

Flowers IPA; guest beers Ⓖ

Village inn overlooking the cricket green, a convenient overnight stop for Stansted Airport, it serves excellent food.

🏚 Q ❀ ⊨ ◖▶ P

ROCHFORD

Golden Lion

35 North Street (N of Market Sq) ☎ (01702) 545487
12-11; 12-10.30 Sun

Fuller's London Pride; Greene King Abbot; guest beers Ⓗ

Long-established free house in a 300-year-old traditional Essex weatherboarded building, much improved by present owners. An impressive range usually includes a mild or other dark beer. Well-behaved dogs welcome. Family room closes at 8pm.

🌙 ❀ ≈ ♣ ⌂

ROWHEDGE

Walnut Tree

Fingringhoe Road (1 mile E
of B1025) OS021216
☎ (01206) 728149
8.30 (8 Thu, 7.30 Fri)-11; 12-3 Sat;
closed Mon & Wed; 12-3, 7.30-10.30
Sun
Beer range varies Ⓗ
Friendly pub on the outskirts
of Colchester where an old
Rayburn stove enhances the
cosy atmosphere. A pool
table, pinball and vinyl juke
box add to its appeal. The
large garden is home to a
goat and chickens.
🏵 ◖◗ ♣ P

SAFFRON WALDEN
Axe
60 Ashdon Road
☎ (01799) 522235
12-2.30, 6-11; 12-10.30 Sun
Greene King IPA, Abbot Ⓗ
Popular, town local in an
extended Victorian building.
The dining room is used for
meetings.
🏵 ◖◗ ⊞ ♣ P ⊞

Old English Gentleman
11 Gold Street (near B184
and B1052)
☎ (01799) 523595
10-11; 12-10.30 Sun
**Black Sheep Best Bitter; Greene
King IPA; Wadworth 6X; guest
beers** Ⓗ
Town-centre beamed pub
with a welcoming
atmosphere, serving a mixed
age range.
🏚 Q 🏵 ♣

SHALFORD
George
The Street (B1053)
☎ (01371) 850207
12-3.30, 6.30-11; 12-3 (closed eve)
Sun
**Adnams Broadside; Greene King IPA;
guest beer** Ⓗ
Friendly, open-plan, beamed
local with large inglenook,
and free from fruit machines
or juke box. Good quality
food represents good value.
🏚 Q 🏵 ◖◗ ▲ P ✂

SIBLE HEDINGHAM
White Horse
39-41 Church Street (400 yds
from A1017, W up Rectory
Road) ☎ (01787) 460742
12-11; 12-10.30 Sun
Greene King IPA Ⓗ
Timber-framed local enjoying
a warm, friendly atmosphere;
children welcome. Darts and
pool played and it fields a
pub football team. Good
food served.
🏚 🏵 ◖◗ ⊞ ▲ ♣ P

SOUTH FAMBRIDGE
Anchor
Fambridge Road (off

Ashingdon Rd between
Rochford and Hockley)
☎ (01702) 203535
11-3, 7-11; 12-4, 7-10.30 Sun
**Greene King Abbot; Nethergate IPA;
guest beers** Ⓗ
Attractive, two-bar pub built
1900, affording views of the
River Crouch and nestled in a
small village. The restaurant
serves good food; pool room.
Q 🏵 ⇔ ◖◗ ⊞ P ✂

SOUTH OCKENDON
Moon under Water
Broxburn Drive (near B1335)
☎ (01708) 855245
11-11; 12-10.30 Sun
**Boddingtons Bitter; Courage
Directors; Theakston Best Bitter;
guest beers** Ⓗ
Vastly-improved, back-street,
estate local (formerly the
Troubadour), restored by JD
Wetherspoon, and unusually,
children are welcome. The
interior colour scheme is
bright yellow and orange.
There are normally two
interesting guest beers
available at excellent low
prices; possibly the cheapest
pub in Essex for food and
drink.
Q 🏵 ◖◗ ♿ ⇔ P ✂ ⊞

SOUTHEND ON SEA
Cork & Cheese
10 Talza Way (below Victoria
Plaza shopping centre)
☎ (01702) 616914
11-11; closed Sun
Nethergate IPA; guest beers Ⓗ
Popular, atmospheric,
subterranean pub run by
friendly staff. The restaurant
upstairs serves substantial
meals weekdays. Local
CAMRA *Pub of the Year* 2000,
it usually stocks at least four
beers.
🏵 ◖⇔ ≢ (Victoria/Central) ♣ ⇔

Liberty Belle
10-12 Marine Parade
☎ (01702) 466936
11-11; 12-10.30 Sun
**Courage Best Bitter; Directors;
guest beer** Ⓗ
Spacious, welcoming, 1903
seafront pub, offering a good
value guest beer plus a cider
or perry. The children's room
at the rear of the pub has
been recently enlarged. Pool,
darts and chess played.
Watch out for the 'flasher' in
the corner.
🏃 🏵 ◖⇔ ≢ (Central) ♣ ⇔ ✂

SOUTHMINSTER
Station Arms
39 Station Road (near
B1020/B1021 jct)
☎ (01621) 772225
12-2.30, 6-11; 12-11 Sat; 12-4,
7-10.30 Sun

**Crouch Vale Best Bitter; Fuller's
London Pride; guest beers** Ⓗ
Friendly weatherboarded pub
that hosts regular beer
festivals. This former East
Anglian CAMRA *Pub of the
Year* serves a variety of real
ales (usually three guests).
Good food is served Thu-Sat
eves in the restaurant. A must
for all serious beer lovers.
🏚 Q 🏵 ◖◗ ≢ ♣ ⇔

ST OSYTH
White Hart
71 Mill Street
☎ (01255) 820318
12-2.30, 7-11 (12-11 summer); 12-
10.30 Sun
Adnams Bitter; guest beers Ⓗ
Once a popular real ale pub
its second set of new owners
are trying to re-establish its
appeal. Located near the
priory in a picturesque
village, the 16th-century
dining room provides an
excellent atmosphere for Sun
lunch. Beer festival held at
Easter.
🏚 🏵 ◖◗ ♣ P

STANSTED
MOUNTFITCHET
Queens Head
3 Lower Street (B1051)
☎ (01279) 812458
11-3, 5.30-11; 12-3, 7-10.30 Sun
**Draught Bass; Greene King IPA;
Tolly Cobbold Original** Ⓗ
Bright, comfortable pub at
the village centre where an
eclectic collection of brass
and old agricultural
implements adorn the walls.
No food Sun.
🏵 ◖⊞ ≢ ♣

Rose & Crown
31 Bentfield Green (1/2 mile
W of B1383)
☎ (01279) 812107
11-3.30, 6-11; 12-3.30, 7-10.30 Sun
Adnams IPA; Young's Bitter Ⓗ
Typical Victorian hamlet
pub: the single large bar is
comfortable and friendly and
well used by the local
community (the landlady
seems to know everybody).
The food is simple but
reliably excellent and very
good value (not served Sun
eve).
🏵 ◖◗ ♣ P

STAPLEFORD TAWNEY
Moletrap
Tawney Common (from
Epping, down Stonards Hill,
left at Fiddlers Hamlet, first
left then right)
☎ (01992) 522394
12-3, 7 (6 summer)-11; 12-4, 7-10.30
Sun
**Fuller's London Pride; guest
beers** Ⓗ

Friendly, low-beamed, old-fashioned alehouse in a rural location, once owned by the inventor of a type of moletrap. Difficult to find, but well worth the effort, this former local CAMRA *Pub of the Year* offers four real ales and good value home-cooked food. ᗰ Q ⇆ ֍ ⊄ ▶ P

STEEPLE

Star Inn
The Street OS938030
☎ (01621) 772646
12-3, 6-11 (12-11 summer Sat); 12-4, 7-10.30 Sun
Crouch Vale IPA; guest beers H
Spacious free house, with caravan/camping facilities at the rear.
ᗰ Q ⇆ ֍ ⊄ ▶ A P ⅍

STISTED

Dolphin
Coggeshall Road (A120, 2 miles E of Braintree)
☎ (01376) 321143
11-3, 6-11; 12-3, 7-10.30 Sun
Ridleys IPA, ESX G
Traditional beamed 15th-century pub with barrels kept on stillage behind the bar. No meals Tue or Sun eves.
ᗰ Q ֍ ⊄ ▶ ♣ P

STOCK

Hoop
21 High Street (B1007)
☎ (01277) 841137
10-11; 12-10.30 Sun
Adnams Bitter; H **guest beers** H/G
Pleasant village local which can be busy (particularly with diners) at weekends. It offers up to eight guest beers (usually five or six on, often local). It hosts a famous May beer festival. Local CAMRA *Pub of the Year* 1998/99.
Q ֍ ⊄ ♣ ⌣

Try also: Bear, 16 The Square (Punch Taverns)

STOW MARIES

Prince of Wales
Woodham Road (2 miles from S Woodham Ferrers, off B1012) OS830993
☎ (01621) 828971
11-11; 12-10.30 Sun
Beer range varies H/G
Popular, friendly village pub, in an attractive 17th-century building. Enjoy the varied beer choice, including Belgian beers, offered by a friendly, knowledgeable staff. Food is varied and excellent value; authentic ovens are used on theme nights. Live music and beer festivals happen during the year.
ᗰ Q ⇆ ֍ ⊄ ▶ ⌣ P

TENDRING

Cherry Tree Inn
Crow Lane (B1035)
☎ (01255) 830200
11-3, 6-11; 12-7 Sun
Adnams Bitter; Greene King IPA, Abbot; guest beers H
This attractive rural pub is situated at a T-junction. Its immense popularity can be put down to fine beer and excellent food. The comfortable and cosy bar adjoins an intimate restaurant. Arnie, the dog, is not the only customer to enjoy the Abbot!
ᗰ ֍ ⊄ ▶ P

THAXTED

Rose & Crown
31 Mill End (visible from B184) ☎ (01371) 831152
12-3, 6-11; 12-4, 7-10.30 Sun
Ridleys IPA; guest beers H
Friendly, well-run local in an historic town with a magnificent church, Guildhall and windmill. It is said to stand on the site of a monastic hostelry. The dining area is cosy and serves excellent food.
ᗰ ֍ ⇌ ⊄ ▶ ⊞ ♣ P

Star
Mill End (B184)
☎ (01371) 830368
11-11; 12-10.30 Sun
Adnams Bitter; Broadside; Draught Bass; Fuller's London Pride H
Popular with locals and visitors alike, it is now open plan, but exposed beams and a vast brick fireplace have been retained. Good value food is served lunchtime and Fri-Sat eves.
ᗰ ֍ ⊄ ▶ ♣ P

THORNWOOD COMMON

Carpenters Arms
Carpenters Arms Lane (B1393, 1 mile from Epping, 2 miles from M11 jct 7)
☎ (01992) 574208
11-3, 6-11; 11-11 Fri & Sat; 12-10.30 Sun
Adnams Broadside; Crouch Vale Best Bitter; McMullen AK; guest beers H
Classic pub of three bars: each has its own character. A pianist plays every Fri eve, and there are regular music nights. Children (and dogs) are welcome. It always has a dark beer on sale (mild and stout alternate), plus a cider in summer. Good quality food is sourced locally as much as possible.
֍ ⊄ ⊞ ⌣ P ⊟

TILLINGHAM

Cap & Feathers

8 South Street (B1021)
☎ (01621) 779212
11-3.30, 6-11 (11-11 summer); 12-4, 7-10.30 Sun
Crouch Vale IPA, Best Bitter, Millennium Gold, seasonal beers; guest beers H
Unspoilt, welcoming 15th-century pub in a picturesque village. A good range of home-cooked food is complemented by a minimum of two guest beers from independent brewers. Comfortable accommodation usually requires early booking.
ᗰ Q ⇆ ֍ ⇌ ⊄ ▶ ♣ ⌣ P

WALTON-ON-THE-NAZE

Royal Marine
3 Old Pier Street (near B1034)
☎ (01255) 674000
11-11; 12-10.30 Sun
Adnams Bitter, Broadside; Marston's Pedigree; guest beers H
Sprawling, elderly pub which has amassed a wealth of memorabilia connected with the sea and the RNLI. There is a small snug and a much larger drinking area. Stalwart supporters of the Walton Folk Festival, it hosts folk nights monthly plus bodhran workshops and jam session Sun. Parking can be tricky.
ᗰ ⊄ ⇌ ♣

WARLEY

Brave Nelson
138 Woodman Road (near B186) ☎ (01277) 211690
12-3, 5.30-11; 12-11 Sat; 12-3.30, 7-10.30 Sun
Greene King IPA; Nethergate Suffolk County; guest beers H
Friendly, comfortable local bearing a nautical theme, a rare local outlet for Nethergate beer. The safe garden hosts summer barbecues; pétanque played. No food Sun.
֍ ⊄ ⊞ ♣ P

WENDENS AMBO

Bell
Royston Road (B1039, towards Royston) OS511364
☎ (01799) 540382
11.30-3, 6-11; 12-3, 7-10.30 Sun
Adnams Bitter; Highgate Dark; H **guest beers** H/G
This small, traditional, friendly local is the social centre of a very pretty village. Local CAMRA *Pub of the Year* 2000.
ᗰ ֍ ⊄ ▶ ⇌ (Audley End) ♣ P

WESTCLIFF-ON-SEA

Hamlet Court
54 Hamlet Court Road
☎ (01702) 391752
11-11; 12-10.30 Sun

CAMRA National Pub Inventory: 'cash register' handpulls, Eagle Inn, Skerne, E. Yorkshire

Courage Directors; Greene King Abbot; John Smith's Bitter; guest beers Ⓗ
A former bank whose popularity, in no small part, is due to the wide range of food and beers. Two guest ales from independent or small brewers are sold at good prices. Regular quiz nights held.
◑▶≉

WHITE RODING
Black Horse
Chelmsford Road (A1060)
☎ (01279) 876322
11.30-3, 5.30-11; 12-3, 7-10.30 Sun
Ridleys IPA, Ⓗ ESX, Rumpus Ⓖ
Village pub with a restaurant serving an extensive menu (no meals Sun eve).
❀◑▶⊞♣P⊬

WIDDINGTON
Fleur de Lys
High Street (1½ miles E of B1383)
☎ (01799) 540659
12-3, 6-11; 12-3, 7-10.30 Sun
Adnams Bitter, Broadside; Greene King IPA; Taylor Landlord Ⓗ
Friendly village local, offering a good choice of ales and meals.
曲⇗❀◑▶♣P

WIVENHOE
Horse & Groom
55 The Cross (B1028)
☎ (01206) 824928
10.30-3, 5.30 (6 Sat)-11; 12-3.30, 7-10.30 Sun

Adnams Bitter, seasonal beers; guest beers Ⓗ
Lively, two-bar local that always has a mild – almost a unique claim in the Tendring peninsula. It makes an ideal starting point to explore historic Wivenhoe.
❀◑▶⊞♣P⊞

Rose & Crown
The Quay (near B1028)
☎ (01206) 826371
11-2.30, 6-11; 12-10.30 Sun
Adnams Bitter; guest beers Ⓗ
This popular, picturesque, quayside pub overlooks the River Colne. Its basic interior has two real fires and there is always the sound of lively conversation. The food is good value for money. Jazz is performed here some summer Suns. Parking can be difficult.
曲Q❀◑▶≉♣

WOODHAM FERRERS
Bell
Main Road (B1418)
☎ (01245) 320443
11-3, 7-11; 12-11 Sat; 12-10.30 Sun
Adnams Bitter; Belvoir Beaver; Ridleys IPA; Taylor Landlord; Wolf Coyote Ⓗ
Victorian pub, renovated and expanded around 1997: a public bar, lounge bar and a restaurant are complemented by a very nice garden.
曲Q❀◑▶⊞♣P

WOODHAM WALTER
Bell

The Street (near B1010)
☎ (01245) 223437
12-3, 7-11; 12-3 (5 summer), 7-10.30 Sun
Greene King IPA; guest beers Ⓗ
Picturesque, 16th-century coaching house, central to the village. Dark oak panelling is complemented by traditional styling. It has a restaurant area and a further lounge which doubles as a family room.
曲Q⇗◑▶P

Cats
Blue Mill Lane (B1010)
OS815076
12-3 (not Mon-Wed), 6-11; 12-3, 7-10.30 Sun
Greene King IPA, Abbot; guest beers Ⓗ
Cosy country pub in attractive gardens affording tranquil views. It masquerades as a country cottage with low beams and warm fires in winter. Difficult to find but well worth the effort. Ploughmans available at lunchtime.
曲Q❀P

WRITTLE
Inn on the Green
57 The Green
☎ (01245) 420266
11-3, 6-11; 11-11 Wed-Sat; 12-10.30 Sun
Mighty Oak Simply the Best; Ⓖ Nethergate IPA; guest beers Ⓗ
Open-plan pub, but with two distinctive drinking areas at either end of the bar. Formerly the Rose & Crown, it is popular with a wide range of customers. Up to four guest ales are sourced from interesting breweries; beer festivals are staged Easter and Autumn.
曲❀◑▶⌂P

Wheatsheaf
70 The Green
☎ (01245) 420695
11-3, 5.30-11; 11-11 Sat; 12-10.30 Sun
Greene King IPA, Abbot; Shepherd Neame Spitfire; guest beer (occasional) Ⓗ
Small, friendly local comprising a public bar and a cosy lounge. Limited parking.
Q❀⊞♣P

INDEPENDENT BREWERIES

Crouch Vale: South Woodham Ferrers
Mighty Oak: Hutton
Railway Tavern: Brightlingsea
Ridleys: Hartford End

The CAMRA National Inventory
Pub interiors of outstanding interest

ENGLAND

Bedfordshire
Broom: Cock
Luton: Painters Arms

Berkshire
Aldworth: Bell
Frilsham: Pot Kiln

Cheshire
Alpraham: Travellers Rest
Barthomley: White Lion
Bollington: Holly Bush
Gawsworth: Harrington Arms
Macclesfield: Castle
Stockton Heath: Red Lion
Wheelock: Commercial

Cornwall
Falmouth: Seven Stars

Cumbria
Broughton Mills: Blacksmith Arms

Derbyshire
Brassington: Olde Gate Inne
Derby: Old Dolphin
Elton: Duke of York
Kirk Ireton: Barley Mow
Wardlow Mires: Three Stags Inn

Devon
Drewsteington: Drewe Arms
Holsworthy: Kings Arms
Luppitt: Luppitt Inn
Topsham: Bridge
Widecombe-in-the-Moor: Rugglestone Inn

Dorset
Pamphill: Vine
Worth Matravers: Square & Compass

Durham
Durham City: Shakespeare, Victoria

Gloucestershire & Bristol
Ampney St Peter: Red Lion
Bristol: Kings Head
Cheltenham: Bath Tavern
Duntisbourne Abbots: Five Mile House
Purton: Berkeley Arms
Willsbridge: Queens Head

Hampshire
Steep: Harrow

Herefordshire
Kington: Olde Tavern
Leintwardine: Sun Inn
Risbury: Hop Pole ('Bert's')

Kent
Broadstairs: Neptunes Hall
Cowden Pound: Queens Arms
Ightham Common: Old House
Snargate: Red Lion

Lancashire
Great Harwood: Victoria
Overton: Ship Hotel
Preston: Black Horse

Leicestershire & Rutland
Medbourne: Horse & Trumpet

Greater London
EC1 Hatton Garden: Olde Mitre
EC4 Blackfriars: Black Friar
WC1 Holborn: Cittie of York, Princess Louise
WC2 Covent Garden: Lamb & Flag, Salisbury
N4 Finsbury Park: Salisbury
N6 Highgate: Flask
N8 Hornsey: Great Northern Railway
NW3 Hampstead: Holly Bush
NW6 Kilburn: Black Lion
NW8 St John's Wood: Crockers Folly
SE1 Southwark: George Inn
SE21 Dulwich: Crown & Greyhound
SW1 Belgravia: Antelope, Paxton's Head
SW1 St James's: Red Lion
W1 Marylebone: Barley Mow
W1 Soho: Argyll Arms
W6 Hammersmith: Dove
W9 Maida Vale: Prince Alfred, Warrington Hotel

Greater Manchester
Altrincham: Railway
Bolton: Howcroft
Eccles: Grapes, Lamb, Royal Oak
Gorton: Plough
Heaton Norris: Nursery Inn
Manchester: Briton's Protection, Circus Tavern, Hare & Hounds, Mr Thomas's, Peveril of the Peak
Marple: Hatters Arms
Middleton: Old Boar's Head
Mossley: Colliers Arms
Rochdale: Cemetery Hotel
Salford: Coach & Horses
Stalybridge: Station Buffet
Stockport: Alexandra, Arden Arms, Queen's Head, Swan With Two Necks
Wigan: Springfield Hotel

Merseyside
Birkenhead: Stork Hotel
Liverpool: Lion, Philharmonic, Prince Arthur, Vines
Lydiate: Scotch Piper

Norfolk
Warham: Three Horseshoes

Northumberland
Berwick-upon-Tweed: Free Trade
Netherton: Star Inn

Nottinghamshire
Arnold: Vale Hotel
Nottingham: Olde Trip to Jerusalem
West Bridgford: Test Match Hotel

Oxfordshire
Bix: Fox
Checkendon: Black Horse

Christmas Common: Fox & Hounds
Steventon: North Star
Stoke Lyne: Peyton Arms
Stoke Row: Crooked Billet
Stoke Talmage: Red Lion
Wantage: Shoulder of Mutton

Shropshire
Halfway House: Seven Stars
Selattyn: Cross Keys
Shrewsbury: Loggerheads
Whitchurch: Plume of Feathers

Somerset
Appley: Globe
Bath: Old Green Tree, Star
Crowcombe: Carew Arms
Faulkland: Tuckers Grave Inn
Huish Episcopi: Rose & Crown ('Eli's')
Midsomer Norton: White Hart
Witham Friary: Seymour Arms

Staffordshire
Tunstall: Vine
High Offley: Anchor

Suffolk
Brent Eleigh: Cock
Bury St Edmunds: Nutshell
Ipswich: Margaret Catchpole
Laxfield: King's Head ('Low House')
Pin Mill: Butt & Oyster

East Sussex
Firle: Ram

West Sussex
The Haven: Blue Ship

Tyne & Wear
Newcastle upon Tyne: Crown Posada

Warwickshire
Five Ways: Case is Altered
Long Itchington: Buck & Bell

West Midlands
Birmingham: Anchor, Bartons Arms, Bellefield, Britannia, British Oak, Market Tavern, Red Lion, Rose Villa Tavern, Samson & Lion, Three Magpies, Villa Tavern, White Swan, Woodman
Bloxwich: Turf Tavern
Dudley: Shakespeare
Rushall: Manor Arms
Sedgley: Beacon
Smethwick: Waterloo Hotel

Wiltshire
Easton Royal: Bruce Arms
Salisbury: Haunch of Venison

Worcestershire
Bretforton: Fleece
Clent: Bell & Cross
Defford: Cider House
Worcester: Paul Pry Inn

Yorkshire (East)
Beverley: White Horse ('Nellie's')
Skerne: Eagle Inn

Yorkshire (North)
Beck Hole: Birch Hall Inn
Boroughbridge: Three Horse Shoes
Harrogate: Gardeners Arms
York: Blue Bell

Yorkshire (West)
Bradford: Cock & Bottle, New Beehive
Heath: King's Arms
Leeds: Adelphi, Cardigan Arms, Garden Gate, Rising Sun, Whitelocks
Wakefield: Redoubt

WALES

Gwent
Grosmont: Cupid's Hill Inn

Mid Wales
Hay-on-Wye: Three Tuns
Llanfihangel-yng-Ngwynfa: Goat
Rhayader: Royal Oak
Welshpool: Grapes

West Wales
Llandovery: Red Lion
Pontfaen: Dyffryn Arms

SCOTLAND

The Borders
Ancrum: Cross Keys

Fife
Kirkcaldy: Feuars Arms

Grampian
Aberdeen: Grill

The Lothians
Dirleton: Castle
Edinburgh: Abbotsford, Bennets Bar, Café Royal, Kenilworth, Leslie's Bar, Oxford Bar

Strathclyde
Glasgow: Horseshoe Bar, Old Toll Bar, Steps Bar
Lochgilphead: Commercial ('The Comm')
Paisley: Bull
Renton: Central Bar
Shettleston: Portland Arms
Uddingston: Rowan Tree

Tayside
Dundee: Clep, Speedwell

NORTHERN IRELAND

County Antrim
Ahoghill: Gillistown House
Ballycastle: House of McDonnell
Ballyeaston: Carmichael's
Bushmills: Bush House (Charles H Callaghan)

County Armagh
Portadown: Mandeville Arms (McConville's)

Belfast
Crown, Fort Bar (Gilmartin's)

County Fermanagh
Enniskillen: Blake's Bar
Irvinestown: Central Bar
Tempo: J McCormick's

Pubs on the National Inventory that have been chosen for the Guide have a star next to their names. Inventory pubs used as illustrations in the Guide may not necessarily have been selected as entries.

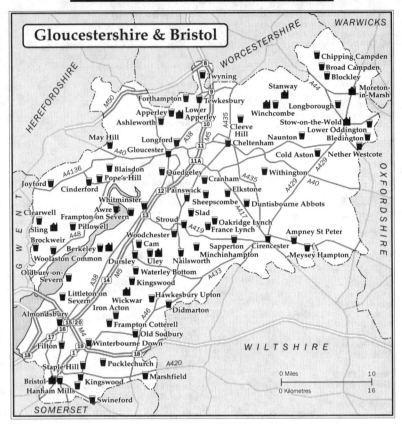

Gloucestershire & Bristol

ALMONDSBURY

Bowl Inn
16 Church Road, Lower
Almondsbury (1/2 mile from
A38 N of M4/M5
interchange)
☎ (01454) 612757
11-3, 5 (6 Sat)-11; 12-3, 7-10.30 Sun
Courage Best Bitter; Smiles Best; Wadworth 6X; guest beers H
Splendid old stone pub/hotel
in a quiet village. Its pleasant
beamed interior features a
central bar. Food and drink
prices are at the top end of
the range and guest beers
have sometimes been
extravagantly priced – check
before ordering.
🏚 Q ✿ 🚑 ◖ P

AMPNEY ST PETER

Red Lion ☆
On A417
☎ (01285) 851596
12-2.30 (not Mon-Fri; 6-11 (10 Mon-Wed); 12-2, 7-10.30 Sun
Hook Norton Best Bitter, seasonal beers *or* **Flowers IPA** H
Superb 400-year-old pub
caught in a time warp where
friendly conversation
prevails. Well-preserved, it
has no counter; service is

from a corner of one of the
two tiny rooms. 🏚 Q ✿ P

APPERLEY

Coal House Inn
Gabb Lane (off B4213)
OS854283
☎ (01452) 780211
11-2.30, 7-11; 12-2, 7-10.30 Sun
**Draught Bass; Wickwar Coopers'
WPA; guest beers** H
Originally a coal wharf, now
a welcoming pub on the
banks of the River Severn
(moorings available).
Q ✿ ◖ 🛏 ▲ ♣ P

ASHLEWORTH

Boat Inn
The Quay OS819251
☎ (01452) 700272
11-2.30 (not winter Wed), 7-11; 12-3,
7-10.30 Sun
Beer range varies G
Delightful old pub beside the
Severn. Owned by the same
family for 400 years, the
interior has hardly changed
for a century. Beers are
mostly from small breweries.
Lunchtime snacks and
moorings available. A runner-
up, national CAMRA *Pub of
the Year 1999*.
Q ✿ ♣ 🖆 P

AWRE

Red Hart
Off A48 Blakeney-Newnham
road OS709080
☎ (01594) 510220
11-3, 6.30 (6 Sat)-11; 12-3, 7-10.30
Sun
**Draught Bass; Freeminer
Speculation; Fuller's London Pride;
guest beers** H
15th-century pub set in
tranquil surroundings near
the River Severn; enjoy the
good atmosphere and
excellent food. The bar
features a well in the middle
of the room. Up to four guest
beers on tap. No lunches
served Mon or eve meal Sun.
✿ 🛏 ◖ P ⌷

BERKELEY

Mariners Arms
Salter Street
☎ (01453) 811822
11-11; 12-10.30 Sun
**Berkeley seasonal beers; Courage
Best Bitter; Smiles seasonal
beers** H
Built in 1490 as a nunnery, it
became a pub during the
Reformation. A friendly,
three-bar pub with a skittle
alley. It hosts live music Sat.
🏚 Q ✿ ◖ 🍺 ♣ 🖆 P

BLAISDON
Red Hart Inn
2 miles off A40 or A48
OS702168 ☎ (01452) 830477
12-3, 6-11; 12-3, 7-10.30
Bath Barnstormer; Hook Norton Best Bitter; RCH East Street Cream; Taylor Golden Best; guest beers H
Attractive pub at the heart of the village, employing an adventurous guest beer policy. Children's certificate – well-behaved children are welcome. A large outdoor area hosts barbecues; also good home-cooked food served. Twice Gloucestershire CAMRA *Pub of the Year*.
🏭 Q 🏵 🌗 ⌷ ♣ P

BLEDINGTON
Kings Head
Off B4450 OS243228
☎ (01608) 658365
11-2.30, 6-11; 12-2.30, 7-10.30 Sun
Hook Norton Best Bitter; Wadworth 6X; guest beers H
Delightful, convivial, 16th-century, stone inn overlooking the village green. It specialises in food – booking essential at weekends. Cider is sold in summer.
🏭 Q 🏵 🛏 🌗 🍴 ⌷ ♣ 🍽 P

BLOCKLEY
Great Western Arms
Station Road (B4479)
☎ (01386) 700362
11.30-2.30 (3 Sat), 6.30 (6 Sat)-11; 12-3, 7-10.30 Sun
Hook Norton Best Bitter, Old Hooky; guest beers H
Situated in a picturesque Cotswold village, this two-bar pub was once a blacksmith's, but was originally built for navvies building the nearby railway, from which the pub takes its name.
Q 🏵 🌗 ⌷ 🍴 ♣ P

BRISTOL
Annexe Inn
Seymour Road, Bishopston (100 yds from A38, along Nevil Road)
☎ (0117) 949 3931
11.30-2.30, 6-11; 11.30-11 Sat; 12-10.30 Sun
Draught Bass; Boddingtons Bitter; Courage Best Bitter; Marston's Pedigree; Smiles Best; guest beers H
Single-storey building converted from two skittle alleys, near the county cricket ground. The enclosed garden and conservatory are suitable for families. Excellent bar food or restaurant meals available (not served Sun). Sparklers are removed on request.
🐜 🏵 🌗 ♣

Bag O'Nails
141 St George's Road (near College Green)
☎ (0117) 940 6776
12-2.15, 5.30-11; 12-11 Fri & Sat; 12-10.30 Sun
Draught Bass; Fuller's London Pride; guest beers H
Small gaslit pub, a few minutes walk from the city centre where up to four guest ales change regularly. It also stocks a large selection of bottle-conditioned beers and foreign ales, plus a few continental beers on draught. Home-made soup served Mon-Fri. Bristol CAMRA *Pub of the Year 2000*. Q

Bell
21 Alfred Place, Kingsdown (near sports centre)
☎ (0117) 907 7563
12-2.30, 5.30-11; 12-11Sat; 12-3.30, 7-10.30 Sun
RCH Pitchfork; Uley Old Spot; Wickwar BOB H
Welcoming local in the Kingsdown area since 1875. Candlelight creates a cosy atmosphere eves. It attracts a mix of locals and students; bar snacks are served lunchtime. The beer range may vary. Q

Brewery Tap
6-10 Colston Street (next to Smiles Brewery)
☎ (0117) 921 3668
11-11; 7-10.30 Sun
Smiles BA, Golden, Best, Heritage, seasonal beers H
Smiles Brewery tap, winner of CAMRA's 1991 *Best New Pub* award. Its two rooms (one no-smoking) are imaginatively decorated with wood panelling, tiled floors and a slate bar. The toilets are up a steep flight of stairs.
Q ⌷ 🌗 ✄

Bridge Inn
16 Passage Street (near former Courage brewery by the river)
☎ (0117) 949 9967
11-11; 12-10.30 Sun
Bath SPA, Gem, Barnstormer H
Small corner pub on a busy street next to the River Avon and close to the station. Reputed to be Bristol's smallest public house, it has replaced Courage Best with Bath SPA, since the adjacent brewery closed in 1999.
🌗 ⇌ (Temple Meads)

Cambridge Arms
Coldharbour Road, Redland
☎ (0117) 973 5754
11-11; 12-10.30 Sun
Draught Bass; Butcombe Bitter; Courage Georges BA, Best Bitter; Fuller's London Pride; Smiles Best H
Large free house with single L-shaped bar, but wood and

stained glass partitions and small nooks accommodate drinkers seeking a more intimate atmosphere. The enclosed garden is child-friendly; a short walk from Clifton Downs.
🏵 ⌷ P

Hare on the Hill
41 Thomas Street North, Kingsdown
☎ (0117) 908 1982
12-2.30, 5-11; 12-11 Fri & Sat; 12-10.30 Sun
Bath SPA, Gem, Barnstormer; guest beer H
Busy, friendly, local set on a steep hill overlooking Stokes Croft area. Bath Ales original outlet, it was the local CAMRA *Pub of the Year* in 1998.
⌷ ♣

Highbury Vaults
164 St Michael's Hill, Kingsdown (near maternity hospital)
☎ (0117) 973 2203
12-11; 12-10.30 Sun
Brains SA; Smiles Golden, Best, Heritage, seasonal beers; guest beers H
Smiles-owned, two-bar pub, whose narrow frontage conceals a Tardis-like interior. A panelled back bar leads to several rooms, plus a heated semi-covered garden with plenty of seating. The small front bar is mainly used by locals. Toilets are at the foot of steep stairs. Eve meals served Mon-Fri.
Q 🏵 ⌷ 🌗

Horts City Tavern
49 Broad Street (near Grand Hotel)
☎ (0117) 925 2520
11-11(1am Fri & Sat); 12-10.30 Sun
Abbey Bellringer; Draught Bass; Courage Best Bitter; guest beers H
This large city-centre pub boasts a lively atmosphere. Up to five regularly changing guest beers are usually sourced from local breweries. It also offers a selection of over 50 malt whiskies and a daily menu with a wide range of freshly-prepared food at reasonable prices (no food Sun eve). Monthly beer festivals held.
🏵 ⌷ 🍴 🍽 ✄

Kellaway Arms
138-140 Kellaway Avenue, Horfield
☎ (0117) 949 7548
11.30-2.30 (3 Fri), 6-11; 11-11 Sat; 12-3, 7-10.30 Sun
Banks's Original; Courage Best Bitter; Wells Bombardier; H
Traditional, friendly, two-bar local near Horfield Common, comprising a deceptively large public bar, a

comfortable smaller lounge plus a sizeable garden. Ten years in this *Guide*.
Q ❀ ◖ ⊟ ♣

Kings Head

60 Victoria Street (between Temple Meads and centre)
☎ (0117) 927 7860
11-3 (not Sat). 5 (7.30 Sat)-11; 11-11 Wed-Fri; 12-3, 7-10.30 Sun
Draught Bass; Courage Best Bitter; Smiles BA Ⓗ
Small, unspoilt city pub, with a superb bar back. A licensed premises since the mid-17th century, the 'tramcar' seating area was installed in 1860. Weekday lunches.
◖ ≠ (Temple Meads)

Old Stillage

147 Church Road, Redfield (A420, between city centre and Kingswood)
☎ (0117) 941 1385
12 (11 Sat)-11; 12-10.30 Sun
Draught Bass; Ringwood Best Bitter; guest beer (occasional) Ⓗ
Lively pub, serving a varied clientele. The friendly staff have received customer service awards. Sport is often on TV. The guest beer is sometimes (but not always) served via a cask breather. Food is served until 7pm.
◖ ≠ (Lawrence Hill) ♣ ⊞

Post Office Tavern

17 Westbury Hill, Westbury-on-Trym
☎ (0117) 940 1233
11-11; 12-3, 7-10.30 Sun
Draught Bass; Ⓖ **Courage Best Bitter; Otter Bitter; Smiles Best; Wadworth 6X;** Ⓗ **guest beers** Ⓗ/Ⓖ
Pleasant pub bearing a Post Office theme. A small but expanding menu is supplemented by a variety of home-made pizzas. Wickwar BOB is sold as Pot Bitter. A dress code applies.
◖ ▮ ✶

Prince of Wales

5 Gloucester Road, Bishopston
☎ (0117) 924 5552
11-11; 12-10.30 Sun
Bath SPA; Butcombe Bitter; Courage Directors Ⓗ
Busy, two-bar pub where the good value lunches are popular with shoppers and students. Stained glass windows and partitions add to its traditional atmosphere.
Q ❀ ◖ ≠ (Redland/Montpelier)

Prince of Wales

84 Stoke Lane, Westbury-on-Trym (off A4018)
☎ (0117) 962 3715
11-3, 5.30 (5 Fri)-11; 11-11 Sat; 12-4, 7-10.30 Sun
Draught Bass; Bath SPA; Courage Best Bitter; Fuller's London Pride; Smiles Best; guest beers Ⓗ

This popular, friendly free house features a pleasant garden where boules is played. Boys Bitter is Courage Georges BA rebadged. A good selection of wines is sold. No-smoking area is available at lunchtime. ❀ ◖ ✶

Railway Tavern

Station Road, Fishponds (near Safeways)
☎ (0117) 965 8774
12-11; 12-3, 7-11 Mon; 12-10.30 Sun
Ind Coope Burton Ale; Marston's Pedigree; Tetley Bitter; guest beer Ⓗ
Local with a spacious single bar and a skittle alley, close to the Bristol-Bath cycle track. The walls are adorned with railway memorabilia. Guest beers come from the Tapster's Choice range.
❀ ◖ ♣

Reckless Engineer

Temple Gate (opp Temple Meads station)
☎ (0117) 929 0425
11.30 (7.30 Sat)-11; 12-10.30 Sun
Beer range varies Ⓗ
Bare-boarded alehouse with a friendly atmosphere. Card-carrying CAMRA members and postal and railway workers in uniform get free admission to see live rock bands, who perform every Sat and sometimes Fri.
◖ ≠ (Temple Meads)

Red Lion

206 Whitehall Road, Whitehall ☎ (0117) 952 0171
11-11; 12-10.30 Sun
Wadworth IPA, 6X, seasonal beers; guest beer Ⓗ
A new landlady was promoted from within and has maintained the excellent beer quality. A real community pub, it often features live music or special events. Badger Tanglefoot is a frequent guest ale.
◖ ▮ ≠ (Lawrence Hill) ♣

Robert Fitzharding

24 Cannon Street, Bedminster
☎ (0117) 966 2794
11-11; 12-10.30 Sun
Draught Bass; Boddingtons Bitter; Butcombe Bitter; Courage Directors; Theakston Best Bitter; guest beers Ⓗ
Former furniture store converted by Wetherspoon's into a thriving pub; a single bar featuring much wood panelling and stained glass, plenty of books and a fair-sized no-smoking area. Two guest beers and food served all day add to the appeal.
Q ◖ ▮ ♿ ☺ ✶

Shakespeare Tavern

68 Prince Street (200 yds

from centre)
☎ (0117) 929 7695
11-11; 12-10.30 Sun
Draught Bass; Courage Best Bitter; Greene King IPA, Abbot; Smiles Best; guest beer Ⓗ
Originally a cider house, this oak-panelled, bare-boarded alehouse dates from 1775. It stands close to the Arnolfini and docks area. The walls are adorned with nautical memorabilia. It serves good value food for the area.
❀ ◖ ▲ ♣

Sugar Loaf

51 St Mark's Road, Easton
☎ (0117) 939 4498
11-11; 12-10.30 Sun
Greene King Abbot; Tetley Bitter Ⓗ
In the heart of Easton, close to some of the finest spice shops in the city, this friendly community pub features a games room as well as two drinking areas, one of which is quiet. The pub name derives from the slave trade era. The house beer is Moles.
❀ ◖ ≠ (Stapleton Rd) ☺

Victoria

20 Chock Lane, Westbury-on-Trym
☎ (0117) 950 0441
12-3, 5.30-11; 12-3, 7-10.30 Sun
Adnams Broadside; Draught Bass; Wadworth IPA, 6X; Ⓗ **seasonal beers** Ⓗ/Ⓟ
Hidden down a quiet lane, this comfortably furnished pub, built in the 1700s, was once a courthouse. Eve food is served until 8pm, but pizzas (with a take-away facility) until 10.
❀ ◖ ▮ ♣ ✶

Try also: **Hope & Anchor**, Jacob Wells Rd (Free); **Old Fox Inn**, Fox Rd, Eastville (Free); **Princess of Wales**, Westbourne Grove (Free); **St George's Hall**, Church Rd, Bedfield (Wetherspoon's)

BROAD CAMPDEN

Bakers Arms

Off B4081, at NW end of village ☎ (01386) 840515
11.30-2.30, 6.30 (6 summer)-11; 12-3, 7-10.30 Sun
Donnington SBA; Hook Norton Best Bitter; Taylor Landlord; guest beers Ⓗ
Fine, old, village local, boasting Cotswold stone walls, exposed oak beams and two open fires. Monthly (3rd Tue) folk music staged. The garden includes a children's play area.
♨ Q ❀ ◖ ♣ ☺ P

BROCKWEIR

Brockweir Country Inn

Off A466, over bridge
OS540011
☎ (01291) 689548
12-3, 6-11; 12-11 Sat; 12-3, 7-10.30 Sun

Draught Bass; Hook Norton Best Bitter; guest beers Ⓗ

On the county border in the Wye Valley, an unspoilt pub whose beams came from a ship built in the village. Popular with walkers; Tintern Abbey and Offa's Dyke are nearby. Good, home-cooked food is available.
🏚 🏕 🍴 🍺 ☕ ♿ 👶 ♣ ☂ P

CAM

Berkeley Arms
High Street
☎ (01453) 542424
11-3, 5-11; 11-11 Fri & Sat; 12-10.30 Sun

Flowers Original; Wickwar BOB; guest beer Ⓗ

Friendly local, built in 1890. The imposing Stroud Brewery tiled frontage includes an impressive gilded Berkeley family crest. It fields quiz, skittles and darts teams. It hosts a beer festival early May. 🏕 🍺 ♣

CHELTENHAM

Adam & Eve
8 Townsend Street (near Tesco superstore)
☎ (01242) 690030
10.30-3, 5-11; 10.30-11 Sat; 12-3, 7-10.30 Sun

Arkells 2B, 3B, Kingsdown, seasonal beers Ⓗ

Unpretentious, no-frills, terraced local, 15 minutes' walk from the town centre. A public bar and small comfortable lounge provide a strong community focus.
Q 👶 ♣

Bayshill Inn
85 St Georges Place
☎ (01242) 524388
11-3, 5-11; 11-11 Fri & Sat (may vary summer); 12-3, 7-10.30 Sun

Badger Tanglefoot; Mayhem's Oddas Light; Wadworth IPA, 6X; guest beers Ⓗ

Friendly town-centre local, refurbished and extended to include a comfortable lounge, but retaining the 'public bar' area. Serving good value food, it gets busy at lunchtime.
Q 🏕 🍺 ♣ ☕

Hewlett Arms
Harp Hill
☎ (01242) 228600
11-2.30 (3 Thu & Fri; 5 Sat), 6-11; 12-5, 7-10.30 Sun

Beer range varies Ⓗ

Comfortable, relaxed pub, fronted by a large garden, on the outskirts of town towards the racecourse; handy for the

football ground. A good range of food is available (not served Sun eve).
🏕 🍺 P ✂

Kemble Brewery Inn
27 Fairview Street (off ring road)
☎ (01242) 243446
11.30-2.30 (3 Fri), 5.30-11; 11.30-11 (may close for 1 hour) Sat; 12-4, 7-10.30 Sun

Archers Village, Best Bitter, Golden; guest beer Ⓗ

Small, but deservedly popular back-street local; hard to find, but worth the effort. The only Archers tied house in the area, it offers good value, home-made food (not served Sun eve). It has a walled garden at the rear.
🏕 🍺

National Hunt
Benhall Ave (signed off A40 nr Benhall roundabout)
☎ (01242) 527461
11-11; 12-10.30 Sun

Boddingtons Bitter; Wadworth 6X; guest beers Ⓗ

Behind the 1960s estate pub façade lies an oasis of real ale in the desert of western Cheltenham; offering up to seven guest ales. It holds beer festivals twice a year. No food Sun eve.
🏕 🍺 P

Royal Union
37 Hatherley Street, Tivoli (off A40, nr Westall Green roundabout)
☎ (01242) 224686
12-11; 12-10.30 Sun

Tetley Bitter; guest beers Ⓗ

This back-street local has a strikingly decorated snug in contrast with the traditional bar area. The skittle alley is in the bar and can be noisy. Sun lunch must be booked. Minchew's cider is sold in summer. 🏕 🚂 ♣ ☕

Try also: **Brown Jug**, Bath Rd (Wadworth)

CHIPPING CAMPDEN

Volunteer Inn
Lower High Street
☎ (01386) 840688
11.30-3, 5-11; 12-3, 7-10.30 Sun

Hook Norton Best Bitter; North Cotswold Genesis; Stanway Stanney Bitter; guest beers Ⓗ

Stone inn with a courtyard and a pleasant garden, west of the village centre, at the end of the Cotswold Way. An inn since 1709, photographs of past village scenes are displayed in the lounge.
🏚 Q 🏕 🍺 🍴 👶 ♣ ☕

CINDERFORD

Forge Hammer

115 Victoria Street (off Valley Rd) OS652132
☎ (01594) 826662
12-3, 7-11; 12-11 Fri, Sat & summer; 12-10.30 Sun

Beer range varies Ⓗ

Friendly local on the outskirts of town. It hosts an annual beer festival in June.
🏚 🚌 🏕 🍴 ♣ P

CIRENCESTER

Golden Cross
20 Blackjack Street (near Corinium Museum)
☎ (01285) 652137
11-3, 6-11; 11-11 Sat; 12-10.30 Sun

Arkells 2B, 3B, seasonal beers Ⓗ

Gimmick-free pub relying on friendly and efficient service and good company. It has a full-sized snooker table; families welcome in the skittle alley when not in use.
🏚 🚌 🏕 🍺 🍴 ♿ ☂ ♣

Twelve Bells
12 Lewis Lane
☎ (01285) 644549
11-11; 12-10.30 Sun

Beer range varies Ⓗ

Beer drinkers' haven, lovingly resurrected by the owner/landlord, with a lively front bar and quieter, panelled rooms at the rear. Five guest beers (300 a year), include a local session beer. Excellent food is served from a good value, wide-ranging menu.
🏚 🚌 🏕 🍴 ♿ ☂ P

Try also: **Bathurst Arms**, North Cerney (Free)

CLEARWELL

Lamb
The Cross (Newland Road)
☎ (01594) 835441
12-3 (not Mon-Thu), 6-11; 7-10.30 closed lunch Sun

Freeminer Bitter, guest beers Ⓖ

With a small cosy bar and a larger lounge, the Lamb features bitter from the nearby Freeminer Brewery, plus at least one guest ale, often from an independent.
🏚 Q 🏕 ♿ ♣ ☕ P

CLEEVE HILL

High Roost
Cleeve Hill (B4632, top of hill)
☎ (01242) 672010
11.30-3, 7-11; 12-5, 7-10.30 Sun

Goff's Knight Rider; Hook Norton Best Bitter Ⓗ

One-bar pub affording superb views over the Severn Vale, reached by a flight of steps. Facilities include a TV, juke box, dartboard and bar skittles. It is handy for walkers on the Cotswold Way. 🏕 🍺 🍴 ♣ P ✂

COLD ASTON

Plough

OS129198 ☎ (01451) 821459

11-2.30, 6.30-11; 12-3, 7-10.30 Sun

Adnams Bitter; Hook Norton Best Bitter; Theakston Best Bitter Ⓗ

Small, 17th-century, stone-flagged pub with low beams; often busy, with a good food trade.

🏚 🕸 ◖ ► 🖚 🛦 ♣ P

CRANHAM

Black Horse Inn

Off A46 OS895130

☎ (01452) 812217

11.45-3, 6.30-11; 12-3, 6.30-10.30 Sun

Boddingtons Bitter; Flowers Original; Hook Norton Best Bitter; Marston's Pedigree; Wickwar BOB Ⓗ

17th-century inn at the heart of a small stone Cotswold village. Bumper portions of home-cooked food make this a popular destination for walkers and motorists. No food Sun eve. Quoits played.

🏚 Q 🕸 ◖ ► 🖚 ♣ P

DIDMARTON

Kings Arms

The Street (A433)

☎ (01454) 238245

12-3, 6-11; 12-3, 7-10.30 Sun

Theakston XB; Uley Hogshead; guest beers Ⓗ

A low-key exterior belies the warm, welcoming interior of this well refurbished 17th-century coaching inn. It was leased from the Beaufort family in 1760 for 1,000 years at 6 pence a year. Excellent restaurant .

🏚 Q 🕸 🖚 ◖ ♣ P

DUNTISBOURNE ABBOTS

Five Mile House ☆

On old A417; leave new road at Centurion Services OS978090 ☎ (01285) 821432

12-3, 6-11; 12-3, 7-10.30 Sun

Marston's Bitter; Taylor Landlord; guest beer Ⓗ

Beautifully resurrected old pub where the tiny bar interior is Grade II listed. A wonderful curved settle forms the wall of a small snug. It has a smart, deservedly popular restaurant, and a no-smoking cellar bar.

🏚 Q 🕸 ◖ ► P 🍴

DURSLEY

Old Spot Inn

Hill Road (next to bus station)

☎ (01453) 542870

11-3. 5-11; 11-11 Fri & Sat; 12-10.30 Sun

Banks's Bitter Marston's Pedigree; Uley Old Ric; guest beers Ⓗ

Excellent free house; built in 1776 as a farm cottage, it has been a pub for 100 years. Lovingly refurbished by the owner it is a real local, popular with walkers. Folk music is performed on Wed. Try the good value Old Ric sausages. Runner-up CAMRA national *Pub of the Year* 1998.

🏚 🕸 ◖ ► 🍴

ELKSTONE

Highwayman

Beech Pike (off A417)
OS965107

☎ (01285) 821221

11-2.30, 6-11; 12-2.30, 7-10.30 Sun

Arkells 2B, 3B, Kingsdown Ⓗ

Comfortable, 400-year-old roadhouse on the Ermine Way. There are roaring log fires, low ceilings and several rooms off the main bar. The extensive menu features some unusual dishes; children's portions available.

🏚 Q 🕸 ◖ ► 🖚 P

FILTON

Ratepayers Arms

Filton Recreation Centre, Elm Park (off A38, by police station)

☎ (0117) 908 2265

12-2 (11.30-2.30 Thu, Fri & Sat), 6.30-11; 12-2, 7-10.30 Sun

Butcombe Bitter; Ind Coope Burton Ale; Smiles Best; Wickwar BOB Ⓗ

Comfortable, well laid-out bar in the recreation centre, open to the public. Facilities include a skittle alley, darts and a snooker room. Free of any tie, it supports local breweries.

Q 🖚 🚲 (Abbeywood) ♣ P

FORTHAMPTON

Lower Lode Inn

OS878317

☎ (01684) 293224

11-3 (not winter Tue), 6-11; closed Mon; 11-3, 6-11 Sun

Donnington BB; Goff's Jouster; Oakhill Bitter; guest beers Ⓗ

15th-century brick pub on the River Severn, licensed since 1590. Approach roads are liable to flooding in winter; moorings available. A ferry operates from the Tewkesbury side of the river Easter to mid-Sept.

🏚 Q 🛏 🕸 🖚 ◖ ► 🖚 🛦 ♣ P 🍴

FRAMPTON COTTERELL

Rising Sun

43 Ryecroft Road

☎ (01454) 772330

11.30-3, 7 (5 Thu-Sat)-11; 11-11 Sat; 12-3, 7-10.30 Sun

Draught Bass; Butcombe Bitter; Wadworth 6X; Wickwar Coopers'

WPA, BOB; guest beer Ⓗ

Popular local with a skittle alley, an upper level dining area and a genuine free house, where local brewers are well supported.

🕸 ◖ ♣ ► P 🍴

FRAMPTON-ON-SEVERN

Bell Inn

The Green (near M5 jct 13)

☎ (01452) 740346

11-3, 6-11; 11-11 Sat and summer; 12-10.30 Sun

Abbey Bellringer; Flowers Original; Greene King IPA Ⓗ

Three-storey Georgian inn overlooking England's largest village green with cricket square. The large garden is ideal for children and barbecues. High quality home-cooked food includes frequent themed evenings. It lies on national cycle route 41 and is close to the canal.

🏚 🕸 🖚 ◖ ► 🚲 🛦 ♣ P 🍴

FRANCE LYNCH

King's Head

OS903035

☎ (01453) 882225

12-3 (4 Sat), 6-11; 12-4, 7-10.30 Sun

Archers Best Bitter; Hook Norton Best Bitter; guest beers Ⓗ

Friendly, single-bar pub at the heart of a compact village of winding streets. The superb newly-reclaimed garden has a children's play area. The village name denotes former Huguenot connections. No food Sun eve. A crêche is provided Fri eve.

🏚 Q 🍴 🕸 ◖ ► 🛦 ♣ P

GLOUCESTER

Black Swan Inn

68-70 Southgate Street

☎ (01452) 523642

11-11; 12-3, 7-10.30 Sun

Berkeley Severn-Up; Donnington BB; Wickwar Old Arnold; guest beers Ⓗ

Mid-19th century listed building between the city centre and historic docks. Six cask ales include a house ale from an undisclosed local brewer; the cider is Black Rat from Moles. Fine accommodation and excellent home-cooked food (not served Sun).

🕸 🖚 ◖ ► 🖚 ⏻

England's Glory

66-68 London Road

☎ (01452) 302948

11.30-2.30, 5 (6 Sat)-11; 12-3, 7-10.30 Sun

Badger Tanglefoot; Mayhem's Oddas Light; Wadworth IPA, 6X, seasonal beers Ⓗ

Popular community pub, enjoying growing reputation for food. It boasts a double skittle alley.

🏰 🌭 🍺 🚪 🍴 👤 🚻 ♿ 🥪 ♣ P ✗

Hogshead
3 Brunswick Road
☎ (01452) 382080
11-11; 12-10.30 Sun
**Boddingtons Bitter; Caledonian 80/-;
guest beers** H
Modern pub, opened in
1999, within the shell of a
former print works. It serves
up to five guest beers and
food (all day). A beer festival
is staged twice a year.
Wheelchair WC.
🍺 🚪 ♿ 🥪

Try also: **Linden Tree**,
Bristol Rd (Wadworth);
Whitesmiths Arms,
Southgate St (Arkells)

HANHAM MILLS
Old Lock & Weir
From Hanham go to foot of
Abbots Rd, turn right on
Ferry Rd
☎ (0117) 967 3793
11-11; 12-10.30 Sun
**Draught Bass; Exmoor Gold, Stag;
Marston's Pedigree** H
Split-level stone free house
mentioned in Conan Doyle's
Micah Clark; local CAMRA
Pub of the Year 1996. The
house bitter is supplied by an
undisclosed brewer. It has its
own riverboat which can be
booked, plus a large riverside
patio. Booking recommended
for meals (not served Sun
eve). Q 🌭 🍺 🚪 ♣ P

HAWKESBURY UPTON
Beaufort Arms
High Street (near A433 turn
off A46)
☎ (01454) 238217
12-3, 5.30-11; 12-11 Sat; 12-10.30
Sun
Wickwar BOB; guest beers H
Excellent, two-bar pub with a
skittle alley. The stables
dining area offers a good
menu. Note the collection of
pub and brewery
memorabilia. A great base for
hiking/cycling trips.
🏰 Q 🌭 🍺 🚪 🍴 🥪 👐 P ✗

IRON ACTON
Rose & Crown
High Street (off B4058)
☎ (01454) 228423
5 (6 Sat)-11; 12-3, 7-10.30 Sun
**Draught Bass; Flowers IPA;
Marston's Pedigree; Uley Old Spot,
Pig's Ear** H
Friendly local, in the village
centre, dating from the
1680s. A free house, with two
bars full of banter, it
concentrates on drink so no
food is sold; a rare local
outlet for Uley beers.
🏰 Q 🌭 🚪 🍴 ♣

JOYFORD
Dog & Muffler
Between B4228 and B4432
OS579133
☎ (01594) 832444
11-3, 7-11; 12-3, 7-10.30 Sun
**Freeminer Speculation; Samuel
Smith OBB** H
Lovely old traditional
country pub set at the heart
of the Forest of Dean;
difficult to find but worth the
trouble. The large gardens
include a play area for
children. Good food.
Q 🌭 🚐 🍺 🚪 ♿ 🏕 ♣ P

KINGSWOOD
Dinneywicks Inn
The Chippings
☎ (01453) 843328
11.30-2.30, 6 (5 Fri)-11; 11.30-11 Sun;
12-3, 7-10.30 Sun
**Draught Bass; Wadworth IPA, 6X,
Farmers Glory; seasonal beers** H
An imposing three-storey
building, this friendly one-
bar pub is named after a
neaby hill that was a horses'
burial ground in the civil
war. It enjoys a strong local
following and serves home-
made meals.
🌭 🍺 🚪 ♣

KINGSWOOD (BRISTOL)
Highwayman
Hill Street (A420, 1/2 mile
from centre)
☎ (0117) 967 1613
11.30-2.30 (3 Sat), 6.30-11; 12-4,
7-10.30 Sun
**Ind Coope Burton Ale; Smiles Best;
Tetley Bitter** H
Friendly, single-bar
roadside pub where beams
and stone walls enhance
its coachhouse style.
Popular with all ages, crib
and skittles are played. The
meals are good value. The
no-smoking area is available
lunchtimes only. It has a
well-appointed family room
and safe garden.
🏕 🌭 🍺 ♣ P ✗

LITTLETON ON SEVERN
White Hart
Signed from B4461
☎ (01454) 412275
12-2.30, 5-11; 12-11 Sat; 12-10.30
Sun
**Draught Bass; Smiles Golden, Best,
Heritage, seasonal beers; Young's
Special** H
Large country inn with
flagstone floors, inglenooks
and simple, understated,
traditional decor. Try a 'room
crawl' through the various
drinking areas off the main
bar. The family room doubles
as the no-smoking area; large
garden.
🏰 Q 🏕 🌭 🚐 🍺 🚪 ♣ P ✗

LONGBOROUGH
Coach & Horses
Off A424
☎ (01451) 830325
11-3, 7-11; 12-3, 7-10.30 Sun
Donnington XXX, BB H
Friendly, one-bar pub in a
quiet village with Morris
dancing connections.
Firefighting mementoes
reflect the proximity of the
Fire Services College. Parking
can be difficult.
🏰 Q 🌭 ♣

Try also: **Coach & Horses**,
Ganborough (Donnington)

LONGFORD
Queens Head
84 Tewkesbury Road (A38)
☎ (01452) 301882
11-3, 5.30 (6 Sat)-11; 12-3.30,
7-10.30 Sun
**Draught Bass; Boddingtons Bitter;
Hook Norton Best Bitter; Marston's
Pedigree; Morland Old Speckled
Hen; Wadworth 6X** H
Pleasant, 18th-century inn
on the edge of Gloucester. Its
stone-flagged public bar area
has been retained while the
dining area has been
extended. It enjoys a fine
reputation for good (booking
essential eves). Colourful
flower baskets adorn the
outside in summer.
🏰 🌭 🍺 🚪 🍴 P

LOWER ODDINGTON
Fox Inn
Off A436
☎ (01451) 870555
12-3, 6.30-11; 12-3, 7-10.30 Sun
**Badger Tanglefoot; Hook Norton
Best Bitter; guest beer** H
Spacious, 15th-century stone
inn, with a relaxed, pleasant
bar area, that boasts a
flagstone floor (not the
original) and a large open
fire. A friendly welcome
awaits those who enjoy a
thoughtful beer range and an
imaginative menu.
🏰 Q 🌭 🍺 ♣ P

MARSHFIELD
Catherine Wheel
High Street
☎ (01225) 892220
11-3 (not Mon), 6-11; 12-3, 7-10.30
Sun
Courage Best Bitter; G **Wadworth
6X; guest beers** H
Superbly restored Georgian
pub at the centre of the
village. Two guest beers
available.
🏰 🌭 🚐 🍺 P

Lord Nelson Inn
High Street
☎ (01225) 891820
12-2.30, 6-11.30; 12-4, 7-10.30 Sun

Draught Bass; Fuller's London Pride; Greene King Abbot; Worthington Bitter H
Big comfortable Cotswold stone pub set at the end of the pretty village High Street. Eve meals served Tue-Sat.
🏨 🍴 ⇋ ◖ 🚲 🅿️

MAY HILL

Glasshouse Inn
Off A40 W of Huntley
OS710213
☎ (01452) 830529
11.30-3, 6.30-11; 12-3, 7-10.30 Sun
Draught Bass; Butcombe Bitter; guest beers G
Unspoilt pub where a new extension blends in well with the original bar. The small garden drinking area features a bench beneath an arched yew hedge.
🏨 Q ⊛ ◖ ♣ 🅿️

MEYSEY HAMPTON

Masons Arms
28 High Street OS119998
☎ (01285) 850164
11.30-2.45 (11-3 Sat), 6-11; 12-4, 7-10.30 (not winter eve) Sun
Draught Bass; Tetley Bitter; guest beers H
Grade II listed, 17th-century village inn, enjoying a picturesque setting on the village green. Thoughtfully refurbished, to retain a rustic feel, it offers a good range of freshly-prepared food (not served Sun).
🏨 ⊛ 🍴 ◖ ⇋ ♣ 🅿️

MINCHINHAMPTON

Ragged Cot
Cirencester Road, Hyde
OS887012
☎ (01453) 884643
11-2.30, 6-11; 12-3, 7-10.30 Sun
Draught Bass; Taylor Landlord; Theakston Best Bitter; Uley Old Spot H
Busy, comfortable free house in open countryside near Minchinhampton Common and Gatcombe Park. Nearly 100 malt whiskies are stocked. Booking is advisable for meals. An excellent base for touring the area, it is reputedly inhabited by a female ghost.
🏨 Q ⊛ 🍴 ◖ ♣ 🅿️

NAILSWORTH

George Inn
Newmarket (1/2 mile up hill from bus station) OS839997
☎ (01453) 833228
11-3, 6-11; 12-3, 7-10.30 Sun
Archers Village; Draught Bass; Taylor Landlord; Uley Old Spot H
Stone pub with a friendly atmosphere, looking southwards over the valley above Nailsworth.

Imaginative food (chicken piri-piri is the house speciality) is cooked by an award-winning chef (booking essential). Limited parking.
Q ⊛ ◖ ♣ 🅿️

NAUNTON

Black Horse Inn
Off B4068 OS119234
☎ (01451) 850565
11-3, 6-11; 12-3, 7-10.30 Sun
Donnington BB, SBA H
Traditional stone pub in an unspoilt village; a handy centre for exploring the Cotswolds, it is popular with walkers. Attractive features include flagstone flooring, a black oak-beamed bar and built-in oak pews. The old snug is now a dining room.
Q ⊛ 🏨 ◖ Å ♣ 🅿️

NETHER WESTCOTE

New Inn
OS225205
☎ (01993) 830827
11-3, 6-11; 11-11 Sat; 12-10.30 Sun
Morrells Best Bitter, Varsity, Graduate; guest beers H
Hidden away on the north side of the village, just inside the county boundary, this was for long the only Morrell's pub in the county. No food Sun eve or Mon.
🏨 Q ⊛ ◖ Å 🅿️

OAKRIDGE LYNCH

Butchers Arms
North edge of village
OS915038
☎ (01285) 760371
11-3, 6-11; 12-4, 7-10.30 Sun
Archers Best Bitter; Greene King Abbot; Taylor Landlord; Tetley Bitter H
Popular, stone two-bar local whose restaurant opens Wed-Sat, and Sun lunch, although food is available in the bar at all times except Sun eve.
🏨 Q ⅀ ⊛ 🍴 ◖ ⊟ Å ♣ 🅿️

OLDBURY ON SEVERN

Anchor Inn
Church Road
☎ (01454) 413331
11.30-2.30, 6.30-11; 11.30-11 Sat; 12-10.30 Sun
Draught Bass; G Black Sheep Bitter; Butcombe Bitter; Theakston Best Bitter, H Old Peculier; G guest beer H
Traditional, two-bar country pub with a no-smoking dining room. Pétanque is played in the pleasant garden. The pub is deservedly popular for its fine food.
🏨 Q ⊛ ◖ ⊟ ♣ ⇔ 🅿️

OLD SODBURY

Dog Inn

Badminton Road
☎ (01454) 312006
11.30-11; 12-3, 7-10.30 Sun
Fuller's London Pride; Marston's Pedigree; Wadworth 6X; Wickwar BOB H
Welcoming country pub, popular with locals and visitors alike, bearing a traditional decor of stone, beams and wood in its large lounge, smaller rooms and skittle alley. A big garden has benches and a play area. Food dominates at weekends.
🏨 ⊛ ◖ ♣ 🅿️ ✠

PAINSWICK

Royal Oak
St Mary's Street (S of A46)
OS868098
☎ (01452) 813129
11-3, 6-11; 12-3, 7-10.30 Sun
Flowers Original; Hook Norton Best Bitter; Tetley Bitter; Wadworth 6X H
Compact, friendly 16th-century town pub: two comfortable bars, one has a display of vintage vehicles made from matchsticks, while the pleasant courtyard displays old pub and brewery signs. No food Sun.
Q ⊛ ◖ ⊟ Å

PILLOWELL

Swan
400 yds east of B4234
OS625065
☎ (01594) 562477
12-2 (3 Sat; closed Mon), 7-11; 12-3, 7-10.30 Sun
Wickwar Coopers' WPA, BOB; guest beers H
Comfortable, friendly pub, situated in the heart of the Forest of Dean. It stocks over 50 speciality cheeses from all over the West Country, served with salads and home-made bread and pickles.
🏨 Q ⇔ 🅿️

POPE'S HILL

Greyhound
Off A48 at Elton Corner
OS686141
☎ (01452) 760344
11-3, 6-11; 12-3, 7-10.30 Sun
Freeminer Gold Standard; Taylor Landlord; guest beers H
Friendly local with a good atmosphere, serving a range of good value meals.
🏨 ⅀ ⊛ ◖ Å ♣ 🅿️

PUCKLECHURCH

Rose & Crown
68 Parkfield Road
☎ (01117) 937 2351
11.30-3, 6-11; 12-4, 7-10.30 Sun
Draught Bass; Wadworth IPA, 6X, seasonal or guest beers H
Large, attractive, two-bar local comprising a small

public bar and a bigger lounge, plus a no-smoking restaurant. Located near the Bristol-Bath cyclepath, it has a large garden. Good food served (except Mon eve).

🏠 🌢 ◐▶ ♣ P ⊁

Star Inn
37 Castle Street
☎ (0117) 937 2391
11-11; 12-10.30 Sun
Draught Bass; Ⓖ **Marston's Pedigree** Ⓗ
Village local – a real focal point of the community. Bass is brought from the cellar in a jug; and there are three draught ciders. The pub is L-shaped, with one corner given over to the good value meals service (no food Sun eve).

🌢 ◐▶ ♣ ⌂ P ⊁

QUEDGELEY
Little Thatch Hotel
141 Bristol Road (B4008)
☎ (01452) 720687
12-2.30 (closed Sat), 6.45-11; 12-2.30, 6.45-10.30 Sun
Beer range varies Ⓗ
Wonderfully preserved building of 1351 now with a modern hotel extension. Legend has it that Anne Boleyn stayed in 1535 while Henry VIII visited strongly Catholic Gloucester. Three small brewery beers are always available.

🌢 🚪 ◐▶ P

SAPPERTON
Daneway Inn
West of village OS939034
☎ (01285) 760297
11-2.30, 6.30-11; 11-3 (summer), 6.30-11 Sat; 12-3 (5 summer), 7-10.30 Sun
Wadworth IPA, 6X, seasonal beers Ⓗ
Lovely old pub, built in 1784 for canal workers, near one end of the now disused Sapperton Tunnel. The comfortable lounge is dominated by a magnificent fireplace with Dutch carving. It is popular with walkers. It boasts a large garden and no-smoking room for families.

🏠 Q 🌢 ◐▶ Å P ⊁

SHEEPSCOMBE
Butchers Arms
Signed off A46 and B4070 OS892104
☎ (01452) 812113
11.30-3, 6.30 (6 Fri & Sat)-11; 12-3.30, 7-10.30 Sun
Hook Norton Best Bitter; Uley Old Spot; guest beers Ⓗ
Large, 17th-century village pub with a restaurant area, furnished in modern, but comfortable country-style.

Note the interesting carved pub sign: it is thought butchering went on here when Henry VIII hunted deer in the valley. Quoits played.

🏠 Q 🌢 ◐▶ ♣ P ⊁ 🔔

SLAD
Woolpack
On B4070 ☎ (01452) 813429
12 (11 summer)-3, 6-11; 12-3.30, 7-10.30 Sun
Uley Bitter, Old Spot, Pig's Ear; guest beer Ⓗ
Authentic popular 16th-century pub clinging to the side of Slad valley affording splendid views. It was made famous by the late *Cider with Rosie* author Laurie Lee. An excellent range of home-cooked food served (not Sun eve). Small car park.

🏠 Q 🐌 🌢 ◐▶ 🍴 ♣ ⌂ P ⊁

STAPLE HILL
Crown Inn
14 High Street
☎ (0117) 975 3608
11-11; 12-10.30 Sun
Draught Bass; Brain's Bitter, SA or Buckley's Rev. James; Butcombe Best Bitter; guest beer Ⓗ
Friendly, busy community pub, it has a children's play area in the garden and a big screen TV for certain sports occasions. A raised area is used primarily for serving food. A regular live music venue, it can get smoky.

🌢 ◐ ♣ P

Humper's Off-Licence
26 Soundwell Road
☎ (0117) 956 5525
12-2, 5-10.30 (11-11 summer Sat); 12-2, 5-10.30 (11-11 summer Sat)
Draught Bass; Butcombe Bitter; Smiles Best; Wickwar BOB; Ⓗ **guest beers** Ⓖ
Unusual, small, street-corner off-licence with always guests available, an extensive range of bottled beers and up to four real ciders, all at reasonable prices.

Q ⌂

Staple Hill Oak
83-86 High Street (A4175)
☎ (0117) 956 8543
10.30-11; 12-10.30 Sun
Draught Bass; Boddingtons Bitter; Butcombe Bitter; Courage Directors; Theakston Best Bitter; guest beers Ⓗ
Large, atmospheric Wetherspoon's conversion of an old furniture store; it benefits from a good local customer base, attracting all ages. Food is served all day.

Q 🌢 ◐▶ 🚪 ⌂ ⊁ 🔔

STROUD
Golden Fleece

Nelson Street
☎ (01453) 764850
5 (11.30 Sat)-11; 12-10.30 Sun
Draught Bass; Boddingtons Bitter; Greene King Abbot; Wadworth 6X Ⓗ
Stroud's jazz and blues pub; one main bar with two alcoves leading off where musical instruments and jazz memorabilia decorate the walls. Live music is performed Thu. Lunch is served at weekends.

🏠 🥤 ♣

Try also: Lord John, Russell St (Wetherspoon's)

SWINEFORD
Swan Inn
Bath Road (A431, Bitton road) ☎ (0117) 932 3101
11-3, 5-11; 12-3, 7-10.30 Sun
Draught Bass; Ⓖ **Buctombe Bitter; Courage George's BA, Best Bitter; guest beer** Ⓗ
Traditional roadside village pub with a main bar and a no-smoking dining area. It is popular for food (not served Sun eve; must book Sun lunch). It lies close to the River Avon.

🏠 🌢 ◐▶ P

TEWKESBURY
Olde Bear Inne
68 High Street (A38)
☎ (01684) 292202
11-11; 12-10.30 Sun
Greenalls Bitter; Marston's Pedigree; Wadworth 6X; Ⓗ **guest beers** Ⓐ
The oldest inn in the county, dating from 1308, it features rambling bar areas, one with leatherwork on the ceiling dated to 1600. A pleasant terrace overlooks the garden and the River Avon (moorings available). No food Sun eve.

🏠 🌢 ◐▶ 🚪 Å ♣ ⊁

White Bear
Bredon Road (off High St)
☎ (01684) 296614
11-11; 12-10.30 Sun
Wye Valley Hereford Bitter; guest beers Ⓗ
Lively, friendly, one-bar pub run by convivial hosts and selling the cheapest pint in town. Venue of CAMRA's Tewkesbury Winter Ale Festival (Feb).

🌢 Å ♣ ⌂ P

TWYNING
Village Inn
The Green OS902367
☎ (01684) 293500
11-2.30, 7-11; 12-2.30, 7-10.30 Sun
Greene King IPA; Tetley Bitter; guest beers Ⓗ
Attractive, one-bar pub circa 1457, overlooking the village

green. Its skittle alley is
popular.
🏠Q🐾◑▷▲♣P

ULEY
Old Crown Inn
The Green
☎ (01453) 860502
11.30-2.30 (11-3 Sat), 7-11; 12-3,
7-10.30 Sun
Uley Bitter, Pig's Ear; guest beers Ⓗ
Single-bar, village pub built
in 1638 as farm cottages.
Recently improved, it has an
upstairs games room. Close
to Uley Brewery and the
Cotswold Way, it is popular
with walkers.
🐾🛏◑▷♣P

WATERLEY BOTTOM
New Inn
Signed from North Nibley
OS758964
☎ (01453) 543659
12-2.30 (not Mon), 6 (7 Mon)-11; 12-11
Sat; 12-3, 7-10.30 Sun
**Berkeley Dicky Pearce; Cotleigh
Tawny; Greene King Abbot; guest
beers** Ⓗ
Large free house standing in
a beautiful setting,
surrounded by steep hills.
The house beer, WB, is a
variation of Cotleigh Harrier
SPA. The attractive garden
has a children's play area. No
food Mon.
🏠Q🐾◑▷🍴♣🍽P

WHITMINSTER
Old Forge
Bristol Road (A38 S end of
village)
☎ (01452) 741306
11-3, 5.30-11; 11-11 Sat; 12-4,
7-10.30 Sun
**Exmoor Ale, Gold; Uley Old Ric;
guest beer** Ⓗ
15th-century building that
was a pub in the 18th
century but not again until
the 1980s, having been a
forge early in the 20th
century. Enjoy good food in
a convivial atmopshere (no
food Sun eve or Mon).
Q🐾◑▷▲🍽P✂

WINCHCOMBE
Bell Inn
Gretton Road
☎ (01242) 602205
11-11; 12-10.30 Sun
**Donnington BB, SBA; Eldridge Pope
Royal Oak; Greene King IPA, Abbot;
guest beers** Ⓗ
Former Donnington pub,
now a free house; its two
adjoining bars are warm and
welcoming.
🏠🐾🛏♣P

Try also: Plaisterers Arms,
Abbey Tce (Ushers)

Choosing Pubs
Pubs in the Good Beer Guide are chosen by
CAMRA members and branches. There is
no payment for entry, and pubs are
inspected on a regular basis by personal
visits, not sent a questionnaire once a year,
as is the case with some pub guides.
CAMRA branches monitor all the pubs in
their areas, and the choice of pubs for the
Guide is often the result of voting at
branch meetings. However,
recommendations from readers are warmly
welcomed and will be passed on to the
relevant CAMRA branch: please use the
form at the back of the Guide.

WINTERBOURNE DOWN
Cross Hands
Down Road (Harcombe Hill
jct)
☎ (01454) 850077
12 (11 Sat)-11; 12-10.30 Sun
**Draught Bass; Courage Best Bitter;
Smiles BA; Wickwar BOB; guest
beers** Ⓗ
Village local, right on a road
junction, hence its name. Its
sewing machine collection is
notable. It hosts live music
Fri. 🏠🐾♣🍽

WITHINGTON
Kings Head
On Yanworth road OS036153
☎ (01242) 890216
11-2.30, 6-11; 12-3, 7-10.30 Sun
**Hook Norton Best Bitter; Wickwar
BOB** Ⓖ
Unspoilt village local, hidden
away down a side road; it has
been in the same family for
over 80 years.
Q🐾🍴♣🍽P

WOODCHESTER
Ram Inn
Station Road (signed from
A46)
☎ (01453) 873329
11-11; 12-10.30 Sun
**Archers Best Bitter; Freeminer
Bitter, Speculation; John Smith's
Bitter; Theakston Old Peculier;
guest beers** Ⓗ
A recently extended
conservatory, overlooking
the valley, enhances this
charming pub that celebrates
its 400th birthday in 2001. It
offers three ever-changing
guest beers (over 400 per
year).
🏠Q🐾◑▷♿▲♣🍽P

Royal Oak
Church Road, North
Woodchester (signed from
A46)

☎ (01453) 872735
11-3, 5.30-11; 11-11 Sat; 12-10.30
Sun
**Archers Best Bitter; Berkeley Old
Friend; Smiles Bitter; Uley Old Spot;
Wychwood Special** Ⓗ
Pretty, whitewashed, 17th-
century inn comprising two
elegant bars; this lively,
friendly local attracts people
from miles around to sample
its imaginative, freshly-
cooked food. Children are
welcome in the dining area.
🏠Q🐾◑▷🍴♣P

WOOLASTON COMMON
Rising Sun
The Common (1 mile off A48
at Woolaston) OS590009
☎ (01594) 529282
12-2.30 (not Wed), 6.30-11; 12-3,
7-10.30 Sun
**Freeminer Bitter; Fuller's London
Pride; Hook Norton Best Bitter** Ⓗ
Lovely country pub affording
excellent views, off the
beaten track but it is well
worth finding. The home-
produced meals are
recommended (not served
Wed).
Q🐾◑▷▲P

The Battle for Britain's Mild
Clive Alexander on saving a beer style

MILD is a traditional British beer (called 'light' in Scotland) often made with darker crystal malts and less hops than bitter beers. It is usually around 3 to 3.5 per cent ABV and lower in strength than best bitters. Some brewers produce light or pale milds, such as Timothy Taylor and Wadworth: these can be similar to a light bitter and are often marketed as such. On the other hand, some milds are strong – up to 6 per cent ABV. These include Gales Festival, Sarah Hughes Ruby and Kelham Island Bete Noire. There are around 130 different milds brewed every year, although some are only available at beer festivals.

But this classic beer is hard to find in much of the country, the South-east in particular. One reason is that mild has become a fashion victim and is wrongly seen as being a weak, watery, down-market beer. In these image-conscious days, the affluent and upwardly mobile wouldn't be seen dead drinking it, though in mild's traditional working-class heartlands this image is quite often a positive selling point.

Is there a grain of truth in the old canard that mild is the preserve of the working class and flat-capped, whippet-owning Northerners? Certainly not. Mild is rare in the North-east but common in the North-west and Midlands, and has pockets of considerable popularity in Wales. It is gaining a foothold in parts of the South-east. Clearly there is a demand, even if only in some areas, from a large cult minority.

CAMRA has a similiar marketing problem with mild to the one it had promoting ale in general to a sceptical public in the 1970s. But mild has one big advantage today – a large, educated, discriminating sector of drinkers just waiting to be sold the product in the right way, at the right price. And here we come to another problem: greedy publicans. Witness the lack of success that mild has in much of the South-east, where publicans sell it at roughly the same prices as draught bitters of 5 per alcohol. Is it any wonder that it doesn't sell well in these pubs? The outlets that do succeed with mild sell vast amounts at considerably less – 20-25 per cent – than bitters and promote it as a session ale. It is clear that mild needs marketing.

CAMRA has set up a Light and Dark Task Group to specifically tackle this problem. Three years ago, a Mad about Mild campaign was launched with posters, leaflets and support material. The subsequent three May Mild campaigns were enthusiastically taken up by many publicans and enterprising chains such as Wetherspoons, with highly encouraging results. The key is to persuade brewers to make the product and, even more important, get publicans to stock it.

Between 1998 and 1999 almost a score of new milds were brewed and there were only a handful of casualties. In fact, more milds were brewed in 1998 and '99 than for many years. The key is to turn the new and occasional brews in to regular high performers and to encourage all brewers to promote their milds.

If your pub doesn't sell mild, ask your landlord to put it on. Better still, join CAMRA and have even more fun going Mad about Mild in local pubs and at beer festivals, while having the satisfaction of helping to support an historic beer style.

● The 2000 Champion Beer of Britain is a dark mild: Moorhouses Black Cat.

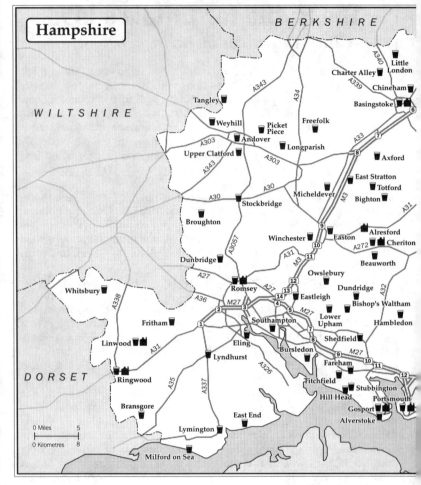

Hampshire

BERKSHIRE

WILTSHIRE

Little London

Charter Alley

Chineham

Basingstoke

Tangley

Weyhill

Picket Piece

Freefolk

Andover

Upper Clatford

Longparish

Axford

East Stratton

Totford

Micheldever

Bighton

Stockbridge

Broughton

Alresford

Winchester

Easton

Cheriton

Beauworth

Dunbridge

Owslebury

Dundridge

Whitsbury

Romsey

Eastleigh

Bishop's Waltham

Hambledon

Fritham

Southampton

Lower Upham

Linwood

Eling

Shedfield

Lyndhurst

Bursledon

Fareham

Ringwood

Titchfield

Stubbington

Portsmouth

Bransgore

Hill Head

Gosport

East End

Alverstoke

Lymington

Milford on Sea

DORSET

0 Miles 5
0 Kilometres 8

ALDERSHOT
Garden Gate
4 Church Lane East
☎ (01252) 321051
11.30-3, 5.30-11; 11-11 Sat; 12-4,
6.30-10.30 Sun
**Greene King IPA, Abbot, seasonal
beers** Ⓗ
Small, but good quality local,
just off the town centre. A
'U'-shaped bar separates the
darts area from a more quiet
drinking area; always friendly
and relaxing.
🏠 🛏 ◑ ▶ ≉ ♣

Red Lion
Ash Road (E end of Manor
Park, A323)
☎ (01252) 403503
12-2, 5-11; 12-11 Wed-Sat; 12-4,
7-10.30 Sun
Beer range varies Ⓗ
Traditional pub with a
secluded garden, open fires
and a relaxed atmosphere but
no juke box or pool table.
Three times local CAMRA
Pub of the Year and runner-up

for Wessex in 1999. Lunches
served Tue-Fri.
🏠 Q 🛏 ◑ ▶ ≉ ♣ P 🛏

Royal Staff
37a Mount Pleasant Road (off
A323 High St/Ash Rd)
☎ (01252) 408012
12-3, 5-11; 12-11 Sat; 12-10.30 Sun
**Fuller's Chiswick, London Pride,
ESB, seasonal beers; guest beers** Ⓗ
Beautifully refurbished in
Victorian style, this back-
street local has a comfortable,
lively single bar, with a
strong community
atmosphere and a good
children's garden. Handy for
Aldershot Town FC. The
guest beers are supplied by
Fuller's. Q 🛏 ◑ ≉ ♣

ALTON
Eight Bells
Church Street (off High Rd)
10-11; 12-10.30 Sun
**Ballard's Best Bitter; Fuller's
London Pride; Hogs Back TEA; guest
beers** Ⓗ

Built in 1640 to serve the
Alton-Odiham turnpike, this
pub has been revitalised with
an enterprising range of
beers, often from Ballards
and Hogs Back, including
milds.
Q 🛏 ≉ ♣

French Horn
The Butts (off A31 S end of
town)
☎ (01420) 83269
11-2.30, 5.30 (6 Sat)-11; 12-3,
7-10.30 Sun
**Courage Best Bitter; Ushers Best
Bitter, Founders, seasonal beers** Ⓗ
This 17th-century town pub
overlooks ancient archery
butts. Quiet, despite its size,
exposed beams and walls,
brasses and a tankard
collection lend atmosphere
while an aviary and skittle
alley add interest.
🏠 Q 🛏 ◑ ▶ P

ALVERSTOKE
Alverbank

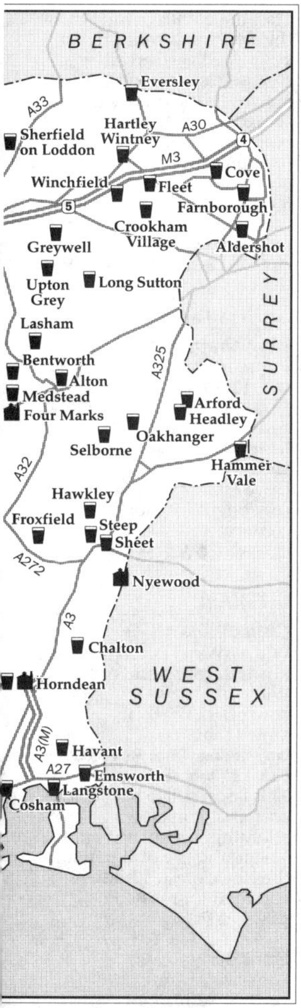
BERKSHIRE
Eversley
A33
Hartley Wintney
A30
Sherfield on Loddon
M3
4
Cove
Winchfield
Fleet
5
Farnborough
Crookham Village
Greywell
Aldershot
Upton Grey
Long Sutton
SURREY
Lasham
A325
Bentworth
Alton
Medstead
Arford
Headley
Four Marks
Oakhanger
Selborne
Hammer Vale
A32
Hawkley
Froxfield
Steep
Sheet
A272
Nyewood
A3
Chalton
WEST SUSSEX
Horndean
A3(M)
Havant
A27
Emsworth
Langstone
Cosham

Stokes Bay Road
☎ (023) 9251 0005
11-11; 12-10.30 Sun
Beer range varies Ⓗ
Victorian country house hotel bar in an attractive setting overlooking Stokes Bay. Once a haunt of Lillie Langtry, it is now licensed for weddings. Up to five real ales from independents and micros, plus a house ale (Ringwood Best Bitter rebadged).
⛰ ❀ ⛟ ◖◗ ⛺ P

ANDOVER

Blacksmiths Arms
134 New Street
☎ (01264) 352881
12-2 (not Tue), 5-11; 11.30-11 Sat; 12-10.30 Sun
Brains Bitter; Fuller's London Pride; Taylor Landlord; guest beer Ⓗ
Classic, two-bar pub; look out for the cricketing and horse-racing memorabilia in the lounge bar.
❀ ⊞ ♣ P

Foresters Arms
2 London Street
☎ (01264) 323580
11-11; 12-10.30 sun
Greene King IPA; Ruddles Best Bitter Ⓗ
One of the few remaining traditional town pubs in Andover with a large, boisterous public bar and a smaller cosy lounge. Good value food is served lunchtime Mon-Sat.
◖ ⊞

Station Hotel
63 Bridge Street
☎ (01264) 336585
11-2.30, 5.30-11; 11-11 Fri & Sat; 12-10.30 Sun
Hampshire Strong's Best Bitter; Ringwood Fortyniner Ⓗ
Despite its name, the hotel is some distance from Andover station. Its imposing entrance leads to two contrasting bars.
❀ ⛟ ◖ ⊞ ♿ ♣ P

ARFORD

Crown
Arford Road (B3002)
☎ (01428) 712150
11-3 6-11; 12-3, 7-10.30 Sun
Fuller's London Pride; Greene King Abbot; guest beers Ⓗ
Traditional village pub: a single bar with many nooks and crannies; beamed and cosy.
⛰ Q ❀ ◖◗ P

AXFORD

Crown
Farleigh Road (B3046, Basingstoke-Alresford road)
☎ (01256) 389492
12-2.30, 6-11; 12-3, 7-10.30 Sun
Fuller's London Pride; Greene King Abbot; guest beers Ⓗ
Small attractive country pub at the northern edge of Candover Valley. The restaurant boasts a Last Supper tapestry. Local brewery Triple fff supplies two guest beers and a house ale, Axford Best.
⛰ Q ❀ ◖◗ ⊞ ♣ P 🍺

BASINGSTOKE

Basingstoke & North Hampshire Cricket Club
Mays Bounty, Fairfields Road (county cricket ground, S of centre)
☎ (01256) 473646
12-2.30, 5.30 (6 Sat)-11; (12-11 summer Sat); 12-10.30 Sun
Beckett's Old Town Bitter; Fuller's London Pride; Ringwood Best Bitter; guest beers Ⓗ
Sports and social club with a pub ambience employing an enthusiastic real ale policy. Regional winner of CAMRA *Club of the Year* 1997; card-carrying CAMRA members welcome (except during County Cricket week in June when normal restrictions apply).
❀ ◖ ♣ P ⍻

Bounty Inn
81 Bounty Road (S edge of town, opp. All Saints church)
☎ (01256) 320071
11-2.30, 5.30-11; 11-11 Sat & summer; 12-10.30 Sun
Courage Best Bitter; Ushers Best Bitter, Founders, seasonal beers Ⓗ
Cosy, 18th-century inn on the site of the old cattle market, close to the county cricket ground. A rare survivor of 1960s redevelopment, the pub attracts a wide variety of customers.
⛰ 🐴 ◖◗ ⊞ ♣ P ⍻

Queen's Arms
Bunnian Place (by station)
☎ (01256) 465488
11-3, 5-11; 11-11 Sat; 12-3, 7-10.30 Sun
Courage Best Bitter, Directors; Theakston XB; Wadworth 6X; guest beer Ⓗ
Refurbished Victorian local, popular with office workers, but drawing a strong contingent of locals. A rare, older-style gem, it stands on the edge of the town-centre re-development.
❀ ◖ ⥈ ♣

BEAUWORTH

Milburys
S of A272, 1 mile beyond Beauworth Hamlet OS570246
☎ (01962) 771248
10.30-2.30 (3.30 Sat), 6-11; 12-2.30, 7-10.30 Sun
Hampshire King Alfred's; Pride of Romsey; Triple fff, Dazed and Confused; guest beer Ⓗ
Remote, 18th-century inn where flagstones, beams and changing levels abound. A massive 250-year-old treadmill and 300ft well feature in one bar. The house bitter is brewed by Triple fff. The food range is generous (as are portions) and includes Sun morning brunch. Skittle alley available.
⛰ Q 🐴 ❀ ⛟ ◖◗ ⛺ ♣ ◒ P ⍻

BENTWORTH

Sun Inn
Off A339
☎ (01420) 562338
12-3, 6-11; 12-10.30 Sun
Cheriton Pots Ale; Courage Best Bitter; Ringwood Best Bitter; Stonehenge Pigswill; guest beers Ⓗ
17th-century inn of three adjoining rooms, each with a log fire. It offers a good home-cooked menu and provides a selection of local micro-breweries' beers (three

guests). The family room is also used for meals.
♔ Q ♉ ❀ ◖◗ P

BIGHTON

Three Horseshoes
Take B3046 from New Alresford OS615344
☎ (01962) 732859
12-2.30 (not Mon), 5.30 (6 Sat)-11; 12-3, 7-10.30 Sun
Gale's Butser, HSB H
Delightful rural local; a pub since 1615, the public bar has large plain tables and a country crafts collection. Cosy, relaxing lounge.
♔ Q ❀ ◖◗ ⊟ ♣ P

BISHOP'S WALTHAM

Bunch of Grapes
St Peter's Street (off High St)
☎ (01489) 892935
10-2, 6-11; 12-2, 7-10.30 Sun
Courage Best Bitter; G **Ushers Best Bitter, seasonal beers** H
Situated in a narrow medieval street leading to the parish church, this small pub has been run by the same family since 1913. The interior is unspoilt by time; worth finding for its originality and genuine welcome.
Q ❀ ⊟ ♣

BRANSGORE

Three Tuns
Ringwood Road (1$^1/_2$ mile N of A35 at Hinton)
☎ (01425) 672232
11-2.30, 6-11; 12-3, 7-10.30 Sun
Gale's HSB; Hampshire Strong's Best Bitter; Ringwood Fortyniner; guest beer H
Picturesque, 17th-century traditional thatched inn near the Dorset county boundary. A central bar serves several drinking and dining areas, boasting oak beams and open fireplaces. Attractive gardens benefit from the quiet rural setting.
♔ Q ❀ ◖◗ ♿ P ⍁

BROUGHTON

Tally Ho!
High Street
☎ (01794) 301280
11-2.30 (3 Sat), 6-11; 12-3, 7-10.30 Sun
Cheriton Pots Ale; Ringwood True Glory; guest beer H
Once a Georgian doctor's house, now an architecturally fine free house. A walkers' pub (it stands on the Clarendon Way), it offers a good range of food (not served Tue eve), much home made. The centre of village life, chat and activity.
♔ Q ❀ ◖◗ ⊟ ♣

BURSLEDON

Jolly Sailor
Lands End Road (park at station, follow signed path)
☎ (023) 8040 5557
11-11; 12-10.30 Sun
Badger Dorset Best, IPA, Tanglefoot; Gale's HSB; guest beer H
Cosy, multi-roomed, waterside pub overlooking Hamble River. Enjoy excellent hospitality and views across the busy marina from the gardens, covered jetty and most rooms. The comprehensive menu suits all tastes.
Q ❀ ◖◗ ⊟ ≠ ⍁

Linden Tree
School Road (off A27/A3025)
☎ (023) 8040 2356
11-2.30, 6-11; 11-11 Fri & Sat; 12-3, 7-10.30 sun
Draught Bass; Wadworth IPA, 6X; seasonal beers (occasional) H
This comfortable, homely, one-bar pub has a large secure garden with play area and a terrace with vines and flowers for summer enjoyment. In winter the real fire adds to the warm welcome. Half the bar is laid out for lunches Mon-Sat.
♔ ❀ ◖ ♣ P

CHALTON

Red Lion
☎ (023) 9259 2246
11-3, 6-11; 12-3, 7-10.30 sun
Gale's Butser, GB, HSB, seasonal beers; guest beers H
Reputed to be the oldest pub in Hampshire it was built in 1147 and became a pub in 1503. The thatched building nestles cosily in the South Downs. The public bar boasts a large inglenook fireplace. No meals Sun eve.
♔ ❀ ◖◗ ⊟ P ⊞

CHARTER ALLEY

White Hart
White Hart Lane (1 mile W of A340)
☎ (01256) 850048
12-2.30 (3 Sat), 7-11; 12-3, 7-10.30 Sun
Morrells Bitter, Varsity; guest beer H
Spacious village pub, with a large skittle alley in the public bar and separate eating areas (no food Mon eve). ♔ Q ❀ ◖◗ ⊟ ♣ ⌓ P ⊓

CHERITON

Flower Pots
SW of centre
☎ (01962) 771318
12-2.30, 6-11; 12-3, 7-10.30 Sun
Cheriton Pots Ale, Best Bitter, Diggers Gold, seasonal beers G

Traditional village inn where the art of conversation is still king. The beer, served straight from the cask, is brewed in the brewhouse across the yard. A barn has been converted to provide high quality accommodation. Wholesome food; Wed eve is curry night prepared by a guest chef; no food Sun eve.
♔ Q ♉ ❀ ⛼ ◖◗ ⊟ ⛺ ♣ P

CHINEHAM

Chineham Arms
Hanmore Road
☎ (01256) 356404
11.30-3; 11.30-11 Fri & Sat; 12-10.30 Sun
Fuller's London Pride, ESB, seasonal beers H
Large estate-type pub, with a very bright interior and a big conservatory.
♔ Q ❀ ◖◗ ♿ P ⍁ ⊓

COSHAM

Churchillian
Widley Walk, Portsdown Hill Road (B2150, near Fort Widley)
☎ (023) 9237 1803
11-11; 12-10.30 Sun
Draught Bass; Gibbs Mew Salisbury, Bishop's Tipple H
This large, single bar stands on top of Portsdown Hill affording superb views of the Solent, the Isle of Wight and the New Forest. Children admitted for meals.
♔ ❀ ◖◗ P

Salisbury
Lonsdale Avenue
☎ (023) 9236 2346
12 (5.30 Mon)-11; 12-10.30 Sun
Wadworth IPA, 6X, seasonal beers H
Imposing 1930s United Breweries building, set in a residential part of town. This friendly pub, with a large public bar and smaller, comfortable lounge, is one of only a few Wadworth's houses in the area.
❀ ◖◗ ⊟ ≠ ♣ P

COVE

Old Courthouse
80 Cove Road (B3014)
☎ (01252) 543031
11-11; 12-10.30 Sun
Draught Bass; Fuller's London Pride, ESB; Hancock's HB; Worthington Bitter; guest beers H
16th-century inn whose extensive horseshoe bar attracts a wide age range. Refurbishment has revealed historic beams. Home-cooked food (not served Sun eve) leads to a happy mix of diners and drinkers.
❀ ◖◗ ♿ ≠ (Farnborough) P

CROOKHAM VILLAGE
Black Horse
The Street
☎ (01252) 616434
11-2.30 (3 Fri & Sat). 5.30-11; 12-3, 7-10.30 Sun

Draught Bass; Courage Best Bitter; Hogs Back Tea *or* seasonal beer; Wadworth 6X Ⓗ

Excellent, beamed village pub providing a friendly atmosphere, good beers and food (Mon-Sat), it is handy for walks along the nearby Basingstoke Canal.
Q ☸ ◖ ♣ P

DUNBRIDGE
Mill Arms
Barley Mill (B3084, by station)
☎ (01794) 340401
11 (12 winter)-3, 6-11; 12-3, 7-10.30 Sun

Hampshire Mottisfont Meddler; Itchen Valley Olde Test Tickler; guest beers Ⓗ

Named after local landowners, not a mill, this large pub comprises an L-shaped lounge (great fire, papers, magazines), a skittle alley (sometimes live music or theatre) and a conservatory. Enjoy the relaxed atmosphere and good food. Cider sold in summer. It hosts a ticket-only beer festival (end Sept) when pub is otherwise closed. ⚌ Q ⛻ ☸ ⌑ ◖ ⊟ ⅋ ⇌ ♣ ⌂ P ⊟

DUNDRIDGE
Hampshire Bowman
Dundridge Lane (1¹/₂ miles off B3035) OS578185
☎ (01489) 892940
11-2.30 (3 Sat), 6-11; 12-3, 7-10.30 Sun

Archers Village, Golden; Ringwood Fortyniner; guest beer (occasional) Ⓖ

Remote basic, no-frills country pub along a winding single track lane. A small serving counter, with casks stillaged behind the bar, in one traditional, brick-floored bar. An informal meeting of classic motorcycles is held most Sun lunchtimes. No food Sun eve or Mon. Cider in summer.
⚌ Q ☸ ◖ Å ♣ ⌂ P

EAST END (LYMINGTON)
East End Arms
Main Road (2¹/₂ miles E of Lymington) OS362968
☎ (01590) 626223
11-3, 6-11; 12-9 Sun

Ringwood Best Bitter, Fortyniner; guest beer Ⓖ

Simple. unspoilt rural pub in a quiet backwater. The traditional public bar is preferred by the friendly locals; a pleasant homely dining/lounge bar serves good quality food (not on Sun eve or Mon). It stands near Solent Way long distance footpath.
⚌ Q ☸ ◖ ⅋ ⇌ ♣ P

EAST STRATTON
Northbrook Arms
☎ (01962) 774150
11-3, 6-11; 12-3, 7-10.30 Sun

Gale's GB, HSB; guest beers Ⓗ

Spacious open-plan pub boasting extensive gardens opposite where volleyball and boules can be played. There is also a skittle alley. A good stop for walkers.
⚌ Q ☸ ⌑ ◖ ⅋ ⅊ ♣ P

EASTLEIGH
Hogshead
18-20 High Street
☎ (023) 8065 2554
11-11; 12-10.30 Sun

Boddingtons Bitter; Brakspear Bitter; Gale's HSB; Wadworth 6X; Ⓗ **guest beers** Ⓖ

Typical Hogshead shop conversion: lots of flagstones, reclaimed brick pillars, pine room dividers etc, comfortably done. It upholds the usual Hogshead marketing policy – four-pint jugs, beer taster glasses and various special offers. Children's certificate. ◖ ⅋ ⅊ ⇌ ♣ ⌂ ⅌

EASTON
Cricketers
Off B3047
☎ (01962) 779353
12-2.30 (3 Wed-Sat), 6-11; 12-3, 7-10.30 (12-10.30 summer) Sun

Draught Bass; Otter Ale; Ringwood Best Bitter; guest beers Ⓗ

Comfortable pub, ofering a changing range of guest beers and excellent food (not served Sun eve). The decor owes much to cricket, and a wide range of reference books can be consulted.
⚌ ☸ ⌑ ◖ ♣ P ⅌

EMSWORTH
Coal Exchange
21 South Street
☎ (01243) 375866
10.30-3, 5.30-11; 10.30-11 Sat; 12-10.30 Sun

Gale's Butser, GB, HSB, seasonal beers; guest beers Ⓗ

Popular, single bar pub near the town square. The name derives from its earlier use as a place to exchange local produce with coal brought in by sea. Emsworth harbour, popular with yachtsmen, is nearby. Note the unusual green-tiled frontage.
⚌ ☸ ◖ ⇌ ♣

EVERSLEY
White Hart
The Street (A327, Reading road) ☎ (0118) 973 2817
11-11; 12-10.30 Sun

Courage Best Bitter, Directors; Fuller's London Pride Ⓗ

Small, 17th-century gem of a country pub: low, beamed ceilings and log fires feature in the cosy front and middle bars; the back bar is more basic, and used for darts, etc.
⚌ Q ☸ ⌑ ⊟ ♣ P

FAREHAM
White Horse
44 North Wallington (¹/₂ mile from Delme roundabout)
☎ (01329) 235197
11-11; 12-4.30, 7-10.30 Sun

Winchester Old Chapel, Buckland Best Bitter, Hole Hertford, Blakes Gosport; Ⓗ **Theakston Mild;** Ⓖ **guest beers** Ⓗ

Small, old-style, cosy village local of two bars; the outside seating area is alongside River Wallington. It is accessible by footbridge from the High Street car park. Meals available Tue-Sat, specialising in seafood. ⚌ Q ☸ ◖ ♣

FARNBOROUGH
Alexandra
74 Victoria Road (near clockhouse roundabout)
☎ (01252) 519964
11-11; 12-10.30 Sun

Ushers Best Bitter, Founders, seasonal beers Ⓗ

This large, welcoming, friendly bar is developing a growing reputation for quality. Relaxing and comfortable, it provides an ideal escape from the nearby shopping centre.
☸ ◖ ⅊ ⇌ ♣ P ⊟

Prince of Wales
184 Rectory Road OS877564
☎ (01252) 545578
11.30-2.30, 5.30-11; 12-3.30, 7-10.30 Sun

Badger Dorset Best, Tanglefoot; Fuller's London Pride; Hogs Back TEA; guest beers Ⓗ

Renowned free house where a comfortable, convivial, village atmosphere and a perfect mix of beers are assured; regular beers are served in the main bar and guests, including a reduced price session beer, in the back snug. No food Sun; occasional cider sold in summer. Local CAMRA *Pub of the Year* 2000.
Q ☸ ◖ ⇌ (North) P

FLEET
Prince Arthur

238 Fleet Road
☎ (01252) 622660
10.30-11; 12-10.30 Sun
Courage Directors; Hogs Back TEA; Ringwood Fortyniner; Theakston Best Bitter; guest beers Ⓗ
Welcome addition to the Fleet scene. An excellent atmosphere prevails in an often crowded environment, including a large no-smoking area. Relatively new, but it seems to have been around for years.
Q ✿ ◖ 🍴 ఈ ⊁ ⊞

FREEFOLK
Watership Down
Off B3400
☎ (01256) 892254
11.30-3, 6-11; 12-3.30, 7-10.30 Sun
Archers Best Bitter; Brakspear Bitter; guest beers Ⓗ
Welcoming, single-bar pub, affectionately as the 'Jerry'. Usually three guest beers on, including a mild, sourced from small breweries. A no-smoking conservatory is available for diners.
🏠 ✿ ◖▶ ♣ P ⊁ 🏷

FRITHAM
Royal Oak
1 mile S of B3078 OS232141
☎ (023) 8081 2606
11-3, 6-11; 11-11 Sat (and summer Fri); 12-10.30 Sun
Ringwood Best Bitter, True Glory, Fortyniner; guest beer (occasional) Ⓖ
Tiny, thatched pub at the end of a New Forest track, comprising three small bars. The Royal Oak is the centre for all forest and country activities. Lunches are just soup and ploughmans-style but high quality. The back bar offers a full meal 'supper club' winter Mon and Tue.
🏠 Q ✿ ▲ ♣ 🏷

FROXFIELD
Trooper
Alton Road (3 miles from Petersfield) OS727273
☎ (01730) 827923
12-3, 6-11; 12-3, 7-10.30 Sun
Ringwood Best Bitter, Fortyniner; guest beers Ⓗ
Remote but friendly free house whose atmosphere is enhanced by candlelight. An extensive food menu is always available. Live entertainment staged monthly.
🏠 Q ✿ ◖▶ P

Try also: **White Horse**, Priors Dean (Free)

GOSPORT
Clarence Tavern
1 Clarence Road

☎ (023) 9253 9726
11-11; 12-10.30 Sun
Winchester Old Chapel, Buckland Best Bitter, Hole Hearted, Blakes Gosport, seasonal beers; guest beers Ⓗ
Formerly a club, which reopened as a pub in March 1999. A rectangular main bar area is linked by a short passage to the newly built old chapel which houses a brewery at the far end, and an upstairs restaurant. No meals Sun eve.
🏠 Q ✿ ◖▶ P ⊁

Five Alls
75 Forton Road
☎ (023) 1252 9773
10-11; 12-10.30 Sun
Draught Bass; guest beer Ⓗ
Two-roomed local hosting regular quiz nights. The guest comes from the Tisbury Brewery range.
✿ 🍴 ♣

Queens Hotel
143 Queens Road
☎ (023) 9258 2645
11.30-2.30, 7-11; 11.30-11 Sat; 12-3, 7-10.30 Sun
Badger Tanglefoot; Black Sheep Special; Oakham JHB; guest beers Ⓗ
Award-winning pub, hidden away in the back streets, but known nationally. There are three drinking areas, the focal point being an old open fire with an elegant, carved wood surround. Real cider is sold summer.
🏠 ♣ ◌

Windsor Castle
33 St Thomas's Road
☎ (023) 9251 0410
11-11; 12-10.30 Sun
Gales Butser, GB, Winter Brew, HSB Ⓗ
Community pub with a large, recently refurbished room and a smaller pool room; see the enormous range of elephants behind the bar.
✿ ఈ ♣ P

GREYWELL
Fox & Goose
The Street
☎ (01256) 702062
11-11; 12-10.30 Sun
Courage Best Bitter; Gibbs Mew Bishop's Tipple; guest beers Ⓗ
16th-century inn, a short distance from Basingstoke Canal in a good walking area. A large field behind the pub is used for events. Children welcome if dining.
🏠 ✿ ◖▶ ▲ ♣ P 🏷

HAMBLEDON
Bat & Ball
Hyden Farm Lane, Clanfield (2½ miles from village)

OS677167
☎ (023) 9263 2692
11.30-3, 6-11; 12-11 Sat; 12-4, 7-10.30 Sun
Gale's Butser, GB, HSB Ⓗ
Known as the cradle of modern cricket and set high on Broadhalfpenny Down, this was once the home of famous matches between the local team and All-England. The bar is full of memorabilia of the great game. Note the parish boundary marked on the floor.
🏠 ✿ ◖▶ ఈ ♣ P

HAMMER VALE
Prince of Wales
Hammer Lane 1 mile S off A3
OS868326
☎ (01428) 652600
12-3, 6-11; 12-3 Sat; 12-10.30 Sun
Gales Butser, GB, HSB, seasonal beer or guest beer Ⓖ
Built in 1927, the pub is set deep in a scenic wooded valley. Inside, a long bar, with its fine old stillage, serves two drinking areas and a no-smoking eating area (no meals Sun eve). Outside, is a large children's play area and patio seating.
🏠 Q ✿ ◖▶ ⚄ ▲ ♣ P

HARTLEY WINTNEY
Waggon & Horses
High Street (A30)
☎ (01252) 842119
11-11; 12-3, 7-10.30 Sun
Courage Best Bitter; Gale's HSB; Ⓗ **Wadworth 6X;** Ⓖ **guest beers** Ⓗ
Welcoming village-cenre pub: a lively public bar and a quieter lounge; the winner of many local CAMRA awards. The landlord serves good food.
🏠 Q ✿ ◖ 🍴 ♣

HAVANT
Old House at Home
2 South Street
☎ (023) 9248 3464
11-11; 12-10.30 Sun
Gale's Butser, GB, HSB, seasonal beers; guest beers Ⓗ
One of the oldest buildings in town, having survived the fire of 1760. This popular, two-bar pub, hidden behind the church, is reputed to have shown the last dancing bear in England. Unusually, the lounge is larger than the public bar. It hosts live music Sat eves.
🏠 ✿ ◖ 🍴 ⇌ ♣ ⊁ 🏷

HAWKLEY
Hawkley Inn
Pococks Lane OS747291
☎ (01730) 827205
12-2.30 (3 Sat), 6-11; 12-3, 7-10.30 Sun

Beer range varies H
Popular free house in a
village, well off the beaten
track. Furnished in an
individual style (note the
moose head), it offers six ales
from independent breweries.
Live music is performed Fri or
Sat in winter. The landlord
sells his own cider. No food
Sun eve.
🏭 Q 🕸 ◖ ▶ ⌂

HEADLEY
Hollybush
High Street
☎ (01428) 712211
11-3, 6-11; 11-11 Sat (& summer Fri);
12-4, 7-10.30 (2-10.30 summer) Sun
**Courage Best Bitter; Ushers Best
Bitter, Founders, seasonal beers** H
Comfortable, welcoming,
Victorian pub with period
decor where a central bar
serves various eating and
drinking areas. A regular bus
service runs from Farnham
and Haslemere.
Q 🐎 ◖ ▶ P ⌲

HILL HEAD
Osborne View
67 Hill Head Road
☎ (01329) 664623
11-11; 12-10.30 Sun
**Badger IPA, Dorset Best,
Tanglefoot, seasonal beers; guest
beers** H
Large, open-plan bar on three
levels; steps lead down to the
garden and beach, affording
panoramic views of the
Solent. Although the
emphasis is on food, there is
plenty of room for drinkers.
🏭 Q 🕸 ◖ ▶ ▲ P ⌲

HORNDEAN
Brewers Arms
1 Five Heads Road
☎ (023) 9259 1325
12-2 (4 Sat; not Mon); 5 (6 Sat)-11;
12-3, 7-10.30 Sun
**Draught Bass; Courage Directors;
Fuller's London Pride; Ringwood
Best Bitter; guest beers** H
Traditional village local, just
off the main road: two
contrasting bars in a 1950s
brick-tiled pub. Two guest
beers are sold at weekends.
Q 🕸 🟥 ♣ P

LANGSTONE
Old Ship
Langstone Road OS731160
☎ (023) 9247 1719
11-11; 12-10.30 Sun
**Gale's Butser, GB, HSB, seasonal
beers; guest beers** H
This large pub on the shore
of Langstone harbour bears a
strong nautical theme. The
single bar is divided into
several drinking areas.
Interesting walks nearby,

include the course of the Old
Hayling Island branch line.
🏭 🕸 ◖ ▶ & ▲ P ⌲

LASHAM
Royal Oak
Off A339
☎ (01256) 381213
11-3, 6-11; 12-3, 7-10.30 Sun
**Fuller's London Pride; Hogs Back
TEA; Ringwood Best Bitter; guest
beers** H
Attractive pub with a
welcoming garden alongside
the church in a pretty village
setting. The pub stocks
interesting guest beers; the
house beer is brewed by
Beckett's.
🏭 🕸 ◖ ▶ 🟥 ♣ P

LINWOOD
Red Shoot Inn
Toms Lane (3 miles E of
A338, Ellingham Cross)
OS187094
☎ (01425) 475792
11-3, 6-11; 11-11 Sat & summer;
12-10.30 Sun
**Red Shoot Forest Gold, Tom's
Tipple; Wadworth IPA, 6X, Farmer's
Glory, seasonal beers** H
Rambling inn in the heart of
the forest (only served by
narrow roads). The micro-
brewery is visible from the
bar, where several multi-level
areas break up the space. It
hosts a music quiz (Thu eve),
live rock (Sun) plus beer
festivals (April and Oct).
🏭 🐎 🕸 ◖ ▶ ▲ P

LITTLE LONDON
Plough Inn
Silchester Road (1 mile off
A340, S of Tadley)
☎ (01256) 850628
12-2.30, 6-11; 12-3, 6-10.30 Sun
Ringwood Best Bitter, True Glory, H
Porter XXXX; guest beers G
Small, attractive country pub
with a pleasant garden. An
interesting range of up to
four guest beers are served
from the cask; filled
baguettes are usually
available.
🏭 Q 🐎 🕸 ♣ P

LONGPARISH
Cricketers
On B3048 (off A303, E of
Andover)
☎ (01264) 720335
12-3 (not Mon), 6-11; 12-11 Sat;
12-10.30 Sun
**Wadworth IPA, 6X, seasonal
beers** H
Close to Longparish
cricket ground in the
heart of the village. This two-
bar pub serves its local
community well. No food
Sun eve.
🕸 ◖ ▶ ♣ P ⊞

LONG SUTTON
Four Horseshoes
Winchester Road
☎ (01256) 862488
12-2.30, 6.30-11; 12-3, 7-10.30 Sun
**Gales Butser, GB, HSB, seasonal
beers** H
Wonderful rural retreat with
an attractive, covered
verandah. The friendly,
comfortable bar is dominated
by a central fireplace. The
former airfield nearby ran
secret wartime operations; it
is now a helicopter station.
Pétanque played.
🏭 Q 🕸 🟥 ◖ ▶ ▲ P

LOWER UPHAM
Woodman Inn
Winchester Road (B2177)
☎ (01489) 860270
11-2.30, 7-11; 11.30-5, 7-10.30 Sat;
12-5.30, 7-10.30 Sun
**Greene King XX Mild, IPA, Abbot;
guest beer** H
Welcoming, part 17th-
century inn with two cosy,
contrasting bars where some
180 whiskies are stocked.
Sandwiches and ploughmans
are available Mon-Sat
lunchtimes. Tue eve quiz
held.
🏭 Q 🕸 🟥 ♣ P ⊟

LYMINGTON (PENNINGTON)
Musketeer
26 North Street, Pennington
(off A337)
☎ (01590) 676527
11.30-2.30 (3.30 Sat), 5.30-11; 12-3,
7-10.30 Sun
**Brakspear Special; Ringwood Best
Bitter, Fortyniner; guest beers** H
Imposing brick-and-tile
building at the village centre,
with a large comfortable bar
in manorial style. The same
friendly family has run the
pub since 1980, in this *Guide*
throughout. An excellent
menu offers home-cooked
specials (not served Sun).
🏭 Q 🐎 🕸 ◖ ▶ P

LYNDHURST (BANK)
Oak
Pinkney Lane (off A35, 1¼
miles SW of Lyndhurst)
OS286072
☎ (023) 8028 2350
11.30-2.30 (3 Sat), 6-11; 12-3, 7-
10.30 Sun
**Draught Bass; Holden's Special
Bitter; Ringwood Best Bitter; guest
beers** P
18th-century building in a
New Forest hamlet,
frequented by walkers and
ponies. The beamed bar is
cosy and characterful, and is
a popular choice for good
quality, home-made meals.
🏭 🕸 🟥 ◖ ▶ ▲ ♣ P

MEDSTEAD
Castle of Comfort
Castle Street (2 miles N of
A31 at Four Marks)
OS655373
☎ (01420) 562112
11-2.30 (3 Sat), 6-11; 12-3, 7-10.30
Sun
**Courage Best Bitter; Ushers Best
Bitter, Founders, seasonal beers** Ⓗ
Attractive, friendly, unspoilt,
17th-century village local,
with two bars. The
Watercress steam line runs
nearby. ♨ Q ❀ ◖▣ ⇌ ♣ P

MICHELDEVER
Half Moon Spread Eagle
Winchester Road
☎ (01962) 774339
12-3, 6-11; 12-3, 7.30-10.30 Sun
**Greene King XX Mild, IPA, Abbot;
guest beer** Ⓗ
Friendly village pub: one
main bar area, plus two
further seating areas (one
serves as the restaurant). It
was renamed the Dever
Arms, but has now reverted
to its original name.
Q ❀ ◖▣ ♣ P

MILFORD ON SEA
Red Lion
32 High Street
☎ (01590) 642236
11.30-2.30, 6-11; 12-3, 7-10.30 Sun
**Brakspear Bitter or Hampshire
Strong's Best Bitter; Flowers
Original; Fuller's London Pride;
Ringwood True Glory** Ⓗ
This 1740s village-centre pub
has been neatly extended to
include two adjoining
houses, and recently
refurbished. A games alcove
is used for darts and pool; the
no-smoking dining area
serves an extensive menu.
Close to the beach, it
provides good views of the
Needles. ♨ Q ❀ ⇌ ◖▣ ઇ Å ♣ P ⅌

OAKHANGER
Red Lion
The Street (off B3004)
☎ (01420) 472232
11-3, 6-11; 12-3, 7-10.30 Sun
**Courage Best Bitter, Directors;
guest beers** Ⓗ
Excellent village local where
a traditional public bar and a
restaurant area are
dominated by luxuriant hop
vines, a real fire, a massive
framed pike and often dogs.
A superb garden, with fruit
trees and bushes, leads to a
children's play area.
♨ Q ❀ ◖▣ ♣ P

OWSLEBURY
Ship Inn
Off B2177, 1½ miles N of
Marwell Zoo
☎ (01962) 777358
11-3, 6-11 (11-11 summer Sat);
12-10.30 Sun
**Greene King XX Mild, IPA; guest
beers** Ⓗ
Busy, welcoming, two-bar
country inn displaying
sporting memorabilia in the
main bar; the Mess-Deck bar
bears a nautical theme.
Home-style cooking
combines pub favourites and
a bistro-style menu. The large
garden has a patio and play
areas.
♨ Q ❀ ◖▶ ▣ ♣ P ▦

PICKET PIECE
Wyke Down Country Pub
Follow brown camping signs
from A303
☎ (01264) 352048
12-3, 6-11; 12-3, 7-10.30 Sun
**Ringwood Best Bitter; True Glory;
guest beer** Ⓗ
Something for all the family
on this farm complex
comprising a
caravan/campsite, golf range
and outdoor pool. The pub is
based on a large barn
conversion with a restaurant
and games rooms. Excellent
food is served in both bar
and restaurant.
♨ 🛏 ❀ ◖▶ ઇ Å ♣ P

PORTSMOUTH
Connaught Arms
119 Guildford Road, Fratton
☎ (023) 9264 6455
11.30-2.30, 6-11; 11.30-11 Fri & Sat;
12-4, 7-10.30 Sun
**Caledonian Deuchars IPA; guest
beers** Ⓗ
One-bar 'Brewer's Tudor'
corner pub. Ales are an
excellent accompaniment for
the truly delicious home-
made pasties with a plethora
of different fillings served in
the raised dining area. Very
popular, especially at
weekends.
❀ ◖ ⇌ (Fratton) ♣ ⏚

Florence Arms
18-20 Florence Road,
Southsea (between
Clarendon Rd and sea front)
☎ (023) 9287 5700
12-11; 12-10.30 Sun
**Morland Old Speckled Hen;
Packhorse Old Pompey; Young's
Bitter, Special; guest beers**
(occasional) Ⓗ
Surprisingly large pub, with a
tiled façade, it was built in
1924 to serve a residential
area, midway between
Southsea shopping centre
and the South Parade pier.
The largest of the three bars
doubles as a function room;
often hosting live acoustic

music. The public bar has
table football. Weekday eve
meals and Sun lunch served.
Q ◖ ▣ ♣ ⏚

Fifth Hampshire Volunteer Arms
74 Albert Road, Southsea
(200 yd E of Kings Theatre)
☎ (023) 9282 7161
12-11; 12-10.30 Sun
Gale's GB, HSB, seasonal beers Ⓗ
A quiet lounge, featuring
military memorabilia
contrasts with a lively public
bar with TV, darts, rock
music juke box and a rare
collection of hard hats.
Q ▣ ♣

Florist
324 Fratton Road, Fratton
☎ (023) 9282 0289
11-2.30, 6-11; 11-11 Sat; 12-10.30
Sun
**Wadworth IPA, 6X, seasonal beer or
guest beer** Ⓗ
This Cogswell-designed
Grade II listed two-bar
'Tudorbethan' house has
been altered. However, its
original brewery mosaic and
stained glass windows are
now displayed on the walls
inside. Still a gem.
Q ઇ ⇌ (Fratton) ♣

Isambard Kingdom Brunel
2 Guildhall Walk (opp.
Guildhall)
☎ (023) 9229 5112
10-11; 12-10.30 Sun
**Boddingtons Bitter; Courage
Directors; Hop Back Summer
Lightning; Theakston Best Bitter,
XB; guest beers** Ⓗ
This recently refurbished
one-bar conversion of the old
Portsmouth & Gosport Gas
Co. office now boasts a raised
seating area. It sports a new
colour scheme but the ever-
helpful, cheerful staff remain
the same.
Q ❀ ◖▶ ઇ ⇌ ⏚ ⅌

Old Oyster House
291 Locksway Road, Milton,
Southsea (off A288, near
University's Langstone site)
☎ (023) 9282 7456
4 (12 Fri & Sat)-11; 12-10.30 Sun
Beer range varies Ⓗ
Spacious, traditional drinkers'
pub, where five real ales and
a scrumpy are always
available. It stands by the
only remaining section of the
Portsea Canal.
❀ ♣ ⏚

Red White & Blue
150 Fawcett Road, Southsea
☎ (023) 9278 0013
11-11; 12-10.30 Sun
**Gale's Butser, GB, HSB; guest
beers** Ⓗ
Compact, street-corner local,
with eclectic decor. A wide

range of board games includes Uckers. Canada Day (1 July) is celebrated on the nearest Sat with Canadian breakfast and moose milk. Sat lunch served. Children's certificate until 8pm. The guest beers are supplied by Gales.

≉ (Fratton) ♣

Rose in June

102 Milton Road, Copnor (100 yds N of prison)
☎ (023) 9282 4191
12-3, 6.30-11; 12-11 Fri & Sat; 12-10.30 Sun
Fuller's London Pride; Gale's HSB; guest beers Ⓗ
Two-bar local that hosts many community events, including raffles, a jug club, quizzes and occasional live music. The large garden has swings.

Q ❀ ☐ ♣ ♣

Royal Marines Artillery Tavern

58 Cromwell Road, Eastney, Southsea (opp. former Royal Marine Barracks)
☎ (023) 9282 0896
10.30-11; 12-10.30 Sun
Gale's Butser, HSB; guest beers Ⓗ
The RMA features a lively public bar where the choice of games include Shut the Box, Uckers and Connect Four, together with a selection of newspapers. A quiet lounge leads to the only permanent skittle alley in the city. Children's certificate.

Q ❀ ☐ ▲ ♣

Sir Loin of Beef

152 Highland Road, Eastney, Southsea (opp. police station)
☎ (023) 9282 0115
11-11; 12-10.30 Sun
Hop Back Summer Lightning; Ringwood Old Thumper; guest beers Ⓗ
Friendly, true free house, close to the Royal Marines Museum; the large public bar bears a submarine theme. Six guest beers often include a mild. ▲ ♣ ⌂

Sir Robert Peel

Astley Street (near law courts)
☎ (023) 9234 5708
11.45-3.30 (4.30 Sat), 7-11; 12-4.30, 7-10.30 Sun
Ringwood Best Bitter; guest beers Ⓗ
1960s estate pub; an oasis among the tower blocks, this friendly free house is worth seeking out, even though it is in need of renovation. No food Sun. Thatcher's cider is available occasionally.

❀ ☐ ᴋ ≉ ♣ ⌂ P

Try also: **Eldon Arms**, Eldon St (Eldridge Pope)

RINGWOOD

Inn on the Furlong

12 Meeting House Lane (opp. Tourist Information office)
☎ (01425) 475139
11-11; 12-4.30, 7-10.30 Sun
Ringwood Best Bitter, Fortyniner, Old Thumper, seasonal beers; guest beers (occasional) Ⓗ
Lively, town-centre drinking house divided into several areas: a main bar, two small snugs and a conservatory/dining/family room. Daily newspapers are available. Ringwood Brewery's flagship pub.

ᴍ ❀ ☐ ⊞

ROMSEY

Abbey Hotel

11 Church Street
☎ (01794) 513360
11-2.30 (3 summer), 6-11; 12-3, 7-10.30 Sun
Courage Best Bitter, Directors Ⓗ
Conversation rules in the Victorian bar of this attractive, late 19th-century pub. The nearest to Romsey Abbey. Its function rooms are frequented by several local societies. All food is home-prepared (not served Sun eve – quiz night).

ᴍ Q ❀ ᴋ ☐ ▮ ≉ P

Tudor Rose

3 Cornmarket
☎ (01794) 512126
10-11; 12-4, 7-10.30 Sun
Courage Best Bitter, Directors Ⓗ
This 15th-century building served as a Guildhall and a brothel before settling down as a pub. The single bar boasts a handsome fireplace. No food Sun.

ᴍ ❀ ☐ ≉ ♣

SELBORNE

Selborne Arms

High Street (B3006, Alton road)
☎ (01420) 511247
11-3, 5.30-11; 11-11 Fri & Sat; 12-10.30 Sun
Courage Best Bitter, Directors; Ringwood Best Bitter; guest beers Ⓗ
A beer house from 1878 in the village made famous by Gilbert White. A massive real fire and church pew seating lend character. Two gardens, home to an aviary and animals, lead on to the Zig Zag walk. Often very crowded in summer.

ᴍ Q ᴋ ❀ ☐ ♣ P

SHEDFIELD

Wheatsheaf

Botley Road (A334)
☎ (01329) 833024
11-11; 12-10.30 Sun
Cheriton Pots Ale; Hop Back Summer Lightning; Mansfield Four Seasons; Ringwood Best Bitter; guest beers Ⓖ
Proudly traditional roadside free house with two cosy bars and a tidy garden. The ales (including two weekly guests) are dispensed from a cooled stillage. Good value home-cooked lunches served.

Q ❀ ☐ ♣ P

SHEET

Queens Head

Sheet Village Green
☎ (01730) 264204
11-2.30, 5.30-11; 11-3, 6-11 Sat; 12-3, 7-10.30 Sun
Brakspear Bitter; Fuller's London Pride; Hampshire Strong's Best Bitter; Wadworth 6X Ⓗ
Typical local, next to the village green and church. The public bar, nearly 400 years old, attracts all ages.

ᴍ Q ❀ ☐ ▮ ☐ ♣ P

SHERFIELD ON LODDON

White Hart

Old Reading Road (100 yds off A33)
☎ (01256) 882280
11-2.30, 6-11; 12-3, 7-10.30 Sun
Beckett's Original; Courage Best Bitter, Directors Ⓗ
Large, open-plan rooms in a very traditional country pub interior dating from the 18th century.

ᴍ Q ❀ ☐ ▮ ᴋ P

SOUTHAMPTON

Bevois Castle

63 Onslow Road, Bevois Valley
☎ (023) 8033 0350
11-11; 12-10.30 Sun
Courage Best Bitter, Directors; Eldridge Pope's Traditional; Theakston Best Bitter; guest beer Ⓗ
Recently refurbished, welcoming one-bar pub, named after a Southampton mythological hero, Sir Bevis of Hamtun. Good value home-cooked meals are complemented by summer barbecues. An annual beer festival is held at the end of May.

ᴍ ❀ ☐ ▮ ♣ P ⊟

Bitter Virtue Off-licence

70 Cambridge Road, Portswood (off The Avenue)
☎ (023) 8055 4881
10.30-8 (closed Mon & Tue); 10.30-2 Sun
Brakspear seasonal beers; Hop Back Summer Lightning, seasonal beers; guest beers Ⓖ
Southampton's only real ale shop stocks over 250 bottle-conditioned beers. British and Belgian beers are a

speciality, but it also has beers from many other countries as well as bottled ciders and perries.

Crown Inn
9 Highcrown Street, Highfield
☎ (023) 8031 5033
11-11; 12-10.30 Sun
Archers Best Bitter; Flowers Original; Fuller's London Pride; Hampshire Strong's Best Bitter; Wadworth 6X Ⓗ
Busy, one-bar pub, close to the University and the common, popular with students and locals alike. The covered patio area now sports gas heating to enable year-round use. Popular with diners (tables can be booked), but essentially still a drinkers' pub.
🏮 ◖ P

Duke of Wellington
36 Bugle Street (near Tudor House Museum)
☎ (023) 8033 9222
11-11; 12-10.30 Sun
Adnams Bitter; Ringwood Best Bitter, Ⓗ XXXX Porter; Ⓖ Wadworth IPA, 6X, Ⓗ Farmers Glory; Ⓖ guest beer Ⓗ
Reputedly Southampton's oldest pub, with parts dating back to the 13th century. The menu, served all day, is comprehensive and good value. An ideal stop on a walk round the City Walls.
🏮 ◖ ◗ ♣ ♣

Freemantle Arms
31 Albany Road
☎ (023) 8032 0759
10.30-3, 6-11; 10.30-11 Fri & Sat; 12-10.30 Sun
Greene King XX Mild, IPA; Ruddles County Ⓗ
Friendly, single-bar local in a quiet cul-de-sac. This ex-Winchester Brewery pub, recently taken over by Greene King from Marston's, retains its fine etched Marston's windows.
🏮 ≠ (Millbrook) ♣

Grove Tavern
68-70 Swift Road, Woolston
☎ (023) 8032 2918
12-3, 7-11; 12-11 Fri & Sat; 12-10.30 Sun
Fuller's London Pride; guest beers Ⓗ
Situated in a residential area near Woolston's shipyards, this former Brickwood's pub is a paradigm of that brewery's once common three-bar style. Snacks are available all sessions. The garden is home to rabbits, guinea pigs and an owl.
🏮 ⚏ ♣ P

Ice House
180 Warren Avenue

☎ (023) 8034 6880
11-11; 2-10.30 Sun
Courage Best Bitter; Wadworth 6X, Ⓗ
Popular, two-bar local near the general hospital, built on the site of an ice pit. The landlord is an enthusiastic photographer; some of his work adorns the lounge bar.
🏮 ⚏ ♣

New Inn
16 Bevois Valley Road
☎ (023) 8022 8437
11-11; 12-10.30 Sun
Gale's Butser, GB, HSB, seasonal beers; guest beers Ⓗ
Superb, single-bar town local, dedicated to the discerning imbiber, with a range of Belgian and German bottled beers and over 100 malt whiskies. Excellent home-cooked food is served. Occasional beer festivals held.
🏮 ◖ ◗ ⊞

Park Inn
37 Carlisle Road, Shirley (off Shirley High St)
☎ (023) 8078 7835
11.30-3, 5-11; 11.30-11 Fri; 11-11 Sat; 12-10.30 Sun
Badger Tanglefoot; Wadworth IPA, 6X; guest beers Ⓗ
This splendid community local supports various teams. The one central bar manages to maintain a good marriage of public and lounge atmospheres. Famous locally for its belly-busting baguettes, it hosts a regular Sun quiz and meat draw.
🏮 ◖ ♣

Platform Tavern
Town Quay (opp. ferry terminals)
☎ (023) 8033 7232
12-11; 12-10.30 Sun
Fuller's London Pride; guest beer Ⓗ
Built in 1873, incorporating part of the original town wall (circa 1350), a small single flagstoned floor bar is connected by a metal spiral staircase to an upstairs pool room. Frequent live music; blues Thu eve, jazz Sun lunch, when drink prices are raised to cover music costs. May close Sat eve for functions.
◖ ◗

Richmond Inn
108 Portswood Road, Portswood
☎ (023) 8055 4523
11-11; 12-10.30 Sun
Greene King XX Mild, IPA; guest beers Ⓗ
Two-bar traditional town pub: a comfortable lounge bar, a boisterous public and a pleasant, secluded garden. At least two guest real ales are

supplied by Greene King.
🏮 ⚏ ≠ (St Denys) ♣

Salisbury Arms
126 Shirley High Street, Shirley ☎ (023) 8077 4624
10-11; 12-3, 7-10.30 Sun
Greene King IPA, Abbot; Ruddles County; guest beer Ⓗ
Comfortable, single-bar, street-corner pub; a back room is used for dining and can be booked for skittles. Dating from the 1860s it is an ex-Winchester Brewery pub. Lunchtime snacks served Mon-Sat, plus a traditional roast on Sun (book). ♣ ⊞

Waterloo Arms
101 Waterloo Road, Freemantle
☎ (023) 8022 0022
12-11; 12-10.30 Sun
Hop Back GFB, Best Bitter, Entire Stout, Thunderstorm, Summer Lightning, seasonal beers; guest beers Ⓗ
Welcoming, one-bar local with an enclosed patio garden. It hosts a beer festival each Spring and Autumn. A bottled foreign beer selection, good value food, regular quiz (Tue) and occasional live music are added attractions.
🏮 ◖ ◗ ≠ (Millbrook) ♣

Wellington Arms
56 Park Road, Freemantle
☎ (023) 8022 7356
11.30-2.30 (3 Fri), 5.30 (5 Fri, 6 Sat)-11; 12-4, 6.30-10.30 Sun
Fuller's London Pride, ESB; Hampshire Pride of Romsey; Ringwood Best Bitter, Fortyniner, Old Thumper; guest beers Ⓗ
This genuine free house comprising two bars and a restaurant, is a treasure trove of Iron Duke memorabilia. It stocks draught Belgian beers and a good selection of wines. No food Sun eve.
Q 🏮 ◖ ◗ ≠ (Central/Millbrook)

STEEP

Harrow Inn ☆
Halfway between the villages of Steep and Sheet OS751251
☎ (01730) 262685
12-2.30 (11-3 Sat), 6-11; 12-3, 7-10.30 Sun
Ballard's Trotton; Cheriton Pots Ale, Diggers Gold; Ringwood Best Bitter Ⓖ
Wonderful old pub in a little lane; two small bars are both warmed by open fires. In the same family for three generations, it has remained totally unspoilt. The menu is limited, but the portions generous, the toilets are on the other side of the lane from the pub!
🏮 Q 🏮 ◖ ◗ ⚏ ♣ ⌣ P

STOCKBRIDGE
Three Cups Inn
High Street
☎ (01264) 810527
12-2, 5-11; 12-2, 7-10.30 Sun
Draught Bass; Fuller's London Pride; guest beer Ⓗ
This 15th-century coaching inn beside the River Test closed as a pub between 1910 and 1996, and was variously used as a builder's yard, tea shop and undertakers. No food Sun eve.
🛏 ✿ ⇔ ◖ ♣ ⇖ P

STUBBINGTON
Golden Bowler
122 Stubbington Lane
☎ (01329) 662845
11-11; 12-10.30 Sun
Draught Bass; guest beers Ⓗ
Modern free house, formerly a spacious 19th-century detached house. The present owner has been here for 20 years. A large open-plan bar, plus a restaurant; there is also a small family room that doubles as a function room.
✿ ◖ ▶ ⅍

TANGLEY
Cricketers Arms
Tangley Bottom (signed at crossroads in Tangley)
OS322528
☎ (01264) 730283
11-3 (not Mon-Fri), 6-11; 12-3, 7-10.30 Sun
Draught Bass; Cheriton Pots Ale Ⓖ
Remote,16th-century drovers inn. A large dining room at the rear serves good quality home cooking, including pizzas (book weekends). Look out for the old rack that holds the barrels.
🛏 Q ✿ ◖ ▶ ⅋ P

TITCHFIELD
Bugle Hotel
The Square
☎ (01329) 841888
11-11; 12-11 Sun
Fuller's London Pride; Gale's HSB; Ringwood Best Bitter; guest beers Ⓗ
Old village coaching inn, now an hotel with a popular bar, eating areas and a function room.
🛏 Q ✿ ⇔ ◖ ▲ ♣ P

Queens Head
The High Street
☎ (01329) 842154
11-3.30, 6.30-11; 11-11 Sat; 11-10.30 Sun
Flowers Original; Fuller's London Pride; Morland Old Speckled Hen; guest beer Ⓗ
Characterful village pub with a fairly small cosy bar area; the original saloon bar has been turned into a

restaurant. Indian curry nights are a popular feature.
Q ✿ 🐕 ✿ ⇔ ◖ ▶ & ▲ P

Wheatsheaf
East Street
☎ (01329) 842965
12-3, 6-11; 12-11 Fri; 12-3, 7-10.30 Sun
Fuller's London Pride; Woodforde's Wherry; guest beers Ⓗ
Unspoilt village local; a small snug has board games and dominoes, another room is used for eating and drinking.
🛏 Q ✿ ✿ ◖ ▲ ♣ P

TOTFORD
Woolpack
On B3046, between Candovers and Alresford
☎ (01962) 732101
11.30-3, 6-11; 12-10.30 Sun
Cheriton Pots Ale; Palmers Best Bitter; guest beer (summer) Ⓗ
Nice 16th-century flint and stone inn, set in a tiny rural hamlet on the Wayfarers Walk. Local places of interest include the lost village of Abbotstone, the Watercress steam railway line and the Grange, one of Europe's great neo-classical monuments.
🛏 Q 🐕 ✿ ⇔ ◖ ▶ & P

UPPER CLATFORD
Crook & Shears
Off A343, S of Andover
☎ (01264) 361543
12-3, 6-11; 12-3, 7-10.30 Sun
Flowers Original; Fuller's London Pride; guest beers Ⓗ
This attractive 17th-century village pub has recently undergone refurbishment, but retains two rooms and a small dining area. At least one beer from Ringwood is always available and good quality food is served. The skittle alley can be booked for functions. Parking can be awkward.
🛏 Q ✿ ✿ ◖ ♣

UPTON GREY
Hoddington Arms
Bidden Road, Upton Grey (4 miles E of A339, 2 miles W of A32) OS701483
☎ (01256) 862371
11.30-2.30 (12-3 Sat), 6-11; 12-3, 7-10.30 Sun
Greene King IPA, Abbot; Ruddles Best Bitter Ⓗ
Grade II listed building in a pretty village surrounded by farmland. One room houses a bar billiards table and a shove-ha'penny slate. Two restaurants, at either end of the pub offer fresh fish and game (no food Sun eve).
🛏 Q 🐕 ✿ ◖ ♣ P ⅍ ⊞

WEYHILL
Weyhill Fair
On A342, 3 miles W of Andover
☎ (01264) 773631
11.15-3, 6 (5 Fri)-11; 12-3, 7-10.30 Sun
Fuller's Chiswick, London Pride, seasonal beers; guest beers Ⓗ
Popular free house serving a constantly changing range of beers and good home-cooked food (no meals Sun eve). Families welcome in the no-smoking area. A large field provides camping for beer, music and cycling themed events. On a good bus route, this regular CAMRA award-winner is not to be missed.
Q ✿ ◖ ▲ ♣ P ⅍ ⊟

WHITSBURY
Cartwheel
OS129188
☎ (01725) 518362
11-2.30 (3 Fri & Sat), 6-11; 12-3, 7-10.30 Sun
Adnams Broadside; Ringwood Best Bitter; guest beers Ⓗ
Idyllic village pub in a pair of Grade II listed cottages. A lofty beamed main bar has a discrete games bar off, with darts and pool. It serves an interesting menu (not winter Mon eve). This good downland walking area has a dense footpath network around the village.
🛏 Q 🐕 ✿ ◖ ▶ 🍺 ♣ ⇖ P

WINCHESTER
Bell
83 St Cross Road (extreme S edge of city)
☎ (01962) 865284
11-3, 5-11; 11-11 Fri & Sat; 12-4, 7-10.30 Sun
Greene King IPA, Triumph; guest or seasonal beer Ⓗ
Comfortable, traditional pub; a quiet lounge for conversation contrasts with the busy, cosmopolitan public bar. The Bell adjoins the 12th-century Hospital of St Cross – England's oldest almshouse. The River Itchen footpath offers lovely walks. No eve meals Tue or Sun.
🛏 Q ✿ ◖ ▶ 🍺 ♣ P

Black Boy
Wharf Hill (off Chesil St, B3330)
☎ (01962) 861754
11-3, 6-11; 12-3, 7-10.30 Sun
Cheriton Pots Ale; Ringwood Best Bitter Ⓗ
Thriving free house serving only locally-brewed real ales, including beers from Hop Back and Triple fff. On a raised terrace across the Itchen from Wolvesey Palace, it has somewhat surreal

CAMRA National Pub Inventory: The Balsck Horse, Clapton-in-Gordano, Somerset

decor. Many games are played in the games/family room. No food Sun eve or Mon.

🏚 🐎 🕷 ◖ ♣ ⊞

Green Man
53 Southgate Street (370 yds S of High St)
☎ (01962) 865429
11.30-3, 6-11; 12-3, 7-10.30 Sun
Greene King IPA, Abbot; guest beers H
Prominent street-corner pub, on the edge of the city centre. A big square island bar serves many drinking areas/booths, but the layout may alter in 2001. It has a skittle alley/meeting room. Handy for the cinema opposite. Eve meals served weekdays.

🏚 ◖ ⇌ ♣ ⊞

Hyde Tavern
57 Hyde Street, Hyde
☎ (01962) 862592
12-2.30, 5-11; 12-3, 6-11 Sat; 12-3, 7-10 Sun
Greene King IPA, seasonal or guest beer H
Very small, two-room pub in a medieval building. The bar is below street level – beware beams and uneven floors. King Alfred's last resting-place is somewhere in the ruins of Hyde Abbey, just behind the pub. Be prepared

to join in with conversation here.
Q ⊞ ⇌ ⊞

St James Tavern
3 Romsey Road (near B3040/B3049 jct)
☎ (01962) 861288
11-2.30, 5.30-11; 11-11 Sat; 12-3, 7-10.30 Sun
Butcombe Bitter; Wadworth IPA, 6X, Farmer's Glory, Summersault (summer), seasonal beers H
Raised above street level on an acute terrace corner, it boasts lofty ceilings, light wood decor and Winchester's last pub bar billiards table. Popular with students and hospital staff, there is a wide selection of good-value food available all sessions except Sun eve.

🕷 ◖ ⇌ ♣ ⅍

Wykeham Arms
75 Kingsgate Street
☎ (01962) 853834
11-11; 12-10.30 Sun
Draught Bass; Gale's Butser, GB, HSB H
Rambling, many-roomed pub near the Cathedral Close and Winchester College. It has held virtually every good pub and food award. Cosy and conversational, the interior is a riot of nick-nacks, curios and antiquities. Fine food and wine – meals served

Mon-Sat. 🏚 Q 🕷 🛏 ◖ ▶

WINCHFIELD

Barley Mow
The Hurst
☎ (01252) 617490
12-3, 5.30-11 (12-11 summer Sat); 12-3, 7-10.30 Sun
Courage Best Bitter; Ushers Best Bitter, seasonal beers; guest beer H
Cosy turn-of-the-century rural pub, with good dining facilities. It stands near the terminal point for narrow boat trips on the Basingstoke Canal. Has its own cricket ground which is available for hire.

🏚 Q 🕷 ◖ ▶ ♣ P

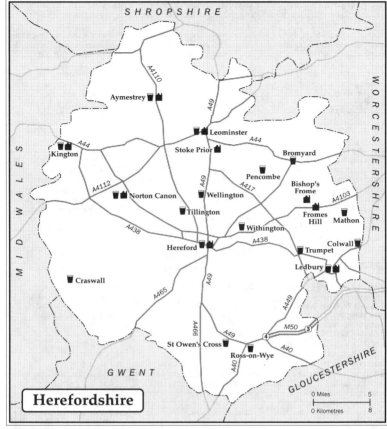

Herefordshire

AYMESTREY

Riverside Inn
On A4110
☎ (01568) 708440
11-11; 12-10.30 Sun
Woodhampton Red Kite, Jack Snipe, Kingfisher, Wagtail (summer)**, Ravenshead Stout** (winter) Ⓗ
Riverside inn that acts as the tap for nearby Woodhampton Brewery. An impessive fireplace, beams and comfortable furnishings dominate in a pub that has a good reputation for food; an extensive elaborate menu is offered. Accommodation is in a converted stable annexe.
🏨 Q ❀ 🛏 ◗ ▲ ♣ P

BROMYARD

Bay Horse
21 High Street
☎ (01885) 482600
11-3, 5.30-11; 12-3.30, 7-10.30 Sun
Hobsons Best Bitter; Marston's Pedigree; guest beers Ⓗ
High Street pub where the wood-panelled bar, with a fireplace and bay windows, has an intimate feel. Cider sold in summer.
❀ ◗ ▶ ⇔ P

Rose & Lion
5 New Road
☎ (01885) 482381
11-3, 6-11; 11-11 Sat; 12-10.30 Sun
Wye Valley Bitter, Butty Bach, seasonal beers Ⓗ
Honest, unpretentious local of real character. Very well run by a friendly landlady, this pub sets the standard for Bromyard. It retains many original features and great charm in its bars and games room. Folk music performed Sun eve.
Q ❀ 🗗 ♣ P

COLWALL

Chase Inn
Chase Road, Upper Colwall
(off B4218, at upper hairpin bend signed 'British Camp')
☎ (01684) 540266
12-2.30 (not Tue), 6-11; 12-2, 7-10.30 Sun
Donnington BB, SBA; Hobsons Best Bitter; Wye Valley seasonal beers Ⓗ
Two-bar pub: cosy lounge and friendly public bar, and a garden giving nice views across the county towards the Welsh mountains. A limited but very satisfying lunch menu is served. No food Tue or Sun. Well worth the 25-minute walk from the station.
Q ❀ ◗ P

CRASWALL

Bulls Head
On back road between Hay-on-Wye and Milchaelchurch
OS278360
☎ (01981) 510616
11-11; 12-4 (not eve) Sun
Wye Valley Butty Bach; guest beers (summer) Ⓖ
Superlative example of an isolated rural alehouse, despite the addition of a dining room. The unspoilt bar – resplendent with hearth, latch door, settles and serving hatch – is timeless. Great food and fabulous scenery; it is located in the shadow of Black Hill.
🏨 Q ⛺ ❀ 🛏 ◗ ▶ 🗗 ▲ ⇔ P

HEREFORD

Barrels
69 St Owen Street
☎ (01432) 274968
11-11; 12-10.30 Sun
Wye Valley Bitter, HPA, Brew 69, seasonal beers; guest beers Ⓗ

This award-winning pub, retaining several rooms, is popular with all ages, especially fans of live TV sport. A beer festival held every Aug Bank Holiday. The tap for Wye Valley Brewery (take outs available), it enjoys a strong cult following.
✿ ⊟ ⇌ ♣ ⌓

Goodbodys
45 West Street
☎ (01432) 265894
11-11; 12-3 Sun
Wye Valley HPA, Dorothy Goodbody's Wholesome Stout, seasonal beers Ⓗ
16th-century black and white building – Wye Valley's latest acquisition. It unashamedly caters for city diners who are discerning with their beer. The lounge areas downstairs and restaurant area upstairs offer a pleasant ambience.
♔ Q ◖ ◗ ♿ P

Lichfield Vaults
11 Church Street
☎ (01432) 267994
11-11; 12-10.30 Sun
Marston's Pedigree; Tetley Bitter; guest beers Ⓗ
Festival Alehouse and long-standing *Guide* entry, always stocking an eclectic range of beers. Shoppers, tourists and workers flock here in daytime; it appeals to a younger crowd at night. Bare boards, TV and a juke box are features of this single bar, located in an alley near the Cathedral.
✿ ◖ ♣ ⌓

Three Elms
1 Canon Pyon Road
☎ (01432) 273338
11-11; 12-10.30 Sun
Flowers Original; Marston's Pedigree; Tetley Bitter; guest beers Ⓗ
On first inspection, ths is perhaps an unlikely award-winning city pub, but an enthusiastic staff ensures this pub caters for all tastes. A play area and pleasant surroundings are a bonus in this oasis on the edge of the city. Popular with families, it is convenient for the racecourse.
♘ ✿ ◖ ◗ ♿ P

Victory
88 St Owen Street
☎ (01432) 274998
11-11; 12-10.30 Sun
Flannery's Celtic Ale; Spinning Dog Chase Your Tail; Wye Valley Butty Bach, HPA; guest beers Ⓗ
Hereford's newest brewery, Spinning Dog, began brewing at the Victory in Spring 2000. The pub is decked out as a sailing galleon, with a lively locals bar at the front and a quieter area to the back, with a balcony and crow's nest. The tiny brewhouse is at the rear of the pub. Eve meals served weekdays 5-7. Live music Thu and Sun eves.
♔ Q ♘ ✿ ◗ ♿ ♣ ⌓

Volunteer
21 Harold Street (opp. TA centre)
☎ (01432) 276189
11-11; 12-10.30 Sun
Draught Bass; Fuller's London Pride or guest beer; Greene King Abbot; Worthington Bitter Ⓗ
Lively, contemporary community pub and Hereford's premier cider outlet. Many of the locals are artists and musicians who organise events at the pub including a monthly folk session (second Wed) and a jazz brunch (summer Sun). Delicious home-cooked food, using fresh local ingredients, is served 11-5 daily (braille menu available); children welcome.
♔ Q ✿ ♿ ♣ ⌓

KINGTON

Old Fogey
37 High Street
☎ (01544) 230685
10.30-11; 12-10.30 Sun
Banks's Bitter; Hobson's Town Crier; Wood Shropshire Lad; guest beer Ⓗ
Friendly High Street pub of great character where a single bar nestles behind an unusual entrance. No frills, it is typical of Kington with much that is unspoilt.
✿ ♣

Olde Tavern ☆
22 Victoria Road
☎ (01544) 231384
11.30-2.30 (not Mon-Fri), 7.30-11; 12-2.30, 7.30-10.30 Sun
Ansells Bitter Ⓗ
Kington's link with the past – this repeated award-winner has two bars frozen in time. Adorned with many curios, this archetypal 19th-century town pub is definitely one for the connoisseur.
Q ⊟ ♣

Queens Head
Bridge Street
☎ (01544) 231106
11-11; 12-10.30 Sun
Dunn Plowman Early Riser; guest beer Ⓗ
A frequent choice for those who enjoy Dunn Plowman beers, this two-bar corner pub has a basic bar with some relatively unspoilt original features, and a more conventional lounge. No food Mon. ♔ ✿ 🛏 ◖ ◗ ▲ ♣ P

LEDBURY

Horseshoe Inn
Homend
☎ (01531) 632770
12-11; 12-10.30 Sun
Flowers IPA; Hobson's Best Bitter; guest beers Ⓗ
A large set of stone steps gives access to a pleasant single bar where many original features have survived a past refurbishment; a cosy feel and some charm add to its character. It is the best port of call for guest beers in town.
♔ ✿ 🛏 ◖ ⇌ ♣

Prince of Wales
Church Lane
☎ (01531) 632250
11-11; 12-10.30 Sun
Banks's Original, Bitter; guest beer Ⓗ
Tucked away in a beautiful narrow cobbled street, this 16th-century timbered pub has been partially knocked through. Always bustling with locals and visitors alike, it is a key folk music venue (Wed eve), and popular for pub games. No-smoking area available at lunchtime.
✿ ◖ ⊟ ⇌ ♣ ⌓ ⚟

Talbot Inn
New Street
☎ (01531) 632963
11.30-3, 5-11; 11.30-11 Sat; 12-4; 7-10.30 Sun
Fuller's London Pride; Banks's Bitter; guest beer Ⓗ
The atmosphere is that of a town pub combined with a small country hotel – very easy-going. A number of bars with discrete nooks and crannies are set around a central bar. Note the splendid inglenook in the main bar area. The restaurant serves good food. Guest ciders sold.
♔ 🛏 ◖ ◗ ♣ ⌓ P

LEOMINSTER

Black Horse
74 South Street
☎ (01568) 611946
11-2.30, 6-11; 11-11 Sat; 12-3, 7-10.30 sun
Hobson's Town Crier; Marches Best Bitter; guest beers Ⓗ
Two-bar free house, Marches' Brewery tap, where a lively public bar contrasts with a quieter lounge bar, divided into two drinking areas. The restaurant serves reasonably-priced home-cooked meals (no food Sun eve). In this *Guide* for 13 consecutive years.
✿ ◖ ◗ ♿ ♣ P

Grape Vaults
4 Broad Street
☎ (01568) 611404
11-3, 5-11; 11-4, 6-11 Sat; 12-4, 6.30-10.30 Sun

Banks's Original; Marston's Bitter, Pedigree; guest beer Ⓗ
A dull façade conceals a real treasure of a pub: one very small bar and a larger one with a real fire. No TV, radio music or fruit machines disturb the conversation here. Listed in this *Guide* for 13 consecutive years, it is a must to visit. The guest beer is sourced locally.
🏚 Q ◖▶

MATHON
Cliffe Arms
On Colwall-Cradley road
OS737458
☎ (01886) 880782
12-3 (not Mon), 6.30 (7 Mon)-11; 12-3, 7-10.30 Sun
Hobson's Best Bitter; guest beers Ⓗ
Black and white pub, parts of which date back to the 1400s. The lounge is divided into three areas. The function room is in a converted barn. No food Sun eve or Mon; the menu is based on organically-grown ingredients.
🏚 ❀ ◖▶ ዿ ♣ P

NORTON CANON
Three Horseshoes Inn
On A480
☎ (01544) 318375
11-3, 6-11; 12-3, 7-10.30 Sun
Shoes Norton Ale, Canon Bitter Ⓗ
This quiet rural roadside inn, home to Shoe's Brewery, was Hereford CAMRA *Pub of the Year* 1999. Two contrasting bars: a community-focussed public and a small lounge with old sofas and a piano; always friendly. Light lunches are available in summer. It boasts is own orchard and shooting gallery.
🏚 Q ❀ 🏠 ⚔ ♣ P

PENCOMBE
Wheelwrights Arms
☎ (01885) 400358
12-3, 6.30-11; 12-2.30, 7-10.30 Sun
Greene King Abbot; Morrells Varsity; Taylor Landlord; Thwaites Bitter;

Wood Special Bitter; guest beer Ⓗ
Much improved village local, now serving a good selection of ales, this pub richly deserves its first entry in this *Guide*.
🏚 Q ⛏ ❀ 🏠 ◖▶ ♣ P

ROSS-ON-WYE
Crown & Sceptre
Market Place, Broad Street
☎ (01989) 562765
11-11; 12-10.30 Sun
Archers Best Bitter; Shepherd Neame Spitfire; Greene King Abbot; guest beers Ⓗ
The premier pub in Ross – an otherwise disappointing town for beer. Open-plan, with one long bar, the place can get very popular. It suits all ages but is favoured by the young at weekends. Never quiet, always friendly, it hosts a beer festival at Easter.
🏚 ❀ ◖▶ ♣ ⛝

ST OWENS CROSS
New Inn
At (A4173/B4521 jct)
☎ (01989) 730274
12-2.30 (3 Sat), 6-11; 12-3, 7-10 Sun
Draught Bass; Tetley Bitter; Wadworth 6X; guest beers Ⓗ
Two-bar, 16th-century black and white roadside pub where hanging baskets are a summer feature. One bar acts as a restaurant (good food) the other a locals' bar. The accommodation includes four-poster beds.
🏚 Q ♣ 🏠 ◖▶ ♣ P

TILLINGTON
Bell Inn
Tillington Road
☎ (01432) 760395
12-3, 6-11; 12-11 Sat; 12-4, 7-10.30 Sun
Draught Bass; Fuller's London Pride; Wye Valley Butty Bach Ⓗ
Refurbished village inn that has kept its community spirit. Choose between the real public bar and plush lounge. It is very geared to families, with a garden and

patio area and a restaurant (no meals Sun eve).
🏚 Q ❀ ◖▶ ⚔ ⚔ ♣ ⛝ P

TRUMPET
Trumpet Inn
At A417/A438 crossroads
☎ (01531) 670277
11.30-3, 6-11; 12-3, 6-10.30 Sun
Castle Eden Ale, IPA; Flowers IPA; guest beer Ⓗ
Reinvigorated beacon at a major road junction. After a sympathetic refurbishment, it is still very much a black and white-timbered pub, albeit with some modern trappings in its bar and dining area. Camping and caravans on site (10% discount for CAMRA members).
🏚 Q ❀ ◖▶ ⚔ ♣ P

WELLINGTON
Wellington
☎ (01432) 830367
11.30-2.30, 6-11; 12-3, 7-10.30 Sun
Draught Bass; Hancock's HB; Shepherd Neame Spitfire; guest beer Ⓗ
Wellington Bomber is a house beer brewed by Marches Ales for this excellent community-focused pub that welcomes travellers. The lively public bar contrasts with the well-appointed dining room at the rear.
🏚 ❀ ◖▶ ⚔ ⚔ ♣ P

WITHINGTON
Cross Keys Inn
On A465
☎ (01432) 820616
7 (12 Sat)-11; 12-4.30, 7-10.30 Sun
Greene King Abbot; Hobson's Best Bitter; Wye Valley Butty Bach; guest beer Ⓗ
No-frills roadside local, recently sold by Whitbread to the longstanding landlord, this is now a genuine free house, selling a good selection of real ales. Dogs are welcome.
🏚 Q ❀ ⚔ ♣ P

Heritage Pubs
The pubs chosen as illustrations in the Guide are taken from CAMRA's National Inventory. These are pubs with unspoilt interiors that need to be preserved for future generations. The illustrations are used as examples of pubs on the inventory and may not necessarily have been chosen for inclusion in the Guide for beer quality. A pub on the inventory that has been chosen as a full entry carries a star next to its name. It has not been possible always to place pub illustrations in the counties where the pubs are sited.

INDEPENDENT BREWERIES
Dunn Plowman: Kington
Fromes Hill: Fromes Hill
Frome Valley: Bishop's Frome
Ledbury: Ledbury
Marches: Leominster
Shoes: Norton Cannon
SP Sporting Ales: Stoke Prior
Spinning Dog: Hereford
Woodhampton: Aymestrey
Wye Valley: Hereford

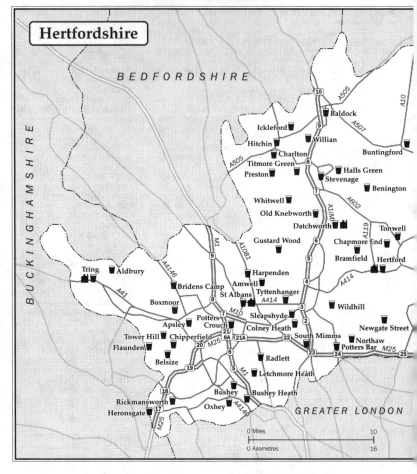

Hertfordshire

BEDFORDSHIRE

BUCKINGHAMSHIRE

Baldock
Ickleford
Hitchin
Willian
Charlton
Buntingford
Titmore Green
Preston
Halls Green
Stevenage
Benington
Whitwell
Old Knebworth
Datchworth
Tonwell
Gustard Wood
Chapmore End
Bramfield
Hertford
Tring
Aldbury
Harpenden
Bridens Camp
Amwell
St Albans
Tyttenhanger
Boxmoor
Sleapshyde
Wildhill
Apsley
Potters Crouch
Colney Heath
Tower Hill
Chipperfield
Newgate Street
Flaunden
South Mimms
Northaw
Potters Bar
Belsize
Radlett
Letchmore Heath
Rickmansworth
Bushey
Bushey Heath
Heronsgate
Oxhey
GREATER LONDON

0 Miles 10
0 Kilometres 16

ALDBURY

Greyhound Inn
Stocks Road
☎ (01442) 851228
11-11; 12-10.30 Sun
Badger IPA, Dorset Best, Tanglefoot, seasonal beers H
Attractive pub in a picturesque village close to Ashridge Estate (NT). A traditional, unspoilt public bar is dominated by a huge fireplace. The house beer comes from the Gribble Brewery in Sussex. The family room doubles as a no-smoking area. No food Sun eve.
♨ ⚘ ⇔ ◖◗ ⊞ ♿ ♣ P ⌿

AMWELL

Elephant & Castle
Amwell Lane (left fork at top of Brewhouse Hill) OS167133
☎ (01582) 832175
12-3, 5.30-11; 12-11 Sat; 12-10.30 Sun
Greene King IPA, Abbot; Ruddles Best Bitter; guest beer H
Friendly, popular 18th-

century pub in a peaceful setting, out of the way and beautifully situated, boasting two large gardens. See the 200-foot well in the bar and open wood-burning suspended fires. Eve meals Tue-Sat; good food.
♨ ⚘ ◖◗ ♣ P

APSLEY

White Lion
44 London Road
☎ (01442) 268948
11-11; 12-10.30 Sun
Fuller's London Pride, ESB, seasonal beers H
Lively, busy, street-corner pub with a friendly landlord and a nice atmosphere. Limited parking. ⚘ ◖ ⇌ P

BALDOCK

Cock
43 High Street
☎ (01462) 892366
11.30-2 (not Mon, Tue or Thu), 5-11; 11.30-11 Sat; 12-4, 7-10.30 Sun
Greene King XX Mild, IPA, Abbot;

guest beer H
Former 17th-century inn retaining an authentic beamed interior and open log fire; a popular local.
♨ ⚘ ◖ ♿ ⇌ ♣ ⊞

BARKWAY

Tally Ho
London Road (signed from A10)
☎ (01763) 848389
11.30-3, 5.30-11; 12-11 Sat; 12-3, 7-10.30 Sun
Beer range varies H
This welcoming roadside pub is North Herts' newest free house. The ever-changing range of beer complements the variety of home-cooked food on offer (not served Sun eve). A separate (no-smoking) restaurant and snug are popular with locals. Local CAMRA's *Most Improved Pub* 2000. ♨ ⚘ ◖◗ ⇔ P

BELSIZE

Plough

Dunny Lane (Sarratt-Chipperfield road) OS034008
☎ (01923) 262800
11-3, 5.30-11; 12-3, 7-10.30 Sun
Greene King IPA; guest beer Ⓗ
Friendly pub with a no-smoking dining area. The garden is popular on summer days, and the pub has a children's certificate. Good home-cooked specials include at least one vegetarian dish (no meals Sun eve).
🏚 🕸 ◖ ▌ ♣ P

BENINGTON
Lordship Arms
42 Whempstead Road (3 miles E of Stevenage via B1037) OS308227
☎ (01438) 869665
12-3, 6-11; 12-3, 7-10.30 Sun
Fuller's London Pride; McMullen AK; Young's Special; guest beers Ⓗ
Excellent free house serving guest beers from small breweries far and wide, plus a large range of fruit wines and a cider. Telephone

memorabilia adorns the pub. Local CAMRA *Pub of the Year* 1997 and '99.
🕸 🍀 ◖ P ⊟

BISHOP'S STORTFORD
Half Moon
31 North Street
☎ (01279) 834500
11-11; 12-3, 7-10.30 Sun
Adnams Broadside; Tap & Spile Premium; guest beers Ⓗ
'Spit and sawdust' pub dating from the 17th century hosting live music alternate Weds. It is usually otherwise quiet, but can be busy eves. Six guest beers to choose from.
🏚 Q 🕸 ◖ 🍴 ≈ ♣ ◖ ✄

BOXMOOR
Boxmoor Vintners (off licence)
25-27 St Johns Road
☎ (01442) 252171
9.30-1, 4.30-9.30; 12-2, 7-9 (Sun & Bank Hols)
Beer range varies Ⓗ
A friendly welcome awaits in the only off-licence in the area with draught ales (three handpumps). It also stocks a good and unusual selection of British bottled beers.
≈ (Hemel Hempstead)

BRAMFIELD
Grandison Arms
18 Bury Lane
☎ (01992) 582564
11-3 (4 Sat), 5.30 (7 Sat)-11 (closed Mon); 11-11 summer Sat); 12-4 (closed eve) Sun
Flowers IPA; Fuller's London Pride; Shepherd Neame Spitfire; guest beer Ⓗ
Two-bar village pub: the larger bar has an extensive dining area. A large, stylish patio houses a marquee. A popular watering-hole for walkers.
🏚 🕸 ◖ ▌ 🍴 ♣ P

BRIDENS CAMP
Crown & Sceptre
Red Lion Lane (off A4146)
☎ (01442) 253250
12-3, 5.30 (6 Sat)-11, (12-11 summer Sat); 12-3, 7-10.30 (12-10.30 summer) Sun
Greene King IPA, Abbot; guest beers Ⓗ
Popular country pub in a small village with a very relaxed atmosphere. The excellent menu is changed weekly.
🏚 🐄 🕸 ◖ ▌ ♣ P

BUNTINGFORD
Crown
17 High Street
☎ (01763) 271422
12-3, 5.30-11; 12-11 Sat; 12-3.30, 7-10.30 Sun

Courage Best Bitter; Mauldons Best Bitter; Wadworth 6X; guest beers Ⓗ
Popular, town-centre pub with a large front bar and a small cosy back bar. Children are welcome in the covered patio and secluded garden. Theme nights, offering speciality foods, are held regularly. Local CAMRA *Best Community Pub* 2000.
🐄 🕸 ◖ ▌

BUSHEY
Queen's Arms
Sparrows Herne
☎ (020) 838 62940
11-11; 12-10.30 Sun
Benskins BB; guest beer (occasional) Ⓗ
Revitalized, hospitable, two-bar pub. The public bar can be a haven from the over-friendly pub dog. The guest beer will become more regular if trade continues to improve. No meals Sun.
🏚 🕸 ◖ ▌ ♣ P

Swan
25 Park Road (off A411)
☎ (020) 895 02256
11-11; 12-10.30 Sun
Benskins BB; Ind Coope Burton Ale; Young's Bitter Ⓗ
Classic, back-street, one-bar boozer, virtually unchanged since its first appearance in this *Guide* in 1974.
🕸 ♣

BUSHEY HEATH
Black Boy
19 Windmill Street (off A412)
☎ (020) 895 02230
11.30-3, 5.30-11; 11-11 Fri; 12-11 Sat; 12-4, 7-10.30 Sun
Adnams Bitter; Benskins BB; guest beers Ⓗ
Three times a winner of the local CAMRA *Pub of the Year* award; a friendly pub with up to five beers on tap, it is popular for food (not served Sun eve).
🕸 ◖ ▌ P

CHAPMORE END
Woodman
30 Chapmore End (off B158, 1/4m SW of A602) OS328164
☎ (01920) 463143
12-3, 6-11; 12-3.30, 7-10.30 Sun
Greene King IPA, Abbot; guest beers (occasional) Ⓖ
Traditional, two-bar country pub with a cellar behind the bar serving cooled beer from the cask in splendid condition; try a pint of 'mix'. Lunches (Mon-Sat) range from sandwiches to Balti. A large garden houses a mini zoo and children's play area. Darts and pétanque teams are based here.
🏚 Q 🕸 ◖ 🍴 ♣ P ⊞

CHARLTON
Windmill
Charlton Road
☎ (01462) 432096
12-3, 5-11; 12-11 Fri & Sat; 12-3, 7-10.30 Sun
Wells IPA, Bombardier; guest beers Ⓗ
Village pub near the River Hiz with resident ducks. Good home-cooked food.
🏠 Q ❀ ◖ ♣ P 🖟

CHIPPERFIELD
Royal Oak
1 The Street
☎ (01923) 266537
12-3, 6-11; 12-3, 7-10.30 Sun
Draught Bass; Ⓗ **Young's Bitter, Special; guest beer** Ⓗ/Ⓖ
Immaculate pub, very friendly; 19 years in this *Guide*. Highly polished wood and brass abound. Good home-prepared food served Mon-Sat (eves by arrangement).
🏠 Q ❀ ♣ P

COLNEY HEATH
Crooked Billet
88 High Street
☎ (01727) 822128
11-2.30, 5.30-11; 11-11 Thu-Sat; 12-10.30 Sun
Greene King IPA; Courage Directors; guest beers Ⓗ
Cottage-style pub, over 200 years old, refurbished in keeping with its origins. The large garden area is suitable for children; popular with walkers. Eve meals Fri and Sat.
🏠 ❀ ◖ ▶ P

DATCHWORTH
Tilbury
1 Watton Road (1 mile E of B197 at Woolmer Green)
OS270183
☎ (01438) 812496
11-3, 5-11; 11-11 Thu-Sat; 12-10.30 Sun
Museum Five Hides, Hop Pit; guest beers Ⓗ
Welcoming, two-bar pub just off the village green. The Museum beers are brewed by the landlord himself. The public bar displays a graveyard of keg breweriana. Good, home-cooked food available (not served Sun eve); no-smoking area is available for diners.
Q ❀ ◖ ▶ ⊟ ♲ Å P

FLAUNDEN
Bricklayers Arms
Hogpits Bottom
☎ (01442) 833322
12-3, 6-11; 12-3, 6-10.30 Sun
Marston's Pedigree; Fuller's London Pride; Ringwood Old Thumper; guest beers Ⓗ
Smart, food-oriented country

pub, which is still drinker-friendly, set in beautiful countryside with a pleasant garden. Four ever-changing guest beers and excellent food served.
🏠 Q ❀ ◖ ♣ P

GREEN TYE
Prince of Wales
☎ (01279) 842517
12-2.45, 5.30-11; 12-11 Sat; 12-11 Sun
Green Tye IPA, Wheelbarrow, seasonal beers; McMullen AK; guest beers Ⓗ
Local CAMRA *Pub of the Year 2000*: a small, traditional village pub, popular with walkers and cyclists. The attached Green Tye Brewery, opened in Oct 1999, normally provides two regular beers, plus seasonal additions.
🏠 ❀ ◖ ♣ P

GUSTARD WOOD
Cross Keys
Ballslough Hill (off B651, 1 mile N of Wheathampstead)
OS174165
☎ (01582) 832165
11-3, 6 (5.30 Fri & Sat)-11; 12-4.30, 7-10.30 Sun
Fuller's London Pride; Greene King IPA; guest beers Ⓗ
Charming, original, roses around the door, 17th-century country pub serving reasonably priced home-made food. Ideal for ramblers. One roomy bar, plus side rooms for children and non-smokers. It is run by friendly staff.
🏠 Q ざ ❀ ◖ ♣ P ⅙

HALLS GREEN
Rising Sun
21 Halls Green (Weston Road; minor road to Cromer)
OS275287
☎ (01462) 790487
11-2.30, 6-11; 12-3, 7-10.30 Sun
Draught Bass; Courage Directors; McMullen AK, Country, Gladstone, seasonal beers Ⓗ
Lovely single-bar country pub, east of Stevenage. An enormous garden has a children's play area and pétanque pitch. Home-cooked food is available daily; the conservatory acts as a restaurant (booking essential). Local CAMRA *1998 Pub of the Year.*
🏠 ❀ ◖ ▶ ♣ P 🖟

HARPENDEN
Carpenters Arms
Cravells Road, Southdown (off A1081)
☎ (01582) 460311
11-3, 5.30-11; 12-3, 7-10.30 Sun
Courage Best Bitter; Ruddles

County; Webster's Yorkshire Bitter; guest beer Ⓗ
Charming, friendly, 200-year old pub where guest beers often come from small independent breweries. Motoring memorabilia adorns the walls. No food Sun.
🏠 Q ❀ ◖ P

Cross Keys
39 High Street
☎ (01582) 763989
11.30-2.30, 5-11; 12-3, 7-10.30 Sun
Boddingtons Bitter; Brakspear Bitter; Fuller's London Pride; Taylor Landlord Ⓗ
300-year-old pub, well preserved despite attempts to extend it. Notable features are the pewter bar top, flagstoned floor, tankards hanging from oak beams and walls adorned with pictures of old Harpenden.
🏠 Q ❀ ◖ ➤

HERONSGATE
Land of Liberty, Peace & Plenty
Long Lane (900 yds from M25 Jct 17) OS023949
☎ (01923) 282226
12-11; 12-10.30 Sun
Brakspear Special; Courage Best Bitter; Young's Bitter, Special; guest beers Ⓗ
Superb country free house, a short hop from the motorway. Two guest beers from micros are supplemented by an unusual range of six Belgian beers on draught. Home-cooked lunches served; 24 hours notice required for eves.
❀ ♣ 🕭 P 🖟

HERTFORD
Old Cross Tavern
8 St Andrew Street
☎ (01992) 583133
11.30-11; 12-10.30 Sun
Fuller's London Pride; Ⓗ **guest beers** Ⓗ/Ⓖ
Opened May 1999 and won the local CAMRA *Pub of the Year* that year; a comfortable welcoming town pub of great character for real ale and real pub connoisseurs. The house beer 'Laugh & Titter' is brewed by Mighty Oak; guests come from micro/craft brewers near and far. No food Sun.
Q ❀ ◖ ➤ (North/East) 🕭

White Horse
33 Castle Street
☎ (01992) 501950
11-3, 5.30-11; 11-11 Fri & Sat; 12-10.30 Sun
Fuller's Chiswick, London Pride, ESB, seasonal beers; Adnams Bitter; guest beers Ⓗ
Former tap of the Dark Horse

Brewery, now owned by Fullers. Old timber-framed buildings have been turned into two bars; the upstairs rooms are no-smoking. The food range has become more interesting with the ownership change (eve meals Mon-Thu); four guest beers on tap, cider in summer.

曲 Q ☎ ◖ ▶ 母 ⇌ (North/East) ⌣ ⌇

HIGH WYCH
Rising Sun
1 mile W of A1184
☎ (01279) 724099
12-2.30 (3 Sat), 5.30 (5 Fri &) Sat)-11; 12-3, 7-11 Sun
Courage Best Bitter; guest beer Ⓖ
Affectionately known as 'Sid's' after its longstanding landlord, and still run by his family; a very friendly, cosy local.
曲 Q ☎ ❀ 母 P

HITCHIN
Victoria
1 Ickleford Road
☎ (01462) 432682
12-3, 5-11; 12-11 Sat; 12-4, 7-10.30 Sun
Greene King IPA, Abbot, seasonal or guest beer Ⓗ
Lively local, close to the town centre.
❀ ◖ ⇌ ♣ P ⊞

ICKLEFORD
Plume of Feathers
Upper Green (400 yds from A600 down Turnpike Lane)
☎ (01462) 432729
11-3, 6-11; 12-5, 7-10.30 Sun
Boddingtons Bitter; Flowers IPA; Fuller's London Pride; Wadworth 6X; guest beers Ⓗ
Friendly, unspoilt pub, run by two sisters for the last five years. Good quality home-cooked food. Lively, but not noisy.
❀ ◖ ♣ P

LETCHMORE HEATH
Three Horeshoes
The Green
☎ (01923) 856084
11-3, 5.30-11; 11-11 Fri & Sat; 12-10.30 Sun
Benskins BB; Marston's Pedigree; Morland Old Speckled Hen; Tetley Bitter Ⓗ
Two-bar 17th-century pub facing the pond and village green. The flagstoned public and cosy beamed lounge both sport a horsey theme. Eve meals Tue-Sat.
曲 Q ❀ ◖ ▶ 母 P

NEWGATE STREET
Coach & Horses
61 Newgate Street Village
☎ (01707) 872326

11-11; 12-10.30 Sun
Greene King IPA; Marston's Pedigree; guest beer Ⓗ
Genuinely old, ivy-covered pub next to the church. Run by gregarious landlord, it is a venue for various clubs. No eve meals Sun.
曲 Q ❀ ◖ ▶ P

NORTHAW
Two Brewers
1 Northaw Road
☎ (01707) 652420
11-11; 12-4, 7-10.30 Sun
Adnams Bitter; Greene King IPA; Ind Coope Burton Ale; Marston's Pedigree; Tetley Bitter Ⓗ
Old village pub next to the church, with one bar divided into several areas maintaining an intimate atmosphere. Window boxes make a colourful display in summer. Children welcome in the dining area.
曲 ❀ ◖ ♣ P

NUTHAMPSTEAD
Woodman Inn
Signed off A10 OS413346
☎ (01763) 848328
11-3.30, 5.30-11; 11-11 Sat; 12-4, 7-10.30 Sun
Adnams Bitter; Greene King IPA; guest beers Ⓗ
17th-century inn, offering good food and accommodation. Note the World War II memorabilia of the USAF 398th bomber group and the memorial outside. Duxford Imperial War Museum is a local attraction. Good, varied menu (not served Sun eve).
曲 Q ❀ ⇌ ◖ ▶ P ⊟

OLD KNEBWORTH
Lytton Arms
Park Lane OS229202
☎ (01438) 812312
11-3, 5-11; 11-11 Fri & Sat; 12-10.30 Sun
Draught Bass; Fuller's London Pride; Theakston Best Bitter; guest beers Ⓗ
This 19th-century Lutyens pub overlooks the Knebworth estate. The nine ever-changing guest beers are complemented by house beers from Millennium Brewing Co., plus bottled foreign beers, malt whiskies and varying cider.
曲 Q ❀ ◖ 占 ♣ ⌣ P ⌇

OXHEY
Victoria
39 Chalk Hill
☎ (01923) 227993
11-3, 5.30-11; 11-11 Sat; 12-10.30 Sun
Benskins BB; guest beer Ⓗ
Two-bar pub with a comfortable public bar and a two-level lounge. Regular

quiz nights held.
❀ ◖ 母 ⇌ (Bushey) ♣ P

POTTERS BAR
Cask & Stillage
23 High Street (1 min walk from Canada Life landmark at A1000/A111 jct)
☎ (01707) 652192
12-11; 12-10.30 Sun
Ind Coope Burton Ale; Tetley Bitter; guest beers Ⓗ
An interesting choice of ales (three guests) are well-looked after here. One through-bar is nicely sectioned off; the display cabinets are worth a look. Disco Fri eve.
❀ ◖ ♣ P

POTTERS CROUCH
Holly Bush
Bedmond Lane (off A4147)
OS116053
☎ (01727) 851792
11.30 (12 Sat)-2.30, 6 (7 Sat)-11; 12-2.30, 7-10.30 Sun
Fuller's Chiswick, London Pride, ESB Ⓗ
Attractive, early 18th-century pub in rural surroundings, boasting large oak tables and period chairs. Good lunchtime snacks served Mon-Sat. The landlord is a top Fuller's Cellarman.
曲 Q ❀ P ⊞

PRESTON
Red Lion
The Green
☎ (01462) 459585
12-3, 5.30-11 (hours vary Sat); 12-3, 7-10.30 Sun
Greene King IPA; guest beers Ⓗ
Home-cooked food is served daily at this village-owned pub with a large garden. Local CAMRA *Pub of the Year* 2000.
曲 ❀ ◖ ▶ 占 ♣ P

RADLETT
Cat & Fiddle
14 Cobden Hill, Watling Street (A5183)
☎ (01923) 469523
11-11; 12-10.30 Sun
Adnams Bitter; Greene King IPA; Young's Special; guest beer Ⓗ
This 18th-century pub boasts many connected oak-panelled bars, decorated with china cats and bric-a-brac.
Q ❀ ◖ ⇌ ♣ P

RICKMANSWORTH
Fox & Hounds
183 High Street
☎ (01923) 441119
11-11; 12-10.30 Sun
Courage Best Bitter, Directors; guest beer Ⓗ
Traditional, two-roomed town pub where the

The Good Beer Guide 2001

comfortable public bar provides a good contrast to the more sedate lounge. Ask what guest beer is on, as it may not be obvious.
🏠 Q 🍴 ◑ 🍺 ⇌ ⊖ ♣ P

Whip & Collar
Uxbridge Road, Mill End
☎ (01923) 774946
11-3, 5.30-11; 12-3, 7-10.30 Sun
Fuller's London Pride; Greene King IPA; Marston's Pedigree; Ⓗ guest beer Ⓖ
Popular pub run on traditional lines. Food is served either in the bar or a no-smoking conservatory (children welcome for meals). There are two garden areas, one with a river running through it.
🏠 🍴 ◑ P

ST ALBANS
Cock
48 St Peters Street
☎ (01727) 854816
11-11; 12-10.30 Sun
Draught Bass; Greene King IPA, Abbot; guest beers Ⓗ
Pleasant town-centre pub dating back to 1620. Eve meals served Mon to Thu (until 8pm).
🏠 🍴 ◑ ▶ ⇌ (City) ♣

Farmers Boy
134 London Road
☎ (01727) 766702
11-11; 12-10.30 Sun
Verulam Special, IPA, Farmers Joy, seasonal beers Ⓗ
Cosy one-bar pub, home of Verulam Brewery. Local CAMRA Pub of the Year 1998. Home-made food is served all day.
🏠 🍴 ◑ ▶ ⇌ (City)

Farriers Arms
35 Lower Dagnall Street (off A5183)
☎ (01727) 851025
12-2.30 (3 Sat), 5.30 (7 Sat)-11; 12-3, 7-10.30 Sun
McMullen AK, Country, Gladstone, seasonal beers Ⓗ
Perennial entry in this Guide: a classic, quiet, back-street local – unless a major sports event is on the TV. Opening times may vary at weekends. Lunches served weekdays.
Q ◑ ♣

Garibaldi
61 Albert Steet
☎ (01727) 855046
12 (11 Sat)-11; 12-10.30 Sun
Fuller's Chiswick, London Pride, ESB, seasonal beers; guest beers Ⓗ
Traditional, friendly, side-street local serving home-made lunches Tue-Sun.
🍴 🍴 ◑ ⇌ (Abbey) ♣ ½

Lower Red Lion
36 Fishpool Street

☎ (01727) 855669
12-2.30, 5.30-11; 12-11 Sat; 12-3, 7-10.30 Sun
Fuller's London Pride; Oakham JHB; guest beers Ⓗ
17th-century genuine free house stocking five guest beers from micro-breweries. Two unspoilt bars and a garden serve as the venue for beer festivals in May and Aug. Good B&B.
🏠 Q 🍴 🍴 ◑ P

Mermaid
98 Hatfield Road
☎ (01727) 854487
11.30-11; 12-10.30 Sun
Adnams Best Bitter; Everards Beacon, Tiger; guest beers Ⓗ
Former Everards pub now owned by the Englishe Inns and serving two guest beers; lunches Mon-Fri. Live bands once a month; backgammon and Go played Tue and Wed respectively.
🍴 ◑ ⇌ (City) ♣ P

SAWBRIDGEWORTH
Gate
81 London Road (Harlow side of mini-roundabouts on A1184)
☎ (01279) 722313
11.30-3, 5.30-11; 11.30-11 Fri & Sat; 12-3, 7-10.30 Sun
Beer range varies Ⓗ
Named after the town's Parsonage Gate, this 18th-century pub serves up to nine beers at any one time, including a B&T house beer. The back bar is young and lively with pool, darts and TV. No food Sun. A micro-brewery is due to open next to the small car park. Cider in summer.
Q 🍴 ◑ ▲ ⇌ ♣ ⌂ P ☐

SLEAPSHYDE
Plough
Off A414 via Smallford Rd and Sleapshyde Lane
☎ (01727) 823720
11.30-2.30, 5.30-11; 11-3, 6-11 Sat; 12-3, 7-10.30 Sun
Fuller's London Pride; Greene King Abbot; Tetley Bitter Ⓗ
Old village pub featuring beams and an inglenook, which hosts popular games nights.
🍴 🍴 🍴 ◑ ♣ P

SOUTH MIMMS
Black Horse
65 Blackhorse Lane (off B556 near A1/M25 jct)
☎ (01707) 642174
11-3, 5.30-11; 11-11 Fri & Sat; 12-10.30 Sun
Greene King IPA, Abbot; guest beer Ⓗ
Classic public bar, home to a thriving darts team, plus a

cosy saloon with classic decor and a pleasant garden.
🏠 🍴 ◑ 🍺 ♣ P

STEVENAGE
Marquis of Lorne
132 High Street, Old Town
☎ (01438) 729154
11-11; 12-10.30 Sun
Greene King Martha Greene, XX Mild, IPA, Abbot; guest beers Ⓗ
Town local drawing an older clientele; a friendly 17th-century coaching inn.
🍴 ◑ 🍺 ⇌ ♣ P

TITMORE GREEN
Hermit of Redcoats
☎ (01438) 351444
11-11; 12-10.30 Sun
Greene King IPA, Abbot; Morland Old Speckled Hen Ⓗ
Traditional country pub, much extended, named after a local wealthy eccentric who lived as a recluse in his mansion for 25 years. Wild hops grow in the garden.
🏠 🍴 ◑ ▶ ⇌ ♣ P½

TONWELL
Robin Hood & Little John
14 Ware Road
☎ (01920) 463352
12-2.30 (3 Sat), 5.30-11; (closed lunch) 7-10.30 Sun
Beer range varies Ⓗ
Excellent village pub that attracts local and passing trade; one bar on split levels creating separate areas. An interesting choice of up to four real ales constantly changes. A no-smoking restaurant annexe, open to children, offers a varied menu.
🏠 🍴 🍴 ◑ ▶ P

TOWER HILL (CHIPPERFIELD)
Boot
Between Bovingdon and Chipperfield
☎ (01442) 833155
11-11; 12-10.30 Sun
Adnams Bitter; Benskins BB; Fuller's London Pride; guest beer Ⓗ
Wonderful old country pub with an extensive garden. Drawings, photographs and a collection of hats decorate the friendly bars, which can be very busy at weekends, but always comfortable. The two bars each stock different ales. Book Sun lunch. Live music Wed. 🏠 🍴 ◑ ▶ P

TRING
Kings Arms
King Street (near Natural History Museum)
☎ (01442) 823318

146

HERTFORDSHIRE

CAMRA National Pub Inventory: Bell, Aldworth, Berkshire

12 -2.30 (3 Fri; 11.30-3 Sat), 7-11; 12-4, 7-10.30 Sun

Adnams Bitter; Wadworth 6X; guest beers H

Superb, wood-panelled, back-street free house which has long championed the cause of independent brewers. It offers an extensive menu of home-cooked food; no-smoking area available at lunchtime.

Robin Hood
11 Brook Street (on roundabout at Hemel end of town)
☎ (01442) 824912
11-2.30 (3 Sat), 5.30 (6.30 Sat)-11; 12-3, 7-10.30 Sun

Fuller's Chiswick, London Pride, ESB, seasonal beers H

Very friendly 'London-style' pub in a country town. Gleaming brasses and awards adorn the walls. The excellent menu includes the best seafood for miles around.

TYTTENHANGER GREEN
Plough
Off A414, via Highfield Lane
☎ (01727) 857777
11.30-2.30 (11-3 Sat), 6-11; 12-3, 7-10.30 Sun

Fuller's London Pride, ESB; guest beers H

Popular country pub with an ever-changing range of four guest beers, renowned for its good value lunches. Children welcome in the conservatory and large garden. Note the impressive collection of bottled beers on display.

WALTHAM CROSS
Vault
160 High Street (opp McDonalds in shopping centre)

☎ (01992) 631600
11-11; 12-10.30 Sun

Beer range varies H

Free house in a former bank premises, stocking six beers, mainly from micros. Children are admitted until 7pm. Live music Thu; disco Fri.

WARE
Crooked Billet
140 Musley Hill
☎ (01920) 462516
12-2.30 (not Mon), 6-11; 12-11 Sat; 12-10.30 Sun

Greene King XX Mild or seasonal beer, IPA, Abbot H

Friendly local, well worth finding.

WARESIDE
Chequers Inn
On B1004 (Much Hadham-Ware road)
☎ (01920) 467010
12-3, 6-11; 12-11 Sat; 12-10.30 Sun

Adnams Broadside; Green Tye Treacle Miner; guest beers H

Friendly 15th-century, two-bar pub with a lounge, whose house beer is brewed by Dark Horse. The restaurant at the rear doubles as a function room; live jazz performed Sun eve.

WHITWELL
Maidens Head
67 High Street
☎ (01438) 871392
11.30-3 (4 Sat), 5 (6 Sat)-11; 12-3, 7-10.30 Sun

McMullen AK, Country; guest beers H

Village pub of character serving home-cooked food (not Mon eve). The landlord and locals offer a friendly welcome at this 1996

CAMRA *East Anglian Pub of the Year*, McMullen *Master Cellarman* award-winner 1992-99.

WILDHILL
Woodman
45 Wild Hill Road (between A1000 and B158) OS265068
☎ (01707) 642618
11.30-2.30, 5.30-11; 12-2.30, 7-10.30 Sun

Greene King IPA, Abbot; McMullen AK; guest beers H

Gem of a pub which always offers a warm welcome and a good range of competitively-priced guest beers. Former local CAMRA *Pub of the Year*. No food Sun.

WILLIAN
Three Horseshoes
Baldock Lane (tiny lane opp the church, 1 mile A1(M) jct 9) OS225308
☎ (01462) 685713
11-11; 12-10.30 Sun

Greene King IPA, Abbot, seasonal beers; guest beers H

Comfortable, friendly, single-bar pub, popular with locals. Good value food, music eves, darts and bridge tournaments are regular features. Local CAMRA *Best Community Pub* 1999.

INDEPENDENT BREWERIES

Dark Horse: Hertford

Green Tye: Much Hadham

McMullen: Hertford

Tring: Tring

Verulam: St Albans

147

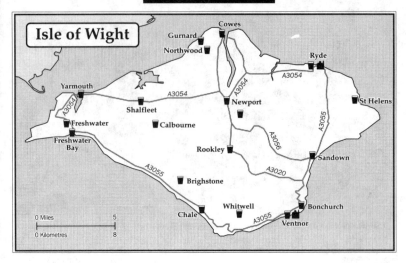

BONCHURCH

Bonchurch Inn
The Chute (off Sandown
Road) ☎ (01983) 852611
11-3, 6.30-11; 12-3, 7-10.30 Sun
Courage Best Bitter, Directors G
Superbly preserved stone pub
tucked away in a Dickensian
courtyard. Italian food
served.
Q ☎ ⊛ ⇔ ◑ ⊟ & ♣ ⌣

BRIGHSTONE

Countryman
Limerstone Road
☎ (01983) 740616
11-3, 7-11 (11-11 summer); 12-3,
7-10.30 Sun
**Badger Dorset Best, Tanglefoot;
Goddards Special; Ringwood Best
Bitter** H
Spacious, friendly, country
roadhouse with a large
lounge bar. This good family
pub enjoys a reputation for
good food and is a CAMRA
regular finalist in the local
Pub of the Year.
🏚 Q ☎ ⊛ ◑ ▲ ♣ P ⌣

CALBOURNE

Blacksmiths Arms
Park Cross, Calbourne Road
(B3401 Carisbrooke road)
☎ (01983) 529265
11-3, 6-11 (11-11 summer); 12-10.30
Sun
Beer range varies H
Traditional CAMRA runner-
up *Pub of the Year* 1997, it
series a diverse range of
British and imported beers;
popular for its German food. It
affords panoramic views of
Parkhurst forest.
🏚 Q ☎ ⊛ ◑ ▲ ♣ P ⌣

CHALE

Wight Mouse
Church Place, Newport Road

(B3399) ☎ (01983) 730431
11-11; 12-10.30 Sun
**Boddingtons Bitter; Fuller's London
Pride; Gale's HSB; Marston's
Pedigree; Morland Old Speckled
Hen; Wadworth 6X** H
Very busy, old stone pub
with an adjoining hotel, near
Blackgang Chine theme park.
This award-winning family
and whisky pub has
extensive facilities. 🏚 Q ☎
⊛ ⇔ ◑ & ▲ ♣ P ⌣

COWES

Anchor Inn
1 High Street
☎ (01983) 292823
11-11; 12-10.30 Sun
**Badger Tanglefoot; Flowers Original;
Fuller's London Pride; Goddards
Fuggle-Dee-Dum; Wadworth 6X;
guest beers** H
Extended town pub, very
popular with locals and
yachtsmen it offers live
music and good food.
🏚 ⊛ ⇔ ◑ ▶

Kingston Arms
176 Newport Road
☎ (01983) 293393
11-3, 6-11; 11-11 Fri, Sat & Mon; 12-4,
7-10.30 Sun
Gale's HSB; guest beers H
Large, friendly local, offering
home cooking.
🏚 ☎ ⊛ ⇔ ◑ ⊟ ♣ ⌣ P

Try also: Union Inn, Watch
House Lane (Gales)

FRESHWATER

Prince of Wales
Princes Road
☎ (01983) 753535
11-11; 12-10.30 Sun
**Boddingtons Bitter; Brains Dark;
Brakspear Special; Ringwood
Fortyniner** H
This former Whitbread
house, now in the free trade,

lies near the town centre. A
pleasant, unspoilt town pub
with a strong local following.
⊛ ▶ ⊟ & ▲ ♣ P ⊟

Try also: Highdown Inn,
Highdown Lane (Ushers)

FRESHWATER BAY

Fat Cat Bar
Sandpipers, Coastguard Lane
☎ (01983) 753634
11-3, 6-11; 12-3, 6-10.30 Sun
Beer range varies H
Hotel with a public bar and
family room, conveniently
situated, stocking an ever-
changing variety of ales.
🏚 Q ☎ ⊛ ⇔ ◑ & P ⌣

GURNARD

Woodvale Hotel
1 Princes Esplanade
☎ (01983) 292037
11-11; 12-10.30 Sun
**Badger Tanglefoot; Draught Bass;
Flowers Original; Fuller's London
Pride; Greene King Abbot** H
Superbly located, seafront
pub, where the large garden
gives sunset views over the
Solent. Live music staged and
pétanque played. The first
floor bar has a balcony.
🏚 ☎ ⊛ ⇔ ◑ ▶ ♣

NEWPORT

Bargemans Rest
Little London Quay (follow
signs from dual carriageway)
☎ (01983) 525828
11-11; 12-10.30 Sun
**Badger IPA, Dorset Best,
Tanglefoot; guest beers** H
Huge riverside pub, formerly
a warehouse and squash club,
it boasts interesting
memorabilia and an
appealing atmosphere. It
stages regular live
entertainment and offers fine

ISLE OF WIGHT

food and a good beer range.
♿ ✤ ◖▸ P

Railway Medina
1 Sea Street
☎ (01983) 528303
11-11; 12-10.30 Sun
Courage Directors; Gale's HSB; Webster's Green Label; guest beers Ⓗ
Back-street corner local, full of character, a long-term *Guide* entry. Railway memorabilia adorn the walls; great atmosphere.
🏨 ♿ ◖▸ 🍴 ✤

Try also: **Hogshead**, High St (Whitbread); **Prince of Wales**, South St (Ushers)

NORTHWOOD
Travellers Joy
85 Pallance Road (A3020 Yarmouth road out of Cowes)
☎ (01983) 298024
11-2.30, 5-11; 11-11 Fri & Sat; 12-3, 7-10.30 Sun
Goddards Special; guest beers Ⓗ
Well-supported beer exhibition house and regular local CAMRA award winner. Eight handpumps give a good beer choice. The garden houses a children's play area and pets corner. Traditional home-cooked food.
🏨 ♿ ✤ ◖▸ 🅰 ✤ ➾ P ✂

ROOKLEY
Chequers Inn
Chequers Inn Road (off A3020) ☎ (01983) 840314
11-11; 12-10.30 Sun
Courage Best Bitter, Directors; Gale's HSB; Morland Old Speckled Hen; John Smith's Bitter Ⓗ
Country pub at the heart of the island: a lounge bar, large restaurant, flagstoned public bar and a spacious children's play area. It serves an extensive menu of home-cooked dishes.
🏨 ♿ ✤ ◖▸ 🍴 🅰 ✤ P ✂

RYDE
Fowlers (Wetherspoon's)
41-43 Union Street
☎ (01983) 812112
11-11; 12-10.30 Sun
Courage Directors; Hop Back Summer Lightning; Theakston Best Bitter; Ventnor Golden Bitter; guest beers Ⓗ
Typical, one-bar Wetherspoon's conversion from an old established clothes shop. Good pub grub.
Q ◖▸ ➾ (Esplanade) ⊞

Lake Huron
51 Upton Road
☎ (01983) 563512
11-11; 12-10.30 Sun
Beer range varies Ⓗ

Unusually well-preserved coaching inn, away from the town centre, now a lively, welcoming local.
🍴 ✂

Simeon Arms
21 Simeon Street
☎ (01983) 614954
11-3, 6-11; 11-11 Sat; 12-10.30 Sun
Courage Best Bitter, Directors; guest beer Ⓗ
Tucked-away local in a back street near the seafront, with a deceptively large interior; an active participant in pub leagues. Eve meals served in summer.
♿ ✤ ◖▸ ➾ (Esplanade) ✤

Try also: **Hole in the Wall**, St John's Rd (Ushers)

ST HELENS
Vine Inn
Upper Green Road
☎ (01983) 872337
11-11; 12-10.30 Sun
Fuller's London Pride; Greene King Abbot; guest beers Ⓗ
Village local on the top side of the green, overlooking the cricket pitch. The grill room majors in locally-caught fresh fish and lobster.
♿ ✤ ◖▸ 🅰 ✤

SANDOWN
Castle
12-14 Fitzroy Street
☎ (01983) 403169
11-3, 7-11; 11-11 Sat; 12-3, 7-10.30 Sun
Ventnor Golden Bitter; guest beers Ⓗ
This excellent town free house and local fields five darts teams; crib and pétanque also played. Always has five real ales on offer.
♿ ✤ ◖▸ ➾ ✤

Caulkheads
42 Avenue Road (Ryde Road)
☎ (01983) 403878
11-11; 12-10.30 Sun
Boddingtons Bitter; Flowers Original; Greene King Abbot; guest beers Ⓗ
Whitbread *Pub of the Year* 1999; spacious with facilities for all. It is renowned for its food, 'early risers' breakfasts, and five guest beers.
♿ ✤ ◖▸ 🅰 ➾ P ✂

SHALFLEET
New Inn
Main Road
☎ (01983) 531314
12-3, 6-11; (12-11 summer); 12-3, 6-10.30 Sun
Draught Bass; Ventnor Golden Bitter; Wadworth 6X; guest beers Ⓗ
Unspoilt ancient stone inn. A short stroll from the quay, popular with islanders and

visiting yachtsmen for its extensive seafood menu.
🏨 ♿ ✤ ◖▸ 🅰 ✤ P ✂

VENTNOR
Crab & Lobster Tap
Grove Road (by central car park and Heritage Centre)
☎ (01983) 852311
10.30-11; 12-10.30 Sun
Ventnor Golden Bitter; guest beers Ⓗ
Interesting town pub displaying an abundance of memorabilia. Eve meals at weekends.
◖▸ ✤

Volunteer
30 Victoria Street
☎ (01983) 852537
11-11; 12-10.30 Sun
Badger Dorset Best, Tanglefoot; Ventnor Golden Bitter, Oyster Stout; guest beers Ⓗ
Traditional, friendly town local, renovated to preserve its original character. This regular local CAMRA *Pub of the Year* finalist hosts a fine October mini-fest.
🏨 Q ✤

Try also: **Four Seasons**, Wroxhall (Free); **Spyglass**, Esplanade (Free)

WHITWELL
White Horse
High Street
☎ (01983) 730375
11-3, 6-11 (11-11 summer); 12-3, 6-10.30 Sun
Badger Dorset Best, Tanglefoot; Greene King Abbot; Ventnor Golden Bitter; guest beers Ⓗ
Built in 1454, one of the oldest established inns on the island, this thatched, stone pub boasts an extensive menu and a large garden.
🏨 ♿ ✤ ◖▸ ♿ ✤ 🍴 P ✂

Try also: **Buddle Inn**, St Catherines Rd (Whitbread)

YARMOUTH
Wheatsheaf Inn
Bridge Road
☎ (01983) 760456
11-11; 12-10.30 Sun
Brakspear Special; Flowers Original; Goddards Fuggle-Dee-Dum; Morland Old Speckled Hen; Wadworth 6X Ⓗ
Old coaching house, now with additional rooms, it is spacious and comfortable for families. Good value food.
🏨 Q ♿ ✤ ◖▸ 🍴 ✤

INDEPENDENT BREWERIES

Goddards: Ryde
Ventnor: Ventnor

149

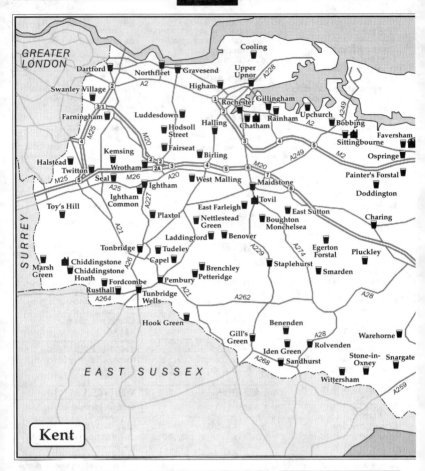

GREATER LONDON

Cooling
Dartford · Northfleet · Gravesend
Upper Upnor
Swanley Village
Rochester · Gillingham
Higham
Farningham
Rainham · Upchurch
Luddesdown
Halling · Chatham · Bobbing
Hodsoll Street
Faversham
Fairseat · Birling
Sittingbourne
Kemsing
Ospringe
Halstead · Wrotham
West Malling · Maidstone
Twitton
Painter's Forstal
Seal · Ightham
Toy's Hill
Ightham Common
Tovil · Doddington
Plaxtol · East Farleigh · East Sutton
Charing
Nettlestead Green · Boughton Monchelsea
Laddingford · Benover
Egerton Forstal · Pluckley
Tonbridge · Tudeley
Staplehurst · Smarden
Chiddingstone · Capel
Marsh Green
Chiddingstone Hoath · Fordcombe · Brenchley · Petteridge
Rusthall · Pembury
Tunbridge Wells

SURREY

Hook Green
Benenden · Warehorne
Gill's Green
Iden Green · Rolvenden
Stone-in-Oxney · Snargate
Sandhurst
Wittersham

EAST SUSSEX

Kent

ASHFORD

South Eastern Tavern
79 Torrington Road
☎ (01233) 621344
11 (4 Sat)-11; 12-3, 7-10.30 Sun
Shepherd Neame Master Brew Bitter H
Superb, welcoming, back-street local with an L-shaped bar and high ceiling adorned with hops.
🏠 ♨ ⇌ ♣ P

BADLESMERE

Red Lion
Ashford Road
☎ (01233) 740320
12-3, 6-11; 12-11 Fri & Sat; 12-10.30 Sun
Fuller's London Pride; Greene King XX Mild, Abbot; Shepherd Neame Master Brew Bitter; guest beers H
Free house offering a wide range of beer including some from local micro-breweries and Johnson's cider. Live music Fri. No meals Sun eve.
🏠 ♨ ◑ ▶ ▲ ♣ ⌂ P

BENENDEN

King William IV
The Street
☎ (01580) 240636
11-3, 5-11; 11-11 Sat; 12-10.30 Sun
Shepherd Neame Master Brew Bitter, Spitfire or seasonal beers H
Village-centre pub of two contrasting bars; good food is served in the saloon. The large garden has plentiful seating.
🏠 ♨ ◑ ▶ ♨ ♣ P

BENOVER

Woolpack Inn
Benover Road (B2162, 1 mile S of Yalding) OS704483
☎ (01892) 730356
11-2.30, 6-11 (11-11 summer Sat); 12-3, 7-10.30 (12-10.30 summer) Sun
Shepherd Neame Master Brew Bitter, Best Bitter, Spitfire, Bishops Finger, seasonal beers H
A warm welcome and good food are always assured at this 15th-century country inn, where brick floors are a feature.
🏠 Q ♨ ◑ ▶ ♣ P

BIRLING

Nevill Bull
1 Ryarsh Road
☎ (01732) 843193
11-3, 5-11; 11-11 Sat; 12-10.30 Sun
Tetley Bitter; Wadworth 6X; guest beer H
Cosy village pub and restaurant named after local landowners of old. The guest beer is normally from a Kent micro.
🏠 ♨ ◑ ▶ ♿ ♣ P

BISHOPSBOURNE

Mermaid Inn
☎ (01227) 830581
12-3, 6-11; 12-3, 7-10.30 Sun
Shepherd Neame Master Brew Bitter H
Attractive, typically Kentish village pub, well worth a short detour from the A2. An unpretentious, yet comfortable gem.
🏠 Q ♨ ◑ ♨

BOBBING

Halfway House
Sheppey Way

150

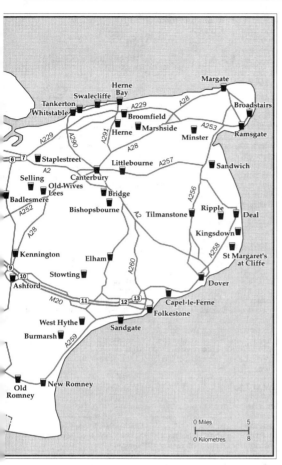

Excellent village local.
♨ Q ♣ P

BROADSTAIRS

Lord Nelson
11 Nelson Place
☎ (01843) 861210
11-11; 12-10.30 Sun
Greene King IPA, Triumph, Abbot; guest beer Ⓗ
Welcoming local, a short walk up from the harbour. Its name commemorates the anchoring of HMS Victory with Nelson's body on board in the bay in 1805.
☎ ❀ ♣ P

Neptune's Hall ☆
1-3 Harbour Street
☎ (01843) 861400
11-11; 12-10.30 Sun
Shepherd Neame Master Brew Bitter, Spitfire, seasonal beers Ⓗ
This traditional boatmen's pub, built in 1815, was Grade II listed after a storm of protests by the regulars. Well worth seeking out.
Q ❀ ◑ ⇌ ♣

BROOMFIELD

Huntsman & Horn
Margate Road (off A299)
OS198667
☎ (01227) 365995
11-11; 12-10.30 Sun
Benskins BB; guest beer Ⓗ
Cosy, 18th-century Grade II listed pub. The restaurant has a children's certificate. Bat and Trap played. No eve meals winter Sun.
♨ ❀ ◑ ▶ ♣ P

BURMARSH

Shepherd & Crook
Shear Way, Thorndyke Road
☎ (01233) 872336
11-2.30; 7-11; 12-2.30, 7-10.30 Sun
Adnams Bitter; Shepherd Neame Master Brew Bitter; guest beer Ⓗ
Welcoming, 18th-century traditional free house. Muskets and other memorabilia are featured in the lounge. Eve meals Tue-Sat.
♨ Q ☎ ❀ ◑ ⊟ ♣ P

CANTERBURY

Eight Bells
34 London Road
☎ (01227) 454794
4.30 (11 Fri & Sat)-11; 12-10.30 Sun
Greene King IPA; Young's Bitter, Special; guest beer Ⓗ
Small, no-frills single room pub, in the suburb of St. Dunstans. The Sun lunches are good value (no other meals served). The clientele varies from die-hard regulars to American tourists and all are made to feel welcome by the cheery tenants. A

☎ (01795) 423825
11-3, 5.30-11; 11-11 Fri & Sat;
12-10.30 Sun
Courage Best Bitter; Shepherd Neame Master Brew Bitter; guest beers Ⓗ
Free house on the old Maidstone-Sheerness road. Enjoy the friendly atmosphere in the main bar and restaurant. Wheelchair WC. No eve meals Tue, bookings essential Sun eve.
❀ ◑ ▶ ▲ ♣ P

BOUGHTON MONCHELSEA

Red House
Hermitage Lane, Wierton (S off B2163, down Wierton Lane and East Hall Hill)
OS783488
☎ (01622) 743986
12-3 (not Tue), 7-11; 12-11 Sat; 12-10.30 Sun
Everards Tiger; Otter Bitter; guest beers Ⓗ
Traditional free house offering a warm welcome with four changing guest ales and a wide selection of bottled beers and fruit wines;

several drinking areas to choose from.
♨ ☎ ❀ ◑ ▶ ▲ ♣ ⌂ P ⊟

Try also: **Cock Inn**, Heath Rd (Young's)

BRENCHLEY

Bull
High Street
☎ (01892) 722701
11.30-3, 5-11; 11-4, 6-11 Sat; 12-4, 7-10.30 Sun
Greene King IPA, Abbot; Harveys BB; guest beer Ⓗ
Welcoming, Victorian local at the centre of an attractive village. The single bar is divided into three distinct areas, plus a conservatory at the rear.
♨ ❀ ⇌ ◑ ▶ ♣

BRIDGE

Plough & Harrow
86 High Street
☎ (01227) 830455
11-3, 6-11; 11-11 Sat; 12-3, 7-10.30 Sun
Shepherd Neame Master Brew Bitter Ⓗ

local gem.
Q ❀ ⚭ ≈ (West) ♣

Thomas Ingoldsby
5-9 Burgate
☎ (01227) 463339
10-11; 12-10.30 Sun
Courage Directors; Shepherd Neame Spitfire; Theakston Best Bitter; guest beers Ⓗ
Spacious, open-plan pub, a typical Wetherspoon's where food is served all day.
Q ◖▶ ₺ ≈ (East) ✄

Westgate Inn
1-3 North Lane
☎ (01227) 464329
10-11; 12-10.30 Sun
Boddingtons Bitter; Courage Directors; Shepherd Neame Spitfire; Theakston Best Bitter; guest beer Ⓗ
The drinking area is divided into numerous alcoves, in another excellent Wetherspoon's conversion.
Q ❀ ◖▶ ₺ ≈ (West) ✄ ▣

Try also: Unicorn, St Dunstans St (Whitbread Pub Partnership)

CAPEL
Dovecote
Alders Road (off A228, follow brown tourist signs)
☎ (01892) 835966
12-3 (4 Sat); 6-11; 12-4, 7-10.30 Sun
Harveys BB; King & Barnes Sussex; Larkins Chiddingstone; guest beers Ⓖ
Cosy local in a tiny hamlet, featuring one long bar, bare brick walls and beamed ceilings. Gravity-dispensed beers are kept in a temperature-controlled room behind the bar.
⚭ Q ❀ ◖▶ ♣ ◌ ▣

CAPEL-LE-FERNE
Lighthouse Inn
Old Dover Road (off B2011)
☎ (01303) 223300
11-3, 5.30-11; 11-11 Sat; 12-10.30 Sun
Greene King IPA, Abbot Ⓗ
Renovated former country club, high on the cliffs overlooking the Dover straits. The original lighthouse sits above the main entrance. It has a family bar/diner and a restaurant serving a high quality menu.
Q ⛺ ⚭ ◖▶ ₺ ▲ P ✄

Royal Oak
New Dover Road (B2011 E of village)
☎ (01303) 244787
11.30-3 (4 Sat), 6 (7 Sat)-11; 12-4, 8-10.30 Sun
Shepherd Neame Master Brew Bitter; guest beers Ⓗ
This cosy 17th-century free house has a snug bar on an

upper level. It stands behind the famous white cliffs overlooking France. No meals Wed eve.
⚭ Q ❀ ◖▶ ▲ ♣ P

CHARING
Bowl Inn
Egg Hill Road (Five Lanes jct)
OS950514
☎ (01233) 712256
5-11; 12-11 Fri & Sat; 12-10.30 Sun
Fuller's London Pride; guest beers Ⓗ
Remote, but friendly and welcoming, 16th-century pub, a regular CAMRA award-winner. It always has three guest beers. The large garden has camping facilities.
⚭ ❀ ▲ ♣ P ✄

CHATHAM
Little Crown
346 High Street
☎ (01634) 844144
11-11; 12-10.30 Sun
Adnams Bitter; Fuller's London Pride; Greene King IPA Ⓗ
Friendly local, near the main shopping area. Photographs of old Chatham decorate the walls. Good value home-cooked food served (not Sat).
⚭ ❀ ◖▶ ≈ ♣

New Inn
291 Luton Road
☎ (01634) 302700
12-3, 6-11; 12-11 Sat; 12-10.30 Sun
Beer range varies
Boisterous pub on Chatham's outskirts, catering for young people.
◖ ♣

Ropemakers Arms
70 New Road (A2)
☎ (01634) 402121
12-3 (not Sat), 7-11; 12-3, 7-10.30 Sun
Goacher's Light; guest beers Ⓗ
Friendly pub decorated with an interesting mural of a dockyard shed by a local artist. No food Sun.
◖ ≈ ♣

Try also: Tap'n'Tin, Railway St (Brewpub)

CHIDDINGSTONE HOATH
Rock Inn
Hoath Corner (1½ miles S of Chiddingstone via Wellers Town) OS497431
☎ (01892) 870296
11.30-3, 6-11 (closed Mon); 12-3, 7-10.30 Sun
Larkins Traditional, Best Bitter (summer), **Porter** (winter) Ⓗ
Old timber-framed rural building featuring a brick floor, irregular beams and unusual handpumps. Ringing the Bull played. No food Sun eves.

⚭ Q ❀ ◖▶ ♣ P

COOLING
Horseshoe & Castle
The Street
☎ (01634) 221691
11.30-3, 6-11; 12-4, 7-10.30 Sun
Adnams Bitter; Draught Bass; guest beers Ⓗ
Quiet country pub in a small village claiming literary connections with Dickens and Shakespeare. A good menu includes seafood as a speciality (eve meals Tue-Sun).
⚭ ❀ ⚭ ◖▶ ♣ P

DARTFORD
Paper Moon
55 High Street
☎ (01322) 281127
10-11; 12-10.30 Sun
Boddingtons Bitter; Courage Directors; Shepherd Neame Spitfire; Theakston Best Bitter; guest beers Ⓗ
Corner pub in a converted bank, serving a wide range of guest beers. Its friendly, welcoming atmosphere makes it popular with regulars.
Q ◖▶ ₺ ≈ ✄ ▣

Tiger
28 St Albans Road (off A226, East Hill)
☎ (01322) 293688
11-11; 12-10.30 Sun
Courage Best Bitter; Shepherd Neame Master Brew Bitter; guest beers Ⓗ
Small, cosy, side-street pub fielding darts, pool and football teams. The guest beer is often from local micro-breweries. Weekday lunches served.
◖ ♣ ♣

Try also: Rose, Overy St (Free)

DEAL
Admiral Penn
79 Beach Street
☎ (01304) 374279
11-3 (not Mon-Fri), 6-11 Sat; closed Sun
Draught Bass; Fuller's London Pride; Wells Bombardier Ⓗ
Smart seafront bar displaying nautical memorabilia. It stocks a notable range of continental spirits and liqueurs.
⚭ ≈

Alma
126 West Street
☎ (01304) 360244
10-3, 6-11; 12-3, 7-10.30 Sun
Shepherd Neame Master Brew Bitter; guest beers Ⓗ
Superb free house serving three guest ales (over 600 different beers in the last few

years). Home to numerous darts/pool/bar billiards teams, it was local CAMRA *Pub of the Year* 1999.

🏵 ≈ ♣

Deal Hoy
16 Duke Street
☎ (01304) 363972
12-3 (not Mon-Tue), 6-11; 11-11 Fri & Sat; 12-10.30 Sun
Shepherd Neame Master Brew Bitter, Spitfire, Bishops Finger, seasonal beers Ⓗ
Small, busy, back-street pub, with a wide screen TV for sports fans. A beer festival over Aug Bank Holiday is a new venture.

🏵 ⓓ ≈

Saracens Head
1 Alfred Square
☎ (01304) 381650
11-11; 12-10.30 Sun
Shepherd Neame Master Brew Bitter, Spitfire, Bishops Finger Ⓗ
Traditional street-corner pub, well supported by the many teams that represent it.

🏵 ≈ ♣

Ship
141 Middle Street
☎ (01304) 372222
11-11; 12-10.30 Sun
Draught Bass; Fuller's ESB; Shepherd Neame Master Brew Bitter; Swale Kentish Pride; guest beer Ⓗ
Traditional pub of distinct drinking areas, including a secluded back room. A regular outlet for Swale Brewery, which often provides the guest beer.

🏚 ≈

DODDINGTON

Chequers
The Street OS935573
11-3.45, 7-11; 11-11 Fri & Sat; 12-3, 7-10.30 Sun
Shepherd Neame Master Brew Bitter, Bishops Finger, seasonal beers Ⓗ
Ever-popular, friendly village pub: a large saloon bar, cosy public and an adjoining family room. Previous regional CAMRA *Pub of the Year*.

🏚 Q ⬧ 🏵 ⓓ 🍴 ♣ P

DOVER

Blakes
52 Castle Street (100 yds from Market Sq)
☎ (01304) 202194
12-3 (not winter Sat), 6-11; closed lunch, 6-10.30 May-Oct Sun
Draught Bass; Fuller's London Pride; Taylor Landlord; Wells Bombardier Ⓗ
Small basement bar/restaurant in a mid 19th-century terrace. Popular with the business community and

cross-channel travellers, it also retains a local following. Wide selection of whiskies stocked.

🏵 🛏 ⓓ ▌ ≈ (Priory) ✂

Flotilla & Firkin
1 Bench Street (off A20, York St. roundabout)
☎ (01304) 204488
11-11; 12-10.30 Sun
Ind Coope Burton Ale; Marston's Pedigree; Tetley Bitter Ⓗ
Formerly the Dover Tavern Alehouse, now heavily themed, but affording the hospitality of a traditional local. Popular with both tourists and locals, children are welcome until 6pm.

🏵 ⓓ ≈ (Priory)

Golden Lion
11 Priory Street (A256/B2011 jct)
☎ (01304) 202919
11-11; 12-10.30 Sun
Adnams Bitter; Greene King IPA; Marston's Pedigree Ⓗ
Newly redecorated town-centre local, very much a drinkers' pub.

≈ (Priory) ♣

Mogul
Chapel Place (near A256/A20 jct)
☎ (01304) 205072
11-11; 12-10.30 Sun
Beer range varies Ⓗ
The recent introduction of stillage and a woodburner has enhanced the friendly ambiance of this traditional two-bar local. Old brewery posters and photos of Dover and Imperial India adorn the wall.

🏚 Q 🏵 ≈ (Priory) ♣ ➲ ✂

Old Endeavour
124 London Road
☎ (01304) 204417
11-11 12-10.30 Sun
Shepherd Neame Master Brew Bitter; seasonal beers Ⓗ
Busy local that hosts occasional music nights; a local motorbike club meets here.

🏵 ⓓ ♣

EAST FARLEIGH

Bull Inn
Lower Road
☎ (01622) 726282
11-11; 12-10.30 Sun
Adnams Bitter; Boddingtons Bitter; Flowers Original; Fuller's London Pride; Tetley Bitter; guest beer Ⓗ
Vibrant community pub; the large comfortable bar is popular with all ages. Live music Sun eves draws a crowd. Good food.

🏚 ⬧ 🏵 ⓓ 🦽 ▲ ≈ P ✂

Victory
Farleigh Bridge (by station)

☎ (01622) 726591
11-11; 12-10.30 Sun
Goacher's Best Dark; Tetley Bitter; guest beer Ⓗ
Friendly pub where the garden overlooks the River Medway.

⬧ 🏵 ⓓ ▲ ≈ ♣ P

EAST SUTTON

Shant Hotel
Charlton Lane (off A274)
☎ (01622) 842235
11-11; 12-3, 7-11 Sun
Rother Valley Level Best; Young's Special; guest beers Ⓗ
Formerly the Prince of Wales, the Shant is set in beautiful countryside. A warm welcome awaits at this popular hostelry, with its comfortable, low-beamed bar/dining area; copious amounts of excellent food always available.

🏚 Q 🏵 🛏 ⓓ 🦽 ▲ P ✂ 🍴

EGERTON FORSTAL

Queen's Arms
OS893464
☎ (01233) 756386
12-2.30, 5.30-11; 12-11 Fri, Sat & summer); 12-10.30 Sun
Goacher's Mild; Shepherd Neame Master Brew Bitter; guest beers Ⓗ
Hard-to-find village local, but worth the effort. The house beer is brewed by Rother Valley and one of the guest ales normally comes from Kent Garden Brewery. Real cider may be stocked in summer. Eve meals Tue-Sat.

🏚 🏵 ⓓ P

ELHAM

Rose & Crown
High Street
☎ (01303) 840226
11-3, 6-11; 12-3, 7-10.30 Sun
Bateman XB; Rother Valley Level Best; guest beers Ⓗ
Large, 16th-century inn, extended in 1740. Good food is served in both bar and restaurant. Baroness Orczy's Scarlet Pimpernel was based on a regular customer. Good accommodation is in a converted stable block. Fresh fish specials feature daily.

🏚 Q ⬧ 🏵 🛏 ⓓ P

FAIRSEAT

Vigo
Gravesend Road (A227, approx 2 miles from Wrotham and Trottiscliffe)
☎ (01732) 822547
11-3 (not Mon), 7-11; 12-3, 7-10.30 Sun
Bateman XXXB; Harveys XX Mild, BB; Young's Bitter; guest beers Ⓗ
Unpretentious old rural pub, housing one of the few Dadlums (indoor skittles)

tables in Kent.
🚶 Q ♣ P ⊭ ⍐

FARNINGHAM

Chequers
87 High Street (250 yds from
A20)
☎ (01322) 865222
11-11; 12-10.30 Sun
**Fuller's London Pride; Gales HSB;
Oakham JHB; Taylor Landlord; guest
beers** Ⓗ
Welcoming, comfortable,
popular corner pub in a
charming village. Good value
food is well-presented (not
served Sun). ❀ ◖ ♣ ⊞

FAVERSHAM

Crown & Anchor
41 The Mall
☎ (01795) 532812
10.30-3, 5.30-11; 10.30-4, 6.30-11
Sat; 12-3, 7-10.30 Sun
**Shepherd Neame Master Brew
Bitter** Ⓗ
True, friendly local, serving
genuine Goulash; the
Hungarian landlord is the
longest serving in Faversham.
◖ ⇌ ♣

Elephant
31 The Mall
☎ (01795) 590157
12 (11 Fri & Sat)-11; 12-10.30 Sun
Greene King IPA; guest beers Ⓗ
Good, friendly pub stocking
four regular guest beers, a
mild is normally available.
Eve meals Wed-Sat; the no-
smoking restaurant must be
booked.
🚶 ❀ ◖ ⇌ ♣

Shipwrights Arms
Hollowshore (from
Davington turn right at the
pub's sign into Ham Rd, left
at bottom, then right)
☎ (01795) 590088
12-3, 6-11; 11-11 Sat & summer; 12-
10.30 Sun
**Goacher's Mild; Kent Garden Corn
Rose; Shepherd Neame Master Brew
Bitter; guest beer** Ⓖ
Lonely outpost of real ale,
affording superb views over
creeks and marsh. It
generates its own electricity.
The Shipwrecked house beer
is from Goacher's, while in
summer cider from Pawley
Farm is stocked. Meals served
Wed-Sun.
🚶 ❀ ◖ ▲ ♣ ⌂ P ⊭

Sun Inn
10 West Street
☎ (01795) 535098
11-11; 12-10.30 Sun
**Shepherd Neame Master Brew
Bitter, Spitfire, seasonal beers** Ⓗ
Historic town-centre house,
formerly two separate pubs.
Quiet at lunchtimes, it gets
busy eves.
🚶 ❀ ◖ ⇌ ♣

Windmill Inn
Canterbury Road, Preston
(A2)
☎ (01795) 536505
11.30-3.30, 6-11; 11.30-11 Sat;
12-10.30 Sun
**Shepherd Neame Master Brew
Bitter, seasonal beers** Ⓗ
Friendly, two-bar pub
retaining many original
features. It is well worth the
walk from the town centre. It
stands opposite Faversham
Town football ground. No
food Sun.
🚶 Q ❀ 🚶 ◖ ▶ ⊡ ⇌ ♣ P

FOLKESTONE

Clifton Hotel
Clifton Gardens, The Leas
(opp. Leas Cliff Hall)
☎ (01303) 851231
11-3, 5.45-11; 11.30-3, 6.30-10.30
Sun
Draught Bass Ⓗ
This large Victorian hotel,
replete with high ceilings and
'olde-worlde' charm, serves
the best Bass in town.
🚶 ⌕ 🚶 ◖ ▶

Lifeboat
42 North Street
☎ (01303) 243958
11-11; 12-10.30 Sun
**Draught Bass; Fuller's London Pride;
guest beers** Ⓗ
Welcoming back-street local
near the harbour. Lunches
served Wed-Sun.
❀ ◖ ▶ ♣

Try also: Wetherspoon's,
Rendezvous St

FORDCOMBE

Chafford Arms
Spring Hill (B2188)
☎ (01892) 740267
11.45-3, 6.30-11; 11-11 Sat; 12-4,
7-10.30 Sun
Larkins Traditional; guest beer Ⓗ
Attractive, roomy tile-hung
Victorian building, close to
the village green. Popular
with diners – fish is a
speciality (eve meals Tue-Sat).
Pleasant gardens.
🚶 ❀ ◖ ▶ ♣ P

GILLINGHAM

Barge
63 Layfield Road
☎ (01634) 850485
7 (12 Sat)-11; 12-10.30 (12-4, 7-10.30
winter) Sun
House beer Ⓗ
The pub is candlelit by night
and affords a view of the
River Medway from the
garden by day. A single bar
town house, its interior
resembles decks below decks.
Folk club held Mon eve. Joshua
Ale is brewed by local brewer
Flagship.
❀ ♣

Dog & Bone
21 Jeffrey Street
☎ (01634) 576829
11-11; 12-10.30 sun
Beer range varies Ⓗ
This busy, town-centre house
has undergone major
renovation, with a new
conservatory and a flagstone
floor. Four handpumps
dispense many unusual ales.
It hosts a charity beer festival
in July.
🚶 ❀ ◖ ▶ ⇌ ♣

Roseneath
79 Arden Street
☎ (01634) 852553
11.30-11; 12-10.30 Sun
Beer range varies Ⓗ
Single bar mid-terraced
property that can get busy by
late eve. Six handpumps offer
a choice of ales to suit all
tastes. Large garden.
❀ ⇌ ♣

Upper Gillingham
Conservative Club
541 Canterbury Street
☎ (01634) 851403
11-2.30, 6.45-11; 11-3, 6.30-11 Sat;
12-2.30, 7-10.30 Sun
**Shepherd Neame Master Brew
Bitter; guest beers** Ⓗ
A warm welcome is assured
in this friendly club. A
spacious bar area serves
competitively-priced ales.
Show this *Guide* or current
CAMRA membership to be
signed in.
♣ P

Will Adams
73 Saxton Street
☎ (01634) 575902
12-4 (not Mon-Fri), 7-11; 12-4, 7-10.30
Sun
**Fuller's London Pride; guest
beers** Ⓗ
Single bar local whose
interior depicts the life and
times of Will Adams, local
shipbuilder and adventurer.
Busy late eve, but a friendly
welcome given.
❀ ⇌ ♣ ⌂

Try also: Frog & Toad, Burnt
Oak Tce (Free); **King George
V**, Prospect Row, Brompton
(Free)

GILLS GREEN

Wellington Arms
Gills Green (off A229, N of
Hawkhurst)
☎ (01580) 753119
11-11; 12-10.30 Sun
Harveys BB; guest beers Ⓗ
Popular, busy,
weatherboarded free house
attracting a good
mix of locals and diners
(good food is served all day);
families welcome. Worth
finding.
🚶 ❀ ◖ ▶ ♣ P

GRAVESEND

Jolly Drayman
1 Love Lane, Wellington Street
☎ (01474) 352355
11.30-3, 6-11; 12-3, 7-11 Sat; 12-3, 7-10.30 Sun
Morland Old Speckled Hen; guest beers Ⓗ
Part of the former Wellington Brewery: a comfortable lounge in a town-centre pub with low beamed ceilings. Lunches served Tue-Fri, barbecues summer weekends.
🏠 ◖ ⇌ ♣ P

Somerset Arms
10 Darnley Road (near station)
☎ (01474) 533837
11-11 (midnight Thu-Sat); 12-4, 7.30-10.30 Sun
Beer range varies Ⓗ
Quaint traditional pub featuring wooden pews. Discos held Thu-Sun eves. No food Sun.
◖ ⇌ ⊞

Windmill
45 Shrubbery Road
☎ (01474) 352242
11-11; 12-10.30 Sun
Burtonwood Best Bitter; Wadworth 6X; guest beers Ⓗ
Comfortable village-style pub with three bars, near the town centre. Popular with all ages, it boasts award-winning gardens.
Q 🏠 ◖ ⊞ ⇌ ♣ P

Try also: Echo, Echo Sq (Free)

HALLING

Homeward Bound
72 High Street
☎ (01634) 240743
12-3, 7-11; 12-3, 7-10.30 Sun
Shepherd Neame Master Brew Bitter Ⓗ
Refurbished village local with a friendly atmosphere. The Medway Triumph Club meets here Tue eve.
🏠 🏠 ⇌ ♣ P

HALSTEAD

Rose & Crown
Otford Lane (1 mile W of A224) OS489611
☎ (01959) 533120
11.30-11; 12-10.30 Sun
Courage Best Bitter; Harveys seasonal beers; Larkins Traditional; guest beers Ⓗ
200-year-old, flint-faced two-bar pub serving three ever-changing guest beers. Children are welcome in the games room; Bat and Trap played. Weekday lunches served.
🏠 Q ➳ 🏠 ◖ ⊞ ♣ P

Try also: Harrow, Knockholt (Shepherd Neame)

HERNE

Smugglers Inn
1 School Lane
☎ (01227) 741395
11-3.30, 6-11; 11-11 Sat; 12-10.30 Sun
Shepherd Neame Master Brew Bitter, Spitfire, seasonal beers Ⓗ
Traditional village pub of two lively bars attracting a family clientele.
🏠 ◖ ⊞ ♣

HERNE BAY

Four Fathoms
2 High Street
☎ (01227) 374987
11-11; 12-10.30 Sun
Shepherd Neame Master Brew Bitter Ⓗ
Spacious, one-bar pub. The family room has two pool tables. Unusual arched windows reflect the style of those in the nearby Victorian station.
➳ ⇌ ♣

Saxon Shore
78-80 Central Parade
☎ (01227) 370316
10-11; 12-10.30 Sun
Boddingtons Bitter; Courage Directors; Shepherd Neame Spitfire; Theakston Best Bitter; guest beers Ⓗ
Seafront Wetherspoon's between the famous Victorian clocktower and recently refurbished bandstand that hosts frequent concerts.
Q ➳ 🏠 ◖ ⊞ ⇌ ✂ ⊞

HIGHAM

Stonehorse Inn
Dillywood Lane (200 yds from B2000)
☎ (01634) 722046
11-3, 6-11 11-11 Fri & Sat; 12-3, 7-10.30 Sun
Courage Best Bitter; guest beers Ⓗ
Quiet rural pub on the edge of Strood comprising two unspoilt bars. A regular outlet for Flagship beers, food is served 12-2 Mon-Fri and 7-9 Wed-Sat. 🏠 Q 🏠 ◖ ⊞ ♣ P

HODSOLL STREET

Green Man
☎ (01732) 823575
11-2.30 (11.30-3 Sat), 6.30-11; 12-3, 7-10.30 Sun
Marston's Pedigree; Shepherd Neame Master Brew Bitter; Wadworth 6X; guest beers Ⓗ
Picturesque local in a tiny hamlet; renowned for the quality of its food (no eve meals Sun or Mon Oct-April).
🏠 🏠 ◖ ▶ P

HOOK GREEN

Elephants Head
Furnace Lane (B2169)
☎ (01892) 890279
11-3, 5-11; 12-3, 6-11 (11-11 summer Sat), 12-3, 7-10.30 Sun
Harveys Pale Ale, BB, Armada, seasonal beers Ⓗ
Stone-built, 15th-century pub in an isolated position, with a large garden. A good selection of home-made meals is complemented by a Sun carvery.
🏠 Q 🏠 ◖ ▶ ♣ P

IDEN GREEN (BENENDEN)

Woodcock Inn
Woodcock Lane (1 mile S of Benenden, left towards Standen St., first left) OS807313
☎ (01580) 240009
11-11; 12-10.30 Sun
Greene King IPA, Abbot; Harveys BB; Rother Valley Level Best; guest beer Ⓗ
Weatherboarded pub, on the edge of Standen Wood, difficult to find but well worth the effort. The pub is divided into a main bar and a dining area serving generous platefuls of good food. The bar is idyllic on a winter's eve with armchairs by a fire.
🏠 Q ◖ ▶ P

IGHTHAM

Chequers
The Street
☎ (01732) 882396
11-3, 6-11; 12-3, 7-10.30 Sun
Greene King IPA, Abbot, seasonal beers Ⓗ
Traditional, one-bar village local with a restaurant.
🏠 🏠 ◖ ⊞ ▲ P

IGHTHAM COMMON

Old House ☆
Redwell Lane (½ mile SW of Ightham village between A25 and A227) OS590559
☎ (01732) 882383
12-3 (not Mon-Fri), 7 (9 Tue)-11; 12-3, 7-10.30 Sun
Daleside Shrimpers; Ⓖ **Flowers IPA;** Ⓗ **Otter Bitter; guest beers** Ⓖ
Genuine, unspoilt country pub, difficult to find without a pub sign. A large open fireplace graces the main bar; a recently retired faithful cash register adorns the side room.
🏠 Q ⊞ ▲ P

KEMSING

Rising Sun
Cotmans Ash Lane, Woodlands OS563599
☎ (01959) 522683
11-3, 6-11; 12-3, 7-10.30 Sun

Beer range varies H
The main bar area is a converted hunting lodge offering a step back in time. An ideal country pub for families in summer with its lovely outdoor area. Up to five constantly rotating guest beers often come from small brewers; cider in summer.
🏚 Q 🎠 🛏 ⬢ 🍴 ⬥ ✦ ⌣ P ⊟

KENNINGTON
Golden Ball
Canterbury Road
☎ (01233) 621728
11-3, 6-11; 11-11 Sat; 12-10.30 Sun
Shepherd Neame Master Brew Bitter, Spitfire, Bishops Finger, seasonal beers H
Friendly, two-bar local on the outskirts of Ashford. Bat and Trap played.
🎠 🍴 ⬢ ⬥ ✦ P

KINGSDOWN
King's Head
Upper Street
☎ (01304) 373915
5-11; 12-3, 7-11 Sat; 12-3, 7-10.30 Sun
Draught Bass; Hancock's HB; Wells Bombardier H
Recently refurbished, smart village local, in a narrow street leading down to the beach. Parking difficult. Booking recommended for meals (served Wed-Sun).
Q 🎠 🎀 🍴 ⬢

LADDINGFORD
Chequers
OS690481
☎ (01622) 871266
12-3, 5-11; 11-11 Sat; 12-10.30 Sun
Adnams Bitter; Fuller's London Pride; King & Barnes Sussex H
Pretty, 15th-century village pub, featuring low oak beams and a Kentish peg-tiled roof, large garden and patio. The landlord supports local village events, and holds an annual beer festival. 🏚 Q 🎀
🎀 🍴 ⬤ (Beltring) ✦ P

LITTLEBOURNE
King William IV
4 High Street
☎ (01227) 721244
11-11; 11-10.30 Sun
Draught Bass; Shepherd Neame Master Brew Bitter; guest beers H
Attractive village inn offering accommodation and good food in the heart of the Garden of England.
🏚 🎀 🎀 🍴 ⬤ ✦ P

LUDDESDOWN
Cock
Henley Street OS664672
☎ (01474) 814208
12-11; 12-10.30 Sun

Adnams Bitter, Broadside; Goacher's Mild; Young's Special; H guest beers H/G
Independently-owned two-bar free house, where a new conservatory provides extra space. The convivial atmosphere is encouraged by an hospitable landlord who stocks a large selection of real ales and ciders. It stands less than a mile from Sole Street station by footpath across fields.
🏚 Q 🎀 🍴 ⬢ ✦ ⌣ P ⊞

MAIDSTONE
Flowerpot
96 Sandling Road (A224)
☎ (01622) 757705
11.30-3, 5.30-11; 11.30-11 Sat; 12-10.30 Sun
Courage Best Bitter; Ruddles County; Shepherd Neame Master Brew Bitter; guest beers (occasional) H
Cosy, corner local recently well refurbished hosting regular live music; Sky sports shown. Bar staff help create a warm, friendly atmosphere.
🏚 🎀 ⬤ ⬥ ⬤ (East) ✦

Pilot
25-27 Upper Stone Street (A229)
☎ (01622) 691162
11-3, 6 (7 Sat)-11; 12-3, 7-10.30 Sun
Harveys XX Mild, BB, Armada, seasonal beers H
This Grade II listed building is a regular *Guide* entry, comprising three distinct drinking areas (one is quiet). Note the water jug and hat collections. Pétanque, pool and darts played. Home-cooked food includes pizzas made to order. No meals Sun when live music is performed.
🏚 Q 🎀 ⬤ ⬤ ✦

Rifle Volunteers
28 Wyatt Street
☎ (01622) 758891
11-3, 6-11; 11-4, 7-11 Sat; 12-3, 7-10.30 sun
Goacher's Mild, Light, Crown Imperial Stout H
A Goacher's tied house, an original and unchanged corner pub where beer and conversation rule. Toy soldiers are used as tokens for 'beer in the wood'.
Q 🎀 ⬤ (East) ✦

Swan Inn
2 County Road
☎ (01622) 751264
11-11; 12-10.30 Sun
Shepherd Neame Master Brew Bitter, Best Bitter, Bishops Finger H
Welcoming, street-corner local that wins regular awards for cellarmanship. Pétanque played. 🎀 ⬤ ⬤ ⬤ (East) ✦ ⊟

Try also: Royal Paper Mill, Old Tovil Rd, Tovil (Goacher's)

MARGATE
Orb
243 Ramsgate Road (A254, just past QEQM Hospital)
☎ (01843) 220663
11-11; 12-10.30 Sun
Shepherd Neame Master Brew Bitter, Best Bitter H
Old, friendly out-of-town local built as a farm dwelling in 1498. It has been sympathetically extended over the years to include a larger bar area and games room.
🏚 🎀 ⬤ ✦ P

Try also: Spread Eagle, Victoria Rd (Free)

MARSH GREEN
Wheatsheaf
On B2028, Edenbridge-Lingfield Road
☎ (01732) 864091
11-11; 12-3, 7-10.30 (12-10.30 summer) Sun
Harveys Mild, BB; guest beers H
Spacious pub of many drinking areas, featuring old photographs on the walls and much pine woodwork. It offers a wide range of up to seven guest beers, plus a big choice of snacks and home-cooked meals. The no-smoking area is the family room.
🏚 Q 🎠 🎀 ⬤ ⬥ ✦ ⌣ P ⊬

MARSHSIDE
Gate
☎ (01227) 860498
11-2.30 (3 Sat), 6-11; 12-4, 7-10.30 Sun
Shepherd Neame Master Brew Bitter, Spitfire, seasonal beers G
This attractive, friendly pub has appeared in 25 editions of this *Guide*, due to the dedication to ale of its licensee. No food winter lunchtime; no-smoking area available at lunchtime only.
🏚 Q 🎠 🎀 ⬤ ⬢ ✦ P ⊬

MINSTER (THANET)
New Inn
2 Tothill Street
☎ (01843) 821294
11.30-3, 5-11; 11.30-11 Fri & Sat; 12-10.30 Sun
Greene King IPA, Abbot; guest beers H
Delightful one-bar village local oozing with warmth and atmosphere. Note the rustic brass and stained glass 'Cobbs' windows. The large garden has an aviary, and children's adventure play

area. Good food comes in ample portions (not Mon, or Sun eve).

🏚 🕸 🕻 🌓 ⇌ ♣ ⌣ P

NETTLESTEAD GREEN
Hop Pole Inn
Maidstone Road
☎ (01622) 812133
11-3, 6-11; 11-11 Sat; 12-10.30 (6 winter) Sun
Harveys BB; guest beers Ⓗ
Single bar pub where a beamed ceiling and open fires provide a warm setting. An eclectic array of artefacts feature spitfires and hop memorabilia. A moat surrounds the new conservatory which enhances the dining area and affords a view to the garden and waterfall.
🕸 🕻 🌓 ♣ P

NEW ROMNEY
Prince of Wales
Fairfield Road
☎ (01797) 362012
12-3, 6 (5 Thu)-11; 11-11 Fri & Sat; 12-3, 7-10.30 Sun
Ind Coope Burton Ale; Shepherd Neame Master Brew Bitter; guest beer Ⓗ
Rare outlet for Burton Ale. The pub is just a short walk from the RHDR light railway station. Crib, pool and darts are played.
🏚 🕸 🕮 Å ♣

NORTHFLEET
Earl Grey
177 Vale Road (off Perry St, near Cygnet Centre)
☎ (01474) 365240
11-2.30, 4.30-11; 11-11 Thu-Sat; 12-10.30 Sun
Shepherd Neame Master Brew Bitter, Spitfire, Bishops Finger, seasonal beers Ⓗ
18th-century flint-faced hostelry, this community pub has a friendly atmosphere and attractive garden.
🕸 ♣ P

Rose
Rose Street (on small estate by station)
☎ (01474) 365791
11-11; 12-3, 7-10.30 Sun
Shepherd Neame Master Brew Bitter Ⓗ
The Rose continues as a local with strong community links; expect a friendly welcome in this cosy one-bar pub.
🕸 🕭 ⇌ ♣

OLD ROMNEY
Rose & Crown Inn
Swamp Road (off A259)
☎ (01797) 367500
11.30-11; 12-10.30 Sun
Bateman Mild; Greene King IPA, Abbot; Fuller's London Pride; guest beers Ⓗ
Attractive village inn affording a good view across the marsh, with a large safe garden. It is a rare outlet for cider (Biddenden) and mild.
🏚 🕸 🍴 🕻 🌓 ♣ ⌣ P ⅊

OLD WIVES LEES
Star Inn
Selling Road
☎ (01227) 730213
5 (12 Sat)-11; 12-3, 7-10.30 Sun
Shepherd Neame Master Brew Bitter; guest beer Ⓗ
Village pub, enjoying a new lease of life after being threatened with closure. The successful efforts of the village action group are an inspiration to all other villages facing the loss of their only pub.
Q 🕸 🕮 ♣ P

OSPRINGE
Anchor
33 Ospringe Street
☎ (01795) 532085
12-2, 6.30-11; 12-11 Sat; 12-4, 7-10.30 Sun
Shepherd Neame Master Brew Bitter Ⓗ
Three-bar local on the busy A2, 100 yards from the Maison Dieu, an ancient traveller's rest used during the crusades. Note the unusual painted decor in all the bars.
🏚 🕭 🕸 ♣

PAINTER'S FORSTAL
Alma
OSC992589
☎ (01795) 533835
10.30-3, 6-11; 12-3, 7-10.30 Sun
Shepherd Neame Master Brew Bitter, Spitfire, seasonal beers Ⓗ
Popular village pub serving excellent food (eve meals Tue-Sat). The small public bar is popular with local drinkers, while the larger saloon bar is mainly used by diners.
🕸 🕻 🌓 🕮 Å ♣ P

PEMBURY
Black Horse
12 High Street
☎ (01892) 822141
11-11; 12-3, 7-10.30 Sun
King & Barnes Sussex; Ruddles County; Young's Special; guest beer Ⓗ
Classic old-fashioned village-centre pub, with a central bar and a good selection of pews. Very lively, at the heart of the community, it serves a varied and extensive bar menu (not Sun eve); popular seafood restaurant in the

grounds. Black Horse Bitter comes from an undisclosed brewery.
🏚 Q 🕸 🕻 🌓

PETTERIDGE
Hopbine
Petteridge Lane OS668413
☎ (01892) 722561
12-2.30 (11-2.30 Sat), 6-11; 12-3, 7-10.30 Sun
King & Barnes Mild, Sussex, Old Ale, Festive, seasonal beers Ⓗ
Attractive brick and weatherboarded pub, built into the side of a hill. The L-shaped bar is divided into two sections by a central fireplace. A friendly welcome is assured in this characterful country pub, the only King & Barnes house in Kent. No food Wed.
🏚 Q 🕸 🕻 🌓 ♣ ⌣ P

PLAXTOL
Golding Hop
Sheet Hill (signed from A227, 1/2 mile N of village)
OS600547
☎ (01732) 882150
11-3, 6 (5.30 Fri)-11; 11-11 Sat; 12-4, 7-10.30 Sun
Adnams Bitter; Young's Special; guest beers Ⓖ
An absolute gem: a cottage-like, whitewashed pub nestling in a valley. An excellent range of beers and ciders can be enjoyed in four rooms on three levels. Bar-billiards and pétanque played. Eve meals Wed-Sun.
🏚 Q 🕸 🕻 🌓 Å ⌣ P

Try also: Kentish Rifleman, Dunks Green (Free)

PLUCKLEY
Dering Arms
Station Road (1½ miles from centre, near station)
☎ (01233) 840371
11.30-3, 6-11; 12-3, 7-10.30 Sun
Goacher's Dark Ⓗ
This old former hunting lodge displays the local Dering-style windows and flagstone floors. The house beer is brewed by Goacher's. The menu specialises in fish dishes (no food Sun eve or Mon).
🏚 Q 🕸 🛏 🕻 🌓 ⇌ P

Try also: Blacksmith's Arms, Smarden Rd (Free)

RAINHAM
Mackland Arms
213 Station Road (500 yds N of station)
☎ (01634) 232178
10-11; 12-10.30 Sun
Shepherd Neame Master Brew Bitter, Best Bitter, Spitfire,

seasonal beers Ⓗ
Mid-terrace, L-shaped bar; a
real local.
≠ ♣

Try also: Rose, High St
(Shepherd Neame)

RAMSGATE

Artillery Arms
36 West Cliff Road
☎ (01843) 853282
12-11; 12-10.30 Sun
Beer range varies Ⓗ
Superb little Victorian pub
whose attractive leaded glass
bow windows depict soldiers
and cannon of the
Napoleonic Wars. With an
emphasis on real ale,
doorstep sandwiches and real
cider add to its appeal.
Thanet CAMRA *Pub of the
Year.*
▲ ᗡ

Australian Arms
45 Ashburnham Road
☎ (01843) 591489
11-11; 12-10.30 Sun
**Courage Directors; Fuller's London
Pride; Gale's HSB** Ⓗ
Busy local that has seen its
flint-based building altered
and extended over the years
to give more bar space.
Children's certificate.
⏁ ❀ ▲ ≠ ♣

Churchill Tavern
18-20 The Paragon (opp.
Motor Museum)
☎ (01843) 587862
11.30-11; 12-10.30 Sun
**Courage Directors; Fuller's London
Pride; Ringwood Old Thumper;
Taylor Landlord; Theakston Old
Peculier; guest beer** Ⓖ
Busy clifftop pub, popular
with locals, visitors and
foreign students from the
nearby language schools.
Rebuilt and refurbished in
the late 1980s in the style of
a country pub. The
handpumps may mislead; all
ales are served from the cask.
🏰 ᗡ ▲ ♣

Montefiore Arms
1 Trinity Place (100 yds from
A255/B2054 jct)
☎ (01843) 593265
12-2.30 (not Wed; 12-4.30 Sat), 7-11;
12-3, 7-10.30 Sun
Tolly Cobbold Original; guest beer Ⓗ
Busy, back-street local that
started out as two cottages. It
is named after legendary
centenarian and
philanthropist, Sir Moses
Montefiore, who lived in the
town. Regular theme nights
held.
≠ (Dumpton Pk)

Southwood Tavern
119 Southwood Road
☎ (01843) 595272

12 (5.30 Mon)-11; 12-10.30 Sun
**Courage Best Bitter; Shepherd
Neame Spitfire; guest beer** Ⓗ
Extended back-street 19th-
century local in the
Southwood district of town,
the nearest pub to Ramsgate
football ground.
🏰 ▲ ≠ ♣ P

St Lawrence Tavern
High Street, St Lawrence
☎ (01843) 592337
11-11; 12-10.30 Sun
Courage Best Bitter; guest beers Ⓗ
Busy pub built in 1969, it was
known as the White Horse
until a full refurbishment by
owners Whitbread and
Thorley Taverns in 1998,
which has given it a
continental feel.
❀ ᗡ ▶ ▲ ≠ ♣ P

RIPPLE

Plough Inn
Church Lane
☎ (01304) 360209
11-4, 6-11; 11-11 Sat; 12-10.30 Sun
**Fuller's London Pride, ESB;
Shepherd Neame Master Brew
Bitter, Spitfire; guest beers** Ⓗ
Attractive, one-bar, beamed,
18th century village inn,
serving an interesting
selection of home-made food
and country wines. Friendly
and welcoming; children
may use the restaurant area.
🏰 ❀ ⇌ ᗡ ▶ P

ROCHESTER

Greyhound
68 Rochester Avenue
☎ (01634) 844120
4 (12 Fri & Sat)-11; 12-10.30 Sun
**Shepherd Neame Master Brew
Bitter; Spitfire or seasonal beers** Ⓗ
Late Victorian terraced local
in a quiet back street: a basic
public bar, but the lounge bar
boasts a coal range and
chaises-longues; quiet,
relaxing and friendly
atmosphere.
🏰 ❀ ⊞ ≠ ♣

Man of Kent Ale House
6-8 John Street (near police
station)
☎ (01634) 818771
12-11; 12-10.30 Sun
**Goacher's Gold Star; Larkins
Traditional; guest beers** Ⓗ
Seven handpumps offer a
range of ales from Kent
micro-breweries. It also stocks
draught Kentish cider and
perry, as well as local wine,
and a range of draught and
bottled German beers. Note
the rare original frontage.
🏰 ❀ ≠ ♣ ᗡ

ROLVENDEN

Star
30 High Street (A28)

☎ (01580) 241369
11-11; 12-10.30 Sun
**Harveys XX Mild, BB; Ruddles Best
Bitter, County; guest beer** Ⓗ
Ancient village inn,
originally a workhouse,
where families are welcome.
A varied menu includes daily
specials; barbecues held in
summer. Quiz Mon and free
pool Wed. Near Kent & E.
Sussex railway, this is a rare
outlet for mild.
🏰 ❀ ᗡ ▶ ♣

RUSTHALL

White Hart
Lower Green Road (2 miles
W of Tunbridge Wells)
☎ (01892) 523076
12-3, 6-11; 11-11 Sat; 12-3, 7-10.30
Sun
**Harveys BB; Tetley Bitter; guest
beer** Ⓗ
Pleasant village local where
hops decorate the bar, and
old photographs and
artefacts are scattered
throughout.
🏰 Q ❀ ♣ P

SANDGATE

Clarendon
Brewers Hill
☎ (01303) 248684
11.45-3, 6-11; 12-3, 7-10.30 Sun
**Shepherd Neame Master Brew
Bitter, Spitfire, Bishops Finger,
seasonal beers** Ⓗ
Timeless, two-bar pub on a
footpath off Sandgate
Esplanade. Enjoy the home-
cooked food and Channel
views. No food Sun eve.
🏰 Q ❀ ᗡ ▶ ♣ ⊟

SANDHURST

Harrier
Link Hill, Rye Road (A268,
1 mile E of village)
☎ (01580) 850323
11.30-2.30, 5-11 (closed Tue); 12-4,
7-10.30 Sun
**Harveys BB; Rother Valley Level
Best; guest beers** Ⓗ
Welcoming roadhouse: a
basic public bar and a cosy
saloon with a dining area. An
excellent menu (served at all
times) specialises in Oriental
and fish dishes. Families
welcome; large garden.
🏰 ❀ ᗡ ▶ ⟟ ♣ P

SANDWICH

George & Dragon
24 Fisher Street (near
quayside and tollbridge)
☎ (01304) 613106
11-3, 6-11; 12-3, 7-10.30 Sun
**Shepherd Neame Master Brew
Bitter, Spitfire, seasonal beers;
guest beer** Ⓗ
Very much a restaurant, but
with a food-free area at the
front near the bar. Modern

decor provides a contrast in one of the town's many ancient buildings. Good food (pizzas only served Sun eve). 🏮 ◖▶ ⇌

Try also: Crispin, High St (Bass)

SEAL
Five Bells
25 Church Street (100 yds N of A25)
☎ (01732) 761503
11.30-11; 12-10.30 Sun
Fuller's London Pride; Greene King IPA; Harveys BB; guest beers Ⓗ
Small, back-street pub, formerly three cottages, with one low-ceilinged bar. The hospitable landlord has much improved the appeal of this house. No food Sun.
Q ◖ ♣

SELLING
Rose & Crown
Perry Wood (1 mile S of village) OS042552
☎ (01227) 752214
11-3, 6.30-11; 12-3, 7-10.30 Sun
Adnams Bitter; Goacher's Mild or Dark; Harveys BB; guest beer Ⓗ
Beautiful pub located high up in the middle of the isolated Perry Wood on the North Downs. Popular with walkers, it has won countless awards for its garden (Bat & Trap played). Well regarded for its food (eve meals served Tue-Sat).
🏮 ⬎ 🏮 ◖▶ 🗡 ♣ P

SITTINGBOURNE
Fountain
Station Street
☎ (01795) 472015
11-3, 5.30-11; 11-11 Fri & Sat; 12-10.30 Sun
Shepherd Neame Master Brew Bitter Ⓗ
Spacious welcoming pub, the nearest to Sittingbourne's steam railway.
🏮 🏮 ◖ ⇌ P

Old Oak
68 East Street
☎ (01795) 472685
10.30-2.30, 7-11; 12-2.30, 7-10.30 Sun
Flowers IPA; guest beer Ⓗ
Friendly, unspoilt local near the town centre, offering an ever-changing guest ale and good value home-cooked meals. Joint winner of local CAMRA *Pub of the Year* 1998.
⬎ 🏮 ◖▶ ⇌ ♣ 🗡

Red Lion
58 High Street
☎ (01795) 472706
11-3, 6-11; 11-11 Fri; 12-3, 7-10.30 Sun
Fuller's London Pride; guest

beers Ⓗ
This former coaching inn stocks a fine range of ales, usually six on tap, including one from the local Swale Brewery.
🏮 🏮 ◖▶ ⇌ ♣ P 🗡

SMARDEN
Bell
Smarden Lane (signed from Headcorn) OS870470
☎ (01233) 770283
11.30-3, 6-11; 12-11 Sat; 12-10.30 Sun
Fuller's London Pride; Harveys Pale Ale; Marston's Pedigree; Shepherd Neame Master Brew Bitter; Wadworth 6X Ⓗ
Large, tile-hung country pub dating from 1630. Low beams and open fires in winter provide a warm welcome. A no-smoking bar is generally used by evening diners. A large, secluded garden adds to its appeal. Classic car meetings are held regularly. Bell Ale is Whitbread Trophy rebadged.
🏮 Q ⬎ 🏮 ◖▶ ♣ ↺ P 🗡

SNARGATE
Red Lion ☆
On B2080, 1 mile from Appledore station
☎ (01797) 344648
11-3, 7-11; 12-3, 7-10.30 Sun
Goacher's Light; Rother Valley Level Best; guest beers Ⓖ
Beautiful pub dating from 1540, highly commended in the CAMRA National *Pub of the Year* awards; known locally as Doris's.
🏮 Q 🏮 ♣ ↺ P

ST MARGARETS AT CLIFFE
Smugglers
High Street
☎ (01304) 853404
12-3, 5-11; 12-11 Sat; 12-4.30, 7-10.30 Sun
Greene King IPA; Theakston Best Bitter; guest beers Ⓗ
Compact, single-bar pub and restaurant set in a 19th-century terrace. Guest beers are normally available weekends only. Mexican food is a speciality.
🏮 ◖▶

STAPLEHURST
Lord Raglan
Chart Hill Road (off A229, 1 mile N at Cross at Hand)
☎ (01622) 843747
12-3, 6-11; 12-4 (closed eve) Sun
Goacher's Light; Harveys BB; guest beers Ⓗ
Unspoilt, roadside pub set amongst orchards and open farmland. The bar is bedecked with hops, and log

fires provide a warm welcome. It enjoys a justifiable reputation for its home-cooked food. Large garden; children welcome.
🏮 Q 🏮 ◖▶ P

STAPLESTREET
Three Horseshoes
46 Staplestreet OS080601
☎ (01227) 750842
12-3, 5-11; 12-11 Fri & Sat; 12-3, 5-10.30 Sun
Shepherd Neame Master Brew Bitter, Spitfire, seasonal beers Ⓖ
Traditional country pub – a classic local and a rare outlet for beers served straight from the cask. Local Crippledick cider is sold in bottles to take away. Meals served Tue-Sat.
🏮 Q 🏮 ◖▶ ♣ P

STONE-IN-OXNEY
Crown
Follow signs from Appledore on B2080 OS939277
☎ (01233) 758789
12-3, 6-11; closed Mon; 12-5 Sun
Shepherd Neame Master Brew Bitter; guest beer Ⓗ
Cosy, friendly village food pub near Saxon Shore way. Comprising two bars and a pool room, it boasts an inglenook. An extra ale is stocked in summer. No food Sun.
🏮 🏮 ◖▶ ♿ P

STOWTING
Tiger Inn
Turn off B2068 $1^1/_2$ miles N of M20 jct 11 OS121414
☎ (01303) 862130
12-2.30 (3 Sat), 7-11; 12-3, 7-10.30 Sun
Everards Tiger; Fuller's London Pride; Shepherd Neame Master Brew Bitter; Theakston Old Peculier; guest beer Ⓗ
Lovely inn, run by local villagers. Renowned for its excellent home-cooked food and Mon night jazz. It is a good stop for North Downs Way walkers.
🏮 Q ⬎ 🏮 ◖▶ ♣ P

SWALECLIFFE
Eddery's
100 St Johns Road
☎ (01227) 792428
11-11; 12-10.30 Sun
Courage Directors; Shepherd Neame Master Brew Bitter; Young's Bitter, Special Ⓗ
Roadhouse bearing a sporting theme: big screen sports shown. A good range of food includes healthy 'Heartbeat' scheme options. Pétanque played. 🏮 ⬎ 🏮 ◖▶ ♿ ⚓ ⇌ (Chestfield & Swalecliffe) ♣ P

SWANLEY VILLAGE

Lamb
Swanley Village Road
☎ (01322) 669921
12-2.30, 5.30-11; 12-3, 7-11 Sat;
12-3, 7.30-10.30 Sun
**Shepherd Neame Master Brew
Bitter, Spitfire, Bishops Finger,
seasonal beers** ⊞
Cosy, popular, village local in
a country setting. Eve meals
served Fri and Sat. Limited
parking. ♨ ❀ ◖ ᵭ ♣ P

TANKERTON

Marine
33 Marine Parade
☎ (01227) 272672
11-11; 12-10.30 Sun
**Shepherd Neame Master Brew
Bitter, Spitfire, seasonal beers** ⊞
Attractive hotel overlooking
the Thames estuary. Popular
for weddings and special
events. The comfortable bar
welcomes locals as well as
hotel guests.
Q ☎ ❀ ♫ ◖ ᴅ ᵭ Å ♣ P ⅍

TILMANSTONE

Ravens
Upper Street (off A256)
☎ (01304) 617337
11.30-3, 6.30-11; 12-3, 6.30-10.30
Sun
Beer range varies ⊞
Attractive village pub, a
single large bar serving
excellent food and home-
made cakes. Quiz nights and
a skittle alley are added
attractions. Popular with
walkers and cyclists, it is set
in pleasant surroundings.
Q ❀ ◖ ᴅ ♣ P

TONBRIDGE

New Drum
54 Lavender Hill (off A26)
☎ (01732) 365044
11-11; 12-10.30 Sun
**Fuller's London Pride; Harveys BB;
Larkins Traditional; guest beers** ⊞
Friendly, family-run pub in a
residential back street, with
usually six ales available.
❀ ♣

Stags Head
9 Stafford Road (by market
behind castle)
☎ (01732) 352017
11-3, 6-11; 11-11 Fri & Sat; 12-3,
7-10.30 Sun
**Hook Norton Generation; Oakham
JHB; Taylor Golden Best;
Woodforde's Wherry; guest beer** ⊞
Tucked out of the way, but
well worth finding, this
single bar pub has a homely
feel. The landlord is an
horologist, so clocks feature.
❀ ≈ ♣ P

Try also: Ivy House, High St
(Free)

Very Wonderful Hooden Horse
59 Pembury Road
☎ (01732) 366080
12-2.30, 6-11.30; 12-11.30 Fri & Sat;
12-10.30 Sun
**Greene King IPA, Abbot; guest
beers** ⊞
Wonderfully basic, two-
roomed pub attracting a
lively clientele, displaying
interesting memorabilia. It
specialises in Mexican food.
❀ ◖ ᴅ ≈

TOYS HILL

Fox & Hounds
Turn off A25 in Brasted, 2
miles OS471520
☎ (01732) 750328
11.30 (12 winter)-2.30 (3 Sat), 6-11;
12-3, 7-10.30 Sun
Greene King IPA, Abbot ⊞
Simple but attractive,
isolated, unmodernised pub
with a single bar, surrounded
by NT woodland. It is
furnished as a homely lounge
complete with a piano and
current magazines. Popular
with ramblers; lunchtime
snacks served.
♨ Q ❀ ♣ P

TUDELEY

Poacher at Tudeley
Hartlake Bridge Road (N off
B2017 from Tonbridge)
OS622461
☎ (01732) 358934
12-3, 6-11; 12-3, 7-10.30 Sun
Harveys BB; guest beers ⊞
Roomy, comfortable bar and
an equally spacious
restaurant, situated away
from the village in pleasant
rural surroundings. The
garden has a play area for
children.
♨ ❀ ◖ ᴅ P

TUNBRIDGE WELLS

Bedford
2 High Street (opp. station)
☎ (01892) 526580
11-11; 12-10.30 Sun
**Greene King IPA, Abbot, seasonal or
guest beers** ⊞
Single-bar tavern with six
handpumps always in use. It
is popular with office workers
and shoppers during the day,
commuters and regulars eves.
No food Sun.
◖ ≈ ♣

Rose & Crown
47 Grosvenor Road (near
Tesco's)
☎ (01892) 522427
10.30-2.30, 5-11; 10.30-11 Fri & Sat;
12-3, 7-10.30 Sun
**Boddingtons Best Bitter; Brains
Dark; Greene King IPA; Wadworth
6X; guest beers** ⊞
Town-centre pub divided by
partitions, taken away at

lunchtime to form one large
bar; it reverts to lounge and
public eves. Very popular at
lunchtime, for its good range
of food.
♨ Q ◖ ᴅ ≈ ♣

Windmill Tavern
32 North Street
☎ (01892) 530827
11-2.30, 5-11; 11-11 Sat; 12-10.30
Sun
**Harveys BB; Swale Kentish Pride;
guest beers** ⊞
Attractive Victorian pub in a
small back street. Note the
glazed bricks façade with
relief design. The small L-
shaped room houses a pool
table. Weekday meals served
(not Tue eve).
♨ ❀ ◖ ᴅ

Try also: Opera House, Mt
Pleasant Rd (J D
Wetherspoon)

TWITTON

Rising Sun
Twitton Lane (1 mile W of
Otford along Pilgrims Way)
☎ (01959) 525489
4 (12 Fri & Sat)-11; 12-10.30 Sun
**Greene King IPA, Triumph; guest
beers** ⊞
Small, friendly bar, near
Danes Hollow battleground.
Games include darts, Bat &
Trap and Shut the Box.
Lunches served Sat and Sun,
steak night Fri eve. The
garden affords splendid views
of the Darent Valley towards
Shoreham.
♨ ❀ ♣

UPCHURCH

Brown Jug
76 Horsham Lane OS842675
☎ (01634) 235287
11-2.30 (3 Sat), 6-11; 12-3, 7-10.30
Sun
**Shepherd Neame Master Brew
Bitter** ⊞
On the edge of Upchurch
village, the Brown Jug is a
two-bar pub displaying an
extensive collection of jugs,
as befits its name. The
landlord is now in his 35th
year at the pub.
♨ ☎ ❀ ⊟ ♣ P

UPPER UPNOR

Kings Arms
2 High Street (follow
signs for Upnor Castle from
Strood)
☎ (01634) 717490
11-11; 12-10.30 Sun
Beer range varies ⊞
Busy village local serving
good value food; a regular
outlet for Flagship beers. No
food Sun eves. Bat and Trap
and pétanque played.
♨ ❀ ◖ ᴅ ⊟ ♣ P

CAMRA National Pub Inventory: Mary McBride's, Cushdendun, Co Antrim

Tudor Rose
29 High Street
☎ (01634) 715305
11-4, 7-11; 12-3.30, 7-10.30 Sun
Young's Bitter, Special; guest beers H
This friendly, multi-roomed pub next to Upnor Castle overlooks the river Medway and the former dockyard. Good value food is served (not Sun or Mon eve). It hosts an annual May Day Bank Holiday beer festival.
🏨 🛏 🎄 🌙 ♣ ♣

WAREHORNE
Worlds Wonder
Kenardington Road (B2067)
☎ (01233) 732431
11.30-2.30, 6.30-11; closed Mon; 12-3, 7-10.30 Sun
Bateman Mild, XXXB; Rother Valley Level Best; guest beers (summer) H
Friendly free house that welcomes families. Near the rare breeds farm at Woodchurch. Sunday roast lunch is recommended.
🏨 🎄 🌙 ♣ Å ♣ P

WEST HYTHE
Boltolph's Bridge Inn
☎ (01303) 267346
11.30-2.30, 6-11; 11.30-3, 7-11 Sat; 12-4, 7-10.30 Sun
Greene King IPA; G **guest beers** H/G
Welcoming, isolated pub using gravity dispense for most ales.
🏨 🎄 🌙 ♣ P

WEST MALLING
Lobster Pot
47 Swan Street
☎ (01732) 843265
12-3; 6 (5 Fri)-11; 12-4, 7-10.30 Sun

Adnams Bitter; guest beers H
Always six interesting beers on at this local CAMRA *Pub of the Year* 1999. The upstairs restaurant doubles as a meeting room or indoor bowling alley. Highly recommended. No food Sun eve.
🏨 🎄 🌙 🌺

WHITSTABLE
New Inn
30 Woodlawn Street
☎ (01227) 264746
11-11; 12-4, 7-10.30 Sun
Shepherd Neame Master Brew Bitter H
Popular community pub serving a diverse clientele.
🌺 ♣

Ship Centurion
111 High Street
☎ (01227) 264740
11-11; 12-10.30 Sun
Adnams Bitter; Cains Mild; guest beers H
Busy, central, one-bar pub where home-cooked bar food is served all day using local and organic produce whenever possible; the menu includes authentic German sausages and goulash. The conservatory has Sky TV.
🛏 🌙 🌺 🕮 🔊

WITTERSHAM
Swan Inn
1 Swan Street (B2082, Tenterden-Rye Road)
☎ (01797) 270913
11-11; 12-10.30 Sun
Goacher's Light; Greene King Triumph H
Friendly local at the village centre, originally an old drovers' pub. Guest beers

often include a mild. This free house hosts live music Fri eve and Sun afternoon, also events such as conker championships. No food Tue.
🏨 🎄 🌙 🕮 ♣ ⌂ P

WROTHAM
Rose & Crown
High Street
☎ (01732) 882409
11-3, 5.30 (6 Sat)-11; 12-3, 7-10.30 Sun
Shepherd Neame Best Bitter, Spitfire, Bishops Finger, seasonal beers H
Pleasant small village pub, hosting lots of local activities, such as golf society and indoor bowls; also the home of local Morris dancers. An excellent range of food is served.
🏨 🎄 🌙 ♣ P

Try also: Three Post Boys, The Square (Greene King)

INDEPENDENT BREWERIES

Ales of Kent: Chatham

Flagship: Chatham

Goacher's: Tovil

Kent Garden: Faversham

Larkins: Chiddingstone

Shepherd Neame: Faversham

Swale: Sittingbourne

Tap'n'Tin: Chatham

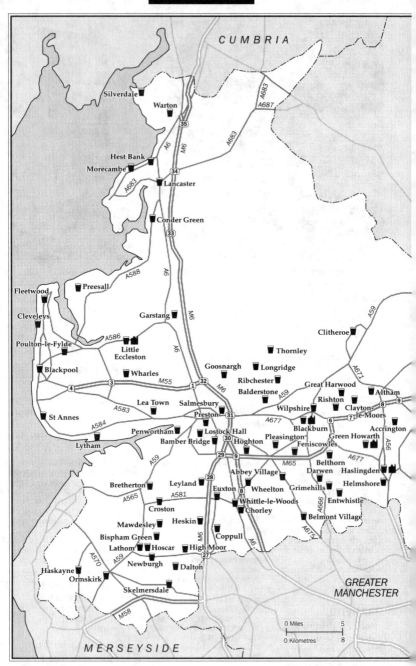

Silverdale
Warton
35
A687
A683
Hest Bank
Morecambe
34
Lancaster
A683
A6
M6
Conder Green
33
A588
A6
Preesall
Fleetwood
Garstang
M6
Cleveleys
A586
Poulton-le-Fylde
Little Eccleston
Clitheroe
A671
A59
Blackpool
4
3
M55
A6
Wharles
1
32
M6
Thornley
Goosnargh
Longridge
Great Harwood
Altham
Lea Town
A583
Ribchester
Rishton
8
9
St Annes
Salmesbury
Balderstone
A59
Wilpshire
Clayton-le-Moors
A584
Preston
31
A677
6
7
Penwortham
Lostock Hall
Blackburn
Accrington
Lytham
Bamber Bridge
Hoghton
Pleasington
Green Howarth
A56
A59
29
30
9
Feniscowles
A677
M65
Belthorn
Abbey Village
Darwen
Haslingden
Bretherton
Leyland
28
Euxton
8
Wheelton
Grimehills
Helmshore
A565
A581
Whittle-le-Woods
Entwhistle
Croston
Chorley
A666
Mawdesley
Heskin
Belmont Village
Bispham Green
M6
Coppull
A675
Lathom
Hoscar
High Moor
A6
Haskayne
A570
A59
Newburgh
Dalton
27
Ormskirk
Skelmersdale
GREATER MANCHESTER
M58
0 Miles 5
0 Kilometres 8
MERSEYSIDE

ABBEY VILLAGE

Hare & Hounds
129 Bolton Road (A675/Dole
Lane jct)
☎ (01254) 830334
12-2.30, 5-11; 12-11 Sat; 12-10.30
Sun
**Boddingtons Bitter; Taylor Landlord;
guest beers** Ⓗ
Busy moorland pub at the
top end of the village.

Drawing a good friendly mix
of locals and passing trade, it
is handy for easy walks
around reservoirs.
🏔 🏠 ◖ 🍺 ♣ P

ACCRINGTON

Arden Inn
85 Abbey Street (A680)
☎ (01254) 385971
12-11; 12-10.30 Sun

**Boddingtons Bitter; Lees Bitter;
guest beers** Ⓗ
Friendly, popular, family-run
town-centre pub; it is mostly
open plan, with one good-
sized room, useful for
meetings. The pool table is
well used.
🚲 ♣

Globe Inn
183 Blackburn Road (A679)

Lancashire

NORTH YORKSHIRE

Salterforth

Black Lane Ends

Briercliffe
Barrowford

Foulridge

Colne

Laneshaw Bridge

Burnley

Cliviger

WEST YORKSHIRE

Victoria

Manchester Road (A680)
☎ (01254) 237727
3 (1 Fri; 12 Sat)-11; 12-10.30 Sun
Thwaites Mild, Bitter H
Open-plan pub; one large U-shaped room with a pool table. ♣

Whitakers Arms

322 Burnley Road (A679)
☎ (01254) 392999
11-11; 12-10.30 Sun
Beer range varies H
Open-plan pub/restaurant specialising in Turkish cuisine. Three changing guest beers and a pool table are added attractions. ◖ ▶ ♣ P

Try also: Brooks Club, Infant St (Free)

ALTHAM

Walton Arms

Burnley Road (A678)
☎ (01282) 774444
11.30-3; 5.30-11; 12-11 Sat; 12-10.30 Sun
Jennings Bitter, Cumberland Ale H
Food-oriented pub, with a number of alcoves for more private drinks and meals.
❀ ⊞

BALDERSTONE

Myerscough

Whalley Road (A59)
☎ (01254) 812222
12-3, 5-11; 12-11 Sat; 12-10.30 Sun
Robinson's Hatters Mild, Hartleys XB, Best Bitter, Frederics, H **Old Tom** (winter) G
Country inn near the Samlesbury aerodrome entrance with a cosy wood-panelled lounge and small no-smoking room. Quality meals finish at 9.30 (served all day Sun). Look outside for the psychopathic Great Dane called Winston.
🛏 Q ⛲ ❀ ⇋ P ⊀

BAMBER BRIDGE

Olde Original Withy Trees

157 Station Road (B6258)
☎ (01772) 330396
11-11; 12-10.30 Sun
Burtonwood Bitter; guest beer H
Lively, former 17th-century farmhouse, reputedly the oldest building in the village. It has a strong darts following and a fine children's play area. A large screen TV and a quiz night Mon also feature.
❀ ⇌ ♣ P

BARROWFORD

Old Bridge Inn

146 Gisburn Road (A682)
☎ (01282) 613983
3 (7 Tue; 2 Fri; 11 Sat)-11; 12-10.30 Sun

Robinson's Old Stockport, Best Bitter H
Lively village local on the Pendle Way. Robinson's Hartleys XB and Old Tom are also occasionally stocked. Quiz night includes a free supper.
🛏 ❀ ♣ P

BELMONT VILLAGE

Black Dog Inn

2 Church Street (A675)
☎ (01204) 811218
12-4 (3 Mon-Wed), 7-11; 12-4, 6.30-10.30 Sun
Holt Mild, Bitter H
Homely, traditional multi-roomed village pub, decorated with antiques. Eve meals available for residents (Mon-Tue). No mobile phones allowed; it is a must for classical music fans.
🛏 Q ⛲ ❀ ◖ ♣ P

BELTHORN

Dog Inn

Belthorn Road (off B6232)
☎ (01254) 690794
12-3, 5-11; 12-11 Sat; 12-10.30 Sun
Black Sheep Best Bitter; Boddingtons Bitter; Marston's Pedigree H
Recently refurbished village local with a restaurant. The stone-flagged bar area is warmed by a very warm fire in winter. An additional ale is put on during busy periods.
🛏 ❀ P

BISPHAM GREEN

Eagle & Child

Malt Kiln Lane (off B5246)
☎ (01257) 462297
12-3, 5.30-11; 12-10.30 Sun
Moorhouse's Black Cat; Thwaites Bitter; guest beers H
Outstanding, 16th-century village local featuring antique furniture and stone-flagged floors. Renowned for its award-winning food, it has its own bowling green and hosts an annual beer festival at Whitsun.
🛏 Q ⛲ ❀ ◖ ▶ ⌣ P ⊀

BLACKBURN

Gibraltar

1 Gibraltar Street (off A677)
☎ (01254) 51691
12-4 (5 Fri; not Tue), 7-11; 12-11 Sat; 12-10.30 Sun
Thwaites Mild, Bitter H
Popular welcoming local where various charities benefit from fundraising. Handy for Corporation Park and East Lancs Cricket Ground. ♿ ♣

Malt & Hops

1 Barton Street (off A674)
☎ (01254) 699453

☎ (01254) 875207
5 (12 Wed-Sat)-11; 12-10.30 Sun
Beer range varies H
Local where the publican listens to what the customer wants to drink and reacts well to changing demand; up to three real ales on offer. An area is set aside for pool and darts in this open-plan pub.
♿ ⇌

10 (11 Sat)-11 (1am Thu-Sat); 12-10.30 Sun

Boddingtons Bitter; Flowers Original; Marston's Pedigree; guest beers H
Good town-centre pub attracting students weekdays and lunchtimes, all ages eves and weekends. It offers wholesome meals and some good guest beers on tap.
⚑ ◑ ⟐ ⭑ ≋ ♣

Navigation Inn
Canal Street, Mill Hill (bridge No 96A Leeds/Liverpool Canal)
☎ (01254) 53230
10.30-11; 12-10.30 Sun
Thwaites Mild, Bitter H
Popular, characterful local run by one of the town's longest-serving landladies; a warm welcome is assured. It is within walking distance of the Rovers' ground.
⚑ ≋ (Mill Hill) ♣

Sir Charles Napier
10 Limbrick
☎ (01254) 52928
11-11 (12 Thu; 1am Fri-Sat); 12-10.30 Sun
Thwaites Bitter, seasonal beers H
Busy outlet, just out of the centre, stocking a rare Thwaites seasonal ale. Live music at the weekends tends to be rock oriented. Good range of snacks available.
⚑ ≋ ♣

BLACK LANE ENDS
Hare & Hounds
Skipton Old Road (follow golf club signs from Colne, approx 1 mile further)
OS929432 ☎ (01282) 863070
12-11; 12-10.30 Sun
Black Sheep Best Bitter; Taylor Golden Best, Landlord; Tetley Bitter; guest beer H
Refurbished country pub on the Yorkshire border; extremely popular with diners for its extensive menu (served all day). Phone for directions if lost!
⚑ ⚑ ◑ ▶ P

BLACKPOOL
Highlands Hotel
206 Queens Promenade, Bispham (near tram station)
☎ (01253) 354877
12-11; 12-10.30 Sun
Thwaites Bitter H
This seafront hotel, popular with locals, has a games room.
⚑ ⚑ ◑ ⊖ (Bispham) ♣ P ✄

Raikes Hall
16 Liverpool Road (off A583, Church St) ☎ (01253) 757971
11.30-11; 12-10.30 Sun
Draught Bass; Stones Bitter; guest beers H

This 240-year-old, Grade II listed building boasts a champion bowling green. The traditionally-styled large room displays pictures of early 20th-century breweries. The meals are good value, as are the regular 'happy hours'. Wheelchair WC and good access to the garden.
⚑ ◑ ▶ ⚑ ⭑ P

Ramsden Arms Hotel
204 Talbot Road (near the North station)
☎ (01253) 623215
10.30-11; 12-10.30 Sun
Boddingtons Bitter; Ind Coope Burton Ale; Marston's Pedigree; Tetley Bitter; guest beer H
The traditional oak-panelled interior displays a collection of mugs and stuffed deer heads.
⚑ ⚑ ⚑ ≋ (North) ♣ P

Saddle Inn
286 Whitegate Drive (A583, near Oxford Sq)
☎ (01253) 798900
12 (11.30 Sat)-11; 12-10.30 Sun
Draught Bass; Hancock's HB; Worthington Bitter; guest beers H
Blackpool's oldest pub (established 1770) has cosy wood-panelled rooms showing pictures of sporting heroes. The garden has a play area for children. The reasonably priced menu includes daily specials (see the blackboard).
⚑ Q ⚑ ◑ ⭑ P ✄

Shovels
260 Common Edge Road, Marton (B5261, 1/2 a mile from A5230 jct)
☎ (01253) 762702
11.30-11; 12-10.30 Sun
Beer range varies H
Large suburban pub serving an excellent menu and four ever-changing beers, usually from micros or brew pubs. It hosts an annual beer festival (Oct) and has a games area.
⚑ ⚑ ◑ ⭑ ⚑ ♣ P ✄

Wheatsheaf
194-196 Talbot Road (50 yds from North station)
☎ (01253) 625062
10.30-11; 12-10.30 Sun
Theakston Mild, Best Bitter, Old Peculier; guest beer H
Characterful, down-to-earth local replete with giant fish, flags, mannequins, wartime posters and a chandelier. An absolute gem.
⚑ ≋ (North) ♣

BRETHERTON
Blue Anchor
South Road (B5247)
☎ (01772) 600270
11.30-3, 5-11; 11.30-11 Fri & Sat; 12-10.30 Sun

Boddingtons Bitter; guest beers H
Well-kept village inn, with a large garden, serving excellent value meals (all day Sat and Sun) and interesting guest beers.
⚑ ⚑ ◑ ♣ ⚑ P

BRIERCLIFFE
Hare & Hounds
1 Halifax Road
☎ (01282) 423268
11-11; 12-10.30 Sun
Thwaites Bitter, seasonal beers H
Village pub on a crossroads, comprising a smart lounge with a games room to the side and large eating area at the rear.
⚑ ◑ ▶ P

BURNLEY
Coal Clough
41 Coal Clough Lane (200 yds E of M65 jct 10)
☎ (01282) 423226
11-11; 12-10.30 Sun
Boddingtons Bitter; Worthington Bitter; guest beer H
This end-of-terrace community local is always busy and friendly. The Masseys Bitter is specially brewed by Bass Museum to an old local brewery recipe. It hosts folk music Tue and a quiz Wed. It is a regular Bass and CAMRA award-winner.
⚑ ≋ (Barracks) ♣

Garden Bar
131-133 St James Street
☎ (01282) 414895
11-11; 12-10.30 Sun
Lees Bitter H
Spacious, open-plan room with a smaller games room. It hosts discos and entertainment eves; quiet conversation is the norm at lunchtime.
⚑ ◑ ⚑ ≋ (Central)

Ighten Leigh Social Club
389 Padiham Road (M65 jct 10 towards Padiham)
☎ (01282) 422306
1-3.30, 7-11; 12-11 Fri-Sat; 12-10.30 Sun
Moorhouse's Premier, Pride of Pendle or seasonal beers H
Large well-established private club with a pub atmosphere at the front and large screen TV and snooker at the rear. CAMRA members welcome; there may be a small entrance charge for guests.
⚑ ⚑ ◑ ⚑ ≋ (Barracks) ♣ P ⊟

Sparrow Hawk Hotel
Church Street (A682)
☎ (01282) 421551
11-11; 12-10.30 Sun
Moorhouse's Premier, Pendle Witches Brew; Theakston Best

Bitter; Wells Bombardier; guest beers [H]
Hotel bar and games room enjoying an excellent atmosphere, it always has three guest beers – usually from micro-breweries. Lively at weekends with entertainment, it also hosts large beer festivals (especially at Easter). A regular CAMRA award-winner.
⋈ ◖ ▸ ♿ ⇌ (Central) ♣ P 🍴

CHORLEY

Malt 'n' Hops
50-52 Friday Street (E of station)
☎ (01257) 260967
12-11; 12-10.30 Sun
Boddingtons Bitter; Cains Mild; Moorhouse's Pendle Witches Brew; Taylor Landlord; guest beers [H]
Single-bar pub of character, furnished with Victoriana. It is handy for the station. Up to five guest beers regularly on tap. ⇌

Plough
139 Pall Mall (B5251)
☎ (01257) 271958
11-4, 7-11; 12-4, 7-10.30 Sun
Banks's Original, Bitter [H]
Thriving two-room local with a comfortable split-level lounge bar and a games room.
⊞ ♿ ♣ P 🍴

Potters Arms
42 Brooke Street (off A6)
☎ (01257) 267954
12-11; 12-3.30, 7-11 Sat; 12-4, 7-10.30 Sun
Boddingtons Bitter; Moorhouse's Premier; Tetley Bitter [H]
Traditional local near the ring road. The central bar serves the game areas and the comfortable lounges. Note the collection of photographs from the world of entertainment.
⇌ ♣ P

Prince of Wales
9-11 Cowling Brow
☎ (01257) 413239
11-11; 12-10.30 Sun
Jennings Mild, Bitter, Cumberland Ale, Sneck Lifter [H]
A large lounge, a traditional tap room, a games room and a snug with real fire make up this pub, close to the Leeds-Liverpool Canal.
⋈ ❀ ⊞ ♣

CLAYTON-LE-MOORS

Albion Ale House
243 Whalley Road (A680)
☎ (01254) 238585
5 (12 Wed-Sat)-11; 12-10.30 Sun
Porter Mild, Bitter, Rossendale, Porter, Sunshine, seasonal beers [H]
Open-plan pub on the Leeds-Liverpool Canal. The patio

area is used for the annual cider festival at Easter and beer festival in summer.
Q ♣ ⇗ P

CLEVELEYS

Victoria
Victoria Road West
☎ (01253) 853306
11-11; 12-10.30 Sun
Samuel Smith OBB [H]
Oustanding local with a restaurant (children welcome) and a games room.
Q ❀ ◖ ▸ ♿ ⊖ ♣ ⇗ P ⤬

CLITHEROE

New Inn
Parsons Lane (B6243)
☎ (01200) 423312
11 (10.30 Sat)-11; 12-10.30 Sun
Moorhouse's Black Cat, Premier; guest beers [H]
Friendly local, opposite the castle. Each of its four rooms has an open fire which are always lit on cold days.
⋈ Q ⏴ ❀ ♠ ⇌ ♣ P

Swan & Royal
Castle Street (B6243)
☎ (01200) 423130
12-11 (midnight Fri & Sat); 12-10.30 Sun
Jennings Mild, Bitter, Cumberland Ale, Cocker Hoop, seasonal beers [H]
Refurbished town-centre pub, now owned by Jennings; its open-plan layout displays the building's history in a warm and pleasing decor.
⋈ Q ◖ ▸ ⇌

CLIVIGER

Queen
412 Burnley Road (A646)
☎ (01282) 436712
1-11; 12-10.30 Sun
John Smith's Bitter; Webster's Green Label; guest beers [H]
Small, two-roomed roadside local whose friendly regulars enjoy quiet conversation. The three guest beers usually come from micro-breweries. View the fascinating collection of old photographs. ⋈ Q ⊞ ♠ ♣

COLNE

Golden Ball
Burnley Road (A56)
☎ (01282) 861862
11.30-3.30, 7-11; 11.30-11 Fri & Sat; 12-10.30 Sun
Tayor Landlord; Tetley Mild, Bitter; guest beers [H]
Recently refurbished pub in an area with little choice of real ale. Good food is served lunchtimes (until 7 at weekends). ❀ ◖ ♣ P

CONDER GREEN

Stork

On A588 near Glasson
☎ (01524) 751234
11-11; 12-10.30 Sun
Boddingtons Bitter; guest beers [H]
Long, beamed building with several small rooms (children welcome) and, down a level, the main bar and restaurant. It is handy for the Lune Estuary Path. A house beer is brewed by Whitbread.
⋈ ❀ ⋈ ◖ ▸ ♠ P

COPPULL

Red Herring
Mill Lane (off B5251)
☎ (01257) 470130
12-11; 12-10.30 Sun
Beer range varies [H]
Former mill offices converted to a one-room pub, serving a house beer from Moorhouse's. CAMRA West Lancs *Pub of the Year*.
⋈ ❀ ◖ ♣ P

CROSTON

Black Horse
Westhead Road (A581)
☎ (01772) 600338
11.30-11; 12-10.30 Sun
Black Sheep Best Bitter; Courage Directors; Hancock's HB; Moorhouse's Premier; Theakston Mild, Best Bitter [H]
Popular village local, well known for its good value food and twice-yearly beer festivals. Croston is twinned with Azay-le-Rideau, and Anglo-French pastimes are covered with both a bowling green and a boules pitch.
❀ ◖ ▸ ⇌ ♣ P

Lord Nelson
Out Lane (A581)
☎ (01772) 600387
12-11; 12-10.30 Sun
Boddingtons Bitter; Cains Bitter; Tetley Bitter; Worthington Bitter [H]
Pleasantly situated pub, facing on to what was once the village green. For many years a *Guide* regular when it was a Higson's outpost, it is somehow appropriate that Cains Bitter is now available.
⋈ ❀ ◖ ▸ ⇌ ♣ P

DALTON

Beacon Inn
3 Beacon Lane (Upholland-Newburgh Road)
☎ (01695) 632607
12-11; 12-3, 7-10.30 Sun
Jennings Mild, Bitter, Cumberland Ale [H]
Large roadside pub, close to Ashurst Beacon and handy for the Beacon Country Park and golf course. It has a restaurant upstairs. ◖ P

DARWEN

Black Horse Hotel

72 Redearth Road (off A666)
☎ (01254) 873040
12-11; 12-10.30 Sun
Holt Bitter; Moorhouse's Black Cat; guest beer ℍ
Small, multi-roomed, friendly family local. 🐈 ♣

Bowling Green
386 Bolton Road (A666)
☎ (01254) 702148
11.30-4, 7-11; 11.30-11 Fri & Sat; 12-10.30 Sun
John Smith's Bitter; Theakston Mild; Webster's Yorkshire Bitter; guest beer ℍ
Three-storey building whose stables are used for Sunday barbecues in summer. This excellent family local has a good games following.
🏚 Q 🐈 🕽 ♣ P

Greenfield
Lower Barn Street
☎ (01254) 703945
12-3, 5.30-11; 12-11 Fri & Sat; 12-10.30 Sun
Boddingtons Bitter; Taylor Landlord; Thwaites Mild, Bitter; guest beer ℍ
Open-plan pub, next to the Sough Tunnel, it serves good value food (all day Sun until 7; no meals Tue). The four guest beers feature stout or porter regularly.
Q 🐈 🕽 ▶

Pub
210 Duckworth Street (A666)
☎ (01254) 708404
11-11; 12-10.30 Sun
Thwaites Bitter; guest beers ℍ
This succinctly-named, refurbished free house stands just off the town centre. Four changing guest beers are complemented by a foreign ale. 🐈 🕽 ⇌ ♣ P

ENTWISTLE
Strawbury Duck
Overshores Road (by station, signed on Edgworth-Darwen old road)
☎ (01204) 852013
11-11; 12-10.30 Sun
Boddingtons Bitter; Moorhouse's Pendle Witches Brew; Taylor Landlord; guest beers ℍ
Sympathetically refurbished and enlarged old hotel situated in a peaceful rural spot; a haunt for real ale drinkers and walkers.
🏚 Q 🐈 🐈 ⇌ 🕽 ⇌ ♣ P ✂

EUXTON
Travellers Rest
Dawbers Lane (A581 off A49)
☎ (01257) 451184
12-3, 6-11; 12-11 Sat; 12-10.30 Sun
Draught Bass; Greenalls Bitter; Marston's Pedigree ℍ
Traditional pub, set in the heart of the countryside; it serves excellent food. The snug offers traditional games;

the garden has a children's play area.
Q 🐈 🐈 🕽 ▶ 🖾 ♣ P ✂

FENISCOWLES
Feildens Arms
673 Preston Old Road (A674/A6062 jct)
☎ (01254) 200988
12-11; 12-10.30 Sun
Barnsley Bitter; Boddingtons Bitter; Chester's Mild; Flowers IPA; guest beers ℍ
Local community pub retaining a small vault. It caters for all ages and is busy at weekends. Meals served Tue-Sun. 🏚 Q 🐈 🐈 🕽
⇌ (Pleasington) ♣ P

FLEETWOOD
North Euston Hotel
The Esplanade
☎ (01253) 876525
11-11; 12-10.30 Sun
Boddingtons Bitter; Courage Directors; Theakston Best Bitter; Webster's Yorkshire Bitter; guest beers ℍ
Large hotel lounge bar providing a commanding view of the river Wyre and Morecambe Bay. The family room and no-smoking areas both close at 7.30pm.
🐈 🖾 🐈 ⇌ (Ferry) ✂

Wyre Lounge Bar
Marine Hall, The Esplanade
☎ (01253) 771141
12-4, 7-11; 12-4, 7-10.30 Sun
Courage Directors; Moorhouse's Premier, Pendle Witches Brew; John Smith's Magnet; guest beers ℍ
Quiet lounge bar, part of the Marine Hall entertainment complex, overlooking the Wyre Estuary. It hosts Fleetwood's beer festival.
Q 🐈 ⇌ (Ferry) P ✂

FOULRIDGE
Hare & Hounds
Skipton Old Road (off A56)
☎ (01282) 864235
12-3, 7-11; 12-10.30 Sun
Tetley Bitter; guest beer ℍ
Three-roomed roadside pub near the Leeds & Liverpool Canal. The house beer is brewed by Moorhouse's. It hit national headlines by being named scruffiest pub in the country by the *News of the World* in 1993 – it has improved since! Meals served all day Sun, until 9.30pm.
🏚 🐈 🐈 🕽 🖈 ♣ P

GARSTANG
Royal Oak
Market Place
☎ (01995) 603318
11-3 (4 Thu), 6-11; 11-11 Fri & Sat; 12-10.30 Sun
Robinson's Hatters Mild, Hartleys

XB, Best Bitter ℍ
17th-century coaching inn with intimate drinking areas.
🏚 Q 🐈 🐈 🖾 🕽 ▶ 🖈 ♣ P

GOOSNARGH
Grapes
Church Lane (off B5269)
☎ (01772) 865234
11.30-3, 7-11; 11.30-11 Thu-Sat & summer; 12-10.30 Sun
Boddingtons Bitter; Tetley Mild, Bitter; Theakston Best Bitter; guest beers ℍ
Attractive village free house close to the village green and church. Enjoy the wonderful real fire on cold nights. Amenities include a children's room, pool room and bowling green, a cobbled drinking area outside pub, as well as a garden to the rear. It is near the reputedly haunted Chingle Hall. Eve meals Wed-Sun. 🏚 🐈 🐈 🕽 ▶ 🖾 ♣

GREAT HARWOOD
Duke of Wellington
Towngate (off B6535)
☎ (01254) 885979
11-11; 12-10.30 Sun
Courage Directors; Theakston Best Bitter, Old Peculier ℍ
Very successfully renovated pub on the town hall square; this fine old building boasts much exposed stonework in the atmospheric lounge that has booth seating. Wheelchair WC. ♿ ⚤ ♣

Royal Hotel
Station Road (off B6535)
☎ (01254) 883541
12-1.30 (3 Sat), 7-11; 12-3, 7-10.30 Sun
Beer range varies ℍ
Victorian, open-plan pub stocking up to five guest beers, usually from small independents, plus a good selection of bottled beers from various countries. Car park is for hotel residents only. Q 🐈 🖾 ⚤ P 🍴

GREEN HOWARTH
Red Lion Hotel
6 Moorgate (from Blackburn Rd, 1¼ miles up Willows Lane)
☎ (01254) 233194
12-3, 7-11; 12-11 Fri & Sat; 12-10.30 Sun
Picks Moorgate Mild, Bedlam Bitter, Lions Pride ℍ
Family-run pub, home of Picks micro-brewery, which also stocks a weekend special brew. The traditional lounge has a games area. 🐈 🕽 ♣ P 🍴

GRIMEHILLS (DARWEN)
Crown & Thistle
Roman Road

☎ (01254) 702624
12-2.30 (not Mon). 6-11; 12-11 Fri &
Sat; 12-10.30 Sun

**Boddingtons Bitter; Tetley Bitter;
guest beer** Ⓗ

Pub where staff strive for
quality and customer care,
and has built a good
reputation for excellent food;
always welcoming.
🏚 Q ❀ ◖ ▶ P

HASKAYNE
Kings Arms
Delf Lane (A5147)
☎ (01704) 840245
12-11; 12-10.30 Sun

Tetley Mild, Bitter; guest beer Ⓗ

Traditional four-roomed pub,
serving good value home-
cooked food using fresh
produce. The four real fires
helped it win local CAMRA's
Winter *Pub of the Year*
1998/99 and 1999/2000.
Food is served all day until
7pm. 🏚 Q ❀ ☎ ◖ ▶ ♣ P

HASLINGDEN
Griffin Inn
86 Hud Rake (off A680)
☎ (01706) 214021
12-11; 12-10.30 Sun

**Porter Mild, Bitter, Rossendale,
Porter, Sunshine, seasonal beers** Ⓗ

Home of Dave Porter's micro-
brewery; great for service and
conversation. The bar area
retains some character whilst
good views can be enjoyed
from the lounge. Q ♣

HELMSHORE
Robin Hood
280 Holcombe Road (B6214)
☎ (01706) 213180
12-2 (not Mon-Thu), 4-11; 1-11 Sat;
1-10.30 Sun

Tetley Bitter; guest beer Ⓗ

This small community pub
lies amongst the remnants of
Lancashire's cotton industry,
close to the Helmshore
Textile Museum. The pub has
been partially opened out but
retains rooms with separate
identities. The landlord is
fanatical about ornamental
ducks which adorn almost
every nook and cranny. A
second beer is supplied by
Phoenix. 🏚 ❀ ♣

HESKIN
Farmers Arms
Wood Lane (B5250)
☎ (01257) 451276
12-11; 12-10.30 Sun

**Boddingtons Bitter; Castle Eden Ale;
Flowers IPA; Taylor Landlord; guest
beer** Ⓗ

Family-run country pub with
an emphasis on food (served
12-9.30) but which retains a
public bar for drinkers.
Families are welcome (large

play area); it is handy for
Camelot Theme Park.
❀ ⬠ ◖ ▶ ⬡ & ⚥ ♣ P

HEST BANK
Hest Bank
2 Hest Bank Lane (over canal
from A5105)
☎ (01524) 824339
11.30-11; 12-10.30 Sun

**Boddingtons Bitter; Marston's
Pedigree; Robinson's Best Bitter;
guest beer** Ⓗ

Greatly extended in the
1980s leaving intact two
older rooms (one a lounge,
the other for games) and a
lantern window. It is popular
both as a local and as an
eating house. Canalside
garden.
🏚 Q ❀ ◖ ▶ ⬡ ⚥ ♣ P ⚲

HIGH MOOR
Rigbye Arms
2 Whittle Lane (off B5246)
☎ (01257) 462354
12-3, 5.30-11; 12-11 Sat, 12-10.30
Sun

**Ind Coope Burton Ale; Marston's
Pedigree; Morland Old Speckled
Hen; Tetley Mild, Bitter** Ⓗ

Smart, but remote, rural pub,
famed for its outstanding
food. It has a well-kept
bowling green and a
Victorian postbox set into its
wall.
🏚 ◖ ▶ ⬠ P

HOGHTON
Royal Oak
Blackburn Old Road, Riley
Green (A675/A6061 jct)
☎ (01254) 201445
11-3, 5.30-11; 11-11 Sat; 12-10.30
Sun

**Thwaites Mild, Bitter, seasonal
beers** Ⓗ

Traditional, low-ceilinged
country pub: several cosy
drinking areas and a dining
area popular for meals.
🏚 Q ☎ ❀ ◖ ▶ & P ⚲

HOSCAR
Railway Tavern
Hoscar Moss Road (by
station) OS468116
☎ (01704) 892369
12-3 (not Mon), 5-11; 12-11 Wed-Sat;
12-10.30 Sun

**Jennings Bitter; Tetley Dark Mild,
Bitter; guest beers** Ⓗ

Superb, unspoilt rural local,
popular with cyclists and
railway enthusiasts, serving
excellent home-cooked local
food. It has a good public bar
and many coal fires warm
your visit; if still cold, try one
of the 30 malt whiskies.
There is a pleasant garden to
relax in, on summer days.
🏚 Q ☎ ❀ ◖ ▶ ⬠ & ⚥
⚞ (Hoscar Moss) ♣ P

LANCASTER
Bobbin
8 Chapel Street (opp. bus
station)
☎ (01524) 32606
11-11; 12-10.30 Sun

**Everards Tiger; Wadworth 6X; guest
beer** Ⓗ

Revamped in 1997 on a
cotton industry theme, the
Bobbin hosts live music Thu;
a big screen TV is on most
eves. & ♣

George & Dragon
24 St George's Quay (off A6)
☎ (01524) 844739
11-11; 12-10.30 Sun

**Brains SA; Tetley Bitter; guest
beer** Ⓗ

Narrow, single-bar pub, near
the Maritime Museum, with
a boules pitch.
❀ ◖ ⚞ P

Horse & Farrier
14 Brock Street (off A6)
☎ (01524) 63491
11-11; 12-10.30 Sun

Thwaites Bitter Ⓗ

Small gimmick-free bar next
to a bookies, mainly
frequented by regulars.
❀ ⚞ ♣

John O'Gaunt
35 Market Street (off A6)
☎ (01524) 65356
11-3 (5 Sat), 6 (7 Sat)-11; 11-11 Thu &
Fri; 12-4, 7-10.30 Sun

**Boddingtons Bitter; Ind Coope
Burton Ale; Jennings Bitter; Tetley
Bitter; guest beers** Ⓗ

Small busy pub with a
handsome original frontage.
Frequent live music is
performed. Guest beers often
include one from Barnsley
Brewery. Lunches served
Mon-Sat (snacks Sun).
❀ ◖ ⚞ ♣

Yorkshire House
2 Parliament Street (near fire
station)
☎ (01524) 64679
7-11; 7-10.30 Sun

**Boddingtons Bitter; Everards
Tiger** Ⓗ

On the fringe of the town
centre, the single bar is
decorated with film posters.
A large upstairs room hosts
live music weekends and
Irish folk Mon.
🏚 ❀

LANESHAWBRIDGE
Emmot Arms
Keighley Road (A6068,
approx 2 miles from Colne)
☎ (01282) 863366
12-3, 5.30-11; 12-11 Sat; 12-10.30
Sun

**Boddingtons Bitter; Tetley Mild,
Bitter; guest beer** Ⓗ

Village pub offering good
food, near the Wycoller

Country Park.
🏚 ⊛ ⊨ ◖ ▸ ♣ P

LATHOM

Ship Inn
4 Wheat Lane (off A5209,
over canal swing bridge)
☎ (01704) 893117
11.30-3, 5-11; 11.30-11 Fri & Sat;
12-10.30 Sun
**Moorhouse's Black Cat, Pendle
Witches Brew; Taylor Landlord;
Theakston Best Bitter, Old Peculier;
guest beers** Ⓗ
Situated on the
Leeds/Liverpool Canal,
locally known as the 'Blood
Tub', from when canal boats
delivered the ingedients for
the famous Lancashire black
pudding, this excellent free
house offers traditional
home-cooked food. The beer
range includes five guests
and a house beer. Local
CAMRA *Pub of the Year* 1999.
Eve meals Mon-Thu.
Q ⊛ ◖ ▸ ≈ (Burscough Jct) P

LEA TOWN

Salwick Club
Lea Lane (on BNFL site; East
Gate) OS476312
☎ (01772) 764077
12-2 (not Sat), 7-11; 12-10.30 Sun
Beer range varies Ⓗ
Large club boasting two
function rooms (extensions
available), one of which has a
full size dance floor. The beer
is a single guest that is
changed regularly. Two
snooker tables, and good
value food are additional
attractions. Show this *Guide*
or CAMRA card for
admission. No meals Sat
lunch or Mon and Tue eves.
⊛ ◖ ▸ 㐂 ▲ ♣ P 🖥

Smith's Arms (Slip Inn)
Lea Lane (opp. BNFL East
Gate) OS476312
☎ (01772) 726906
12-2, 4-11; 12-11 Fri & Sat; 12-10.30
Sun
Thwaites Best Mild, Bitter Ⓗ
Splendid country pub which
has not had to resort to food
domination, although the
meals are good value. A
courtesy car is offered to
locals. It has recently
acquired camping space in an
adjacent field. Local CAMRA
Pub of the Season winner.
Note the lack of pumpclips.
🏚 ⊛ ◖ ▲ ♣ P

LEYLAND

Eagle & Child
Church Road (B5248)
☎ (01772) 433531
11.45-11; 12-10.30 Sun
**Burtonwood Bitter, seasonal beers;
guest beers** Ⓗ
Ancient inn near the historic

cross: one long bar is divided
into several drinking areas.
Weekday lunches served. It
stands opposite a bowling
green.
⊛ ◖ ♣ P

LITTLE ECCLESTON

Cartford Hotel
Cartford Lane (1/2 mile off
A586, next to toll bridge)
☎ (01995) 670166
12-3, 7 (6.30 summer)-11; 12-10.30
Sun
Beer range varies Ⓗ
Popular, friendly riverside
free house where four guest
beers are complemented by
two from the adjoining Hart
Brewery. Good value bar food
includes a take-away pizza
service. Local CAMRA *Pub of
the Year* 2000.
🏚 Q ⊛ ⊨ ◖ 㐂 ♣ ⌂ P

LONGRIDGE

Alston Arms
Inglewhite Road (off B5269)
☎ (01772) 783331
11.30-11; 12-10.30 Sun
**John Smith's Bitter; Theakston Mild,
Best Bitter; guest beers** Ⓗ
Comfortable pub on the
Chipping side of the
town. The garden is home
to several animals and a
double decker bus. Steak
nights are a feature. Enjoy
wonderful views of the
Ribble Valley from the
conservatory. A 'glow in the
dark' pool table and a 5p play
bandit are unusual
attractions.
🏚 Q ⌂ ⊛ ◖ ▲ ♣ P

Old Oak
111 Preston Road
(B6243/B6244 jct)
☎ (01772) 783648
12-3, 5-11; 12-11 Fri & Sat; 12-10.30
Sun
**Theakston Mild, Best Bitter; guest
beers** Ⓗ
Welcoming community local
with real wood settles, a
comfortable lounge off the
bar area and a games room.
The no-smoking area is
available lunchtimes. No
food Tue. The guest beer
changes daily. It hosts a giant
onion competition!
🏚 ⊛ ◖ ♣ P ⊬ 🖥

White Bull
1A Higher Road (off B5269)
☎ (01772) 783198
5 (12 Fri & Sat)-11; 12-10.30 Sun
**Theakston Best Bitter; guest
beers** Ⓗ
Roomy, lively pub at the top
of the village; the games
room benefits from a
spectacular view. Quiz Thu; a
DJ is in residence Fri, Sat and
Sun eves.
🏚 ◖ ▸ ▲ ♣ P

LOSTOCK HALL

Victoria
Watkin Lane (B5254)
☎ (01772) 335338
11-11; 12-10.30 Sun
John Smith's Bitter; guest beers Ⓗ
Large pub set back from the
main road; a true community
local comprising a
comfortable lounge, and a
spacious public bar which is
big on games. Two guest
beers are always available,
usually high gravity. No food
Mon.
⊛ ◖ ▸ ⊞ ≈ ♣ P

LYTHAM

Hole in One
Forest Drive (off B5261 in
Hall Park Estate)
☎ (01253) 730598
11.30-3, 5-11; 11.30-11 Fri & Sat;
12-10.30 Sun
Thwaites Bitter Ⓗ
Large, modern local, popular
early eve; its decor reflects
the local golfing amenities.
Home-cooked food is served
during the day and early eve,
when a no-smoking area is
available. There is a good
spacious public bar-cum-
games room.
⊛ ◖ ▸ ⊞ 㐂 ♣ P

Taps
12 Henry Street (behind
Clifton Arms Hotel)
☎ (01253) 736226
11-11; 12-10.30 Sun
Beer range varies Ⓗ
Converted from ostlers
cottages over 100 years ago,
this basic but cosy alehouse is
popular throughout the year.
The cask cider varies and
there is always a cask mild
amongst the nine on tap; a
brisk trade keeps the ale
fresh. No food Sun.
🏚 Q ⊛ ◖ 㐂 ≈ ⌂

MAWDESLEY

Black Bull
Hall Lane (off B5246)
OS499151
☎ (01704) 822202
12-11; 12-10.30 Sun
**Greenalls Bitter; Taylor Landlord;
guest beers** Ⓗ
400-year-old, stone country
pub, displaying prize-
winning hanging baskets all
year round. Food is served all
day Sun, but not Mon eve.
The garden houses a boules
pitch.
🏚 ⌂ ⊛ ◖ 㐂 ♣ P ⊬

Robin Hood
Bluestone Lane (off B5250)
OS506163
☎ (01704) 822275
11.30-3, 5-11; 11-11 Sat; 12-10.30
Sun
Boddingtons Bitter; Castle Eden Ale;

Flowers IPA; Taylor Landlord; guest beers Ⓗ
Food-oriented, isolated country pub at the crossroads between Croston, Eccleston and Mawdesley with six ales always on tap.
♘ ❀ ◐ ◑ P ⊬

MORECAMBE

Dog & Partridge
19 Bare Lane (B5275)
☎ (01524) 426246
11-11; 12-10.30 Sun
Boddingtons Bitter; Taylor Landlord; guest beers Ⓗ
Large local with a single, divided bar, mostly carpeted. This former Hogshead is still selling a range of Whitbread-supplied ales, but also others from independents, such as Dent.
◐ ◑ ≹ (Bare Lane) ♣ P

Smugglers' Den
56 Poulton Road (near police station)
☎ (01524) 421684
11-3, 7-11; 12-10.30 Sun
Boddingtons Bitter; Tetley Bitter; guest beer Ⓗ
Stained glass and nautical knick-knacks remind customers of this low-beamed, stone-floored pub's past. The garden houses caged birds.
♨ ❀ ♣ P

NEWBURGH

Red Lion Hotel
9 The Green (A5209)
☎ (01257) 462336
11-11, 12-10.30 Sun
Burtonwood Bitter; guest beers Ⓗ
Extensively renovated and expanded but retaining its village local charm, the Red Lion is popular for food and large screen TV sports. It hosts an annual beer festival (Aug).
🛏 ◐ ◑ ♿ ⊬

ORMSKIRK

Hayfield
22 County Road (A59)
☎ (01695) 571157
12-11, 12-10.30 Sun
Beer range varies Ⓗ
Large, comfortable, modern pub serving up to ten real ales in a friendly atmosphere. Good value food is also available.
❀ ◐ ◑ ♿ ≹ P ▯

Queens Head
30 Moor Street (near bus station)
☎ (01695) 574380
12-11; 12-10.30 Sun
Beer range varies Ⓗ
Festival Alehouse in the town centre, serving up to four guest beers, popular with students. No food Sun.
Q ❀ ◐ ≹

PENWORTHAM

St Teresa's Social Centre
Queensway (off A59)
☎ (01772) 743523
7.30 (3 Sat)-11; 3-10.30 Sun
Flowers IPA; Ind Cope Burton Ale; Tetley Mild, Bitter; guest beers Ⓗ
Thriving catholic club comprising a games room, lounge and a function room – each with its own bar (12 handpumps in total). Entry for CAMRA members is on production of a card; non-members are charged £1 (six visits allowed).
♘ ⊞ ♿ ♣ P

PLEASINGTON

Butlers Arms
Victoria Road
☎ (01254) 201561
12-2.30, 6-11; 12-11 Sat & summer; 12-10.30 Sun
Marston's Pedigree; Theakston Bitter; guest beer Ⓗ
Originally a farm, circa 1790 that sold its own ale, the beer range now includes an extra guest in summer, plus a mild. Good quality home-cooked food is served (eve meals Tue-Sat). Own bowling green.
♨ Q ♘ ❀ ◐ ◑ ♣ P

POULTON-LE-FYLDE

Thatched House
12 Ball Street (by St Chads church)
11-11; 12-10.30 Sun
Boddingtons Bitter; guest beers Ⓗ
Always busy eves, this pub fills to the point of overflow when a football match is on. Quiet moments can be enjoyed during the day. No children admitted.
♨ Q ⊞ ♿ ≹

PREESALL

Black Bull
192 Park Lane (B5377)
☎ (01253) 810294
12-3 (not Mon), 6-11; 12-3, 7-10.30 Sun
Tetley Mild, Bitter; guest beers Ⓗ
Low-beamed, multi-roomed rural village-centre pub. A loyal local clientele enjoys excellent food (not served Mon).
Q ❀ ◐ ◑ ♣ P ⊬

PRESTON

Ashton Institute & Social Club
10-12 Wellington Road, Ashton (by Sacred Heart church)
☎ (01772) 726582
7 (4 Fri & Sat)-11; 12-10.30 Sun
Boddingtons Bitter; Worthington Bitter; guest beers Ⓗ
Lively club in a residential area, worth the effort to find, as its interesting guest beers always include a mild. West Pennines CAMRA *Club of the Year* 1998/99, it hosts an annual beer fest (late Oct) and fields a keen golfing society. Show this *Guide* or CAMRA card to be signed in.
♣

Black Horse ☆
166 Friargate (near market)
☎ (01772) 204855
10.30-11; 7-10.30 (closed lunch) Sun
Robinson's Hatters Mild, Old Stockport, Hartleys XB, Best Bitter, Frederics, Old Tom Ⓗ
Classic pub with two rooms off a large tiled bar. Note the hall of mirrors, wood panelling and other original features in this listed building.
≹

Flax & Firkin at the Corn Exchange
Lune Street (off Ringway, A59)
☎ (01772) 880046
11-11; 12-10.30 Sun
Boddingtons Bitter; Ind Coope Burton Ale; Tetley Bitter Ⓗ
Formerly the oldest part of the public hall, now a spacious Firkin pub; note the sculpture outside commemorating the corn riots of 1842 in Preston. A large TV is popular for sports; table soccer, Jenga and Connect Four also played. Home-made soups and pies available. Limited parking.
❀ ◐ ◑ ♿ ≹ ♣ ⌓ P

Greyfriar
144 Friargate (Ringway jct)
☎ (01772) 558542
11-11; 12-10.30 Sun
Boddingtons Bitter; Courage Directors; Theakston Best Bitter; Thwaites Mild; guest beers Ⓗ
This large modern pub is a Wetherspoon's success story. It provides comfortable surroundings and a wider range of guest beers than most pubs in the group – usually five, often rarely available brews.
Q ◐ ◑ ♿ ≹ ⊬ ⊞

Hogshead (Moss Cottage)
99 Fylde Road (A583)
☎ (01772) 252870
11-11; 12-10.30 Sun
Boddingtons Bitter; Tetley Bitter; guest beers Ⓗ
Spacious, detached former doctor's surgery converted to a pub in 1995, a local CAMRA award-winner. It is close to the university but attracts a wide ranging

clientele. Up to 12 guest beers on tap but they can be expensive. The cellar is visible from the drinking area.

❀ ◑ ▸ ᕃ ᔓ

Limekiln

288 Aqueduct Street (off A583)

☎ (01772) 493247

11-11; 12-10.30 Sun

Banks's Original, Bitter Ⓗ

Down-to-earth, one-roomed pub, at the end of the Lancaster-Preston Canal. It fields a keen fishing club and soccer team.

❀ ♣ P 🗄

Mitre Tavern

90-91 Moor Lane (A5071/A6 jct)

☎ (01772) 251918

12-3, 6.30-11; 12-10.30 Sun

Boddingtons Bitter; Tetley Bitter; guest beers Ⓗ

Welcoming pub with a refurbished lounge and a traditional games room. Guest beers are changed weekly (usually two on); good value meals (not served Sat) include a curry night.

◑ ⊞ ♣ P

Moorbrook Inn

370 North Road (A6 jct)

☎ (01772) 201127

4-11; 12-3, 7-10.30 Sun

Thwaites Bitter Ⓗ

Small, homely, wood-panelled local with two small rooms off the main bar area. Folk music is performed Fri eve. It boasts a collection of pewter tankards and a large range of malt whiskies.

Q ❀ ♣

New Britannia

6 Heatley Street (off Friargate)

☎ (01772) 253424

11-3 (4 Sat), 6-11; 7-10.30 (closed lunch) Sun

Boddingtons Bitter; Castle Eden Ale; Marston's Pedigree; Wadworth 6X; guest beers Ⓗ

Small, friendly, single-bar, town-centre pub featuring etched Britannia windows. It is close to the university.

❀ ◑ ≈ ♣ ᔓ

INDEPENDENT BREWERIES

Hart: Little Ecclestone

Moorhouse's: Burnley

Picks: Green Howarth

Pictish: Rochdale

Porter: Haslingden

Three B's: Blackburn

Thwaites: Blackburn

Old Black Bull

35 Friargate (Ringway jct)

☎ (01772) 823397

10.30-11; 12-10.30 Sun

Boddingtons Bitter; Cains Bitter; guest beers Ⓗ

Large Tudor-fronted, town-centre pub: a small front vault, a games area and a large lounge offer up to seven guest beers. Big screen TV is popular on match days.

❀ ◑ ⊞ ≈ ♣

Olde Dog & Partridge

44 Friargate (off Ringway)

☎ (01772) 252217

11-2.30 (3 Sat), 6 (7 Bank Hols)-11; 12-3, 6.30-10.30 Sun

Fuller's London Pride; Highgate Dark; Worthington Bitter; guest beers Ⓗ

Attracting a varied clientele, but well-known as a bikers' pub, where impressive motorbikes are often parked outside in summer. Excellent value basic lunches are served Mon-Sat. Local CAMRA *Pub of the Season* winner, it is decorated with military memorabilia. A DJ entertains Sun eve.

◑ ≈ ♣

Real Ale Shop

47 Lovat Road (off A6, N of centre)

☎ (01772) 201591

11-2, 5-10; 12-2, 6-10 Sun

Beer range varies Ⓗ

Hard to find, this off-licence stocks a wide choice of specialist bottled beers, up to four draught ales and Thatcher's cider.

ᔓ

Varsity

140a Church Street (near Guildhall)

☎ (01772) 253730

11-11; 12-10.30 Sun

Banks's Bitter; Marston's Pedigree Ⓗ

Town-centre bar, on four levels, formerly a Conservative Club, it is now primarily a young person's venue that can be very busy weekend eves, when smart dress is required. It hosts regular live entertainment and has a large screen TV. Food is served all day.

◑ ▸ ᕃ ≈ 🗄

RIBCHESTER

Cross Keys Hotel

Fleet Street Lane (B6245)

☎ (01254) 878353

12-2.30, 5-11; 12-10.30 Sun

Moorhouse's Black Cat, Premier; guest beers Ⓗ

Traditional coaching inn and restaurant on a sharp bend on the Longridge road. Now operating as a true free house, it offers an expanding

range of beers, and supports local breweries. Enjoy good views of the Ribble valley, and occasional folk music.

🏮 ❀ ◑ ▸ ▲ ♣ ᔓ P

RISHTON

Rishton Arms

Station Road (off A678)

☎ (01254) 886396

7 (12 Sat)-11; 12-10.30 Sun

Thwaites Mild, Bitter, seasonal beers Ⓗ

Large, comfortable and well-supported local next to the station.

≈ ♣ P

SALTERFORTH

Anchor Inn

Salterforth Lane (off B6383)

☎ (01282) 813186

12-11; 12-10.30 Sun

Courage Directors; Ruddles Best Bitter; John Smith's Bitter; Theakston Best Bitter Ⓗ

Welcome stop on the Leeds-Liverpool Canal, the Anchor boasts an impressive array of stalactites in the cellar (tours by arrangement with the landlord). A guest beer is likely to be added to the range.

🏮 ❀ ◑ ᕃ ▲ ♣ P

SAMLESBURY

New Hall Tavern

Cuerdale Lane (1/2 mile from M6 jct 31, opp. Samlesbury Brewery)

☎ (01772) 877217

11.30-11; 12-10.30 Sun

Boddingtons Bitter; guest beers Ⓗ

Welcoming country pub at a rural crossroads, recently refurbished. Three guest beers are always on tap, changing at least twice weekly. Traditional home-cooked food is served at reasonable prices (all day Sun until 9pm). 🏮 ⭍ ❀ ◑ ▲ ♣ P ⅄

SILVERDALE

Woodlands

Woodlands Drive (off Cove Rd, by cemetery)

☎ (01524) 701655

12-3 (not Mon-Fri), 7-11; 12-3, 7-10.30 Sun

Beer range varies Ⓗ

Former country house, circa 1858, on the edge of Eaves Wood, being restored by an enthusiastic owner. Through the stunning entrance hall and another room lies a cosy bar; enjoy the great views across the bay. It draws a mainly local clientele. Two cask beers on tap plus a house ale from Mansfield.

🏮 Q ⭍ ❀ ▲ ♣ P 🗄

CAMRA National Pub Inventory: The Old Green Tree, Bath, Somerset

SKELMERSDALE

Tawd Vale Inn
11 Berry Street (old town, off School Lane)
☎ (01695) 733294
1-5, 7-11; 12-3, 7-10.30 Sun
John Smith's Bitter; guest beers H
Friendly, family-run local which takes its name from a former colliery. Popular with a wide range of customers, but it can get smoky. The pub is home to a pet goose and a beermat-catching dog!
🌼 ♣ P

ST ANNES

Victoria Hotel
Church Road (off B5233)
☎ (01253) 721041
11-11; 12-10.30 Sun
Boddingtons Bitter; Cains Bitter; Courage Best Bitter; Theakston Best Bitter; guest beers H
Large, traditional local attracting a varied clientele. Regular live music (lounge bar) and a large games room are attractions. Ever-popular, it is a proper community pub. Eve meals served 5-7pm.
🌼 ◖▯ 🍴 ♿ ♣ P

THORNLEY

Derby Arms
Chipping Lane
☎ (01772) 782623

12-3, 6-11 (midnight supper licence); 12-10.30 sun
Greenalls Bitter; guest beer H
Smart, oak-panelled and beamed 18th-century coaching inn. Its four lounge areas are popular with diners – very food oriented, but the beer is not neglected; the guest is selected from a limited list. Local specialist sauces are sold. Note the collection of sporting items displayed.
🌼 Q ⛺ 🌼 ◖▯ 🍴 ♿ ♣ P

WARTON

George Washington
Main Street
☎ (01524) 732865
11-11; 12-10.30 Sun
Draught Bass; Boddingtons Bitter; Flowers IPA; guest beer H
Renovated (and renamed) in 1998, modernised and partly opened-out, the decor features Washington, who had a tenuous connection with Warton.
🌼 ⛺ 🌼 ◖▯ ♿ ⚓ ♣ P

WHARLES

Eagle & Child
1 Church Road (3 miles NE of Kirkham) OS448356
☎ (01772) 690312
7-11; 12-4, 7-10.30 Sun
Beer range varies H
Unspoilt country free house under a thatched roof; the beamed lounge bar is furnished with a number of old settles.
🌼 Q 🌼 ♣ P

WHEELTON

Dressers Arms
Briars Brow (near A674)
☎ (01254) 830041
11-11; 12-10.30 Sun
Boddingtons Bitter; Tetley Bitter; Worthington Bitter; Taylor Landlord; guest beers H
Multi-roomed stone pub with a Chinese restaurant on the first floor. A comfortable bar and lounge are complemented by a games room and snug. Up to four changing guest beers on tap. Meals served all day Sun until 8pm.
🌼 ⛺ 🌼 ◖▯ ♿ ♣ P ✂

Red Lion
196 Blackburn Road (off A674) ☎ (01254) 830378
12-11; 12-10.30 Sun
Theakston Best Bitter; guest beers H
Popular, village pub with a split-level interior, comfortable bar and a games room, a short walk from the Leeds-Liverpool Canal. Meals served Fri eve, plus Sat and Sun.
🌼 ◖▯ ♣ P

WHITTLE-LE-WOODS

Royal Oak
216 Chorley Old Road (off A6) ☎ (01257) 276485
2.30-11; 12-10.30 Sun
John Smith's Bitter; Wells Bombardier; guest beer H
Small, single-bar, terraced village local, this friendly pub is popular with locals and visitors alike; the haunt of mature motor cycle enthusiasts it stocks a good selection of malt whiskies. Note the splendid Nuttalls windows. Not to be missed.
🌼 Q 🌼 ♣

WILPSHIRE

Bulls Head Hotel
779 Whalley New Road (A666 from Blackburn towards Whalley, 1/2 mile from Brownhill roundabout)
☎ (01254) 248274
11-11; 12-10.30 Sun
Boddingtons Bitter; Flowers Original; Marston's Pedigree; guest beers H
Spacious pub where a large menu complements the six guest beers. The mix of age groups makes this pub a very active and attractive venue for all.
Q 🌼 ◖▯ ♿ ⇌ ♣ P ✂

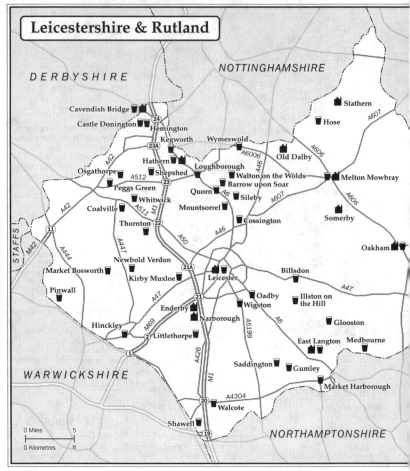

Leicestershire & Rutland

DERBYSHIRE

NOTTINGHAMSHIRE

Cavendish Bridge
Castle Donington
Hemington
Kegworth
Wymeswold
Stathern
Hose
Old Dalby
Hathern
Loughborough
Osgathorpe
Shepshed
Walton on the Wolds
Melton Mowbray
Peggs Green
Barrow upon Soar
Whitwick
Quorn
Sileby
Coalville
Mountsorrel
Somerby
Thornton
Cossington
Newbold Verdon
Oakham
Market Bosworth
Kirby Muxloe
Leicester
Billsdon
Pinwall
Oadby
Illston on the Hill
Enderby
Wigston
Hinckley
Narborough
Glooston
Littlethorpe
East Langton
Medbourne
Saddington
Gumley
Market Harborough
Walcote
Shawell

WARWICKSHIRE

NORTHAMPTONSHIRE

STAFFS

0 Miles 5
0 Kilometres 8

BARROW ON SOAR

Navigation
Mill Lane
☎ (01509) 412842
11-3, 5.30-11; 11-11 Sat; 12-3, 7-10.30 Sun
Belvoir Mild, Star Bitter; Marston's Pedigree; Tetley Bitter; guest beers H
Busy, village canalside pub, where guest beers are usually from local microbreweries. No weekend lunches but barbecues in summer.
⚰ Q ⏱ 👁 🍽 ♣

BILLESDON

New Greyhound
2 Market Place (old A47)
☎ (0116) 259 6226
12-2, 5.30-11; 12-11 Sat; 12-3.30, 7-10.30 Sun
Banks's Original; Marston's Bitter, Pedigree H
Overlooking the old market square, this no-nonsense local offers a warm friendly welcome to passing trade; a

typical two-roomed village pub.
Q ⏱ 👁 ♣ 🍽

CASTLE DONINGTON

Cross Keys
90 Bondgate
☎ (01332) 812214
12-2.30 (not Mon), 5-11; 12-11 Sat; 12-10.30 Sun
Draught Bass; Marston's Pedigree; Theakston Best Bitter; guest beers H
Traditional, two-roomed pub, home to two local rugby teams. Note the original Offilers Brewery etched windows. Regular 'happy hours' early eve.
⚰ ❀ 👁 ♣ P

CAVENDISH BRIDGE

Old Crown
400 yds off A6 at Trent Bridge
☎ (01332) 792392
11-3, 5-11; 12-4.30, 7-10.30 Sun
Draught Bass; Marston's Pedigree; guest beers H
Friendly, atmospheric village

pub boasting a collection of several hundred water jugs hanging from the lounge ceiling. Home-cooked lunches, three guest beers and a guest cider add to its appeal. A gem.
❀ ♣ 🍽 P

COALVILLE

Stamford and Warrington
72 High Street
☎ (01530) 833278
10.30-3, 7-11; 12-3, 7-10.30 Sun
Marston's Pedigree H
Two-roomed pub with a bar and smoke room, formerly a coaching inn frequented by the Earls of Stamford and Warrington.
Q ❀ 🍽 ♣

COSSINGTON

Royal Oak
105 Main Street
☎ (01509) 813937
12-3 (not Mon; 4 Sat); 6-11; 12-3, 7-10.30 Sun

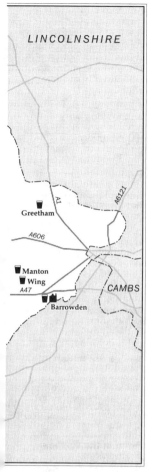

Everards Beacon, Tiger; guest beers Ⓗ
Small, well refurbished village local with a wood-panelled interior: one L-shaped room with plain wood furniture, plus a conservatory. The guest beers come from Everards Old English Ale Club. Popular with diners; long alley skittles played.
Q ❀ ◖ ▷ ♣ P

EAST LANGTON
Bell Inn
Main Street
☎ (01858) 545278
11.30-2.30 (3.30 Sat), 7 (5 Fri; 6 Sat)-11; 12-4, 7-10.30 Sun
Greene King IPA, Abbot; Langton Caudle Bitter, Bowler; Ⓗ guest beers Ⓖ
Listed building circa 16th century, featuring a pretty walled garden, very low beams and an open log fire. Langton Brewery has recently started production in a micro-brewery situated in

buildings behind the Bell.
🏚 Q ❀ 🚲 ◖ ▷ P

GLOOSTON
Old Barn Inn
Main Street
☎ (01858) 545215
12-2.30 (not Mon), 7-11; 12-3, 7-10.30 Sun
Greene King IPA; guest beers Ⓗ
16th-century rural inn set in the heart of Leicestershire's hunting country. Low oak beams and an open fire add to the welcoming ambience. Three constantly changing guest beers are usually available; award-winning food is served in both the bar and restaurant (no meals Sun eve).
🏚 Q ❀ 🚲 ◖ ▷ P

GUMLEY
Bell Inn
2 Main Street
☎ (0116) 279 2476
11-3, 5.30-11; 12-3, 7-10.30 Sun
Boddingtons Bitter; Everards Tiger; Greene King IPA; guest beers Ⓗ
Early 19th-century free house, popular with local rural and commuting urban clientele. An extensive patio garden to the rear is unsuitable for children or dogs. The beamed interior comprises an L-shaped bar and a no-smoking restaurant (no meals Sun eve).
🏚 Q ◖ ▷ ♣ P

HATHERN
Three Crowns
Wide Lane (off A6)
☎ (01509) 842233
12-2.30, 5.30-11; 12-11 Sat; 12-3, 7-10.30 Sun
Draught Bass; M&B Mild; Worthington Bitter; guest beer Ⓗ
Popular village local: three rooms, a skittle alley and a large garden (pétanque played).
🏚 Q ❀ 🖼 ▲ ♣ P ⚥ ⊟

HEMINGTON
Jolly Sailor
21 Main Street
☎ (01332) 810448
11-11; 12-10.30 Sun
Draught Bass; Greene King Abbot; M&B Mild; Mansfield Bitter; Marston's Pedigree; guest beers Ⓗ
Small, two-roomed heavily timbered village pub where artefacts adorn the walls and ceilings. Four guest beers on offer plus cider in summer.
🏚 Q 🚍 ❀ ◖ ♣ ⊕ P

HINCKLEY
Railway Hotel
Station Road (opp. station)
☎ (01455) 615285

11-11; 11.30-3.30, 7-11 Sat; 12-3.30, 7-10.30 Sun
Banks's Original; Marston's Bitter, Pedigree Ⓗ
Spacious local whose basic bar is adorned with railway pictures. The comfortable lounge hosts occasional live music and the conservatory has a pool table.
Q 🚍 ❀ 🚲 ◖ ≢ ♣ P

HOSE
Black Horse
21 Bolton Lane
☎ (01949) 860336
12-2.30 (not Tue); 7-11; 12-4, 7-10.30 Sun
Brains Mild; Castle Eden Bitter; Home Bitter; guest beers Ⓗ
Basic, but comfortable, village local: an unspoilt bar, a traditional lounge and a wood-panelled restaurant serving a menu based on local produce.
❀ ◖ 🖼 ⅙ ♣ P

Rose & Crown
43 Bolton Lane
☎ (01949) 60424
12-2.30; 7 (5 Fri)-11; 12-3.30, 7.30-10.30 Sun
Greene King IPA, Abbot; guest beers Ⓗ
Cosy, split-room village pub in the Vale of Belvoir, that attracts locals and visitors alike. It may close weekday lunchtime in winter. One of the three guest beers is always a mild.
🏚 ❀ ◖ ⅙ ▲ ♣

ILLSTON ON THE HILL
Fox & Goose
Main Street (off B6047, near Billesdon)
☎ (0116) 259 6340
12-2.30 (not Mon-Tue or Wed-Thu winter), 5.30 (7-Mon)-11; 12-2.30, 7-10.30 Sun
Everards Beacon, Tiger, Original; guest beer Ⓗ
A gem: a cosy, unchanged village pub with a timeless feel, displaying a collection of local mementoes and hunting memorabilia. Tucked away, but it is well worth seeking out. Self-catering holiday flat available.
🏚 Q ❀ 🚍 🖼 ♣

KEGWORTH
Red Lion
24 High Street
☎ (01509) 672466
11-11; 12-10.30 Sun
Adnams Bitter; Banks's Original; Caledonian Deuchars IPA; Marston's Pedigree; guest beers Ⓗ
Characterful pub comprising four simply decorated rooms. The large garden has a children's play area;

The Good Beer Guide 2001

pétanque and skittles also played. Regularly changing cider usually available and good food is served.
🏚 Q ☞ ⚙ ◑ ▶ 🛏 ⅃ ♣ ⌂ P ⅄

KIRBY MUXLOE
Royal Oak
35 Main Street
☎ (0116) 239 3166
11-2.30, 5.30-11; 11-3, 6-11 Sat; 12-3, 7-10.30 Sun
Adnams Bitter; Everards Beacon, Tiger; guest beers Ⓗ
Modern exterior conceals a comfortable, traditionally-styled lounge bar and a restaurant, popular with both locals and business folk at lunchtime. Guest beers come from the Everards Old English Ale Club.
⚙ ◑ ▶ P

LEICESTER
Ale Wagon
27 Rutland Street
☎ (0116) 262 3330
11-11; 12-10.30 Sun
Hoskins & Oldfield HOB Bitter, EXS; guest beers (occasional) Ⓗ
Formerly the Queens, this became the first Hoskins & Oldfield tied house in 1999. Restored to its 1930s interior with two rooms and a central bar, it is popular with beer drinkers visiting the city. Six Hoskins beers are usually on tap; bottle-conditioned cider sold. ≠ ⅄

Black Horse
1 Foxon Street (on Braunstone Gate)
☎ (0116) 254 0030
12-3, 5-11; 12-11 Fri & Sat; 12-4, 7-10.30 Sun
Everards Beacon, Tiger; guest beers Ⓗ
Small beer drinkers' pub, popular with students. Its two rooms and central bar have been untouched by refurbishment. Guest beers are from Everards Old English Ale Club. ♣

Hat & Beaver
60 Highcross Street
☎ (0116) 262 2157
12-11; 12-3, 7-10.30 Sun
Hardys & Hansons Best Mild, Best Bitter, Classic Ⓗ
Basic, two-roomed local with a relaxed atmosphere, one of Leicester's few remaining traditional pubs. It is handy for the Shires shopping centre. Well-filled good value cobs are available at lunchtime (not Sun). TV in the bar, and Devil among the Tailors played. ♣

Leicester Gateway
52 Gateway Street (near University)

☎ (0116) 255 7319
11-11; 12-10.30 Sun
Bateman XB; Castle Rock Hemlock; Fuller's London Pride; guest beers Ⓗ
Pleasant one-roomed pub, converted from a hosiery factory into a large comfortable bar (check out the ladies underwear displayed). Up to five guest beers, plus a mild is always available. A good varied menu is served until 8pm (6pm Sun).
◑ ▶ 🛏 ⌂ P ⅄

Talbot
4 Thurcaston Road (road access from Loughborough Road only)
☎ (0116) 266 2280
11-2.30 (4 Sat), 6 (6.30 Sat)-11; 12-4, 7-10.30 Sun
Ansells Mild, Bitter; Marston's Pedigree; guest beers Ⓗ
Friendly local of historical interest in the heart of old Belgrave, convenient for Belgrave Hall Museum, Abbey Pumping Station, and the Great Central Steam Railway (Leicester North). No food Sun.
🏚 ⚙ ◑ ♣ P

Tom Hoskins
131-133 Beaumanor Road
☎ (0116) 261 1008
11-11; 12-10.30 Sun
Hoskins Bitter, Tom's Gold, seasonal beers; M&B Mild; guest beers Ⓗ
Tom Hoskins brewery tap. A two-roomed popular local. Closure of brewery means pub and beer range may change. Handy for the Great Central Steam Railway (Leicester North), and the new space centre. Weekday lunches.
Q ☞ ⚙ ◑ 🛏 🛏 ♣ P

Vaults
1 Wellington Street (near Fenwicks)
☎ (0116) 255 5506
5 (12 Fri & Sat)-11; 12-3, 7-11 Sun
Beer range varies Ⓗ
Cellar bar with a friendly atmosphere selling beers from micro-brewers. Customers from far and near enjoy the changing beers from seven handpumps. Live music Sat and Sun when an entrance fee is sometimes charged.
≠ ⌂ ⅄

LITTLETHORPE
Plough Inn
7 Station Road
☎ (0116) 286 2383
11-2.30 (3 Sat), 6-11; 12-3, 7-10.30 Sun
Everards Beacon, Tiger, Original, seasonal beers; guest beers Ⓗ

Thatched village local where the cosy lounge, bar and dining area are free from juke box or machines. Its food and hospitality attracts a wide range of customers. Long alley skittles by arrangement. Guest beers come from Everards Old English Ale Club. No food Sun eve. Q ⚙ ◑ ▶ 🛏
≠ (Narborough) ♣ P

LOUGHBOROUGH
Albion
Canal Bank
☎ (01509) 213952
11-3 (4 Sat), 6-11; 12-3, 7-10.30 Sun
Shepherd Neame Master Brew Bitter; Samuel Smith OBB; guest beer Ⓗ
Tranquil, canalside pub with a bar, darts room and a quiet lounge serving good value beer and home-cooked food. Outside drinking is on the canal bank or patio. The beer range includes a mild.
Q ⚙ ◑ ▶ 🛏 ≠ ♣ P

Boat Inn
Meadow Lane
☎ (01509) 214578
11-3, 5-11; 11-11 Fri & Sat; 12-10.30 Sun
Banks's Original; Marston's Bitter, Pedigree Ⓗ
Cosmopolitan canalside pub on the edge of town, where a friendly welcome is assured. It is popular with boaters in summer (moorings available).
⚙ ◑ 🛏 ≠ ♣ P 🛏

Swan in the Rushes
21 The Rushes
☎ (01509) 217014
11-11; 12-10.30 Sun
Archers Golden; Marston's Pedigree; Taylor Landlord; Tetley Bitter; guest beers Ⓗ
Traditional two-roomed free house with a dining room/no-smoking area. The six guest beers always include a mild and often a Castle Rock brew. Good food is complemented by a range of real coffees and malts. Regular live music is played in the function room. Eve meals served weekdays. 🏚 Q
☞ ⚙ 🛏 ◑ ▶ ♣ ⌂ P 🛏

Tap & Mallet
36 Nottingham Road
☎ (01509) 210028
11.30-2.30, 5-11; 11.30-11 Sat; 12-10.30 Sun
Courage Best Bitter; Marston's Pedigree; Theakston Mild; guest beers Ⓗ
Genuine free house between the town centre and the station, serving up to six guest beers mostly from an interesting range of micro-breweries; the Theakston's Mild is often replaced by a

174

micro mild. The large garden has a children's play area.

🏚 Q 🏵 🍴 ⇌ ♣ 🍷

MARKET BOSWORTH
Red Lion
1 Park Street
☎ (01455) 291713
11-2.30, 7-11; 11-11 Sat; 12-3,
7-10.30 Sun

Banks's Original, Bitter; Camerons Bitter; Marston's Pedigree; Theakston XB, Old Peculier; guest beers Ⓗ

Grade II listed building housing a split-level, L-shaped pub. With over 150 guest ales each year, it is popular with both locals and visitors to the nearby Bosworth Battlefield site, the railway and Ashby Canal.

🏚 🏵 🛏 🍴 🍴 ♣ P

MARKET HARBOROUGH (LITTLE BOWDEN)
Cherry Tree
Church Walk, Kettering Road
☎ (01858) 463525
12-2.30, 5-11; 11-11 Fri & Sat;
12-10.30 Sun

Everards Beacon, Tiger, Original; guest beers Ⓗ

Spacious pub featuring low beams, a thatched roof and many small seating areas; although it is in Little Bowden, it feels part of the adjoining Market Harborough community. No meals Sun eve.

🏵 🍴 🍴 ♣ P ⚲

MEDBOURNE
Horse & Trumpet ☆
12 The Old Green
7-11; 12-2.30, 7-10.30 Sun

Bateman XB; Greene King IPA Ⓗ

Classic, basic, unspoilt pub; a free house since the early 1970s, this former Watney's house still displays an illuminated Red Barrel pub sign. In the same family since 1939, this beer-drinkers' pub is well worth a visit.

🏚 Q 🐫 🏵 ♣

Nevill Arms
12 Waterfall Way
☎ (01858) 565288
12-2.30, 6-11; 12-3, 7-10.30 Sun

Adnams Bitter; Fuller's London Pride; guest beers Ⓗ

The initials MGN over the door are those of Captain Nevill, who was heir to the nearby Holt estate when this former coaching inn was rebuilt in 1863 after a fire. Outside, the banks of Medbourne brook abound with ducks; inside a log fire burns in the large inglenook.

🏚 🏵 🛏 🍴 ♣ P

MELTON MOWBRAY
Boat Inn
57 Burton Street
☎ (01664) 560518
12-2 (Sat & summer only), 5-11; 11-2,
5-11 Fri; 12-3, 7-10.30 Sun

Burtonwood Bitter, Top Hat; guest beer Ⓗ

One roomed traditional pub with open fires.

🏚 Q ⇌ ♣

Crown
10 Burton Street
☎ (01664) 564682
11-3.30, 7.30-11; 11-11 Sat; 12-3,
7.30-10.30 Sun

Everards Beacon, Tiger, Original, seasonal beers; guest beers Ⓗ

Friendly two-roomed town pub, run by a long-serving landlord. Popular with office workers and shoppers at lunchtime, it attracts all ages at night.

🏚 🐫 🏵 🍴 ⇌ ♣

Mash Tub
58 Nottingham Street
☎ (01664) 410051
11-3, 6-11; 11-11 Sat; 12-4, 7-10.30
Sun

Banks's Original, Bitter Ⓗ

Single bar, split-level town pub serving good value lunches (not on Sun).

🏚 🍴 ⇌ 🍷

MOUNTSORREL
Lindens Hotel
22 Halstead Road
11-4, 6-11; 11-11 Fri & Sat; 12-10.30
Sun

Everards Beacon, Tiger, Original or guest beer Ⓗ

Country house, built in 1901 as a family home and converted to a pub in 1951. It has a large lounge lined with bookcases, a bar, pool room and a restaurant. The extensive gardens have a play area for children and a pétanque piste.

🏚 Q 🐫 🏵 🍴 🍴 🍴 ♣ P

Waterside
Sileby Road
☎ (0116) 230 2750
11-2.30, 6-11; 12-3.30, 7-10.30 (12-
10.30 summer) Sun

Everards Beacon, Tiger, Original; guest beer Ⓗ

Riverside pub next to Mountsorrel lock comprising a large lounge/dining area, plus a small snug. Boats can be moored nearby.

Q 🏵 🍴 🍴 🕭 P

NEWBOLD VERDON
Jubilee
80 Main Street
☎ (01455) 822698
7 (6 Wed)-11; 2.30-11 Fri; 11-11 Sat;
12-10.30 Sun

Marston's Bitter, Pedigree Ⓗ

Very community-minded, friendly two-roomed village local; this cosy, unspoilt, no-frills pub extends a warm welcome to all.

🏚 🏵 ♣ P

OADBY
Black Dog
23 London Road
☎ (0116) 271 2233
12 (11 Fri & Sat)-11; 12-10.30 Sun

Banks's Original, Bitter Ⓟ

Georgian two-roomed, street-corner pub with no-frills, but twice winner of Wolverhampton & Dudley Brewery *Best Kept Cellar* competition (1998 and '99). Limited parking.

🏵 🍴 ♣ P 🕭

Cow & Plough
Stoughton Farm Park, Gartree Road (follow Farmworld signs from A6)
☎ (0116) 272 0852
5 (12 Sat)-9; 12-4, 7-9 Sun

Fuller's London Pride; Hoskins & Oldfield HOB Bitter, Leatherbritches Steaming Billy, Bitter; guest beers Ⓗ

Its atmospheric vaults are adorned with breweriana. Ever-changing guest beers usually come from independent breweries at this 1998 East Midlands CAMRA *Pub of the Year*.

Q 🐫 🏵 🕭 ♣ 🍷 P ⚲

OSGATHORPE
Storey Arms
41 Main Street
☎ (01530) 224166
12-3, 7.30-11; 12-3, 7.30-10.30 Sun

Banks's Original, Bitter; Marston's Pedigree; guest beers Ⓗ

Traditional country pub with a 1960s-style bar and lounge; darts and pool are played in the bar. It hosts barbecues in the garden in summer and occasional live music (Sat).

🏚 Q 🏵 🍴 🕭 ♣ P

Royal Oak
20 Main Street
☎ (01530) 222443
12-3 (not Mon-Fri), 7-11; 12-3, 7-10.30
Sun

M&B Mild; Marston's Bitter, Pedigree Ⓗ

Quiet village local where assorted memorabilia adorn the bar and there is a nice floral beer garden. Accommodation in purpose-built chalets is handy for East Midlands airport.

🏚 Q 🐫 🏵 🍴 🕭 ♣ P

PEGGS GREEN
New Inn
Clay Lane (B587, 200 yds from A512 at Griffydam roundabout)

☎ (01530) 222293

12-2 (not Mon-Wed, 12-3 Sat), 5.30 (6.30 Sat)-11; 12-3, 7-10.30 Sun

Draught Bass; M&B Mild; Marston's Pedigree Ⓗ

Traditional village pub of several rooms offering a good Irish welcome and occasional folk nights. Summer lunchtime opening hours may vary.

⚞ Q ⌛ ⊞ ♣ P

PINWALL

Red Lion

Main Road (B4116, 1 mile from A5)

☎ (01827) 712223

11-11; 12-10.30 Sun

Banks's Original; Draught Bass; Marston's Pedigree; Taylor Landlord; guest beers Ⓗ

Rural, cosy local unspoilt by the restaurant and hotel to the rear. Pinwall is not shown on most maps. Home-cooked meals served Mon-Sat.

⚞ Q ❀ ⚑ ◖❱ P

QUORN

Blacksmiths Arms

29 Meeting Street

☎ (01509) 412751

12-2 (11-2.30 Sat), 5.30-11; 12-3, 7-10.30 Sun

Marston's Bitter, Pedigree Ⓗ

Busy village local: a low-beamed bar and cosy snug.

⚞ Q ⚑ ♣

SADDINGTON

Queen's Head

Main Street

☎ (0116) 240 2536

11-3, 5.30-11; 12-3, 7-10.30 Sun

Adnams Bitter; Everards Beacon, Tiger; guest beers Ⓗ

Discover lovely views of the Laughton Valley and Saddington Reservoir from the garden or conservatory-style restaurant, hiding behind the standard façade of this village local. Guest beers are from Everards Old English Ale Club. No meals Sun eve. ⚞ Q ❀ ◖❱ P

SHAWELL

White Swan

Main Street

☎ (01788) 860357

12-2.30 (not Sat)-11; closed Mon; 12-2.30 (closed eve) Sun

Adnams Bitter; Marston's Pedigree Ⓗ

Olde-worlde village pub featuring wood panelling, real fires and a quality restaurant. ⚞ Q ❀ ◖❱ ♣ P ▯

SHEPSHED

Bull & Bush

61 Sullington Road

☎ (01509) 506783

12-3, 5.30-11; 12-4, 7-10.30 Sun

Banks's Original; Marston's Pedigree Ⓗ

This traditional, unspoilt local stocks a good range of malts. It has a large garden that hosts summer barbecues.

❀ ♣ P

SILEBY

Free Trade

11 Cossington Road

☎ (01509) 814494

11.30-2, 5.30-11; 11.30-3, 6.30-11 Sat; 12-3, 7-10.30 Sun

Everards Beacon, Tiger, Original, seasonal beers Ⓗ

Popular thatched local, catering for all ages with a garden and pétanque court to the rear. Booking advised for Sun lunch.

⚞ Q ❀ ◖ ⇒ P

THORNTON

Bricklayers Arms

213 Main Street

☎ (01530) 230808

12-3, 6-11; 11-11 Sat; 12-10.30 Sun

Everards Tiger; guest beers Ⓗ

Unspoilt, traditional, village local, partly dating from the 16th-century, with a basic quarry-tiled bar area and a comfortable lounge. It overlooks Thornton Trout Fisheries. Guest beers are from Everards Old English Ale Club. No food Sun eve or Mon.

⚞ Q ❀ ◖❱ P

WALCOTE

Black Horse

Lutterworth Road (A4304, 1 mile E of MI jct 20)

☎ (01455) 552684

12-2 (not Mon-Thu or Sat), 7 (5.30 Fri, 6.30 Sat)-11; 12-3, 6.30-10.30 Sun

Greene King Abbot; Hoskins & Oldfield HOB Bitter; Oakham JHB; Taylor Landlord; guest beers Ⓗ

Single bar free house serving home-cooked Thai food and beers from independent breweries. Well worth the one mile detour from the M1. ❀ ◖❱ P

WALTON ON THE WOLDS

Anchor

2 Loughborough Road

☎ (01509) 880018

12-3, 5.30-11; 12-3, 7-10.30 Sun

Marston's Bitter, Pedigree; Taylor Landlord; guest beers Ⓗ

Single-roomed village local, featuring a garden at the front, patio plus a grass area at the rear (pétanque played). Excellent food is available, with occasional themed nights staged (no meals Sun eve). Q ❀ ◖❱ ♣ ⏴ P

WHITWICK

Lady Jane

Hall Lane

☎ (01530) 836889

12-3, 6-11; 12-3, 6-10.30 Sun

Marston's Pedigree; guest beer Ⓗ

Estate pub built in the 1960s; comprising two rooms. Entertainment is staged in the lounge Sat eve; the usual pub games are played in the spacious bar of this community pub.

Q ❀ ⚲ P

Three Horseshoes

11 Leicester Road

☎ (01530) 837311

11-3, 6.30-11; 12-2, 7-10.30 Sun

Draught Bass; M&B Mild; guest beer (occasional) Ⓗ

Unspoilt traditional alehouse known locally as Polly's with a basic bar and a tiny smoke room containing wood-backed pews.

⚞ Q ❀ ⚑ ♣ P

WIGSTON

Star & Garter

114 Leicester Road

☎ (0116) 288 2450

11-2.30, 5-11; 11-11 Sat; 12-3, 7-10.30 Sun

Everards Beacon, Tiger; guest beer Ⓗ

Friendly, two-roomed pub, catering for all ages, in a wood-panelled bar and a cosy, beamed lounge. Long alley skittles played (by arrangement). The guest beer is from Everards Old English Ale Club.

❀ ◖ ⚑ ♣ P

WYMESWOLD

Three Crowns

45 Far Street

☎ (01509) 880153

11.30-3, 5.30 (6 Sat)-11; 12-3, 7-10.30 Sun

Adnams Bitter; Marston's Pedigree; guest beers Ⓗ

Friendly village local with beamed ceilings in the bar and a split-level snug/lounge. Locals are always on the piste (pétanque) or doing the Telegraph crossword. Two guest beers, one is always from a micro, often the local Belvoir Brewery.

⚞ Q ❀ ◖ ⚑ ♣ P

Rutland

BARROWDEN

Exeter Arms

28 Main Street (1 mile off A47)

☎ (01572) 747247

12-2.30, 6-11; 12-3, 7-10.30 Sun

Blencowe Toy Boys, Young Boys, Big Boys, Strong Boys, seasonal beers; guest beers Ⓗ

CAMRA National Pub Inventory: The Ship Hotel, Overton, Lancashire

Stone pub in an idyllic setting on the village green opposite the duck pond; one long room with oak beams. Cider sold in summer; Blencowe beers are brewed here.
🏚 ❀ ⇌ ◖❒ ♣ ⛄ P

GREETHAM
Plough
23 Main Street (B5668)
☎ (01572) 813613
11-3, 5-11; 11-11 Fri & Sat; 12-10.30 Sun
Grainstore Cooking, Triple B, Ten Fifty; guest beer H
Welcoming village local which is connected to Grainstore Brewery. Guest beers are often seasonals from Grainstore. Baguettes are sold by the inch!
🐾 ❀ ◖❒ Å ♣ P

MANTON
Horse & Jockey
2 St Mary's Road (off A6003)
☎ (01572) 737335
11-3, 7-11; 12-3, 7-10.30 Sun
Mansfield Riding Bitter H
250-year-old village local on the Rutland Water cycle route; it gets very popular in summer.
🏚 Q ⇌ ◖❒ ⛃ ♣ P

OAKHAM
Grainstore Brewery Tap
Station Approach (off A606)
☎ (01572) 770065
11-2.30, 6-11; 11-11 Fri & Sat; 12-2.30, 7-10.30 Sun
Grainstore Cooking, Triple B, Ten Fifty, seasonal beers; guest beers H
Refurbished grain warehouse (see the original grain ladder); the brewery is housed above the bar. Guest beers are often seasonal beers from the brewery. Traditional dispense is used at one end of bar, swan necks at the other. Wheelchair WC.
❀ ◖❹ ≈ ♣ P ⛉

Try also: Wheatsheaf, Northgate (Everards)

WING
Cuckoo
3 Top Street
☎ (01572) 737340
11.30-3 (not Tue), 6.30-11; 12-4, 7-10.30 Sun
Fuller's London Pride; Marston's Pedigree; guest beers H

17th-century village local with a thatched roof and whitewashed walls. A warm welcome awaits in this unspoilt free house, where the beer range includes a house beer from Mauldons and an occasional mild. Boules played. Curry is a speciality; no food Tue.
🏚 Q ❀ ◖❒ ♣ P

INDEPENDENT BREWERIES

Belvoir: Old Dalby
Blencowe: Barrowden
Brewsters: Stathern
Everards: Narborough
Featherstone: Enderby
Grainstore: Oakham
Hoskins & Oldfield: Leicester
John O'Gaunt: Melton Mowbray
Langton: East Langton
Parish: Somerby
Shardlow: Cavendish Bridge
Shepherd: Lutterworth
Wicked Hathern: Hathern

Beer Festival Calendar 2001

CAMRA stages a large number of beer festivals every year. They are brilliant shop windows for cask beer and give drinkers the opportunity to sample beers from independent brewers rare to individual localities. Beer festivals are enormous fun, many offering good food and live entertainment and, where possible, facilities for families. Some seasonal festivals specialise in spring, autumn and winter ales. Festivals range in size from small local ones, to large regional ones, and the Campaign's two national festivals: for winter beers in January and the Great British in August, which features around 500 beers. The list below offers just a sample of the festivals planned for 2001. For up-to-date information contact the CAMRA web-site: **www.camra.org.uk** or, by joining CAMRA (use form at the back of the Guide), you will receive the Campaign's monthly newspaper What's Brewing, which lists every festival on a month-by-month basis.

JANUARY
Great British Winter Beer Festival, Manchester
Cambridge winter festival
Hitchin winter festival
St Neots winter festival

FEBRUARY
Bradford
Bristol
Dover
Rotherham

MARCH
Darlington spring festival
Hitchin
Leeds
London Drinker

APRIL
Bury St Edmunds
Dunstable
Newcastle
Paisley

MAY
Alloa
Cambridge
Colchester
Doncaster
Glenrothes
Ongar
Woodchurch, nr Ashford, Kent*

JUNE
Devizes
Thurrock
Woodchurch, nr Ashford, Kent*
(date not finalised: check with CAMRA)

JULY
Bishop Auckland*
Canterbury

Chelmsford
Clacton
Cotswolds
Derby

AUGUST
Great British Beer Festival, London
Barnsley
Bishop Auckland* (date not finalised: check with CAMRA)
Larling (Norfolk)
Peterborough

SEPTEMBER
Chappel (Essex)
Darlington
Hull
Ipswich
Keighley
Maidstone
St Albans
Sheffield
Troon

OCTOBER
Alloa
Bedford
Gravesend
Huddersfield
Middlesbrough
Norwich
Wakefield

NOVEMBER
Aberdeen
Barnsley winter festival
Rochford

DECEMBER
Pig's Ear (East London)
Ipswich winter festival

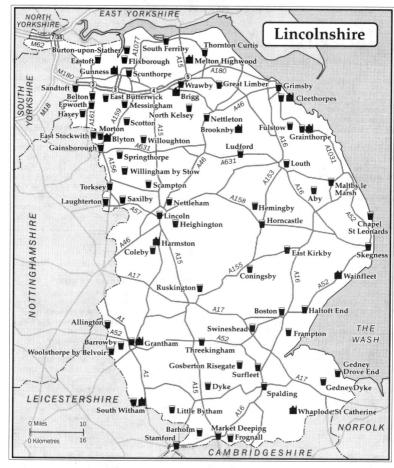

Lincolnshire

ABY

Railway Tavern
Main Road
☎ (01507) 480676
12-3, 7-11 (closed Tue Jan-Easter);
12-3, 7-10.30 Sun
Adnams Bitter; Everards Tiger; guest beer H
Friendly village pub serving splendid home-cooked food, it offers a warm welcome in its open bar and adjoining games room. Twice regional finalist for the Homefire *Pub of the Year*. Note the display of rural and railway memorabilia.
ﾑﾑ ❀ ◑ ♣ P ⊬

Try also: Vine, S Thoresby (Bateman)

ALLINGTON

Welby Arms
The Green
☎ (01400) 281361
12-2.30, 6-11; 12-4, 6-10.30 Sun
Draught Bass; John Smith's Bitter; Taylor Landlord; guest beers H
Popular village pub with a

large bar area, offering a friendly welcome, plus good home-cooked food in the restaurant.
ﾑﾑ Q ❀ ⇔ ◑ ▷ ♿ P

BARHOLM

Five Horseshoes
On lane just up from sharp bend on main street
☎ (01778) 560238
5 (12 Sat)-11; 12-10.30 Sun
Adnams Broadside; Fuller's London Pride; Theakston XB; guest beers H
Traditional 18th-century building of local barnack stone in a quiet hamlet. Note the Javan wood carving above bar. A creeper-covered patio and large garden with bouncy castle for children attract families; pétanque played.
ﾑﾑ Q ⌂ ❀ ▲ ♣ P ⊞

BARROWBY

White Swan
High Road (2 miles from Grantham)
☎ (01476) 562375

11.30-11; 12-10.30 Sun
Boddingtons Bitter; Courage Directors; Ruddles Best Bitter; guest beer (occasional) H
Close to the village green, the pub retains two bars: the small lounge is quiet and comfortable, whilst the larger bar area has pool and darts.
Q ❀ ◑ ♣ P

BELTON

Crown Inn
Stockhill, Churchtown
☎ (01427) 872834
4 (12 Sat)-11; 12-10.30 Sun
John Smith's Bitter; Theakston Best Bitter; guest beer H
Quaint, family-run local, hidden away behind the church, enjoying a friendly and relaxed atmosphere. The landlord organises the annual Belton wheelbarrow race.
ﾑﾑ ❀ P ⊟

BOSTON

Ball House
Wainfleet Road (A52, 1 mile

from centre)
☎ (01205) 364478
11-3, 6.30-11; 12-3, 7-10.30 Sun
Draught Bass; Bateman Mild, XB, XXXB Ⓗ
Mock-Tudor pub, boasting award-winning floral displays and excellent home-cooked food (booking advisable weekends). Sited on a former cannonball store – hence the unusual name.
🏨 ❀ ◖ ▶ ⌖ ♣ P

Britannia Inn
4 Church Street (near Assembly Rooms)
☎ (01205) 365178
11-11; 12-10.30 Sun
Draught Bass; Bateman XB Ⓗ
Busy, traditional town-centre pub, one of the oldest in Boston, retaining many old features. The garden overlooks the Haven River. No food Sun.
🏨 ❀ ◖ ⌖ ♣

Coach & Horses
86 Main Ridge
☎ (01205) 362301
5 (6 Fri)-11; 11-3, 7-11 Sat; 12-3, 7-10.30 Sun
Bateman XB, XXXB Ⓗ
Small, one-roomed local offering a genuinely friendly pub atmosphere, near the football ground. Dominoes, darts and pool played.
🏨 ♣

Cowbridge
Horncastle Road, Cowbridge (B1183 N of town)
☎ (01205) 362597
11-3, 6-11; 12-4, 7-10.30 Sun
Home Mild, Bitter; guest beers Ⓗ
Friendly pub with a restaurant leading off the smaller bar, serving well-priced food. Handy for Boston Golf Club.
❀ ◖ ⌖ P

Eagle
144 West Street (near station)
☎ (01205) 361116
11-2.30, 6 (5 Thu)-11; 11-11 Fri & Sat; 12-11 Sun
Adnams Broadside; Banks's Bitter; Taylor Landlord; guest beer Ⓗ
Town pub stocking an interesting range of ever-changing guest beers. The function room hosts a number of societies, including Boston Folk Club.
🏨 ❀ ⌖ ≋ ♣ ⌂

Ship Tavern
Custom House Lane (off South Sq)
☎ (01205) 358156
11-11; 12-10.30 Sun
Bateman Mild, XB; Greene King IPA; guest beers Ⓗ
Converted last year to a one-roomed pub with a pool area, the pub is now a lot more spacious, and retains a mix of

wooden pews and cushioned bench seating; the farmhouse table is still intact.
❀ ≋ ♣

BURTON-ON-STATHER

Ferry House
Stather Road (follow campsite signs through village)
☎ (01724) 721299
12-4.30 (not Mon-Fri); 7-11 (extended hours Sat in summer); 12-10.30 Sun
Beer range varies Ⓗ
Large, single-roomed village pub, divided into discrete drinking areas, situated alongside the River Trent. Children are welcome in the large garden; tables on the river bank are perfect for watching the ships go by. Outdoor entertainment performed summer Sat eves.
❀ ⛺ ♣ P

CHAPEL ST LEONARDS

Ship
109 Sea Road (1/2 mile from seafront)
☎ (01754) 872640
12-3.30, 7-11; 12-3.30, 7-10.30 Sun
Bateman Mild, XB, Victory; guest beers (occasional) Ⓗ
Cheerful, welcoming local, popular with regulars and tourists alike. The full Bateman range is sometimes available in summer.
🏨 ❀ ◖ ⛺ ♣ P

CLEETHORPES

Crow's Nest Hotel
Balmoral Road
☎ (01472) 698867
11-3, 6-11; 12-3, 7-10.30 Sun
Samuel Smith OBB Ⓗ
Welcoming estate pub: comfortable lounge and spacious bar; winner of Sam Smith's 1999 national *Cellar* award. This pub proves that quality beats quantity – only one beer but worth a visit! A classic example of 1950s pub architecture.
Q ❀ ⌖ ⊞ P ⠼

Gardens Bar, Winter Gardens
Kingsway
☎ (01472) 692925
12 (11 summer)-4, 6.45-11; 12-4, 6.45-10.30 Sun
Bateman XB; Highwood Tom Wood Best Bitter; Theakston XB Ⓗ
Public lounge at the front of the Winter Gardens complex. Food is available in the conservatory, plus Sun lunches in the Floral Suite. Home of the Cleethorpes' Beer Festival. ◖ ▶ P

No. 2 Refreshment Room
Station Approach

☎ (01472) 697951
12-11; 12-10.30 Sun
John Smith's Magnet; Mansfield Mild; guest beers Ⓗ
Small local on the station forecourt, serving guest beers at excellent prices. ≋

Willys Pub and Brewery
17 High Cliff Road
☎ (01472) 602145
11-11; 12-10.30 Sun
Bateman XB; Willy's Original; guest beers Ⓗ
Local CAMRA *Pub of the 90s*, ever-present in this *Guide* since opening. The brewery can be observed from the bar. Excellent wholesome lunches are served at reasonable prices. A seaside gem.
◖ ≋

COLEBY

Tempest Arms
Hill Rise (off A607, 7 miles S of Lincoln)
☎ (01522) 810287
11.30-2.30, 6.30-11; 12-3, 7-10.30 Sun
Bateman XB; guest beers Ⓗ
At the centre of village life, a recent regional winner of a national *Community Pub* award this pub stands on the Viking Way, affording panoramic views over the Vale of Trent. Excellent bar meals; a small cosy restaurant is available for private bookings (no food Mon eve).
❀ ◖ ⌖ ♣ P

CONINGSBY

Leagate Inn
Leagate Road (B1192, E of village, off A153)
☎ (01526) 342370
11-3, 7-10.30 (6-11 Fri & Sat); 12-10.30 Sun
Marston's Pedigree; Theakston XB; guest beers Ⓗ
Historic pub, a 16th-century coaching inn; a contemporary yew tree stands next to an old gibbet. It also boasts a priest hole and antique furnishings. Excellent food is based on local produce.
🏨 Q ⛺ ❀ ⌂ ◖ ▶ ♣ P

DYKE

Wishing Well Inn
Main Street
☎ (01778) 422970
11-3, 6-11; 11-3, 7-10.30 Sun
Everards Tiger; Greene King Abbot; guest beers Ⓗ
Busy village pub, nearing 2001 guest beers served over the last six years. It enjoys a reputation for good food but this does not detract from the 'village local' atmosphere. A house beer, Going Down Well, is also on tap. Annual

beer festival held August.

🏨 🏕 🛏 ◖ ▮ ⌸ ♿ ▲ ♣ P

EAST BUTTERWICK

Dog & Gun
High Street (signed from A18)
☎ (01724) 783419
7 (5 Thu & Fri; 12 Sat)-11; 12-10.30 Sun

John Smith's Bitter; DarkTribe Dixie's Mild, Galleon or Bigfoot Genesis Ⓗ
Basic but welcoming village local by the River Trent; three rooms are served from a single bar. The mild is now a permanent feature. Other DarkTribe/Bigfoot beers are rotated on the third handpump as available.
🏨 ♣ P

EAST KIRKBY

Red Lion
Main Road
☎ (01790) 763406
12-2.30, 7-11; 12-3, 7-10.30 Sun

Draught Bass; Broadstone Best Bitter; guest beers Ⓗ
Popular pub, adorned with clocks and breweriana, close to an air museum and wartime airfield.
🏨 🛏 🏕 ◖ ▮ ⌸ ▲ ♣ P

EAST STOCKWITH

Ferry House Inn
24 Front Street
☎ (01427) 615276
11.30-3, 7-11; 12-4, 7-10.30 Sun

Bigfoot Genesis; John Smith's Bitter; Webster's Yorkshire Bitter; guest beer Ⓗ
Excellent pub catering for all ages, serving home-produced food at all times (except Mon eve) and local Bigfoot beer.
🏨 🏕 🛏 ◖ ▮ ♣ P

EASTOFT

River Don
Sampson Street (off A18 via Crowle/A161)
☎ (01724) 798040
12-2 (not Tue), 7-11; 12-5, 7-11 Sat; 12-5, 7-10.30 Sun

Barnsley Bitter; John Smith's Bitter; guest beers Ⓗ
Refurbished village local decorated with rural artefacts. The single large room has distinct drinking areas. Good value 'hot skillet' meals are available (not Sun eve). Guest beers come mainly from Yorkshire independents. It hosts regular party evenings and ferret racing.
🏨 🏕 ◖ ▮ ♣ P

EPWORTH

Red Lion Hotel
Market Place
☎ (01427) 872208
11-11; 12-10.30 Sun

Ind Coope Burton Ale; Tetley Bitter; guest beer Ⓗ
Residential, olde-worlde coaching inn serving good food in the bar, or delightful restaurant, from an extensive menu (sizzling steaks a speciality). The conservatory doubles as a family room.
🏨 🛏 🛏 ◖ ▮ P ✂

Try also: Queens Head (John Smith's)

FLIXBOROUGH

Flixborough Inn
1 High Street
☎ (01724) 863082
11-3, 5-11; 12-10.30 Sun

Beer range varies Ⓗ
Comfortable village local, strong on food and guest beers (three), it has a quiet lounge and public bar separated by a restaurant area. Families welcome for meals.
🏨 🏕 ◖ ▮ ⌸ ⌸ ♣ P

FRAMPTON

Moores Arms
Church End (take A16 1 mile E, from Kirton roundabout to Marsh)
☎ (01205) 722408
11.30-3, 6-11; 11.30-11 Sat; 12-10.30 Sun

Draught Bass; Bateman XB; guest beer Ⓗ
Very attractive, friendly village pub, dating back to the 1690s. Close to marshes and the famous Frampton RSPB reserve, it is popular with birdwatchers and walkers. An extensive, home-cooked menu is served in the bar and restaurant. Very family friendly.
🏨 🏕 ◖ ▮ ⌸ ⌸

FROGNALL

Goat
155 Spalding Road (B1525, 1½ miles E of Market Deeping)
☎ (01778) 347629
11-2.30 (3 Sat), 6-11; 12-3, 6.30-10.30 Sun

Adnams Bitter; guest beers Ⓗ
Spacious pub dating from the 1640s with a large garden featuring a play area for under-fives. It always has a good range of beers from micro-breweries (over 1275 served to date). Two dining areas offer good value food.
🏨 Q 🛏 🏕 🏕 ◖ ▮ ⌸ ▲ P

FULSTOW

Cross Keys
Main Street
☎ (01507) 363223
11-3, 7 (5.30 Wed-Fri)-11; (5.30-11 Wed-Fri); 11-11 Sat; 11-11 Sun

Draught Bass; John Smith's Bitter; Morland Old Speckled Hen; Theakston Mild; guest beers Ⓗ
Comfortable, welcoming village local, that serves excellent home-cooked meals in the dining room. Guest beers change regularly.
🏨 Q 🏕 ◖ ▮ ♣ P

GAINSBOROUGH

Eight Jolly Brewers
Ship Court, Silver Street
☎ (01427) 677128
11-11; 12-10.30 Sun

Caledonian Deuchars IPA; Highwood Tom Wood Best Bitter; Taylor Landlord; guest beers Ⓗ
Real ale haven serving nine beers at all times; twice runner-up for CAMRA *Pub of the Year*: a small bar and upstairs lounge, plus a food bar (no meals Wed).
Q ◖ ♣ ⌂ ✂ 🍴

GEDNEY DROVE END

New Inn
Main Road (follow B1359 off A17)
☎ (01406) 550389
12-4 (not Mon-Fri), 7-11; 12-4, 7-10.30 Sun

Elgood's Cambridge Bitter Ⓗ
This comfortable, welcoming pub, run by the same family for 23 years, houses a collection of porcelain pigs. A stall in the car park supplies freshly-grown produce from the landlord's smallholding. Booking essential for all meals.
🏨 Q 🏕 ◖ ▮ ⌸ ♣ ▲ P

GEDNEY DYKE

Chequers
Main Street (follow B1359 off A17)
☎ (01406) 362666
12-2, 7-11; 12-3, 7-10.30 Sun

Adnams Bitter; Elgood's Black Dog Mild; Everards Tiger; Greene King Abbot; Ⓗ
Country pub and restaurant serving top quality food. Dating from 1795, it lies in a quiet Fenland village and is well worth seeking out.
🏨 Q 🏕 ◖ ▮ P

GOSBERTON RISEGATE

Duke of York
106 Risegate Road (B1397, 1½ miles from Gosberton)
☎ (01775) 840193
12-11; 12-4, 7-10.30 Sun

Bateman XB; John Smith's Bitter; guest beers Ⓗ
Friendly, lively village local with a widespread reputation for good value beer and food. The multi-roomed interior includes a no-smoking dining room (no food Mon). The garden has a

The Good Beer Guide 2001

large play area.

🏠 🕯️ ◖ ▲ ♣ P

GRAINTHORPE

Black Horse
Mill Lane
☎ (01472) 388229
11-2 (12-3 Sat), 7-11; 12-3, 7-10.30 Sun

Donoghue Mollys Mild, Danny Boy Bitter, seasonal beers H
Thriving village local, popular with all ages and home of the recently established Donoghue's Brewery. Good value food and a warm welcome are assured.

🏠 Q 🕯️ ◖ ▶ ◲ P

GRANTHAM

Blue Pig
9 Vine Street
☎ (01476) 563704
11 (10.30 Sat)-11; 12-10.30 Sun

Castle Eden Ale; Flower's Original; Taylor Landlord; guest beer (occasional) H
Lovely olde-worlde pub boasting inglenook seating and a wealth of beams. Good home-cooked food at reasonable prices means this pub is often busy. Note the collection of pigs and other artefacts.

🏠 🕯️ ◖ ◲

Nobody Inn
North Street (near Asda)
☎ (01476) 565288
12-11; 12-10.30 Sun

Everards Tiger; guest beers H
This lively one-bar pub, run by one of Grantham's youngest licensees, attracts a good mix of customers. Big screen Sky TV sports, pool and darts feature.

≈ ♣

Shirleycroft Hotel
Harrowby Road (off A52 to Boston)
☎ (01476) 563260
11-11; 12-10.30 Sun

Draught Bass; Bateman XB; guest beer H
Victorian hotel, set back from the road, in its own grounds. One large drinking area has seating in a variety of nooks and crannies. A restaurant and American Diner serve a range of good value home-cooked food.

🕯️ ⇦ ◖ P

GREAT LIMBER

New Inn
High Street (A18)
☎ (01469) 560257
11-3, 6.30-11; 11-11 Fri & Sat; 12-10.30 Sun

Boddingtons Bitter; Samuel Smith OBB; Worthington Bitter; guest beer H

Quiet pub on the main road through the village, popular for its good food, served in the lounge. The traditional public bar is favoured by locals.

🏠 Q 🕯️ ⇦ ◖ ▶ ◲ ♣ P

GRIMSBY

Swigs
21 Osborne Street
☎ (01472) 354773
11-11; 7-10.30 Sun

Bateman XB; Willy's Original; guest beers H
Second outlet for Willy's of Cleethorpes; it serves excellent food at lunchtime (Mon-Sat) and is lively eves. Popular with locals and students, it has appeared annually in this *Guide* since 1991. ◖ ≈ (Town)

Tap & Spile
Haven Mill, Garth Lane (behind Freshney Place shopping centre)
☎ (01472) 357493
12-4, 7-11; 12-11 Fri & Sat; 12-4, 7-10.30 Sun

Beer range varies H
Excellent conversion of the ground floor of a renovated Victorian flour mill, offering a friendly welcome to all and up to eight beers. Regular music nights include folk and acoustic blues. Local CAMRA *Pub of the Year*.
≈ (Town) ♣ ○

Tivoli Tavern
14 Old Market Place
☎ (01472) 246911
11-11; 12-10.30 Sun

Draught Bass; Highgate Dark; Worthington Bitter H
Good honest drinkers' pub – no fancy gimmicks or themes, just an oasis of calm when escaping the nearby shopping centre. The award-winning National Fishing Heritage Centre is a ten-minute walk away.
≈ (Town)

Yarborough Hotel
29 Bethlehem Street (next to station)
☎ (01472) 268283
11-11; 12-10.30 Sun

Bateman Mild; Courage Directors; Theakston Best Bitter; guest beers H
Spacious and popular with all ages, this typical Wetherspoon's pub is well used at all times. Food served all day; no music. Local CAMRA *Pub of the Year* 1998 and '99.
Q 🕯️ ◖ ▶ & ≈ (Town) ○ ⚲ ⊞

HALTOFT END

Castle
Wainfleet Road (A52, 2 miles

NE of Boston)
☎ (01205) 760393
11-11; 12-10.30 Sun

Bateman Mild, XB; guest beer H
Friendly, roadside local that serves excellent value meals and has a large adventure playground for children.
🏠 Q 🕯️ ⇦ ◖ ▶ ♣ P

HAXEY

Loco
31 Church Street
☎ (01427) 752879
7-11; 12-4, 7-10.30 Sun

John Smith's Bitter; guest beer H
Friendly free house in a small village, this former Co-op has been transformed, with the front end of a steam loco set into a wall and a display of railway memorabilia. It hosts occasional gourmet eves and has featured on Yorkshire TV as an unusual pub.
🏃 ⇦ ▶ & ♣ ⚲

Try also: King's Arms (John Smith's)

HEIGHINGTON

Butcher & Beast
High Street
☎ (01522) 790386
11-4, 7-11; 11-11 Sat; 12-10.30 Sun

Draught Bass; Bateman XB, Valiant, XXXB; guest beer H
Popular local in a commuter village, its picturesque setting includes award-winning floral displays. Several drinking areas are normally well populated; note the beer engine behind the bar.
🏠 🏃 🕯️ ◖ & ♣ P ⊟

HEMINGBY

Coach & Horses
Church Lane (between A158/A153)
☎ (01507) 578280
12-2 (not Mon or Tue), 7 (6 Wed-Fri)-11; 12-3, 7-10.30 Sun

Bateman Mild, XB; guest beer H
Friendly, popular village local; the pleasant, cosy interior has a low beamed ceiling. The well-kept beer, food and good atmosphere make this pub worth a visit. Eve meals Wed-Sat.
🏠 Q 🕯️ ◖ ▲ ♣ P

HORNCASTLE

Admiral Rodney Hotel
North Street
☎ (01507) 523131
11-3, 5.30-11; 11-11 Sat; 11-10.30 Sun

Courage Directors; John Smith's Bitter H
Lively town-centre pub adjoining an hotel; the bar bears a maritime theme.
🕯️ ⇦ ◖ ▶ & P

182

LAUGHTERTON

Friendship Inn
Main Road
☎ (01427) 718681
11.30-2.30 (3 Sat), 6-11; 12-3, 7-10.30 Sun
Marston's Pedigree; guest beer 🄷
Comfortable village pub, comprising games, lounge and dining areas, serving home-cooked food. It also has its own caravan site and squash club. Live music performed Sun and alternate Fri eves. The house beer, Friendship Bitter, is of undisclosed local origin.
♨ ❀ ◖ ◗ ⛺ ♣ P

LINCOLN

Cornhill Vaults
Exchange Arcade, Cornhill
☎ (01522) 535113
11-11; 2-10.30 Sun
Samuel Smith OBB 🄷
19th-century, historic, city-centre cellar with the atmosphere of a village pub. An interesting menu of home-cooked food caters for vegetarians and vegans and changes frequently. An excellent juke box is switched on after 3pm; pool, darts and table football played.
♞ ◖ ⇌ (Central) ♣ 🚭

Dog & Bone
10 John Street (off Monks Rd, past college)
☎ (01522) 522403
12-3, 7-11; 12-3, 7-10.30 Sun
Bateman XB, Valiant, XXXB, seasonal beers 🄷
This pleasant and friendly one-roomed pub, displaying an array of old relics and Bateman's memorabilia, is popular with students. Lunchtime snacks served.
♨ ❀ ♿ ⇌ ♣ P 🍺

Golden Eagle
21 High Street (1 mile from centre)
☎ (01522) 521058
11-3, 5-11; 11-11 Fri & Sat; 12-10.30 Sun
Banks's Bitter; Bateman XB; Taylor Landlord; guest beers 🄷
Independent oasis in a sea of big brewery pubs in the south of the city. The boisterous public bar complements the quieter lounge. At least three interesting guest beers are on tap at any time. Now part of the Tynemill Group, it is handy for Lincoln City FC.
❀ ◖ ⊞ ♿ ♣ ⛵ P

Jolly Brewer
26 Broadgate
☎ (01522) 528583
11-11; 12-10.30 Sun
Draught Bass; Theakston XB; guest beers 🄷
Art Deco style, long-standing *Guide* entry of several distinctive drinking areas. Offering four varying guest beers at all times it is very popular, especially at weekends; good value Sun lunch served.
♨ ❀ ◖ ⇌ ⛵ P ♣

Lord Tennyson
72 Rasen Lane
☎ (01522) 889262
11-2.30, 5.30-11; 12-2.30, 7-10.30 Sun
Draught Bass; Tetley Bitter; guest beer 🄷
Named after the Lincolnshire Poet Laureate, this pub is close to the uphill tourist area but retains a local feel. Good value pub food includes special offers. The guest beer is from the Tapster's Choice range.
❀ ◖ ◗ ♣ P

Peacock
Wragby Road
☎ (01522) 524703
11.30-11; 12-10.30 Sun
Hardys & Hansons Mild, Best Bitter, Classic, seasonal beers 🄷
This friendly local can be lively at times. Good value food includes 'two for the price of one' offers.
♨ ❀ ◖ ◗ ♣ P

Post Office Sports & Social Club
Maitland Block, Dunkirk Road (off Burton Rd)
☎ (01522) 524050
11-3 (4 Sat), 7-11; 12-4, 7-10.30 Sun
John Smith's Bitter; guest beer 🄷
No-frills club, with the emphasis on beer during the week, becoming more family oriented at the weekend. Club prices prevail. Show a CAMRA membership card or this *Guide* to obtain entry.
♣ P

Queen in the West
12-14 Moor Street (off A57, Carholme road)
☎ (01522) 880123
12-3, 5.30-11; 11-11 Fri & Sat; 12-5, 7-10.30 Sun
Draught Bass; Morland Old Speckled Hen; Shepherd Neame Spitfire; John Smith's Bitter; Theakston XB; Wells Bombardier; guest beers 🄷
This two-room street-corner pub is a regular *Guide* entry, reflecting its commitment to real ale with eight beers usually available. Busy eves, quieter lunchtimes when good food is served (Mon-Fri).
◖ ⊞ ♣

Ritz
High Street (by St Marks shopping centre)
☎ (01522) 512103
11-11; 12-10.30 Sun
Bateman Mild, XXXB; Boddingtons Bitter; Courage Directors; Theakston Best Bitter; guest beers 🄷
Sensitive Wetherspoon's conversion of a former cinema in Art Deco style. It cannot be missed at night due to a riot of turquoise and pink neon, but inside a quiet, comfortable atmosphere pervades. The split-level drinking area features pictures of past film stars.
Q ◖ ◗ ♿ ⇌ 🚭

Sippers
26 Melville Street (near bus and rail stations)
☎ (01522) 527612
11-2, 5 (4 Fri; 7 Sat)-11; 7-10.30 (closed lunch) Sun
Courage Directors; Marston's Pedigree; Morland Old Speckled Hen; John Smith's Bitter; Theakston Mild; guest beers 🄷
Comfortable, two-roomed corner pub with a nice display of nautical items, offering two guest beers from independent brewers plus good value food (not served Sun or Sat eve). Deservedly a regular *Guide* entry.
◖ ◗ ⇌

Strugglers
83 Westgate (NW of castle)
☎ (01522) 535023
11.30-3, 5-11; 11.30-11 Fri & Sat; 12-10.30 Sun
Draught Bass; Marston's Pedigree; guest beers 🄷
Recently refurbished, and now back to its former glory, this pub has regained its previous loyal following. The bustling bar contrasts with the cosy snug. This pub is not child-friendly.
♨ Q ❀ ◖ ⊞ ♣

Varsity
20 Guildhall Street
☎ (01522) 544938
11-11; 12-10.30 Sun
Banks's Bitter; Marston's Pedigree 🄷
Recent open-plan conversion of the former main post office building in the centre of the city. It draws a mixed clientele during the day, but is noisy and popular with younger people eves. Food is served until 10pm (8pm Fri and Sat).
❀ ◖ ◗ ⇌ 🚭 🍺

Victoria
6 Union Road
☎ (01522) 536048
11-11; 12-10.30 Sun
Bateman XB; Everard's Old Original; Taylor Landlord; guest beers 🄷
A *Guide* regular, this back-street local behind the castle, is a gem, now a Tynemill pub. Food is served until 8.45pm weekdays. The beer

range usually features some of the many local micro-breweries' beers and a guest mild.

Q ❀ ◖▮ ☕ ⌂

LITTLE BYTHAM

Willoughby Arms
Station Road
☎ (01787) 410276
12-2, 5-11; 12-11 Sat; 12-10.30 Sun
Bateman XB; guest beers Ⓗ
Pub affording lovely rural views: a lounge bar, games room and a cellar bar, the venue for live music Fri and Sat. Good home-cooked food is served in the lounge or restaurant. The house beer is supplied by Newby Wyke. Beer fests held Bank holiday weekends.

🚶 ❀ 🛏 ◖▮ ♣ P ⛾

LOUTH

Masons Arms
Cornmarket
☎ (01507) 609525
11 (9.30 for coffee)-11; 12-10.30 Sun
Bateman Mild, XB, XXXB; Marston's Pedigree; Taylor Landlord; guest beer Ⓗ
18th-century posting inn located in the market square; a quiet comfortable lounge (children welcome until 9pm) and a wood-panelled bar. Good quality food is served in the lounge and upstairs restaurant.

Q 🛏 ◖▮ ▮ ♿

Newmarket Inn
133 Newmarket
☎ (01507) 605146
7-11; 12-3, 7-10.30 Sun
Castle Eden Ale; Highwood Tom Wood Shepherds Delight; guest beer Ⓗ
Cosy, two-roomed pub, popular with locals and theatre-goers alike, it is nicely decorated and without a juke box. Tennysons Tipple is a house beer from Highwood.

Q ❀

Wheatsheaf
62 Westgate
☎ (01507) 603159
11-3, 5-11; 11-11 Sat; 12-4, 7-10.30 (12-10.30 summer) Sun
Boddingtons Bitter; Flowers Original; Tipsy Toad Ale; guest beers Ⓗ
Popular pub dating from 1612, situated by St James church spire. A 'beer and bangers' event is held in May at this Louth CAMRA *Pub of the Year* 1999.

🚶 🛏 ❀ ◖P⛾

White Horse
Kenwick Road (A157, 1 mile from centre)
☎ (01507) 60331
11.30-3, 6-11; 12-3, 7-11 Sun

Draught Bass; Fuller's London Pride; Highwood Tom Wood Best Bitter Ⓗ
Fish is a speciality in the dining area; bar meals are also served. Outside bars open in the garden in summer; pool is played in the main bar.

❀ ◖ ♣ P

Woolpack
Riverhead
☎ (01507) 606568
11-3 (not Mon), 5-11; 11-11 Sat; 12-4, 7-10.30 Sun
Bateman Mild, XB, XXXB; Greene King Triumph; seasonal beers Ⓗ
Dating from the 18th-century, this welcoming local stands at the head of the Louth canal. Friendly staff, no loud music and traditional English home-cooking add to its appeal; Sun lunch is highly recommended (no food Sun eve or Mon). Louth CAMRA *Pub of the Year* 1997, '98 and 2000.

🚶 Q ❀ ◖▮ ♣ P

LUDFORD

White Hart Inn
Magna Mile
☎ (01507) 313489
12-5 (not Mon-Fri), 7-11; 12-5, 7-10.30 Sun
Greene King Abbot; Wells Bombardier; guest beers Ⓗ
Spacious, comfortable village pub with a pool room.

🚶 ❀ 🛏 ◖▮ ▮ A P

MALTBY-LE-MARSH

Crown Inn
Beesby Road (50 yds from A157/A1104 jct)
☎ (01507) 450349
11-3, 7-11 (closed Mon); 12-3, 7-10.30 Sun
Bateman XB, XXXB; guest beers Ⓗ
Picturesque, 18th-century, creeper-covered village inn. Inside the beams and walls are adorned with china jugs, sauce boats and other unusual knick-knacks. A reasonably-priced menu includes daily specials.

Q ❀ ◖▮ A P

MARKET DEEPING

Bull
The Market Place
☎ (01778) 343320
11-11; 12-10.30 Sun
Adnams Bitter; Everards Tiger; Old Original; guest beers Ⓗ
16th-century coaching inn: a front bar with an eating area, and a snug bar, the Dug Out, is down two steps at the back. It is named after a Papal Bull relating to Crowland Abbey across the Fen.

⛴ ❀ ◖ A ♣

Vine
19 Church Street
☎ (01778) 342387
11.30-2, 5.30-11; 11.30-5, 6.30-11 Sat; 12-3, 7-10.30 Sun
Wells Bombardier, Eagle; guest beer Ⓗ
This friendly local was originally a Victorian prep school; a busy front bar and a cosy lounge. Ask to see the model train set.

🚶 Q ❀ ♿ A ♣ P ⛾

MESSINGHAM

Horn Inn
High Street
☎ (01724) 762426
11-11; 12-10.30 Sun
John Smith's Bitter; guest beers Ⓗ
Friendly, roadside village local, attractively refurbished and extended. A strong emphasis is placed on home-cooked food; the central bar serves several discrete drinking areas. Brasses, pictures and photographs enhance the rural decor. Children welcome if dining (eve meals Thu-Sat). Two guest beers generally available. Wheelchair WC.

🚶 ❀ ◖▮ ♿ P

Try also: **Bird in the Barley**, Northfield Rd (Banks's)

MORTON

Crooked Billet
Crooked Billet Street (1 mile N of Gainsborough)
☎ (01427) 612584
11-11; 12-10.30 Sun
Fuller's London Pride; guest beers Ⓗ
Friendly village local whose landlord is keen to promote real ale. A games room with Sky TV and juke box, and two quieter rooms are served by a central bar with a drinking area. Occasional live music.

🚶 Q ◖▮ ▮ ♿ ♣

NETTLEHAM

Black Horse
Chapel Lane
☎ (01522) 750702
11.30-3 (4.30 Sat), 6-11; 12-5.30, 7-10.30 Sun
Bateman XB; Brains Dark; Highwood Tom Wood Best Bitter; Tetley Bitter; Theakston Best Bitter; guest beers Ⓗ
Attractive stone, mid-18th-century pub, with later alterations, it stands off the village green in the village centre. A large stone fireplace features in the lounge. Constantly changing guest beers, and live music eves (usually Tue) add interest. Eve meals finish at 8pm.

🚶 Q ◖▮ ▮ ♿ ♣

LINCOLNSHIRE

NETTLETON

Salutation Inn
Church Street
☎ (01472) 851228
12-3, 6-11; 12-3, 6-10.30 Sun
Draught Bass; Highwood Tom Wood Best Bitter; Taylor Landlord; Wadworth 6X; guest beers (occasional) H
A homely, relaxed atmosphere exists in this L-shaped room where good food is served and children are welcome. ❀ ◖ ▶ ♠ P

NORTH KELSEY

Butchers Arms
Middle Street
☎ (01652) 678002
4-11; 12-11 Sat; 12-10.30 Sun
Highwood Tom Wood Best Bitter, Tom Wood Harvest Bitter; Tom Wood Bomber County, guest beers (summer) H
Refurbished village local, a single room noted for its real fire, it is effectively the Highwood brewery tap.
▦ Q ❀ ♣ P

Try also: Queens Head, North Kelsey Moor (Free)

RUSKINGTON

Black Bull
10 Rectory Road
☎ (01526) 832032
11.30-2.30 (3 Fri & Sat); 6.30-11; 12-3, 7-10.30 Sun
Draught Bass; Bateman XB; guest beers (occasional) H
Comfortable, friendly, thriving village local with lively atmosphere, especially during Wed eve quiz nights. Note the quaint sculptures over the front entrance. Booking advised for Sun lunch and eve meals (no food Sun eve).
▦ ◖ ▶ ♿ ⚲ ♣ P

SANDTOFT

Reindeer Inn
☎ (01724) 710774
12-4 (not Mon-Thu), 6 (7 Fri & Sat)-11; 12-4, 7-10.30 Sun
John Smith's Bitter; Worthington Bitter; guest beers (occasional) H
Cosy, inviting country pub serving traditional, home-cooked food; very popular at weekends.
▦ ❀ ◖ ▶ P ✗

SAXILBY

Anglers
65 High Street
☎ (01522) 702200
11.30-2.30, 6 (5 Fr; 7 Sat)-11; 12-3, 7-10.30 Sun
Home Bitter; Theakston Best Bitter; guest beer H
Very much the village local,

table skittles are often played at lunchtime and other games teams are well supported. The name derives from anglers who once crowded the banks of the nearby Foss Dyke.
◲ ⚲ ♣ P

SCAMPTON

Dambusters Inn
High Street (B1398)
☎ (01522) 731333
12-3, 6-11; 12-3, 7-11 Sun
Greene King IPA, Abbot; guest beers (summer) H
Recently-opened village pub, with a heritage museum dedicated to the 617 Dambusters Squadron who were based at RAF Scampton. Rare archive material is displayed and aviation artwork is for sale.
▦ Q ◖ ▶ P

SCOTTON

Three Horseshoes
Westgate
☎ (01724) 763129
12-3 (not Mon-Fri), 7-11; 12-3, 7-10.30 Sun
Greene King IPA; John Smith's Bitter; guest beer H
Unspoilt village pub of three rooms, one is for games.
▦ Q ❀ ♣ P

Try also: White Swan, Scotter (Free)

SCUNTHORPE

Beckwood
Holme Lane, Bottesford (signed from A18)
☎ (01724) 856342
12-3, 6 (5 Fri)-11; 11-11 Sat; 12-10.30 Sun
Tom Wood Harvest Bitter; guest beer H
Estate pub whose plain exterior conceals a cosy, welcoming interior of a comfortable lounge and refurbished public bar. A regular outlet for local Highwood beers. Eve meals served Fri and Sat 6-8pm.
Q ❀ ◖ ▶ ♣ P

Blue Bell
Oswald Road
☎ (01724) 863291
11-11; 12-10.30 Sun
Courage Directors; John Smith's Bitter; Theakston Best Bitter; guest beers H
Wetherspoon's-style conversion of three former shop units. It offers three guest beers and food until 9pm. Very popular Fri and Sat eves. Q ❀ ◖ ▶ ♿ ⚲ P ✗

Honest Lawyer
Oswald Road
☎ (01724) 849906

11-11; 7-10.30 Sun
Beer range varies H
Small ground-floor bar with an upstairs drinking area. Seven handpumps provide an ever-changing selection of ales. ⚲

Malt Shovel
219 Ashby High Street, Ashby
☎ (01724) 843318
11-11; 12-10.30 Sun
Barnsley Bitter; Courage Directors; John Smith's Bitter; Theakston Old Peculier; Webster's Yorkshire Bitter; guest beers H
Converted snooker hall, located in busy shopping area, featuring country-style decor with oak beams and floral furnishings, and serving good value meals. Guest beers come from independent brewers. Licensed snooker facilities have been retained next door. ❀ ◖ ▶

Queen Bess
Derwent Road, Ashby (near A18/Grange Lane S jct)
☎ (01724) 840827
11.30-3.30 (4 Sat), 6-11; 12-3, 7-10.30 Sun
Samuel Smith OBB H
1960s estate pub drawing a loyal local following to its comfortable lounge and public bars. It has a large concert room and serves the best Sam Smith's in town.
▦ Q ❀ ◲ ♣ P

Try also: Riveter, Henderson Ave (Old Mill)

SKEGNESS

Vine Hotel
Vine Road, Seacroft (1 mile S of centre, off Drummond Rd)
☎ (01754) 763018
10-3, 6-11; 11-3, 6-10.30 Sun
Bateman Mild, XB, XXXB, seasonal beers H
Very attractive hotel, standing in peaceful surroundings away from the bustle of the resort. There are hints of a Tennyson connection and tales of smugglers and ghostly revenue men.
▦ Q ⚘ ▦ ◖ ▶ ◲ ♣ P

SOUTH FERRIBY

Nelthorpe Arms
School Lane (off A1077 to Barton)
☎ (01652) 635235
12-3, 6-11; 12-11 Sat; 12-4, 7-10 Sun
Bateman Mild or Theakston Mild; Tetley Bitter; guest beers H
Welcoming village local dating back to the 17th century: a smart well-appointed lounge/dining area and a rustic bar. Popular with walkers and cyclists.

185

lies close to the Viking Way. Live music performed Sat eve. The two guest beers come from independents.
🚪 Q ✿ 🛏 🌙 ⊟ ♣ P

Try also: **Hope & Anchor**, Sluice Rd (Mansfield)

SOUTH WITHAM

Blue Cow
26 Main Street
☎ (01572) 768432
12-3, 5-11; 11-11 Fri & Sat; 12-10.30 Sun
Blue Cow Thirwells Bitter, Cuddy Ale (occasional), **Premium** Ⓗ
Friendly local village pub serving beers brewed on the premises by the landlord. A stone-walled tap room leads into the panelled restaurant. A good choice of competitively priced food is served at all times; the buffet style lunches are popular.
🚪 Q 🌙 ⊟ & ♣ P

SPALDING

Birds
108 Halmer Gate (follow A151 off A16 bypass, heading into town)
☎ (01775) 723329
11-11; 12-10.30 Sun
Greene King IPA, Abbot; guest beer Ⓗ
Large, estate-style pub recently refurbished, part of the Hungry Horse brand, popular with the locals.
✿ 🌙 & ♣ P ✂

Lincoln Arms
4 Bridge Street
☎ (01775) 722691
11-3 (3.30 Sat), 7-11; 12-3, 7-10.30 Sun
Mansfield Mild, Riding Bitter, Bitter, seasonal beers Ⓗ
Traditional, 18th-century riverside local with a friendly atmosphere.
🛏 ≈ ♣

Lincolnshire Poacher
11 Double Street
☎ (01775) 766490
11-3, 5-11; 11-11 Sat; 12-3, 7-10.30 Sun
Theakston Best Bitter, XB, Old Peculier (winter); **guest beers** Ⓗ
Curiously owned by Hoskins but does not sell their beers. However it always offers four guest beers, with over 100 last year alone. This pleasant riverside pub attracts a lively clientele.
✿ 🛏 🌙 ≈

Try also: **Red Lion Hotel**, Market Place (Free)

SPRINGTHORPE

New Inn
16 Hill Road

☎ (01427) 838254
7-11 (closed Mon & Tue); 12-2, 7-10.30 Sun
Bateman XXXB; Marston's Pedigree Ⓗ
Very restricted opening hours (ring to check), but well worth the effort – if only to meet the infamous singing landlord. Eve meals may be booked.
🚪 Q 🌙 ⊟ P ⊟

STAMFORD

Green Man
29 Scotgate
☎ (01780) 753598
11-11; 12-10.30 Sun
Theakston Best Bitter; guest beers Ⓗ
Friendly local, a short walk from the town centre. An L-shaped, split-level, one bar pub, it always has several guest beers on tap, often from micro-breweries. Two cask ciders are always available and sometimes a perry (gravity dispense). No food Sun.
🚪 🌙 🛏 🌙 ≈ ⊖ ⊟

Lord Burghley
17 Broad Street
☎ (01780) 763426
11-11; 12-10.30 Sun
Draught Bass; Fuller's London Pride; Greene King Abbot; Worthington Bitter; guest beer Ⓗ
Five-roomed, friendly local in a traditional stone building. Occasional folk events are held in summer. A wide spectrum of the public uses the pub. Burghley House on the south side of Stamford, is open to the public.
🚪 Q 🌙 ≈ ♣

Periwig
Red Lion Square
☎ (01780) 762169
11-11; 12-10.30 Sun
Oakham JHB; John Smith's Bitter; Theakston XB; guest beer Ⓗ
Refurbished pub, featuring a large split-level bar; the upstairs balcony and room are popular with students. No food Sun.
🌙 ≈

Try also: **Crown Hotel**, Red Lion Sq (Free); **Daniel Lambert**, St Leonard's St (Free)

SURFLEET

Crown
6 Gosberton Road (B1356, opp. church)
☎ (01775) 680466
5-11; 12-3, 7-11 Sat; 12-3, 7-11 Sun
Bateman XB Ⓗ
Greatly refurbished and expanded, this comfortable pub boasts sofas, rocking chairs and open fires. It

serves regular bar snacks; more elaborate meals by arrangement.
🚪 Q P

Mermaid
2 Gosberton Road (B1356 near bridge)
☎ (01775) 680275
11.30-3, 6.30-11; 12-3, 7-10.30 Sun
Adnams Broadside; John Smith's Bitter; guest beers Ⓗ
In a former brewery on the River Glen this pub offers a warm atmosphere and great value meals in the bars and restaurant. Some visitors find the food too dominant eves and weekends. The large garden is ideal for children.
🚪 Q ✿ 🛏 🌙 P

SWINESHEAD

Wheatsheaf Hotel
Market Place
☎ (01205) 820349
12-2.30, 6-11; 12-11 Sat; 12-3, 7-10.30 Sun
Bateman XB; guest beers Ⓗ
Traditional two-bar pub in the village centre, offering excellent food in the bar or restaurant (not served Mon).
🚪 Q ✿ 🌙 ♣ P

THEDDLETHORPE

Kings Head
Mill Road (signed from coastal road, A1031)
☎ (01507) 338655
12-3, 7-11; 12-3, 7-10.30 Sun
Greene King IPA; guest beers Ⓗ
Modernised 16th-century thatched cottage pub of two oak-beamed rooms; one has a very low ceiling, so watch your head. A large garden has a children's play area with bouncy castle and climbing frame.
🚪 Q ✿ 🌙 ♣

THORNTON CURTIS

Thornton Hunt Inn
17 Main Street (A1077)
☎ (01469) 531252
12-3, 6.30-11; 12-3, 7-10.30 Sun
Taylor Landlord; Tetley Bitter; guest beer Ⓗ
One comfortable, attractively furnished room. The excellent and extensive range of home-cooked food draws diners from far and wide, especially at weekends. The guest beer is from Highwood. Children are welcome; there is a children's garden and 'fun trail'. ✿ 🛏 🌙 P

THREEKINGHAM

Three Kings Inn
Salters Way (100 yds S of A52)
☎ (01529) 240249
11-3, 7-11; 12-3, 7-10.30 Sun
Draught Bass; Black Sheep Best

CAMRA National Pub Inventory: Five Mile House, Duntisbourne Abbots, Gloucester

Bitter; Worthington Bitter Ⓗ
Welcoming village pub
standing close to the site of
the 9th century battleground
of Stow Green where
reputedly three Danish
chieftains were killed, hence
the names of the village and
pub – look for the effigies
above the entrance.
🏚 🕸 🌓 ▶ 🍴 ♣ P

TORKSEY

Castle Inn
Station Road (off A156, near
golf course)
☎ (01427) 718212
12-2 (not Tue), 6-11; 12-11 Sat; 12-
10.30 Sun
Home Bitter; guest beer
(summer) Ⓗ
Former Victorian farmhouse
and station hotel, now a
comfortable village inn
retaining lounge and public
bars. Good local facilities for
golf and fishing. Home-
cooked food includes a
weekly special.
🏚 Q 🕸 ⇔ 🌓 ▶ 🍴 🅰 ♣ P 🍴

WILLINGHAM-BY-STOW

Half Moon Inn
23 High Street
☎ (01427) 788340
12-2 (not Mon-Wed), 7-11; 12-3,
7-10.30 Sun
Castle Eden Ale; guest beers Ⓗ
Two-bar village inn, offering
a welcoming atmosphere and

good bar meals (fish & chip
night last Fri of month).
🏚 Q 🕸 🌓 ▶ 🍴 ♣ 🍴

Try also: Fox & Hounds
(Free)

WILLOUGHTON

Stirrup
1 Templefield Road
☎ (01427) 668270
12-3, 7-11; 12-3, 7-10.30 Sun
John Smith's Bitter; guest beer Ⓗ
Fine old stone pub drawing a
strong local following.
Interesting beers are always
on offer.
🏚 🕸 P

WOOLSTHORPE BY BELVOIR

Rutland Arms
Woolsthorpe Wharf,
Sedgebrook Road (1 mile E of
Belvoir Castle)
☎ (01476) 870111
12-3, 6-11; 11-11 Sat; 12-10.30 Sun
Draught Bass; Fuller's London Pride;
Tetley Bitter Ⓗ
Two-roomed country pub
next to the Grantham-
Nottingham Canal, very
popular with anglers and
walkers – it gets very busy in
summer. Campers and
caravanners are welcome.
Fresh home-cooked meals
served.
🏚 Q 🐎 🕸 🌓 ▶ 🍴 ♿ 🅰 ♣ P 🍴

WRAWBY

Jolly Miller
Brigg Road (A18)
☎ (01652) 655658
12-2, 5-11; 12-11 Sat; 12-10.30 Sun
Highwood Tom Wood Harvest Bitter;
guest beers Ⓗ
Small, single-room pub
fitted-out in comfortable
country inn style. It hosts
musical entertainment most
Sat eves. The pub grounds
include facilities for caravans.
🏚 🕸 ⇔ 🌓 ▶ 🅰 ♣ P 🍴

INDEPENDENT BREWERIES

Bateman: Wainfleet

Bigfoot: Blyton Carr

Bluebell: Whaplode St.
Catherine

Blue Cow: South Witham

DarkTribe: Gunness

Donoghue: Grainthorpe

Duffield: Harmston

Highwood: Melton
Highwood

King & Smart: Brookenby

Newby Wyke: Grantham

Oldershaw: Grantham

Orchard: Brigg

Willy's: Cleethorpes

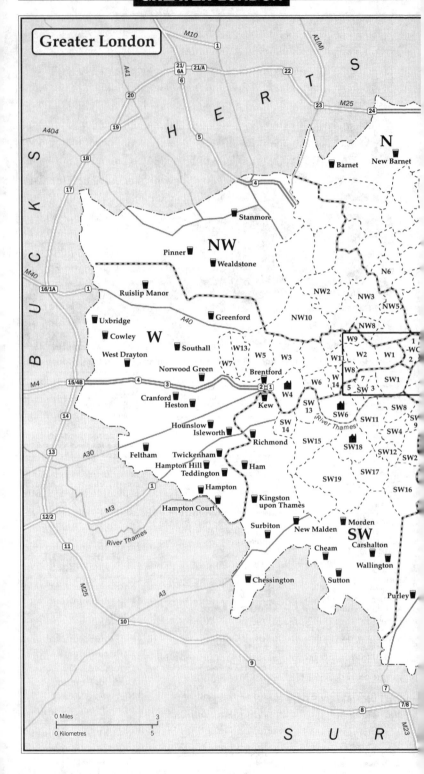

Greater London

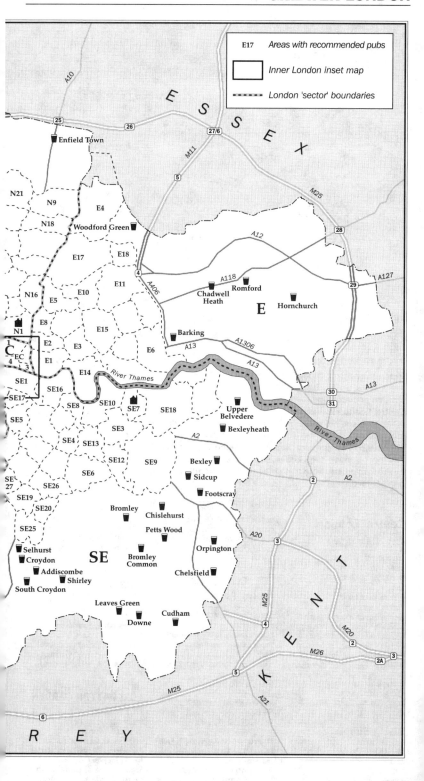

E17   *Areas with recommended pubs*

Inner London inset map

London 'sector' boundaries

E S S E X

Enfield Town

N21

N9

E4

N18

Woodford Green

E17

E18

N16

E11

E5

E10

A118

Chadwell Heath

Romford

E

Hornchurch

E8

N1

E15

Barking

1

C

EC

4 3

E2

E3

E6

A1306

E1

E14

River Thames

A13

A13

SE1

SE16

30

31

SE17

SE8

SE10

SE7

SE18

Upper Belvedere

SE5

Bexleyheath

SE4

SE13

SE3

A2

River Thames

SE12

SE9

Bexley

SE6

Sidcup

SE 27

SE26

Footscray

SE19

SE20

Bromley

Chislehurst

SE25

Petts Wood

Orpington

Selhurst

SE

Croydon

Bromley Common

Chelsfield

Addiscombe

Shirley

South Croydon

Leaves Green

Cudham

Downe

K E N T

R E Y

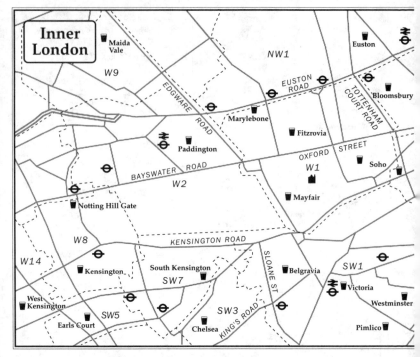

Inner London

Greater London is divided into seven areas: Central, East, North, North-West, South-East, South West and West, reflecting the London postal boundaries.

Central London includes EC1 to EC4 and WC1 and WC2. The other six areas have their pubs listed in numerical order (E1, E4, etc) followed in alphabetical order by the outlying areas which do not have postal numbers (Barking, Hornchurch, and so on).

The Inner London map, above, shows the area roughly covered by the Circle Line. Note that some regions straddle more than one postal district.

Central London

EC1: BARBICAN

Leopard
33 Seward Street
☎ (020) 7253 3587
11-11 closed Sat & Sun
Beer range varies H
Pub with a well-deserved following amongst locals, city workers and many from further afield. The large conservatory is complemented by a small courtyard garden. Very busy early eve, it supports local micros and serves an imaginative menu.
🏠 ⊛ ◖ ▶ ⇌ (Barbican/Old St) ⊖

Rising Sun
38 Cloth Fair
☎ (020) 7726 6671
11.30-11; 12-3, 7-11 Sat; 12-10.30 Sun
Samuel Smith OBB H
Back-street local in the heart

of the city. Carved wooden panels and pew seats add to the impression of a traditional London pub.
◖ ▶ ⇌ ⊖ ♣

EC1: CLERKENWELL

Crown Tavern
43 Clerkenwell Green
☎ (020) 7250 0757
11-11 (6 Sat); closed Sun
Fuller's London Pride; Tetley Bitter; Young's Bitter; guest beers H
Ex-Nicholson's pub with 'Heritage' status. Try to spot the snob screen.
◖ ⊖ (Farringdon)

Jerusalem Tavern
55 Britton Street
☎ (020) 7450 4281
11-11; closed Sat & Sun
St. Peter's Best Bitter, Extra, Fruit Beer, Wheat Beer, Strong Ale, seasonal beers A
Busy pub with an unusual layout; competition is high for the tiny raised seating

area. London's only St. Peter's tied house, it offers the full range of the brewery's bottled beers.
🏠 Q ⊛ ◖ ⇌ (Farringdon) ⊖

Sekforde Arms
34 Sekforde Street
☎ (020) 7253 3251
11-11; 12-4 Sun
Young's Bitter, Special, seasonal beers H
Small, wedge-shaped local near Clerkenwell Green.
🏠 ⛵ ⊛ ◖ ▶ ⇌ (Farringdon) ⊖ ♣

EC1: HATTON GARDEN

Old Mitre
9 Ely Place
☎ (020) 7405 4751
11-11; closed Sat & Sun
Friary Meux BB; Ind Coope Burton Ale; Tetley Bitter H
Small, two-bar pub that must be the hardest in London to find, but worth a visit to see

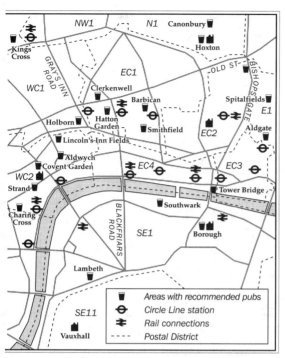

On the map:
- NW1
- Kings Cross
- N1 — Canonbury
- Hoxton
- GRAY'S INN ROAD
- OLD ST
- EC1
- WC1
- Clerkenwell
- Barbican
- Spitalfields
- E1
- BISHOPSGATE
- Holborn
- Hatton Garden
- Smithfield
- Aldgate
- EC2
- Lincoln's-Inn Fields
- Aldwych
- Covent Garden
- WC2
- EC4
- EC3
- Strand
- Tower Bridge
- Charing Cross
- Southwark
- BLACKFRIARS ROAD
- SE1
- Borough
- Lambeth
- SE11
- Vauxhall

Legend:
- Areas with recommended pubs
- Circle Line station
- Rail connections
- ---- Postal District

the 18th-century wood panelling.
Q ⊞ ⊖ (Chancery Lane)

EC1: SMITHFIELD
Melton Mowbray
14 High Holborn
☎ (020) 7405 7077
11-11; closed Sat & Sun
Fuller's Chiswick, London Pride, ESB, seasonal beers Ⓗ
Fuller's Ale & Pie house opposite the Prudential building. This refurbished commercial premises features lots of wood panelling and a gallery bar. Popular with local office workers.
⌾ ⍲ ⟋ ⇌ (Farringdon)
⊖ (Chancery Lane) ⊞

EC3: CITY
Lamb Tavern
10-12 Leadenhall Market
☎ (020) 7626 2454
11-9; closed Sat & Sun
Young's Bitter; Special, seasonal beers Ⓗ
Popular, friendly pub at the heart of the magnificent Leadenhall market.
⍲ ⇌ (Fenchurch St/Liverpool St)
⊖ (Monument) ⌿

Swan
Ship Tavern Passage, 78-80 Gracechurch Street
☎ (020) 7283 7712
11-9; closed Sat & Sun
Fuller's Chiswick, London Pride, ESB, seasonal beers Ⓗ
Small, popular pub with bars

on the ground and first floors. Busy lunch and early eves, occasionally stays open later if business is brisk.
⍲ ⇌ (Fenchurch St)
⊖ (Monument) ⊞

Three Lords
27 Minories
☎ (020) 7481 4249
11-11; closed Sat & Sun
Young's Bitter, Special, seasonal beers Ⓗ
Refurbished pub in a semi-modern block, with a comfortable basement bar.
Q ⍲ ⇌ (Fenchurch St)
⊖ (Aldgate/Tower Gateway)

EC4: CITY
Bell
29 Bush Lane
☎ (020) 7626 7560
11-10; closed Sat & Sun
Courage Directors; Shepherd Neame Spitfire Ⓗ
The pub is reputedly one of the oldest small pubs in the City of London and survived the Great Fire of London.
Q ⇌ (Cannon St) ⊖

Harrow
22 Whitefriars Street
☎ (020) 7427 0911
11-11; closed Sat & Sun
Draught Bass; Fuller's London Pride Ⓗ
Recently refurbished split-level single bar, off busy Fleet Street.
⍲ ⇌ (Blackfriars) ⊖

WC1: BLOOMSBURY
Calthorpe Arms
252 Grays Inn Road
☎ (020) 7278 4732
11-11; 12-10.30 Sun
Young's Bitter, Special, seasonal beers Ⓗ
Friendly, single-bar, corner pub that is popular with locals and office workers alike. The upstairs dining room is open lunchtimes; eve meals on request. ⌾ ⍲ ⇌ (Kings Cross) ⊖ (Russell Sq)

Kings Arms
11a Northington Street
☎ (020) 7405 9107
11-11; closed Sat & Sun
Greene King IPA; Marston's Pedigree; Wadworth 6X Ⓗ
This one-bar corner pub retains many of the better features from its days under Charringtons and is a welcome retreat from the bustle of nearby Grays Inn Road.
⌾ ⊖ (Russell Sq) ♣

Lamb
94 Lamb's Conduit Street
☎ (020) 7405 0713
11-11; 12-3.30, 7-10.30 Sun
Young's Bitter, Special, Winter Warmer Ⓗ
Attractive Grade II listed building furnished with green upholstery, snob screens and a snug to suit non-smokers. The pub also boasts a working music hall polyphon. The upstairs dining room serves excellent food Sun-Fri.
Q ⌾ ⍲ ⊖ (Russell Sq) ♣ ⌿

Old Monk
39-41 Grays Inn Road
☎ (020) 7831 0714
11-11; closed Sat & Sun
Adnams Bitter; Courage Directors; Fuller's London Pride; Greene King IPA Ⓗ
Very busy early eve, the range of beers in this converted wine bar can change, and may run down Fri eve. ⍲ ⊖ (Chancery Lane)

Pakenham Arms
1 Pakenham Street
☎ (020) 7837 6933
9am-1.30am
Fuller's London Pride, ESB; Harveys BB; Young's Bitter Ⓗ
This large friendly pub is popular with locals, office and postal workers. It serves six real ales, two on gravity. It has a licence extension from 9am to 1.30am every day, and serves breakfast, lunch and dinner.
⌾ ⍲ ⟋ ⊖ (Russell Sq) ♣

Rugby Tavern
19 Great James' Street
☎ (020) 7405 1384

191

The Good Beer Guide 2001

11-11 (12-3, 6-11 Sat summer); closed Sun

Shepherd Neame Master Brew Bitter, Best Bitter, Spitfire, seasonal beers H
Recently refurbished, one-bar pub serving local residents and the business community. It fields a regular darts team.
🍺 ◖ ▮ ⊖ (Russell Sq) ♣

Swan
7 Comso Place
☎ (020) 7837 6223
11-11; 12-10.30 Sun
Courage Directors; Greene King Abbot; Theakston Best Bitter, Old Peculier; guest beers H
One-bar, wood-panelled pub in a busy hotel and restaurant district. It regularly has two guest ales and serves food at all times.
◖ ▮ ⊖ (Russell Sq)

WC1: HOLBORN
Cittie of Yorke
22 High Holborn
☎ (020) 7242 7670
11.30 (12 Sat); closed Sun
Samuel Smith OBB H
Step into the back bar which resembles a baronial hall and be impressed by the vaulted ceiling, long bar, screenwork, booths and massive vats. A front bar, panelled and more intimate, lies above an extensive cellar bar. 🏛 Q 🍺
◖ ▮ ⊖ (Chancery Lane)

Overdraught's
6 Dane Street
☎ (020) 7405 6087
11.30-11; closed Sun
Thwaites Best Bitter; Forge Smithy; guest beer H
Small street-corner pub with a downstairs bar where you can usually be guaranteed at least one beer that's unusual for the area.
◖ ♣

Penderel's Oak
283-288 High Holborn
☎ (020) 7242 5669
11-11; 12-10.30 Sun
Boddingtons Bitter; Courage Directors; Fuller's London Pride; Theakston Best Bitter; guest beers H
Huge Wetherspoon's conversion with bars at ground floor and basement levels. Despite the size there are clear distinctions between the various drinking areas. A children's certificate operates weekends.
Q 🍺 ◖ ▮ ⊖ ⊬ ⊞

Three Cups
21-22 Sandland Street
☎ (020) 7831 4302
11-11; closed Sat & Sun
Young's Bitter, Special, seasonal beers H
Close to Grays Inn, this busy,

one-bar pub also has an upstairs room. It attracts a varied, convivial clientele.
🍺 ◖ ⊖

WC2: ALDWYCH
George IV
28 Portugal Street
☎ (020) 7831 3221
11-11; closed Sat & Sun
Draught Bass; Fuller's London Pride H
Impressive corner pub near the LSE and the Peacock Theatre. Note the large sign for Hoare and Co's Three Guinea Stout.
◖ ▮ ⊖ (Holborn)

WC2: CHARING CROSS
Lemon Tree
4 Bedfordbury
☎ (020) 7831 1391
11-11; 12-10.30 Sun
Courage Best Bitter; Shepherd Neame Spitfire H
Friendly pub, popular with staff from the Coliseum Theatre (home of the English National Opera). Sun lunch is a speciality.
◖ ▮ ≈ ⊖

Marquis of Granby
51 Chandos Place
☎ (020) 7836 7657
11-11; 12-10.30 Sun
Adnams Bitter; Marston's Pedigree; guest beers H
Narrow wedge-shaped pub with church-style partitions.
Q ◖ ▮ ≈ ⊖

Ship & Shovell
1-3 Craven Passage
☎ (020) 7839 1311
11-11; 12-9 Sat; closed Sun
Badger IPA, Dorset Best, Golden Champion, Tanglefoot H
Now a pub of two halves, as an extension has been opened on the opposite side of the passage, it is named after Sir Cloudesley Shovell who was shipwrecked off the Scilly Isles in the 18th century.
◖ ≈ ⊖ (Embankment)

WC2: COVENT GARDEN
Cross Keys
31 Endell Street
☎ (020) 7836 5185
11-11; 12-10.30 Sun
Courage Best Bitter, Directors; Marston's Pedigree H
Popular pub bedecked in greenery outside, while the interior houses much bric-a-brac including Beatles memorabilia.
Q ◖ ⊖

Hogshead
23 Wellington Street
☎ (020) 7836 6930
11-11; 12-8 Sun

Beer range varies H
Popular corner pub, handy for the Lyceum Theatre, London Transport Museum and all the other Covent Garden attractions.
◖ ≈ (Charing Cross)

Lamb & Flag
33 Rose Street
☎ (020) 7497 9504
11-11 (10.45 Fri & Sat); 12-10.30 Sun
Courage Best Bitter, Directors; Greene King IPA; Marston's Pedigree H
Historic pub, reputedly the oldest in Covent Garden, known at one time as the 'Bucket of Blood' because of prize fighting. It had connections with Samuel Butler and John Dryden who was mugged outside. Live jazz upstairs Sun eve.
≈ (Charing Cross) ⊖

Sun
21 Drury Lane
☎ (020) 7240 2489
11-11; closed Sun
Beer range varies H
Small, friendly pub which has now reverted to its original name. Toasted sandwiches are a speciality.
Q ⊖

WC2: HOLBORN
Newton Arms
31 Newton Street
☎ (020) 7242 8497
11-11; 11-3, 7-11 Sat; closed Sun
Adnams Bitter; Marston's Pedigree H
Friendly, modern pub in a 1960s office block. Weekday meals served.
◖ ▮ ⊖

WC2: LINCOLN'S INN FIELDS
Knights Templar
95 Chancery Lane
☎ (020) 7831 2660
11-11; 12-10.30 Sun
Boddingtons Bitter; Courage Directors; Fuller's London Pride; Theakston Best Bitter; guest beers H
High-ceilinged Wetherspoon's in a former bank, decorated in marble and gold. Raised no-smoking area at rear. It has possibly the most spacious ladies loos in London. A Woolwich cash machine is provided for customers.
Q ◖ ▮ 👵 ⊬ ⊞

Seven Stars
53 Carey Street
☎ (020) 7242 8521
11-11; closed Sat & Sun
Courage Best Bitter, Directors; Fuller's London Pride; Wells Bombardier; Young's Bitter; guest beer (occasional) H

Opened as the Leg & Seven
Stars in 1602, this unspoilt
pub is popular with the legal
profession. Toilets are
approached via a suicidally
steep staircase behind the
bar. May close early if quiet.
Q ◖ ⊖ (Temple)

WC2: SOHO
Moon Under Water
105-107 Charing Cross Road
☎ (020) 7287 6039
11-11; 12-10.30 Sun
**Boddingtons Bitter; Courage
Directors; Fuller's London Pride;
Theakston Best Bitter; guest
beers** H
Enormous Wetherspoon's
pub in the former premises of
the Marquee Club. A lift
serves the pub's three levels.
◖ ▶ ⑆ ⊖ (Leicester Sq) ⊞

WC2: STRAND
Edgar Wallace
40 Essex Street
☎ (020) 7353 3120
11-11; closed Sat & Sun
**Adnams Bitter; Boddingtons Bitter;
Flowers Original; Wadworth 6X;
Wells Bombardier; guest beers** H
Popular pub, and listed
building, named after the
author and playwright, close
to Temple Bar.
◖ ⊖ (Temple)

East London
E1: ALDGATE
Castle
44 Commercial Road
☎ (020) 7481 2361
11-11; closed Sat & Sun
**Courage Best Bitter, Directors;
Webster's Yorkshire Bitter; guest
beer** H
A beautiful mirrored wooden
bar, a back room and upstairs
games room in a building of
architectural merit; well
worth a visit. Try the salt
beef.
◖ ⊖ (East) ♣

E1: SPITALFIELDS
Pride of Spitalfields
3 Heneage Street
☎ (020) 7247 8933
11-11; 12-10.30 Sun
**Fuller's London Pride, ESB, seasonal
beers; guest beers** H
Busy, single-bar local also
used by the business
community. It features
photos of old East End
scenes, old bottles and
chamber pots. Good value
beer and handy for the curry
houses in Brick Lane.
🏠 ❀ ◖ ⊖ (Aldgate E)

E2: BETHNAL GREEN
Approach Tavern
47 Approach Road
☎ (020) 7980 2321
12 (11 Sat)-11; 12-10.30 Sun
**Adnams Bitter; Fuller's London
Pride; Marston's Pedigree;
Wadworth 6X** H
Very popular, friendly pub
with a spacious patio area in
front and an art gallery on
the first floor.
🏠 ❀ ◖ ▶ ≈ ⊖ ♣

Camdens Head
456 Bethnal Green Road
☎ (020) 7613 4263
11-11; 12-10.30 Sun
**Boddingtons Bitter; Courage
Directors; Theakston Best Bitter;
guest beers** H
Small, friendly local, part of
the Wetherspoon group, with
a shady, paved courtyard at
the rear. Q ❀ ◖ ▶ ≈ ⊖ ⊁ ⊞

E3: BOW
Coburn Arms
8 Coburn Road
☎ (020) 7980 3793
11-11; 12-10.30 Sun
**Young's Bitter, Special, seasonal
beers** H
Young's pub in a side street,
well served by public
transport. Popular with locals
who help create a warm
atmosphere.
◖ ▶ ⑆ ⊖ (Bow Rd) ♣

E4: CHINGFORD
Bull & Crown
The Green, Kings Head Hill
☎ (020) 8529 5773
11-11; 12-10.30 Sun
Ridleys IPA; Tetley Bitter H
Spacious two-bar pub, selling
possibly the cheapest pint for
miles around. A popular
music venue.
❀ 🏠 ◖ ⊞ ⑆ ≈ P

Kings Ford
250-252 Chingford Mount
Road
☎ (020) 8523 9365
11-11; 12-10.30 Sun
**Boddingtons Bitter; Courage
Directors; guest beers** H
Popular pub in the middle of
a bustling shopping area; it
gets very busy weekend eves
and frequently stocks up to
four guest ales. Q ◖ ▶ ⑆ ⊁ ⊞

Kings Head
26 Kings Head Hill
☎ (020) 8529 1655
11-11; 12-10.30 Sun
Beer range varies H
Hilltop pub, next to the
police station, now owned by
Punch Taverns, but has a
three-year contract for guest
ales. It features a central
island bar. ❀ ◖ ▶ ≈ P

E5: CLAPTON
Anchor & Hope
15 High Hill Ferry (off Mt.
Pleasant Lane/Big Hill)
☎ (020) 8806 1730
11-3, 5.30 (6 Sat)-11; 12-4, 7-10.30
Sun
Fuller's London Pride, ESB H
Popular riverside pub, local
CAMRA *Pub of the Year* 1999.
The landlord is approaching
his 50th year behind the bar
here.
❀ ≈

Princess of Wales
146 Lea Bridge Road
☎ (020) 8533 3463
11-11; 12-10.30 Sun
**Young's Bitter, Special, seasonal
beers** H
Large riverside pub; spot the
herons, but watch out for
cyclists.
Q ❀ ◖ ▶ ⊞ ≈ ♣ P

E6: EAST HAM
Millers Well
419-423 Barking Road
☎ (020) 8471 8404
11-11; 12-10.30 Sun
**Courage Directors; Greene King
Abbot; Shepherd Neame Spitfire;
Theakston Old Peculier; Wadworth
6X; guest beers** H
Spacious Wetherspoon's pub
opened in 1993; converted
from a wine bar, and
extended into shop premises
next door in 1997. Decorated
in typical JDW style with old
photos and information
boards. Six regular and two
guest beers on handpump
and St Peter's bottled beers.
Q ◖ ▶ ⊖ ⊁ ⊞

E8: HACKNEY
Prince Arthur
95 Forest Road
☎ (020) 7254 3439
11.30-11; 11.30-4, 7-11 Sat; 12-4,
7-10.30 Sun
**Adnams Bitter; Fuller's London
Pride; Greene King Abbot** H
Popular with locals and well
worth seeking out. This very
friendly side-street pub is in
its 18th consecutive year in
the *Guide*.
🏠 ❀ ◖ ▶ ≈ (Central) ♣

E10: LEYTON
Drum
557 Lea Bridge Road
☎ (020) 8539 6577
11-11; 12-10.30 Sun
**Courage Directors; Theakston Best
Bitter; guest beer** H
Untypical Wetherspoon's
house divided into areas, it is
small for this chain; a
popular local. Q ❀ ◖ ▶
≈ (Walthamstow Central) ⊖ ⊁ ⊞

William IV
816 High Road
☎ (020) 8556 2460
11-11; 12-10.30 Sun

Fuller's London Pride, ESB;
Woodforde's Wherry; guest beers Ⓗ
Large traditionally decorated
East End pub with a relaxed
atmosphere. Committed to
good real ale – don't let the
wine bar signs put you off.
🏠🍴◑ ▶

Birkbeck Tavern
45 Langthorne Road
☎ (020) 8539 2584
11-11; 12-10.30 Sun
Courage Best Bitter; guest beers Ⓗ
Extensive 19th-century
building where two bars offer
a very wide range of guest
beers, in a back street near
Leyton station. 🏠 🍴 ⊖ ♣

North Star
24 Browning Road
☎ (020) 8532 2421
11-11; 12-10.30 Sun
Draught Bass; Fuller's London Pride;
guest beers Ⓗ
Decorated with railway items
to commemorate the North
Star – a steam loco, it stands
in a quiet conservation area
best reached on foot from the
station. 🚶 🏠 ◑ 🍴 ⊖

Try also: Walnut Tree, High
Rd (Wetherspoon's)

E11: WANSTEAD
Duke of Edinburgh
79 Nightingale Lane
☎ (020) 8989 0014
11-11; 12-10.30 Sun
Adnams Bitter; Young's Bitter; guest
beers Ⓗ
Excellent local that caters for
all ages.
Q ◑ ▶ ⊖ (Snaresbrook) ♣

E14: LIMEHOUSE
Grapes
76 Narrow Street
☎ (020) 7987 4396
12-3, 5.30 (7 Sat)-11; 12-3, 7-10.30
Sun
Adnams Bitter; Ind Coope Burton
Ale; Marston's Pedigree Ⓗ
Small, comfortable pub:
downstairs a narrow panelled
bar and a restaurant
(specialising in seafood)
above. Enjoy spectacular
views from the riverside deck.
🚶 Q 🏠 ◑ ▶ ⇌ ⊖ (DLR) ♣

E14: WESTFERRY
Oporto Tavern
43 West India Dock Road
☎ (020) 7987 3620
11-11; 12-10.30 Sun
Beer range varies Ⓗ
Down-to-earth local on the
edge of docklands. Weekday
lunches served.
🏠 ◑ ⊖ (DLR) ♣

E15: STRATFORD
Golden Grove

146-148 The Grove
☎ (020) 8519 0750
11-11; 12-10.30 Sun
Boddingtons Bitter; Shepherd
Neame Spitfire; Theakston Best
Bitter; guest beers Ⓗ
Very popular town-centre
pub where food is available
all day.
Q 🏠 ◑ 🍴 ♿ ⇌ ⊖ ⏚ P ⊬ ⊞

King Edward VII
47 Broadway
☎ (020) 8221 98419
12-11; 12-10.30 Sun
Badger Tanglefoot; Draught Bass;
Fuller's London Pride; Shepherd
Neame Bishop's Finger Ⓗ
Large two-bar pub;
previously, (and still by
many) called the Prussia, but
understandably the name
was changed. Meals served
12-7.
🏠 ◑ ▶ ⇌ ⊖ (DLR)

E17: WALTHAMSTOW
Flowerpot
128 Wood Street
☎ (020) 8223 9941
12 (11 Sat)-11; 12-10.30 Sun
Draught Bass Ⓗ
This old-fashioned local is a
long-standing *Guide* entry.
🏠 ⇌ (Wood St.)

Village
31 Orford Road
☎ (020) 8521 8892
11-11; 12-10.30 Sun
Beer range varies Ⓗ
Pleasant local with a quiet
snug. Popular at weekends, it
has a large paved garden. No
food Mon.
🚶 Q ⏟ 🏠 ◑ ⇌ (Central) ⊖

E18: SOUTH WOODFORD
George
70 High Road
☎ (020) 8532 2441
12-11; 12-10.30 Sun
Draught Bass; Fuller's London
Pride Ⓗ
18th-century building
comprising a long L-shaped
drinking area and a pleasant
eating area away from the
main bar. Piped music, but
generally a quiet pub on a
busy main road, offering
good wheelchair access.
Weekend meals served 12-5.
🏠 ◑ ▶ ♿ ⊖ P

BARKING
Britannia
1 Church Road (near A123)
☎ (020) 8594 1305
11-3, 5-11; 11-11 Sat; 12-10.30 Sun
Young's Bitter, Special, Winter
Warmer, seasonal beers Ⓗ
Young's East London
outpost: a spacious saloon
and a basic public bar. Note
the caryatids on the outside

of the pub – a now rare
example in East London.
Local CAMRA *Pub of the Year*
2000.
🏠 ◑ ▶ ⏚ ⇌ ⊖ ♣ P

CHADWELL HEATH
Eva Hart
1128 High Road (A118)
☎ (020) 8597 1069
11-11; 12-10.30 Sun
Boddingtons Bitter; Courage
Directors; Shepherd Neame Spitfire;
Theakston Best Bitter; guest
beers Ⓗ
Converted police station,
now a Wetherspoon's
featuring a raised no-
smoking/eating area, plus a
balcony. The present
management is keen on guest
beers, stocking up to four
including a regional brew
(normally from Greene King
or Ridley).
Q 🏠 ◑ ▶ ♿ ⇌ P ⊬ ⊞

HORNCHURCH
Chequers
North Street (near A124)
☎ (01708) 442094
11-11; 11-3, 5.30-11 Fri & Sat; 12-4,
7-10.30 Sun
Friary Meux BB; Young's Bitter;
guest beers Ⓗ
Small, traditional, local on a
traffic island. It offers
excellent value beers
including a house beer from
Ind Coope. It is always busy
especially on darts nights.
Local CAMRA *Pub of the Year*
1997, '98 and '99.
◑ ⇌ (Emerson Pk) ♣ P

ROMFORD
Moon & Stars
99-103 South Street (near
A125)
☎ (01708) 730117
10-11; 12-10.30 Sun
Boddingtons Bitter; Courage
Directors; Greene King Abbot;
Theakston Best Bitter; guest
beers Ⓗ
Popular with all ages; families
are welcome in the outside
drinking area.
Q 🏠 ◑ ▶ ⇌ ⊬ ⊞

WOODFORD GREEN
Cricketers
299-301 High Road (A11)
☎ (020) 8504 2734
11-3, 5.30-11; 11-11 Fri & Sat; 12-
10.30 Sun
McMullen AK, Country, Gladstone,
seasonal beers Ⓗ
Comfortable, friendly two-
bar local stocking the full
range of Mac's beers
including seasonal brews. It
stands close to the famous
statue of Sir Winston
Churchill on the green.
🏠 ◑ ⏚ P

Travellers Friend
496-498 High Road (A104)
☎ (020) 8504 2435
11-11; 12-4, 7-10.30 Sun
Courage Best Bitter, Directors; Fuller's London Pride; Greene King Abbot; Ridleys IPA; guest beers (occasional) H
Small, friendly, local boasting wood panelling and snob screens. Run by a friendly couple who have never sold keg bitter. Good value meals. Limited parking. Try your luck at Perudo, a Peruvian dice game. Q ♦ ╆ P

Try also: Hogshead, Cranbrook Rd, Ilford (Hogshead)

North London

N1: CANONBURY
Compton Arms
4 Compton Avenue
☎ (020) 7359 6883
11-11; 12-10.30 Sun
Greene King Martha Greene, IPA, Abbot H
Country pub in London: a small, cottage-style local in a side street comprising a front bar with a small room behind. Sky TV is on a large screen for sport; it can get very busy at weekends. No eve meals Tue. ✿ ◖ ▶
≢ (Highbury & Islington) ⊖

Marquess Tavern
32 Canonbury Street
☎ (020) 7354 2974
11-11; 12-10.30 Sun
Young's Bitter, Special, seasonal beers H
Grand Victorian bar with public, saloon and food areas (meals 12-9.30, not Sun). Its fine interior was preserved by Young's when they took over in 1979. ✿ ✿ ◖ ▶ ≢ (Essex Rd) ⊖ (Highbury & Islington) ♣

N1: HOXTON
Wenlock Arms
26 Wenlock Road
☎ (020) 7608 3406
12-11; 12-10.30 Sun
Beer range varies H
Lively street-corner local for a new century; up to eight ales on tap including a mild. Live jazz and the famous salt-beef 'sandwedges' are added attractions.
✿ ≢ (Old St) ⊖ ♣ ⌣

N6: HIGHGATE
Flask Tavern
77 Highgate West Hill
☎ (020) 8340 7260
11-11; 12-10.30 Sun
Adnams Bitter; Greene King Abbot; Marston's Bitter; Morland Old Speckled Hen; Tetley Bitter; Young's Bitter H

Very attractive, 17th-century pub of various small rooms on different levels with flagstone floors; previously used by both famous and infamous London characters. The large heated outside drinking area is always very popular. ✿ ✿ ◖ ▶ ⊖ (Highgate/Archway) ♣

Gatehouse
1 North Road
☎ (020) 8340 8054
11-11; 12-10.30 Sun
Draught Bass; Courage Directors; Greene King Abbot; Shepherd Neame Spitfire; Theakston Best Bitter; guest beers H
Traditional pub, a well-established part of Highgate village life. The pub and its site are steeped in local history dating back to the 14th century and boasts two active ghosts. The pub's theatre stages regular performances. ✿ Q ✿ ◖ ▶ & ⊖ (Archway) ╆ ⊞

N9: LOWER EDMONTON
Beehive
24 Little Bury Street
☎ (020) 8360 4358
12 (11 summer)-11; 12-10.30 Sun
Adnams Bitter; Ansells Bitter; Tetley Bitter; guest beer H
Friendly 1930s local in a residential area comprising one large comfortable bar. Eve meals served 6-8 except Sun when lunch is available 12-5.30.
✿ ◖ ▶ ♣ P

N16: STOKE NEWINGTON
Rochester Castle
145 Stoke Newington High Street
☎ (020) 7249 6016
11-11; 12-10.30 Sun
Boddingtons Bitter; Courage Directors; Fuller's London Pride; Greene King Abbot; Hop Back Summer Lightning; guest beers H
Large friendly local featuring alcove seating, the original (listed) tilework on the walls and a doorstep mosaic. Food served all day (until 9.30 Sun).
Q ✿ ◖ ▶ ✿ ♣ ╆ ⊞

N18: UPPER EDMONTON
Gilpins Bell
50-54 Fore Street
☎ (020) 8884 2744
11-11; 12-10.30 Sun
Boddingtons Bitter; Courage Directors; Shepherd Neame Spitfire; Theakston Best Bitter; guest beers H
Large pub of several distinct drinking areas, including a family section, it features

portraits of the Cecil family, once large local landowners. It gets packed shoulder to shoulder when nearby Spurs are playing at home; door staff on duty at weekends. Wheelchair WC.
✿ Q ✿ ✿ ◖ ▶ & P ╆ ⊞

N21: WINCHMORE HILL
Dog & Duck
74 Hoppers Road
☎ (020) 8886 1987
11-11; 12-10.30 Sun
Boddingtons Bitter; Greene King IPA; Wadworth 6X; Young's Special H
Friendly, back-street local recently refurbished without any loss of character. Loyal regulars enjoy the enclosed garden, playing shove ha'penny and watching TV sport. ✿ ✿ ≢ (Palmers Green/Winchmore Hill) ♣

Half Moon
749 Green Lanes
☎ (020) 8360 5410
11-11; 12-10.30 Sun
Draught Bass; Courage Best Bitter, Directors; Greene King IPA; guest beers H
Long, narrow shop conversion, popular with locals.
◖ ▶ ≢

Orange Tree
18 Highfield Road
☎ (020) 8360 4853
12-11; 12-10.30 Sun
Greene King IPA; guest beers H
Popular local hideaway, just off Green Lanes serving reasonably priced, good value meals (booking advised). A big screen TV is provided for sport; occasional live music. The large garden has a play area and barbecue. Local CAMRA *Pub of the Year* 1999 and 2000. ✿ ◖ ♣

BARNET
Albion
74 Union Street
☎ (020) 8441 2841
11-11 (11-2.30, 4.30-11 Mon & Tue Jan-March); 12-10.30 Sun
Greene King IPA, Abbot; Ind Coope Burton Ale H
Small, welcoming local, tucked away off the High Street. Formerly two cottages, the Albion retains the feel of a two-bar pub. It retains an outside gents' toilet.
✿ ⊖ (High Barnet) ♣ ⌣ P

Barnet Conservative Club
33 High Street
☎ (020) 8449 0400
11-3, 6-11; 12-3, 7-10.30 Sun
Greene King IPA; guest beer H
Spacious, two-bar High Street club, the front bar is for

members only, a warm welcome is extended to card-carrying CAMRA members and bearers of this *Guide*. Guest beers may not always be available.
Q ⊖ (High Barnet) ♣ P

King William IV
18 Hadley Highstone, Hadley
☎ (020) 8449 6728
11-3, 5.30-11 (11-11 Mon, Wed & Sat summer); 12-4, 7-10.30 (12-10.30 summer) Sun
Adnams Bitter; Benskins BB; Hook Norton Best Bitter; Ind Coope Burton Ale; guest beer (occasional) ℍ
Country-style, 17th-century inn on the very edge of London, close to Hadley Common, site of the Battle of Barnet. Quiet and characterful with warm, intimate drinking areas, it has a new restaurant at the rear. A house ale, Hadley Bitter, is brewed by Ushers.
🏭 Q 🏵 ◖ ▶

Olde Mitre
58 High Street
☎ (020) 8449 6582
11-11; 12-10.30 Sun
Adnams Bitter; Ind Coope Burton Ale; Tetley Bitter; guest beers ℍ
Grade II-listed, 17th-century, wood-panelled, former coaching inn, now an ale house. One bar serves three split-level drinking areas. TV for sport. Eve meals served Mon-Fri 5-7.
◖ ▶ ⊖ (High Barnet) ♣ P

NEW BARNET
Hadley Hotel
113 Hadley Road
☎ (020) 8449 0161
11-11; 12-10.30 Sun
Fuller's London Pride; Marston's Pedigree; Morland Old Speckled Hen ℍ
Comfortable Victorian hotel hidden away in leafy suburbia; ideal after a stroll through Hadley Woods. Note the recent mural in the snug depicting the Battle of Barnet. No food Sun; eve meals available Thu-Sat. 🏵 🛏 ◖ ▶

ENFIELD TOWN
Old Wheatsheaf
3 Windmill Hill
☎ (020) 8363 0516
11-11; 12-2, 7-10.30 Sun
Adnams Bitter; Benskins BB; Tetley Bitter; guest beers ℍ
Expensive, traditional two-bar pub with notable floral displays and a body-building gym at the rear. Pictures of old Enfield decorate the saloon bar. Weekday lunches served.
◖ 🍴 ≈ (Enfield Chase) ♣

North West London
NW1: EUSTON
Head of Steam
1 Eversholt Street
☎ (020) 7388 2224
11-11; 12-10.30 Sun
Beer range varies ℍ
Unusual pub at the front of Euston station. Opened in its present form in 1995, it is full of railway memorabilia and transport models, most of which are for sale. Monthly beer festivals and Sky TV (not intrusive) feature in CAMRA's North London *Pub of the Year* 1999. Eve meals 5-8, Mon-Fri. No food Sun.
◖ ▶ ≈ ⊖ ♣ ◡ ⌣ 🍴 ▶

NW1: KING'S CROSS
Euston Flyer
83-87 Euston Road
☎ (020) 7383 0856
11-11; 12-6 Sun
Fuller's Chiswick, London Pride, ESB, seasonal beers; guest beer ℍ/ⓖ
Large open-plan pub divided into different sections, opened in 1998. It can sometimes be boisterous eves and hosts occasional beer festivals; large screen Sky TV. Closed some Sat eves in football season. Meals served all day until 9 (7 Sat and Sun). ◖ ▶ 🪑 ≈ ⊖ 🍴

NW2: CRICKLEWOOD
Beaten Docket
50-56 Cricklewood Broadway
☎ (020) 8450 2972
11-11; 12-10.30 Sun
Courage Directors; Greene King Abbot; Theakston Best Bitter; guest beers ℍ
Nothing like the losing ticket after which it's named, this Wetherspoon's is something of a beacon in an area not known for quality ale.
Q 🏵 ◖ ▶ 🪑 ≈ 🍴

NW3: BELSIZE PARK
Washington
50 Englands Lane
☎ (020) 7722 6118
11-11; 12-10.30 Sun
Ind Coope Burton Ale; Marston's Pedigree; Tetley Bitter; Young's Bitter; guest beers ℍ
Magnificent Victorian pub boasting its original tiling, etched glass and mirrors. Home to several sports teams and the Hampstead Comedy Club (Sat). It opens 10am weekdays for breakfast.
🏵 ◖ ▶ ⊖ ♣

NW3: HAMPSTEAD
Duke of Hamilton
23-25 New End

☎ (020) 7794 0258
12-midnight (no entry after 11pm); 12-10.30 Sun
Fuller's London Pride, ESB; guest beer ℍ
Friendly, single bar pub just off busy Heath Street, popular with locals, sports fans and patrons of the New End Theatre next door. Local CAMRA *Pub of the Year* 1997, it offers good value for the area.
Q 🏵 ⊖ ◡ 🍴

NW5: KENTISH TOWN
Pineapple
51 Leverton Street
☎ (020) 7209 4911
12 (11 Sat)-11; 12-10.30 Sun
Boddingtons Bitter; Brakspear Bitter; Marston's Pedigree ℍ
Unchanging, family-run, cosy, back-street oasis with a loyal following.
≈ ⊖ ♣

NW8: ST. JOHNS WOOD
Clifton
96 Clifton Hill
☎ (020) 7624 5233
11-11; 12-10.30 Sun
Adnams Bitter; Greene King Abbot; Marston's Pedigree; Tetley Bitter; guest beer ℍ
Wonderful villa-style pub with a bar and two other rooms, although it originally had four. Built as a house in 1837, it became a pub in 1894. Lots of wood and an unusual Temperance Society mirror feature; Sky TV in one room. Weekend food available all day.
🏵 ◖ ▶ ♣

NW10: HARLESDEN
Coliseum
26 Manor Park Road
☎ (020) 8961 6570
11-11; 12-10.30 Sun
Boddingtons Bitter; Courage Directors; Shepherd Neame Spitfire; Theakston Best Bitter; guest beers ℍ
Imaginative conversion of a former cinema, the original Art Deco 1929 version achieved fame in its own right in *The Blue Lamp*. Q 🏵 ◖ ▶ 🪑 ≈ (Willesden Jct) ⊖ 🍴

Grand Junction Arms
Acton Lane
☎ (020) 8965 5670
11-11; (1am Fri; 12.30am Sat); 12-10.30 Sun
Young's Bitter, Special, seasonal beers ℍ
With moorings on the Grand Union Canal and a large garden, this spacious pub has three contrasting bars. No admission after 10.30 Fri or Sat, when there is live music in the back bar, and late

night snacks. Children's certificate.

🕭 🍺▌ 🏧 🖶 P

PINNER

Queens Head
31 High Street
☎ (020) 8868 9844

11-3.30, 5-11; 12-3.30, 7-10.30 Sun

Adnams Bitter; Benskins BB; Fuller's London Pride; Greene King Abbot; Tetley Bitter; Young's Special Ⓗ

Grade II listed building, the oldest pub in Pinner, where parts date back to1540, although an alehouse is believed to have been on this site since the first Pinner fair in 1336. Well worth a visit. Non-smoking area available at lunchtime.

🚰 Q 🕭 🍺▌ P 🍴

Try also: **Oddfellows**, Waxwell Lane (Carlsberg-Tetley)

STANMORE

Malthouse
7 Stanmore Hill
☎ (020) 8420 7265

4-11 (midnight Wed & Thu); 12-10.30 Sun

Beer range varies Ⓗ

Recently given a makeover by the licensee and regulars, this pub is still the most enterprising in the area. A true community pub, it offers beers from far and wide and theme eves on Sat, usually with free food.

🚇

Vine
154 Stanmore Hill
☎ (020) 8954 4676

12-11; 12-10.30 Sun

Adnams Bitter; Ind Coope Burton Ale; Tetley Bitter; guest beers Ⓗ

Old coaching inn at the top of Stanmore Hill where separate drinking areas have been retained despite just the one bar.

🕭 🍺▌ 🍀 P

WEALDSTONE

Royal Oak
60 Peel Road
☎ (020) 8427 3122

12-11; 12-10.30 Sun

Adnams Bitter; Ind Coope Burton Ale; Tetley Bitter; guest beers Ⓗ

The public bar has been lost in the recent refurbishment, but this 1930s pub is still a haven in a town that is becoming drowned in fake 'Oirish' bars. Pleasant conservatory to the rear. Limited parking. 🍺▌ ≋ (Harrow & Wealdstone) 🚇 🍀 P

Try also: **Sarsen Stone**, High St (Wetherspoon's)

South East London

SE1: BOROUGH

George Inn ☆
77 Borough High Street
☎ (020) 7407 2056

11-11; !2-10.30 Sun

Boddingtons Bitter; Greene King Abbot; Flowers Original; Fuller's London Pride; guest beer Ⓗ

Large galleried coaching inn rebuilt in the 17th century and now owned by the National Trust. The old bedrooms have been converted to dining rooms. Restoration Ale is brewed for the pub by Crouch Vale. No food Sun eve. Q 🕭 🍺▌ 🏧 ≋ (London Bridge) 🚇 🍀

Market Porter
9 Stoney Street
☎ (020) 7407 2495

11-11; 12-10.30 Sun

Beer range varies Ⓗ

Large, friendly wood-panelled pub overlooking Borough market. Up to eight real ales available at any one time; it has served over 1000 in the last two years, mainly from micro-breweries.
🍺▌≋ (London Bridge) 🚇

Royal Oak
44 Tabard Street
☎ (020) 7357 7173

11-11; closed Sat & Sun

Harveys XX Mild, Pale Ale, BB, Armada, seasonal beers Ⓗ

The only Harvey's pub in London, tricky to find but worth it, for the traditional decor and lack of music or machines. Q 🍺▌ 🏧 ≋ (London Bridge) 🚇 🍀

Shipwrights Arms
88 Tooley Stret
☎ (020) 7378 1486

11-11; 12-10.30 Sun

Beer range varies Ⓗ

Large free house close to Tower Bridge and the tourist attractions on Tooley Street. Andy Bishop's Bitter (brewed for the pub by Crouch Vale) is usually available.
🍺▌≋ (London Bridge) 🚇

Wheatsheaf
6 Stoney Street
☎ (020) 7407 1514

11-11

Beer range varies Ⓗ

Small, unpretentious, back-street market pub – worth a visit. English/Irish bands perform first Sun of the month, otherwise closed Sun. Revised Thameslink 2000 plans have removed the threat of demolition.
🍺▌≋ (London Bridge) 🚇

SE1: LAMBETH

Windmill

44 Lambeth High Street
☎ (020) 7735 1698

11-9; closed Sat & Sun

Courage Best Bitter; Tetley Bitter Ⓗ

Attractive pub near Lambeth Bridge, hidden behind the fire station. It gets very busy at lunchtime. 🚇 🍺▌
≋ (Vauxhall) 🚇 (Lambeth N)

SE1: SOUTHWARK

Mad Hatter Hotel
3-7 Stamford Street
☎ (020) 7401 9222

11-11; 12-10.30 Sun

Fuler's Chiswick, London Pride, ESB Ⓗ

This is an excellent conversion by Fuller's of an old office building into a traditional pub and hotel. Note the nice collection of hats. Good quality food at reasonable prices. 🛏 🍺▌ ♿
≋ (Blackfriars) 🚇 🍴

SE1: TOWER BRIDGE

Pommelers Rest
196-198 Tower Bridge Road
☎ (020) 7378 1399

11-11; 12-10.30 Sun

Boddingtons Bitter; Courage Directors; Fuller's London Pride; Theakston Best Bitter; guest beers Ⓗ

Wetherspoon's pub with a family room (open until 9) close to Tower Bridge. Food served all day.
Q 🐕 🍺▌ ≋ (London Bridge) 🚇 ♨

SE3: BLACKHEATH

Hare & Billet
1a Eliot Cottages
☎ (020) 8852 2352

11-11; 12-10.30 Sun

Adnams Bitter; Boddingtons Bitter; Flowers Original; Wadworth 6X; guest beers Ⓗ/Ⓖ

Medium-sized Hogshead pub on the village side of Blackheath, overlooking one of the ponds. No-smoking area closes at 9.
Q 🍺▌ ≋ 🍴

SE4: CROFTON PARK

Brockley Jack
410 Brockley Road
☎ (020) 8699 3966

12-11; 12-10.30 Sun

Greene King IPA, Abbot; guest beers Ⓗ

Large coaching inn acquired by Greene King from the Magic Pub Company. With a fringe theatre at the side it attracts a mixed clientele. Wierd wicker and brass is suspended everywhere. Well worth a visit. 🕭 🍺▌ ≋ 🍀

SE5: CAMBERWELL

Fox on the Hill

149 Denmark Hill
☎ (020) 7738 4756
11-11; 12-10.30 Sun
Boddingtons Bitter; Courage Directors; Greene King Abbot; Shepherd Neame Spitfire; Theakston Best Bitter; guest beers Ⓗ
Large, brick Wetherspoon's pub near Kings College Hospital, featuring extensive paved and planted areas to the front and rear. The London Eye, some three miles away, can clearly be seen from the front gardens. Cider stocked in summer.
Q ⛲ ❀ ◖▶ ᕐ ≈ (Denmark Hill) ᗡ P ✄

SE6: CATFORD
Catford Ram
9 Winslade Way
☎ (020) 8690 6206
11-11; 12-10.30 Sun
Young's Bitter, Special, Winter Warmer Ⓗ
Modernised and now more spacious, local in Catford shopping centre, run by a friendly management; excellent food. Near the Lewisham theatre, home of the Catford Beer Festival.
◖▶ ᕐ ≈ ♣

SE8: DEPTFORD
Dog & Bell
116 Prince Street
☎ (020) 8692 5664
12-11; 12-10.30 Sun
Fuller's London Pride, ESB; guest beers Ⓗ
Very popular back-street local, twice SE London CAMRA *Pub of the Year*, stocking a good range of guest beers and whiskies; reputedly haunted.
Q ❀ ◖▶ ≈ ♣ ⊞

SE9: ELTHAM
Howerd Club
447 Rochester Way
☎ (020) 8856 7212
12-3 (not Mon-Fri), 7.30-11; 12-2.30, 7.30-10.30 Sun
Fuller's London Pride; Shepherd Neame Master Brew Bitter; guest beers Ⓗ
Former CAMRA National *Club of the Year* attached to St Barnabas church hall. Popular with the local community who warmly welcome visitors. The guest beer changes regularly.
Q ❀ ≈

SE10: GREENWICH
Ashburnham Arms
25 Ashburnham Grove
☎ (020) 8692 2007
12-3, 6-11; 12-3, 7-10.30 Sun
Shepherd Neame Master Brew Bitter, Best Bitter, Spitfire, seasonal beers Ⓗ

Cosy, award-winning Shepherd Neame pub, a short walk from the station. Eve meals available Tue and Fri. Attractions include bar billiards and a regular quiz (Tue).
❀ ◖▶ ≈ ⊖ (DLR) ♣

Plume of Feathers
19 Park Vista
☎ (020) 8858 0533
12-11; 12-10.30 Sun
Adnams Bitter; Boddingtons Bitter; Morland Old Speckled Hen; Webster's Yorkshire Bitter; guest beers Ⓗ
Oldest pub in Greenwich, next to the park and handy for the observatory, National Maritime Museum and Royal Naval College. Its walled garden is ideal for children. ❀ ◖▶ ≈ (Maze Hill)

Trafalgar Tavern
Park Row
☎ (020) 8858 2437
11.30-11; 12-10.30 Sun
Courage Best Bitter, Directors; Morlands Old Speckled Hen; guest beer Ⓗ
Large, Regency-style riverside pub built in 1836 bearing a naval theme. A former Evening Standard *Pub of the Year*. Eve meals served Tue-Sat. ᨀ ᕐ ◖▶ ᗡ ≈ (Maze Hill) ⊖ (Cutty Sark DLR)

SE10: NORTH GREENWICH
Pilot
68 River Way
☎ (020) 8858 5910
11-11 (midnight Fri & Sat); 12-10.30 Sun
Fuller's London Pride, ESB; Young's Special Ⓗ
Built in 1801, this pub has been given a new lease of life as the closest pub to the Millennium Dome. The licensee was one of the first to be awarded a *Cask Marque*.
ᨀ ᕐ ❀ ➡ ◖▶ P ✄ ⊞

SE12: LEE
Crown
117 Burnt Ash Hill
☎ (020) 8857 6607
11-11; 12-10.30 Sun
Young's Bitter, Special, seasonal beers Ⓗ
Attractive pub in a residential area, just off the South Circular road. The verandah at the front overlooks the paved drinking area.
❀ ◖▶ ≈ ♣ P

SE13: LEWISHAM
Hogshead
354 Lewisham High Street
☎ (020) 8690 2054
11-11; 12-10.30 Sun
Boddingtons Bitter; Marston's

Pedigree; Ⓗ **guest beers** Ⓗ/Ⓖ
Small, attractive pub north of Lewisham Hospital. It offers friendly, efficient service in comfortable, well-maintained surroundings. Barbecues held in the garden in summer.
❀ ◖▶ ≈ (Ladywell) ♣

SE16: ROTHERHITHE
Mayflower
117 Rotherhithe Street
☎ (020) 7237 4088
12-11; 12-10.30 Sun
Greene King IPA, Triumph, Abbot, guest beer Ⓗ
Historic 17th-century riverside pub, from which the Pilgrim Fathers are reputed to have set sail for America. Enjoy superb views from the jetty drinking area. No food Mon or Sun eve.
❀ ◖▶ ⊖

SE17: WALWORTH
Beehive
60-62 Carter Street
☎ (020) 7703 4992
11-11; 12-10.30 Sun
Courage Best Bitter, Directors; Fuller's London Pride; Wadworth 6X Ⓗ
Fine, solid back-street local offering a warm welcome. Note the large selection of malt whiskies. Within walking distance of Kennington Park it is deservedly popular and well worth the search.
❀ ◖▶ ≈ (Elephant & Castle) ⊖ (Kennington)

SE18: WOOLWICH
Prince Albert (Rose's)
49 Hare Street
☎ (020) 8854 1538
11-11; 12-3 Sun
Beer range varies Ⓗ
Outstanding wood-panelled pub near the ferry roundabout. Good value hot and cold snacks are available throughout the day. A rare venue for bar billiards. Real cider is available weekends.
≈ (Arsenal) ♣ ᗡ ⊟

SE19: CRYSTAL PALACE
Occasional Half
2 Anerley Hill
☎ (020) 8778 8211
11-11; 12-10.30 Sun
Courage Best Bitter; Flowers Original; Young's Bitter; guest beer Ⓗ
Lively, spacious pub serving a good selection of food. An area is set aside for non-smokers from 12-7. Occasional real ale festivals held.
❀ ◖▶ ᕐ ≈ ✄

SE19: GIPSY HILL
Railway Bell
14 Cawnpore Street
☎ (020) 8670 2844
11-3, 5.30 (6 Sat)-11; 12-3, 6-10.30 Sun

Young's Bitter, Special Ⓗ
Popular with diners at lunchtime; more cosmopolitan eves; barbecues in summer. Hidden in the back streets near the station, the pub recently won a brewery award for its food.
🏶 🍺 ▲ ⇌ ♣

SE20: PENGE
Moon & Stars
164-166 High Street
☎ (020) 8776 5680
11-11; 12-10.30 Sun

Boddingtons Bitter; Courage Directors; Theakston Best Bitter; guest beers Ⓗ
Large Wetherspoon's pub with a local feel. Three guest beers always available, it hosts a beer festival in spring and autumn. Next to Sainsbury's superstore it is always busy. Weston's Old Rosie cider always available.
Q 🏶 🍺 ▶ ♿ ⇌ (Penge E/Kent House) ⊖ (Beckenham Rd Tramlink) 🍺 P ✂

SE25: SOUTH NORWOOD
Alliance
91 High Street
☎ (020) 8653 3604
11-11; 12-10.30 Sun

Courage Best Bitter; guest beers Ⓗ
Traditional, very popular street-corner pub near the station with a long, rather narrow bar. Food (served weekdays) includes 'real' sausages. May close Sat afternoons during football season.
🍺 ⇌ (Norwood Jct) ♣

Clifton Arms
21 Clifton Road
☎ (020) 8771 2443
12 (11 Sat)-11; 12-10.30 Sun

Adnams Bitter; Fuller's London Pride; Greene King IPA; guest beers Ⓗ
Traditional street-corner pub close to Selhurst Park football ground; very busy before and after matches. Guest beers, often including a mild, come from small independent brewers. No food Sun. 🏶 🍺 ⇌ (Selhurst/Norwood Jct) ⊞

Portmanor
1 Portland Road (A215)
☎ (020) 8655 1308
11-11; 12-10.30 Sun

Courage Best Bitter; Fuller's London Pride; Greene King Abbot; guest beers Ⓗ
Well-patronised free house

with an adventurous guest beer policy of supporting micro-breweries at reasonable prices. The bar menu is geared to suit all tastes or visit the comfortable upstairs Manor Restaurant. Sun eve meals end at 7.
🏶 🍺 ▶ ⇌ (Norwood Jct) ⊖ (Harrington Rd Tramlink)

SE26: UPPER SYDENHAM
Dulwich Wood House
39 Sydenham Hill
☎ (020) 8693 5666
11-11; 12-10.30 Sun

Young's Bitter, Special, seasonal beers Ⓗ
Traditional local run by friendly staff and management. A boules piste features in the large garden which has a children's play area; also home to a golfing society. Enjoy good views of London from the car park. Buses 63 and 202 stop outside. Q 🏶 🍺 🍺 ⇌ (Sydenham Hill) ♣ P

SE27: WEST NORWOOD
Hope Tavern
49 Norwood High Street
☎ (020) 8670 2035
11-11; 12-10.30 Sun

Young's Bitter, Special, seasonal beers Ⓗ
Friendly corner local with a central bar; one of Young's longest-held pubs.
🏶 🍺 ⇌

ADDISCOMBE
Claret Free House
5a Bingham Corner, Lower Addiscombe Road (A222)
☎ (020) 8656 7452
11.30-11; 12-10.30 Sun

Palmers IPA; Shepherd Neame Spitfire; guest beers Ⓗ
Only 50 yards from the new tram stop stands this small, single-bar free house where the emphasis is on quality, quantity and conversation. The owners are enthusiastic supporters of small independent breweries and always offer three or four guest beers which change regularly.
⊖ (Addiscombe Tramlink)

BEXLEY
Cork & Cask (off-licence)
3 Bourne Parade, Bourne Road
☎ (01322) 528884
11-2, 4-10; 10-10 Sat; 12-3, 7-10 Sun

Beer range varies Ⓖ
Off-licence with usually five real ales and two real ciders available (range varies), plus an excellent selection of

British and foreign bottled beers. Over 650 different real ales sold in five years. Containers sold.
⇌ 🍺

Kings Head
65 Bexley High Street
☎ (01322) 526112
11-11; 11-4, 6-11 Sat; 12-4, 7-10.30 Sun

Courage Best Bitter; Greene King IPA, Abbot Ⓗ
Historic, 16th-century, timber-framed building boasting genuine oak beams, at the heart of old Bexley village; a very popular, welcoming pub.
🏶 🍺 ⇌ P

BEXLEYHEATH
Robin Hood & Little John
78 Lion Road
☎ (020) 8303 1128
11-2.30, 5.30 (7 Sat)-11; 12-4, 7-10.30 Sun

Courage Best Bitter; Flagship Futtock; Shepherd Neame Spitfire; Taylor Landlord; guest beers Ⓗ
Friendly, back-street local with a drinking area on the forecourt. Enjoy the daily themed lunches (Mon-Sat) sitting at tables made from old sewing machines. Over 21s only admitted. Bexley CAMRA *Pub of the Year* 2000.
🏶 🍺

Royal Oak (Polly Clean Stairs)
Mount Road
☎ (020) 8303 4454
11-3, 6-11; 11-11 Sat; 12-3, 7-10.30 Sun

Courage Best Bitter; guest beers Ⓗ
Attractive, historic weather-boarded building with horse-brasses, plates and tankards hanging from the ceiling. This country pub was overtaken by 1930s housing estates. Choose from lots of different seating areas. Children only allowed in the garden. Q 🏶 P

Try also: **Jolly Millers,** Mayplace Road West (Free)

BROMLEY
Bitter End (off-licence)
139 Masons Hill
☎ (020) 8466 6083
12-3 (not Mon), 5-10 (9 Mon); 11-10 Sat; 12-2, 7-9 Sun

Beer range varies Ⓖ
Off-licence offering a wide range of cask ales and ciders: typically four or five ales and three or four ciders in the week, more at weekends. It also sells an excellent range of bottled beers from Britain and abroad. Containers also sold. ⇌ (South) 🍺

199

Bricklayers Arms
141-143 Masons Hill
☎ (020) 8460 4552
11-3.30 (3 Sat), 5.30 (5 Fri; 7 Sat)-11; 11-3, 7-10.30 Sun
Shepherd Neame Master Brew Bitter, Best Bitter, Spitfire, Bishops Finger Ⓗ
Lively local on the busy A21 out of Bromley. A good choice of food is served lunchtime; eve meals must be booked.
❀ ◖ ≈ (South)

Bromley Labour Club
HG Wells Centre, St. Marks Road
☎ (020) 8460 7409
11-11, 12-10.30 Sun
Shepherd Neame Master Brew Bitter; guest beers Ⓗ
Very friendly social club, close to Bromley South station. Non-members need to be signed in; CAMRA members are requested to show membership cards.
❀ ≈ (South) ♣ ⚬

Red Lion
10 North Road
☎ (020) 8460 2691
11-11, 12-10.30 Sun
Beards Best Bitter; Harveys BB; Greene King Abbot; guest beers Ⓗ
Back-street local with a very friendly staff; a recent SE London CAMRA *Pub of the Year*. The TV is only used for major sports events. Eve meals finish at 7pm; no food Sun. Look out for the original tiling as you enter.
Q ❀ ◖ ≈ (North) ♣

BROMLEY COMMON
Bird in Hand
62 Gravel Road, Keston (near Bromley bus garage)
☎ (020) 8462 1083
11-11; 12-10.30 Sun
Courage Best Bitter; guest beers Ⓗ
Lovely, comfortable back-street pub stocking three guest beers, favouring regional brewers. ❀ ◖

Two Doves
37 Oakley Road, Keston (off A21)
☎ (020) 8462 1627
12-3, 5.30 (5 Mon & Fri; 6 Sat)-11; 12-3, 7-10.30 Sun
Draught Bass; Courage Best Bitter; Young's Bitter; guest beers Ⓗ
Very homely pub on the edge of Bromley Common and woods, where there is always a friendly welcome in comfortable surroundings. A good selection of guest beers is served in rotation. Bus 320 stops outside.
Q ❀ ◖

CHELSFIELD
Five Bells
Church Road (1 mile from

M25 jct 4)
☎ (01689) 821044
11-3, 6-11; 12-4, 7-10.30 Sun
Courage Best Bitter; guest beer Ⓗ
In the same family for over 65 years, this unspoilt village local draws a very friendly crowd and has an excellent and adventurous real ale policy. Good value food with a speedy service.
Q ❀ ◖ ◗ P

Kent Hounds
Well Hill (off A224)
OS497643
☎ (01959) 534288
11-2.30, 5.30-11; 12-3, 7-10.30 Sun
Courage Best Bitter, Directors; Marston's Pedigree; Shepherd Neame Master Brew Bitter Ⓗ
Simple village pub where the rather cluttered interior includes a collection of key fobs hanging from the ceiling. Good value food (groups should book in advance).
⚏ ❀ ◖ ◗ P

CHISLEHURST
Bull's Head
Royal Parade (A208)
☎ (020) 8467 1727
11-11; 12-10.30 Sun
Young's Bitter, Special, seasonal beers Ⓗ
Very pleasant, spacious Young's pub and hotel. No hot food in the lounge bar just sandwiches and snacks (no meals Sun eve). Voted Kent CAMRA Town *Pub of the Year* 1999.
Q ◗ ❀ ⚏ ⚬ ◖ ◗ P ⚬

Sydney Arms
Old Perry Street
☎ (020) 8467 3025
11-3, 5.30-11; 11-11 Fri & Sat; 12-10.30 Sun
Courage Best Bitter, Directors; guest beers Ⓗ
Pleasant, traditional pub in a smart area, convenient for Scadbury Park nature reserve.
❀ ◖ ◗ P

CROYDON
Dog & Bull
24 Surrey Street (off High Street)
☎ (020) 8667 9718
11-11; 12-10.30 Sun
Young's Bitter; Special, seasonal beers Ⓗ
Popular market street pub in a Grade II listed building with a large garden. In 1995 the pub and market, which has a royal charter were visited by Prince Charles. Food served until 9pm.
Q ❀ ◖ ◗ ≈ (East/West) ⊖ (George St/Church St Tramlink) ♣

Hogshead
60 High Street (A235)

☎ (020) 8667 0684
11-11; 12-10.30 Sun
Boddingtons Bitter; Flowers Original; Fuller's London Pride; Wadworth 6X; Ⓗ **guest beers** Ⓖ/Ⓗ
Conversion of a former bank to provide drinking areas on two floors. Bare boards and stone floors contrast with metal ventilation ducting. Popular eves, when it can get noisy. Meals served 12-8.
◖ ◗ ≈ (East/West) ⊖ (George St/Church St Tramlink) ⚬

Princess Royal
22 Longley Road (off A213/A235)
☎ (020) 8240 0046
11-3, 5.30 (8 Sat)-11; 11-11 Fri; 12-3, 8-10.30 Sun
Greene King XX Mild, IPA, Triumph, Abbot, seasonal beers; Ruddles County Ⓗ
Small, one-bar pub with a warm welcome enhanced by a log fire in winter. Food is served till 10.30 (not Sun eve). Jugs hang from the ceiling and limited edition plates top the bar. No fruit machines. The garden features a fish pond.
⚏ Q ❀ ◖ ◗ ≈ (West) ♣

Royal Standard
1 Sheldon Street (off High St)
☎ (020) 8688 9749
11.30-11; 12-10.30 Sun
Fuller's Chiswick, London Pride, ESB, seasonal beers Ⓗ
Small, back-street corner pub in the old town, dwarfed by a multi-storey car park. One central bar serves three rooms; the garden across the road is almost under the A232 flyover. Q ❀ ◖ ◗
≈ (East/West) ⊖ (Church St/George St Tramlink) ♣

CUDHAM
Blacksmiths Arms
Cudham Lane South (near Biggin Hill) OS445601
☎ (01959) 572678
11-11; 12-10.30 Sun
Courage Best Bitter, Directors; Fuller's London Pride; Shepherd Neame Spitfire; guest beers Ⓗ
Spacious country pub on the border of Greater London and Kent, with a pleasant atmosphere. Classic car enthusiasts gather here (first Sun each month).
⚏ Q ❀ ◖ ◗ ⚒ P ⚬

DOWNE
George & Dragon
26 High Street
☎ (01689) 889031
12-3, 5.30-11; 12-11 Fri & Sat; 12-10.30 Sun
Draught Bass; Fuller's London Pride; Hancock's HB Ⓗ
Very comfortable pub in a conservation village in lovely

countryside, convenient for Darwin's Downe House. Very popular for meals (not served Sun eve). The house beer is M&B Brew XI rebadged.
🏚 🕸 🌣 ◖ ✦

Queens Head
25 High Street
☎ (01689) 852145
11-11; 12-10.30 Sun
Ind Coope Burton Ale; Young's Bitter; guest beer H
Very popular village local where the large public bar is good for ramblers. A comfortable saloon bar, very nice children's room and a dining room complete this traditional pub. No meals Sun eve. 🏚 Q 🐸 🕸 🌣 ◖ 🍴 ✦ ✂

FOOTSCRAY

Seven Stars
Footscray High Street
☎ (020) 8300 2043
11.30-11; 12-5 (closed eve) Sun
Adnams Bitter; Draught Bass; Greene King IPA H
16th-century pub retaining many original features.
🕸 ◖ P

LEAVES GREEN

Kings Arms
Leaves Green Road (A233, N of Biggin Hill)
☎ (01959) 572514
11-11; 12-10.30 Sun
Courage Best Bitter; Harveys BB; Young's Special H
One of the oldest pubs in the borough, with parts dating to the 15th century. Beer is expensive, but it is well worth a visit. Its 'olde-worlde' charm is somewhat marred by constant background music.
🏚 🕸 ◖ 🌣 🍴 ⚘ ✦ P

ORPINGTON

Cricketers
93 Chislehurst Road
☎ (01689) 812648
12-3, 5-11; 12-11 Sat; 12-10.30 Sun
Adnams Broadside; guest beers H
Friendly pub with a large family room. It usually serves a range of Adnams beers.
🐸 🕸 P

PETTS WOOD

Sovereign of the Seas
109-111 Queensway
☎ (01689) 891606
11-11; 12-10.30 Sun
Boddingtons Bitter; Courage Directors; Shepherd Neame Spitfire; Theakston Best Bitter; guest beers H
One-bar Wetherspoon's serving the community, featuring beer festivals and cheap beer promotions.
Q 🕸 ◖ 🌣 ⚘ ⇆ 🌣 ✂

PURLEY

Foxley Hatch
8-9 Russell Hill Parade, Russell Hill Road (A23, one-way system)
☎ (020) 8963 9307
11-11; 12-10.30 Sun
Boddingtons Bitter; Courage Directors; Greene King Abbot; Theakston Best Bitter; guest beers H
A smaller Wetherspoon's pub serving a predominantly local trade. The L-shaped bar is decorated with pictures of old Purley (once known as Foxley) whilst the rear 'snug' displays pictures of foxes. It offers regular price promotions and beer festivals.
Q ◖ ◗ ⚘ ⇆ 🌣 ✂ 🌣

SELHURST

Two Brewers
221 Gloucester Road (off A213)
☎ (020) 8684 3544
11-11; 12-10.30 Sun
Shepherd Neame Master Brew Bitter, Best Bitter, Spitfire, Bishops Finger H
Fine, low-ceilinged community pub which feels like a country inn. One central bar serves several drinking areas. A rare outlet in the area for Shep's ales; note: a cask breather is used on seasonal beers. No food weekends.
🕸 ◖ ⇆ ⚘

SHIRLEY

Orchard
116 Orchard Way (off A232)
☎ (020) 8777 9011
12-3, 5.30-11; 12-11 Sat; 12-3, 7.30-10.30 Sun
Harveys BB; guest beers H
Roomy, comfortable interior in a 1970s estate pub. A rare mix of a modern local with a traditional feel, but not the easiest place to find by public transport. Even so, a good retreat in a suburban desert. No food Sun.
◖ ⚘ P

Sandrock
152 Upper Shirley Road
☎ (020) 8662 1931
11.30-11; 12-10.30 Sun
Draught Bass; Fuller's London Pride H
Friendly atmosphere in a large but cosy pub with a popular restaurant (children's meals available).
🕸 ◖ ◗ ⊖ (Coombe Lane Tramlink) P ✂

SIDCUP

Alma
10 Alma Road

☎ (020) 8300 3208
11-2.30, 6-11; 11-11 Fri & Sat; 12-3, 7-10.30 Sun
Courage Best Bitter; Shepherd Neame Spitfire; Young's Bitter H
Popular, back-street local, recently redecorated. It is popular with commuters early eve. Parking for four cars only.
Q 🕸 ◖ ⚘ ⚘ P

Try also: Hog's Head, High St (Hogshead)

SOUTH CROYDON

Rail View
188 Selsdon Road (off A235)
☎ (020) 8688 2315
11-11; 12-10.30 Sun
Adnams Bitter; Fuller's London Pride; Hancock's HB; Young's Special; Young' Special guest beers H
A warm welcome awaits the visitor to this local; enjoy a game of crib or dominoes in the public bar or a chat in the comfortable lounge, which displays pictures of the railway steam era.
🕸 ◖ 🌣 ⇆ ⚘ P

UPPER BELVEDERE

Royal Standard
39 Nuxley Road
☎ (01322) 432774
11-11; 12-10.30 Sun
Draught Bass; Fuller's London Pride; Greene King IPA; guest beers H
Single bar with a conservatory for families, popular at weekends and bank holidays. Large screen TV is on for sport (no sound). Food is served Mon-Thu 12-3, 6-8; Fri-Sun 12-5. The guest beers are often seasonal or 'one-offs' from smaller breweries. 🐸 🕸 ◖ ◗ P

South West London

SW1: BELGRAVIA

Star Tavern
6 Belgrave Mews West
☎ (020) 7235 3019
11.30-11; 11.30-3, 6.30-11 Sat; 12-3, 7-10.30 Sun
Fuller's Chiswick, London Pride, ESB H
Famous mews pub which has been in all editions of this *Guide*. It has a small bar plus an upstairs bar which doubles as a function room. Excellent food. Not easy to find, but worth the effort. West London CAMRA *Pub of the Year* 2000.
◖ ◗ ⊖ (Hyde Pk Cnr) ⊞

SW1: PIMLICO

Jugged Hare
172 Vauxhall Bridge Road
☎ (020) 7828 1543

11-11; 12-10.30 Sun
Fuller's Chiswick, London Pride, ESB; seasonal beers; guest beer H
Smart, former Natwest bank with an upstairs balcony, close to the Warwick Way shops. No food Friday eve.
◖▮ ⇌ (Victoria) ⊖ ⊞

Morpeth Arms
58 Millbank
☎ (020) 7834 6442
11-11; 12-10.30 Sun
Young's Bitter, Special, seasonal beers H
Imposing Victorian corner pub near the river, facing the MI6 building. A smart, comfortable lounge decorated in traditional style, plus a small no-smoking snug at the rear.
Q ❀ ◖▮ ◐
⇌ (Vauxhall) ⊖ ⊬

Royal Oak
2 Regency Street
☎ (020) 7834 7046
11-11; 12-6 Sun
Young's Bitter, Special, seasonal beers H
Victorian pub, saved from demolition, situated on the apex of two streets. It features hanging floral baskets in summer. ◖▮ ⇌ (Victoria) ⊖ (St James Pk/Pimlico)

Try also: Pimlico Tram, Charlwood St (Greene King)

SW1: VICTORIA
Wetherspoon's
Victoria Island, Victoria Station
☎ (020) 7931 0445
11-11; 12-10.30 Sun
Boddingtons Bitter; Courage Directors; Fuller's London Pride; Theakston Best Bitter; guest beers H
The ultimate station waiting room providing a full view of the departure board. Football colours are not admitted.
◖▮ ⇌ ⊖ ⊞

Try also: Willow Walk, 25 Wilton Rd (J D Wetherspoon)

SW1: WESTMINSTER
Buckingham Arms
62 Petty France
☎ (020) 7222 3386
11-11; 12-5.30, Sun
Young's Bitter, Special, seasonal beers H
Popular Silver Selection pub with a long mirrored bar. A corridor drinking area behind the bar houses a TV. ⇌ (Victoria) ⊖ (St James Pk/Pimlico)

Sanctuary House
33 Tothill Street
☎ (020) 7799 4044
11-11; 12-10.30 Sun

Fuller's Chiswick, London Pride, ESB, seasonal beers H
Spacious Fuller's Ale and Pie house, part of an hotel in a building reputedly used by MI5 during the 1939-45 war.
⛺ ◖▮ ◐ ⇌ (Victoria) ⊖ (St James Pk) ⊞

Westminster Arms
9 Storeys Gate
☎ (020) 7222 8520
11-11 (8 Sat); 12-6 Sun
Draught Bass; Brakspear Bitter; guest beers H
Small pub near Parliament Square with a downstairs wine bar and a first-floor restaurant. Used by many MPs, the pub has a division bell.
◖▮ ⊖ ⊞

SW2: BRIXTON
Crown & Sceptre
2 Streatham Hill
☎ (020) 8671 0843
11-11; 12-10.30 Sun
Boddingtons Bitter; Courage Directors; Hop Back Summer Lightning; Theakston Best Bitter; guest beers H
Early Wetherspoon's conversion which has mellowed into a characterful pub. The Hop Back fans ensure a fast turnover for the beer. Q ❀ ◖▮ ⇌ (Streatham Hill) P ⊬

SW3: CHELSEA
Blenheim
27 Cale Street
☎ (020) 7349 0056
11-11; 12-10.30 Sun
Badger IPA, Dorset Best, Tanglefoot H
Spacious, one-bar pub with pine fittings and an ornate skylight.
❀ ◖▮ ♣

Coopers Arms
87 Flood Street
☎ (020) 7376 3120
11-11; 12-10.30 Sun
Young's Bitter, Special, seasonal beers H
Lively back-street corner pub with a basic, open-plan bar.
⛺ Q ◖▮ ⊖ (Sloane Sq)

Queens's Head
27 Tryon Street
☎ (020) 7589 0262
11-11; 12-10.30 Sun
Courage Best Bitter, Directors H
Predominantly gay bar to the rear; locals favour the quieter front bar.
❀ ◖▮ ⊖ (Sloane Sq)

Surprise
6 Christchurch Terrace
☎ (020) 7349 1821
12-11; 12-10.30 Sun
Draught Bass; Fuller's London Pride; guest beer H

Warm local, lost in the heart of a residential area; worth seeking out.
❀ ⊖ (Sloane Sq) ♣

SW4: CLAPHAM
Bread & Roses
68 Clapham Manor Street
☎ (020) 7498 1779
11-11; 12-10.30 Sun
Adnams Bitter; guest beer (occasional) H
Unusual, modern interior of bright pastel coloured walls; well designed for families and with facilities for disabled, in a helpful, welcoming atmosphere. No-smoking restrictions lifted at 6pm.
⛺ ❀ ◖▮ ⇌ (High St) ⊖ (North/Common) ⊬

Rose & Crown
2 The Polygon, Clapham Old Town
☎ (020) 7720 8265
11.30-11; 12-10.30 Sun
Greene King IPA, Abbot; Morland Old Speckled Hen; guest beers H
Unspoilt traditional alehouse. A compact, L-shaped bar area is divided by pillars and wood partitions. Low ceilings create an intimate atmosphere. It enjoys regular local trade. Guest beers come from the Beer Seller list. Eve meals Mon-Thu.
❀ ◖▮ ⊖ (Common)

SW5: EARLS COURT
Blackbird
209 Earls Court Road
☎ (020) 7835 1855
11-11; 12-10.30 Sun
Fuller's Chiswick, London Pride, ESB, seasonal beers H
Traditional Fuller's Ale & Pie house in a former bank, serving wholesome pub fare; a large horseshoe front bar and a cosier seating area behind. ◖▮ ⊖ ⊞

SW6: PARSONS GREEN
Duke of Cumberland
235 New Kings Road
☎ (020) 7736 2777
11-11; 12-10.30 Sun
Young's Bitter, Special, seasonal beers H
Facing the south side of the green, this large Victorian pub is very decorative and boasts an ornamental tiled wall and two real fires. The former rear public bar has been knocked through. Eve meals Mon-Thu. Table football played.
◖▮ ⊖ ♣

White Horse
1 Parsons Green
☎ (020) 7736 2115
11-11; 12-10.30 Sun
Draught Bass; Harveys BB; Highgate

Dark; Rooster's Yankee; guest beers Ⓗ
Large, busy, upmarket pub facing the green, with an outdoor terrace in front and a new dining area at the rear. An excellent range of bottled beers include all available Trappist beers. The Old Ale Festival (Nov) is one of many annual events.
🏚 Q ❀ ◖ ▶ ⊖ ⊞

SW7: SOUTH KENSINGTON
Anglesea Arms
15 Selwood Terrace
☎ (020) 7373 7960
11-11; 12-10.30 Sun
Adnams Bitter, Broadside; Brakspear Bitter, Special; Fuller's London Pride; guest beers Ⓗ
Popular, upmarket pub with a dining room and front patio. It boasts connections with Charles Dickens and D H Lawrence. ❀ ◖ ▶ ⊖ ⊞

SW8: SOUTH LAMBETH
Priory Arms
83 Lansdowne Way
☎ (020) 7622 1884
11-11; 12-10.30 Sun
Adnams Bitter, Broadside; Harveys BB; guest beers Ⓗ
The best free house for miles, serving two regularly changing guest beers from micro-breweries, plus a selection of foreign bottled beers. It hosts a German beer festival (Oct). This increasingly popular single-bar pub is four times winner of SW London CAMRA *Pub of the Year*.
❀ ◖ ⊖ (Stockwell) ⇔ 🖬 ⊞

Surprise
16 Southville
☎ (020) 7622 4623
11-11; 12-10.30 Sun
Young's Bitter, Special, seasonal beers Ⓗ
Peacefully situated in a cul-de-sac, next to Larkhall Park, the pub comprises a small but airy L-shaped drinking area around a friendly bar, with a quiet room behind decorated with skilful caricatures of regulars. Eve meals Mon-Fri; no lunches winter weekends.
🏚 Q ❀ ◖ ▶ ⊖ (Stockwell)

SW9: BRIXTON
Trinity Arms
45 Trinity Gardens
☎ (020) 7274 4544
11-11; 12-10.30 Sun
Young's Bitter, Special, seasonal beers Ⓗ
Attractive, one-bar pub, close to Brixton market in a quiet area, serving some of the best pints around. Q ❀ ◖ ⇌ ⊖

SW9: CLAPHAM NORTH
Landor
70 Landor Road
☎ (020) 7274 4386
11-11; 12-10.30 Sun
Greene King IPA; Shepherd Neame Spitfire; Wells Bombardier Ⓗ
Extensive, Victorian pub where the handsome mahogany carved features include a mirror behind the bar; sailing paraphernalia hangs from the ceiling. A theatre upstairs presents shows most eves.
◖ ▶ ⇌ (High St) ⊖

SW11: BATTERSEA
Castle
115 Battersea High Street
☎ (020) 7228 8181
12-11; 12-10.30 Sun
Young's Bitter, Special, seasonal beers Ⓗ
Refurbished 1960s pub: the interior is like a café bar, but the atmosphere is of a pub. The large conservatory houses many plants. Q ❀ ◖ ▶

SW12: BALHAM
Grove
39 Oldridge Road
☎ (020) 8673 6531
12-11; 12-10.30 Sun
Young's Bitter, Special Ⓗ
Large pub, built on the site of an old cycle racing track. It serves the best pint of Young's in SW12.
❀ 🕀 ⇌ (Clapham South)

Moon Under Water
194 Balham High Road
☎ (020) 8673 0535
11-11; 12-10.30 Sun
Boddingtons Bitter; Courage Directors; Hop Back Summer Lightning; Theakston Best Bitter; guest beers Ⓗ
Good, down-to-earth boozer with efficient service for such a busy pub. Move to the rear no-smoking section for a quieter pint.
Q ◖ ▶ ⇌ ⊖ ⇔ ⊬ ⊞

SW13: BARNES
Coach & Horses
27 Barnes High Street
☎ (020) 8876 2695
11-11; 12-10.30 Sun
Young's Bitter, Special, Winter Warmer Ⓗ
Superb, homely former coaching inn, with a 'village' feel. Notable etched windows at the front, and a children-friendly garden with a boules pitch add to its appeal. Barbecues are popular. Local CAMRA *Pub of the Year* 1998.
❀ ◖ ⇌ (Barnes Bridge)

Rose of Denmark
28 Cross Street

☎ (020) 8392 1761
11-11; 12-10.30 Sun
Brakspear Bitter; Taylor Landlord; Woodforde's Wherry Ⓗ
Street-corner local, tucked away but worth seeking out. It is comfortable and surprisingly roomy. The name derives from the nickname of Queen Alexandra, wife of Edward VII. Food comprises basket meals, served all hours.
❀ ◖ ▶ ⇌ (Barnes Bridge) ♣

SW14: EAST SHEEN
Hare & Hounds
216 Upper Richmond Road West
☎ (020) 8876 4304
11-11; 12-10.30 Sun
Young's Bitter, Special, Winter Warmer Ⓗ
Large, comfortable, oak-panelled lounge, with a full-size snooker table in a rear saloon. Childrens' play area in the large walled garden. Wide choice of food.
🏚 ❀ ◖ ▶ 🕀 ⇌ (Mortlake) ♣

SW15: PUTNEY
Railway
202 Upper Richmond Road
☎ (020) 8788 8190
11-11; 12-10.30 Sun
Boddingtons Bitter; Courage Directors; Shepherd Neame Spitfire; Theakston Best Bitter; guest beers Ⓗ
Standard Wetherpoon's comforts, spread over two floors. Note the model railway suspended from the ceiling! The upstairs bar often stocks a different guest beer.
Q ◖ ▶ ⇌ ⊖ (E Putney) ⇔ ⊬ ⊞

SW16: STREATHAM COMMON
Pied Bull
498 Streatham High Road
☎ (020) 8764 4003
11-11; 12-10.30 Sun
Young's Bitter, Special, seasonal beers Ⓗ
Imposing, comfortable pub near the common, with a traditional atmosphere drawing a regular following. Some facilities currently unavailable due to refurbishment.
🏚 Q ❀ ◖ ▶ 🕀 ⇌ ♣ P

SW16: STREATHAM HILL
Hogshead
68-70 Streatham High Road
☎ (020) 8696 7587
11-11; 12-10.30 Sun
Boddingtons Bitter; Flowers Original; Ⓗ guest beers Ⓗ/Ⓖ
Friendly pub, stocking a good range of guest beers. Different floor levels enhance

the varied drinking areas. Good quality food is unobtrusively served.

🏃 ◖▶ ⛄ ⇌ ☺ ⚂

SW17: SUMMERSTOWN

Leather Bottle
538 Garratt Lane
☎ (020) 8946 2309
11-11; 12-10.30 Sun
Young's Bitter, Special, seasonal beers Ⓗ
17th-century, split-level pub, notable for its Dutch-style roof and and large garden; almost a country pub in town, it can get very busy. Barbecues in summer. Family room available until 7pm.
🏃 Q ☕ 🍴 ◖ ⇌ (Earlsfield) P

Prince of Wales
646 Garratt Lane
☎ (020) 8946 2628
11-11; 12-4, 7-10.30 Sun
Young's Bitter, Special, seasonal beers Ⓗ
Three-roomed local, on the corner of busy Garratt Lane, and handy for Wimbledon Greyhound Stadium. Note the handsome tiled exterior. Weekday lunches served.
🏃 ☕ 🍴 ◖ ⚂ ♣ P

SW18: WANDSWORTH

Cats Back
86 Point Pleasant
☎ (020) 8877 0818
12-3, 5.30-11; 11-11 Fri & Sat; 12-10.30 Sun
O'Hanlon's Blakeley's Best, seasonal beers Ⓗ
Small back-street local displaying a remarkable collection of artefacts. It stands near the Thames and the east end of Wandsworth Park. Weekday lunches.
🏃 🍴 ◖

Grapes
39 Fairfield Street
☎ (020) 8877 0756
11-11; 12-10.30 Sun
Young's Bitter, Special Ⓗ
Small single-bar pub with wood-panelled walls – note the mirrors along one side. It dates as a beer shop from at least 1833. Weekday lunches served. 🍴 ◖ ⇌ (Town) ♣

Old Sergeant
104 Garratt Lane
☎ (020) 8874 4099
11-11; 12-10.30 Sun
Young's Bitter, Special Ⓗ
Very welcoming local which has changed little over the years. A long-standing, much respected landlord always makes customers welcome. Weekday lunches. 🍴 ◖ ⚂ ♣

Queen Adelaide
35 Putney Bridge Road
☎ (020) 8874 1695

11-11; 12-10.30 Sun
Young's Bitter, Special, Winter Warmer Ⓗ
Large, friendly local, close to Wandsworth Park. a main bar area and a larger room with Sky TV. Proper Chinese food was recently introduced at lunchtimes (except Sun); (no eve meals Sun). It boasts a particularly fine large garden. 🍴 ◖ ▶ ⊝ (E Putney) ♣

Rose & Crown
138 Wandsworth High Street
☎ (020) 8871 4497
11-11; 12-10.30 Sun
Courage Directors; Theakston Best Bitter; Taylor Landlord; guest beers Ⓗ
Reopened after extensive refurbishment and reverting to its original name, late in 1998. A Wetherspoon's house, it has a central bar and distinct areas in a variety of colours and seating. Local history panels and a mosaic from local artist Gail Farnesi feature. Three guest beers.
Q 🍴 ◖ ▶ ⇌ (Town) ♣ ⊞

SW19: MERTON

Princess of Wales
98 Morden Road
☎ (020) 8542 0573
11-3, 5-11; 11-11 Fri & Sat; 12-10.30 Sun
Young's Bitter, Special, seasonal beers Ⓗ
Main road local with two drinking areas, but no longer a public; fairly quiet and airy. The pub has two large friendly dogs. Eve meals served weekdays only.
🏃 🍴 ◖ ▶ ⊝ (S Wimbledon) (Morden Rd Tramlink) P

SW19: SOUTH WIMBLEDON

Sultan
78 Norman Road
☎ (020) 8542 4532
12-11; 12-10.30 Sun
Hop Back GFB, Entire Stout, Summer Lightning, Thunderstorm, seasonal beers Ⓗ
1950s back-street pub which attracts both local custom and those on a pilgrimage to Hop Back's only London pub. Barbecues held in summer, and an annual beer festival. The Sultan's name refers to a 19th-century racehorse not a potentate. 🍴 ♿
⊝ (S Wimbledon/Colliers Wood)

SW19: WIMBLEDON

Crooked Billet
15 Crooked Billet
☎ (020) 8946 4942
11-11; 12-10.30 Sun
Young's Bitter, Special, seasonal beers Ⓗ

Large, comfortable, inn dating from 1509, on the fringes of the common. The restaurant at the rear serves excellent meals and wines.
🏃 Q ☕ 🍴 ◖ ▶ ♣

Hand in Hand
7 Crooked Billet
☎ (020) 8946 5720
11-11; 12-10.30 Sun
Young's Bitter, Special, seasonal beers Ⓗ
One of two pubs left on a tiny road which once contained four. Over 21s only admitted in summer, when the small green outside doubles as a garden extension.
🏃 Q ☕ 🍴 ◖ ▶ ♣ ⚂

Try also: Rose & Crown, High St, Wimbledon Village (Young's)

CARSHALTON

Railway Tavern
47 North Street
☎ (020) 8669 8016
12-2.30, 5-11; 11-11 Sat; 12-10.30 Sun
Fuller's London Pride, ESB Ⓗ
Friendly corner local, near the station, decorated with railway memorabilia. The landlord is a Fuller's *Master Cellarman*. The pub fields two marbles teams. 🍴 ◖ ⇌ ♣

Windsor Castle
378 Carshalton Road
(A232/B271 jct)
☎ (020) 8669 1191
11-11; 12-10.30 Sun
Draught Bass; Fuller's London Pride; Hancock's HB; guest beers Ⓗ
Single-bar pub with a restaurant one end. Over 1700 guest beers have been sold; it offers four pint jugs for the price of three. No eve meals Sun.
🍴 ◖ ▶ ♿ ⇌ (Beeches) ♣ P

CHEAM

Claret Free House
33 The Broadway (A4023)
☎ (020) 8715 9002
11.30-11; 12-10.30 Sun
Cottage Champflower; Shepherd Neame Master Brew Bitter; guest beers Ⓗ
Smart bar in the main shopping street. Recently refurbished to high standard and fully air-conditioned it features light wood panelling and scrubbed wood floors. Booking is advisable for the restaurant upstairs.
◖ ▶ ⇌

Prince of Wales
28 Malden Road
☎ (020) 8641 8106
11 (12 Sat)-11; 12-10.30 Sun
Adnams Bitter; Fuller's London

Pride; Tetley Bitter Ⓗ
Not central, but easily accessible, this spacious local caters for most tastes and is well worth seeking out.
🐕 ❀ ◑ ▶ ♿ ♣ ✄

CHESSINGTON
North Star
271 Hook Road (A243)
☎ (020) 8391 9811
12-11; 12-10.30 Sun
Adnams Bitter; Draught Bass; Fuller's London Pride Ⓗ
Large community pub, now open-plan, with the accent on food (not served Sun eve). Wheelchair WC.
Q ❀ ◑ ▶ ♿ ♣ P

KEW
Coach & Horses
8 Kew Green
☎ (020) 8940 1208
11-11; 12-10.30 Sun
Young's Bitter, Special, seasonal beers Ⓗ
Coaching inn on the edge of Kew Green; a single bar pub plus another room. There is a garden to the rear, pavement seating at the front. Home-cooked food is good quality and comes in generous portions (not served Sun eve). Families welcome.
🏠 Q ❀ 🛏 ◑ ▶ ≉ (Bridge/Gardens) ⊖ ♣ P

Greyhound
82 Kew Green
☎ (020) 8940 0071
11-11; 12-10.30 Sun
Courage Best Bitter, guest beers Ⓗ
This 19th-century pub overlooking Kew Green features wood panelling and an original fireplace in the front bar area, retained during a 1996 renovation. Children welcome in the rear dining area. Up to three guest beers on tap. No food Sun eve. ❀ ◑ ▶ ≉ (Bridge)

KINGSTON
Canbury Arms
49 Canbury Park Road
☎ (020) 8288 1882
11-11; 12-10.30 Sun
Courage Best Bitter, Directors; guest beers Ⓗ
Community pub where the accent is on live music (Fri and Sat eves) and televised sport; Sun night is quiz night. It offers a constantly changing range of up to four guest beers at the stronger end of the spectrum. Real cider rotates weekly.
❀ ≉ ♣ ♻ P ⊟

Druid's Head
2-3 Market Place
☎ (020) 8546 0723
11-11; 12-10.30 Sun

Boddingtons Bitter; Brakspear Bitter; Shepherd Neame Spitfire; Wadworth 6X; Ⓗ guest beers Ⓗ/Ⓖ
Large Hogshead in typical style, extended from an historic pub into adjoining premises, featuring split-level bars on both floors. The Druid's Bar retains some original features and stocks up to four guest beers. No-smoking restrictions in the raised bar area apply Sun-Thu.
🏠 Q ◑ ▶ ♿ ≉ ♻ ✄

Kelly Arms
2 Glenthorne Road
☎ (020) 8296 9815
11-11; 12-10.30 Sun
Courage Best Bitter; guest beers Ⓗ
Traditional local pub hidden in back streets, but worth seeking out. It serves a mixed clientele, with TV for sports events and a Sun night quiz. Limited parking.
❀ ◑ ▶ ♣ P

Park Tavern
19 New Road (near Richmond Park Kingston gate)
10.30-11; 12-10.30 Sun
Brakspear Special; Young's Bitter; guest beers Ⓗ
Tucked-away local, perfect for a constitutional after a walk in the nearby Richmond Park. Interesting guest beers and a mixed clientele make this a hidden gem. Dogs welcome – biscuits and bowls are kept behind the bar.
🏠 Q ♣ ♣

Willoughby Arms
47 Willoughby Road
☎ (020) 8546 4236
10.30-11; 12-10.30 Sun
Flowers Original; Fuller's London Pride; Taylor Landlord guest beers Ⓗ
Recently extended and redecorated this back-street local hosts occasional beer festivals. Eric Clapton and the Yardbirds rehearsed upstairs in the 1960s. Guest beer is sold at a reduced price Sun; a real drinker's pub.
❀ ♣

Wych Elm
93 Elm Road
☎ (020) 8546 3271
11-3, 5-11; 11-11 Sat; 12-3, 7-10.30 Sun
Fuller's Chiswick, London Pride, ESB, seasonal beers Ⓗ
One of only two Fuller's pubs in Kingston: a two-room layout that includes a public bar. The pleasant garden hosts occasional barbecues. Home-cooked meals are served Mon-Sat.
Q ❀ ◑ 🍴 ♣

MORDEN
Lady St Helier
33 Aberconway Road
☎ (020) 8540 2818
11-11; 12-10.30 Sun
Boddingtons Bitter; Courage Directors; Shepherd Neame Spitfire; Theakston Best Bitter; guest beers Ⓗ
Large Wetherspoon's opposite the tube station, re-named as a result of a competition amongst the customers, after the nearby housing estate (for years the largest in Europe). It can be smokey.
◑ ▶ ♿ ⊖ P ✄ ⊞

NEW MALDEN
Woodies
Thetford Road
☎ (020) 8949 5824
11-11; 12-10.30 Sun
Adnams Broadside; Flowers Original; Fuller's London Pride; Young's Bitter, Special; guest beers Ⓗ
Former cricket pavilion displaying much sporting and entertainment memorabilia. Children welcome in raised area if eating.
🏠 Q ❀ ◑ ♿ ♣ P

RICHMOND
Duke of York
29 Kew Road
☎ (020) 8332 6749
11-11; 12-10.30 Sun
Marston's Pedigree; Tetley Bitter; guest beers Ⓗ
Up to five beers from regional brewers guest at this town-centre Festival Ale House, now under Punch Taverns control; four-pint jugs are available. The landlord was national runner-up for the 1999 Tetley award.
◑ ≉ ⊖ ♣

Red Cow
59 Sheen Road
☎ (020) 8940 2511
11-11; 12-10.30 Sun
Young's Bitter, Special, seasonal beers Ⓗ
Locally popular, single bar pub, a short walk from the shops. Good lunches and eve meals (served until 8.30 weekdays). Overnight accommodation is a new facility.
🏠 🛏 ◑ ▶ ≉ ⊖ ♣

Watermans Arms
12 Water Lane
☎ (020) 8940 2893
11-3, 5.30-11; 11-11 Sat; 12-10.30 Sun
Young's Bitter, Special, Winter Warmer Ⓗ
Small, Victorian two-roomed pub in a cobbled stone lane

leading to the river. The upstairs function hosts impromptu music Mon eve. Try the games – horsey-horsey, shut-the-box, and shove ha'penny. No food Mon.

🏚 🍺 ≈ ⊖ ♣

White Cross
Riverside, Water Lane
☎ (020) 8940 6844
11-11; 12-10.30 Sun
Young's Bitter, Triple A, Special, seasonal beers Ⓗ
Extremely popular, prominent Thames-side pub in an unrivalled setting. The riverside terrace is open in summer and sunny winter weekends, river level permitting. Plastic glasses used for outdoor drinking.

🏚 🏮 🍺 ≈ ⊖

Try also: **Old Ship Inn**, King St (Young's)

SURBITON
Lamb Inn
73 Brighton Road (A243)
☎ (020) 8390 9229
11-11; 12-10.30 Sun
Greene King IPA; Marston's Pedigree; Young's Special, guest beer Ⓗ
Small, one-bar local with a new lease of life under caring licensees who offer a regularly changing guest beer. A pleasant patio and garden hosts occasional barbecues; quiz night Tue, karaoke first Sat in the month. Home-cooked lunches.

🏮 🍺 ♣

Waggon & Horses
1 Surbiton Hill Road (A240)
11-2.30, 5-11; 12-11 Sat; 12-10.30 Sun
Young's Bitter, Special, seasonal beers Ⓗ
Large, traditional pub of several drinking areas, yet remaining welcoming. Local and regional CAMRA *Pub of the Year* 1998 and '99. Barbecues held in summer; Thai lunches Sun.

Q 🏮 🍺🕮 ≈ ♣

SUTTON
Little Windsor
13 Greyhound Road (off A232)
☎ (020) 8643 2574
11-11; 12-10.30 Sun
Fuller's Chiswick, London Pride, ESB, seasonal beers; guest beers Ⓗ
Originally the Windsor Castle, this small back-street local is well worth finding. Five pumps give choice and quality in a friendly atmosphere.

🏮 🍺 ≈ ♣

New Town
7 Lind Road (off A232)
☎ (020) 8770 2072
12-3, 5-11; 12-11 Fri & Sat; 12-10.30 Sun
Young's Bitter, Special, seasonal beers Ⓗ
Two bars remain in this spacious, traditionally designed pub which has undergone sympathetic alteration. Situated in an area well served with good pubs. No eve meals Sun.

🍺 🏮 🕮 🍺 ≈ ♣ ✂

WALLINGTON
Duke's Head
6 Manor Road (A232)
☎ (020) 8401 7410
11-11; 12-10.30 Sun
Young's Bitter, Special, seasonal beers Ⓗ
Traditional pub, with a small hotel extension, in an attractive setting on the edge of Wallington Green which serves as an outdoor drinking area in summer.

🏚 Q 🏮 🍺🕮 🛆 ≈ ♣ P

West London
W1: FITZROVIA
Duke of York
47 Rathbone Street
☎ (020) 7636 7065
11-11 (5 Sat); closed Sun
Greene King IPA; Abbot; guest beer Ⓗ
Friendly back-street pub just off Oxford Street, popular with local workers.

🍺 ⊖ (Tottenham Ct Rd)

Hogshead
72 Grafton Way
☎ (020) 7387 7923
11 (12 Sat)-11; closed Sun
Boddingtons Bitter; Brakspear Bitter; Wadworth 6X; guest beers Ⓖ/Ⓗ
Comfortable new Hogshead pub popular with office workers and locals. One of very few West End pubs to have draught cider.

Q 🍺🕮 ⊖ (Warren St) ⌣

Jack Horner
236 Tottenham Court Road
☎ (020) 7636 2868
11-11; closed Sun
Fuller's Chiswick, London Pride, ESB, seasonal beers Ⓗ
Large Fuller's Ale & Pie house, handy for the electronics retailers in Tottenham Ct Road.

🍺 🛆 ⊖ (Tottenham Ct Rd)

King & Queen
1 Foley Street
☎ (020) 7636 5619
11-11; 12-10.30 Sun
Adnams Extra; Courage Directors; Ruddles Best Bitter; guest beer Ⓗ
Late Victorian corner pub

with an interesting exterior but the interior is not original. Frequented by staff of Middlesex Hospital and office workers.

🍺 ⊖ (Goodge St)

Try also: **Hope**, Tottenham St (Whitbread)

W1: MARYLEBONE
Beehive
7 Homer Street
☎ (020) 7262 6851
11-3, 5.30-11; 11-11 Fri & Sat; 12-10.30 Sun
Boddingtons Bitter; Fuller's London Pride Ⓗ
Back-street local which has been in many editions of this *Guide*; one of the smallest pubs in W1.

🍺 ≈ ⊖

Carpenters Arms
12 Seymour Place
☎ (020) 7723 1050
11-11; 12-10.30 Sun
Fuller's London Pride; Webster's Yorkshire Bitter; guest beers Ⓗ
Busy, popular pub in a back street near Marble Arch.

🍺🕮 ⊖ (Marble Arch)

Duke of York
65 Harrowby Street
☎ (020) 7262 9129
11-11; 12-10.30 Sun
Draught Bass; Hancock's HB; guest beers Ⓗ
Ornate Victorian corner pub displaying much sporting memorabilia. Try the Goan restaurant upstairs.

🍺🕮 ⊖

Golden Eagle
59 Marylebone Lane
☎ (020) 7935 3228
11-11; 12-10.30 Sun
Brakspear Bitter; Fuller's London Pride; guest beers Ⓗ
Small, traditional pub offering two guest ales from regional brewers. A pianist performs Thu and Fri eves. Lunchtime snacks include the famous Biggles sausages.

⊖ (Bond St)

Turners Arms
26 Crawford Street
☎ (020) 7724 4504
11-11; 12-10.30 Sun
Young's Bitter, Special; guest beers Ⓗ
Small one-roomed traditional pub recently refurbished under new ownership. Worth a visit. Guest beers are sourced from micro-breweries.

≈ ⊖ ♣ 🍴

Wargrave Arms
40 Brendon Street
☎ (020) 7723 0559
11-11; 12-10.30 Sun
Young's Bitter, Special Ⓗ

Narrow corner pub built in 1866. One of the Finch's pubs acquired by Young's.
◑ ▶ ⇌ ⊖

W1: MAYFAIR
Fuller's Ale Lodge
11 Avery Row
☎ (020) 7629 1643
11-11; 12-5 Sat; closed Sun
Fuller's London Pride, ESB, seasonal beers Ⓗ
In a narrow street, sandwiched between Claridge's hotel and New Bond St. A *Master Cellarman* ensures Fuller's ales are served in best condition. A dress code applies.
◑ ⊖ (Bond St) ⊞

Guinea
30 Bruton Place
☎ (020) 7409 1728
11 (6.30 Sat)-11; closed Sun
Young's Bitter, Special, seasonal beers Ⓗ
Small, historic back-street pub with its own top-class restaurant.
Q ◑ ▶ ⊖ (Bond St/Green Pk)

Hogshead
11-13 Dering Street
☎ (020) 7629 0531
11-11; 12-11 Sat; closed Sun
Adnams Bitter; Boddingtons Bitter; Brakspear Bitter; Fuller's London Pride; Wadworth 6X; Ⓗ **guest beers** Ⓗ/Ⓖ
Alehouse in the best Hogshead tradition, serving up to three guest ales on gravity – the largest selection in the area – plus usually two ciders. Food served until 9pm (8pm Fri/Sat). A welcome haven from the Oxford St bustle. Over 21s only; no football shirts.
◑ ▶ ⅙ ⊖ (Bond St) ⌣ ✄

Old Monk
24-26 Maddox Street
11-11; closed Sat & Sun
Fuller's London Pride; Theakston Best Bitter; guest beers Ⓗ
Large city-centre establishment, opened in 1999. Screens give some privacy.
◑ ▶ ⊖ (Oxford Circus)

Windmill
6-8 Mill Street
☎ (020) 7491 8050
11-11 (4 Sat); closed Sun
Young's Bitter, Special, seasonal beers Ⓗ
Former nightclub, now a two-bar pub comfortably furnished, featuring wood panelling and decorative ceilings and frieze. Food is served in the lower back bar and the upstairs restaurant.
Q ◑ ▶ ⊖ (Oxford Circus)

W1: SOHO
Kings Arms
23 Poland Street
☎ (020) 7734 5907
11-11; 12-10.30 Sun
Courage Directors; Theakston Best Bitter Ⓗ
Popular gay pub, more mixed at lunch times and frequented by tourists. The Druids reformed here in 1781 and the present landlord is to be inducted as an honorary Druid.
◑ ▶ ⊖ (Oxford Circus)

W2: PADDINGTON
Archery Tavern
4 Bathurst Street
☎ (020) 7402 4916
11-11; 12-10.30 sun
Badger IPA, Dorset Best, Tanglefoot Ⓗ
Wood-panelled pub, next to a mews with a working stables, decorated with an archery theme.
◑ ▶ ⇌ ⊖ ♣

W3: ACTON
Duke of York
86 Steyne Road
☎ (020) 8992 0463
11.30-11; 12-10.30 Sun
Brakspear Bitter; Courage Best Bitter; Fuller's London Pride Ⓗ
One-bar, back-street local with a room for diners and meetings. Beware the karaoke Thu eve.
Q ⛢ ❀ ◑ ▶ ♣

Kings Head
214 High Street
☎ (020) 8992 0282
11-11; 12-10.30 Sun
Fuller's Chiswick, London Pride, ESB, seasonal beers Ⓗ
Imposing corner local: a vibrant, friendly single bar.
❀ ◑ ▶ ♣

W4: CHISWICK
Bell & Crown
11-13 Thames Street, Strand-on-the-Green
☎ (020) 8994 4164
11-11; 12-10.30 Sun
Fuller's Chiswick, London Pride, ESB Ⓗ
Riverside pub boasting two conservatories.
❀ ◑ ▶ ⇌ (Kew Bridge)

Old Pack Horse
434 Chiswick High Road
☎ (020) 8995 0647
11-11; 12-10.30 Sun
Fuller's Chiswick, London Pride, ESB, seasonal beers Ⓗ
Impressive corner pub featuring much ornate woodwork. Thai food is served Mon-Sat. ❀ ◑ ▶
⇌ (Gunnersbury) ⊖ (Park)

W5: EALING
Castle
36 St Mary's Road
☎ (020) 8567 3285
11-11; 12-10.30 Sun
Fuller's Chiswick, London Pride, ESB; seasonal beers Ⓗ
Local opposite Thames Valley University; its traditional exterior belies a sympathetic (and long overdue) re-furbishment. ❀ ◑ ▶ ⅙ ⊖ (South)

Duffy's
124 Pitshanger Lane
☎ (020) 8998 6810
11-11; 12-10.30 Sun
Draught Bass; Fuller's London Pride; Greene King Abbot; Hancock's HB; Young's Bitter Ⓗ
Comfortable single bar pub with two distinct drinking areas and a restaurant. ◑ ▶

Plough
297 Northfield Avenue
☎ (020) 8567 1416
11-11; 12-10.30 Sun
Fuller's Chiswick, London Pride, ESB Ⓗ
Comfortable, two-bar pub in Little Ealing. The interior was refurbished in 1991 following a fire. ❀ ◑ ▶ ⊞ ⊖ (Northfields) P

Red Lion
13 St Mary's Road
☎ (020) 8567 2541
11-11; 12-10.30 Sun
Fuller's Chiswick, London Pride, ESB, seasonal beers Ⓗ
Single bar institution near Ealing Film Studio, from which it derives its alternative name, Stage Six. The walls are lined with film memorabilia and there is an award-winning terrace-style garden. Q ❀ ◑ ▶ ⇌ (Broadway) ⊖ (South)

Try also: Rose & Crown, Church Place (Fuller's)

W6: HAMMERSMITH
Andover Arms
57 Aldensley Road
☎ (020) 8741 9794
11-11; 12-3.30, 7-10.30 Sun
Fuller's Chiswick, London Pride, ESB, seasonal beers Ⓗ
Pleasant, two-bar local in Brackenbury village – well hidden, but worth seeking out. Excellent Thai food served, plus traditional lunches (no food Sun).
◑ ▶ ⊖ (Ravenscourt Pk) ⊞

Brook Green Hotel
170 Shepherd's Bush Road
☎ (020) 7603 2516
11-11; 12-10.30 Sun
Young's Bitter, Special, seasonal beers Ⓗ
Spacious Victorian corner-pub opposite Brook Green. It has been recently extensively

refurbished, incorporating a large cellar bar and reinstating the hotel rooms. A handy place to stay if visiting Olympia.
🏵 ⇌ ◑ ⊖

Salutation
154 King Street
☎ (020) 8748 3668
11-11; 12-10.30 Sun
Fuller's Chiswick, London Pride, ESB; guest beer Ⓗ
Edwardian purpose-built pub with a marvellous tiled exterior. Inside it's a spacious one-roomed comfortable place with separate drinking areas. A small conservatory and a garden, unusual for the area, add to its appeal. No food Sun eve.
🏵 ◑ ⊖ (Ravenscourt Pk)

W7: HANWELL
Dolphin
13 Lower Boston Road
☎ (020) 8840 0850
12-11; 12-10.30 Sun
Brakspear Bitter; Fuller's London Pride; Marston's Pedigree; Morland Old Speckled Hen; Wadworth 6X Ⓗ
Transformed from the former White Hart, this pub stands by the green of old Hanwell village. An oasis for discerning diners and drinkers, the predominantly wood decor is complemented by various brewery artefacts. No food Mon. Q ◑ ➽ ♣ ✁

W8: KENSINGTON
Britannia
1 Allen Street
☎ (020) 7937 6905
11-11; 12-10.30 Sun
Young's Bitter, Special, seasonal beers Ⓗ
Friendly local, just off Kensington High Street, which has been in all editions of this *Guide*. The conservatory is a no-smoking area at lunchtime.
◑ ⊖ (High St)
Churchill Arms
119 Kensington Church Street
☎ (020) 7727 4242
11-11; 12-10.30 Sun
Fuller's Chiswick, London Pride, ESB, seasonal beers Ⓗ
Busy, popular, pub filled with bric-a-brac. The landlord has justly won many pub awards.
Q ◑ ⊖ (Notting Hill Gate) ⊞

W8: NOTTING HILL GATE
Uxbridge Arms
13 Uxbridge Street
☎ (020) 7727 7326
11-11; 12-10.30 Sun
Brakspear Special; Fuller's London Pride; guest beers Ⓗ
Intimate local, just off the

main shopping area.
Q 🏵 ⊖

W9: MAIDA VALE
Warrington Hotel ☆
93 Warrington Crescent
☎ (020) 7286 2929
11-11; 12-10.30 Sun
Brakspear Special; Fuller's London Pride, ESB; Young's Special; guest beer Ⓗ
Superb example of a Victorian 'gin palace', built in 1859 with florid Art Nouveau decor and an impressive staircase. Thai restaurant upstairs.
◑ ⊖ (Warwick Ave)

Warwick Castle
6 Warwick Place
☎ (020) 7286 6868
11-11; 12-10.30 Sun
Draught Bass; Fullers's London Pride Ⓗ
Local near Little Venice. Note the clock and print of Paddington station. Eve meals served 6-8.
◑ ⊖ (Warwick Ave)

W11: BAYSWATER
Cock & Bottle
17 Needham Road
☎ (020) 7229 1550
12-11; 12-10.30 Sun
Brakspear Bitter; Marston's Pedigree Ⓗ
Pleasant, friendly corner pub retaining some ornate features; well worth visiting.
🏵 ◑ ⊖ (Notting Hill Gate)

W13: WEST EALING
Drayton Court
2 The Avenue
☎ (020) 8997 1019
11-11; 12-10.30 Sun
Fuller's Chiswick, London Pride, ESB, seasonal beers; guest beer (occasional) Ⓗ
Popular large local where facilities include separate bars, a function room, a big garden, a theatre downstairs and conference facilities upstairs, set behind a splendid neo-gothic exterior.
🏵 ◑ ▮ ⌂ ₺ ➽

W14: WEST KENSINGTON
Seven Stars
253 North End Road
☎ (020) 7385 3571
11-11; 12-10.30 Sun
Fuller's London Pride, ESB Ⓗ
Spacious Art Deco pub: two drinking areas plus a garden patio where barbecues are sometimes held.
🏵 ◑ ⊖

BRENTFORD
Brewery Tap

47 Catherine Wheel Road
☎ (020) 8560 5200
11-11; 12-10.30 Sun
Fuller's London Pride, ESB, seasonal beers Ⓗ
Popular, lively local (currently under threat from developers) off the High Street and close to the Grand Union Canal. It features three elevated bar areas and regular live music: jazz Tue and Thu; blues Fri; pianist Sat; folk Sun. Good value lunches.
🏵 ◑ ⇌ ♣

Magpie & Crown
128 High Street
☎ (020) 8560 5658
11-11; 12-10.30 Sun
Beer range varies Ⓗ
Mock-Tudor single-bar pub opposite the magistrates' court. This basic, friendly local serves four constantly changing beers from independent and micro-brewers plus a good selection of continental bottled beers. Local CAMRA *Pub of the Year* 1999.
🏵 ⇌ ♣ ⌂ ⏛

COWLEY
Paddington Packet Boat
High Road
☎ (01895) 442392
12-11; 12-10.30 Sun
Fuller's Chiswick, London Pride, ESB Ⓗ
Large 200-year-old, friendly local that boasts some original fittings and mirrors alongside plenty of memorabilia, much of it connected with the old packet-boat service to Paddington on the nearby canal. No food Sun eve but lunch served until 4pm.
🏨 🏵 ➽ ◑ ₺ ♣ P

CRANFORD
Jolly Gardeners
177 High Street
☎ (020) 8897 6996
11-11; 12-10.30 Sun
Tetley Bitter; guest beer Ⓗ
Cosy, two-room local where two real fires keep drinkers warm in winter, whilst swings and slides keep children amused on sunny days. The guest beer, from the south or south-west, is unusual for area. Accommodation weekdays only.
🏨 🏵 ➽ ◑ ♣ P

FELTHAM
Moon on the Square
30 The Centre, High Street
☎ (020) 8893 1293
11-11; 12-10.30 Sun
Boddingtons Bitter; Courage

Directors; Theakston Best Bitter; guest beers H
Spacious, popular, town-centre pub, where photos and panels depict bygone Feltham and local history. An oasis in this area for regular guest beers from independent breweries. Q ◑ ▶ & ⇌ ⅍ ⊞

GREENFORD
Bridge Hotel
Western Avenue (A40/A4127 jct)
☎ (020) 5866 6246
11-11; 12-10.30 Sun
Young's Bitter, Special, Winter Warmer H
Friendly pub by the A40 fly-over, which serves the adjacent hotel, restaurant and conference centre. No meals at weekends.
❀ ⇚ ◑ ▶ & ⇌ ⊖ ♣ P

HAM
Fox & Goose
327 Petersham Road
☎ (020) 8940 8178
11-11; 12-10.30 Sun
Young's Bitter, Special H
Small, very cosy local with an unusual orange-tiled façade close to historic Ham House and Richmond Park, the pub has a large garden.
Q ❀

HAMPTON
Jolly Coopers
16 High Street
☎ (020) 8979 3384
11-3, 5-11; 11-11 Sat; 12-10.30 Sun
Brakspear Bitter; Courage Best Bitter; Marston's Pedigree; Wells Bombardier; Young's Bitter H
Cosy pub, recently redecorated, with lots of paraphernalia, run by friendly staff. A plaque lists the landlords back to 1727. It hosts a regular music quiz. Eve meals are served in the restaurant. ◑ ▶ & ⇌ P

White Hart
70 High Street
☎ (020) 8979 5352
11-3, 5.30-11; 11.30-11 Sat; 12-10.30 Sun
Greene King Abbot; Tetley Bitter; guest beers H
True free house in mock-Tudor style featuring a big log fire and a collection of chamber pots. Always eight real beers on tap, many from small breweries. The Thai restaurant upstairs is closed Mon even when it is used by Hampton Chess Club.
⇚ ❀ ◑ ▶

HAMPTON COURT
Kings Arms
Lion Gate, Hampton Court

Road
☎ (020) 8977 1729
11-11; 12-10.30 Sun
Badger IPA, Dorset Best, Tanglefoot, seasonal beers H
Imposing historic pub whose three bars include a well-frequented public; note the mosaic-floored lounge area. Meals are very popular, including afternoon teas in the tourist season.
◑ ▶ ⊞ ⇌ ♣

HAMPTON HILL
Roebuck
72 Hampton Road
☎ (020) 8255 8133
11-11; 12-4, 7-10.30 Sun
Badger Dorset Best; guest beer H
Comfortable, corner local with bare boards and an ever-growing collection of bric-a-brac – much of it bearing a naval connection. Formerly a Watneys pub, now a true free house where the guest beer is changed monthly.
⇘ ❀ ⇚ ♣

HESTON
Robert Inn
366 Great West Road
☎ (020) 8570 6261
11-11; 12-10.30 Sun
Fuller's Chiswick, London Pride, ESB H
Formerly known as the Master Robert (a name retained for the adjacent motel), a useful refreshment stop en-route to Heathrow Airport.
⇚ ◑ ⊖ (Hounslow W) ♣ P

HOUNSLOW
Cross Lances
236 Hanworth Road (A314)
☎ (020) 8570 4174
11-11; 12-10.30 Sun
Fuller's London Pride, ESB H
Early Victorian tiled local retaining a refurbished public bar. Popular for its huge meals, it hosts regular cribbage eves, and outdoor jazz on Bank Holiday Sun.
❀ ◑ ▶ ⊞ ⇌ ♣ P

ISLEWORTH
Coach & Horses
183 London Road (A315)
☎ (020) 8560 1447
11-11 (midnight Wed, Fri & Sat); 12-10.30 Sun
Young's Bitter, Special, seasonal beers H
17th-century coaching inn, mentioned in Dickens *Oliver Twist*. It stages regular live music (jazz/folk) and has an authentic Thai restaurant. A good friendly atmosphere and a family garden add to its appeal. ⇘ ❀ ◑ ▶ ⊞ &
⇌ (Syon Lane) ♣ P

NORWOOD GREEN
Red Lion
92-94 Linkfield Road (near station)
☎ (020) 8560 1457
11-11; 12-10.30 Sun
Brakspear Bitter; Flowers IPA; Marston's Pedigree; guest beers H
Substantial pub, hidden away in a quiet terrace. The original pub was built in the 19th century to serve the local factory workers. Live music Sat eve and Sun afternoon.
❀ ◑ ⊞ & ⇌ ♣

Plough
Tentelow Lane (A4127)
☎ (020) 8574 1945
11-11; 12-10.30 Sun
Fuller's Chiswick, London Pride, ESB H
Recently restored externally, even the non-standard Fuller, Smith & Turner Chiswick Ales signwriting was 'regilded'. One of the oldest pubs in the area it dates back to the 1600s, with its origins in the 14th century. Food available weekdays.
❀ ◑ ▶ ♣ P

Try also: Lamb, Norwood Rd (Courage)

RUISLIP MANOR
J J Moons
12 Victoria Road
☎ (01895) 622373
11-11; 12-10.30 Sun
Boddingtons Bitter; Courage Directors; Fuller's London Pride; Shepherd Neame Spitfire; Theakston Best Bitter; guest beers H
Conventional Wetherspoon's (a former Woolworth's conversion). Now well established (same manager for eight years) and deservedly popular. No car park but 'pay and display' at rear.
Q ◑ ▶ & ⊖ ⅍ ⊞

SOUTHALL
Beaconsfield Arms
63-67 West End Road (off A4020)
☎ (020) 8574 8135
11-11; 12-10.30 Sun
Draught Bass; Greene King Abbot; Scanlon's Spike; guest beers H
Unusually situated, halfway down a residential street, but not visible from either end, this campaigning local is the last bastion of cask mild in West London, well worth seeking out before a curry on the Broadway.
❀ ⇌ ♣ P ⊟

Three Horseshoes
2 High Street
☎ (020) 8574 2001

CAMRA National Pub Inventory: Cross Keys, Selattyn, Shropshire

11-11; 12-10.30 Sun
Draught Bass; Flowers IPA; Wadworth 6X H
Built in 1922, this pub was part of the Royal Brewery's Brentford estate and replaced an earlier pub on the same site which took its name from the smithy opposite. Get your beer from the public, but you may prefer the private or saloon bars to sup your pint. No food Sun.
◑ 🍴 ⇌ ♣

TEDDINGTON
Lion
27 Wick Road
☎ (020) 8977 6631
12-11; 12-10.30 Sun
Greene King Abbot; Wadworth 6X; Young's Bitter; guest beer H
Large single-bar local, excellently refurbished by a CAMRA award-winning landlord, now attracting a wider custom. Excellent meals (to 9pm eves) and a large garden make it well worth finding.
🚲 ⊛ ◑ ⇌ (Hampton Wick)

Queen Dowager
49 North Lane
☎ (020) 8977 2583
11-11; 12-10.30 Sun
Young's Bitter, Special, seasonal beers H
Pleasant, quiet, local just off the main street and convenient for car parks, it is popular with staff at the nearby National Physical Laboratory. A surprisingly large garden extends round behind the pub.
Q ⊛ ◑ 🍴 ⇌ ♣

Try also: Builders Arms, Field Lane (Nomura)

TWICKENHAM
Eel Pie
9-11 Church Street
☎ (020) 8891 1717
11-11; 12-10.30 Sun
Badger IPA, Dorset Best, Tanglefoot, seasonal beers, guest beer H
In an historic street off the town centre, this perenially popular pub enjoys a reputation for high quality weekday lunches. The guest beer usually comes from the Gribble Inn at Oving, Sussex. Inch's Stonehouse cider available.
◑ ⇌ ♣ ⌂

Prince Albert
30 Hampton Road
☎ (020) 8894 3963
11-11; 12-10.30 Sun
Fuller's Chiswick, London Pride, ESB, seasonal beers H
Small Victorian pub, recently renovated and extended, popular with rugby fans on match days. Live blues music performed most Sat eves. No eve meals Sun.
⊛ ◑ ▶ ⇌ (Strawberry Hill)

Prince Blucher
124 The Green
☎ (020) 8894 1824
11-11; 12-10.30 Sun
Fuller's Chiswick, London Pride, ESB, seasonal beers H
Large, family-oriented pub with a childrens' play area in the sizeable garden, which hosts summer barbecues. Very busy for weeked TV football and rugby. No meals Sun eve.
⊛ ◑ ▶ ⇌ (Strawberry Hill)

Try also: Old Anchor, Richmond Road (Young's)

UXBRIDGE
Load of Hay
Villier Street
☎ (01895) 234676
11-3, 5.30 (7 Sat)-11; 12-3, 7-10.30 Sun
Crown Buckley Best Bitter; guest beers H
It's worth pushing past the regulars to the front bar – it's a little gem. Micros feature strongly in the changing range of three guest beers, the excellent quality of which is matched by the food (booking advised Fri); no meals Sun eve.
Q ☕ ⊛ ◑ ▶ ♣ P ⚲

WEST DRAYTON
De Burgh Arms
Station Approach, High Street
☎ (01895) 432823
12 (11 Fri & Sat)-11; 12-10.30 Sun
Beer range varies H
Next to the station, this large pub is a 17th-century Grade II listed building. All pumps have sparklers, but bar staff willingly remove them on request to serve any of the six beers usually available. Full menu available 12 to 9.45 (6.45 Sun).
⊛ ◑ ▶ ♿ ⇌ ⌂ P

INDEPENDENT BREWERIES

Freedom: SW6
Fuller's: W4
London Bridge: SE1
Mash: W1
Meantime: SE7
Pacific Oriental: EC2
Pitfield: N1
Soho: WC2
Young's: SW18

Hops on a bus

CAMRA is firmly opposed to drinking and driving. The Good Beer Guide lists bus information phone lines for Britain, Northern Ireland and the offshore islands.
National Bus Hotline 0870 608 2608

ENGLAND

Bedfordshire & Luton Bedfordshire CC 01234 228337; Luton UA 01582 404074.

Berkshire Bracknell Forest BC 01344 424938; Reading BC/Wokingham BC 0118 959 4000; Newbury UA 01635 40743; Windsor & Maidenhead RBC 01753 524144.

Buckinghamshire & Milton Keynes UA: 0345 382000.

Cambridgeshire & Peterborough City 01223 717740.

Cheshire: Cheshire CC: 01244 602666; Halton BC: 0151 471 7384; Warrington BC 01925 444250.

Cornwall: 01209 719988.

Cumbria: 01228 606000.

Derbyshire & Derby City 01332 292200.

Devon Devon CC: 01392 382800; Plymouth: 01752 222666; Torbay UA: 01803 613226.

Dorset Dorset CC: 01305 783645; Bournemouth BC: 01202 557272; Poole BC: 01202 673555.

Durham Durham CC: 0191 383 3337; Darlington BC: 01325 384573; Hartlepool BC: 01429 523555; Stockton-on-Tees BC: 01642 444777.

Essex Essex CC, Southend BC & Thurrock/Grays BC: 0345 000333.

Gloucestershire & Bristol Glos CC: 01452 425543; Bristol City & S Glos UA: 0117 955 5111

Hampshire Hants CC: 01962 846924; Portsmouth City: 0239 265 0967; Southampton City: 0238 055 3011.

Herefordshire & Worcestershire 0345 125436.

Hertfordshire 0345 244344.

Isle of Wight 01983 823710.

Kent Kent CC & Medway UA: 0345 696996.

Lancashire Lancs CC, Blackburn with Darwen BC & Blackpool BC: 01257 241693.

Leicestershire & Rutland Leicestershire: 0116 251 1411; Rutland CC: 01572 758290.

Lincolnshire Lincolnshire CC: 01522 553135; N Lincs (Scunthorpe) UA: 01522 532424; NE Lincs (Grimsby) DC: 01472 358646.

Greater London All London boroughs: 0207 222 1234.

Greater Manchester 0161 228 7811.

Merseyside 0151 236 7676.

Norfolk 0500 626116.

Northamptonshire 01604 751431.

Northumberland 01670 751431.

Nottinghamshire & Nottingham City 0115 924 0000.

Oxfordshire 01865 711312/01865 772250.

Shropshire & Telford & Wrekin UA 0345 056785.

Somerset Somerst CC: 01823 272033; Bath & NE Somerset UA: 0117 955 5111; N Somerset (Weston-super-Mare) UA: 0117 955 5111.

Staffordshire & City of Stoke on Trent 01785 223344.

Suffolk 0645 583358.

Surrey 01737 223000.

Sussex East Sussex CC: 01273 474747; West Sussex CC: 0345 959099; Brighton & Hove UA: 01273 886200/01273 674881.

Tyne & Wear 0191 232 5325.

Warwickshire 01926 414140.

West Midlands 0121 200 2700.

Wiltshire Wiltshire CC: 0345 090899; Swindon BC: 01793 428428.

Yorkshire Yorkshire North CC: 01325 468771; Middlesbrough & Redcar & Cleveland BC & Stockton BC: 01642 444777; York City: 01904 624161; Yorkshire South: 01709 515151; Yorkshire West: 0113 245 7676.

WALES

Glamorgan Bridgend UA: 01656 647093; Caerphilly UA: 01495 235223; Cardiff UA: 0292 087 3252/0292 039 6521; Merthyr Tydfil UA: 01685 385539; Neath & Port Talbot UA: 01792 222718/01792 580580; Rhondda Cynon Taff UA: 01443 494700/01443 682671; Swansea UA: 01792 636348/01792 580580; Vale of Glamorgan: 01446 704687/01292 039 6521.

Gwent 01495 355444.

Mid Wales 01597 826643/01970 617951.

North East Wales Denbighshire UA: 01824 706968; Flintshire UA: 01352 704035; Wrexham UA: 01978 266166.

North West Wales Isle of Anglesey UA: 01248 752459/01248 750444; Conwy UA: 01492 575412; Gwynedd UA: 01286 679525.

West Wales Carmarthenshire UA: 01267 231817; Ceredigion UA: 01545 572504/01970 617951; Pembrokeshire UA: 01437 775227.

SCOTLAND

Borders 01835 825123/01896 752237.

Central Clackmannanshire UA: 01786 446474; Falkirk UA: 01324 504724.

Dumfries & Galloway 0345 090510.

Fife 01592 416060.

Grampian & Aberdeen 01224 637047.

Highlands & Islands Highlands UA: 01463 702695/01463 239292; Orkney: 01856 873535/01463 702695; Shetlands: 01595 694100; Western Isles UA: 01851 703773/01463 702695.

Lothians 0131 225 3858.

Strathclyde 0141 332 7133.

Tayside Angus UA: 01307 461775; Dundee City: 01382 433125; Perth & Kinross UA: 0845 301 1130

NORTHERN IRELAND
Belfast 0289 024 6485; Ulster area 0289 033 3000.

CHANNEL ISLANDS
Alderney: 01481 823760; Guernsey: 01481 43400; Jersey: 01534 21201.

ISLE OF MAN
IoM Transport: 01624 662525.

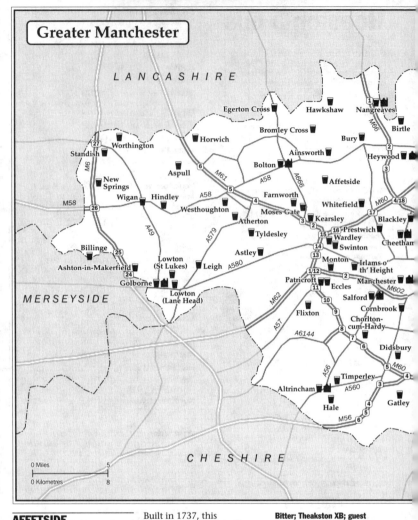

Greater Manchester

AFFETSIDE

Pack Horse

52 Watling Street (2 miles
NW of Walshaw) OS755136
☎ (01204) 883802

11.30-3, 7 (6 Fri)-11; 11-11 Sat;
12-10.30 Sun

**Hyde's Anvil Light, Bitter, P
seasonal beers** H

Country pub affording
panoramic views, on the
course of a Roman road. Parts
of the pub are said to date
from the 15th century.
Lunches served daily but eve
meals Fri only (6-8).

AINSWORTH

Duke William

Wells Street (off B6196 2½
miles W of Bury) OS763103
☎ (01204) 524726

12-11; 12-10.30 Sun

**Boddingtons Bitter; Lees Bitter;
Taylor Landlord** H

Built in 1737, this
community-focused village
local is a hidden gem. It has a
good reputation for its home-
cooked food.

ALTRINCHAM

Old Market Tavern

Old Market Place
☎ (0161) 927 7062

12-11; 12-10.30 Sun

Beer range varies H

Originally a 19th-century
coaching inn; an ever-
changing range of up to 10
ales and four ciders are
complemented by a good
choice of Belgian beers, and
good food.

Orange Tree

13-15 Old Market Place
☎ (0161) 928 2600

11.45-11; 12-10.30 Sun

Marston's Pedigree; Ruddles Best

**Bitter; Theakston XB; guest
beers** H

Friendly, family-run local.
Note the old photos of local
interest including long-gone
pubs. An extensive range of
good food is available until
9pm.

ASHTON-IN-MAKERFIELD

Sir Thomas Gerard

8 Gerard Street
☎ (01942) 713519

11-11; 12-10.30 Sun

**Boddingtons Bitter; Courage
Directors; Theakston Best Bitter;
Thwaites Mild; guest beers** H

Wetherspoon's conversion of
a former supermarket; one of
the few cask outlets left in
this keg wilderness.

ASHTON-UNDER-LYNE

Caledonia Hotel

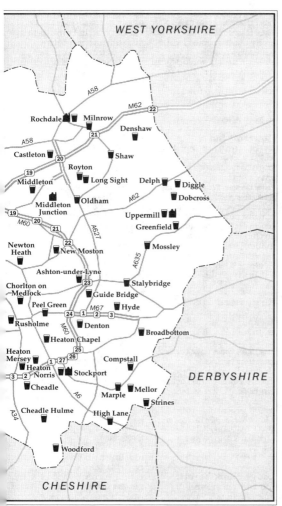

WEST YORKSHIRE

Rochdale • Milnrow
M62 [22]
Denshaw
A58
[21]
Castleton • Shaw
[20]
Royton
[19] Long Sight
Middleton • Delph • Diggle
A62 • Dobcross
Oldham
Middleton
Junction
Uppermill
[19]
M60 [20]
[21] Greenfield
Newton A627
Heath [22] New Moston Mossley
A635
Ashton-under-Lyne
[23] Stalybridge
Chorlton on
Medlock • Guide Bridge
Peel Green M67 • Hyde
[24] 1 2
Rusholme 3 Broadbottom
M60 • Denton
Heaton Chapel
Heaton [25]
Mersey [26] Compstall
1 [27]
Heaton DERBYSHIRE
3 2 Norris • Stockport
Cheadle
A6 • Mellor
Marple • Strines
Cheadle Hulme
A34 High Lane

CHESHIRE

• Woodford

55-57 Ratcliffe Road (between B5238 and B5239)
☎ (01942) 830285
7-11; 12-10.30 Sun
Burtonwood Bitter; guest beer Ⓗ
Open-plan local, slightly off the beaten track; the two halves of the pub retain their separate identities. Note the fine fireplace in the lounge.
🏾 🐎 🌸 ♣

ASTLEY

Cart & Horses
221 Manchester Road
☎ (01942) 870751
12-11; 12-10.30 Sun
Holt Mild, Bitter Ⓗ
Local roadside pub in an unusual position. A classic pub frontage leads into a lounge, raised no-smoking room and a sporting tap room.
🍺 ♣ P ⚬

ATHERTON

Atherton Arms
6 Tyldesley Road
☎ (01942) 882885
12-11; 12-10.30 Sun
Holt Mild, Bitter Ⓗ
A large central bar serves three distinct areas: a tap room with pool and snooker tables; a large lounge with several seating areas and a hall leading to a concert room.
🍺 ♿ ⇌ ♣ P

Pendle Witch
2-4 Warburton Place
☎ (01942) 884537
12-11 12-10.30 Sun
Moorhouse's Black Cat, Premier, Pendle Witches Brew, seasonal beers; guest beers Ⓗ
Off the main road, down an alley two town houses have been converted to create a popular Moorhouse's one-room pub with more standing room than seating. It also has pleasant outside drinking areas; worth seeking out. 🌸 ♣

Wheatsheaf
48 Market Street
☎ (01942) 883948
11.30-3.30, 7-11; 11.30-11 Fri & Sat; 12-10.30 Sun
Lees GB Mild, Bitter Ⓗ
Recently refurbished, the pub retains two front lounges boasting etched windows and its vestibule entrances. A popular meeting place for local societies. Q ◖ ▶ ♣

BILLINGE

Holts Arms (Foot)
Crank Road (opp. hospital)
☎ (01695) 622705
12-11; 12-10.30 Sun
Burtonwood Bitter guest beers Ⓗ

---

13 Warrington Street
☎ (0161) 339 7177
11-11; 12-4, 7-10.30 Sun
Robinson's Hatters Mild, Best Bitter, Frederic's Ⓗ
Three-storey town-centre pub, recently well refurbished to create three distinct drinking areas and a raised dining area. Dark-stained wood and tartan fabrics lend a warm feel to a friendly, sociable atmosphere. Good home-made food (eve meals Tue-Sat).
🌸 🛏 ◖▶ ⇌ P

Dog & Pheasant
528 Oldham Road
☎ (0161) 330 4894
12-11; 12-10.30 Sun
Banks's Mild; Marston's Bitter, Pedigree, HBC Ⓗ
Popular, friendly local, near Medlock Valley Country Park. It serves good value food (not Tue or Sun eves).
🏾 🌸 ◖ ▶ P

Oddfellows Arms
Kings Road, Hurst
☎ (0161) 330 3656
11-11; 12-10.30 Sun
Robinson's Hatters Mild, Best Bitter, Old Tom (winter) Ⓗ
Lively, comfortable and sociable, this five-roomed, street-corner local is an established *Guide* entry. Many original features remain including the magnificent bar, snug, and vault/lounge. 🌸 ♣ ⚬

Witchwood
152 Old Street
☎ (0161) 344 0321
12-11; 12-10.30 Sun
John Smith's Bitter; Theakston Best Bitter; guest beers Ⓗ
Lively, two-bar pub, known as a venue for good live music. ⇌

ASPULL

New Inn

1721 listed building of low ceilings and old beams. It is reputed to have once housed the local hospital mortuary. It has its own bowling green.

🏚 Q ⌨ ◖ ▮ ➕ ♣ P ✄

BIRTLE

Pack Horse Inn
Elbut Lane (N of B6222 near Jericho) OS836125
☎ (0161) 764 3620
11.30-11; 12-10.30 sun
Lees GB Mild, Bitter, seasonal beers Ⓗ

Cosy rural pub, dating from the 18th century. A conservatory has been added and the old barn converted to accommodate the restaurant and lounge areas. Meals served 12-9.30.

🏚 ⌨ ◖ ▮ ▲ P

BLACKLEY

Duke of Wellington
36 Weardale Road, Higher Blackley (off A6104, 3/4 mile from A576)
☎ (0161) 720 6809
11-11; 11-4, 7-11 Sat; 12-4, 7-10.30 Sun
Holt Mild, Bitter Ⓗ

Holt's largest sales of mild are achieved in this well-proportioned mock-Tudor house. It comprises a vault, snug and a large lounge and tends to be busy, often bustling. Look out for the brass war memorial and the stunning bar.

Q ⌨ ♣

BOLTON

Dog & Partridge
26 Manor Street
☎ (01204) 388596
5 (12 Fri & Sat)-11; 12-10.30 Sun
Thwaites Bitter, seasonal beers Ⓗ
Enterprising, unspoilt local just off the town centre. It offers a convivial atmosphere and a wide range of social activities. Note Cornbrook window in the 'music room'.

⌨ ⇌ ♣ 🍴

Hen & Chickens
143 Deansgate (near bus station)
☎ (01204) 389836
11.30-11; 7.30-10.30 Sun
Greenalls Mild, Bitter; guest beers Ⓗ
Friendly, town-centre local with a central bar. Winner of various awards, including the local CAMRA *Pub of the Year*, it stocks three changing guest beers. No food Sun.

◖ ⇌

Hope & Anchor
747 Chorley Old Road (B6226)
☎ (01204) 842650

3 (12 Sat)-11; 12-10.30 Sun
Tetley Mild, Bitter; Lees Bitter; Taylor Landlord Ⓗ
Lively, multi-roomed local with a welcoming atmosphere, known locally as 'the Little Cocker' (close to Doffcocker Lodge nature reserve). The pub fields several darts and dominoes teams.

🏚 ⌨ ⌨ ⌨ ♣ P

Howcroft Inn ☆
36 Pool Street (off Topp Way, A673)
☎ (01204) 526814
12-11; 12-10.30 Sun
Taylor Landlord; Tetley Mild, Bitter; guest beers Ⓗ
Exceptional, unpretentious pub just outside the town centre. Its large bowling green hosts an annual Autumn beer festival. Bank Top beers are a regular feature. Excellent value Sun lunches (served 12-5).

🏚 ⌨ ◖ ♣ ⌣ P

Kings Head
52-56 Junction Road (off A676)
☎ (01204) 62609
12-11; 12-10.30 Sun
Tetley Mild, Bitter; Taylor Landlord; guest beers Ⓗ
Grade II listed building, mainly 18th-century, but re-furbished in 1991 to provide three drinking areas (one with a York stone floor) and a long bar. A bowling green at the rear is available for hire. Bank Top beers are often available.

⌨ ◖ ▮ ♣ P

Lodge Bank Tavern
260 Bridgeman Street (1/2 mile off Thynne Street, B9999)
☎ (01204) 531946
12-11 (12.30-4.30, 7.30-11 winter); 12-10.30 Sun
Lees GB Mild, Bitter, seasonal beers Ⓗ
Friendly local just outside the town centre, opposite 'Bobby Heywood's' park.

⌨ ⌨ ⇌ ♣ P

Lord Clyde
109 Folds Road (A676)
☎ (01204) 521705
11-11; 12-10.30 Sun
Hyde's Anvil Light, Dark, Ⓟ Jekyll's Gold Ⓗ
Traditional, multi-roomed pub near the town centre: a small L-shaped tap room, a small room at the rear and a larger lounge with pool table. Children welcome until 7pm.

🛏 ⌨ ◖ ⌨ ♣ P 🍴

Man & Scythe
6-8 Churchgate
☎ (01204) 527267
11-11; 12-10.30 Sun

Boddingtons Bitter; Flowers IPA, Original; Holt Bitter; guest beers Ⓗ
The fifth Earl of Derby spent his last hours here before being executed. Ask to see the 12th-century cellar. Excellent good value food.

⌨ ⌨ ♣ ♣

Try also: Varsity, Churchgate (Banks)

BROADBOTTOM

Cheshire Cheese
65 Lower Market Street
☎ (01457) 762339
6 (4 Sat)-11; 12-10.30 Sun
Thwaites Mild, Bitter; Yates 1884 Bitter; guest beers Ⓗ
Popular, end-of-terrace friendly pub, on the Etherow Valley Way walk. It is the only local outlet for Hoegaarden.

🏚 ⌨ ▲ ⇌ ♣

BROMLEY CROSS

Flag Inn
50 Hardmans Lane (off B6472, Darwin Rd)
☎ (01204) 302236
11-11; 12-10.30 Sun
Boddingtons Bitter; Dent Bitter; guest beers Ⓗ
At this attractive, stone-flagged Whitbread managed house, the imaginative guest beers change weekly.

🏚 ⌨ ◖

BURY

Blue Bell
840 Manchester Road (A56, near Blackford Bridge)
☎ (0161) 766 2496
11.30-11; 12-10.30 Sun
Holt Mild, Bitter Ⓗ
Large, three-roomed pub with a traditional vault, run by an amiable host. Frequented by mature Man U fans, the comfortable lounge is the haunt of friendly locals.

⌨ ⌨ ♣ P

Dusty Miller
87 Crostons Road (B6213/B6214 jct)
☎ (0161) 764 1124
2 (12 Fri & Sat)-11; 12-10.30 Sun
Moorhouse's Black Cat, Premier, Pendle Witches Brew; guest beers Ⓗ
Two-roomed local with a central bar, at a busy road junction (parking limited). A glassed-over courtyard is pleasant in summer.

⌨ ⊖

Old Blue Bell
2 Bell Lane (B621/B622 jct)
☎ (0161) 761 3674
12-11; 12-10.30 Sun
Holt Mild, Bitter Ⓗ
Prominent building at a busy

road junction, this traditional, comfortable, multi-roomed pub hosts live music Sat afternoon, Thu and Sun eves; children welcome until 6pm. Q ⊞ ⊖ ♣

Try also: Arthur Inn, Bolton Rd (Porter); **Rose & Crown**, Manchester Old Rd (Free)

CASTLETON
Blue Pits Inn
842 Manchester Road (A664)
☎ (01706) 632151
12-4 (5 Fri & Sat), 7.30-11; 12-4, 7-10.30 Sun
Lees GB Mild, Bitter ⊞
Friendly local in a former railway building which once served as a mortuary. The three distinct drinking areas now offer a much warmer atmosphere. Former winner of J W Lees *Best-Kept Cellar* award. ⇌ ♣ P

CHEADLE
Queens Arms
177 Stockport Road (100 yds W of M60, jct 2)
☎ (0161) 428 3081
12 (3 Mon)-11; 12-10.30 Sun
Robinson's Hatters Mild, Old Stockport, Best Bitter ⊞
Unpretentious, three-roomed local near the AA centre. Families are welcome until 8.30 in the rear lounge and large garden which contains play equipment.
🏚 ⛵ ✿ P ⊁ ⊟

CHEADLE HULME
Church
90 Ravenoak Road (A5149)
☎ (0161) 485 1897
11-11; 12-10.30 Sun
Robinson's Hatters Mild, Old Stockport, Hartleys XB (occasional), **Best Bitter** ⊞
Attractive, cottage-style pub where both the comfortable lounges feature real fires. The small traditional vault feels like a totally different pub. No meals Sun eve.
🏚 Q ✿ ◖ ⊞ ⇌ ♣ P

King's Hall
13 Station Road
☎ (0161) 485 1555
11-11; 12-10.30 Sun
Boddingtons Bitter; Courage Directors; Theakston Best Bitter; guest beers ⊞
Typical Wetherspoon's conversion, turning a former Chinese restaurant into an attractive modern pub. The conservatory at the rear is a no-smoking area. It is popular with all ages, particularly younger drinkers eves. Dress restrictions apply at times.
Q ✿ ◖ ⚲ ⇌ ⊁

CHEETHAM
Queen's Arms
4-6 Honey Street (off A665)
☎ (0161) 834 4239
12-11; 12-10.30 Sun
Phoenix Bantam; Taylor Landlord; guest beers ⊞
Welcoming, two-roomed free house, boasting a large garden, barbecue and children's play area at the rear, that gives a panoramic view of Manchester across the Irk Valley. Six guest beers are complemented by a selection of Belgian draught and bottled beers. Note the original Empress Brewery tiling on the front.
🏚 ⛵ ✿ ◖ ▶ ⇌ (Victoria) ⊖ ♣

CHORLTON-CUM-HARDY
Beech Inn
72 Beech Road
☎ (0161) 881 1180
11-11; 12-10.30 Sun
Boddingtons Bitter; Flowers Original; Morland Old Speckled Hen; Taylor Best Bitter, Landlord; Whitbread Trophy ⊞
Thriving, three-roomed pub, just off the village green; no food, no music, no gimmicks.
Q ✿ ⊞ ♣

Marble Beer House
57 Manchester Road
☎ (0161) 881 9206
12-11; 12-10.30 Sun
Marble Bitter, Liberty IPA, McKenna's Revenge Porter; guest beer ⊞
This continental-style café/bar with pavement seating, stocks a good range of bottled Belgian and German beer. Their own beers are brewed in Manchester. Soup and sandwiches available lunchtime. Q ✿

CHORLTON-ON-MEDLOCK
Hogshead
421-423 Oxford Road (B5117)
☎ (0161) 273 1490
11 (12 Sat)-11; 12-10.30 Sun
Boddingtons Bitter; Wadworth 6X; ⊞ **guest beers** ⊞/Ⓖ
This striking building is a recent addition to the busy Oxford Road near the university. The usual Hogshead interior: the upstairs bar is strictly no-smoking. It gets busy in term-time and also attracts customers from the local hospitals. ◖ ▶ ⅙ ⊖ ⊁

COMPSTALL
Andrew Arms
George Street

☎ (0161) 427 2281
11.30-11; 12-10.30 Sun
Robinson's Hatters Mild, Best Bitter ⊞
Detached stone pub next to the chapel in an attractive village close to Etherow Park nature reserve.
🏚 ✿ ◖ ⊞ ♣ P

CORNBROOK
Hope Inn
297 Chester Road
11-5, 7.30-11; 12-5, 7-10.30 Sun
Hyde's Anvil Light, Bitter, Ⓟ **seasonal beers** ⊞
Rare example of a surviving Manchester stand-up, street-corner local: telly, lots of chat, and a crossword library characterize this pub.
⇌ (Deansgate) ⊖ (G.Mex) ♣ ⊟

DELPH
Royal Oak (Th'heights)
Broad Lane, Heights (1 mile above Denshaw Road)
OS982090
☎ (01457) 874460
7-11; 12-4, 7-10.30 Sun
Boddingtons Bitter; Coach House Gunpowder Mild; guest beers ⊞
Isolated, 250-year-old stone pub on a packhorse route, overlooking the Tame Valley; a cosy bar and three rooms. Good, home-cooked food (Fri-Sun eve plus Sun lunch in summer) often features home-bred beef and pork. The house beer is brewed by Moorhouse's.
🏚 Q ✿ ▶ P

DENSHAW
Black Horse Inn
2-4 The Culvert, Oldham Road (A672, 2 miles from M62 jct 22)
☎ (01457) 874375
12-3, 6-11; 12-11 Sat; 12-10.30 Sun
Banks's Original, Bitter; Taylor Landlord; guest beers ⊞
Attractive 17th-century, stone pub, in a row of terraced cottages, comprising a cosy L-shaped bar area and two rooms. It offers a wide range of home-cooked food.
⛵ ✿ ◖ ▶ ▲ P ⊁ ⊟

Try also: Junction, Rochdale Rd (Lees)

DENTON
Lowes Arms
301 Hyde Road
☎ (0161) 336 3069
12-11; 12-10.30 Sun
Boddingtons Bitter; guest beers ⊞
Imposing former home-brewpub; under inspired management it has turned from a dilapidated boozer into a thriving, hospitable

pub. Up to four guest beers, always come from independent breweries.
❀ ◖ ▶ ⊟ ♣ P

Red Lion
1 Stockport Road
☎ (0161) 337 8032
11-11; 11-4, 7-11 Sat; 12-4, 7-10.30 Sun

Hyde's Anvil Light, Bitter Ⓗ
Brick pub displaying an attractive façade at a busy junction: one large main room, plus a cosy front lounge. This is a thriving centre for the local community. Q ♣

DIDSBURY

Fletcher Moss
1 William Street
☎ (0161) 438 0073
12-11; 12-10.30 Sun

Hyde's Anvil Dark, Bitter, Jekyll's Gold, seasonal beers Ⓗ
Recently extended to include a spacious new conservatory, it is one of the few village pubs that is not a food-driven operation, but retains a strong local identity.
& P

Hogshead
653A Wilmslow Road (B5093)
☎ (0161) 448 7875
12-11; 12-10.30 Sun

Boddingtons Bitter; Tetley Bitter; Wadworth 6X; Ⓗ **Marston's Pedigree; guest beers** Ⓖ/Ⓗ
Purpose-built new café-bar in typical Hogshead style where much use is made of bare brickwork and wood. It stocks up to 14 beers (four may be gravity dispense).
❀ ◖ ▶ & ⌣ ⚲

DIGGLE

Diggle Hotel
Station Houses (1/2 mile off A670) OS011081
☎ (01457) 872741
12-3, 5-11; 12-11 Sat; 12-3, 5-10.30 Sun

Boddingtons Bitter; Taylor Golden Best, Landlord; guest beer Ⓗ
Family-run stone pub, in a pleasant hamlet. It lies close to the Standedge canal tunnel under the Pennines and comprises a bar area and two rooms with an accent on home-cooked food (served all day Sat).
❀ ⇌ ◖ ▶ P

DOBCROSS

Navigation
Wool Road (A670)
☎ (01457) 872418
11.30-3, 5-11; 11.30-11 Sat; 12-10.30 Sun

Banks's Original, Bitter; Camerons Bitter; seasonal beers Ⓗ

Next to the Huddersfield narrow canal, this stone pub was built in 1806 to slake the thirsts of the navvies cutting the Stondedge tunnel under the Pennines. The open-plan lounge is a shrine to brass band music.; live concerts staged summer Suns. Good home-cooked food.
❀ ◖ ▶ P

Swan Inn (Top House)
The Square
☎ (01457) 873451
12-3, 5-11; 12-3; 7-10.30 Sun

Moorhouse's Pendle Witches Brew; Phoenix Best Bitter, Thirsty Moon, Wobbly Bob, seasonal beers; Theakston Mild, Best Bitter Ⓗ
This stone village local circa 1765 boasts an interesting history. The renovated bar area has a flagged floor and serves three distinct drinking areas. Good value, home-cooked food includes Indian dishes.
⚏ Q ❀ ◖ ▶ ⌣

ECCLES

Lamb Hotel ☆
33 Regent Street (A57, by Metrolink terminus)
☎ (0161) 789 3882
11.30-11; 12-10.30 Sun

Holt Mild, Bitter Ⓗ
Archetypal Edwardian Holt's house, featuring splendid Art Nouveau tiling, glazing and ornate woodwork. The largest of its four rooms is dominated by a full-sized billiard table.
Q ⊟ ⇌ ⊖ ♣ P

Try also: Wellington, Church St (Holt)

EGERTON

Cross Guns
Blackburn Road (A666)
☎ (01204) 303341
12-11; 12-10.30 Sun

Bank Top Brydge Bitter; Black Sheep Best Bitter; Boddingtons Bitter; Tetley Bitter; guest beer Ⓗ
Victorian local where a friendly welcome is assured; small pool room, TV corner and a larger dining area (most meals are home-cooked).
⚏ Q ❀ ◖ ▶ P ⌣

FARNWORTH

Britannia
34 King Street (off A6053, opp. bus station)
☎ (01204) 571629
11-11; 12-10.30 Sun

Boddingtons Bitter; Moorhouse's Premier; Whitbread Trophy; guest beers Ⓗ
Extremely popular town-centre pub with a large basic vault and a smaller lounge. It

hosts mini beer festivals (may and Aug Bank Hols) in a specially covered outdoor bar area. Excellent value lunches.
❀ ◖ ⇌ ♣

FLIXTON

Church Inn
34 Church Road (B5123, near station)
☎ (0161) 748 2158
11-11; 12-10.30 Sun

Cains Bitter; Greenalls Mild, Bitter; guest beer Ⓗ
Former schoolhouse and courtroom, now a comfortably furnished pub with various seating areas.
⚏ ❀ ◖ ▶ ⇌ ♣ P

GATLEY

Gothic Bar
61a Church Road (off A560)
☎ (0161) 491 1966
12-11; 12-10.30 Sun

Cains Mild, Bitter, FA, seasonal beers; guest beer Ⓗ
Single-roomed pub converted from a former chapel, this is Cains only tied house in Greater Manchester. Try the interesting range of home-cooked food, including vegetarian options; eve meals served Thu & Fri, 5-8.
Q ❀ ◖ ▶ ⇌ ♣ ⌣

GOLBORNE

Railway
131 High Street
☎ (01942) 728202
12 (11 Sat)-11; 12-10.30 Sun

Theakston Mild; Sarah's Hop House Bitter, seasonal beers; guest beers Ⓗ
After many months of delays and mishaps the Railway now boasts the only brewery in the area. Live music (Fri) and a Beer Club make this a very popular pub. A central bar serves both the games room and lounge.
⚏ ⇌ ⌣ P ⚲

GREENFIELD

King William IV
134 Chew Valley Road (A669 Ladhill Lane jct)
☎ (01457) 873933
11.30-11; 12-10.30 Sun

Draught Bass; Highgate Dark; Tetley Bitter; Worthington Bitter; guest beers Ⓗ
Detached stone pub on a main road at the village centre, with a cosy, friendly interior where locals meet to discuss village life, uninterrupted by a juke box. Handy for walks over the Saddleworth Hills.
❀ ◖ ⇌ ♣ P

Railway
11 Shaw Hall Bank Road

(opp. station)
☎ (01457) 872307
5 (12 Fri & Sat)-11; 12-10.30 Sun
John Smith's Bitter; Taylor Golden Best, Landlord; guest beers Ⓗ
Friendly village local with a central bar and games area; note the collection of old Saddleworth photos in the public bar. Live music is performed Thu and Fri eves and Sun afternoon.
🏚 🛏 🍺 🏃 ≈ ♣ P

GUIDE BRIDGE
Boundary
2 Audenshaw Road
☎ (0161) 330 1677
11-11; 12-10.30 Sun
Phoenix Old Oak; John Smith's Bitter; guest beers Ⓗ
Friendly, welcoming local pub by Ashton canal and railway station. Canal boat trips by horse-drawn narrow boat are organised here. Good value food and an annual beer festival in June are added attractions.
◖ ◗ 🍺 ≈ ♣ P

HALE
Railway
128-130 Ashley Road (opp. station)
☎ (0161) 941 5367
11-11; 12-10.30 Sun
Robinson's Hatters Mild, Hartleys XB, Best Bitter Ⓗ
Reputedly haunted, but friendly and unspoilt, this 1930s multi-roomed local retains much wood panelling. No food Sun.
Q 🍺 ◖ 🍺 🏃 ≈ ⊖ (Altrincham) ♣

HAWKSHAW
Red Lion
81 Ramsbottom Road (A676)
OS753150
☎ (01204) 856600
12-3, 6-11; 12-10.30 Sun
Jennings Bitter, Cumberland Ale; guest beer Ⓗ
Attractive, single-roomed, stone pub set in a picturesque area. Freshly prepared, home-made food is available at the bar whilst a more extensive menu is served in the restaurant.
🛏 ◖ ◗ P

HEATON CHAPEL
Hinds Head
Manchester Road (A626)
☎ (0161) 431 9301
11.30-11; 12-10.30 Sun
Castle Eden Ale; Fuller's London Pride; Marston's Pedigree; Taylor Landlord; Thwaites Bitter; guest beer Ⓗ
Smart, attractive, cottage-style pub with a conservatory restaurant and a lounge

divided into distinct areas to give an intimate feel. Well respected for its excellent food (not Sun eve), it boasts the best pub garden in the area.
Q 🍺 ◖ ◗ 🏃 P

HEATON MERSEY
Griffin
552 Didsbury Road (A5145)
☎ (0161) 443 4077
12-11; 12-10.30 Sun
Holt Mild, Bitter Ⓗ
Often very busy, this multi-roomed main road local is dominated by its superb mahogany and etched glass bar.
🍺 ◖ ≈ (E Didsbury) P ⤨

HEATON NORRIS
Nursery ☆
Green Lane (off A6)
☎ (0161) 432 2044
11.30-3, 5.30-11; 11.30-11 Sat; 12-10.30 Sun
Hyde's Anvil Mild, Bitter, Ⓟ **Jekyll's Gold, seasonal beers** Ⓗ
Unspoilt,1930s pub, well-hidden in a pleasant suburban area, where a good choice of rooms includes a superb wood-panelled lounge. It has a bowling green at the rear. Excellent food (set lunches only Sun); children welcome if dining.
🍺 ◖ ♣ P 🍴

HEYWOOD
Wishing Well
89 York Street (A58)
☎ (01706) 620923
12-11; 12-10.30 Sun
Jennings Cumberland Ale; Moorhouse's Premier, Pendle Witches Brew; Phoenix Hopwood; Taylor Landlord; guest beers Ⓗ
This popular free house and restaurant serves up to ten real ales, including house beers from Moorhouse's and Phoenix.
◖ P 🍴

HIGH LANE
Royal Oak
Buxton Road (A6)
☎ (01663) 762380
12-3, 5.30-11; 11-11 Sat & summer; 12-10.30 Sun
Burtonwood Bitter; guest beers Ⓗ
On the busy A6, the Royal Oak offers lots of activities.
🏚 🍺 ◖ ◗ ♣ P

HINDLEY
Wiganer
44 Wigan Road (A577)
☎ (01942) 208884
12-11; 12-10.30 Sun
Boddingtons Bitter; Yates Bitter; guest beer (occasional) Ⓗ
Formerly known as Sir Robert

Peel, the new name relates to Wigan RLFC whose memorabilia are festooned around the open-plan pub. It serves good value lunches.
◖ ≈ ♣ P

HORWICH
Crown Hotel
1 Chorley New Road (A673/B6226 jct)
☎ (01204) 690926
11-11; 12-10.30 Sun
Holt Mild, Bitter Ⓗ
This large pub is open plan, except for the vault which houses a pool table. A handy stopping-off place for visits to the local beauty spot at Rivington.
🏚 ⛟ 🍺 ◖ 🍺 🏃 ♣ P

HYDE
Cotton Bale
21-25 Market Place
☎ (0161) 830 0380
11-11; 12-10.30 Sun
Boddingtons Bitter; Courage Directors; Thwaites Mild; guest beers Ⓗ
This large pub on two levels stands in the bustling market area of town. Converted from a shop in typical Wetherspoon's style.
Q ◖ 🏃 ≈ (Central) ⤨

Sportsman Inn
57 Mottram Road
☎ (0161) 368 5000
11-11; 12-10.30 Sun
Plassey Bitter; Taylor Landlord; Whim Magic Mushroom Mild, Hartington Bitter; guest beer Ⓗ
Brilliant, spacious local that has a risen from the ashes to become a thriving hub of the community. Regional CAMRA *Pub of the Year*, its three pleasant rooms house a snooker table and log end dartboard. 🏚 Q 🍺 ◖ 🍺 ≈ (Newton/Central) ♣ ⌂ P 🍴

White Hart
47 Old Road, Newton
☎ (0161) 368 1602
11.30-11; 12-10.30 Sun
Robinson's Hatters Mild, Best Bitter Ⓟ
Warm, friendly local near a large textile factory and surrounded by back-to-back houses. Its almost unchanged multi-roomed layout is set around a central bar; desrvedly popular.
🏚 Q 🍺 ≈ (Flowery Field) ♣

White Lion
7 Market Place
☎ (0161) 368 2948
11-11; 11-5, 7-11 Sat; 12-4, 8-10.30 Sun
Robinson's Hatters Mild, Best Bitter, Ⓟ **Old Tom** (winter) Ⓗ
Perpetually busy, this two-roomed town-centre pub gets

packed on market days. It boasts a noteworthy long bar in the tap room.
◖ ⊕ ≠ (Central) ♣

IRLAMS O' TH' HEIGHT
Wellington
345 Bolton Road (A6, old road)
☎ (0161) 745 8288
11-11; 12-10.30 Sun
Holt Mild, Bitter Ⓗ
1960s pub with a large square lounge and a comfortable snug to the side; the vault is at the rear of the bar. The main entrance is up steep steps, with wheelchair access round the left-hand side.
Q ⊕ ♣ P

KEARSLEY
Clock Face
63-65 Old Hall Street
☎ (01204) 400292
4 (3 Fri)-11; 12-5, 7-11 Sat; 12-4.30, 7-10.30 Sun
Holt Bitter; Tetley Mild, Bitter Ⓗ
Basic, traditional local that serves a dedicated loyal band of customers. Note the original working clock on the façade, over 70 years old.
🕰 🏵 ≠ ♣

LEIGH
Musketeer
15 Lord Street
☎ (01942) 701913
11-11; 12-10.30 Sun
Boddingtons Mild, Bitter; guest beers Ⓗ
Notable features here include the see-through juke box in the lounge, the tiled area in front of the bar, and the RL photographs in the tap room. A haven in a town running out of real beer pubs.
◖ ◗ ⊕ ♣

LONGSIGHT
Sir Edwin Chadwick
587 Stockport Road (A6, near A6010 jct)
☎ (0161) 256 2806
11-11; 12-10.30 Sun
Boddingtons Bitter; Courage Directors; Theakston Best Bitter; guest beers Ⓗ
The landlord is committed to keeping two guest beers at all times in this Wetherspoon's pub which is full of locals. Comfy chairs by the door are appreciated by older customers. It also boasts two outside drinking areas.
Q 🏵 ◖ ⟨ ♿ ⌖ ⊞

LOWTON (LANE HEAD)
Red Lion
324 Newton Road
☎ (01942) 671429
12-3.30, 6-11; 12-11 Fri & Sat;

12-10.30 Sun
Greenalls Mild, Bitter; Marston's Pedigree; Tetley Bitter; guest beers Ⓗ
This large popular local comprises three lounge areas, a games room and a bowling green. It is a good base for Haydock Park and Pennington Flash. Children welcome until 9pm.
🏵 🚃 ◖ ◗ ⊕ ♣ P

LOWTON (ST LUKES)
Hare & Hounds
1 Golborne Road
☎ (01942) 728387
12-11; 12-10.30 Sun
Tetley Mild, Bitter; guest beers Ⓗ
A low-beamed entrance opens out into a large multi-area pub; from the tap room to the children's play room it is popular with all ages.
🏵 ◖ ◗ P ⌖

MANCHESTER CITY CENTRE
Bar Fringe
8 Swan Street (A62/A665 jct)
☎ (0161) 835 3815
12-11; 12-10.30 Sun
Bank Top seasonal beers; Marble seasonal beers Ⓗ
City-centre 'Brown Bar', based on the North European formula, serving a wide bottled range and Belgian draught beers. Ephemera abounds in this eccentric bar. Meals served 12-8 (6 weekends). 🏵 ◖ ≠ (Victoria)
⊖ (Market St) ♣

Beer House
6 Angel Street (off A664, near A665 jct)
☎ (0161) 839 7019
11.30-11; 12-10.30 Sun
Moorhouse's Pendle Witches Brew; Taylor Landlord; Thwaites Bitter; guest beers Ⓗ
A change of licensee, but undiminished in its appeal, it boasts 14 handpumps in the downstairs bar (two for cider); there is always a guest mild, plus Belgian beers in draught and in bottle. Food promotions represent good value.
🏵 ◖ ≠ (Victoria) ⊖ ♣ ⌂ P

Castle
66 Oldham Street (near A62/A665 jct)
☎ (0161) 236 2945
12-11; 12-10.30 Sun
Robinson's Hatters Mild, Dark Mild, Old Stockport, Hartleys XB, Best Bitter, Frederics, Old Tom Ⓗ
Larger than it would first appear; behind the tiled façade and mosaic floor entrance lie a front room with an original tiled bar, a snug and a games room. This is Robinson's only city outlet,

offering all seven ales.
⊕ 🏵 (Piccadilly) ⊖ (Piccadilly Gdns)

Circus Tavern ☆
86 Portland Street
☎ (0161) 236 5818
12-11; 12-4 (closed eve) Sun
Tetley Bitter Ⓗ
One of Britain's most unspoilt, traditional pubs, this tiny two-roomed house is a Manchester institution. Its intimacy encourages conversation and since it is so small it may shut its doors when full at weekends. Q ≠ (Piccadilly)
⊖ (Piccadilly Gdns)

City Arms
48 Kennedy Street
11.30-11; 11.30-3, 7-11 Sat; closed Sun
Tetley Bitter; guest beers Ⓗ
Deservedly popular, it is much frequented by the business community; good value food is served promptly. This listed building bears a noteworthy frontage. ◖ ≠ (Oxford Rd)
⊖ (St Peters Sq)

Grey Horse
80 Portland Street
☎ (0161) 236 1874
11-11; 12-10.30 Sun
Hyde's Anvil Mild, Bitter, Jekyll's Gold Ⓗ
This much-loved, city-centre haunt, is now back to its best. The compact single-room is ideal for a drink and a chat.
⊖ (Piccadilly) ≠ (Piccadilly Gdns)

Hare & Hounds ☆
46 Shudehill
☎ (0161) 832 4737
11-11; 12-10.30 Sun
Holt Bitter; Tetley Bitter Ⓗ
Smart, city-centre pub with all the feel of a local; extensive tiling, polished wood and mirrors surround a central lobby with a vault at the front and a lounge at the back. It is often lively with older customers enjoying a piano singalong.
🏵 ⊕ ≠ (Victoria) ⊖ ♣

Hogshead
64-66 High Street (opp. Arndale Market Hall)
☎ (0161) 832 4824
12-11; 12-10.30 Sun
Banks's Bitter; Boddingtons Bitter; Marston's Pedigree; Taylor Landlord; Wadworth 6X; guest beers Ⓗ/Ⓖ
Popular bare-boarded beer emporium of several distinct drinking areas. Busy at lunchtimes and weekends, it is handy for city-centre shopping and the numerous Indian cafés. Meals served 12-9 (8 Fri and Sat). 🕰
◖ ◗ ≠ (Victoria) ⊖ (Market St)
♣ ⌂ ⌖

Jolly Angler
47 Ducie Street
☎ (0161) 236 5307
12-3, 5.30-11; 12-11 Sat; 12-10.30 Sun
Hyde's Anvil Mild, Bitter, Jekyll's Gold, seasonal beers H
Tiny two-roomed pub in a maze of one-way back streets between Piccadilly Station and a retail park. Well worth finding, it is quiet in the afternoon, livelier eves. A mild is sometimes available.
🚃 ≠ (Piccadilly) ⊖ ♣

Lass o'Gowrie
36 Charles Street
☎ (0161) 273 6932
11-11; 12-10.30 Sun
Lass o'Gowrie Log 35, Log 42; Marston's Pedigree; Taylor Landlord; Wadworth 6X H
Former Hogshead, this brew-pub is spectaculary clad in original Threlfalls tilework. The open-plan interior retains a large snug.
◖ ᕁ ≠ (Oxford Rd) ᗒ P ⊁

Marble Arch
73 Rochdale Road, Collyhurst (A664)
☎ (0161) 832 5914
11.30 (12 Sat)-11; closed Sun
Marble N/4 Bitter, Bitter, Liberty IPA, McKenna's Revenge Porter, seasonal beers; guest beers H
First made its reputation as a pioneering free house, but now concentrates on beers from its own on-site brewery. Apart from the beer and food (11.30-8 weekdays), the pub is remarkable for its late Victorian interior, including a sloping mosaic floor. Guest beers appear at weekend.
◖ ▮ ≠ (Victoria) ⊖

Old Monkey
90-92 Portland Street (Princess St jct)
☎ (0161) 236 3787
11.30-11; 12-10.30 Sun
Holt Mild, Bitter H
Two-storey pub; the ground-floor bar displays photographs of old Manchester in the heyday of the cotton trade; the upstairs lounge, with its own bar counter is plusher and quieter. Weekday lunches served. ◖ ᕁ ≠ (Piccadilly/Oxford Rd) ⊖ (Piccadilly Gdns)

Peveril of the Peak ☆
27 Great Bridgewater Street
☎ (0161) 236 6364
12-3, 5.30 (7 Sat)-11; 7-10.30 (closed lunch) Sun
Boddingtons Bitter; Tetley Bitter; Theakston Best Bitter; guest beer H
A superb tiled exterior together with woodwork and stained glass in the bar make this almost triangular pub a classic. 🚃 ◖ ᕁ ≠ (Oxford Rd) ⊖ (St Peters Sq) ♣

Pot of Beer
36 New Mount Street (off Rochdale Road, A664)
☎ (0161) 834 8579
12-11; closed Sun
Boddingtons Bitter; Robinson's Dark Mild; H **guest beers** H/G
Hidden in a maze of narrow streets, this tiny free house is well worth seeking out. The bar and lounge are divided by a half-height wall. Polish food is a main feature of the menu (served 12-9 most days).
ᗒ 🌐 ◖ ▮ ≠ (Victoria) ⊖ ᗕ

Rain Bar
80 Great Bridgewater Street
☎ (0161) 235 6500
11-11; 12-10.30 Sun
Lees GB Mild, Bitter, Moonraker, seasonal beers H
This former umbrella factory was converted into a pub in 1999. The patio (with heaters) overlooks the Rochdale Canal; it is surrounded by trendy flats. Weekend breakfasts served from 9am. 🌐 ◖ ▮ ᕁ ≠ (Oxford Rd) ⊖ (St Peters Sq)

Sand Bar
120 Grosvenor Street, All Saints
☎ (0161) 273 3141
11 (12.30 Sat)-11; 5-10.30 Sun
Phoenix Bantam; Wells Bombardier; guest beers H
Enterprising, independently-run café bar featuring ever-changing guest beers from local micros and a wide range of foreign beers in bottle and on draught; German imports are a speciality.
◖ ≠ (Oxford Rd)

Smithfield Hotel & Bar
37 Swan Street (A665, S of A664 jct)
☎ (0161) 839 4424
12-11; 12-10.30 Sun
Greene King XX Dark Mild; H **guest beers** H/G
A northern quarter pub, always worth visiting, especially for its ever-changing range of new beers from new micros. Seven handpumps are supplemented by jugs from the cellar during beer festivals. Good value food.
🛏 ◖ ▮ ≠ (Victoria) ⊖ ♣

White Lion
43 Liverpool Road, Castlefield
☎ (0161) 832 7373
11.30-11; 12-10.30 Sun
Boddingtons Bitter; Taylor Landlord; guest beers H
Pub at the heart of the rejuvenated Castlefield area, close to the canal basins and museums. Good food is all made on the premises; the curries are highly

recommended (no meals Fri eve). 🌐 ◖ ᕁ ≠ (Deansgate) ⊖ (G.Mex)

Try also: Britons Protection, Gt Bridgewater St (Tetley); **Sinclair's,** Cathedral Gates (Samuel Smith); **White House,** Gt Ancoats St (Free)

Railway
223 Stockport Road, Rose Hill
☎ (0161) 427 2146
11.45-11; 12-10.30 Sun
Robinson's Hatters Mild, Best Bitter H
This impressive, spacious pub opened alongside Rose Hill railway station in 1878. It has an open-plan layout, with two large comfortable rooms. A good local catering for all, it serves tasty lunches. Children welcome until 5pm. 🌐 ◖ ᕁ ≠ (Rose Hill) P

Oddfellows Arms
73 Moor End Road (2 miles from Marple Bridge on back New Mills road)
☎ (0161) 449 7826
11-3, 5.30-11 (closed Mon); 12-3, 7-10.30 Sun
Adnams Bitter; Marston's Bitter, Pedigree; guest beers H
Elegant, three-storey building, sympathetically altered internally, in a picture postcard setting. It places a strong accent on quality food and an excellent choice of beers.
🚃 Q 🌐 ◖ ▮ ᕁ P ⊟

Crown
52 Rochdale Road
☎ (0161) 654 9174
11-11; 12-10.30 Sun
Lees GB Mild, Bitter H
End-of-terrace pub, recently extended, where one bar serves a large lounge full of bric-à-brac and horse brasses, and a plush, comfortable snug. It is busy and popular. ♣ P

Tandle Hill Tavern
Thornham Fold, Thornham Lane (1 mile off A671 or A664, along unmetalled road) OS898091
☎ (01706) 345297
7 (5 summer)-11; 12-11 Sat; 12-10.30 Sun
Lees GB Mild, Bitter, Moonraker (winter) H
True gem, set in a small farming community in a country park. One main room and a small snug give an atmosphere which is always warm and welcoming. Soup and sandwiches usually

available lunchtimes.
🏠 Q 🍴 🏕

MILNROW

Crown & Shuttle
170 Rochdale Road (A640)
☎ (01706) 648259
12-11; 12-10.30 Sun
Lees GB Mild, Bitter Ⓗ
Traditional pub, popular with
locals and homeward-bound
workers. Usually busy, with a
friendly atmosphere, the
three rooms provide a
homely feel. Ask to see the
landlord's military museum
in the upstairs room.
🍴 ♣ P

MONTON

Park Hotel
142 Monton Road (B5229)
☎ (0161) 787 8608
11-11; 12-10.30 Sun
Holt Mild, Bitter Ⓗ
1960s local, recently
enlarged, so the spacious
vault and lounge are
complemented by a now
roomy 'snug' displaying
canal and mining
memorabilia. 🏕 🍴 ♣ P

MOSES GATE (FARNWORTH)

Railway Hotel
Egerton Street (off B6053)
☎ (01204) 571858
12 (11.30 Sat)-11; 12-10.30 Sun
Holt Mild, Bitter Ⓗ
A central bar services this
large, open-aspect pub; the
vault is to the left, while a
small semi-partitioned area
next to the lounge houses a
pool table. Live acts perform
Sun. Q ≈ ♣

MOSSLEY

Church Inn
82 Stockport Road
☎ (01457) 832021
11-11; 12-10.30 Sun
John Smith's Bitter; guest beers Ⓗ
Cosy, friendly local doing
well the job it was designed
to. Traditional layout of
lounge, snug and tap room
providing good views across
the valley; a good no-
nonsense pub. Q ♣ P

Rising Sun
235 Stockport Road (1 mile N
of Top Mossley on A670)
☎ (01457) 834436
6-11; 12-10.30 Sun
**Black Sheep Best Bitter; Taylor
Landlord; guest beers** Ⓗ
Stone terraced pub affording
good views over the Tame
Valley. Q ♣ P

Try also: Tollemache Arms,
425 Manchester Rd
(Robinson's)

NANGREAVES

Lord Raglan
Mount Pleasant
☎ (0161) 764 6680
12-3, 7-11; 12-10.30 Sun
**Leyden Nanny Flyer, Raglan Sleeve;
Theakston Old Peculier; guest
beers** Ⓗ
This charming country inn is
the home of the new Leyden
Brewery, and stocks several
Belgian beers. Renowned for
its good food (served 12-9
Sun). 🏕 ◑ 🍺 P

NEW MOSTON

New Moston
52-54 Belgrave Road (off
A663)
☎ (0161) 682 8265
12-4.30, 7-11; 12-11 Fri & Sat;
12-10.30 sun
**Banks's Bitter; Camerons
Strongarm; guest beer** Ⓗ
Busy community local in a
residential backwater behind
Failsworth station; a
traditional vault and large
lounge. 🍴 ≈ (Failsworth) ♣

NEW SPRINGS

Colliers Arms
192 Wigan Road (A52138)
☎ (01942) 831171
1.30-5.30 (not Thu), 7.30-11; 12-4.45,
7.30-10.30 Sun
Burtonwood Bitter; guest beer Ⓗ
Unspoilt, 17th-century pub
just up the hill from the
Leeds-Liverpool Canal. The
outdoor drinking area is in
the tiny car park. Q 🏕 ♣ P

NEWTON HEATH

Railway Hotel
82 Dean Lane (off A62, opp.
station)
☎ (0161) 681 8199
12-11; 12-10.30 Sun
Holt Mild, Bitter Ⓟ
Imposing double-fronted
Victorian house; it has a
popular vault and a large
main bar featuring some
original locomotive etched
windows and wall tiling.
🍴 ≈ (Dean Lane) ♣

OLDHAM

Dog & Partridge
376 Roundthorn Road,
Roundthorn (off B6194)
☎ (0161) 624 3335
7 (4 Fri; 12.30 Sat)-11; 12-10.30 Sun
Lees GB Mild, Bitter Ⓗ
Typical, three-roomed village
local run by a popular, long-
serving licensee. The olde-
worlde pub features beamed
ceilings and comfortable
surroundings. ♣ P

Hawthorne Inn
365 Rondthorn Road,
Roundthorn (off B6194)

☎ (0161) 624 5767
12-11; 12-10.30 Sun
Cains Bitter; guest beers Ⓗ
Friendly, family-oriented
village local where the large
open-plan interior includes a
separate games room. The
extensive garden is popular
in summer. The pub hosts an
annual brass band contest on
Whit Fri. No food Mon.
🏕 🚲 ◑ ♣ P

Tommyfield
51 Henshaw Street (opp.
Tommyfield market)
☎ (0161) 652 8648
11-11; 12-10.30 Sun
**Lees GB Mild, Bitter, seasonal
beers** Ⓗ
Welcoming, friendly, town-
centre pub opposite the
famous market. Each of the
two rooms has a bar.
🏕 ◑ 🍴 ♣ P

PATRICROFT

Queens Arms
Green Lane (B5231, near
station)
☎ (0161) 789 2019
7 (5 Fri; 12 Sat)-11; 12-10.30 Sun
Boddingtons Bitter; guest beer Ⓗ
The first railway pub in the
world where recent
alterations have been carried
out sympathetically. Off the
beaten track, its location is
the reason for the eve-only
opening during the week.
This three-room pub has a
distinct community feel.
🏕 🍴 ≈ ♣ P

Stanley Arms
295 Liverpool Road (A57)
☎ (0161) 788 8801
12-11; 12-10.30 Sun
Holt Mild, Bitter Ⓗ
Small corner local, built in
1880. The bar faces the front
vault, with the rear of the
pub served by a hatch in the
entrance corridor.
Q 🍴 ≈ ♣ P

Try also: White Lion,
Liverpool Rd (Holt)

PEEL GREEN

Grapes Hotel
439 Liverpool Road (A57)
☎ (0161) 789 6971
11-11; 12-10.30 Sun
Holt Mild, Bitter Ⓗ
Listed Edwardian
monumental pub with many
original features intact:
mahogany, etched glass and
extensive tiling adorn its four
rooms and spacious lobby.
The room beyond the bar
houses a pool table.
Q 🍴 ≈ ♣ P

Try also: Ellesmere, King
William St, Winton (Holt)

PRESTWICH

Woodthorpe Hotel
Bury Old Road (A665/A6064 jct)
☎ (0161) 795 0032
11.30-11; 12-10.30 Sun
Holt Mild, Bitter H
Impressive old manor house, formally the residence of the Holt brewing family. Well converted, many original features have been retained. No food Sat.
🎍 ❀ 🚄 🌙 ⊖ (Heaton Pk)

ROCHDALE

Albion
600 Whitworth Road (A671, 1 mile from centre)
☎ (01706) 648540
5 (12 Sat)-11; 12-11 Sun
Taylor Mild, Best Bitter; Tetley Bitter; guest beers H
Multi-roomed local, comfortable and welcoming, whose landlord is highly regarded for superb ale and food. This traditional pub enjoys a strong following.
🍴 ❀ 🌙

Britannia Inn
4 Lomax Street (near A671/A58 roundabout)
☎ (01706) 710662
12-11; 12-10.30 Sun
Lees Bitter, seasonal beers H
Run by the longest serving landlord in Rochdale, the best room is notable for its carved wooden fireplace. Weekday meals served.
❀ 🚄 🌙 🌒 ♣

Cask & Feather
1 Oldham Road
☎ (01706) 711476
11-11; 11-10.30 Sun
McGuinness Feather Plucker Mild, Best Bitter, Junction Bitter, Tommy Todd Porter H
Large, one-room traditional pub that brews its own ales. Famous also for excellent food and live entertainment it attracts a mixed clientele.
🌙 ⇌

Healey Hotel
172 Shawclough Road, Healey (B6377)
☎ (01706) 645453
12 (3 Tue & Wed)-11; 12-10.30 Sun
Robinson's Best Bitter, Old Tom (winter) H
Pleasant country-style pub bearing many original features, including some tilework. It is handy for Healey Dell nature reserve. The pub has its own pétanque team.
Q ⇌ ❀ ♣ ✄

Merry Monk
234 College Road (near A6060/B6222 jct)
☎ (01706) 646919

Banks's Bitter; Marston's Pedigree; guest beers H
Friendly unpretentious local free house, selling a good range of beers. A free juke box and an unusual Ring the Bull game add to its appeal.
♣ P

Reed Hotel
Reed Hill (off pedestriansed Yorkshire St)
☎ (01706) 646696
11-11; 11-10.30 Sun
Banks's Bitter H
Over 200 years old this pub was originally a coaching inn; multi-roomed and comfortable it has notable Phoenix Brewery windows. No food Tue or Sun.
🍴 ❀ 🚄 🌙 ♣ P ✄ 🗇

Success to the Plough
179 Bolton Road, Marland (A58, 2 miles from centre)
☎ (01706) 633270
12-11; 12-5, 7-10.30 Sun
Lees GB Mild, Bitter, seasonal beers H
This imposing, detached redbrick pub has a deceptively spacious interior. There is a popular bowling green at the rear. Weekday lunches.
❀ 🌙 P

Try also: **Cemetery**, Bury Rd (Free)

ROYTON

Dog & Partridge
148 Middleton Road
☎ (0161) 628 4198
12-11; 12-10.30 Sun
Lees GB Mild, Bitter H
Out of town-centre boozer where a warm welcome is always guaranteed. It stocks an excellent selection of malt whiskies.
❀ ♣

Railway Hotel
1 Oldham Road
☎ (0161) 624 2793
12-11; 12-10.30 Sun
Lees GB Mild, Bitter H
Large pub, dominating the main town-centre junction, comprising three distinct drinking areas; a large, busy vault, a larger central lounge and a smaller snug. Table football played.
🌙 🍴 ♣

RUSHOLME

Albert
5 Walmer Street (off Wilmslow Rd, B5117)
☎ (0161) 224 7705
11-11; 12-10.30 Sun
Hyde's Anvil Bitter, Jekyll's Gold H
Friendly, two-bar local within a few yards of Manchester's

famous 'Curry Mile'. It attracts a regular multi-cultural clientele.
♣ P

Osborne House
32 Victory Street (off Wilmslow Rd, B5117)
☎ (0161) 224 9534
11.30-11; 12-10.30 Sun
Hyde's Anvil Mild, Bitter H
Welcoming, back-street local, refurbished in alehouse style a couple of years ago where one central bar serves various drinking areas. It handy for the local curry houses.
♣ P

SALFORD

Crescent
18-20 Crescent (A6, near University)
☎ (0161) 736 5600
11.30-11; 12-10.30 Sun
Rooster's Special; John Smith's Bitter; guest beers H
The Crescent offers seven ever-changing guests including a mild, plus a good value, inventive menu. A central bar serves three rooms; the vault hosts beer and cider festivals. A corridor leads to a new, attractive walled garden. No eve meals Sat or Sun. 🍴 Q ❀ 🌙
⇌ (Crescent) ♣ 🍽 P

King's Arms
11 Bloom Street (off A6, opp. A34 jct)
☎ (0161) 832 0167
12-11; 12-17 Sun
Bridgewater Navigator; Hyde's Anvil Jekyll's Gold; guest beers H
Imposing, angular free house, just off the beaten track, but near the new Bridgewater Brewery. Live music is a feature of the large crescent-shaped main room, with folk (Tue) and Jazz (Wed). Meals served 12-9. Pitching Green organic perry is stocked.
🌙 ⇌ (Central) 🍽

Olde Nelson
285 Chapel Street (A6, opp. cathedral)
☎ (0161) 281 9607
12 (11 Sat)-11; 12-10.30 Sun
Boddingtons Bitter; Lees Bitter; Tetley Dark Mild H
Attractive, Victorian hotel notable for its ornamental exterior. A large, popular corner vault houses a large screen TV for important matches. The entry corridor opens to a lobby and finally a plush rear lounge.
🍴 ⇌ (Central) ♣

Union Tavern
105 Liverpool Street (parallel to and between A6/A57)
☎ (0161) 736 2885
11.30-11; 12-10.30 Sun

Holt Mild, Bitter H
Isolated local, run by friendly staff, surrounded by industrial buildings. This basic, no-frills outlet, with added charm, fields several darts teams.
🍺 ♿ ⇌ (Crescent) ♣ P

Welcome
Robert Hall Street (off A5066, near B5461 jct)
☎ (0161) 872 6040
12-4, 7.30-11; 12-3, 7-10.30 Sun
Lees GB Mild, Bitter P
Ex-Wilson's 1970s pub, a worthy spiritual successor to the original Welcome: a comfortable lounge, busy games room and a well-used function room. One of the brewery's favourite houses, run by the doyenne of Salford landladies. Q ❀ 🍺 ⊖ (Exchange Quay/Salford Quays) ♣ P

SHAW
Black Horse Hotel
203a Rochdale Road (B6194, 1/2 mile from centre)
☎ (01706) 847173
3.30 (12 Sat)-11; 12-10.30 Sun
Lees GB Mild, Bitter H
Traditional, friendly stone-built pub with a comfortable lounge and a vault.
🍺 ♣ P

STALYBRIDGE
Station Buffet Bar ☆
Platform 1, Stalybridge Station, Rassbottom Street
☎ (0161) 303 0007
11-11; 12-10.30 Sun
Boddingtons Bitter; Flowers IPA; Wadworth 6X; guest beers H
Ever-improving premier free house decorated in a restrained manner throughout the four rooms. It offers up to six guest beers from independent breweries, plus an occasional cider and hosts frequent beer festivals.
🏨 Q ❀ 🍷 ⇌ 🍺 P

STANDISH
Boars Head
Wigan Road (A49/A5106 jct)
☎ (01942) 749747
11-3, 5.30-11; 11.30-11 Sat; 12-3, 7-10.30 Sun
Burtonwood Bitter, Top Hat; guest beers H
Old coaching house with a history dating back to 1271. Its bowling green is in use Easter-Oct. Good value lunches served.
🏨 ❀ 🍷 P

Dog & Partridge
33 School Lane (A5209)
☎ (01257) 401218
11-11; 12-10.30 Sun
Boddingtons Bitter; Tetley Mild,

Bitter; guest beers H
Friendly pub, popular for watching sport on TV.
Q ❀ ♣ P

Globe
94 High Street (A49)
☎ (01257) 400759
11.30-11; 12-10.30 Sun
Beer range varies H
Large, roadside, traditional local with a children's certificate.
Q 🍷 🍷 ♣ P ✗

Horseshoe
1 Wigan Road (A49)
☎ (01257) 400716
12-11; 12-10.30 Sun
Burtonwood Bitter; guest beer H
Locals' pub, much improved by a recent refurbishment; it is popular for games and good value home-cooked food. Limited parking.
Q 🍷 ♣ P

STOCKPORT
Armoury
31-33 Shaw Heath
☎ (0161) 480 5055
11-11; 12-10.30 Sun
Robinson's Hatters Mild, Best Bitter, Old Tom G
Unspoilt 1920s pub near the site of a former garrison. Its three rooms, include a traditional vault and a comfortable lounge; the family room (upstairs) opens at lunchtime.
🍷 ❀ 🛏 🍺 ⇌ ♣

Blossoms
2 Buxton Road, Heaviley (A6/Bramhall Lane jct)
☎ (0161) 477 2397
12-3, 5-11; 12-11 Sat; 12-10.30 Sun
Robinson's Hatters Mild, Best Bitter, H **Old Tom** G
Superb traditional local of three rooms (plus a large upstairs meeting room) and a single bar; an ideal place for a quiet, relaxing drink. Local CAMRA *Pub of the Year* 1998. No food Sun.
Q 🍷 ♣ P

Olde Woolpack
70 Brinksway (A560, near M60 jct 11)
☎ (0161) 429 6621
11.30-3, 5-11; 11.30-11 Fri; 11.30-4.30, 7.30-11 Sat; 12-10.30 Sun
Marston's Pedigree; Theakston Best Bitter; guest beers H
This thriving, multi-roomed free house is overshadowed by a giant blue pyramid. Comfortable and welcoming; local CAMRA *Pub of the Year* 1999. Three ever-changing guest beers always include one mild.
🍷 🍺 ♣ P

Red Bull
14 Middle Hillgate

☎ (0161) 480 2087
11.30-11, 12-3, 7-10.30 Sun
Robinson's Hatters Mild, Best Bitter H
A warren of interconnecting areas and rooms, including a flagged tap room, and an eclectic mix of furniture give the Red Bull an unforced rustic feel. The home-made food (served weekdays) has won awards. Tiny car park.
Q 🍷 ⇌ P

Spread Eagle
31 Lower Hillgate
☎ (0161) 480 7057
12-11, 12-10.30 Sun
Robinson's Hatters Mild, Best Bitter P
At last the Robinson's brewery tap makes the *Guide*: never an architectural gem, but keen licensees have made this a welcoming and enjoyable local, patronised by regulars, brewery workers and shoppers. Food is restricted to sandwiches and the landlord's superb home-made curries.
❀ 🍷 ⇌ ♣ 🍴

Swan with Two Necks
☆
36 Princes Street (opp. Merseyway shopping precinct)
☎ (0161) 480 2341
11-11, 12-4 (closed eves) Sun
Robinson's Hatters Mild, Best Bitter, Frederics H
An oasis of calm from the bustle of the town centre, situated just behind Woolworth's, this busy, oak-panelled, multi-roomed, Art Deco pub was last refurbished in the 1920s. Try the lasagne made with Robinson's Old Tom (no food Sun).
Q 🍷 🍺 ♣

Tiviot
Tiviot Dale (near A560/B6167 jct)
☎ (0161) 480 4109
11-11, 12-3, 7-10.30 Sun
Robinson's Hatters Mild, Best Bitter, P **Old Tom** (winter) G
This comfortable pub is a haven for shoppers from nearby Merseyway. A central bar serves four rooms including a games room with table football. A warm welcome is assured from the friendly licensees and staff. No food Sun. 🍷 🍺 ♣ 🍴

STRINES
Sportsman
105 Strines Road (1 mile from Marple on New Mills Rd)
☎ (0161) 427 2888
11.30-3, 5.30-11; 11.30-11 Sat; 12-10.30 Sun
Boddingtons Bitter; Cains Mild, Bitter; guest beer H

Welcoming country pu of two rooms affording impressive views over the Mellor: a comfortable lounge and vault. Good value home-cooked food and a pleasant garden are added attractions.
🏚 Q 🕿 🌣 🌓 🖳 & 🛦 ⇌ (limited service) ♣ P 🗗

Try also: Royal Oak, Strines Rd (Robinson's)

SWINTON

Park Inn
137 Worsley Road (A572, between A6 and A580)
☎ (0161) 794 4296
12-11; 12-10.30 Sun
Holt Mild, Bitter H
Old local with a more recent façade; the large lounge was formerly two rooms – also a front L-shaped vault and a tiny snug served via a hatch at the rear.
🖳 ♣

White Lion
242 Manchester Road (A6/A572 jct)
☎ (0161) 288 0434
12-4, 7-11; 12-4, 7-10.30 Sun
Robinson's Hatters Mild, Old Stockport, Best Bitter H
18th-century pub, much altered though comfortable, it comprises a spacious vault and two lounges. The back room is dedicated to memorabilia of the Swinton Lions RL team whose ground once stood nearby. Children welcome until 7pm.
🕿 🌣 🌓 🖳 ⇌ ♣ P

White Swan
186 Worsley Road (near A572/A580 jct)
☎ (0161) 794 1504
12-11; 12-10.30 Sun
Holt Mild, Bitter H
Pleasant, roomy pub, built in the late 1920s boasting splendid wood panelling in the main room. The former billiards room is used for families Sun (until 7pm); the front vault is popular.
🕿 🌣 🌓 🖳 ♣ P

Try also: Football, Swinton Hall Rd (Tetley); **Lord Nelson**, Bolton Rd (Holt)

TIMPERLEY

Quarry Bank Inn
Bloomsbury Lane
☎ (0161) 980 4345
11.30-11; 12-10.30 Sun
Hyde's Anvil Mild, Bitter, seasonal beers H
Thriving, popular, suburban pub on the edge of the old village centre: a popular vault and a quieter lounge with restaurant area (no food Sun

eve). It has a well-used bowling green.
Q 🕿 🌣 🌓 🖳 & ♣ P

TYLDESLEY

Half Moon
115-117 Elliot Street
☎ (01942) 873206
11-11; 12-10.30 Sun
Holt Bitter; guest beers H
Town-centre local with a low-ceilinged lounge bar and a pool/games room. A good variety of guest beers is stocked.
🌣 ♣

Mort Arms
235-237 Elliot Street
☎ (01942) 873206
11-4 (4.30, Sat), 7-11; 12-10.30 Sun
Holt Mild, Bitter H
Smart, comfortable lounge, part panelled, it features a bowed bar and etched glass.
🖳 ♣

UPPERMILL

Cross Keys
Off Running Hill Gate (off A670)
☎ (01457) 874626
11-11; 12-10.30 Sun
Lees GB Mild, Bitter, Moonraker, seasonal beers H
Attractive, 18th-century stone building overlooking Saddleworth church. The public bar has a stone-flagged floor and a Yorkshire range. The centre for many activities, including mountain rescue, it hosts folk nights Wed and Sun in the barn. Children's certificate.
🏚 Q 🕿 🌣 🌓 🖳 ♣ P

WARDLEY

Morning Star
520 Manchester Road (A6, 3/4 mile W of Swinton)
☎ (0161) 794 4927
12-11; 12-10.30 Sun
Holt Mild, Bitter H
Popular with locals and visitors alike, this busy pub on the outskirts of Swinton is run by a friendly staff. On entry, one experiences a warm, comfortable relaxing atmosphere.
🌣 🌓 ⇌ (Moorside) ♣ P

Try also: Pied Piper, Eastham Way, Walkden (Robinson's)

WESTHOUGHTON

White Lion
2 Market Street (B5235, by town hall)
☎ (01942) 811991
11-11; 12-10.30 Sun
Holt Mild, Bitter H
Good, unpretentious town-centre local of typical Holt

character. Restored tiles, woodwork and etched glass add to the distinctive flavour of this multi-roomed pub.
🌣 ♣ P

WHITEFIELD

Coach & Horses
71 Bury Old Road (A665)
☎ (0161) 798 8897
12-11; 12-10.30 Sun
Holt Mild, Bitter H
Traditional local displaying all the characteristics of the original 1880s building. There is a deceptively large lounge off the bar area, plus a tap room and a snug.
Q 🌣 ⊖ (Besses o' th' Barn) ♣ P

Eagle & Child
Higher Lane (near A665/A56 jct)
☎ (0161) 766 3024
12-11; 12-10.30 Sun
Holt Mild, Bitter H
Large, black and white pub, set back from the road. It has a large L-shaped main bar with a cosy side room. The well-kept bowling green at the rear is very popular in summer.
🌣 🌓 ⊖ (Besses o' th' Barn) ♣ P

WIGAN

Beer Engine
69 Poolstock (ring road)
☎ (01942) 321820
11-11; 12-10.30 Sun
Moorhouse's Pendle Witches Brew; John Smith's Bitter; guest beers H
Community pub with large lounge and function room that hosts an annual Beer & Pie Festival (Oct). Meals served 12-6 daily. It has its own bowling green.
🌣 🌓 🖳 & ⇌ (North Western/Wallgate) P

Bold Hotel
161 Poolstock Lane, Worsley Mesnes
☎ (01942) 241095
2-4.30, 7-11; 12-3, 7-10.30 sun
Burtonwood Bitter; guest beer H
Small friendly local, just outside the town centre. See the excellent collection of rugby league memorabilia in the tap room. 🖳 ♣

Bowling Green
106-108 Wigan Lane
☎ (01942) 516004
12-11; 12-10.30 Sun
Caledonian Deuchars IPA; Lees Bitter; John Smith's Bitter; Theakston Mild; guest beers H
A separate vault is a rarity in Wigan, enjoy it at this convivial watering-hole, winner of the local CAMRA 1999 *Pub of the Year*, plus many seasonal awards. Daily newspapers available.
🏚 🌣 & ♣ 🗗

CAMRA National Pub Inventory: sign at the Olde Gate, Brassington, Derbyshire

Brockett Arms
Mesnes Road
☎ (01942) 820372
11-11; 12-10.30 Sun
Shepherd Neame Spitfire; Tetley Bitter; Theakston Best Bitter; Thwaites Mild; guest beers H
Open-plan pub, now part of the Wetherspoon's empire, with a comfortable, relaxing atmosphere. It stands just outside the town centre.
Q ◑ ▶ ♿ P ⏤ ⊞

Millstone
67 Wigan Lane
☎ (01942) 245999
3.30 (12 Fri & Sat)-11; 12-10.30 Sun
Thwaites Bitter H
Warm, friendly watering-hole, popular with domino enthusiasts, it is one of the very few local Thwaites outlets.
🏵 ◑ ♿ ♣

Moon Under Water
5-7a Market Place
☎ (01942) 323437
11-11; 12-10.30 Sun
Cains Mild; Courage Directors; Shepherd Neame Spitfire; guest beers H
Situated right in the centre of town, it is very popular at weekends. Q ◑ ▶ ♿ ⇌ (North Western/Wallgate) ⏤ ⊞

Old Pear Tree
44 Frog Lane (400 yds from bus station)
☎ (01942) 243617
12-11; 12-10.30 Sun
Burtonwood Bitter; guest beer H
Traditional coaching-style

house, a comfortable and well-presented pub.
🏠 🏵 ◑ ▶ ⬚ ⇌ (North Western/Wallgate) ♣ P

Orwell
Wigan Pier Complex, Wallgate
☎ (01942) 323034
11-11 (varies winter); 12-10.30 Sun
Beer range varies H
Attractively refurbished pub at the centre of the Wigan Pier complex, by the Leeds-Liverpool canal. A cobbled area is used for outdoor drinking. 🍺 🏵 ◑ ▶ ⇌ (North Western/Wallgate) ♣ P ⏤

Try also: Swan & Railway, 80 Wallgate (Banks)

WOODFORD
Davenport Arms (Thief's Neck)
550 Chester Road (A5102)
☎ (0161) 439 2435
11-3.30, 5.15-11; 11-11 Sat; 12-3, 7-10.30 Sun
Robinson's Hatters Mild, Best Bitter, Old Tom H
Superb, unspoilt multi-roomed farmhouse pub on the edge of suburbia. The licence has been held by the same family for 70 years. Children welcome at lunchtime in the no-smoking snug and the large, attractive garden. Other Robinson's beers may be available.
🏠 Q 🍺 🏵 ◑ ⬚ ♣ P ⏤

WORTHINGTON
Crown
19-20 Platt Lane (between A49 and A5106)
☎ (01257) 421354
11-11; 12-10.30 Sun
Boddingtons Bitter; Tetley Bitter; guest beers H
A large, mahogany-panelled bar area and antique furniture feature in this warm, welcoming rural hostelry. Just outside Standish, it benefits from views of surrounding farmland. It boasts an excellent restaurant, plus a games room. A mild is always available.
🏠 🏵 🛏 ◑ ▶ ♣ P

INDEPENDENT BREWERIES

Altrincham: Altrincham
Bank Top: Bolton
Bridgewater: Salford
Holt: Cheetham
Hydes: Manchester
Lees: Middleton Junction
Marble: Manchester
Mash & Air: Manchester
McGuinness: Rochdale
Leyden: Nangreaves
Old Pint Pot: Salford
Phoenix: Heywood
Robinson's: Stockport
Saddleworth: Uppermill
Sarah's Hop House: Golborne

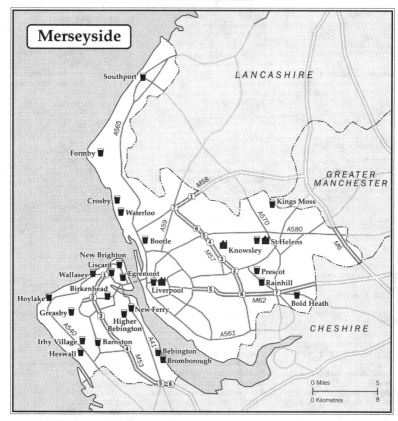

Merseyside

LANCASHIRE

GREATER MANCHESTER

Southport

Formby

Crosby
Waterloo
Bootle
New Brighton
Liscard
Wallasey
Egremont
Birkenhead
Hoylake
Greasby
New Ferry
Higher Bebington
Irby Village
Barnston
Heswall
Bebington
Bromborough

Kings Moss
St Helens
Knowsley
Prescot
Rainhill
Liverpool
Bold Heath

CHESHIRE

0 Miles 5
0 Kilometres 8

BARNSTON VILLAGE

Fox & Hounds
107 Banston Road
☎ (0151) 648 7685
11-11; 12-10.30 Sun
Ruddles County; Theakston Best Bitter; Webster's Yorkshire Bitter; guest beer Ⓗ
Built in 1911 on the site of an 18th-century pub: a lounge, tiled bar and a snug, offering real home-cooked pub grub. The courtyard makes a welcome resting point during the local CAMRA 13 Pubs Walk in summer.
🏔 Q 🛏 🕮 ◖🍴 ♣ P

BEBINGTON

Rose & Crown
57 The Village (opp. Town Hall)
☎ (0151) 643 1312
11.30-11; 12-10.30 Sun
Thwaites Best Bitter Ⓗ
Bustling, friendly, multi-roomed pub, built in 1732. It is popular with office workers and shoppers at lunchtime, local residents at night. Weekday lunches served. Limited parking.
Q ◖🍴 ≒ ♣ P

BIRKENHEAD

Crown Ale House
128 Conway Street (by Europa Centre)
☎ (0151) 647 0589
11-11; 12-10.30 Sun
Cains Bitter; Greenalls Mild, Bitter; guest beers Ⓗ
Multi-roomed, listed building, boasting fine old bar fittings. A previous CAMRA *Pub of the Year* under Greenalls management. Family room closes at 5pm.
🛏 🕮 ◖🍴 ≒ (Conway Pk) ♣

Dispensary
20 Chester Street (near ferry terminal)
☎ (0151) 650 0676
11.30-11; 12-10.30 Sun
Cains Mild, Bitter, seasonal beers; guest beers Ⓗ
Superbly refurbished Cain's tied house; the ceiling over the bar has been removed to show a central glass apex. Local CAMRA *Pub of the Year* 2000. Weekday lunches; live music performed Thu.
🕮 ◖ ≒ (Hamilton Sq) 🔲

BOLD HEATH

Griffin
184 Warrington Road (A57 near Rainhill)
☎ (0151) 424 5143
12-11; 12-10.30 Sun
Beer range varies Ⓗ
Attractive country pub with a large garden that caters for families and serves food all day and a single guest beer.
🕮 ◖ 🍴 ♿ ♣ P ⅟

BOOTLE

Cat & Fiddle
St Martins House, Stanley Road
☎ (0151) 922 9561
11.30-11; 12-10.30 Sun
Cains Bitter; guest beer Ⓗ
Friendly, lively, recently refurbished pub aimed at the over 25s. It hosts live music Thu and disco Fri and Sat. Eve meals served weekdays (5.7); no food Sun.
◖ ▶ ≒ (New Strand)

Maggies
Bridle Road
☎ (0151) 284 7028
11.30-11; 12-10.30 Sun
Thwaites Bitter Ⓗ
Spacious, friendly, local with a widescreen TV and a games room.
🛏 ◖ ♿ P

Wild Rose
2a Triad Centre, Stanley Road
(A567, by New Strand
shopping centre)
☎ (0151) 922 0828
11-11; 12-10.30 Sun
Cains Mild; guest beers H
Wetherspoon's pub, used by
office workers and shoppers
during the day and locals
eves.
Q ◑ & ≠ (New Strand)

BROMBOROUGH
Dibbinsdale Inn
Dibbinsdale Road
☎ (0151) 334 5171
11 (11.30 Sat)-11; 12-10.30 Sun
**Banks's Original, Bitter; Camerons
Bitter; Marston's Pedigree; guest
beers** H
Attractive village inn dating
from 1835: an open-plan bar
and restaurant, offering a
wide selection of food with a
specials board. Quiz night
and live music are regular
events.
≠ ◑ & ≠ P ⌂

CROSBY
Crosby
75 Liverpool Road (A565)
☎ (0151) 924 2574
11-11; 12-10.30 Sun
**Fuller's London Pride; Greene King
Abbot** H
Ex-Hogshead, now serving
just two deservedly popular
real ales, this large single-
roomed pub is used by sports
enthusiasts at weekends
owing to its three screen TVs.
Weekend lunches served,
plus an early eve meal on Sat
(5-7). ❀ ◑ & ≠ (Blundellsands/
Crosby)

Crow's Nest
63 Victoria Road (A565)
☎ (0151) 931 2268
11.30-11; 12-10.30 Sun
Cains Bitter; guest beer H
Proper local; small and
friendly, it boasts a public
bar, lounge and tiny snug. A
lively buzz of conversation
thrives in all the rooms.
Sample the guest beer early
in the week as it tends to run
out. Q ❀ ⊞ ≠ (Blundellsands/
Crosby) P

EGREMONT
Egremont Ferry
48 Tobin Street
☎ (0151) 639 3205
11-11; 12-10.30 Sun
**Cains Bitter; John Smith's Bitter;
guest beers** H
The 'Eggy' is a Porterhouse
pub, affording fine views
across the Mersey. The split-
level interior and upstairs
extension both feature
wooden floors and
traditional alehouse decor.

An outdoor area on the
promenade lets you take in
the sea air. Weekend meals
served all day until 7pm.
❀ ◑ ▶

Try also: **Brighton**, Brighton
St (Courage)

FORMBY
Freshfield Hotel
1 Massams Lane, Freshfield
(1/2 mile from B5424)
☎ (01704) 874871
12-11; 12-10.30 Sun
**Boddingtons Bitter; Castle Eden Ale;
Flowers IPA; Fuller's London Pride;
Moorhouse's Black Cat; guest
beers** H
Popular suburban local where
twelve real ales are always
available, many from smaller
independent brewers. A local
guitar club meets here. It can
be busy at weekends. No
children.
≠ Q ❀ ◑ ≠ (Freshfield) P

GREASBY
Irby Mill
Mill Lane
☎ (0151) 604 0194
12-11; 12-10.30 Sun
**Cains Traditional Bitter; Jennings
Bitter, Snecklifter; Taylor Landlord;
Theakston Best Bitter; guest
beers** H
Traditional country pub built
in 1980 on an ancient mill
site. Two rooms, linked by a
narrow bar, are full of
characters and friendly
banter. A former regional
CAMRA *Pub of the Year*. Eve
meals served weekdays (5-8).
Q ❀ ◑ P

HESWALL
Dee View Inn
Dee View Road
☎ (0151) 342 2320
12-11; 12-10.30 Sun
**Boddingtons Bitter; Cains
Traditional Bitter; Taylor Landlord;
Tetley Bitter; guest beers** H
Excellent single-bar
traditional pub on a hairpin
bend, opposite the war
memorial. It offers six
handpumped ales, including
guests. ≠ ❀ ♣ P

Johnny Pye
Pye Road (behind bus staton)
☎ (0151) 342 8215
11-11; 12-10.30 Sun
**Banks's Original; Cains; Camerons
Bitter** H
A welcome addition to the
village's pubs; enjoy the
friendly atmosphere and
excellent pub food. The large
screen TV for sports fans can
be avoided in the quiet L-
shaped lounge. Eve meals
finish at 8; no food Sun eve.
❀ ◑ & ▶ P ✂ ⌂

HIGHER BEBINGTON
Travellers Rest
169 Mount Road
☎ (0151) 608 2988
12-11; 12-10.30 Sun
**Boddingtons Bitter; Cains Bitter;
Flowers Original; Greene King Abbot;
Taylor Landlord; guest beers** H
Friendly village inn dating
from 1720, Wirral CAMRA
Pub of the Year 1998 and '99.
A central bar serves an open-
plan lounge and a no-
smoking room. Good value
food (not served Sun).
≠ Q ◑ & ♣ ✂

HOYLAKE
Hoylake Lights
52 Market Street (near
station)
☎ (0151) 632 1209
11-11; 12-10.30 Sun
**Cains Mild; Courage Directors;
Tetley Bitter; Theakston Best Bitter;
guest beer** H
This long, open-plan pub
results from recent stylish
conversion of a shop by
Wetherspoon's, deservedly
popular.
Q ◑ ▶ ≠ ○ ✂ ⊞

IRBY VILLAGE
Shippons Inn
8a Thingwall Road
☎ (0151) 648 0449
11-11; 12-10.30 Sun
**Banks's Original, Bitter; Camerons
Strongarm; Marston's Pedigree;
guest beer** H
Traditional village pub,
converted in 1994 from an
18th-century farm building,
retaining an inglenook.
Attractions include folk
music (Mon), a lively quiz
(Wed) and imaginative
theme nights. Try the well-
filled baguettes.
Q ❀ ◑ & P

KINGS MOSS
Colliers Arms
37 Pimbo Road (off B5205,
Rainford Road, near Billinge)
☎ (01744) 892894
12-11; 12-10.30 Sun
Beer range varies H
Off the beaten track this
1850 village pub has a stone-
flagged floor and an
attractive garden. Good
home-cooked food is
complemented by up to three
guest beers.
≠ Q ❀ ◑ ⊞ & ♣ P ✂

LISCARD
Stanley's
83 Seaview Road
☎ (0151) 639 9736
11-11; 12-10.30 Sun
**Theakston Best Btter; guest
beers** H

Wallasey's newest pub is proving to be a success on both the beer and food front. A good atmosphere is created by a mix of clientele and friendly staff. Superb exotic menu (eve meals Thu-Sat, 6-8.30).

◖▶&⊖P

LIVERPOOL: *CENTRE*

Baltic Fleet
33a Wapping
☎ (0151) 709 3116
11.30-11; 12-10.30 Sun
Cains Mild, Traditional Bitter; guest beers Ⓗ
Well-known 'flat-iron' pub opposite the Albert Dock, bearing a nautical theme. House beers, produced by the local Passageway Brewery, vary summer and winter. High quality food is served Tue-Sun. 🚇Q◖▶⊖ (James St) ⌂P✄

Cambridge
51 Mulberry Street
11.30 (12 Sat)-11; 12-10.30 Sun
Burtonwood Bitter, Top Hat; guest beers Ⓗ
Split-level, lively pub on the Liverpool University campus. This Forshaw's Alehouse is closed until 6pm on some weekends during university vacations.

❀♣

Cracke
13 Rice Street (off Hope St, between the two cathedrals)
☎ (0151) 709 4171
11-11; 12-10.30 Sun
Cains Bitter; Marston's Pedigree; Phoenix Oak Bitter, Wobbly Bob; guest beers Ⓗ
Hospitable, multi-roomed pub whose garden has recently reopened. Good value food includes traditional and vegetarian breakfasts, and a curry night (Thu 5-7.30). Two real ciders are on gravity dispense. Q❀ ◖⊞≠ (Lime St) ⊖ (Central) ⌂

Dispensary
87 Renshaw Street
☎ (0151) 709 2160
11-11; 12-10.30 Sun
Cains Mild, Bitter, FA, seasonal beers; guest beers Ⓗ
Traditional Victorian corner local ensuring a friendly welcome and great atmosphere. Regional *Pub of the Year* 1999 and CAMRA/English Heritage *Pub Refurbishment* award-winner. Good value food is served until 7pm. ◖▶≠ (Lime St) ⊖ (Central)

Doctor Duncan
St Johns House, St Johns Lane
☎ (0151) 709 5100

11.30-11; 12-10.30 Sun
Cains Mild, Bitter, FA, seasonal beers; guest beers Ⓗ
A warm welcome is assured from the friendly staff at this local CAMRA *Pub of the Year*. One main bar serves several rooms, including a classic Victorian tiled room. Four ever-changing guests and a house beer complement the Cains' range. Top quality food is served until 7pm. The family room is designated as the no-smoking area. Q❀❀◖▶≠ (Lime St) ⊖ (Central)✄⊞

Everyman
5-9 Hope Street (beneath Everyman Theatre)
☎ (0151) 709 4776
12-2am; closed Sun
Beer range varies Ⓗ
Popular for food at lunchtime and with theatregoers eves, it stocks up to four guest beers. Candlelight and fresh flowers add to the atmosphere. Light meals continue until midnight.
◖▶⌂

Globe
17 Cases Street (opp. Central station)
☎ (0151) 709 5060
11-11; 12-10.30 Sun
Cains Mild, Bitter Ⓗ
Friendly pub where a sloping floor tests customers' sobriety. Favoured 1960s music is played loud at times. ≠ (Lime St) ⊖ (Central)

Hogshead
18-20 North John Street
☎ (0151) 236 8760
11-11 (2am Fri & Sat); 12-10.30 Sun
Beer range varies Ⓗ/Ⓖ
Large, modern, Hogshead theme pub, popular with office workers at lunchtime and nightclubbers eves. Up to nine guest beers available.
◖▶&

Lion Tavern ☆
67 Moorfields
☎ (0151) 236 1734
11-11; 12-10.30 Sun
Lees Bitter; Taylor Landlord Ⓗ
The smallest of Liverpool's classic Victorian pubs: a feast of wood, glass and tiles, crowned by an unusual dome in the rear lounge. One bar has an Irish flavour and serves a mix of locals and business folk.
◖⊞ ⊖ (Moorfields)

Peter Kavanaghs
2-6 Egerton Street
☎ (0151) 709 8443
12-11; 12-10.30 Sun
Cains Bitter; Greene King Abbot; guest beer Ⓗ
Multi-roomed pub with a

strong sense of community. Historic photographs, paintings and bric-à-brac add atmosphere.
Q◖

Pig & Whistle
12 Covent Garden
☎ (0151) 236 4760
11.30-11; closed Sun
Marston's Pedigree Ⓗ
Victorian pub, popular with the business community; three comfortable rooms on three floors. The upstairs bar opens at lunchtime. No food at weekends.
◖⊖ (Moorfields/James St)

Post Office
2 Great Newton Street
☎ (0151) 707 1005
12-11; 12-10.30 Sun
Cains Bitter; guest beers Ⓗ
Friendly Victorian pub, popular with students, hospital and university staff as well as locals. Good value lunches served.
❀◖⊞≠ (Lime St)

Poste House
23 Cumberland Street
☎ (0151) 236 4130
11-11; 12-10.30 Sun
Cains Mild, Bitter Ⓗ
Small, two-storey pub with a lively, friendly atmosphere, offering excellent value lunches on weekdays.
◖≠ (Lime St) ⊖ (Moorfields)

Roscoe Head
26 Roscoe Street
☎ (0151) 709 4490
11.30-11; 12-10.30 Sun
Jennings Bitter; Morland Old Speckled Hen Ⓗ
Friendly, popular traditional pub where three rooms are served by a single bar. It is an ever-present *Guide* entry.
◖≠ (Lime St) ⊖ (Central)

Ship & Mitre
133 Dale Street
☎ (0151) 236 0859
11.30 (12.30 Sat)-11; 2.30-10.30 Sun
Hyde's Anvil Dark Mild, Bitter; guest beers Ⓗ
Friendly pub where gaslighting picks out its Art Deco features. It offers an ever-changing range of up to ten guest beers, plus popular quarterly beer festivals. Good value lunches are served weekdays. Q◖≠ (Lime St) ⊖ (Moorfields) ♣⌂⊟

Vernon Arms
69 Dale Street
☎ (0151) 236 4525
11.30 (12 Sat)-11; closed Sun
Coach House Gunpowder Mild; guest beers Ⓗ
Friendly pub popular with the business community, serving usually six ever-changing guest beers, one is

often from Liverpool Brewing Co. Excellent value meals are served until 7pm.
◖▐ ≠ (Lime St) ⊖ (Moorfields)

Wetherspoon's
1 Charlotte Row
☎ (0151) 709 4802
11-11; 12-10.30 Sun
Cains Mild; guest beers Ⓗ
Spacious, modern pub, providing Wetherspoon's usual range of cask ales and guests. It hosts beer festivals and serves good value food until late.
Q ◖▐ & ✂ ⊞

White Star
4 Rainford Gardens
☎ (0151) 231 6861
11.30-11; 12-10.30 Sun
Cains Bitter; guest beers Ⓗ
Traditional pub in the Matthew Street area. A friendly atmosphere prevails in the bar area with a quieter, comfortable rear lounge, ideal for relaxing and admiring the huge Bass mirror. ≠ (Lime St)
⊖ (Moorfields/(Central))

LIVERPOOL: *EAST*
Clubmoor
119 Townsend Lane, Anfield
☎ (0151) 260 8170
12-11; 12-10.30 Sun
Cains Mild, Bitter Ⓗ
Handsome, detached pub on the main road with a large lounge and a small public bar. It is handy for Liverpool and Everton football grounds.
❀ ⊟ ♣

Derby Lodge
Roby Road, Huyton
☎ (0151) 443 0932
12-11; 12-10.30 Sun
Beer range varies Ⓗ
Attractive pub/restaurant with a large lounge. Food is served all day until 10pm (10.30 Fri and Sat). The garden affords good views.
Q ❀ ⇔ ◖▐ & ≠ (Roby) P

Edinburgh
4 Sandown Lane, Wavertree
☎ (0151) 475 2648
12-11; 12-10.30 Sun
Cains Mild, Traditional Bitter, FA; guest beers Ⓗ
Traditional-style alehouse popular with locals for its friendly, efficient service. Cosy little gem.

Willowbank
329 Smithdown Road, Wavertree (A562)
☎ (0151) 733 5782
11-11; 12-10.30 Sun
Beer range varies Ⓗ
Festival Alehouse, popular with locals and students stocking an ever-changing

range of up to eleven real ales. It publishes it own newsletter. Eve meals finish at 7pm.
❀ ◖▐ ⊟ ♣

LIVERPOOL: *NORTH*
Raven
72 Walton Vale (A59)
☎ (0151) 524 1255
11-11; 12-10.30 Sun
Cains Mild; guest beers Ⓗ
This Wetherspoon's pub has a large no-smoking area; bustling and friendly. Food is available all day until 10pm (9.30 Sun).
Q ◖▐ & ≠ (Orrell Pk) ✂

LIVERPOOL: *SOUTH*
Allerton Hall (Pub in the Park)
Clarke Gardens, Springwood Avenue
☎ (0151) 494 2664
11.30-11; 12-10.30 Sun
Cains Bitter; guest beers Ⓗ
This Grade II listed building has been refurbished as a pub/restaurant: an attractive comfortable multi-roomed interior, plus an extensive garden and play area.
⏚ ❀ ◖▐ & ≠ (Allerton) P ✂

Brewery Tap
Stanhope Street
☎ (0151) 709 2129
11-11; 12-10.30 Sun
Cains Mild, Bitter, FA, seasonal beers; guest beers Ⓗ
This busy brewery tap is used as a base for Cains' brewery tours. Note the extensive range of breweriana on display. Up to three guest ales are served in a friendly atmosphere.
❀ ◖P

NEW BRIGHTON
Telegraph
25-27 Mount Pleasant Road
☎ (0151) 639 1508
11.30-11; 12-10.30 Sun
Boddingtons Bitter; Cains Bitter; Castle Eden Bitter; guest beer Ⓗ
Bar and two small lounges, but the conservatory is the main lounge here. Olde-worlde decor features in this lively, friendly, pub. Eve meals served Wed-Fri, 5.30-7.30.
❀ ◖▐ & ♣ P

Try also: Albion, Albion St (John Smith's)

NEW FERRY
Cleveland Arms
31 Bebington Road
☎ (0151) 645 2847
11.30-11; 12-10.30 Sun
Thwaites Best Mild, Bitter Ⓗ
Popular, friendly, open-plan

local in a pedestrianised area. Pool and darts played.
≠ (Bebington) ♣ P

PRESCOT
Clock Face
54 Derby Street (A57)
☎ (0151) 292 4121
11-11; 12-10.30 Sun
Thwaites Bitter Ⓗ
Attractive pub on the edge of the town; this private house, converted in the 1980s enjoys a relaxed, friendly atmosphere. Eve meals finish at 8pm.
Q ❀ ◖▐ & ≠ P

Sun Inn
11 Derby Street (A57)
12-11; 12-10.30 Sun
Beer range varies Ⓗ
Spacious, welcoming, historic pub over 200 years old. A real fire warms the 'Mayor's Parlour'.
Q ≈ ♣ ♣

RAINHILL
Manor Farm
Mill Lane (off M62, jct 7)
☎ (0151) 430 0335
12-11; 12.30-10.30 Sun
Burtonwood Bitter; guest beer Ⓗ
Attractive, 15th-century manor farmhouse, popular with families for its characterful spacious interior and extensive play area outside. Excellent meals are served all day in the upstairs restaurant.
⏚ ❀ ◖P

SOUTHPORT
Blakes Hotel and Pizza Bar
19 Queens Road
☎ (01704) 500811
4 (12 Sat)-11; 12-10.30 Sun
Adnams Bitter; Camerons Strongarm; Moorhouse's Black Cat, Pride of Pendle, Pendle Witches Brew; Taylor Landlord Ⓗ
Well-known and popular locals' bar with an excellent reputation for its home-made pizza. Nine cask beers are always available.
❀ ⇔ ▐ ≠ P

Bold Arms
59-61 Botanic Road, Churchtown
☎ (01704) 228192
11.30-11; 12-10.30 Sun
Tetley Dark Mild, Bitter; Taylor Landlord; guest beer Ⓗ
17th-century coaching house set in the historic village of Churchtown.
⏚ ⏚ ❀ ◖▐ ⊟ & P

Falstaff
68 King Street
☎ (01704) 501116
11.30-11; 12-10.30 Sun

CAMRA National Pub Inventory: Seven Stars, Falmouth, Cornwall

Courage Directors; Theakston Mild, Best Bitter; Wells Bombardier; guest beers Ⓗ
Town-centre house, transformed from an ordinary pub doing poor trade into one of the busiest, selling the best beer in town. Excellent meals are good value. Q ❀ ◑ ◗ ♿ ≠ ♣

London
14 Windsor Road
☎ (01704) 542885
12-11; 12-10.30 Sun
Barnsley Bitter; Old Tom Ⓗ
Popular community pub, slightly out of the town centre area.
🐴 ❀ ◑ ≠ ♣ P

Up Steps
20 Upper Aughton Road, Birkdale
☎ (01704) 569245
11.30-11; 12-10.30 Sun
Coach House Coachman's Best Bitter, Dick Turpin, Gingernut, Posthorn; Theakston Mild, Best Bitter Ⓗ
Traditional street-corner local, once the pub where Red Rum went for a pint! It fields darts, dominoes and quiz teams. The only local outlet for Coach House beers.
❀ ≠ (Birkdale) ♣ P

Wetherspoon's
93-97 Lord Street
☎ (01704) 530217
11-11; 12-10.30 Sun
Boddingtons Bitter; Cains Mild; Courage Directors; Theakston Best Bitter; guest beer Ⓗ
Typical Wetherspoon's format in a former 19th-century furniture emporium and department store.
Q ◑ ◗ ♿ ≠ ⊬ ⊞

ST. HELENS

Abbey Hotel
11 Hard Lane, Dentons Green
☎ (01744) 28609
12-11; 12-10.30 Sun
Holt Mild, Bitter Ⓗ
Spacious, former coach house, over 100 years old, located on the edge of the town. The pub has four rooms.
Q 🐴 ♣ P

Beecham's Bar & Brewery
Water Street (A58, off Westfield St, near clock tower)
☎ (01744) 623420
12-11; closed Sun
Beechams Bitter, Stout, seasonal beers; Thwaites Bitter, Chairman's, Daniel's Hammer Ⓗ
Bar and brewery in the ex-Beecham's Powders offices, now part of St. Helens College. The students learn brewing and bar management. Opening times can vary.
♿ ≠ (Central) ♣ ⊬

WALLASEY

Farmers Arms
225 Wallasey Village
☎ (0151) 638 2110
11.30-11; 12-10.30 Sun
Cains Bitter; Tetley Bitter; Theakston Best Bitter; guest beer Ⓗ
A front bar, side snug and a back lounge; previous local CAMRA *Pub of the Year*. The guest beer pump is in the bar. Weekday lunches include Chinese stir-fries.
◑ ⊟ ≠ (Grove Rd)

WATERLOO

Volunteer Canteen
45 East Street
☎ (0151) 928 6594
11-11; 12-10.30 Sun
Cains Bitter Ⓗ
Small, friendly, two-bar pub, with table service available in the lounge. Note the interesting display of local photographs. Q ≠

INDEPENDENT BREWERIES

Beecham's: St. Helens
Cains: Liverpool
Cambrinus: Knowsley
Liverpool: Liverpool
Passageway: Liverpool

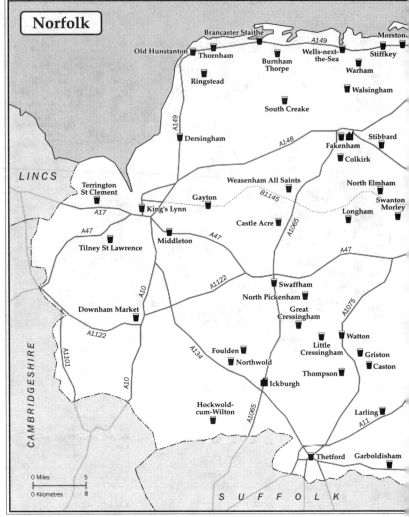

Norfolk

(Map of Norfolk showing locations including: Brancaster Staithe, Old Hunstanton, Thornham, Morston, Wells-next-the-Sea, Stiffkey, Burnham Thorpe, Warham, Ringstead, Walsingham, South Creake, Dersingham, Fakenham, Stibbard, Colkirk, Weasenham All Saints, North Elmham, Terrington St Clement, Gayton, Swanton Morley, King's Lynn, Castle Acre, Longham, Middleton, Tilney St Lawrence, Swaffham, North Pickenham, Great Cressingham, Downham Market, Watton, Foulden, Little Cressingham, Griston, Northwold, Caston, Thompson, Ickburgh, Hockwold-cum-Wilton, Larling, Thetford, Garboldisham)

LINCS
CAMBRIDGESHIRE
SUFFOLK

0 Miles 5
0 Kilometres 8

ALDBOROUGH

Black Boys
The Green (1 mile from A140 Aylsham-Cromer Road)
☎ (01263) 768086
12-3, 7-11; (closed winter Mon); 12-3, 7-10.30 Sun
Greene King IPA; guest beer Ⓗ
Quiet country pub in a picturesque rural village by the green.
🏚 Q 🕭 ◑ ▶ ᴕ ♣ P

ASHWELLTHORPE

White Horse
49-55 The Street (former B1135, ½ mile from B1113)
☎ (01508) 489721
12-3 (not Mon, 4 Sat), 5.30-11; 12-3, 7-10.30 Sun
Fuller's London Pride; Woodforde's Wherry; guest beers Ⓗ
Quiet, comfortable village-centre pub boasting original

beams and a collection of posters. 🏚 Q 🕭 ◑ ▶ ♣ P

ATTLEBOROUGH

Griffin Hotel
Church Street
☎ (01953) 452149
10.30-3, 5.30-11; 10.30-11 Fri & Sat; 12-3, 7-10.30 Sun
Greene King Abbot; Wolf Best Bitter, Coyote, Granny Wouldn't Like It; guest beer Ⓗ
Characterful coaching inn sporting original oak beams; two bars and a dining area.
🛏 ◑ ▶ 🍴 ⅄ ≠ P

AYLSHAM

Black Boys
Market Place
☎ (01263) 732122
11-11; 12-3, 7-10.30 Sun
Courage Directors; Greene King IPA; Woodforde's Wherry; guest beer

(occasional) Ⓗ
Large town-centre pub, dating from 1650. Note the original beams and fascinating old photos. No food Wed. 🕭 🛏 ◑ ≠ (Bure Valley narrow guage) ⌣ P

BINTREE

Royal Oak
The Street
☎ (01362) 683326
11-3, 5.30-11; 12-3, 7-10.30 Sun
Adnams Bitter; Greene King Abbot; guest beers Ⓗ
Early 19th-century alehouse that draws a broad mix of clientele (notwithstanding the old drayman ghost in the cellar). A warm, welcoming ambience is enhanced by a large open fireplace and the landlady's home-made food (not served Sun eve).
🏚 🕭 ◑ ▶ ♣ P

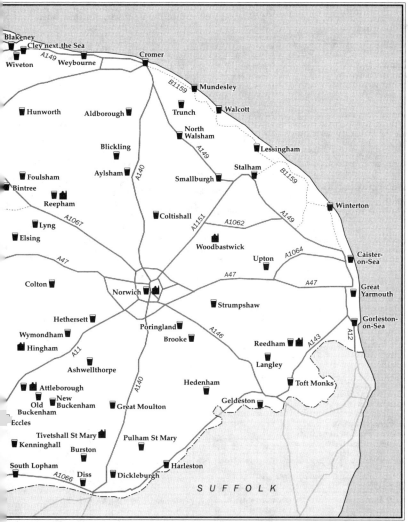

BLAKENEY

Manor Hotel

The Quay (E end)
☎ (01263) 740376

11-2.30, 6-11; 12-3, 6-10.30 Sun

Adnams Bitter, guest beer H

Hotel bar overlooking the
quay and salt marshes in a
popular area for walkers and
birdwatchers. Good value
food. Q ❀ ⇔ ◖ ▷ P

BLICKLING

Buckinghamshire Arms

On B1354, just outside
Aylsham ☎ (01263) 732133

12-3, 6-11; 12-3, 7-10.30 Sun

**Greene King IPA, Abbot; guest
beers** H

Unspoilt pub next to
Blickling Hall. A delightful
snug complements a bar with
a real fire; good food.
🏚 Q ❀ ⇔ ◖ ▷ P

BRANCASTER STAITHE

Jolly Sailors

Main Road (A149)
☎ (01485) 210314

11-11; 12-10.30 Sun

**Greene King IPA; Woodforde's
Wherry; guest beers** H

Traditional pub in a coastal
village near a harbour, much
loved by birdwatchers, it
opens at 8am for breakfast. It
sells cider in summer.
🏚 Q ➤ ❀ ◖ ▷ ⑤ ㄥ ▲ ♣ ⌂ P ⅍

Try also: White Horse, Main
Rd (Free)

BROOKE

White Lion

49 The Street OS289992
☎ (01508) 550443

12-3 (not Mon), 5.30-11; 12-11 Sat;
12-10.30 Sun

Adnams Bitter; Greene King IPA;
guest beers H

Attractive thatched pub in an
idyllic setting opposite the
meres (ponds). This friendly
local is notable for the low
ceilings, part clay-tiled floor
and long narrow bar.
🏚 ❀ ◖ ▷ ♣ P

BURNHAM THORPE

Lord Nelson

Walsingham Road
☎ (01328) 738241

11-3 (2.30 winter), 6-11; 12-3, 7-10.30
(closed winter eve) Sun

Greene King XX Mild (summer), **IPA,**
Abbot; Woodforde's Wherry,
Nelson's Revenge G

Popular pub displaying
Nelson memorabilia. All beer
is brought from the tap
room. Live music performed
Fri. The large garden has
children's activities.
🏚 Q ➤ ❀ ◖ ▷ ⑤ ♣ P ⅍

Try also: Hoste Arms, Burnham Mkt (Free); Crown, Stanhoe (Elgood's)

BURSTON

Crown Inn
Crown Green
☎ (01379) 741257
12-2.30 (3 Fri & Sat), 5.30-11; 12-3, 6.30-10.30 Sun
Adnams Bitter; guest beers Ⓖ
17th-century beamed pub; the public bar has recently been altered but not lost any of its charm. It has a bowling green. 🔥 Q ❀ ◐ ◑ ⊟ ♿ ⛺ ♣ P

CAISTER ON SEA

Ship
2 Victoria Street
☎ (01493) 728008
11-11; 12-10.30 Sun
Flowers IPA; Greene King IPA; Marston's Old Speckled Hen; Whitbread Best Bitter Ⓗ
Close to the beach so it gets busy in summer, this single bar is divided into several drinking areas and has a pleasant courtyard. Limited parking. 🔥 🐴 ❀ ◐ ⛺ P

CASTLE ACRE

Ostrich
Stocks Green
☎ (01760) 755398
12-3 , 7-11; 12-3, 7-10.30 Sun
Greene King XX Mild, IPA, Abbot, seasonal beers Ⓗ
16th-century coaching inn set in an attractive medieval village. The superb menu includes a vegetarian option; families are catered for.
🔥 Q 🐴 ❀ 🛏 ◐ ◑ ♿ ⛺ P

CASTON

Red Lion
The Green
☎ (01953) 488236
11.30-2.30, 5-11; 11.30-11 Sat; 12-10.30 Sun
Beer range varies Ⓗ
This 19th-century flintknapped pub is noted for its comprehensive range of food and friendly atmosphere. The house beer, Eds Ale is brewed locally by Wolf. Q ❀ ◐ ◑ ⊟ ⛺ P

CLEY-NEXT-THE-SEA

Three Swallows
☎ (01263) 740526
11.30-2.30, 6-11 (11.30-11 summer); 12-3, 7-10.30 Sun
Greene King IPA, Abbot; guest beer Ⓗ
Friendly old inn with a notable bar; once it looked across a busy harbour, now silted up, but still giving spectacular views. Handy for Cley bird reserve.
🔥 Q ❀ 🛏 ◐ ◑ ♣ P

COLKIRK

Crown
Crown Road
☎ (01328) 862172
11-2.30, 6-11; 12-3, 7-10.30 Sun
Greene King XX Mild, IPA, Abbot, seasonal beer or guest beer Ⓗ
Two-roomed pub with a dining area serving good value food; a friendly village local. 🔥 ❀ ◐ ◑ ♣ P

COLTISHALL

Railway Inn
8 Station Road (B1150)
☎ (01603) 738316
11-11; 12-10.30 Sun
Adnams Bitter; guest beer Ⓗ
Friendly local in large grounds. Built in 1720, it was originally known as the New Inn, until the arrival of the railway around 1840.
🔥 🐴 ❀ ◐ ◑ ⛺ ⇌ (Bure Valley narrow guage) ♣ P

COLTON

Ugly Bug
High House Farm Lane
☎ (01603) 880794
12-3, 5.30 (6 Sat)-11; 12-3, 7-10.30 Sun
Beer range varies Ⓗ
Formerly a barn this pub has been sympathetically restored; farm implements adorn the walls and ceiling. The beers include four guests and a house ale from Iceni. No meals Sun eve.
🐴 ❀ ◐ ◑ ♣ P

CROMER

Anglia Court Hotel
Runton Road
☎ (01263) 512443
11-11; 12-10.30 Sun
Woodforde's Wherry; Ⓖ **guest beers** (summer) Ⓗ
Smugglers Bar on the ground floor of a clifftop hotel.
Q 🐴 ❀ 🛏 ◐ ◑ ♿ ⛺ ⇌ P

Red Lion Hotel
Brooke Street
☎ (01263) 514964
11-11; 12-10.30 Sun
Adnams Bitter; Draught Bass; Fuller's London Pride; Greene King Abbot; guest beers Ⓗ
Family-run free house and hotel affording sea views. The rich mahogany fittings in the Edwardian public bar compliment the flint and brick interior. 🛏 ◐ ◑ ⛺ ⇌ P

DERSINGHAM

Feathers Hotel
Manor Road
☎ (01485) 540207
11-2.30, 5.30-11 (11-11 summer Sat); 12-3, 7-10.30 Sun
Adnams Bitter; Draught Bass; guest beer Ⓗ
Comfortable, three-bar hotel on the Sandringham estate. The extensive gardens include a play area.
🔥 Q ❀ 🛏 ◐ ◑ P

DICKLEBURGH

Crown
The Street
☎ (01379) 741475
12-3, 7-11; 12-11 Sat; 12-10.30 Sun
Greene King IPA; guest beer Ⓗ
Heavily-beamed, single bar ex-coaching inn featuring flagstoned floor, open fireplace and wooden settles. A house beer is stocked. No meals served Sun eve or Wed.
🔥 ❀ ◐ ◑ ⛺ ♣ P

DISS

Cock Inn
Fair Green, Denmark Street
☎ (01379) 643633
11.30-3, 11.30-11 Fri & Sat; 12-10.30 Sun
Adnams Bitter; Woodforde's Wherry; Taylor Landlord; guest beer Ⓗ
Small, two-bar pub with stone-flagged floors.
🔥 ❀ ♣ P

DOWNHAM MARKET

Live & Let Live
22 London Road
☎ (01366) 383933
12-2 (not Wed), 7-11 (hours vary winter); 12-10.30 Sun
Beer range varies Ⓗ
Town pub serving two ever-changing beers from independent breweries in a split-level bar. Pool and other team games played; live music at weekends; can get busy. Meals served in summer. ❀ 🛏 ◐ ⇌ ♣

Try also: Crown, Bridge St (Free)

ECCLES

Old Railway Tavern (Eccles Tap)
Station Road OS018899
12-2.30 (not Mon-Thu), 5.30-11; 12-2.30 (may extend), 7-10.30 Sun
Adnams Bitter; Greene King IPA Ⓗ
Rural drinkers' gem stubbornly resisting so-called progress. 🔥 Q ❀ ⇌ (Eccles Rd. – limited service) P ▯

ELSING

Mermaid
Church Street
☎ (01362) 637640
12-3, 6-11; 12-3, 7-10.30 Sun
Adnams Bitter; Greene King Abbot; Woodforde's Wherry; guest beer Ⓗ
Beamed, 17th-century village local, but welcoming custom from a wide area. This rural free house fields local league darts and pool teams, while a

piano enhances the pub atmosphere.
🏠 ☕ ◑ ♣ P ⊟

FAKENHAM

Bull
Bridge Street
☎ (01328) 862560
11-3, 7-11; 11-11 Thu-Sat; 12-3, 7-10.30 Sun
Blanchfield Black Bull Mild, Best Bitter, Hi-Hop, Raging Bull Ⓗ
Home to Blanchfield Brewery, a comfortable three-roomed pub.
Q ☕ ◑ Å ♣ P

Star
44 Oak Street
☎ (01328) 862895
11-2.30, 7-11; 12-3, 7-10.30 Sun
Tolly Cobbold Original; guest beer Ⓗ
Single bar town local, this listed building, which dates back to the 16th century has a pool room and a large enclosed garden.
Q ☕ Å ♣ P

FOULDEN

White Hart Inn
White Hart Street
☎ (01366) 328638
11-3, 6-11; 12-5 Sun
Greene King IPA, Abbot Ⓗ
Friendly country village pub comprising several drinking/eating areas; the old bar has bare boards. Home-cooked food.
🏠 Q ☕ ⇔ ◑ ⅙ ♣ P

FOULSHAM

Queens Head
2 High Street
☎ (01362) 683339
11-3, 7-11; 12-3, 7-10.30 Sun
Adnams Bitter; Woodforde's Wherry; guest beers Ⓗ
Old pictures depict a well established pub in a farming village as it remains today. Its bowling green is popular. An extensive menu is based on local produce.
🏠 ☕ ◑ ♣ P

GARBOLDISHAM

Fox Inn
The Street
☎ (01953) 688151
11.30-2.30, 5-11; 11.30-11 Sat; 12-10.30 Sun
Adnams Bitter; Greene King IPA; Shepherd Neame Spitfire; guest beer Ⓗ
17th-century pub, the interior of which has been opened up to create a large, but segregated, bar where the emphasis is on food. A woodburner stands in the inglenook. No food Sun eve.
🏠 ☕ ◑ ♣ P ⊞

GAYTON

Crown
Lynn Road
☎ (01553) 636252
11.30-2.30, 6 (5.30 Fri)-11; 11-3, 6-11 Sat; 12-3, 7-10.30 Sun
Greene King XX Mild, IPA, Triumph, Abbot Ⓗ
Local at the heart of village life enjoying a growing reputation for food. It has a pleasant garden for summer drinking. 🏠 Q ☕ ◑ ♣ P

GELDESTON

Wherry
7 The Street
☎ (01508) 518371
11-3, 7-11; 12-3, 7-10.30 Sun
Adnams Bitter, Broadside, seasonal beers Ⓗ
Wonderful brick-built, two-bar local with a good atmosphere. The classic public bar boasts a clay-tiled floor, with a larger main bar at the rear; good food does not dominate.
🏠 Q ☕ ◑ ⅙ Å ♣ P

GORLESTON

Dock Tavern
Dock Tavern Lane
☎ (01493) 442255
12-11; 12-10.30 Sun
Adnams Broadside; Elgood's Black Dog Mild; Fuller's London Pride; Greene King IPA; guest beers Ⓗ
L-shaped bar featuring an upside-down rowing boat cut in half over the bar. Up to four guest ales on tap. ☕

GREAT CRESSINGHAM

Windmill
Water End (off A1065 4 miles S of Swaffham)
☎ (01760) 756232
11-3, 6-11; 12-3, 6.30-10.30 Sun
Adnams Bitter, Broadside; Draught Bass; guest beers Ⓗ
17th-century free house with at least 10 drinking/eating areas. Food is popular and good value. The house beer (Windy Miller) is from Bass.
🏠 Q ⇆ ☕ ◑ ⅙ Å ♣ P

GREAT MOULTON

Fox & Hounds
Frith Way
☎ (01379) 677506
11-2.30 (not Mon or Tue), 7-11; 12-10.30 Sun
Adnams Bitter; Draught Bass; guest beer (summer) Ⓗ
Single bar village pub with a large number of comfy sofas. The restaurant is run by a Spanish chef (no food Mon eve). 🏠 ☕ ◑ Å ♣ P

GREAT YARMOUTH

Red Herring

24-25 Havelock Road (near town wall)
☎ (01493) 853384
11.30-3, 6-11; 12-3, 7-10.30 Sun
Adnams Bitter; Elgood's Black Dog Mild; guest beers Ⓗ
Good quality Victorian local, with a commitment to quality in an area not renowned for real ale (four guests on tap).
◑ Å ♣ P ⊞

GRISTON

Waggon & Horses
Church Road (take B1108 from A1075 between Thetford and Watton)
☎ (01953) 883847
11-3, 6.30-11; 12-3, 7-10.30 Sun
Greene King IPA, Abbot, guest beers Ⓗ
17th-century pub with a cosy atmosphere serving an excellent range of real ales; the guest beers are always changing. A good menu includes daily specials.
Q ☕ ◑ ⅙ P ⅟

HARLESTON

Cherry Tree
74 London Road
☎ (01379) 852345
12-2.30, 6-11; 7-10.30 Sun
Adnams Bitter Ⓗ
Deceptively small edge-of-town local with a large garden and a good atmosphere – no food Mon.
🏠 Q ☕ ◑ ⊟ ⅙ ♣ P

Duke William
28 Redenhall Road
☎ (01379) 853183
11-11; 12-5.30, 7-10.30 Sun
Adnams Bitter; Courage Best Bitter, Directors; Woodforde's Wherry; guest beers (summer) Ⓗ
Traditional, small town pub: two comfortable bars and a good, no-frills atmosphere.
🏠 ☕ ⊟

HEDENHAM

Mermaid
Norwich Road
☎ (01508) 482480
12-3, 7 (5 Fri)-11; 12-4, 7-10.30 (may extend) Sun
Greene King IPA; Tindall Mild, Ale; guest beer Ⓗ
300-year-old former coaching inn. This timber-framed building, with brick floors and real fires, is well worth visiting for the Tindall ales.
🏠 ☕ ◑ ♣ P ⅟

HETHERSETT

King's Head
36 Old Norwich Road
☎ (01603) 810206
11-2.30, 5.30 (5 Fri)-11; 12-3, 7-10.30 Sun
Greene King Abbot; Marston's

Pedigree; John Smith's Bitter;
Woodforde's Wherry Ⓗ
Bustling, friendly, rural pub
on the outskirts of the
village: a characterful interior
complete with inglenooks, a
no-smoking dining area and
a snug. No food Sun eve.
♨ Q ☜ 🕸 ◖ D ♣ P

HOCKWOLD-CUM-WILTON

Red Lion
114 Main Street
☎ (01842) 828875
12-2.30, 6-11; 12-11 Sat; 12-10.30
Sun
Greene King IPA; guest beers Ⓗ
Thriving village local,
opposite a small green. Busy
at times due to its good food
and beer. 🕸 ◖ D P

HUNWORTH

Hunny Bell
The Green
☎ (01263) 712300
11-3, 5.30-11; 12-5, 7-10.30 Sun
Adnams Bitter; Greene King IPA, Ⓖ
Abbot; Ⓗ Woodforde's Wherry;
guest beer Ⓖ
Single bar plus a dining
room, with lots of beams and
brickwork in a picturesque
setting by the village green.
♨ Q 🕸 ◖ D ♿ ♣ P

KENNINGHALL

Red Lion
East Church Street
☎ (01953) 887849
12-3, 6.30-11; 12-11 Sat; 12-10.30
Sun
Greene King XX Mild, IPA, Triumph,
Ⓗ Abbot; Ⓖ Ruddles Best Bitter Ⓗ
400-year-old pub,
sympathetically refurbished,
to include lots of wood and a
quarry-tiled floor. Only one
bar, but with a number of
drinking areas, including a
snug.
♨ Q 🕸 ⌂ ◖ D ♣ P ⊞

KING'S LYNN

Fenman
Blackfriars Road
☎ (01553) 761889
11-11; 12-3, 7-10.30 Sun
Greene King IPA, Abbot; guest
beer Ⓗ
Modern, one-room bar with a
pool table, opposite the
station.
🕸 ≈ ♣

London Porterhouse
78 London Road
☎ (01553) 766842
12-3, 6-11; 12-11 Fri & Sat; 12-10.30
Sun
Greene King IPA, Abbot Ⓖ
Small, popular bar near the
Southgates, serving beer from
casks behind the bar.
🕸 ≈ ♣

Ouse Amateur Sailing Club
Ferry Lane (off King St)
☎ (01553) 772239
11.30-4, 7-11; 11.30-11 Fri; 12-4,
8.30-10.30 Sun
Bateman XB, XXB; guest beers Ⓖ
Popular, cosy club with a
verandah overlooking the
river; CAMRA National *Club
of the Year* 1998. Show
CAMRA membership or this
Guide for entry. No food Sun.
♨ 🕸 ◖ ♣ ⌂

Stuart House Hotel
35 Goodwins Road
☎ (01553) 772169
12-2, 7 (6 Fri)-11; 12-2, 7-10.30 Sun
Beer range varies Ⓗ
Welcoming bar in a
privately-owned hotel.
Regular events include live
music and a summer beer
festival.
♨ 🕸 ⌂ ◖ D P

White Horse
9 Wootton Road
☎ (01553) 763258
11-3, 5.30-11; 11-11 Fri & Sat; 12-3, 7-
10.30 Sun
Greene King IPA; Morland Old
Speckled Hen; guest beer Ⓗ
Lively, traditional, two-bar
drinkers' pub near the
Gaywood Clock. ♣ P

Try also: Crossways, Sth
Everard St (Greene King)

LANGLEY

Beauchamp Arms
Buckenham Ferry (between
Claxton and Langley village)
OS350043
☎ (01508) 480247
12-3, 7-11; 11-11 Sat & summer;
12-10.30 Sun
Greene King IPA; Woodforde's
Wherry, Great Eastern (summer);
guest beer Ⓗ
Large, multi-roomed free
house in a remote
location on the south bank
of the River Yare. Extensive
recent refurbishment has
enhanced the cosy
atmosphere. Extensive boat
moorings are free for
customers. Good home-
cooked food served.
♨ ☜ 🕸 ⌂ ◖ D ♿ ♣ P

LARLING

Angel
Norwich Road (A11, 1 mile
from Snetterton racetrack)
☎ (01953) 717963
11-11; 12-10.30 Sun
Adnams Bitter; guest beers Ⓗ
Don't pass by this pub on the
road from Norwich to
London. Packed with local
atmosphere, it offers
interesting ales and friendly
chat.
♨ 🕸 ⌂ ◖ D ⊟ ⚑ P ⊟

LESSINGHAM

Star
School Road (off A149)
☎ (01692) 580510
1-3, 7 (5 summer)-11; 11-3, 12-10.30
Sun
Greene King IPA; guest beers Ⓗ
Small friendly local with a
caravan site in the garden.
♨ Q ☜ 🕸 ⌂ ◖ D ♿ ♣ P ✂
⊟

LITTLE CRESSINGHAM

White Horse
Watton Road (off B1108,
3 miles W of Watton)
☎ (01953) 883434
12-3, 7-11; 12-3, 7-10.30 Sun
Flowers Original; guest beer Ⓗ
17th-century inn, popular
with ramblers. Good home-
cooked food includes a
selection of Balti dishes.
♨ 🕸 ◖ D ⚑ ♣ P

LONGHAM

White Horse
Wendling Road OS939157
☎ (01362) 687464
12-2.30 (not Mon; may extend), 6.30-
11; 12-3, 6.30-10.30 Sun
Woodforde's Wherry; guest beers Ⓗ
Comfortable brick and flint
pub in the village centre,
with a wood-burning stove.
This good community local
displays local crafts for sale.
♨ 🕸 ◖ D ♣ P ⊟

LYNG

Fox & Hounds
The Street
☎ (01603) 872316
12-3, 5-11; 12-11 Sat; 12-4, 7-10.30
Sun
Greene King IPA, Abbot;
Woodforde's Wherry; Wells
Bombardier; guest beers Ⓗ
Early 18th-century village
pub: the bar is heavily
beamed with a low ceiling
and large open log fire.
They host regular jazz/folk
nights and achieve a good
balance of drinking and
eating.
♨ ☜ 🕸 ◖ D ⚑ ♣ P ✂

MIDDLETON

Gate Inn
Fair Green (1/2 mile N of A47
in Fair Green village)
☎ (01553) 840518
12-2.30, 7 (5.30 Fri)-11; 12-3, 7-10.30
Sun
Greene King IPA; guest beers Ⓗ
Popular pub with a recently
added eating area, well
known for good value food –
Fri fish night is highly
recommended (no eve meals
Mon). The pub is one mile
east of the famous Hardwick
roundabout.
♨ Q 🕸 ◖ D ♣ P

MORSTON
Anchor
The Street
☎ (01263) 740791
11-3, 7-11 (11-11 summer); 12-10.30 Sun
Woodforde's Wherry H
A real local welcome is assured in this unspoilt pub where a new extension blends well with the original building. Seal trips, popular with holidaymakers, can be booked here. Meals served all day in summer; winter eve meals Fri-Sun. Morston Mud is a house beer.
🏨 Q 🕙 🌜 🍴 ♿ Å ♣ P

MUNDESLEY
Royal Hotel
Paston Road
☎ (01263) 720096
11-3, 6-11; 12-3, 6-10.30 Sun
Adnams Bitter; Greene King IPA, Abbot; guest beer H
Hotel whose Nelson Bar has a comfortable olde-worlde charm enhanced by an inglenook, leather chairs and Lord Nelson memorabilia.
🏨 Q 🛏 🌜 🍴 🕙 Å P

NEW BUCKENHAM
King's Head
Market Place
☎ (01953) 860487
12-2.30 (3.30 Sat), 7-11; 12-3.30, 7-10.30 Sun
Adnams Bitter; Draught Bass; Iceni Fine Soft Day H
Village local, set on the green: a carpeted front lounge leads through to a tiled and flagstoned public bar. A good range of food, includes a vegetarian menu (no food Mon).
🏨 Q 🌜 🛏 🕙 Å ♣

NORTH ELMHAM
Railway Freehouse
40 Station Road
☎ (01362) 668300
11-2.30, 6-11; 11-11 Fri, Sat & summer; 12-10.30 Sun
Beer range varies H
Former railway hotel, now one bar divided to give comfy seating around an open log fire. A changing selection of local and regional ales is on offer.
🏨 🌜 🕙 ♿ ♣ P

NORTH PICKENHAM
Blue Lion
Hillside (3 miles S of Swaffham)
☎ (01760) 440289
11-11; 12-10.30 Sun
Greene King IPA; Wells Eagle; Woodforde's Great Eastern; guest beer H
Delightful rural pub, close to

the Peddars Way footpath. It has a friendly, relaxed atmosphere. Meals served 11-10.30pm.
🏨 Q 🌜 🌜 🕙 🍴 ♿ Å ♣ P

NORTH WALSHAM
Orchard Gardens
Mundesley Road
☎ (01692) 405152
12-11; 12-10.30 Sun
Courage Directors; guest beers H
Lively local pub that places a keen emphasis on real ale with an annual beer festival in May and up to four guest beers. Note the bicycle hanging from the ceiling. Children allowed in the rear conservatory. 🌜 ♣ ♣ P

NORTHWOLD
Crown Inn
30 High Street
☎ (01366) 727317
12-2.30, 6-11; 11.30-11 Sat; 12-3, 7-10.30 Sun
Greene King IPA, Abbot; guest beers H
Popular, busy village local offering good value food plus live music most Fris.
🏨 🌜 🕙 ♣ P

NORWICH
Alexandra
16 Stafford Street
☎ (01603) 627772
10.30-11; 12-10.30 Sun
Chalk Hill Tap, CHB, Flintknapper's Mild; guest beers H
A real back-street local extending a friendly welcome to all: two bars with a pool table in one. 🏨 Q 🌜 🍴 🍴

Beehive
30 Leopold Road
☎ (01603) 451628
11-3.30, 5.30-11; 11-11 Sat; 12-3.30, 7-10.30 Sun
Draught Bass; Courage Best Bitter; Wolf Best Bitter; Woodforde's Mardler's Mild; guest beers H
Friendly local: two comfortable bars and a garden. Q 🌜 🕙 ♣ P

Champion
101 Chapelfield Road
☎ (01603) 765611
10.30-11; 12-10.30 Sun
Greene King IPA, Abbot; guest beers H
Former Whitbread pub, now a free house serving a house beer (brewer varies); Evening News *Pub of the Year* 1999. Lunchtime snacks. ♣

Coach & Horses
82 Thorpe Road (400 yds from station)
☎ (01603) 477077
11-11; 12-10.30 Sun
Boddingtons Bitter; Chalk Hill Tap, CHB, Dreadnought, Flinknapper's

Mild, Old Tackle; Taylor Landlord; guest beers H
Home of Chalk Hill Brewery, visible at the rear of this large pub which has an interesting balcony and a timber herringbone floor. Often hosts live music Sats and can be busy on matchdays.
🏨 🌜 🕙 ⇌ ♣ 🍴 P

Cottage
9 Silver Road
☎ (01603) 441461
12-11; 12-10.30 Sun
Buffy's Bitter, India Pale Ale; Tetley Bitter H
Residential area pub with one modernised bar. 🌜

Dyers Arms
2-4 Lawson Road
☎ (01603) 787237
10.30-2.30, 6.30-11; 10.30-4, 7-11 Fri & Sat; 12-3, 7.30-10.30 Sun
Adnams Bitter; Draught Bass; Taylor Landlord H
Cosy corner pub with friendly staff, popular with locals. Q 🌜 ♿ ♣ P 🍴

Eaton Cottage
75 Mount Pleasant
☎ (01603) 453048
11-11; 12-10.30 Sun
Adnams Bitter; Fuller's London Pride; Marston's Pedigree; Stones Bitter; guest beers H
Popular local where two bars are connected by a long, winding corridor. A rare example of an off-sales snug survives here. Live music played some eves; piano in the lounge bar. The house beer is from Wolf.
🌜 🍴 ♣ P

Fat Cat
49 West End Street
☎ (01603) 624364
12 (11 Sat)-11; 12-10.30 Sun
Adnams Bitter; Hopback Summer Lightning; Greene King Abbot; Taylor Landlord; Woodforde's Wherry H
National CAMRA *Pub of the Year* 1998; the beer range here is vast with 12 beers on handpump, many more on gravity, kept in tap room visible from the main bar. Foreign (bottled and draught) beers are also stocked. A beer drinkers' paradise.
🌜 ♣ 🍴 🍴

Gardeners Arms
2-8 Timber Hill
☎ (01603) 621447
10.30-11; 12-10.30 Sun
Adnams Bitter; Draught Bass; Boddingtons Bitter; Greene King Abbot; guest beers H
Deceptively large, city-centre hostelry drawing a lunchtime shoppers/office clientele and a much younger eve scene, when the no-smoking area is no longer available. No food Sun. 🌜 🕙 ♣ ✄

King Edward VII
63 Aylsham Road
☎ (01603) 403703
5 (12 Sat)-11; 12-10.30 Sun
Beer range varies Ⓗ
Large roadside pub enjoying
vastly improved support for
real ale; the three guest beers
come from local micro-
brewers, sometimes chosen
by the locals. The large
garden has three drinking
areas. Kingfisher cider is
occasionally stocked.
🏠 ♣ ⌂ P

King's Arms
22 Hall Road (near bus
station) ☎ (01603) 766361
11-11; 12-10.30 Sun
**Adnams Bitter, Broadside; Greene
King Abbot; Wolf Coyote; guest
beers** Ⓗ
CAMRA East Anglian *Pub of
the Year* 1999, it offers a
superb range of ever-
changing regional ales (eight
guests) in a former Greene
King hostelry. Traditional
Czech, Dutch and Iceni
lagers are also available.
🏠 ♣ ⌂ ✦

Ribs of Beef
24 Wensum Street (near
Anglican Cathedral)
☎ (01603) 619517
10.30-11; 11-11 Sun
**Adnams Bitter; Fuller's London
Pride; guest beers** Ⓗ
Riverside pub offering free
mooring. Friendly staff help
make it popular with all ages.
The house beer, Ribcracker is
supplied by Woodforde's.
🍺 ◖⊞

Rosary Tavern
95 Rosary Road, Thorpe
Hamlet
☎ (01603) 666287
11.30-11; 12-10.30 Sun
Adnams Bitter; guest beers Ⓗ
Square pub, on a hill
overlooking the city, a good
conversational pub. The six
guest beers usually include
Bateman XB and
Woodforde's Wherry. The
family room opens summer.
🍺 🏠 ◖✦♣ ⌂ P

Trafford Arms
61 Grove Road
☎ (01603) 628466
11-11; 12-10.30 Sun
**Adnams Bitter; Boddingtons Bitter;
Tetley Bitter; Woodforde's Mardler's
Mild; guest beers** Ⓗ
Open-plan pub serving the
local community that holds a
beer festival every Feb. No-
smoking area available at
lunchtime. Barley Boy is a
house beer from
Woodforde's. ◖♣ ⌂ ✦

Vine
7 Dove Street
☎ (01603) 629258

10.30-11; 12-10.30 Sun
**Adnams Bitter, Extra, Broadside,
seasonal beers** Ⓗ
The smallest pub in the city,
off the market place. 🏠 ♣

Wig & Pen
6 Palace Plain (St Martins)
☎ (01603) 625891
11.30 (12 Sat)-11; 12-4.30 Sun
**Adnams Bitter; Boddingtons Bitter;
Buffy's Bitter; guest beers** Ⓗ
Busy local serving a changing
range of guest ales, situated
near the Law Courts. A 16th-
century beamed building
offering an excellent choice
of food. Limited parking.
🏠 ◖▶ ♣ P

Try also: Billy Bluelight,
Hall Rd (Woodforde's)

OLD BUCKENHAM
Ox & Plough
The Green
☎ (01953) 860004
12-3, 6.30-11.30; 12-11.30 Sat; 12-3,
7-11 (12-11 summer) Sun
**Adnams Bitter; Woodforde's
Wherry** Ⓗ
Single-bar pub overlooking a
large village green; a cosy
sitting area houses an eclectic
mix of knicks-knacks; the
rear bar area has a pool table
and juke box. Popular with
locals. 🏘 🏠 ◖▶ P

OLD HUNSTANTON
Ancient Mariner
Golf Course Road
☎ (01485) 534411
11-3, 6-11; 11-11 Sat & summer;
12-10.30 Sun
**Adnams Bitter, Broadside; Draught
Bass; guest beer** Ⓗ
Large, busy pub attached to
the Le Strange Arms Hotel.
Family friendly, it has a large
conservatory and gardens
running down to the beach.
🏘 🍺 🏠 ⇔ ◖▶ ♿ P

PORINGLAND
Royal Oak
44 The Street
☎ (01508) 493734
12-2, 6-11; 12-11 Sat; 12-3, 7-10.30
Sun
**Adnams Bitter; Woodforde's Wherry,
guest beers** Ⓗ
Rare example of an alehouse
in rural Norfolk; no food but
a commitment to real ale.
The single bar has several
alcoves. It holds an annual
beer festival. 🏠 ♣ P

PULHAM ST. MARY
King's Head
☎ (01379) 676318
11.30-3, 5.30-11; 11-11 summer;
12-10.30 Sun
**Adnams Bitter; Buffy's Bitter; guest
beers** Ⓗ

Single cosy bar in a village
pub offering good value food.
The large garden has a play
area.
🏘 🏠 🍺 ◖▶ 🅰 P ✦

REEDHAM
Railway Tavern
17 The Havaker
☎ (01493) 700340
11-3, 6-11 (11-11 summer); 12-10.30
Sun
**Humpty Dumpty Little Sharpie, Un
Petit Deux Petit, Claude Hamilton,
seasonal beers; guest beers** Ⓗ
Characterful inn with its own
brewery. It hosts regular beer
festivals with special train
services laid on. The beer
range is matched by a
connoisseur collection of
malt whiskies, plus cider in
summer. 🏘 Q 🏠 ⇔ ◖▶ 🍺
♿ 🅰 ⇌ ♣ ⌂ P ⊞

Try also: Lord Nelson, Quay
(Free)

REEPHAM
Kings Arms
Market Place
☎ (01603) 870345
11.30-3, 5.30-11; 11-11 Sat; 12-3,
7-10.30 Sun
**Adnams Bitter; Draught Bass;
Fuller's London Pride; Greene King
Abbot; Woodforde's Wherry** Ⓗ
This village-centre, listed pub
boasts much exposed
brickwork and beams and
three real fires.
🏘 🏠 ◖▶ 🍺 ♣ P

RINGSTEAD
Gin Trap Inn
High Street
☎ (01485) 525264
11.30-2.30, 7 (6.30 summer)-11; 12-
2.30, 7-10.30 Sun
**Adnams Bitter; Greene King Abbot;
Woodforde's Norfolk Nog; guest
beers** (summer) Ⓗ
Classic village local;
good food is served in a split-
level bar enhanced by a
roaring log fire and a
fearsome collection
of animal traps. The house
beer comes from
Woodforde's.
🏘 🏠 ⇔ ◖▶ ♣ P

SMALLBURGH
Crown
North Walsham Road (A149)
☎ (01692) 536314
12-3 (4 Sat), 5.30 (7 Sat)-11; 12-3,
7-10.30 Sun
**Greene King Abbot; Flowers IPA;
Tetley Bitter; guest beers** Ⓗ
Comfortable, two-bar village
pub and restaurant in a
thatched, beamed 15th-
century building with a nice
garden.
🏘 Q 🏠 ⇔ ◖▶ 🅰 ♣ P

SOUTH CREAKE
Ostrich Inn
11 Fakenham Road
☎ (01328) 823320
12-3, 7 (6.30 Fri & Sat)-11; 12-3,
7-10.30 Sun
**Greene King IPA, Abbot;
Woodforde's Wherry, Nelson's
Revenge; guest beers** Ⓗ
Narrow single-bar village
local taking its name from
the crest of the Coke family
of Holkham. There is a
partitioned dining area
which operates with a supper
licence (until midnight).
🍴 ⊛ Å ♣ P

SOUTH LOPHAM
White Horse
The Street
☎ (01379) 687252
11-3, 6-11; 12-3, 6-11 Sun
**Adnams Bitter; Greene King IPA;
guest beer** Ⓗ
17th-century food-oriented
pub featuring beams,
exposed brick, an inglenook
and bare boards in a cosy
atmosphere. Childrens' play
area at the rear.
🍴 Q ⊛ ◖ ▶ ♣ P ⅙ ⊟ ⊞

STALHAM
Swan
High Street
☎ (01692) 581482
11-11; 12-10.30 Sun
**Adnams Bitter, Broadside; Bateman
XXXB** Ⓗ
Comfortable, friendly, two-
bar local in a small town.
🍴 Q ⊛ ◖ ▶ ⊟ Å ♣ P

STIBBARD
Ordnance Arms
Guist Bottom
☎ (01328) 829471
11-3 (not Mon-Fri), 5.30-11; 12-3,
7-10.30 Sun
**Draught Bass; Greene King IPA;
guest beer** (summer) Ⓗ
Unspoilt, three bar pub with
a pool table in one room. The
Thai restaurant at the rear of
the building has a good
reputation locally (open Tue-
Sat eves) only. 🍴 ⊛ ♣ P

STIFFKEY
Red Lion
44 Wells Road
☎ (01328) 830552
11-3, 6 (7 winter)-11; 12-3, 7-10.30
Sun
Adnams Bitter; Greene King Abbot;
Ⓗ **Woodforde's Wherry;** Ⓖ **guest
beer** Ⓗ
Beamed building of several
drinking areas: a friendly
local. 🍴 ⏁ ⊛ ◖ ▶ ⅙ Å ♣ P ⅙

STRUMPSHAW
Shoulder of Mutton

Norwich Road
☎ (01603) 712274
11-11; 12-10.30 Sun
**Adnams Bitter, Broadside, seasonal
beers; Greene King IPA; guest
beers** Ⓗ
Set back from the road, with
two distinct areas for
drinking and dining
(emphasis on home-cooked
food). The large garden at the
rear and pétanque courts are
an unusual bonus. No meals
Sun eve. 🍴 ⊛ ◖ ▶ ♣ P

Try also: **Huntsman**,
Norwich Rd (Free)

SWAFFHAM
George Hotel
Station Street (A1065)
☎ (01760) 721238
11-2.30, 6.30-11; 12-2, 7-10.30 Sun
Greene King IPA, Abbot Ⓗ
Split-level public bar in a
town-centre hotel, a popular
meeting place, it serves an
unusual menu.
Q ⊯ ◖ ▶ ♣ P

SWANTON MORLEY
Darby's
1-2 Elsing Road
☎ (01362) 637647
11-3, 6-11, 11.30-11 Sat; 12-10.30
Sun
**Adnams Bitter, Broadside; Badger
Tanglefoot; Greene King IPA, Abbot;
Woodforde's Wherry; guest beers** Ⓗ
Old farm cottages converted
attractively into a multi-area
pub, making good use of the
original brick and beamed
interiors. The accent on
regional ales is proving
popular in this rural family
free house. The imaginative
menu is mostly home-made.
🍴 ⏁ ⊛ ⊯ ◖ ▶ ⅙ Å ♣ P ⅙

TERRINGTON ST CLEMENTS
County Arms
Marshland Street
☎ (01553) 828511
12-3 (not Mon-Fri), 7-11; 12-3, 7-10.30
Sun
Greene King IPA, Abbot Ⓗ
Three-bar local, a true
drinkers' pub, it is pleasant
and comfortable. ⊛ P

THETFORD
Albion
93-95 Castle Street
☎ (01842) 752796
11-2.30 (3 Fri & Sat), 6 (5 Fri)-11; 12-3,
7-10.30 Sun
Greene King IPA, Abbot; guest beers
(occasional) Ⓗ
Former flint cottages in the
old part of town where a
warm welcome and good
value ale are assured in a
traditional drinkers' pub.
🍴 ⊛ ♣ P ⊞

Kings Head
27 White Hart Street (near
Ancient House museum)
☎ (01842) 753050
11-11; 12-10.30 Sun
**Greene King XX Mild, IPA, Abbot;
guest beers** Ⓗ
Old coaching inn, now a
thriving two-roomed
drinkers' pub with a friendly,
down-to-earth atmosphere.
The only mild outlet in town,
it also has the widest range of
beers (up to three guests). It
hosts a beer festival in June.
⊛ ⇌ ♣ P

THOMPSON
Chequers
Griston Road OS923969
☎ (01953) 483360
11.30-2.30, 6.30-11; 12-3, 6.30-10.30
Sun
**Adnams Bitter; Fuller's London
Pride; Wolf Best Bitter; guest
beers** Ⓗ
16th-century thatched inn
featuring several drinking
and eating areas. On the
Peddars Way footpath, it is
ideal for walkers.
🍴 Q ⊛ ◖ ▶ ♣ P ⅙

THORNHAM
Lifeboat
Ship Lane ☎ (01485) 512236
11-11; 12-10.30 Sun
**Adnams Bitter; Greene King IPA,
Abbot; Woodforde's Wherry; guest
beers** Ⓗ
16th-century smugglers'
alehouse transformed into a
large, busy pub on the edge
of the saltmarsh; popular in
summer.
🍴 Q ⏁ ⊛ ⊯ ◖ ▶ ♣ ⌂ P

Try also: **White Horse**,
Holme-next-the-Sea (Pubmaster)

TILNEY ST LAWRENCE
Buck Inn
2 Church Road
☎ (01945) 880839
12-3 (not Mon-Fri), 7-11; 12-3, 7-10.30
Sun
**Elgood's Black Dog Mild,
Cambridge** Ⓗ
Pleasant Fenland village pub,
a community local with a
room for diners. Bar billiards
played. 🍴 ⊛ ⊯ ◖ ▶ ♣ P

TOFT MONKS
Toft Lion
Yarmouth Road (A143)
☎ (01502) 677702
11.30-2.30, 5-11; 12-3.30, 7-10.30
Sun
**Adnams Bitter, Broadside; guest
beers** Ⓗ
Good local on the main road.
Note the collections of
matchboxes and jugs. A
warm welcome and good
quality home-cooking awaits,

with a good selection of board games by the fireside.
🏚 ❀ 🖛 ◖ Ġ Å ♣ P

TRUNCH

Crown
Front Street
☎ (01263) 722341
12-2.30 (3 summer), 6-11; 12-3, 7-10.30 (12-10.30 summer) Sun
Greene King IPA; Shepherd Neame Spitfire; guest beer Ⓗ
One-roomed pub whose friendly landlord holds a beer festival every Aug.
🏚 Q ❀ ♣ P

UPTON

White Horse
17 Chapel Road
☎ (01493) 750696
11-11; 12-10.30 Sun
Adnams Bitter, Broadside; St. Peter's Best Bitter; guest beers Ⓗ
Traditional friendly village local near the Broads. The food is excellent value – try the fish and chips (Fri).
🏚 Q ❀ ◖ Å ♣ P

WALCOTT

Lighthouse
Coast Road (B1159)
☎ (01692) 650371
11-3, 6-11 (11-11 summer Sat); 12-10.30 Sun
Adnams Bitter; Tetley Bitter; guest beers Ⓗ
Friendly pub, popular with visitors and locals alike offering good value food, including local fish.
🏚 Q ➷ ❀ 🖛 ◖ Å ♣ ᴄ P ⊁ ⊞

WALSINGHAM

Bull
Common Place, Shirehall Plain ☎ (01328) 820333
11-3, 6-11; 11-11 Sat; 12-3, 7-10.30 Sun
Boddingtons Bitter; Flowers IPA, Original; Marton's Pedigree; Tolly Cobbold Original (summer) Ⓗ
15th-century pub close to the shrine, displaying interesting artefacts. Well worth a visit. Eve meals served in the restaurant.
🏚 ❀ 🖛 ◖ ▶ P

WARHAM

Three Horseshoes ☆
Bridge Street
☎ (01328) 710547
11.30-2.30, 6-11; 12-3, 6-10.30 Sun
Greene King IPA; Woodforde's Wherry; guest beer Ⓗ
Genuine 1920s pub with a sympathetic extension. The home-cooked meals are based on local specialities. This pub is a gem. Some beers are served under gravity.
🏚 Q ❀ 🖛 ◖ ▶ 🖸 Ġ Å ♣ P ⊁

WATTON

Breckland Wines (off-licence)
80 High Street
☎ (01953) 881592
9-9; 9-9 Sun
Beer range varies
Excellent selection of bottled beers (many are bottle-conditioned), but no draught ale sold.

WEASENHAM ALL SAINTS

Ostrich
Cross Roads (A1065)
☎ (01328) 838221
11.30-2.30 (not Mon or Tue), 7-11; 12-3, 7-10.30 Sun
Adnams Bitter; guest beer (occasional) Ⓗ
Cosy, one-bar, village local. A guest beer is put on at busy periods. 🏚 Q ❀ ♣ P

WELLS-NEXT-THE-SEA

Crown Hotel
The Buttlands
☎ (01328) 710209
11-2.30, 6-11; 12-2.30, 7-10.30 Sun
Adnams Bitter; Draught Bass; guest beer Ⓗ
Smart but friendly hotel, famed for its menu. The place for a relaxing drink or lazy holiday.
🏚 Q ➷ ❀ 🖛 ◖ ▶ Å ⇌ ♣ P

Edinburgh
Station Road
☎ (01328) 710120
11-2.30 (3 Fri), 7, (6.30 Sat)-11; 12-3, 7-10.30 Sun
Draught Bass; Hancock's HB; guest beer Ⓗ
Friendly local serving an excellent range of guest ales in its long, single bar. The top area is reserved for food (no lunches Thu).
🏚 ❀ 🖛 ◖ ▶ 🖸

WEYBOURNE

Ship
The Street
☎ (01263) 588721
12-3 (not Mon), 7-11; 11-11 Sat & summer; 12-4.30; 7-10.30 Sun
Greene King IPA, Abbot; guest beer Ⓗ
One large bar, with a pool table in a separate area and a small dining room. This 19th-century brick and flint building features Steward & Patteson windows. An additional guest beer is stocked in summer.
🏚 ❀ ◖ ▶ Å ⇌ (N. Norfolk coastal railway) ♣ P

WINTERTON

Fishermans Return
The Lane
☎ (01493) 393305

11-2.30, 6.30-11; 11-11 Sat; 12-10.30 Sun
Greene King Triumph; Woodforde's Mardlers Mild, Wherry, Ⓗ **Norfolk Nog;** Ⓖ **guest beers** Ⓗ
300-year-old flint and brick building, with wood panelling in the main bar, run by a longstanding landlord and lady. Meals include local fish and game. One of the guest beers is often from Mauldon's.
🏚 Q ➷ ❀ 🖛 ◖ ▶ Å ♣ ᴄ P ⊁

WIVETON

Bell
Blakeney Road
☎ (01263) 740101
11-3, 6-11; 12-3, 7-10.30 Sun
Beer range varies Ⓗ
Large single-bar pub with a conservatory where children are welcome. Car enthusiasts note the Jaguar engine displayed in an inglenook. Beers are brewed specially for the pub by the City of Cambridge Brewery.
🏚 Q ❀ 🖛 ◖ ▶ Å P 🖸

WYMONDHAM

Feathers
13 Town Green (W of centre)
☎ (01953) 605675
11-3, 7-11; 12-3, 7-10.30 Sun
Adnams Bitter; Greene King Abbot; Marston's Pedigree; guest beers Ⓗ
This welcoming pub, embellished with agricultural memorabilia, has the most extensive range of real ales in town. The house beer is brewed by Bass. ❀ ◖ ▶ ♣ P

Beer site
Keep in touch with
CAMRA:
www.camra.org.uk

INDEPENDENT BREWERIES

Blanchfield: Fakenham

Blue Moon: Hingham

Buffy's: Tivetshall St. Mary

Chalk Hill: Norwich

Humpty Dumpty: Reedham

Iceni: Ickburgh

Reepham: Reepham

Tindall: Ditchingham

Wolf: Attleborough

Woodforde's: Woodbastwick

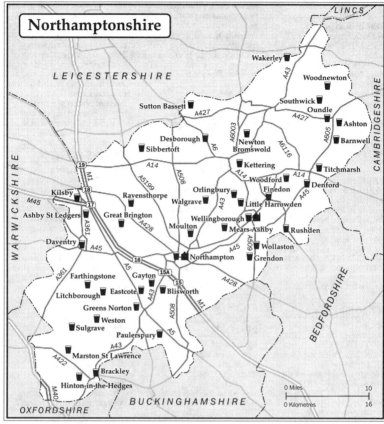

Northamptonshire

LINCS
LEICESTERSHIRE
WARWICKSHIRE
CAMBRIDGESHIRE
BEDFORDSHIRE
BUCKINGHAMSHIRE
OXFORDSHIRE

Wakerley
Woodnewton
Southwick
Oundle
Ashton
Barnwell
Sutton Bassett
Desborough
Sibbertoft
Newton Bromswold
Kettering
Titchmarsh
Kilsby
Ravensthorpe
Orlingbury
Woodford
Denford
Ashby St Ledgers
Great Brington
Walgrave
Finedon
Little Harrowden
Moulton
Wellingborough
Daventry
Mears Ashby
Rushden
Northampton
Wollaston
Grendon
Farthingstone
Gayton
Litchborough
Eastcote
Blisworth
Greens Norton
Weston
Sulgrave
Paulerspury
Marston St Lawrence
Brackley
Hinton-in-the-Hedges

0 Miles 10
0 Kilometres 16

ASHBY ST LEDGER

Old Coach House
Main Street (off A361)
☎ (01788) 890349
12-3, 6-11; 12-11 Sat; 12-11 Sun
Everards Original; Flowers Original; Fuller's London Pride; guest beers H
Popular pub all year round: real fires provide a warm winter welcome and a large garden is used for summer barbecues. The extensive menu of fine food is recommended.
🏠 Q 🕸 🛏 🕽 🍴 ♣ P

ASHTON

Chequered Skipper
The Green (1 mile off A605 Oundle roundabout)
☎ (01832) 273494
11.30-3, 6-11; 11.30-11 Sat; 12-10.30 Sun
Beer range varies H
A traditional thatched exterior hides a modern interior with a flagstone bar top and leaded windows, well restored following a disastrous fire three years ago. It has an exceptional outdoor drinking area; the annual world conker

championship takes place on the green in Oct.
Q 🕸 🕽 🚻 ♣ P

BARNWELL

Montagu Arms
300 yds off A605
☎ (01832) 273726
12-3, 6-11; 11-11 Sat; 12-10.30 Sun
Adnams Bitter, Broadside; Flowers IPA, Original; guest beer H
In a quiet village, this reputedly haunted 16th-century stone pub has low ceilings, lots of exposed timbers and a no-smoking restaurant. Large gardens include a children's play area and crazy golf. Occasional beer festivals held.
🏠 Q 🕸 🛏 🕽 🚻 🏕 ⇌ ⊖ P

BLISWORTH

Royal Oak
1 Chapel Lane
☎ (01604) 858372
12-2.30; 5-11; 11-11 Fri & Sat; 12-10.30 Sun
Draught Bass; Courage Directors; Everards Tiger; Hook Norton Best Bitter; Wadworth 6X; guest beers H
Traditional village pub with an inglenook in the snug and

old oak beams. It always has six real ales on tap.
🏠 Q 🕸 🕽 P

BRACKLEY

Greyhound
131 High Street
☎ (01280) 703331
11-3, 7-11; 12-10.30 Sun
Beer range varies H
Ever-changing guest ales in this traditional town-centre pub make it a must to visit. The whisky range is extensive, too, with over 40 malts. Mexican food is a speciality.
🏠 🕽 ♣ 🍽

Red Lion
11 Market Place
☎ (01280) 702228
11-11; 12-10.30 Sun
Wells Eagle, Bombardier; guest beer H
Pub built in Northants ironstone, tucked away behind the town hall. A drinker's pub, the front bar has TV and pool; the rear bar has a dining area, leading to the covered patio and a stage for live bands.
🏠 🕸 🛏 🕽 ♣

The Good Beer Guide 2001

DAVENTRY

Coach & Horses
Warwick Street
☎ (01327) 876692
11-2.30, 5 (4.30 Fri)-11; 12-3, 7-11
Sat; 12-3, 7-10.30 Sun
Greene King Abbot; Ind Coope Burton Ale; Tetley Bitter; guest beers Ⓗ
Just off the town centre, this pub has a welcoming open fire, wooden floors and stone walls. Weekday lunches served. A New Orleans jazz band plays alternate Thu.
🍴 Q ❀ ◑ ♣

Dun Cow
2-4 Brook Street
☎ (01327) 871545
11-11; 12-10.30 Sun
Draught Bass; Tetley Bitter; Flowers Original Ⓗ
Early 17th-century coaching inn with an unspoilt snug and a gallery bar that acts as a function room. Sun roasts served.
🍴 Q ❀ ◑ ⊟ ♣ P

DENFORD

Cock
High Street (off A45/A14)
☎ (01832) 732565
12-3, 5.30-11; 12-4, 6.30-11 Sat;
12-4, 7-10.30 Sun
Boddingtons Bitter; Flowers IPA; guest beer Ⓗ
Picturesque pub dating from 1593. Once a coaching inn, the bar now occupies a former boot shop and blacksmith's; the beamed main bar offers Northants skittles. The Memsahib Restaurant opens Wed-Sat 7-9 where meals are cooked by an award-winning curry chef. Sun lunch also served.
🍴 Q ❀ ▶ ♣

DESBOROUGH

George
79 High Street
☎ (01536) 760271
11-4, 6-11; 11-11 Fri & Sat; 12-.10.30
Sun
Everards Beacon, Tiger Ⓗ
Former coaching inn built in the 18th-century out of local ironstone; now an opened-out bar/lounge. The covered yard hosts Northants skittle teams; also a pigeon club, football, crib and dom teams meet here. Live music performed on occasional Sat eve. 🍴 ☕ 🐾 ⊟ ♣ P

EASTCOTE

Eastcote Arms
6 Gayton Road (off A5, 2 miles N of Towcester)
☎ (01327) 830731
12-2.30 (not Mon), 6-11; 12-3, 7-10.30
Sun

Adnams Bitter; Fuller's London Pride; Greene King IPA; guest beers Ⓗ
Friendly honest service in a quality pub featuring traditional coat hooks along the bar. Eve meals served Fri and Sat. Beware the low beams in doorways. Families welcome.
🍴 Q ❀ ◑ ▶ ♿ P

FARTHINGSTONE

Kings Arms
Main Street
☎ (01327) 361604
12-2 (not Mon-Fri), 7-11; 12-2, 7-10.30
Sun
Hook Norton Best Bitter; guest beers Ⓗ
18th-century, listed village pub: a comfortable armchair lounge area, an L-shaped bar and games room with Northants skittles. A landscaped garden and good, home-cooked food at weekends make it worth a visit. It specialises in traditional British cheeses.
🍴 Q ❀ ◑ ♣ P

FINEDON

Prince of Wales
Well Street (off High St, A6/A510)
☎ (01933) 680226
11-3, 7-11; 12-3, 7-10.30 Sun
Greene King IPA, Triumph, Abbot, guest beer Ⓗ
Stone and brick built local at the heart of a small town. This three-roomed house was recently taken over by Greene King from Marston's but the landlord has been in residence for over 20 years.
Q ⊟ ♣ P

GAYTON

Eykyn Arms
20 High Street
☎ (01604) 858361
11.30-2, 5-11; 11.30-3, 7-11 Sat;
12-3, 7-10.30 Sun
Adnams Bitter; Mansfield Bitter, Old Baily; Wells Eagle; guest beer (occasional) Ⓗ
Well-frequented village local, comprising a lounge at the front, a bar at the back with a games area at one end and a large conservatory for non-smokers. This mobile phone-free pub is named after Captain Eykyn. No lunches served Mon. 🍴 Q ❀ ☕ 🐾 ◑
▶ ⊟ ♿ ▲ ♣ P ✂ 🍴

GREAT BRINGTON

Fox & Hounds
Main Street (2 miles from A428)
☎ (01604) 770651
11-11; 12-10.30 Sun
Butcombe Bitter; Greene King IPA,

Abbot; Marston's Pedigree; Morland Old Speckled Hen; guest beers Ⓗ
350-year-old coaching inn boasting flagstoned floors, original beams and some wood panelling. The olde-worlde style pub is split into three areas, with log fires, a good atmosphere and a view of casks in the cellar. Guest beers are often seasonal brews. The car park is 200 yds after the pub, down back lane. 🍴 Q ❀ ◑ ▶ ♣ P

GREENS NORTON

Butchers Arms
10 High Street (signed from A43) ☎ (01327) 350488
12-3, 5-11; 12-11 Fri & Sat; 12-10.30
Sun
Ruddles County; Morland Old Speckled Hen Ⓗ
Excellent food, live music, a relaxed atmosphere, a good selection of malt whiskies and individual bottled wines are added attractions here.
Q ❀ ◑ ▶ ⊟ ♿ ♣ P

GRENDON

Half Moon
42 Main Road (off A45 at Earls Barton exit)
☎ (01933) 663263
12-2.30 (3 Sat), 6-11; 12.30-3,
7-10.30 Sun
Wells Eagle; guest beers Ⓗ
17th-century, oak-beamed country pub: friendly and relaxed with a warm welcome. 🍴 ❀ ◑ ♣ P ✂

HINTON-IN-THE-HEDGES

Crewe Arms
☎ (01280) 703314
12-2.30, 7-11; 12-2.30, 7-10.30 Sun
Hook Norton Best Bitter; Marston's Pedigree Ⓗ
Welcome stone-built local with a restaurant, at the heart of a small hamlet. Pool and darts are played in the games room. A function room is housed in a barn to the rear. Well worth seeking out.
🍴 Q ❀ ◑ ▶ ♣ P

KETTERING

Park House
Holdenby (off A14, S of town) ☎ (01536) 523377
11-11; 12-10.30 Sun
Banks's Original, Bitter Ⓗ
Large modern pub near the cinema and Tesco's providing a comfortable post-shopping refuge. The ground-floor bar is divided into smaller areas; the restaurant is upstairs (stair lift available).
❀ ◑ ▶ ♿ P ✂ 🍴

Piper
Windmill Avenue (off old A6)

240

☎ (01536) 513870
11-3 (4 Sat), 6-11; 12-10.30 Sun
Theakston Mild, Best Bitter, XB, Old Peculier; guest beers H
Close to Wicksteed Park, this 1950s pub features a plush lounge bar and popular games bar.
🏮 ◑ ♣ P

Try also: Shirehorse, Newland St (Carlsberg-Tetley)

KILSBY
George
11-13 Watling Stret (A5/A361 jct)
☎ (01788) 822229
11.30-3, 6-11; 12-10.30 Sun
Draught Bass; Greene King IPA, Abbot; Marston's Pedigree; guest beers H
Attractive village pub, ideal for a break from the A5. The wood-panelled lounge is complemented by a long back bar and an open-plan dining area. No meals Sun eve.
Q 🏮 ⇔ ◑ ◨ ♣ P ⅄

LITCHBOROUGH
Old Red Lion
4 Banbury Road
☎ (01327) 830250
11-3, 6.30-11; 12-3, 6.30-10.30 Sun
Banks's Bitter; Marston's Pedigree; Morrells Varsity H
No change here – thank goodness: this delightful, genuine pub of flagstones and beams is a must to visit. Pool, darts and Northants skittles are played in separate rooms. It offers friendly service and good quality and value food.
🏮 Q 🏮 ◑ ♣ P ⊟

LITTLE HARROWDEN
Lamb Inn
Orlingbury Road
☎ (01933) 673300
11-2.30, 7-11; 12-3, 7-10.30 Sun
Adnams Broadside; Wells Eagle, Bombardier; guest beers H
Welcoming stone village pub where the beamed lounge has a very popular eating area off to one side, serving an imaginative menu. Northants skittles played in the bar. No meals alternate Sun eves (quiz night).
Q 🏮 ◑ ♣ P ⊞

MARSTON ST LAWRENCE
Marston Inn
1¹/₂ miles off B4525
☎ (01295) 711906
12-3 (not Mon), 7 (6 Sat)-11; 12-3, 7-10.30 Sun
Hook Norton Best Bitter, Old Hooky, seasonal beers H
A cosy atmosphere prevails in

this no-nonsense village local of three small rooms; one is a no-smoking dining room serving an extensive menu. Children welcome in the large garden which also caters for campers.
🏮 Q 🏮 ◑ ◨ 🅰 ♣ ⌁ P ⅄

MEARS ASHBY
Griffins Head
Wilby Road
☎ (01604) 812945
11.30-2.30, 5.30-11; 12-3, 6.30-11 Sat; 12-10.30 Sun
Everards Beacon, Tiger; Marston's Pedigree; Wells Eagle; guest beers H
Busy pub whose bar is home to Northants skittles and darts, the cosy lounge has an inglenook.
🏮 Q 🏮 ◑ ◨ ♣ P

MOULTON
Telegraph
31 West Street (off A43)
☎ (01604) 644188
11.30-3 (not Mon), 6.30-11; 12-4, 6.30-10.30 Sun
Draught Bass; John Smith's Bitter; Marston's Pedigree; Morland Old Speckled Hen; guest beer H
Traditional stone pub featuring beams in its bar and lounge. Adjacent to Moulton Agricultural College, the landlord has served here for 25 years. Bar billiards played. Lunches served Tue-Fri.
🏮 Q 🏮 ◑ ◨ ⅃ ♣ P

NEWTON BROMSWOLD
Swan
6 Church Lane (off A6, S of Rushden)
☎ (01933) 413506
11-3 (not Mon), 5 (5.30 Sat)-11; 12-3, 7-10.30 Sun
Greene King IPA, Abbot; guest beer H
Idyllic, quiet country pub on the Bedfordshire border, an ideal halt for walkers and cyclists. This unspoilt two-roomed village pub fields men's and ladies' skittles teams and hosts regular events. Good value food.
🏮 Q 🏮 ◑ ◨ ♣ P

NORTHAMPTON
Crown & Cushion
276 Wellingborough Road
☎ (01604) 633937
11-11; 12-10.30 Sun
Banks's Bitter H
L-shaped, street-corner community pub selling one beer in superb form. The garden contains playground facilities.
🏮 ♣ ⊟

Duke of Edinburgh
3 Adelaide Street

☎ (01604) 637903
12-2.30 (3 Fri), 5-11; 11-11 Sat; 12-3, 7-10.30 Sun
Wells Eagle, Bombardier; guest beer H
Fairly small, L-shaped back-street local, built circa 1840. A friendly atmosphere makes strangers feel welcome. It hosts a disco Fri eves, live music Sat eves.
🏮 ♣ ⊞

Malt Shovel Tavern
121 Bridge Street (facing Carlsberg brewery)
☎ (01604) 234212
11.30-3, 5-11; 12-4, 7-10.30 Sun
Banks's Bitter; Castle Eden Ale; Fuller's London Pride; Frog Island Natterjack; guest beers H
This pub, displaying much breweriana, offers friendly service, free from machines, sparklers and noise. A cosy, warm, traditional pub its garden is hidden from the road. Regular beer festivals held and imported bottled beers are stocked. Current local CAMRA *Pub of the Year*. Eve meals end at 7pm.
Q 🏮 ◑ ◔ ♿ ⇌ ♣ ⌁

Racehorse
15 Abington Square
☎ (01604) 631997
11-11; 12-10.30 Sun
Mansfield Bitter; guest beer H
Busy, town-centre community pub which attracts younger people eves to hear occasional live bands. Five guest beers are always on sale.
🏮 ♣ P

Victoria Inn
2 Poole Street (N of centre)
☎ (01604) 633660
11.30-2.30, 5.30-11; 11.30-11 Fri & Sat; 12-10.30 Sun
Adnams Bitter; Greene King Abbot; guest beers (occasional) H
Smallish Victorian corner pub hosting two quiz nights and bar billiards matches. Situated close to the former racecourse, it is frequented by sports players after games, as well as a mixed local crowd.
♣

Wootton Workingmen's Club
23 High Street (near M1 jct 15)
☎ (01604) 761863
12-2.30 (not Thu), 7-11; 12-11 Sat; 12-3, 7-10.30 Sun
Greene King IPA; guest beers H
Formerly the Red Lion, this club has a real pub atmosphere. The five ever-changing guest beers are chosen by the knowledgeable steward. There is a lounge, games room and concert room with a large screen TV. CIU restrictions apply at this

CAMRA East Midlands *Club of the Year* 1997.
♣ P

ORLINGBURY

Queens Arms
11 Isham Road (off A509/A43)
☎ (01933) 678258
12-2.30, 6-11; 12-11 Sat; 12-10.30 Sun
Draught Bass; Cains Mild; Marston's Pedigree; Tetley Bitter; guest beers H
Very friendly village pub offering four changing guest ales. The enterprising landlord and lady operate a real ale club, and host an annual beer festival. Local CAMRA *Pub of the Year* runner-up 1999.
Q ❀ ♣ P

OUNDLE

Rose & Crown
11 Market Place
☎ (01832) 273284
11 (8am Thu)-11; 12-10.30 sun
Mansfield Riding Bitter, Bitter; Marston's Pedigree; guest beer H
Two-roomed, town centre pub: the lounge bar is split-level with a dining area leading on to a patio; stunning views of Oundle's historic spire can be enjoyed from this suntrap. It stocks an extensive range of malt whiskies. The bar is a magnet for younger customers. No eve meals Fri or Sun; breakfast served Thu.
🏨 ❀ ◗ ♿

PAULERSPURY

Barley Mow
53 High Street
☎ (01327) 811260
12-2.30, 7-11; 11-11 Fri & Sat; 12-10.30 Sun
Vale Notley Ale; Marston's Pedigree; guest beers H
Welcoming village local with an L-shaped bar and games room, reputedly haunted by a ghost called Rebecca. There is a play area in the garden.
🏨 Q ❀ ♣ P

RAVENSTHORPE

Chequers
Church Lane (off High St, 1¹/₂ miles off A428)
☎ (01604) 770379
12-3, 6-11; 12-11 Sat; 12-3, 7-10.30 Sun
Fuller's London Pride; Thwaites Bitter; guest beers H
Friendly local free house, popular with walkers and cyclists offering good value food and two changing guest beers. Northants skittles played in the games room; the cosy L-shaped bar is

replete with beams and bric-a-brac.
Q ❀ ◗ ♣ P

RUSHDEN

Rushden Historical Transport Society
Rushden Station, Station Approach
☎ (01933) 318988
12-3 (not Mon-Fri), 7.30-11; 12-2.30, 7.30-10.30 Sun
Fuller's London Pride; Hop Back Summer Lightning; guest beers H
Midland railway station saved by the Society in 1985, now a working railway once again. Visit the gaslit private bar and museum housing transport memorabilia. The carriage on the platform is used as no-smoking room. A mecca for micro-brewery's beers. Temporary membership is available.
🏨 Q ❀ ♣ P ⚹ 🍺

SIBBERTOFT

Red Lion
Welland Rise
☎ (01858) 880011
12-3 (not Mon or Tue), 6.30-11; 12-3, 7-10.30 Sun
Draught Bass; Everards Tiger; guest beer H
Busy village pub, two miles from the site of the Battle of Naseby. It enjoys a reputation for good food served in the restaurant and bar.
Q ❀ 🛏 ◗ P

SOUTHWICK

Shuckborough Arms
Main Street
☎ (01832) 274007
12-2 (not Mon or Tue), 6-11; 12-3, 7-10.30 Sun
Fuller's London Pride; Marston's Pedigree; guest beer H
Cosy village local, dating from the 16th century. A through-bar has games and eating areas at one end and a large fireplace and a drinking area at the other. It stands by a cricket pitch, close to Southwick Hall. Eve meals Wed-Sun.
🏨 Q ⛵ ❀ ◗ ♿ ♣ P

SULGRAVE

Star
Manor Road
☎ (01295) 760389
11-2.30, (12-3 summer), 6-11; 12-5, 7-10.30 Sun
Hook Norton Best Bitter, Old Hooky, seasonal beers H
Stone pub next to Sulgrave Manor, birthplace of George Washington. An excellent choice of meals is served in the restaurant. Children are unwelcome. 🏨 Q ❀ 🛏 ◗ P

SUTTON BASSETT

Queens Head
Main Street
☎ (01858) 463530
11.45-2.30, 6.30-11; 12-2.30, 7-10.30 Sun
Adnams Bitter; Taylor Best Bitter; guest beer H
Late 19th-century, two-roomed village pub, overlooking the Welland valley. Italian dishes are a speciality in the Amalfi Restaurant upstairs (also served in the bar).
🏨 Q ❀ ◗ ♣ P ⚹

TITCHMARSH

Dog & Partridge
6 High Street (off A605)
☎ (01832) 732546
12-2, 6-11; 12-2, 7-10.30 Sun
Wells Eagle, seasonal beers; guest beers H
Warm, friendly village local where Northamptonshire skittles are played. Very close to Nene valley, it is handy for walks, the marina, nature reserve and fishing. Regular *Guide* entry for over 10 years.
🏨 ❀ ♿ ♣ P 🍺

WAKERLEY

Exeter Arms
Main Street
☎ (01572) 747817
12-3 (not Mon), 6-11; 12-3, 7-10.30 Sun
Bateman XB; Marston's Pedigree; guest beer H
17th-century stone pub where the comfortable lounge is warmed by a wood-burning stove. Access for wheelchairs is via the side entrance. Within easy reach of Rutland Water and Peterborough, it is close to Wakerley Great Woods. No food Mon.
🏨 Q ❀ 🛏 ◗ ♿ ♠ P

WALGRAVE

Royal Oak
Zion Hill (off A43)
☎ (01604) 781248
12-3, 6-11; 12-3, 6-10.30 Sun
Adnams Bitter; Boddingtons Bitter; guest beers H
Popular village pub featuring a large front bar, plus a smaller bar and weekend restaurant to the rear. A Northants skittles room is in an outbuilding.
Q ❀ ◗ ♣ P ⚹

WELLINGBOROUGH

Vivian Arms
153 Knox Road (near station)
☎ (01933) 223660
11-11; 12-10.30 Sun
Wells Eagle; guest beers H
Traditional, back-street local

CAMRA National Pub Inventory: Victoria, Durham

with a small cosy lounge, a wood-panelled bar and a large games room. This friendly pub, with piped music in only one room, has featured in most editions of this *Guide*. Large garden.
🏰 Q 🏵 🍴 ≠ ♣ P

Wellingborough Old Grammarians Association
46 Oxford Street
☎ (01933) 226188
12-3, 7-11; 12-11 Fri & Sat; 12-10.30 Sun
Hook Norton Best Bitter, Old Hooky; Wells Eagle; guest beers Ⓗ
This sports and social club caters for most outdoor games. Slightly faded but friendly, the town-centre three-roomed club has TV in the lounge. Access is from the rear car park (stair lift for wheelchairs), press the voicecom button. Open to all; regular visitors will be asked to join the club.
🕼 ♦ 🖴 P

WESTON
Crown
2 Helmdon Road
☎ (01295) 760310
12-2.30 (not Mon), 6-11; 12-2.30, 7-10.30 (closed winter eve) Sun
Beer range varies Ⓗ
Stone-built family-run local with a quarry-tiled floor in the bar and lounge. The games room offers pool and darts, and there is a no-smoking family dining room.

An out of the way, but welcoming pub that is well worth seeking out.
🏰 Q 🏵 🕼 ♦ ♣ P ⅍

WOLLASTON
Boot
35 High Street
☎ (01933) 664270
11.30-1.30 (not Mon-Thu), 6-11; 12-11 Fri & Sat; 12-2.30, 7-10.30 Sun
Greene King IPA; Marston's Pedigree; Tetley Bitter; guest beers Ⓗ
Refurbished local retaining very few original features: one large room is split into three sections, plus a games room at the back; very much a local. Live blues bands perform regularly.
♣ P

Crispin Arms
14 Hinwick Road
☎ (01933) 664303
12-11; 12-10.30 Sun
Flowers IPA; Fuller's London Pride; Greene King Abbot; Shepherd Neame Best Bitter; Theakston Best Bitter; guest beer Ⓗ
Two-roomed local serving up to six real ales. It gets very busy early eve with workers, and later with village locals. Unchanged by the new

INDEPENDENT BREWERIES

Cannon: Wellingborough
Frog Island: Northampton

landlady who extends a warm welcome to all.
🏰 Q 🏵 P

WOODFORD
Dukes Arms
83 High Street (off A604/A510)
☎ (01832) 732224
12-2, 7-11; 12-2, 7-10.30 Sun
Banks's Bitter; Fuller's London Pride; Taylor Landlord; Wadworth 6X Ⓗ
Picturesque pub that overlooks the green, named after the Duke of Wellington, who was a frequent visitor to this pretty village. It comprises two wood-panelled bars, a games room with Northants skittles, plus an upstairs restaurant. Runner-up in a1995 local newspaper *Pub of Year* competition.
🏰 Q 🏵 🕼 ♦ 🍴 & ♣ P

WOODNEWTON
White Swan Inn
22 Main Street
☎ (01780) 470381
12-4.30, 7-11; 12-4.30, 7-10.30 Sun
Fuller's London Pride; Oakham JHB; guest beers Ⓗ
Welcoming, 200-year-old village free house consisting of a single long room and a restaurant serving excellent fresh food; a rare outlet for Rockingham Ales. Families are welcome. Ask about the local historical link to Coco the Clown. Pétanque played.
Q 🏵 🕼 ♦ & ♣ P 🏠

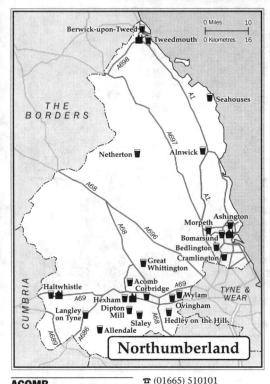

Berwick-upon-Tweed
Tweedmouth

0 Miles 10
0 Kilometres 16

THE
BORDERS

Seahouses

Netherton
Alnwick

Ashington
Morpeth
Bomarsund
Bedlington
Great
Whittington
Cramlington

Haltwhistle
Acomb
Corbridge
A69
Wylam
TYNE &
WEAR
Hexham
Ovingham
Langley
on Tyne
Dipton
Mill
Slaley
Hedley on the Hill
Allendale

Northumberland

ACOMB

Miners Arms
Main Street
☎ (01434) 603909
5 (12 summer)-11; 12-10.30 Sun
**Durham White Velvet; Federation
Buchanan's Best Bitter; Mansfield
Four Seasons; Yates Bitter; guest
beers** Ⓗ
Unspoilt village pub, a free
house since 1750. Well worth
a visit. The house beer is
brewed by Big Lamp. Meals
served in summer.
🏨 Q ❀ ◖ ▶ 🖫

ALLENDALE

King's Head Hotel
Market Place
☎ (01434) 683681
11-11; 12-10.30 Sun
**Greene King Abbot; Jennings
Cumberland Ale; Tetley Bitter;
Theakston Best Bitter; guest
beers** Ⓗ
Set in a conservation area at
the heart of an attractive
small town, this former
coaching inn is popular with
residents and visitors for
quality real ales and food.
The absence of a juke box
and gaming machines adds
to the convivial atmosphere.
🏨 Q 🏨 ◖ ▶ ♣

ALNWICK

Hotspur Hotel
Bondgate Without

☎ (01665) 510101
11.30-3, 5.30-11; 12-10.30 Sun
**Black Sheep Best Bitter;
Northumberland Castles; guest
beers** Ⓗ
Roomy hotel bar in the
middle of Alnwick. The range
of beers may vary and
summer weekend evenings
can be more productive for
the independent beer hunter
than winter weekdays. The
bar lies beyond a larger inner
courtyard opening on to
Bondgate Without.
🏨 ◖ ▶

John Bull
12 Howick Street
☎ (01665) 602055
12 (11 Sat)-3, 7 (5 Fri)-11; 12-3,
7-10.30 Sun
**Draught Bass; Tetley Bitter; guest
beers** Ⓗ
Smart, quiet pub in the
middle of a terrace of houses
stocking two constantly
changing guest beers. It also
specialises in malt whiskies.
Q ❀ ♣

ASHINGTON

Black Diamond Inn
29 South View
☎ (01670) 851500
11-11; 12-10.30 Sun
House beer Ⓗ
The mining history of what
was once called the largest pit
village in the world is well
represented in the

photographs which line the
walls of the bar. This room
also contains a proper red
phone box. The lounge/diner
is quiet and comfortable. No
eve meals Sun. The house
beer, Black Diamond, is
brewed by Northumberland.
🏨 ◖ ▶ 🖫 &

Bubbles Wine Bar
58A Station Road
☎ (01670) 850800
11-11; 12-10.30 Sun
Beer range varies Ⓗ
The name's unlikely but the
beer's good and pub's fine.
Just off the paved shopping
centre this pub usually stocks
a beer from Northumberland
Brewery. Live music Thu and
Sat eves. A good find in what
was once a beer desert.
❀ ◖

BEDLINGTON

Grapes
68 Front Street West
☎ (01670) 822936
11-3, 7-11; 11-11 Sat; 12-3, 7-10.30
Sun
Beer range varies Ⓗ
One guest beer is regularly
available in a bar featuring
sporting pictures.
❀ ♣ P

Northumberland Arms
112 Front Street East
☎ (01670) 822754
11-3.30 (not Mon-Tue), 7-11; 11-11
Thu-Sat; 12-10.30 Sun
Beer range varies Ⓗ
Warm and welcoming pub
offering a good range of
constantly changing guest
beers. There is a room for
pool and an upstairs function
room.
◖ ♣

BERWICK UPON TWEED

Barrels
Bridge Street
☎ (01289) 308013
11-11; 12-10.30 Sun
**Boddingtons Bitter; Border
Rampart; Flowers Original; guest
beers** Ⓗ
Excellent, two-roomed pub
with an additional cellar bar
beside Berwick's Jacobean
bridge. It is renowned for
excellence on three fronts:
superb food, fine beer and
good entertainment. It has a
wine bar atmosphere, but a
constant supply of
independent beers (local and
national) provides interest for
all.
◖ ⇶

Foxtons
Hide Hill
☎ (01289) 303939
11-11; 12-10.30 Sun
Caledonian Deuchars IPA, 80/-;

guest beer Ⓗ
Wine bar-type establishment
at the heart of Berwick,
where good food and fine
beer are guaranteed. This
place has succeeded where
most other pubs in central
Berwick have failed,
providing a range of
independent cask beers. Do
not be put off by the wine
bar ambience, this place is
worth a visit.
◖▶≠

Leaping Salmon
Bankhill
☎ (01289) 303184
11-11; 12-10.30 Sun
Boddingtons Bitter; guest beers Ⓗ
This Wetherspoon's outlet
occupies a prominent whitewashed building at the end
of the 'new' bridge. Up to
four beers and several
comfortable seating areas are
Wetherspoon's trademarks.
Q◖▶≠⑫

BOMARSUND

Cat & Sawdust
Earth Balance, West
Sleekburn Farm ($^3/_4$ mile N of
A189, spine road, and A1147
intersection) OS273843
☎ (01670) 822112
11-3; 12-4 Sat; 12-4 Sun (summer
hours vary)
Beer range varies Ⓗ
A diverse range of customers
drop into this small, friendly
Northumberland Brewery
tap, opened in 1998. Part of
the 220-acre environmentally
sustainable Earth Balance
community site, it has
sawdust on the floor, a dart
board and piano. Two of the
brewery's beers are available
at all times.
Q❀♿♣P

CORBRIDGE

Black Bull
Middle Street
☎ (01434) 632261
11-11; 12-10.30 Sun
Boddingtons Bitter; Castle Eden Ale;
Flowers Original; Wadworth 6X Ⓗ
Spacious, comfortable, L-
shaped bar with an
additional restaurant area
serving meals all day.
♨❀◖▶≠P⑫

Dyvels
Station Road
☎ (01434) 633633
4 (12 Sat)-11; 12-4, 7-10.30 Sun
Draught Bass; Black Sheep Best
Bitter; guest beers Ⓗ
Very friendly local, an ideal
base for exploring Hadrian's
Wall. ♨❀⇌≠♣P⑫

CRAMLINGTON

Plough

Middle Farm Buildings
☎ (01670) 737633
11-3, 6-11; 11-11 Thu-Sat; 12-10.30
Sun
Theakston XB; guest beers Ⓗ
Popular pub created from
former farm buildings
standing at the heart of an
old village. The lounge and
unusual gingan provide
plentiful comfortable sitting
space, whilst the slightly
smaller bar may be entered
from the garden. The three
guest beers change regularly.
Children welcome 12-3 in
the gingan, when smoking is
prohibited.
⤶❀◖⑫≠P⑂

DIPTON MILL

Dipton Mill
Dipton Mill Road
☎ (01434) 606577
12-2.30, 6-11; 12-4.30, 7-10.30 Sun
Hexhamshire Devil's Elbow, Shire
Bitter, Devil's Water, Whapweasel;
Tetley Bitter Ⓗ
The tap for the Hexhamshire
Brewery: a small low-
ceilinged pub with a large
garden. Popular in summer.
The bar billiards room
doubles as a children's room.
The pub has won awards
from the local CAMRA
branch, and for its selection
of cheeses.
♨Q❀◖▶Å♣⑫

GREAT WHITTINGTON

Queens Head Inn
☎ (01434) 672267
12-2.30 (not Mon), 6-11; 12-3, 7-10.30
Sun
Black Sheep Best Bitter; Hambleton
Bitter Ⓗ
This inn, dating from the
15th-century, is reputed to be
the oldest in the county. Four
handpumps serve a variety of
guest beers; the house beer is
brewed by Hambleton. A
warm welcome is assured.
The extensive food menu is
based on local produce.
♨Q◖▶P

HALTWHISTLE

Black Bull
Market Square
☎ (01434) 320463
11-3 (not Mon), 7-11; 12-3, 7-10.30
Sun
Beer range varies Ⓗ
Superb pub boasting open
fires, beams, horsebrasses and
a welcoming staff; a small
low-ceilinged bar is the focal
point. Already a showcase for
the finest independent
breweries, at time of writing
the owner was producing
experimental brews from a
purpose-built on-site
brewery.
♨Q

HEDLEY ON THE HILL

Feathers
☎ (01661) 843607
12-3 (not Mon-Thu), 6-11; 12-3,
7-10.30 Sun
Boddingtons Bitter; guest beers Ⓗ
Splendid country pub in a
lofty hilltop location. Real
fires in both the bar and the
lounge give a cosy feel which
is enhanced by the warm
welcome. Quality food is
offered to accompany the
range of three guest beers.
♨Q❀▶P≠

HEXHAM

Forum
Market Place
☎ (01434) 609190
11-11; 12-10.30 Sun
Boddingtons Bitter; Courage
Directors; Theakston Best Bitter;
guest beers Ⓗ
Recently converted cinema,
that incorporates its original
Art Deco style. A large feature
window has replaced the
cinema screen in this long,
narrow building. Handy for
the market square and
Abbey. Q◖▶≠⑂⊞

Tap & Spile
Battle Hill
☎ (01434) 602039
11-11; 12-3, 7-10.30 Sun
Theakston Best Bitter; guest
beers Ⓗ
Busy, popular pub with a
reputation for its
continuously changing
selection of beers (five
guests). It hosts regular live
music, with a strong
emphasis on
Northumberland traditional
styles, plus blues nights. At
the time of the survey over
800 different beers have been
sold at this flagship Tap and
Spile. Q◖≠

LANGLEY ON TYNE

Carts Bog Inn
On A686
☎ (01434) 684338
12-3, 7-11; 12-3, 7-10.30 Sun
Marston's Pedigree; Theakston Best
Bitter; guest beers Ⓗ
Interesting free house, in the
same family for several
generations, built in 1730 on
the site of an ancient (1521)
brewery. The guest beers are
supplied by local micros. Can
get busy Sun lunch.
♨Q⤶❀◖▶♿♣P

MORPETH

Joiners Arms
3 Wansbeck Street
☎ (01670) 513540
11-11; 12-10.30 Sun
Draught Bass; Tetley Bitter; guest
beers Ⓗ

This friendly pub offers a small plain bar containing a collection of stuffed birds in glass cases. Guest beers are served from the lounge which has a view of the river. A pleasant place for a refreshing drink after crossing the bridge. ⌂ ≠

Tap & Spile
Manchester Street
☎ (01670) 513894
12-2.30, 4.30-11; 11-11 Fri & Sat; 12-10.30 Sun
Beer range varies H
Award-winning, popular community pub next to the bus station. Eight handpumps provide a good choice of real ales. It acts as the unofficial practice rooms of the local pipe and fiddle society.
⌂ ◖ ≠ ♣ ○

NETHERTON
Star Inn ☆
Off B634 from Rothbury
☎ (01669) 630238
12-1.30, 7-10.30 (11 Fri & Sat); winter hours may vary; 12-1.30, 7-10.30 Sun
Castle Eden Ale G
This unspoilt gem, unchanged for the last 80 years, is the only pub in Northumberland to have been in every edition of this *Guide*. This classic pub is set in beautiful countryside. The beer is served on gravity direct from the cellar and a warm welcome is assured.
Q ⊛ P

OVINGHAM
Bridge End Inn
West Road
☎ (01661) 832219

12 (Tue; 4 Sat)-11; 12-3, 7-10.30 Sun
Stones Bitter; Taylor Landlord; Tetley Bitter; guest beer H
Comfortable, old-style pub with a bar and lounge which doubles occasionally as a music room. A friendly welcome is assured. Handy for walks in picturesque Whittle Dene.
⌂ Q ⌂ ⌂ ≠ (Prudhoe) ♣ P

SEAHOUSES
Olde Ship Hotel
Main Street
☎ (01665) 720200
11-4, 6-11; 11-11 Fri, Sat & summer; 12-10.30 Sun
Draught Bass; Ruddles Best Bitter; Theakston Best Bitter; guest beers (summer) H
First licensed in 1812, this homely two-star hotel, originally a farmhouse, has been owned by the same family since 1910. The saloon and cabin bars are crammed full of local seafaring memorabilia and nautical equipment. ⌂ Q ⌂ ⌂ ◖ Å P

SLALEY
Travellers Rest
On B6306, 1 mile N of village, 4 miles S of Hexham
☎ (01434) 673231
11-11; 12-10.30 Sun
Boddingtons Bitter; guest beers H
Although licensed for over 100 years, this welcoming inn, with several distinct cosy areas within one room, started life in the 16th century as a farmhouse. Living up to its name, it offers a restaurant and extensive play facilities for children outside. No food Sun eve. ⌂ ⊛ ⌂ ◖ D P

TWEEDMOUTH
Angel
Brewery Bank
☎ (01289) 303030
11-11; 12-10.30 Sun
Border Farne Island Pale Ale, Rampart; Northumberland Castles; guest beers H
Formerly owned by Border Brewery, the Angel is now the only guaranteed outlet in Berwick for Border Beers. A two-roomed pub, with a pool table and central bar, it can get busy on match days, despite Berwick's average attendance of 300. All supporters seem to call in. ⊛ ≠ P

WYLAM
Boathouse
Station Road
☎ (01661) 853431
12 (11 Fri & Sat)-11; 12-10.30 Sun
Beer range varies H
Well-appointed, friendly pub in a prime location, adjoining a country railway station and bridge over the River Tyne. It offers up to eight beers in an ever-changing range. Families welcome. Bar meals served at weekends. ⌂ Q ⌂ ⊛ ◖ ≠

INDEPENDENT BREWERIES

Border: Tweedmouth

Hexhamshire: Hexham

Northumberland: Bomarsund

CAMRA National Pub Inventory: Fleece, Bretforton, Worcestershire

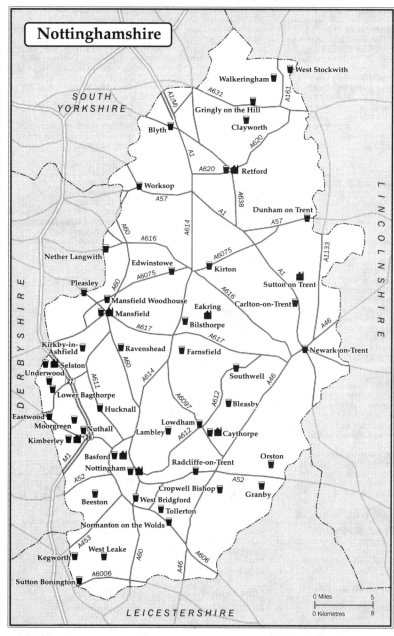

Nottinghamshire

SOUTH YORKSHIRE

West Stockwith

Walkeringham

Gringly on the Hill

Clayworth

Blyth

Retford

Worksop

Dunham on Trent

Nether Langwith

Edwinstowe

Kirton

Sutton on Trent

Pleasley

Mansfield Woodhouse

Eakring

Carlton-on-Trent

Mansfield

Bilsthorpe

Kirkby-in-Ashfield

Ravenshead

Farnsfield

Newark-on-Trent

Underwood

Selston

Southwell

Lower Bagthorpe

Bleasby

Eastwood

Hucknall

Lowdham

Moorgreen

Nuthall

Lambley

Caythorpe

Kimberley

Orston

Basford

Radcliffe-on-Trent

Nottingham

Cropwell Bishop

Granby

Beeston

West Bridgford

Tollerton

Normanton on the Wolds

West Leake

Kegworth

Sutton Bonington

DERBYSHIRE

LINCOLNSHIRE

LEICESTERSHIRE

0 Miles 5
0 Kilometres 8

BASFORD

Horse & Groom

462 Radford Road (near ring road)
☎ (0115) 970 3777
11-11; 12-10.30 Sun
Draught Bass; Belvoir Star Bitter; Courage Directors; Wells Bombardier; guest beers Ⓗ
Pleasant, friendly local, once Shipstone's brewery tap, it now stocks an interesting range of guest beers.
🏠 🍺 🚪

BEESTON

Commercial Inn

19 Wollaton Road
☎ (0115) 917 8994
12-11; 12-10.30 Sun
Hardys & Hansons Best Mild, Best Bitter Ⓟ **Classic, seasonal beers** Ⓗ
Comfortable, friendly, two-roomed local; the beer from the electric fonts is the real stuff.
🕸 🍺 🚃 ♣ P

Victoria Hotel

Dovecoat Lane (by station)
☎ (0115) 925 4049
11-11; 12-10.30 Sun
Bateman XB; Caledonian Deuchars IPA; Castle Rock Hemlock; Everards Tiger; guest beers Ⓗ
Busy, four-roomed Victorian architectural gem: excellent food is served and over 100 whiskies stocked; the cider varies. Live music.
🏠 Q 🕸 🍺 🚪 ♿ 🚃 ☕ P

BILSTHORPE

Stanton Arms
Mickledale Lane (off A614)
☎ (01623) 870234
12-4, 7-11; 12-11 Fri & Sat; 12-10.30 Sun
Barnsley Bitter, Old Tom Ⓗ
Large estate pub in a former pit village comprising a lounge, public bar with pool table and a large function room. Reasonably priced meals served.
⌂ ◐◑ ⊟ P

BLEASBY

Waggon & Horses
Gypsy Lane (1 mile S of station)
☎ (01636) 830283
12-2.30 (not Mon), 6-11; 12-3, 7-10.30 Sun
Banks's Bitter; Marston's Pedigree Ⓗ
Once a simple farmhouse, this unassuming village local enjoys a rural setting overlooking the church. Within its whitewashed walls there is a lounge, cosy bar, pool room and children's area with lots of space for them at the rear. Snacks usually available.
⌂ ❀ ⊟ ▲

BLYTH

Angel Inn
Bawtry Road (1 mile from A1)
☎ (01909) 591213
11.30-2.30, 6-11; 12-3, 7-10.30 Sun
Hardys & Hansons Best Mild, Best Bitter Ⓗ
Very busy old inn that places an emphasis on good value meals. Huge fires are lit throughout the winter.
⌂ 🛏 ◐◑ ♿ ♣ P

CARLTON-ON-TRENT

Great Northern
Ossington Road (other side of A1 from the village)
☎ (01636) 821348
12-3, 5-11; 12-11 Fri & Sat; 12-10.30 Sun
Beer range varies Ⓗ
Two-bar village pub which gained its name from its proximity to the East Coast main line. An area is set aside for meals, plus there is a large children's room and outside play area. Note the railway artefacts and bottled beer collection.
⌂ ♞ ❀ ◐◑ ▲ ♣ P ⊡

CAYTHORPE

Black Horse
29 Main Street (1 mile S of Lowdham station)
☎ (0115) 966 3520
11.45-2.30 (not Mon), 5.30-11; 12-3, 7 (8 winter)-10.30 Sun
Beer range varies Ⓗ
All that a village inn should be, dating back over 300 years and reputedly once a haunt of Dick Turpin. Accomplished home cooking makes good use of fresh seasonal ingredients, particularly fish and can be enjoyed with a pint of Caythorpe beer brewed on the premises. Booking for eve meals (not served Sun) is essential.
⌂ Q ❀ ◐◑ ⊟ ♣ P

Try also: Old Volunteer (Hardys & Hansons)

CLAYWORTH

Blacksmiths Arms
Town Street
☎ (01777) 818171
11.30-3, 6-11; 12-3, 7-10.30 Sun
Stones Bitter; Worthington Bitter; guest beers Ⓗ
Smart village pub with a first class restaurant.
⌂ Q ❀ ◐◑ ♿ P ⊘ ⊡

CROPWELL BISHOP

Wheatsheaf
11 Nottingham Road
☎ (0115) 989 2247
11-11; 12-10.30 Sun
Banks's Original; Mansfield Mild, Bitter, Marston's Pedigree Ⓗ
Village local, with three drinking areas, dating back 500 years and reputedly haunted. Chinese banquets can be booked for parties of 10 or more in an upstairs room. ❀ ⊟ ♣ P

DUNHAM ON TRENT

Bridge Inn
Main Street
☎ (01777) 228385
12-3, 5-11; 11-11 Sat; 12-10.30 Sun
Stumbling Bitter; guest beers Ⓗ
Roadside pub close to Dunham toll bridge. Stumbling is a house beer brewed by Broadstone.
⌂ ❀ 🛏 ◐◑ ♿ ♣ P ⊡

EASTWOOD

Greasley Castle
1 Castle Street
☎ (01773) 761080
10.30-11; 12-10.30 Sun
Hardys & Hansons Best Mild, Best Bitter Ⓟ
One-roomed Victorian corner local displaying a large collection of colliery plates. It hosts live music Fri and Sun eves. Lunchtime snacks available; it may close weekday afternoons. ❀ ♣

EDWINSTOWE

Forest Lodge Hotel
2-4 Church Street
☎ (01623) 824443
12-3, 5-11; 12-11 Sat; 12-10.30 Sun
Theakston XB, Old Peculier; guest beers Ⓗ
17th-century coaching inn, well restored; it makes an excellent base from which to explore the nearby historic Sherwood Forest. A *Real Fire Pub of the Year* finalist. Discount given to CAMRA members for accommodation. The house beer is by Kelham Island.
⌂ ❀ 🛏 ◐◑ ♿ P

FARNSFIELD

Red Lion
Main Street
☎ (01623) 882304
11-3, 6.30-11; 12-3, 6.30-10.30 Sun
Mansfield Mild, Riding Bitter, Bitter; Marston's Pedigree Ⓗ
Friendly, family-run local on the main road through the village, with an excellent restaurant (eve meals Tue-Sat). ⌂ Q ❀ ◐◑ P ⊡ ⊞

GRANBY

Marquis of Granby
Dragon Street
☎ (01949) 850461
7.30-11; 7.30-10.30 Sun
Belvoir Mild; Marston's Bitter Ⓗ
Small village local in the Vale of Belvoir dating back to 1760 or earlier, it is believed to be the original Marquis of Granby pub. This calm and cosy refuge serves local beers including a house ale from Belvoir. Note only open eves.
⌂ Q ◑ ⊟ ♿ ♣ P ⊡

GRINGLY ON THE HILL

Blue Bell
High Street
☎ (01777) 817406
6 (12 Sat)-11; 12-10.30 Sun
Marston's Pedigree; Tetley Bitter; guest beers Ⓗ
Quiet village local that features an interesting American restaurant.
⌂ Q ♞ ❀ ◑ P ⊡

HUCKNALL

Pilgrim Oak
44-46 High Street
☎ (0115) 963 2539
10.30-11; 12-10.30 Sun
Draught Bass; Courage Directors; Theakston Best Bitter; guest beers Ⓗ
Wetherspoon's outlet converted from a Co-op store into a comfortable town-centre pub. Meals are served all day until 10pm (9.30 Sun). Q ◐◑ ♿ ⇌ (Robin Hood Line) P ⊘ ⊞

KEGWORTH

Station Hotel

Station Road (1½ miles from the Leicestershire village)
☎ (01509) 672252
12-3, 6-11; 12-3, 7-10.30 Sun
Courage Directors; Marston's Pedigree; guest beers H
Railway hotel circa 1857, still offering accommodation. The upstairs restaurant offers an *à la carte* menu, including a vegetarian choice. This quaint hotel has three bars and a garden affording excellent views.
🏨 ✿ 🛏 ◑ 🍴 ⌂ P

KIMBERLEY
Nelson & Railway
12 Station Road (opp. brewery)
☎ (0115) 938 2177
10.30-3, 5-11; 10.30-11 Thu-Sat; 12-10.30 Sun
Hardys & Hansons Best Bitter, H/P **Classic, seasonal beers** H
Friendly, two-roomed Victorian pub where the beamed lounge acts as the dining area (Sun lunch served 12-6). The landlord has been here for 30 years.
✿ 🛏 ◑ 🍴 ♣ P

Queens Head
34 Main Street
☎ (0115) 938 2117
10.30-11; 12-10.30 Sun
Hardys & Hansons Best Mild, Best Bitter P
Popular corner pub up a small flight of steps. Note the large collection of old bottles. The upstairs lounge hosts live music Mon, Fri and Sat eves. Breakfast is served from 10.30 and bar food until 3pm.
🍴 ♣

Stag Inn
67 Nottingham Road
☎ (0115) 938 3151
5 (2 Sat)-11; 12-10.30 Sun
Boddingtons Bitter; Greenalls Mild, Bitter; Marston's Pedigree; guest beer H
Popular, 16th-century local featuring a low beamed ceiling and settles. The large garden has a play area. Constantly changing guest beer.
Q ✿ 🍴 ♣ P

KIRKBY-IN-ASHFIELD
Countryman
Park Lane (B6018, S of town, between Selston and Kirkby)
☎ (01623) 752314
11-11; 12-10.30 Sun
Draught Bass; Theakston Mild, Best Bitter, XB, seasonal beers; guest beers H
Friendly 18th-century roadside inn of two rooms with beamed ceilings. Child-friendly it has a play area and bouncy castle. The menu includes home-cooked daily

specials (no food Sun eve or Mon). A welcome is given to all, including bikers and hikers. Live music Fri eve.
🏨 ✿ ◑ 🍴 ♿ ♣ ⌂ P

KIRTON
Fox at Kirton
Main Street (A6075)
☎ (01623) 860502
11-3.30, 6-11; 12-3.30, 7-10.30 Sun
Boddingtons Bitter; Flowers Original; guest beers H
The Fox is a late Victorian inn standing in over four acres of gardens and paddocks, in a farming village. Permanent bouncy castle and play equipment so families are welcome, as are campers and caravanners. The beer range includes Glentworth ales.
✿ 🛏 ◑ 🍴 Å ♣ P ✗

LAMBLEY
Robin Hood & Little John
82 Main Street
☎ (0115) 931 2531
11-3 (12-5 Sat), 6-11; 12-5, 7-10.30 Sun
Home Mild, Bitter; Mansfield Riding Bitter, Bitter; Marston's Pedigree H
Popular drinkers' pub, thought to be the oldest in the village. Originally it was a W H Hutchinson's & Sons house.
🏨 Q ✿ ◑ 🍴 ♣ P

LOWDHAM
World's End
Plough Lane (off Ton Lane, off A6097))
☎ (0115) 966 3857
12-3, 5.30 (6 Sat)-11; 12-5, 7-10.30 Sun
Marston's Pedigree; guest beer H
Tucked away (look out for the flagpole), this attractive white-painted village local is bedecked with flower baskets and tubs in summer. Inside, first rate home cooking can be enjoyed in the comfortable open-plan lounge bar and dining area (no meals Sun eve).
🏨 Q ✿ ◑ Å ♿ P

LOWER BAGTHORPE
Dixies Arms
School Road (off B600 at Underwood)
☎ (01773) 810505
2 (12 Sat)-11; 12-10.30 Sun
Home Mild, Bitter; Theakston Best Bitter; guest beer H
250-year-old, beamed country inn with a tap room, a snug, a lounge and a spacious children's play area. It supports its own football team, pigeon club and Morris dancing club; a true village

local. Live bands play most Sat eves.
🏨 ✿ 🛏 Å ♣ P

MANSFIELD
Bold Forester
Botany Avenue
☎ (01623) 632970
11-11; 12-10.30 Sun
Boddingtons Bitter; Castle Eden Ale; Flowers Original; Greene King Abbot; Marston's Pedigree; Wadworth 6X H
Large, new pub with 12 beers, including six guests always available. Built in traditional style, it incorporates many interesting features but has no juke box or children's play area. It hosts live bands Sun eve, regular quiz nights and an annual beer festival.
✿ ◑ 🍴 ♿ ♣ ⌂ P ✗

Plough Inn
180 Nottingham Road (A60 ½ mile S of town centre and station)
☎ (01623) 623031
11-11; 12-10.30 Sun
Boddingtons Bitter; Flowers Original; Marston's Pedigree; Wadworth 6X; guest beers H
Large, one-roomed pub on a busy road where eight real ales are always available. Customers and staff are friendly. Big screen TV; good food is served until 9pm (not available Thu eve during the live music session).
✿ ◑ 🍴 ♿ ⇌ P

Railway Inn
9 Station Street (200 yds from the Robin Hood line station)
☎ (01623) 623086
11-11; 12-10.30 Sun
Bateman XB, XXXB H
Very reasonable prices on both beer and home-cooked food are upheld by the long term tenants. Close to main shopping centre, the inn has a pool room.
Q 🚲 ✿ ◑ ♣ 🍴

Reindeer Inn
Southwell Road West
☎ (01623) 651180
11-11; 12-10.30 Sun
Mansfield Bitter, seasonal beers; Marston's Pedigree H
Large, modern pub with a games room, public and saloon bars with a restaurant area.
✿ ◑ 🍴 ♣ P

Try also: **Ram**, Littleworth (Mansfield)

MANSFIELD WOODHOUSE
Greyhound Inn
82 High Street
☎ (01623) 464403

12-11; 12-3, 7-10.30 Sun
**Courage Directors; Home Mild,
Bitter; Mansfield Bitter; guest
beers** H
Friendly village local in a
central location comprising a
lounge and a tap room with a
pool table and darts. Close to
the Robin Hood railway line.
✿ 🍴 ⇌ ♣ P

MOORGREEN
Horse & Groom
Church Road (B600)
☎ (01773) 713417
11-11; 12-10.30 Sun
**Hardys & Hansons Best Bitter,
Classic, seasonal beers** H
17th-century country pub:
one large L-shaped room
with a popular restaurant
upstairs; it is close to
Beauvale Abbey and Robin
Hood Well. The large garden
is well-equipped.
🏚 ✿ ◖ ▶ P ⚥

NETHER LANGWITH
Jug & Glass
Queens Walk (A632)
☎ (01623) 742283
11.30-4, 7-11; 12-4, 7-10.30 Sun
**Hardys & Hansons Best Bitter,
Classic, seasonal beers** H
Popular, historic village pub
standing by a stream; two
rooms and a restaurant (open
Thu-Sat eves and Sun lunch).
🏚 ◖ ▶ 🍴 & ♣ P

NEWARK-ON-TRENT
Fox & Crown
4-6 Appletongate
☎ (01636) 605820
11-11; 12-10.30 Sun
**Castle Rock Hemlock; Everards
Tiger; Hook Norton Best Bitter;
Marston's Pedigree; guest beers** H
Popular town pub, twice
winner of local CAMRA *Pub
of the Season*. It offers an
excellent range of beer and
hosts regular brewery and
theme nights, plus occasional
live music. Good value food.
◖ ▶ & ⇌ (Castle/Northgate)
↺ ⚥

Mailcoach
13 London Road
☎ (01636) 605164
11.30-3, 5.30-11; 11.30-11 Sat; 12-3,
7-10.30 Sun
**Boddingtons Bitter; Flowers IPA,
Original; guest beers** H
Large room divided into
three areas serving excellent
home-cooked food. Regular
live music sessions are staged,
plus two beer festivals a year.
Cider stocked in summer.
🏚 ✿ ◖ ⇌ (Castle) ↺ P

Newcastle Arms
34 George Street
☎ (01636) 705098
12-4, 7-11; 12-2.30, 5-11 Tue-Thu;

12-4, 7-11 Sun
**Home Mild, Bitter; Ruddles Best
Bitter; Wells Bombardier; guest
beer** H
This traditional Victorian
local has a basic bar and a
comfortable lounge.
✿ 🍴 ⇌ (Northgate) ♣

Old Malt Shovel
25 Northgate
☎ (01636) 702036
11.30-3, 6 (7 Mon & Tue)-11; 12-4,
7-10.30 Sun
**Adnams Broadsde; Everards Tiger;
Taylor Landlord; guest beers** H
One room pub on the site of
a 16th-century bakery. The
garden room restaurant (no
food Mon or Tue eve)
specialises in Portuguese and
Mexican dishes; steak night
Wed. The house beer comes
from Rudgate. The pub has a
covered long alley skittles
pitch. 🏚 ✿ ◖ ▶ & ⇌ (Castle/
Northgate) ♣

Wing Tavern
Market Place
☎ (01636) 702689
11-3.30, 7-11; 12-3, 7-10.30 Sun
**Theakston Best Bitter, XB, Old
Peculier** H
Untouched, secluded town-
centre pub, just off the
market square. Inside it is
basic in nature, comprising a
main bar, pool room and a
small family room. Outside a
paved area has the church as
a backdrop.
🌿 ✿ 🍴 ⇌ (Castle/Northgate) ♣

NEWINGTON
Ship
Newington Road (off A614,
on Misson road) OS667940
☎ (01302) 710334
12-11; 12-10.30 Sun
**Courage Directors; Tetley Bitter;
Theakston Best Bitter, Old
Peculier** H
Old pub by the River Idle,
popular with fishermen.
Once the tap for the
Newington brewery
it is now very food-oriented,
with a good vegetarian
choice.
✿ ◖ ▶ & P

NORMANTON ON THE WOLDS
Plough
Old Melton Road (off A606)
☎ (0115) 937 2401
11.30-3, 5.30-11; 11-11 Fri & Sat;
12-4, 7.30-10.30 Sun
**Courage Directors; John Smith's
Magnet; Theakston Best Bitter** H
Traditional rural pub with
two lounges and a
restaurant. Pub league
pétanque is played in the
large garden. Eve meals
served Tue-Sat.
🏚 Q ✿ ◖ ▶ & ↺ P

NOTTINGHAM
Bell
18 Angel Row
☎ (0115) 947 5241
10.30-11; 12-3, 7-10.30 Sun
**Draught Bass; Black Sheep Special,
Riggwelter; Brains SA; Jennings
Mild, Bitter; Ruddles County; guest
beers** H
Historic wood-panelled inn
dating back to 1437, offering
a wide selection of ales. Live
jazz is performed in the back
bar Sun lunch and several
eves.
Q ✿ ◖ ⇌ 🍴

Bunkers Hill Inn
36-38 Hockley (next to the
new National Ice Centre)
☎ (0115) 910 0114
11-11; 12-10.30 Sun
Beer range varies H
Ten constantly changing real
ales, specialising in small and
micro-brewers are served in
this genuine family-owned
and -run pub, converted
from former bank premises
by the owner. Very popular.
◖ & ⇌ ↺

Forest Tavern
257 Mansfield Road
☎ (0115) 947 5650
4 (12 Fri & Sat)-11; 12-10.30 Sun
**Castle Rock Hemlock; Greene King
Abbot; Marston's Pedigree;
Woodforde's Wherry; guest beer** H
Continental-style bar
stocking draught and bottled
European beers. Food,
including a Tapas menu, is
served all day. Live bands
perform at the Maze behind
the pub (open until 2am
Mon-Sat).
◖ ▶ ↺

Gladstone Hotel
45 Loscoe Road,Carrington
☎ (0115) 960 3256
5.30-11; 12-3, 7-11 Sat; 12-3, 7-10.30
Sun
**Marston's Pedigree; Wadworth
6X** H
Small very friendly, two-
roomed back-street boozer,
circa 1880, serving the local
community. The public bar
displays sporting
memorabilia, whilst the
lounge is decorated with the
landlord's knick-knacks and
an expanding library. A
house beer is also sold.
✿ ♣

Golden Fleece
105 Mansfield Road
☎ (0115) 947 2843
11-11; 12-10.30 Sun
Draught Bass; G **Cains Mild;
Flowers Original, Marston's
Pedigree; Young's Special; guest
beers** H
Two-bar pub on three levels
serving a constantly
changing range of guest

beers. Table football and pinball played. Home-made food includes vegetarian dishes; meals served 11-8 (12-4 Sun). The roof garden is an unusual feature.
🏵 ◖ ▷ ♣

Lincolnshire Poacher
161 Mansfield Road (uphill from Victoria Centre)
☎ (0115) 941 1584
11-11; 12-10.30 Sun
Bateman XB, XXXB; Marston's Pedigree; Taylor Landlord; guest beers Ⓗ
Deservedly popular, traditional-style pub with wood floors. It always offers several rapidly changing guest beers plus an interesting, varied menu (eve meals served Tue-Thu until 8pm). The pub is 'twinned' with a bar in Amsterdam.
Q 🏵 ◖ ▷ ♣ ⚌

March Hare
248 Carlton Road, Sneinton
☎ (0115) 950 4328
11-2.30, 6-11; 12-2.30, 7-10.30 Sun
Courage Directors; John Smith's Bitter Ⓗ
Built in 1958 and still run by the original landlord, it draws a mixed clientele, which includes a pool team. Hot food is served Mon-Fri; the menu is one of the best value in town. Q ◖ ▷ ♣ P

Olde Trip to Jerusalem
☆
1 Brewhouse Yard, Castle Rock
☎ (0115) 947 3171
11-11; 12-10.30 Sun
Hardys & Hansons Best Mild, Best Bitter, Classic, seasonal beers Ⓗ
Reputedly Nottingham's oldest pub, claiming to go back to 1189; a must for the first time visitor to the city. Many of the rooms are dug out of the sandstone rock, and its attractions include a haunted galley, the History of Nottingham tapestry and Ring the Bull games. Meals served 11 (12 Sun)-6.
🏚 Q 🏵 ◖ ▷ ♣

Portland Arms
24 Portland Road, Radford
☎ (0115) 942 0181
11-3, 6-11; 12-11 Sat; 12-10.30 Sun
Hardy & Hansons Best Mild, Best Bitter, Classic, seasonal beers Ⓗ
Warm, friendly local in the student area. It stages live music Wed and Sat and caters for a wide age range. Facilities include pool, Sky TV sport, a weekly quiz (Tue) and a traditional roast on Sunday. 🏵 ◖ ♣

Queens Hotel
2 Arkwrght Street (opp. station)

☎ (0115) 953 2288
11-11; 12-10.30 Sun
Boddingtons Bitter; Flowers Original; Worthington Bitter; guest beers Ⓗ
Victorian, street-corner pub with a friendly atmosphere. The bar and lounge have separate entrances.
🚪 ◖ ⇌ P

Red Lion
21 Alfreton Road (off Canning Circus, 1 mile N of centre)
☎ (0115) 952 0309
11.30 (11 Sat)-11; 12-10.30 Sun
Adnams Bitter; Greene King Abbot; Marston's Pedigree; guest beers Ⓗ
This good local serves a home-made three-course lunch on Sun, plus competitive food deals during the week. A choice of eight beers, Sky TV sport, and a rooftop patio are added attractions.
Q 🏵 ◖ ⚓

Vat & Fiddle
12-14 Queensbridge Road (near station)
☎ (0115) 985 0611
11-11; 12-10.30 Sun
Beer range varies Ⓗ
This single-room pub is the Castle Rock Brewery tap, serving four of its handpulled beers, plus six ever-changing guests. It also has 80 malt whiskies on offer and an extensive range of vodkas. Snacks usually available.
Q 🏵 ⚓ ⇌

NUTHALL
Three Ponds
Nottingham Road (near M1, jct 26)
☎ (0115) 938 3170
11-11; 12-10.30 Sun
Hardys & Hansons Best Mild, Best Bitter, Classic, seasonal beers Ⓗ
Busy roadside hostelry comprising three spacious open-plan rooms. The large garden has a children's play area and the unused skittle alley serves as sheltered outdoor area.
🏵 ◖ ▷ P ▦

ORSTON
Durham Ox
Church Street
☎ (01949) 850059
12 (11 Sat)-3, 6-11; 12-10.30 Sun
Highwood Tom Wood Best Bitter; Home Bitter; Marston's Pedigree; John Smith's Bitter; Theakston Best Bitter Ⓗ
Pleasant, split-room, country pub with a garden and pavement café areas. Both table and long alley skittles are played. Filled rolls are made to order. Vale of

Belvoir CAMRA *Pub of the Year.*
🏚 Q 🏵 ⚓ ♣ P

PLEASLEY
Olde Plough
Chesterfield Road North (A617)
☎ (01623) 810386
11.30-3, 5.30-11; 11-11 Sat; 12-3, 7-10.30 Sun
Marston's Bitter, Pedigree, HBC Ⓗ
Busy but friendly open-plan pub that has been extensively renovated. The menu is varied, with daily specials offering good value (no meals Sun eve); quiz nights Tue and Sun. 🏵 ◖ ▷ ♣ P

RADCLIFFE ON TRENT
Royal Oak
Main Road
☎ (0115) 933 3798
11-11; 12-10.30 Sun
Castle Eden Ale; Marston's Pedigree; Morland Old Speckled Hen; Taylor Landlord; guest beers Ⓗ
Convivial village local with a comfortable lounge and a boisterous bar, serving up to eight cask ales.
🏚 🏵 ⚐ ⇌ ♣ P

RAVENSHEAD
Sherwood Ranger Inn
Chapel Lane ($\frac{1}{2}$ mile S of B6020, between Larch Farm and Blidworth) OSSK5654
☎ (01623) 793040
12-3, 5-11; 12-11 Fri & Sat; 12-10.30 Sun
Hardys & Hansons Best Bitter, seasonal beers Ⓗ
Attractive 1960s-style suburban pub, with an open lawn affording views over open countryside. A lounge, public bar and games room with pool table complete the amenities. Fresh-filled cobs available lunchtime. It hosts an annual bonfire and fireworks event in Nov.
🏃 🏵 ⚐ ♣ P

Try also: Little John, Main Road (Mansfield)

RETFORD
Anchor Inn
Carolgate (opp. fire station
☎ (01777) 703241
11-11; 12-10.30 Sun
Adnams Bitter; Castle Eden Ale; Flowers IPA; Marston's Pedigree; Wadworth 6X; guest beers Ⓗ
Attractive, town-centre pub, popular for its home-made food and changing range of beers. A friendly welcome is guaranteed. Q 🏵 ◖ ⚓ ⇌ P ⊟

Clinton Arms
24 Albert Road (near canal basin)

☎ (01777) 702703
11-11; 12-10.30 Sun
Courage Directors; Wells Bombardier; John Smith's Bitter; guest beers Ⓗ
Attractive, three-roomed town pub where the atmosphere varies according to the time of day and events in progress. A wide screen TV for sports fans, regular live music (rock/blues), a games room and an outdoor play area are added attractions. Meals are served until 7pm.
🍴 🏵 ◖▶ ⊞ ⌂ ♣ ♣ P ⑪

Market Hotel
West Carr Road
☎ (01777) 703278
11-3, 6-11; 11-11 Sat; 12-4, 7-10.30 Sun
Adnams Bitter; Camerons Strongarm; Marston's Pedigree; guest beers Ⓗ
Close to the station, this old, traditional free house has been owned by the same family for 40 years. It offers excellent food (not served Sun eve) and five regularly changing guest ales. A pub to suit all ages; children welcome.
Q 🏵 ◖▶ ⊞ ⌂ ▲ ⇌ P ⑪

Whitehouses Inn
London Road
☎ (01777) 703703
11-3.30, 5-11; 11.30-11 Sat; 12-10.30 Sun
Boddingtons Bitter; Caledonian 80/-; Castle Eden Ale; guest beers Ⓗ
Lively family pub stocking a selection of guest beers, and serving quality food at reasonable prices. A friendly welcome is assured from all the staff.
🏵 ◖▶ ▲ ♣ P

SELSTON
Horse & Jockey
Church Lane (off B6018)
☎ (01773) 781012
12-2.30, 5-11; 12-7.10.30 Sun
Draught Bass; Ⓗ **Greene King Abbot; Taylor Landlord;** Ⓖ **Whim Magic Mushroom Mild;** Ⓗ **guest beers** Ⓗ/Ⓖ
Welcoming, family-run village local dating back to 1664. Low beamed ceilings and flagstone floors feature in its four rooms; pool and darts are played in the top room. Local CAMRA *Pub of the Season* winter 1999/2000. Wed is folk night, Sun quiz night. The family room is open weekday lunchtimes; children's portions of main meals served.
🍴 Q 🍴 🏵 ◖⊞ ♣ ⌂ P

SOUTHWELL
Old Coach House
69 Easthorpe (A612, just

before the Minster)
☎ (01636) 813289
5 (4 Fri; 12 Sat)-11; 12-10.30 Sun
Beer range varies Ⓗ
Busy corner local where there's at least five beers available, always including a mild, mostly from independents. A homely atmosphere is enhanced by no less than three real fires and a large collection of board games. Cider sold in summer.
🍴 🏵 ▲ ♣ ⌂

SUTTON BONNINGTON
Anchor Inn
16 Bollards Lane
☎ (01509) 673648
7 (12 Sat)-11; 12-10.30 Sun
Banks's Original; Marston's Pedigree; guest beer Ⓗ
150-year-old, one-bar, split-level pub, originally a butchers shop. It reputedly has a resident ghost – Mr Bollard, hence the name of the lane. The pub, which bears a nautical theme, fields a football team. Lunchtime snacks available.
🍴 Q 🏵 ◖♣ P ⑪

TOLLERTON
Air Hostess
Stanstead Avenue (off A606)
☎ (0115) 937 2485
11.30-3, 5.30-11; 11.30-4, 6.30-11 Sat; 12-3, 7-10.30 Sun
Courage Directors; Ruddles County; guest beers Ⓗ
1960s two-roomed pub, it is very popular with a varied local clientele. An aviation theme is obvious from the photos and pictures. The pub has keen pétanque players. The good menu includes a vegetarian choice.
Q 🏵 ◖⊞ ♣ P

UNDERWOOD
Red Lion
Church Lane, Bagthorpe (off B600)
☎ (01773) 810482
12-3, 5.30-11; 12-11 Sat; 12-10.30 Sun
Boddingtons Bitter; Flowers Original; Marston's Pedigree; guest beer Ⓗ
300-year-old, beamed, friendly village pub with an eating area where children are welcome, plus a large garden and play area (barbecues held in summer).
🏵 ◖▶ P

WALKERINGHAM
Three Horseshoes
High Street
☎ (01427) 890959
11.30-3, 7-11; 12-4, 7-10.30 Sun
Draught Bass; Stones Bitter;

Worthington Bitter; guest beer Ⓗ
This village pub, catering for locals and visitors alike, enjoys a good reputation for its home-cooked food served in the bar or restaurant. It is also noted for its award-winning flower displays. No meals Sun eve or Mon.
Q ◖▶ ⌂ ▲ ♣ P ⑪

WEST BRIDGFORD
Meadow Covert
Alford Road, Edwalton (near Edwalton Golf Club)
☎ (0115) 923 2074
11-11; 12-10.30 Sun
Hardys & Hansons Best Bitter, Classic, seasonal beers Ⓗ
Comfortable lounge; the bar has two pool tables and a big screen TV. The garden has a children's play area.
🏵 ◖▶ ⊞ ⌂ ♣ P

Stratford Haven
2 Stratford Road
☎ (0115) 982 5981
10.30-11; 12-10.30 Sun
Adnams Bitter; Bateman XB; Caledonian Deuchars IPA; Castle Rock Hemlock; Hook Norton Old Hooky; Marston's Pedigree Ⓗ
Handily located for cricket matches, it is just up the road from Trent Bridge. This new Tynemill pub is proving to be the most popular in the area. No meals Sun eve.
🏵 ◖▶ ✂

WEST LEAKE
Star Inn
Melton Lane
☎ (01509) 852233
11-2.30, 6-11; 10-3, 6-11 Sat; 12-3.30, 7-10.30 Sun
Draught Bass; guest beers Ⓗ
Old, traditional, pub dating back well over 200 years: three rooms include a family room and restaurant. Large garden.
🍴 Q ⏚ 🏵 ◖⌂ ♣ P

WEST STOCKWITH
Waterfront
Canal Lane

INDEPENDENT BREWERIES

Alcazar: Basford
Broadstone: Retford
Castle Rock: Nottingham
Caythorpe: Caythorpe
Hardys & Hansons: Kimberley
Holland: Kimberley
Leadmill: Selston
Mallard: Nottingham
Mansfield: Mansfield
Maypole: Eakring
Springhead: Sutton-on-Trent

☎ (01427) 891223
11-11; 12-10.30 Sun
John Smith's Bitter; guest beers Ⓗ
Village pub, overlooking the marina on the Trent – popular with boaters in summer. It stocks five guest beers and hosts an Easter beer festival.
🛏 🐕 ☏ ⌂ ◗ ♿ ᴀ ♣ ⌂ P
✂ 🏠

WORKSOP

Greendale Oak
Norfolk Street (off the market square)
☎ (01909) 475280
12-11; 12-4, 7-10.30 Sun

Stones Bitter; Theakston Mild; guest beers Ⓗ
Small, cosy, gaslit, mid-terrace pub built in 1790; it fields keen darts and dominoes teams and serves good food.
Q ❀ ◗ ᴀ ♣ P

Mallard
Station Approach
☎ (01909) 530757
2 (12 Sat)-11; 12-3, (closed eve) Sun
Beer range varies Ⓗ
Small, genuine free house on the station platform, serving constantly changing beers from small breweries (over 400 per year) plus a wide

range of foreign bottled beer. Occasional beer festivals are held in the cellar bar.
❀ ᴀ ⇌ ⌂ P 🏠

Newcastle Arms
88 Carlton Road
☎ (01909) 485384
11-2.30, 5.30-11; 11-11 Fri & Sat;
12-3, 7-10.30 Sun
Home Bitter; Theakston Best Bitter; guest beers Ⓗ
Comfortable, traditional local, popular with all ages; it can be busy at times. Guest beers often include local products. Traditional food includes a daily special and Sun lunches. ❀ ◗ ᴀ ⇌ ♣

CAMRA National Pub Inventory: Ye Old Tavern, Kington, Herefordshire

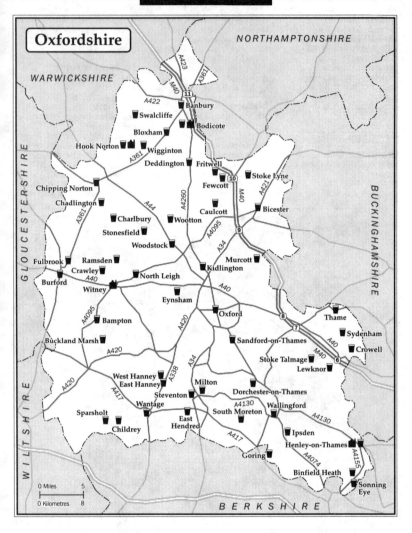

Oxfordshire

NORTHAMPTONSHIRE

WARWICKSHIRE

A423
A361
M40
11 Banbury
A422 Swalcliffe
Bodicote
Bloxham
Hook Norton Wigginton
Deddington Fritwell
A361 Fewcott 10 Stoke Lyne
Chipping Norton M40 A421
Chadlington Caulcott Bicester
Charlbury Wootton A4095
Stonesfield A44 A4260 9
Woodstock A34
Fulbrook Ramsden Murcott
Crawley A40 Kidlington
Burford North Leigh
Witney A40 8
Eynsham 7
A4095 Oxford Thame
A420 Sydenham
Bampton A34 Crowell
Buckland Marsh Sandford-on-Thames A40 6
A420 Stoke Talmage M40
West Hanney Lewknor
East Hanney A338 Milton
Steventon Dorchester-on-Thames
Sparsholt A417 Wantage A4130 Wallingford A4130
Childrey East Hendred South Moreton
A417 Ipsden
Goring Henley-on-Thames
Binfield Heath A4074 A4155
Sonning Eye

GLOUCESTERSHIRE

BUCKINGHAMSHIRE

WILTSHIRE

0 Miles 5
0 Kilometres 8

BERKSHIRE

BAMPTON

Morris Clown
High Street
☎ (01993) 850217
12-2 (not Mon-Wed), 5-11; 12-11 Sat;
12-5, 7-10.30 Sun
**Courage Best Bitter; Wychwood
Shires; guest beer** Ⓗ
Welcoming local warmed by
a large open fire in winter.
The pub is 800 years old and
its name reflects the village's
history of Morris dancing.
🏨 ❀ ♣ P

Try also: Elephant & Castle,
Bridge St (Free)

BANBURY

Bell Inn
12 Middleton Road (near
station)
☎ (01295) 253169
12-3, 7-11; 12-11 Sat; 12-4,

8-10.30 Sun
**Highgate Dark; Worthington Bitter;
guest beers** Ⓗ
Popular, community two-bar
pub, serving weekday
lunches. Aunt Sally is played
in summer. 🏨 ❀ Ⓒ 🍴 ≠ ♣ P

Olde Reindeer
47 Parsons Street (near
Market Sq)
☎ (01295) 264031
11-11 (10 Mon); closed Sun
**Hook Norton Mild, Best Bitter,
Generation, Old Hooky; guest
beers** Ⓗ
Superb, 15th-century former
coaching inn; visit the
Jacobean globe room which
is fully wood panelled. A
relaxed venue with quiet
music where tidy dress is
required. No under 21s
admitted. The food is all
home cooked.
🏨 ❀ Ⓒ 🍴 P

BICESTER

Swan
13 Church Street
☎ (01869) 369035
11.30-11; 12-10.30 Sun
**Greene King IPA, Abbot, guest
beers** Ⓗ
Friendly, unspoilt two-bar,
market town pub serving
well-priced food. Piped
contemporary music is the
norm here; live music most
Sat. Eve meals served Sun-
Thu.
🏨 🚪 Ⓒ 🍴 ≠ ♣ ⌂

BINFIELD HEATH

Bottle & Glass
Harpsden Road (off A4155,
1/2 mile NE of centre)
☎ (01491) 575755
11-4, 6-11; 12-4, 7-10.30 Sun
Brakspear Bitter, Old, Special Ⓗ
Picturesque, thatched,

beamed, 17th-century, country pub with a flagstoned floor in its main bar and a large garden. Home-cooked food includes vegetarian options (no meals Sun eve).

Q ❀ ◑ ▮ P ✕

BLOXHAM

Elephant & Castle
Humber Street (off A361)
☎ (01295) 720383
11-3, 5-11; 11-11 Sat; 12-10.30 Sun
Hook Norton Best Bitter; guest beers Ⓗ
A convivial welcome awaits at this 16th-century coaching inn, a community-based Hook Norton pub, run by the present landlord for 26 years. Aunt Sally, bar billiards and shove-ha'penny are played here and add plenty of character. A guest cider is sold in summer. No food Sun.

🏠 Q ❀ ◑ ▮ ♣ ◠ P

Red Lion
High Street (A361)
☎ (01295) 720352
11.30-2.30, 7-11; 12-3, 7-10.30 Sun
Adnams Bitter; Wadworth 6X; guest beers Ⓗ
Friendly, two-bar pub that follows a popular guest beer programme. The large garden includes a children's play area. It draws a good mix of ages, diners, and drinkers. Special events and regular offers on meals are added attractions.

🏠 Q ❀ ◑ ▮ ▱ ▲ ≈ ♣

BODICOTE

Plough
9 High Street
☎ (01295) 262327
11-2.30, 6-11; 12-3, 7-10.30 Sun
Bodicote Bitter, No. 9, Triple X (winter)**, seasonal beers** Ⓗ
Pleasant, friendly village pub, with its own brewery. Home-cooked food is served in the lounge/dining room; meals are cooked to order Sun. Beer festivals are held first weekend in Feb and Aug.

🏠 ❀ ◑ ▮ ▱ ♣

BUCKLAND MARSH

Trout at Tadpole Bridge
Off A420 to Bampton
OS335004
☎ (01367) 870382
11.30-3, 6-11; 12-4, 7-10.30 (not winter eve) Sun
Archers Village; Fuller's London Pride; guest beers Ⓗ
This 17th-century stone building has been a Thames pub for over 100 years. It boasts a stone floor and

original beams. With its pleasant garden running right to the river's edge, the Trout is a great starting point for a walk on the Thames path; recommended for its meals. Wheelchair WC.

🏠 Q ⟲ ❀ ◑ ▮ ▱ ▲ ♣ P

BURFORD

Lamb
Sheep Street
☎ (01993) 823155
11-2.30, 6-11; 12-3, 7-10.30 Sun
Badger Dorset Best; Hook Norton Best Bitter; Wadworth 6X Ⓗ
Cosy, flagstoned bar in a comfortable 15th-century hotel, offering friendly service and four real fires.

🏠 Q ❀ ⇌ ◑ ▱

Try also: Royal Oak, Witney St (Wadworth)

CAULCOTT

Horse & Groom
Lower Heyford Road
☎ (01869) 343257
11-3 (4 Sat), 6-11; 12-3, 7-10.30 Sun
Hook Norton Best Bitter; guest beers Ⓗ
With three constantly changing guest beers (about 150 each year), this charming, thatched pub, in its rural setting, is a haven for local real ale enthusiasts. An interesting range of home-cooked specials and O'Hagan's sausages are served in the bar and restaurant.

🏠 Q ❀ ◑ ▮

CHADLINGTON

Tite Inn
Mill End
☎ (01608) 676475
12-2.30, 6.30-11; closed Mon; 12-3, 7-10.30 Sun
Archers Village; Fuller's London Pride; Young's Special; guest beers Ⓗ
Cotswold stone free house affording fine views from an attractive garden. Well-behaved children and walkers are welcome. The garden room opens in summer. Excellent, freshly prepared food is served in the dining area.

🏠 Q ❀ ◑ ▮ ▱ ▲ ◠ P

CHARLBURY

Rose & Crown
Market Street
☎ (01608) 810103
12 -11; 11-11 Sat; 12-10.30 Sun
Archers Village; guest beers Ⓗ
Popular, town-centre pub attracting all ages, with an excellent rotation of guest beers, plus a good choice of Belgian bottled beers. Walkers are welcome to eat

their own food here. A pool room and patio courtyard add to its appeal.

🏠 ❀ ▲ ≈ ♣

CHILDREY

Hatchet
High Street
☎ (01235) 751213
12-2.30 (3 Sat), 7-11; 12-3.30, 7-10.30 Sun
Morland Original; guest beers Ⓗ
Lively, very friendly open-plan local in a picturesque downland setting, serving an interesting range of ever-changing guest beers that almost always includes a mild.

❀ ◑ ▮ ▱ ♣ P

CHIPPING NORTON

Chequers
Goddards Lane (next to theatre)
☎ (01608) 644717
11-11, 12-10.30 Sun
Fuller's Chiswick, London Pride, ESB, seasonal beers Ⓗ
This award-winning pub is popular with all ages. It has four seating areas and a no-smoking restaurant serving Thai and daily specials. Meals are also available at the bar; Sun meals served 12-5.

🏠 Q ◑ ▮ ♣ P

Oxford House
18 Horsefair (opp. police station)
☎ (01608) 642918
11.30-3, 5-11; 12-3, 5-10.30 Sun
Draught Bass; Greene King Abbot; Hook Norton Best Bitter; guest beers Ⓗ
A recent 'retro' revamp has led to a single bar with a covered patio area as a restaurant. A popular early eve venue, a different beer is promoted daily between 5 and 7pm. Skittle alley can be booked. Aunt Sally is played in summer (Thu). The menu offers English and Italian cuisine.

🏠 Q ⇌ ◑ ▮ ♣

CRAWLEY

Crawley Inn
Foxburrow Lane
☎ (01993) 708930
Lunchtime varies; 6-11; 11-11 Fri & Sat; 12-10.30 Sun
Goff's Jouster, Vale Notley Ale; guest beers Ⓖ
Wherever you look in this two-bar pub you will find the unexpected – whether it be bar stools, puppets, six absinthes on sale, or wonderful murals, all making a visit to the Crawley Inn unforgettable. Be prepared for anything including 'wild' games on Sun. A cider is

usually available.
🏚 Q 🕸 🕪 ▶ 🛓 ♣ 🖰 P

CROWELL

Shepherds Crook
The Green (off B4009
between Chinnor and M40
jct 6) OS744997
☎ (01844) 351431
11.30-3, 5-11; 11-11 Sat; 12-5,
7-10.30 (12-10.30 summer) Sun
**Batham Best Bitter; Donnington BB;
Hook Norton Best Bitter; Taylor
Landlord; guest beers** Ⓗ
Comfortable country inn,
lying under the Chiltern
Ridge near a point-to-point
course. It offers an interesting
range of beers, plus a good
value home-cooked menu
specialising in fish dishes
(vegetarian choice also
available).
🏚 Q 🕸 🕪 ▶ P

DEDDINGTON

Crown & Tuns
New Street (B4260)
☎ (01869) 337371
11-3, 6-11; 12-3, 7-10.30 Sun
**Hook Norton Mild, Best Bitter, Old
Hooky, seasonal beers** Ⓗ
Recently renovated 16th-
century coaching inn. In
every edition of this *Guide*, it
caters for all age groups,
families included, and will
extend opening times when
required.
🏚 🕸 🕪 ♣

DORCHESTER-ON-THAMES

Chequers
20 Bridge End (off High St,
off A4074; from S turn sharp
left after bridge)
☎ (01865) 340015
12-2 (not Mon or Wed, 12-3 Sat), 7-11;
12-3, 7-10.30 Sun
**Courage Best Bitter; Hook Norton
Best Bitter; Wadworth IPA; guest
beer** (occasional) Ⓖ
Genuine, 17th-century local
in an attractive village which
boasts an historic abbey. Lots
of games played, including
Aunt Sally (summer Fri).
Handy for walkers and the
Rivers Thames and Thame.
🏚 Q 🐾 🕸 🛏 ♣ P ⚞

EAST HANNEY

Black Horse
Main Street (200 yds from
Hanney Cross Rd, off A338)
☎ (01235) 868212
12-2.30, 5.30 (6 winter)-11; closed
Mon; 12-4, 6-11 Sun
**Brakspear Bitter; Hook Norton Best
Bitter; guest beer** Ⓗ
Whitewashed free house in
an attractive Vale village with
a pleasant garden. The
spacious, comfortable bar,
with a no-smoking dining

area at one end, offers a
varied and interesting range
of beers, plus German
cuisine. Q 🕸 🕪 ▶ ♣ P

EAST HENDRED

Eyston Arms
High Street
☎ (01235) 833320
12-3 (not Mon-Thu), 7-11; 12-10.30
Sun
**Courage Best Bitter; Wadworth 6X;
guest beers** Ⓗ
Cosy, traditional, village local
boasting original beams and
a quaint inglenook. The
landlord is enthusiastic about
guest beers and has featured
more than 500 in under four
years. Friendly clientele; lots
of games available.
🏚 🕸 ♣ P

EYNSHAM

Queens Head
17 Queen Street
☎ (01865) 881229
12-3, 6-11; 12-11 Sat; 12-3, 7-10.30
Sun
**Greene King IPA, Triumph; guest
beer** Ⓗ
Friendly, 18th-century inn
comprising two bars: a quiet
public bar and a more vibrant
lounge. Railway memorabilia
adorns both. The guest is
taken from the Greene King
list. 🏚 🕸 ♣ 🕪 🍴 ᴧ ♣

FEWCOTT

White Lion
Fritwell Road (off A43 at
Ardley, near M40 jct 10)
☎ (01869) 346639
7 (11 Sat)-11; 12-4, 7-10.30 Sun
Beer range varies Ⓗ
An excellent and varied range
of beers, usually including
micros, is always on offer at
this friendly, 18th-century
village pub. Popular with
locals, there is a strong
emphasis on games and sport
– pool, darts, dominoes and
Aunt Sally; Ardley United
Football Club is based here.
🏚 🕸 ♣ P

FRITWELL

Kings Head
92 East Street
☎ (01869) 346738
12-3, 7-11; 12-4 (closed eve) Sun
**Hook Norton Best Bitter; Wychwood
Shires, seasonal beers** Ⓗ
17th-century Cotswold stone
pub where generous home-
cooked meals are served in
the bar and dining room;
families welcome. No eve
meals Sun or Tue.
🏚 🕸 🕪 ♣ P

FULBROOK

Masons Arms

Shipton Road (A361 Burford
road)
☎ (01993) 822354
12-2, 6.30-11; closed Mon; 12-3,
7-10.30 Sun
**Hook Norton Best Bitter; Wadworth
6X;** Ⓗ **guest beers** Ⓖ
Welcoming, 200-year-old
village pub featuring bars
with original beams and a
large open fire. Good value
food includes local game
dishes. It is about 10
minutes' walk from Burford.
🏚 Q 🕸 🕪 ♣ ⚞

GORING

Catherine Wheel
Station Road (off B4009,
High St)
☎ (01491) 872379
11.30-2.30, 5-11; 12-4, 7-10.30 Sun
**Brakspear Mild, Bitter, Old, Special,
seasonal beers** Ⓗ
Old, beamed pub boasting a
lovely inglenook fireplace.
Children are welcome in the
'Forge Bar', which was once a
blacksmith's shop, and the
large, safe garden. Good
value, home-cooked food
includes daily specials (no
meals Sun eve).
Accommodation is in a
nearby cottage.
🏚 Q 🕸 🛏 🕪 ▶ 🛓 ⇌ ♣

John Barleycorn
Manor Road (off B4009, High
St)
☎ (01491) 872509
10-2.30, 6-11; 12-3, 7-10.30 Sun
**Brakspear Bitter, Special, seasonal
beers** Ⓗ
Many-roomed, low-beamed
pub with a cosy lounge. An
extensive, good-value menu
includes daily specials
(children allowed in the
lounge/restaurant). Close to
the River Thames and the
Ridgeway long distance
footpath, it is popular with
tourists.
Q 🕸 🛏 🕪 ▶ 🛓 ⇌ ♣

HENLEY-ON-THAMES

Bird in Hand
61 Greys Road (off A4155)
☎ (01491) 575775
11.30-2.30, 5-11; 11.30-11 Sat;
12-10.30 Sun
**Brakspear Mild, Bitter; Fuller's
London Pride; guest beers** Ⓗ
Friendly, one-bar, town local:
Henley's only real ale free
house. Visit the large garden
with aviary, pond and pets –
it is safe for children. The two
guest beers are often from
micros. Weekday lunches
served.
Q 🕸 🕪 🛓 ⇌ ♣

Saracen's Head
129 Greys Road (off A4155;
up hill 1/2 mile SW of
A4130/A4155 jct)

☎ (01491) 575929
11-2.30 (3 Sat), 5.30-11; 12-10.30 Sun
Brakspear Mild, Bitter, Old, Special H
A friendly welcome awaits in this popular and busy local which has an emphasis on pub games. It enters teams in the local league for darts, crib and pool. Home-cooked snacks are always available.
🏠 🕸 🚅 ▲ ♣ P

HOOK NORTON
Pear Tree
Scotland End (near brewery)
☎ (01608) 737482
11.30-2.30, 6-11; 11.30-11 Sat; 12-4, 7-10 Sun
Hook Norton Mild, Best Bitter, Generation, Old Hooky, seasonal beers H
Effectively the brewery tap, this small, 18th-century one-roomed brick-faced pub features log fires and exposed beams. Home-cooked bar food (not served Sun eve) is reasonably priced. It epitomises the English country pub for locals and visitors.
🏠 Q 🕸 🚅 ◖ ▶ 🚻 ▲ ♣ P

Sun Inn
High Street
☎ (01608) 737570
11-3, 7-11; 12-3, 7-10.30 Sun
Hook Norton Mild, Best Bitter, Generation, Old Hooky, seasonal beers; guest beers H
Two pubs have been well combined to provide roomy drinking and dining areas. Good food is all freshly cooked to order.
🏠 Q 🕸 🚅 ◖ ▶ 🚻 ▲ ♣ P

IPSDEN
King William IV
Hailey E off A4074 at crossroads, (signed to Well Place, left at next crossroads) OS643858
☎ (01491) 681845
11-2.30, 6-11; 12-3, 7-10.30 Sun
Brakspear Mild, Bitter, Old, Special, seasonal beers G
Country pub in an idyllic setting benefitting from lovely views. Hard to find, but you are amply rewarded by the quality and range of Brakspear's beers and its food. Popular with hikers, due to its close proximity to the Ridgeway long distance footpath (1¹/₂ miles).
🏠 Q 🐕 🕸 ◖ ▶ ⌐ P ⚲

KIDLINGTON
Kings Arms
4 The Moors
☎ (01865) 373004
11-2.30, 6-11; 11-11 Sat; 12-10.30 Sun
Greene King IPA; Ind Coope Burton

Ale; Marston's Pedigree; guest beer H
Popular local comprising two small bars and a covered courtyard. It serves good cheap lunchtime meals. An occasional beer festival is held.
🕸 ◖ 🍴 ♣ P

LEWKNOR
Olde Leathern Bottel
1 High Street (off B4009, near M40 jct 6)
☎ (01844) 351482
11-2.30, 6-11; 12-3, 7-10.30 Sun
Brakspear Bitter, Old, Special, seasonal beers H
Comfortable, inviting, family-run village pub with a large inglenook and low beams. The extensive well-kept garden has a children's play area. An excellent range of home-cooked food (with vegetarian options), is reasonably priced and caters for all tastes.
🏠 🐕 🕸 ◖ ▶ 🍴 🚻 ♣ P ⚲

MILTON (NEAR ABINGDON)
Admiral Benbow
44 High Street
☎ (01235) 831344
11-2.30, 5 (7 Sat)-11; 12-3, 7-10.30 Sun
Morrells Bitter H
No-frills village local, often loud and smoky. Named after Admiral Benbow, the 17th-century adventurer, whose portrait hangs in the bar. Weekday lunchtime meals available.
🕸 ◖ ♣

MURCOTT
Nut Tree Inn
Main Street
☎ (01865) 331253
11-3, 6.30-11; 12-3, 6.30-10.30 Sun
Wadworth IPA, 6X; guest beer H
Picturesque village local run by a very welcoming landlord. Although food plays a major role, the drinker is not overlooked (no food Sun). It stocks a good range of guest beers, plus a house beer from Wychwood. The conservatory is the family room.
🏠 Q 🐕 🕸 ◖ ▶ 🚻 ♣ P ⚲

NORTH LEIGH
Woodman
New Yatt Road (off A4095, Witney-Woodstock road)
☎ (01993) 881790
12-2.30, 6-11; 12-10.30 Sun
Hook Norton Best Bitter; Wadworth 6X; guest beers H
Small, friendly, village pub serving freshly cooked home-made food (no eve meals

Mon). The large terrace and garden are the site for popular beer festivals (Easter and Aug bank hols), now in their twelfth year.
🏠 🕸 🚅 ◖ ▶ ♣ P

OXFORD
Angel & Greyhound
30 St Clements Street
☎ (01865) 242660
11-11; 12-10.30 Sun
Young's Bitter, Special, Winter Warmer or guest beer H
Popular local meeting place just outside the city centre, with a friendly, relaxed atmosphere. Bar billiards and board games played. No meals Sun eve.
🏠 Q 🕸 ◖ ▶ ♣

Butchers Arms
5 Wilberforce Street, Headington
☎ (01865) 761252
11.30-2.30, 5.30-11; 11.30-11 Fri & Sat; 12-10.30 Sun
Fuller's Chiswick, London Pride, ESB, seasonal beers H
Busy, friendly, back-street local where the single bar displays a collection of football tickets. It boasts a heated patio area. Not far from Headington centre, it is worth the bus ride from the city. Weekday lunchtime meals available.
🏠 🕸 ◖ ♣

Harcourt Arms
1-2 Cranham Terrace (off Walton St, down Jericho St)
☎ (01865) 310630
12-2.30 (3 Fri & Sat), 5.30-11; 12-3, 7-10.30 Sun
Fuller's Chiswick, London Pride, ESB H
Atmospheric dimly-lit pub that displays modern art prints. Board games are popular. It also sells Fuller's 1845 bottled-conditioned beer.
🏠 🕸 ◖ ▶ 🚻 ♣

Hobgoblin
108 St Aldates
☎ (01865) 250201
11-11; 12-10.30 Sun
Wychwood Shires; guest beers H
Lively, city-centre pub opposite the Town Hall, serving an impressive range of guest beers. Popular with students – special offers are often available. Good value food is served until 6pm (4pm Sun).
◖ ⚖

Lamb & Flag
12 St Giles
☎ (01865) 515787
12-11; 12-10.30 Sun
Brakspear Bitter; Hook Norton Old Hooky; Theakston Old Peculier; guest beers H

The Good Beer Guide 2001

Historic 13th-century inn, now run by St John's College as a free house. Bar snacks are usually available.

Marlborough House
60 Western Road
☎ (01865) 243617
11.30-2.30, 6-11; 11.30-11 Sat; 12-10.30 Sun
Benskins BB; Greene King IPA Ⓗ
Small, friendly back-street pub, popular with students and locals alike. It has a pool room upstairs and hosts live music Wed eve.
◖♣

Old Ale House
163 Iffley Road
☎ (01865) 245290
12-11; 12-10.30 Sun
Morrells Bitter, Varsity; guest beers Ⓗ
Small, three roomed, split-level Victorian pub, recently restyled as one of Morrells' ale house brand with enough paraphernalia to fill a skip. High prices, but free monkey nuts. Food is served all sessions. It was formerly called the Fir Tree.
◖▶⌂

Old Tom
101 St Aldates
☎ (01865) 243034
10.30-11; 12-10.30 Sun
Morrells Bitter, Varsity, Graduate, seasonal beers Ⓗ
Small, narrow, 17th-century pub, popular with all. Recently revived, it takes its name from the bells at Christ Church College. A no-smoking area is available at lunchtime.
Q❀◖◐≠

Prince of Wales
73 Church Way, Iffley
☎ (01865) 778543
11.30-3, 6-11; 12-3, 7-10.30 Sun
Badger Tanglefoot; Wadworth IPA, 6X; Farmers Glory, seasonal beers; guest beers Ⓗ
Attractive village local usually offering eight ales, two miles from the city centre. No food Sun eve.
❀◖⌂P

Rose & Crown
14 North Parade Avenue (off Banbury road), 1/2 mile N of centre)
☎ (01865) 510551
11-3, 5 (6 Sat)-11; 12-4, 7-10.30 Sun
Adnams Bitter; Ind Coope Burton Ale Ⓗ
Excellent Victorian local of two rooms and a corridor drinking area with a serving hatch, plus a heated rear covered garden. A pub for conversation, frequented by town and gown alike, it is run by friendly staff.
🏚Q❀◖▶

258

Turf Tavern
4 Bath Place
☎ (01865) 243735
11-11; 12-10.30 Sun
Archers Golden; Brakspear Special; Caledonian Deuchars IPA; Flowers Original; guest beers Ⓗ
Historic, famous and popular 600-year-old pub, boasting three large gardens, approached down alleyways amongst college buildings. It usually has 11 beers on tap. Meals available 12-8 daily, with a fast service.
Q❀◖▶⌂≠

Wharf House
14 Butterwyke Place, St Ebbes (Thames St/Speedwell St jct)
☎ (01865) 246752
11-3, 5.30-11; 11-11 Sat; 12-4, 7-10.30 Sun
Hook Norton Best Bitter; RCH Pitchfork; guest beers Ⓗ
True free house, offering two constantly changing guest beers, a superb range of Belgian beers, plus real cider and perry. A mixed clientele enjoys this down-to-earth boozer, where the ambience varies according to the time of day.
❀≠⌂P

Try also: **Grog Shop** (off licence), Walton St (Free)

RAMSDEN
Royal Oak
High Street (off B4022, Witney-Charlbury road)
OS356153
☎ (01993) 868213
11.30-3, 6.30-11; 12-3, 7-10.30 Sun
Archers Golden; Ⓗ **Fuller's ESB; Goff's White Knight;** Ⓖ **Hook Norton Best Bitter** Ⓗ
Attractive, quiet, friendly 17th-century coaching inn within easy reach of Oxford, Cheltenham and the Cotswolds. Exposed beams, stone walls, and a welcoming log fire are attractive features. Popular with walkers, it is accessible from several circular routes. Well-regarded for its meals, based on local produce.
🏚Q❀🛏◖&P🍴

SANDFORD-ON-THAMES
Fox
25 Henley Road
☎ (01865) 777803
12-3, 6.30-11; 12-3, 7-10.30 Sun
Morrells Bitter, Varsity, Ⓗ/Ⓖ **seasonal beers** Ⓗ
Long-standing *Guide* entry selling the cheapest and best Morrells in the area; ask for gravity beer. 🏚Q❀🍺♣P

SONNING EYE
Flowing Spring

Henley Road (A4155, 2 miles E of Caversham)
☎ (0118) 969 3207
11.30 (11 Sat)-11; 12-10.30 Sun
Fuller's Chiswick, London Pride, ESB, seasonal beers Ⓗ
Traditional pub, recently improved by a sympathetic extension and verandah with extra seating. A variety of events are staged in the pleasant garden. Good food at reasonable prices includes excellent Sun lunches; eve meals served Tue-Sat.
🏚Q🛏❀◖▲♣P≠

SOUTH MORETON
Crown
High Street (off A4130, 1 mile E of Didcot)
☎ (01235) 812262
11-3, 5.30-11; 12-3, 7-10.30 Sun
Adnams Bitter; Badger Tanglefoot; Wadworth IPA, 6X; Ⓗ **guest beer** Ⓖ
This village local is deservedly popular for meals which include vegetarian choices. A regularly changing guest beer is served from casks behind the bar. Families are welcome throughout this pub, the best there is closest to Didcot.
🏚🛏❀◖♣P

SPARSHOLT
Star
Watery Lane
☎ (01235) 751539
12-3, 6-11; 11-11 Sat; 12-10.30 Sun
Butts Barbus Barbus; Morland Original; guest beers Ⓗ
Friendly, traditional village free house where a strong horse-racing theme reflects the interest of the surrounding community. Camping is possible in the garden, by arrangement.
🛏❀🛏◖&▲♣P≠

STEVENTON
Cherry Tree
33 High Street
☎ (01235) 831222
11.30-2.30, 5-11; 11-11 Fri & Sat; 12-10.30 Sun
Red Shoot Tom's Tipple; Wadworth IPA, 6X, Farmers Glory; guest beers Ⓗ
Large old rambling pub which has been subjected to discreet modernisation. Its two pleasant, comfortable bars and dining area cater for a varied clientele. Aunt Sally played.
🏚❀◖♣P

STOKE LYNE
Peyton Arms ☆
1/2 mile off B4100, near Bicester
☎ (01869) 345285
12-2.30 (not Mon or Tue), 6.30 (6 Fri &

Sat)-11; 12-2.30, 7-10.30 Sun
Hook Norton Mild, Best Bitter, Generation, Old Hooky, seasonal beers; G
Very peaceful, small village pub whose two simple bars have remained largely unchanged in decades and offer a bygone retreat from the 21st century. Aunt Sally is played in summer.
🏚Q🕸🅰♣P

STOKE TALMAGE
Red Lion ☆
Off A40 at Tetsworth
OS681994
☎ (01844) 281651
12-2 (not Mon-Thu), 6-11; 12-2.30, 7-10.30 Sun
Beer range varies H
Old-fashioned, down-to-earth country pub where everyone is made welcome and asked to join in. Children can enjoy the adjacent farm, with small domestic animals. Three beers are stocked in winter, and four in summer – usually one from a local micro.
🏚Q🌂🕸🅰♣🅿⊟

STONESFIELD
Black Head
Church Street
☎ (01993) 891616
11-3, 5.30-11; 11-11 Fri & Sat; 12-10.30 Sun
Courage Best Bitter; guest beers H
Two-bar pub: the front bar is the larger, with pool table and darts, while the back bar is quieter and more cosy. A busy, friendly pub, it offers guest beers not usually available locally, and is a rare outlet for beers from the nearby Wychwood Brewery.
🏚🕸🍴◗🅰♣🅿

SWALCLIFFE
Stag's Head
The Green (B4035, 6 miles W of Banbury)
☎ (01295) 780232
11.30-2.30 (not Mon; 11.30-3 Sat), 6.30-11; 12-3, 7-10.30 Sun
Brakspear Bitter; Hook Norton Best Bitter; guest beers H
This 15th-century picturesque thatched pub in a classic Oxfordshire village is comfortably furnished in traditional style. It features an imaginative, humorous menu, and an attractive terraced garden. A warm welcome is assured in both bars.
🏚Q🕸◗♣🅿

SYDENHAM
Crown
Sydenham Road (off B4445, between Thame and

Chinnor, near M40 jct 6)
OS729018
☎ (01844) 351634
12-3, 6-11; Sun hours vary
Morrells Bitter, Varsity; guest beers H
Dating from 1680 in a quiet farming village off the beaten track, the cosy, low-beamed single large bar offers good food from snacks to a full à la carte menu. Eve meals served Tue-Sat.
🏚Q🕸◗♣🅿

THAME
Swan Hotel
9 Upper High Street
☎ (01844) 261211
11-11; 12-10.30 Sun
Brakspear Bitter; Hook Norton Best Bitter; guest beers H
Welcoming, market town hotel, featuring unusual furniture and fittings, and a two constantly changing guest beers. Note the Tudor painted ceiling in the excellent restaurant. Bar meals are also available.
🏚🍴◗

Try also: Abingdon Arms, Cornmarket (Free)

WALLINGFORD
Kings Head
2 St Martin's Street (A329, near A4130 jct)
☎ (01491) 838309
11-11; 12-10.30 Sun
Brakspear Bitter, seasonal beers H
Popular, one-bar, modern, town-centre pub where families are welcome until 4pm. ♣🅿

WANTAGE
Abingdon Arms
87 Grove Street (A338)
☎ (01235) 763957
12.30 (11.30 Fri)-2.30; 7-11; 12-4.30, 7-10.30 Sun
Greene King Abbot, Triumph; Morland Original H
Welcoming traditional pub where a quiet, relaxing atmosphere prevails. A fenced garden area is ideal for young children. Close to the town centre. Sandwiches are usually available.
🏚Q🕸♣🅿

Royal Oak
Newbury Street (near Market Place)
☎ (01235) 763129
12-2.30 (not Mon-Thu), 5.30 (7 Sat)-11; 12-2, 7-10.30 Sun
Draught Bass; G **Wadworth 6X;** H/G **West Berkshire Maggs' Mild,** G **Dr Hexter's Wedding Ale, Dr Hexter's Healer;** H/G **guest beers** G
Popular, lively free house, where varied clientele

celebrate beer with a knowledgeable landlord. CAMRA Regional *Pub of the Year* 1999. West Berkshire Brewery predominate here. Lunch available Fri.
🍴🍷

Try also: **Volunteer**, Station Rd, Grove (Hook Norton)

WEST HANNEY
Lamb Inn
School Road (off A338)
☎ (01235) 868917
11-3, 6-11; 12-3, 7-10.30 Sun
Draught Bass; Oakham JHB; Shepherd Neame Spitfire; Young's Special; guest beers H
Excellent free house where the landlord provides tasting notes on beers. Deservedly popular, it serves good food. Its August Bank Holiday beer festival is now well established. It hosts live jazz every fortnight. Local CAMRA *Pub of the Year* 1997 and '99. Limited parking.
Q🕸◗🅿

WIGGINTON
White Swan Inn
Pretty Bush Lane (off A361, follow signs for waterfowl sanctuary)
☎ (01608) 737669
12-11; 12-3, 7-10.30 Sun
Hook Norton Mild, Best Bitter; guest beers H
Traditional stone country pub with a quarry-tiled bar area. An interesting menu features O'Hagan's sausages. Walkers, children and pets are all welcome. Cider is sold in summer.
🏚Q🕸◗♣🍷🅿

WOODSTOCK
Queen's Own
59 Oxford Street
☎ (01993) 813582
12-2.30, 6-11; 12-11 Sat; 12-10.30 Sun
Ushers Best Bitter, Founders, seasonal beers H
Friendly, single-bar pub welcoming to locals and visitors alike.
🏚🕸◗♣

Try also: Rose & Crown, Oxford St (Morrells)

WOOTTON (NEAR WOODSTOCK)
Killingworth Castle
Glympton Road (B4027, N of Woodstock)
☎ (01993) 811401
12-2.30,6.30-11; 12-3, 7-10.30 Sun
Morland Original; Ruddles Best Bitter; guest beers H
Picturesque, 17th-century inn with a long, spacious bar

CAMRA National Pub Inventory: Olde Trip to Jerusalem, Nottingham

featuring simple wooden
furniture, candles on the
tables and a log fire.
There is a small family
room, plus a games room
with a pool table. Welcoming
licensees maintain
high standards. Local folk
and professional jazz eves
staged.
🏠 Q ♿ 🐕 🍴 ◖◗ & ▲ ♣ P

260

INDEPENDENT BREWERIES

Brakspear: Henley-on-Thames

Hook Norton: Hook Norton

Plough Inn: Bodicote

Wychwood: Witney

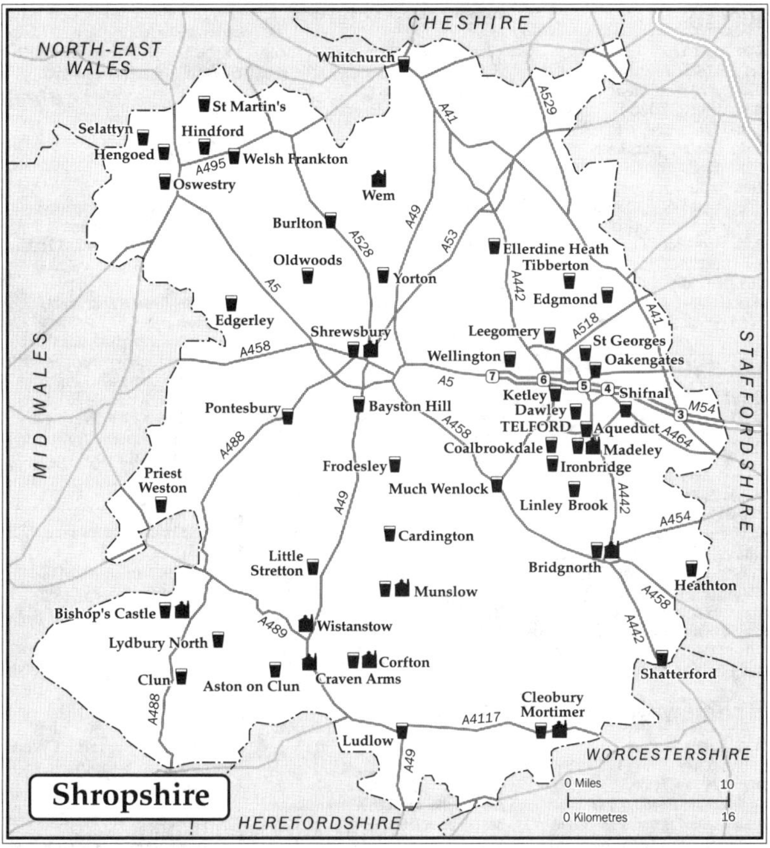

ASTON ON CLUN

Kangaroo

On B4368, off A49, 2 miles W of Craven Arms OS503981
☎ (01588) 660263
12-3 (not Mon & Tue), 7-11; 12-11 Fri & Sat; 12-10.30 Sun
Wells Bombardier; guest beers Ⓗ
Cosy village pub with warm, friendly atmosphere. It has a games room and large garden. Home-cooked menu includes occasional international themed eves. Roo Brew comes from Six Bells Brewery.
⩩ ❀ ◐ ◑ ⊟ ♿ ⇌ (Broome) ♣ P ⍻

BAYSTON HILL

Compasses

Hereford Road (A49)
☎ (01743) 872921
5 (12 Fri & Sat)-11; 12-10.30 Sun
Draught Bass; M&B Brew XI; guest beers Ⓗ
Traditional pub retaining a separate snug and bar. The garden overlooking the village green is suitable for families. An occasional cider is stocked.
Q ❀ ⊟ ♿ ♣ P ⍻

BISHOPS CASTLE

Castle Hotel

Market Square
☎ (01588) 638403
12-2.30, 6.30-11; 12-10.30 Sun
Draught Bass; Hobsons Best Bitter; Six Bells Big Nev's; guest beer Ⓗ
Fine country town hotel: a snug bar boasting original woodwork, a larger room off and a public bar. Excellent home-cooked food served. It has a large, pleasant garden.
⩩ Q ❀ ⛟ ◐ ◑ ♣ P

Six Bells

Church Street
☎ (01588) 630144
12-2.30 (not Mon or winter Tue), 5-11; 12-11 Sat; 12-10.30 Sun
Six Bells Big Nev's, Marathon, Cloud Nine, seasonal beer Ⓗ
This 17th-century coaching inn is the tap for the Six Bells Brewery. A friendly local, it enjoys a solid reputation for intresting home-cooked food (lunch Thu-Sun, eves Fri & Sat). Shropshire CAMRA *Pub of the Year* 1999 and regional winner 2000. Cider in summer.
⩩ Q ❀ ◐ ◑ ♿ ♣ ⍾ P

BRIDGNORTH

Bear

Northgate (in Hightown)
☎ (01746) 763250
11-2.30 (10-3 Fri & Sat), 5 (6 Sat)-11; 12-2.30, 7-10.30 Sun
Batham Mild, Best Bitter; Boddingtons Bitter; guest beers Ⓗ
Comfortable town pub, with two lounges, attracting adult drinkers. Good food lunchtimes and gourmet nights (Thu). Local beers feature as guests.
Q ❀ ⛟ ◐ ♿ ▲ ⇌ (SVR) P

Railwaymans Arms

Platform 1, Bridgnorth Railway Station, Hollybush Road (SVR station)
☎ (01746) 763461
12-2 (11-3.30 summer), 7-11; 11-11 Sat; 12-10.30 Sun
Batham Mild, Best Bitter; guest beers Ⓗ
Bar in the old station buildings, the older part is the original railway refreshment rooms. Displaying much railway memorabilia, it is a haunt for the railway's volunteers.
⩩ Q ❀ ♿ ⇌ (SVR) ♣ ⍾ P

BURLTON

Burlton Inn

On A528 Shrewsbury-Ellesmere road near B4397 jct
☎ (01939) 270284

11-3, 6-11; 12-3.30, 7-10.30 Sun

Banks's Bitter; guest beers H

Attractive country pub near the North Shropshire lakes offering a wide selection of home-made food based on local produce. Three constantly changing guest ales provide an interesting selection.
🏚 Q 🖛 🕕 🗈 🛦 ♣ P

CARDINGTON

Royal Oak

☎ (01694) 771266

12-2.30, 7-11 (closed Mon); 12-2.30, 7-10.30 Sun

Draught Bass; Hobsons Best Bitter; Marston's Pedigree; Wood Shropshire Lad H

At the eastern edge of the village, giving views across rolling countryside, this attractive, low-beamed pub features a huge open fireplace and wooden settles. No meals Sun eve.
🏚 Q 🛞 🕕 🛦 ♣ P 🚭

CLEOBURY MORTIMER

Old Lion Inn

Lower Street (A4117)
☎ (01299) 270085

4 (12 Sat)-11; 12-10.30 Sun

Hobsons Best Bitter, Town Crier, Old Henry; guest beers H

Old pub, comprising a lounge with a raised dining area, plus a small bar. The main outlet for Hobsons beer. The meals are mostly based on local produce (lunches served weekends, no eve meals Sun).
🏚 🕕 🛦 ♣

CLUN

White Horse

The Square
☎ (01588) 640305

11.30-3, 6.30-11; 12-4, 7-10.30 Sun

Theakston Best Bitter; guest beer H

Comfortable local at the centre of a timeless village, with a single L-shaped bar. A good range of board games is provided to welcome families. The food is home made. One local guest beer plus one other on tap. Secluded garden.
🏚 🛞 🕕 ♣

CORFTON

Sun Inn

On B4368, Bridgnorth-Craven Arms road
☎ (01584) 861239

11-2.30, 6-11; 12-3, 7-10.30 Sun

Corvedale Norman's Pride; guest beers H

17th-century family-run inn with award-winning facilities for customers with disabilities. Set in scenic Corvedale, the pub acts as a tourist information point, and serves a wide range of good value meals. The garden houses a micro-brewery. Children's certificate. 🏚 Q 🕕 🗈 🖧 🛦 ⌂ ♣ P 🚭 🗂

EDGERLEY

Royal Hill

W of A5 at Nescliffe
OS352175 ☎ (01743) 741242

12-2 (not winter; 12-3 Sat), 6.30-11; 12-2, 7-10.30 Sun

Salopian Shropshire Gold, Minsterley Ale H

Single-bar, 17th-century riverside pub, popular with anglers and canoeists. There's a traditional bar with wooden seats and open fire and a more comfortable living room-style lounge. The garden affords views across the River Severn.
🏚 Q 🍺 🛞 🖧 🛦 ♣ P

EDGMOND

Lion

1 Newport Road (1/4 mile off B5062) ☎ (01952) 813036

12-3 (not Mon-Fri), 6-11; (11-11 summer Sat); 12-10.30 Sun

Tap & Spile Best Bitter; Worthington Bitter; guest beer H

Village pub frequented by all ages with a bar lounge and no-smoking dining area. The large garden houses an aviary. Good food on a varying menu at very reasonable prices is served weekend lunches and Tue-Sat eve. 🏚 🛞 🕕 🗄 P

ELLERDINE HEATH

Royal Oak

Midway between A442 and A53 OS603226
☎ (01952) 250300

12-3, 5-11; 11-11 Sat; 12-3, 7-10.30 Sun

Hanby Drawwell; Hobsons Best Bitter; Shepherd Neame Spitfire; guest beers H

Popular country pub that offers excellent value food and beer. Also known as the 'Tiddlywink', possibly due to its small size. No food Tue.
🏚 🛞 🕕 🛦 ♣ ⌂ P

FRODESLEY

Swan Inn

☎ (01694) 731208

7 (6 Fri)-11; 12-2.30, 7-7.30 Sun

Boddingtons Bitter; Hook Norton Best Bitter; Worthington Bitter; guest beer H

Welcoming village local

where the bar is divided into separate drinking areas. Close to the South Shropshire hills; walkers are welcome. Eve meals served Wed-Sat 7-9.
🏚 🛞 🕽 🛦 ♣ P

HEATHTON

Old Gate

Between B4176 and A458 near Halfpenny Green
OS814923 ☎ (01746) 710431

12-2.30 (not Mon), 6.30-11; 12-3, 6.30-10.30 Sun

Enville Ale; Greene King Abbot; Tetley Bitter H

Busy, country pub, off the beaten track: two rooms with exposed beams and log fires. Families welcome – the large garden has a children's play area. An exceptional menu is based on local produce.
🏚 🛞 🕕 🛦 ⌂ P

HENGOED

Last Inn

Off B4579 3 miles N of Oswestry OS680979
☎ (01691) 659747

7-11; 12-3, 7-10.30 Sun

Boddingtons Bitter; guest beers H

Rural pub in attractive Welsh borderland, offering a varied selection of guest beers. Families are well provided for; good food is served Wed-Mon eve and Sun lunch.
🏚 Q 🍺 🕽 ♣ ⌂ P

HINDFORD

Jack Mytton Inn

☎ (01691) 679861

12-3, 6-11 (12-11 summer); closed winter Mon; 12-3, 6-10.30 Sun

Beer range varies H

Cosy rural hostelry on the popular Llangollen Canal. A former farmhouse, it is named after an infamous, flamboyant local landowner and known locally as 'Mad Jacks'. A large garden, three ales and an extensive well-appointed restaurant are added attractions.
🏚 Q 🛞 🕕 🖧 🛦 P

LINLEY BROOK

Pheasant

Britons Lane (off B4373, Bridgnorth-Broseley road)
OS680979
☎ (01746) 762260

12-2.30 (3 Sat), 6.30 (7 winter)-11; 12-3, 6.30 (7 summer)-10.30 Sun

Beer range varies H

In an idyllic rural setting and committed to real ale, this inn is described by the landlord as a throwback in time. Over the years, out went the juke box, in came bar billiards.
🏚 Q 🛞 🕕 ♣ P

LITTLE STRETTON
Ragleth
Ludlow Road (parallel to A49)
☎ (01694) 722711
12-2.30, 6-11; 12-11 Sat; 12-10.30 Sun
Brains Bitter; Hobsons Best Bitter; guest beers Ⓗ
In walking country, this 17th-century inn permits dogs, boots and children in the bar which has an inglenook, dark woodwork and a brick and tiled floor. A lounge and restaurant, 70 malt whiskies and attractive garden add to its appeal.
🏚 Q 🏶 ◑ ▶ 🏳 Å ♣ P

LUDLOW
Charlton Arms Hotel
Ludford Bridge
☎ (01584) 872813
12-3, 6.30-11; 12-11 Sat; 12-10.30 Sun
Hobsons Best Bitter; guest beers Ⓗ
Smart, country town hotel towards the edge of Ludlow. Its garden overlooks the River Teme. Five guest beers include local brews; perry stocked in summer.
🏚 🏶 ⇌ ◑ ◖ 🚋 ♣ ⌂ P 🏳

Nelson Inn
Rocks Green (A4117 Kidderminster road)
☎ (01584) 872908
12-3 (not Tue), 7-11; 12-11 Fri & Sat; 12-10.30 Sun
Banks's Original; Flowers Original; guest beers Ⓗ
Two-roomed local; the lounge displays musical instruments for use by locals taking part in spontaneous weekend music sessions. The public bar offers four-ring quoits. Three guest beers on tap, plus cider in summer.
🏚 🏶 ◑ Å ≈ ♣ ⌂ P 🏳

LYDBURY NORTH
Powis Arms
☎ (01588) 680254
12-2 (not Mon), 12-3 Sat), 7-11; 12-3, 7-10.30 Sun
Six Bells Big Nev's; Tetley Bitter; guest beer Ⓗ
Friendly pub in a village close to Bishops Castle. Run by two sisters who put a lot of effort into cooking and presenting meals, which include speciality nights, served in an attractive dining room. ⇌ ◑ ▶ 🏳 Å P

MUCH WENLOCK
George & Dragon
2 High Street (opp. Spar shop) ☎ (01952) 727312
12-2.30, 6-11 (12-11 school hols); 12-2.30, 7-10.30 Sun
Hook Norton Best Bitter; guest beers Ⓗ

Popular, unspoilt local offering an ever-changing range of guest beers from Shropshire and beyond. Good food is served in the bar and restaurant (phone for eve meal times). An unassuming frontage leads into a traditional bar.
Q ◑ ▶ ♣

MUNSLOW
Crown Inn
On B4368, Bridgnorth-Craven Arms road
☎ (01584) 841205
12-2.30, 7-11; 12-3, 7-10.30 Sun
Crown Butcher's Best; Shepherd Neame Spitfire Ⓗ
Old Hundred house inn with an unspoilt Tudor interior, and a warm, welcoming atmosphere. See the micro-brewery next to the bar. An excellent menu, using only fresh ingredients, features French and Thai dishes. Facilities include a secluded garden and children's certificate. 🏚 🏶 ⇌ ◑ ▶ ♣ P

OLD WOODS
Romping Cat
☎ (01939) 290273
11-3 (not Wed or Fri, 12.30-3.30 Sat), 7-10.30; 12-2.30, 7-10.30 Sun
Boddingtons Bitter; Fuller's London Pride; Greene King Abbot; guest beers Ⓗ
Rural pub, popular with locals and townspeople. Well known locally for the quality and variety of its beers.
🏚 Q 🏶 ♣ P 🏳

OSWESTRY
Black Gate
7 Salop Road
☎ (01691) 653168
12-3 (not Thu), 6.30-11; 12-3, 7-10.30 Sun
Thwaites Mild, Bitter, Chairman's; guest beers Ⓗ
Dated 1612 this Grade II listed timber-framed free house stands just outside the erstwhile town wall gate. It has only been a pub since 1995, comprising a timber-floored bar and cosy lounge.
Q ♣

PONTESBURY
Horseshoes Inn
Minsterley Road
☎ (01743) 790278
12-3, 6-11; 12-4, 7-10.30 Sun
Castle Eden Ale; Fuller's London Pride; guest beers Ⓗ
Busy, friendly local in a large village, conveniently placed for walking in the south Shropshire hills. Very active in local games leagues, it stocks two guest beers.
🏶 ◑ ▶ ♣ P

PRIEST WESTON
Miners Arms
OS293973
☎ (01938) 561352
11-4, 7-11; 12-4, 7-10.30 Sun
Fuller's London Pride; Six Bells Big Nev's; Worthington Bitter Ⓗ
Remote country pub, still largely unspoilt. Very much a community pub it also draws walkers visiting the nearby stone circle. Don't miss the indoor well. It hosts monthly folk singing (first Wed).
🏚 🏶 ◑ 🚋 Å ♣ P

SELLATTYN
Cross Keys ☆
Glyn Road (B4519, Ceiriog road, 3 miles N of Oswestry)
☎ (01691) 650247
12-3, 7-11; 12-3, 7-10.30 Sun
Banks's Original, Bitter Ⓗ
Superb, 17th-century truly local village hostelry of small rooms, convenient for Offa's Dyke footpath. Opening hours may vary.
🏚 Q 🐕 🏶 ⇌ Å ♣ P

SHATTERFORD
Red Lion
Bridgnorth Road (A442)
☎ (01299) 861221
11.30-2.30, 6.30-11; 12-3, 7-10.30 Sun
Banks's Original, Bitter; Ⓟ
Batham Best Bitter; guest beers Ⓗ
Smart, family-owned free house: two bars (one no-smoking) and restaurant. It enjoys a justified reputation for superb food to suit all tastes from sandwiches to chef's specials and fresh fish. Wheelchair WC.
🏚 Q 🏶 ◑ ▶ 🚋 P 🍴

SHIFNAL
White Hart
4 High Street
☎ (01952) 461161
12-3, 6-11; 12-11 Fri & Sat; 12-10.30 Sun
Ansells Bitter; Enville Chainmaker Mild, Simpkiss Bitter, Ale; Ind Coope Burton Ale; guest beers Ⓗ
This attractive half-timbered 17th-century inn always features strongly in local CAMRA polls. Also noted for home-prepared lunches, the pub is a rare outlet for Chainmaker Mild.
🏶 ◑ ≈ ♣ ⌂ P

SHREWSBURY
Admiral Benbow
24 Swan Hill
☎ (01743) 352796
12-3 (not Mon or Tue), 7-11, 12-11 Sat; closed lunch, 7-10.30 Sun
Greene King Abbot; guest beers Ⓗ
17th-century listed building named after a local historical

figure. The L-shaped bar is popular with motorcycle enthusiasts, ale drinkers and regulars. The cobbled courtyard is popular in summer. Up to five guest beers. 🏨 🏶 ◖🛏 ⟐ �· ⚓ ✠

Albert Hotel
Smithfield Road
☎ (01743) 358198
11-11; 12-3, 8-10.30 Sun
Banks's Original, Bitter; Camerons Strongarm; Marston's Pedigree; guest beer H
Ideally placed for both rail and bus stations; a small lounge area lies off the public bar. It hosts regular special events, including clairvoyant eves. ◖🛏 ⟐ ⚓ �· ⟐ 🗗

Armoury
Victoria Avenue
☎ (01743) 340525
12-11; 12-10.30 Sun
Boddingtons Bitter; Wadworth 6X; Wood Shropshire Lad; guest beers H
The building served as an armoury in 1806; it was moved to its present site in 1922. In 1995 it was renovated and renamed the Armoury. A spacious, large single room is furnished with large tables and chairs, displaying local memorabilia.
🏨 Q ◖🛏 ⚃ �· ⚓

Boat House
New Street, Port Hill
☎ (01743) 362965
11-11; 12-10.30 Sun
Boddingtons Bitter; Flowers IPA; Greene King Abbot; guest beers H
Hogshead pub which can be reached by footbridge from Quarry Park. Its terraced garden overlooks the River Severn. Guest beers include a local offering; also a good selection of Belgian beers, plus an extensive wine list.
🏨 Q 🏶 ◖🛏 �· ⚓ ⟐ P ✠

Coach & Horses
Swan Hill
☎ (01743) 365661
11-11; 12-10.30 Sun
Draught Bass; guest beers H
Unspoilt Victorian pub with a wood-panelled bar. The sympathetically extended lounge acts as a lunchtime restaurant (booked parties only eves). The Goodalls Gold house beer is from Salopian. Q ◖🛏 �· ⟐

Dolphin
48 St Michael Street
☎ (01743) 350419
5 (3 Fri & Sat); 5-10.30 Sun
Beer range varies H
Early gaslit drinking house boasting a porticoed entrance and its original layout. Up to five ales and an occasional cider stocked, plus a good

range of specialist coffee.
Q ⚃⚐🛏 ⟐ ⟐

Loggerheads ☆
1 Church Street
☎ (01743) 355457
11-11; 12-3, 7-10.30 (varies summer) Sun
Banks's Original, Bitter; Draught Bass; Camerons Strongarm; guest beers H
Popular town-centre local of four distinct rooms: the public bar is easily the smallest in town; don't miss the gentleman's room.
Q ◖🛏 ⚃� �·⚓ 🗗

Nags Head
22 Wyle Cop
☎ (01743) 362455
11.30-11; 12-10.30 Sun
Draught Bass; guest beers H
Often lively, reputedly haunted, historic house of considerable architectural interest. Three guest beers come mainly from Carlsberg-Tetley. 🏶 ⊖ ⚓

Try also: Olde Bucks Head, The Mount (Bass)

ST MARTINS
Greyhound Inn
Overton Road (B5069)
☎ (01691) 774307
12-11; 12-10.30 Sun
Banks's Original; Morland Old Speckled Hen; Webster's Yorkshire Bitter H
Delightful, refurbished, popular rural pub. The bar displays artefacts from the local closed Ifton Colliery. The extensive outdoor play area affords views of the Welsh hills. The home-made meals are popular.
🏨 Q 🏶 ◖🛏 ⚃ 🖎 A ⚓ P

TELFORD: AQUEDUCT
Britannia
Aqueduct Road
☎ (01952) 591488
12-3, 6-11; 11.30-11 Sat; 12-3.30, 7-10.30 Sun
Banks's Original, Bitter, seasonal beers P **guest beers** H
Deceptively large, two-roomed pub circa 1860, which serves the community with regular charity events. Bank's and Marston's Festival range sold. The venue for local historical society meetings.
Q 🏶 ⚃🖎 A ⚓ P 🗗

COALBROOKDALE
Coalbrookdale Inn
12 Wellington Road (near Museum of Iron)
☎ (01952) 433953
12-3, 6-11; 12-3, 7-10.30 Sun
Courage Directors; Fuller's London Pride; guest beers H

Excellent traditional pub, the deserving winner of many awards, it offers a superb extensive range of beer in a convivial atmosphere. Mouth-watering international menu (not served Sun). Winter fires, summer flowers. Small car park.
🏨 ⚘ 🏶 ◖🛏 ⚓ ⟐ P ✠

PAWLEY
Three Crowns
Hinksay Road (off B4373, at Finger Rd garage)
☎ (01952) 590868
11.30-3 (4 Sat), 6.30-11; 12-3, 7.30-10.30 Sun
Marston's Bitter, Pedigree, HBC H
Small town pub with just the one room, part of which is given over to darts and pool. The pub is close to Telford Town Park with good lakeside walks and nature trails. 🏶 ◖ A ⚓ P

IRONBRIDGE
Golden Ball
1 Newbridge Road (off B4373 at Jockey Bank)
☎ (01952) 432179
12-3, 6-11; 12-3, 7-10.30 Sun
Courage Directors; Marston's Pedigree; Ruddles Best Bitter H
Traditional pub: lots of beams and fireplaces, and boasting panoramic views. Handy for the museum site. It serves good quality and value food. No juke box or game machines but occasional live music. The house beer, Ironmaster is from the Crown brew-pub. A retreat from the modern world. 🏨 🏶 🖎 ◖🛏 ⚓ P 🗗

Robin Hood
33 Waterloo Street (B4373)
☎ (01952) 433100
11.30-3, 6.30-11; 11-11 Sat; 12-10.30 Sun
Banks's Original; Theakston XB; guest beers H
This friendly, attractive two-bar pub keeps six real ales and regularly features Shropshire beers; a 2000 local CAMRA *Pub of the Season* winner. A riverside location, and good food are attractions.
🏶 🖎 ◖🛏 ⟐ P ✠

KETLEY
Compasses Inn
Beverley Road (off B5061)
☎ (01952) 617997
11-11; 12-10.30 Sun
Banks's Original; Enville Saaz; Marston's Pedigree; Salopian Golden Thread; guest beers (occasional) H
Family-run free house. A varied reasonably-priced menu caters for all tastes,

including vegetarian. It hosts weekend entertainment.
♨ ◖◗ ⊟ ♣ P ⊓

Pear Tree Bridge Inn
Holyhead Road (B5061, between A442 and A518)
☎ (01952) 414526
12-4 (not Mon-Fri), 6 (7 Sat)-11; 12-4, 7-10.30 Sun
Worthington Bitter; guest beers [H]
A warm welcome is assured at this one-roomed pub, where a friendly husband and wife team have taken the pub from closure to become a local CAMRA award-winning real ale house. Up to six real ales offered.
Q ♿ ⇌ (Oakengates) ♣ P

LEEGOMERY

Malt Shovel
Hadley Park Road (off A442)
☎ (01952) 242963
12-2.30, 5-11; 12-3, 7-10.30 Sun
Banks's Bitter; Camerons Bitter; Ind Coope Burton Ale; Marston's Pedigree [H]
Traditional pub where conversation is the loudest noise. It offers a varied home-cooked menu at reasonable prices, weekdays. A pub to relax in, winner of a local CAMRA award.
♨ Q ❀ ◖ ⊟ ♣ P ⊓

MADELEY

Forresters Arms
41 High Street (off A442)
☎ (01952) 581767
12-3, 6-11; 12-11 Fri & Sat; 12-10.30 Sun
Draught Bass; Worthington Bitter; guest beers [H]
Refurbished in recent years, after being gutted by fire, its two intimate bars are adorned with bric-à-brac and photographs of old Madeley. Close to Blists Hill Museum.
♨ ❀ ◖ ▲ ♣ P

Royal Oak
High Street (off A442)
☎ (01952) 585598
12-4 (not Mon-Thu), 5-11; 12-4, 7-10.30 Sun
Draught Bass; Burtonwood Top Hat; Castle Eden Bitter; Worthington Bitter; guest beers [H]
Locals' pub with a strong leaning towards darts and a small, intimate lounge. Lively conversation is the norm. Handy for nearby Blists Hill Museum. ♨ ⊟ ♿ ▲ ♣ P

OAKENGATES

Crown Inn
Market Street
☎ (01952) 610888
12-3, 7-11; 12-11 Thu-Sat; 12-3.30, 7-10.30 Sun
Hobsons Best Bitter; guest beers [H]
A traditional wood-floored market town pub of three distinct drinking areas. It offers 250-300 different beers per year and hosts a new beers festival, twice a year featuring 29 handpulls. Live music Thu eve. ♨ ⚲ ❀ ⊟ ⇌ (Oakengates) ♣ ⌓ P ⊁

ST GEORGES

Albion
Station Hill (between Oakengates and St Georges)
☎ (01952) 614193
12-2.30, 5-11; 12-4, 7-11 Sat; 12-4, 7-10.30 Sun
Banks's Original; Marston's Bitter, Pedigree; seasonal beers [H]
Excellent example of a traditional one-bar local where friendly staff and regulars create a wonderful atmosphere. The picturesque garden overlooks the Shropshire plain.
❀ 🛏 ⇌ (Oakengates) ♣ P

St Georges Sports & Social Club
Church Road
☎ (01952) 612911
7 (12 Sat)-11; 12-4, 7-10.30 Sun
Banks's Original, Bitter; Enville Ale; guest beers [H]
Large, popular club that fields numerous teams. Comfortable and welcoming, it was voted regional CAMRA *Club of the Year* 1997. Guest beers are usually locally sourced. Entry on production of this *Guide* or a CAMRA card.
❀ ♿ ♣ P

WELLINGTON

Cock Hotel
Holyhead Road (B5061)
☎ (01952) 244954
4 (12 Thu-Sat)-11; 12-3, 7-10.30 Sun
Bateman Mild; Hobsons Best Bitter; guest beers [H]
An 18th-century former coaching inn, the Cock is a classic English ale house. An independent free house, it stocks up to eight real ales in its traditional bar. CAMRA local *Pub of the Year* 1998, '99 and 2000. ♨ Q ❀ 🛏 ⊟ ⇌ (Wellington) ♣ P ⊁ ⊓

TIBBERTON

Sutherland Arms
High Street (1 mile off B5062)
☎ (01952) 550533
12-2.30, 6-11; 12-11 Sat; 12-10.30 Sun
Banks's Original; Marston's Bitter, Pedigree, HBC [H]
Typical village pub with various drinking areas and a dining area. It is a cosmopolitan pub, very popular with students. It offers an excellent selection of malt whiskies and good value food (eve meals Tue-Sat). ♨ ❀ ◖◗ ⊟ ♣ P

WELSH FRANKTON

Narrow Boat Inn
Ellesmere Road (A495 Oswestry road)
☎ (01691) 661051
11-3, 6-11; 12-3, 6-10.30 Sun
Beer range varies [H]
Rural, former canal house, alongside Llangollen Canal. Waterways exhibits provide the theme. Boats available to hire from the adjacent boatyard.
♨ Q ❀ ◖◗ ▲ P

WHITCHURCH

Red Cow
5 Pepper Street
☎ (01948) 664681
10-11; 12-10.30 Sun
Draught Bass; Worthington Bitter; guest beer [H]
Friendly pub down a side-street off the High Street, popular with locals and boaters from the canal. Three drinking areas, include a pool room. ♨ ❀ ⇌ ♣

YORTON

Railway Inn
Near station
☎ (01939) 220240
11.30-3, 6.30-11; 12-3.30, 7-10.30 Sun
Wood Parish, Special, Shropshire Lad; Salopian Golden Thread; Wadworth 6X; [H] **guest beers** [H]/[G]
Friendly pub in the same family for over 60 years. A simple bar contrasts with the well-appointed lounge which displays many trophies.
♨ Q ❀ ⇌ (Request Stop) P

INDEPENDENT BREWERIES

All Nations: Madeley (Future in doubt)

Corvedale: Crofton

Crown Inn: Munslow

Hanby: Wem

Hobsons: Cleobury Mortimer

Salopian: Shrewsbury

Six Bells: Bishop's Castle

Three Tuns: Bishop's Castle

Wood: Wistantow

Worfield: Bridgnorth

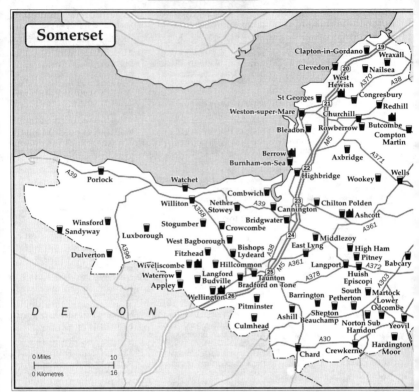

Somerset

Clapton-in-Gordano · Wraxall **19**
Clevedon **20** · Nailsea
West Hewish · A370 · A38
St Georges · Congresbury · Redhill
Weston-super-Mare **21** · Churchill
Bleadon · Rowberrow · Butcombe
Berrow · Compton Martin
Burnham-on-Sea **22** · Axbridge · A371
Highbridge · Wookey · Wells
Watchet · Combwich · A39 · Chilton Polden
Williton · Nether Stowey · Cannington **23** · Ashcott
Porlock · Stogumber · Bridgwater · A361
Winsford · Crowcombe · Middlezoy
Sandyway · Luxborough · West Bagborough **24** · East Lyng · High Ham
Dulverton · Fitzhead · Bishops Lydeard · Pitney · Babcary
Wiveliscombe · Hillcommon · Langport · Huish Episcopi
Waterrow · Langford Budville · Taunton **25** · South Petherton · Martock
Appley · Bradford on Tone · Barrington · Lower Odcombe
Wellington **26** · Pitminster · Shepton Beauchamp · Yeovil
Ashill · Norton Sub Hamdon
Culmhead · A30 · Hardington Moor
Chard · Crewkerne

D E V O N

0 Miles 10
0 Kilometres 16

APPLEY

Globe Inn ☆
2¹/₂ miles N of A38 at White Ball Hill OS071215
☎ (01823) 672327
11-2.30 (not Mon), 6.30-11; 12-3, 7-10.30 Sun

Cotleigh Tawny; guest beer [H]
Wonderful old inn, hidden away in the hills of the Devon border. Several cosy rooms lead off the brick-floored corridor bar area; one for diners, a second for families. The food is first class. Cider sold in summer.
🏔 Q 🛏 🕭 🌜 🍺 🌳 ♣ ⌂ P

ASHCOTT

Ring O'Bells
High Street (off A39)
☎ (01458) 210232
12-2.30, 7-11; 12-2.30, 7-10.30 Sun

Beer range varies [H]
Popular, multi-level village pub with a cosy bar area. The same superb, award-winning food is served here and in the restaurant. At least one beer comes from Moor Beer Co, plus two guests from micro-breweries.
🛏 🕭 🌜 🍺 ♿ ♣ ⌂ P

ASHILL

Square & Compass ☆
Windmill Hill (A358)

☎ (01823) 480467
12-3, 6.30-11; 12-3, 7-10.30 Sun

Exmoor Ale, Gold; guest beers [H]
Inviting, friendly country pub, where an excellent menu offers a wide choice of home-made food. Enjoy local walks nearby and the large garden.
🏔 Q 🛏 🌜 🍺 🅰 P

AXBRIDGE

Lamb
The Square
☎ (01934) 732253
11-11; 12-10.30 Sun

Butcombe Bitter, Gold; Wadworth 6X [H]
15th-century coaching inn at the centre of an historic market town. There are several beamed drinking areas, a dining room and a terraced garden.
Q 🌜 🛏 🌜 ♣

BABCARY

Red Lion
Main Street (signed off A37, 2 miles from A303)
☎ (01458) 223230
12-3, 5.30-11; 12-3, 7-10.30 Sun

Draught Bass; Otter Bitter, [H] **Bright;** [G] **guest beers** [H]
Typical village pub: a stone-flagged public bar and a cosy lounge bar with settles. Built of local stone under a

thatched roof, it has a nice garden at the rear. Eve meals served Tue-Sat.
Q 🌜 🕭 🍺 🌳 ♣ P

BARRINGTON

Royal Oak
Off B3168 between Ilminster and Curry Rivel
☎ (01460) 53455
12-3, 5.30-11; 11-11 Sat; 12-10.30 Sun

Fuller's London Pride; Greene King Abbot; Young's Bitter or Special [H]
Busy, traditional village pub where a lively atmosphere prevails. A lounge bar, public bar, games room and skittle alley make this pub popular with the local community.
🏔 🌜 🕭 🍺 🌳 ♣ ⌂ P

BATH

Bell
103 Walcot Street
☎ (01225) 460426
11.30-11; 12-3, 7-10.30 Sun

Abbey Bellringer, Bath Barnstormer; Courage Best Bitter; Fuller's London Pride; Smiles Best; guest beers [H]
Open-plan bar with a Bohemian atmosphere, renowned for its live music at least three times a week.
🌜 ⇌ ♣

Coeur de Lion
17 Northumberland Place

GLOUCESTERSHIRE & BRISTOL

WILTSHIRE

Keynsham
Saltford
Kelston
Chew Magna
Bath
Timsbury
Wellow
Norton St Philip
Hinton Blewitt
Midsomer Norton
Oakhill
Leigh upon Mendip
Rudge
Faulkland
Chelynch
Doulting
Wanstrow
West Cranmore
Witham Friary
East Woodlands
Frome
Bruton
Lovington
Bayford
Sparkford
Wincanton
Corton Denham

DORSET

☎ (01225) 463568
11-11; 12-8 Sun
Draught Bass; guest beers H
Reputably the smallest pub in Bath, featuring a large stained/frosted glass window. Three guest beers. ◖≢ (Spa)

Cross Keys Inn
Midford Road, Combe Down (B3110)
☎ (01225) 832002
11-2.30, 6-11; 11-3, 7-11 Sat; 12-3, 7-10.30 Sun
Courage Best Bitter; Gibbs Mew Bishops Tipple; Ushers Best Bitter, Founders, seasonal beers H
Attractive Bath stone roadhouse-type pub on the southern edge of the city, comprising two traditional bars. An aviary is a feature of the walled garden. Good value food available.
🚶🏠⊛◖▯⊟&P⌿🖫

Curfew
11 Cleveland Place West
☎ (01225) 424210
11-2.30, 5-11; 12-11 Sat; 12-10.30 Sun
Draught Bass; Badger Tanglefoot; Wadworth 6X; guest beer H
Pub with old wooden decor downstairs, plus an unusual, comfortable upstairs room furnished with sofas. A small, unexpected, vine-covered garden area is a bonus.
⊛◖♣

Hop Pole
Albion Buildings, Upper Bristol Road
☎ (01225) 446327
12-3, 5-11; 12-11 Fri & Sat; 12-10.30 Sun
Bath SPA, Gem, Barnstormer, seasonal beers (occasional) H
Popular pub, frequented by students, visitors and locals. Bath Ales second pub, sympathetically renovated, it is situated close to Victoria Park and the River Avon. A variety of foreign bottled beers is stocked, along with bottled organic cider.
🚶⊛◖♣

Lambretta's
10 North Parade
☎ (01225) 464650
11-11; 12-10.30 Sun
Abbey Bellringer; Banks's Bitter; Draught Bass; Marston's Pedigree; Smiles Best; guest beer H
Town-centre pub featuring wood panelling, bare boards, and a scooter in a glass case.
🏠◖≢(Spa)♣

Old Farmhouse
1 Landsdown Road
☎ (01225) 316162
12-11; 12-10.30 Sun
Abbey Bellringer; Badger Tanglefoot; Draught Bass; Butcombe Bitter; Wadworth IPA, 6X H
Friendly pub next to Abbey Ales Brewery. It hosts jazz nights several eves a week. Note the Symonds Brewery glasswork above the bar.
🚶⊛◖P

Old Green Tree ☆
12 Green Street
11-11 7-10.30 (closed lunch) Sun
Bath Barnstormer; Oakhill Black Magic Stout; RCH Pitchfork; Wickwar BOB; guest beers H
Lovely, city-centre classic, this pub has three wood panelled rooms, usually crowded. The beers are local. A gem.
Q≢(Spa)

Pulteney Arms
Daniel Street
☎ (01225) 463923
11.30-3, 5.30-11; 11-11 Sat; 12-10.30 Sun
Draught Bass; Smiles Best; Ushers Best Bitter; Wadworth 6X; guest beer H
Handsome Georgian corner pub, to which the Bath rugby crowd bring a lively atmosphere.
🚶⊛◖▯≢(Spa)♣

Ram
20 Claverton Bldgs, Widcombe (over footbridge from station)
☎ (01225) 421938
11-2.30, 5-11; 11-11 Fri & Sat; 12-7 Sun

Draught Bass; Smiles Best; Ushers Best Bitter H
Large, friendly local with warm wood panelling.
◖≢⌂

BAYFORD

Unicorn Inn
Off A303
☎ (01963) 32324
12-3, 7-11; 12-2 (closed eve) Sun
Butcombe Bitter; guest beers H
Coaching inn with flagstone floors and a log burning stove. The no-smoking dining area serves good food and a selection of wines.
🚶Q⊛🍴◖▯⌂P

BISHOPS LYDEARD

Lethbridge Arms
Gore Square (off A358 Taunton-Williton road)
☎ (01823) 432234
11-2.30, 6-11; 11-11 Sat; 12-10.30 Sun
Cotleigh Tawny; Marston's Pedigree; guest beer H
Large, 16th-century former coaching inn, offering a wide choice of home-cooked food. Popular with visitors to the nearby West Somerset Railway, children are welcome. Skittles played.
🚶⊛🍴◖⊟≢(West Somerset Railway)♣⌂P⌿

BLEADON

Queens Arms
Celtic Way (300 yds from A370, S of Weston-S-Mare)
☎ (01934) 812080
11-2.30, 5.30-11; 11-11 Sat; 12-10.30 Sun
Draught Bass; Badger Tanglefoot; Butcombe Bitter; G **Palmers BB,** H **IPA; Ringwood Old Thumper; guest beer** G
Now back as a free house after some time under Smiles' ownership and offering up to six beers from regional and independent breweries. An attractive and atmospheric low-beamed inn it is popular with locals and West Mendips walkers.
🚶Q⊛◖▯♣⌂P⌿

BRADFORD ON TONE

White Horse Inn
Off A38, between Taunton and Wellington
☎ (01823) 461239
11.30-3, 5-11; 12-3, 7-10-30 Sun
Cotleigh Tawny; Barn Owl; Juwards Bitter H
Set in the centre of a pretty village this pub has a large garden and a restaurant serving good food. The outbuildings house a post office/store.
Q⊛◖P

BRIDGWATER

Fountain Inn

West Quay (by Town Bridge)
☎ (01278) 424115
11-3, 6-11; 11-11 Fri & Sat; 12-3, 7-10-30 Sun
Badger Tanglefoot; Butcombe Bitter; Red Shoot Forest Gold; Wadworth IPA, 6X, seasonal beers; guest beers Ⓗ
One-room riverside pub serving up to seven ales; a friendly town-centre local where pictures of the town in days gone-by adorn the walls. Bar snacks available.
⇌ ♿ ♣

BRUTON

Royal Oak Inn

21-25 Coombe Street (B3081, Shepton Mallet road)
☎ (01749) 812215
12-2, 6-11; 12-3, 7-10-30 Sun
Butcombe Bitter; guest beers Ⓗ
This friendly free house keeps a house beer from Bath Ales (Sharpe's Brew) and serves good value food. There is plenty of room in the open plan bar. Limited parking.
Q ♘ ⛟ ◖◗ ⇌ ♣ P ⚟

BURNHAM-ON-SEA

Rosewood

Love Lane
☎ (01278) 780246
11-11; 12-10.30 Sun
Greene King Martha Greene, IPA, Abbot Ⓗ
Large roadside pub revamped as a Hungry Horse outlet. The bar has been divided into two areas: a food area with a bar where children are admitted, and a bar area with a sports theme featuring pool table, darts and a pull-down TV screen. Meals served all day.
❀ ◖◗ ♿ ▲ ♣ P ⚟

CANNINGTON

Malt Shovel Inn

Blackmoor Lane, Bradley Green (off A39, E of Cannington)
☎ (01278) 653432
11.30-3, 6.30 (7 winter)-11; 12-3, 7-10.30 Sun
Cotleigh Tawny; Exmoor Fox; guest beers Ⓗ
Family-run free house overlooking the Quantocks, boasting a large garden. No meals winter Sun eves.
♨ Q ♘ ❀ ⛟ ◖◗ ♿ ⌓ P

CHARD

Bell & Crown

Combe Street, Crimchard
☎ (01460) 62470
11-2.30 (not Mon), 7-11; 12-3, 7-10.30 Sun
Otter Bitter, Ale; guest beers Ⓗ
Gas lighting gives this popular local a good atmosphere. Value for money food and occasional beer festivals are added attractions. Eve meals served Tue-Sat.
Q ❀ ◖◗ ♣ P

CHELYNCH

Poachers Pocket

$1/2$ mile N of A361 at Doulting OS648438
☎ (01749) 880220
12-3, 6-11; 12-3, 7-10.30 Sun
Butcombe Bitter; Oakhill Best Bitter; Wadworth 6X; guest beer Ⓗ
Part 14th-century pub in a small village; a popular local. The large garden is well patronised.
♨ Q ❀ ◖◗ ♿ ♣ ⌓ P

CHEW MAGNA

Bear & Swan

13 South Parade
☎ (01275) 331100
11-11; 12-6 (closed eve) Sun
Butcombe Bitter; Courage Best Bitter; Otter Bitter Ⓖ
Extensively refurbished and strong on food, the pub also takes beer seriously, using proper cooling equipment. No eve meals Sun. Rare local Otter outlet.
♨ Q ❀ ◖◗

Try also: Pony & Trap, Newtown (Ushers)

CHILTON POLDEN

Toby Inn

Chilton Polden Hill (A39, 6 miles E of Bridgwater)
☎ (01278) 722202
12-3 (not winter Mon), 6-11; 12-3, 7-10.30
Cotleigh Tawny; Otter Bitter; guest beer (occasional) Ⓗ
Old wayside pub: a small, split-level bar and restaurant area, whose features include an inglenook, beams and natural stone walls. The restaurant/bar hosts monthly jazz sessions and offers good value home-cooked food.
Q ❀ ◖◗ ▲ P

Try also: Red Tile, Middle Rd, Cossington (Butcombe)

CHURCHILL

Crown Inn

The Batch, Skinners Lane (small lane S of A38/A368 jct)
☎ (01934) 852995
11.30-11 (may close Mon/Tue afternoon); 12-10.30 Sun
Draught Bass; Palmers IPA; RCH Hewish IPA, PG Steam; guest beers Ⓖ
This unspoilt stone pub of character supports small West Country breweries. Welcoming log fires burn in the two stone-floored bars. Good food. The house beer Batch Bitter is Cotleigh Harrier rebadged.
♨ Q ❀ ◖ ▲ P

CLAPTON-IN-GORDANO

Black Horse

Clevedon Lane OS472739
☎ (01275) 842105
11-3, 6-11; 11-11 Fri & Sat; 12-3, 7-10.30
Draught Bass; Ⓗ **Courage Best Bitter; Smiles Best; Webster's Yorkshire Bitter** Ⓖ
Delightful stone village local, dating from the 14th century. Flagstoned floors, beams and outdoor drinking areas add to its appeal; it can be busy, despite its relatively remote location. No food Sun.
♨ Q ♘ ❀ ◖ ♣ ⌓ P

CLEVEDON

Little Harp

Elton Road (near seafront)
☎ (01275) 343739
10.30-11; 12-10.30 Sun
Greene King IPA, Abbot; guest beer Ⓗ
Large, open-plan pub with a central bar, affording good views over the Severn to Wales. Food is served all day.
♘ ❀ ◖◗ ♣ P ⚟ ⊞

COMBWICH

Old Ship Inn

Ship Lane
☎ (01278) 652348
12-3, 7-11; 12-3, 7-10.30 Sun
Courage Directors; Oakhill Best Bitter; Teignworthy Reel Ale; guest beers Ⓗ
Old village pub in a lane leading down to the River Parret. A free house, it has a split-level, single bar/restaurant with inglenook and beams, sympathetically modernised, plus a skittle alley where children are admitted.
♨ Q ❀ ◖◗ P

COMPTON MARTIN

Ring O' Bells

Bath Road (A368)
☎ (01761) 221284
11.30-3, 6.30-11; 12-3, 7-10.30 Sun
Butcombe Bitter, Gold; Ⓗ **Wadworth 6X;** Ⓖ **guest beer** Ⓗ
Superb country inn which offers something for everyone; excellent, good value food complements the beer. Large garden and family room.
♨ Q ♘ ❀ ◖◗ ▲ ♣ P

CONGRESBURY

Plough

High Street (off A370)

☎ (01934) 832475
11-2.30, 5-11; 11-11 Sat; 12-4,
7-10.30 Sun
Draught Bass; P **Butcombe Bitter;** H **guest beers** P
Believed to be around 300 years old, the Plough has a part-flagstoned floor. Although the interior has been altered, it retains several drinking areas. Table skittles and shove-ha'penny played.
🚶 🌸 ♣ 👄 P

CORTON DENHAM
Queens Arms Inn
3 miles from A303, E of Sparkford
☎ (01963) 220317
12-2.30, 6.30-11; 11.30-2.30, 6-11 Sat & Summer; 12-3 (closed eve) Sun
Arkells BB; Cotleigh Tawny; guest beers H
The best selection of guest beers in this corner of Somerset; see the board in the lounge for the list. Excellent food served, too.
🚶 Q 🌸 🛏 👄 🌂 P

CREWKERNE
Crown
34 South Street
☎ (01460) 72464
6.30-11; 12-3, 7-10.30 Sun
Ringwood Old Thumper; guest beers H
17th-century former coaching inn with two bars, refurbished in traditional style. Good value B&B is offered.
🚶 🛏 🌂 ♣

CROWCOMBE
Carew Arms ☆
Signed from A358
☎ (01984) 618631
11.30-3, 6-11; 12.30-3, 7-11 Sun
Exmoor Ale; guest beers G
Unspoilt village pub; its flagstoned public bar is a good base for visiting the Quantocks. Good food and accommodation make it worth a visit.
🚶 Q 🐂 🌸 🛏 👄 🌂 👄 P

CULMHEAD
Holman Clavel
Through Blagdon Hill from Taunton, left at crossroads
☎ (01823) 421432
12-3, 5 (6 Sat)-11; 12-3, 7-10.30 Sun
Butcombe Bitter, Gold; guest beers H
14th-century, traditional, oak-beamed inn reputedly haunted by a resident ghost. A warm welcome is assured.
🚶 Q 🐂 🌸 👄 🅰 ♣ 👄 P ✂

DOULTING
Abbey Barn Inn
On A361, about 1 mile E of

Shepton Mallet
☎ (01749) 880321
12-2.30, 6-11; 12-2.30, 7-10.30 Sun
Draught Bass; Oakhill Best Bitter; Otter Bitter; guest beer (summer) H
Friendly, well-run pub of two comfortable bars, plus a skittle alley, named after a medieval tithe barn nearby.
🚶 🌸 👄 👄 🌂 👄

DULVERTON
Rock House Inn
1 Jury Road
☎ (013982) 323131
11-3, 6-11; 12-3, 7-10.30 (11 summer) Sun
Exmoor Ale; Flowers Original; Wadworth 6X; guest beers H
Traditional, welcoming, old stone pub at the top of this bustling edge-of-Exmoor town has competitively-priced beers. No food Tue.
🚶 Q 🐂 👄 🅰 ♣ 👄

EAST LYNG
Rose &Crown
On A361, 6 miles E of Taunton ☎ (01823) 698235
11-2.30, 6.30-11; 12-3, 7-10.30 Sun
Butcombe Bitter, Gold; Eldridge Pope Royal Oak H
This old village local has a timeless quality enhanced by comfortable antique furniture and a large stone fireplace. An extensive menu is available at all times; attractive garden.
🚶 Q 🌸 🛏 👄 🌂 ♣ P ✂

EAST WOODLANDS
Horse & Groom
1 mile SE of A361/B3092 jct OS792445
☎ (01373) 462802
11.30-2.30 (not Mon), 6.30-11; 12-3, 7-10.30 Sun
Butcombe Bitter; Wadworth 6X; guest beers G
17th-century inn on the western edge of the Longleat estate; a cosy bar with open fireplace and a flagstoned floor, plus a small dining room (no meals Sun eve or Mon). Two guest beers stocked. 🚶 Q 🌸 👄 🅰 ♣ P

FAULKLAND
Tuckers Grave ☆
On A366, 1 mile E of village
☎ (01373) 834230
11-3, 6-11; 12-3, 7-10.30 Sun
Draught Bass; Butcombe Bitter G
Built on the site of a suicide in 1747, this has been an inn for over 200 years. Consisting of three rooms, there is no bar; the beer is set up in a bay window. Enjoy the wonderful view from the garden. Popular with cyclists.
🚶 Q 🌸 🅰 ♣ 👄 P

FITZHEAD
Fitzhead Inn
Off B3187 at Milverton OS285124
☎ (01823) 400667
12-2.30, 7-11; 12-2.30, 7-10.30 Sun
Cotleigh Tawny; guest beer H
Cosy, village pub, used by regulars as well as visitors who are attracted by its good quality food.
🚶 Q 👄 🅰 👄

FROME
Griffin
Milk Street
☎ (01373) 467766
5 (11 Sat)-11; 12-10.30 Sun
Milk St Alchemy, Nicks, Zig Zag, Beer!; guest beer H
Bare, basic and popular, serving excellent beers from the attached Milk St Brewery.
🚶 🌸 ≈ ♣ 🍺

HARDINGTON MOOR
Royal Oak Inn
Moor Lane (off A30)
☎ (01935) 862354
12-2.30 (not Mon), 7-11; 12-2.30, 7-10.30 Sun
Butcombe Bitter; guest beers H
Former farmhouse offering a good choice of snacks and meals (not served Mon). Two parrots preside over this friendly pub.
🚶 Q 🌸 👄 ♣ 👄 P

HIGH HAM
Kings Head
Main Street (left off B3153 between Langport and Somerton)
☎ (01458) 250628
12-30.3 (not Mon, Wed or Fri), 6.30-11; 12-3, 7-10.30 Sun
Beer range varies H
Friendly village pub that offers something for everyone. All the real ales are sold at the same price.
🚶 🐂 🌸 👄 👄 🌂 ♣ P

HIGHBRIDGE
Coopers Arms
Market Street
☎ (01278) 783562
11-3.30, 5-11; 11-11 Fri & Sat; 12-3.30, 7.30-10.30 Sun
Adnams Broadside; Fuller's London Pride; RCH East Street Cream; guest beers H
Large pub where six ales are normally available (one is a house beer); two lounge areas and a bar with a skittle alley, pool table and dartboard.
🌸 🌂 🅰 ≈ ♣ P

HILLCOMMON
Royal Oak Inn
On B3227 between Taunton and Milverton

The Good Beer Guide 2001

☎ (01823) 400295
11.30-2.30, 7 (6 Fri)-11; 12-2.30,
7-10.30 Sun

Cotleigh Tawny; Exmoor Ale; guest beer ⓗ
This free house has a large garden and serves good food.
Q ⊛ ◑ ▶ ⓠ ⚓ P

HINTON BLEWITT
Ring of Bells
About 2 miles from A37 at Temple Cloud
☎ (01761) 452239
11-3.30, 5 (6 Sat)-11; 12-3, 7-10.30 Sun

Abbey Bellringer; Wadworth 6X; guest beers ⓗ
In a secluded village this small, friendly local offers an enterprising range of guest beers and good food; also cider in summer. Well worth the detour.
⚏ Q ⊛ ◑ ▶ ⚓ ⌂ P

HUISH EPISCOPI
Rose & Crown (Eli's) ☆
On A372, 1 mile E of Langport
☎ (01458) 250494
11.30-2.30, 5.30-11; 12-10.30 Sun

Draught Bass; Teignworthy Reel Ale; guest beers ⓗ
Completely unchanged, four-roomed pub with an open bar area, home-cooked snacks available.
Q ⚏ ⊛ ◑ ⚓ Å ⚓ ⌂ P

KELSTON
Old Crown
Bath Road (A431, 3 miles from Bath)
☎ (01225) 423032
11.30-2.30, 5-11; 11.30-11 Sat; 12-10.30 Sun

Draught Bass; Butcombe Bitter, Gold; Smiles Best; Wadworth 6X ⓗ
Superb, low-ceilinged, flagstoned pub owned by Butcombe Brewery. A friendly atmosphere and superb value home-cooked food are its hallmarks. The car park lies across a busy road. No children admitted. Eve meals served Tue-Sat.
⚏ Q ⊛ ⌧ ◑ ▶ P

KEYNSHAM
Ship Inn
93 Temple Street
☎ (0117) 986 9841
12-3, 6.30-11; 12-11 Sat; 12-10.30 Sun

Abbey Bellringer; Draught Bass; Courage Best Bitter; Worthington Bitter; guest beers ⓗ
Excellent ale house with a large main bar and a smaller lounge, plus a dining area for its popular food. It is frequented by keen darts and shove-ha'penny players. Usually two or three local

guest beers on tap. Small car park and garden.
⊛ ◑ ▶ ≈ ⚓ P ⊞

LANGFORD BUDVILLE
Martlet Inn
1/2 mile off B3187, between Wellington and Milverton
☎ (01823) 400262
12-2.30 (not Mon), 7-11; 12-3, 7-10.30 Sun

Cotleigh Tawny, Barn Owl; Exmoor Ale; guest beer (summer) ⓗ
Welcoming old village inn with an increasing reputation for good food. The main bar area has flagstones and a wood-burning stove with a second stove in the upper bar. The skittles alley doubles as a family room.
⚏ Q ⚏ ⊛ ◑ ▶ ⚓ P ⚐

LANGPORT
Black Swan Hotel
North Street
☎ (01458) 250355
11-2.30, 6-11; 12-4, 7-10.30 Sun

Exmoor Hart; Fuller's London Pride; guest beer ⓗ
Popular converted coaching inn comprising two bars, a restaurant and a function room for skittles. Home-cooked food is provided from a comprehensive menu.
Q ⊛ ◑ ▶ ⌧ ⌦ Å ⚓ ⌂ P

LEIGH UPON MENDIP
Bell
High Street
☎ (01373) 812316
12-3, 7-11; 12-3, 7-10.30 Sun

Draught Bass; Butcombe Bitter; Wadworth IPA, 6X; guest beer ⓗ
Much altered and extended village inn, now comfortably furnished, it places an emphasis on food trade. It has a restaurant, but food is served throughout the pub.
⚏ ⊛ ◑ ▶ ⌦ ⚓ P

LOWER ODCOMBE
Masons Arms
41 Lower Odcombe (off Yeovil-Montacute road at Greensleeves Nursery)
☎ (01935) 862591
12-3 (not Mon/Tue), 7-11; 12-3, 7-10.30 Sun

Butcombe Bitter; Otter Bright; guest beers ⓗ
Thatched pub, built in local hamstone, 500 years old; a true local, it is unpretentious, friendly and welcoming. It hosts an annual beer festival (Sept) and guest beers tend to be from West Country brewers. It boasts two skittle alleys.
⊛ ◑ ▶ Å ⚓ ⌂ P

LUXBOROUGH
Royal Oak of Luxborough
2 miles N of B3224
OS983378
☎ (01984) 640319
11-2.30, 6-11; 12-3, 7-10.30 Sun

Cotleigh Tawny; Exmoor Gold; Flowers IPA; guest beers ⓗ
Large rambling pub extended into the cottage next door to add a dining area. Well-kept beers are enhanced by the aroma of excellent food and real fires. This gem lies hidden away in the folds of Exmoor National Park.
⚏ Q ⚏ ⊛ ⌦ ◑ ▶ Å ⌂ P

MARTOCK
Nags Head
East Street (off B3165 at Pinnacle)
☎ (01935) 823432
12-2.30 (not Mon), 6-11; 12-3, 7-10.30 Sun

Otter Bitter; guest beers ⓗ
Traditional village pub offering home-cooked food and good value B&B in a self-contained annexe. No food Mon. Skittles played.
⊛ ⌦ ◑ ▶ ⌧ Å ⚓ P ⚐

MIDDLEZOY
George Inn
42 Main Road (1 mile from A372/A361 jct)
☎ (01823) 698215
12-2.30 (3 Sat; not Mon), 7-11; 12-3, 7-10.30 Sun

Butcombe Bitter; Hop Back Summer Lightning; guest beers ⓗ
17th-century, traditional village pub on the Somerset Levels, a favourite with anglers and birdwatchers. Home-cooked food (not served Sun eve) includes daily specials. Somerset CAMRA *Pub of the Year* 2000.
⚏ Q ⊛ ⌦ ◑ ▶ P ⚐

MIDSOMER NORTON
White Hart ☆
The Island
☎ (01761) 418270
11-11; 12-10.30 Sun

Draught Bass; Butcombe Bitter Ⓖ
Inside a slightly tatty exterior lies a superb multi-roomed Victorian pub. This is a classic.
Q ⚏ ⊛ ◑ ⚓ ⌂

NAILSEA
Blue Flame
West End OS449690
☎ (01275) 856910
12-3 (5 Sat), 6-11; 12-5, 7-10.30 Sun

Draught Bass; Fuller's London Pride; Smiles Best, Heritage; guest beer (summer) Ⓖ
On the outskirts of town, this is a wonderfully unspoilt and

270

SOMERSET

friendly cottage-style pub. The large pleasant garden hosts barbecues in summer. Guest beers are usually from local micro-breweries.
🚶 Q 🐾 🌸 ▲ ♣ ⌂ P

NETHER STOWEY

Rose & Crown
St Mary Street (off A39, Bridgwater-Minehead road)
☎ (01278) 732265
12-11; 12-5 Sun
Cotleigh Barn Owl; Cottage Golden Arrow; Moor Withy Cutter; guest beers Ⓗ
Welcoming 16th-century coaching inn at the village centre; the public bar and lounge enjoy a strong local following. The restaurant is open Wed-Sun serving local and home-grown produce.
🌸 🚐 ◁ ▶ 🍴 ⌂

NORTON ST PHILIP

Fleur de Lys
On B3110, about 1 1/2 miles from A36 jct
☎ (01373) 834333
11-3, 5-11; 11-11 Sat; 12-3, 7-10.30 Sun
Draught Bass; Oakhill Best Bitter; Worthington Bitter Ⓗ
This ancient stone building has been extensively but sympathetically refurbished. The re-sited bar is on the site of the old passageway through which the pub ghost reputedly passed on his way to the gallows.
🚶 Q ◁ ▶ ♣ ⌂ P

NORTON SUB HAMDON

Lord Nelson
Rectory Lane (1 1/2 miles S of A303)
☎ (01935) 881473
12-2.30, 6.30-11; 12-11 Sat; 12-10.30 Sun
Teignworthy Reel Ale; Worthington Bitter; guest beers Ⓗ
Converted hamstone farmhouse sympathetically refurbished; this popular village pub offers an extensive menu and interesting guest beers, along with regular live music.
🚶 🌸 ◁ ▶ ♣ ⌂ P ✗

PITMINSTER

Queens Arms
3 miles S of Taunton off B3170 OS219192
☎ (01823) 421529
11-11; 12-11 Sun
Cotleigh Tawny; Exmoor Gold; Juwards Premium; Otter Bitter Ⓗ
Cosy village pub selling locally brewed beers. The main bar is divided by a wood-burning stove. Home-made food is served in

the bar and restaurant (no food Sun eve).
🚶 Q 🐾 🌸 🚐 ◁ ▶ P

PITNEY

Halfway House
Pitney Hill (B3153)
☎ (01458) 252513
11.30-3, 5.30-11; 12-3.30, 7-10.30 Sun
Butcombe Bitter; Cotleigh Tawny; Hop Back Summer Lightning; Otter Bright; Teignworthy Reel Ale; guest beers Ⓖ
An absolute gem: this old village pub features flagstone floors and basic furniture. It usually stocks six-nine ales, mainly from West Country micros, plus Wilkins cider in summer. The home-cooked food includes superb curries (no food Sun).
🚶 Q ◁ ▶ ▲ ⌂ P

PORLOCK

Ship Inn
High Street (A39, foot of Porlock Hill)
☎ (01643) 862507
10.30-11; 12-11 Sun
Draught Bass; Cotleigh Barn Owl; Courage Best Bitter; guest beers Ⓗ
This picturesque, historic thatched inn dates from the 13th century. It is within walking distance of both sea and moor. The bar boasts a stone floor and handsome beer engine; also a games room. Wheelchair WC.
🚶 Q 🐾 🌸 🚐 ◁ ▶ ♿ ▲ ♣ ⌂ P

REDHILL

Bungalow Inn
Winford Lane (1/2 mile off A38, S of Bristol Airport) OS513640
☎ (01275) 472386
12-3, 6-11; 12-11 Fri & Sat; 12-10.30 Sun
Draught Bass; Ⓟ **Butcombe Bitter; Wadworth IPA, 6X** Ⓗ
Pub with two cosy bars and a well-equipped children's room; (beware fake handpumps in the function room).
🚶 🌸 ◁ ▶ ▲ ♣ P

Try also: Princes Motto, Barow Gurney (Free)

ROWBERROW

Swan Inn
Signed off A38 S of Churchill
☎ (01934) 852371
12-3, 6-11; 12-3, 7-10.30 Sun
Draught Bass; Butcombe Bitter, Gold; Wadworth 6X Ⓗ
Quiet, secluded country pub with two large bars, popular for food, it offers varied good quality snacks and meals (no meals Sun eve). The large outdoor area opposite is

suitable for families in summer.
🚶 Q 🌸 ◁ ▶ ⌂ P

RUDGE

Full Moon
Turn off A36 at Bell, Standerwick OS829518
☎ (01373) 830936
12-11; 12-10.30 Sun
Draught Bass; Butcombe Bitter; Fuller's London Pride Ⓗ
17th-century country pub with extensive restaurants and garden.
🚶 Q 🌸 🚐 ◁ ▶ ♿ ▲ ♣ ⌂ P ✗

ST GEORGES

Woolpack
Shepherds Way (near M5 jct 21) ☎ (01934) 521670
12-2.30 (3 Sat), 6-11; 12-3, 7-10.30 Sun
Oakhill Best Bitter; guest beers Ⓗ
This 17th-century coaching inn was once a woolpacking station. Warm and friendly, it is well used by locals. It serves at least three guest beers plus a wide range of meals at reasonable prices.
🚶 Q 🌸 ◁ ▶ ▲ ⇌ (Worle Parkway) ♣ P

SALTFORD

Bird in Hand
58 High Street (400 yds off A4)
☎ (01225) 873335
11-3, 6.30-11; 11-3.30, 6-11 Fri & Sat; 12-3.30, 6.30-10.30
Abbey Bellringer; Draught Bass; Courage Best Bitter; Smiles BA Ⓗ
Popular pub, alongside the River Avon and Bristol-Bath cycle track. A no-smoking conservatory-style dining room offers excellent views and an extensive good value menu.
Q 🌸 ◁ ▶ ♣ ⌂ P

SANDYWAY

Sportsman's Inn
Between Withypool and N Molton OS793333
☎ (01643) 831109
12-3, 6.30-11; 12-3, 7-10.30 Sun
Exmoor Ale, Fox, Beast; guest beers Ⓗ
Welcoming, roomy inn, high on Exmoor where beers come mainly from Exmoor Brewery. Cider stocked in summer.
🚶 Q 🌸 🚐 ◁ ▶ ♣ ⌂ P

SHEPTON BEAUCHAMP

Duke of York
North Street
☎ (01460) 240314
12-3, 7-11; 12-11 Sat; 12-3, 7-10.30 Sun
Draught Bass; Butcombe Gold; Teignworthy Reel Ale; Worthington

Bitter; guest beers Ⓗ
400-year-old village pub,
with a real ale-drinking
parrot! A warm, friendly
welcome is guaranteed in the
spacious bar with wood-
burning stove. An ever-
changing game menu
includes partridge served in
local cider sauce.
🏰 ✿ ❀ ◖ ◗ ♿ ⚓ ♣ ⌂ P

SOUTH PETHERTON

Brewers Arms
18 St James Street (1/2 mile
off A303)
☎ (01460) 241887
11.30-2.30, 6-11; 12-3, 7-10.30 Sun
Otter Bitter; Worthington Bitter;
guest beers Ⓗ
17th-century coaching inn in
a picturesque hamstone
village. A pleasant enclosed
courtyard, an excellent range
of home-cooked food and an
annual beer festival (late
May) add to its appeal.
🏰 ✿ ◖ ◗ ⚓ ♣ ⌂

SPARKFORD

Sparkford Inn
High Street (off A303)
☎ (01963) 440218
11-11; 12-10.30 Sun
Draught Bass; Otter Bitter; guest
beers Ⓗ
Large 15th-century coaching
inn and restaurant. Several
drinking areas include a
family area and quiet corners.
Cider is sold in summer.
🏰 Q ✿ ❀ ◖ ◗ ⚓ ♣ ⌂ P ⅄

STOGUMBER

White Horse
High Street
☎ (01984) 656277
11.30-3, 6-11; 12-3, 7-10.30 Sun
Cotleigh Tawny; Otter Bitter; guest
beers Ⓗ
Village-centre pub serving
traditional food at reasonable
prices, a mile from West
Somerset Railway.
🏰 Q ✿ ❀ ◖ ◗ P

TAUNTON

Eagle
46 South Street (400 yds S of
East Reach)
☎ (01823) 275713
11.30-2.30 (not Mon; 11-3 Sat); 12-
3.30, 7-10.30 Sun
Smiles Best; guest beers Ⓗ
Traditional Victorian pub;
one room but divided into
eating, bar and games areas.
🏰 Q ✿ ◖ ◗ ♣ P

Harpoon Louies
75 Station Road (400 yds
from station)
☎ (01823) 324404
6-12; 7-11 Sun
Beer range varies Ⓗ
Bar/restaurant serving

excellent food and seasonal
beers from Cotleigh, Cottage,
Hop Back and Otter. Late
hours apply for diners only.
◗ ≠

Masons Arms
Magdelene Street
☎ (01823) 288916
10.30-3, 5 (6 Sat)-11; 12-3, 7-10.30
Sun
Draught Bass; Exe Valley Bitter;
Juwards Bitter; guest beers Ⓗ
Traditional, town-centre pub
with a central fireplace in a
300-year-old building which
opened as a beer house in
1855. Bar food – all home-
cooked – is always available.
Q ❀ ⊯ ◖ ◗ ♣

Try also: Hawkridge Arms,
Riverside (Badger); Perkin
Warbeck, East St (Free)

TIMSBURY

Seven Stars
North Road
☎ (01761) 470398
12-3, 6-11; 12-11 Sat; 12-3, 7-10.30
Sun
Gibbs Mew Bishops Tipple; Ushers
Best Bitter, Founders, seasonal
beer Ⓗ
Warm, friendly, village local,
this deceptively large pub has
been well refurbished inside
and out. It has a large garden
with a boules pitch. No meals
Sun eve.
🏰 ❀ ◖ ◗ ♿ ♣ P ⅄

WANSTROW

Pub at Wanstrow
Station Road
☎ (01749) 850455
12-3 (not Mon), 6.30-11; 12-3, 7-10.30
Sun
Beer range varies Ⓗ/Ⓖ
First-class pub belying its
simple name, run by a
landlord who previously ran
a Sussex CAMRA Pub of the
Year. Well worth the visit.
🏰 Q ◖ ◗ ♿ ♣ ⌂ P

WATCHET

Star Inn
Mill Lane
☎ (01984) 631367
11.30-3, 6.30-11; 12-3, 7-11 Sun
Cotleigh Tawny; Oakhill Best Bitter;
guest beers Ⓗ
Built in 1680 as three
cottages where low ceilings
enhance a cosy atmosphere.
🏰 ⏛ ❀ ◖ ◗ ♿ ≈ (WSR) P

WATERROW

Rock Inn
On B3227 between
Wiveliscombe and Bampton
☎ (01984) 623293
11-3, 6-11; 12-3, 7-10.30 Sun
Cotleigh Tawny; Exmoor Gold Ⓗ
Old inn set in a rockface, well

known for its interesting
menu, served at all times.
🏰 Q ◖ ◗ ♿ ⚓ P

WELLINGTON

Cottage Inn
31 Champford Lane
☎ (01823) 664650
11-3, 6-11; 12-3, 7-10.30 Sun
Fuller's London Pride; Greene King
Abbot; Juwards Bitter; guest beer Ⓗ
Comfortable local, handily
placed for the local
theatre/cinema. With skittles,
darts and a Carnival Club,
there always seems to be
something going on. It offers
good value lunches (no food
Sun). Limited parking.
❀ ◖ ◗ ♣ P

WELLOW

Fox & Badger
Railway Lane (2 miles W of
B3110 at Hinton
Charterhouse) OS741583
☎ (01225) 832293
11.30-2.30, 6-11; 11-11 Fri & Sat;
12-10.30 Sun
Draught Bass; Butcombe Bitter;
Tetley Bitter; Wadworth 6X; guest
beer Ⓗ
Wellow's only pub, a two-bar
local where, unusually, the
public bar is carpeted and the
lounge bar is flagstoned. Can
be difficult to park.
🏰 Q ❀ ◖ ◗ ⊟ ♣ ⌂

WELLS

Britannia Inn
Bath Road (B3139)
☎ (01749) 672033
12-3, 5-11; 11-11 Sat; 12-3, 7-10.30
Sun
Butcombe Bitter; Courage Best
Bitter; Oakhill Best Bitter; guest
beers Ⓗ
Popular two-bar local serving
a housing estate. Eve meals
served Fri and Sat.
⏛ ❀ ◖ ◗ ♣ P

City Arms
69 High Street
☎ (01749) 673916
10-11; 12-10.30 Sun
Butcombe Bitter; Cotleigh Harrier;
Greene King Abbot; Ind Coope
Burton Ale; Smiles Golden; guest
beers Ⓗ
Superb old city-centre pub set
around a courtyard; part of
the building used to be the
local jail. Smart, but cosy and
friendly. ❀ ◖ ◗ ♣ ⅄

WEST BAGBOROUGH

Rising Sun Inn
Off A358 OS171334
☎ (01823) 337035
12-3, 7-11 (closed Mon); 12-4 (closed
eve) Sun
Butcombe Bitter; Cotleigh Tawny; Ⓗ
RCH Pitchfork; Ⓖ guest beer Ⓗ
Cosy, 16th-century village

inn, set in the Quantock Hills. It serves good home-cooked food (booking advised) and Lanes cider.
🚶Q◖▶⌂

WEST CRANMORE
Strode Arms
E of Shepton Mallet, S of A361
☎ (01749) 880450
11.30-2.30, 6.30-11; 12-3, 7-10.30 Sun
Flowers IPA; Marston's Pedigree; Oakhill Bitter; guest beers Ⓗ
Lovely village pub overlooking a pond. Ring for Sun lunch opening as may be closed; no meals winter Sun eve. 🚶Q🐾≢(E Somerset Railway)⌂P

WESTON-SUPER-MARE
Dragon Inn
15 Meadow Street (near main pier) ☎ (01934) 621304
10-11; 12-10.30 Sun
Boddingtons Bitter; Butcombe Bitter; Courage Directors; Exmoor Stag; RCH Pitchfork; guest beers Ⓗ
This Wetherspoon's outlet is a popular meeting place as it is centrally situated, close to the seafront and shops. Meals are available all day.
Q🐾◖▶♿≢⌂✦▥

Off the Rails
Station Approach, Station Road ☎ (01934) 415109
10-11; 12-10.30 Sun
Beer range varies Ⓗ
Single-roomed pub, doubling as station buffet. It stages a range of regular events for its strong local following and provides a free juke box. The beer range varies (two ales winter, three in summer), RCH and Oakhill feature often. Å≢P

Regency
22-24 Lower Church Road (opp. Weston College, near seafront)
☎ (01934) 633406
11-11; 12-10.30 Sun
Draught Bass; Bath Gem; Boddingtons Bitter; Courage Best Bitter; Wadworth 6X; guest beer Ⓗ
One bar, plus a pool room in this friendly pub. The lunches are good value and quality. The guest beer is always from an independent or local brewery. 🐾◖Å♣

WILLITON
Foresters Arms
55 Long Street (A39)
☎ (01984) 632508
11-11; 12-10.30 Sun
Cotleigh Harrier, Tawny; guest beer Ⓗ
Modernised, 17th-century

coaching inn comprising two bars and a dining room, a short walk from West Somerset Railway. 🚶🐾🛌◖ ▶🚪≢(WSR)⌂P🏳

WINCANTON
Bear Inn
12 Market Place
☎ (01963) 32581
11-11; 12-10.30 Sun
Draught Bass; Greene King Abbot; Ringwood Best Bitter Ⓗ
Large former coaching inn: one main bar and substantial games and function rooms; it stocks a selection of bottled Belgian beers. A good range of food includes a children's menu and take-aways.
🚶Q🛌◖▶♣P

Try also: Miller's Inn, Silver St (Free)

WINSFORD
Royal Oak Inn
At foot of Winsford Hill
☎ (01643) 851455
11-3, 7-11; 12-3, 7-10.30 (11 summer) Sun
Cotleigh Barn Owl; Exmoor Ale; guest beer Ⓗ
Thatched, ancient inn in one of Exmoor's most popular villages, an ideal base for exploring the National Park.
🚶Q🐾🛌◖▶ÅP

Beer site
Keep in touch with CAMRA:
www.camra.org.uk

WITHAM FRIARY
Seymour Arms ☆
Off B3092, by old station OS745410
☎ (01749) 850742
11-3, 6-11; 12-3, 7-10.30 Sun
Ushers Best Bitter; guest beer (occasional) Ⓗ
Old village local, unspoilt by progress. A central serving hatch and fine garden are notable features.
🚶Q♣⌂P

WIVELISCOMBE
Bear Inn
10 North Street
☎ (01984) 623537
11-3, 5-11; 11-11 Fri & Sat; 12-10.30 Sun
Cotleigh Tawny; Exmoor Gold; guest beers Ⓗ

Former 17th-century coaching house with a friendly bar and a family dining room serving good home-cooked food. Beer lover's weekends are organised in conjunction with local breweries; local farm cider is served in summer. The house beer is brewed by Cotleigh. Good children's play area.
🚶🐾🛌◖▶Å♣⌂P

WOOKEY
Burcott Inn
Follow B3139 W from Wells
☎ (01749) 673874
11.30-2.30, 6-11; 12-3, 7-10.30 Sun
Beer range varies Ⓗ
This friendly, roadside house boasts ever-changing ales, a games room and a large walled garden shaded by trees.
🚶Q🐾◖▶♿Å♣P

WRAXALL
Old Barn
Bristol Road (in grounds of Wraxall House off B3130)
☎ (01275) 819011
11.30-3, 5-11; 11.30-11 Fri & Sat (may vary); 12-3, 7-10.30 Sun
Draught Bass; Bath Gem; Courage Best Bitter; Mole's Best Bitter; Smiles Best; guest beer Ⓖ
On entering this secluded pub in the grounds of Wraxall House you cannot miss the array of casks behind the bar. This converted barn has plenty of space inside and a pleasant outdoor area.
🚶Q🐾◖Å♣⌂P

YEOVIL
Great Western
47 Camborne Grove (by Pen Mill station)
☎ (01935) 431051
12-2 (not Mon), 7-11; 12-3, 7-10.30 Sun
Wadworth IPA, 6X; seasonal beers; guest beer Ⓗ
Friendly local serving good value bar food. Old railway items decorate the bar.
🐾◖▶≢(Pen Mill)♣

INDEPENDENT BREWERIES
Abbey Ales: Bath
Ash Vine: Frome
Berrow: Berrow
Butcombe: Butcombe
Cotleigh: Wiveliscombe
Cottage: Lovington
Exmoor: Wiveliscombe
Juwards: Wellington
Milk Street: Frome
Moor: Ashcott
Oakhill: Oakhill
RCH: West Hewish**

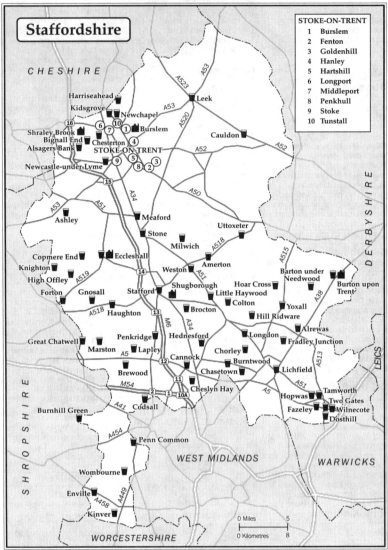

Staffordshire

STOKE-ON-TRENT

1. Burslem
2. Fenton
3. Goldenhill
4. Hanley
5. Hartshill
6. Longport
7. Middleport
8. Penkhull
9. Stoke
10. Tunstall

CHESHIRE

Harriseahead
Kidsgrove
Newchapel
Leek
Shraley Brook
Bignall End
Alsagers Bank
Chesterton
Burslem
STOKE-ON-TRENT
Newcastle-under-Lyme
Cauldon

DERBYSHIRE

Ashley
Meaford
Stone
Milwich
Uttoxeter
Copmere End
Eccleshall
Knighton
Weston
Amerton
High Offley
Barton under Needwood
Forton
Gnosall
Stafford
Shugborough
Hoar Cross
Burton upon Trent
Haughton
Brocton
Little Haywood
Colton
Yoxall
Hill Ridware
Great Chatwell
Penkridge
Hednesford
Longdon
Alrewas
Marston
Lapley
Chorley
Fradley Junction
Brewood
Cannock
Burntwood
Lichfield
Chasetown
Cheslyn Hay
Hopwas
Tamworth
Burnhill Green
Codsall
Two Gates
Fazeley
Wilnecote
Dosthill
Penn Common

SHROPSHIRE

WEST MIDLANDS
WARWICKS

Wombourne
Enville
Kinver

LEICS

0 Miles 5
0 Kilometres 8

WORCESTERSHIRE

ALREWAS

George & Dragon
120 Main Street
☎ (01283) 791476
11.30-2.30 (3 Sat), 5-11; 12-3,
7-10.30 Sun

**Banks's Bitter; Camerons
Strongarm; Marston's Pedigree** H
Popular village-centre local,
close to the Trent & Mersey
canal. No food served Sun.
Q ❀ ◖ ▌ P ⊞

Try also: **Crown**, Post Office
Rd (Free)

ALSAGERS BANK

Gresley Arms
High Street (B5367, 3 miles
NW of Newcastle)
☎ (01782) 720297

6-11, 12-3, 7-11 Sat; 12-3, 7-10.30
Sun

Stones Bitter; guest beers H
Welcoming multi-roomed
village pub offering three
ever-changing guest ales from
independent brewers. A
superb view and children's
play area are assets of the
garden. Lunches served at
weekends.
Q ❀ ❀ ▌ ◖ ⊞ ♿ ♣ P

Try also: **Railway**,
Halmerend (Burtonwood)

AMERTON

Plough
On A518
☎ (01889) 270308
11-11; 12-10.30 Sun
Banks's Bitter; Marston's Pedigree;

guest beers H
Agreeable country inn,
opposite Amerton Farm.
Meals are served in the
dining room. The large
garden has a children's play
area.
▥ ☎ ❀ ⇔ ◖ ▌ ⊞ ⚲ ♣ P

ASHLEY

Robin Hood
Lower Road (from
Loggerheads, take B5026 for
3/4 mile, turn left into Lower
Rd)
☎ (01630) 672237
6 (5.30 Fri)-11; 12-11 Sat; 12-10.30
Sun

**Bank's Original, Bitter; guest
beer** H
Traditional pub with oak
beams, an open fire and a

friendly clientele. An authentic Thai restaurant is open Wed-Sat.
🏠 ▶ P

BARTON UNDER NEEDWOOD
Shoulder of Mutton
16 Main Street
☎ (01283) 712568
11-3, 5-11; 11-11 Fri & Sat; 12-10.30 Sun

Draught Bass; Marston's Pedigree; Worthington Bitter; guest beers ⒣
Two-roomed, part 17th-century inn at the centre of the village where ever-changing guest beers are chosen by the manageress. Low ceilings, and real fires ensure a warm welcome and home-made food is always available. A landscaped outdoor drinking space includes a children's play area.
🏠 ❀ ◖ ▶ 🍴 P

BIGNALL END
Plough
2 Ravens Lane (B5500, 1/2 mile E of Audley)
☎ (01782) 720469
12-3, 7-11; 12-11 Fri & Sat; 12-10.30 Sun

Banks's Bitter; guest beers ⒣
Popular roadside hostelry, catering for local and passing trade in a traditional bar and a split-level lounge. An ever-changing range of guest ales and excellent value meals are the norm at this Potteries CAMRA *Pub of the Year* 1995.
❀ ◖ ▶ 🍴

BREWOOD
Swan
Market Square
☎ (01902) 850330
12-2.30 (3 Fri; 4 Sat), 7-11; 12-4, 7-10.30 Sun

Mansfield Riding Bitter; Marston's Pedigree; Theakston XB; guest beers ⒣
Comfortable village-centre pub with low-beamed ceilings, where two cosy snugs are complemented by a skittle alley upstairs. Local CAMRA *Pub of the Year* 1999. No food Sun. ◖ ♣ P

BROCTON
Chetwynd Arms
Cannock Road (A34)
☎ (01785) 661089
11-11; 12-10.30 Sun

Banks's Original, Bitter, Marston's Pedigree; guest beers ⒣
On the north-western edge of Cannock Chase, this popular pub has a thriving, unspoilt bar, a comfortable lounge and an outdoor children's play area. Q ❀ ◖ ▶ 🍴 ♣ P 🍺

BURNHILL GREEN
Dartmouth Arms
Snowdon Road OS787006
☎ (01746) 783268
12-3, 6-11; 12-3, 6-10.30 Sun

Hobsons Best Bitter, Town Crier ⒣
Isolated old pub on the Shropshire border. Its age is hidden beneath wisteria outside; oak beams and a sympathetic renovation inside. A welcome Hobsons' outlet in the area. A no-smoking area is set aside for lunchtime meals.
🏠 Q ❀ ◖ ▶ P

BURNTWOOD
Drill Inn
Springlestyche Lane (first left after Nags Head from Swan Island)
☎ (01543) 674092
12-11; 12-4, 6-11 Mon; 12-10.30 Sun

Marston's Pedigree or Morland Old Speckled Hen; Tetley Bitter; guest beer ⒣
Pub in a rural setting, with a spacious lounge.
❀ ◖ ♣ P

White Swan
2 Cannock Road
☎ (01543) 675937
5 (12 Sat)-11; 12-3.30, 7-10.30 Sun

Ansells Bitter; Ind Coope Burton Ale; guest beers ⒣
Comfortable, friendly, single-roomed local.
Q P

BURTON ON TRENT
Alfred
51 Derby Street
☎ (01283) 562178
11-3, 6-11; 11-11 Fri & Sat; 12-3, 7-10.30 Sun

Burton Bridge XL, Bridge Bitter, Porter, Festival Ale, seasonal beers; guest beers ⒣
Friendly, three-roomed pub with an open bar and a lounge divided into three areas, plus a games room. Families are welcome at this 1999 Staffordshire CAMRA *Pub of the Year*.
❀ 🏠 ◖ ▶ 🍴 ♣ P

Bass Museum (Burton Bar)
Horninglow Street
☎ (01283) 511000 (ext. 3513)
11-7 (6 Sat); 12-5 Sun

Draught Bass; ⒣/Ⓟ **Victoria Ale, Offilers, Joules 2B, P2 Stout** ⒣
Bar inside the Bass Museum where shire horses and steam engines are on show. Free admission for current card-carrying CAMRA members.
Q 🐎 ❀ 🍴 🚻 ⇌ ♣ P

Burton Bridge Inn
24 Bridge Street (end of Trent Bridge, A511)
☎ (01283) 536596

11.30-2.15, 5.30-11; 12-2, 7-10.30 Sun

Burton Bridge Bitter, Festival Ale, Old Expensive, seasonal beers; guest beers ⒣
Recently refurbished and extended brewery tap that attracts a varied clientele; skittles played. No food Sun; the guest beers are available Sun.
🏠 Q ❀ ◖ ♣

Derby Inn
17 Derby Road
☎ (01283) 543674
11-3, 5.30-11; 11-11 Fri & Sat; 12-3, 7-10.30 Sun

Marston's Pedigree ⒣
Friendly local with a small wood-panelled lounge and a lively bar displaying railway memorabilia. Local fruit, veg, eggs and cheese are sold at weekends in the bar. Well worth a visit.
Q 🍴 ⇌ ♣ P

Devonshire Arms
89 Station Street (opp. former Ind Coope Brewery)
☎ (01283) 562392
11-2.30, 5.30-11; 11-11 Fri & Sat; 12-3, 7-10.30 Sun

Burton Bridge XL, Bridge Bitter, Stairway to Heaven, Top Dog Stout; guest beers ⒣
Comfortable, congenial pub for conversation over excellent locally-brewed beers. One of Burton's oldest pubs, now owned by Bridge Brewery, it stocks a range of continental bottled beers. It hosts monthly themed food eves.
❀ ◖ ⇌ ♣ P 🍴

Thomas Sykes
Anglesey Road (1 mile from station, towards Branston)
☎ (01283) 510246
11.30-2.30, 5 (7 Sat)-11; 11.30-11 Fri; 12-2.30, 7-10.30 Sun

Draught Bass; Marston's Pedigree; guest beers ⒣
Set in the former stables of the Heritage Brewery, this listed building contains many artefacts from former local breweries.
Q 🍴 ⇌ P

Try also: **Anglesey Arms**, Bearwood Hill Rd (Marston's); **Lord Burton**, High St (Free)

CANNOCK
Stumble Inn
264 Walsall Road, Bridge Town (off A5)
☎ (01543) 502077
12-3, 6-11 (midnight Sat); 12-10.30 Sun

Banks's Original; Marston's Pedigree, Taylor Landlord; guest beers ⒣
Comfortable, one-roomed

pub, offering live music Fri and regularly changing guest beers. P

CAULDON
Yew Tree Inn
Off A52/A523
☎ (01538) 308348
11-3, 6-11; 12-3, 7-10.30 Sun
Draught Bass; Burton Bridge Bridge Bitter; Mansfield Riding Mild Ⓗ
Characterful pub full of antiques and artefacts, including working polyphons, pianolas and grandfather clocks. Snacks are always available, try the pickled eggs. Q ⌂ ❀ Ⓖ Å ♣

CHASETOWN
Junction
High Street
☎ (01543) 686240
12-4 (not Mon-Fri), 7 (5 Fri)-11 Sat; 12-4, 7-10.30 Sun
Banks's Bitter; M&B Brew XI; Marston's Pedigree; guest beers Ⓗ
Traditionally-run, one-roomed local dating from the 1850s, undisturbed by juke box or electronic games. ❀

Uxbridge Arms
2 Church Street
☎ (01543) 674853
12-3 (11 Fri & Sat); 12-10.30 Sun
Draught Bass; Highgate Dark; guest beers Ⓗ
Busy, two-roomed local dating from the mid-19th century where the guest ales are constantly changing. No food Sun eve. ◖ Ⅾ ⊞ ♣ P

CHESLYN HAY
Woodman Inn
Littlewood Lane (off A34)
☎ (01922) 413686
12-3, 6.30-11; 11-11 Sat; 12.30-3.30, 7-10.30 Sun
Marston's Pedigree; Theakston Best Bitter, XB; guest beers Ⓗ
Welcoming village pub and restaurant offering a relaxed atmosphere in comfortable surroundings. ⌂ ❀ ◖ Ⅾ ⊞ ⅙ ⇌ (Landywood) ♣ P ⅍

CHESTERTON
Black Horse
Sutton Street (off B5500)
☎ (01782) 561313
12-3 (5 Sat), 7-11; 12-3, 7-10.30 Sun
Tetley Bitter; guest beers Ⓗ
Corner local with a traditional bar and com-fortable lounge, this former Alton Derby Ales house retains a full set of etched windows. Hollows Bitter house beer is brewed by Coach House. ❀ ◖ Ⅾ ⅙ ♣ P

CHORLEY
Malt Shovel

Green Lane
☎ (01543) 685277
7-11; 12-3, 7-10.30 Sun
Ansells Mild, Bitter; Tetley Bitter; guest beer Ⓗ
200-year-old traditional village local, where you can join in the old-fashioned singalong (first Sat of the month). Guest ales change two or three times a week. ⌂ Q ❀ ⊞ Å ♣ P

CODSALL
Codsall Station
Chapel Lane
☎ (01902) 847061
11.30-2.30, 5-11; 11-11 Sat; 12-10.30 Sun
Holden's Mild, XB, Special Bitter; guest beers Ⓗ
Sensitive restoration by Holden's of Grade II listed station buildings; railway memorabilia is displayed around the pub. Railway Bitter is brewed by Holden's for the pub. A drinkers' pub worth visiting, it is a short train ride from Wolverhampton. ⌂ Q ⌂ ❀ ◖ Ⅾ ⇌ P

COLTON
Greyhound
Bellamour Lane
☎ (01889) 586769
12-3 (not winter Mon-Thu), 7-11; 4.30-11 Fri; 12-11 Sat; 12-11 Sun
Banks's Original, Bitter; guest beers Ⓗ
Classic, unspoilt village pub with an attractive garden for outdoor drinking. ⌂ ❀ ◖ Ⅾ ♣ P

COPMERE END
Star
1¹/₂ miles W of Eccleshall)
OS803294
☎ (01785) 850279
12-3, 6-11; 12-11 Sat; 12-3, 7-10.30 Sun
Draught Bass; guest beer Ⓗ
Cosy, traditional country pub, opposite Cop Mere, popular with walkers, cyclists and anglers. Occasional auctions are held for summer produce. No food Sun eve. ⌂ Q ❀ ◖ Å ♣ P

DOSTHILL
Fox
105 High Street
☎ (01827) 280847
12-3, 5-11; 12-3, 7-10.30 Sun
Ansells Mild; Draught Bass; Tetley Bitter; guest beers Ⓗ
Excellent local which has lost nothing since winning the local CAMRA *Pub of the Year* award in 1997. Up to five guest beers are available, as is a range of fruit wines and an excellent choice of food

served at the bar and in the restaurant (check if serving Sun eve). Q ❀ ◖ Ⅾ ⊞ ♣ P

ECCLESHALL
George
Castle Street
☎ (01785) 850300
11-11 (midnight supper licence), 12-10.30 Sun
Eccleshall Slaters Bitter, Original, Top Totty, Premium, Supreme, seasonal beers; guest beers (occasional) Ⓗ
Originally a coaching inn, this town-centre hotel has nine luxurious bedrooms and a bistro. Eccleshall's first brewery for over a century opened behind the George in 1995; seven cask beers are usually on sale. Local CAMRA *Pub of the Year* 1997. ⌂ ⌂ ❀ ⇌ ◖ Ⅾ Å P

ENVILLE
Cat Inn
Bridgnorth Road (A458)
☎ (01384) 872209
12-3, 7 (6 Wed-Fri)-11; closed Sun
Enville Ale; Everards Beacon; guest beers Ⓗ
The nearest outlet to Enville Brewery. This part 16th-century inn has four rooms, one of which is dedicated to games. The food is highly recommended (no eve meals Sun). ⌂ Q ❀ ◖ Ⅾ ♣ P

FAZELEY
Three Horseshoes
New Street (near B5404/A4091 jct)
☎ (01827) 289754
12-3, 6.30-11; 12-10.30 Sun
Draught Bass; M&B Mild; Marston's Pedigree Ⓗ
Busy, traditional, back-street local. ⌂ ❀ Å ♣

FORTON
Swan at Forton
Eccleshall Road (off A41, 1 mile along A519)
☎ (01952) 812169
12-3, 6-11; 12-10.30 Sun
Boddingtons Bitter; Flowers IPA; guest beers Ⓗ
Family-friendly, 18th-century coaching inn, incorporating a mini-craft centre display. The conservatory accommodates an extensive restaurant, but it is otherwise comparatively unrefurbished. The accommodation (nine rooms) is in a converted barn. ⌂ ❀ ⇌ ◖ Ⅾ Å P

FRADLEY JUNCTION
Swan Inn
OS140140
☎ (01283) 790330

11-3, 6-11; 12-2.30, 7-10.30 Sun
Ansells Bitter; Ind Coope Burton Ale; Marston's Pedigree H
Unspoilt, two-roomed canalside pub at the junction of the Trent & Mersey and Coventry canals, benefitting from a beautiful rural setting popular with boaters, walkers and cyclists in summer; there is a caravan park nearby.
🛏 ❀ ◖ ▶ P

GNOSALL

Royal Oak
Newport Road
☎ (01785) 822362
12-3, 6-11; 12-3, 7-10.30 Sun
Greene King Abbot; Ind Coope Burton Ale; Tetley Bitter; guest beer H
Popular village local; the garden has a lawned area, swings and a climbing frame. It offers a carvery Sat eve and Sun lunch in an upstairs function room.
🛏 ❀ ◖ ▶ ⊕ ♣ P

GREAT CHATWELL

Red Lion
2 miles E of A41, near Newport OS792143
☎ (01952) 691366
6 (11 Sat)-11; 12-10.30 Sun
Draught Bass; Everards Beacon, Tiger; Worthington Bitter; guest beers H
Friendly, family-run, country pub offering a range of guest beers. It has an excellent play area in the garden for children, who are also welcome in the lounge. Good value food is served in the bar and restaurant.
🛏 ⛺ ❀ ◖ ▶ ⊕ ▲ ♣ P ☖

HARRISEAHEAD

Royal Oak
42 High Street
☎ (01782) 513362
12-3 (not Mon-Fri), 7-11; 12-3, 7-10.30 Sun
Courage Directors; John Smith's Bitter; guest beers H
Busy, genuine free house in a semi-rural location on the Kidsgrove side of Mow Cop (NT) where a smallish bar and a larger lounge cater for all ages. The background music is difficult to hear above the conversation.
⊕ ♣ P ☖

HAUGHTON

Bell
Newport Road (A518)
☎ (01785) 780301
11.30-2.30, 6-11; 12-3, 7-10.30 Sun
Banks's Original; Marston's Pedigree; guest beer H
Homely village free house, where an L-shaped room is split into two distinct bar

areas, with various collections on display. The garden has a large lawned area with a fishpond.
🛏 ❀ ◖ ▲ ♣ P

HEDNESFORD

Queens Arms
37 Hill Street (off A460)
☎ (01543) 878437
12-3, 6.30-11; 12-3, 7-10.30 Sun
Draught Bass; Highgate Dark; Worthington Bitter P
This comfortable, two-roomed pub, popular with locals, serves good value lunches.
Q ❀ ◖ ⊕ ♣ P

HIGH OFFLEY

Anchor*
Peggs Lane, Old Lea
(by bridge 42 of Shropshire Union Canal) OS775256
☎ (01785) 284569
Summer: 11-3, 6-11; 12-3, 7-10.30 Sun; Winter: 11-3 Fri only, 7-11 Fri & Sat; 12-3 Sun
Marston's Pedigree (summer); **Wadworth 6X** H/G
Originally called the Sebastopol, this classic, basic, two-bar pub is not easily found by road. Behind the unspoilt bar is a canalware gift shop. Local CAMRA *Pub of the Year* 2000.
🛏 Q ❀ ⊕ ▲ ♣ ⌂ P

HILL RIDWARE

Chadwick Arms
☎ (01543) 490552
11.30-3, 6-11 (closed winter Mon); 12-3, 7-10.30 Sun
Banks's Bitter; Marston's Pedigree; guest beer H
Rural pub in a quiet village, close to the River Trent.
Q ❀ ▶ ⅏ ♣ P

HOAR CROSS

Meynell Ingram Arms
OS133234
☎ (01283) 575202
12-11; 12-10.30 Sun
Marston's Pedigree; Shepherd Neame Spitfire; Taylor Landlord H
16th-century pub in a rural village setting. The two cosy unspoilt rooms have real fires in winter. A varied menu is served in the bar and restaurant/function room.
🛏 Q ❀ ◖ ▶ ♣ P

HOPWAS

Red Lion
Lichfield Road
☎ (01827) 62514
11.30-2.30 (3 Sat), 6-11; 12-3, 7-10.30 Sun
Ansells Mild, P **Bitter; Marston's Pedigree; guest beer** H
Friendly, pub with a safe, canalside garden. Beware the

humpback bridge when leaving.
❀ ◖ ▶ ⊕ ♣ P

KIDSGROVE

Blue Bell
25 Hardingswood
☎ (01782) 744052
7.30-11; 1-3.30, 7-11 Sat; 12-3.30, 7.30 (7 summer)-10.30 Sun
Thwaites Bitter; guest beers H
Genuine free house of four small rooms in a canalside location, the beers change rapidly here, serving over 500 in two years; always a real cider and more than 20 Belgian beers in stock. No TV, juke box, pool or bandits disturb the atmosphere of this CAMRA Potteries *Pub of the Year* 1999.
Q ❀ ➤ ⌂ P ⊬

KINVER

Cross
Church Hill
☎ (01384) 872435
12-4, 7-11; 12-11 Fri & Sat; 12-3, 7-10.30 Sun
Banks's Hansons Mild, Bitter; P **Marston's Pedigree** H
Friendly two-roomed local, just off the high street and handy for boats on the Staffs and Worcs Canal.
🛏 ❀ ♣ ⌂ P ☖

Old White Harte Hotel
111 High Street
☎ (01384) 872305
11.30-11; 12-10.30 Sun
Banks's Original, Bitter; P **Marston's Pedigree, seasonal beers** H
This old village-centre pub is popular with diners. It has a pleasant garden at the rear.
❀ ◖ ▶ P ☖

Plough & Harrow
High Street
☎ (01384) 872659
7 (12 Sat)-11; 12-10.30 Sun
Batham Mild, Best Bitter, XXX H
Two-roomed pub, popular with walkers and campers as well as locals. Food is available at weekends only; cider sold in summer.
❀ ◖ ▶ ⊕ ♣ ⌂ P

Whittington
On A449, S of A458 jct
☎ (01384) 872110
11.30-11; 12-10.30 Sun
Banks's Original, Bitter; Marston's Pedigree, seasonal beers H
Converted 14th-century manor house visited by Charles II after the Battle of Worcester, it boasts panelled walls, moulded ceilings and walled Tudor garden. Live jazz performed Tue eve, boules played. Meals are served all day.
🛏 Q ❀ ◖ ▶ ♣ P ☖

KNIGHTON

Haberdashers Arms
Between Adbaston and Knighton OS753276
☎ (01785) 280650
12.30-11 (may close afternoon); 12-10.30 Sun
Banks's Original, Bitter; guest beer Ⓗ
Welcoming, traditional, four-roomed early Victorian community pub, saved from closure in 1997. Its large garden is often used for events. Local CAMRA *Pub of the Year* 1999.
🏰 Q 🐕 ☀ 🏠 ♣ P ♿

LAPLEY

Vaughan Arms
Bickford Road (1¹/₂ miles N of A5 near Penkridge) OS874130
☎ (01785) 840325
12.30-2.30 (not Mon), 7-11; 12-3, 6.30-11 Sat; 12-3, 7-10.30 Sun
Banks's Original; Marston's Bitter, Pedigree; guest beers Ⓗ
Friendly village pub which caters for diners, it was named aftrer the Vaughan family who resided at Lapley Hall. The pub was originally located 200 yards from its current site, but moved in the 1890s due to complaints by Hall residents of rowdiness at closing times.
🏰 ☀ ◖▶ ♿ 🏠 ♣ P

LEEK

Den Engel
23-25 St Edward Street
☎ (01538) 373751
12-3 (not Mon-Thu), 7 (5 Wed-Fri)-11; 12-3, 7-10.30 Sun
Beer range varies Ⓗ
Authentic Belgian-style single-room bar with waiter service. Huge windows make for bright sunny lunchtimes. A large range of draught and bottled beers are always served in the correct glass; it also stocks various Genevers. A Flemish restaurant upstairs offers beer-based specialities (lunches Fri and Sat; eve meals Wed-Sat). ◖▶ ⌂

Wilkes Head
16 St Edward Street
☎ (01538) 383616
11-11; 12-10.30 Sun
Whim Magic Mushroom Mild, Hartington Bitter, Hartington IPA; guest beers Ⓗ
Whim tied house: three small rooms where lively and robust conversation is the norm. It offers regularly changing guest ales and cider. 🐕 ☀ ⌂

LICHFIELD

Earl of Lichfield Arms

10 Conduit Street
☎ (01543) 251020
11-11; 12-3, 7-10.30 Sun
Banks's Original, Bitter; Marston's Pedigree Ⓗ
Popular, bare-boarded bar on the corner of the market place, known locally as the Drum. The enclosed beer garden at the rear is a welcome retreat in summer. Good value food is served Mon-Sat. ☀ ◖ ≠ (City)

George & Dragon
28 Beacon Street
☎ (01543) 263554
12-11; 12-3.30, 5-10.30 Sun
Banks's Original, Bitter; Ⓟ
Marston's Pedigree Ⓗ
Friendly, two-roomed local close to the Cathedral; well worth finding.
Q ☀ 🏠 ≠ (City) ♣ P ♿

Hogshead
12-14 Tamworth Street (near Three Spires shopping precinct)
☎ (01543) 258925
11-11; 12-10.30 Sun
Boddingtons Bitter; Marston's Pedigree; Tetley Bitter; Wadworth 6X; Ⓗ **guest beers** Ⓗ/Ⓖ
Recent development in typical Hogshead style, however the pub is about to be refurbished in 1930s Art Deco style. Very busy Fri and Sat eves, therefore meals are not available at these times and smoking restrictions are lifted. Usually two or three guest beers available.
◖ ♿ ≠ (City) ✂

Queens Head
Queen Street
☎ (01543) 410932
12-11; 12-3, 7-10.30 Sun
Adnams Bitter; Marston's Pedigree; Taylor Landlord; guest beers Ⓗ
Traditional Victorian pub, converted into a one-roomed Marston's 'Ale House' with a convivial atmosphere. A superb selection of cheeses is always available; no meals Sun. Q ◖ ≠ (City) ♣

LITTLE HAYWOOD

Red Lion
Main Road
☎ (01889) 881314
4 (12 Fri & Sat)-11; 12-10.30 Sun
Marston's Bitter, Pedigree Ⓗ
Lively village pub, very much a community local, it boasts an award-winning garden. Specially brewed monthly brews from Marston's, Banks and Camerons are also stocked. 🏰 ☀ 🏠 ♿ ♣ P

LONGDON

Swan with Two Necks
40 Brook End, Armitage (off A51)

☎ (01543) 490251
12-2.30, 7-11; 12-3, 7-11 Sat; 12-3, 7-10.30 Sun
Ansells Bitter; Ind Coope Burton Ale; guest beers Ⓗ
400-year-old, beamed village pub with a stone-flagged bar, a comfortable lounge and a restaurant (open Fri and Sat eve) serving fine food. There is also an extensive bar menu – try the superb cod and chips. 🏰 Q ☀ ◖ ▶ P

MARSTON

Fox
Birchmore Lane (1 mile NW of Wheaton Aston) OS835140
☎ (01785) 840729
Beer range varies Ⓗ
Remote, country free house with a relaxed homely atmosphere. Up to six beers available, plus ciders in summer.
🏰 ♿ ♣ ⌂

MEAFORD

George & Dragon
On A34, N of Stone, 100 yds S of A34/A51 jct
☎ (01785) 818497
11-11; 12-10.30 Sun
Burtonwood Bitter, Top Hat; guest beer Ⓗ
Main road inn with a spacious, wood-panelled lounge bar. Eve meals and Sun lunch are served in the first-floor restaurant. Burtonwood *Pub of the Year* area winner for the last two years.
☀ ◖ ▶ ♿ ♿ ♣ P

MILWICH

Green Man
Sandon Lane (B5027)
☎ (01889) 505310
12-2 (not Mon-Wed), 5-11; 12-11 Sat; 12-10.30 Sun
Draught Bass; Worthington Bitter; guest beer Ⓗ
Welcoming village pub, well situated for hikers. A list of landlords since 1792 is displayed in the bar.
🏰 ☀ ◖ ♿ ♣ P

NEWCASTLE-UNDER-LYME

Albert Inn
1 Brindley Street (off A34/A523 ring road)
☎ (01782) 615525
11-3 (not Tue-Thu), 5-11; 12-11 Fri; 11-4, 7-11 Sat; 12-3.30, 7-10.30 Sun
Burtonwood Bitter, Top Hat Ⓗ
Traditional corner local where a friendly atmosphere helps attract all ages. ♣

Ironmarket
21 Ironmarket

☎ (01782) 713131
11-11; 12-10.30 Sun
Boddingtons Bitter; Marston's Pedigree; Titanic Premium; Ⓗ **guest beers** Ⓗ/Ⓖ
Hogshead Alehouse offering the widest range of beers in the town centre. It can get extremely busy Fri and Sat eve. CAMRA Potteries *Pub of the Year* 1998. It opens 10am for breakfast; eve meals finish at 8 (not served Sun).
◑▶ & ⌂

Olde Smithy
102 Albert Street
☎ (01782) 840729
12-11; 12-10.30 Sun
Everards Beacon, Tiger; guest beers Ⓗ
Free house with a large public bar, lounge, and games room, situated just out of the town centre and convenient for the New Victoria theatre. No food served Wed; usually three guest beers on tap.
◑ ⊡ ♣

NEWCHAPEL
Grapes
2 Station Road
☎ (01782) 783815
12-3 (not Mon-Fri), 7-11; 12-3, 7-10.30 Sun
Greenalls Bitter; Greene King Abbot; Marston's Pedigree; guest beer Ⓗ
Busy public bar and two lounges frequented by a social, sporting clientele. Still largely surrounded by fields, a regular bus service stops close by.
❀ ⊡ ♣ P

PENKRIDGE
Boat
Cannock Road (by Staffs & Worcs Canal)
☎ (01785) 714178
12-3.30, 5.30-11; 11-11 Sat; 12-10.30 Sun
Ansells Bitter; Marston's Pedigree; Morland Old Speckled Hen Ⓗ
This canalside pub is especially popular in summer. No meals Sun eve.
⚓ ❀ ◑▶ & ♣ P

Try also: **Star,** Market Place (Banks's)

PENN COMMON
Barley Mow
Pennwood Lane (off Wakeley Hill) OS949902
☎ (01902) 333510
12-2.30, 6-11; 12-11 Sat; 12-10.30 Sun
Banks's Original; Greene King IPA, Abbot; Ind Coope Burton Ale; guest beer Ⓗ
Recently extended pub where the original building dates from the 1630s. Very

welcoming and offering good food, has a garden and play area. Handy for Penn Golf Course.
❀ ◑▶ P

STAFFORD
Bird in Hand
Victoria Square, Mill Street (opp. Crown Court)
☎ (01785) 252198
11-11; 12-10.30 Sun
Courage Directors; Ruddles Best Bitter; John Smith's Bitter; Worthington Bitter Ⓗ
Justifiably popular town-centre pub, a rarity in having retained separate rooms. The bar, snug, games room and lounge satisfy clientele of all ages. It hosts two beer festivals a year.
⚓ ❀ ◑▶ ⊡ ⇌ ♣

Hogshead
Unit 3, Earl Street
☎ (01785) 241560
11-11; 12-10.30 Sun
Banks's Bitter; Boddingtons Bitter; guest beers Ⓗ
Conversion of the old County education offices have given a spacious comfortable pub, typical of the Hogshead chain. It has improved the choice of beers available in the town centre, but can be noisy late eve.
❀ ◑▶ & ⇌ ⌂ ✂

Stafford Arms
Railway Street (opp. station)
☎ (01785) 253313
12-11; 12-4, 7-10.30 Sun
Draught Bass; Titanic Best Bitter, Premium, White Star, guest beers Ⓗ
Now owned by Punch Taverns, but still one of the best choices of beer in town. It hosts occasional beer festivals; no meals in winter. Biddenden cider is sometimes available.
Q ❀ ⚓ ◑▶ ⇌ ♣ ⌂ P ✂

Tap & Spile
59 Peel Terrace (off B5066, 1 mile from centre)
☎ (01785) 223563
4.30 (12 Fri & Sat)-11; 12-10.30 Sun
Beer range varies Ⓗ
This 1994 sympathetic conversion to a Tap & Spile has greatly improved choice in northern Stafford, with up to eight guest beers on at once. Regular quizzes and free bar billiards add to its appeal.
⚓ ❀ ♣ ⌂ ✂

STOKE ON TRENT: BURSLEM
Vine
Hamil Road
11-11; 12-10.30 Sun
Courage Best Bitter, Directors;

guest beers Ⓗ
1930s pub converted in recent years to one room, but retaining a friendly, local atmosphere. It is popular with football fans due to its proximity to Vale Park, home of Port Vale FC. ♣

Try also: **Olde Smithy,** Moorland Rd (Free)

FENTON
Malt 'n' Hops
295 King Street
☎ (01782) 313406
12-3, 7-11; 12-3, 7-10.30 Sun
Courage Directors; Theakston Mild; guest beers Ⓗ
Excellent example of a true free house, one of the very few in the city. The range of four guests, normally from small independent brewers, is frequently changed; also Belgian beers available.
⇌ (Longton)

Try also: **Potter,** King St (Free)

GOLDENHILL
Cushion
230 Broadfield Road (off A50 at Red Lion, right at T-jct)
☎ (01782) 783388
5 (3 Fri)-11; 12-5, 7-11 Sat; 12-10.30 Sun
Greenalls Bitter; Marston's Pedigree; guest beer Ⓗ
Small, well-refurbished pub now a free house: one bar, but it gives the impression of two rooms and offers a remarkably rural outlook for a town pub. Experienced owners involve this popular pub in local affairs.
❀ ♣ P

HANLEY
Golden Cup
65 Old Town Road (off Potteries Way ring road, A50)
☎ (01782) 212405
11.30-11; 12-4, 7-10.30 Sun
Draught Bass; Ruddles County Ⓗ
Friendly local, the last beer house in Hanley to obtain a liquor licence. Splendid bar fittings and the ornate Edwardian exterior proclaims 'Bass only'. It runs a thriving pensioners club and was voted *Community Pub of the Year* 1998.
❀ ◑ ♣

Hogshead Ale House
2-6 Percy Street
☎ (01782) 209585
11-11; 12-10.30 Sun
Boddingtons Bitter; Titanic Premum; Wadworth 6X; guest beers Ⓗ
Large city-centre house with eight handpumped beers and four on gravity, plus a huge

range of Belgian bottled beers; the cider varies. Handy for the new cultural quarter. ◖❍ ⌂

Try also: **Reginald Mitchell**, Tontine St (Wetherspoon's)

HARTSHILL

Old House at Home
544 Hartshill Road (A52 Newcastle road)
☎ (01782) 610985
4.30 (12 Sat)-11; 12-5, 7-10.30 Sun
Draught Bass; Ind Coope Burton Ale; Marston's Pedigree; Tetley Bitter Ⓗ
Main road pub comprising a comfortable lounge and a basic bar, with an emphasis on games and quizzes.
⚘ ⊞ ♣

LONGPORT

Packhorse Inn
8 Station Street (A527)
☎ (01782) 577322
11-11; 12-10.30 Sun
Marston's Pedigree; Theakston Best Bitter; guest beers Ⓗ
Old canalside pub with a converted stable block to the rear. The single bar has a dining area off, where excellent value meals are served. ⚘ ◖❍ ⇌ (Longport) ♣

MIDDLEPORT

White Swan
107 Newport Lane (B5051)
☎ (01782) 813639
11-11; 11-4, 7-11 Sat; 12-3, 7-10.30 Sun
Boddingtons Bitter; Chester's Mild; Flowers Original; Wadworth 6X; guest beers Ⓗ
A real gem; this popular, friendly Potteries back-street local is very much part of the local community and boasts its own golf society.
⚒ ⇌ (Longport) ♣

PENKHULL

Greyhound Inn
Manor Court Street
☎ (01782) 848978
11-3, 5.30-11; 11-11 Fri & Sat; 12-10.30 Sun
Marston's Pedigree; Moorland Old Speckled Hen; Tetley Bitter; guest beer Ⓗ
The public bar was built in 1540 as the manor courthouse of Newcastle-under-Lyme. Enlarged in 1704, this pub has a genuine local feel and was voted *Community Pub of the Year* 1999. Children allowed in for meals; the menu includes kangaroo steaks. Eve meals served Tue-Sat.
⚒ Q ⚘ ◖❍ ⊞ ♣ P

Marquis of Granby
St Thomas Place

☎ (01782) 847025
11.45-11; 12-10.30 Sun
Banks's Original, Bitter; Marston's Pedigree, HBC Ⓗ
Imposing red brick building opposite the village square and church, it has a comfortable lounge, friendly bar and excellent garden. The food is good value.
⚘ ◖ ⊞ ♣ P ⊞

STOKE

Corky's
405 London Road, West End
☎ (01782) 413421
11-11 12-3, 7-10.30 Sun
Banks's Original, Bitter; Marston's Pedigree Ⓗ
Large but friendly pub; it has two distinct areas serving authentic Thai food (not Tue), also a snooker room with two full-sized tables.
⚘ ◖ ❍ ♣

Grey's Corner
9 Hartshill Road
☎ (01782) 746550
11-11; 11-4, 7-11 Sat; 11-4, 7-10.30 Sun
Banks's Orignal; Camerons Bitter; Marston's Pedigree; Taylor Landlord Ⓗ
Town-centre local on two levels, serving excellent lunches. It boasts a particularly fine patio area.
⚘ ◖ ⇌ ♣

Wheatsheaf
84-92 Church Street
☎ (01782) 747462
11-11; 12-10.30 Sun
Draught Bass; Courage Directors; Theakston Best Bitter; guest beers Ⓗ
Large, modern, pub built on the site of an old coaching inn, with a typical Wetherspoon's interior. It can get busy on Sat when Stoke City are at home. Handy for visiting Spode and Mintons Potteries, it has drastically increased the range of real ale in the town centre.
Q ◖ ❍ ⇌ ⌂ ✗ ⊞

TUNSTALL

Paradise
42 Paradise Street (off Tower Sq)
☎ (01782) 833266
12-11; 12-4.30, 8-10.30 Sun
Courage Directors; Ind Coope Burton Ale; Thwaites Bitter Ⓗ
Friendly, welcoming town-centre pub with a single U-shaped room, close to a main bus route.
⚒ ♣

White Hart
43 Roundwell Street
☎ (01782) 835817
11-11; 12-4.30, 7.30-10.30 Sun

Marston's Bitter, Pedigree Ⓗ
A real local community pub where the atmosphere and beer attract customers from miles around. It hosts regular karaoke (Sat) and occasional barbecues in summer. ⚘

STONE

Red Lion
25 High Street
☎ (01785) 814500
11-11; 12-10.30 Sun
Boddingtons Bitter; Everards Tiger; guest beers Ⓗ
Deceptively large central pub with a narrow frontage: a spacious public bar at the back and a small, quieter lounge overlooking the pedestrianised High Street.
⚘ ⊞ ⚘ ♣ P

Star
21 Stafford Street (by Trent and Mersey Canal)
☎ (01785) 813096
11-11; 12-10.30 Sun
Banks's Original, Bitter; Marston's Pedigree; guest beers Ⓗ
Dating from 1568, this canalside pub is located on thirteen floor levels, yet various extensions have not affected the original bar.
⚒ ⚘ ◖ ❍ ⊞ P ⊟

Swan
18 Stafford Street (by Trent and Mersey Canal)
☎ (01785) 819414
11-11; 12-10.30 Sun
Coach House Joule Old Priory, Victory; guest beers Ⓗ
This 18th-century canal warehouse was converted to a pub in the mid-19th century. Restored in 1999 to become Stone's leading free house, it stocks eight cask beers and two ciders. Meals served Tue-Sat. The house beer is also brewed by Coach House for Joule's of Stone.
⚒ ⚘ ◖ ⚘ ⌂

TAMWORTH

Albert
32 Albert Road (near station)
☎ (01827) 64694
5-11; 12-3, 7-11 Sat; 12-3, 7-10.30 Sun
Banks's Original, Bitter; Morrells Varsity; guest beers Ⓗ
Popular local where a warm welcome is guaranteed, handy for the station. A previous local CAMRA *Pub of the Year* winner, the guest beer is often a seasonal beer from Banks's or Marston's.
⚘ ⊞ ⚘ ⇌ ♣ P ⊟

White Lion
Aldergate (next to Council Offices)
☎ (01827) 64630
11-11; 12-10.30 Sun

Banks's Original, Bitter; Marston's Pedigree; guest beer [H]
Lively, two-roomed, town-centre pub, popular with all ages; it gets busy at weekends. The restaurant is recommended, especially for Sunday roasts.
◖ ⅙ ⇌ P

Try also: Globe Hotel, Lower Gungate (Bass); Jail House Rock Café, Lichfield St (Free)

TWO GATES
Bulls Head
Watling Street
☎ (01827) 287820
12-2.30 (3 Sat), 6.30-11; 12-2.30, 7-10.30 Sun
Banks's Original; Marston's Pedigree [H]
Popular local featuring a comfortable bar and lounge, serving good value food Mon-Sat.
Q ❀ ◖ 🍺 ⇌ (Wilnecote) ♣ P

UTTOXETER
Roebuck
Dove Bank (A518)
☎ (01889) 565563
11-2, 5-11; 11-11 Fri & Sat; 12-3, 7-10.30 Sun
Theakston Best Bitter, XB; guest beers [H]
With three guests, this pub offers the best choice of beer in town. Popular with locals, it dates from the 17th century and was once a beer retailing premises, becoming a pub 100 years ago. The outdoor drinking area is not suitable for children.
❀ ⇔ ◖ 🍺 ▲ ⇌ ♣ P

Smithfield Hotel
37 High Street
☎ (01889) 562682
11-3, 7-11; 12-4, 7-10.30 Sun
Burtonwood Bitter, Top Hat; guest beer [H]
Named the Plume of Feathers from 1627, this street-corner pub was renamed a century ago. It has been restored by the present award-winning licensee.
⇔ ◖ ▶ 🍺 ▲ ♣

Vaults
Market Place
☎ (01889) 562997
11-3, 5.30-11; 11-3.30, 5-11 Fri; 11-4, 7-11 Sat; 12-3, 7-10.30 Sun
Draught Bass; Marston's Pedigree [H]
Friendly, unspoilt, three-room pub, boasting a large bottled bar collection. Bar skittles played in the room next to the bar.
🍺 ▲ ⇌ ♣

WESTON
Woolpack

The Green
☎ (01889) 270238
11.30-3, 5.30-11; 11.30-11 Fri & Sat; 12-10.30 Sun
Banks's Original, Bitter, Marston's Pedigree [H]
This 17th-century inn on the green has retained its local trade while attracting more diners. No food Sun eve.
🍺 ❀ ◖ ▶ 🍺 ♣ P

WILNECOTE
Prince of Wales
70 Hockley Road
☎ (01827) 280013
12-3, 7-11; 12-3, 7-10.30 Sun
Theakston Best Bitter, XB; guest beers [H]
Typically five real ales are available here, together with a good range of single malts. A number of the guest beers are from Scotland.
Q ❀ 🍺 ♣ P

WOMBOURNE
New Inn
1 Station Road (¹/₂ mile from A459/A463 jct)
☎ (01902) 892037
11-3, 5.30-11; 11-11 Thu-Sat; 12-4, 7-10.30 Sun
Banks's Original, Bitter, seasonal beers [P]
Large roadhouse close to the village centre; children are welcome in the well-equipped garden. No food Sun.
❀ ◖ 🍺 ♣ P 🛏

YOXALL
Crown Inn
Main Street
☎ (01543) 472551
11.30-3, 5.30-11; 11.30-11 Sat; 12-10.30 Sun
Marston's Pedigree, [H]
Welcoming traditional pub with a dining area in the smart lounge.
🛏 ❀ ◖ ▶ 🍺 ⅙ ▲ ♣ P

INDEPENDENT BREWERIES

Bevvied Bull: Burton upon Trent
Burton Bridge: Burton upon Trent
Eccleshall: Eccleshall
Marston's: Burton upon Trent
Old Cottage: Burton upon Trent
Shraley Brook: Shraley Brook
Shugborough: Shugborough
Titanic: Burslem

CAMRA National Pub Inventory: Tap House, Shrwesbury, Shropshire

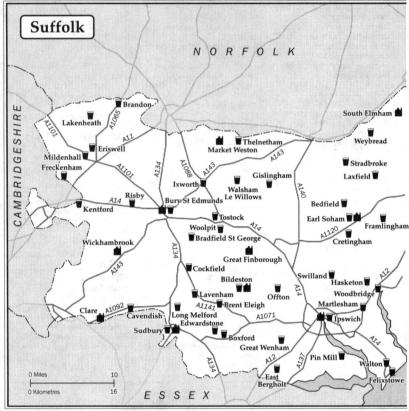

ALDEBURGH

Mill Inn
Market Cross Place
☎ (01728) 452563
11-3, 5-11; 11-11 Fri , Sat & summer;
12-3, 7-10.30 Sun
Adnams Bitter, Broadside, seasonal beers Ⓗ
Popular with both locals and tourist alike, the Mill's fresh fish is recommended.
🏠 ◐ 🅳 Å

White Hart
222 High Street
☎ (01728) 453205
11.30-11; 12-10.30 Sun
Adnams Bitter, Broadside, seasonal beers Ⓗ
Single room pub, busy with locals and visitors.
🏠 ❀ 🖂 Å ♣ Ⓗ

BECCLES

Bear & Bells
Old Market
☎ (01502) 712291
11-3, 5.30-11; 12-3, 7-10.30 Sun
Adnams Bitter; Greene King IPA, Abbot; guest beer Ⓗ
Comfortable Victorian pub near the river, renowned for good ales and wholesome food (not served Sun).
Q ◐ 🅳 ≠

BEDFIELD

Crown
Church Lane (head N from Earl Soham)
☎ (01728) 628431
11.30-3 (may vary), 6-11 ; 12-4, 7-10.30 Sun
Greene King IPA Ⓗ
Off the beaten track, this pub is worth seeking out for its cosy feel and warm welcome. No food Tue.
🏠 ❀ ◐ Å ♣ P ✂

BILDESTON

Kings Head
132 High Street (B1115, Hadleigh-Stowmarket Road)
☎ (01449) 741434
12-3, 5-11 (closed winter Mon) 11-11 Sat & summer; 12-10.30 Sun
Beer range varies Ⓗ
Brewing on site as the Brettvale Brewery Co since 1996, now known as the Kings Head Brewery, this large village centre inn has a single bar layout. It hosts live music at weekends and an annual beer festival in May (40 beers). 🖂 ◐ ♣ P

BOXFORD

White Hart
Broad Street
☎ (01787) 211071
12-3, 6-11; 12-3, 7-10.30 Sun
Adnams Broadside; Greene King IPA; guest beers Ⓗ
Timber-framed free house in the village centre, away from the main road. A changing range of guest beers is complemented by a varied menu.
🏠 ❀ ◐ 🅳 ♣ P

BRADFIELD ST GEORGE

Fox & Hounds
Felsham Road
☎ (01284) 386379
11.30-3, 5.30-11; closed Mon; 12-3, 7-10.30 Sun
Buffy's Bitter; Nethergate Suffolk County; Greene King IPA; guest beer Ⓗ
Recently free of tie, this pub has been refurbished retaining a practical public bar and offering a full restaurant service in the comfortable lounge (eve meals Wed-Sat). Guest beers are sourced locally. Outside the village centre it is close to the historic coppiced woodlands of the Suffolk Wildlife Trust.
Q ❀ ◐ 🅳 Ⓗ P

BRANDON

Five Bells
Market Hill
☎ (01842) 813472
11-11; 12-10.30 Sun
Greene King IPA, Abbot H
Ancient, flint-faced building,
well situated at the corner of
the market square. Local
trade is lively, fielding games
teams. Booking essential for
eve meals.
🕸 ◖ ▶ 🛏 ≈ ♣ P

BRENT ELEIGH

Cock ☆
Lavenham Road OS941478
☎ (01787) 247371
12-3, 6-11; 12-3, 7-10.30 Sun
**Adnams Bitter, Broadside; Greene
King IPA; Nethergate Priory Mild** H
Absolute gem: thatched,
unspoilt and at peace with
the world.
🏚 Q 🕸 🛏 ◖ ♣ ☍ P

BUNGAY

Chequers Inn
23 Bridge Street
☎ (01986) 893579
11-11; 12-10.30 Sun
**Adnams Bitter; Fuller's London
Pride; Taylor Landlord; guest
beers** H

Popular, 17th-century inn,
serving up to six guest ales,
with usually a dark ale
available. It hosts impromptu
music nights (Sun) and an
annual beer festival (Oct).
🏚 🕸 ◖ ▲ P 🎟

Green Dragon
29 Broad Street
☎ (01986) 892681
11-3, 5-11; 11-11 Fri & Sat; 12-10.30
Sun
**Adnams Bitter; Green Dragon
Chaucer, Bridge Street,** H **Dragon,
seasonal beers** G
Green Dragon beer is brewed
at the rear of this spacious
twin-bar inn with a dining
room/family area.
🏚 🛏 🕸 ◖ ▶ 🛏 ▲ ♣ P

BURY ST EDMUNDS

Greyhound
28 Eastgate Street
☎ (01284) 752358
11-11; 12-10.30 Sun
Greene King IPA, Abbot H
Friendly, edge-of-town pub
displaying many photos of
old town pubs.
🕸 ☍ P

Queens Head
39 Churchgate Street
☎ (01284) 761554
11-11; 12-10.30 Sun
**Adnams Broadside; Ind Coope
Burton Ale; Nethergate IPA; Tetley
Bitter; guest beer** H
Lively, town-centre pub
boasting a large conservatory
and games room with pool
table. The bar has recently
been extended and
redecorated.
🕸 ◖ ▶ ♣ 🎟 🎟

Rising Sun
98 Risbygate Street
☎ (01284) 701460
11-3, 6-11; 11-11 (Wed, Fri & Sat);
12-4, 7-10.30 Sun
**Greene King XX Mild, IPA, Abbot,
guest beer** H
Unspoilt 16th-century
beamed pub with a no-
smoking restaurant.
🏚 ◖ P

Rose & Crown
48 Whiting Street (fronts on
to Westgate St.)
☎ (01284) 755934
11.30-11; 11-3, 7-11 Sat; 12-2.30,
7-10.30 Sun
**Greene King XX Mild, IPA, Abbot,
seasonal beers** H
Highly recommended, this
family-run, unspoilt town
local is within sight of the
brewery. Good value lunches.
A mild stronghold!
🛏 ◖ 🎟 ♣ 🎟

BUTLEY

Oyster
Orford Road (B1084)

☎ (01394) 450790
11.30-3, 6-11; 11-11 Sat; 12-3,
7-10.30 Sun
Adnams Bitter, Broadside H
Unspoilt pub, beamed
throughout and displaying
memorabilia of local history
and its nautical links. A
motorcycle club meets here
regularly. The varied menu
features locally-caught fish.
🏚 Q 🕸 ◖ ▶ 🛏 ▲ ♣ P

CARLTON COLVILLE

Bell Inn
The Street (off B1384)
☎ (01502) 582873
11-3, 4-11; 11-11 Fri, Sat & Summer;
12-10.30 Sun
**Green Jack Bitter, Grass Hopper,
Orange Wheat, Golden Sickle, Gone
Fishing, seasonal beers; guest
beers** H
Spacious, open-plan inn
owned by Green Jack
Brewery with a restaurant
area serving good quality
food. The no-smoking area
doubles as a family room.
🏚 Q 🛏 🕸 ◖ ▶ 🛏 ▲ P 🎟

CAVENDISH

Bull
High Street
☎ (01787) 280245
11-3, 6-11; 12-3, 7-10.30 Sun
**Adnams Bitter, Broadside, seasonal
beers** H
Friendly village pub dating
from 1530, enjoying an
excellent reputation for food
(booking necessary for
weekend eves and Sun
lunch). 🏚 Q 🕸 🛏 ◖ ▶ P

CHILLESFORD

Froize Inn
The Street
☎ (01394) 450282
12-3, 6-11, 12-11 Sat; 12-10.30 Sun
Beer range varies H
Popular award-winning pub
with excellent food and beer;
local guest beers often
feature. The pub is named
after a local version of a
pancake called a froize.
Q 🕸 🛏 ◖ ▶ 🛏 ▲ ♣ P

COCKFIELD

Three Horseshoes
Stowes Hill
☎ (01284) 828177
12-3, 5.30-11; 12-3, 6.30-10.30 Sun
**Greene King IPA; Mauldons
Moletrap; guest beer** H
Part-thatched, 14th-century
free house; the lounge-cum-
restaurant features exposed
crown post and timbers.
Home-cooked food in
generous portions at
affordable prices is served in
the no-smoking dining room
(no meals Tue).
🏚 🕸 ◖ ▶ ▲ ♣ ☍ P

CRETINGHAM
Bell
The Street
☎ (01728) 685419
11-2.30 (3 Sat), 6-11; 12-10.30 Sun
Adnams Bitter; Woodforde's Wherry; guest beer Ⓗ
Oak-beamed pub in the village centre offering home-cooked meals based on local produce. The small snug bar is a delight.
▨ Q ❀ 🞄 🞄 D ♣ P ⚥

DUNWICH
Ship Inn
St James Street
☎ (01728) 648219
11-3, (3.30 Sat), 6-11; 12-3.30, 7-10.30 Sun (may open longer summer)
Adnams Bitter, Broadside, seasonal beer Ⓗ
One of the few buildings left in this once important and thriving town where most have now been lost to the sea. Flagged floor and open fire are features of the main bar; children are welcome in the conservatory/restaurant and large garden.
▨ Q ⚞ ❀ 🞄 🞄 D ♣ P

EARL SOHAM
Victoria
On A1120
☎ (01728) 685758
11.30-3, 5.30-11; 12-3, 7-10.30 Sun
Earl Soham Gannet Mild, Victoria, Albert, Sir Roger's Porter Ⓗ
This pub appeals to all: no airs and graces, it is renowned for its basic, but friendly atmosphere. Fresh local produce is used to offer an excellent choice of meals.
▨ Q ❀ 🞄 D ♣ P

EAST BERGHOLT
Hare & Hounds
Heath Road
☎ (01206) 298438
12-2.30, 5-11; 12-2.30, 6-10.30 Sun
Adnams Bitter, Broadside; Ⓗ **guest beers** Ⓖ
Fine, 15th-century pub retaining a pargetted ceiling (deep plaster relief), circa 1590, in the lounge. Guest beers come mainly from local breweries. No food Tue.
▨ Q ⚞ ❀ 🞄 D 🞄 🞄 ♣ P

Royal Oak (Dickey)
East End
☎ (01206) 298221
12-2.30 (3 Sat), 5.30 (6 Sat)-11; 12-3, 7-10.30 Sun
Greene King IPA, Abbot, seasonal beers; Ruddles County Ⓗ
Excellent rural pub which may be difficult to find (follow signs to Grange campsite). The friendly single bar is well-supported by locals, whilst the snug bar

has recently re-opened. Pétanque played.
▨ Q ❀ 🞄 A ♣ P ⚥

EDWARDSTONE
White Horse
Mill Green OS951429
☎ (01787) 211211
12-2 (not Mon), 6.30-11; 12-3, 7-10.30 Sun
Greene King IPA; guest beers Ⓗ
Off the beaten track (OS map necessary) this two-bar rural free house boasts a wide selection of pub games and a fine collection of enamel signs. Always a guest mild on tap. No food Mon.
▨ Q ❀ 🞄 D 🞄 A ♣ P

ERISWELL
Chequers
The Street
☎ (01638) 532478
11-11; 12-10.30 Sun
Greene King IPA, Abbot Ⓖ
19th-century, flint-faced pub in a country estate village. Although food-oriented it is becoming more welcoming for just drinkers. Enjoy the Breckland walks nearby.
Q ❀ 🞄 D P ⚥

FELIXSTOWE
Victoria
Felixstowe Ferry
☎ (01394) 271636
11-3, 6-11; 12-3, 6-10.30 Sun
Adnams Bitter, Broadside; Greene King IPA Ⓗ
Cosy, welcoming pub close to the Deben River estuary. The upstairs no-smoking room/restaurant offers a splendid view of the North Sea and coastline while the car park gives access to walks along the sea defences. An excellent menu includes daily fish specials.
▨ ⚞ ❀ 🞄 D 🞄 A ♣ P ⚥

FRAMLINGHAM
Station
Station Road
☎ (01728) 723455
12-3, 5-11; 12-3, 7-10.30 Sun
Earl Soham Gannet Mild, Victoria, Albert, Sir Roger's Porter Ⓗ
Homely furnished pub whose basic decor reflects the railway era. Note the rare five pump font on the bar. An ideal place to drink in this historic market town.
▨ Q ❀ 🞄 D ♣ P

FRECKENHAM
Golden Boar
The Street (B1102, 2 1/2 miles from A11 at Mildenhall)
☎ (01638) 723000
11.30-11; 12-4, 7-10.30 Sun
Adnams Bitter, Broadside; Elgood's

Black Dog Mild; guest beers Ⓗ
16th-century beamed former coaching inn, where an original fireplace was recently exposed after extensive sympathetic refurbishment. An excellent value, home-cooked menu incorporates fresh ingredients and daily changing specials (booking advised).
▨ ❀ ⚞ 🞄 D 🞄 ♣ P

GISLINGHAM
Six Bells
High Street
☎ (01379) 783349
12-3, 7-11; 12-3, 7-10.30 Sun
Adnams Bitter; guest beer Ⓗ
Spacious village-centre pub which supports local micro-breweries. Excellent home-made food from an interesting menu is served Tue-Sun.
⚞ ❀ 🞄 D 🞄 A ♣ P

GREAT WENHAM
Queens Head
Capel St Mary Road (off B1070) ☎ (01473) 310590
12-2.30, 6-11; 12-2.30, 7-10.30 Sun
Greene King IPA; guest beers Ⓗ
Attractive, mid 19th-century country pub of character, popular with locals, walkers and cyclists in summer. The well-designed no-smoking dining room, recently opened, has quickly gained acclaim for its curry menu.
▨ Q ❀ 🞄 D ♣ P

HASKETON
Turks Head
Low Road OS247506
☎ (01394) 382584
12-3, 6-11; 12-3, 7-10.30 Sun
Tolly Cobbold Mild, Original, seasonal beers; guest beers Ⓗ
Attractive beamed, friendly village local. A new conservatory overlooks a secluded garden. It offers good home-cooked food, plus theme nights (no food Sun eve or Mon).
▨ ❀ 🞄 D 🞄 A ♣ P

IPSWICH
Dales
Dales Road
☎ (01473) 250024
11-2.30, 4-30 (6.30 Sat)-11; 12-3.30, 7-10.30 Sun
Adnams Bitter; Draught Bass; Tolly Cobbold Mild, Bitter; guest beers Ⓗ
Modern, two-bar pub with a comfortable lounge, on a quiet housing estate. Good value meals.
❀ 🞄 D 🞄 ♣ P

Fat Cat
288 Spring Road
☎ (01473) 726524

12-11; 11-11 Sat; 12-10.30 Sun

Adnams Bitter; Wells Bombardier; H **Woodforde's Wherry,** H/G **Nog;** H **guest beers** H/G

Furnished in typical Victorian working class fashion with wood floors and bench seating and decorated with tin advertising signs and posters, this Suffolk CAMRA *Pub of the Year* 1998 has 20 ales on tap, several from local breweries.

Q 🏤 ➤ (Derby Rd) ⌂ ⊞

Greyhound

9 Henley Road
☎ (01473) 252105

11-2.30, 5-11; 11-11 Sat; 12-10.30 Sun

Adnams Mild, Bitter, Broadside, seasonal beers; guest beers H

Busy community pub enjoying a good reputation for food; a traditional style public bar and larger lounge.

Q 🏤 🌰 ◗ ⊞ ♣ P ⊞

Milestone Brewhouse (Mulberry Tree)

5 Woodbridge Road (opp Odeon) ☎ (01473) 252425

12-3, 5-11; 12-11 Fri & Sat; 12-10.30 Sun

Boddingtons Bitter; Everard's Tiger; Greene King IPA, Abbot; Tolly Cobbold Original H **guest beers** H/G

Large, busy pub, mainly open-plan, it has some discrete seating areas. A popular venue for local bands it hosts live music Thu, Fri and Sat eves. A range of gravity-served beers is kept in the tap room. No eve meals Thu-Sun. 🏤 🌰 ◗ ▮ ⌂ P 🛏

Woolpack

11 Tuddenham Road
☎ (01473) 253059

11-3, 5-11; 12-10.30 Sun

Adnams Bitter; Ind Coope Burton Ale; Tolly Cobbold Bitter, Original, IPA H

Interesting old red-brick building on the outskirts of the town centre: its three bars include a tiny front bar.

🏤 Q ◗ ▮ ♣ P

IXWORTH

Greyhound

49 High Street
☎ (01359) 230887

11-3, 6-11; 12-3, 7-10.30 Sun

Greene King XX Mild, IPA, Abbot, seasonal beers H

Three-bar local retaining a marvellously intimate snug. The lively public bar fields good games teams.

▮ Å ♣ P

KENTFORD

Cock

Bury Road
☎ (01638) 750360

11.30-3, 6-11; 11-11 Sat; 12-4, 7-10.30 Sun

Greene King IPA, Abbot, seasonal beers; guest beers H

Much more ancient than appears outside. Note the superb carved beams in one bar. Its three large rooms (one is a restaurant) retain the atmosphere of a good community pub.

🏤 🌰 ◗ ▮ ⊞ ⇌ (Kennett) P

LAKENHEATH

Brewers Tap

54 High Street
☎ (01842) 862328

11-11; 12-4.30, 7-10.30 Sun

Nethergate Suffolk County; guest beers H

Under threat of closure until the present landlord established a real ale theme three years ago, this is now a busy pub. Book for eve meals. The house beer is provided by Payn of Ramsey.

🌰 ◗ ▮ ♣

Half Moon

4 High Street
☎ (01842) 861484

11-3 (4 Sat), 6-11; 12-4, 7-10.30 Sun

Greene King XX Mild, IPA, Abbot; guest beers H

All-purpose local on the outskirts of a large village. It retains a nice two-bar layout with an off-sales hatch between. The guest beers are from Greene King's list.

🏤 Q 🌰 ◗ ▮ ⊞ ⌂ P 🛏

LAVENHAM

Angel

Market Place
☎ (01787) 247388

11-11; 12-10.30 Sun

Adnams Bitter; Greene King IPA; Nethergate Bitter; Woodforde's Wherry H

This award-winning 15th-century inn overlooks Lavenham's market square and Guildhall. The restaurant and bar have a refined yet relaxing atmosphere, serving good food from local ingredients. The guest rooms are characterful.

🏤 Q 🌰 🛏 ◗ ▮ P

LAXFIELD

Kings Head (Low House)

Gorams Mill Lane (off B1117, below churchyard)
☎ (01986) 798395

11-3, 6-11; 11-11 Tue; 12-4, 7-10.30 Sun

Adnams Bitter, Broadside; Greene King IPA, Abbot; guest beers G

Classic pub without a bar; the beer is served from the tap room to be savoured in a warren of rooms and outside drinking areas. Not to be

missed – a gem.

🏤 Q 🛎 🌰 ◗ ▮ Å ♣ ⌂ P

Royal Oak

High Street
☎ (01986) 798446

11-3 (not Mon), 6-11; 11-11 Fri & Sat; 12-10.30 Sun

Adnams Bitter; guest beers H

A regularly changing selection of guest beers, often from local micros, is complemented by generous food portions from an extensive menu. No meals Sun eve or Mon. 🏤 ◗ ▮ Å

LONG MELFORD

George & Dragon

Hall Street
☎ (01787) 371285

11.30-11; 12-10.30 Sun

Greene King IPA, Abbot H

Family-run, former coaching inn with a lounge-style single bar and a restaurant serving an interesting menu. Still a good drinking pub hosting live music (folk and blues) Wed eve.

🏤 🌰 🛏 ◗ ▮ P 🛏

LOWESTOFT

Oak Tavern

Crown Street West (off B1074) ☎ (01502) 537246

10.30-11; 12-10.30 Sun

Greene King Abbot; guest beers H

Large, open-plan pub, popular with football, darts and pool teams. The house beer is brewed by Woodforde's and a range of Belgian bottled-beers is stocked. 🌰 ⇌ ♣ P

Triangle Tavern

29 St. Peter's Street (opp Triangle Market Place)
☎ (01502) 582711

11-11; 12-10.30 Sun

Green Jack Bitter, Grass Hopper, Orange Wheat, Golden Sickle, Gone Fishing, seasonal beers; guest beers H

Popular, town-centre pub with contrasting bars, owned by Green Jack Brewery. It hosts weekly live music in the front bar, and seasonal beer festivals.

🏤 ▮ ⇌ ⌂

Welcome

182 London Road North
☎ (01502) 585500

10.30-4, 7.30-11; 12-4, 7.30-10.30 Sun

Adnams Bitter, Broadside; Greene King Abbot; guest beers H

Aptly named town-centre local, a single bar displaying old Lowestoft memorabilia.

⇌ ♣

MARTLESHAM

Black Tiles

Main Road (100 yds from

A12 roundabout)
☎ (01473) 610298
11-11; 12-10.30 Sun
Adnams Bitter, Broadside; guest beer Ⓗ
Originally a 1940s teashop, now a popular family pub with a continental feel, this all-day food venue has a lounge and satellite TV/cocktail bars, a restaurant and no-smoking conservatory. A pleasant garden and pond, plus children's play area are added attractions.
🚶 Q ⛵ 🏵 ◖▶ 🕭 P ⊁

MILDENHALL

Queens Arms
Queensway (follow signs for West Row)
☎ (01638) 713657
11-3, 7-11; 12-3, 7-10.30 Sun
Greene King XX Mild (winter), **IPA; guest beers** Ⓗ
Cosy, one-roomed pub on the outskirts of town drawing good local trade, but newcomers are made welcome. Limited menu of home-cooked food available; pizzas available to eat in or take away. Limited parking.
🏵 🕭 ◖▶ ♣ P

OFFTON

Limeburners
Willisham Road
☎ (01473) 658318
12-2 (not Mon). 5-11; 11-11 Sat; 12-4, 7-10.30 Sun
Adnams Bitter; Wells Eagle; guest beer Ⓗ
Friendly, two-bar local with a large garden; named after a local limekiln. Sun is buskers' night. No meals Thu eve.
🏵 ◖▶ ♣ P

PIN MILL

Butt & Oyster
☎ (01473) 780764
11-3, 7-11; 11-11 Sat & summer; 12-10.30 Sun
Tolly Cobbold Bitter Ⓖ **Original, IPA, Old** Ⓗ
Classic riverside pub boasting high-backed wooden settles and views over the Orwell. It has deservedly appeared in every edition of this *Guide*.
🚶 Q 🏵 ◖▶ ♣ P

RISBY

White Horse
Newmarket Road OS790660
☎ (01284) 810686
11-11; 11-3, 6-11 Mon; 12-10.30 Sun
Beer range varies Ⓗ
Large 18th-century roadside pub serving good home-made food. A giant outdoor draughts board and an indoor ghost add interest. 1999 Suffolk CAMRA *Pub of*

the Year: a genuine free house.
🚶 🏵 🍴 ◖▶ 🍺 & ♣ P ⊁

SNAPE

Golden Key
Priory Road
☎ (01728) 688510
11-3, 6-11; 12-3, 7-10.30 Sun
Adnams Bitter, Broadside, seasonal beers Ⓗ
Close by the famous Maltings concert hall; fine food and high-backed settles before a roaring fire add to its appeal.
🚶 Q 🏵 🍴 ◖▶ P

SOUTHWOLD

Harbour Inn
Blackshore
☎ (01502) 722381
11-11; 12-10.30 Sun
Adnams Bitter, Broadside, seasonal beers Ⓗ
Cosy riverside pub which now has a restaurant. Children's play area; dogs welcome too!
🚶 Q ⛵ 🏵 ◖▶ Å ♣ P ⊞

Lord Nelson
East Street
☎ (01502) 722079
11-11; 12-10.30 Sun
Adnams Bitter, seasonal beers Ⓗ
Nelson memorabilia abounds in this busy town pub near the cliffs. Children welcome in the side room.
🚶 🏵 ◖▶ Å ⊞

Sole Bay
7 East Green
☎ (01502) 724736
11-11; 12-10.30 Sun
Adnams Bitter, Broadside, seasonal beers Ⓗ
Single room pub by the lighthouse, often a subject for local artists.
🍴 ◖▶ Å ♣

STRADBROKE

Queens Head
Queens Street
☎ (01379) 384384
11.30-3, 6.30-11; 12-3.30, 7-10.30 Sun
Adnams Bitter; Greene King IPA; Woodforde's Wherry; guest beer (weekend) Ⓗ
A Victorian frontage hides a 16th-century interior displaying naval memorabilia. A jazz and beer festival is staged in May. Weekday lunches and guest ales represent good value.
🚶 🏵 ◖▶ P

White Hart
Church Street
☎ (01379) 384310
11-3, 7-11; 12-3, 7-10.30 Sun
Adnams Bitter; Flowers IPA; guest beer (occasional) Ⓗ
Locals' pub in a 16th-century

building, recently saved from closure after a vigorous campaign. Own bowling green.
🚶 🏵 ◖▶ ♣ P

SUDBURY

Waggon & Horses
Acton Square
☎ (01787) 312147
11-3, 6.30 (5 Fri)-11; 12-3, 7.30-10.30 Sun
Greene King IPA, Abbot; guest beer Ⓗ
Back-street local comprising several drinking areas, it hosts regular themed food events.
🚶 Q ⛵ 🏵 🍴 ◖▶ ⇆ ♣ ⊞

SWILLAND

Moon & Mushroom (Half Moon)
High Road
☎ (01473) 785320
11-2.30, 6-11; closed Mon; 12-3, 7-10.30 Sun
Buffy's Hopleaf; Green Jack Grass Hopper, Golden Sickle; Nethergate Umbel Ale, Woodforde's Wherry, Norfolk Nog Ⓖ
Extremely popular, out-of-the-way pub that attracts all types. The landlord offers a true welcome to all customers. Features include a cosy fire and oak beams; try a game of shove-ha'penny or a freshly cooked meal (not served Sun eve).
🚶 Q 🏵 ◖▶ ♣ P

THEBERTON

Lion
The Street
☎ (01728) 830185
11-2.30, 6-11; 12-3, 7-10.30 Sun
Adnams Bitter; guest beers Ⓗ
Popular village local offering three guest beers, usually from East Anglia, and live jazz first Sun in the month.
🚶 🏵 ◖▶ Å ♣ P

THELNETHAM

White Horse
Hopton Road
☎ (01379) 898298
11-3, 5-11; 11-11 Sat; 12-3, 7-10.30 Sun
Adnams Bitter; Fuller's London Pride; Greene King IPA; Nethergate Golden Gate; guest beers Ⓗ
Lovely, remote rural free house serving a local beer range with house specials brewed by Old Chimneys in neighbouring Market Weston. The safe garden provides a summer dining area; an extensive menu is served in the cosy restaurant.
🚶 🏵 ◖▶ ♣ P

TOSTOCK

Gardeners Arms

Church Road
☎ (01359) 270460
11.30-2.30, 7-11; 12-3, 7-10.30 Sun
Greene King IPA, Abbot, seasonal beers H
Fine old building retaining many original beams, set near a peaceful village green. The public bar has a stone floor; the lounge has a large fireplace and dining area. Pool played in this popular pub. Eve meals served Wed-Sun; no lunches Sun.
🏚 🕸 🌙 🍺 ♣ P ⊞

WALBERSWICK

Bell Inn
Ferry Road
☎ (01502) 723109
11-3, 6-11 (11-11 summer); 12-3.30, 7-10.30 Sun
Adnams Bitter, Broadside, seasonal beers H
Classic 600-year-old seaside inn, multi-roomed with high settles and worn flags in the main bar; always popular.
🏚 Q 🕸 🛏 🌙 🍺 ♣

WALSHAM LE WILLOWS

Six Bells
Sumner Road
☎ (01359) 259726
11.30-2.30, 5.30 (6.30 Sat)-11; 12-2, 7-10.30 Sun
Greene King XX Mild, IPA, Abbot, seasonal or guest beer H
Former wool merchant's house in the centre of a pretty village, partly dating from the 16th century. The main bar features heavily carved timbers and a large inglenook; two more bars and a games room complete the accommodation. A simple alehouse menu is served lunch and early eve.
🏚 Q 🕸 🛏 🌙 🍺 ♣ P ⊞

WALTON

Half Moon
303 Walton High Street
☎ (01394) 216009
12-2.30, 5-11; 12-11 Sat; 12-3, 7-10.30 Sun
Adnams Bitter, Broadside, guest beer H
Traditional, two-bar drinkers' pub, retaining a small basic public bar, popular with local dart players and cribbage teams, plus a larger lounge. No fruit machines, food or music intrude.
🏚 Q 🕸 🍺 ♣ P

WANGFORD

Angel Inn
39 High Street (off A12 bypass) ☎ (01502) 578636
12-3, 6-11 (12-11 summer); 12-3, 7-10.30 (12-10.30 summer) Sun
Fuller's London Pride; Wolf Best Bitter; guest beer H

300-year-old coaching inn, well modernised, employing much brick, bare board and exposed timber, in a pleasant village set back from the A12.
🏚 Q 🛏 🕸 🛏 🌙 ▲ ♣ P ⊁

Plough
London Road
☎ (01502) 578239
11-2.30 (3.30 Sat), 7-11; 12-3.30, 7-10.30 Sun
Adnams Bitter, Broadside, G **seasonal beers** H
Rare outlet for gravity-dispensed beer; cut off from the village by the busy A12, but it is easy to find.
🏚 Q 🕸 🌙 ▲ ♣ P

WENHASTON

Star
Hall Road
☎ (01502) 478240
11-3, 6-11; 12-3, 7-10.30 Sun
Adnams Bitter, seasonal beers G
Village local where beer is served from cooling cabinets behind the bar. Large garden. No food Mon.
🏚 Q 🛏 🕸 🌙 ▲ ♣ P

WESTLETON

White Horse Inn
Darsham Road
☎ (01728) 648222
12-3, 7-11; 12-4, 7-10.30 Sun
Adnams Bitter, Broadside, seasonal beers H
Brick-built village local next to the green and duck pond; a popular halt for walkers and birdwatchers.
🏚 Q 🕸 🛏 🌙 ♣ P

WEYBREAD

Crown Inn
The Street
☎ (01379) 586710
11-11; 12-10.30 Sun
Greene King IPA, Abbot; guest beer H
Two-roomed Victorian local, offering a warm welcome and a varying choice of local and regional beers.
🏚 🕸 🛏 🌙 ♣ P

WOODBRIDGE

Anchor
16-19 Quay Street (opp station)
☎ (01394) 382649
12-11; 12-10.30 Sun
Greene King XX Mild, IPA, Abbot; guest beers (occasional) H
Small, intimate front bar connects with lower dining rooms behind. A naval and nautical theme runs throughout, without being overdone. Very popular in summer, it is a rare outlet for mild in Woodbridge. No eve meals Sun.
🏚 🛏 🕸 🌙 ⇒ ♣ ⊁ 🍺

Old Bell & Steelyard
103 New Street
☎ (01394) 382933
11-3 (4 Sat), 6-11; 12-4, 7-10.30 Sun
Greene King IPA, Abbot; guest beer H
Fortunately this ancient inn has been restored back into a more basic style of pub. Although mostly knocked through, it does retain several different drinking areas. Exposed beams and tiled floors give the main serving area much character. Meals available at all times.
🏚 🛏 🕸 🌙 🍺 ⇒ ♣ P ⊁

WOOLPIT

Bull Inn
The Street (off A14, Bury-Stowmarket road)
☎ (01359) 240393
11-3, 6-11; 12-3, 7-10.30 Sun
Young's Best Bitter, seasonal beer; guest beer H
Warm, friendly, family-run inn and restaurant. The large pleasant garden and play area make it ideal for families. Meals come in generous platefuls and include daily home-cooked specials. Sun lunch is recommended (no food Sun eve). B & B is of a high standard.
Q 🛏 🕸 🛏 🌙 🍺 ♣ P

INDEPENDENT BREWERIES

Adnams: Southwold

Bartram's: Thurston

Cox & Holbrook: Great Finborough

Earl Soham: Earl Soham

Green Dragon: Bungay

Green Jack: Oulton Broad

Greene King: Bury St Edmonds

Kings Head: Bildeston

Lidstones: Wickhambrook

Mauldons: Sudbury

Nethergate: Clare

Old Cannon: Bury St Edmonds

Old Chimneys: Market Weston

St Peter's: South Elmham

Tolly Cobbold: Ipswich

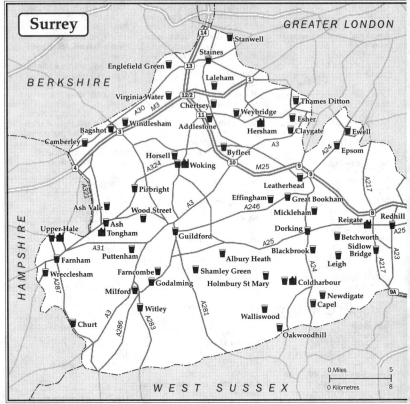

Surrey

GREATER LONDON

BERKSHIRE

Stanwell

14

Staines

Englefield Green

13

Laleham

1

Virginia Water

12/2

Chertsey

Weybridge

Thames Ditton

11

Esher

Windlesham

Addlestone

Hersham

Claygate

Bagshot

3

Ewell

Camberley

Byfleet

A3

Epsom

Horsell

Woking

10

M25

9

A24

Leatherhead

9

Pirbright

Effingham

Great Bookham

A246

Ash Vale

Wood Street

Mickleham

8

Reigate

Redhill

Upper Hale

A3

Dorking

Betchworth

A25

Ash

Guildford

Sidlow

Tongham

A25

Bridge

A31

Puttenham

Blackbrook

Leigh

A23

Farnham

Albury Heath

A24

A217

Wrecclesham

Farncombe

Shamley Green

Coldharbour

Milford

Godalming

Holmbury St Mary

Newdigate

9A

Witley

Capel

A281

Walliswood

Churt

A286

A283

Oakwoodhill

WEST SUSSEX

0 Miles 5
0 Kilometres 8

ADDLESTONE

Queens Arms
107 Church Road (B3121)
☎ (01932) 847845
11-3, 5.30-11; 11-11 Sat; 12-3,
7-10.30 Sun
**Courage Best Bitter; Young's Bitter,
Special** H
Small former Ashby (Staines)
Brewery house, built 1867,
on the B3121, heading west
out of town. Mainly a pub for
local people but everybody is
assured of a friendly
welcome.
❀ ◗ ♣ P

Waggon & Horses
43 Simplemarsh Road (off
A318)
☎ (01932) 828488
11-11; 12-10.30 Sun
**Gibbs Mew Bishops Tipple; Ushers
Best Bitter, seasonal beers** H
Family local on the edge of
the town, worth seeking out.
The U-shaped drinking area
boasts two cuckoo clocks.
Ushers *Pubs in Bloom* winner
in previous years. It hosts live
music Thu, and a quiz Tue
eve; eve meals served Thu
Sat.
♨ ❀ ◗ ♣ P

Try also: Station House,
Station Rd (Greene King)

ALBURY HEATH

William IV
Little London OS066467
☎ (01483) 202685
11-3, 5.30-11; 12-3, 7-10.30 Sun
**Flowers IPA; Hogs Back Hop Garden
Gold; Wadworth 6X; guest beers** H
Lovely 16th-century country
pub replete with beams,
flagstones, and a large
fireplace. Three distinct areas
are served from the single
bar. The two guest beers
change every couple of
months. Eve meals served
Tue-Sat. ♨ Q ❀ ◗ ⊞ ♣ P

ASH

Dover Arms
31 Guildford Road (A323)
☎ (01252) 326025
11-3, 6-11; 12-4, 7-10.30 Sun
Beer range varies H
200-year-old roadside inn
comprising two very
contrasting bars: the
public/games bar can be
boisterous, whilst the saloon
is quieter and more geared to
dining; family friendly.
❀ ◗ ▶ ⊞ ♿ ⇌ ♣ P

ASH VALE

Houstons
72 Vale Road (A321)

☎ (01252) 325535
11-11; 12-10.30 Sun
**Greene King IPA; Hogs Back TEA;
Tetley Bitter** H
Comfortable, lively,
enterprising, single bar
roadside pub with a southern
US influence as portrayed on
the large mural outside.
Twice monthly special Sat
eve feasts are produced in
genuine Texan style, with
slow roasting oven.
♿ ❀ ◗ ▶ ⇌ ♣ P

BAGSHOT

Foresters Arms
173 London Road (A30)
☎ (01276) 472038
12-2.30, 6-11; 12-3, 7-10.30 Sun
**Courage Best Bitter; Fuller's London
Pride; Greene King IPA; Hogs Back
TEA; guest beers** H
Small, pleasant local, where
three connected seating areas
are set around three sides of
the bar. It offers a wide range
of beers, and popular
traditional food. The
adjoining skittle alley can be
hired.
❀ ◗ ▶ ♣ P

BETCHWORTH

Dolphin Inn
The Street (off A25)

Courage Best Bitter; Fuller's London Pride; guest beers Ⓗ
Classic free house that stocks seven rapidly rotating guests. A real pub in every sense with two real fires, solid tables and chairs and 18th-century timbers. The art of conversation is very much alive and mobile phones are banned. The conservatory is a recent addition.
🚧 Q ❀ ◖▶ P ⊞

CAMBERLEY
Crown
469 London Road (A30)
☎ (01276) 709376
12-11; 12-4, 7-10.30 Sun
Courage Best Bitter; guest beer Ⓗ
Popular local, renowned for the excellent quality of its three cask ales, and wide selection of good food (weekdays) at fair prices. The guest beer is frequently from one of several small breweries in the area, and one of Smiles' brews is always available too. 🚧 ❀ 🛏 ◖▶ ◖
⇒ (Blackwater)♣ P

CAPEL
Crown
98 The Street
☎ (01306) 711130
11-2.30, 5-11; 11-11 Sat; 12-10.30 Sun
Fuller's London Pride; guest beers Ⓗ
Traditional village pub used by all ages. The split-level front bar has pool and the area behind the back bar is used by families, diners and drinkers. Normally three frequently changing guest beers include two from the brewer's list and one from an independent, usually Cottage.
🖘 ❀ ◖▶ ♣ P ⊀

CATERHAM
Clifton Arms
110 Chaldon Road (B2031)
☎ (01883) 343525
11-2.30, 5.30-11; 11-3, 6-11 Sat; 12-10.30 Sun
Morland Old Speckled Hen; Young's Bitter; guest beers Ⓗ
Various collections and photos are a feature of the main bar, while the small back bar tends to be used for food and opens into an area that hosts music and occasional dinner dances. The two guests change regularly. Lunches served Sun-Fri, eve meals Tue-Sat.
❀ ◖▶ 🖘 P

King & Queen
34 High Street (B2030)
☎ (01883) 345438
11-11; 12-10.30 Sun

Fuller's Chiswick. London Pride, ESB Ⓗ
The middle bar has a high ceiling and large inglenook with a small eating area at the back. There is also a front bar and a room at the side for darts. The food includes authentic oriental dishes (no meals Sun eve).
🚧 ❀ ◖▶ ♣ P

CHERTSEY
Coach & Horses
14 St Annes Road
☎ (01932) 563085
12-11; 12-3, 7-10.30 Sun
Fuller's Chiswick, London Pride, ESB, seasonal beers Ⓗ
A warm welcome awaits all at this tile-hung pub. It is attractively floodlit on dark winter eves, while hanging baskets brighten it up in summer. No food weekends, or Mon eve.
❀ 🛏 ◖▶ ♣ P ⊞

Crown
7 London Street
☎ (01932) 564657
11-11; 12-10.30 Sun
Young's Bitter, Special, Winter Warmer Ⓗ
Imposing Victorian inn near the town centre. Although there is a TV in the bar, the emphasis is on conversation, which is pleasantly interrupted by the grandfather clock. The conservatory is a recent addition.
🚧 Q 🖘 ❀ 🛏 ◖▶ ⅄ ⇒ P

CHURT
Crossways
Churt Road (A287)
☎ (01428) 714323
11-3.30, 5-11; 11-11 Fri & Sat; 12-4, 7-10.30 Sun
Cheriton Best Bitter; Courage Best Bitter; Ⓗ Ringwood Fortyniner; guest beers Ⓖ
A friendly welcome, a relaxed atmosphere, filled only with conversation, and a grand choice of beer (300 guests a year) await here. There are also three or four real ciders on stillage behind the bar. This was the 1999 Surrey CAMRA *Pub of the Year*. No food Sun.
Q ❀ ◖▶ 🖽 ⅄ ♠ ♣ ⊂ P

CLAYGATE
Foley Arms
Foley Road
☎ (01372) 463431
11-11; 12-10.30 Sun
Young's Bitter, Special, Winter Warmer Ⓗ
Comfortable two-bar Victorian village pub. A children's play area takes up part of the large garden.

☎ (01737) 842288
11-3, 5.30-11; 11-11 Sat; 12-10.30 Sun
Young's Bitter, Special, Winter Warmer Ⓗ
Friendly, 16th-century village pub with a flagstone floor and two wood-burning inglenooks. In a very attractive spot, it stands opposite the village church and blacksmith's.
🚧 Q ❀ ◖▶ ♣ P

BLACKBROOK
Plough at Blackbrook
Blackbrook Road (off A24, S of Dorking)
☎ (01306) 886603
11-2.30 (3 Sat), 6-11; 12-3, 7-10.30 Sun
King & Barnes Sussex, seasonal beer Ⓗ
Genuine country pub, well known for its good food and award-winning cellar. Enjoy the two comfortable bars and the small but tidy garden. No meals Sun eve.
Q ❀ ◖▶ P

BYFLEET
Plough
104 High Road (off A245)
☎ (01932) 353257
11-3, 5-11; 12-3, 7-10.30 Sun

Light meals served eves (not Sun).

♨ Q ❀ ◖ ❶ ❷ ≈ ♣ P

Griffin

58 Common Road
☎ (01372) 463799
11-11; 12-10.30 Sun
Badger Dorset Best; Fuller's London Pride; Pilgrim Surrey Bitter; guest beer Ⓗ

Popular 1920s back-street local: a lively public bar and a quieter, comfortable L-shaped lounge with bench seating. Note the Mann, Crossman & Paulin windows. Eve meals served Fri.

♨ Q ❀ ◖ ❹ ♣ P

Swan

2 Hare Lane
☎ (01372) 462582
11-11; 12-10.30 Sun
Draught Bass; Courage Best Bitter; Fuller's London Pride; Marston's Pedigree Ⓗ

Early 20th-century pub with a Thai restaurant. The single bar is decorated in brasserie style. It boasts strong cricketing connections – the Leverets play on the green opposite.

◖ ❶ ≈ P

COLDHARBOUR

Plough Inn

Coldharbour Lane (Leith Hill-Dorking road) OS152441
☎ (01306) 711793
11.30-3, 6-11; 11.30-11 Sat; 12-10.30 Sun
Badger Tanglefoot; Hogs Back TEA; Leith Hill Crooked Furrow, Tallywhacker; Ringwood Old Thumper; guest beers Ⓗ

In good walking country near Leith Hill, this pub can become very busy in the summer. The bar features ten handpumps, one dispenses Biddenden cider. The tiny Leith Hill Brewery is on the premises.

♨ Q ☙ ❀ ⛺ ◖ ❶ ⛄ P

DORKING

Bush

10 Horsham Road (A2003)
☎ (01306) 889830
12-2.30 (3 Sat), 6-11; 12-3, 7-10.30 Sun
Brakspear Bitter; Greene King IPA; guest beer Ⓗ

Good, single bar local away from the town centre. There is a covered patio and garden at the back. The pub fields a marbles team. The guest beer is usually from a small brewery. Eve meals Tue-Sat.

❀ ◖ ❶ ♣

Cricketers

81 South Street (A25, one-way system)
☎ (01306) 889938

12-11; 12-10.30 Sun
Fuller's Chiswick, London Pride, ESB, seasonal beers Ⓗ

Small one-bar local which features a large etched mirror with a cricketing motif. The patio garden is pleasant in summer. No food Sun.

❀ ◖ ♣

Kings Arms

45 West Street (A25, one-way system)
☎ (01306) 883361
11-11; 12-3, 7-10.30 Sun
Fuller's London Pride; Greene King IPA; Wadworth 6X; Young's Special; guest beer Ⓗ

Originally built as three farmworkers' cottages in 1405, later becoming a coaching inn, the pub retains some beams and wood panelling. It stages live music Sun eve and a quiz Mon eve. The guest beer is usually from a small brewery. Eve meals Tue-Sat. Limited parking.

❀ ◖ ❶ ♿ ≈ (West) P

Queen's Head

Horsham Road (A25, one-way system)
☎ (01306) 883041
11-11; 12-10.30 Sun
Fuller's Chiswick, London Pride, ESB Ⓗ

Attractive tile-hung, family-run pub. The single bar has two dartboards and a pool table as well as a TV for the main sports events. No food Sun. Very limited parking.

❀ ◖ ♣ P ⊞

Try also: **Bulls Head**, South St (Gales)

EFFINGHAM

Plough

Orestan Lane
☎ (01372) 458121
11-2.45 (3 Sat), 6-11; 12-3, 7-10.30 Sun
Young's Bitter, Special, Winter Warmer Ⓗ

Delightful retreat, frequently very busy with diners early eve and at weekends. A good enclosed garden at the rear has children's swings etc.

Q ❀ ◖ ❶ P

ENGLEFIELD GREEN

Beehive

34 Middle Hill (off A30, Egham Hill)
☎ (01784) 431621
11-11; 12-10.30 Sun
Gale's GB, HSB; Hop Back Summer Lightning; guest beers Ⓗ

A good beer range (three guests) is stocked at this friendly village local on the slopes of Egham Hill. Built in 1870, and not changed much since, it hosts beer festivals late spring and Aug Bank

---

Holidays. Cider is sold in summer. An extensive menu is served 12-5.

♨ ❀ ◖ ♣ P

EPSOM

Barley Mow

Pikes Hill (off A2022)
☎ (01372) 721044
11-11; 12-10.30 Sun
Fuller's Chiswick, London Pride, ESB Ⓗ

Pleasant pub: its single large bar is attractively decorated and features many nooks and seating areas. It hosts a curry night (Tue) and steak night (Thu), no food Sun eve. The spacious garden is secluded.

♨ ❀ ◖ ❶ ♿ ♣ ⊞

Railway Guard

48 Church Road (off A2022)
☎ (01372) 721143
11-11; 12-10.30 Sun
Hop Back Summer Lightning; Fuller's London Pride; Taylor Landlord; guest beers Ⓗ

Beer-drinker's pub, stocking a frequently-changing range of beers, it is popular with students at weekends, but not rowdy. It boasts an hexagonal rotating pool table. A wide range of single malt whiskies and weekday lunches are also on offer. Local CAMRA *Pub of the Year* 2000.

❀ ◖ ♣ ⊞

ESHER

Albert Arms

82 High Street (A307)
☎ (01372) 465290
11-11; 12-10.30 Sun
Boddingtons Bitter; Brakspear Special; Fuller's London Pride; Young's Bitter; guest beer Ⓗ

Family-owned and -run free house that gets busy on race days – Sandown Park is nearby. A two-bar pub, it also has a dining area (no food Sun eve).

Q ◖ ❶ ❹

EWELL

Eight Bells

78 Kingston Road
☎ (020) 8393 9973
11.30-11; 12-10.30 Sun
Greene King IPA, Abbot; guest beers Ⓗ

Friendly Edwardian pub with a large bar area. Unobtrusive background music is played most of the time, with live music Sat eve. Eve meals finish at 8pm.

♨ ❀ ◖ ❶ ♿ ≈ (West) ♣ P

FARNCOMBE

Cricketers

37 Nightingale Road (over level crossing, away from

centre)
☎ (01483) 420273
12-3, 5.30-11; 11-11 Sat; 12-10.30 Sun

Fuller's Chiswick, London Pride, ESB, seasonal beers H
Originally kept by one Julius Caesar of Surrey and England cricket fame, it still features all things cricket, from bails to bats and pads. Proud to be 12 successive years in this *Guide*. No eve meals Sun.
🏚 🍺 ▶ ≈ ♣ ✂ 🖵

FARNHAM
Lamb
43 Abbey Street (near Farnham Maltings off A287)
☎ (01252) 714133
11-2.30, 5-11; 11-11 Fri & Sat; 12-10.30 Sun

Shepherd Neame Best Bitter, Spitfire, seasonal beers H
Small and comfortable, off the town centre, the Lamb appeals to all ages on the basis of beer, good food and live music (Fri). Two real fires add to the cosiness in winter, whilst in summer the rooftop terrace garden can be a suntrap.
🚶 🏚 🍺 ▶ ≈ ♣

Queens Head
9 The Borough (on A287/A325, one-way system)
☎ (01252) 726524
11-11; 12-10.30 Sun

Gale's Butser, GB, HSB, seasonal beers; guest beer H
Historic, town-centre pub owned by Gale's since 1888. It attracts a loyal local following, as well as being popular with shoppers and visitors to Farnham. It stands a short walk from the castle. No food Sun.
🚶 🏚 🍺 🖵 ≈ ♣ 🖵

Shepherd & Flock
22 Moor Park Lane (off A31, N of Farnham)
☎ (01252) 716675
11-3, 5.30-11; 11-11 Fri & Sat; 12-10.30 Sun

Courage Best Bitter; Fuller's London Pride; Gale's HSB; Hogs Back TEA; Ringwood Old Thumper; guest beers H
A single, long bar leads to a dining/drinking seating area at one end, occasional TV-viewing occurs in the more traditional other end. Smoking is permitted throughout, relieved by a clean-air system. The garden is child-friendly.
🏚 🍺 ▶ P

William Cobbett
4 Bridge Square, Abbey Street (A287, by Farnham Maltings)
☎ (01252) 726628
11-11; 12-10.30 Sun

Courage Best Bitter, Directors;

Theakston Old Peculier; guest beers H
Birthplace of the 19th-century radical whose name it bears, this is a young person's venue and the music can be loud. Multi-roomed, it also boasts covered outside drinking area to the rear.
🏚 🍺 ▶ ≈ ♣ P

GODALMING
Anchor
110 Ockford Road (A3100, signed Milford from inner relief road)
☎ (01483) 417085
12-2.30 (3 Sat), 5.30 (6 Sat)-11; 12-3, 7-10.30 Sun

Badger Tanglefoot; Brakspear Bitter; Gale's HSB; Hop Back Summer Lightning; guest beers H
On the edge of town, elevated above the road, with an L-shaped bar, this free house stocks a genuine range of guest beers. It attracts a mainly younger clientele eves who enjoy sometimes loud music. Parking is difficult.
🏚 🍺 ♣ P

Red Lion
1 Mill Lane (High St jct)
☎ (01483) 415207
11 (12 Sat)-3, 6.30-11; 12-3, 7-10.30 Sun

Courage Best Bitter; guest beers H
Large town pub of two contrasting bars: the saloon is potentially sedate, whilst the large public/games bar can be lively. It usually sells two guest beers of an unusual nature, plus interesting bottled beers. No food Sun eve.
Q 🍺 ▶ 🖳 ♿ ≈ ♣ 🖵

GREAT BOOKHAM
Anchor
161 Lower Road (off A246, via Eastwick Rd)
☎ (01372) 452429
11-3, 5.30-11; 12-3, 7-10.30 Sun

Courage Best Bitter, Directors; guest beers H
500-year-old Grade II listed local; cosy and welcoming with an island bar, it is traditionally decorated with exposed brickwork, oak beams and a large inglenook. No food Sun.
🚶 Q 🏚 🍺 ♣ P

GUILDFORD
Plough
16 Park Street (one-way system, anti-clockwise from station)
☎ (01483) 570167
11-11; 12-10.30 Sun

Fuller's London Pride; Tetley Bitter; Young's Special H
One of the last of Guildford's traditional pubs, it stands in

marked contrast to recent town-centre developments. Its small, single bar is often crowded.
≈ ♣ 🖵

Varsity Sports Bar
Egerton Road (off A3, opp. County Hospital)
☎ (01483) 505271
11-11; 12-10.30 Sun

Beer range varies H
Off-campus, this recently refurbished University sports bar is open to the public and used extensively by non-students. It stocks three regularly changing beers and hosts festivals: bottled beers in the Spring and cask ales in the Autumn. Opening hours might vary outside term-time. No food Sun eve.
🍺 ▶ P

Try also: **Cricketers**, Aldershot Rd, Rydes Hill (Inntrepreneur)

HOLMBURY ST MARY
King's Head
Pitland Street (50 yds off B2126)
☎ (01306) 730282
11-3, 6-11; 11-11 Sat & summer; 12-10.30 Sun

Fuller's London Pride; Hogs Back TEA; Ringwood Best Bitter; guest beers H
Lively local at the foot of wooded Holmbury Hill, popular with ramblers. No meals Sun eve.
🚶 🏚 🍺 ▶ ♣ P

HORSELL
Plough
Cheapside, South Road OS996599
☎ (01483) 714105
11-3, 5-11; 11-11 Sat; 12-4, 7-10.30 Sun

Fuller's London Pride; ; Greene King IPA; Young's Special; guest beers H
Enjoying a rural setting on the edge of Horsell Common in good walking territory, the Plough is set back from the road and easily missed, which would be a pity given both the beers (guests are often from Beckett's and Sharp's) and the excellent quality food. No meals Sun eve.
🚶 🏚 🍺 ▶ P

LALEHAM
Feathers
The Broadway (B377)
☎ (01784) 453561
11-11; 12-10.30 Sun

Courage Best Bitter; Fuller's London Pride; Morland Old Speckled Hen; guest beers H
Friendly village local, a short walk from the Thames. An

excellent beer range includes two frequently-changing independent guests, complemented by regular beer festivals. Good pub food is served all day until 9.30. Local CAMRA *Pub of the Year* 1999.

🏨 🏵 🕪 🅰 ♣ P

LEATHERHEAD
Hogshead (Penny Black)
5 North Street
☎ (01372) 386719
11-11; 12-10.30 Sun
Boddingtons Bitter; Flowers Original; Fuller's London Pride; Marston's Pedigree; Wadworth 6X; Ⓗ guest beers Ⓗ/Ⓖ
Converted from an old post office, hence its name, this pub has been redecorated in café-bar style with a painted ceiling, exposed brick pillars and walls with some wood panelling.

🏨 🏵 🕪 🖑 ⇌ ✄

LEIGH
Plough
Church Road
☎ (01306) 611348
11-11; 12-10.30 Sun
King & Barnes Sussex, Broadwood, Festive, seasonal beer Ⓗ
Two-bar village inn, enjoying an attractive position near the church. The Victorian public (with many games) contrasts with the 15th-century lounge bar/restaurant (the very good food is sold throughout).

Q 🏵 🕪 ⊟ ♣ P

MICKLEHAM
King William IV
Byttom Hill (off A24, southbound) OS174538
☎ (01372) 372590
11-3, 6-11; 12-3, 7-10.30 Sun
Adnams Bitter; Badger Dorset Best; Hogs Back TEA; guest beers Ⓗ
Charming, 18th-century pub, perched on a rocky hillside, where its popular stepped garden affords views across to Norbury Park. It is much frequented by diners, but access may be difficult for the infirm. No food Mon eve.
🏨 Q 🏵 🕪 P

Running Horses
Old London Road (B2209)
☎ (01372) 372279
11.30-3, 5.30-11; 12-3.30, 7-10.30 Sun
Friary Meux BB; Fuller's London Pride; Greene King Abbot; Young's Bitter; guest beer Ⓗ
16th-century, listed coaching inn, named in 1828 after a run-off of the Derby. The dining area to the rear is converted from stables,

where racehorses were once kept and offers a wide ranging menu (booking is recommended); no food Sun eve.
🏨 🏵 🛏 🕪 🖑

MILFORD
Red Lion
Old Portsmouth Road
(A3100, near A286 jct)
☎ (01483) 424342
11-2.3,0 5.30-11; 11-11 Sat; 12-3, 6-10.30 Sun
Gale's Butser, GB, HSB, seasonal beers; guest beer (occasional) Ⓗ
Gale's Horndean Inn, where a considerable emphasis is placed on food, but this large roadside pub maintains a good pub atmosphere in its public bar and games area, skittle alley and function room. No meals Sun eve.
Q 🏵 🕪 ⊟ 🖑 P

NEWCHAPEL
Blacksmiths Head
Newchapel Road (B2028, near Lingfield)
☎ (01342) 833697
11-3, 5.30-11; 12-3, 6-11 Sat; 12-3, 6-10.30 Sun
Brakspear Bitter; Fuller's London Pride, ESB; guest beer Ⓗ
Close to the imposing Mormon Temple, this pub, originally with three rooms, has been opened out into a single bar with a restaurant area featuring a menu with a Spanish element (no food Mon). The guest beer changes weekly.
🏨 Q 🏵 🕪 🅰 ♣ P

NEWDIGATE
Surrey Oaks
Parkgate Road, Parkgate OS205436
☎ (01306) 631200
11.30-2.30 (3 Sat), 5.30 (6 Sat)-11; 12-3, 7-10.30 Sun
Adnam's Bitter; Fuller's London Pride; guest beers Ⓗ
This old, attractive country inn is usually full of friendly locals. The one bar serves a number of distinct drinking areas with a restaurant part serving good food (eve meals Tue-Sat). The lovely garden has doves flying around. The beer range is impressive and often features unusual ales.
🏨 Q 🏵 🕪 ♣ ⊝ P

OAKWOOD HILL
Punchbowl
Oakwood Hill Lane (off A29)
☎ (01306) 627249
11-3; 12-10.30 Sun
Badger Dorset Best, Tanglefoot; guest beer Ⓗ
Attractive, tile-hung building, parts of which date from the

14th century. The lounge features a large inglenook and stone flags; the public bar offers games. Good home-cooked food is served (no meals Sun eve). The guest beer is often from the Gribble Brewery.
🏨 🏵 🕪 ⊟ ♣ P ⊞

OXTED
George
52 High Street, Old Oxted (off A25)
☎ (01883) 713453
11-11; 12-10.30 Sun
Badger IPA, Dorset Best, Tanglefoot Ⓗ
Comfortable 500-year-old pub featuring three drinking areas. Well known for good food at reasonable prices, it is often busy.
🏨 Q 🏵 🕪 P

PIRBRIGHT
Royal Oak
Aldershot Road (A324)
☎ (01483) 232466
11-11; 12-10.30 Sun
Flowers IPA, Original; guest beers Ⓗ
400 years old in a superb setting by a stream, the pub has a massive garden to quieten even the most energetic of children. Other attractions include six guest beers, low beams, separate drinking areas, three real fires, clay pigeon and cask ale clubs, plus a monthly quiz.
🏨 Q 🏵 🕪 🖑 🅰 P ✄

PUTTENHAM
Good Intent
62 The Street (off B3000)
☎ (01483) 810387
11-2.30, 6-11; 11-11 Sat; 12-10.30 Sun
Courage Best Bitter; Greene King Abbot; Theakston Old Peculier; Young's Bitter, Special; guest beer Ⓗ
Excellent free house in a pretty village, it is popular with walkers (and their dogs) from the North Downs Way. Diners appreciate 'newspaper' fish and chips (Wed); eve meals Tue-Sat.
🏨 🏵 🕪 🅰 ♣ ⊝ P

REDHILL
Garland
5 Brighton Road (A23)
☎ (01737) 760377
11-11; 12-3, 7-10.30 Sun
Harveys XX Mild, Sussex Pale Ale, BB, Armada, seasonal beers Ⓗ
The huge collection of clowns is not immediately obvious but is a feature of this Victorian local just off the town centre. Darts is very popular but does not intrude.

Eve meals served Wed-Sun.
🕸 ◖ ▌ ≋ ♣ ♠

Hatch
44 Hatchlands Road (A25 towards Reigate)
☎ (01737) 764593
12-3, 5.30-11; 12-3, 7.30-10.30 Sun
Shepherd Neame Master Brew Bitter, Spitfire, Bishops Finger, seasonal beers Ⓗ
This smart, friendly, stone-clad local boasts an impressive floral display on the front patio. Inside, the busy but relaxed single bar has several drinking areas decorated with Edwardian music hall prints and a collection of copper pans. The food is good.
🕸 ◖ ▌ ♠

Sun
17-21 London Road (A25)
☎ (01737) 766886
11-11; 12-10.30 Sun
Courage Directors; Greene King Abbot; Hogs Back TEA; Shepherd Neame Spitfire; Wadworth 6X; guest beers Ⓗ
Large glass-fronted Wetherspoon's outlet, just off the shopping centre, whose walls tell the story of famous local residents and events.
Q ◖ ▌ ≋ ⌂ ⚲ ⊞

Try also: Home Cottage, Redstone Hill (Young's)

Bricklayers Arms
The Green (B2128)
☎ (01483) 898377
11-11; 12-10.30 Sun
Arundel Best Bitter; Courage Best Bitter; Gales HSB; guest beers Ⓗ
Rare example of what Surrey pubs used to be like; dominated by a magnificent public bar and imposing real fire. It lies tucked away on the edge of the village green in good walking territory. Guests are likely to include the Arundel range. ⚏ 🕸 ♣ P

Three Horseshoes
Ironbottom (off A217)
☎ (01293) 862315
12-2.30 (3 Sat), 5.30-11; 12-3, 7-10.30 Sun
Fuller's London Pride, ESB, seasonal beer; Harvey's BB; Young's Bitter, Special; guest beer Ⓗ
Sympathetically extended, this comfortable rural inn offers good value and excellent quality beer and lunchtime food. The guest beer changes frequently.
⚏ Q ☙ 🕸 ⚕ ◖ ♣ P

Angel

24 High Street (A308)
☎ (01784) 452509
11-11; 12-10.30 Sun
Courage Best Bitter; Hogs Back Hair of the Hog; Ushers Best Bitter; guest beers Ⓗ
Welcoming and comfortable town-centre inn that can trace its origins to the 14th century. The well-kept range features up to five beers; the food is excellent value.
🕸 ⚕ ◖ ▌ ≋

Bells
124 Church Street (off B376)
☎ (01784) 454240
11-11; 12-10.30 Sun
Young's Bitter, Special, seasonal beers Ⓗ
Attractive and comfortable pub in the old and quieter part of town, close to the river; it enjoys a good local following.
Q 🕸 ◖ ▌ ♿

Hobgoblin
14 Church Street (off A308)
☎ (01784) 452012
12-11; 12-10.30 Sun
Wychwood Shires, Special, Hobgoblin, seasonal beers; guest beer Ⓗ
Popular, single-bar pub near the town centre, serving an ever-changing guest beer to a young clientele, who like the modern music mix (at high volume) eves. Weekday lunches served.
⚏ 🕸 ◖ ≋

Old Red Lion
Leacroft (off Kingston Road, 250 yds E of station)
☎ (01784) 453355
11-3, 5-11; 11-11 Sat; 12-3.30, 7-10.30 Sun
Courage Best Bitter; Fuller's London Pride, seasonal beers Ⓗ
Attractive pub dating from the 17th century where a single, central bar is surrounded by a comfortable, well-decorated drinking area with a games room off to the side. Prices are a bit higher than other local pubs, but it is in a quiet spot, off the main road. No food Sun; a Young's beer is always stocked.
Q 🕸 ◖ ≋ ♣ P

Wheatsheaf
Park Road (B378)
☎ (01784) 253372
11-11; 11-10.30 Sun
Courage Best Bitter, Directors; guest beers Ⓗ
Popular corner pub in a part of Stanwell that retains its village atmosphere, despite being close to Heathrow airport. It has two small drinking areas (children only admitted to the garden). No

food Sat eve or Sun.
🕸 ◖ ▌ P

George & Dragon
High Street (off B364)
☎ (020) 8398 2206
11-11; 12-10.30 Sun
Draught Bass; Brakspear Bitter; Courage Best Bitter Ⓗ
Set off the road in its own car park, the pub retains the atmosphere of a village local. Its wood-panelled interior is divided into a number of areas, including one for children. It hosts live jazz monthly.
Q ☙ 🕸 ◖ ≋ P ⚲

Ball & Wicket
104 Upper Hale Road (A3016)
☎ (01252) 735278
4 (12 Sat)-11; 12-3, 7-10.30 Sun
B&T Dragonslayer; Courage Best Bitter; Hale & Hearty Upper Ale, Wicket Bitter, seasonal beers; Wadworth 6X Ⓗ
Brew-pub whose rapidly growing reputation is attracting ale-lovers from far and wide, but still manages to retain its image as a local. It stands opposite Hale CC and cricket is reflected in the beer names. The owner also runs an American-style brew-pub in Woking.
⚏ 🕸 P

Black Prince
147 Upper Hale Road (A3016)
☎ (01252) 714530
12-11; 12-3, 6-11 Sat; 12-3, 6-10.30 Sun
Fuller's Chiswick, London Pride, seasonal beers Ⓗ
A warm welcome awaits in this cosy, two-bar pub. A dining room is adjacent to the main bar and pool and darts are played in the lounge. The garden features a safe children's play area. A top-notch Indian restaurant is just a few doors away.
⚏ Q 🕸 P

Rose & Olive Branch
Callow Hill ($1/2$ mile N of Christchurch Rd, B389)
OS993689
☎ (01344) 843713
11-3, 5.30 (6 Sat)-11; 12-5, 7-10.30 Sun
Greene King Abbot; Ruddles Best Bitter; Wadworth 6X Ⓗ
Comfortable, cosy country pub, slightly out of the way, but well worth the trip. It offers an extensive range of good quality food. The name refers to a Civil War treaty when the Cavaliers gave a rose and the Roundheads an

olive branch.
Q ✿ ◖ ▶ P

WALLISWOOD
Scarlett Arms
Walliswood Green Road
OS119382
☎ (01306) 627243
11-2.30, 5.30-11; 12-3, 7-10.30 Sun
King & Barnes Mild, Sussex, Festive, seasonal beers Ⓗ
This beautiful old, whitewashed building, formerly two 17th-century cottages, became a pub in 1907. Two small rooms lead off the bar; the rear one, behind the impressive fireplace, is for games. Local CAMRA *Pub of the Year* 2000; it serves good food plus cider in summer.
🏠 Q ✿ ◖ ▶ ♣ ⌂ P

WEYBRIDGE
Jolly Farmer
40 Princes Road (off A317)
☎ (01932) 856873
10.30-3, 5.30-11; 10.30-11 Sat; 12-4, 7-10.30 Sun
Fuller's London Pride; Hop Back Best Bitter, Summer Lightning, seasonal beers Ⓗ
Comfortable well-patronised and friendly back-street local where a single L-shaped bar is surrounded by upholstered bench seats, and has a low, beamed ceiling.
✿ ◖

Prince of Wales
11 Cross Road, Oatlands
☎ (01932) 852082
10.30-11; 12-10.30 Sun
Adnams Bitter; Draught Bass; Boddingtons Bitter; Fuller's London Pride; Tetley Bitter Ⓗ
This quite large local is hidden just off the main road but noticeable by its impressive floral display decorating the front. It has three bars with two main areas: a large open fire at one end, and a restaurant adjoining the other. Small car park.
🏠 Q ✿ ◖ ▶ P ⊞

WINDLESHAM
Half Moon
Church Road (from A30 take School Lane, then first right)
☎ (01276) 473329
11-3; 5.30-11 (11-11 summer, if busy); 12-4, 7-10.30 Sun
Brakspear Bitter; Fuller's London Pride; Hop Back Summer Lightning; Ringwood Fortyniner; Theakston Old Peculier; guest beers Ⓗ
This attractive free house has been run by the Sturt family since 1904. Popular for the range and quality of its beers and food (no meals Sun eve), it boasts an extensive

garden/play area with prize floral displays. Children's certificate.
🏠 Q ✿ ◖ ▶ ⅃ ⌂ P

Try also: Surrey Cricketers, Chertsey Rd (Waverley Inns)

WITLEY
Star Inn
Petworth Road (A283)
☎ (01428) 684656
11-11; 12-3, 7-10.30 Sun
Friary Meux BB; guest beers Ⓗ
Two-bar village pub, dating from the 17th century. The attractive beamed lounge bar features an inglenook. The restaurant is a conservatory extension in which children are welcome. It employs an imaginative guest beer policy.
✿ ◖ ♣ P

Try also: White Hart, Petworth Rd (Shepherd Neame)

WOKING
Wetherspoons
51-57 Chertsey Road
☎ (01483) 722818
11-11; 12-10.30 Sun
Courage Directors; Hogs Back TEA; Theakston Best Bitter; guest beers Ⓗ
Easily one of the best in the chain and usually stocking three or four imaginative guest beers, it is large, open plan and often very busy at weekends. Difficult to imagine that there was ever a Woking centre without it.
Q ◖ ▶ ⅃ ≠ ⌂ ⅃ ⊞

WOOD STREET
Royal Oak
89 Oak Hill OS958510
☎ (01483) 235137
11-3 (3.30 Sat), 5-11; 12-3.30, 7-10.30 Sun
Courage Best Bitter; Hogs Back TEA; guest beers Ⓗ
This legendary free house has just passed its 1000th beer. It offers four guests of the impossible-to-guess kind, one of which is always a mild. A friendly welcome is assured, especially from Oliver the

Red Burmese cat. Local CAMRA *Pub of the Year* 1998.
✿ ◖ ♣ ⌂ P

WRECCLESHAM
Bat & Ball
15 Bat & Ball Lane, Boundstone (off Upper Bourne Lane via Sandrock Hill) OS834444
☎ (01252) 792108
12-11; 12-10.30 Sun
Boddingtons Bitter; Brakspear Bitter; Fuller's London Pride; guest beers Ⓗ
Lovely free house, somewhat isolated, on the Bourne stream. It can be difficult to find, but is always worth the effort. Extremely popular with diners and families, but the quality of the beer is never compromised. Ballards Strong Old Ale is served on gravity when available. No food Sun eve.
⅃ ✿ ◖ ⅃ P

Sandrock
Sandrock Hill Road (off B3384) OS830444
☎ (01252) 715865
11-11; 12-10.30 Sun
Batham Best Bitter; Brakspear Bitter; Cheriton Pots Ale; Enville Ale; guest beers Ⓗ
First-class free house serving a great range of beers at their best. Comfortable, welcoming and well managed, this pub attracts a wide range of customers. Beer festivals are held in a marquee in the garden. Not to be missed. No food Sun.
🏠 Q ⅃ ✿ ◖ ♣ P

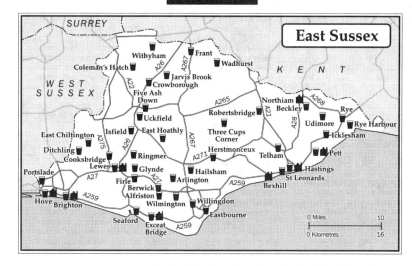

East Sussex

ALFRISTON

Old Smugglers Inne
Waterloo Square
☎ (01323) 870241
11-2.30, 6.30-11; 12-3.30, 7.30-9 Sun
Harveys BB, Old; Old Forge Pett Progress H
Pub with two names – it is also known locally as the Market Cross. It retains much character in the main bar and has a rambling set of other small rooms featuring beams and low ceilings. Reputedly haunted by two ghosts, it is frequented by walkers on the South Downs Way.
Q ✿ ❀ ◑ ▶ & ✁

Try also: Wingrove (Free)

ARLINGTON

Old Oak Inn
Just outside village on Hailsham-Wilmington road OS558078
☎ (01323) 482072
11-3, 6-11; 12-3, 7-10.30 Sun
Badger Dorset Best; Harveys BB; guest beer G
Cosy, quiet pub near Abbots Wood and Arlington Stadium, it is ideal for a quiet drink and a meal in its comfy longe and restaurant. Eve meals served Tue-Sat.
⚅ Q ❀ ◑ ▶ P 🍺

BECKLEY

Rose & Crown
Northiam Road
(B2188/B2165 jct)
☎ (01797) 252161
11-3, 5.30-11; 11-11 Fri & Sat; 12-11 Sun
Adnams Broadside; Harveys BB; Hook Norton Best Bitter guest beers H
Spacious, family pub, affording fine views from the garden. Beers from distant breweries are always available along with an excellent menu.
⚅ Q ❀ ◑ ▶ ♣ P

BERWICK

Cricketers Arms
S of A27, just off Drusilla's roundabout OS519053
☎ (01323) 870469
11-3, 6-11 (11-11 summer Sat); 12-10.30 Sun
Harveys BB, seasonal beers G
Fine old house (once two cottages) where time has stood still. Winner of Sussex CAMRA *Pub of the Year* and Harvey's *Cellar of the Year* 1997. Its large garden is ideal for walkers. A good range of excellent food is served in generous helpings.
⚅ Q ❀ ◑ ▶ & P

BRIGHTON

Basketmakers Arms
12 Gloucester Road
☎ (01273) 689006
11-3, 5.30 (5 Tue & Thu)-11; 11-11 Fri & Sat; 12-10.30 Sun
Gale's Butser, GB, HSB, Festival Mild, seasonal beers; guest beers H
Deservedly popular, street-corner pub where a good choice of whiskies is on offer; busy at weekends. Eve meals served weekdays.
◑ ▶ ≉ 🍴

Cleveland
27 Cleveland Road (opp. Blakers Park)
☎ (01273) 502396
11.30-11; 12-10.30 Sun
Marston's Pedigree; Theakston Best Bitter; Wadworth 6X; Young's Special; guest beers H
Welcoming local set in a residential area. The bar is covered with paintings by local artists which are for sale. Live music is staged once a month.
❀ ◑ ♣

Constant Service
96 Islingword Road
☎ (01273) 607058
12-11; 12-10.30 Sun
Harveys BB, Armada, seasonal beers; Wadworth 6X H
Pleasant corner pub where the walls are adorned with prints of old Brighton and waterworks memorabilia.
⚅ ❀

Evening Star
55-56 Surrey Street (near station)
☎ (01273) 328931
11.30 (11 Sat)-11; 12-10.30 Sun
Dark Star Skinner's Pale Ale, Skinner's Golden Gate Bitter, Dark Star, seasonal beers; guest beers H
Home of the Dark Star Brewery, this friendly pub has nine pumps dispensing an ever-changing selection of house beers, guest beers and usually two ciders. Regular live music performed.
❀ ◑ ≉ 🍴

Greys
105 Southover Street
☎ (01273) 680734
11-3, 5.30-11; 11-11 Sat; 12-10.30 Sun
Beer range varies H
This busy corner pub hosts live music every Mon eve. There is a regular house beer from Bewery on Sea and it is noted for its high quality food, served Tue-Sun lunch and Tue-Thu eves.
❀ ◑ ▶

Hand in Hand
33 Upper St James's Street
☎ (01273) 602521
11-3, 5.30-11; 11-11 Sat; 12-10.30 Sun

Kemptown Brighton Bitter, Bitter, Olde Trout, SID, Old Grumpy; guest beers Ⓗ
Compact home of Kemptown Brewery, with unusual decor: the walls are covered with extracts from old newspapers and historic local pictures, whilst ties adorn the ceiling. An occasional cider is stocked.
◖ ⏥

Lord Nelson
36 Trafalgar Street
☎ (01273) 695872
11-11; 12-10.30 Sun
Harveys XX Mild, Pale Ale, BB, Armada, seasonal beers Ⓗ
Deservedly popular two-bar pub where children are welcome until early eve. Quiz night Tue; it is home to many sporting societies. No food Sun.
⚏ ❀ ◖ ⇜

Park Crescent
39 Park Crescent Terrace
☎ (01273) 604993
3 (12 Sat)-11; 12-10.30 Sun
King & Barnes Broadwood, Festive, seasonal beers Ⓗ
Popular with students, this pub offers a cosmopolitan feeling; children are welcome early eve. A wide-ranging menu includes a daily special plus Sunday lunch; coffee and newspapers also available. No meals Sun eve.
❀ ▶ ⏥

Prestonville
64 Hamilton Road
☎ (01273) 701007
5 (4 Fri; 11 Sat)-11; 12-10.30 Sun
Gale's Butser, GB, HSB, Festival Mild, seasonal beers; guest beers Ⓗ
Welcoming corner pub in an 18th-century development. It has undergone a revival since new management took over in 1997, and is worth going out of the way to find. An extended lunch service is offered at weekends, but no eve meals.
Q ❀ ◖⊞

Prince Arthur
38 Dean Street (off Western Road)
☎ (01273) 203472
12-11; 12-10.30 Sun
Fuller's London Pride; Harveys BB Ⓗ
Single-bar, town-centre local with a conservatory, near the main shopping area.
Q ⇜ ⏥

Pump House
Behind Hannington's store
11-11; 12-10.30 Sun
Draught Bass; Harveys BB; Courage Directors Ⓗ
Carefully refurbished pub at the heart of the Lanes area; ideal for shopping. ◖ ♿ ⚹

Ranelagh Arms
2-4 High Street
☎ (01273) 681634
10.30-11; 12-10.30 Sun
Fuller's London Pride; Wells Bombardier; Young's Special Ⓗ
Small, one-bar pub filled with musical memorabilia, plus a collection of coins above the bar. A popular venue for live music Sun lunch and eve and the occasional Thu.
❀ ◖ ▶

Stag Inn
33 Upper Bedford Street
☎ (01273) 609676
11-11; 12-10.30 Sun
Shepherd Neame Master Brew Bitter, Spitfire, Bishops Finger, seasonal beers Ⓗ
New home for Brighton's 'sausage pub' with a spacious seating area by a long narrow bar. Note the Watney and Whitbread keg fonts that do not dispense the said beer, but are an example of the landlord's sense of humour. No eve meals Sun.
❀ ◖ ♣

Try also: Hop Poles, Middle St (Greene King)

COLEMANS HATCH
Hatch Inn
B2210 signed to Wych Cross
OS452334
☎ (01342) 822363
11.30-2.30, 5.30-11 (11.30-11 summer Sat); 12-10.30 Sun
Larkins Traditional; Harveys BB, seasonal beers; guest beer Ⓗ
This single-bar pub features beams and hops. It is good to see local small brewers supported; Biddenden cider also sold. Watch out for low beams on the way to the toilets and beware of crowds at weekends. Eve meals served Tue-Sat. Limited parking.
⚏ ❀ ◖ ⏥ P

COOKSBRIDGE
Pumphouse
Next to the station
☎ (01273) 400528
11-11; 12-10.30 Sun
Harveys BB; guest beer Ⓗ
Quiet, two-bar pub and restaurant, with an extensive menu, that hosts live music every Fri eve.
Q ◖ ▶ ⇜ P

CROWBOROUGH
Coopers Arms
Coopers Lane, St Johns (from Crowborough Cross follow St John's Road, 1/2 mile)
OS507316
☎ (01892) 654796
12-2.30 (not Mon), 6-11; 12-3, 7-11 Sat; 12-3, 7-10.30 Sun

Harveys BB; Shepherd Neame Master Brew Bitter Ⓗ
Traditional community local on the edge of Ashdown Forest, in the same family for 25 years, it has one main long bar where conversation predominates, plus a games room. Home-made lunches, including authentic Indian dishes, are served Tue-Sat.
Q ❀ ◖ ♣ P

DITCHLING
White Horse
16 West Street
☎ (01273) 842006
11-11; 12-10.30 Sun
Harveys BB; guest beers Ⓗ
Welcoming village pub with a resident ghost, it stands near the foot of Ditchling Beacon, the village church is oposite and Ann of Cleeves' house is nearby.
⚏ ❀ ◖ ♣ P

EAST CHILTINGTON
Jolly Sportsman
Chapel Lane (off B2116)
OS372153
☎ (01273) 890400
12-2.30, 6.30-11 (not Mon eve); 12-4 (closed eve) Sun
Beer range varies Ⓖ
Bistro-style pub/restaurant, serving well-regarded food. Off the beaten track, this pub also acts as a local polling station and general community centre.
⚏ Q ❀ ◖ ▶ ⏥ P ⊟

EAST HOATHLY
Kings Head
1 High Street (off A22)
☎ (01825) 840238
11-4, 6-11; 12-4, 7-10.30 Sun
Fuller's London Pride; Harveys BB; guest beers Ⓗ
Ivy-clad village-centre meeting place where the large bar is divided in two, and there is a restaurant/games room. The guests tend to be stronger beers from a variety of breweries. Small car park.
Q ⇋ ❀ ◖ ♣ P

Try also: Foresters (Harveys)

EASTBOURNE
Alexandra Arms
433 Seaside (A259, 2 miles E of centre)
☎ (01323) 720913
11.30-3, 5-11; 12-3, 7-11 Sun
Beards Best Bitter; Greene King IPA, Triumph, Abbot, seasonal beers; Harveys BB; guest beers Ⓗ
Comfortable, well-run local which usually has 10 beers on tap. Features include monthly curry nights, bar billiards and a weekly quiz.

The house beer is from Arundel Brewery. No food Mon eve.
🏠🏵🍺🍀 P

Buccaneer
10 Compton Street (next to Congress Theatre and Winter Gardens)
☎ (01323) 732829
11-11; 7-10.30 Sun
Ind Coope Burton Ale; Marston's Pedigree; Tetley Bitter; guest beers Ⓗ
To celebrate the pub's recent century it was converted from a polystyrene pirate ship to a Festival Ale House. Situated at the heart of Eastbourne's theatreland, it is popular with actors, and also tennis players when events are taking place in Devonshire Park. No-smoking area available until 8pm.
🍺🍀 🍴

Hurst Arms
76 Willingdon Road (A22, 1¹⁄₂ miles N of centre)
☎ (01323) 721762
11-11; 7-10.30 Sun
Harveys BB, Old, Armada Ⓗ
A *Guide* regular since 1978; this imposing Victorian local houses a large public bar and a smaller saloon. It was probably named after the Hurst Mill which stood nearby. It hosts a general knowledge quiz Sun.
Q 🏵 🍴

Lamb Inn
High Street, Old Town (A259, 1 mile W of centre)
☎ (01323) 720545
10.30-3, 5.30-11; 10.30-11 Fri & Sat; 12-4, 7-10.30 Sun
Harveys XX Mild, Pale Ale, BB, Old, Armada, seasonal beers Ⓗ
Beamed Harvey's show house where each of its three distinctive bar areas is on a different level. The cellar dates from 1290 and a passage used to lead to the church next door (cellar tours by arrangement). It is convenient for Gildredge Park and the Towner Art Gallery and Museum.
Q 🏵 🍺 ≈

EXCEAT BRIDGE
Golden Galleon
On A529
☎ (01323) 892247
11-11; 12-10.30 (3.30 winter) Sun
Cuckmere Haven Best Bitter, Guv'nor, Golden Peace, seasonal beers; Ⓗ **guest beers** Ⓗ/Ⓖ
Nestling on the bank of the Cuckmere, this pub provides home-brewed ales from a former telephone exchange, and first class food with an Italian flavour. A bar

extension provides a no-smoking area at busy periods.
🏠 Q 🍺🏵🍺🍴 P 🍴

FIRLE
Ram ☆
The Street
☎ (01273) 858222
11.30-11; 12-10.30 Sun
Harveys BB; guest beers Ⓗ
Time has passed the Ram by; it retains a farmhouse kitchen atmosphere with dangling hops, plus two other rooms. Interesting food and at least three real ales from independent breweries are the norm here.
🏠 Q 🍺🏵🍺🍴🍀 P 🍴

FIVE ASH DOWN
Firemans Arms
400 yds off Uckfield bypass, on old A26
☎ (01825) 732191
11.30-3, 6-11; 11-11 Sat; 12-3, 7-10.30 Sun
Greene King IPA; Harveys BB; guest beers Ⓗ
Busy local, run by a steam railway enthusiast, who hosts a steam engine rally on New Year's day. A good range of bar food is available (not Tue eve).
🏠🏵🍺🍺🍴🍀🍴 P 🍴

FRANT
Abergavenny Arms
Frant Road (A267)
☎ (01892) 750233
11.30-3, 5.30-11; 11.30-11 Sat; 12-10.30 Sun
Fuller's London Pride; Harveys BB; Rother Valley Level Best; guest beers Ⓗ
Large, split-level free house that dates back to 1450; usually five beers available.
🏠🏵🍺🍺🍴🍀 P 🍴

GLYNDE
Trevor Arms
The Street
☎ (01273) 858208
11-11; 12-10.30 Sun
Harveys Pale Ale, BB, seasonal beers Ⓗ
Traditional, unspoilt local tucked away in the South Downs, at the centre of village life. Two bars cater for a wide spread of customers.
Q 🍺🏵🍺≈🍀 P 🍴

HAILSHAM
Grenadier
67 High Street (NW of centre)
☎ (01323) 842152
10-11; 12-10.30 Sun
Harveys XX Mild, BB, Armada, seasonal beers Ⓗ
Spacious, Victorian town pub comprising a busy public bar and a saloon/lounge. It is a

major fund-raiser in Hailsham for Guide Dogs – see the pictures over the bar; the Milk and Ale Club is the charity group, based around a core of regulars.
🍺🏵🍺🍴🍺🍀 P

HASTINGS
Jenny Lind
69 High Street, Old Town
☎ (01424) 421392
11-11 (midnight Fri & Sat); 12-10.30 Sun
Hook Norton Best Bitter; Old Forge Pett Progress; Taylor Landlord; guest beers Ⓗ
Popular two-bar pub in the heart of Hastings historic old town, recently refurbished. It hosts live music and offers local ales.
🏠🍺🏵🍺🍴 A

HERSTMONCEUX
Brewers Arms
Gardener Street
☎ (01323) 832226
11-2.30, 6-11; 12-3, 7-10.30 Sun
Greene King IPA, Triumph; Harveys BB; Ⓗ **guest beers** Ⓖ
Cosy, two-bar pub with a friendly welcoming atmosphere, displaying lots of clocks and curios. Special events include food theme nights, games and wine tasting. No food Tue. The large garden is a bonus.
🏠🏵🍺🍀 P

Welcome Stranger
Chapel Row (E of village)
☎ (01323) 832119
12-3 (not Mon-Fri), 7-11; 12-3, 7-10.30 Sun
Harveys BB, Old; guest beer (occasional) Ⓗ
Fine example of an unspoilt village pub, known locally as the 'Kicking Donkey', it has been in the same family for 90 years. Beer is served through a hatch into a small bar room. 🏠 Q 🏵 A 🍀 P

HOVE
Cliftonville Inn
98-101 George Street
☎ (01273) 726969
11-11; 12-10.30 Sun
Courage Directors; Hop Back Summer Lightning; Shepherd Neame Spitfire; Theakston Best Bitter; guest beers Ⓗ
Busy, comfortable Wetherspoon's pub in the main shopping street, known for offering the lowest beer prices in the area. Look out for frequent beer festivals featuring many independent breweries. Meals are served all day. Q 🍺🍺 ≈ 🍴 ⊞

Eclipse
33 Montgomery Street (S of

railway, between Hove and Aldrington)
☎ (01273) 272212
11-3, 5-11; 11-11 Sat; 12-10.30 Sun
Harveys XX Mild, Pale Ale, BB, seasonal beers H
Very much a two-bar pub; the larger public houses the pool table and darts whilst the small, panelled saloon lends itself to comfort and conversation. Excellent value food includes huge steaks (eve meals Tue-Sat). 🛏 ⊛ 🍴 ▶ 🍺 ♿ ≠ (Aldrington/Hove) ♣

ICKLESHAM
Queens Head
Parsonage Lane (off A259)
☎ (01424) 814552
11-11; 12-5, 7-10.30 Sun
Beer range varies H
Welcoming country inn with a great menu and up to six beers. Superb views and a fine collection of farm tools add to its appeal. Well worth finding, it gets busy at mealtimes.
🛏 Q ⊛ 🍴 ♣ ⌂ P ✂ 🎁

ISFIELD
Laughing Fish
Station Road (W of A26, 2 miles S of Uckfield)
☎ (01825) 750349
11.30-3, 5.30-11; 11-11 Sat; 12-4, 7-10.30 (12-10.30 summer) Sun
Greene King IPA or Abbot; Harveys BB, Old; guest beer H
Victorian village local near Bentley Wildfowl Reserve and the Lavender Line. A stream runs through the pub's cellar.
🛏 ⇝ ⊛ 🍴 ♣ P ✂

JARVIS BROOK
Wheatsheaf
Mount Pleasant (by Crowborough Station)
☎ (10892) 663756
12-3, 5-11; 11-11 Fri & Sat; 12-4, 7-10.30 Sun
Harveys Pale Ale, BB, seasonal beers H
Unspoilt pub of three distinct rooms; their layout dates back to the 1880s. Old photographs and the history of the pub adorn the walls of the 'middle bar'. This white weatherboarded pub is worth seeking out. No food Sun.
🛏 Q ⊛ 🍴 ≠ (Crowborough) ♣ P

LEWES
Black Horse
55 Western Road
☎ (01273) 473653
11-2.30, 5.30 (6 Sat)-11; 12-2.30, 7-10.30 Sun
Greene King IPA, Triumph; Harveys BB; guest beers H
This former coaching inn,

now owned by Greene King, features two contrasting bars; the public has a fascinating collection of old photographs and a CAMRA mirror, the smaller lounge is a quiet oasis of calm.The Sussex game Toad in the Hole is played.
Q ⊛ 🖼 ◀ 🍴 ≠ ♣

Gardeners Arms
46 Cliffe High Street
☎ (01273) 474808
11-11; 12-10.30 Sun
Harveys BB, guest beers H
Good, basic, two-bar free house, where eight handpumps feature an ever-changing range from a wide range of breweries. Two real ciders are also available.
◀ ≠ ⌂ 🎁

Lewes Arms
Mount Place
☎ (01273) 473152
11-11; 12-10.30 Sun
Greene King Abbot; Harveys BB, Old H
This historic, curved-fronted pub is built into the castle ramparts. A folk club meets in the small upstairs function room. Well behaved children are allowed in the games room. Toad in the Hole is played.
🛏 Q ◀ 🍺 ≠ ♣

Snowdrop Inn
South Street
☎ (01273) 471018
11-11; 12-10.30 Sun
Fuller's ESB; Harvey's BB, Old; Hop Back Summer Lightning H
Popular busy pub with a single bar on the ground floor, and a seating area upstairs; it bears a highly individual decor both inside and out. The excellent menu has a vegetarian bias.
⊛ ◀ ▶

Try also: Elephant & Castle, White Hill (Free)

PETT
Royal Oak
Pett Road
☎ (01424) 812515
11-3, 6-11; 12-3, 6-10.30 Sun
Harveys BB; Young's Special; guest beers H
Large pub, split into three areas where a large fire, excellent home-cooked food and four beers are the main attractions. The guest beers tend to be strong.
🛏 Q 🐾 ⊛ ◀ 🍺 A P

Try also: Two Sawyers, Pett Rd (Free)

PORTSLADE
Stanley Arms
47 Wolseley Road (400 yds N

of station, along footpath)
☎ (01273) 701590
1 (12 Fri & Sat)-11; 12-10.30 Sun
Beer range varies H
Lively, friendly, local with a relaxed ambience, hosting live music some weekends. An ever-changing ale range from small breweries is complemented by a selection of Belgian bottled beers. A beer festival (Sept) is an annual event at this local CAMRA *Pub of the Year* 1999.
🛏 ⊛ ≠ (Fishersgate) ♣ ⌂ 🎁

RINGMER
Cock Inn
Uckfield Road (A26, Lewes road)
☎ (01273) 812040
11-3, 6-11; 12-3, 7-10.30 Sun
Harveys XX Mild or Old, BB; guest beers H
Small, traditional bar plus rooms for eating; an extensive bar menu is served. The large inglenook is an attractive feature.
🛏 🐾 ⊛ ◀ 🍺 P ✂

ROBERTSBRIDGE
Ostrich
Station Road
☎ (01580) 881737
11-11; 11-10.30 Sun
Adnams Bitter; Harveys BB; guest beers H
Former station hotel, now a good spacious free house boasting a games room and a tropical garden. Basic snacks are available.
🛏 🐾 ⊛ ≠ P

RYE
Ypres Castle
Gun Gardens (behind Ypres Tower)
☎ (01797) 223248
12-11; 12-10.30 Sun
Adnams Broadside; Harveys XX Mild; Old Forge Pett Progress; guest beers H
Not immediately obvious, this unspoilt pub is well worth seeking out (access is on foot only). Affording superb views of the harbour, it stands near Rye's most picturesque parts. Fresh local fish, meat and game are specialities. The safe gardens include a boules piste.
🛏 Q ⊛ ◀ 🍺 ≠ ♣ ⌂ ✂

RYE HARBOUR
Inkerman Arms
Harbour Road (off A259)
☎ (01797) 222464
12-3, 7-11 (closed winter Mon); 12-3, 7-10.30 (not winter eve) Sun
Greene King Triumph; Old Forge Pett Progress; Rother Valley Level Best; guest beers H
Quiet, friendly, traditional

pub with secluded dining areas, specialising in fish. The large garden has a boules piste; it stands next to Rye Harbour nature reserve. Local micros are favoured as beer suppliers.

🏔 Q ❀ ◖▶ ຯ ♣ P ⊬

SEAFORD

Boot

16 South Street
☎ (01323) 895454
10-11; 12-10.30 Sun
Flowers Original; Harveys BB; guest beers Ⓗ
Large bar with plush furnishings in a friendly local, down a back street; background music is played. It has a children's certificate and wide food menu. ◖▶ ≋

ST LEONARDS

Bull

530 Bexhill Road (A259 near Bexhill)
☎ (01424) 424984
12-3, 6-11; 12-4, 7-10.30 Sun
Shepherd Neame Master Brew Bitter, Best Bitter, Spitfire, Bishops Finger or seasonal beer Ⓗ
Welcoming roadside pub serving a good menu (book at weekends; no food Sun eve). It is handy for Glyne Gap shops.
🏔 Q ◖▶ ຯ ♣ P

Dripping Spring

34 Tower Road (1 mile N of Warrior Sq.)
☎ (01424) 434055
12-3, 5-11; 11-11 Fri & Sat; 12-3, 7-10.30 Sun
Fuller's London Pride; Goacher's Light; Oakhill Bitter; guest beers Ⓗ
Superb family-run pub with six beers available (over 1200 to date). It hosts a quiz Sun eve. Winner of Sussex CAMRA *Pub of the Year* award 1999.
❀ ຯ ≋ (Warrior Sq) ♣

Duke

48 Duke Road, Silverhill
☎ (01424) 436241
11-11; 12-10.30 Sun
Fuller's London Pride, ESB; Greene King IPA; Harveys BB; guest beers Ⓗ
Traditional, busy street-corner local with a cosy, welcoming atmosphere in its two bars. Excellent beer range. Q ❀ ⊟ຯ ♣

Horse & Groom

Mercatoria Street
☎ (01424) 420612
11-3.30, 5-11; 12-4, 7-10.30 Sun
Harveys Pale Ale, BB; Wells Bombardier; guest beers Ⓗ
Smart pub with an unusual horseshoe bar, it gets busy at weekends. The 1829 listed building lies in the heart of

old St Leonards. No food Sun. The restaurant and accommodation are new additions.
🏔 Q ❀ ◖▷ ຯ ◖ ≋ (Warrior Sq)

TELHAM

Black Horse

Hastings Road (A2100, Battle road)
☎ (01424) 773109
11-3, 6-11; 12-3, 7-10.30 Sun
Shepherd Neame Master Brew Bitter, Spitfire, Bishops Finger, seasonal beers Ⓗ
This pub has a skittle alley in the attic and two boule pistes outside. An annual music festival is held in a marquee spring Bank Holiday. Good food served.
🏔 ❀ ◖▶ ♣ P

THREE CUPS CORNER

Three Cups Inn

On B2096 between Heathfield and Battle
☎ (01435) 830252
11-3, 6-11; 12-2, 7-10.30 Sun
Greene King IPA; Harveys BB; guest beers Ⓗ
Ex-Beards house, now in the Greene King estate, this little country pub is a super one to find out in the sticks, but hurry, it may change!
🏔 Q ຯ ❀ ◖▶ ♣ P

UCKFIELD

Alma

Framfield Road (B2102, E of centre)
☎ (01825) 762232
11-2.30, 6-11; 12-2, 7-10.30 Sun
Harveys XX Mild, Pale Ale, BB, Old, Armada, seasonal beers Ⓗ
The best pub in which to sample the full Harvey's range in the area. The traditional public bar and comfortable saloon have been run by the same family for generations. Small garden. No food Sun. The family room doubles as a no-smoking area.
Q ຯ ❀ ◖⊟ ຯ ≋ ♣ P ⊬ ⊟

UDIMORE

Kings Head

On B2089, W of village
☎ (01424) 882349
11-4, 5.30-11; 12-4, 7-10.30 Sun
Harveys BB; guest beers Ⓗ
Built in 1535, this traditional village alehouse boasts beams, open fires, wood floors, and a no-smoking dining room serving home-cooked food. Scenic walks nearby.
🏔 Q ❀ ◖▶ ຯ ⚓ ♣ P

WADHURST

Rock Robin

Station Hill (opp. station)
OS622330
☎ (01892) 783776
11-11; 12-10.30 Sun
Harveys BB; guest beers Ⓗ
Large pub, providing at least six real ales; the restaurant serves a wide range of meals at all times.
🏔 Q ຯ ❀ ◖▶ ≋ ♣ P

WILLINGDON

Red Lion Inn

99 Wish Hill
☎ (01323) 502062
11-3, 5-11 (11-11 summer Sat); 12-3, 7-10.30 Sun
King & Barnes Sussex, Broadwood, Festive, seasonal beers Ⓗ
Local village pub, with a family room and bar billiards available. ❀ ◖▶ ♣ ▱ P ⊬

Wheatsheaf

Church Street (400 yds off A22)
☎ (01323) 502069
11-3, 5-11; 12-3, 7-10.30 Sun
Courage Best Bitter, Directors; Greene King Abbot; Shepherd Neame Spitfire; Young's Special Ⓗ
Interesting old pub, licensed since the mid-19th century, previously two cottages. Good pub fare is prepared on the premises and served in the bar and restaurant (no eve meal Sun). Q ❀ ◖▶ ♣ P

WILMINGTON

Giants Rest

On A27, Polegate-Lewes road
☎ (01323) 870207
11-11; 12-10.30 Sun
Harveys BB; Hop Back Summer Lightning; Taylor Landlord Ⓗ
This fine village free house is well used by locals and walkers; it stands near the Long Man landmark. Interesting home-cooked food comes from an award-winning kitchen.
🏔 ❀ ◖▶ ຯ ⚓ ♣ ▱ P ⊬

WITHYHAM

Dorset Arms

on B2110
☎ (01892) 770278
11-3, 6-11; 12-3, 7-10.30 Sun
Harveys Pale Ale, BB, seasonal beers Ⓗ
Picturesque, 17th-century village pub; its unspoilt timbered bar is warmed by a log fire. Children are allowed in the lounge and restaurant. Excellent bar meals are cooked by the landlady (no food Sun eve or Mon).
🏔 ❀ ◖▶ P

West Sussex

AMBERLEY

Sportsman

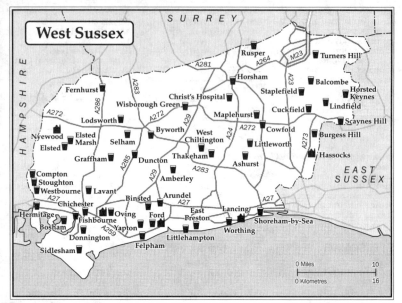

West Sussex

Rackham Road
☎ (01978) 831787
11-2.30 (3 Sat), 6-11; 12-10.30 Sun
Fuller's London Pride; Young's Bitter; guest beer Ⓗ
Convivial three-bar village pub affording fine views over the Wildbrooks. Home of the Miserable Old Buggers Club, its house beer (Miserable Old Bugger) is brewed by Spinnaker Ales. A revolving hexagonal pool table and good food are added attractions.
🏚 Q ❀ ◑ ▶ 🍴 ⇔ P

ARUNDEL

Kings Arms
36 Tarrant Street
☎ (01903) 882312
11-3, 5.30-11; 11-11 Sat; 12-10.30 Sun
Fuller's London Pride; Young's Special; guest beers Ⓗ
Established around 1625 this unspoilt, traditional pub is located just off the centre, nestling below the RC cathedral in a quieter part of town. A Hop Back beer is always on tap.
❀ ◑ ▢ ▲ ⇌ ♣

Swan
27 High Street
☎ (01903) 882314
11-11; 12-10.30 Sun
Arundel Best Bitter, Gold; Fuller's London Pride; guest beer Ⓗ
Popular respected hotel close to the castle in the centre of this historic town. There is a choice of good bar food and an excellent *à la carte* restaurant. Children are allowed in the lounge.
🛏 ◑ ▶ ▲ ⇌

ASHURST

Fountain
☎ (01403) 710219
11.30-2.30 (3 Sat), 6-11; 12-3, 7-10.30 Sun
Fuller's London Pride; Harveys BB; Shepherd Neame Master Brew Bitter; Ⓗ **guest beers** Ⓖ
Built in 1570, this is an excellent country pub. Good food is available, but it remains primarily a beer pub.
🏚 Q ❀ ◑ ▶ ▲ ♣ P

BALCOMBE

Cowdray Arms
London Road (B2036/B2110 jct)
☎ (01444) 811280
11-3, 5.30-11; 12-3, 7-10.30 Sun
Greene King IPA, Abbot; Harveys BB; guest beers Ⓗ
1998 North Sussex CAMRA *Pub of the Year*, this popular roadside pub is a regular halt for London to Brighton car runs. A large no-smoking conservatory is available for diners, offering a good range of reasonably-priced food (Sun meals served 12-7). Children's certificate.
Q ❀ ◑ ▶ ♣ P

BINSTED

Black Horse
Binsted Lane (off A27/B2132)
OS980064
☎ (01243) 551213
11-3, 6-11; 12-3, 7-10.30 Sun
Courage Directors; Gale's GB, HSB; Harveys BB; Hop Back Summer Lightning; guest beers Ⓗ
Off the beaten track, set amid lovely countryside, this

welcoming pub offers excellent food in the bar or conservatory/restaurant. Over 20 different varieties of sweets, sold by weight, are an addition to the more usual pub attractions.
🏚 Q ❀ ◑ ▶ & ♣ P

BOSHAM

White Swan
Station Road (A259 at Swan roundabout)
☎ (01243) 576086
12-3, 5-11; 12-4.30, 6-11 Sat; 12-4.30, 6.30-10.30 Sun
Ballard's Best Bitter; Ringwood Old Thumper; John Smith's Bitter; Young's Bitter, Special; guest beer Ⓗ
An inn for 300 years, this friendly roadside local has been extended over time and now boasts a restaurant and a skittle alley in part of a former bakery. An old fireplace recently uncovered blends well with the bare brick and timbers. A focus of the community; local fish is a speciality.
🏚 Q ❀ ◑ ▶ & ▲ ⇌ ♣ P 🍴

BURGESS HILL

Watermill
1 Leylands Road, Worlds End (150 yds E of Wivelsfield station)
☎ (01444) 235517
11-11; 12-10.30 Sun
Shepherd Neame Spitfire; Young's Bitter, Special Ⓗ
Large friendly local on the edge of town, with a fair-sized garden, it offers a varied menu (not Sun eve).
Q ❀ ◑ ▶ ⇌ (Wivelsfield)

BYWORTH

Black Horse Inn
100 yds from A283
OS985212
☎ (01798) 342424
11-2.30 (3 Sat), 6-11; 12-3, 7-10.30
Sun

Arundel Gold; Badger IPA; Fuller's London Pride; guest beer Ⓗ
Unspoilt, welcoming rural pub (circa 1791) where the bar area features a log fire, bare floorboards and traditional games; eating areas include an Elizabethan dining room (children welcome). Good views can be enjoyed from the pleasant garden.
🏚 Q ❀ ◖ ▸ Å ♣ P

CHICHESTER

Coach & Horses
125 St Pancras (600 yds E of market cross)
☎ (01243) 782313
11-2.30, 6-11; 12-3, 7-10.30 Sun

King & Barnes Mild, Sussex, Festive, seasonal beers Ⓗ
Traditional local on the edge of the city centre. Attractively refurbished it offers a genuinely friendly welcome, plus good value lunches. The large garden is a pleasant refuge.
🏚 Q ❀ ◖ ♣

Try also: **Chequers**, Oving Rd (Free)

CHRIST'S HOSPITAL

Bax Castle
Two Mile Ash ($1/2$ mile W of Southwater village)
OS148272
☎ (01403) 738369
11.30-2.30 (3 Sat), 6-11; 12-3, 7-10.30 Sun

Draught Bass; Brakspear Bitter; Fuller's London Pride; Harveys BB; guest beers Ⓗ
Set behind a former railway bridge, this pub is popular with walkers on the Downs Link. Its large safe garden has a play area for children, and there is also a good family room. No eve meals winter Sun.
🏚 Q ➴ ❀ ◖ ▸ P

COMPTON

Coach & Horses
The Square (B2146)
☎ (023) 9263 1288
11-2.30 (3 Sat), 6-11; 12-3, 7-10.30 Sun

Fuller's ESB; guest beers Ⓗ
16th-century pub in a charming downland village, surrounded by excellent walking country. The large front bar has two open fires. There is also a smaller rear bar, a restaurant (closed Sun

eve and Mon) and a skittle alley. Guest beers (at least four) normally come from small independents.
🏚 Q ❀ ◖ ▸ ♣

COWFOLD

Hare & Hounds
Henfield Road (A281)
☎ (01403) 865354
11.30-3, 6-11; 12-3, 7-10.30 Sun

Greene King IPA; Harveys BB; King & Barnes Sussex; Tetley Bitter; guest beers Ⓗ
Victorian village local, refurbished in 1995 using timber from gale-damaged trees from nearby Leonardslee Gardens. No eve meals winter Mon.
🏚 ❀ ◖ ▸ ♣ P

CUCKFIELD

White Harte
South Street
☎ (01444) 413454
11-3, 6-11; 12-3, 7-10.30 Sun

King & Barnes Sussex, Broadwood, Old, Festive, seasonal beers Ⓗ
Two-bar village local with a basic public bar, not at all 'twee'; a long-standing *Guide* entry.
🏚 Q ❀ ◖ ◲ P

DONNINGTON

Blacksmiths Arms
Selsey Road (B2201, 2 miles S of Chichester)
☎ (01243) 783999
11-3, 6-11 (11-11 summer Fri & Sat); 12-4, 7-10.30 (12-10.30 summer) Sun

Winchester Old Chapel, Hole Hearted, Blake's Gosport Bitter, seasonal beers; guest beer Ⓗ
17th-century part Grade II listed pub, the most eastern of the Winchester alehouses, serving their own fine beers and superb food. Cosy, in a cottage style, it has a large, safe garden full of things for children to do. Deservedly popular; book early for the monthly themed food nights.
🏚 ❀ ◖ ▸ ♣ ◲ P

DUNCTON

Cricketers
Main Road (A285, $1^1/2$ miles S of Petworth)
☎ (01798) 342473
11-2.30, 6-11; 12-3, 7-10.30 (not winter eves) Sun

Archers Golden; Friary Meux BB; guest beers Ⓗ
Cosy bar whose imposing inglenook is used for roasting chestnuts in season. The large award-winning garden is safe for children. Real cider and barbecues feature in summer. Good quality food and a skittle alley add interest. No mobile phones

allowed. Local CAMRA *Pub of the Year* 1996 and '99. Eve meals served Tue-Sat.
🏚 Q ❀ ◖ ▸ Å P

EAST PRESTON

Fletcher Arms
Station Road, Rustington (next to Angmering station)
☎ (01903) 784858
11-11; 12-10.30 Sun

Adnams Broadside; Fuller's London Pride; Greene King Abbot; Marston's Pedigree; Ringwood Best Bitter; guest beer Ⓗ
Welcoming, community pub, next to the station. A boules piste, summer barbecues, children's play area and pets corner enliven the garden. The function room doubles as a family room; live music performed at weekends.
🏚 ❀ ➴ ◖ ▸ ◲ Å
➳ (Angmering) ♣ ◔ P

Try also: **Henty Arms**, Ferring (Pubmaster)

ELSTED

Three Horseshoes
Between Harting and Midhurst
☎ (01730) 825746
11-2.30, 6-11; 12-3, 7-10.30 (not winter eve) Sun

Ballard's Best Bitter; Cheriton Pots Ale; Fuller's London Pride; Taylor Landlord; guest beers Ⓗ
Traditional village pub with parts dating from 1540; oak beamed and brick floored. The huge garden affords magnificent views of the South Downs. Good quality home-cooked food is a speciality; Inches cider is sold in summer.
🏚 Q ❀ ◖ ▸ ♣ ◔ P

Try also: **Ship**, South Harting (Free)

ELSTED MARSH

Elsted Inn
Off A272, near old railway bridge OS834207
☎ (01730) 813662
11.30-3, 5.30 (6 Sat)-11; 12-3, 6-10.30 Sun

Ballard's Best Bitter, Nyewood Gold; Cheriton Pots Ale; Fuller's London Pride; Gales GB; guest beers Ⓗ
Popular country pub, originally serving the former Elsted station, two miles outside the village. Note the genuine Victorian decor. An extensive range of good, home-cooked food is served in the cosy bars and restaurant.
🏚 Q ❀ ➴ ◖ ▸ ♣ P

FELPHAM

Old Barn

42 Felpham Road (near Butlin's)
☎ (01243) 821564
11-11; 12-10.30 Sun
Gale's GB; Hop Back Summer Lightning; Ringwood Best Bitter; guest beers ⚏
Busy, one-bar pub with distinctive areas: a cosy locals' section at the front, but the rest tends to be boisterous. TVs are only switched on for sport; games machines are quiet. A pool table and dartboard are at the rear; the bar billiards table is a pleasant addition. Meals include all-day breakfasts (served until 7pm).
⚙ ◖ ♣ P

FERNHURST
Kings Arms
Midhurst Road (A286, 1 mile S of village)
☎ (01428) 652005
11-3, 5.30 (6.30 Sat)-11; 12-3, (closed eve) Sun
Otter Bright; Triple fff Dazed and Confused; guest beers ⚏
Cosy, 17th-century true free house and restaurant specialising in fish and game meals; it is popular with locals, diners and walkers. The house beer comes from Brewery on Sea; guest beers from small independent brewers.
⚏ Q ⚙ ◖ ▸ ⚹ ▲ P ⚟

Red Lion
The Green (1/4 mile E of A286 crossroads)
☎ (01428)653304
11-3, 5-11;12-3, 7-10.30 Sun
Hogs Back TEA; King & Barnes Sussex; guest beers ⚏
17th-century pub overlooking the village green with a pleasant secluded garden. Up to four guest beers from small local breweries are available, whilst the menu features home-made pies and other traditional meals. May close Sun eve in winter. Boules played.
⚏ Q ⚞ ⚙ ◖ ♣ P ⚟

Try also: Lickfold Inn, Lickfold (Free)

FISHBOURNE
Woolpack Inn
71 Fishbourne Road (A259)
☎ (01243) 785707
11-11; 12-10.30 Sun
Adnams Bitter; Greene King IPA, Abbot; Young's Bitter; guest beers ⚏
This striking 1930s roadhouse provides a true community focus. The modern interior retains distinct spaces, including a smart dining area (no food

Sun eve). The fine garden hosts summer barbecues.
⚙ ⛝ ◖ ▸ ⚹ ♣ P

FORD
Shaky Doo
Ford Road
☎ (01903) 882244
11-11 (midnight supper licence); 12-10.30 Sun
Young's Special; guest beers ⚏
Formerly the Arundel Arms, this early Victorian station hotel is a welcome new entry. London beers feature alongside local micros in a pub with a real local atmosphere. Irish (keg) Guinness is available.
⚙ ⛝ ◖ ▸ ▲ ♣ P

GRAFFHAM
Forester's Arms
☎ (01798) 867202
11-2.30, 5.30-11;12-3, 7-10.30 Sun
Cheriton Pots Ale; guest beers ⚏
Fine village free house only a mile off the South Downs Way offering wholesome English fare. Its attractions include an inglenook, a pleasant garden, and three ever-changing guest beers from independent brewers.
⚏ Q ⚙ ◖ ▸ ▲ P

Try also: White Horse (Free)

HERMITAGE
Sussex Brewery
36 Main Road (A259, 1/2 mile E of Emsworth)
☎ (01243) 371533
11-11; 12-10.30 Sun
Badger Dorset Best; Young's Bitter, Special; guest beers ⚏
Cosy, bare-boarded local with open fires where a good range of guest beers includes Hermitage Best brewed by Poole. A speciality sausage menu is available in the bar and restaurant.
⚏ Q ⚙ ◖ ▸ ⚹ (Emsworth) P ⚟

HORSHAM
Bedford
3 Station Road (behind station)
☎ (01403) 253128
11.30-3, 5-11; 11.30-11 Fri & Sat; 12-2.30, 7-10.30 Sun
Fuller's London Pride; King & Barnes Sussex; guest beers ⚏
Spacious pub drawing a local and passing trade, it has a comfortable, refurbished public bar offering large screen TV sports, two pool tables, darts and occasional live music. These facilities are complemented by a quieter saloon bar and a landscaped patio.
⚏ Q ⚙ ◖ ⚹ P

Malt Shovel
15 Springfield Road (Albion Way jct)
☎ (01403) 254543
11-11; 12-10.30 Sun
Boddingtons Bitter; Flowers Original; Gale's GB; guest beers ⚏/⚏
Traditional pub where the emphasis is on real ale and real food; it stocks six beers and a cider on handpump, plus three beers on gravity. Friendly, helpful staff will let you try a taster before you order your beer. Meals served 12-7 (6.30 Sun).
⚏ ⚙ ◖ ▸ ⚹ ♣ ⛀ P

HORSTED KEYNES
Green Man
The Green (access via B2028 or A275) OS385283
☎ (01825) 790656
11.30-3, 5.30 (6 Sat)-11; 12-3, 7-10.30 (hours may vary summer) Sun
Greene King IPA, Abbot; Harveys BB ⚏
Popular village pub next to the village green, and close to the Bluebell Railway. The no-smoking restaurant area serves good home-cooked food.
⚏ ⚙ ◖ ♣ P

LAVANT
Earl of March
Lavant Road (A286, 2 miles N of Chichester)
☎ (01243) 774751
10.30-3, 6 (5.30 summer)-11; 12-3, 7-10.30 Sun
Draught Bass; Cottage Golden Arrow; Ringwood Old Thumper; guest beers ⚏
Friendly village pub affording fine downland views from the garden, close to the historic Goodwood motor racing circuit. Good food features game and fish, in generous home-cooked portions. Children's certificate; live music is staged every Thu eve. Three guest beers are the norm here.
⚙ ◖ ▸ ♣ ⛀ P

LINDFIELD
Linden Tree
47 High Street
☎ (01444) 482995
11-3, 6-11; 12-3, 7-10.30 Sun
Arundel Best Bitter; Marston's Pedigree; Ringwood Old Thumper; guest beers ⚏
Friendly free house situated in a picturesque village, where there are always six real ales available. Weekday lunches served. ⚏ Q ⚙ ◖

LITTLEHAMPTON
Dewdrop

96 Wick Street
☎ (01903) 716459
10.30-3, 5.30-11; 10.30-11 Sat; 12-10.30 Sun
Gales's GB, HSB; guest beer H
Interesting 'time warp' local in a row of terraced houses.
🍺 ♣

Try also: **George**, Surrey St (Wetherspoon's)

LITTLEWORTH
Windmill
Littleworth Lane (from either A24 or A272, head for Partridge Green) OS193205
☎ (01403) 710308
11.30-3, 5.30-11; 12-3, 7-10.30 Sun
King & Barnes Sussex, seasonal beers H
Welcoming country local pub, with thriving traditional public bar. Cask mild is served using a cask breather. No food Sun eve.
🍺 Q 🕮 ◑ ▶ P

LODSWORTH
Half Way Bridge Inn
Half Way Bridge (A272, 1 mile S of village)
☎ (01798) 861281
11-3, 6-11; 12-3, 7-10.30 (not winter eve) Sun
Cheriton Pots Ale; Fuller's London Pride; Gale's HSB; Harveys Old; guest beers H
Multi-roomed, 18th-century coaching stop, serving good home-made food (book at weekends). Children over the age of ten are welcome in the dining room and front garden. Weston's scrumpy cider is sold.
🍺 Q 🕮 ◑ ♣ ➷ P

Try also: **Hollist Arms** (Free)

MAPLEHURST
White Horse
Park Lane OS190246
☎ (01403) 891208
12 -2.30 (3 Sat), 6-11; 12-3, 7-10.30 Sun
Harveys BB; Weltons Dorking Pride; guest beers H
Friendly country pub affording good views from the garden. Very popular, it always has several guest beers and ciders available and the excellent food represents good value. The landlord is an avid classic car enthusiast. Children's certificate.
🍺 Q 🎋 🕮 ◑ ♣ ➷ P ⚥

OVING
Gribble Inn
Gribble Lane
☎ (01243) 786893
11-3, 6-11 (11-11 summer); 12-3, 7-10.30 (12-10.30 summer) Sun
Gribble Fursty Ferret, Ale, Reg's

Tipple, Plucking Pheasant, Porterhouse, Pig's Ear, seasonal beers H
This 16th-century, thatched pub is home to Gribble's award-winning beers (production can be viewed in the brewhouse adjoining the skittle alley). A meeting place for the local folk-song club (among others), it also hosts monthly jazz nights. A mobile phone-free zone.
🍺 Q 🎋 🕮 ◑ ▶ ✆ ♣ ➷ P ⚥

RUSPER
Plough
High Street
☎ (01293) 871215
11.30-2.30 (3 Sat), 6-11; 12-3, 7-10.30 Sun
Courage Directors; Fuller's London Pride; King & Barnes Sussex; guest beer H
Traditional, beamed, one-bar pub with a reinstated stone floor in front of the bar; parts date back to the 15th century. Good food; a large garden and bar billiards add to its appeal. A cask breather may be used on slow selling beers (not the regular brews).
🍺 🕮 ◑ ▶ ♣ ➷

SCAYNES HILL
Sloop
Sloop Lane
☎ (01444) 831219
12-3, 6-11; 12-3, 7-10.30 (12-10.30 summer) Sun
Greene King XX Mild, IPA, Abbot, Triumph, seasonal beers; guest beer H
Unspoilt, two-bar rural pub with an emphasis on food in the saloon bar; traditional farming clientele frequent the public bar where bar billiards and darts are played. Hearty country food carries a New England influence (no meals Sun eve). This pub next to the Ouse Canal boasts three gardens.
🍺 🕮 ◑ ▶ 🍺 ♣ P

SELHAM
Three Moles
1 mile S of A272, midway between Midhurst and Petworth OS935206
☎ (01798) 861303
12-2, 5.30-11; 11.30-11 Sat; 12-10.30 Sun
King & Barnes Mild, Sussex, seasonal beers; guest beers H
Very traditional pub run by a lively landlady; no food or slot machines but singsongs happen on the first Sat of each month. This free house runs a cyber-café Mon-Wed; bar billiards and shove-ha'penny played.
🍺 Q 🕮 ♣ P

SHOREHAM BY SEA
Buckingham Arms
35-37 Brunswick Road
☎ (01273) 453660
11-11; 12-10.30 Sun
Harveys BB; Hop Back Summer Lightning; Ringwood True Glory; guest beers H
Former coaching inn, now a 'Sir Loyne of Beef' free house, selling up to six guest beers at realistic prices and frequent special offers. Buck Brew is usually Shepherd Neame Master Brew Bitter rebadged. Weekday lunches served.
🕮 ◑ ⇌ P

Green Jacket
225 Upper Shoreham Road
☎ (01273) 452556
11.30-3, 6-11; 11.30-11 Sat; 12-10.30 Sun
Draught Bass; Harveys BB; guest beers H
Large busy local where the guest beer range changes weekly. Good food is mostly home made (eve meals served Wed-Sat). It has a large, pleasant patio and garden where boules can be played.
🍺 Q 🕮 ◑ ▶ ⇌ ♣ P

Lazy Toad
88 High Street
☎ (01273) 441622
11-11; 12-10.30 Sun
Badger Tanglefoot; Gale's Festival Mild; Greene King Abbot; Shepherd Neame Spitfire; guest beers G
This ex-wine bar and conservative club serves its ales from a range of casks on stillage behind the bar. It is festooned with Frog & Toad paraphernalia.
Q ◑ ⇌

Red Lion Inn
Old Shoreham Road
☎ (01273) 453171
11.30-3, 5.30-11; 11.30-11 Sat; 12-10.30 Sun
Courage Best Bitter, Directors; Harveys BB; guest beers H
Ever-popular free house stocking at least five guest beers a week; it is home to the Adur beer festival (Easter) and a smaller one in Sept. Good food can be eaten in a no-smoking area. It stands close to the ancient tollbridge.
🍺 Q 🕮 ◑ ▶ P

Royal Sovereign
6 Middle Street (by Marlipins Museum)
☎ (01273) 453518
11-11; 12-10.30 Sun
Badger Tanglefoot; Brakspear Special; Castle Eden Ale; Flowers Original; Fuller's London Pride; King & Barnes Sussex H
Classic, back-street, purpose-built pub featuring green

United Brewery tiling and leaded windows, it has good food and a friendly ambience. The caricatures on the wall are of customers from the 1960s. Challenge the beer-mat catching dog.
🍴Q ◖⇥ P

Try also: Crabtree, Buckingham Rd (Gale's)

SIDLESHAM
Crab & Lobster
Mill Lane (750 yds off B2145) OS862973
☎ (01243) 641233
11-3, 6-11; 12-3, 7-10.30 (not winter eve) Sun
Arundel Best; Badger IPA; Cottage seasonal beers; Gale's GB; Itchen Valley Fagin's Ⓗ
Two-bar, 15th-century village inn, on the edge of Pagham Harbour, popular with walkers and ornithologists. Home-cooked food includes crab and lobster salads in summer.
🍴Q 🏠 ◖◗ P

STAPLEFIELD
Jolly Tanners
Handcross Road
☎ (01444) 400335
11-3, 5.30-11; 11-11 Sat; 12-10.30 Sun
Fuller's Chiswick, London Pride; Harveys BB; guest beer Ⓗ
Busy, popular, two-bar pub with a large garden close to the cricket field, serving a good selection of food. It is one mile south of Nymans Gardens (NT). There is always a mild on handpump.
🍴Q 🏠 ◖◗ ⌂ P

STOUGHTON
Hare & Hounds
Off B2146 through Walderton OS801114
☎ (01705) 631433
11-11; 12-10.30 Sun
Draught Bass; Gale's GB, HSB; Harveys BB; Taylor Landlord; Young's Bitter Ⓗ
Secluded, 350-year-old, classic Sussex flint building, in an area of outstanding natural beauty. Enjoy fine views from the gardens and good value, home-made food including fresh local seafood and game. Time stands still as you relax at this pub, 26 years in this *Guide*.
🍴Q 🏠 ◖◗ P

THAKEHAM
White Lion
The Street (300 yds from B2139) OS108174
☎ (01798) 813141
11-3.30; 5.30-11 (hours may extend); 12-4, 6.30-10.30 Sun

Flowers Original; Harveys BB; guest beers Ⓗ
Unspoilt, 500-year-old village pub that boasts an historic interior with old passageways underneath. The landlord attracts many customers for his repartee!
🍴Q 🏠 ◖◗ ♣ P

TURNERS HILL
Crown
East Street (B2028/B2110 jct)
☎ (01342) 715218
11-3, 5.30-11; 11-11 Sat; 12-10.30 Sun
Morland Old Speckled Hen; guest beers Ⓗ
Spacious one-bar pub and restaurant featuring an open fire and beams. It hosts regular themed beer festivals and offers a large range of sausages on its menu.
🍴Q 🏠 ◖◗ ♣ P

Punchbowl
Selsfield Road (B2028, 1/4 mile S of B2110 jct) OS343349
☎ (01342) 715416
11-3, 6-11; 12-3, 7-10.30 Sun
Shepherd Neame Master Brew Bitter, Best Bitter, Bishops Finger, seasonal beers Ⓗ
Roadside Shepherd Neame house on the village outskirts, set on a hillside commanding views across the countryside. It opens 8.30am for breakfast Wed-Sat; no eve meals Sun.
🍴🏠 ◖◗ P

WEST CHILTINGTON
Five Bells
Smock Alley OS091172
☎ (01798) 812143
11-3, 6-11; 12-3, 7-10.30 Sun
King & Barnes Sussex; guest beers Ⓗ
An admirable ever-changing range of ales usually includes a mild. A pleasant bar is complemented by a spacious conservatory and an enticing menu (not served Sun eve).
🍴Q 🏠 ◖◗ ♣ ⌂ P

WESTBOURNE
Good Intent
North Street
☎ (01243) 372656
11-2.30, 5-11; 11-11 Fri & Sat; 12-3, 7-10.30 Sun
Ansells Mild; Friary Meux BB; Greene King IPA; Ind Coope Burton Ale; guest beer Ⓗ
Friendly, two-bar, 16th-century village local where the lounge was once a bakery. An enclosed garden has an aviary and swings. The food range includes pizzas to eat in or take away (no meals Sun). The guest beer comes from Tisbury

Brewery or Tapster's Choice range. Pool played.
🍴🏠 ◖◗ ⊟ ♣ P

WISBOROUGH GREEN
Cricketers Arms
Loxwood Road
☎ (01403) 700369
11-2.30 (3 Sat), 5.30 (6 Sat)-11; 12-3, 7-10.30 Sun
Cheriton Pots Ale; Fuller's London Pride; Wadworth 6X; guest beer Ⓗ
Pleasant country pub where wood block floors and a wealth of beams set off a central fireplace with a wood burning stove. Home of English motor mowing racing, with monthly events. Cider sold in summer. Opens all day for some cricket matches and other village occasions.
🍴Q 🏠 ◖◗ ⌂ P

WORTHING
Alexandra
28 Lyndhurst Road
☎ (01903) 234833
11-11; 12-10.30 Sun
Draught Bass; Boddingtons Bitter; Harveys BB; guest beer Ⓗ
Unspoilt two-bar corner local with a pool room.
🍴Q 🏠 ◖◗ ⇥ (East) ♣

Charles Dickens
56 Heene Road (just N of seafront)
☎ (01903) 603791
11-3, 5.30-11; 11-11 Fri & Sat; 12-10.30 Sun
Draught Bass; Harveys BB; Hop Back Summer Lightning; Shepherd Neame Spitfire; Taylor Landlord; guest beers Ⓗ
New free house, sympathetically renovated and refurbished to provide a bar area, lounge and dining area on the first floor, with further seating and a games room downstairs. Children are welcome away from the bar.
🏠 ◖◗ ♣ ✂

Cricketers
66 Broadwater Street West
☎ (01903) 233369
11-3, 6-11; 11-11 Fri & Sat; 12-10.30 Sun
Draught Bass; Fuller's London Pride; Harvey's BB; Wells Bombardier; Young's Special Ⓗ
Excellent pub next to Broadwater Green with a large garden. A separate dining area ensures that the bar retains a traditional public bar feel. Occasional beer festivals held. Eve meals served Wed-Sat.
🍴🏠 ◖◗ ♣ ♣

George & Dragon
1 High Street, Tarring
☎ (01903) 202497

CAMRA National Pub Inventory: Crown Liquor Saloon, Belfast

11-3, 5.30-11; 11-11 Fri & Sat;
12-10.30 Sun
Hop Back Summer Lightning; John Smith's Bitter; guest beers H
Dating from 1610, this is a fine example of a thriving single-bar community local that has managed to provide modern facilities without losing the warmth, cosiness and feel of a traditional, multi-roomed pub. No food Sun.
Q ❀ ◑ ≹ (West) ♣ P

O'Connor's Bar
1 Newlands Road
☎ (01903) 601000
11-3 (not Mon), 6-11; 11-11 Fri & Sat;
12-3, 7-10.30 Sun
Harveys BB, seasonal beers; Hop Back Summer Lightning, seasonal beers; Shepherd Neame Spitfire; guest beers H
Not mock-Irish despite the name this renovated, one-bar pub bears eclectic decor. Features include Thai food, real cider, original artwork from a local college and a range of bottle-conditioned ales (including Hop Back and Heather Ales). Local CAMRA *Pub of the Year* 1999. Lunches served at weekends only. Limited parking.
◑ ◗ ≹ (Central) ♣ ⌂ P

Richard Cobden
2 Cobden Road
☎ (01903) 236856
11-3, 5.30-11; 11-11 Fri & Sat;
12-3.30, 7-10.30 Sun
Beer range varies H
Welcoming traditional street-corner local that hosts folk music (Thu) and Morris dancing. No food Sun.
❀ ◑ ≹ (Central) ♣ ⊟

Selden Arms
41 Lyndhurst Road
☎ (01903) 234854
11 (12 Sat)-11; 12-10.30 Sun
Ringwood Fortyniner; guest beers H
Small, friendly, one-bar

As a result of the sale of King & Barnes to Hall & Woodhouse and uncertainty over the future of K&B beers, some CAMRA branches in Sussex did not submit K&B pubs for the Guide. Since then Hall & Woodhouse has confirmed that some K&B beers will be matched for sale in former King & Barnes pubs. See Badger and Gribble Inn in the Breweries section.

community local stocking up to five constantly changing guest beers from small breweries, including one dark beer. Reasonably-priced food is served (not Sun eve). Children (and dogs) welcome.
♨ Q ◑ ◗ ≹ (Central) ♣

Swan
79 High Street (opp. Safeways)
☎ (01903) 232923
11-2.30, 6-11; 11-11 Sat & Sun;
12-10.30 Sun
Draught Bass; Greene King Abbot; Harveys BB; Shepherd Neame Spitfire; guest beers H
Popular town pub where a warm welcome is guaranteed. One large comfortable bar with two fires and a restaurant area where children are welcome at lunchtimes; eve meals only available in summer. Live music some eves.
♨ ❀ ◑ ≹ (Central) ♣

Try also: **Vine**, Tarring High St (Badger Inns)

YAPTON
Lamb Inn
Bilsham Road (B2132)
☎ (01243) 551232
11-3, 5.30 (5 Fri, 6 Sat)-11; 12-4.30, 6.30-10.30 Sun
Greene King Abbot; Harveys BB; guest beer H

Friendly roadside pub on the southern edge of the village. The large garden houses play equipment, an animal enclosure and boules courts. The new restaurant is no-smoking. An excellent community pub.
♨ Q ❀ ◑ ◗ ◱ ら ♣ P

Maypole Inn
Maypole Lane (off B2132, 1/2 mile N of village)) OS978041
☎ (01243) 551417
11-3, 5.30-11; (11-11 Fri & Sat in summer); 12-3, 5.30-10.30 Sun
Ringwood Best Bitter; guest beers H
Family-run pub with a rural atmosphere, tucked down a lane away from the village centre. It boasts a cosy lounge with two fires, a large public bar (children's certificate) and a skittle alley. Up to five guest beers change regularly.
♨ Q ❀ ◑ ◱ ら ▲ ♣ ⌂ P

INDEPENDENT BREWERIES

(EAST SUSSEX)
Cuckmere Haven: Exceat Bridge
Dark Star: Brighton
First Inn Last Out: Hastings
Forge: Hastings
Harveys: Lewes
Hedgehog and Hogshead: Hove
Kemptown: Brighton
Rother Valley: Northiam
White: Bexhill

(WEST SUSSEX)
Arundel: Ford
Ballard's: Nyewood
Brewery on Sea: Lancing
Gribble Inn: Oving
Rectory: Hassocks

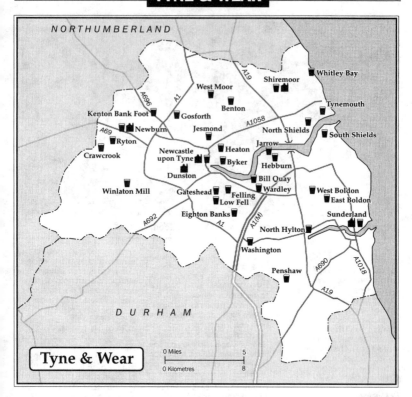

Tyne & Wear

N O R T H U M B E R L A N D

D U R H A M

0 Miles 5
0 Kilometres 8

BENTON

Benton Ale House
Front Street, Longbenton
(near Metro)
☎ (0191) 266 1512
11-11; 12-10.30 Sun
**Banks's Bitter; Camerons Bitter,
Strongarm; Marston's Pedigree** H
Large multi-roomed pub with
a welcoming seating and
standing area to the front
and a more lively games area
to the rear.
◖ ▶ ⊖ (Four Lane Ends) P ▤

BILL QUAY

Albion Inn
Reay Street (foot of hill, on
river bank)
☎ (0191) 469 2418
4-11; 11-11 Sat & summer; 12-10.30
Sun
Beer range varies H
Lively,community pub with
an opened-out interior. The
beer range usually features
one or more local micros.
The garden offers views of
Tyneside's industrial
heartland. Children welcome
in the conservatory until
7.30. ♨ ⛴ ⚘ ⊖ (Pelaw) ⇦ P

BYKER

Cluny
36 Lime Street

☎ (0191) 230 4475
11-11 (12.30-3.30, 5.30-11 Mon);
12-10.30 Sun
**Banks's Bitter, Original; Mordue
Geordie Pride, Workie Ticket,
seasonal beers; guest beers** H
Fine redevelopment of an old
(1870s) warehouse into a
pub-cum-art gallery offering
good beer, interesting food
and the chance to view works
by local artists. Much use has
been made of original
features in a sympathetic
refit. The pub faces Byker
City Farm.
◖ ▶ ⚙ ⊖ (Manors) ▤

Cumberland Arms
Byker Buildings (off Byker
Bank near Byker bridges)
☎ (0191) 265 6151
12-11; 12-10.30 Sun
Beer range varies G
Wonderfully unspoilt two-
roomed pub with at least four
beers available, mainly from
local micro-breweries. A
friendly welcome is
guaranteed, it is frequented
by morris and sword dancers.
Live music upstairs most
nights.
♨ ⛴ ⚙ ⚐ ⊖ ➕ P

Fighting Cocks
127 Albion Row
☎ (0191) 265 2106
4 (11 Fri & Sat)-11; 7-10.30 Sun

**Castle Eden Ale; Everards Tiger;
Four Rivers Hadrian, Centurion** H
Very much a community pub
with a loyal group of
regulars. The Sun eve music
sessions attract performers
from all round the area.
Good river views to be had
from the windows of this
much-improved basic pub.
⇦ ▤

Free Trade Inn
St Lawrence Road
☎ (0191) 265 5764
11-11; 12-10.30 Sun
**Mordue Five Bridge Bitter, Geordie
Pride, Workie Ticket, seasonal
beers; Theakston Best Bitter** H
This small popular, busy pub
looks upriver towards the
Newcastle bridges. Very keen
regulars, friendly staff, and
well-kept beers combine to
produce a pub that's always
worth visiting. ♨ ⚘

Tyne
1 Maling Street
☎ (0191) 265 2550
11-11; 12-10.30 Sun
**Black Sheep Best Bitter; Durham
Magus, seasonal beers; Mordue
Workie Ticket, seasonal beers;
Taylor Landlord** H
Small, single-roomed pub
under Glasshouse Bridge. The
beer quality brings in the
crowds, so it can get very

busy. Live music Wed eve and Suns. Barbecues held on summer Suns. ❀

CRAWCROOK

Rising Sun
Bank Top (1/2 mile S of main crossroads)
☎ (0191) 413 3316
11.30-11; 12-10.30 Sun
Boddingtons Bitter; Castle Eden Ale; Mordue Workie Ticket; guest beers Ⓗ
Recent refurbishment has given a spacious feel, whilst excellent food and ale ensure there is something for everyone in this lively community local.
❀ ◖❩ ♣ P

EAST BOLDON

Black Bull
98 Front Street
☎ (0191) 536 3769
11-11; 12-10.30 Sun
Courage Directors; McEwan 80/-; Wells Bombardier Ⓗ
Terraced single-roomed village pub, with linked bar and lounge areas. It specialises in cheap, good quality meals.
◖❩ ♣ P ⊞

Grey Horse
Front Street
☎ (0191) 536 4186
11-11; 12-10.30 Sun
Morland Old Speckled Hen; Ruddles Best Bitter; John Smith's Magnet; Wells Bombardier Ⓗ
Large village pub; a former coaching inn with mock Tudor exterior.
Q ❀ ◖❩ ⬚ ≩ ♣ ⊞

EIGHTON BANKS

Lambton Arms
Rockcliffe Way
☎ (0191) 487 8137
11-11; 12-10.30 Sun
Beer range varies Ⓗ
Four handpumps guarantee a regular choice of real ale from a selection of seven. This friendly pub provides good eating and drinking facilities and an excellent view of surrounding countryside. Meals served all day.
❀ ◖❩ P ⊁

FELLING

Old Fox
10-12 Carlisle Street
☎ (0191) 420 0357
12-11; 12-10.30 Sun
Banks's Bitter; Bateman XB; guest beers Ⓗ
Cheerful, well-appointed local, serving good value bar meals all day, plus up to three guest beers.
⬚ ❀ ⬚ ◖❩ ⊖ ♣

GATESHEAD

Borough Arms
82 Bensham Road (through subway from Metro interchange)
☎ (0191) 478 13234
11-3, 7-11; 12-10.30 Sun
Draught Bass; guest beers Ⓗ
Solid, stone built pub featuring an opened-out interior and three, usually interesting, guest beers. This lively social centre stands close to town-centre shops and transport. Folk night alternate Thu.
⬚ ◖❩ ♣ P

GOSFORTH

County Hotel
High Street
☎ (0191) 285 6919
12 (11 Fri & Sat)-11; 12-3, 7-10.30 Sun
Courage Directors; Marston's Pedigree; Morland Old Speckled Hen; McEwan 80/-; Theakston Best Bitter; Wells Bombardier; guest beers Ⓗ
Long L-shaped bar, plus a small, comfortable back room on a busy High Street.
Q ◖❩ ⊖ (S Gosforth) ⌣ P

HEATON

Chillingham
Chillingham Road
☎ (0191) 265 5915
11-11; 12-10.30 Sun
Black Sheep Best Bitter; Mordue Workie Ticket; Theakston Best Bitter; guest beers Ⓗ
Roadside pub of two large rooms: the bar has a pool room leading off, while the lounge is more restful. Both rooms can get very full, especially at the start of term (lots of students). Note the interesting mirrors. Lunch served until 5 Sat.
◖❩ ⬚ ⬚ ⊖ (Chillingham Rd) P

HEBBURN

Clock
Victoria Road West
☎ (0191) 424 1134
11-11; 12-10.30 Sun
Beer range varies Ⓗ
Large, one-roomed bar; very noisy and popular. It derives its name from its large roof-mounted clock.
⊖ (Jarrow) P

Dougies Tavern
Blackett Street
☎ (0191) 428 4800
11.30-11; 12-10.30 Sun
Beer range varies Ⓗ
Warm, friendly, pub, catering for all. Traditional yet lively, it hosts live music Thu eve. Food is a speciality, particularly Sun. A children's certificate, secure play area and garden make it popular

with families. Mordue seasonal beers stocked.
⬚ ❀ ◖❩ ⬚ ⊖ (Jarrow) ♣ P

JARROW

Ben Lomond
Grange Road West
☎ (0191) 483 3839
11-11; 12-10.30 Sun
Castle Eden Nimmos XXXX; Courage Directors; Theakston Best Bitter; guest beers Ⓗ
Typical town-centre Wetherspoon's: good food, free from juke boxes, bandits, etc. Its open-plan design includes several partitioned areas in the main bar.
Q ◖❩ ⊖ ⊁ ⊞

JESMOND

Collingwood Arms
Brandling Village
☎ (0191) 281 1271
12-11; 12-10.30 Sun
Courage Directors; Taylor Landlord; Theakston Best Bitter; Wells Bombardier; guest beers Ⓗ
Long, narrow, pub with sitting areas at each end. In an area popular with students, the pub is often very busy.
❀ ◖❩ ⊖ P

KENTON BANK FOOT

Twin Farms
22 Main Road
☎ (0191) 286 1263
11-11; 12-10.30 Sun
Mordue Workie Ticket; Taylor Landlord; guest beers Ⓗ
Large pub and restaurant where various areas offer a choice of seating. This interesting pub stands in its own grounds between the city and airport.
⬚ ❀ ◖❩ ⬚ ⊖ (Bank Foot) P

LOW FELL

Aletaster
706 Durham Road (Chowdene Bank jct)
☎ (0191) 487 0770
12 (11 Sat)-11; 12-10.30 Sun
Courage Directors; Mordue Workie Ticket, Radgie Gadgie; Theakston Best Bitter; guest beers Ⓗ
In appearance, a typical S&N T&J Bernard pub, but more committed to real ale and cider than most. Its range of regular real ales, imaginative guests and occasional beer festivals plus friendly staff make it extremely popular. Regular live music.
❀ ⌣ P

NEWBURN

Keelman
Grange Road
☎ (0191) 267 0772
11-11; 12-10.30 Sun

Big Lamp Bitter, Prince Bishop Ale, Premium, seasonal beers H
Grade II listed former water pumping station that now houses the Big Lamp brewery and tap. It has built a strong following who enjoy the warm, friendly atmosphere and picturesque location.
❀ ⇌ ◑ ◗ ♿ P

NEWCASTLE-UPON-TYNE

Bacchus
High Bridge
☎ (0191) 232 6451
11.30-11; 7-10.30 Sun
Mordue Workie Ticket; Stones Bitter; Tetley Bitter; guest beers H
Spacious, two-roomed city-centre pub: the front bar looks out on to the street, the back room has a smaller seating area leading off. Lunches are very popular (not served Sun).
◑ ⇌ ⊖ (Monument)

Bodega
125 Westgate Road
☎ (0191) 221 1552
11-11; 12-10.30 Sun
Big Lamp Prince Bishop; Durham Magus; Mordue Workie Ticket; Theakston Best Bitter; guest beers H
This popular pub can get very busy, especially on match days. Two stained glass ceiling domes remain from the original building which was rebuilt a few years ago. The house beer No. 9 is Mordue's Geordie Pride rebadged.
◑ ⇌ ⊖ (Central/St James)

Bridge Hotel
Castle Square
☎ (0191) 232 6400
11-11; 12-10.30 Sun
Black Sheep Best Bitter; Mordue Workie Ticket; guest beers H
Large pub, standing by the high level bridge; the garden overlooks the river and old town walls. The single room offers various sitting and standing areas; the upstairs room hosts a long-established folk club.
❀ ◑ ⇌ ⊖ (Central)

Crown Posada
33 Side
☎ (0191) 232 1269
11 (12 Sat)-11; 12-3, 7-10.30 Sun
Castle Eden Conciliation Ale; Jennings Bitter; guest beers H
Absolute gem, boasting fine stained glass and an interesting ceiling. A small snug and larger sitting area are joined by a very narrow bar area. Can get very busy, but it is always worth visiting.
Q ⇌ ⊖ (Central/Monument)

Duke of Wellington
High Bridge
☎ (0191) 261 8852
11 (12 Sat)-11; 12-10.30 Sun
Ind Coope Burton Ale; Marston's Pedigree; Tetley Bitter; guest beers H
Single room pub stocking a rapidly changing selection of guest beers and hosting frequent beer festivals; can be very busy. No food Sun.
◑ ⇌ ⊖ (Monument)

Head of Steam
2 Neville Street
☎ (0191) 232 4379
11-11; 12-10.30 Sun
Draught Bass; Black Sheep Best Bitter; guest beers H
Modern basement bar attracting a varied clientele and serving a good value Sun lunch.
⇌ ⊖ (Central)

Hotspur
103 Percy Street
☎ (0191) 232 4352
11-11; 12-10.30 Sun
Courage Directors; McEwan 80/-; Theakston Best Bitter, Old Peculier; guest beers H
Single-roomed pub facing the Haymarket bus station, stocking an interesting selection of guest beers. Near the university, it is popular with students, but also shoppers and office workers.
❀ ◑ ◗ ⊖ (Haymarket)

New Bridge
2 Argyle Street
☎ (0191) 232 1020
11-11; 12-10.30 Sun
Beer range varies H
Ideal spot for a pint after a film at the nearby cinema complex. Regular visits are recommended to try the varied beers on offers. Tasty meals are also available as take-aways.
◑ ⊖ (Manors)

Tilleys
Westgate Road
☎ (0191) 232 0692
11.30-11; 7-10.30 (12-10.30 if NUFC at home) Sun
Jennings Bitter, Cumberland Ale, Sneck Lifter, seasonal beers H
The only outlet in the area regaularly serving a range of Jennings beers. Its proximity to the College of the Performing Arts and the Tyne Theatre ensures an interesting mix of customers. No food Sun.
◑ ⇌ ⊖ (Central/ St James)

NORTH HYLTON

Shipwrights Hotel
Ferryboat Lane (off A1231, Sunderland road)
☎ (0191) 549 5139
11-4, 5-11; 12-3, 7-10.30 Sun
Marston's Pedigree; guest beers H
Former ship chandlers' and post office, this 350-year-old pub is full of character; a *Guide* entry for 24 years. It serves traditional and more unusual food in a quiet, comfortable atmosphere.
⇌ ◑ ◗ P

NORTH SHIELDS

Magnesia Bank
1 Camden Street
☎ (0191) 257 4831
11-11; 12-10.30 Sun
Beer range varies H
Very popular town-centre pub, recently refurbished. Noted for its food and live music – national *Live Music Pub of the Year* 1999. Seven handpumps dispense a constantly changing range of beers including a Durham brew; it is the official Mordue brewery tap.
◑ ◗ ⊖ ⚡ 🚭 ▢

PENSHAW

Grey Horse
Old Penshaw Village (800 yds off A183)
☎ (0191) 584 4882
11-11; 12-10.30 Sun
Tetley Bitter H
This long-standing *Guide* entry is popular with locals and resting visitors from Penshaw Monument and local walks. Children welcome.
Q ❀ ◑ ◗ P ▢

Prospect
Victoria Terrace (A183)
☎ (0191) 584 4001
12-3, 6.30-11; 12-3, 7-10.30 Sun
Worthington Bitter; Theakston XB; guest beers H
Warm and friendly, this popular pub returns to the *Guide*. Drawing a good mix of locals and visitors, it is ideal for a family meal or a resting place for a drink after tackling Penshaw Monument.
Q ◑ ◗ ⊟ ♿ ♣ P ▢

RYTON

Olde Cross
Old Village ($^{1}/_{2}$ mile N of B6317)
☎ (0191) 413 4689
11.30-2 (not winter Mon), 4.30-11; 11-11 Sat; 12-10.30 Sun
Courage Directors; guest beers H
Welcoming hostelry, occupying a picturesque setting on the village green. It offers a choice of bar meals or the Italian restaurant upstairs, plus up to three guest beers. Handy for walks on Ryton Willows.
❀ ◑ ◗ P

SHIREMOOR

Shiremoor Farm
Middle Engine Lane
☎ (0191) 257 6302
11-11; 12-10.30 Sun
Mordue Workie Ticket; Taylor Landlord; guest beers Ⓗ
Extensively refurbished and extended, this excellent Fitzgerald free house now has designated no-smoking areas, and a new restaurant; a popular lunchtime venue.
Q ⌂ ❀ ◖▶ & P ⌘

SOUTH SHIELDS

Alum Ale House
River Drive (next to ferry landing)
☎ (0191) 427 7245
11-11; 12-10.30 Sun
Banks's Bitter; Camerons Strongarm Marston's Pedigree; guest beers Ⓗ
Small, popular, pub, a regular 'waiting room' for the ferry to North Shields. Panelled walls, a bare wood floor and a copper-topped bar complement the friendly atmosphere and warm welcome. Buskers' night Thu; quiz Sun eve. ⊖ ⊓

Bamburgh
175 Bamburgh Ave (Coast road, opp. Leas)
☎ (0191) 427 5523
11-11; 12-10.30 Sun
Black Sheep Best Bitter; Boddingtons Bitter; Flowers Original; Jennings Cumberland Ale; Tetley Bitter; guest beers Ⓗ
Large, open-plan pub run by very pleasant staff. On the coast road to Sunderland, it enjoys wonderful views of the sea and distant harbour piers. Very popular (especially for summer meals), it draws a good mix of locals and visitors.
❀ ◖▶ & ♣

Beacon Inn
100 Greens Place (Lawe Top, close to Roman fort)
☎ (0191) 456 2876
11-11; 12-10.30 Sun
Marston's Pedigree; Stones Bitter; Tetley Bitter; guest beer Ⓗ
Pleasant, open-plan pub, affording panoramic views over the mouth of the Tyne. Popular with tourists and locals, it is well known for its wide choice of good value meals (eve meals Mon-Fri). Friendly staff.
Q ❀ ◖▶ ▲ ⊖ ♣ P ⊓

Chichester Arms
Chichester Road (A194/B1298 jct)
☎ (0191) 420 0127
11-11; 12-10.30 Sun
Ind Coope Burton Ale; Tetley Bitter; guest beers Ⓗ
Spacious, street-corner local at a busy bus and Metro interchange. Friendly, helpful staff.
⌂ ◖🍴 ⊖ (Chichester) ♣

Dolly Peel
137 Commercial Road (near market place)
☎ (0191) 427 1441
11-11; 12-3, 7-10.30 Sun
Black Sheep Best Bitter; Courage Directors; Fuller's London Pride; Taylor Landlord; guest beers Ⓗ
Pleasant award-winning public house run by a friendly landlord and staff. The bar retains the nostalgic feel of a traditional old Shields river pub; it is named after a local fishwife.
Q ❀ ⊟ &

Riverside
3 Commercial Road
☎ (0191) 455 2328
12-11; 12-3, 7-10.30 Sun
Black Sheep Special; Courage Directors; Taylor Landlord; Theakston Best Bitter; guest beers Ⓗ
Deservedly popular local CAMRA *Pub of the Year*, at the heart of the Mill Dam area. Renowned for its friendly atmosphere and efficient, cheerful staff it stocks an ever-changing range of guest ales and ciders, offering some rarities. ⊖ ⌂

Stags Head
45 Fowler Street (400 yds N of Town Hall)
☎ (0191) 456 9174
11-11; 12-10.30 Sun
Draught Bass; Stones Bitter; Worthington Bitter Ⓗ
Unspoilt, town-centre pub displaying interesting old photographs of the town. Can get crowded at weekends, but there is more space in upstairs bar. ⊖

Steamboat
51 Mill Dam
☎ (0191) 454 0134
12-11; 12-10.30 Sun
Marston's Pedigree; Stones Bitter; Tetley Bitter; guest beer Ⓗ
Popular pub near the Customs House. Its wood-panelled walls are covered with shipping artefacts, flags and other bric-à-brac.
⊖ ⊞

SUNDERLAND

Fitzgeralds
10-12 Green Terrace
☎ (0191) 567 0852
11-11; 12-10.30 Sun
Beer range varies Ⓗ
Split-level free house near the university, offering the largest selection of ales in the area. Ten frequently changing guest ales are supplemented by numerous beer festivals making it extremely popular – hence door control staff operate at weekends. Meals served 12-3, 4.30-6.30.
❀ ◖▶ ≢

Harbour View
Harbour View, Roker
☎ (0191) 567 1402
11-11; 12-10.30 Sun
Draught Bass; guest beers Ⓗ
Popular, street-corner pub overlooking the marina, on the main coast road. Guest ales include regular offerings from local micro-breweries with strong support for Darwin Brewery beers. Busy on Sunderland matchdays despite the football ground moving away. ❀

Ropery
Webster's Bank, Deptford
☎ (0191) 514 7171
7-11; 7-11 Sun
Castle Eden Ale; Nimmos XXXX; guest beer Ⓗ
Circa 1793, the building stands on the site of the first patent ropeworks on the River Wear. The entertainments licence extends to outside (live music several times a week). Free transport to other local pubs provided at weekends. A friendly pub, offering good value food.
❀ ◖▶ & P ⊓

Saltgrass
36 Ayres Quay, Deptford
☎ (0191) 565 7229
11-11; 12-10.30 Sun
Draught Bass; Marston's Pedigree; guest beers Ⓗ
Two-roomed ex-Vaux pub close to the former shipyard: a small tap room bears a nautical theme, while a roaring fire warms the comfortable lounge. Free transport to other local pubs at weekends. No food Sun eve.
♨ ◖▶ & ⊞

Tap & Barrel
Salem Street, Hendon
☎ (0191) 514 2810
4 (12 Sat)-11; 12-10.30 Sun
Beer range varies Ⓗ
Traditional ale house on the edge of the city centre: three rooms all featuring bare floorboards and exposed brickwork. It stocks up to six ever-changing guest ales and hosts occasional beer festivals.
♨ Q ≢ ♣

William Jameson
30-32 Fawcett Street
☎ (0191) 514 5016
11-11; 12-10.30 Sun
Boddingtons Bitter; Castle Eden Nimmos XXXX; Courage Directors;

Theakston Best Bitter; guest beers H
Former 'Binns' department store, refurbished by Wetherspoon's into a vast air-conditioned pub offering food all day, cheap drinks and numerous beer festivals. Very busy on matchdays when the hard-pressed staff try their best to satisfy demand.
Q ◑ ▶ & ≋ ♻ ⅙ ▦

TYNEMOUTH
Copperfields
Hotspur Street
☎ (0191) 293 6666
12-11; 12-10.30 Sun
Theakston Best Bitter; guest beers H
This comfortable bar is part of the splendid Grand Hotel which overlooks Longsands Beach. There is no sea-view from the bar, but drinks may be taken into the hotel lounge at the front. Friendly, courteous bar staff offer one or two guest beers. Eve meals for non-residents finish at 7.
⇔ ◑ ▶ & ⊖ P

Cumberland Arms
Front Street
☎ (0191) 257 1820
11-11; 12-10.30 Sun
McEwan 80/-; Theakston Best Bitter; guest beers H
A small front bar with a nautical theme greets the visitor stepping inside from the village's main street. A larger upper level, with its own bar, offers more seating, plus a patio. No food Sun. A warm and friendly pub.
🏔 ❀ ◑ ⊞ ⊖ ♣

Fitzpatrick's
29 Front Street
☎ (0191) 257 8596
11-11; 12-10.30 Sun
Beer range varies H
Large, comfortable bar with two distinct drinking areas, which gets very busy as it is close to the priory and beach. Two or three guest beers usually on tap. ❀ ◑ ▶ ⊖

Tynemouth Lodge
Tynemouth Road
☎ (0191) 257 8956
11-11; 12-10.30 Sun
Draught Bass; Belhaven 80/-; Caledonian Deuchars IPA; guest beer (occasional) H

INDEPENDENT BREWERIES

Big Lamp: Newburn
Darwin: Sunderland
Federation: Dunston
Four Rivers: Newcastle (in receivership)
Mordue: Shiremoor

18th-century free house; a no-nonsense pub where a warm welcome is assured. One of the few traditional public houses remaining, it boasts the highest sales of draught Bass on Tyneside.
🏔 Q ❀ ⊖ ♻ P

Try also: Turks Head, Front St (T&J Bernard)

WARDLEY
Green
White Mare Pool
(B1288/A184 jct)
☎ (0191) 495 0171
11-11; 12-10.30 Sun
Castle Eden Nimmos XXXX; Ruddles County; Taylor Landlord; guest beers H
Landmark building at a major road intersection. A member of the respected Sir John Fitzgerald's chain, with a busy public bar, large restful lounge and popular dining room, it offers friendly service and a good atmosphere throughout. Guest beers often come from micro-breweries. Meals served 12-9.
❀ ◑ ▶ ⊞ & P

WASHINGTON
Sandpiper
Easby Road, Biddick (follow signs for District 7)
☎ (0191) 415 1733
11-11; 12-10.30 Sun
Boddingtons Bitter; Castle Eden Ale; Wadworth 6X; guest beers H
Modern estate pub: a large comfortable lounge and a smaller public bar, stocking up to seven ales.
❀ ◑ ▶ ⊞ & ♣ P

Steps
47-49a Spout Lane
☎ (0191) 415 1733
11-11; 12-10.30 Sun
Beer range varies H
Comfortable, friendly locals' lounge bar in the old village, recently extended and remodelled. Three continually changing ales on sale. It is popular with young people at weekends. ◑

WEST BOLDON
Black Horse
Rectory Bank
☎ (0191) 536 1814
11-11; 12-10.30 Sun
Castle Eden Ale; Flowers Original; Morland Old Speckled Hen; guest beer H
Large pub near the parish church, specialising in good quality meals; most of the pub is dedicated to an eating area, leaving a small public bar. It can get very busy.
◑ ▶ ⊞ ♣ P

Heritage Pubs
The pubs chosen as illustrations in the Guide are taken from CAMRA's National Inventory. These are pubs with unspoilt interiors that need to be preserved for future generations. The illustrations are used as examples of pubs on the inventory and may not necessarily have been chosen for inclusion in the Guide

---

WEST MOOR
George Stephenson
Great Lime Road
☎ (0191) 268 1073
12-11; 12-10.30 Sun
Beer range varies H
Well refurbished pub in the shadow of the East Coast railway line. It hosts popular music nights (Wed and Sat) featuring local bands. The frequently changing beer range usually includes a local brew.
❀ P ⍟

WHITLEY BAY
Briardene
7 The Links (coast road, N of centre)
☎ (0191) 252 0926
11-11 (public bar may close afternoons); 12-10.30 Sun
Black Sheep Best Bitter; Mordue Workie Ticket; Theakston Best Bitter; guest beers H
Impressive roadside lounge bar with a smaller public bar to the rear. Very popular for its food and with families, it stocks a constantly changing selection of wide-ranging guest beers. Several beer festivals are held each year.
🐾 ❀ ◑ ▶ ⊞ & ♣ P ⅙

WINLATON MILL
Golden Lion
Spa Well Road (A694)
☎ (0191) 414 5840
12 (6 Mon)-11; 12-10.30 Sun
Ruddles County; Courage Directors; Theakston Best Bitter; guest beer (summer) H
Lively, friendly two-roomed pub, popular with local residents. Its restaurant is expected to reopen by time of publication. Well located for the scenic Derwent Walk, along an old railway track.
❀ P ⍟

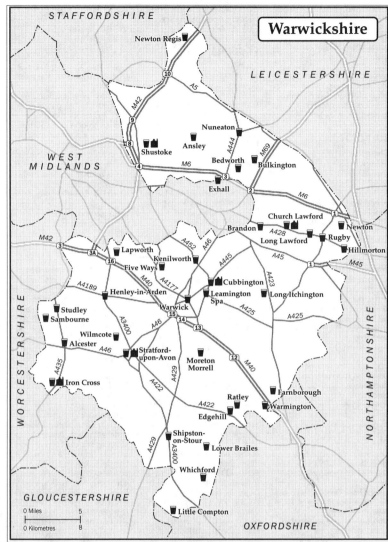

Warwickshire

STAFFORDSHIRE

LEICESTERSHIRE

Newton Regis

WEST MIDLANDS

Shustoke
Ansley
Nuneaton
Bedworth
Bulkington
Exhall

Church Lawford
Newton
Brandon
Long Lawford
Rugby
Hillmorton

Lapworth
Kenilworth
Five Ways
Cubbington
Henley-in-Arden
Leamington Spa
Long Itchington

Studley
Sambourne
Warwick

Wilmcote
Alcester
Stratford-upon-Avon
Moreton Morrell

WORCESTERSHIRE

Iron Cross
Ratley
Farnborough
Warmington
Edgehill

Shipston-on-Stour
Lower Brailes

Whichford

NORTHAMPTONSHIRE

0 Miles 5
0 Kilometres 8

Little Compton

GLOUCESTERSHIRE

OXFORDSHIRE

ALCESTER

Holly Bush
37 Henley Street
☎ (01789) 762482
12-3, 6-11; 12-11 Sat; 12-4, 7-10.30 Sun
Adnams Broadside; Cannon Royall Fruiterer's Mild; Uley Bitter; guest beers Ⓗ
Revived, traditional pub, tucked away behind the Town Hall offering three guest ales and hosting occasional beer festivals in the function hall and large garden. A regular folk club meets here.
Q ☞ ❀ ◖ ▶ ⊟ ♣ ⊁

Three Tuns
34 High Street
☎ (01789) 762626
12-11; 12-10.30 Sun

Goff's Jouster; Hobsons Best Bitter; guest beers Ⓗ
Central, single-room pub with a flagstoned floor. No food or music, but up to seven ales available, specialising in local micro-breweries.
Q ♣

ANSLEY

Lord Nelson Inn
Birmingham Road (B4112)
☎ (024) 7639 2305
12-2.30, 5.30-11; 12-11 Sat; 12-10.30 Sun
Draught Bass; M&B Brew XI; guest beers Ⓗ
Roadside pub/restaurant bearing a nautical feel in its friendly locals' bar and popular lounge. The restaurant opens Mon-Sat

eves and Sun lunch.
♨ ❀ ◖ ▶ ⊟ ♣ P

BEDWORTH

White Swan
All Saints Square
☎ (024) 7631 2164
11-11; 12-10.30 Sun
Wells Eagle, Bombardier Ⓗ
Large, town-centre pub, comprising a pleasantly refurbished lounge and a smaller bar/games room. No food Sun.
❀ ◖ ⊟ ⇌ ♣

Try also: White Horse Inn, Mill St (Free)

BRANDON

Royal Oak
Station Road (off A428, next

to rail line)

☎ (024) 7654 2304

12-2.30, 6-11; 12-11 Sat; 12-10.30 Sun

Ansells Bitter; Draught Bass; Tetley Bitter; guest beers Ⓗ

Multi-level village pub that gets crowded some nights. The food area provides a view of an old well (from a long-gone on-site brewery).

🕸 ◖ ▮ 🍺 ও 🅰 ♣ P

BULKINGTON

Chequers

Chequers Street

☎ (024) 7631 2182

12-3, 7-11; 12-11 Fri & Sat; 12-10.30 Sun

Draught Bass; M& B Mild, Brew XI; guest beers Ⓗ

One-room village free house split into three areas, all served from the same bar.

🏚 🕸 ♣ P

Weavers Arms

12 Long Street, Ryton (off Wolvey Rd)

☎ (024) 7631 4415

12-3, 6 (5.30 Fri)-11; 12-3.30, 7-10.30 Sun

Draught Bass; M& B Mild, Brew XI; guest beers Ⓗ

Well-known two-room free house where its popular, traditional bar has been extended to give a small games area. No food Sun or Mon.

🏚 🕸 ◖ ▮ ♣

CHURCH LAWFORD

Old Smithy

1 Green Lane (off A428, 4 miles from Rugby)

11-3, 5.30-11; 11-11 Sat; 12-10.30 Sun

Draught Bass; Frankton Bagby Anvil Ale; Greene King IPA, Abbot; Tetley Bitter; guest beers Ⓗ

Friendly village pub that caters for everyone with separate restaurant and games rooms, and a children's play area. It features seven or more cask ales, including a range from the on-site Frankton Bagby Brewery.

🏚 🕸 ◖ ▮ ও ♣ P

CUBBINGTON

Queens Head

20 Queen Street

☎ (01926) 429949

12-11; 12-10.30 Sun

Ansells Mild, Bitter; Draught Bass; guest beer Ⓗ

Sparse-looking, three-roomed Victorian local, but it has a very friendly atmosphere with good conversation. Home to an active angling club, darts teams and folk music (Tue eve). Major sporting events are shown on

a large screen TV. The guest beer changes frequently.

Q 🕸 ◖ ▮ ♣ P

EDGEHILL

Castle

☎ (01295) 670255

11.15-2.30, 6.15-11; 12-3, 6.30-10.30 Sun

Hook Norton Best Bitter, Old Hooky; guest beer (occasional) Ⓗ

Interesting pub boasting outstanding views; it was built as a round tower in 1742 from local stone. A wooden drawbridge links the 70-ft tower to a smaller square tower. A lovely garden overlooks the site of a Civil War battle; Aunt Sally played. The accommodation is in three self-catering apartments.

🏚 🕸 ⛫ ◖ ▮ ▮ ♣ ⌣ P

EXHALL

Boat

188 Blackhorse Road

☎ (024) 7636 1438

12-3, 7-11; 12-11 Sat; 12-3, 7-10.30 Sun

Ansells Mild, Bitter; guest beers Ⓗ

18th-century pub, full of character near the canal (Sutton Stop), little altered in recent years. 🏚 🕸 ♣ P

FARNBOROUGH

Butcher's Arms

Main Street (off A423, Southam and Banbury road)

☎ (01295) 690615

12-4, 7-11; 12-4, 7-10.30 Sun

Draught Bass; Hook Norton Best Bitter; guest beers Ⓗ

Fine old village pub, built of local ironstone. The food in both the bar and the restaurant is of high quality. Families are made especially welcome; the garden has space for the children to explore in summertime, away from the cars.

🏚 Q 🕸 ◖ ▮ ♣ P

FIVE WAYS

Case is Altered ☆

Case Lane (off the Claverdon road at A4141/A4177 roundabout)

☎ (01926) 484206

12 (11.30 Sat)-2.30, 6-11; 12-2, 7-10.30 Sun

Brains Dark; Flowers Original; Greene King IPA, Ⓖ **guest beer** Ⓗ

350-year-old, unspoilt little gem, full of atmosphere and character. No children, dogs, music, food or mobiles – just good ale and conversation. The bar billiards table still takes pre-decimal coins. The homely lounge opens weekends.

🏚 Q ♣ P

HENLEY-IN-ARDEN

White Swan

100 High Street

☎ (01564) 792623

11-11; 12-10.30 Sun

Ansells Mild; Marston's Pedigree; Morland Old Speckled Hen; guest beers Ⓗ

Friendly, characterful, coaching house partly dating back to the 14th century, serving good value food in the lounge or restaurant. It is reputedly haunted by a housemaid who was hanged at the gallows for murder. It hosts regular live jazz and quiz eves.

🕸 ⛫ ◖ ▮ 🅰 ≈ ♣ P

HILLMORTON

Bell

High Street (A428)

☎ (01788) 544465

12-11; 12-10.30 Sun

Draught Bass; M&B Brew XI Ⓗ

Traditional boozer; the public bar has games, while the new restaurant has added another dimension to this popular pub. The Bass is always excellent.

🕸 ◖ ▮ ▮ ♣ P ⊬

IRON CROSS

Queens Head & Fat God's Brewery

On B4088 (old A435)

☎ (01386) 871012

11 (12 winter)-11; 12-10.30 Sun

Fat God's Bitter, Morris Dancer, Porter of the Vale, Thunder & Lightning, seasonal beers Ⓗ

Lively pub with a strong commitment to the local community and good causes. The home of Fat God's Brewery, it was the local CAMRA *Pub of the Year* 1999. It hosts a festival in June, with 30 beers stocked over a week. Try the bread, made using Fat God's yeast. Families welcome.

🏚 🕸 ◖ ▮ ও ▮ ⌣ P

Try also: Coach & Horses, Harvington (Free)

KENILWORTH

Clarendon House Hotel

6 High Street (near A429/A452 jct)

☎ (01926) 857668

11-11; 12-10.30 Sun

Greene King IPA, Abbot; Hook Norton Best Bitter; guest beers Ⓗ

Traditional inn, parts of which date back to the 15th century, but now refurbished in a more modern style with a bar and brasserie. Two changing guest beers are served by attentive staff.

🕸 ⛫ ◖ ▮ P

Old Bakery Hotel
12 High Street (near A429/A452 jct)
☎ (01926) 864111
12-2.30 (not Mon-Fri), 5-11; 12-2.30, 5-10.30 Sun
Fuller's London Pride; Hook Norton Best Bitter; Jennings Cumberland Ale [H]
Attractively restored and extended, 17th-century family-run hotel, formerly a bakery. A peaceful and comfortable bar welcomes residents and visitors alike. Friendly and courteous service awaits in a picturesque area of this small town, close to castle.
Q ❀ 🛏 P

Royal Oak
36 New Street (main Coventry road)
☎ (01926) 853201
6-11; 12-10.30 Sun
Marston's Bitter, Pedigree [H]
Small, cosy local in the old part of town; it sometimes stages folk and other music sessions weekday eves.
🔥 ❀ ⊟ ♿ ♣

LAPWORTH

Navigation
Old Warwick Road (B4439)
☎ (01564) 783337
11-2.30, 5.30-11; 11-11 Sat; 12-10.30 Sun
Draught Bass; Highgate Dark; M&B Brew XI; guest beers [H]
Excellent canalside pub stocking interesting guest beers for the area. A traditional, unspoilt bar and small cosy lounge are complemented by a well-designed extension for the popular home-cooked food. The cider varies.
🔥 Q ❀ ◑ ◗ ⊟ ⛺ ⇌ ⌓ P

LEAMINGTON SPA

Brunswick
67 Brunswick Street
☎ (01926) 425896
3 (12 Fri & Sat)-11; 12-10.30 Sun
Marston's Pedigree; guest beer [H]
1960s pub in the old town area, south of the canal. One large bar features a pool table one end and a fish tank at the other. Photos recall Frank Whittle, inventor of the jet engine, who lived locally. A pets corner is housed in the garden – children welcome until early eve.
❀ ⇌ P

Red House
113 Radford Road
☎ (01926) 881725
11.30-3.30, 5-11; 11.30-11 Fri & Sat; 12-10.30 Sun
Draught Bass; Greene King Abbot; M&B Brew XI; Worthington Bitter; guest beers [H]
Unusually busy local where drinking is accompanied by good conversation. The Cheese Society will be pleased to sample any rare cheeses. Large garden.
Q ❀ ♣

LITTLE COMPTON

Red Lion
Off A44
☎ (01608) 674397
12-2.30, 6-11; 12-3, 7-10.30 Sun
Donnington BB, SBA [H]
Cotswold stone local, heavily involved in the community. Two chefs ensure good food quality. Handy for visiting the Rollright Stones, it is Donnington's only tied house in Warwickshire. Aunt Sally played.
🔥 ❀ 🛏 ◑ ◗ ⊟ ♣ P

LONG ITCHINGTON

Harvester Inn
Church Road
☎ (01926) 812698
11-3, 6-11; 12-10.30 Sun
Hook Norton Best Bitter, Old Hooky; guest beer [H]
Friendly, popular family-run genuine free house with two bars (one is dominated by a pool table) and a dining room. Note that this is *the* Harvester not part of the Harvester chain.
◑ ◗ ⛺ ♣ P

LONG LAWFORD

Country Inn
29 Main Street
☎ (01788) 565188
12-2.30 (3.30 Sat), 6-11; 12-11 Fri; 12-3.30, 7-10.30 Sun
Greene King IPA; M&B Mild, Brew XI; guest beers [H]
Friendly, single-bar village free house, boasting oak beams, a flagstone floor and a log fire. It has a games room and a quality restaurant.
🔥 🐴 ❀ ◑ ◗ ♣ P

Sheaf & Sickle
Coventry Road (A428, 1½ miles from Rugby)
☎ (01788) 544622
12-2.30, 6-11; 12-11 Sat; 12-10.30 Sun
Ansells Mild, Bitter; Tetley Bitter; guest beer [H]
Friendly local, with a quiet snug and a busy bar. It offers a good choice of guests and hosts occasional beer festivals. The quality restaurant is very popular, as are the well-priced bar snacks.
❀ ◑ ◗ ♿ ♣ P

LOWER BRAILES

George Hotel
High Street
☎ (01608) 685223
12-11; 12-10.30 Sun
Hook Norton Mild, Best Bitter, Generation, seasonal beers [H]
Grade II listed coaching inn with elements from the 16th to 18th centuries. Sympathetically refurbished, it enjoys a thriving local trade and stages frequent live music. The restaurant often hosts theme evenings (Indian, Mexican etc). Aunt Sally is played here.
🔥 Q 🐴 ❀ 🛏 ◑ ◗ ⊟ ♿ ⛺ ♣ P

MORETON MORRELL

Black Horse
☎ (01926) 651231
11.30-3, 6.30-11; 12-3, 7-10.30 Sun
Hook Norton Best Bitter; guest beer [H]
Village local within easy reach of the M40, deserving of greater support. The guest beer is usually from a small independent brewery. Enjoy the peaceful garden. Good value filled rolls are recommended.
Q ❀ ⛺

NEWTON

Stag & Pheasant
Main Street
☎ (01788) 860326
12-3 , 6-11; 12-4, 7-10.30 Sun
Banks's Original, Bitter; guest beer [H]
Traditional, thatched cosy village local, reputed to be the oldest A-frame building in Warwickshire. Formerly a farmhouse where there are reputedly strange goings on in the cellar; a thirsty ghost?
Q ❀ ◑ ◗ ♿ ♣ P ⊔

NEWTON REGIS

Queen's Head
Main Road
☎ (01827) 830271
11-2.30, 6-11; 12-2.30, 7-10.30 Sun
Draught Bass; M&B Brew XI; Highgate Dark; guest beer [H]
16th-century village pub, where guest beers from regional and micro-breweries change approximately fortnightly.
🔥 ❀ ◑ ◗ ⊟ ♣ P

NUNEATON

Bull
Bull Street, Attleborough
☎ (024) 7638 6626
12-3, 5-11; 12-11 Fri & Sat; 12-10.30 Sun
Beer range varies [H]
Well used, friendly pub whose interior is crammed with bric-a-brac and old village pictures. 🔥 ❀ ♣ P

Felix Holt
3 Stratford Street

☎ (024) 7634 7785
11-11; 12-10.30 Sun
Beer range varies Ⓗ
Large, town-centre Wetherspoon's pub that can get busy at weekends.
Q ◑ ▮ & ⇌ ⅍ ▣

Fox Inn
The Square, Attleborough
☎ (024) 7638 3290
11-11; 12-10.30 Sun
Mansfield Riding Mild, Bitter Ⓗ
Well-appointed, two-room local situated in the heart of the 'village'. No food Sat eve or Sun.
❀ ◑ ▮ 🖰 & ♣ ▣

Try also: **Attleborough Arms**, Highfield Rd (Free)

RATLEY
Rose & Crown
☎ (01295) 678148
12-2.30, 6-11; 12-2.30, 6-10.30 Sun
Badger Tanglefoot; Wells Eagle, Bombardier; guest beers Ⓗ
Wonderful old stone pub with a well-deserved reputation for its beers. Set in beautiful countryside in a secluded village, this family-run local is reputedly haunted by a Roundhead ghost from the nearby battle of Edgehill. The garden houses an Aunt Sally.
🏚 Q 🛏 ❀ ◑ ▮ & ▲ ♣ ⅍

RUGBY
Alexandra Arms
72 James Street (near multi-storey car park)
☎ (01788) 587660
11.30-3, 5-11; 11.30-11 Fri & Sat; 12-10.30 Sun
Ansells Bitter; Greene King Abbot; Marston's Pedigree; guest beers Ⓗ
Busy, friendly local just off the town centre with a comfortable, traditional lounge bar and a games room. It offers rapidly changing guest beers and good value bar food. Rugby CAMRA *Pub of the Year* 1998 and '99, it hosts occasional beer festivals. Cider sold in summer.
Q ❀ ◑ ▮ ⇌ ♣ 🖰

Raglan Arms
30 Dunchurch Road (opp Rugby School playing fields)
☎ (01788) 544441
12-3 (not Thu), 7-11; 12-11 Fri; 11-11 Sat; 12-10.30 Sun
Banks's Hanson's Mild; Greene King Abbot; Marston's Bitter, Pedigree; guest beers Ⓗ
Excellent local offering a good atmosphere and up to seven real ales. Twice previous winner of Rugby CAMRA *Pub of the Year*, it is a rare outlet for Hanson's Mild.
Q ❀ ◑ ▮ ♣ P

Three Horseshoes Hotel
22 Sheep Street
☎ (01788) 544585
11-2.30, 7-11; 7-11 Sun
Greene King IPA, Abbot; guest beers Ⓗ
Spacious, 18th-century former coaching inn in the town centre, providing a quiet drinking area and eating areas. Its recently increased range of handpumps regularly feature Frankton Bagby beers. Discount on accommodation for CAMRA members. Limited parking.
🏚 🛏 ◑ P

Victoria
1 Lower Hillmorton Road
☎ (01788) 544374
12-2.30, 6-11; 12-11 Sat; 12-2.30, 7-10.30 Sun
Cottage Champflower; guest beers Ⓗ
Triangular shaped pub: front bar and a comfortable lounge decorated in Victorian style. Guest beers include local Frankton Bagby and Church End brews. This friendly pub is popular with locals. No food Sun.
◑ 🖰 ⇌

SAMBOURNE
Green Dragon
The Village Green (between A435 and A441)
☎ (01527) 892465
11-3, 6-11; 5.30-11 Fri; 12-3, 7-10.30 Sun
Draught Bass; Hancock's HB; M&B Brew XI Ⓗ
Overlooking the green, this attractive, 17th-century inn offers two bars and a restaurant. Oak beams, brasses and pewter add to its character and it enjoys a good reputation for food. Modern en-suite accommodation is also available.
🏚 Q ❀ 🛏 ◑ P

SHIPSTON-ON-STOUR
Black Horse
Station Road (Ilmington road)
☎ (01608) 661617
12-3.30, 7-11; 12-2.30, 7-10.30 Sun
Greene King Abbot; Tetley Bitter; guest beers Ⓗ
An ancient pub in an ancient town, once a bustling seaport but now sadly landlocked. This friendly pub sells good value home-cooked food and an enterprising selection of guest beers.
🏚 Q 🛏 ❀ ◑ 🖰 P

Try also: **Bird-in-Hand**, Newbold (Hook Norton)

SHUSTOKE
Griffin Inn
Coleshill Road, Church End (B4116, on sharp bend)
☎ (01675) 481205
12-2.30, 7-11; 12-2.30, 7-10.30 Sun
Highgate Mild; Marston's Pedigree; Theakston Old Peculier; guest beers Ⓗ
Old country village inn, full of warmth from log fires and low beamed ceilings. It usually stocks ten real ales, always one from the Church End Brewery next door. Great food is served daily except Sun. A must.
🏚 Q 🛏 ❀ ◑ P

STRATFORD UPON AVON
Pen & Parchment
Bridgefoot (next to canal on the gyratory system)
☎ (01789) 297697
11-11; 12-10.30 Sun
Boddingtons Bitter; Flowers Original; Marston's Pedigree; Taylor Landlord; Wadworth 6X; guest beers Ⓗ
18th-century town-centre pub, part of the Hogshead chain. Serving a wide and rapidly changing range of ales, it actively promotes real ales. Try a 'Bat' – four $1/3$ pint measures of ale, or a four-pint jug for the price of three on selected beers.
❀ 🛏 ◑ ▮ ⇌ ↻ ⅍

Queen's Head
53 Ely Street
☎ (01789) 204914
11-11; 12-10.30 Sun
Draught Bass; Highgate Saddlers; M&B Brew XI; guest beers Ⓗ
Lively 18th-century town pub with exposed beams, flagstone floors and real fires. A *Guide* entry for many years. Cider is sold in summer.
🏚 ❀ 🛏 ◑ ▲ ♣ ↻ ▣

Try also: **Cox's Yard**, Bridgefoot (Brew pub); **Salmon Tail**, Evesham Rd (Free)

STUDLEY
Little Lark
108 Alcester Road (A435/Toms Town Lane jct)
☎ (01527) 853105
12-3, 6-11; 12-11 Sat; 12-3, 6.30-10.30 Sun
Ushers Best Bitter, Founders, seasonal beers Ⓗ
This friendly, street-corner pub bears a newspaper theme. Good food and ale make it popular with residents and local workers alike. There is a real fire in one of the three rooms.
🏚 ◑ ▮ ♣ ↻

CAMRA National Pub Inventory: Biggin Hall, Coventry, West Midlands

WARMINGTON

Plough Inn
Church Hill (off B4100,
6 miles NW of Banbury)
☎ (01295) 690666
12-3 (not Mon-Fri), 5.30-11; 12-3,
7-10.30 Sun
**Hook Norton Best Bitter; Marston's
Pedigree; guest beer** H
Small, friendly, traditional
stone village local. The low-
ceilinged drinking area is
dominated by a large
fireplace with a copper hood.
The village is on the side of
Edge Hill, one of
Warwickshire's most
prominent landmarks.
Guest beer is often from a
local brewery. No food Sun
eve.
🛏 ✿ ◑ ◗ ♣ P

WARWICK

Cape of Good Hope
66 Lower Cape
☎ (01926) 498138
12-3, 6-11; 12-11 Fri; 12-3, 6-10.30
Sun
**Boddingtons Bitter; Tetley Bitter;
guest beer** H
Well-known canalside pub,
built soon after the canal
opened; the front bar is only
a few feet from the water.
The rear lounge features a
painting explaining the
origin of the name. It is busy
with local factory and office
workers at lunchtimes. It
serves a good value and
extensive menu. The house

beer is from Weatheroak.
✿ ◑ ◗ 🍴 P

Globe Hotel
10 Theatre Street (off Market
Place)
☎ (01926) 492044
11-11; 12-3, 7-11 Sun
**Fuller's London Pride; M&B Brew XI;
guest beer** H
Grade II listed building in the
town centre, a convenient
place to rest on market days
in the comfortable lounge
bar. Children welcome until
7pm. Eve meals are served in
the restaurant (no meals Sun
eve).
✿ 🛏 ◑ ◗ ≠

Old Fourpenny Shop
27 Crompton Street (near
racecourse)
☎ (01926) 491360
12-2.30 (3 Fri & Sat), 5.30 (5 Fri, 6 Sat)-
11; 12-3, 6-10.30 Sun
M&B Brew XI; guest beers H
Its 10th consecutive *Guide*
entry, it stocks six real ales,
five of which are guests and
can change on a daily basis;
RCH Pitchfork is a regular
favourite guest. Good quality
home-cooked food is
available in the bar or
restaurant (no lunches Sun).
🛏 ◑ ◗ P

WHICHFORD

Norman Knight
Facing village green
☎ (01608) 684621
12-2.30, 7-11; 12-2.30, 7-10.30 Sun

**Hook Norton Best Bitter; guest
beers** H
Traditional village pub,
boasting stone-flagged floors
and exposed timbers, named
after John de Mohun who is
buried in the village church.
It has a holiday cottage to let
and caravan field. Eve meals
served Fri and Sat. Aunt Sally
and shove-ha'penny played.
🛏 ✿ 🛏 ◑ ◗ 🚻 ⅄ ♣ P

WILMCOTE

Masons Arms
Aston Cantlow Road
☎ (01789) 297416
11-11; 12-10.30 Sun
**Black Sheep Best Bitter; Hook
Norton Best Bitter; guest beer**
(occasional) H
Traditional village pub with
real fires and a pleasant
conservatory/dining area.
The Hook Norton is
renowned for both its quality
and value.
🛏 Q ✿ 🛏 ◑ ◗ ⅄ ≠ ♣ P

INDEPENDENT
BREWERIES

Church End: Shustoke

Cox's Yard: Stratford
upon Avon

Frankton Bagby: Church
Lawford

Queens Head: Iron Cross

Warwickshire:
Cubbington

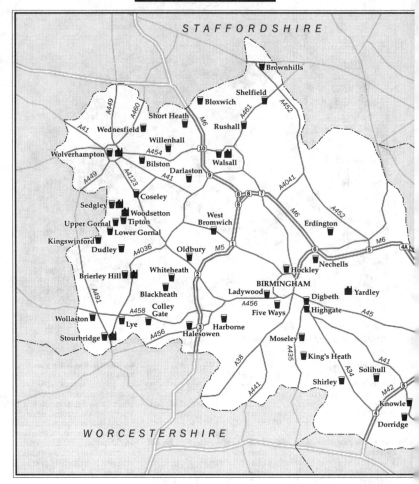

STAFFORDSHIRE

Brownhills

Shelfield
Bloxwich
Short Heath
Rushall
Wednesfield
Willenhall
Wolverhampton
Bilston
Walsall
Darlaston
Coseley
Sedgley
Woodsetton
Upper Gornal
Tipton
West Bromwich
Erdington
Lower Gornal
Kingswinford
Dudley
Oldbury
Hockley
Nechells
Whiteheath
Brierley Hill
BIRMINGHAM
Blackheath
Ladywood
Digbeth
Yardley
Colley Gate
Five Ways
Highgate
Wollaston
Lye
Harborne
Stourbridge
Halesowen
Moseley
King's Heath
Solihull
Shirley
Knowle
Dorridge

WORCESTERSHIRE

ALLESLEY

Rainbow Inn
73 Birmingham Road (off A45)
☎ (024) 7640 2888
11-11; 12-3, 6-10.30 Sun
Courage Best Bitter, Directors; Rainbow Piddlebrook, Firecracker, seasonal beers; guest beers H
Lively old village-centre pub on the outskirts of Coventry. It is central to community events including the Village festival. It stocks occasional guest beers and seasonal specials, from the new Rainbow Brewery in the stables at rear.
Q ❀ ◐ ▶ ⌘ ♣ P

BARSTON

Bulls Head
Barston Lane
☎ (01675) 442830
11-2.30, 5.30-11; 11-11 Sat; 12-10.30 Sun
M&B Brew XI; Draught Bass; guest beers H
Genuine village local, with

parts dating back to the 15th-century, it is a loyal supporter of independent breweries. Solihull CAMRA *Pub of the Year* 2000.
♨ Q ❀ ◐ ▶ P

BILSTON

Olde White Rose
20 Lichfield Street
☎ (01902) 498339
12-11; 12-3.30, 7-10.30 Sun
Beer range varies H
Popular, one-room pub, serving up to twelve ever-changing beers, plus good value food all day (no meals Sun eve). Local CAMRA Town *Pub of the Year* 1999.
❀ ◐ ▶ ❤ ⇋ 🍴

Try also: Trumpet, 58 High St (Holden's)

BIRMINGHAM: CITY CENTRE

Bennetts
8 Bennetts Hill (off New St)
☎ (0121) 643 9293

11-11; 12-10.30 Sun
Banks's Bitter; Marston's Pedigree H
Former classical Victorian bank that has been converted with a stylish interior; popular with office workers.
◐ ▶ ⇋ (Snow Hill/New St)

Figure of Eight
236-239 Broad Street
☎ (0121) 633 0917
10.30-11; 12-10.30 Sun
Boddingtons Bitter; Courage Directors; Theakston Mild, Bitter; guest beers H
Typical Wetherspoon's pub at the heart of Broad Street nightlife; it stocks an excellent range of up to ten guest beers.
❀ ◐ ▶ ♿ ⇋ (Five Ways) 🍴

Hogshead
29a Newhall Street
☎ (0121) 200 2453
12-11; closed Sun
Boddingtons Bitter; Enville Bitter; H **guest beers** H/G
Newish Hogshead selling an excellent, constantly-

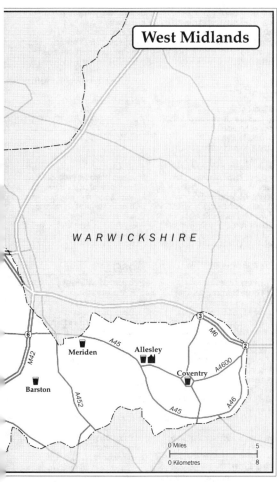

West Midlands

WARWICKSHIRE

Meriden
Allesley
Coventry
Barston

0 Miles 5
0 Kilometres 8

---

changing range from micros
and regional breweries alike;
it is especially busy at
weekends. Meals served 12-9
(8 Sat); no food Sun. A
variety of drinking areas
make much use of wood in
the decor. Very friendly.
◖ ▶ ≈ (Snow Hill) ♣ ☖ ✄

Old Fox
54 Hurst Street (opp.
Hippodrome)
☎ (0121) 622 5080
11.30-11; 12-10.30 Sun
**Ansells Mild; Marston's Pedigree;
Morland Old Speckled Hen; Tetley
Bitter; guest beers** Ⓗ
Traditional pub, convenient
for the Chinese Quarter.
Tables and chairs are put
outside on the pavement
when weather permits. Two
rooms are served by an island
bar. No food Sun eve.
❀ ◖ ▶ ≈ (New St)

Old Joint Stock
4 Temple Row West (opp.
Cathedral)
☎ (0121) 200 1892

11-11; closed Sun
**Fuller's Chiswick, London Pride,
ESB; guest beers** Ⓗ
Former Grade II listed bank,
converted into a drinking
haven, serving shoppers and
office workers. One of the
guest beers is normally from
Beowulf. Wheelchair access is
via the outside drinking area.
❀ ◖ ▶ ♿ ≈ (New St/Snow Hill) ▣

Slurping Toad
Hurst Street (near
Hippodrome)
☎ (0121) 633 9584
11-11; 12-10.30 Sun
Beer range varies Ⓗ
Trendy pub in the
redeveloping area of
Birmingham, featuring bare
timbers and bookshelves.
Meals served 12-8.
Wheelchair WC.
◖ ▶ ♿ ≈ (New St)

Tap & Spile
Regency Wharf, Gas Street
(off Broad St)
☎ (0121) 632 5602
11-11; 12-10.30 Sun

**Draught Bass; Bateman XB;
Everards Tiger; Fuller's London
Pride; Highgate Dark; Tap & Spile
Premium** Ⓗ
Cosy, two-bar pub, in a
converted canalside building,
arranged on split levels; the
bottom bar looks out on to
the canal. Stocking a large
range of real ales, it is one of
the few pubs in Birmingham
selling real cider. ◖ ☖

DIGBETH

Anchor ☆
308 Bradford Street (behind
coach station)
☎ (0121) 622 4516
11-11; 12-10.30 Sun
**Ansells Mild; Tetley Bitter; guest
beers** Ⓗ
Victorian corner pub
boasting three rooms, served
from a central bar. It hosts
regular beer festivals and a
changing range of guest beers
and bottled beers from
around the world feature in
this local CAMRA *Pub of the
Year* 1998.
❀ ◖ ▶ ≈ (New St/ Moor St) ♣

Horans Tavern
92 Floodgate Street
☎ (0121) 643 3851
11-11; 12-3 (closed eve) Sun
Ansells Mild; guest beers Ⓗ
Genuine Irish pub, within
the Irish Quarter, serving
some unusual beers from
around the country. The
clientele is mixed but a
friendly atmosphere prevails
in the cosy back room and
open-plan bar.
Q ◖ ▶ ♣

White Swan ☆
276 Bradford Street
☎ (0121) 622 2586
11-3, 4.15-11; 12-3, 7-10.30 Sun
Banks's Original, Bitter Ⓗ
Ornately decorated two-
roomed pub serving a mix of
customers in the Irish
Quarter.
◖ ≈ (Moor St)

Woodman ☆
106 Albert Street (opp. Old
Curzon St station)
☎ (0121) 643 1959
11-11; 12-10.30 Sun
**Ansells Mild; Tetley Bitter; guest
beers** Ⓗ
A gem of a pub in a
redeveloping area of the city.
The interior decor has
remained unchanged for
almost a century. A friendly
atmosphere, with no dress
restrictions, makes it a
popular local.
◖ ▶ ▣ ≈ (Moor St)

ERDINGTON

Lad in the Lane
28 Bromford Lane (400 yds N

of A38)

☎ (0121) 377 7471

11-11; 11-2.30, 5.30-11 Tue; 11-2.30, 5-11 Wed; 12-3, 7-10.30 Sun

Ansells Mild; Marston's Pedigree; Tetley Bitter Ⓗ

Splendid, 14th-century building, magnificently renovated. The large lounge is split and there is a small, basic bar. The extensive garden is very popular in summer. No food Sun.

🏵 ◖🍴 ♣ P

FIVE WAYS

White Swan

57 Grosvenor Street West (near Tesco's)

☎ (0121) 643 6064

11.30-2.30 (3 Sat), 5 (7 Sat)-11; 12-3, 7-10.30 Sun

Ansells Mild, Bitter; Greene King Abbot; Marston's Pedigree; Tetley Bitter Ⓗ

The last unspoilt pub in this part of Birmingham; a traditional unpretentious two-bar house, decorated in Victorian style; the public bar has pool and darts. It is close to Brindley Place office and restaurant complex.

◖🍴 🚲 ⇌ (Five Ways)

HARBORNE

Bell

11 Old Church Road

☎ (0121) 427 0934

12-11; 12-10.30 Sun

Beer range varies Ⓗ

This part-18th-century friendly local lies on consecrated ground: one small central bar, with a lounge and a public seating area serves two guest beers. It has a bowling green.

Q 🏵 ◖🚲

White Horse

2 York Street

☎ (0121) 427 6023

11-11; 12-10.30 Sun

Marston's Pedigree; Tetley Bitter; guest beers Ⓗ

Typical Festival Alehouse with wooden floorboards and fittings. It is friendly and compact, so can get busy at times. Ever-changing beers (seven guests) feature many from smaller independent and regional breweries.

◖🚲 ⇌

HIGHGATE

Lamp Tavern

257 Barford Street

☎ (0121) 622 2599

12-11; 12-6 Sun

Church End Gravediggers; Everards Tiger; Marston's Pedigree; Morland Old Speckled Hen; Stanway Stanney Bitter; guest beer (Fri) Ⓗ

Popular pub serving a wide-ranging clientele with an

excellent choice of ales; it is still the only regular local outlet to try Stanway beer. Regular live music is staged in the back room. Previous Birmingham CAMRA *Pub of the Year.* ◖🚲

HOCKLEY

Black Eagle

16 Factory Road (near Soho House Museum)

☎ (0121) 523 4008

11.30-3, 5.30-11; 11.30-11 Fri; 12-3, 7-11 Sat; 12-3, 7-10.30 Sun

Ansells Mild, Bitter; Marston's Pedigree; Taylor Landlord; guest beers Ⓗ

Excellent food is served at this current local CAMRA *Pub of the Year.* Rebuilt in 1895, it retains most of the original features. It regularly offers beers from the local Beowulf Brewery

🏵 ◖🍴 ⊖ (Benson Rd)

Church Inn

22 Great Hampton Street (A41 from centre)

☎ (0121) 515 1851

11.45-11; 12-3, 6-11 Sat; closed Sun

Batham Best Bitter; Burton Bridge Old Expensive; Morland Old Speckled Hen; guest beer Ⓗ

Excellent, old-fashioned pub, close to the city centre, renowned for good food in very large portions. It also offers an impressive selection of some 70 whiskies. The room off the bar is open on request and is a real gem.

◖🍴🚲 ⇌ (Jewellery Qtr/Snow Hill) ⊖ (St Pauls)

Red Lion

94-95 Waterstone Lane (off A4540)

☎ (0121) 236 8371

12-11; 12-10.30 Sun

Banks's Original, Bitter Ⓟ

Two-roomed pub in Birmingham's famous Jewellery Quarter. Note the mirrored wall and bar back and elaborate etched windows. Popular with locals, it gets busy early eve.

🚲🚲 ⇌ (Jewellery Qtr)

White House

99 New John Street West

☎ (0121) 523 0782

11-11; 12-10.30 Sun

M&B Mild, Brew XI; guest beer Ⓗ

Old-fashioned estate local, simply furnished, it represents very good value for money.

🏵 ◖ ⇌ (Jewellery Qtr) ⊖ ♣

KINGS HEATH

Pavilions

229 Alcester Road South

☎ (0121) 441 3286

12-3, 5-11; 12-11 Fri & Sat; 12-10.30 Sun

Banks's Bitter; Marston's Pedigree Ⓗ

Modern, two-roomed pub inside an 1860 building. The interior has been designed with style and its traditional ambience does not feel contrived. It is popular with a wide age range.

🏵Q ◖🍴🚲 P 🏠

LADYWOOD

Fiddle & Bone

4 Sheepcote Street

☎ (0121) 200 2223

11-11; 12-10.30 Sun

Marston's Pedigree; Theakston Best Bitter, Old Peculier; guest beer Ⓗ

Spacious but friendly four-bar pub-cum-restaurant on the canal. Nightly live music specialises in Jazz, Blues and South American.

Q 🏵🏵 ◖🚲 ⇌ P

MOSELEY

Prince of Wales

118 Alcester Road

☎ (0121) 449 4198

11-11; 12-10.30 Sun

Ansells Mild; Marston's Pedigree; Ind Coope Burton Ale Ⓗ

Cosy, three-roomed pub, little changed since 1900, it is popular with the local community.

Q 🏵🏵 ♣

Station

7 High Street, Kings Heath

☎ (0121) 444 1257

11-11; 12-10.30 Sun

Ind Coope Burton Ale; Tetley Bitter; guest beer (occasional) Ⓗ

This friendly local draws a mixed clientele. Live music is sometimes performed. A room is set aside for sporting events.

◖🚲

NECHELLS

Villa Tavern ☆

307 Nechells Park Road

☎ (0121) 682 9862

11.30-2.30, 5.30-11; 11.30-11 Fri & Sat; 12-3, 7-10.30 Sun

Ansells Mild, Bitter; Marston's Pedigree; Tetley Bitter Ⓗ

Late Victorian pub boasting a beautiful interior; note the stained glass bow window in the lounge. The three rooms (bar, lounge and function room) are served by a single bar. Good value weekday lunches available.

Q ◖🚲 ⇌ (Aston) ♣ P

BLACKHEATH

Waterfall

132 Waterfall Lane, Cradley Heath

☎ (0121) 561 3499

12-3, 5-11; 12-11 Fri & Sat; 12-10.30 Sun

Batham Best Bitter; Enville Ale; Holden's Special; Hook Norton Old Hooky; Marston's Pedigree; guest beers H
Free house, overlooking a steep hill, with a front lounge and public bar behind (use side entrance). Around ten real ales and a varying cider attract drinkers and diners from afar; it enjoys a busy weekday lunch trade. ⊛ ◖◗ 〓 ♿ 〓 (Old Hill) ♣ ◔ P ✂

BLOXWICH
Sir Robert Peel
104 Bell Lane
☎ (01922) 470921
12-2.30, 5-11; 12-11 Fri & Sat; 12-10.30 Sun
Banks's Original; P Courage Directors; guest beer H
Large Victorian roadside pub: a friendly, comfortable public bar at the front with a plusher lounge at the rear. The restaurants serve good value food, which is also available in the lounge (no meals Sun eve).
🏨 ⊛ ◖◗ 〓 ⊟ ♿ 〓 ♣ P

Turf Tavern ☆
13 Wolverhampton Road
☎ (01922) 407745
12-3, 7-11; 12-2.30, 7-10.30 Sun
Holden's Mild, XB; guest beer H
Known locally as Tinky's this three-roomed pub is in a time warp, unaltered for decades; basic but characterful.
🏨 Q ⊛ 〓 〓

BRIERLEY HILL
Rose & Crown
161 Bank Street (200 yds from Town Hall)
☎ (01384) 77825
12.30 (12 Sat)-3, 7-11; 12-3, 7-10.30 Sun
Holdens Mild, Bitter, H/P Special H
Friendly local near Merry Hill shopping centre and the waterfront complex. It has a games-oriented bar and comfortable lounge decorated with regulars' holiday souvenirs.
⊛ 〓 ♣ P

Vine (Bull & Bladder)
10 Delph Road (off A4100)
☎ (01384) 78293
12-11; 12-10.30 Sun
Batham Mild, Bitter, XXX H
Great Black Country brewery tap at the top of the 'Delph run' and handy for Merry Hill shopping centre. Note the award-winning extension into the former butcher's shop next door. Dudley CAMRA Pub of the Year 1996. Weekday lunches served.
🏨 Q ⏳ ⊛ ◖ 〓 ♣ P

Try also: Bell, Delph Rd;

Black Horse, Delph Rd (Free)

BROWNHILLS
Royal Oak
68 Chester Road (A452)
☎ (01543) 452089
12-3 (3.30 Sat), 6-11; 12-3.30, 6-10.30 Sun
Ansells Mild, Bitter; Greene King IPA, Abbot; Ind Coope Burton Ale; Tetley Bitter; guest beer H
Known locally as the Middle Oak it was Walsall CAMRA Pub of the Year 1998 and '99. This large pub has been refurbished and now reflects the Art Deco theme present when it was built. Regularly changing guest beers are an added attraction.
🏨 ⊛ ◖◗ 〓 ♣ P

COLLEY GATE
Round of Beef
33 Windmill Hill (A458)
☎ (01384) 567646
11 (10.30 Fri)-11; 12-3, 7-10.30 Sun
Banks's Original, Bitter H
Comfortable, modernised and friendly local on the brow of a hill. The vibrant locals' bar is very much Sky sports TV and games oriented, whilst the lounge offers a more relaxed atmosphere. It has special hours throughout the week for cheaper drinking sessions.
Q ⊛ 〓 ♣ P ⊟

Why Not
Why Not Street (1/2 mile from foot of Windmill Hill, A458)
☎ (01384) 561019
12-3, 6-11; 12-11 Sat; 12-3, 7-10.30 Sun
Batham Best Bitter; guest beers H
Tucked away in a side street, the central bar serves a lounge that is popular with drinkers, together with a couple of smaller rooms favoured by diners.
🏨 ⊛ ◖◗ ♣

COSELEY
Painter's Arms
Avenue Road (off A4123 at Roseville)
☎ (01902) 883095
12-11; 12-4, 7-10.30 Sun
Holden's Mild, Bitter, P Special H
Lively pub just outside 'the village', handily placed for the station and Wolverhampton Canal. No food Sun.
⏳ ⊛ ◖ 〓 P ⊟

White House
1 Daisy Street (B4163)
☎ (01902) 402703
11-3, 6-11; 12-3, 7-10.30 Sun
Ansells Mild; Greene King Abbot; Tetley Bitter; guest beers H
Family-run free house,

notable for its good value food (not served Sun). It usually stocks two proper guest ales.
🏨 ⊛ ◖◗ 〓 ♣

COVENTRY
Biggin Hall
214 Binley Road (A427, 2½ miles E of centre)
☎ (024) 7645 1046
10.30-11; 12-10.30 Sun
Banks's Original, Bitter; Marston's Pedigree; guest beer H
Built in the 1920s, this distinctive pub retains some original features, including the oak panelling in the rear lounge. The pub has a pleasant bar and attracts drinkers of all ages. Separate pool room.
Q ⊛ ◖ 〓 ♣ P

Boat
31 Shilton Lane (near Sowe Common)
☎ (024) 7661 3572
12-3, 7-11; 12-11 Sat; 12-10.30 (varies) Sun
Draught Bass; M&B Brew XI H
Unspoilt pub on the outskirts of the city with a traditional bar, quieter lounge and a pool room. Weekday lunches served.
🏨 ⊛ ◖ ♣ P

Caludon
St Austell Road, Wyken (1/2 mile from A4600, Ansty road)
OS371798
☎ (024) 7645 3669
12-3, 6 (6.30 Sat)-11; 12-3, 7-10.30 Sun
Ansells Mild, Bitter; Tetley Bitter; guest beers H
This friendly, popular, two-roomed estate pub fields darts and domino teams and stages social nights. Good value meals include home-cooked specials (no food Sun eve). The garden has a play area.
⊛ ◖◗ 〓 ♣ P

Chestnut Tree
113 Craven Street (vehicle access from Hearsall Lane, B4101)
☎ (024) 7667 5830
12 (11 Sat)-11; 12-10.30 Sun
Courage Directors; John Smith's Bitter; guest beers H
Set in a conservation area, this pub stocks over 160 malt whiskies, plus two guest beers – one is normally from a micro-brewery. The name comes from the large tree in the rear patio. No food Sun eve or Tue.
Q ⊛ ◖◗ 〓 ♣ P

Craven Arms
58 Craven Street, Chapelfields (1 mile from centre, off B4106)

☎ (024) 7671 5308
11-11; 12-4, 7-10.30 Sun
Brains Bitter; Flowers Original; guest beers H
Popular community pub in the old watchmaking area of the city.
🏠 ❀ ◖ ▶

Flying Standard
2-10 Trinity Street (off Broadgate)
☎ (024) 7655 5726
11-11; 11-11 Sun
Banks's Bitter; Boddingtons Bitter; Courage Directors; guest beers H
Multi-levelled city-centre Wetherspoon's pub set over two floors, both with no-smoking areas. The upstairs garden terrace is an unusual feature. The pub's name reflects the local car industry.
Q ❀ ◖ ▶ ♿ ✕ ▦

Gatehouse Tavern
46 Hill Street (by inner ring road, near Belgrade Theatre)
☎ (024) 7663 0140
11-3, 5-11; 11-11 Thu-Sat; 12-4, 7-11 Sun
Draught Bass; Fuller's London Pride; guest beers
Small, popular pub, built by the landlord in an old mill gatehouse. It boasts the largest garden in the city centre. Guest beers are usually from Church End Brewery. No meals Sat eve or Sun. ❀ ◖ ▶

Herald
Sir Henry Parkes Road, Canley (off A45)
☎ (024) 7667 3266
11-11; 12-10.30 Sun
Beer range varies H
Comfortable local with a circular lounge, plus a bar with large screen TV, a pool table and darts. It offers two changing guest beers and excellent value bar meals (no food Sun eve).
❀ ◖ ▶ ⊟ ⇌ (Canley) ♣ P

Jolly Collier
568 Woodway Lane
☎ (024) 7661 2904
12-4.30, 7-11; 12-4, 7-10.30 Sun
Draught Bass; Courage Directors; John Smith's Bitter; guest beer H
Friendly local tucked away at the end of a lane close to the motorway and canal: a cosy lounge with an adjoining central bar. The spacious garden has a play area.
❀ ♣ P

Malt Shovel
93 Spon End, Chapelfields (B4101, 1/4 mile from inner ring road, jct 7)
☎ (024) 7622 0204
12-11; 12-10.30 Sun
Donnington SBA; Tetley Bitter; guest beers H
Comfortable pub, where

three wood-panelled bar areas are served from a central bar. Note the landlord's arts works which adorn the walls, particularly the large painting of medieval Coventry. Live music Fri and Sat nights is performed in the 'tent'. Guest beers usually come from Church End Brewery.
🏠 ❀ ◖ P

Nursery Tavern
38-39 Lord Street, Chapelfields (1 mile W of centre, off Allesley old road)
☎ (024) 7667 4530
11-11; 12-10.30 Sun
Banks's Original; Courage Best Bitter; Everards Tiger; John Smith's Bitter; guest beer H
Friendly, three-roomed community pub with an ever-changing range of guest beers. Noted for its thriving rugby and Formula One fan clubs and its support of traditional pub games. Beer festivals held annually in June and December.
Q ≿ ❀ ◖ ♣ ⌂

Old Windmill
22 Spon Street
☎ (024) 7625 2183
11-11; 12-3, 7-10.30 Sun
Banks's Bitter; Courage Directors; Marston's Pedigree; Morland Old Speckled Hen; guest beers H
Multi-roomed, 16th century pub in the city centre conservation area, handy for the newly opened Sky Dome complex. Look out for the old brewhouse towards the rear. It hosts occasional beer festivals.
🏠 ◖ ⇌ ♣

Royal Oak
22 Earlsdon Street, Earlsdon
☎ (024) 7667 4140
5-11; 12-3, 7-10.30 Sun
Ansells Mild; Draught Bass; Tetley Bitter; guest beers H
Busy pub employing table service at peak periods. Note the slate bar top and clock and the award-winning patio.
🏠 Q ❀

DARLASTON

Fallings Heath Tavern
248 Walsall Road (A4038)
☎ (0121) 526 3403
12-3, 7.15-11; 12-2.30, 7.30-10.30 Sun
Ansells Mild, Bitter; guest beer H
Friendly, three-roomed local, notable for the pig memorabilia in the bar.
Q ≿ ❀ ⊟ ♣ P ⊟

DORRIDGE

Forest Hotel
Station Approach
☎ (01564) 772120

11-2.30, 5.30-11; 12-2.30, 7-10.30 Sun
Draught Bass; guest beer H
19th-century hotel: three bars and a restaurant attract a varied clientele, and gets busy at weekends. No food Sun eve.
❀ 🛏 ◖ ▶ ⊟ ⇌ P

Railway
Grange Road
☎ (01564) 773531
11-3, 4.30-11; (11-11 summer); 11-3, 4.30-10.30 Sun
Draught Bass; M&B Brew XI; guest beers H
Popular pub that has been run by the same family for almost a century. Food is good value, with game a speciality in season. Solihull CAMRA *Pub of the Year* 1999.
🏠 Q ❀ ◖ ▶ 🛏 ⇌ ♣ P

DUDLEY

Full Moon
58-60 High Street
☎ (01384) 212294
10-11; 12-10.30 Sun
Banks's Original; Boddingtons Bitter; Courage Directors; Enville Ale; Theakston Best Bitter; guest beers H
Huge Wetherspoon's shop conversion in the town centre, recently refurbished.
Q ◖ ▶ ♿ ⌂ ✕ ▦

Lamp Tavern
116 High Street (A459)
☎ (01384) 254129
12-11; 12-10.30 Sun
Batham Mild, Bitter, XXX H
Lively local with a sympathetically refurbished bar and a comfortable lounge. The former Queens Cross Brewery at the rear now houses a room for functions and live music.
🏠 ❀ 🛏 ◖ ▶ ♿ ♣ P ✕

HALESOWEN

Hawne Tavern
76 Attwood Street, Hawne (200 yds from A458)
☎ (0121) 602 2601
12-2.30, 5-11; 12-11 Sat; 12-10.30 Sun
Banks's Original, Bitter; ℗ guest beers H
Traditional local, hidden in a side street. The central bar serves a cosy lounge, together with a larger games oriented bar area. Pool is played in the bar.
❀ ◖ ▶ ♣ P

Porters Ale House
Birmingham Street
☎ (0121) 550 1548
11-11; 12-3, 7-10.30 Sun
Beer range varies H
Comfortable town-centre hostelry opposite the local leisure centre, it is popular

with office workers, shoppers and students alike. A good value home-cooked menu is served Mon-Sat. Normally three real ales are available including the house bitter – a Greenalls brew.
❀ ◖ P

Waggon & Horses
21 Stourbridge Road (A458)
☎ (0121) 550 4989
12-11; 12-10.30 Sun
Batham Best Bitter; Enville Ale; guest beers Ⓗ
Long established *Guide* regular, where fourteen ever-changing real ales are complemented by a wide range of fruit wines. It attracts customers from far and wide.
♣ ⌣

KINGSWINFORD

Park
182 Cot Lane (500 yds from A4101)
☎ (01384) 287178
12-11; 12-3, 7-10.30 Sun
Ansells Bitter; Batham Best Bitter; guest beer Ⓗ
Popular, two-roomed pub close to Broadfield House Glass Museum.
❀ ⌷ ♣ P

Union
Water Street (off A4101/A491))
☎ (01384) 830668
12-3 (4.30 Sat), 7-11; 12-3.30, 7-10.30 Sun
Banks's Original, Bitter Ⓟ
This small, friendly local, hidden in a side street, has won the brewery's *Garden of the Year* award for the last two years.
❀ ♣ P 🍺

KNOWLE

Vaults
St John's Close (off High St)
☎ (01564) 773656
12-2.30, 5-11; 12-11 Sat; 12-10.30 Sun
Ansells Mild; Eldridge Pope Hardy Country; Ind Coope Burton Ale; Tetley Bitter; guest beers Ⓗ
Popular pub in a picturesque village, it holds occasional beer festivals and an annual pickled onion competition! No food Sun.
◖ ♣ ⌣

LOWER GORNAL

Fountain Inn
8 Temple Street (A4175, off A459)
☎ (01384) 242777
12-3, 6-11; 12-11 Sat; 12-4, 7-10.30 Sun
Enville Ale; Everards Tiger, Original; Holden's Special; guest beers Ⓗ
Genuine Black Country free

house serving nine real ales, bottled Belgian ales and a large selection of fruit wines as well as up to three proper ciders. It hosts beer festivals twice yearly.
❀ ◖ ♣ ⌣

LYE

Fox
8 Green Lane (off A4036)
☎ (01384) 898614
11-11; 12-10.30 Sun
Banks's Original, Bitter; Ⓟ
Marston's Pedigree Ⓗ
Traditional Black Country side-street pub whose public bar is popular with sports fans (the pub fields a football team). There is also a small comfortable lounge.
❀ ⌷ ≒ ≉ P 🍺

MERIDEN

Queens Head
Old Road OS250820
☎ (01676) 522256
12-11; 12-3, 7-10.30 Sun
Draught Bass; M&B Brew XI; guest beer Ⓗ
Comfortable, single-bar pub, just off the Coventry road on outskirts of town. No food Sun.
❀ ◖ Å P

OLDBURY

Fountain
Albion Street (off A457)
☎ (0121) 544 6892
12-11; 12-5, 6.30-11 Sat; 12-4, 7-10.30 sun
Banks's Mild, Bitter Ⓟ
Cosy local in a quiet side street, just off the No. 87 bus route. Pool played here.
🛏 ♣ P 🍺

RUSHALL

Farmers Boy
Barns Lane
☎ (01922) 629660
11 (4 Wed & Thu)-11; 12-10.30 Sun
Ansells Mild, Bitter Ⓗ
Friendly community pub, offering traditional pub games, a cosy lounge and a large bar with an adjoining children's area. Meals represent excellent value.
❀ ◖ ◗ ⌷ ♣ P

SEDGLEY

Beacon Hotel ☆
129 Bilston Street (A463)
☎ (01902) 883380
12-2.30 (3 Sat), 5.30 (6 Sat)-10.45 (11 Fri & Sat); 12-3, 7-10.30 Sun
Hughes Pale Amber, Sedgley Surprise, Dark Ruby; guest beer Ⓗ
Faithfully restored Victorian brewery tap whose four rooms surround a tiny snob-screened island bar. No bandits or piped muzak spoil

the atmosphere.
Q 🛏 ❀ ♣ P

Try also: Clifton, High St (Wetherspoon's)

SHELFIELD

Four Crosses
1 Green Lane (off A461)
☎ (01922) 682518
12 (11.30 Sat)-11; 12-3, 7-10.30 Sun
Banks's Original, Bitter; Ⓟ
Marston's Pedigree; guest beers Ⓗ
Imposing pub on a crossroads: a traditional, bright saloon bar displays photographs of the pub's origins as a blacksmiths; part of the pub is at least 300 years old. It has a comfortable lounge and a 'passageway' for children. The garden is popular in summer. ❀ ⌷ ♣ P

SHIRLEY

Bernie's Real Ale Off-Licence
Cranmore Boulevard (off A34)
☎ (0121) 744 2827
12-2 (not Mon), 6-10; 12-2, 7-9.30 Sun
Beer range varies Ⓗ/Ⓟ
Excellent off-licence run by CAMRA members, offering normally six ales from micros and independent breweries. Well worth finding; try before you buy with sampling glasses.

SHORT HEATH

Duke of Cambridge
82 Coltham Road
☎ (01922) 408895
12-3.30, 7.30-11; 12-3.30, 7.30-10.30 Sun
Highgate Dark, Ⓟ **Morland Old Speckled Hen;** Ⓗ **Worthington Bitter;** Ⓟ **guest beers** Ⓗ
Cosy and friendly, this former 17th-century farmhouse became a pub in the 1820s. A particular feature is the collection of toy vehicles displayed in both bars. A warm welcome awaits you. 🛏 Q 🛏 ⌷ ⅙ ♣ P

SOLIHULL

Golden Lion
Warwick Road
☎ (0121) 704 1567
11-11; 12-3, 7-10.30 Sun
John Smith's Bitter; Wells Bombardier; guest beers Ⓗ
Improved spacious three-roomed pub, serving good value food and changing guest beer, close to the town centre. Live jazz is performed Sun lunch. Eve meals finish at 7pm. The prices are good for this area.
❀ ◖ ⌷ ♣ P

Harvester

Tanhouse Farm Road (800 yds from A45/B425 jct)
☎ (0121) 742 0770
12-2.30 (3 Fri & Sat), 6-11; 12-3.30, 7-10.30 Sun
John Smith's Bitter; guest beers Ⓗ
Corner estate pub, featuring a large bar and a comfortable lounge. It hosts regular quiz nights, live entertainment (Wed) and occasional charity events, with a good community spirit. Children are welcome until 9pm and can use the play equipment in the large garden. The guest beer changes regularly. No eve meals Sun.
🏵 ◖ ⬚ ♣ P

STOURBRIDGE
Hogshead
21-26 Foster Street (off ring road, near bus and train stations)
☎ (01384) 370140
12-11; 12-10.30 Sun
Boddingtons Bitter; Enville White; Marston's Pedigree; guest beers Ⓗ
Large, single room: a long bar where various seating areas on two levels and wooden floors add character. There is a TV and low background music. It hosts a regular quiz (Tue). Price reductions for CAMRA members. The cider range varies. A well-priced menu includes adventurous specials.
🏵 ◖ ▸ ♿ ➤ (Town) ⟲ ✄

New Inn
2 Cherry Street (off B4186, via Glebe Lane)
☎ (01384) 393323
2 (12 Sat)-11; 12-10.30 Sun
Ansells Mild; Enville Ale; Greene King IPA, Abbot; Marston's Pedigree Ⓗ
Popular, two-roomed local in a residential area; its latest feature is the international buffet bar offering a larger selection of dishes. Lunch available Sat; no food Sun.
🏵 ▸ ⬚ ♣ P

Plough & Harrow
107 Worcester Street
☎ (01384) 397218
12-2.30 (not Mon-Fri), 6 (7 Mon-Thu)-11; 12-3, 7-10.30 Sun
Ansells Bitter; Enville White; Ind Coope Burton Ale; Marston's Pedigree; guest beer Ⓗ
Welcoming pub near a large park. It has many alcoves and plenty of coat-hanging space.
🏠 🏵 ♣

Red Lion
Lion Street (off ring road)
☎ (01384) 397563
12-3, 7-11; 11-11 Sat; 12-3, 7-10.30 Sun
Draught Bass; Enville White; guest beers Ⓗ
Popular, two-roomed pub

with an additional room used as a Tapas bar. It holds regular quiz nights for charity. No meals Sun eve or Mon.
🏠 🏵 ◖ ◖ ▸ ⬚ ♣

Seven Stars
21 Brook Road, Oldswinford (B4186, opp. station)
☎ (01384) 394483
11-11; 12-10.30 Sun
Batham Best Bitter; Theakston Best Bitter, XB; guest beers Ⓗ
Bustling, friendly pub that can get very busy; two large rooms plus a restaurant, with the same excellent menu served throughout. It boasts a fine carved wood back-bar fitting and an outdoor heated courtyard.
🏵 ◖ ▸ ➤ (Junction) P

Shrubbery Cottage
28 Heath Lane, Oldswinford (B4186, 1/4 mile W of A491 jct)
☎ (01384) 377598
12-11; 12-3, 7-10.30 (12-10.30 summer) Sun
Holden's Mild, Bitter, Special, XB or guest beer Ⓗ
Black Country brewery-owned pub dedicated to good ale and conversation; no games or loud music disturb the small L-shaped lounge or rear extension.
🏵 ◖ ➤ (Junction) ⟲ P

TIPTON
Crown & Cushion
2 Gospel Oak Road (A4037/A461 jct)
☎ (0121) 556 0635
12-11; 12-10.30 Sun
Ansells Mild; Tetley Bitter; guest beers Ⓗ
Imposing, three-roomed hostelry, overlooking the Ocker Hill traffic island. The bar has an unusual rotating pool table. A function room is available but beware – it is reputedly haunted! 🏠 ⬚ ⊖ (Wednesbury/Gt Western St) ♣ P

Port 'n' Ale
178 Horseley Heath (A461, 300 yds from Gt Bridge bus station)
☎ (0121) 557 7249
12.30-3, 5-11, 12-11 Sat; 12-4.30, 7-10.30 Sun
Greene King IPA, Triumph, Abbot; Moorhouses Pendle Witches Brew; RCH Pitchfork; guest beers Ⓗ
Three-roomed free house on the main West Bromwich-Dudley road. At least one real cider is available, along with a good range of malt whiskies. Regular live R&B is staged. Eve meals served 5-8.
🏵 ◖ ▸ ⬚ 🅐 ➤ (Dudley Port) ♣ ⟲ P

Rising Sun

116 Horseley Road (off A461, 1/4 mile from Gt Bridge bus station)
☎ (0121) 520 7033
12-2.30 (3 Sat), 5-11; 12-3, 7-10.30 Sun
Banks's Original, Bitter; RCH Pitchfork; guest beers Ⓗ
Local CAMRA *Pub of the Year* three years running, this superb free house clinched the national award for 1999. It offers four guests including a mild, plus real cider and a good range of malt whiskies. It hosts a quiz ever other Tue eve; charity events include a beer festival (Aug Bank Hol).
🏠 🏵 ◖ ⬚ ➤ ♣ ⟲ 🅗

UPPER GORNAL
Britannia Inn
109 Kent Street (A459)
☎ (01902) 883253
12-3, 7-11; 12-11 Sat; 12-5, 7-10.30 Sun
Batham Mild, Best Bitter, XXX Ⓗ
Built in 1780, with a late 19th-century tap room, where beer is served from handpumps set against the wall. Conversation predominates in a serene atmosphere. The colourful garden is worth visiting in summer.
🏠 Q 🏵 ⬚ ♣ ✄

WALSALL
Lane Arms
169 Wolverhampton Road West, Bentley (400 yds W of M6 jct 10)
☎ (01922) 623490
12-3, 5-11; 12-11 Fri & Sat; 12-10.30 Sun
Highgate Dark, Bitter, Saddlers, Old Ale; guest beer (occasional) Ⓗ
Large, multi-roomed 1930s-style roadhouse serving good value food (not on Sun). It hosts occasional beer festivals in the garden. The pub has its own football team, fishing club and pigeon fanciers' club. 🏠 Q 🏵 ◖ ⬚ ♣ P

New Birchills Tavern
15 Birchills Street
☎ (01922) 722599
11.30-3, 5.30 (6 Sat)-11; 12-3, 5.30-10.30 Sun
Banks's Original, Bitter; Ⓟ
Marston's Pedigree; guest beer Ⓗ
Small, modernised, one-roomed Victorian pub with a conservatory restaurant. Although a successful food pub it still manages to function as a great back-street local. Cosy and comfortable, but strictly no T-shirts or trainers. ♿ ➤ P 🅗

Rising Sun
90 Ablewell Street (A34, just outside centre)
☎ (01922) 626575

12-11; 12-10.30 Sun
Highgate Dark, Saddlers, seasonal beers H
Constructed over 100 years ago but altered radically inside, this pub hosts discos Thu-Sat (Sat is devoted to rock music).
🏰 🏵 ◖ ⧦ ♣

Rose & Crown
55 Old Birchills, Birchills (off A34, near Canal Museum)
☎ (01922) 720533
12-11; 12-10.30 Sun
Highgate Dark, Bitter Saddlers; guest beer H
The pub dates from 1901 when it was built on the site of an 18th-century coaching inn; a splendid example of traditional bustling public bar plus a quieter snug/family room with a pool table.
🏰 🐂 🕽 ♣

Tap & Spile
John Street (near Magistrates' court)
☎ (01922) 627660
11-3, 5.30-11; 11-11 Fri & Sat; 12-3, 7-10.30 Sun
Wells Eagle; guest beers H
Friendly, Victorian two-bar pub known locally as the 'Pretty Bricks'. It offers good value menus (not served Mon eve or Sun), plus up to seven guest ales.
🏰 🏵 ◖ ▶ 🕽 ⧦

Victoria
23 Lower Rushall Street
☎ (01922) 725848
12-11; 12-3, 7.30-10.30 Sun
Everards Tiger; Greene King IPA, Abbot; Marston's Pedigree; Taylor Dark Mild; guest beers H
This popular two-roomed pub, with cosy front and back rooms, offers excellent bar food. The defunct tower brewery at the rear now serves as living quarters. A visit is strongly recommended; up to six guest beers make it all the more worthwhile.
🏰 🏵 ◖ 🕽 ⧦

Wharf
Town Wharf, Wolverhampton Street
☎ (01922) 613100
11-11 (1am Thu-Sat); 12-10.30 Sun
Highgate Saddlers, seasonal beers H
Next to the new art gallery, this modern open-plan pub is mainly frequented by younger drinkers. If affords good views over the wharf with access in summer months. 🏵 ◖ & ⧦ P

White Horse
Green Lane, Birchills (A34, ½ mile from centre)
☎ (01922) 631272

11.30-3, 5-11; 11.30-11 Fri & Sat; 12 (varies)-10.30 Sun
Banks's Original, Bitter P
Comfortable, L-shaped bar with a cracking small snug at rear; worth a visit.
◖ 🕽 ⧦ P 🍴

White Lion
150 Sandwell Street, Caldmore (in shadow of Little London flats)
☎ (01922) 628542
12-3, 6-11; 12-11 Sat; 12-4.30, 7-10.30 Sun
Adnams Bitter; Ansells Mild, Bitter; Greene King IPA; Ind Coope Burton Ale; Marston's Pedigree; guest beer H
Large, popular, Victorian corner house with a sloping floor in the bar. A comfortable lounge and basic games room and good value meals complete the facilities.
🏵 ◖ 🕽 ♣

WEDNESFIELD
Pyle Cock
Rookery Street
☎ (01902) 732125
11-11; 12-4, 7-10.30 Sun
Banks's Original, Bitter, P **seasonal beers** H
Splendid local: a traditional bar with wooden settles and etched windows, plus a cosy smoke room; no food, no frills but a warm welcome is assured.
Q 🖾 🕽 P

Vine
35 Lichfield Road (A4124 over canal bridge from centre)
☎ (01902) 732529
11-3, 7-11; 12-3, 7-10.30 Sun
Flowers IPA; guest beers H
Unspoilt inter-war pub of three rooms, each with a coal fire. A friendly welcome awaits both locals and visitors.
🏰 🏵 ◖ 🕽 ⌂ P

WEST BROMWICH
Old Crown
56 Sandwell Road (near A41/A4031 jct)
☎ (0121) 525 4600
12-4, 5 (6 Sat)-11; 12-4, 7-10.30 Sun
Beer range varies H
Though locally famous for its excellent Indian food, this compact side-street pub also has plenty to offer the drinker, with three rotating guest beers and mulled wine available. No food Sun or Sat lunch.
◖ ▶ ⊖ (Dartmouth St) 🍴

Royal Oak
14 Newton Street (off A4031 one-way system)
☎ (0121) 588 2318
5 (12 Sat)-11; 12-4, 7-10.30 Sun

M&B Mild, Brew XI; guest beers H
Friendly, two-roomed corner pub with constantly changing guest beers; quiz night Thu.
Q 🕽 ♣

Vine
Roebuck Street
☎ (0121) 553 2866
11.30-2.30, 5-11; 11.30-11 Fri & Sat; 12-10.30 Sun
Beer range varies H
Vastly extended corner pub, near the metro line. Home-made Asian food and a spectacular Indian barbecue is now available every evening (all day weekends). Busy when Albion play at home.
🏵 ◖ ▶ ⧦ (Galton Bridge) ⊖ (Kenrick Pk)

Wheatsheaf
379 High Street, Carters' Green
☎ (0121) 553 4221
11-11; 12-3, 7-10.30 Sun
Holden's Mild, P **Bitter;** P/H **Special; guest beer** H
Busy local with a basic bar and a comfortable lounge; the landlord teaches practical cellarmanship skills for the local college. Sunday lunch must be booked. Small car park.
🏵 ◖ 🕽 ⊖ (Dartmouth St) ♣ P 🍴

WHITEHEATH
Whiteheath Tavern
400 Birchfield Lane, Oldbury (near M5 jct 2)
☎ (0121) 552 3603
12-3.30 (not Tue-Fri), 8-11; 12-3.30, 8-10.30 Sun
Ansells Mild, Bitter; H **Banks's Original** P
Friendly, old-fashioned local on the main Oldbury-Blackheath road.
🕽 ⧦ (Rowley Regis) ♣

WILLENHALL
Falcon Inn
78 Gomer Street West (400 yds from centre, behind high rise block)
☎ (01902) 633378
12-11; 12-10.30 Sun
Fuller's ESB; Greene King Abbot; Hydes Anvil Mild, Bitter; RCH Pitchfork; guest beers H
Two-roomed 1930s pub, with 10 handpumps in the bar, offering a wide range of good value beers and malt whiskies. Current beers are listed on a blackboard in the lounge.
Q 🏵 🕽 ♣ ✕ 🍴

Ring o'Bells
John Street (opp. police station)
☎ (01902) 606164
11-11; 12-3, 7-10.30 Sun

Banks's Original, Bitter ℗
Comfortable, single-roomed pub with a quarry-tiled floor.
⚘ ♣

WOLLASTON

Princess
115 Bridgnorth Road (A458)
☎ (01384) 443687
11-11; 12-3.30, 7-10.30 Sun
Banks's Original; Wadworth 6X; Wells Bombardier; guest beers Ⓗ
Former M&B house, now owned by Enterprise Inns, following the acquisition of Gibbs Mew. Refurbished in a traditional manner, it appeals to all ages. Good quality meals are reasonably priced.
⚘ ◖▶ & P

Unicorn
145 Bridgnorth Road (A458)
☎ (01384) 394823
12 (11 Fri & Sat)-11; 12-4, 7-10.30 Sun
Batham Mild, Best Bitter, seasonal beers Ⓗ
Former brewhouse (still standing at the side of the pub), this basic drinking house is popular with all ages and genuinely unspoilt by progress.
Q ⚘ ⊟ P

WOLVERHAMPTON

Chindit
113 Merridale Road (towards Bantock Park from Chapel Ash)
☎ (01902) 425582
12-3, 5-11; 11-11 Sat; 12-3, 7-10.30 Sun
Greene King IPA; guest beers Ⓗ
Popular local with a public bar and lounge hosting occasional acoustic eves. Chindits were soldiers of the First Staffs Regiment who fought in Burma.
⊟ ♣

Clarendon Hotel
Chapel Ash (next to Banks's Brewery)
☎ (01902) 420587
11-11; 12-10.30 Sun
Banks's Bitter, ℗ **seasonal beers** Ⓗ
Popular brewery tap with a large split-level lounge; the smaller smoke room has its own bar and is quieter. It gets busy for all Wolves home games. Breakfast is served from 8am; eve meals are served weekdays (until 8pm).
⟿ ◖▶ P ⊟

Hogshead
186 Stafford Street
☎ (01902) 717955
11-11; 12-10.30 Sun
Boddingtons Bitter; Wadworth 6X; ♣ **guest beers** Ⓗ/Ⓖ
Popular town-centre pub with raised seating areas and two no-smoking areas; note the leaded skylight above the

bar. Up to 10 ales are usually on tap.
◖▶ ⇌ ⊖ (St Georges) ⚐

Homestead
Lodge Road, Oxley (off A449 at Goodyear island)
☎ (01902) 787357
12-2.30, 6-11; 12-3, 7-11 Sat; 12-3, 7-10.30 Sun
John Smith's Bitter; Tetley Bitter; guest beers Ⓗ
Large, two-roomed suburban pub where families are welcome (large outdoor children's play area available). It serves good home-cooked food and is one of the few Wolverhampton pubs to offer accommodation.
⚘ ⟿ ◖▶ ⊟ ♣ P

Kearney's
90 Chapel Ash (A41, near A454)
☎ (01902) 421880
11-3, 5.30-11; 12-3, 7-10.30 Sun
Banks's Hanson's Mild, Bitter, seasonal beer or guest beer Ⓗ
Set in an attractive terrace, this pub (formerly the Combermere Arms) boasts three rooms, a covered patio and a garden. Try the award-winning sandwiches. A regulars' pub which welcomes newcomers.
⚘ ⊟

Mitre
Lower Green, Tettenhall Road
☎ (01902) 567890
12-2.30 (not Mon), 5.30-11; 12-11 Fri & Sat; 12-10.30 Sun
Banks's Bitter; Draught Bass; Greene King IPA Ⓗ
Spacious, two-roomed local on the green at the bottom of the rock.
⚘ ◖▶

Moon Under Water
Lichfield Street (opp. Grand Theatre)
☎ (01902) 422447
11-11; 12-10.30 Sun
Banks's Original; Courage Directors; Theakston Best Bitter; guest beers Ⓗ
This large bar has some small panelled areas for a more intimate pint. It attracts all ages and gets very busy at weekends.
Q ⟿ ◖▶ ⚐ ⊞

Newhampton
Riches Street, Whitmore Reans (off A41)
☎ (01902) 745773
11-11; 12-10.30 Sun
Courage Best Bitter, Directors; Marston's Pedigree; Wells Bombardier Ⓗ
Busy, corner local attracting a mixed clientele to three distinctly different rooms. The large garden has a

children's play area and a bowling green. The function room is used as a music venue. The newly-refurbished bowls pavilion is also used for functions. The meals are all home-cooked, only hotpot is on the menu Sun eve.
🍴 ⚘ ◖▶ ♣ ⌂ ⊟ ⊞

Quarterhouse
Compton Road, Chapel Ash (A454)
12-2.30, 5-11; 12-11 Sat; 12-10.30 Sun
Banks's Original, Bitter, ℗ **seasonal beers** Ⓗ
A friendly atmosphere prevails in this one-roomed local that hosts live music Thu eves.
⚘ P ⊟

Roebuck
384 Penn Road, Penn (A449, 3 miles from centre)
☎ (01902) 331307
11-11; 12-3, 7.30-10.30 Sun
Banks's Original, Bitter, ℗ **seasonal beers; Marston's Pedigree** Ⓗ
Elongated pub of three distinct areas including small alcoves which, with the stained glass and tiles, help to create a traditional feel. A rear hatch serves the garden and children's play area. Good value food.
⚘ ◖▶ P ⊟

Royal Oak
70 Compton Road (A454)
☎ (01902) 422845
11-11; 12-10.30 Sun
Banks's Original, Bitter Ⓗ
Pleasant, extended 19th-century local with a warm welcome for all. Popular with students, it can be noisy on music eves. ⚘ ◖▶ P ⊟

Shoulder of Mutton
Wood Road, Tettenhall Wood
☎ (01902) 756672
11.30-3, 5.30-11; 11.30-11 Sat; 12-10.30 Sun
Banks's Original, Bitter; ℗ **seasonal beers; Marston's Pedigree** Ⓗ
Large, modern pub with a beamed interior: one long bar in the lounge, plus three smaller partitioned seating areas. Good, home-cooked food is available Mon-Sat.
⚘ ◖▶ ♣ P ⊟

Stamford Arms
Lime Street, Pennfields
☎ (01902) 424178
11-11; 12-10.30 Sun
Banks's Original, Bitter ℗
Corner local where three rooms are served by a single bar with a hatch. Note the tiled entrance.
⊟ ♣ ⊟

Swan

CAMRA National Pub Inventory: artefact in Mandeville Arms (McConville's), Portadown, Co Armagh

Bridgnorth Road, Compton
☎ (01902) 754736
11-11; 12-10.30 Sun
Banks's Original, Bitter Ⓟ
Victorian pub with a small public bar, a snug and a larger lounge. 🏚️🏡♣P🚭

Tap & Spile
35 Princess Street
☎ (01902) 713319
11-11; 12-10.30 Sun
Banks's Original; Tap & Spile Premium; guest beers Ⓗ
Small, town-centre pub comprising an open bar area and a small snug. Busy at

lunchtimes and weekends, it usually has six cask ales on tap.
🏚️🐾◖🕭⭥⊖👌

Wheatsheaf Hotel
Market Street (next to police station)
11 (10.30 Sat)-11; 12-3, 7-10.30 Sun
Banks's Original, Bitter Ⓟ
Traditional town-centre pub: three rooms and a conservatory; some of the smoke room seats retain a bell-push at the back (no longer in use).
🏚️🏡⭥⊖🚭

INDEPENDENT BREWERIES

Banks's: Wolverhampton

Batham: Brierley Hill

Beowulf: Yardley

Enville: Stourbridge

Highgate: Walsall

Holden's: Woodsetton

Hughes: Sedgley

Rainbow: Allesley

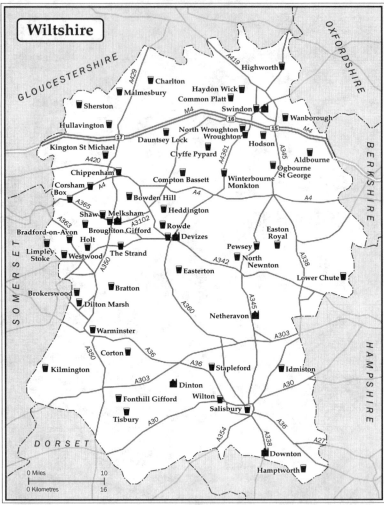

Wiltshire

(Map of Wiltshire showing neighbouring counties OXFORDSHIRE, GLOUCESTERSHIRE, BERKSHIRE, HAMPSHIRE, DORSET, SOMERSET and pub locations)

Highworth

Charlton
Malmesbury
Haydon Wick
Common Platt
Sherston
Swindon
Wanborough
Hullavington
North Wroughton
Wroughton
Hodson
Kington St Michael
Dauntsey Lock
Clyffe Pypard
Aldbourne
Ogbourne
St George
Chippenham
Compton Bassett
Winterbourne
Monkton
Corsham
Box
Bowden Hill
Shaw Melksham
Heddington
Bradford-on-Avon
Broughton Gifford
Rowde
Easton
Royal
Holt
Devizes
Limpley
Stoke
Westwood
The Strand
Pewsey
North
Newnton
Easterton
Lower Chute
Brokerswood
Bratton
Dilton Marsh
Netheravon
Warminster
Corton
Stapleford
Idmiston
Kilmington
Dinton
Fonthill Gifford
Wilton
Salisbury
Tisbury
Downton
Hamptworth

0 Miles 10
0 Kilometres 16

ALDBOURNE

Blue Boar
The Green (off B4192)
☎ (01672) 540237
11.30-3, 6-11 (11-11.30 summer);
12-10.30 Sun
Wadworth IPA, 6X, seasonal beers H
Ancient, beamed bar in a cosy pub overlooking the village green. It featured in a 1970s *Dr Who* episode.
※ ◑ ♣ ♠

BOWDEN HILL

Rising Sun
32 Bowden Hill (1 mile E of Lacock)
☎ (01249) 730363
11.30-3 (not winter Mon), 6-11;
12-10.30 Sun
Mole's Tap Bitter; Best Bitter; Brew 97; guest beer (occasional) H
Attractive, 17th-century single bar inn affording spectacular views over the

Avon Vale from the large garden. Mole's Brewery tap, it hosts live music Wed eve. No food Sun eve or Mon.
曲 Q ※ ◑ ♣ ♠ P

Try also: Bell (Free)

BOX

Quarrymans Arms
Box Hill (off A4)
☎ (01225) 743569
11-3, 6-11; 11-11 Fri-Sat; 12-10.30 Sun
Butcombe Bitter; Mole's Best Bitter; Wadworth 6X; guest beer (occasional) H
Excellent village pub built over the old stone mines near Bath. Enjoy the superb views over the valley. Well hidden in the lanes; ring for directions. ※ 曲 ◑ ♣ ♠ P

BRADFORD ON AVON

Beehive

263 Trowbridge Road (by canal bridge)
☎ (01225) 863620
12-2.30, 7-11; 12-3, 7-10.30 Sun
Butcombe Bitter; H **guest beers** H/G
Friendly pub by the canal stocking a constantly changing variety of guest beers. The large garden is suitable for families; very popular in summer and with diners. Lunches served Wed-Mon; eve meals Mon-Sat.
曲 Q ※ ◑ ♣ ♠ P

Rising Sun
231 Winsley Road
☎ (01225) 862354
12-11; 12-10.30 Sun
Archers Village, Golden Bitter H
Basic, old fashioned, friendly local on the outskirts of the town. This is a rare Archer's outlet in this part of the country.
曲 ※ ◑ ♣ ♠ ◔ ◻

Three Horseshoes
55 Frome Road (near station)
☎ (01225) 865876
11-11; 12-4, 7-11 Sun
Abbey Bellringer; Butcombe Bitter; Courage Best Bitter; Wadworth 6X; Wells Bombardier Ⓗ
Friendly pub, just a short walk from the town's historic Tythe Barn.
🏠 🏵 ◑ ▶ 🔥 ♣ P

BRATTON
Duke
☎ (01380) 830242
11.30-3, 7-11.30; 11.30-11.30 Sat; 12-3, 7-10.30 Sun
Courage Best Bitter; Mole's Best Bitter; guest beer Ⓗ
Busy village pub on the edge of Salisbury Plain. Excellent Mole's beers, good food and rooms enhance a hearty walking weekend.
🏵 🖼 ◑ ▶ 🔥 ♠ ♣ P

BROKERSWOOD
Kicking Donkey
Follow signs to Woodland Park from A36 or A350 OS833519
☎ (01373) 823250
11.30-2.30 (3 Sat), 6.30-11; 12-10.30 Sun
Oakhill Best Bitter; Stonehenge Danish Dynamite; Wadworth 6X; guest beer Ⓗ
17th-century country inn with exposed beams, brasses, etc, divided into three drinking areas and a restaurant. The popular garden caters well, with seating for 200, children's play equipment and a bouncy castle all summer.
🏠 Q 🏵 ◑ ▶ 🔥 ⟵ P

BROUGHTON GIFFORD
Bell on the Common
2 miles W of Melksham, off B3107
☎ (01225) 782309
11-2.30, 6.30-11; 11-11 Fri & Sat; 12-10.30 Sun
Wadworth IPA, 6X, seasonal beers Ⓗ
Lovely two-bar pub overlooking the common; one smart bar/restaurant, the other has wooden settles and an open fire. Good garden for summer, where boules is played.
🏠 ◑ ▶ 🔥 ♣ P

CHARLTON
Horse & Groom
The Street (B4040, Malmesbury-Cricklade road)
☎ (01666) 823904
12-3, 7-11; 12-11 Sat; 12-10.30 Sun
Archers Village; Wadworth 6X; guest beer Ⓗ
Attractive Cotswold stone country inn, fronted by a

lawn; a roomy public bar, plus a smaller bar that serves the restaurant (good menu).
🏠 Q 🏵 🖼 ◑ ▶ 🔥 P

CHIPPENHAM
Old Road Tavern
Old Road
☎ (01249) 652094
11-4, 5.45-11; 11-11 Fri & Sat; 12-10.30 Sun
Courage Best Bitter; Ruddles County; Wadworth 6X Ⓗ
Basic, unpretentious local, popular with Morris dancers. No food Sun.
🐕 🏵 ◑ ⟵ ♣

CLYFFE PYPARD
Godard Arms
Wood Street OS074769
☎ (01793) 731386
12-2.30, 7-11; 12-11 Sat; 12-10.30 Sun
Wadworth 6X; guest beers Ⓗ
Picturesque village pub on split levels, serving quality food and an interesting range of guest ales. It stages regular live music. Skittles played.
🏠 Q 🏵 🖼 ◑ ▶ 🍴 ♣ P

COMMON PLATT
Foresters Arms
Near Swindon OS110868
☎ (01793) 770615
11.30-3, 5.30-11; 12-3, 7-10.30 Sun
Archers Best Bitter; Courage Best Bitter; Wadworth 6X Ⓗ
Very busy pub comprising a large lounge area and a small bar; food oriented, it can get very crowded, but maintains a friendly atmosphere. This former village local is now on the outskirts of a new housing estate. Small car park. No food Sun eve.
🏠 🏵 ◑ ▶ 🍴 ♣ P

COMPTON BASSETT
White Horse
☎ (01249) 813118
11-3, 5-11; 12-3, 7-11 Sun
Badger Tanglefoot; Wadworth 6X; guest beers Ⓗ
Traditional country inn with two bars and a restaurant, situated close to a golf course and cycle track. It has a skittle alley. 🏠 Q 🏵 🖼 ◑ ▶ 🍴 🔥 ♣ ⟵ P ✍

CORSHAM
Two Pigs
38 Pickwick
☎ (01249) 712515
7-11; 12-2.30, 7-10.30 Sun
Stonehenge Pigswill; guest beers Ⓗ
Large, single-bar pub that hosts live blues music Mon eve (over 21s only). The 'sty', a covered seating area, is in use during the summer; other features include flagstone

floors and wood-panelled walls.
🏠 🏵 🔥

CORTON
Dove Inn
Off A36 OS934406
☎ (01985) 850109
12-3 (3.30 Sat), 6.30-11; 12-4, 7-10.30 Sun
Brakspear Bitter; Oakhill Best Bitter; Fuller's London Pride; guest beers Ⓗ
This hidden-away pub is well worth searching out. Considerably extended, a warm welcome is assured at this country pub which offers a choice of beers and an exciting menu, plus accommodation that is adapted for disabled guests.
🏠 Q 🏵 🖼 ◑ ▶ 🔥 ⟵ P ✍

Try also: **Prince Leopold,** Upton Lovell (Free)

DAUNTSEY LOCK
Peterborough Arms
On B4069, Lyneham-Chippenham road
☎ (01249) 890409
11-2.30 (3 Sat), 6-11; 12-3.30, 7-10.30 Sun
Archers Best Bitter; Wadworth 6X; guest beer Ⓗ
Friendly free house with a cosy lounge and a log fire, serving an excellent range of home-cooked food. Children are welcome in the extensive grass play area and the skittle alley.
🏠 Q 🐕 🏵 ◑ ▶ ♣ P

DEVIZES
British Lion
Estcourt Street
☎ (01380) 720665
11-11; 12-10.30 Sun
Beer range varies Ⓗ/Ⓖ
Basic, down-to-earth pub, stocking the widest range of real ales in town; there is always a special offer on big jugs. The lawned garden has swings for children.
🏵 ♣ ⟵ P

Fox & Hounds
Nursteed
☎ (01380) 723789
11-3, 7-11; 12-3, 7-10.30 Sun
Wadworth IPA, 6X Ⓗ
This thatched pub features regularly on Wadworth calendars. Its long interior includes a restaurant area.
Q 🏵 ◑ ▶ ♣ P

Hare & Hounds
Hare & Hounds Street
☎ (01380) 723231
11-3, 7-11; 12-3, 7-10.30 Sun
Wadworth IPA, 6X, seasonal beers Ⓗ
What you see is what you

get: a friendly, back-street local that's been a *Guide* regular since the 1980s. No food Sun.

🏚 Q 🕸 ◑ ♣ P

DILTON MARSH

Prince of Wales

94 High Street (B3099)
☎ (01373) 865487
11.30 (12 Fri)-2.30 (3 Sat); 12-3, 7-10.30 Sun
Fuller's London Pride; Wadworth 6X; Wells Eagle, Bombardier; guest beer Ⓗ

Family-owned, traditional friendly local; skittles, crib and pool played, plus a quiz every Sun eve.

Q 🕸 ◑ 👤 ➳ ♣ P

EASTERTON

Royal Oak

11 High Street (B3098)
☎ (01380) 812343
11-3, 5.30-11; 12-3, 7-10.30 Sun
Wadworth IPA, 6X; guest beers Ⓗ
Popular, 16th-century thatched village pub, with some modern extensions. The saloon bar doubles as the dining area for excellent home-cooked meals.

🏚 Q 🍃 🕸 ◑ ▶ 🍴 👤 ♣ P

EASTON ROYAL

Bruce Arms

Easton Road (B3087)
☎ (01672) 810216
11-2.30 (3 Sat), 6-11; 12-3, 7-10.30 Sun
Butts; Wadworth 6X; guest beer (summer) Ⓗ
Fine, basic, country pub with plenty of character. It is popular with locals – who are friendly.

🏚 Q 🍃 🕸 ⚔ ♣ P

FONTHILL GIFFORD

Beckford Arms

1½ miles SE of B3089 at Hindon on Tisbury road OS930311
☎ (01747) 870385
11.45-11; 12-10.30 Sun
Greene King Abbot; Hop Back Best Bitter; guest beers Ⓗ
17th-century former Lord Beckford's inn, this large building has a public bar with usual games, a cosy lounge, a dining area and a garden room. Attractively furnished with old pieces, it is spacious yet intimate. Good quality food.

🏚 🍃 🕸 🛏 ◑ ▶ ♣ P

HAMPTWORTH

Cuckoo

☎ (01794) 390302
11.30-2.30, 6-11; 11.30-11 Sat; 12-10.30 Sun
Badger Tanglefoot; Cheriton Pots

Ale; Hop Back GFB, Summer Lightning; Wadworth 6X; guest beer Ⓖ
Traditional thatched country pub on the edge of the New Forest. Four small bars cater for all, including non-smokers. A peaceful garden has an area for children to play and adults to have peace. It stocks up to four guest beers in summer. Wessex CAMRA *Pub of the Year 1999*.

🏚 Q 🍃 🕸 ◑ ▶ ♣ 🍴 P ✕

HAYDON WICK

Manor Farm

Near Swindon
☎ (01793) 705222
11-11; 12-10.30 Sun
Banks's Original, Bitter; Marston's Pedigree Ⓗ
Old farmhouse, sympathetically converted and extended. It offers a wide food menu.

🏚 Q 🕸 ◑ ▶ 👤 P 🍴

HEDDINGTON

Ivy

Stockley Road (2 miles off A4 from Calne)
☎ (01380) 850276
12-3, 6.30-11; 12-11 Sat; 12-10.30 Sun
Wadworth IPA, 6X, seasonal beers Ⓖ
Picturesque, thatched village local, originally three 15th-century cottages. Choose from the varied selection of food on the menu board (eve meals Thu-Sat).

🏚 Q 🕸 ◑ ▶ ♣ P 🍴

HIGHWORTH

Wine Cellar

High Street
☎ (01793) 763828
7 (5.30 Wed & Thu; 1 Fri; 12 Sat); 12-5, 7-10.30 Sun
Archers Village, Best Bitter; guest beers Ⓖ
Long, single cellar bar stocking a good variety of wines and whiskies. It hosts occasional live music. Beer discount for CAMRA members.

♣ 🍴

Try also: **Jesmond House Hotel** (Archers)

HODSON

Calley Arms

Off B4005
☎ (01793) 740350
12-2.30 (not Mon; 11.30-3 Sat), 6.30-11 Tue-Fri; 12-2, 7-10.30 Sun
Wadworth IPA; guest beers Ⓗ
Welcoming pub in a rural setting: a large bar with a raised dining area. It stocks a large range of malt whiskies

and English country wines. No food Sun eve or Mon.

🏚 🕸 ◑ ▶ 🍴 P

HOLT

Tollgate

Ham Green
☎ (01225) 782326
11.30-2.30, 6.30-11 (closed Mon); 12-2.30 (closed eve) Sun
Beer range varies Ⓗ
18th-century inn, in a pretty village where the main thrust is on good quality food and beer (the range changes fortnightly).

🏚 Q 🕸 ◑ ▶ P ✕

HULLAVINGTON

Queens Head

23 The Street (off A429 Malmesbury-Chippenham road)
☎ (01666) 837221
12-3 (not Mon), 7-11; 12-11 Sat; 12-10.30 Sun
Archers Village; Fuller's London Pride; guest beer Ⓗ
Open-plan pub with real fires and a skittle alley. A children's menu is available 6-7.30.

🏚 Q 🕸 🛏 ◑ ▶ 👤 ♣ P

IDMISTON

Earl of Normanton

Tidworth Road (A338, 5 miles S of A303 jct)
11-3, 6-11; 12-3, 7-10.30 Sun
Cheriton Pots Ale, Best Bitter; Hop Back Summer Lightning; guest beers Ⓗ
Roadside local in an idyllic setting; its elevated garden affords superb view of Bourne Valley. Locally renowned for excellent food, it makes a perfect stop on the busy A338.

🏚 Q 🕸 🛏 ◑ ▶ ♣ P

KILMINGTON

Red Lion Inn

On B3092, 2½ miles N of A303 near Mere
☎ (01985) 844263
11.30-3, 6.30-11; 12-3.30, 7-10.30 Sun
Butcombe Bitter; guest beers Ⓗ
Welcoming, unspoilt, single-bar pub, over 400 years old. It nestles in the lee of the South Wilts Downs, near Stourhead Gardens. Serving good value lunches it is popular with walkers.

🏚 Q 🕸 🛏 ◑ ▶ 🍴 P ✕ 🍴

KINGTON ST MICHAEL

Jolly Huntsman

High Street
☎ (01249) 750305
11.30-2.30, 6.30 (5.30 Fri)-11; 12-3, 7-10.30 Sun
Badger Tanglefoot; Draught Bass;

Tetley Bitter; Wadworth 6X; Wickwar BOB Ⓗ
Friendly village local with a good choice of real ales and good food.
🏠 🛏 🕩 ♿ ⚿ P

LIMPLEY STOKE
Hop Pole
Woods Hill
☎ (01225) 723134
11-3, 6-11; 12-3, 7-10.30 Sun
Draught Bass; Butcombe Bitter; Courage Best Bitter; guest beers Ⓗ
Traditional village local: a cosy oak-panelled public bar and a lounge set out with tables for dining. The large garden overlooks the Avon Valley. Boules and skittles played.
Q 🛏 🏵 🕩 ⊞ ♿ ⚿ ⇌ P ⚲

LOWER CHUTE
Hatchet
About 5 miles N of A303 and Weyhill OS312532
☎ (01264) 730229
11.30-3, 6-11; 12-4, 7-10.30 Sun
Greene King IPA, Triumph; guest beers Ⓗ
14th-century thatched village pub, originally a barn and two cottages, this absolute gem is well worth finding, especially for the food which is good value and quality.
🏠 Q 🏵 🛏 🕩 ♣ ⏷ P

MALMESBURY
Three Cups
The Triangle
☎ (01666) 823278
11-2.30, 6-11; 11-11 Sat; 12-10.30 Sun
Brakspear Bitter; guest beers Ⓗ
Friendly local close to the Abbey comprising a busy public bar and a quiet lounge. Guest beers are constantly changing; Thatcher's cider is available most of the time. Limited parking, but only five minutes walk from the town centre.
🏠 Q 🏵 🕩 ⊞ ♣ ⏷ P

Whole Hog
8 Market Cross
☎ (01666) 825845
11-11; 12-10.30 Sun
Archers Best Bitter; Wadworth 6X; two guest beers Ⓗ
Converted old cottage hospital with a bar and restaurant (no meals Sun eve).
🕩 ♣ ⏷ ⚲

Try also: **Red Bull**, Sherston Rd (Free); **Rose & Crown**, High St (Ushers)

MELKSHAM
Red Lion

3 The City
☎ (01225) 702960
11-2.30, 5 (6 Sat)-11; 11-11 Fri; 12-3, 7-10.30 Sun
Draught Bass; Bath Gem; Church End Gravediggers; guest beer Ⓗ
Popular, friendly local, claimed to be the oldest pub in Wiltshire, dating back to the 13th century. A rare local outlet for mild ales, it offers a frequently changing guest beer. Lunches served Mon-Fri.
Q 🏵 🕩 ♿ ⇌ ♣ P

NORTH NEWTON
Woodbridge Inn
On A345 Pewsey-Upavon road
☎ (01980) 630266
12-11; 12-10.30 Sun
Wadworth IPA, 6X, Farmers Glory; guest beer Ⓗ
Pleasant, welcoming inn on the busy A345, parts of which date from the 17th century. Good food is served in a no-smoking restaurant. French boules piste available in the large garden.
🏠 🏵 🛏 🕩 ⚿ ⏷ P

NORTH WROUGHTON
Check Inn
Woodland View (old Devizes road next to M4)
☎ (01793) 845584
11.30-3.30, 6.30-11; 11.30-11 Sat; 12-10.30 Sun
Beer range varies Ⓗ
Genuine free house serving six real ales; this ex-roadside local has been cut off by the M4. A single-bar pub it boasts a big garden and stocks a good range of Czech, Belgian, German and British bottled beers, plus Leffe Blond on draught.
🏠 🏵 🕩 ♣ ⏷ P

OGBOURNE ST GEORGE
Old Crown
Marlborough Road (signed off A346)
☎ (01672) 841445
11.30-2.30, 6-11; 12-3, 7-10.30 Sun
Wadworth 6X; guest beer Ⓗ
Cosy, food-oriented, carpeted bar, by the site of a former rail station. Note the 90ft well in the restaurant.
🏵 🛏 🕩 ⚿ ♣ ⏷ P ⚲

PEWSEY
Coopers Arms
37-39 Ball Road (off B3087) OS170595
☎ (01672) 562495
12-2, 6-11 (closed winter eves); 12-4, 7-10.30 Sun
Oakhill Mendip Gold; Wadworth 6X; guest beers Ⓗ
Character aplenty in this thatched out-of-the-way gem,

where live music, comedy and quiz nights add to the overall ambience.
🏠 🛏 🏵 ⚿ ⇌ P

ROWDE
George & Dragon
High Street
☎ (01380) 723053
12-3, 7-11; 12-3, 7-10.30 Sun
Beer range varies Ⓗ
Welcoming, historic pub well-known for its excellent food (booking advisable); no food Mon. Three guest beers available.
🏠 Q 🏵 🕩 ♿ ⚿ ♣ P

SALISBURY
Barley Mow
71 Greencroft Street (200 yds from Salisbury Arts Centre)
☎ (01722) 505225
4 (12 Sat)-11; 12-10.30 Sun
Hop Back GFB, Summer Lightning; guest beer Ⓗ
Originally two cottages that became a pub in 1742 – one large L-shaped bar is run jointly by three Mancunians who create a good atmosphere. Nearby is a public green with swings.
🏠 ♣

Bird in Hand
North Street
☎ (01722) 327238
10-11; 12-10.30 Sun
Draught Bass; Hardy Pope's Traditional; Ind Coope Burton Ale Ⓗ
Edwardian street-corner local, fielding teams in local pool and darts leagues.
🛏 ⇌ ♣ ⏷

Deacons Alms
118 Fisherton Street
☎ (01722) 504723
5 (4 Fri, 12 Sat)-11; 12-10.30 Sun
Hop Back GFB; guest beers Ⓗ
Popular town pub, five minutes' walk from the city centre. Two bars, only one with real ale, allow the choice between TV and table football or conversation. Guest beers are generally from micros and constantly changing. 🏠 🛏 ⇌ 🍺

Devizes Inn
53 Devizes Road (A360)
☎ (01722) 327842
4.30 (2 Fri; 12 Sat)-11; 12-10.30 Sun
Hop Back GFB, Summer Lightning; guest beer Ⓗ
Comfortable, two-bar, friendly local which until the early 1950s was a fish and chip shop plus off-licence. Now a tourist board recommended free house, it offers 10% discount to CAMRA members.
🏵 🛏 ⊞ ⇌ ♣ P

Queens Arms
9 Ivy Street (next to Brown St

car park)
☎ (01722) 341053
11-3, 5-11; 11-11 Sat & summer; 12-10.30 Sun

Ushers Best Bitter; guest beer Ⓗ
This reputedly haunted 14th-century pub claims the city's longest continuous licence. Named after Queen Elizabeth I, see the entrance canopy that has a preservation order on it. This city-centre local hosts monthly live bands (Fri).
🏚 ⊯ ◖ ⇌ ♣ P

Royal George
17 Bedwin Street
☎ (01722) 327782
11-11; 12-10.30 Sun

Adnams Bitter; Gales HSB; Wadworth 6X Ⓗ
Grade II listed pub boasting low beams, one of which came from a ship of the same name. This friendly city pub has the feel of a country inn.
🏚 ⊯ ◖ ♣ P

Tom Brown's
225 Wilton Road
☎ (01722) 335918
12-3 (not Mon-Fri), 6-11 Sat; 12-3, 7-10.30 sun

Goldfinch Tom Browns Midnight Sun, Flashman's Clout, Midnight Blinder Ⓗ
Community pub, popular with locals, that fields darts and pool league teams. Other games available on request or just enjoy the conversation.
♣

Village
33 Wilton Road (A36 near St Pauls roundabout)
☎ (01722) 329707
12 (4 Mon)-11; 12-5, 7-10.30 Sun

Abbey Bellringer; Taylor Landlord Ⓗ **guest beers** Ⓖ/Ⓗ
Friendly corner local where a collection of railwayana features loco horns on which 'time' is called. It specialises in beers unusual for the area; many guests are customer requests.
⇌ ♣

Wyndham Arms
27 Escourt Road (near swimming pool)
☎ (01722) 331026
4.30 (3 Fri; 12 Sat)-11; 12-10.30 Sun

Hop Back GFB, Best Bitter, Thunderstorm, Summer Lightning, seasonal beers; guest beers Ⓗ
Built as an hotel in 1860 and owned by Folliotts Brewery, in 1986 it became the first home of Hop Back Brewery – now an enviable pub appealing to people from all walks of life.
Q ⛺ ♣ ⊁

SHAW
Golden Fleece

Folly Lane
☎ (01225) 702050
11.30-2.30 (3 Sat), 6-11; 12-3, 7-10.30 Sun

Butcombe Bitter, Gold; Marston's Pedigree; Wickwar BOB Ⓗ
Old coaching inn, servng good, traditional food. The garden out the back overlooks the village cricket pitch.
⛺ ◖ 🦽 ♿ ♣ P

SHERSTON
Rattlebone Inn
Church Street (B4040)
☎ (01666) 840871
11-11; 12-10.30 Sun

Greene King Abbot; Smiles Best; guest beers Ⓗ
Attractive 16th-century pub, named after a local hero, where a six-sided pool table, skittles and boules provide good entertainment. A good, varied menu completes its appeal. Draught beers include Rattlebone SPA.
🏚 Q ⛺ ◖ 🍴 🦽 ♿ ♣ P

STAPLEFORD
Pelican Inn
Warminster Road (A36)
☎ (01722) 790241
11-2.30 (3 Sat), 6-11; 12-3, 7-10.30 Sun

Greene King Abbot; Otter Bitter; Ringwood Best Bitter; guest beer Ⓗ
This 18th-century pub takes its name from a galleon of that name which went on to become Drake's Golden Hind. Serving excellent value food and ale, it retains a true pub feel. The large safe garden has swings and a slide.
🏚 Q ⛺ ⊯ ◖ 🦽 ♿ ♣ P

SWINDON
Duke of Wellington
27 Eastcote Hill
☎ (01793) 534180
12-2, 6.30-11; 12-11 Sat; 12-3, 7-10.30 Sun

Arkell's 2B, 3B, seasonal beers Ⓖ
The only Arkells' pub to serve beer on gravity, it has a small bar and an even smaller snug. Sun lunch available.
🏚 ⛺ ⇌ ♣

Glue Pot
5 Emlyn Square
☎ (01793) 523935
11-11; 12-3, 7-10.30 Sun

Archers Village, Best Bitter, Golden; guest beer Ⓗ
Small, no-frills, one-bar boozer, built in the mid-19th century as part of Brunel's railway village. High-backed wooden seats create several small booths. Busy at weekends. Weekday lunches served.
Q ⛺ ◖ ⇌ ♣

Plough
26 Devizes Road
☎ (01793) 535603
12-2.30, 6-11; 12-11 Fri; 11-11 Sat; 12-3, 7.30-10.30 Sun

Arkell's 2B, 3B Ⓗ
Friendly traditional local with a small bar and adjoining lounge. ♣

Riflemans Hotel
42 Regent Street
☎ (01793) 529240
11-11; 12-3 (closed eve) Sun

Banks's Original, Bitter Ⓗ
'Hotel' is a misnomer for this large single-bar pub with a restaurant extension. Its town-centre location provides varied clientele depending on the time of day. Meals served 11.30-7.
⛺ ◖ 🦽 ⇌ P ⊁ 🍴

Savoy
38-40 Regent Street
☎ (01793) 533970
10.30-11; 12-10.30 Sun

Archers Best Bitter; Boddingtons Bitter; Courage Directors; Theakston Best Bitter; Wadworth 6X; guest beers Ⓗ
Large converted ex-cinema, providing a single bar and split-level seating. The four guest beers are constantly changing. Q ◖ 🦽 ⇌ 👜 ⊁ 🍴

TISBURY
South Western Hotel
Station Road
☎ (01747) 870160
11.30-3, 6-11; 11.30-11 Fri & Sat; 12-3, 7-10.30 Sun

Tisbury seasonal beers Ⓗ
Victorian railway inn of several drinking areas. It acts as the tap for Tisbury Brewery and usually has three of their beers on. It features railway memorabilia and items of local interest. Good value food (not served Thu).
🏚 Q ⛺ ⊯ ◖ 🦽 ⇌ ♣ P

WANBOROUGH
Plough
High Street
☎ (01793) 790523
12-2.30, 5-11; 12-11 Fri; 12-3, 6-11 Sat; 12-3, 7-10.30 Sun

Archers Village; Draught Bass; Fuller's London Pride; Wadworth 6X; guest beer Ⓗ
Listed, 17th-century thatched pub featuring beams, stone walls, and log fires. Try the Harrow 100 yards away, under the same ownership, but carrying a different beer range. Weekday lunches served; eve meals Mon-Sat.
🏚 Q ⛺ ◖ ♣ P

WARMINSTER
Yew Tree
174 Boreham Road

☎ (01985) 212335
11-11 (12-2.30, 5.30-11 winter); 12-10.30 Sun
Ringwood Best Bitter; guest beers H
Pleasant, 200-year-old pub on the outskirts of Warminster where a friendly welcome is assured. A wide and varied choice of real ales (four guests) is always available. Eve meals on request.
❀ ⇔ ◖ & P

WESTWOOD
New Inn
☎ (01225) 863123
10.30-2.30, 6-11; 12-3, 7-10.30 Sun
Draught Bass; H **Hop Back Best Bitter;** G **Wadworth 6X;** H **guest beers** G
Nice old village lcal with two log fires. The landlord used to live in Salisbury so Hop Back beers are a favourite.
🏠 ⌂ ◖ ▯ P ⌿

WILTON
Bear
12 West Street (50 yds from market square)
☎ (01722) 742398
11.30-2.30, 4.30-11; 11-3, 5.30-11 Sat; 12-3, 5-10.30 Sun
Badger Dorset Best H

This warmly decorated single room bar, dating from the 16th century, offers a cosy fire in winter and a beer garden in summer. There is an alcove with a pool table, juke box and gaming machine.
🏠 ❀ ♣

Bell
Shaftesbury Road (A30, $^1/_2$ mile from traffic lights towards Shaftesbury)
☎ (01722) 743121
11-2.30, 6-11; 11-11 Sat; 12-3, 7-10.30 Sun
Draught Bass; Greene King IPA; Worthington Bitter; guest beer H
Cosy, intimate local supporting activities and charities within the town. It dates from the early 17th century, so low ceilings and interesting nooks and crannies abound.
🏠 Q ☎ ❀ ⇔ ♣ P

WINTERBOURNE MONKTON
New Inn
Follow signs for village off A4361, N of Avebury
☎ (01672) 539240
11-3, 6-11; 12-3, 7-10.30 (all day if busy) Sun

Archers Village, Marley's Ghost; Wadworth 6X; guest beer H
Friendly local with a cosy bar and restaurant area. The garden has a large children's play area. No food Sun eve.
🏠 ❀ ⇔ ◖ ▯ & ▲ ♣ P

WROUGHTON
Carters Rest
High Street (A4361, Swindon-Avebury road)
☎ (01793) 812288
11-11; 12-10.30 Sun
Archers Village, Best Bitter, Golden Bitter, guest beer H
Friendly, two-roomed Edwardian pub, refurbished in down-to-earth style. The no-frills public bar and friendly staff appeal to its local clientele.
🏠 ❀ ◖ ▱ ♣ P

CAMRA National Pub Inventory: The Three Stags Heads, Wardlow Mires, Derbyshire

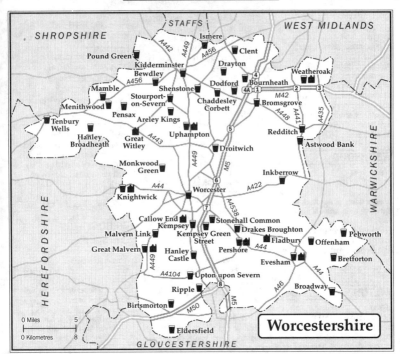

Worcestershire

0 Miles 5
0 Kilometres 8

ARELEY KINGS

King's Arms
19 Redhouse Road (off
B4196) ☎ (01299) 827132
12-3, 6-11, 12-11 Fri & Sat; 12-10.30
Sun
Banks's Original, Ⓗ **Bitter;** Ⓟ **guest
beer** Ⓗ
Friendly, cosy village local
with an L-shaped bar and
restaurant. It has a garden
and bowling green at the
back. ⚘ ◖ ♣ P 🏠

ASTWOOD BANK

Why Not
The Ridgeway (A44, 1 mile S
of village)
☎ (01527) 893566
11-2.30, 6-11; 12-3, 7-10.30 Sun
**Boddingtons Bitter; Brains Dark;
Wadworth 6X** Ⓗ
Friendly, country pub
comprising a small bar and a
larger lounge; children's
certificate. Booking for meals
is advisable, no food Sun eve.
🏯 ⚘ ◖ 🅳 ♿ ♣ Å ♣ 🍴

BEWDLEY

Black Boy
50 Wyre Hill (follow Sandy
Bank from B4194 at Welch
Gate) ☎ (01299) 403523
12-3, 7-11; 12-3, 7-10.30 Sun
**Banks's Original, Bitter; Marston's
Pedigree, seasonal beers** Ⓗ
Comfortable, three-roomed
local, a steep climb from the
town. Well-behaved children
may be allowed in the games

room when not in use.
🏯 Q ⚘ 🅳 ♣

Cock & Magpie
Severnside North
☎ (01299) 403748
11-11 (11-4, 6-11 winter); 12-10.30
(12-4, 7-10.30 winter) Sun
Banks's Original, Bitter Ⓟ
Small, two-roomed local
fronting the river; summer
drinking often spills out into
the road, while in winter
floods can be hazardous.
Q 🅳 ≠ (SVR) ♣ 🍴

Little Pack Horse
High Street (B4194)
☎ (01299) 403762
10.30-3, 6-11; 10.30-11 Sat;
10.30-10.30 Sun
**Ushers Best Bitter, Founders,
seasonal beers** Ⓗ
A central bar serves two
rooms, with a third further
back, full of old settles and a
variety of seats. It is full of
nooks and crannies with
quirky memorabilia.
🏯 🐕 ⚘ ◖ 🅳 ≠ (SVR) ♣ 🍴

Tipplers
Bewdley Beer Agency, 70
Load Street
☎ (01299) 402254
10-10; 12-3, 6-10 Sun
**Hobson's Town Crier; Hook Norton
Old Hooky; Malvern Hills Black Pear;
guest beer** Ⓗ
Real ale off licence in the
town centre, also stocking a
range of bottled and foreign
beers, plus Westons Old Rosie
cider in summer. ≠ (SVR) ⚲

Try also: **George Hotel,** Load
St (Carlsberg-Tetley);
Woodcolliers Arms, Welch
Gate (Free)

BIRTSMORTON

Farmers Arms
Birts Street (off B4208)
☎ (01684) 833308
11-2.30, 6-11 (11 -11 summer Sat);
12-3, 7-10.30 Sun (12-10.30 summer)
Sun
**Hook Norton Best Bitter, Old Hooky;
guest beer** Ⓗ
Black and white country
pub, tucked away down a
quiet lane: a small lounge
with low beams and larger
bar with a stone-flagged
floor. The garden has swings
and fine views of the
Malvern Hills.
🏯 Q ⚘ ◖ ♣ P

BOURNHEATH

Nailers Arms
Doctors Hill (off Stourbridge
Road) ☎ (01527) 873045
12-3, 6-11; 12-11 Sat & summer;
12-10.30 Sun
Enville White; guest beers Ⓗ
This newly refurbished
pub has a wine bar feel
in the lounge, but a proper
public bar. Innovative food is
served and at least three real
ales. It boasts a large garden
area.
🏯 ⚘ ◖ 🅳 ♿ P 🍴

Try also: **Gate,** Dodford Rd
(Smiles)

BRETFORTON

Fleece ☆
The Cross (near church, signed off B4035)
☎ (01386) 831173
11-3, 6-11; 11-11 Sat; 12-3, 6.30-10.30 (12-10.30 summer) Sun
Hook Norton Best Bitter; M&B Brew XI; Uley Old Spot; guest beers H
Famous old NT pub whose interior has been untouched for centuries, featuring inglenooks, antique furniture and a world-famous pewter collection. The large garden/orchard is great for families.
🏛 Q ❀ ◑ ▶ ⚓ ♣ ⌂

Try also: Thatch Tavern, Honeybourne (Free)

BROADWAY

Crown & Trumpet
Church Street (Snowshill road) ☎ (01386) 853202
11-2.30 (3 summer), 5-11; 11-11 Sat; 12-3.30, 6-10.30 Sun
Boddingtons Bitter; Flowers IPA, Original; Stanway Stanney Bitter, seasonal beers H
Comfortable 17th-century Cotswold inn with oak beams. It keeps an unusual range of pub games. The menu offers seasonal dishes and local produce. Stanway brews Cotteswold Gold in summer exclusively for the pub. 🏛 ❀ ⚓ ◑ ▶ ⚓ ♣ P

BROMSGROVE

Golden Cross Hotel
20 High Street
☎ (01527) 870005
11-11; 12-10.30 Sun
Theakston Best Bitter; Wyre Piddle in the Hole, In the Wind; guest beers H
Typical Wetherspoon's house, spacious and open plan, it usually stocks six ales or more. Very busy and noisy eves, lunchtimes are more relaxed. Cheap food is available. ◑ ▶ ♿ P ✂ ⊞

Ladybird
2 Finstall Road, Aston Fields (by station)
☎ (01527) 878014
11-11; 12-10.30 Sun
Batham Best Bitter; Hobson's Best Bitter; guest beers H
Formerly the Dragoon and saved from closure in 1997, it is now completely refurbished with pine panelling. The comfortable lounge has a no-smoking dining area serving good value food. ❀ ◑ ▶ ⚓ ≈ P

Try also: Crown, Catshill (Free)

CHADDESLEY CORBETT

Swan
High Street
☎ (01562) 777302
11-3, 6-11; 11-11 Sat; 12-3, 7-10.30 Sun
Batham Mild, Best Bitter, XXX H
Friendly old village pub built in 1606, with a popular bar, large lounge and a restaurant. It hosts regular jazz on Thu eve. No food Mon.
🏛 ❀ ◑ ▶ ⚓ ♣ ⌂ P

CLENT

Bell & Cross ☆
Holy Cross (off A491)
☎ (01562) 730319
12-3, 6-11; 12-10.30 Sun
Banks's Original, Bitter; Marston's Pedigree; guest beers H
Traditional, cosy pub with one of the most unspoilt interiors in Worcestershire: five small rooms each having an individual character, many with real fires. Eve meals Tue-Sat.
🏛 Q ❀ ◑ ▶ ⚓ ♣ P ✂

DODFORD

Dodford Inn
Whinfield Road (off A448)
OS939729
☎ (01527) 832470
12-3, 7-11; 12-3, 7-10.30 Sun
Banks's Original; Theakston Best Bitter; guest beers H
Friendly pub with a single bar, lost in beautiful countryside. Guest beers are usually sourced from independent breweries. It hosts a folk/beer festival in summer. Children's certificate.
🏛 ❀ ◑ ▶ ⚓ ♣ ⌂ P ✂

DRAKES BROUGHTON

Plough & Harrow
Worcester Road (A44 between Worcester and Pershore) ☎ (01905) 841041
11-30-3, 6-11; 11-11 Fri & Sat; 12-10.30 Sun
Draught Bass; Flowers Original; guest beers H
Large roadside black and white pub boasting a strong food reputation. The public bar accommodates drinkers, while the large, comfortable lounge bar offers open fires and sofas as well as a dining area. The guest beer changes weekly. 🏛 ❀ ◑ ▶ ⚓ ♿ P

DRAYTON

Robin Hood
Drayton Road (off B4188)
OS906758
☎ (01562) 730255
12-3, 5.30-11; 12-11 Sat; 12-10.30 Sun
Ansells Bitter; guest beers H

Small tidy bar and a comfortable lounge featuring inglenook seating and exposed beams. It stocks Bulmers cider and up to four guest beers. It has a children's animal farm at the rear.
🏛 Q ❀ ◑ ▶ ⚓ ⌂ P

Try also: Queens, Belbroughton (Marston's)

DROITWICH

Gardeners Arms
47 Vines Lane
☎ (01905) 772936
12 (11 Fri & Sat summer)-11; 12-10.30 Sun
Banks's Hanson's Mild, P **Original,** H **Bitter;** P **Marston's Pedigree** H
Tidy, cosy, two-roomed pub that lies next to Vines Park, the River Salwarpe and the Droitwich Barge Canal. The garden has a children's play area. Weston's Old Rosie sold in summer. No food Mon.
❀ ◑ ▶ ⚓ ♣ ⌂ P ⊞

Railway Inn
Kidderminster Road (from A38, Westlands island, towards centre)
☎ (01905) 770056
12-11; 12-3, 7-10.30 (12-10.30 summer) Sun
Banks's Original; Marston's Bitter, Pedigree; guest beers H
Small, two-roomed canalside pub with rooms adorned with railway memorabilia and a model railway. Good value meals are all freshly prepared. A large roof-top patio overlooks the restored canal basin. ❀ ◑ ▶ ≈ ♣ P

ELDERSFIELD

Greyhound
Lime Street (off B4211)
OS815304
☎ (01452) 840381
11.30-2.30 (3 Sat), 6 (7 Mon)-11; 12-3, 7-10.30 Sun
Butcombe Bitter; Wadworth 6X; guest beer G
Unspoilt, traditional country pub: a small cosy lounge bar has a real fire and games, plus a skittle alley-cum-function room. No food Mon. 🏛 Q ❀ ◑ ▶ ⚓ ♣ P

EVESHAM

Green Dragon
Oat Street (near library)
☎ (01386) 446337
11-11 (midnight Thu; 1am Fri & Sat); 6.30-10.30 (closed lunch) Sun
Evesham Asum Ale, Asum Gold, seasonal beers H
Busy, town-centre pub in a 16th-century building, the home of Evesham Brewery. It has a large games area and a cosy lounge/dining room (no food Sun). Live rock and

blues Fri eve – an admission charge applies. ◑ 🍴 ⬛ ≈ ♣

Try also: **Trumpet**, Merstow Green (Hook Norton)

GREAT MALVERN

Malvern Hills Hotel
Wynds Point (A449/B4232 jct) ☎ (01684) 564787
11-11; 12-10.30 Sun
Marston"s Bitter, Pedigree; Morrells Varsity H
Upmarket retreat on the Malvern Hills near British Camp; walkers and children are welcome. Open early morning for coffees, etc.
🏚 🌺 🛏 ◑ 🍴 ➤ P ⅟

Red Lion
4 St Anns Road
☎ (01684) 569787
12-3, 6-11.30; 12-11.30 Sat; 12-10.30 Sun
Banks's Original, Bitter; Marston's Pedigree H
Pleasant town pub with a large patio. Children are welcome at lunchtime. An imaginative range of food is all cooked freshly to order.
🌺 ◑ ≈

HANLEY BROADHEATH

Fox Inn
On B4204 ☎ (01886) 853219
12-3 (summer only), 6-11; 12-5, 7-10.30 Sun
Batham Best Bitter; Hobson's Best Bitter H
Large country pub comprising a beamed lounge bar, a dining area and a small snug that doubles as the family room. Another bar is dedicated to pub games. Interesting menu served.
🏚 ➤ 🌺 🛏 ◑ 🍴 ♣ P ⅟

HANLEY CASTLE

Three Kings
Church End (off B4211)
☎ (01684) 592686
12-3 (may vary), 7-11; 12-3, 7-10.30 Sun
Butcombe Bitter; Thwaites Bitter; guest beers H
Unspoilt village pub, almost a century in the same family. Three distinct drinking areas are all warmed by real fires. Live music is played in Nell's Bar Sun eves.
🏚 Q ➤ 🌺 🛏 ◑ 🍴 ♣ 🛒

INKBERROW

Old Bull
Village Green OS14573
☎ (01386) 792428
12-3, 5.30-11; 12-11 Sat; 12-10.30 Sun
Flowers Original; Wadworth 6X; guest beer H
Half-timbered pub with flagstoned floors, believed to

be almost 500 years old. The cosy lounge has open fires and a welcoming atmosphere; children's certificate. 🏚 Q ➤ 🌺 ◑ 🍴 P

ISMERE

Old Waggon & Horses
Stourbridge Road (A451)
☎ (01562) 700298
11.30-3.30, 6-11; 12-3, 7-11 Sun
Banks's Original, Bitter; P
Marston's Pedigree; guest beer H
Early 19th-century carriers' pub, a stopping-off point on the Kidderminster to Stourbridge Road. A characterful pub: the bar has etched windows and an old-fashioned bar front; the comfy lounge has plenty of seating. The dining area off the lounge admits children.
🏚 Q 🌺 ◑ 🍴 ♣ P 🍴

KEMPSEY

Walter de Cantelupe
The Main Road
☎ (01905) 820572
12-2, 6-11 (closed Mon); 12-2, 7-10.30 Sun
Malvern Hills Black Pear; Marston's Bitter; Taylor Landlord; guest beers H
Attractive free house in a large village, three miles out of Worcester. It keeps a high quality selection of beers whilst superb food is served from a regularly changing menu; the Ploughman's is particularly spectacular.
🏚 🌺 🛏 ◑ P 🍴

KEMPSEY GREEN STREET

Huntsman Inn
Green Street (from A38 at Kempsey, via Post Office Lane; 2 miles)
☎ (01905) 820336
12-3, 6-11; 12-4, 7-10.30 Sun
Batham Best Bitter; Everards Beacon, Tiger H
Comfortable, homely pub that is popular with locals, serving three quality ales not found for miles around. It enjoys a strong food trade and has a skittle alley.
🏚 🌺 ◑ 🍴 ♣ P

KIDDERMINSTER

Boar's Head (Tap House)
39 Worcester Street (near Glades arena Sports Centre)
☎ (01562) 862450
12-11, 12-10.30 Sun
Banks's Original, Bitter; Camerons Strongarm; Marston's Pedigree; guest beers H
Town-centre pub with individuality; the main bar leads to a covered courtyard, heated when cold for year-

round use; this has a bottle bar for busier nights. The lounge is quieter. No food Sun. 🏚 🌺 ◑ ≈ (BR/SVR) ♣

Hare & Hounds
120 Stourbridge Road (1 mile from centre, towards Stourbridge)
☎ (01562) 753897
11-11, 12-10.30 Sun
Banks's Original; Enville Bitter; Taylor Landlord; Theakston Bitter; guest beers H
Main road, single-bar pub; Wetherspoon's has transformed a closed pub into a consistently busy local. No children inside, but garden area with a single exit is great for parents
Q 🌺 ◑ 🍴 ♿ P 🍴 🎦

King & Castle
SVR Station, Comberton Hill (next to main station)
☎ (01562) 747505
11-3, 5-11; 11-11 Sat; 12-10.30 Sun
Ansells Mild; Batham Best Bitter; Wyre Piddle Royal Piddle; guest beers H
At the Kidderminster terminus of the Severn Valley Railway, this elegant pub is a recreation of a 1930s station buffet and bar. It welcomes children (away from the bar) until 9pm. Shops, when the railway is running, and a wheelchair WC are on station concourse. 🏚 Q 🌺 ◑ 🍴 ♿ ≈ (BR/SVR) 🛒 P

Try also: **Cricketers**, Lorne St (Banks's)

KNIGHTWICK

Talbot
200 yds off A44
☎ (01886) 821235
11-11; 12-10.30 Sun
Hobson's Best Bitter; Teme Valley T'Other, This, That, Wot? H
Pretty, family-owned hotel, home of the Teme Valley Brewery. The beer uses hops from the estate of the Clift family who also own the hotel; the restaurant uses local organic produce.
🏚 🌺 ◑ 🍴 ♣ 🛒 P

MALVERN LINK

New Inn
105 Lower Howsell road
☎ (01886) 832359
11-11; 12-10.30 Sun
Banks's Original, Bitter; P
Marston's Pedigree H
This community pub is home to many teams, including cricket. It holds a fête day last Sat in June; bonfire and fireworks in Nov. Children are welcome in the lounge, with a large play area in the garden. Eve meals can be booked. 🌺 ◑ 🍴 ♣ P 🍴

Swan Inn

Newland (off A449)
☎ (01886) 832224
11-3, 7 (6 summer)-11; 12-3, 7-10.30 Sun

Hobson's Best Bitter; Hook Norton Best Bitter; Shepherd Neame Spitfire; guest beer (summer) H

Nice country pub on the edge of common land, popular with local business people at lunch time for its varied menu with international influences. No food winter Tue eves. ♨ Q ✿ ◑ ▶ P

MAMBLE

Sun & Slipper

1/4 mile off A456
☎ (01299) 832018
12-3, 6.30-11 (closed Mon); 12-3, 7-10.30 Sun

Banks's Original, Bitter; Hobson's Best Bitter; guest beer H

Two-roomed pub in the village centre; the small, cosy bar is decorated with hops and brasses and has a pool table. Guest ales come from local independents. The craft centre nearby is worth a visit.
♨ ✿ ◑ ▲ ♣ P ⎕

MENITHWOOD

Cross Keys Inn

1 mile off B4202 OS709690
☎ (01584) 881425
11-3, 6-11; 11-11 Thu-Sat; 12-10.30 Sun

Marston's Bitter, Pedigree; guest beer H

Busy, rural village pub, popular with locals and visitors. The single bar offers different areas to sit and drink in a friendly atmosphere. Sandwiches and baltis are always available.
♨ ✿ ♣ P

MONKWOOD GREEN

Fox

Follow signs for Wichenford out of Hallow OS803601
☎ (01886) 889123
6-11, 11-11 Sat; 11-10.30 Sun

Cannon Royall Fruiterer's Mild, Arrowhead, Buckshot, seasonal beers H

Classic country pub where you will find open fires, exposed beams and a warm welcome. Real cider is supplied by local producer, Barkers. ♨ ✿ ◑ ▲ ♣ ⊃ P

OFFENHAM

Bridge Inn

Boat Lane (follow signs for river) ☎ (01386) 446565
11-11; 12-10.30 Sun

Bateman XB; Caledonian Deuchars IPA; Hobson's Bitter; guest beers H

Ancient inn with its own moorings and a riverside garden. The bridge was washed away over 300 years ago, and it is known locally as the Boat.
♨ Q ✿ ◑ ▶ ⊞ ♣ P

Try also: Fish & Anchor, Fish & Anchor Crossing (Banks's)

PEBWORTH

Masons Arms

Broad Marston Road
☎ (01789) 720083
12-2, 6-11; 12-3, 7-11 Sat; 12-3, 7-10.30 Sun

Draught Bass; Hook Norton Best Bitter, Old Hooky; guest beer H

Friendly local village pub that boasts the biggest indoor skittle alley in the area in its well-equipped games room. Familes are genuinely welcomed. No food Tue.
Q ➤ ✿ ◑ ▶ ♣ P ⊁

Try also: Ivy, North Littleton (Free)

PENSAX

Bell

On B4202, S of village
☎ (01299) 896677
12-2.30 (not Mon), 5-11; 12-10.30 Sun

Archers Golden; Enville Bitter; guest beers H

Welcoming country pub with a friendly feel. People travel here for the fine ales and food and panoramic views. Guest beers come from a range of mainly local independents. The no-smoking dining room welcomes children.
♨ Q ✿ ◑ ▶ ⊃ P

Try also: Manor Arms, Abberley (Free)

PERSHORE

Brandy Cask

25 Bridge Street
☎ (01386) 552602
11.30-2.30 (3 Sat), 7-11; 12-3, 7-10.30 Sun

Brandy Cask Whistling Joe, Brandysnapper, Ale Mary, John Baker's Original; Courage Directors; Ruddles Best Bitter; guest beers H

Town-centre free house: a large bar and bistro; its attractive gardens stretch to the bank of the Avon. Brandy Cask Brewery stands at rear of the pub. Worcestershire CAMRA *Pub of the Year* 1998.
♨ Q ✿ ◑ ▶

POUND GREEN

Olde New Inn

1/2 mile from B4194 at Button Oak
☎ (01299) 401271
12-3, 7 -11; 12-10.30 Sun

Draught Bass; Theakston Mild; guest beer H

Large country pub with a restaurant and family room, 10 minutes' walk up a steep hill from the Severn Valley Railway at Arley. Several rooms are set around the central bar. Guest beers come from local independents.
➤ ✿ ◑ ▲ ⇌ (Arley SVR) ♣ P

REDDITCH

Woodland Cottage

102 Mount Pleasant
☎ (01527) 402299
11-3, 6-11; 11-11 Sat; 12-3, 7-10.30 Sun

Boddingtons Bitter; Fuller's London Pride; Young's Bitter, Special H

Pleasant, open-plan pub divided into two drinking areas; a bar to the front and a lounge to the rear. The car park affords excellent views. Meals served Tue-Fri. ✿ ◑ P

Try also: Sportsman, Peakman St (M&B)

RIPPLE

Railway Inn

Station Road (B4091)
☎ (01684) 592225
11 (6 Mon)-11; 12-3, 7-10.30 Sun

Malvern Hills Black Pear; guest beers H

Busy village community pub with friendly welcome for all in its small quiet front bar. The large rear function room houses a skittle alley and pool tables.
♨ ➤ ✿ ◑ ▲ ♣ P ⊁

SHENSTONE

Plough

Off A450/A448 OS865735
☎ (01562) 777340
12-3, 6-11; 12-3, 7-10.30 Sun

Batham Mild, Best Bitter, XXX H

Tidy country pub of three drinking areas. Off the beaten track, hidden down country lanes, this drinkers' pub is well worth seeking out.
♨ Q ✿ ⊞ ♿ ♣ P

STONEHALL COMMON

Fruiterer's Arms

From Norton, first left after garden centre, 3 miles OS882489 ☎ (01905) 820462
12-2, 6-11; 12-3, 7-10.30 Sun

Worthington Bitter; guest beers H

Country free house enjoying a strong food trade; a comfortable lounge bar with a restaurant at the rear. It usually stocks three guest beers from smaller brewers. Extensive children's play area. ♨ ✿ ◑ ▶ ♿ P

STOURPORT-ON-SEVERN

Rising Sun

335

50 Lombard Street (opp. fire station)
☎ (01299) 822530
10.30-11; 12-10.30 Sun
Banks's Hanson's Mild, P Original, Bitter; Marston's Pedigree; guest beers H
Locals' canalside pub with a single bar and split-level drinking area, plus a small safe patio area. Meals available Tue-Sat.
🏨 ✸ ◑ ▲ ♣ 🗗

Wheatsheaf
39 High Street
☎ (01299) 822613
10.30-11; 12-10.30 Sun
Banks's Hanson's Mild, Original, Bitter P
Town-centre pub that boasts both a traditional bar and a comfortable lounge, close to the river. Lunchtime snacks available Mon-Sat plus Sun lunches served. Well-behaved children are welcome until 9.30. 🏨 ✸ ◱ ▲ ♣ P 🗗

Try also: **Bird in Hand**, Holly Rd (Whitbread)

TENBURY WELLS
Pembroke Arms
Cross Street
☎ (01584) 810301
12-3, 6-11; 12-11 Sat; 12-11 Sun
Draught Bass; Hobson's Best Bitter H
Ancient spacious black and white coaching inn, recently restored. The large lounge area has the games room to one side.
🏨 Q ✸ ◑ ▲ ♣ P

Ship Inn
Teme Street
☎ (01584) 810269
11-2.30, 7-11; 12-3, 7-10.30 Sun
Hobson's Best Bitter; guest beer H
Market town pub of character: a small bar area one side, and a comfortable lounge where there is an emphasis on food. Large garden.
✸ ⋈ ◑ ▲ P ✄

UPHAMPTON
Fruiterer's Arms
Uphampton Lane (off A449)
OS83969
☎ (01905) 620305
12.30-3, 7-11; 12-3, 7-10.30 Sun
Cannon Royall Fruiterer's Mild, Arrowhead, Buckshot, seasonal beers; John Smith's Bitter H
This excellent, unspoilt, country pub, is home to the Cannon Royall Brewery. It has a cosy, homely lounge and a public bar.
🏨 Q ✸ ◑ ◱ ▲ ♣ P

UPTON UPON SEVERN
White Lion Hotel

21 High Street
☎ (01684) 592551
11-11; 12-10.30 Sun
Beer range varies H
Lounge bar in an attractive, provincial hotel where exposed beams and an open fire contrast with the soft furnishings of the seating area. It has three regularly changing beers on tap.
Q ☡ ✸ ⋈ ◑ ▶ P

Try also: **Little Upton Muggery**, Old St (Ushers)

WEATHEROAK
Coach & Horses
Weatheroak Hill
☎ (01564) 823386
11.30-2.30, 5.30-11; 11.30-11 Fri & Sat; 12-10.30 Sun
Black Sheep Best Bitter; Hook Norton Old Hooky; Weatheroak Light Oak, Weatheroak, Redwood; Wood Special H
Attractive pub where a stone-flagged public bar contrasts with a modern restaurant in a pleasant rural setting. A full range of food is available (not Sun eve) to accompany the eight real ales on tap. Home of Weatheroak Brewery, it was local CAMRA *Pub of the Year* 1999.
🏨 Q ✸ ◑ ◱ ◱ ᴅ ▲ ♣ P

WORCESTER
Bell
35 St Johns
☎ (01905) 424570
11-3, 5.30-11; 11-4, 7-11 Sat; 12-3, 7-10.30 Sun
Cannon Royall Arrowhead; Fuller's London Pride; M&B Brew XI; guest beers H
Friendly 17th-century local with a skittle alley at the rear. Beer, rather than food oriented, two rooms offer a contrast to the busy bar area.
☡ ✸ ♣

Berkeley Arms
School Road, St Johns
☎ (01905) 421427
11-11; 12-3, 7-10.30 Sun
Banks's Hanson's Mild, Original, Bitter P
One of a dying breed of 'no food' pubs and proud of it. It is well worth the trip.
☡ ✸ ◱ ♣ P 🗗

Dragon
51 The Tything
☎ (01905) 25845
12-11; 12-10.30 Sun
Beer range varies H
Busy, listed boozer near the town centre. Always has one mild among a selection of four or five regularly changing ales; the cider varies, too. Live music staged Tue and Sun.
✸ ⇌ (Foregate St) ↻

Olde Talbot
Friar Street (near Cathedral)
☎ (01905) 23573
11.30-11; 12-10.30 Sun
Greene King IPA, Abbot; guest beers H
Large bar featuring bare wood, plus a cosy bar extension where children are welcome. Part of a two-star hotel, it boasts a quality restaurant. 🏨 ☡ ⋈ ◑
⇌ (Foregate St) P

Plough
23 Fish Street, Deansway (next to fire station)
☎ (01905) 21381
12-3, 8-11; closed Mon & Tue; 12-2, 8-10.30 Sun
Shepherd Neame Spitfire; guest beers H
Traditional, two-roomed, early 18th-century free house, with a relaxed atmosphere. Guest beers often come from local micros. ✸ ◑ ⇌ (Foregate St)

Swan with Two Nicks
28 New Street (by Cornmarket)
☎ (01905) 28190
11-11; 7-10.30 Sun
Boddingtons Bitter; guest beers H
Historic city-centre pub, boasting many original features; beware the low beam at the bar. Many guest ales come from local micros, it also offers an impressive range of malts. Good value lunches available. ☡ ◑
⇌ (Shrub Hill/Foregate St) ♣

Try also: **Bush**, Bull Ring (Free); **Lamb & Flag**, The Tything (Banks's); **Mount Pleasant**, London Rd (Whitbread)

INDEPENDENT BREWERIES

Brandy Cask: Pershore

Cannon Royal: Uphampton

Evesham: Evesham

Malvern Hills: Great Malvern

St George's: Callow End

Teme Valley: Knightwick

Weatheroak: Weatheroak

Woodbury: Great Witley

Wyre Piddle: Fladbury

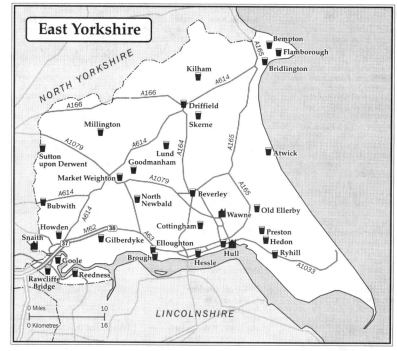

East Yorkshire

Yorkshire (East)

ATWICK

Black Horse
Church Street
☎ (01964) 532691
11.30-4, 6-11; 11.30-11 Sat; 12-10.30 Sun

John Smith's Bitter; guest beer H
Local pub, two miles north of Hornsea, overlooking the village green; this pleasant, three-roomed house has a small restaurant. Limited parking. ❀ ◐ ♣ P

BEMPTON

White Horse Inn
30 High Street
☎ (01262) 850266
11-4 (4.30 Fri & Sat), 7-11; 12-3.30, 7-10.30 Sun

Draught Bass; guest beers H
Former Moors & Robsons house, situated a mile from an RSPB centre and cliffs. Built in 1938, the pub retains its original blue tiled roof. The comfortable, open-plan lounge has period wood panelling; pool room.
🏨 ❀ 🛏 ◐ Å ≠ ♣ P

BEVERLEY

Cornerhouse
2 Norwood (near bus station)
☎ (01482) 882652
12-2.30, 5-11; 11-11 Fri & Sat; 12-10.30 Sun

Greene King Abbot; Taylor Landlord; Tetley Bitter; guest beers H
Totally transformed from a youngsters' hangout to a well-respected pub/café bar serving quality food in colourful air-conditioned surroundings. A recent welcome addition to Beverley's pub scene; curry eve Tue (5-8). ❀ ◐ ▶ P

Grovehill
183 Holme Church Lane (1 mile E of centre)
☎ (01482) 867409
12-2 (not Mon-Thu), 7-11; 11-11 Sat; 12-10.30 Sun

Camerons Bitter; Marston's Bitter H
Built in the 1920s by Moors & Robson this roadside pub has a plain bar and a well-furnished lounge. ❀ 🍺 ♣ P

Rose & Crown
North Bar Without
☎ (01482) 862532
11-3, 5-11; 12-10.30 Sun

Stones Bitter; Theakston Best Bitter; guest beer H
Substantial 'Brewer's Tudor' pub next to North Bar, Westwood and the racecourse. Popular for home-cooked food in the comfortable lounge and smoke room (eve meals until 9). The bar has a pool table.
Q ❀ ◐ ▶ 🍺 ♣ P

Tap & Spile (Sun Inn)
1 Flemingate
☎ (01482) 881547
12-3, 5-11; 12-11 Fri & Sat; 12-10.30 Sun

Big Lamp Bitter; Black Sheep Special; Taylor Landlord; Theakston Old Peculier; guest beers H
Spartan restoration of a medieval timber-framed building, claimed to be Beverley's oldest pub, facing the Minster. No meals Wed. Weston's Old Rosie cider stocked. Regular folk and acoustic music performed.
❀ ≠ ♣ ⌂ ⅄

White Horse Inn (Nellies) ☆
22 Hengate (by bus station)
☎ (01482) 861973
11-11; 12-10.30 Sun

Samuel Smith OBB H
One of Beverley's landmarks. This historic inn offers a multi-roomed interior with gas lighting, stone-flagged floors, coal fires and home cooking. Folk and jazz eves held upstairs. No food Mon. Local CAMRA *Pub of the Year* 1999.
🏨 Q ❀ ◐ 🍺 P ⅄

Woolpack Inn
37 Westwood Road (near Westwood Hospital)
☎ (01482) 867095
4 (12 Fri & Sat)-11; 12-10.30 Sun

Burtonwood Bitter; guest beer H
In a residential street of Victorian houses; read the pub's history in the no-smoking snug. Folk nights second Tue of month. No eve meals Sun. Small garden.
❀ ◐ ⅄

BRIDLINGTON

Old Ship
90 St John Street
☎ (01262) 670466
11-11; 12-4, 7-10.30 Sun
**Webster's Yorkshire Bitter;
Worthington Bitter; guest beer** Ⓗ
Thriving, former Vaux local.
Comfortable drinking areas
include a large bar with a
pool table, a lounge and a
no-smoking snug. Outdoor
play area for children. Eve
meals served 5.30-7.30 Mon-
Sat. Q ❀ ◑ 𝄢 ♣ ✂

Seabirds
6 Fortyfoot (1 mile N of
centre, near rail bridge)
☎ (01262) 674174
12-11; 12-10.30 Sun
**Camerons Bitter, Strongarm
Marston's Pedigree** Ⓗ
Large, well extended pub: the
comfortable bar features
photos of old Bridlington;
whilst the well furnished
lounge is decorated with
seafaring items, it has a
children's certificate.
❀ ◑ 𝄢 ♿ ⚓ ♣ ⍾ P

BROUGH

Buccaneer
47 Station Road
☎ (01482) 667435
12-2.30, 5-11; 12-11 Fri & Sat; 12-3,
7-10.30 Sun
Tetley Bitter; guest beers Ⓗ
Popular village pub by the
station, offering a warm
welcome to its traditional bar
and inviting, comfortable
lounge. ❀ ◑ 𝄢 ≈ ♣ P

BUBWITH

Jug & Bottle
Main Street
☎ (01757) 289707
5 (12 Sat)-10; 12-10 Sun
**Taylor Landlord; Black Sheep Best
Bitter; guest beers** Ⓗ
Off-licence selling draught
beer to take away: always two
Taylor's beers and real cider
available alongside a good
selection of British and
foreign bottled beers. ⍾

COTTINGHAM

Cross Keys
94 Northgate
☎ (01482) 875364
11-11; 12-10.30 Sun
**Marston's Pedigree; Tetley Dark
Mild, Bitter; guest beers** Ⓗ
Open-plan interior with an
area for pool. The outdoor
drinking area is heated. Note
the attractive ceiling dome
above the bar. Eve meals
served 5-7. ❀ ◑ ♿ ≈ ♣ P

Hallgate Tavern
125-127a Hallgate
☎ (01482) 844448

11-11; 12-10.30 Sun
Camerons Bitter, Strongarm Ⓗ
Deceptively large pub near St.
Mary's church with two bars,
a popular pool room and a
no-smoking eating area. Note
the attractive green-tiled
frontage, a legacy of its
former use as a butcher's
shop. Popular at weekends
with younger drinkers for
karaoke, live music and
discos. ❀ ◑ ♿ ≈ ♣ ⍾

DRIFFIELD

Mariner's Arms
47 Eastgate South (near cattle
market) ☎ (01377) 253708
3-11 (11.45 Sat); 12-10.30 Sun
**Burtonwood Bitter, seasonal beers;
guest beer** Ⓗ
Traditional market town
street-corner local that has
retained two rooms; a basic
bar and a more comfortable
lounge with a friendly
atmosphere. ❀ 𝄢 ≈ ♣ P

Old Falcon Inn
57 Market Place
☎ (01377) 255829
11-11; 12-10.30 Sun
John Smith's Bitter; guest beer Ⓗ
Narrow one-roomed pub
with a wood-panelled bar
and comfortable bench
seating. The pool table is
removed at weekends busy.
Guest beers come from
micro-breweries. ≈ ♣

ELLOUGHTON

Half Moon
The Crossroads, Main Street
☎ (01482) 667362
12-3, 6-11; 12-3, 7-10.30 Sun
**Courage Directors; Marston's
Pedigree; John Smith's Bitter; guest
beer** Ⓗ
This traditional bar caters for
local trade and games
players, whilst meals are
served in the large lounge
and restaurant. ❀ ◑ 𝄢 ♣ P

FLAMBOROUGH

Seabirds
Tower Street
☎ (01262) 850242
11.30-3, 7 (6.30 Sat)-11; 12-3,
8-10.30 Sun
John Smith's Bitter; guest beer Ⓗ
Former, two-roomed pub
which has been opened up
slightly, is well known near
and far for its fresh seafood,
varied menu and extensive
wine and whisky selection.
No eve meals winter Sun or
Mon. ▲ ❀ ◑ ⚓ P

GILBERDYKE

Cross Keys Inn
Main Road (B1230, W edge
of village) ☎ (01430) 440310

11-11; 12-10.30 Sun
**Boddingtons Bitter; John Smith's
Bitter; Tetley Bitter; guest beers** Ⓗ
Welcoming pub on the old
A63, now bypassed by the
M62. It enjoys strong support
amongst locals who
appreciate the emphasis on
traditional beer and games.
Draught Hoegaarden Belgian
beer stocked and three
rotating guest ales.
▲ ❀ ♣ ⍾ P

GOODMANHAM

Goodmanham Arms
Main Street
☎ (01430) 873849
12-5 (not Mon-Fri), 7-11 Sat; 12-5,
7-10.30 Sun
**Black Sheep Best Bitter; Theakston
Best Bitter guest beer** Ⓗ
Friendly village pub on the
Wolds Way, opposite the
church. The comfortable bar
features a Victorian fireplace;
the quarry-tiled hallways
leads to the parlour. Outside
gents WC. ▲ Q ❀ ♣ P

GOOLE

Macintosh Arms
13 Aire Street
☎ (01405) 763850
11-11; 12-10.30 Sun
**Bateman XB; Tetley Dark Mild,
Bitter; guest beer** Ⓗ
A busy, sometimes raucous
place where there's always
someone ready to debate
beers or bikes, or give you a
game of doms. Goole
motorcycle club meets here
twice a month. ❀ 𝄢 ≈ ♣ P

Try also: **Old George**, Market
Place (John Smith's)

HEDON

Shakespeare Inn
9 Baxtergate
☎ (01482) 898371
12-11; 12-10.30 Sun
**Tetley Dark Mild, Bitter; Theakston
Best Bitter; Worthington Bitter;
guest beers** Ⓗ
Popular, one-room pub,
serving good quality food (no
eve meals Mon). Extensive
brewery memorabilia is
displayed alongside
photographs of Hedon.
Popular with locals.
▲ ❀ ◑ ♣ P

HESSLE

Darleys
312 Boothferry Road
(A1105/B1232 jct near
Humber Bridge)
☎ (01482) 643121
11-3, 5.30-11; 11-11 Sat; 12-10.30
Sun
**Taylor Landlord; Wadworth 6X;
guest beer** Ⓗ
A substantial Whitbread

'Brewer's Tudor' pub on the old western approach to Hull, it retains a public bar, comfortable lounge and carvery restaurant.
Q 🛏 🍽 🌜 ◑ ⊟ ♣ P 🚭

HOWDEN

Barnes Wallis
Station Road (B1228, 1 mile N of Howden)
☎ (01430) 430639
12-2 (not Mon), 5 (7 Mon)-11; 12-11 Sat; 12-10.30 Sun
Black Sheep Best Bitter; Flowers IPA; Hambleton Bitter; guest beers Ⓗ
Friendly, open-plan pub next to the station stocking guest beers from independent breweries. Its decor reflects a local association with the inventor Barnes Wallis.
⚱ 🍽 ◑ ⊟ ♿ ⇌ ♣ P

HULL

Bay Horse
115-117 Wincolmlee (400 yds N of North Bridge on W bank of River Hull)
☎ (01482) 329227
11-11; 12-10.30 Sun
Bateman Mild, XB, XXXB, seasonal beers; guest beer (occasional) Ⓗ
Cosy, street-corner local, Bateman's only tied house north of the Humber. The public bar contrasts with the spectacular, lofty, stable lounge. Home-cooked food is a speciality. Hull CAMRA *Pub of the Year* 1998 and joint winner 1999.
⚱ ◑ ▶ ⊟ ♿ ♣ P

Cask & Cutter
44 Queen Street (near pier)
☎ (01482) 324886
11-11; 12-4, 7-10.30 (varies summer) Sun
Draught Bass; Highgate Dark; Tetley Bitter; guest beers Ⓗ
Renovated in 1999, the former Oberon maintains its two-roomed layout with a games room to the rear and a wooden-floored comfortable bar at the front. The pub is adorned with maritime artefacts. Up to three guest beers on tap. ◑ ▶ ⊟ ♣

Courts Bar
10 Bowlalley Lane, Old Town
☎ (01482) 226543
11-11; 12-10.30 Sun
Camerons Bitter, Strongarm Ⓗ
Converted Law Society hall in the Land of Green Ginger, popular after work with a mixed clientele. Music throughout the day can be intrusive as there are no quiet areas. A busy circuit pub at weekends. Food is available all day; no-smoking area until 6pm.
◑ ▶ ♿ 🚭 ⊟

Gardeners Arms
35 Cottingham Road
☎ (01482) 342396
11-11; 12-10.30 Sun
Marston's Pedigree; Tetley Bitter; guest beers Ⓗ
Popular, and at times busy, pub near the University. The alehouse-style front room is popular with locals and students, with its dark wood, subdued lighting and brick walls. Up to five guest ales and regular beer festivals held. Meals served 12-6 weekends; weekday eve meals 5-7.
🍽 ◑ ▶ ♿ ♣ P

Kingston Hotel
25 Trinity House Lane, Old Town
☎ (01482) 223993
11-4.30, 7-11; 11-11 Sat; 12-4.30; 7-10.30 Sun
Mansfield Mild, Riding Bitter Ⓗ
Historic town pub overlooking Holy Trinity church, the newly renovated market place and Trinity House. Note the impressive exterior and superb original carved wooden bar back. ♣

Minerva Hotel
Nelson Street, Old Town (near pier and marina)
☎ (01482) 326909
11-11; 12-10.30 Sun
Taylor Landlord; Tetley Bitter; guest beers Ⓗ
Famous pub, built in 1835, overlooking the estuary and what's left of the pier. Superb photos of Humber ferry paddle steamers and shipping displayed. Multi-roomed, it hosts a sea shanty festival (Sept). Eve meals served Mon-Thu. ⚱ Q 🍽 ◑ ▶ ♣

Mission
11-13 Posterngate, Old Town (E of Princes Quay shopping centre) ☎ (01482) 221187
11-11; 12-10.30 Sun
Old Mill Mild, Bitter, Old Curiosity, seasonal beers Ⓗ
Converted seaman's mission, resembling a baronial hall, it includes a minstrel's gallery and a deconsecrated chapel. Handy for the shopping centre. 🛏 ◑ ♿ ⇌ (Paragon) 🚭

Old Blue Bell
Market Place, Old Town (down alley next to covered market) ☎ (01482) 324382
11-11; 12-10.30 Sun
Samuel Smith OBB Ⓗ
Dating from the 1600s, this pub has retained a multi-room interior. A popular meeting place for local societies, it boasts a fine collection of bells. Children welcome in the snug; pool upstairs. No meals Sun.
🍽 ◑ ⊟ ♣

Olde Black Boy
150 High Street, Old Town
☎ (01482) 326516
11-11; 12-10.30 Sun
Tetley Bitter; guest beers Ⓗ
In Hull's Museum Quarter, it retains a bar, wood-panelled front room and two upstairs rooms. Good value food served until 6.30; five guest beers and three ciders/perry; joint winner CAMRA Hull *Pub of the Year* 1999.
⚱ Q ◑ ▶ ⊟ ♣ ⌣

Olde White Hart ☆
25 Silver Street
☎ (01482) 326363
11-11; 12-10.30 Sun
McEwan 80/-; Theakston Best Bitter, Old Peculier; guest beer Ⓗ
16th-century courtyard pub, once the residence where the Governor of Hull resolved to deny Charles I entry to the city. Superb woodwork, sit-in fireplaces and stained glass feature in a sympathetically renovated interior. Eve meals may be booked. Q 🛏 🍽 ◑ ♣

Rugby Tavern
5 Dock Street (behind Brown's bookshop on George St) ☎ (01482) 324759
11-11; 12-10.30 Sun
Samuel Smith OBB Ⓗ
U-shaped one-roomed pub with comfortable seating and a wooden façade. Popular for lunchtime food (Mon-Sat), busy at weekends.
◑ ⇌ (Paragon) ♣

St John's Hotel
10 Queens Road (off Beverley Road, 1 mile N of centre)
☎ (01482) 343669
12-11; 12-10.30 Sun
Mansfield Mild, Riding Bitter, seasonal beers; Marston's Pedigree Ⓗ
Traditional Victorian street-corner pub that retains its separate rooms, including a down-to-earth front corner bar with original gaslight pipes and a quiet back room. Well run, and much loved by regulars. 🛏 🍽 ⊟ ♿ ♣ P

Station Inn
202 Beverley Road
☎ (01482) 341482
12-11; 12-10.30 Sun
Old Mill Bitter, seasonal beers Ⓗ
Old Mill's second pub in Hull, the Station is a two-roomed house, north of the city centre. The tiled front bar and rear lounge/pool room both boast cosy fires. Discos held Fri and Sat in the back room. 🍽 🍽 ♣

Tap & Spile
169-171 Spring Bank
☎ (01482) 323518
12-11; 12-10.30 Sun
Beer range varies Ⓗ

This large street-corner alehouse serves the biggest range of beers in the city, as well as Lindisfarne fruit wines and Weston's Old Rosie cider. Two comfortable areas are set aside for non-smokers. Live music Mon and Tue; Sun lunch served. 🏮 ⌂ ✁

KILHAM
Star Inn
Church Street
☎ (01262) 420619
11-2, 6-11; 12-3 7-10.30 Sun
John Smith's Bitter; Theakston XB; guest beer Ⓗ
Excellent village pub in the heart of the Yorkshire Wolds. It maintains a central bar serving four rooms (three with real fires). It has a high quality restaurant to the rear, offering local produce.
🏚 ᛒ 🏮 (▶ ▲ ♣ P

LUND
Wellington Inn
19 The Green
☎ (01377) 217294
12-3 (not Mon), 7-11; 12-10.30 Sun
Black Sheep Best Bitter; John Smith's Bitter; Taylor Dark Mild, Landlord; guest beer Ⓗ
Attractive inn overlooking the village green. The building was renovated in 1995 and features flagstone floors, open fires and varied drinking areas. Eve meals (Tue-Sat). 🏚 🏮 (▶ P ✁ 🗗

MARKET WEIGHTON
Half Moon Inn
39 High Street
☎ (01430) 872247
5 (12 Fri & Sat)-11; 12-10.30 Sun
Burtonwood Bitter Ⓗ
Former coaching inn in a market town offering a friendly welcome. One long room has a bar area at the rear with a pool table. Popular with younger drinkers at weekends. 🏮 ♣ P

MILLINGTON
Gate Inn
Main Street
☎ (01759) 302045
12-4 (not Mon-Fri), 7-11; 12-4, 7.30-10.30 Sun
Black Sheep Best Bitter; Old Mill Bitter; John Smith's Bitter; Tetley Bitter Ⓗ
Friendly village local in a pretty Yorkshire Wolds setting. Note the old Yorkshire map on the ceiling. Pool room adjoins the single bar. Weekend lunches; no eve meals Sun. 🏚 🏮 🏠 ▶ ♣ P

NORTH NEWBALD
Tiger Inn

The Green
☎ (01430) 827759
12-11; 12-10.30 Sun
Black Sheep Best Bitter; John Smith's Bitter; Taylor Landlord; guest beer Ⓗ
Old village pub of character overlooking a small village green and close to the Wolds Way, welcoming both to families and walkers. The interior features a matchboard ceiling, beams and real fires. A good range of food includes a specials board.
🏚 🏮 🏠 (▶ 🏠 ♣ P

OLD ELLERBY
Blue Bell inn
Crabtree Lane (off A165 on old Hornsea road)
☎ (01964) 562364
12-4.30 (not Mon-Fri), 7-11; 12-4.30, 7-10.30 Sun
Tetley Dark Mild, Bitter; Ind Coope Burton Ale; guest beers Ⓗ
Unspoilt, cosy village local; a one-roomed pub with a low beamed ceiling and much brasswork. The large outside area has seating and an array of flowers in summer. A games room and two ever-changing guest beers add to its appeal. 🏚 🏮 ▲ ♣ P

PRESTON
Cock & Bell
1 Main Street
☎ (01482) 899345
6 (11.30 Thu, Fri & Sat)-11; ; 12-10.30 Sun
Castle Eden Bitter; Tetley Bitter; Wadworth 6X Ⓗ
Comfortable, two-roomed pub: a large room with a real fire and a no-smoking room where pool is played. Large outdoor play area for children. The restaurant opens for Sun lunch; bar meals also served Thu and Fri. 🏚 🏮 ♣ P ✁

RAWCLIFFE BRIDGE
Black Horse
Bridge Lane (Moorends-Rawcliffe Road, between two bridges)
☎ (01405) 839019
12-2 (not Mon-Thu), 6-11 (10.30 Fri & Sat); 12-2, 7-10.30 Sun
Tetley Bitter; guest beer (occasional) Ⓗ
Country pub dating back to 1861: a comfortable lounge, pool and dining rooms. Ask

---
INDEPENDENT BREWERIES
Hull: Hull
Old Mill: Snaith
Wawne: Wawne
---

the licensee about the two ghosts.
🏮 (▶ ▲ ♣ P

REEDNESS
Half Moon Inn
Main Street
☎ (01405) 704484
12-3 (not Tue or Thu), 7-11; 12-11 Sat; 12-10.30 Sun
Ruddles County; Theakston Black Bull; guest beers (summer) Ⓗ
Remote, traditional two-roomed village local close to Blacktoft Sands RSPB reserve. It has an L-shaped public bar, plus a lounge/restaurant where an extensive menu includes special offers on Thu, Fri and Sat eves (lunch served weekends).
🏚 Q 🏮 ▶ 🏠 ▲ ♣ P 🗗

RYEHILL
Crooked Billet
Pitt Lane (400 yds from A1033, E of Thorngumbald)
☎ (01964) 622303
11-11; 12-10.30 Sun
Burtonwood Bitter, Top Hat, guest beer Ⓗ
This 17th-century inn boasts an attractive beamed ceiling and a stone-flagged floor in the lounge and bar area. Note the varied artefacts. No meals Tue eve.
🏚 Q 🏮 (▶ ♣ P

SKERNE
Eagle Inn ☆
Wansford Road
☎ (01377) 252178
12-2 (not Mon-Fri), 7-11; 12-3, 7-10.30 Sun
Camerons Bitter Ⓗ
Classic, unspoilt village local with a basic bar and a front parlour. Drinks are served to your table from a small cellar off the entrance corridor. Beer is dispensed from a Victorian cash register beer engine. Outside WCs.
🏚 Q 🏮 🏠 ♣ P

SUTTON UPON DERWENT
St Vincent Arms
Main Street (follow B1288 past Elvington)
☎ (01904) 608349
11.30-3. 6-11; 12-3, 7-10.30 Sun
Banks's Bitter; Fuller's Chiswick, Ⓗ **ESB;** Ⓖ **John Smith's Bitter; Taylor Landlord; Wells Bombardier; guest beer** Ⓗ
Great food puts this pub on the map at weekends. Nice drinking surroundings for an amazing selection of regular beers; ESB is always served straight from the cask. Nothing is too much trouble.
🏚 ᛒ 🏮 (▶ P

Yorkshire (North)

APPLETREEWICK

New Inn
Main Street
☎ (01756) 720252
12-3 (not Mon), 7-11; 12-3, 7-10.30 Sun

Daleside Nightjar; John Smith's Bitter; Theakston Black Bull H
Friendly Dales pub frequented by locals, hikers and cyclists, stocking a large range of foreign bottled beers. The bar is an L-shaped room with another room across the hall. The gated garden across the road gives fine Dales views. The Dales Way footpath runs nearby. ﹴ Q ❀ ⇔ ◑ ▲ ♣ P

ARKENGARTHDALE

CB Inn
On unclassified road 4 miles NW of Reeth, 1/2 mile past Langthwaite OS000031
☎ (01748) 884567
11-11; (6.30 Mon-Thu, Jan & Feb); 12.10.30 Sun

Black Sheep Best Bitter; Riggwelter; John Smith's Bitter; Theakston Best Bitter H
Rambling, whitewashed 18th-century inn, former home of Charles Bathurst, lead miner and landowner. Low ceilings, wood floors and antique furniture add atmosphere; friendly service and an enticing menu, entirely home-prepared, attract custom.
ﹴ Q ⍭ ❀ ⇔ ◑ ▶ P ⊟

ASKRIGG

Crown Inn
Main Street
☎ (01969) 650298
11-3, 6-11; 11-11 Sat summer; 12-10.30 Sun

Black Sheep Best Bitter, Special; John Smith's Bitter; Theakston Best Bitter; guest beers (summer) H
Large bar area serving several rooms and crannies, popular with locals and visitors, especially for the meals based on fresh produce.
ﹴ Q ❀ ◑ ▶ ♣ P ⊟

BECK HOLE (NEAR GOATHLAND)

Birch Hall Inn ☆
(1 mile N of Goathland)
☎ (01947) 896245
11-3, 7.30-11 (not Mon eve), (11-11 summer); 12-3, 7.30-10.30 Sun

Black Sheep Best Bitter; Theakston Black Bull; guest beers H
Not to be missed: a tiny two-roomed pub in a charming village in *Heartbeat* country, near the North Yorks Moors Railway. Popular with walkers, it is a great place to spend a summer's day.
ﹴ Q ❀ ⇔ ♣

BILBROUGH

Three Hares
Main Street (off A64, York-Leeds road)
☎ (01937) 832128
12-3, 7-11; closed Mon; 12-4 (closed eve) Sun

Black Sheep Best Bitter; Taylor Landlord; guest beers H
200-year-old converted blacksmith's shop with a central bar serving the former snug and bar. High quality food is served in two no-smoking dining rooms.
ﹴ ❀ ◑ ▶ P

BILTON IN AINSTY

Chequers
Off B1224 between York and Wetherby
☎ (01423) 359066
12-2.30, 6-11; 12-11 Sat; 12-4.30, 7-10.30 Sun

Black Sheep Best Bitter; John Smith's Bitter; Theakston Best Bitter; guest beer (occasional) H
Off the beaten track in a historic village, this pub affords commanding views over the countryside. You step down to a comfortable lounge, a bar, and a no-smoking restaurant offering a large choice of meals and snacks (not served Sun eve or Mon). ﹴ ❀ ⇔ ◑ ▶ ♣ P

BIRSTWITH

Station
Station Road
☎ (01423) 770254
11.30-2.30 (not Mon), 5.30-11; 11.30-11 Sat; 12-5, 7-10.30 Sun

Tetley Bitter; guest beer H
Open-plan, traditional Victorian pub with a friendly atmosphere and an attractive restaurant. The guest beer is a Rudgate product.
ﹴ Q ❀ ⇔ ◑ ▶ P

BISHOP MONKTON

Lamb & Flag
Boroughbridge Road
☎ (01765) 677322
12-3, 5.30-11; 12-3, 7-10.30 Sun
Black Sheep Best Bitter; Tetley Bitter; guest beer H
Friendly two-room village inn in a picturesque setting, near the Ripon Canal.
ﹴ Q ❀ ◑ ▶ ♣ P

Masons Arms
St John's Road
☎ (01765) 677427
12-3, 6.30-11; 12-3, 6.30-10.30 Sun
Black Sheep Best Bitter; Daleside Greengrass; Rudgate Battleaxe; Tetley Bitter H
Quiet village pub with a stream running by the front door, teeming with wildlife; a duck race is held Aug Bank Hol. ﹴ Q ⍭ ❀ ◑ ▶ ᐤ ▲ ⇔ P

BISHOPTHORPE

Ebor
46 Main Street
☎ (01904) 706190
11-11; 12-10.30 Sun H
Samuel Smith OBB H
Attractive, two-roomed village pub with a large back garden. Q ❀ ◑ ▶ ⇔ P

BOROUGHBRIDGE

Three Horseshoes ☆
Bridge Street ☎ (01423) 322314
11-3, 5-11; 12-3, 7-10.30 (may extend summer) Sun
Camerons Strongarm; John Smith's Magnet H
This classic hotel has a superb genuine 1930s feel, in the same family for the past century; a wonderful place for friendly conversation.
ﹴ Q ⍭ ⇔ ◑ ▶ ⇔ ▲ ♣ P

BREARTON

Malt Shovel
Off B6165 ☎ (01423) 862929
12-3, 6.30-11; closed Mon; 12-3, 7.30-10.30 Sun
Black Sheep Best Bitter; Daleside Nightjar; Theakston Best Bitter; guest beer H
Unspoilt village pub, dating back to the 16th century with exposed beams and stone, well-known for its home-cooked food (not served Sun eve).
ﹴ Q ⍭ ❀ ◑ ▶ ♣ P

BROMPTON

Crown
Station Road
☎ (01609) 772547
12-3, 7 (5 Fri)-11; 12-11 Sat; 12-10.30 Sun
John Smith's Bitter, Magnet; guest beer H
Pub by the village green, opened out into a single long bar with pool and TV.
ﹴ ◑ ▶ ♣ P

BROMPTON BY SAWDON

Cayley Arms
On A170 ☎ (01723) 859372
11.30-2.30 (not Mon); 5.30-11; 12-3, 7-10.30 Sun
Tetley Bitter; Theakston Best Bitter, XB; guest beer H
Prominent roadside pub with a children's play area. The excellent food includes local specialities including game (booking advisable).
ﹴ Q ⍭ ❀ ◑ ▶ ▲ ♣ P ⊬

BURN

Wheatsheaf

341

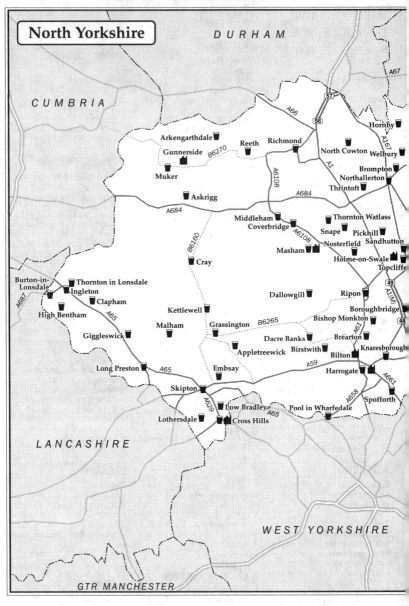

North Yorkshire

DURHAM

CUMBRIA

A67

A66

Hornby

Arkengarthdale
Gunnerside
Muker
Reeth
Richmond
North Cowton
Welbury
Brompton
Northallerton
Thrintoft

Askrigg

A684

Middleham
Coverbridge
Thornton Watlass
Snape
Pickhill
Nosterfield
Sandhutton
Masham
Holme-on-Swale
Topcliffe

B6160

Cray

Burton-in-Lonsdale
Thornton in Lonsdale
Ingleton
Clapham
High Bentham
Giggleswick

Dallowgill
Ripon
Boroughbridge
Bishop Monkton

Kettlewell
Malham
Grassington
B6265
Dacre Banks
Brearton
Appletreewick
Birstwith
Bilton
Knaresborough
Long Preston
A65
Embsay
A59
Harrogate
Skipton
Low Bradley
Pool in Wharfedale
Spofforth
Lothersdale
Cross Hills

LANCASHIRE

WEST YORKSHIRE

GTR MANCHESTER

Main Road (A19)
☎ (01757) 270614
12-11; 12-10.30 Sun
John Smith's Bitter; Taylor Landlord; Tetley Bitter; guest beer H
The exterior of this roadside inn belies the friendly welcome found within. An open hearth compliments the country and railway artefacts which adorn the walls, alongside collections of Dinky toys. The restaurant gets busy Sun (eve meals served Thu-Sat).
🏔 Q ❀ ◑ ▶ ♣ P

BURTON-IN-LONSDALE
Punch Bowl
9 Low Street ☎ (015242) 61568
12-3 (not Mon), 7-11; 12-11 Sat;
12-10.30 Sun
Thwaite's Bitter; Daniel's Hammer H
Village inn, off the main road but worth seeking out, offering good value meals. Bikers welcome. The garden affords lovely views.
🏔 Q ❀ ⇌ ◑ ▶ ▲ ♣ P

CARLTON IN CLEVELAND

CAWOOD
Ferry Inn

Blackwell Ox
Off A172, near Stokesley
☎ (01642) 712287
11.30-3, 6.30 (5.30 Sat & summer)-11;
(11-11 summer Sat); 12-10.30 Sun
Draught Bass; Fuller's London Pride; Worthington Bitter; guest beer H
The only pub in the village: a pleasant central bar with seating areas at different levels; good food (Thai cooking a speciality). Popular with locals, and walkers.
🏔 Q ❧ ❀ ◑ ▶ ▲ ♣ P ✾

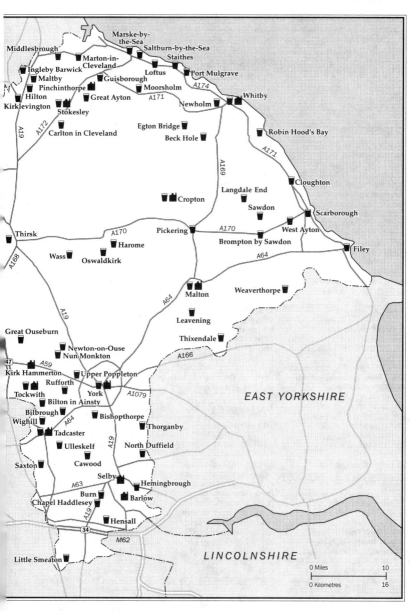

King Street ☎ (01757) 268515
12-3 (not Mon or Tue), 5-11; 12-11 Sat;
12-10.30 Sun
**Black Sheep Special; Camerons
Bitter; Mansfield Bitter; Taylor
Landlord; guest beers** Ⓗ
16th-century inn where there
are several drinking areas
with low beams, settles and
open fires. Outside a terrace
and large garden stand right
on the riverbank. Guest ales
are from local independents.
🏛 Q ➤ ❀ � ⬤ 🌙 ♠ P

CHAPEL HADDLESEY
Jug Inn

Main Street
☎ (01757) 270307
12-3, 6-11; 12-11 Sat; 12-10.30 Sun
Beer range varies Ⓗ
Cosy 250-year-old village
pub: two bars with low
ceilings display a fine
collection of jugs and plates.
'Just for You' is a house beer
supplied by Brown Cow. The
garden leads to the river. Folk
groups meet here.
🏛 Q ❀ � ⬤ 🌙 🚽 ⚘ ♠ P

CLAPHAM
Flying Horseshoe
Next to station OS678733

☎ (015242) 51229
12-4 (not Mon-Thu), 6-11, (11.30-3 (4
Sat), 5.30-11 summer); 12-4, 6-11.30
(supper licence) Sun
**Jennings Cumberland Ale; Tetley
Bitter; guest beers** Ⓗ
Country hotel in extensive
grounds with a comfortable
bar, games room and no-
smoking restaurant. Expect
four real ales with one from
Dent. Llive music is staged.
🏛 ➤ ❀ � ⬤ 🌙 ⚘ ♠ P

New Inn
☎ (015242) 51203
11-3, 7-11; 11-11 Sat; 12-10.30 Sun
Black Sheep Best Bitter; Dent

Bitter; Tetley Bitter; guest beers Ⓗ
Large, 18th-century coaching
inn: two oak-panelled lounge
bars displaying cycling and
caving pictures. Children
welcome in the no-smoking
restaurant. Felbeck Bitter is
Flying Firkin Aviator
rebadged.
🏠 Q 🌐 🚬 ◖❶ ♿ ⚓ ♣ P

CLOUGHTON

Bryherstones Inn
Newlands Road
☎ (01723) 870744
12-3, 6-11; 12-4, 6-10.30 Sun
Taylor Golden Best, Landlord;
Theakston Best Bitter, Old
Peculier Ⓗ
Traditional country inn
within the North Yorks
Moors national park.
Originally a farmhouse with
stables, it was converted to a
four-room pub on three
levels. It is noted locally for
superb home-cooked meals.
🏠 Q 🐾 🌐 ◖❶ ⚓ ♣ P ⚲

COVERBRIDGE

Coverbridge Inn
Two miles W of E Witton on
A6108 ☎ (01969) 623250
11-11; 12-10.30 Sun
Black Sheep Best Bitter; John Smith's
Bitter; Taylor Landlord; Theakston
Best Bitter; guest beers Ⓗ
Cosy, 16th-century inn
featuring an open log fire in
the main bar with bench
seats in the bay window.
Well used by locals, this
friendly pub offers an
extensive menu.
🏠 Q 🐾 🌐 🚬 ◖❶ ♣ P

CRAY

White Lion Inn
☎ (01756) 760262
11.30-11; 12-10.30 Sun
Moorhouse's Premier, Pendle
Witches Brew; guest beers Ⓗ
Traditional stone-flagged pub
below Buckden Pike in lovely
walking country. The main
room boasts original beams
and an open fire. Guest beers
come from Moorhouse's and
Roosters.
🏠 Q 🐾 🌐 🚬 ◖❶ ♣ P ⚲

Try also: George Inn,
Hubberholme (Free)

CROPTON

New Inn
Woolcroft OS755890
☎ (01751) 417330
11-11 (varies winter weekdays); 12-3,
7-10.30 Sun
Cropton King Billy, Two Pints,
Scoresby Stout, Backwoods Bitter,
Monkmans Slaughter, seasonal
beers; Tetley Bitter Ⓗ
Busy, country pub in a
hilltop setting offering a

choice of rooms plus visitor's
centre for the brewery.
🐾 🌐 🚬 ◖❶ ♿ ⚓ ♣ ⌂ P

CROSS HILLS

Old White Bear
6 Keighley Road
☎ (01535) 632115
11.30 (5 Mon)-11; 12-10.30 Sun
Boddingtons Bitter; Old Bear
Bitter Ⓗ
Large , multi-roomed brew
pub, circa 1735, at the heart
of village life. Aunty
Wainwright's Eating 'Ole
serves good value food. The
brewery, in former stables,
uses local well water and
some home-grown hops.
🏠 🌐 ◖❶ ♣ P

Try also: Kings Arms,
Sutton-in-Craven (Whitbread)

DACRE BANKS

Royal Oak
Oak Lane
☎ (01423) 780200
11-3, 5.30-11; 12-3, 7-10.30 Sun
Black Sheep Best Bitter; Daleside
Old Legover; Rudgate Battleaxe;
Tetley Bitter Ⓗ
18th-century inn with views
over Nidderdale. Note the
oak panelling decorated with
amusing rhymes and sayings.
🏠 Q 🐾 🌐 🚬 ◖❶ ♣ P

DALLOWGILL

Drovers Inn
On minor road about 2 miles
W of Laverton OS210720
☎ (01765) 658510
12-3 (3.30 Fri & Sat summer), 7 (6.30
Fri, Sat & summer)-11; closed Mon; 12-3
(3.30 summer), 6.30-10.30 Sun
Black Sheep Best Bitter; Old Mill
Bitter; John Smith's Bitter Ⓗ
Single roomed wayside
country pub, on the edge of
the moors, overlooking the
lower Nidderdale. Popular
with the local farming
community and ramblers, a
rare outlet in this area for Old
Mill beer. 🏠 🌐 ◖❶ ♿ ⚓ ♣ P

EGTON BRIDGE

Horseshoe Hotel
In the valley, 1/4 mile from
station over the river
☎ (01947) 895245
11.30-3, 6.30-11 (11-11 summer);
12-10.30 Sun
John Smith's Bitter; Theakston Best
Bitter; guest beers Ⓗ
Residential hotel, formerly an
18th-century country house,
set in beautiful grounds on
the edge of the River Esk. The
bar features wood pews and a
good fire; good food is served
in the bar and restaurant. Do
not confuse with Egton, the
village at the top of the hill.
🏠 Q 🐾 🌐 🚬 ◖❶ ≈ ♣ P

EMBSAY

Elm Tree
Elm Tree Square
☎ (01756) 790717
11.30-3, 5.30-11; 12-3, 7-10.30 Sun
Goose Eye No-eyed Deer; Tetley
Bitter; guest beers Ⓗ
Popular with locals and
visitors for both the ale and
food; a large main room with
a smaller (no-smoking) side
room with pew-type seats for
diners. Normally three guest
beers stocked. Handy for
Embsay and Bolton Abbey
Steam Railway.
🌐 🚬 ◖❶ ≈ P

FILEY

Imperial Vaults
20-22 Hope Street
☎ (01723) 512185
12-11; 12-10.30 Sun
Boddingtons Bitter; John Smith's
Bitter; Morland Old Speckled Hen;
guest beer Ⓗ
Friendly, two-roomed town-
centre pub. Meals available
until early eve in summer.
🚬 ◖❶ ♿ ≈ ♣

GIGGLESWICK

Black Horse
Church Street
☎ (01729) 822506
12-2.30, 5.30-11; 11-11 Sat; 12-10.30
Sun
Black Sheep Best Bitter; Jennings
Mild; Taylor Landlord; Tetley
Bitter Ⓗ
Quiet, relaxed village local
with a long L-shaped room
for drinking and a 20-seat
restaurant. 🏠 🌐 🚬 ◖❶ P

Try also: Royal Oak, Settle
(Whitbread)

GRASSINGTON

Foresters Arms
20 Main Street
☎ (01756) 752349
11-11; 12-10.30 Sun
Black Sheep Best Bitter;
Boddingtons Bitter; Tetley Mild,
Bitter; guest beers Ⓗ
Old coaching inn in a busy
village centre (parking is
limited). The large bar area
offers good home-cooked
food. 🏠 🌐 🚬 ◖❶ P

Try also: Clarendon Hotel,
Hebden (Free)

GREAT AYTON

Buck
1 West Terrace (A173, near
bridge)
☎ (01642) 722242
11-11; 12-10.30 Sun
Boddingtons Bitter; Flowers
Original; Castle Eden Ale; guest
beer Ⓗ
18th-century coaching inn

YORKSHIRE (NORTH)

by the river in Captain Cook's village. It enjoys a friendly atmosphere and strong local patronage.
Q ⊠ ⊛ ◖▶ ♣ P

Try also: Wainstones Hotel, Gt Broughton (Free)

GREAT OUSEBURN
Crown Inn
Main Street
☎ (01423) 330430
5-11; 11-11 Sat; 12-10.30 Sun
Black Sheep Best Bitter; John Smith's Bitter; guest beers Ⓗ
Attractive, many-roomed village inn. Its reputation for good food draws custom from a wide area, but it is also a popular local. Lunches at weekends. ⚏ Q ⊛ ▶ P

GUISBOROUGH
Anchor Inn
16 Belmongate
☎ (01287) 632715
11-11; 12-10.30 Sun
Samuel Smith OBB Ⓗ
18th-century, cottage-style pub, well refurbished, located on the south-east edge of town. ⚏ Q ⊛ ◖▶

Tap 'n' Spile
Westgate ☎ (01287) 632983
11.30-11; 12-3, 7-10.30 Sun
Beer range varies Ⓗ
Old town-centre pub decorated in traditional style with a no-smoking room at the rear. Q ⊛ ◖ ➳ ⌣ ✂

Three Fiddles
34 Westgate
☎ (01287) 632417
11-11; 12-10.30 Sun
Draught Bass; guest beer Ⓗ
Old coaching inn on the main street: two bars, plus a large garden accessed via a passage. ⚏ Q ⊛ ⇔ ◖ ♣

HAROME
Star Inn
☎ (01439) 770397
12-2.30 (not Mon), 6.30-11; 12-10.30 Sun
Black Sheep Special; John Smith's Bitter; Theakston Best Bitter; guest beer Ⓗ
Historic thatched inn with a formidable reputation for excellent food; a single, characterful lounge bar plus a restaurant. ⚏ ⊛ ◖▶ P

HARROGATE
Coach & Horses
16 West Park
☎ (01423) 568371
11-11; 12-10.30 Sun
Black Sheep Best Bitter; John Smith's Bitter; Tetley Bitter Ⓗ
Very popular, cosy pub near the town centre. ◖▶ ➳

Gardeners's Arms ☆
Bilton Lane (1 mile from A59)
☎ (01423) 506051
12-3, 6 (7 Sat)-11; 12-3, 7-10.30 Sun
Samuel Smith OBB Ⓗ
Ancient pub featuring thick stone walls, wood panelling, a large stone fireplace and a tiny snug. Eve meals available Sept-March (not Wed or Sun). ⚏ Q ⊛ ▶ ♣ P

Old Bell Tavern
6 Royal Parade (opp. Crown Hotel) ☎ (01423) 507930
12-11; 12-10.30 Sun
Black Sheep Best Bitter; Caledonian Deuchars IPA; Taylor Landlord; guest beers Ⓗ
Recently converted from a restaurant to a single room pub with an L-shaped bar, stocking a good selection of Belgian bottled beers. It enjoys a good trade from the nearby conference centre. Eve meals 6-7.30. Q ◖▶ ➳

Shepherd's Dog
141 Otley Road
☎ (01423) 533031
11-11; 12-10.30 Sun
Draught Bass; Stones Bitter Ⓗ
Large pub with many activities catering for locals.
⊛ ◖▶ ♿ ♣ P

Tap 'n' Spile
Tower Street
☎ (01423) 526785
11-11; 12-10.30 Sun
Tap & Spile Premium; guest beers Ⓗ
Three-roomed pub serving up to eight real ales and a cider to a mixed clientele. No food Sun. ◖ ➳ ♣ ⌣ ✂

Try also: Harwood, Station Rd, Pannal (Free)

HEMINGBOROUGH
Crown
Main Street
☎ (01757) 638434
12 (2 Mon)-11; 12-10.30 Sun
Black Sheep Best Bitter; John Smith's Bitter; Tetley Bitter; Wadworth 6X Ⓗ
Next to the 12th-century minster which boasts the

second tallest spire in England, this comprises a comfortable V-shaped bar and adjoining lounge. No food Mon. ⊛ ◖▶ P

HENSALL
Anchor
Main Street
☎ (01977) 661634
6 (5 Wed-Fri)-11; 12-3, 5-11 Sat (may vary); 12-10.30 Sun
John Smith's Bitter; Taylor Landlord; guest beer Ⓗ
Single L-shaped room with a small games area and a long lounge. British and continental beer bottles are displayed. A varied menu and theme nights give a modern touch to the classic rural appearance of this pub. Sun lunch served.
⚏ ⊛ ▶ ⇌ (Limited Service) ♣ P

HIGH BENTHAM
Horse & Farrier
83 Main Street
☎ (015242) 61381
12-2, 6-11; 11-11 Sat; closed Mon); 12-10.30 Sun
Theakston Best Bitter; guest beer Ⓗ
15th-century building, housing a food-oriented pub/restaurant. The extensive bar has quiet corners. Bring your own musical instrument on last Thu of the month.
⚏ ⊛ ◖▶ ▲ P ✂

HILTON
Falcon
Seamer Road
☎ (01642) 592228
11.30-11; 12-10.30 Sun
Flowers Original; guest beers Ⓗ
This smart village inn places a strong emphasis on food and enjoys a growing reputation for quality ales. A single L-shaped bar and a restaurant. ⊛ ◖▶ ♿ P ⊟

HORNBY
Grange Arms
☎ (01609) 881249
11-11; 12-10.30 Sun
Black Sheep Best Bitter; John

INDEPENDENT BREWERIES

Black Dog: Whitby
Black Sheep: Masham
Captain Cook: Stokesley
Cropton: Cropton
Daleside: Harrogate
Franklin's: Bilton
Hambleton: Holme-on-Swale
Malton: Malton
Marston Moor: Kirk Hammerton

North Yorkshire: Pinchinthorpe
Old Bear: Crosshills
Brown Cow: Barlow
Rooster's: Harrogate
Rudgate: Tockwith
Selby: Selby
Samuel Smith: Tadcaster
Swaled Ale: Gunnerside
York: York

The Good Beer Guide 2001

Smith's Bitter; guest beers H
Pleasant, whitewashed village
pub with a linked lounge,
snug, little bar and
restaurant. An excellent
variety of home-cooked food
is available 12-9 daily. There
is always one guest beer from
Durham Brewery.
🏨 ❀ ◖▶ P 🏚

INGLEBY BARWICK

Myton House Farm
Ingleby Way (access from
A1045 and A1044
roundabouts)
☎ (01642) 751308
11-11; 12-10.30 Sun
Camerons Bitter, Strongarm; guest
beer H
Impressive new pub in
farmhouse style, serving
reputedly the biggest housing
estate in Europe between
Thornaby and Yarm. Several
drinking areas surround a
central bar. 🏨 ❀ ◖▶ ♿ P ⅏ 🏚

INGLETON

Wheatsheaf
22 High Street
☎ (015242) 41275
12-11; 12-10.30 Sun
Black Sheep Best Bitter, Special,
Riggwelter; Moorhouse's Pendle
Witches Brew; Theakston Best
Bitter; guest beers H
Pub with a single, long, cosy
bar, handy for the end of the
Waterfalls Walk. Meals come
in large portions served in a
no-smoking dining room.
🏨 ❀ ⇌ ◖▶ ♣ P

KETTLEWELL

Kings Head
☎ (01756) 760242
12-3, 6.30-11; 12-11 Sat; 12-10.30
Sun
Black Sheep Best Bitter, Special,
Riggwelter; Tetley Bitter; guest beer
(summer) H
Three-storey building, tucked
away in the village; its open
interior boasts a large
inglenook., stone floors and
bench seating. An excellent
base for walking, caving and
touring on the Dales Way.
🏨 Q ❀ ⇌ ◖▶ Å ♣ P

Try also: **Fox & Hounds,**
Starbotton (Free)

KIRKLEVINGTON

Crown
Thirsk Road (A67, near A19
Crathorne interchange)
☎ (01642) 780044
5 (12 Sat)-11; 12-10.30 Sun
Boddingtons Bitter; Castle Eden Ale;
Marston's Pedigree; John Smith's
Magnet H
Friendly, welcoming,
roadside pub in a commuter
village: two drinking areas

each with an open fire. All
food is home-prepared and
cooked; lunches served at
weekends (booking
advisable). 🏨 ❀ ◖▶ ♿ ♣ P

KNARESBOROUGH

Beer Ritz (off-licence)
17 Market Place
☎ (01423) 862850
10-10; 11-10 Sun
Beer range varies G
Speciality off-licence, selling
over 300 bottled beers from
around the world as well as
changing cask ales and
ciders. Discount on draught
beers for card-carrying
CAMRA members. ⇌ ◔

Blind Jacks
19 Market Place
☎ (01423) 869148
4 (5.30 Mon, 12 Fri & Sat)-11; 12-10.30
Sun
Black Sheep Best Bitter; Daleside
Greengrass; Taylor Landlord; Village
White Boar; guest beers H
This cosy characterful gem of
an alehouse in a Georgian
building exudes the
traditional atmosphere of an
earlier age. The no-smoking
room is upstairs. Q ⇌ ⅏

Half Moon
1 Abbey Road (off Briggate)
☎ (01423) 862663
5.30 (12 Sat)-11; 12-10.30 Sun
Mansfield Riding Bitter H
Cosy, one-roomed pub
overlooking the Nidd, known
best for its Boxing Day tug of
war with the rival pub across
the river. 🏨 Å ⇌

Marquis of Granby
31 York Place (A59, York
road) ☎ (01423) 862207
11.30-3, 5.30-11; 11.30-11 Wed, Fri &
Sat; 12-10.30 Sun
Samuel Smith OBB H
Solid, welcoming two-
roomed pub, furnished in
Victorian style. No food Sun.
❀ ◖◗ Å ♣ P

LANGDALE END

Moorcock Inn
OS938913
☎ (01723) 882268
11-3, 5.30-11 (closed winter Mon-Tue);
12-3, 7-10.30 (not winter eves) Sun
Beer range varies H
Remote, stone pub
sympathetically renovated,
near a forest drive.
Traditional home-cooked
food; busy in summer.
🏨 Q ❀ ◖▶ Å ♣ P ⅏

LEAVENING

Jolly Farmers
Main Street
☎ (01653) 658276
12-3 (not Mon), 7-11; 12-3, 7-10.30
Sun

John Smith's Bitter; Taylor Landlord;
Tetley Bitter; guest beer H
Award-winning, 17th-century
village local, extended but
retaining the cosiness of the
multi-roomed pub. The
dining room specialises in
excellent game dishes.
🏨 ⛵ ❀ ◖▶ ♣ P 🏚

LITTLE SMEATON

Fox
Main Street
☎ (01977) 620254
12-3, 7-11; 12-10.30 Sun
Black Sheep Best Bitter; John
Smith's Bitter; Taylor Landlord H
Cosy, comfortable free house
with a single L-shaped room,
this traditional village local
stands in an attractive setting
near the River Went. ❀ ♣ P

LOFTUS

White Horse
73 High Street
☎ (01287) 640758
12-11; 12-10.30 Sun
John Smith's Bitter; guest beer H
Located at the east end of the
town: one large room with a
central bar. ❀ ⇌ ♣ P

Try also: **Station,** Station Rd
(Bass)

LONG PRESTON

Maypole Inn
On A65 ☎ (01729) 840219
11-3, 6-11; 11-11 Sat; 12-10.30 Sun
Castle Eden Ale; Moorhouse's
Premier; Taylor Landlord; Tetley
Bitter H
Award-winning pub on the
village green facing the
maypole. Three rooms: a tap-
room, a comfortable lounge
and a dining room serving
good value meals. Saxon
Gold cider stocked.
🏨 Q ❀ ⇌ ◖▶ Å ⇌ ◔ P

LOTHERSDALE

Hare & Hounds
Dale End ☎ (01535) 630977
12-3.30, 6-11; 12-4, 7-10.30 Sun
Tetley Bitter; Theakston Best Bitter;
guest beers H
One of the oldest buildings
in the village; the car park
opposite was once the sheep
market. This welcoming,
two-roomed watering-hole
stands on the Pennine Way.
Pool played; good food.
❀ ◖▶ ♿ P

LOW BRADLEY

Slaters Arms
Crag Lane ☎ (01535) 632179
12-3, 6 (7 winter)-11; 12-3, 7-10.30
Sun
Black Sheep Best Bitter; John
Smith's Bitter; Webster's Green
Label H

346

Whitewashed 16th-century local in a picturesque Aire Valley village. The sympathetically refurbished lounge has retained an inglenook and original beams. The smaller locals' drinking area at the rear affords panoramic views across the valley. Good value meals. ♨ ❀ ◖❙ ♣ P

MALHAM

Lister Arms
Gordale Scar Road
☎ (01729) 830330
12-3, 7-11 (12-11 summer Sat); 12-3, 7-10.30 (12-10.30 summer) Sun
Marston's Pedigree; John Smith's Bitter; Theakston Black Bull; guest beers Ⓗ
Popular village pub, dating from 1702: three distinct areas, plus a pleasant sheltered garden. Two guest beers are usually available, along with a wide range of bottled beers and malt whiskies, plus Thatchers cider in summer.
♨ ❀ ⊨ ◖❙ ▲ ♣ ⟳ P

MALTBY

Pathfinders
High Lane ☎ (01642) 590300
11-11, 12-10.30 Sun
Black Sheep Best Bitter, Special; guest beers Ⓗ
Much-extended village pub with a spacious, split-level, open-plan interior and a strong emphasis on food. Renamed in the 1950s in honour of the RAF Pathfinder squadrons. ❀ ◖❙ ▲ ♣ P

MALTON

Crown Hotel (Suddaby's)
12 Wheelgate
☎ (01653) 692038
11-11; 12-4, 7-10.30 Sun
Malton Double Chance, Crown Bitter, Owd Bob; guest beers Ⓗ
Busy, town-centre pub with a conservatory eating area. Malton brewery is situated in the rear courtyard. Pickwick Porter is the house guest beer. The pub hosts beer festivals in July and Dec.
♨ Q ⇆ ⊨ ◖ ▲ ≉ P

Try also: **Royal Oak**, Old Malton (Free)

MARSKE

Frigate
Hummers Hill Lane (opp. cricket club)
☎ (01642) 484302
11 (12 Sat)-11; 12-5, 7-10.30 Sun
John Smith's Magnet Ⓗ
Well-established estate pub, hosting regular live music and quiz nights. Pool and

darts played in the bar.
Q ❀ ⊞ ≉ ♣ P ⊟

MARTON IN CLEVELAND

Rudds Arms
Stokesley Road (200 yds N of A174/A172 jct)
☎ (01642) 315262
11-11; 12-10.30 Sun
Boddingtons Bitter; Flowers Original; Marston's Pedigree; guest beers Ⓗ
Spacious, open-plan pub, close to the Captain Cook Museum; a very lively meeting place. Foresters Feast menu is available 12-6.30. Entertainment is staged most eves. ◖ ≉ P

MASHAM

Black Sheep Brewery Visitors Centre (Bistro)
Wellgarth
☎ (01765) 689227 or 680101
11-11 (6 Mon); closed Tue in Jan & Feb; 12-6 Sun
Black Sheep Best Bitter, Special, Riggwelter, Yorkshire Square Ale Ⓗ
Large, open-plan bistro with a balcony next to the brewery in a former maltings. A gift shop is also included in the complex where regular daytime tours of the brewery commence. Eve meals Tue-Sat. ❀ ◖❙ ⧖ P

MIDDLEHAM

White Swan
Market Place
☎ (01969) 622093
12-3, 6.30-11; 12-11 Sat; 12-10.30 Sun
Black Sheep Best Bitter, Special; Hambleton Bitter; John Smith's Bitter; guest beers Ⓗ
Inn with a Georgian frontage on the cobbled market place near Richard III's castle. A comfortable stone-flagged bar is complemented by sensitively decorated restaurants serving an imaginative menu of excellent food.
♨ Q ❀ ⊨ ◖❙ ♣ ⊟

MIDDLESBROUGH

Doctor Browns
135 Corporation Road (1/4 mile E of town hall)
☎ (01642) 213213
11.30-11; 12-10.30 Sun
Draught Bass; guest beers Ⓗ
Large, comfortable pub hosting live music Fri and Sat and a quiz Mon. The closest city-centre pub to the football ground, it gets busy on match days.
❀ ◖❙ ⧖ ≉

Hogshead
14 Corporation Road
☎ (01642) 219320

11-11 (opens at 10 Mon-Sat for breakfast); 12-10.30 Sun
Boddingtons Bitter; Wadworth 6X; Ⓗ **guest beers** Ⓗ/Ⓖ
Typical Hogshead pub, popular with office workers and shoppers. Several bottled Belgian beers are available, and the pub holds regular beer festivals. Outside drinking is permitted in the pedestrianised area by the pub. Q ❀ ◖❙ ⧖ ≉ ⟳ ⧖

Isaac Wilson
61 Wilson Street
☎ (01642) 247708
11-11; 12-10.30 Sun
Courage Directors; Theakston Best Bitter; Worthington Bitter; guest beers Ⓗ
Wetherspoon's pub, converted from former county court premises, comfortably furnished with lots of cosy corners. This popular pub gets very busy at weekends. Q ◖❙ ≉ ⧖

Star & Garter
14 Southfield Road
☎ (01642) 245307
11-11; 12-10.30 Sun
Beer range varies Ⓗ
Large pub opposite the University, a former CAMRA *Pub Preservation Award* winner; the licensee also holds several S&N *Cellarmanship* awards. Meals available 11-9; no-smoking area designated for lunchtime only.
Q ❀ ◖❙ ⊞ ≉ P ⧖

MOORSHOLM

Jolly Sailor Inn
On A171, 3/4 mile E of Moorsholm jct
☎ (01287) 660270
11-11; 12-.10.30 Sun
Black Sheep Best Bitter; John Smith's Magnet; guest beers (summer) Ⓗ
Former coaching inn on the main moors road to Whitby. Low beamed ceilings feature in the bar/lounge, and restaurant. Regular live entertainment and special sizzling steak nights are added attractions. ♨ ❀ ◖❙ P

MUKER

Farmers Arms
On B6270 ☎ (01748) 886297
11-3 (extended summer), 7-11; 12-3, 7-10.30 Sun
Castle Eden Nimmos XXXX; John Smith's Bitter; Theakston Best Bitter, Old Peculier Ⓗ
Nice pub for a quiet pint, used by locals of this Dales village, also liked by walkers and daytrippers. Central heating makes the large single room, with its nooks and snug, comfortable on

cold days, the large stone flags on the floor are impressive. Good value pub grub. ⚨ Q ⅏ ❀ ◖▶ ⚓ ♣ P

NEWHOLM

Olde Beehive Inne
Off A171, 2 miles W of Whitby ☎ (01947) 602703
11.30-3, 7-11; 12-3, 7-10.30 Sun
John Smith's Magnet; Theakston Old Peculier; guest beers Ⓗ
Originally a drovers' inn, this authentic beamed village pub is full of character. Note the pub sign written in verse. Good food.
⚨ Q ❀ ◖▶ ♣ P ⅍

NEWTON-ON-OUSE

Blacksmith's Arms
Cherry Tree Ave (head for RAF Linton, 3 miles off A19) ☎ (01347) 848249
12-3 (not Mon-Thu), 5.30-11, 12-11 Sat; 12-10.30 Sun
Banks's Bitter; Camerons Bitter, Strongarm; guest beer Ⓗ
Homely, attractive two-bar village pub popular with anglers. The games room has a pool table and Sky TV. A resident Italian chef produces, pasta, pizzas, steaks and specialities.
⚨ Q ❀ ⇔ ◖▶ ♣ P ⊟

NORTH COWTON

Blacksmith's Arms
Myton Terrace ☎ (01325) 378310
12-3 (not Mon-Fri), 7 -11; 12-3, 7-10.30 Sun
Black Sheep Best Bitter; guest beers Ⓗ
Busy, welcoming pub, with a linked lounge and restaurant, where the emphasis is on meals. Guest beers come from local independent breweries. ⚨ ❀ ◖▶ P

Try also: Arden Arms, Atley Hill (Free)

NORTH DUFFIELD

Kings Arms
Main Street (off A163) ☎ (01757) 288492
4 (12 Sat)-11; 12-10.30 Sun
Black Sheep Best Bitter; Hambleton Stallion; John Smith's Bitter; Taylor Landlord; guest beers Ⓗ
Village pub with an outside play area overlooking the green and duck pond. The friendly landlord offers one of the best selections of real ale in the area. Meals Wed-Sat eve and weekend lunch. ⚨ Q ❀ ◖▶ ♣ P ⅍

NORTHALLERTON

Tanner Hop
2a Friarage Street (off High St towards hospital) ☎ (01609) 778482
7-11 (midnight Thu, 1am Fri); 2-1am Sat; 12-10.30 Sun
Courage Directors; Hambleton Bitter; John Smith's Bitter; guest beers Ⓗ
Busy bar with a wooden floor, enamel signs and paraphernalia, echoing the age of the dance hall from which it was converted. It holds a late music licence. It stocks Belgian fruit beers and stages beer festivals. Cider occasionally available.
▶ ⅃ ♣ ⌂

NOSTERFIELD

Freemasons Arms
On B6267 ☎ (01677) 470548
12-3, 6-11 (closed Mon); 12-3, 7-10.30 Sun
Black Sheep Best Bitter; Taylor Landlord; Tetley Bitter; Theakston Best Bitter; guest beer (occasional) Ⓗ
Excellent roadside country inn, adorned with fascinating military and biking memorabilia. The flagstoned bar area has a cosy open fire. It can get very busy as it is popular for its quality meals. ⚨ ◖▶ P ⊟

NUN MONKTON

Alice Hawthorn
The Green (off A59, York-Harrogate road) ☎ (01423) 330303
12-2, 6-11; 12-10.30 Sun
Camerons Bitter; Marston's Pedigree; Tetley Bitter; guest beers Ⓗ
Cosy country pub offering an excellent range of home-cooked food. Drink with a view of the maypole and duck pond in summer, or huddle round a log fire in winter. The children's play garden is a new attraction. ⚨ ❀ ◖▶ ⚓ ♣ P

OSWALDKIRK

Malt Shovel
OS623790 ☎ (01439) 788461
12-2.30, 6.30-11; 12-3, 7-10.30 Sun
Samuel Smith OBB Ⓗ
Historic, multi-roomed pub built around 1610 as the manor house. Full of character, it boasts much period furniture and welcoming log fires in winter. ⚨ ❀ ◖▶ P

PICKERING

White Swan
Market Place ☎ (01751) 472288
11 (opens 10 for coffee)-3, 6-11; 11-11 Mon & Sat; 12-3, 7-10.30 Sun
Black Sheep Best Bitter, Special; guest beer Ⓗ
Family-run inn with a buzzing, relaxed and informal atmosphere, and friendly, helpful staff who combine a passion for real ale and fine wine with great food. Guest rooms and suites go beyond expectations but are affordably priced. Cider in summer. ⚨ Q ⅏ ❀ ◖▶ ⚓ ⇌ (NYMR)♣ ⌂ P ⅍

PICKHILL

Nags Head
☎ (01845) 567391
11-11; 12-10.30 Sun
Black Sheep Best Bitter; Hambleton Bitter; John Smith's Bitter; Theakston Black Bull; guest beer (occasional) Ⓗ
Friendly village pub that also provides quality accommodation and excellent food, including both vegetarian and game dishes. The stone-flagged bar is separate from the carpeted lounge and has a policy of excluding children after 7.30.
⚨ ❀ ⇔ ◖▶ ⊞ ♣ P

POOL IN WHARFEDALE

Hunters Inn
Harrogate Road (A658) ☎ (0113) 284 1090
11-11; 12-10.30 Sun
Tetley Bitter; Theakston Best Bitter; guest beers Ⓗ
Single room pub, attracting a mixed clientele. A pool table and juke box are at the opposite end to the fireplace. The meals represent good choice and value; nine ales always available.
⚨ ❀ ◖ ♣ P

PORT MULGRAVE

Ship
Rosedale Lane ☎ (01947) 840303
11-11; 12-4, 7-10.30 Sun
John Smith's Magnet; Theakston Black Bull; guest beers Ⓗ
Near the high cliffs and close to the Cleveland Way, this pub bears a nautical theme and enjoys strong local patronage.
⚨ Q ⅏ ❀ ⇔ ◖▶ ⚓ ♣ P

REETH

Kings Arms
High Row (B6270) ☎ (01748) 884259
11-11; 12-10.30 Sun
Black Sheep Best Bitter; John Smith's Bitter; Taylor Landlord; Theakston Old Peculier or Black Sheep Riggwelter Ⓗ
Locals know it as the 'Middle House'. A date stone above the front door testifies to 1734. The large L-shaped bar features an inglenook and

good views down the valley. Good food and accommodation.
🏨 🍴 ⌂ ◖ ▶ Å ♣ ⊞

RICHMOND

Holly Hill Inn
Sleegill (Hudswell road)
☎ (01748) 822192
12-11; 12-10.30 Sun
Black Sheep Best Bitter; Theakston Best Bitter; Taylor Landlord Ⓗ
Warm, cheerful, two-level bar, well-used by locals, with comfortable large bench seats and solid tables. The lounge is next to the new restaurant; also excellent bar food menu and service. Accommodation should be ready by Nov 2000. 🏨 🛏 🍴 ⌂ ◖ ▶ ♣ P ⊞

Try also: **Black Lion**, Finkle St (Pubmaster)

RIPON

Golden Lion
69 Allhallowgate
☎ (01765) 602598
11-3, 7-11 (11-11 summer); 12-3, 7-10.30 Sun
Black Sheep Best Bitter; Hambleton Goldfield; John Smith's Bitter; Theakston Best Bitter; guest beer Ⓗ
Spacious, L-shaped bar, sub-divided into smaller areas, one of which is a restaurant (no meals Sun eve). Naval memorabilia is displayed.
◖ ▶ ♣

One-Eyed Rat
51 Allhallowgate
☎ (01765) 607704
12-3 (4 Sat), 6 (5.30 Fri)-11; 12-3, 7-10.30 Sun
Black Sheep Best Bitter; Taylor Landlord; guest beers Ⓗ
Traditional, popular pub without TV or juke box, close to the city centre, stocking a selection of German bottled beers plus Biddenden cider. Bar billiards played.
🏨 Q 🍴 ♣ ⌣

Wheatsheaf
Harrogate Road (A61)
☎ (01765) 602410
12-3 (not Mon), 7-11; 12-3, 7-10.30 Sun
Tetley Bitter; guest beer Ⓗ
Friendly, old, two-roomed pub on the outskirts of Ripon. 🏨 Q 🍴 ♣ P

ROBIN HOOD'S BAY

Victoria Hotel
Station Road (opp. car park)
☎ (01947) 880205
12-3, 6.30-11; 12-11 Fri, Sat & summer; 12-10.30 Sun
Camerons Bitter, Strongarm; guest beers Ⓗ
Large hotel, built in 1897 on a clifftop overlooking the bay

and village, where all pubs sell real ale. Note the super pumpclip collection derived from guest ales. Cleveland CAMRA *Pub of the Year* 1999.
🏨 Q 🛏 🍴 ⌂ ◖ ▶ ♣ ✂

RUFFORTH

Tankard Inn
Main Street (B1224, 4 miles W of York)
☎ (01904) 738621
11.30-3, 6-11; 11.30-11 Sat; 12-4, 7-10.30 Sun
Samuel Smith OBB Ⓗ
1930s pub retaining some original features; two rooms both have quarter-circle bars, open fires and bench seating. This village pub is well regarded for recreational activities (indoor and out). Large garden. No food Sun eve or Mon. 🏨 🍴 ◖ ▶ ⊞ ♣ P

SALTBURN

Saltburn Cricket, Bowls and Tennis Club
Marske Mill Lane (next to Saltburn Sports Centre)
☎ (01287) 622761
8 (6 summer Sat)-11; 6-11 (12-3, 8-11 winter) Sun
Tetley Bitter; guest beers Ⓗ
Private sports club with its own cricket, bowls and tennis teams; it stays open all day on match days. It consists of a lounge and games room (pool and darts played). The friendly regulars make casual visitors welcome. 🍴 Å ⇌ ♣ P ⊟

Victoria
Dundas Street (near station)
☎ (01287) 624637
11-3, 7-11; 11-11 Sat; 12-10.30 Sun
Black Sheep Special; Ind Coope Burton Ale; John Smith's Magnet; Tetley Bitter; guest beer Ⓗ
The only true pub in a Victorian Quaker town. It has a bar, lounge, and upstairs function room hosting live music Thu and Sun. It can get quite lively weekends and during holiday seasons. No food Mon. ◖ ⊞ Å ⇌ ♣

SANDHUTTON

Kings Arms
On A167
☎ (01845) 587263
12-2.30 (4 Sat, may vary), 6.30-11; 12-4, 6.30-10.30 Sun
John Smith's Bitter; Taylor Landlord; Theakston Best Bitter; Village White Boar Ⓗ
An attractive floral exterior invites you into a warm, comfortable and friendly pub. Restaurant meals, bar meals and snacks always available except Mon.
🏨 Q 🍴 🛏 ◖ ▶ ⊞ Å ♣ P

SAWDON

Anvil Inn
Main Street (off A170)
☎ (01723) 859896
11-11; 12-10.30 Sun
Theakston Best Bitter; guest beers Ⓗ
Friendly, restored blacksmith's shop with a dining area, serving excellent value meals; well worth a detour.
🏨 Q 🛏 🍴 🛏 ◖ ▶ Å ♣ P

SAXTON

Greyhound ☆
Main Street
☎ (01937) 557202
11.30-3, 5.30-11, 11-11 Sat; 12-10.30 Sun
Samuel Smith OBB Ⓗ
Attractive, three-roomed, 13th-century village pub, next to the church. Grade II listed, the tiny cosy bar features a flagged floor. An extensive colourful plate collection decorates the walls throughout. Popular with locals. Enjoy drinks outside in summer surrounded by climbing roses and plants.
🏨 Q 🍴 ♣

SCARBOROUGH

Cellars
35-37 Valley Road
☎ (01723) 367158
7 (11 summer)-11; 12-3, 7-10.30 Sun
Tetley Bitter; guest beers Ⓗ
Local family pub in the cellar of an elegant Victorian building which has been converted to self-contained holiday apartments and a restaurant.
🍴 🛏 ◖ ▶ Å ⇌ P

Highlander
Esplanade (South Cliff)
☎ (01723) 365627
11-11; 12-10.30 Sun
Tetley Bitter; Younger IPA; guest beers Ⓗ
Busy, one-roomed pub with a patio at the front overlooking South Bay. It boasts an extensive range of malt whiskies, plus a showman's steam engine. The WM Clark Mild is brewed by Clarks of Wakefield.
🏨 🍴 🛏 ◖ ⌂ ♿ Å ⇌ ⊟

Hole in the Wall
26-32 Vernon Road
☎ (01723) 373746
11.30-2.30 (3 Sat), 7-11; 12-3, 7-10.30 Sun
Durham seasonal beers; Fuller's ESB; Shepherd Neame Master Brew Bitter; guest beers Ⓗ
Busy, friendly conversational pub near the town centre and spa complex. Vegetarian meals available. Winner of many local CAMRA *Pub of the*

Year awards and *Good Pub Food* guide recommended, it has been in this *Guide* for 17 consecutive years.
Q ✦ ▲ ≉ ♣ ⌂

Indigo Alley
4 North Marine Road
☎ (01723) 381900
12-11; 12-10.30 Sun
Taylor Landlord; guest beers Ⓗ
Lively pub, situated between North Bay and the town centre. It offers six ales and Belgian Leffe beer on draught. Live music is performed – four sessions a week. Local CAMRA *Town Pub of the Year* 1999. ≉

Jolly Roger
27-29 Eastborough
☎ (01723) 351426
12-11; 12-10.30 Sun
Banks's Bitter; Camerons Strongarm; guest beer Ⓗ
Large, attractive one-roomed pub, a popular live music venue. Close to the sea front, its decor is based on a nautical theme. Excellent food is served during the tourist season. A resident ghost and smugglers' tunnel add interest. ⅋ ⇔ ◖ ≉ ♣

Old Scalby Mills Hotel
Scalby Mills Road (by Sea Life Centre)
☎ (01723) 500449
11-11; 12-10.30 Sun
Daleside Old Lubrication, Monkey Wrench; guest beers Ⓗ
Historic 500-year-old building (formerly a watermill) on the Cleveland Way, enjoying views across the bay. Busy in summer. Children's certificate.
Q ⊛ ◖ ⅃ ▲ ♣

Scarborough Arms
1 North Terrace
☎ (01723) 373575
11-11; 12-10.30 Sun
Marston's Pedigree; John Smith's Bitter, Magnet; guest beer Ⓗ
Popular pub, just off the town centre, offering a welcoming atmosphere and excellent value food (eve meals until 8pm).
⊛ ◖ ⅃ ♣ ⊟

Spa
45 Victoria Road
☎ (01723) 372907
11-3, 5-11; 11-11 Fri & Sat; 12-3, 7-10.30 Sun
Black Sheep Special; Tetley Bitter Ⓗ
Traditional, friendly pub catering for all ages and highly rated for pub games. Toasted sandwiches available lunchtimes. ≉ ♣

Tap 'n' Spile
28 Falsgrave Road
☎ (01723) 363837

11-11; 12-10.30 Sun
Everards Tiger; Big Lamp Bitter; Theakston Old Peculier; guest beers Ⓗ
Busy old coaching inn, sympathetically renovated and displaying local memorabilia: three rooms including a no-smoking family lounge and large patio. Excellent value home-cooked food; eve meals served 5-7.
Q ⊛ ◖ ▲ ≉ ⌂ P ⅃

Try also: Alma Inn, Alma Parade (S&N); **Golden Ball**, Sandside (Samuel Smith)

SKIPTON

Narrow Boat
38 Victoria Street (narrow alleyway off Coach St, near canal bridge)
☎ (01756) 797922
12 (11 summer)-11; 12-10.30 Sun
Caledonian Deuchars IPA; Taylor Landlord; guest beers Ⓗ
Excellent, friendly, free house with a no-smoking main bar and a smokers' gallery above. No muzak or machines disturb the conversation. Six rotating guest beers (including a mild) from Northern independents are stocked, alongside foreign bottled beers. Q ⊛ ◖ ≉ ♣ ⅃

Railway
13-15 Carleton Street (opp. Tesco's)
☎ (01756) 793186
11-11; 12-10.30 Sun
Tetley Mild, Bitter; guest beers Ⓗ
Friendly, street-corner local with a traditional, two-roomed layout. The tap room has railway-themed decor and is popular with domino players; the lounge has been recently refurbished. Two guest beers from Tapster's Choice range usually available. ⊟ & ♣

Try also: Albion, Otley St (Punch Taverns)

SNAPE

Castle Arms Inn
☎ (01677) 470270
11-11; 12-10.30 Sun
Black Sheep Best Bitter; Hambleton Bitter; John Smith's Bitter; Taylor Landlord or guest beer Ⓗ
Traditional pub and restaurant in a very pretty village that boasts a fine avenue and arboretum. Note the freestanding inglenook. Quoits played.
⇔ Q ⇔ ◖ ⅃ & ▲ ♣ P

SPOFFORTH

King William IV
Church Hill

☎ (01937) 590293
12-3 (not Mon), 5.30-11; 12-11 Sat; 12-10.30 Sun
John Smith's Bitter; Tetley Bitter; guest beers Ⓗ
Small, friendly, local away from the main road. The cosy beamed tap room is used for darts and dominoes; village bingo is held once a week in the lounge. It has a reputation for good food (not served Mon).
⇔ Q ⊛ ◖ ⅃ & ♣ P

STAITHES

Captain Cook
60 Staithes Lane
☎ (01947) 840200
11-11; 12-10.30 Sun
John Smith's Bitter; Magnet; guest beers Ⓗ
Impressive bank-top pub named after the famous seafarer whose apprenticeship was spent in the village. Guest beers are usually from East Midlands or Lincolnshire micros and often feature beer styles not usually found in this area. Children welcome in the games room. Limited parking.
⇔ Q ⊛ ⇔ ◖ ⅃ & ▲ P ⊟

Cod & Lobster
Slip End ☎ (01947) 840295
12-11; 12-10.30 Sun
Camerons Bitter, Strongarm; Ind Coope Burton Ale Ⓗ
Pub by the harbour that has links with Captain Cook; its long bar displays nautical relics. Note: no vehicular access, use the hilltop car park. ⇔ ⊛ ◖ ♣

STOKESLEY

Spread Eagle
39 High Street (close to Town Hall)
☎ (01642) 710278
11-11; 12-10.30 Sun
Banks's Original; Camerons Strongarm; Marston's Pedigree Ⓗ
Small, unspoilt, town-centre local with a garden leading to the river. Excellent home-cooked food is served all day – good value and popular so book at peak times. In the front room, only the real fire is allowed to smoke.
⇔ Q ⊛ ◖ ⅃ & ⅃ ⊟

White Swan
1 West End
☎ (01642) 710263
11.30-3, 5.30 (7 Sat)-11 (11.30-11 summer Fri & Sat); 12-3, 7-10.30 (12-10.30 summer) Sun
Castle Eden Ale; Daleside Crackshot; Captain Cook Slipway; guest beers Ⓗ
Traditional local with its own brewery which also supplies the guest beer; a recent local

CAMRA *Pub of the Year* and *Perfect Ploughman's* award-winner. Great Yorkshire beer festival is held every Easter to support local independent breweries. No juke box, but some unusual pub games.
⛫ Q ♣ ⚟ ⊓

TADCASTER

Angel & White Horse
Bridge Street
☎ (01937) 835470
11-3.30, 5-11; 12-3.30, 7-10.30 Sun
Samuel Smith OBB Ⓗ
Samuel Smith's brewery tap overlooking the famous brewery shire horse stables. The large open-plan bar features oak panelling and a real fire. ⛫ ❀ ☾ ♣

Try also: Howden Arms, High St (Samuel Smith)

THIRSK

Golden Fleece Hotel
42 Market Place
☎ (01845) 523108
11-3, 6-11; 12-3, 7-10.30 Sun
Hambleton Bitter, Goldfield, Stud Ⓗ
Imposing Georgian hotel overlooking the market place. The quiet, comfortable carpeted bar bears a horse racing theme (Thirsk races). A wide range of food, to suit most tastes and pockets, is available daily in the restaurant. ⛫ Q ⛾ ◗ ⛺ ≠ P

THIXENDALE

Cross Keys
☎ (01377) 288272
12-3, 6-11; 12-3, 7-10.30 Sun
Jennings Bitter; Tetley Bitter; guest beer Ⓗ
Unspoilt, welcoming one-roomed gem nestling at a junction of valleys in the Yorkshire Wolds, popular with walkers and locals alike. Children welcome in the garden. ⛫ ❀ ☾ ◗ ⛺ ♣

THORGANBY

Ferryboat Inn
1 mile NE of Thorganby, at end of lane leading to River Derwent OS697426
☎ (01904) 448224
12-3, 7-11 (hours extended summer weekends); 12-3, 7-10.30 Sun
Old Mill Bitter; guest beer Ⓗ
Quiet pub along a narrow country lane just outside the village; a friendly bar and a new family room. The large garden which runs down to the River Derwent is pretty.
⛫ Q ⛮ ❀ ♿ ⛺ P ⊓

THORNTON WATLASS

Buck Inn
On village green
☎ (01677) 422461
11-3, 5.30-11; 11-11 Sat; 12-10.30 Sun
Black Sheep Best Bitter; John Smith's Bitter; Tetley Bitter; Theakston Best Bitter; guest beer Ⓗ
Attractive pub on the village green: a cosy bar and dining room serving excellent food. Occasional jazz and other music performed. Quoits played.
⛫ ⛮ ❀ ⛾ ☾ ◗ ⊟ ♿ ♣ P ⚟

THORNTON-IN-LONSDALE

Marton Arms
1/4 mile N of A65/A687 jct
☎ (015242) 41281
12-3 (not winter Mon-Thu), 7-11; 12-11 Fri & Sat; 12-10.30 Sun
Beer range varies Ⓗ
Pre-turnpike coaching inn, dated 1679, with a large, comfortable, oak-beamed lounge, a ten-minute walk from the start of the Waterfalls Walk. Eight ever-changing guest beers, plus Weston's Old Rosie cider.
⛫ ❀ ⛾ ☾ ◗ ⛺ ♣ ⌓ P

THRINTOFT

New Inn
☎ (01609) 777060
12-3, 7-11; closed Mon; 12-3, 7-11 Sun
Black Sheep Special; Fuller's London Pride; Worthington Bitter; guest beer Ⓗ
New in name only (built 1776), this relaxed village pub has a good and growing reputation for both beer and food. ⛫ ❀ ☾ ◗ ♣ P

TOCKWITH

Spotted Ox
Westfield Road (off B1224)
☎ (01423) 358387
11-3, 5.30-11; 11-11 Fri & Sat; 12-10.30 Sun
Tetley Bitter; guest beers Ⓗ
Community-focused village local enjoying a good reputation for its extensive menu of almost entirely home-cooked food and daily specials, complemented by the widest range of guest ales for miles around. Eve meals served 6-8.45 (8.30 Sun).
❀ ☾ ◗ ⊟ ♣ P

TOPCLIFFE

Swan
Front Street
☎ (01845) 577207
12-3 (later summer Sat), 7-11; 12-3 (later summer), 7-10.30 Sun
Marston's Pedigree; John Smith's Bitter Ⓗ
Traditional village local of two rooms with a central servery. Try the bar game, 'Baiting the Bull'. ⛫ ♣ P ⚟

ULLESKELF

Ulleskelf Arms
Church Fenton Lane
☎ (01937) 531508
6 (11 Sat)-11; 12-10.30 Sun
Black Sheep Best Bitter; John Smith's Bitter; guest beers Ⓗ
Formerly the Railway Hotel, its garden gives access to the station. Licences to fish in the nearby River Wharfe are on sale here. Accommodation is no longer available. Lunches served weekends.
Q ❀ ◗ ≠ ♣ P

UPPER POPPLETON

Lord Collingwood
The Green (off A59, York-Harrogate road)
☎ (01904) 794388
12 (11 summer)-3, 5.30-11; 12-3, 7-10.30 Sun
Mansfield Riding Bitter, Ⓗ
Attractive village pub overlooking the green. 'Olde-Worlde' in style, it has a single pleasant, L-shaped bar. Popular with local commuters and regulars from the greater York area. No eve meals Sun. ⛫ ❀ ☾ ◗ ≠ ♣ P

WASS

Wombwell Arms
OS555793
☎ (01347) 868280
12-2.30, 7-11; closed Mon; 12-3, 7-10.30 (not winter eve) Sun
Black Sheep Best Bitter; Taylor Landlord; guest beer Ⓗ
Warm, welcoming village inn: a small cosy bar and a good choice of rooms for eating. It hosts occasional live music supper eves.
⛫ Q ⛮ ❀ ⛾ ☾ ◗ ♣ P

WEAVERTHORPE

Star Inn
Turn off A64 at Sherburn traffic lights
☎ (01944) 738273
12-4 (not Mon-Fri), 7-11; 12-4, 7-10.30 Sun
Camerons Bitter; Tetley Bitter; guest beers Ⓗ
This family-owned village inn offers excellent food, freshly prepared on the premises, including a traditional Sun lunch, plus comfortable accommodation. Northern regional beers are featured. No meals Tue eve; late supper licence other eves; lunch also served Sat.
⛫ Q ❀ ⛾ ◗ ⛺ ♣ P ⚟

WELBURY

Duke of Wellington
☎ (01609) 882464
12-3 (not Mon or Tue), 7-11; 12-10.30 Sun
John Smith's Bitter, Magnet; guest

beer H
Busy village pub with a
linked lounge, bar and
restaurant where a mix of
locals and diners makes for
friendly atmosphere.
🏚 ❀ ◑ ♣ P

Try also: Cat & Bagpipes,
East Harlsey (Free)

WEST AYTON
Olde Forge Valley Inn
5 Pickering Road (A170)
☎ (01723) 862146
11.30-11; 12-10.30 Sun
**Camerons Bitter; Tetley Bitter;
guest beer** H
300-year-old coaching inn,
comprising a wood-panelled
lounge bar, a locals' bar and a
restaurant. Popular with
visitors to the North York
Moors national park.
🏚 Q ❧ ❀ 🛏 ◑ ▲ ♣ P

WHITBY
Duke of York
Church Street (at foot of 199
steps to the Abbey)
☎ (01947) 600324
11-11; 12-10.30 Sun
**Black Dog Special; Courage
Directors; John Smith's Bitter; guest
beer** (summer) H
Busy, unspoilt pub with
traditional decor and fine
views of the harbour. Popular
in Folk Week, it is a rare local
outlet for Whitby's Black Dog
Brewery beers (also available
at Henry's Bar). Meals served
all day (12-10). 🛏 ◑ ♿ ⇌

Little Angel
18 Flowergate
☎ (01947) 602514
11-11; 12-10.30 Sun
Tetley Bitter; guest beers H
Grade II listed building,
featuring a 14th-century
internal window. ◑ ❧ ⇌ ♣

Tap 'n' Spile
New Quay Road (opp. bus
and rail stations)
☎ (01947) 603937
12 (11 summer)-11; 12-4, 7-10.30 (12-
10.30 summer) Sun
**Tap & Spile Premium; guest
beers** H
Friendly, three-roomed red
brick pub formerly the Cutty
Sark. It hosts live music four
nights a week and is a mecca
for folk week and the Moor
and Coast weekend. Six guest
beers and two real ciders on
tap. Q ❧ ◑ ⇌ ♣ ◔ ⤧

Try also: Henry's Bar
(Metropole Hotel), West Cliff
(Free)

WIGHILL
White Swan
Main Street

☎ (01937) 832217
12-2.30, 5 (6 Sat)-11; 12-3, 7-10.30
Sun
**Draught Bass; John Smith's Bitter;
Tetley Bitter; Theakston Best
Bitter** H
Small, traditional village pub,
with a coaching inn history.
A passage, separate bars and a
dining room give a homely
atmosphere. The home-made
menu includes special offers
for early eve diners (check
times). 🏚 Q ❧ ❀ ◑ ⤸ P

YORK
Ackhorne
St Martins Lane
☎ (01904) 671421
12-11; 12-10.30 Sun
**Black Sheep Best Bitter; Rooster's
Yankee; guest beers** H
Excellent two-roomed oasis
just off the famous
Micklegate. An interesting
beer range includes three
ever-varying guests. A
friendly welcome for locals
and tourists alike. Eve meals
served Tue-Fri. Q ❀ ◑ ⇌ ♣

Blue Bell ☆
53 Fossgate
☎ (01904) 654904
12-11; 12-10.30 Sun
**Camerons Strongarm; Greene King
Abbot; Marston's Pedigree; Tetley
Bitter; guest beers** H
Smashing little pub with the
last perfectly-surviving
Edwardian interior in York. A
warm welcome is assured in
both small rooms, so be
prepared to linger and savour
the atmosphere. ⤸ ♣ ⊞

Maltings
Tanners Moat (below Lendal
Bridge)
☎ (01904) 655387
11-11; 12-10.30 Sun
**Black Sheep Best Bitter; guest
beers** H
Nationally renowned and a
regular award winner –
including York CAMRA's *Pub
of the Year* 2000. A true free
house and firm champion of
micro-breweries who supply
the six guest beers. Great
value food (served until 4 at
weekends). ◑ ⇌ ♣ ◔

Masons Arms
6 Fishergate
☎ (01904) 646046
11-11; 12-10.30 Sun
John Smith's Bitter; guest beers H
Classic example of 'Brewers'
Tudor' architecture,
sympathetically maintained
and refurbished. The oak
panelling and fireplace came
from York Castle. Is this the
only pub in Britain with a
collection of blowlamps?
Formidable reputation for its
food, served 12-9.30 every
day. ❀ 🛏 ◑ ⤸ P

Minster Inn
24 Marygate (behind the
Museum gardens)
☎ (01904) 624499
11.30-11; 12-10.30 Sun
**Black Sheep Best Bitter; John
Smith's Bitter; guest beers** H
Multi-roomed Edwardian
local: three rooms and a bar
off a central corridor.
Friendly service and
welcoming locals who take
part in a regular programme
of activities and trips. Sited
just outside the old Abbey
walls, this is a comfortable
place for a quick drink or a
long stay with friends.
Q ❀ ⇌ ♣ ⤧

Royal Oak
18 Goodramgate
☎ (01904) 653856
11-11; 12-10.30 Sun
**Ind Coope Burton Ale; Tetley Bitter;
guest beers** H
Small, stylish town pub
comprising three welcoming
rooms off a staggered
corridor. The 'Tudor' look
comes from a revamp by
then owners John J Hunt in
1934. It enjoys a very good
reputation for its food (the
bread is home-baked) which
is served from 11 (12 Sun)-8.
Q ❧ ◑ ⇌ ⤧

Saddle Inn
Main Street, Fulford
☎ (01904) 633317
12-3, 6.30-11; 12-11 Sat; 12-4,
7-10.30 Sun
Banks's Bitter; Camerons Bitter H
Attractive, friendly suburban
local with a tiled entrance
hall, a single L-shaped bar
and a dining area. The
garden has recently been
augmented with four
pétanque terrains – the only
ones in York. No food Mon.
🏚 ❧ ❀ 🛏 ◑ ♿ ♣ P ⬚

Swan Inn
16 Bishopgate Street
☎ (01904) 634968
4 (12 Thu-Sat)-11; 12-10.30 Sun
**Flowers Original; Greene King Abbot;
Taylor Landlord; guest beer** H
Classic, street-corner local,
one of the few pubs in the
York area with a 'West
Riding' layout – a drinking
lobby, plus two self-
contained adjacent rooms
with serveries from the main
bar. This Tetley's Heritage
Inn has a lively atmosphere,
maintained by the hosts, staff
and regulars. 🏚 ❀ ⇌ ♣

Tap 'n' Spile
29 Monkgate
☎ (01904) 656158
11.30-11; 12-10.30 Sun
**Black Sheep Best Bitter; Tap & Spile
Premium; guest beers** H
Imposing, Flemish-style,
19th-century building. The

large, wood-floored bar has a screened-off, raised darts/TV area at one end whilst a more intimate, carpeted lounge area has recently been created at the other. Guest beers often include the much sought-after Rooster range.
🏮 🍺 ♣ ⌂ P

Victoria
1 Heslington Road
☎ (01904) 622295
12-11; 12-10.30 Sun
Old Mill Mild, Bitter, Bullion, seasonal beers H
Large, street-corner pub revitalised by current owners, Old Mill. Essentially open-plan, the comfortable interior is broken up into distinct areas by partitions and pillars. Popular with both students and locals, food is served until 7 (4 Sun).
🏮 🛏 🍺 P

Wellington Inn
47 Alma Terrace
☎ (01904) 645642
11-3 (not Mon), 6-11; 11-5, 7-11 Sat; 12-4, 7-10.30 Sun
Samuel Smith OBB H
Classic, mid 19th-century, terraced local which was originally a beerhouse. The staggered central corridor gives access to a public bar, pool room and a small lounge, each with its own character. The convivial atmosphere makes this pub a pleasure to seek out.
🏚 Q 🛏 🏮 🍺 ♣

York Beer & Wine Shop
28 Sandringham Street (off A19/Fishergate)
☎ (01904) 647136
11 (6 Mon)-10; 6-10 Sun
Black Sheep Best Bitter; Taylor Landlord; guest beers H
Now more than 15 years old and still going strong, offering draught beer and cider to take out in any quantity, plus a large range of British and foreign bottle-conditioned beers. The wines, mouth-watering cheeses and ice-cream also on sale make this the only shop you ever need! ⌂

Yorkshire (South)

AUCKLEY

Eagle & Child
24 Main Street
☎ (01302) 770406
11.30-3, 5-11; 11.30-11 Sat; 12-4, 7-10.30 Sun
Barnsley Bitter; John Smith's Bitter; Theakston Best Bitter; guest beer H
Smart traditional rural pub (beams, plaster and brass abound), whose cosy feel is

fostered by welcoming hosts. A raised dining area serves both families and non-smokers. The guest beer is often from Darwin, but other small brewers also feature.
🏮 🍺 P ⚲

BARNBURGH

Coach & Horses
High Street
☎ (01709) 829306
12-4.30, 7.30-11; 12-3.30, 7-10.30 (12-10.30 summer) Sun
John Smith's Bitter H
Impressive white building overlooking the church: three rooms and a lobby in an unspoilt 1937 pub where glass, brass and polished wood abound, note the *Andy Capp* mural in the tap room.
Q 🏮 ♣ P

BARNBY DUN

Gateway
Station Road
☎ (01302) 882849
12-3 (not Mon), 5.45-11; 12-3, 6.45-10.30 Sun
Barnsley Bitter; John Smith's Bitter guest beers (occasional) H
Hotel, restaurant and bar on the main road into the village. The lounge bar has a friendly, comfortable atmosphere and bar meals are available at lunch time (not Mon). The restaurant is open in the evening (not Sun) and the meals are highly recommended.
🏮 🛏 🍺 🚻 ♣ P

BARNSLEY

Courthouse Station
24 Regent Street
☎ (01226) 779056
11-11; 12-10.30 Sun
Courage Directors; Tetley Bitter; Theakston Best Bitter; guest beers H
Very popular with all ages; the building was once home to the main railway station until 1960, and a court house before then. Information on local history fills the walls. No away fans, plastic glasses used on home match days.
Q 🏮 🍺 🚻 ⚟ (Interchange) ⚲ 🏢

Keresforth Hall
Keresforth Hall Road, Kingstone (800 yds off A6133 down narrow lane)
☎ (01226) 284226
11-2, 7-11; 12-3, 7-10.30 Sun
Beer range varies H
Open countryside views to the west and south are assets to this comfortably furnished main bar lounge with a dining room and a family conservatory. Rebuilt in the 1930s, the pub serves high

quality food and beers from micros. 🍺 🏮 🍺 ♿ P 🏢

Outpost
2 Union Street, Sheffield Road (near Alhambra roundabout on A61)
☎ (01226) 241274
12-4, 7-11; 12-10.30 Sun
Hardys & Hansons Best Bitter P
Two-roomed modern town pub: a comfy lounge with colonial green furnishings and bamboo-type chairs; the locals' tap room has a pool table and large screen TV, useful for soccer fans (home and away) on busy match days. Service is via a hatch in the corridor. Very good value Sun lunches served.
🏮 🚃 ⚟ (Interchange) ♣ P

BAWTRY

Turnpike
High Street
☎ (01302) 711960
11-11; 12-10.30 Sun
Ruddles Bitter, County; John Smith's Bitter H
A pub since 1986 with only one landlord, it stands opposite the market place and is a meeting place for Bawtry's restaurant-goers. Lots of wood panelling, glass and a flagstone floor round the bar add to its appeal. 🏮 🍺

BIRDWELL

Cock Inn
Pilley Hill (off A61)
☎ (01226) 742155
12-3, 7-11; 12-3, 7-11 Sun
Draught Bass; John Smith's Bitter
Popular village inn, stone built with a slate floor and displaying much brassware. No meals Sun eve.
🏚 🏮 🍺 P

BLAXTON

Blue Bell
Thorne Road
☎ (01302) 770424
12-2 (not Mon), 5-11.30 (11 Mon); 11-11 Sat; 12-10.30 Sun
John Smith's Bitter; guest beers H
Smart, airy roadside pub with a dining area serving home-cooked favourites at lunch, and a more varied choice eves. Two changing guest beers; John Smith's Magnet alternates on one pump.
🏚 🍺 ♣ P

BROOMHILL

Old Moor Tavern
Everilgate Road
☎ (01226) 755455
11-11; 12-10.30 Sun
John Smith's Bitter; Marston's Pedigree; guest beers H
Set in the middle of the Wetlands Project and handy

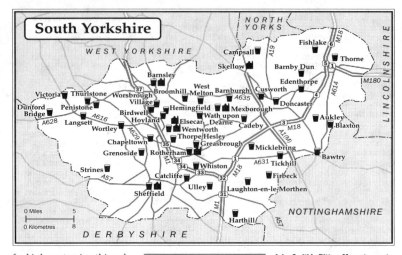

South Yorkshire

for bird sanctuaries, this pub enjoys an excellent reputation for its food.
Q ✿ ◖ ▮ & P

CADEBY
Cadeby Inn
Main Street
☎ (01709) 864009
11.30-11; 12-10.30 Sun
John Smith's Bitter; Samuel Smith OBB; Tetley Bitter; guest beers Ⓗ
Former farmhouse with a small stone-flagged bar, and a homely lounge featuring wood, stone and brass. Renowned for its carvery served in a smart room.
⇢ ✿ ◖ ▮ ♣ P ⚹

CAMPSALL
Old Bells
High Street ☎ (01302) 700423
11.30-3, 6-11; 12-3, 7-10.30 Sun
Black Sheep Best Bitter; John Smith's Bitter Ⓗ
At over 150 years old, this is the oldest pub in Doncaster Borough, comprising a lounge, a small smoke room, plus a tiny snug and two restaurants. It is situated in the old part of the village. Q ✿ ◖ ▮ ⊞ P

CATCLIFFE
Waverley
Brinsworth Road (B6067, 1 mile from M1 jct 33)
☎ (01709) 360906
12-4, 6-11; 11-11 Sat; 12-4, 7-10.30 Sun
Beer range varies Ⓗ
Large, modern, three-roomed genuine free house, featuring up to four ever-changing guest beers, including local micros, it has a large family room and outdoor play area; free children's entertainment Fri and Sat eves is a bonus for parents. ⇘ ✿ ◖ ⊞ & ♣ P

CHAPELTOWN
Commercial
107 Station Road
☎ (0114) 246 9066
12-3, 5.30-11; 12-11 Sat; 12-3, 7-10.30 Sun
Wentworth Venture, WPA, Oatmeal Stout; guest beers Ⓗ
Outstanding pub with something for everyone: good food, ale and cider; quiz nights and folk club; regular beer festivals. Three rooms include a no-smoking snug, and a games room.
Q ✿ ◖ ▮ & ▲ ⇌ ♣ ⌂ P ⚹ ⊟

Prince of Wales
80 Burncross Road
☎ (0114) 246 7725
11-3, 5.30-11; 11-11 Fri; 11-4, 6.30-11 Sat; 12-3, 7-10.30 Sun
John Smith's Bitter; Tetley Bitter; Theakston Best Bitter Ⓗ
Former Ward's pub with a cosy lounge and tap room with darts. A collection of owls above the bar betrays the landlord's football affiliation. Q ✿ ◖ ⇌ P

Wharncliffe Arms
365 Burncross Road
☎ (0114) 246 3807
3 (12 Fri & Sat)-11; 12-10.30 Sun
Boddingtons Bitter; Stones Bitter; guest beers Ⓗ
120-year-old cottage-style pub with a cosy atmosphere. Added attractions include games and quiz nights, home to animals and an aviary. Usually four guest beers on offer.
⇢ Q ✿ ⇌ ♣

CUSWORTH
Mallard
Cusworth Lane (from A638 N of Doncaster, take road to Cusworth Hall)
5 (12 Fri & Sat)-11; 12-10.30 Sun
John Smith's Bitter, Magnet; guest beer Ⓗ
1960s estate pub, popular with locals: a sport-oriented public bar; quiz held in the lounge Thu eve. A guest beer from a local independent brewery is often available.
✿ ⊞ & ▲ ♣ P

DONCASTER
Black Bull
Market Place
☎ (01302) 364309
11-11; 12-10.30 Sun
Barnsley Bitter, IPA; Boddingtons Bitter; John Smith's Bitter; Theakston Best Bitter Ⓗ
Large market pub, popular with traders and shoppers at lunchtime. Multiple TV screens show sport; disco/karaoke on Fri and Sat eves. ✿ ◖ ▮ & ⇌ ♣ ⚹

Leopard
1 West Street
☎ (01302) 363054
11-11; 12-10.30 Sun
Glentworth seasonal beers; John Smith's Bitter; guest beer Ⓗ
Lively, street-corner pub boasting a superb tiled exterior; inside, a large bar/games room, comfortable lounge and an upstairs room hosting regular rock and comedy gigs. Local CAMRA *Pub of the Year* 2000.
✿ ⇌ ♣ P

Masons Arms
Market Place
☎ (01302) 364391
11-4, 7.30-11; 10.30-11 Sat; 12-4.30, 7.30-10.30 Sun; hours may vary
Tetley Dark Mild, Bitter; Taylor Landlord Ⓗ
A perennial in this *Guide*, this traditional market pub is multi-roomed and has a spacious garden. The increased beer range has proved to be a big

attraction.

Q ⊛ ⊟ ⇌ ♣

Plough

8 West Laithe Gate

☎ (01302) 738310

11-11; 12-3, 7-10.30 Sun

Barnsley Bitter; Draught Bass; guest beer (occasional) Ⓗ

One of Doncaster's few unspoilt traditional pubs: a busy public bar, a comfortable lounge and a tiny garden. A locals' pub at the heart of the town.

⊛ ⊟ ⇌ ♣

Salutation

14 South Parade

☎ (01302) 340705

11-11, 12-10.30 Sun

Marston's Pedigree; Tetley Dark Mild, Bitter; guest beers Ⓗ

Still badged as a Tetley Festival Ale House, this former coaching inn is on the road to the racecourse and football ground. Meals served until 7 (4 Sun).

⚏ ⊛ ◖ ⇌ ♣ P

Tut 'n' Shive

West Laithe Gate

☎ (01302) 360300

11-11, 12-10.30 Sun

Black Sheep Best Bitter, Special, Riggwelter; Boddingtons Bitter; Marston's Pedigree; guest beers Ⓗ

With typical Tut 'n' Shive offbeat decor, this pub is popular with younger drinkers. A large screen TV shows sports and its hosts occasional live music. The cider (Addlestones) is served without gas pressure. ◖ ⌂

DUNFORD BRIDGE

Stanhope Arms Inn

☎ (01226) 763104

12.30-3 (not winter Mon), 7-11; 11-11 Sat; 12-10.30 Sun

Black Sheep Best Bitter; Taylor Landlord Ⓗ

Early 19th-century former shooting lodge, situated amidst the spectacular scenery of the Peak District national park, and alongside the Upper Don trail of the Transpennine Trail. Popular with bikers and ramblers. No food Mon. ⊛ ⇨ ◖ ⅅ ⅄ Ⓐ P

EDENTHORPE

Beverley Inn

117 Thorne Road

☎ (01302) 882724

12-3, 5 (6 Sat)-11; 12-3, 7-10.30 Sun

Barnsley Bitter; John Smith's Bitter; Theakston XB; guest beer Ⓗ

Smart hotel where the relaxed atmosphere attracts a mixed clientele, but mostly mature patrons. The emphasis is on good food and beer.

⊛ ⇨ ◖ ⅅ P

FIRBECK

Black Lion

9 New Road

☎ (01709) 812575

12-3.30, 5.30-11; 11-11 Sat; 12-3, 7-10.30 Sun

Barnsley Bitter; Stones Bitter; John Smith's Bitter, Magnet; guest beers Ⓗ

17th-century pub, reputedly haunted whose walls are adorned with photos of locals and celebrities; small snug area. This smart pub in a picturesque village is popular with walkers, offering an extensive menu of home-cooked food.

⚏ ⊛ ⇨ ◖ ⅅ ♣ P

FISHLAKE

Hare & Hounds

Church Street

☎ (01302) 841208

11-4, 7-11; 12-10.30 Sun

Mansfield Bitter; Marston's Pedigree Ⓗ

Traditional village local, with a small bar and a large lounge, close to an historic church and many footpaths for ramblers. Karaoke Sat and Sun eves. ⊛ ⊟ Ⓐ ♣ P

GREASBROUGH

Prince of Wales

9 Potter Hill

☎ (01709) 551358

11-4, 7-11; 12-3, 7-10.30 Sun

John Smith's Bitter; Ⓟ **guest beer** Ⓗ

Friendly corner local: a traditional tap room and comfortable lounge, renowned for its low-priced ever-changing guest beer. Outside drinking is on the pavement. ⊛ ⊟ ♣ ⊟

GRENOSIDE

Cow & Calf

88 Skew Hill Lane ($1/2$ mile from A61) ☎ (0114) 246 8191

11.30-3, 6-11; 11.30-10.30 Sat; 12-10.30 Sun

Samuel Smith OBB Ⓗ

Charming, converted farmhouse in extensive grounds, offering good value ale and food, plus quiz nights twice a week. No eve meals Sun. Q ⅏ ⊛ ◖ ⅅ ♣ P ⅄

HARTHILL

Beehive

16 Union Street (opp. church)

☎ (01909) 770205

12-3 (not Mon), 6 (7 Sat)-11; 12-3, 7-10.30 Sun

Tetley Bitter; Taylor Landlord; guest beer Ⓗ

Traditional, friendly country pub, home of Harthill morris men, it hosts a folk club first

Fri of every month. Three rooms, with a full-sized snooker table in the back room; families welcome if eating. Picturesque village.

⊛ ◖ ⅅ ♣ P

Try also: **Loyal Trooper**, Sheffield Rd, Sth Anston (Tetley)

HEMINGFIELD

Elephant & Castle

Tinglebridge Lane (off M1 jct 36 at B6096)

☎ (01226) 755986

11-11; 12-10.30 Sun

Barge & Barrel Nettlethrasher, Leveller; John Smith's Bitter; Tetley Bitter; guest beer Ⓗ

Welcoming, 17th-century village inn, near the canal and lock, used by locals, walkers and anglers. Opened up from five small rooms into one elongated room, it retains the traditional pub feel. ⊛ ◖ ⅅ ⅄ ⇌ ♣ P ⅄

Lundhill Tavern

Beechhouse Road

☎ (01226) 752283

11-11; 12-10.30 Sun

Barnsley Bitter; John Smith's Bitter; Samuel Smith OBB; guest beers Ⓗ

Probably one of the reasons why fewer people leave Barnsley than any other town in England.

Q ⊛ ⅅ Ⓐ ♣ P

HOYLAND

Furnace Inn

163 Milton Road

☎ (01226) 742000

12 (11.30 Sat)-4, 6.30-11; 12-3, 7-10.30 Sun

Stones Bitter; Tetley Bitter Ⓗ

Previously owned by Ward's, but retaining its charm and character and the landlord's cellarmanship is still superb. It stands next to a fishing pond, complete with ducks and swans – perfect on a sunny afternoon.

⊛ ⇌ (Elsecar & Hoyland) ♣ P ⊟

LANGSETT

Waggon & Horses

INDEPENDENT BREWERIES

Abbeydale: Sheffield
Barnsley: Elsecar
Concertina: Mexborough
Drummonds: Sheffield
Glentworth: Skellow
Kelham Island: Sheffield
Oakwell: Barnsley
Orchard: Barnsley
Wentworth: Wentworth

Manchester Road (A616)
☎ (01226) 763417
12-3, 7-11; 12-3, 7-10.30 Sun
Courage Directors; Theakston Best Bitter Ⓗ
Real ale, real food, real fire, real comfy!
🐜 Q 🐾 🎋 ⊯ ◑ ▶ A P ⊬

LAUGHTON-EN-LE-MORTHEN
Hatfield Arms
19 High Street
☎ (01909) 562681
12-3, 6-11; 12-11 Fri & Sat; 12-10.30 Sun
Boddingtons Bitter; John Smith's Magnet; guest beer (occasional) Ⓗ
Friendly local near the church, apparently haunted by a former landlady in the cellar, this two-roomed main road pub has a lounge and a large tap room and is popular with walkers visiting Roche Abbey. The excellent, good value meals are home made.
◑ ▶ ⊕ ♣ P

St Leger Arms
4 High Street
☎ (01909) 562940
12-11; 12-10.30 Sun
Barnsley Bitter; Boddingtons Bitter; Whitbread Trophy Ⓗ
Friendly local on the main road, reputedly haunted. Very popular with walkers visiting Roche Abbey, it has an outdoor play area. Beams and brasses abound in this old pub, which has a large dining room (families welcome if eating), and a small snug. Good food includes regular curry nights.
🎋 ◑ ▶ ♣ P ⊟

MEXBOROUGH
Concertina Band Club
9a Dolcliffe Road
☎ (01709) 580841
12-4, 7-11; 12-2, 7-10.30 Sun
Concertina Club Bitter, Bengal Tiger, seasonal beers; John Smith's Bitter; guest beer (occasional) Ⓗ
Small, family-owned club which houses its own award-winning micro-brewery. Visitors are made welcome.
⇌ ♣

Falcon
12 Main Street
☎ (01709) 571170
11.30-11; 12-3, 7-10.30 Sun
Old Mill Bitter Ⓗ
Lively town pub: the large lounge area is made more cosy by a number of small raised areas; there is also a tap room. Other beers from the Old Mill range are often also available. 🎋 ⇌ ♣

George & Dragon
81 Church Street (off A6023, near river)

☎ (01709) 584375
12-11; 12-10.30 Sun
John Smith's Bitter; Stones Bitter; Tetley Bitter; guest beers Ⓗ
A former Ward's pub, this is a welcoming building with three rooms and a central bar. The garden and children's play area are popular with families.
🎋 ♿ ♣ P

MICKLEBRING
Plough Inn
Greaves Sike Lane
☎ (01709) 812710
12-2.30, 6.30-11; 12-3, 6.30-10.30 Sun
John Smith's Bitter, Magnet; guest beer Ⓗ
Country pub that is known for its food, close to the M18. Two rooms, including small snug, have been recently refurbished. Approaching from Hellaby/Rotherham, turn sharp right after the phone box for the car park.
🐜 🎋 ◑ ▶ ♣ P

PENISTONE
Cubley Hall
Mortimer Road, Cubley
☎ (01226) 766086
11-11; 12-10.30 Sun
Greene King Abbot; Ind Coope Burton Ale; Tetley Bitter; guest beer Ⓗ
Former gentleman's residence, sympathetically refurbished and offering good food in a comfortable ambience of oak panelling, mosaic tiled floors and elaborate ceiling mouldings. The extensive grounds include a children's play-ground. 🐾 🎋 ⊯ ◑ ▶ P ⊬ ⊞

ROTHERHAM
Limes Hotel
38 Broom Lane, Broom
☎ (01709) 363431
11-11; 12-10.30 Sun
Banks's Original, Bitter; Camerons Strongarm; guest beer Ⓗ
Spacious Victorian residence, sympathetically converted into a pub/hotel. This popular local has a comfortable bar serving an exceptional menu.
⊯ ◑ ▶ P ⊟

Moulders Rest
110-112 Masbrough Street Near (Rotherham FC Millmoor) ☎ (01709) 560095
12-4 (5 Sat), 6 (7 Fri & Sat)-11; 12-5, 7.30-10.30 Sun
John Smith's Bitter; guest beer Ⓗ
Large, main road corner pub with a busy tap room and a though lounge, popular for games. Good value food is served weekdays, and guest beers are competitively

priced.
🎋 ⊯ ◑ ▶ ⊕ ⇌ (Central) ♣ P

Try also: Tut 'n' Shive, Wellgate (Whitbread)

Rhinoceros
35-37 Bridgegate (opp. church) ☎ (01709) 361422
11-11; 12-10.30 Sun
Courage Directors; Theakston Best Bitter; guest beers Ⓗ
Open-plan pub in the town centre, representing good value, a short walk from bus and rail stations. This typical Wetherspoon's pub has a former furniture salesroom; no music, but conversation is appreciated, regular beer festivals held. The no-smoking area is extensive.
Q ◑ ▶ ♿ ⇌ (Central) ⊬ ⊞

Woodman
Midland Road, Masbrough (off A269, opp. bus garage)
☎ (01709) 512128
12-3, 7-11; 7-10.30 Sun
Stones Bitter; guest beer Ⓗ
Friendly, former Bentley's pub with a traditional tap room, a snug lounge and a garden/play area outside. Upstairs a snooker room is for hire. Guest beers are usually from small micros.
🎋 ⊕ ♣

SHEFFIELD: *CENTRAL*
Banker's Draft
1-3 Market Place
☎ (0114) 275 6609
11-11; 12-10.30 Sun
Boddingtons Bitter; Courage Directors; Tetley Bitter; Theakston Best Bitter; guest beers Ⓗ
Converted from a bank, this large central pub appeals to all. Both floors have bars and no-smoking areas. Frequent price promotions and regular beer festivals feature. Meals served all day until 10 (9.30 Sun). Q ♿ ⇌ (Midland)
⊖ (Castle Sq) ♿ ⊬ ⊞

Bath Hotel
66 Victoria Street
☎ (0114) 249 5151
12-3 (not Mon-Wed or Sat), 7-11; 7-10.30 Sun
Tetley Dark Mild, Bitter Ⓗ
This ex-Gilmour's pub is Grade II listed and consists of two rooms and a tiled corridor drinking area. The Bath is the only regular outlet for mild in the city centre. The house beer is brewed by Tetley. Q ⊖ (University) ♣

Fat Cat
23 Alma Street
☎ (0114) 249 4801
12-3, 5.30-11; 12-3, 7-10.30 Sun
Kelham Island Bitter, Pale Rider, seasonal beers; Taylor Landlord; guest beers Ⓗ

Award-winning free house, having sold well over 3000 different beers. The Kelham Island brewhouse and new visitors centre are located nearby. An extensive vegetarian menu and regular beer festivals are added attractions. Eve meals served weekdays 6-7.30. ♨ Q ⌂ ❀ ◖ ▶ ⊖ (Swalesmoor) ⌂ P ✄

Grapes Inn
80-82 Trippet Lane
☎ (0114) 249 0909
12-11 (may close if quiet); closed Sun
Morland Old Speckled Hen; John Smith's Bitter, Magnet; Tetley Bitter Ⓗ
Grade II listed, ex-Gilmour's house: the centre bar serves the snug, main lounge and tiled corridor drinking area. The pool room is to the rear, and an upstairs function room is regularly used by live bands. ⌂ ❀ ≈ (Midland) ⊖ (West St) ♣

Hallamshire Hotel
182 West Street
☎ (0114) 272 9787
11-11; 12-10.30 Sun
Marston's Pedigree; Taylor Landlord; Tetley Bitter; guest beers Ⓗ
Following refurbishment as the first of Tetley's Festival Inns and Taverns, the pleasant wood interior now compliments the Grade II listed frontage. Meals served all day until 7. ❀ ◖ ▶ ♿ ⊖ (West St)

Hogshead
25 Orchard Street, Orchard Square ☎ (0114) 272 1980
11-11; 12-10.30 Sun
Black Sheep Best Bitter; Boddingtons Bitter; Tetley Bitter; Wadworth 6X; Ⓗ **guest beer** Ⓖ
Small, but busy, city-centre alehouse with a guest beer on gravity dispense, this pub has had a recent modern makeover and now offers disabled facilities. The no-smoking bakery opens early (9am) for food and hot drinks; meals served all day until 9. ❀ ◖ ▶ ♿ ≈ (Midland) ⊖ (Cathedral)✄

Red Deer
18 Pitt Street
☎ (0144) 272 2890
11.30-11; 12-3, 7-11 Sat; 7.30-10.30 Sun
Greene King Abbot; Ind Coope Burton Ale; Marston's Pedigree; Taylor Landlord; Tetley Bitter; guest beers Ⓗ
Friendly public house just off the West Street run, popular with university academics and students alike. It offers a large variety of traditional ales and an extensive lunchtime menu.
Q ❀ ◖ ⊖ (West St)

Red Lion
109 Charles Street
☎ (0114) 272 4997
11.30-11; 11.30-3.30, 7-11 Sat; 7-10.30 Sun
Fuller's London Pride; John Smith's Magnet; Stones Bitter Ⓗ
The display of Ward's memorabilia indicates the pub's history. The small snug is popular with regulars whilst a conservatory provides additional drinking space (no smoking at lunchtime).
❀ ◖ ≈ (Midland) ⊖ (Castle Sq)

Rutland Arms
86 Brown Street
☎ (0114) 272 9003
11.30-11; 12-10.30 Sun
Barnsley Bitter or Wentworth IPA; Greene King Abbot; Ind Coope Burton Ale; Marston's Pedigree; Tetley Bitter Ⓗ
Popular cosmoplitan pub in the city's cultural quarter. The striking old Gilmour's frontage is matched by the award-winning garden. Meals served 11.30-7.30 weekdays; 12-2.30 Sat. ❀ ⌂ ◖ ▶ ≈ (Midland) ⊖ (Castle Sq) P

Ship Inn
312 Shalesmoor
☎ (0114) 281 2209
12-3, 7 (5 Fri; 7.30 Sat)-11; 12-3, 7.30-10.30 Sun
Hardys & Hansons Best Bitter, seasonal beers Ⓗ
The impressive Tomlinson's tiled frontage makes a welcome invitation to this friendly, family-run pub, winner of many CAMRA awards and a regular *Guide* entrant.
◖ ⊖ (Shalesmoor) ♣ P ⏢

SHEFFIELD: *EAST*
Carlton
563 Attercliffe Road, Attercliffe ☎ (0114) 244 3287
11 (11.30 Fri)-3, 7 (7.30 Fri & Sat)-11; 7.30-10.30 Sun
Courage Directors; John Smith's Bitter, Magnet Ⓗ
Small friendly pub with a pool room; community sing-a-longs at weekends are accompanied by the landlord at the organ. It has a deceptively narrow frontage in a previously busy shopping area, now near Don Valley Stadium. Worth a visit to enjoy its community atmosphere. ♨ ⊖ (Attercliffe/ Woodbourne Rd) ♣ ⏢

Cocked Hat
75 Worksop Road, Attercliffe
☎ (0114) 244 8332
11-11; 11-3, 7-11 Sat; 12-2, 7-10.30 Sun
Banks's Bitter; Marston's Bitter, Pedigree, HBC Ⓗ
In the shadow of the Don

Valley Stadium, this pub is a rare outlet for real ale and the only Marston's pub in Sheffield. The shelves of this compact and cosy pub boast an impressive beer bottle collection. Bar billiards played. ♨ ❀ ◖ ⊖ (Attercliffe – Technology Park) ♣ ⊞

Gypsy Queen
Drakehouse Lane, Beighton (by Crystal Peaks shopping centre)
☎ (0114) 248 7429
11-11; 12-10.30 Sun
Hardy & Hansons Best Bitter, Classic; Stones Bitter Ⓗ
Modern Hardys & Hansons edge-of-town drinking pub, albeit with a comfortable drinking area. Rustic style decor and a large terrace outside with seating overlooking the main road and wooded valley are features. Meals served 11-10 Mon-Sat, 12-9 Sun.
♨ Q ❀ ◖ ♿ ⊖ (Beighton/ Drakehouse Lane) P

SHEFFIELD: *NORTH*
Cask & Cutler
1 Henry Street, Shalesmoor
☎ (0114) 249 2295
12-2 (not Mon), 5.30-11; 12-11 Fri & Sat; 12-3, 7-10.30 Sun
Beer range varies Ⓗ
Sheffield CAMRA's 1999 *Pub of the Year* and the runner-up in Yorkshire. Continuing champion of small independent brewers, it has offered nearly 3000 beers to date on seven ever-changing handpulls. House brewery is due to open shortly. ♨ Q ❀ ⊖ (Shalesmoor) ⌂ ✄ ⏢

Gardeners Rest
105 Neepsend Lane
☎ (0114) 272 4978
11-11; 12-10.30 Sun
Taylor Golden Best, Porter, Landlord; Ram Tam Ⓗ **guest beers** Ⓗ/Ⓖ
Former Cockayne's house set in a rapidly changing industrial area. A free house since 1998, is has been recently refurbished and extended. A no-smoking dram-shop, a tap room hosting regular live music, a conservatory and riverside garden complete the amenities here. Q ❀ ◖ ♿ ⊖ (Infirmary Rd) ♣ ✄ ⏢

Hillsborough Hotel
54-58 Langsett Road
☎ (0114) 232 2100
6-11 Fri; 12-11 Sat; 12-10.30 Sun
Beer range varies Ⓗ
Renovated and refurbished in 1999; although open as an hotel, the bar which stocks a range of guest beers is restricted to the weekend, but

is well worth a visit. Children welcome on the terrace. Meals served Sat and Sun.
🏨 Q 🏵 🛏 ◖ ● ⊖ (Langsett/Primrose View) P ⊁

New Barrack Tavern
601 Penistone Road, Hillsborough
☎ (0114) 234 9148
12-11; 12-10.30 Sun
Abbeydale Moonshine; Barnsley Bitter; John Smith's Magnet; Wentworth WPA; guest beers Ⓗ
Classic, award-winning three-roomed ex-Gilmour's house where the wide range of beer is complemented by cider and continental beers, both bottled and draught. Good food and a whisky collection add to its appeal. Regular folk and blues music is staged. Eve meals Mon-Fri. 🏨 Q 🏵 ◖ ● ⊖ (Bamforth St) ⇔ P 🍴

Rock House
168-172 Rock Street, Pitsmoor ☎ (0114) 272 4682
1 (not Mon-Thu)-4, 8-11; 1-4, 8-10.30 Sun
John Smith's Bitter, Magnet; guest beer Ⓗ
Friendly, family-run pub, catering for all ages in the local community. The L-shaped main room and sunken snug both bear a Scottish theme, reflecting the landlord's roots; a wide range of whiskies is kept. 🏵 ♣

SHEFFIELD: SOUTH
Archer Road Beer Stop (off-licence)
57 Archer Road (opp. Esporta) ☎ (0114) 255 1356
11 (10.30 Sat)-10; 12-2, 6-10 Sun
Taylor Landlord; guest beers Ⓗ
Small corner shop off-licence stocking up to five draught beers, mainly from local small breweries, plus a wide range of British bottle-conditioned beers and world classics.

Castle Inn
Twentywell Road, Bradway
☎ (0114) 236 2955
11-11; 12-10.30 Sun
Boddingtons Bitter; Marston's Pedigree; Taylor Landlord; Tetley Bitter; guest beers Ⓗ
Traditional country-style pub: two bars and a dining area. Dating from the 1870s, it was previously used as a dormitory by workers who built nearby Totley Tunnel. The new landlord now ensures locals and newcomers receive a very warm welcome!
Q 🏵 ◖ ● 🍴 ⇔ ≈ (Dore) ♣ P

Cremorne
185 London Road

☎ (0114) 255 0126
12-11; 12-3, 7-10.30 Sun
Marston's Pedigree; Tetley Bitter; guest beers Ⓗ
Popular pub in an area with few real ale outlets: a large L-shaped drinking area in stone and bare board style, plus a lower level games area. Four guest beers change weekly. ♣

Old Mother Redcap
Prospect Road, Bradway
☎ (0114) 236 0179
11.30-3.30, 5.30-11; 11-11 Sat; 12-10.30 Sun
Samuel Smith OBB Ⓗ
Modern farmhouse-style building at Bradway bus terminus, with a single L-shaped lounge. Very popular with locals of all ages, it represents extremely good value. Eve meals served Thu and Fri. 🏵 ◖ ● ≈ ♣ P 🍴

Shakespeare
106 Well Road
☎ (0114) 255 3995
12-3.30, 5.30-11; 12-4.30, 7-11 Sun; 12-3, 7-10.30 Sun
Marston's Pedigree; Stones Bitter; Tetley Bitter; guest beer Ⓗ
Very welcoming community pub enjoying loyal local custom, near Heeley City Farm. One bar serving three drinking areas it has been run by the same landlord for 39 years. The guest beer is from the Tapster's Choice range. 🏵 ♣ P

White Lion
615 London Road
☎ (0114) 255 1500
12-11; 12-10.30 Sun
Ind Coope Burton Ale; Marston's Pedigree; Tetley Bitter; guest beers Ⓗ
Grade II listed, former Tetley Heritage Pub and Festival Alehouse. Its many rooms include a tiled corridor, two snugs and a no-smoking lounge. Popular with all ages. 🏵 ♣ ⇔ ⊁

SHEFFIELD: WEST
Ball Inn
171 Crookes
☎ (0114) 266 1211
11-11; 12-10.30 Sun
Boddingtons Bitter; Castle Eden Ale; Flowers Original; Marston's Pedigree; guest beers Ⓗ
Large pub in typical 'alehouse' style with bare floorboards, exposed walls and wood panelling. Several seating areas are set around a central bar; the games area has two pool tables. Often busy with a mix of locals and students. 🏵 ◖ ♣ ⇔

Bell Hagg Inn
3 Manchester Road (A57 Glossop road)

☎ (0114) 230 2082
12-11; 12-10.30 Sun
Banks's Bitter; guest beer Ⓗ
Free house on the edge of the city, built on a hillside affording spectacular views over the Rivelin Valley. An L-shaped lounge is set around the bar, with a smaller room to the rear. The garden has an extensive children's play area. Breakfasts served 7.30-11am. Live jazz last Thu of month. Q 🏵 🛏 ◖ ● P

Cobden View
40 Cobden View Road
☎ (0114) 266 3714
5 (2 Sat)-11; 12-10.30 Sun
Barnsley Bitter, Castle Eden Ale; guest beer Ⓗ
Popular community pub with a through-lounge, small bar area and a games room. Regular activities including quiz nights Mon and Tue and folk on Thu. 🏵 ♣

Noah's Ark
94 Crookes ☎ (0114) 266 3300
12 (11 Sat)-11; 12-10.30 Sun
Boddingtons Bitter; Castle Eden Ale; Flowers IPA; Marston's Pedigree; John Smith's Magnet; Tetley Bitter; guest beers Ⓗ
Extended community pub with an open-plan lounge around a central bar. The original layout can still be discerned from the seating arrangement. Located in a student area, but popular with all ages. Eve meals served 5-7. 🏵 ◖ ♣

Old Heavygate
114 Matlock Road
☎ (0114) 234 0003
2-4 (12-5 Sat), 7-11 (12-11 winter Sat); 12-4, 7-10.30 Sun
Hardys & Hansons Best Bitter; seasonal beers Ⓗ
A former tollhouse and an adjacent cottage dating from 1696 form this popular two-room community pub. Built on a hillside, the spacious tap room is on a higher level than the comfortable lounge. 🏵 ♣ P 🍴

Porter Brook
565 Ecclesall Road
☎ (0114) 266 5765
11-11; 12-10.30 Sun
Boddingtons Bitter; Tetley Bitter; guest beers Ⓗ/Ⓖ
Whitbread Hogshead on the bank of the River Porter: an open-plan bar in typical style with bare floorboards. The best beer range in the area it stocks up to 11 guest ales, hence often crowded especially weekend eves. Meals served all day until 8.30. Q 🏵 ◖ ● ⊁

Walkley Cottage
46 Bolehill Road

☎ (0114) 234 4968
11-11; 12-10.30 Sun
Greene King Abbot ; Marston's Pedigree; Taylor Landlord; Tetley Bitter; guest beer Ⓗ
Popular two-roomed local comprising a spacious lounge and a games room. Guest beers come from micros as well as regional breweries. Quiz night Thu. Eve meals served 6-8. Q ⚶ ◑ 🌓 ⌁ ♣ P

STRINES

Strines Inn
Bradfield Dale, Bradfield (2 miles N of A57, W of Sheffield) OS222906
☎ (0114) 285 1247
11-3, 7-11; 11-11 Sat & summer; 12-10.30 Sun
Mansfield Riding Bitter; Morland Old Speckled Hen Ⓗ
Listed building dating back 700 years and an inn since 1771, it has never been owned by a brewer. Well decorated with wood, brass and stuffed animal heads much in evidence, it is delightfully situated in walking country.
🚲 Q ⚶ 🛏 ◑ 🌓 ♣ P ✉

THORNE

Canal Tavern
South Parade (town side of canal flyover bridge)
☎ (01405) 813688
11.30-3, 5.30-11; 11.30-11 Sat; 12-10.30 Sun
Boddingtons Bitter; John Smith's Bitter; Tetley Bitter; guest beers Ⓗ
Canalside hostelry, popular with boaters, offering a wide range of beers and an extensive menu.
⚶ ◑ 🌓 ⇌ (South) ♣ P

THORPE HESLEY

Masons Arms
106 Thorpe Street (exit M1 jct 35, ½ mile)
☎ (0114) 246 8079
12-3, 6-11; 12-3, 7-10.30 Sun
John Smith's Bitter, Magnet; Theakston Best Bitter; Old Peculier Ⓗ
Attractive single bar, 19th-century village pub near the church. Traditional music Wed and Thu eves is accompanied by a resident pianist. Home to Rotherham Motor Club and South Yorkshire MG club. No food Sun. ⚶ ◑ 🌓 ⅋ ♣ P

THURLSTONE

Huntsman
136 Manchester Road (A628)
☎ (01226) 764892
6 (12 Thu-Sat)-11; 12-10.30 Sun
Beer range varies Ⓗ
Cosy, intimate and comfortable pub featuring

low beamed ceilings and open log fires. It hosts beer festivals in April and Oct. Barnsley CAMRA *Pub of the Year* 1999. Food is served all day Thu-Sun; bookings only Fri and Sat eves.
🚲 ⚶ ◑ 🌓 ⌣ ✉

TICKHILL

Scarbrough Arms
Sunderland Street
☎ (01302) 742977
11-3 (4 Sat), 6-11; 12-3, 7-10.30 Sun
John Smith's Bitter, Magnet; Theakston Old Peculier; guest beers Ⓗ
Popular local: three rooms of differing character. Home-made lunches Tue-Sat include imaginative vegetarian dishes. This traditional stone-built pub was voted local CAMRA *Pub of the Year* 1997-98.
🚲 Q ⚶ ◑ 🌓 ♣ P ⅋

ULLEY

Royal Oak
Turnshaw Road
☎ (0114) 287 2464
11-3, 6-11; 12-3, 6-10.30 Sun
Samuel Smith OBB Ⓗ
Old pub in a picturesque village, replete with lots of brasses, saddles and wooden beams, popular with local farmers, walkers and diners. Over 300 years old this large country pub has extensive gardens and a children's room. Very good value beer and excellent food.
⅏ ⚶ ◑ 🌓 P

VICTORIA

Victoria Inn
On A616 at crossroads OS178055
☎ (01484) 682785
12-2 (not Mon-Thu), 7-11; 12-2, 7-10.30 Sun
Tetley Bitter Ⓗ
Cosy, friendly local, run by the same licensee for almost half a century. Q P

WATH UPON DEARNE

Staithes
Doncaster Road (near new industrial estate)
☎ (01709) 873546
11-11; 12-10.30 Sun
Barnsley Bitter; John Smith's; guest beer Ⓗ
Spacious, comfortable, well-appointed free house displaying interesting artefacts. The popular, extensive, home-cooked menu is good value. ⚶ ◑ 🌓 P

WENTWORTH

George & Dragon
85 Main Street

☎ (01226) 742440
10-11; 10-10.30 Sun
Stones Bitter; Taylor Landlord; guest beers Ⓗ
Open from 10am for breakfast, this cosy country free house in picturesque Wentworth serves a house beer from Wentworth Brewery, Bobby Sweetings Ale. Food includes the famous George's cow pie – a complete meal in one dish! Excellent children's adventure play area. 🚲⚶◑P

Rockingham Arms
Main Street
☎ (01226) 742075
11-11; 12-10.30 Sun
Theakston Best Bitter, Old Peculier; guest beer Ⓗ
Cosy pub in a charming village, that retains a multi-roomed layout around a central bar. Good food and entertainment provided in the barn. Well located for walking in Wentworth Park, it hosts a long-established folk club (Fri). The bowling green and large garden are added attractions.
🚲 Q ⌣ ⚶ 🛏 ◑ 🌓 P

WEST MELTON

Plough Inn
144 Melton High Street (228/229 bus stops directly outside, not Sun)
☎ (01709) 872995
12-11; 12-10.30 Sun
Barnsley Bitter; John Smith's Bitter; guest beer Ⓗ
Large, multi-roomed village pub with a tap room/games room and a conservatory. The landlord encourages a family atmosphere.
⌣ ⚶ ◑ 🌓 ⅋ P

WHISTON

Golden Ball
7 Turner Lane (off High St, next to PO)
☎ (01709) 378200
11.45-11; 12-10.30 Sun
Tetley Bitter; Taylor Landlord; guest beers Ⓗ
Popular 'olde-worlde' pub, in a picture postcard village. Full of charm, it has a pleasant outside drinking area to the front and garden to the rear, near a dyke and manorial barn. Families are welcome up to 9pm if eating. Laurel & Hardy fan club meets here. ⚶ ◑ 🌓 ⅃ ♣ P ✉

WORSBROUGH VILLAGE

Edmunds Arms
25 Worsbrough Village
☎ (01226) 206865
11.30-3 (4 Sat), 6-11; 12-4, 7-10.30 Sun
Samuel Smith OBB Ⓗ

Splendid inn opposite an historic church, comprising a lounge, tap room and restaurant, offering good value food (eve meals Tue-Sat). Q ❀ ◖ ⊟ ♣ P

WORTLEY

Wortley Arms Hotel
Halifax Road (A629)
☎ (0114) 288 2245
11-11; 12-10.30 Sun
Barnsley Bitter; John Smith's Bitter; Taylor Dark Mild, Landlord; Theakston Old Peculier, guest beer H
Rambling old village hostelry, oozing with understated character and charm, featuring an enormous fireplace, wood panelling, and exposed stonework inlaid with a coat of arms. It stands just off the Trans-Pennine trail. A house beer is sold.
🏠 ⛵ ❀ 🛏 ◖ ◗ P ✂

Yorkshire (West)

ABERFORD

Arabian Horse
Main Street
☎ (0113) 281 3312
11-11; 12-10.30 Sun
John Smith's Bitter; Theakston Best Bitter; guest beer H
18th-century inn on the green of one of Leeds' most attractive villages. Friendly, with a warm welcome, it boasts two large open fires. The only pub in Britain with this name. No food Sun.
🏠 ❀ ◖ ⑂ ♣ P

ALLERTON BYWATER

Boat Inn
Boat Lane (off Main Street)
☎ (01977) 552216
12-3, 6-11 (11-11 summer); 12-10.30 Sun
Boat Man in the Boat; Tetley Bitter; guest beers H
Welcoming pub on the River Aire in a former pit village. Run by a former GB Rugby League player, mementoes of whose career adorn the walls. Winner of local CAMRA *Pub of the Season* winter 1999/2000. Always at least one beer from the Boat Brewery, which is situated in the pub car park.
⛵ ❀ ◗ 🖊 P

BARWICK IN ELMET

New Inn
17 Main Street
☎ (0113) 281 2289
11-11; 12-3, 7-10.30 Sun
John Smith's Bitter; guest beers H
Friendly, 18th-century roadside inn, recently extended into adjoining

cottages. A real local with service from a tiny bar and hatchway. Eve meals Tue-Thu 5.45-7.30. Q ◖ ⊟ ♣

BINGLEY

Brown Cow
Ireland Bridge (off A650)
☎ (01274) 569482
11.30-3, 5.30-11; 11.30-11 Sat; 12-10.30 Sun
Taylor Golden Best, Dark Mild, Best Bitter, Landlord, Ram Tam; guest beer H
Attractive riverside pub with a more rural feel than town centre and a relaxed, friendly atmosphere, it is said to be haunted! Jazz nights Mon; quiz nights Tue with bingo and free food. Home-made food is a speciality (not served Mon eve). The guest beer comes from Goose Eye or Black Sheep.
🏠 ❀ ◖ 🖊 & ⇌ P

BRADFORD

Castle Hotel
20 Grattan Road (off Westgate)
☎ (01274) 393166
11.30-11; closed Sun
Fuller's ESB; Mansfield Riding Bitter; Taylor Golden Best, Landlord; guest beers H
This imposing stone pub was built in 1898, complete with castellated battlements. Formerly a Webster's house it now sells a variety of beers in a relaxing atmosphere. A cordial welcome awaits shoppers and regulars to its open-plan interior with a quiet drinking area.
🛏 ⇌ (Forster Sq/Interchange) ♣

Cock & Bottle ☆
93 Barkerend Road (inner ring/Otley rd jct)
☎ (01274) 738446
12-3, 7-11; 12-3, 8-10.30
Taylor Golden Best, Landlord; Tetley Bitter; Theakston Best Bitter, XB H
Newly restored to its former glory, this 19th-century Grade II listed pub is on CAMRA's national inventory of pubs of outstanding historic interest. The multi-roomed interior has an original Victorian bar, stained glass mirrors, woodwork and etched windows. 🏠 ⛵ ◖ ⇌ (Forster Sq/Interchange) ♣ P ✂

Corn Dolly
110 Bolton Road
☎ (01274) 720219
11.30-11; 12-10.30 Sun
Black Sheep Best Bitter; Taylor Landlord; Theakston Best Bitter; guest beers H
White-painted stone pub, opened as the Wharf in 1834 to serve the nearby canal

basin. Open-plan, but with a separate games area, the pub serves four ever-changing guest beers plus a house ale from Moorhouses. Lunchtime snacks. Music Sun eve. Bradford CAMRA *Pub of the Year* 2000. 🏠 ❀ ⇌ (Forster Sq/Interchange) ♣ P

Fighting Cock
21-23 Preston Street
☎ (01274) 726907
11.30-11; 12-10.30 Sun
Black Sheep Special; Greene King Abbot; Old Mill Bitter; Taylor Golden Best, Landlord; Theakston Old Peculier; guest beers H
Drinkers' oasis in an industrial neighbourhood, offering usually 12 ales plus real cider. Home-cooked food served Mon to Sat.
🏠 ❀ ◖ ⛲ 🖊

Goldsborough
1 Captain Street, Bolton Road
☎ (01274) 740138
11.30-11; 12-10.30 Sun
Old Mill Bitter; Taylor Landlord; Tetley Bitter; guest beers H
Originally the Drayman's, it became the Goldsborough in the early 20th century. Popular with sports fans, the spacious bar has a collection of baseball caps, several comfy sofas and a large screen TV. Fine wines also available. ❀ ◖ ⇌ (Forster Sq/Interchange) ♣ P

Haigy's
31 Lumb Lane
☎ (01274) 731644
5 (12 Fri & Sat)-1am; closed Sun
Black Sheep Best Bitter; Greene King Abbot; Tetley Bitter; guest beers H
Lively pub with a late licence, offering a friendly welcome and a good range of beers. The exterior is painted in claret and amber – the colours of nearby Bradford City FC. Guest beers are usually from Ossett Brewery.
❀ ◗ ⇌ (Forster Sq) ♣ P

Melborn Hotel
104 White Abbey Road (B6144, 1/2 mile from centre)
☎ (01274) 726867
1 (2 Wed-Fri, 12 Sat)-11; 12-10.30 Sun
Moorhouse's Premier; Tetley Bitter; guest beers H
Now a Bradford institution, famed for the landlord's dedication to cask ale and live music, this 1930s former Melbourne Brewery hotel attracts both local enthusiasts and those from further afield. Look for the fine collection of Melbourne breweriana.
🏠 ❀ 🛏 ♣ P

New Beehive Inn ☆
171 Westgate (B6144)
☎ (01274) 721784

12-11; 11.30-1am Fri & Sat; 6-10.30 Sun

Goose Eye Bitter; Kelham Island Bitter; Taylor Landlord; guest beers Ⓗ

Friendly, popular multi-roomed bar with a basement skittle alley, now restored to its Edwardian splendour with coal fires and gas lighting. Regular live music. No food Sun. ⚼ Q ⌾ ⇄ ◖Ⓐ ⇌ (Forster Sq) ♣ P

Old Bank

69 Market Street (near City Hall) ☎ (01274) 743680
11-11; 12-10.30 Sun

Boddingtons Bitter; Castle Eden Ale; Flowers Original; Marston's Pedigree; Wadworth 6X; Ⓗ **guest beers** Ⓗ/Ⓖ

Former Barclay's Bank , popular with office workers and shoppers. Well situated, it stocks a good range of ales, plus foreign beers. Antiques and pictures tell the building's history. No smoking area until 7pm. Bradford CAMRA *Pub of the Season* Spring 1998. Meals served 12-9 (7 Fri and Sat). ⚼ Q ◖Ⓓ ⇔ (Interchange/ Forster Sq) ⊬

Steve Biko Bar

D Floor, Richmond Building, University, Richmond Road ☎ (01274) 233257
11 (7 Sat)-11; 7-10.30 Sun

Courage Directors; John Smith's Bitter; Ruddles County; Theakston Best Bitter, XB; guest beers Ⓗ

Open-plan bar within the university building, run by the students' union. A laid-back atmosphere attracts a diverse range of drinkers who mix easily with the students. Can get busy and noisy eves. Reasonably priced food and regular cheap beer promotions. ◖Ⓓ⇌ (Interchange/Forster Sq) P

BRIGHOUSE

Crown

6 Lightcliffe Road, Waring Green (off A644 at the Albion) ☎ (01484) 715436
11-11; 12-10.30 Sun

Courage Directors; Tetley Bitter; Theakston Mild Ⓗ

Friendly local: two rooms off an open-plan area; very popular between 5 and 8pm. ⚼ ♣ P

Red Rooster

123 Elland Road, Brookfoot (A6025) ☎ (01484) 713737
5 (4.30 Fri; 11 Sat)-11; 12-10.30 Sun

Black Sheep Best Bitter; Moorhouse's Pendle Witches Brew; Old Mill Bitter; Rooster's Yankee; guest beers Ⓗ

Popular real ale drinkers' pub,

stocking up to five guest beers. Glasses holding two pints are available for the seriously thirsty. ⚼ ⊛ ♣ ◡ P

BUTTERSHAW

Barley Mow

536 Halifax Road ☎ (01274) 414291
11-11; 12-10.30 Sun

Fuller's ESB; Taylor Landlord; Tetley Bitter; guest beer Ⓗ

Popular , traditional pub with a regularly changing guest beer and a lively atmosphere. ⊛ Ⓐ P

Beehive Inn

583 Halifax Road ☎ (01274) 678550
11-11; 12-10.30 Sun

Tetley Bitter; guest beer Ⓗ

Lively, homely local where children are welcome until 7.30pm. Disco every Fri eve, karaoke Sat eve and Sun lunch. Beehive Bitter is house beer brewed by Tetley. ♣

CALDER GROVE

Navigation

Broadcut Road (400 yds off Denby Dale road over canal bridge) ☎ (01924) 274361
12-11; 12-10.30 Sun

Barge & Barrel Nettlethrasher; Black Stump; Draught Bass Ⓗ

Canalside pub popular with families due to both having a softplay room and outdoor play area. The lounge is for adults only. ⚼ ⌕ ⊛ ◖Ⓓ ⅏ P

CARLTON

Rosebud

22 Westfield Road, Rothwell ☎ (0113) 282 2236
5 (12 Fri & Sat)-11; 12-4.30, 7-10.30 Sun

John Smith's Bitter; Tetley Bitter; guest beers Ⓗ

Welcoming traditional village pub with a tap room, smart lounge and cosy atmosphere. Guest ales are currently from the Tapster's Choice range. ⊛ Ⓐ ♣ P

CASTLEFORD

Garden House

Wheldon Road ☎ (01977) 552934
11.30-11; 12-10.30 Sun

John Smith's Bitter; Tetley Bitter; Worthington Bitter; guest beers Ⓗ

Friendly, two-roomed pub very close to Castleford RL ground. Cheap but wholesome pub food served. ⊛ ◖Ⓓ Ⓐ P

Glass Blower

15 Bank Street ☎ (01977) 520390

11-11; 12-10.30 Sun

Boddingtons Bitter; Courage Directors; John Smith's Bitter; Taylor Landlord; Theakston Best Bitter; guest beers Ⓗ

Typical Wetherspoon's conversion of an old post office. Very keen on real ale from micros and regional breweries. Q ⊛ ◖Ⓓ ⅏ ⇌ ⊬

CHURWELL

Commercial

78 Elland Road (A643) ☎ (0113) 253 2776
12-3, 5.30-11; 12-10.30 Sun

Black Sheep Best Bitter; Tetley Dark Mild, Bitter Ⓗ

Friendly local with a low beamed ceiling. It features a main open-plan area on several levels with a central bar and a small back room; a lower area at one end is mainly used for meals (not served Sun eve or Mon). There is a children's play area outside. ⊛ ◖Ⓓ ♣ P

CLECKHEATON

Marsh

28 Bradford Road (A638 near bus station) ☎ (01274) 872104
11-3 (not Wed), 7-11; 12-4, 7-10.30 Sun

Old Mill Mild, Bitter, Bullion, seasonal beers Ⓗ

A warm welcome is assured in this popular local. Opened out, it has a games area and a raised drinking area. Known some years ago as the 'Waxworks' as it was so quiet, this pub will now make a much livelier impression! ⊛ ♣ P

CROSSROADS

Quarry House Inn

Bingley Road, Lees Moor (1/2 mile from A629/A6033 jct) ☎ (01535) 642239
12-3, 7-11; 12-3, 7-10.30 Sun

Taylor Golden Best, Landlord; Tetley Bitter Ⓗ

Family-run converted farmhouse set in open countryside enjoying extensive views. The bar, a former church pulpit, is set in a small cosy area. Excellent food (30 minute extension eves for diners). Over ten years in this *Guide* and twice winner of local CAMRA *Pub of the Season* award. Families very welcome at all times. Q ◖Ⓓ Ⓐ P

DEWSBURY

Gate Inn

50 Thornhill Road (B6117, S of A644 jct) ☎ (01924) 461897
4 (12 Fri & Sat)-11; 12-10.30 Sun

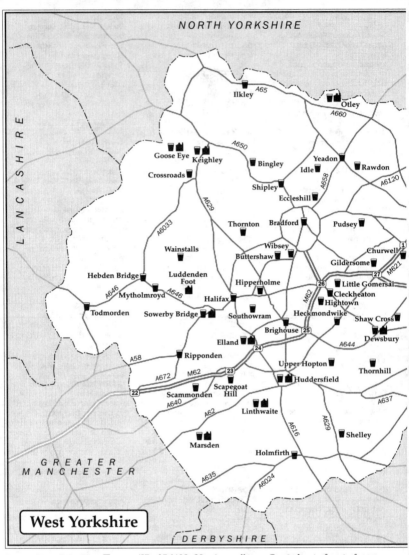

West Yorkshire

Barnsley Bitter; Tetley Bitter Ⓗ
Traditional, three-roomed
pub, in the shadow of a
railway bridge and textile
mills, with strong sporting
associations. 🏠🌸🍴♣ P

John F Kennedy
2 Webster Hill (A644 at inner
ring road jct)
☎ (01924) 455828
8 (7 Fri & Sat)-11; 8-10.30 Sun
Taylor Landlord; guest beer Ⓗ
A pub which evolves slowly
but remains unchanged; it
now boasts a clock but the
limited opening times
remain subject to variation.
The guest beer is usually from
a Yorkshire micro. 🏠🚌♣ P

Leggers
Robinsons Boatyard, Savile
Town Wharf, Mill Street East

(SE of B6409, 20 mins walk
from centre)
☎ (01924) 502846
12-11; 12-10.30 Sun
Everards Tiger; guest beers Ⓗ
First-floor bar with a low
beamed ceiling in the
converted hayloft of
boathorse stables overlooking
a busy canal basin with
residential moorings. Always
has two house beers brewed
on the premises by Sunset
and usually three guest ales.
🏠🌸🍴♣ P

West Riding Licensed Refreshment Rooms
Railway Station, Wellington
Road (inner ring road)
☎ (01924) 459193
11-11; 12-10.30 Sun
Black Sheep Best Bitter; Taylor
Landlord; guest beers Ⓗ

Created out of part of a
Grade II listed station
building (1848) it usually has
six beers on tap with a bias
towards smaller brewers'
products. Platform and car
park access. Eve meals served
Tue and Wed. No-smoking
area available until 6pm.
🏠🌸🍴👥🚌👄 P

ECCLESHILL
Royal Oak
39 Stony Lane, Eccleshill
☎ (01274) 639182
11-11; 12-10.30 Sun
Taylor Landlord; Tetley Mild,
Bitter Ⓗ
Country-style friendly village
local; the comfortable lounge
is the old listed part of the
building. A more recently
built tap room can only be

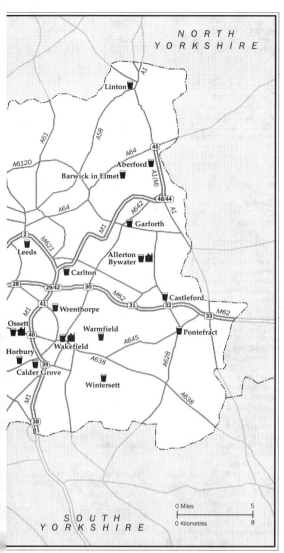

The oldest pub in Garforth, on a main road position. The large lounge boasts an extensive array of brasswork; also a games room and 'Tudor Room'. ✿ ♣ P

GILDERSOME

New Inn
Church Street
☎ (0113) 253 4821
11-3, 5-11; 11-11 Fri & Sat; 12-10.30 Sun

Samuel Smith OBB Ⓗ

Good example of a 1930s pub with original windows and curvy corners, selling value for money beer to its many appreciative customers. The tap room is truly separate and there's a massive well-equipped garden at the back. No food Tue. ✿ ◖ ⊟ P

Old Griffin Head
Branch Road, Town Street
☎ (0113) 253 3159
11.30-3, 5.30-11; 11.30-11 Fri & Sat; 11.30-10.30 Sun

Boddingtons Bitter; Taylor Landlord; Whitbread Trophy Ⓗ

Big, old and whitewashed, the Old Griffin Head is a country-style pub featuring beams, brass and copper artefacts. Well-upholstered settles provide seating in the raised areas. Can get very busy weekend eves. No food Sun. Outdoor seating is in the car park. ✿ ◖ P

GOOSE EYE

Turkey Inn
☎ (01535) 681339
12-3, 5.30-11; 12-5, 7-11 Sat; 12-3, 7-10.30 Sun

Greene King Abbot; Ind Coope Burton Ale; Tetley Bitter; Turkey Bitter; guest beer Ⓗ

200-year-old ex-Aaron King village pub: two comfortable rooms with open fires facing the bar and a pool room to side. Steaks are a speciality in the dining area (no food Mon). Turkey Bitter comes from a new brewhouse at the rear. Irish band monthly (Mon), disco Tue. ♨ ✿ ◖ ♪ ♣ P

HALIFAX

Big Six
10 Horsfall Street, King Cross (off A646) ☎ (01422) 350169
5 (11 Fri & Sat)-11; 12-10.30 Sun

Ind Coope Burton Ale; Tetley Bitter; guest beers Ⓗ

Still has the feel of a multi-roomed Victorian mid-terrace local. Often busy with a wide range of customers, it welcomes dog walkers. The bar billiards table is a rare find in West Yorks. ♨ ✿ ♣

accessed via the gents' toilets. 1999 Vanguard *Cellarman of the Year* award winner.
✿ ⊟ ♣ P

ELLAND

Barge & Barrel
10-20 Park Road (A6026)
☎ (01422) 373623
12-11; 12-10.30 Sun

Barge & Barerel Best Bitter, Nettlethrasher, Leveller; Black Sheep Best Bitter, Special; guest beers Ⓗ

Roomy canalside pub with a central horseshoe-shaped bar and Victorian decor; a meeting place for the Canal Society and ramblers. Usually five of the beers brewed here are available. No food Wed.
♨ ✿ ◖ ⑇ ▲ ♣ ⌣ P ⊞

GARFORTH

Gaping Goose
41 Selby Road
☎ (0113) 286 2127
11.30-11; 12-10.30 Sun

Tetley Mild, Bitter Ⓗ

Golden Fleece
Lindley Road, Blackley (just off M62 jct 24)
☎ (01422) 372704
12-2 (not Tue & Sat), 7-11; 12-2.30, 7-10.30 Sun

Draught Bass; Boddingtons Bitter; Stones Bitter Ⓗ

Hilltop village local dating back to the early 18th century. Next to the cricket pitch, it offers fine views of the local scenery and a display of brassware inside. Popular for business lunches.
⇘ ✿ ◖ P

Shears Inn
Paris Gates, Boys Lane
☎ (01422) 362936
11.45-11; 12-10.30 Sun
Taylor Golden Best, Best Bitter, Landlord, Ram Tam; Theakston Best Bitter; guest beer Ⓗ
Cosy, low-roofed pub with bay window seating, nestling in the valley bottom and overlooked by a large mill complex. Good value, hearty, home-cooked food provides a major attraction at lunchtimes. No food Sun.
♛ ❀ ☾ ≢ ♣ P

Sportsman
Bradford Old Road, Ploughcroft (1/4 mile E of A647) ☎ (01422) 367000
12-2.30, 6-11; 12-midnight Sat; 12-10.30 Sun
Old Mill Bitter; Taylor Landlord; Tetley Bitter; Theakston Old Peculier; guest beer Ⓗ
Hilltop free house affording expansive views, next to an all-weather ski-slope, adventure play area and children's go-kart track. Folk club meets Thu. Quiz night Fri and Sat. The family room doubles as the no-smoking area. ♘ ❀ ☾ ◗ ♣ P ⊘

Tap & Spile
1 Clare Road
☎ (01422) 362692
11-11; 12-10.30 Sun
Big Lamp Bitter; Black Sheep Best Bitter; guest beers Ⓗ
Listed mock-Tudor pub, opened by Ramsdens Brewery between the wars. A recent sympathetic refurbishment has added warmth to the traditional atmosphere of its several drinking areas. Six guest beers usually available. The cider varies. No food Sun. ☾ ♣ ⌓

Three Pigeons Ale House
1 Sun Fold, South Parade (near station)
☎ (01422) 347001
12-11; 12-10.30 Sun
Barge & Barrel Best Bitter; Black Sheep Best Bitter; Taylor Best Bitter, Landlord; guest beers Ⓗ
Small, friendly, hospitable ale house consisting of an octagonal drinking area (note the ceiling mural) with rooms radiating off. Five minutes from the football/rugby ground – fans welcome. Lunches served weekdays; Mon is curry night. Three guest beers on tap. ♛ ❀ ☾ ◗ ≢ ♣

West End
216 Parkinson Lane
☎ (01422) 250559
11-30-11; 12-10.30 Sun
Boddingtons Bitter; Old Mill Bitter; guest beers Ⓗ
A large, partly-raised lounge featuring a mangle, is complemented by pool and games rooms, in this sociable local. ♛ ❀ ♣ P

HEBDEN BRIDGE

Fox & Goose
9 Heptonstall Road (A646 jct)
☎ (01422) 842649
11.30-3, 7-11; 12-3, 7-10.30 Sun
Woodforde's Wherry; guest beers Ⓗ
Traditional, sociable pub, free from juke box or bandits, eleven consecutive years in the *Guide*. All beers are sold at fair prices. Q ❀ ≢ ♣ ⊔

Hare & Hounds
Billy Lane, Chiserley, Old Town (off A6033 at Peckett Well, 1 mile) OS005280
☎ (01422) 842671
7(12 Sat)-11; 12-10.30 Sun
Taylor Golden Best, Best Bitter, Landlord, Ram Tam Ⓗ
Taylor's tied house in a village above Hebden Bridge, known as 'Lane Ends'. Good value weekend lunches; eve meals 7-9 (not Mon).
♛ Q ❀ ⊟ ☾ ◗ ♣ P

Stubbing Wharf
King Street (A646, 1/4 mile W of centre) ☎ (01422) 844107
12-11; 12-10.30 Sun
Boddingtons Bitter; Flowers Original; Greene King IPA; Taylor Landlord; guest beers Ⓗ
Sandwiched between river and canal, this comfortable and spacious pub enjoys a good atmosphere. Up to four guest beers on tap. Canalside seating for fine days.
♛ Q ❀ ☾ ◗ ♣ P

White Lion Hotel
Bridge Gate (A6033)
☎ (01422) 842197
11-11; 12-3, 7-10.30 Sun
Boddingtons Bitter; Castle Eden Ale; Flowers Original; Taylor Landlord; guest beers Ⓗ
Former coaching inn, opened out to offer a mix of styles to a wide-ranging clientele. Wheelchair WC. Good B & B.
♛ ♘ ❀ ⊟ ☾ ◗ ♿ ≢ P ⊘

HECKMONDWIKE

Old Hall
New North Road (1/2 mile NW of the 'Green')
☎ (01924) 404774
11.30-11; 12-10.30 Sun
Samuel Smith OBB Ⓗ
Once home to the scientist Joseph Priestley, this Grade I listed building is said to be haunted. Dating from the 1470s it has a rare acorn ceiling and open gallery. Royal portraits adorn the walls. No eve meals Sun (lunch served 12-5).
❀ ☾ ◗ ♣ P ⊘

HIGHTOWN

Cross Keys
283 Halifax Road (A649, 1 mile NW A62 jct)
☎ (01274) 873294
12-2.30 (not Mon-Wed), 5.30-11; 12-11 Sat; 12-10.30 Sun
Camerons Bitter; Marston's Bitter, Pedigree Ⓗ
Conservatory dining area overlooks the pitch and putt square in summer and has views across the valley of Lands Beck. Disabled access is from the car park; the front door opens into the bar area. Nicely opened up, the pub retains a multi-roomed feel. No meals Mon eve.
❀ ☾ ◗ ♿ P

HIPPERHOLME

Brown Horse Inn
Denholme Gate Road, Coley (A644, 1 mile N of centre)
☎ (01422) 202112
11-11; 12-3, 7-10.30 Sun
Boddingtons Bitter; John Smith's Bitter; Taylor Landlord; Webster's Yorkshire Bitter Ⓗ
Yorkshire's only Brown Horse. The interior is comfortably spacious; food is cooked to order (eve meals Mon-Fri). ❀ ☾ ◗ P

Old White Beare
Village Street, Norwood Green (off A58)
☎ (01274) 676645
11.30-11; 12-10.30 Sun
Boddingtons Bitter; Taylor Best Bitter, Landlord; guest beer Ⓗ
Village pub with a sympathetic restaurant extension. Note the wood-panelled fixed seating in the snug. ❀ ☾ ◗ ♣ P

HOLMFIRTH

Old Bridge Hotel
Market Walk
☎ (01484) 681212
11-11; 11-10.30 Sun
Black Sheep Best Bitter; Taylor Best Bitter, Landlord; Tetley Mild, Bitter; guest beer Ⓗ
Well-appointed, town-centre hotel, convenient for *Summer Wine* country, and the Pennines. Formerly a club, and once a private residence, parts of the building date back to the 1700s. Spacious restaurant or bar food option.
❀ ⊟ ☾ ◗ P

Rose & Crown (Nook)
7 Victoria Square
☎ (01484) 683960
11.30-11; 12-10.30 Sun
Samuel Smith OBB; Taylor Best Bitter, Landlord; Tetley Dark Mild; Bitter; Theakston Best Bitter; guest beer Ⓗ
Timeless town-centre local which puts the beerdrinker at

the top of its list. A regular *Guide* entry for well over 20 years. Several rooms, including one with a new stove. Folk club meets first Thu of each month. 🏨 ☎ ♣

HORBURY

Boons
26 Queen Street
☎ (01924) 274506
11-3, 5-11; 11-11 Fri & Sat; 12-10.30 Sun

Clark's Bitter; John Smith's Bitter; Taylor Landlord; Tetley Bitter; guest beers Ⓗ
Situated in the town centre, a one-roomed pub with a central bar. A good example of how a former keg-only outlet can be turned into a successful real ale venue.
🏨 ❀ 🍺 ♣

HUDDERSFIELD

Fieldhead
219 Quarmby Road, Quarmby
☎ (01484) 654581
4 (12 Fri & Sat)-11; 12-10.30 Sun

Stones Bitter; guest beer Ⓗ
Imposing building in a prominent position overlooking the Colne Valley, it has a horseshoe-shaped bar and several well-furnished, spacious rooms, including a pool room. Live entertainment features fairly regularly. ❀ ♣ P

Head of Steam
St George's Square
☎ (01484) 454533
11-12.30am (2am Fri & Sat); 12-10.30 Sun

Beer range varies Ⓗ
Multi-roomed pub occupying one wing of Huddersfield's Grade I listed railway station. Walls are adorned with railway memorabilia, and regular themed beer festivals are held. Live music mid-week, and meals available at all times. Popular with all, especially students.
❀ 🍺 🅳 ♿ ≈ 🍴

Marsh Liberal Club
Glenfield, 31 New Hey Road, Marsh (A640, 1¹/₂ miles from centre)
☎ (01484) 420152
12-2, 7-11; 12-11 Sat; 12-10.30 Sun

Bateman Mild; Black Sheep Best Bitter; Taylor Best Bitter; Theakston Best Bitter; guest beers Ⓗ
Large, comfortable, stone-built club with a well-deserved reputation for its beer. Three rotating guest beers, usually from micros and an occasional cider, complement the permanent ales. Crown green bowls and snooker are popular. Show this *Guide* or a CAMRA

membership card to be signed in. Wheelchair WC.
❀ ♿ ♣ ⌂ P

Rat & Ratchet
40 Chapel Hill (A616, near ring road) ☎ (01484) 516734
3.30 (12 Wed-Sat)-11; 12-10.30 Sun

Greene King Abbot; Taylor Mild, Best Bitter, Landlord; guest beers Ⓗ
A short stroll from the town centre, this brew pub has a deservedly high reputation among discerning drinkers, and achieved 10 years in this *Guide*. Up to 14 beers on offer, including one brewed on the premises. A popular meeting place for local groups. ❀ 🍺 ≈ ⌂ P

Shoulder of Mutton
11 Neale Road, Lockwood (near A6161/B6108 jct)
☎ (01484) 424835
7 (3 Sat)-11; 12-10.30 Sun

Boddingtons Bitter; Taylor Best Bitter, Landlord; Tetley Mild, Bitter; guest beers Ⓗ
Walnut-panelled pub with warm old fashioned charm and a traditional tap room. There is plenty of conversation, which is not drowned by the legendary juke box. Located in a quiet cobbled corner, off the Meltham road.
❀ ≈ (Lockwood) ♣

Slubbers Arms
1 Halifax Old Road, Hillhouse (off A641, ³/₄ mile from centre)
☎ (01484) 429032
11-3, 7-11; 12-3, 7-10.30 Sun

Marston's Pedigree; Taylor Golden Best, Best Bitter, Landlord; guest beer Ⓗ
Mid-19th-century pub, crammed with memorabilia ranging from the early textile days through to some interesting beer dispensers from the 1960s. Popular with students and folk fans.
🏨 Q ❀ 🍺 ♣ 🍴

Zeneca Recreation Club
509 Leeds Road (A62, 1¹/₂ miles NE of town)
☎ (01484) 421784
12-11; 12-3, 7-10.30 Sun

Taylor Best Bitter; Tetley Bitter; guest beer Ⓗ
Recent CAMRA award-winning club with a spacious, comfortable bar area. An outdoor area is used for watching the sports activities. Show this *Guide* or CAMRA membership to gain entry. Good value, home-cooked lunches (not served Sat). ❀ 🍺 ♣ P 🍴

IDLE

Albion Inn

25 New Line, Greengates (A657) ☎ (01274) 613211
12-11; 12-4, 7-10.30 Sun

Taylor Landlord; Tetley Mild, Bitter Ⓗ
Friendly, two-roomed local on the main Leeds-Keighley road. 🍺 ♣ P

Idle Working Mens' Club
23 High Street
☎ (01274) 613602
12-3 (4 Fri & Sat), 7.30 (7 Fri & Sat)-11; 12-3, 7-10.30 Sun

Tetley Bitter; guest beers Ⓗ
Friendly social club established in this fine stone-fronted building in 1928. It hosts entertainment weekend eves and stocks two guest beers, one in the downstairs games room and one in the lounge. Show this *Guide* or CAMRA membership card to be signed in. ♣

New Inn
58 High Street
☎ (01274) 613161
12-11; 12-10.30 Sun

Taylor Landlord; Tetley Bitter; guest beers Ⓗ
Friendly, 19th-century local, popular with local amateur singers for karaoke Wed and piano nights Fri and Sat. Eve meals served 5.30-7.30 Wed-Fri; children's menu and reductions for senior citizens.
🍺 🅳 ♣ P

ILKLEY

Bar T'at
7 Cuncliffe Road (behind Betty's Tea Rooms)
☎ (01943) 608888
12-11; 12-10.30 Sun

Black Sheep Best Bitter; Caledonian Deuchars IPA; Taylor Landlord; guest beers Ⓗ
Recently converted china shop, at the town centre, on two levels with a no-smoking area downstairs. A good range of foreign bottled beers plus a limited but unusual menu are added features.
Q ❀ 🍺 ≈ ♣ 🍴

Riverside Hotel
Riverside Gardens
☎ (01943) 607338
11-11; 12-10.30 Sun

Samuel Smith OBB; Tetley Bitter; Thwaites Bitter Ⓗ
Set in parkland, this two-roomed hotel bar is comfortable and welcoming for families. It has an outdoor play area and riverside patio.
🏨 Q ❀ 🛏 🍺 ≈ ♣ P

KEIGHLEY

Burlington Arms
Market Street
☎ (01535) 603320
11-11; 12-10.30 Sun

Taylor Golden Best, Best Bitter P
This T-shaped pub, with a games room, offers a bright friendly welcome from both long-standing staff and the locals. Snacks available most lunchtimes. ⊛ ➥ 🍴

Cricketers Arms
Coney Lane
☎ (01535) 669912
11.30-11; 12-10.30 Sun
Moorhouse's Premier; Taylor Golden Best; guest beers H
This small, cosy pub was well refurbished by the former Worth Brewery in 1999. The walls have been taken back to bare stone and one drinking area features tram-style seating with luggage racks. Two guest beers usually come from local micros. ➥ ♣

Friendly
2 Aireworth Street
☎ (01535) 672136
12-11; 12-5, 7-11 Sat; 12-10.30 Sun
Taylor Golden Best, Best Bitter P
Small, end-of-terrace local of two rooms, friendly by name and friendly by nature. 1960s background music is regularly played. 🍴

Globe
Parkwood Street
☎ (01535) 610802
11.30-11; 12-10.30 Sun
Taylor Golden Best, Dark Mild, Best Bitter, Landlord, Ram Tam (occasional) H
Friendly, comfortably furnished house with three open rooms and a bar area. Home to the local sub aqua, swimming and pigeon clubs, the pub is a familiar sight to travellers on Worth Valley Railway which passes close by. ▥ Q ◖ ▮ & ➥ ♣ P

KEIGHLEY TO OXENHOPE AND BACK
Keighley & Worth Valley Railway Buffet Car
Stations at Keighley, Ingrow West, Oakworth, Haworth & Oxenhope
☎ (01535) 645214; talking timetable 647777
Sat, Sun & Bank Hols, March-Oct
Beer range varies H
Volunteer-run steam railway buffet car giving changing views of the Worth valley. The beers are from independent breweries.
Q ▲ ➥ (Keighley) P ⌀ 🍴

Try also: Brewery Arms, Longcroft (Free)

LEEDS: *CITY*
City of Mabgate
45 Mabgate (near bus station)
☎ (0113) 245 7789

11-11; 12-3.30, 7.30-10.30 Sun
Boddingtons Bitter; Taylor Landlord; Whitbread Trophy; guest beers H
Cosy back-street pub, popular with locals and real ale fans alike, comprising a basic public bar and a comfy lounge. A permanent Roosters' beer is available as well as up to four guests, two of which are usually Fuller's London Pride and Adnams Best Bitter. Weekday lunches. ▥ ⊛ ◖ & ⌀

Duck & Drake
43 Kirkgate
☎ (0113) 246 5806
11-11; 12-10.30 Sun
Old Mill Bitter; Taylor Golden Best, Landlord; Theakston Best Bitter, Old Peculier; guest beers H
Basic, two-roomed, wooden-floored ale house, set beside the railway bridge. A wide range of real ales and long-serving friendly staff make this pub popular with old and young alike. Ten successive years in this *Guide*. Live jazz Mon and Thu.
▥ ➥ (City) ♣ ⌀

Palace
Kirkgate
☎ (0113) 244 5882
11-11; 12-10.30 Sun
Ind Coope Burton Ale; Marston's Pedigree; Tetley Dark Mild, Bitter; guest beers H
Tremendously successful pub since its conversion to a Festival Ale House by Allied-Domecq with one of the widest choices of guest beers you will find in the city centre, however, premium prices apply. Enjoy the heated garden. Meals served 12-7 (4 Sun). ⊛ ◖ ♣ ⊞

Prince of Wales
Mill Hill
☎ (0113) 245 2434
11-11; 12-10.30 Sun
Black Sheep Best Bitter; John Smith's Bitter; guest beers H
City-centre retreat from the mediocrity that abounds in this area – with one or two notable exceptions. Two rooms, a pool/TV room with green baize motif and a larger bric-a-brac filled lounge. The outside is usually festooned with floral baskets. Weekday lunches. ▥ ◖ ➥ (City)

Scarbrough Hotel
Bishopgate Street
☎ (0113) 243 4590
11-11; 12-10.30 Sun
Black Sheep Best Bitter; Marston's Pedigree; Tetley Bitter; guest beers H
Busy city-centre pub near the station which retains its original Ind Coope tiled exterior. Occasional beer festivals are held, but offering

---

up to eight guest beers, plus a cider and/or perry, means the pub always has one of the widest selection of ales available. Meals served 12-6.
⊛ ◖ ▮ & ➥ (City) ⌀

Victoria Family & Commercial Hotel
28 Great George Street (behind Town Hall)
☎ (0113) 245 1386
11-11; 12-10.30 Sun
Black Sheep Best Bitter; Marston's Pedigree; Tetley Dark Mild, Bitter; guest beers H
Victorian pub, happily retaining much of its original character; the main room is full of glass and wood and has its traditional alcoves. The two side rooms off the main hallway are open at busy times. Popular at lunch with office workers.
Q ◖ ▮ ➥ (City) ⌀

Whip Inn
Bowers Yard (down alleyway off Duncan St)
☎ (0113) 242 7246
11-11; 12-3, 8-10.30 Sun
Tetley Mild, Bitter H
This fine, uncompromising drinking establishment is Leeds' oldest traditional courtyard pub. It has won awards for the quality of its beer and is one of the few outlets stocking the light version of Tetley Mild. The drinking area is on two levels. ⊛ ➥ (City) ♣

LEEDS: *EAST*
Cross Green
54 Cross Green Lane
☎ (0113) 248 0338
11-11; 12-10.30 Sun
John Smith's Bitter; Tetley Dark Mild, Bitter H
Friendly local boozer.
Q ⌸ & ♣ P

LEEDS: *NORTH*
Chemic Tavern
9 Johnston Street, Woodhouse
☎ (0113) 295 0195
11-11; 12-10.30 Sun
Taylor Landlord; Tetley Bitter; guest beer (occasional) H
Compact two-roomed pub where the low beamed ceiling and traditional decor give a cosy feel. At the front is a comfortable lounge and at the back a public bar.
⌸ ♣ P

New Roscoe
Bristol Street, Sheepscar
☎ (0113) 246 0778
11.30-11; 12-10.30 Sun
Tetley Bitter; guest beer H
This lively, welcoming pub boasts an original Irish theme. See the mural outside

depicting Leeds personalities and the scale model of the late lamented Roscoe in the music room. It hosts live music most eves and a quality talent night Tue. Meals 12-7 Mon-Thu.
❀ ◐◗ ⊞ ♣ P

LEEDS: *SOUTH*

Blooming Rose
19 Burton Row, Hunslet Moor
☎ (0113) 270 0426
11-11; 12-10.30 Sun
Black Sheep Best Bitter; Tetley Bitter; guest beer Ⓗ
Welcoming, suburban local, facing on to Hunslet Moor, popular with drinkers of all ages and backgrounds, particularly at lunchtimes for the wide variety of excellent value meals. The guest beer is usually from a large regional. Summer drinking on the moor is a must.
❀ ◐ ⊞ ♣ P ⚟

Garden Gate ☆
3 Whitfield Place, Hunslet (pedestrian precinct)
☎ (0113) 270 0379
12-11; 12-10.30 Sun
Tetley Bitter Ⓗ
Magnificent Edwardian pub with a central corridor and four rooms off. The original interior displays fine faïence, tiling, mahogany panelling and etched glass. Wonderful architecture combines with a friendly, welcoming, down-to-earth atmosphere. ♨ ⊞ ♣

Grove
Back Row, Holbeck
☎ (0113) 243 9254
12-11; 12-4, 7-11 Sat; 12-10.30 Sun
Courage Directors; Marston's Pedigree; Ruddles County; John Smith's Bitter; Tetley Bitter; Theakston XB Ⓗ
Classic inter-war pb with a tiled West Riding corridor. Multi-roomed, each room has its own 'feel'. Free live music is performed in the back room most nights (ring beforehand to check). Bitter and lager are served in different glasses – a welcome rarity these days! No food Sat. ♨ ❀ ◐ ⊞ ⇌ (City) ♣

LEEDS: *WEST*

Beech Hotel
8 Tong Road, Lower Wortley
☎ (0113) 263 8659
11-11; 12-3, 7-10.30 Sun
Tetley Bitter Ⓗ
Friendly, community local with genuine Irish connections; its Melbourne Brewery exterior features etched windows and mosaic. Inside the main bar area is supplemented by two smaller rooms at the back, decorated with brassware and sports trophies. ⊞ ♣

Beer-Ritz Off-Licence
14 Weetwood Lane, Far Headingley
☎ (0113) 275 3464
10-10; 12-8.30 Sun
Beer range varies Ⓗ
Enterprising specialist off-licence, opposite Bryan's Fish Restaurant, stocking a wide range of beers, many bottle-conditioned, from Britain and overseas; the cider choice varies. ⌓

Eldon
190 Woodhouse Lane (opp. University)
☎ (0113) 245 3387
11-11; 12-10.30 Sun
Marston's Pedigree; Tetley Bitter; guest beers Ⓗ
Festival Ale House, popular with staff and students from the University. Open plan, but a mixture of pillars and a raised area offers some seclusion. Big screen TV. Regular promotions (Mon) and occasional beer festivals; up to four guest beers stocked in term time. ◐◗ ♿

Highland
36 Cavendish Street, Burley (down steps to left of Sentinel Towers on Burley Road)
☎ (0113) 242 8592
11.30-11; 12-10.30 Sun
Tetley Dark Mild, Bitter Ⓗ
Victorian triangular-shaped local that would have once been at the end of a terrace, but now nestles amongst commercial buildings and student flats. The narrow main room has a bar along the middle of one side and there is a games room at one end. ♣

Old Vic
17 Whitecote Hill, Bramley (400 yds from A657/B6157 jct) ☎ (0113) 256 1207
4 (2 Fri; 11 Sat)-11; 12-3, 7-10.30 Sun
Black Sheep Best Bitter; Taylor Landlord; Tetley Bitter; guest beers Ⓗ
Spacious converted vicarage, hence the name. This popular three-roomed free house has a serving area offering two changing guest beers plus a house beer from Coach House.
♨ Q ❀ ⊞ ♿ ♣ P

Sun Inn
153 Town Street, Stanningley, Pudsey
☎ (0113) 257 4894
11.30 (11 Sat)-3, 6 (7 Sat)-11; 1-5, 7-10.30 Sun
Tetley Mild, Bitter; guest beer Ⓗ
Multi-roomed local served from a central bar: the basic tap room with a pool table is entered via the side door. Either side of the front door is a small snug and a dining area leads into a comfortable lounge area. ❀ ◐◗ ⊞ P

West End House
Abbey Road, Kirkstall (A65, $2^{1}/_{2}$ miles from city centre)
☎ (0113) 278 6332
11-11; 12-10.30 Sun
Boddingtons Bitter; Tetley Bitter; guest beers Ⓗ
Stone-built roadside pub, with a split-level lounge, next to a sports centre and close to Kirkstall Abbey. First referred to as an alehouse in 1867, nearby streets are named after its first landlord (Tordoff). Up to four guest beers on tap, one from Theakston. No food Sun eve.
❀ ◐◗ ⇌ (Headingley)

LINTHWAITE

Sair Inn
139 Lane Top (top of Hoyle Ing, off A62) OS100143
☎ (01484) 842370
7 (5 Fri, 12 Sat)-11; 12-10.30 Sun
Linfit Mild, Bitter, Cascade, Special, Autumn Gold, English Guineas Stout, seasonal beers Ⓗ
CAMRA National *Pub of the Year* 1997; a gem of an alehouse dating from the 1800s and a brew pub for the past 16 years. Four rooms warmed by coal fires; one room is quiet for non-smokers. Typically 10 beers are on offer. Popular with locals, groups and coach parties from near and far.
♨ Q ⛐ ❀ ♣ ⌓ ⚟

LINTON

Windmill
Main Street (99 bus route from Leeds or Wetherby)
☎ (01937) 582209
11.30-3, 5-11; 11.30-11 Sat; 12-10.30 Sun
Marston's Pedigree; John Smith's Bitter; Theakston Best Bitter; guest beer Ⓗ
A great stone-built pub in the picturesque village of Linton beside the River Wharfe, often with three roaring fires alight. Two drinking areas with a friendly atmosphere created by a mix of locals and visitors. The restaurant is a must. ♨ ❀ ◐◗ P

LITTLE GOMERSAL

Wheatsheaf
95-96 Gomersal Lane ($^{1}/_{2}$ mile S of A643/A651 jct) OS254205
☎ (01274) 873661
12-3 (not Mon). 5-11; 12-11 Fri & Sat; 12-10.30 Sun

Black Sheep Best Bitter; Tetley
Bitter; guest beer Ⓗ
Former farmhouse licensed in
1858, in a pleasant quasi-
rural setting – it seems to be
back to front upon approach.
Said to be haunted, it retains
a country feel with a three-
roomed interior and
brassware. The house beer is
from Barge and Barrel. No
food Sun eve or Mon.
🛏 ☀ ◑ ♣ P ✲

MARSDEN
Riverhead Brewery Tap
2 Peel Street (off A62)
☎ (01484) 841270
5 (4 Fri; 11 Sat)-11; 12-10.30 Sun
Riverhead Sparth Mild, Butterley
Bitter, Deer Hill Porter, Cupwith
Light, Black Moss Stout, March
Haigh Special, seasonal beers Ⓗ
Village brew pub converted
from a Co-op, whose main
beers are named after local
reservoirs. Popular with
visitors, ramblers and locals,
it is close to many
attractions, including the
Pennine Way, Standedge
Tunnel and Huddersfield
Narrow Canal. Q & ≠ ⌣

MYTHOLMROYD
Hinchliffe Arms
Cragg Vale (off B6138, 1¹/₂
miles S of town)
☎ (01422) 883256
12-2.30, 6-11; 12-10.30 Sun
Ruddles County; Taylor Landlord;
Theakston Best Bitter, Black Bull,
Old Peculier Ⓗ
Small rural hotel with a
comfortable lounge bar and a
dining room in a lovely
riverside setting, next to the
village church. On Calderdale
Way, and close to the
Pennine Way, it is popular
with walkers. Good food (not
served Mon eve).
🍴 ☀ ⌂ ◑ Å P

Shoulder of Mutton
38 New Road (B6138)
☎ (01422) 883165
11.30-3, 7-11; 11.30-11 Sat; 12-10.30
Sun
Black Sheep Best Bitter;
Boddingtons Bitter; Castle Eden Ale;
Flowers IPA; Taylor Landlord; guest
beer Ⓗ
Popular roadside local,
boasting a display of Toby
jugs, china, and a collection
of memorabilia from the
notorious Cragg Vale coiners.
Eve meals 7-8.30 (not served
Tue). ◑ ≠ P ✲

OSSETT
Brewers Pride
Low Mill Road (off Healey
Rd) ☎ (01924) 273865
12-3, 5.30-11; 12-11 Fri & Sat; 12-
10.30 Sun

Ossett Excelsior; Taylor Landlord;
guest beers Ⓗ
Popular true free house,
decorated with old brewery
memorabilia. It is a five-
minute walk from the Calder
& Hebble Canal. Four guests
plus another beer from Ossett
Brewery (behind the pub).
Good choice of home-cooked
lunches (mon-Sat). Local
CAMRA *Pub of the Season*
1999. 🍴 Q 🛏 ☀ ◑ ⌣

Red Lion
73 Dewsbury Road (A629, 1
mile from M1 jct 40)
☎ (01924) 273487
12-11; 12-10.30 Sun
John Smith's Bitter; Tetley Bitter;
guest beers Ⓗ
18th-century inn with a low,
oak-beamed ceiling where
two guest beers are usually
available. Popular for good
value home-cooked meals
(not served Sun or Mon eves).
◑ P

OTLEY
Bay Horse
20 Market Place
☎ (01943) 461122
11-11; 12-10.30 Sun
Tetley Mild, Bitter; guest beers Ⓗ
Busy, two-roomed, town-
centre pub with a corridor
drinking area. Note the
stained glass windows. It
retains an outside gents' WC.
☀ ⊟ ♣

Bowling Green
18 Bondgate (near bus
station) ☎ (01943) 461494
12-4, 7-11; 12-3, 7-11; 12-10.30 Sun
Black Sheep Best Bitter; guest
beers Ⓗ
Prominent pub, comprising
an L-shaped main bar,
packed full of unusual relics –
beware the skeleton by the
pool table! Beers from
Briscoe's, now brewed behind
the pub, are always available.
🍴 ☀ ♣

Junction
44 Bondgate (Charles St jct)
☎ (01943) 463233
11-11; 12-10.30 Sun
Black Sheep Best Bitter; Taylor Best
Bitter, Landlord; Tetley Bitter;
Theakston Old Peculier; guest
beer Ⓗ
Excellent, one-roomed,
street-corner pub, popular
with locals and visitors alike.
Acoustic musicians are
welcome Mon; live music
Tue. Leeds CAMRA *Pub of the
Year* 1999. 🍴 ◑ ♣

PONTEFRACT
Golden Lion
Sessions House Yard (next to
courthouse)
☎ (01977) 702915

12 (11 Fri & Sat)-11; 12-10.30 Sun
John Smith's Bitter; guest beers Ⓗ
Two large bars, recently
refurbished; the public has
pool and darts, whilst the
lounge hosts live music Fri
eve and a quiz Wed.
☀ ≠ (Tanshelf) ♣

Robin Hood Inn
4 Wakefield Road (off A645)
☎ (01977) 702231
11.30-3.30 (4.30 Fri & Sat), 7-11;
12-3.30, 7-10.30 Sun
John Smith's Bitter; Tetley Bitter;
guest beers Ⓗ
End-of-town pub: a busy
public bar with three other
drinking areas. Wakefield
CAMRA *Pub of the Year* 1998.
Lunches served Fri & Sun. 🍴
☀ ◑ ≠ (Tanshelf/Baghill) ♣

Tap & Spile
28 Horsefair (opp. bus
station) ☎ (01977) 793468
12-11; 12-3, 7-10.30 Sun
Beer range varies Ⓗ
Chain alehouse with three
drinking areas of bare
floorboards and brickwork. It
hosts occasional music Thu
eve, plus beer festivals at least
twice a year.
≠ (Baghill/Monkhill) ♣ P

PUDSEY
Butchers Arms
30 Church Lane
☎ (0113) 256 4313
11-11; 12-10.30 Sun
Samuel Smith OBB Ⓗ
One of Pudsey's more mature
drinking establishments, this
sturdy stone pub offers cosy
fires, traditional surroundings
and a warm welcome.
Popular with post office
workers from across the road.
☀ ◑ ♣

Royal
30 Station Street
☎ (0113) 256 4085
11-11; 12-10.30 Sun
Thwaites Bitter Ⓗ
Grand pub, built to serve a
long-gone station, with a
wood-panelled corridor, co-
ordinating twin lounges to
the left and a lively tap to the
right, all boasting old settles
and original fittings. Clubs –
from bikers to ukelele – meet
here. Outside seating is in the
car park. ☀ ⊟ P

RAWDON
Emmott Arms
Town Street (600 yds from
A65/A658 jct)
☎ (0113) 250 6036
11-11; 12-10.30 Sun
Samuel Smith OBB Ⓗ
Old, stone, hilltop local,
affording good views over the
Aire Valley. A comfortable
lounge is complemented by a

traditional tap room; the upstairs function room is also used for Sunday lunches. 🏶 ◖⌂ ♣ P

RIPPONDEN
Old Bridge Inn
Priest Lane (off A58, near B6113 jct)
☎ (01422) 822595
12-3, 5.30-11; 12-11 Sat; 12-10.30 Sun

Black Sheep Best Bitter, Special; Taylor Golden Best, Best Bitter, Landlord; guest beer Ⓗ
Possibly Yorkshire's oldest pub (recorded as early as 1307), in a picturesque setting by a packhorse bridge. Note: only the guest beer pumps are labelled. 🏶 ◖▶ P

SCAMMONDEN
Brown Cow
Saddleworth Road, Deanhead (B6114, 2 1/2 miles S of Barkisland)
☎ (01422) 822227
12-3 (not Mon-Thu), 7-11; 12-3, 7-10.30 Sun

Mansfield Riding Bitter; guest beers Ⓗ
High moorland coaching inn, overlooking Scammonden Water. Popular with cross-Pennine travellers, it features a noteworthy collection of old firefighting equipment and unusual clocks. Well worth a visit, despite the remote location. 🏶Q ➿ 🏶 ◖▶ ▲ ♣ P

SCAPEGOAT HILL
Scape House Inn
13a High Street
☎ (01484) 654144
12-3, 6-11; 12-3, 6-10.30 Sun

Jennings Mild, Bitter, Cumberland Ale, Cocker Hoop, Sneck Lifter Ⓗ
Attractive, 200-year-old pub in an elevated position giving scenic views across the Colne Valley. Its walls are adorned with horse and carriage artefacts, old photos of Huddersfield and a collection of walking sticks. Popular for food, and a rare local outlet for Jennings beers. 🏶🏶 ◖▶ P

SHAW CROSS
Huntsman
Chidswell Lane (400 yds from A653/B6128 jct)
☎ (01924) 275700
12-3, 7 (5 Fri)-11; 12-3, 7-10.30 Sun

Black Sheep Best Bitter; Taylor Landlord; guest beer Ⓗ
Converted from two 17th-century farm cottages, this pub is on the urban fringe, with fine views north towards Leeds. Next to a working farm, and popular with walkers, it boasts a

Yorkshire range and farming bric-a-brac. The house beer is brewed by Highwood. Lunches served Tue-Sat. 🏶🏶 ◖ P

SHELLEY
Three Acres Inn
37-41 Roydhouse (off B6116, near Emley Moor TV mast) OS214124
☎ (01484) 602606
12-3 (not Sat), 7-11; 12-3, 7-10.30 Sun

Adnams Best Bitter; Mansfield Bitter; Marston's Pedigree; Morland Old Speckled Hen; Taylor Landlord; guest beers Ⓗ
Welcoming, turn of the century coaching inn, set in the rolling Pennine countryside. Family owned for 30 years, this terrific hostelry has recently added a delicatessen to complement its reputation as one of the best dining pubs in Britain. 🏶🏶 ➿ ◖▶ P

SHIPLEY
Branch
105 Bradford Road (Otley Rd jct)
☎ (01274) 584495
11.30-11; 12-10.30 Sun

Black Sheep Best Bitter; Ind Coope Burton Ale; Marston's Pedigree; Tetley Bitter; guest beers Ⓗ
Ex-Festival Ale House with a varied clientele and friendly atmosphere. A large rectangular bar dominates the pub, which is decorated with brewery memorabilia. It hosts regular beer festivals. Children allowed in for meals. ◖▶ ➿ P ✄

Fanny's Ale & Cider House
63 Saltaire Road (A657)
☎ (01274) 591419
11.30-3, 5.30-11; 11.30-11 Fri & Sat; 12-10.30 Sun

Taylor Golden Best, Landlord; guest beers Ⓗ
Cosy, nostalgic atmosphere with old brewery memorabilia around the walls of a gaslit lounge. It stocks an excellent range of

Belgian bottled and draught beers. It stands near the historic village of Saltaire. 🏶 ◖ ➿ (Saltaire) ♣ ⌂ P

Shipley Pride
1 Saltaire Road (300 yds from Fox Corner on A657)
☎ (01274) 585341
11.30-11; 12-3, 7-10.30 Sun

Taylor Landlord; Tetley Bitter; guest beers Ⓗ
Two-roomed friendly local, formerly the Old Beehive Hotel, with a central bar. Home-made lunches are a speciality. 🏶 ◖ ➿ ♣ P

Sun Hotel
3 Kirkgate
☎ (01274) 530757
11-11; 12-10.30 Sun

Boddingtons Bitter; Taylor Landlord; Theakston Best Bitter; guest beers Ⓗ
Popular, two-bar, Wetherspoon's pub where two levels are linked by a central staircase. Up to six guest ales, and food available every day until 10pm, all at reasonable prices. Q 🏶 🏶 ◖▶ ♿ ➿ ✄

Victoria Hotel
192 Saltaire Road (A657)
☎ (01274) 585642
11.30-11; 12-10.30 Sun

Boddingtons Bitter; Taylor Landlord; Whitbread Trophy; guest beers Ⓗ
Two-roomed friendly local bearing a Victorian-style decor of stained glass and wood in the lounge; the lively tap room is popular with younger customers. The historic village of Saltaire lies across the main road. 🏶 ◖⌂ ➿ (Saltaire) ♣ P

Try also: **Noble Comb**, Mill Road (Free)

SOUTHOWRAM
Shoulder of Mutton
14 Cain Lane
☎ (01422) 361101
12 (2.30 Wed)-11; 12-10.30 Sun

Greene King Abbot; Ruddles Best Bitter; guest beers Ⓗ
Hilltop village local serving

INDEPENDENT BREWERIES

Barge & Barrel: Elland	**Ossett:** Ossett
Boat: Allerton Bywater	**Rat & Ratchet:** Huddersfield
Briscoe's: Otley	
Clark's: Wakefield	**Riverhead:** Marsden
Fernandes: Wakefield	**Ryburn:** Sowerby Bridge
Goose Eye: Keighley	**Sunset:** Dewbury
Huddersfield: Huddersfield	**Taylor:** Keighley
Kitchen: Huddersfield	**Turkey Inn:** Goose Eye
Linfit: Linthwaite	**West Yorkshire:** Ludenden Foot

changing guest beers. Regular activities include charity quizzes and slide shows. 🏠 ♣

SOWERBY BRIDGE
Alma Inn
Cottonstones, Mill Bank (1¼ miles off A58 at Triangle pub) OS028215 ☎ (01422) 823334
6 (7 winter, 12 Sat)-11; 12-10.30 Sun
Taylor Best Bitter, Landlord; Tetley Bitter; guest beer Ⓗ
Popular, stone-flagged rural pub with commanding views. It stocks 80-plus Belgian bottled beers and hosts annual Belgian, German and other theme weekends, often with appropriate food. No meals Tue eve. 🏠 Q 🐾 ▶ & ♣ ⌂ P

Puzzle Hall Inn
21 Hollins Mill Lane
☎ (01422) 835547
12-11; 12-10.30 Sun
Beer range varies Ⓗ
Former premises of the Puzzle Hall Brewery, this ever-popular inn hosts a wide variety of events, including jazz, live bands, games and curry nights (Wed). 🏠 🐾 ◀ ≈ ♣ ⌂ P

Rams Head Inn
26 Wakefield Road
☎ (01422) 83576
12-2 (5 Sat), 7-11; 12-3, 7-10.30 Sun
Ryburn Best Bitter, Light, Ryedale Bitter, Stabbers, Coiners or Luddite Ⓗ
Home of Ryburn Brewery, housed in the cellar, the pub is popular with all ages. The two rooms have been subdivided and connected to an outside drinking area. Emphasis is on food at lunchtimes. Sing-alongs Sat and Sun eves. Some beers may not have pumpclips. 🏠 🐾 ◀ ♣

THORNHILL
Savile Arms (Church House)
Church Lane (B6117, 2½ miles S of Dewsbury)
☎ (01924) 463738
5-11; 12-4, 7-11 Sat; 12-4, 7-11 Sun
Black Sheep Best Bitter; Old Mill Bitter; Tetley Bitter; guest beers Ⓗ
This 600-year-old pub shares consecrated ground with the adjacent church of St Michael which contains fine Savile family tombs and stained glass dating from the 1400s. The pub features a tropical fish tank and displays of local artists' work. Not suitable for children. 🐾 ♣ P ⊞

THORNTON
Thornton Cricket Club

Hill Top Road (path behind No 104)
☎ (01274) 834585
8 (2 Sat)-11 (closed winter Sat); 8-11 Sun
Taylor Golden Best, Best Bitter, Landlord Ⓗ
A warm welcome awaits in this hilltop haven. On good days catch the spectacular views and the occasional cover drive. Enthusiastic volunteers staff the bar. Show CAMRA membership card or this *Guide* to be signed in. 🐾 ♣

TODMORDEN
Cross Keys
649 Rochdale Road, Walsden (A6033)
☎ (01706) 815185
12-11; 12-10.30 Sun
Black Sheep Best Bitter; Fuller's London Pride; Lees Bitter; Taylor Landlord; guest beers Ⓗ
The bar faces the canal through a pleasant lounge and conservatory extension. A small snug, and a large tap room add extra appeal to this busy local. The beer range normally includes a mild. 🐾 ◀ ▶ ▲ ≈ (Walsden) ♣

Queen Hotel
Rise Lane (by station)
☎ (01706) 811500
11-11; 12-10.30 Sun
Black Sheep Best Bitter; Lees GB Mild, Bitter; Marston's Pedigree; Taylor Landlord; guest beers Ⓗ
Large bar in a hotel which offers many facilities to residents, including a gym, sauna and swimming pool. 🛏 ◀ ▶ & ≈ P

Top Brink
Lumbutts (near disused water mill) OS957235
☎ (01706) 812696
6 (12 Sat)-11; 12-10.30 Sun
Boddingtons Bitter; Castle Eden Ale; Flowers Original; Taylor Landlord; guest beer Ⓗ
Mid 18th-century village inn with an emphasis on food. Dark wood panelling and brassware abound. It stands on the Calderdale Way, close to Mankinholes youth hostel and the Pennine Way. Guest beers come from various micros. Meals served all day Sun. 🐾 ◀ ▶ ▲ P

White Hart
White Hart Fold
☎ (01706) 812198
11-3.30, 7-11; 11.30-11 Fri & Sat; 12-10.30 Sun
Tetley Bitter; guest beers Ⓗ
Imposing 1930s 'Brewer's Tudor'-style pub, popular with all ages. Up to three guest beers available. 🐾 ◀ ▲ ≈ ♣ P

UPPER HOPTON
Freemasons Arms
36 Hopton Hall Lane (B6118)
☎ (01924) 492093
11.30-11; 12-10.30 Sun
Black Sheep Special; Old Mill Bitter; John Smith's Bitter; Taylor Landlord; guest beers Ⓗ
Revitalised country pub and Italian restaurant with fine views to the south from the large conservatory. The house beer is usually from Caledonian Brewery. No food Mon. 🏠 Q 🐾 ▶ & ♣ ⌂ P

WAINSTALLS
Cat i' th' Well Inn
Wainstalls Lane, Lower Saltonstall (¼ mile W of town) OS042285
☎ (01422) 244841
7-11 (12-3, 6-11 Sat & summer); 12-3, 7 (6 summer)-10.30 Sun
Castle Eden Ale; Taylor Golden Best, Best Bitter, Landlord Ⓗ
Comfortable, traditional country inn, set in a picturesque wooded valley. The interior is enhanced by oak panelling which came from a demolished Victorian castle. Popular with walkers. Lunches served Sat; sandwiches Sun. Quiz night Mon. Q 🐾 ♣ P

WAKEFIELD
Albion
94 Stanley Road, Eastmoor
☎ (01924) 376206
11-4, 7-11; 11-11 Fri & Sat; 12-10.30 Sun
Samuel Smith OBB Ⓗ
Impressive, 1930s local at the edge of the town centre. This thriving pub hosts various games and social nights. No meals service, but you may take food in. 🐾 ▥ ≈ (Kirkgate) ♣ P

Fernandes Brewery Tap
The Old Malthouse, 5 Avison Yard, Kirkgate
☎ (01924) 291709
5 (11 Fri & Sat)-11; 12-10.30 Sun
Fernandes Maltshovel Mild, Wakefield Pride, Double Six, guest beers Ⓗ
Old 19th-century malthouse where the top floor maltstore has been converted to the brewery tap featuring an extensive collection of brewery memorabilia, original beams and a cosy atmosphere. There's no strangers in this bar, just friends we have not met yet. Q ◀ ▶ ≈ (Kirkgate) P

Harry's Bar
107b Westgate (near station)
☎ (01924) 373773

12-11; closed Sun

Taylor Landlord; Tetley Bitter; guest beers Ⓗ

Small, one-roomed pub hidden just off Westgate but certainly not aimed at the 'Westgate Crowd'. Good value, home-made meals include a 'healthy option'.
🏚 ❀ ◖ ﴾ ≠ (Westgate)

Kings Arms
Heath Common, Heath (off A6555, Wakefield road)
☎ (01924) 377527
11-3, 5.30-11; 12-10.30 Sun

Clark's Traditional Bitter; Taylor Landlord; Tetley Bitter; guest beer Ⓗ

17th-century pub: three oak-panelled rooms with gas lighting, plus an *à la carte* restaurant and family conservatory. There are extensive gardens to rear and a village green to the front. The guest beers are supplied by Clark's. 🏚 Q ⏵ ❀ ◖ ﴾ P

O'Donoghues
60 George Street (near station) ☎ (01924) 291326
5-11; 1-10.30 Sun

Ossett Silver Link, Excelsior; guest beers Ⓗ

Traditional ale house. Enjoy the warm friendly atmosphere, real log fires and unaltered decor. Traditional live music is played by local musicians. All welcome; wheelchair access is via back door. 🏚 Q ⏵ ﴾ ≠ (Westgate)

Redoubt ☆
28 Horbury Road
☎ (01924) 377485
11.30-11; 12-4, 7-10.30 Sun

Taylor Landlord; Tetley Mild, Bitter Ⓗ

Four-roomed Tetley Heritage house with strong RL connections. This cosy, unspoilt pub offers traditional pub games. Local CAMRA *Pub of the Season* winner 1999.
❀ ﴾ ≠ (Westgate) ♣ P

Six Chimneys
41-43 Kirkgate (off the precinct, near bus station)
☎ (01924) 239449
11-11; 12-10.30 Sun

Boddingtons Bitter; Courage Directors; Tetley Bitter; Theakston Best Bitter; guest beers Ⓗ

Busy, city-centre pub offering a large no-smoking area, free from juke box and fruit machines. Curry night every Thu.
Q ﴾ ≠ (Kirkgate/Westgate) ⌦

Wakefield Labour Club (Red Shed)
18 Vicarage Street (behind market) ☎ (01924) 215626
11-4 (not Mon-Thu), 7-11; 12-4, 7-10.30 Sun

Beer range varies Ⓗ

Small, friendly club, built of wood, stocking beers from small independent breweries, plus a wide range of Belgian beers, and occasional ciders. Finalist in the CAMRA national *Club of the Year* competition 1997, '98 and joint winner 1999.
Q ≠ (Westgate/Kirkgate) ♣ P ⎕

WARMFIELD
Plough
45 Warmfield Lane (400 yds from A655)
☎ (01924) 862007
12-3, 5-11; 12-11 Sat; 12-10.30 Sun

John Smith's Bitter; Theakston Best Bitter; guest beer Ⓗ

Unspoilt, 18th century inn, overlooking the lower Calder Valley, with a low, beamed ceiling. It has been recently sympathetically refurbished by the owner. Good bar meals; a changing Ossett Brewery beer is usually stocked. 🏚 ❀ ◖ ▶ ♣ P

WIBSEY
Gaping Goose
5-6 Slack Bottom Road (off Buttershaw Lane)
☎ (01274) 601701
4 (2 Sat)-11; 12-10.30 Sun

Black Sheep Best Bitter; Tetley Bitter Ⓗ

Intimate village local, well worth seeking out. A comfortable lounge boasts a large display of brassware and pottery, whilst the tap room is games-oriented. Limited parking. ❀ ⌲ ♣ P

WINTERSETT
Angler's Retreat
Ferrytop Lane (between Crofton and Ryhill villages)
OS382157
☎ (01924) 862370

12-3, 7-11; 12-3, 7-10.30 Sun

Barnsley Bitter; Tetley Bitter; Theakston Black Bull, XB; guest beer Ⓗ

Cosy, two-roomed rural pub, handy for anglers and bird watchers visiting the nearby reservoir, country park and heronry centre. Biker-friendly. 🏚 ❀ P

WRENTHORPE
New Pot Oil
Wrenthorpe Road (off A650, 2 miles from M1 jct 41)
☎ (01924) 373133
12-11; 12-10.30 Sun

Tetley Bitter; guest beers Ⓗ

Large village pub with one main room, but plenty of alcoves where you can enjoy a quiet pint. The family room is to the rear. Lunchtime snacks available.
⏵ ❀ ♣ P

YEADON
Albert
High Street
☎ (0113) 250 0420
12-11; 12-4, 7-10.30 Sun

Taylor Landlord; Tetley Mild, Bitter Ⓗ

Friendly corner local, with a long, narrow lounge and a small functional tap room, close to Yeadon Tarn. ♣

Woolpack
18 New Road (A65 between Rawdon and Guiseley)
☎ (0113) 250 6079
11-11; 12-10.30 Sun

Marston's Pedigree; Tetley Bitter; guest beers Ⓗ

Popular, much-enlarged Punch Taverns Festival Alehouse on the busy Leeds-Ilkley road. It stocks five guest beers, plus a cider and occasional perry, lunches served until 5 Sun.
❀ ◖ ♣ ⌂ P

Choosing Pubs

Pubs in the Good Beer Guide are chosen by CAMRA members and branches. There is no payment for entry, and pubs are inspected on a regular basis by personal visits, not sent a questionnaire once a year, as is the case with some pub guides. CAMRA branches monitor all the pubs in their areas, and the choice of pubs for the Guide is often the result of voting at branch meetings. However, recommendations from readers are warmly welcomed and will be passed on to the relevant CAMRA branch: please use the form at the back of the Guide.

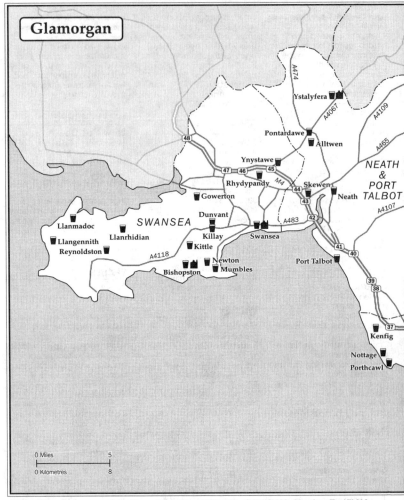

Glamorgan

Ystalyfera
Pontardawe
Alltwen
Ynystawe
Rhydypandy
Gowerton
Skewen
Neath
NEATH & PORT TALBOT
Dunvant
SWANSEA
Killay
Kittle
Swansea
Llanmadoc
Llangennith
Reynoldston
Llanrhidian
Newton
Mumbles
Bishopston
Port Talbot
Kenfig
Nottage
Porthcawl

0 Miles 5
0 Kilometres 8

Authority areas covered: Bridgend UA, Caerphilly UA, Cardiff UA, Merthyr Tydfil UA, Neath & Port Talbot UA, Rhondda, Cynon, Taff UA, Swansea UA, Vale of Glamorgan UA

ABERAMAN

Blaengwawr Inn
373 Cardiff Road
☎ (01685) 871706
11-11; 12-10.30 Sun
Cains Bitter; Worthington Bitter; guest beers Ⓗ
Lively, single bar local, strong on community spirit, with a pleasant atmosphere.
🏠 ♣

ABERCARN

Old Swan
55 Commercial Road
☎ (01495) 243161
4 (11 Fri & Sat)-11; 12-10.30 Sun
Courage Best Bitter; Ⓗ/Ⓖ Ushers seasonal beers Ⓗ
Friendly, single-bar pub with a warm welcome. Courage Best on gravity is a popular choice.
🏠 ♣

ABERCYNON

Royal Oak
Incline Top (off B4059)
OS089956
☎ (01443) 742229
4 (12 Sat)-11; 12-10.30 Sun
Hancock's HB; guest beer Ⓗ
Comfortable, welcoming local sited at the top of the locks of the former Glamorganshire Canal, it is difficult to find but worth it.
🏠 🍴 🅿 🏡 ♣ P

ABERTHIN

Farmers Arms
On A4222 1 mile from Cowbridge traffic lights
☎ (01446) 773429
11.30-11; 12-10.30 Sun
Watkin's OSB; Young's Bitter; guest beers Ⓗ
Pleasant, friendly village pub serving excellent food Tue-

Sat; children's meals and vegetarian dishes are also available.
Q 🏠 🍴 🅿 ♣ P

ALLTWEN

Butchers Arms
Alltwen Hill
☎ (01792) 863100
12-3, 6.30-11; 12-3, 7-10.30 Sun
Courage Directors; Everards Original; John Smith's Bitter Wadworth 6X; guest beer Ⓗ
Large free house in a quiet hillside village; the single bar and restaurant are both popular with diners. Beer prices are expensive for the area. 🏠 🏡 🍴 🅿 P

BEDWELLTY

New Inn
☎ (01443) 831625
12-3.30, 7-11; 12-3 (closed eve) Sun

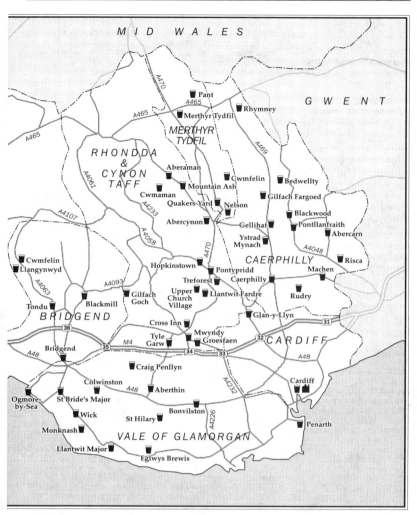

Buckley's Rev. James; Hancock's HB; guest beer (occasional) H
Well-appointed, pleasantly furnished free house, with a plush drinking area and a good restaurant (open Tue-Sat eves).
🏚 🅐 ◗ ▶ P

BISHOPSTON

Joiners Arms
50 Bishopston Road
☎ (01792) 232658
11-11; 12-10.30 Sun
Courage Best Bitter; John Smith's Bitter; Swansea Bishopswood Bitter; Three Cliffs Gold, Original Wood, seasonal beers; guest beers H
Home of Swansea Brewing Co. and 1999 South and Mid Wales CAMRA *Pub of the Year*. This pub is popular with locals and visitors alike. It hosts regular beer festivals and serves good value food; a must.
🏚 Q 🅐 ◗ ▶ ♣ P

BLACKMILL

Ogmore Junction Hotel
On A4061
☎ (01656) 840371
11.30-11; 12-10.30 Sun
Draught Bass; Worthington Bitter; guest beers H
Attractive, old, friendly well-run pub, offering beer exceptional in quality and variety for the area. Local CAMRA *Pub of the Year* 1999. No meals Sun eve.
Q 🅐 ◗ ▶ 🖽 ⅃ ♣ P

BLACKWOOD

Rock & Fountain
St David's Avenue, Woodfieldside (from High St take turn opp. Argos, follow road to river)
☎ (01495) 223907
12 (3 Mon)-11; 12-10.30 Sun
Marston's Pedigree; Worthington Bitter; guest beer H
Traditional friendly pub by

Sirhowy River; recently refurbished. Good food includes genuine home-made chips with meals (no food Sun eve or Mon).
🏚 ◗ ▶ ♣ P

BONVILSTON

Red Lion
On A48 ☎ (01446) 781208
11.30-3, 5-11; 11-11.30 Sat; 12-3, 7-10.30 Sun
Brains Dark, Bitter, SA H
Award-winning village pub on the main road enjoying a good reputation for food (eve meals Tue-Sat).
🅐 ◗ ♣ P

BRIDGEND

Coach
37 Cowbridge Road
☎ (01656) 649321
11.30-11; 12-10.30 Sun
Draught Bass; Worthington Bitter H
Friendly, quiet, award-

winning pub near the college. No meals served Sun eve. 🏾 ◖ ♿ ₮

Famous Penybont Inn
Derwen Road
☎ (01656) 652266
11-11; 12-10.30 Sun
Marston's Pedigree; Tetley Bitter; Wadworth 6X; guest beers Ⓗ
Town-centre pub boasting a cosy, friendly atmosphere, much railway memorabilia and reasonably priced meals. It is handy for the railway and bus stations and shops. Food is served 12-7 daily. Wheelchair WC. ◖ ◗ ♿ ₮

Five Bells Inn
Ewenny Road (at A4063/B4265/A4061 jct)
☎ (01656) 664941
11.30-4, 6-11; 11.30-11 Wed-Sat; 12-10.30 Sun
Draught Bass; Worthington Bitter Ⓗ
Cosy pub at a busy road junction, comprising a spacious comfortable bar, an adjoining games area and a quiet lounge on an upper level. No food Sun.
◖ 🍴 ♿ ₮ P

Haywain
Coychurch Road, Brackla
☎ (01656) 669945
11.30-11; 12-10.30 Sun
Morland Old Speckled Hen; Worthington Bitter; guest beers Ⓗ
This large, bustling estate pub, is popular for lunches. No eve meals served Sun.
🌸 ◖ ◗ ♿ P

Wyndham Arms
Dunraven Place
☎ (01656) 663608
11-11; 12-10.30 Sun
Draught Bass; Brains SA; Courage Directors; Theakston Best Bitter; guest beers Ⓗ
Wetherspoon's revival of a large old town-centre hotel, displaying interesting photographs and paintings of old Bridgend. Meals served 11-10 (12-9.30 Sun). An occasional cider is stocked. Wheelchair WC.
Q ◖ ◗ ♿ ₮ ⌂ ✂ 🏵

CAERPHILLY
Courthouse
Cardiff Road
☎ (029) 2088 8120
11-11; 12-10.30 Sun
Morland Old Speckled Hen; Theakston XB; Wadworth 6X Ⓗ
A traditional, 14th-century Welsh longhouse. The conservatory provides panoramic views over the moat to the castle.
Q 🌸 ◖ ◗ ₮

CARDIFF
BBC Cardiff Club

Llantrisant Road, Llandaff
☎ (029) 2032 2734
12-2.30, 5.30-11; 12-3, 7-10.30 Sun
Brains Bitter; guest beer Ⓗ
Members' club where contrasting rooms are set around a central bar. Entry is the door intercom. Mention CAMRA on arrival to be signed in as a guest. Weekday lunches served.
Q 🌸 ◖ ♿ ♣ ✂

Black Lion
Cardiff Road, Llandaff (A4119/High St. jct)
☎ (029) 2056 7312
11-11; 12-3, 7-10.30 Sun
Brains Dark, Bitter, SA; Buckley's Rev. James Ⓗ
Friendly, traditional pub, near Llandaff Cathedral. The spacious lounge stocks a good range of beers. Brains *Cellarmanship* award winner.
Q ◖ 🍴 ₮ (Fairwater) ♣ 🏵

Butchers Arms
29 Llandaff Road (B4267 off Cowbridge Rd E)
☎ (029) 2022 7927
11-11; 12-3, 7-10.30 Sun
Brains Dark, Bitter, SA Ⓗ
Traditional local: a bright, lively public bar is complemented by a smaller, cosy lounge enjoying a strong local following. It stands next to Chapter Arts Centre.
Q 🍴 ♣

Chapter Arts Centre
Market Road, Canton
☎ (029) 2031 1050
6-11 (midnight Fri); 7-10.30 Sun
Beer range varies Ⓗ
The Arts Centre beat over 200 pubs to be voted Cardiff CAMRA *Pub of the Year;* a stylish, bohemian atmosphere prevails in this former school. An excellent range of malt whiskies and continental beers plus an occasional cider complement the four real ales from independent breweries.
🌸 ◗ ♿ ♣ ⌂ P 🏵

City Arms
10-12 Quay Street
☎ (029) 2022 5258
11-11 (midnight Fri & Sat); 12-10.30 Sun
Brains Dark, Bitter, SA Ⓗ
Traditional Brains' house, much beloved of rugby supporters; it is convenient for Cardiff's Millennium Stadium. No food served on match days; it can get busy when stadium in use. Good value lunches served Mon-Sat. Wheelchair WC.
◖ 🍴 ♿ ₮ (Central) ♣

Cottage
25 St Mary's Street

☎ (029) 2033 7194
Brains Dark, Bitter, SA Ⓗ
11-11; 12-10.30 Sun
This single-bar pub with a long, narrow, split-level interior makes the most of mirrors and space-saving seating arrangements. Note the superb woden frontage. It serves excellent-cooked meals at reasonable prices.
◖ ₮ (Central) 🏵

Ffynnon Wen
Thornhill Road, Thornhill (A469 Caerphilly road)
☎ (029) 2052 2353
11.30-11; 12-10.30 Sun
Banks's Original, Bitter, seasonal beers Ⓗ
Modern pub, built around what was once a farmhouse. A bar, lounge and restaurant make up three distinct areas.
Q 🌸 ◖ ◗ ♿ P 🏵

Maltsters
75 Merthyr Road, Whitchurch
☎ (029) 2061 4326
11-11; 12-10.30 Sun
Brains Dark, Bitter, SA; guest beers (occasional) Ⓗ
Bar and lounge in a traditional pub with a skittle alley at the rear; lively but friendly atmosphere. Meals served 12-6 (3 Sun).
Q 🌸 ◖ 🍴 ♣ 🏵

Newt & Cucumber
Wharton Street
☎ (029) 2022 2114
12-11; closed Sun
Greene King IPA, Abbot; Morland Old Speckled Hen; guest beers Ⓗ
Four guest beers are normally available in this split-level, city-centre pub. No-smoking area available until 5pm.
◖ ◗ ₮ ✂

Three Arches
Heathwood Road, Llanishen
☎ (029) 2075 3831
11-11; 12-10.30 Sun
Brains Dark, Bitter, SA, seasonal beers; Buckley's Rev. James Ⓗ
Large suburban pub comprising three distinct drinking areas and three bars. It is a comfortable place to relax in after a stroll around nearby Roath Park. No meals Sun eve. 🌸 ◖ ◗ 🍴 ♿ ₮ (Heath High Level/Heath Low Level) ♣ P ✂ 🏵

Traders Tavern
6-8 David Street (near prison)
☎ (029) 2023 8795
11-11; 5-11.30 (concert nights only) Sun
Brains Bitter; guest beer Ⓗ
Tucked away behind the Cardiff International Arena, this is the CIA's local and is open till midnight when concerts are staged. This comfortable, colourful, one-bar pub is adorned with CIA

posters. Home-cooked food served.

Q ☺ ◖ ▶ ⇌ (Queen St) ⊞

Vulcan
10 Adam Street, Adamsdown
☎ (029) 2046 1580
11.30-7.30 (11 Mon & Fri; 6 Sat); 12-4 Sun

Brains Dark, Bitter Ⓗ

Although near the city centre, the Vulcan does not draw enough passing trade to justify eve opening. It does however have plenty of loyal regulars, and is a local CAMRA *Pub of the Year* regular. Simply furnished, its lunchtime meals (Mon-Fri) represent excellent value.

◖ ⊞ ⇌ (Queen St) ♣

White Hart
66 James Street (on A4119)
☎ (029) 2047 2561
11-11; 11-3 Sun

Brains Dark, Bitter Ⓗ

Large, single bar, comfortably furnished, with a polished wooden floor; it is well decorated with local and nautical photographs and artefacts. This well-run characterful local stands near an entertainment complex and the Techniquest Centre.

♣ ⇌ (Cardiff Bay)

Y Gasgen
St Johns Square
☎ (029) 2022 1980
12-11 (midnight Fri & Sat); 12-10.30 Sun

Boddingtons Bitter; guest beers Ⓗ

Small, split-level pub serving up to five frequently changing guest beers; a refreshing change from the Brains/Welsh Brewers pubs that dominate the area. It can get busy at weekends; meals served 12-6.

☺ ◖ ♿ ⇌ (Central) ↻

Try also: Goat Major, High St (Brains)

COLWINSTON
Sycamore Tree
Off A48
☎ (01656) 652827
12-3 (not winter Mon or Tue), 6 (6.30 winter)-11; 12-3, 7-10.30 Sun

Beer range varies Ⓗ

Classic village pub in an attractive setting, slightly awkward to find, but well worth the find. It regularly appears in both this *Guide* and CAMRA's *Good Pub Food*. Indoor boules played.

🏛 Q ⛵ ☺ ◖ ▶ ⊞ ♣ P

CRAIG PENLLYN
Barley Mow
1¹/₂ miles N of A48
OS978773
☎ (01446) 772558

12-3 (not Mon), 6-11; 12-3, 7-10.30 Sun

Draught Bass; Hancock's HB; guest beer Ⓗ

This friendly, welcoming pub is popular with locals and visitors alike for its good beer and food. It is reputedly haunted by a ghost that rings a broken electric bell.

🏛 ◖ ▶ ⊞ ♣ P

CROSS INN
Cross Inn
Main Road OS056828
☎ (01443) 223431
12-11; 12-10.30 Sun

Boddingtons Bitter; Brains Bitter; Hancock's HB Ⓗ

Small, friendly, village pub featuring flagstones, bare floorboards and old local photographs. It offers good value home-cooked food.

◖ ♿ ♣ P

CWMAMAN
Falcon Inn
1 Incline Row OS008998
☎ (01685) 873758
11-11; 12-10.30 Sun

Beer range varies Ⓗ

Friendly pub stocking at least three beers at any one time. It was extended recently using wood and stone from a nearby chapel. Hard to find, but well worth the effort.

☺ ◖ ▶ P

CWMFELIN
Cross Inn
Maesteg Road
☎ (01656) 732476
11.45-11; 12-10.30 Sun

Brains Bitter, SA; Buckley's IPA Ⓗ

Friendly local on a busy road, boasting a traditional benched public bar and a smart lounge. Limited parking.

⇌ (Garth) P

DUNVANT
Found Out Inn
Killan Road (up hill towards Three Crosses)
☎ (01792) 203596
12-3.30, 5.30-11; 12-11 Sat; 12-3, 7-10.30 Sun

Flowers Original; Tetley Bitter; guest beer Ⓗ

Village local, rebuilt in the 1960s, whose landlady is keen to promote real ales.

Q ☺ ◖ ▶ ♣ P

EGLWYS BREWIS
Carpenters Arms
Eglwys Brewis Road
☎ (01446) 792063
11 (6.30 Wed)-11; 12-10.30 Sun

Brains Dark, Bitter, SA; guest beer Ⓗ

Lively pub turned from one

of the worst to one of the best pubs in the vale under the new landlord. Gwatkin cider is stocked in summer. Excellent food and family facilities now provided.

🏛 Q ⛵ ☺ ◖ ▶ ⊞ ♿ ▲ ♣ ↻ P ✂

GELLIHAF
Coal Hole
Bryn Road (off main road)
☎ (01443) 830280
12-2.30, 6.30-11; 12-4.30, 7-11; 12-4.30, 7-10.30 Sun

Hancock's HB; guest beer Ⓗ

Popular, friendly, one-bar pub where the dining area, offers good value food (no eve meals Sun). Large play area outside.

☺ ⇌ ◖ ♣ P

GILFACH FARGOED
Capel
Park Place
☎ (01443) 830272
12-4, 7-11; 11-11 Fri & Sat; 12-10.30 Sun

Brains SA; John Smith's Bitter; guest beers Ⓗ

Large, friendly traditional Valleys pub boasting lots of original features. Lunches are served at weekends.

Q ⇌ ◖ ⊞ ⇌ ✂

GILFACH GOCH
Griffin Inn
Hendreforgan (¹/₂ mile off A4093) OS988875
☎ (01443) 672247
7 (12-Sat); 12-10.30 Sun

Brains SA; guest beer (summer) Ⓗ

Traditional, popular local nestled at the bottom of the valley. Well decorated, it displays hunting trophies and rural implements.

☺ ⊞ ♣ P

GLAN-Y-LLYN
Fagins Ale & Chop House
8 Cardiff Road
☎ (029) 2081 1800
12-11; 12-10.30 Sun

Brains Bitter; Cains FA; Caledonian 80/-; Hancock's HB; Shepherd Neame Bishops Finger; Ⓗ **guest beers** Ⓖ/Ⓗ

Popular alehouse serving an ever-changing range of guest beers. Note the sayings in 'Wenglish' dotted around. No meals available Sun eve or Mon.

☺ ◖ ▶ ⇌ (Taffs Well)

GOWERTON
Commercial Hotel
Station Road
☎ (01792) 872072
12-11; 12-3, 6-10.30 (12-10.30 summer) Sun

Brains SA; Buckley's Best Bitter,
seasonal beers [H]
This renovated Victorian
local near the station serves
weekday bar meals.
Q ❀ ◖◗ ⊞ ⅄ ≈ ♣ P

GROESFAEN

Dynevor Arms
Llantrisant Road (A4119)
☎ (029) 2089 0530
11-11; 12-3, 7-10.30 Sun
Draught Bass; Hancock's HB; guest
beer [H]
Large, open-plan roadside
village pub with a dining
area, serving good value
meals (not available Sun eve).
The guest beer is changed
weekly.
❀ ◖◗ ♣ ◌ P

HOPKINSTOWN

Hollybush
Ty Mawr Road
☎ (01443) 402325
11-11; 12-10.30 Sun
Hancock's HB; guest beer [H]
Friendly roadside inn whose
sports-oriented bar is
complemented by a
comfortable lounge. Mid-
Glamorgan CAMRA *Pub of
the Year* 1998 and '99.
◖◗ ⊞ ⅄ & ♣ ◌ P ⊟

KENFIG

Prince of Wales
Maudlam OS804818
☎ (01656) 740356
11.30-4, 6-11; 11.30-11 Fri & Sat;
12-10.30 Sun
Draught Bass; Worthington Bitter;
guest beer [G]
Historic pub boasting
exposed stone walls and a
large open fireplace, the
former town hall of the lost
City of Kenfig. No eve meals
Sun or Mon in winter.
🏠 Q ❀ ◖◗ ⅄ P

KILLAY

Railway Inn
555 Gower Road, Upper
Killay
☎ (01792) 203946
11-11; 12-10.30 Sun
Swansea Bishopswood Bitter,
Original Wood, seasonal beers [H]
Former station waiting rooms
converted into a lounge, bar
and small family room; this
free house is a major outlet
for Swansea Brewery.
Swansea CAMRA *Pub of the
Year* 2000.
🏠 ⅋ ❀ ◖◗ ♣ P

Try also: Village Inn, Killay
Quadrant (Bass)

KITTLE

Beaufort Arms
18 Pennard Road

☎ (01792) 234521
11.30-11; 12-10.30 Sun
Brains SA; Buckley's Best Bitter,
Rev. James, seasonal beers [H]
Reputedly the oldest pub on
Gower, this popular village
local forms the centre of the
community. It is well known
for its food. Large outside
play area to amuse children.
Q ❀ ◖◗ ⊞ ♣ P ⊬

LLANGENNITH

Kings Head
☎ (01792) 386212
11-11; 12-10.30 Sun
Watkin's BB, OSB; guest beers [H]
Historic, stone-walled pub on
the village green. Spectacular
beaches are within walking
distance (for the energetic).
Games room; food is served
all day. The guest beers are
usually Welsh.
Q ❀ ◖◗ ⊞ ⅄ ♣ P

LLANGYNWYD

Corner House
Top of hill (W of A4063)
☎ (01656) 732393
11-11; 12-10.30 Sun
Draught Bass; Brains Bitter, SA;
guest beer [H]
Comfortable, traditional
country pub.
❀ ◖◗ & ⅄ P

Old House (Yr Hew Dŷ)
Top of the hill (W of A4063)
OS858889
☎ (01656) 733310
11-11; 12-10.30 Sun
Flowers IPA, Original; guest
beers [H]
One of Wales' oldest pubs
(1147AD), this thatched
house, full of atmosphere, is
extremely popular and has a
renowned restaurant
(booking advised eves and
Sun). Traditional Mari Lwyd
is performed at New Year. No
meals Sun eve.
🏠 Q ⅋ ❀ ◖◗ ⅄ P

LLANMADOC

Brittania Inn
☎ (01792) 386624
11.30-3.30 (not winter Tue or Wed),
7-11 (11-11 summer); 12-10.30 Sun
Marston's Pedigree; guest beer
(occasional) [H]
17th-century pub benefitting
from excellent views and
good walks nearby. Guest
beers are sold in holiday
periods.
🏠 Q ❀ ⊨ ◖◗ ⊞ ⅄ ♣ P ⊬

LLANRHIDIAN

Greyhound Inn
Oldwalls
☎ (01792) 391027
11-11; 12-10.30 Sun
Draught Bass; Boddingtons Bitter;
Marston's Pedigree; guest beers [H]

Free house, with an excellent
atmosphere, there are usually
at least two guest beers and
the food is popular –
especially local fish. Families
all welcome in the games
room.
🏠 Q ⅋ ❀ ◖◗ ⊞ ⅄ ♣ P ⊬

LLANTWIT FARDRE

Bush Inn
Main Road
☎ (01443) 203958
4 (12 Sat)-11; 12-4, 6.30-10.30 Sun
Hancock's HB; guest beers [H]
This, small, vibrant, single
bar village local is popular
with its loyal, mostly mature
clientele. Small car park.
♣ P

LLANTWIT MAJOR

Kings Head
East Street
☎ (01446) 792697
11-11; 12-10.30 Sun
Brains Dark, Bitter, SA, seasonal
beers; Worthington Bitter [H]
This pub's basic bar and more
comfortable lounge have
been much improved since
being purchased by Brains.
Tiny car park.
🏠 ❀ ◖ ⊞ ⅄ ♣ P

Llantwit Major Social
Club
The Hayes, Colhugh Street
(main beach road)
☎ (01446) 792266
11.30-3.30 (not Wed), 6.30-11; 12-2,
7-10.30 Sun
Hancock's HB; Worthington Bitter;
guest beer [H]
Imposing building, set in its
own grounds. A snooker
room, pool room and thrice-
weekly bingo add to its
appeal. The guest beer is
often from Wye Valley.
Q ⅋ ⅄ ♣ P

MACHEN

White Hart Inn
Nant Ceisiad (100 yds N of
A468 under rail bridge)
OS203892
☎ (01633) 441005
12-3, 6.30-11; 12-3, 6.30-10.30 Sun
Hancock's HB; guest beers [H]
This rambling pub boasts
extensive wood panelling,
some salvaged from a luxury
liner. An enterprising range
of beers is mostly sourced
from micros (three guests). A
good range of food is sold at
reasonable prices.
🏠 Q ❀ ⊨ ◖◗ P

MERTHYR TYDFIL

Tregenna Hotel
Park Terrace
☎ (01685) 723627
12-3, 5.30-11; 12-4, 7-10.30 (eves –
summer only) Sun

Draught Bass; guest beers Ⓗ
Comfortable lounge bar in a
family-run three-star hotel,
ideally placed for exploring
the nearby Brecon Beacons
National Park.
⊨ ◖ ▌ P

MONKNASH

Plough & Harrow

Off B4265
☎ (01656) 890209
12-11; 12-10.30 Sun
Draught Bass; Ⓖ Cottage Golden
Arrow; Hancock's HB; Shepherd
Neame Spitfire; Taylor Landlord;
Worthington Bitter; Ⓗ guest beers
Ⓖ/Ⓗ
This historic pub serves a
wide range of guest beers
from near and far, ensuring
its consistent award-winning
track record. A pub full of
character where good food
and live music enhance its
popularity. Eve meals served
weekdays. Limited parking.
⋈ ❀ ◖ ▌ ♣ ᗡ P

MOUNTAIN ASH

Jeffreys Arms

Jeffrey Street
☎ (01443) 472976
7 (12 Sat)-11; 12-10.30 Sun
Draught Bass; Worthington Bitter;
guest beer Ⓗ
Large village pub with a
sports oriented bar and a
pleasant lounge.
⊞ ♣

MUMBLES

Park Inn

23 Park Street
☎ (01792) 366738
5.30 (12 Sat)-11; 12-11 Sat; 12-10.30
Sun
Marston's Pedigree; Ruddles County;
Worthington Bitter; guest beer Ⓗ
Welcoming, back-street local,
a short walk from the
seafront, popular with locals
and those seeking decent
conversation without
intrusive music or machines.
Swansea CAMRA *Pub of the
Year* 1998.
⋈ Q ♣

West Cross Inn

43 Mumbles Road, West
Cross
☎ (01792) 401143
11-3.30, 5.30-11; 11-11 Sat; 11-10.30
Sun
Flowers Orginal; Wadworth 6X;
Worthington Bitter Ⓗ
Popular pub and restaurant
in a splendid position on the
edge of Swansea Bay, on the
route of the old Mumbles
railway.
Q ❀ ◖ ▌ ᗕ P ⚲

MWYNDY

Barn at Mwyndy

Down lane opp. corner Park
Garage on A4119 OS056816
☎ (01443) 222333
11-11; 12-10.30 Sun
Hancock's HB; guest beers Ⓗ
Converted 16th-century
Welsh long barn decorated
with many rustic implements
and stonework. It comprises
a two-level bar, good
restaurant with a no-smoking
room and conference
facilities. No food Sun eve.
⋈ ❀ ◖ ▌ ᗕ P

NEATH

Highlander

2 Lewis Road
☎ (01639) 633586
12-2.30, 6-11; 12-11 Sat; 12-3.30,
7-10.30 Sun
Draught Bass; Bryn Celyn Buddy
Marvellous; Watkin's OSB;
Worthington Bitter; guest beers Ⓗ
Comfortable one-bar town
pub with an eating area
downstairs plus an upstairs
restaurant. It enjoys a well-
deserved reputation for its
good value food and wide
range of guest ales. No meals
Sun eve.
◖ ▌ ⇌

Star Inn

83 Penydre Neath
☎ (01639) 633586
12.30-11; 12-2.30, 7-10.30 Sun
Draught Bass; Hancock's HB;
Watkin's Whoosh; guest beer Ⓗ
Near Neath RFC, this
comfortable public house has
that feel-good factor. It is
well known locally for its
Bass, served from a 1940s
beer engine.
❀ ◖ ⇌ P

NELSON

Dynevor Arms

Commercial Street , Village
Square
☎ (01443) 450295
11-11; 12-10.30 Sun
Brains Bitter; Hancock's HB Ⓗ
Former brew-pub (and
mortuary), over 200 years
old, with a busy public bar
and comfortable lounge. Live
music is staged Sat eves.
⊞ ♣ P

NEWTON

Newton Inn

New Well Lane (opp garage)
☎ (01792) 362398
12-11; 12-10.30 Sun
Draught Bass; Ⓗ/Ⓖ Fuller's London
Pride; Worthington Bitter Ⓗ
Popular village local offering
good value meals, a quiz
(Mon eve) and a large screen
TV for sporting events. ◖ ▌ ⊞

NOTTAGE

Farmer's Arms

Lougher Row
☎ (01656) 784595
11.30-11; 12-10.30 Sun
Ruddles County; Worthington Bitter;
guest beers Ⓗ
Popular, rambling pub by the
village green, live music most
nights in one bar. No meals
Sun eve.
⋈ ❀ ◖ ▌ ⊞ ⅙ ᗘ P

Swan

West Road
☎ (01656) 782568
11-11; 12-10.30 Sun
Draught Bass; Courage Best Bitter,
Directors; John Smith's Bitter guest
beer Ⓗ
Very popular pub, frequented
especially by locals and rugby
notables. No food Sun.
❀ ◖ ᗘ P

OGMORE BY SEA

Pelican Inn

Ewenny Road
☎ (01656) 880049
11.30-11; 12-11 Sun
Draught Bass; Wadworth 6X;
Worthington Bitter Ⓗ
Welcoming roadside inn
overlooking Ogmore Castle,
it attracts both local and
passing trade. Pizzas are
available at any time.
Q ᗑ ❀ ◖ ▌ ♣ P

PANT

Pant Cad Ifor

By mountain railway
☎ (01685) 723688
11-11; 12-10.30 Sun
Draught Bass; Hancock's HB;
Worthington Bitter; guest beers Ⓗ
Busy village pub, where the
plush bar stocks interesting
guest beers and the
restaurant offers good food.
⋈ ❀ ◖ ▌ P

PENARTH

Royal Hotel

1 Queen Street
☎ (029) 2079 0290
11-11; 12-10.30 Sun
Bullmastiff Gold Brew, Son of a
Bitch, seasonal beers Ⓗ
Street-corner local serving
Bullmastiff beers at
commendably low prices. An
occasional disco or karaoke is
staged at weekends. Booking
is essential for meals.
❀ ⊨ ▌ ⊞ ⇌ (Dingle Rd) ♣

Windsor Hotel

Windsor Road
☎ (029) 2070 2821
12-11; 12-10.30 Sun
Cains Traditional Bitter; Felinfoel
Double Dragon; Hancock's HB; guest
beers Ⓗ
Street-corner local with
a restaurant. Up to three
guest beers feature local
micros.
◖ ⇌ (Dingle Rd)

PONTARDAWE

Pontardawe Inn
123 Herbert Street
☎ (01792) 830791
12-11; 12-10.30 Sun
Buckley's Best Bitter, Rev. James; guest beers Ⓗ
Attractive, two-bar, village inn, with a riverside location. Home to Pontardawe Music Festival it also hosts live music Fri and Sat eves. Boules court at the bar; good food (no meals Tue eve).
❀ ◑ ▶ ⊞ ♿ ♣ P

PONTLLANFRAITH

Crown
Bryn View
☎ (01495) 223404
12-3, 5-11; 12-11 Fri & Sat; 12-3, 7-10.30 Sun
Courage Best Bitter; John Smith's Bitter; guest beers Ⓗ
Two-roomed pub with a basic public bar and a spacious lounge; a haven for golfers and locals alike. With children's play equipment in the garden it gets busy with families on fine summer eves.
❀ ◑ ▶ ⊞ ♣ P ✂

PONTYPRIDD

Llanover Arms
Bridge Street (opp. Ynysangharad Park)
☎ (01443) 403215
12-11; 12-3, 7-10.30 Sun
Brains Dark, Bitter, SA; Worthington Bitter; guest beer Ⓗ
Charismatic town pub full of character.
❀ ⊞ ⇌ ♣ P

PORTHCAWL

Lorelei Hotel
36-38 Esplanade Avenue
☎ (01656) 788342
5 (4 Fri; 12 Sat)-11; 12-3, 7-10.30 Sun
Draught Bass; Ⓖ **Marston's Pedigree; guest beers** Ⓗ
Enterprising bar in a small hotel that hosts several beer festivals a year. Cider is stocked occasionally. Weekend lunches served. Local CAMRA *Pub of the Year* 2000.
❀ ⇌ ◑ ▶ ▲ ♨

Royal Oak
1 South Road
☎ (01656) 782684
11.30-11; 12-10.30 Sun
Draught Bass; Worthington Bitter; guest beer (occasional) Ⓗ
Comfortable, characterful pub on the fringe of the shopping area. No meals served Sun eve.
Q ❀ ◑ ▶ ♿ ▲ P

PORT TALBOT

Lord Caradoc

69-72 Station Road
☎ (01639) 896007
11-11; 12-10.30 Sun
Draught Bass; Brains Dark, SA; Courage Directors; Theakston Best Bitter; guest beers Ⓗ
Spacious, open-plan Wetherspoon's pub with one large L-shaped bar.
Q ❀ ◑ ▶ ♿ ⇌ ♨ P ✂ ⊞

QUAKERS YARD

Glantaff Inn
Cardiff Road
☎ (01443) 410822
12-4, 7-11; 12-4, 7-10.30 Sun
Cain's Bitter; Courage Best Bitter, Directors; John Smith's Bitter; Wells Bombardier; guest beers Ⓗ
Comfortable inn displaying a large collection of water jugs, and boxing memorabilia. It enjoys a warm atmosphere. Good food is served in the upstairs restaurant, with bar meals downstairs (no eve meals Sun).
Q ❀ ◑ ▶ P

REYNOLDSTON

King Arthur Hotel
Higher Green
☎ (01792) 391099
11-11; 12-10.30 Sun
Draught Bass; Felinfoel Double Dragon; Worthington Bitter; guest beers (summer) Ⓗ
Imposing village pub and hotel restaurant popular with both locals and tourists. Arthur's Stone (prehistoric monument) stands on nearby Cefn Bryn Hill. Large outdoor drinking area.
🛏 Q ⏰ ❀ ⇌ ◑ ▶ ⊞ ▲ ♣ P

RHYDYPANDY

Masons Arms
Rhydypandy Road, Morriston (follow signs to hospital then Rhydypandy road for 1½ miles) OSSN6602
☎ (01792) 842535
12-11; 12-10.30 Sun
Courage Best Bitter; Marston's Pedigree; Smiles Best; guest beers Ⓗ
17th-century inn of two bars; it is popular with diners but retains a thriving local following. 🛏 ❀ ◑ ▶ ⊞ ♣ P

RHYMNEY

Farmers Arms
Brewery Row
☎ (01685) 840257
12-11; 12-3, 7-10.30 Sun
Boddingtons Bitter; Brains Bitter; guest beer Ⓗ
Friendly, spacious, comfortable pub and restaurant, traditionally furnished. Bric-a-brac includes Rhymney Brewery memorabilia.
◑ ▶ ⇌ ♣

RISCA

Fox & Hounds
Park Road
☎ (01633) 612937
11-11; 12-10.30 Sun
Beer range varies Ⓗ
Lively pub, overlooking the park, offering an interesting guest beer. It holds a New Year beer festival. The Crumlin stretch of the Monmouthshire Canal passes behind the pub.
❀ ◑ ▶ ♣ P

Railway Tavern
Dan-y-Graig Road
☎ (01633) 600101
11.30-11; 12-10.30 Sun
Draught Bass; Hancock's HB Ⓗ
Small, two-bar town pub: a plush lounge and basic bar serving good food.
❀ ◑ ▶ ⊞ ♣ P

RUDRY

Maenllwyd Inn
At crossroads SE of Rudry
☎ (01222) 888505
11-11; 12-10.30 Sun
Courage Best Bitter, Directors; Theakston XB; guest beer Ⓗ
Characterful, 400-year-old country inn, of stone walls and low beamed ceilings, that has been sympathetically extended. Sample the good food from an extensive menu, and enjoy forest walks nearby.
🛏 Q ⏰ ❀ ◑ ▶ P

SKEWEN

Crown
216 New Road
☎ (01792) 411270
12 (11 Sat)-11; 12-10.30 Sun
Brains Dark, Bitter, SA; Buckley's Best Bitter Ⓗ
Friendly local: upstairs is a snooker room with a bar, and downstairs a public bar and a comfortable lounge.
❀ ⊞ ⇌ ♣

ST BRIDES MAJOR

Farmers Arms
Wick Road
☎ (01656) 880224
12-3, 6-11; 12-10.30 Sun
Courage Directors; Ushers Best Bitter, Founders, seasonal beers Ⓗ
Busy, friendly bar and restaurant, opposite the village pond. Good food is served in both rooms. A justifiably regular *Guide* entry.
🛏 Q ❀ ◑ ▶ P

ST HILARY

Bush Inn
½ mile off A48 near TV mast
☎ (01446) 772745
11.30-11; 12-10.30 Sun

Draught Bass; G Hancock's HB; H Morland Old Speckled Hen G
Pleasant, three-bar pub in a 16th-century village. Excellent bar and restaurant meals are all home-made under the auspices of one French and one Welsh chef. Families welcome. No food Sun eve. Weston's Old Rosie cider is always available.
🏰 Q ✿ ◖ ▮ ⇨ P

SWANSEA

Brynymor Hotel
Brynymor Road
☎ (01792) 466650
11.30-11; 12-10.30 Sun
Ind Coope Burton Ale; Tetley Bitter H
One-roomed pub, where there is an emphasis on games, popular with both locals and students. It is a rare local outlet for Burton Ale. No meals Sun eve.
◖ ▮ ♿ ♣

Eli Jenkins Alehouse
24 Oxford Street (near bus station)
☎ (01792) 630961
11-11; 12-10.30 Sun
Badger Tanglefoot; Draught Bass; Worthington Bitter; guest beers H
This large modern pub with wooden alcoves and niches, is very popular with town-centre diners (eve meals finish at 7.30). Wheelchair WC.
◖ ▮ ♿

Rhyddings Hotel
Brynmill Avenue (near St Helens rugby ground)
☎ (01792) 648885
11-11; 12-10.30 Sun
Smiles Best; Tetley Bitter; guest beer H
Pleasant pub attracting locals and students. The bar is popular for pool. Mirrors and breweriana adorn the walls.
✿ ◖ ▮ ♣

Vivian Arms
6 Gower Road, Sketty
☎ (01792) 516914
12-11; 12-10.30 Sun
Brains Bitter, SA H
A *Guide* stalwart: a traditional two-bar pub, popular with locals. Eve meals served weekdays.
✿ ◖ ▮ ⊞

Westbourne Hotel
11 Bryn-y-mor Road (near the Guildhall)
☎ (01792) 476637
11-11; 12-10.30 Sun
Draught Bass; Hancock's HB; guest beers H
Popular corner pub dislaying a large slate Bass wall plaque. Smoking restrictions in the lounge are lifted at 9pm. Handy for both the football

and rugby grounds.
✿ ◖ ▮ ⊞ ⊁

TONDU

Llynfi Arms
Maesteg Road
☎ (01656) 720010
12 (1 Mon & Tue)-4, 7-11; 12-3, 7-10.30 Sun
Worthington Bitter; H guest beers H/G
Roadside pub with a lively bar and a comfortable lounge encircled by a working model railway. It embraces an adventurous guest beer policy. No meals Sun eve, or Mon-Tue.
◖ ▮ ⊞ ♿ ⇌

TREFOREST

Otley Arms
Forest Road (near station)
☎ (01443) 402033
11-11; 12-10.30 Sun
Bullmastiff Gold Brew; Cains Traditional Bitter; Worthington Bitter; guest beer H
Students' watering-hole, a popular venue for televised sport and keenly priced ales. This multi-roomed pub extends over different levels. Limited parking.
◖ ⇌ ♣ P

TYLE GARW

Boars Head
Coed Cae Lane (600 yds from A473 by level crossing)
☎ (01443) 225400
12-4, 7-11; 12-3, 7-10.30 Sun
Beer range varies H
Unspoilt, simply furnished, traditional local, opposite forest walks. Q ✿ ⊞

UPPER CHURCH VILLAGE

Farmers Arms
St Illtyds Road
☎ (01443) 205766
11-11, 12-10.30 Sun
Draught Bass; Brains Bitter; Hancock's HB H
Small village local with a warm welcome for everyone. Lunches served Mon-Sat.
✿ ◖ P

WICK

Star Inn
Ewenny Road
☎ (01656) 890519
12-3, 5-11 (11-11 summer); 12-5.30, 7-10.30 Sun
Hancock's HB; Worthington Bitter; guest beer H
Comfortable village pub near the coast, an ideal place for a post-beach pint. Well known locally for its first-class food. It has a spacious bar and smaller lounge.
🏰 Q ✿ ◖ ▮ ⊞ ♣ P ⊟

YNYSTAWE

Millers Arms
634 Clydach Road (next to school)
☎ (01792) 842614
11.30-11; 12-10.30 Sun
Flowers Original; Wadworth 6X; guest beers H
Popular roadside pub enjoying a reputation for good food; note the display of unusual teapots.
✿ ◖ ▮ P

YSTALYFERA

Wern Fawr Inn
47 Wern Road (off A4067)
☎ (01639) 843625
7-11; 1-3, 7-10.30 Sun
Bryn Celyn Rave On, CHH, Oh Boy, Buddy Marvellous, Buddy's Delight, seasonal beers; guest beer H
Traditional village local, home of the Bryn Celyn Brewery. Sample the excellent ales in the cosy public bar or the small lounge. 🏰 Q ⊞ ♣ ⊟

YSTRAD MYNACH

Royal Oak
Commercial Street (main road)
☎ (01443) 862345
12-3, 5.30-11; 12-11 Sat; 12-3, 7-10.30 Sun
Draught Bass; Hancock's HB H
Unmistakable 'Brewer's Tudor' pub with notable acid-etched windows. A busy through public bar includes discrete areas. Good food.
✿ ◖ ▮ ⇌ ♣ P

Cask Marque

Pubs that carry the Cask Marque symbol indicate that the licensees have successfully passed a number of tests concerning beer quality, and display plaques to this effect in their outlets. However, these pubs have been chosen independently of Cask Marque by CAMRA.

INDEPENDENT BREWERIES

Brains: Cardiff

Bryn Celyn: Ystalyfera

Bullmastiff: Cardiff

Swansea: Swansea

Tomos Watkin: Swansea

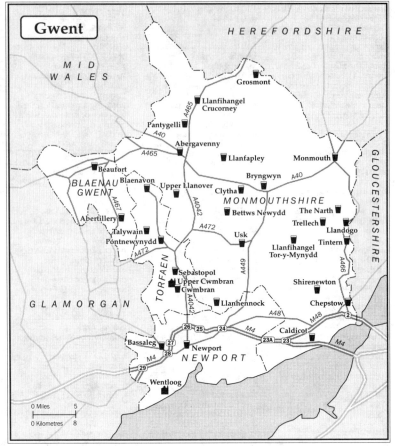

Gwent

HEREFORDSHIRE

MID WALES

Grosmont

Llanfihangel Crucorney

Pantygelli

A40

Abergavenny

A465

Llanfapley

Monmouth

GLOUCESTERSHIRE

Beaufort

BLAENAU GWENT

Blaenavon

Upper Llanover

Clytha

Bryngwyn

A40

A467

A4042

MONMOUTHSHIRE

Bettws Newydd

The Narth

Abertillery

Trellech

Llandogo

Talywain

Pontnewynydd

A472

Usk

Tintern

Llanfihangel Tor-y-Mynydd

A466

TORFAEN

A449

A472

Sebastopol

Upper Cwmbran

Cwmbran

Shirenewton

GLAMORGAN

Llanhennock

Chepstow

A48

2

M48

26 25 24

M4

23A 23

Caldicot

Bassaleg

27

NEWPORT

M4

Newport

28

M4

29

Wentloog

0 Miles 5
0 Kilometres 8

Authority areas covered: Blaenau Gwent UA, Monmouthshire UA, Newport UA, Torfaen UA

ABERGAVENNY

Coach & Horses
41 Cross Street
11-11; 12-3, 7-10.30 Sun
Brains SA; Flowers IPA; Wadworth 6X H
Popular family-run pub, possibly the oldest in town, by the site of a former town gate. The open-plan interior shows lots of wooden beams, some displaying old Whitbread tankards. The fine old fireplace is of Tudor origin.

Somerset Arms
Victoria Street
☎ (01873) 852158
12-11; 12-10.30 Sun
Draught Bass; Worthington Bitter; guest beer H
Friendly corner local, worth the few minutes walk from the town centre. The cosy bar has a welcoming real fire on cold days and the comfortable lounge is where diners can enjoy good home-cooked food. Interesting guest ales to choose from.

Station
37 Brecon Road
☎ (01873) 854759
5 (11 Thu-Sat)-11; 12-4, 7-10.30 Sun
Draught Bass; Hancock's HB; Freeminer Bitter; Tetley Bitter H
Vibrant, traditional pub which, as the name suggests, has old railway connections. Drawing a good mix of customers, it is very much part of the town circuit for drinkers young and old. Limited parking.

ABERTILLERY

Commercial
Market Street
☎ (01495) 212310
12-3, 6.30-11; 12-11 Fri & Sat; 12-10.30 Sun
Worthington Bitter; guest beer H
This popular pub provides a good community focus for a town-centre outlet. The spacious bar has a large TV screen for sports fans while two comfortable rooms at the front and rear offer quieter surroundings and are popular with diners (eve meals Mon-Fri).

BASSALEG

Tredegar Arms
4 Caerphilly Road (1 mile N of M4 jct 28)
☎ (01633) 893247
11-11; 12-10.30 Sun
Brains Bitter; Fuller's London Pride; Greene King Abbot; guest beers H/G
This spacious cask ale house is justifiably popular with drinkers and diners. Several drinking areas include a no-smoking part where children are welcome. The garden also has a play area. Occasional beer festivals held.

BEAUFORT

Rhyd-y-Blew
Rassau Road, Carmeltown
☎ (01495) 308935
12-3, 6.30 (6 Wed, Fri & Sat)-11; 12-3, 7-10.30 Sun
Brains SA; Flowers IPA; Tetley Bitter; guest beer H
The name means 'ford of the hairs' (best ask); this established real ale watering-hole attracts beer-lovers from far and wide. Its multi-level interior is divided into several areas. The extensive menu includes some home-made dishes making it a popular choice for lunch (served Mon-Fri).
🏚 ◑ ♣ P

BETTWS NEWYDD

Black Bear
Village signed off B4598
OS361062
☎ (01873) 880701
11-3 (not Mon), 5-11; 12-10.30 Sun
Beer range varies G
Very welcoming and relaxed pub with a restaurant deserving its good reputation; the three-course 'whatever comes out of the kitchen' choice is excellent value. Late supper licence. The beer range is changed periodically.
🏚 Q ❀ 🍴 ◑ P

BLAENAVON

Cambrian Inn
80-81 Llanover Road (corner of Hill St)
☎ (01495) 790327
6 (1 Fri; 12 Sat)-11; 12-4, 7-10.30 Sun
Draught Bass; Brains Bitter, SA; guest beers H
The epitome of a traditional street-corner pub, with a strong local following but a friendly welcome for visitors. A games room and cosy lounge lead off the bar.
🍺 ♣

Castle Hotel
94 Broad Street
☎ (01495) 792477
11-11; 12-3, 7-10.30 Sun
Beer range varies H
Welcoming, open-plan pub offering the only town-centre accommodation. Normally one beer is on sale at a single competitive price, regardless of strength (usually ABV 4%-plus). Booking is essential for eve meals. It is a handy base for exploring local heritage sites. 🛏 ◑ ♣ P 🍴

Try also: **Pottery**, Llanover Rd (Free)

BRYNGWYN

Cripple Creek Inn
Old Abergavenny Road (off

A40, about a mile from Raglan)
☎ (01291) 690256
12-11; 12-10.30 Sun
Draught Bass; Brains SA; Tetley Bitter H
Pleasant, cosy, pub just off the old Abergavennny road: several drinking areas and a restaurant. Extensive menus are served in the bar and restaurant; with children's and vegetarian options. Table skittles played.
🏚 ❀ ◑ ♣ P ⚥

CALDICOT

Cross Inn
1 Newport Road
☎ (01291) 420692
11-11; 12-10.30 Sun
Draught Bass; Courage Best Bitter; guest beer H
Busy pub at the old crossroads in the village centre (handy for local bus services). The lounge has a pumpclip display and is based around a central fireplace, while the bar is popular for games. Cider sold in summer.
🏚 ❀ 🍺 ♣ 🍷 P

CHEPSTOW

Coach & Horses
Welsh Street (near town arch)
☎ (01291) 622626
12-11; 12-10.30 Sun
Buckley's Best Bitter, Brains SA; Fuller's London Pride; guest beer H
Welcoming, traditional pub, with a split-level interior, that has built up a loyal following among cask ale lovers. Its summer beer festival (July) coincides with the town carnival. Handy for the racecourse and a short stroll from the castle.
❀ 🛏 ◑ ▶ ≋ ♣

CLYTHA

Clytha Arms
On B4598
☎ (01873) 840206
12-3.30 (not Mon), 6-11; 12-11 Sat; 12-3, 7-10.30 Sun
Draught Bass; Caledonian Deuchars IPA; Felinfoel Double Dragon; guest beers H
Multiple award-winning pub and restaurant set in spacious gardens, home to a menagerie of ducks, cats and dogs. Excellent food includes local dishes (no meals Sun eve or Mon).
🏚 Q ❀ 🛏 ◑ ▶ 🍷 P 🍴

CWMBRAN

Commodore Hotel
Mill Lane, Llanyravon (off Llanfrechfa Way, behind Crows Nest pub))
☎ (01633) 484091

11-3, 6-11; 6.30-10.30 Sun
Beer range varies H
Plush family-run hotel. The Pilliners Lounge is ideal for a relaxing drink and excellent bar meals. An *à la carte* menu is served in the Willows Restaurant, while below decks Mary O'Brien's Bar offers a livelier alternative. A good base for local exploration. One or two Brains-Crown Buckley beers usually on tap. ❀ 🛏 ◑ ▶ P

Try also: **Mount Pleasant**, Wesley St (Ushers)

GROSMONT

Angel Inn
On B4347
☎ (01981) 240646
12-2.30, 6-11; 12-11 Sat; 12-10.30 Sun
Buckley's Best Bitter; guest beers H
Comfortable community pub in a village of historic importance. Welcoming atmosphere with some interesting reading for the supine. The midsummer beer festival makes use of the old market hall outside. Cider and accommodation are available in summer. Pétanque played.
Q ❀ 🛏 ◑ ▶ ⚔ ♣ 🍷 P

LLANDOGO

Sloop Inn
On A466
☎ (01594) 530291
12-2.30, 5.30-11; 11.30-11 Sat; 12-6 (12-10.30 summer) Sun
Wye Valley Dorothy Goodbody's Bitter; guest beer H
Pleasant bar with a log fire, and a lounge affording good views of the River Wye make this a good stop on a trip to nearby Tintern Abbey or as a base to explore the beautiful surrounding countryside. Good standard of accommodation.
🏚 ❀ 🛏 ◑ ▶ 🍺 ♣ P

LLANFAPLEY

Red Hart Inn
On B4233 E of Abergavenny
☎ (01873) 780227
12-3; 7-11 closed Mon; 12-3, 7-10.30 Sun
Draught Bass; Cottage Golden Arrow; guest beers (occasional) H
Welcoming family-run pub and restaurant, boasting a prize-winning garden set in a small village set in rolling countryside. The Cottage beers are well established and sometimes include a house special. Enjoy the big log fire in winter and occasional Morris dancing in summer.
🏚 Q ❀ ◑ ♣ P

LLANFIHANGEL CRUCORNEY

Skirrid Inn

Hereford Road (off A465, 4 miles N of Abergavenny)
☎ (01873) 890258
11-3, 6-11; 11-11 Sat & summer; 12-10.30 Sun

Ushers Best Bitter, Founders, seasonal beers Ⓗ

Claiming to be the oldest pub in Wales, solidly built and impressive in scale, it is popular with walkers and visitors to the Black Mountains as well as with locals. Highly praised food, garden, and accommodation complement the beers.

🏨 Q ⊛ ⇋ ◖ 🍴 ⊞ ♣ P

LLANFIHANGEL TOR-Y-MYNYDD

Star Inn

Follow Llansoy signs
OS459023
☎ (01291) 650256
11.30-3, 6.30-11; 12-3, 7-10.30 Sun

Ind Coope Burton Ale; Marston's Pedigree; guest beer Ⓗ

Large, friendly family-run pub, the social centre of this tiny hamlet. An impressive wooden reception desk and a huge log fire greet visitors. An extensive menu is served in the dining area. A camping and caravan site stands in the grounds, plus a cottage to let.

🏨 Q ⊛ ⇋ ◖ 🍴 ⊞ ▲ ♣ P

LLANHENNOCK

Wheatsheaf Inn

Approx 1 mile off main Caerleon-Usk road OS353927
☎ (01633) 420468
11-3, 5-11 (11-11 summer); 12-3, 7-10.30 Sun

Draught Bass; Worthington Bitter; guest beer Ⓗ

Largely unchanged gem of a country pub giving sweeping views of the lower Usk Valley. Interesting guest ales are usually stronger than the regulars. Pétanque is played in fine weather.

🏨 ⊛ ◖ 🍴 ♣ P

MONMOUTH

Green Dragon Inn

St. Thomas's Square
☎ (01600) 712561
11-11; 12-10.30 Sun

Draught Bass; Hancock's HB; Marston's Bitter, Pedigree; guest beer Ⓗ

Comfortable, welcoming pub near the medieval tower bridge. Good quality food makes it popular with diners. Don't miss the cartoon gallery in the toilets! A jazz band plays Wed eves.

Q ⊛ ◖ 🍴 ⊞ ▲ P

Try also: **Griffin Inn**, Whitecross St (Free; **Mayhill Hotel**, Mayhill (Free)

THE NARTH

Trekkers

2 miles E of Trellech, off B4293 OS525064
☎ (01600) 860367
11-3.30, 6-11; 11-11 Sat; 12-10.30 Sun

Felinfoel Bitter; Freeminer Bitter; guest beer Ⓗ

Former pony-trekking centre, in the charming style of a log cabin. Guide books to the many walks of the surrounding picturesque Wye Valley are available. Local and British dishes are a speciality. The skittle alley doubles as a family room.

🏨 ☡ ⊛ ◖ 🍴 ❤ ▲ ♣ P

NEWPORT

George

157 Chepstow Road, Maindee
☎ (01633) 255528
11-11; 12-10.30 Sun

Everards Beacon, Tiger; John Smith's Bitter; guest beer (occasional) Ⓗ

Busy open-plan pub: a spacious interior with a quieter section at the rear. It is a rare local outlet for Everards beers. Sporting events shown on the large TV screen are popular.

⊛ ♣

Godfrey Morgan

Chepstow Road, Maindee
☎ (01633) 221928
11-11; 12-10.30 Sun

Draught Bass; Boddingtons Bitter; Brains Dark, SA; Theakston Best Bitter; Wadworth 6X; guest beers Ⓗ

Attractive Wetherspoon's conversion of a former cinema and bingo hall. The pleasantly decorated, multi-level interior displaying pictures of old film stars and almost forgotten Newport cinemas helps retain a link with its past. Wheelchair access is via the car park entrance.

Q ◖ 🍴 & ❤ ⊞

Hornblower

126 Commercial Street
☎ (01633) 668001
11-11; 12-10.30 Sun

Brains SA; guest beers Ⓗ

Lively, town-centre bar offering an extensive juke box and live music every other Thu. It is full of early bikers' memorabilia. One of the guest beers is always a mild, a beer style which it champions. No children admitted.

≈ ♣ ⌂

Red Lion

47 Stow Hill (500 yds from train and bus stations)
☎ (01633) 264398
11-11; 12-10.30 Sun

John Smith's Bitter; Ushers Best Bitter; seasonal beers Ⓗ

Popular, traditional town-centre pub that attracts a good local following and hosts live music every Fri; it is the home of Newport Folk Club. No children admitted. Lunches served Mon-Sat.

🏨 ⊛ ◖ ≈ ♣

St Julian Inn

Caerleon Road (outskirts of Caerleon)
☎ (01633) 258663
11-11; 12-10.30 Sun

Courage Best Bitter; John Smith's Bitter; guest beer Ⓗ

Very popular, CAMRA award-winning pub giving tranquil views over the River Usk and Caerleon, including the Roman amphitheatre almost opposite. The cosy interior has several adjoining areas, including a wood-panelled lounge, surrounding a central servery.

⊛ ◖ 🍴 ♣ P

Wetherspoon's

10-12 Cambrian Centre, Cambrian Road
☎ (01633) 251752
11-11; 12-10.30 Sun

Draught Bass; Boddingtons Bitter; Brains Dark, SA; Courage Directors; Theakston Best Bitter, XB; guest beers Ⓗ

This large, open-plan pub is popular with all ages. Pictures of old Newport and local celebrities adorn the walls and pillars. It is handy for the station, but not so good for parking. Standard Wetherspoon's pub fare is served.

Q ◖ 🍴 & ≈ ⌂ ⊬ ⊭

Try also: **Old Murenger House**, High St (Samuel Smith); **Ship & Pilot**, Church St, Pill (Free)

PANTYGELLI

Crown Inn

Old Hereford Road (off A465, 4 miles N of Abergavenny)
OS302179
☎ (01873) 853314
11.30-3, 6.30-11; 12-3, 7-10.30 Sun

Draught Bass; Hancock's HB; Felinfoel Double Dragon; Fuller's London Pride; Ⓗ **guest beers** Ⓗ/Ⓖ

Large pub in a tiny hamlet where a flower-decked patio provides panoramic views of the Skirrid Mountain. Lively and friendly, it hosts occasional live music (jazz and folk-rock). Guest beers come from independent breweries. Two miles off the

main road, it is well worth finding.
🏚 ❀ ⇔ ◑ ▶ P

PONTNEWYNYDD
Horseshoe Inn
Hill Street
☎ (01495) 762188
12-11; 12-10.30 Sun
John Smith's Bitter; Ushers Best Bitter, seasonal beers ⊞
Cosy, intimate, pub just off the main road. Pictures of local scenes and a few horseshoes are dotted around the small public bar and lounge (children's certificate). The upper level has a busy games room and Hayloft restaurant, a popular choice for Sun lunch which must be booked.
🐕 ❀ ◑ ⊟ ♣

SEBASTOPOL
Open Hearth
Wern Road (access via South St or Station Rd/Austin Rd)
☎ (01495) 763752
11.30-4, 6-11; 11-11 Sat; 12-4, 7-10.30 Sun
Archer's Golden; Boddingtons Bitter; Greene King Abbot; Hancock's HB; guest beers ⊞
Gwent CAMRA *Pub of the Year,* this welcoming, canalside pub is popular with drinkers and diners alike: up to four guest ales on tap, while excellent food from an extensive menu is augmented by chef's specials. The big garden has a play area and the canal towpath is popular in warm weather.
❀ ◑ ⊟ ♣ P

SHIRENEWTON
Carpenters Arms
Usk Road (B4235)
☎ (01291) 641231
11-3; 6-11; 12-3, 7-10.30 Sun
Flowers IPA; Fuller's London Pride; Marston's Pedigree; Wadworth 6X; guest beers ⊞
Spacious, multi-roomed, 400-year-old country pub boasting its original flagstoned floors and open fires. The building was originally simultaneously a carpenter's, blacksmith's and a pub. It stocks over 50 malt whiskies and serves a good selection of home-cooked food (no meals winter Sun eves).
🏚 Q 🐕 ❀ ◑ ♣ P

Tredegar Arms
The Square
☎ (01291) 641274
12-3 (may vary), 6-11; 12-11 Sat; 12-4, 7-10.30 Sun
Draught Bass; Hancock's HB; Hook Norton Best Bitter; guest beers ⊞
The public bar and games

---

area are popular with locals; there is also a small lounge and dining room displaying a large collection of spoons. In summer the whitewashed pub front is decorated with an attractive floral display. Recommended for its food.
🏚 Q ❀ ⇔ ◑ ▶ ♣ P ⤬

TALYWAIN
Globe Inn
Commercial Road
☎ (01495) 772053
6.30 (11 Sat)-11; 12-4, 7-10.30 Sun
Brains Dark, Bitter; guest beer ⊞
Now run by another locally well-known publican, this friendly pub retains its traditional atmosphere in the cosy bar (with real fire), plus the comfortable lounge which sometimes hosts live music. It holds occasional beer festivals. Pool played and thriving games teams are based here. Occasional cider in summer.
🏚 ❀ ⊟ ♣ ⌂

TINTERN
Cherry Tree Inn
Devauden Road (off A466 at Royal George Hotel)
OS526001
☎ (01291) 689292
11.30-2.30 (not Mon-Tue winter), 6-11; 12-3, 7-10.30 Sun
Hancock's HB Ⓖ
A short walk from the tourist trap of Tintern takes you to the only Welsh pub to appear in every edition of this *Guide.* Just one small room contains a 70-year-old bar billiards table. Beer and cider are served straight from the cask in the adjoining cellar. Limited parking.
🏚 Q ❀ ♣ ⌂ P

TRELLECH
Lion Inn
On B4293, Chepstow-Monmouth road
☎ (01600) 860322
11-3, 6 (7 Mon, 6.30 Sat)-11; 12-3 (closed eve) Sun
Draught Bass; Bath SPA; guest beers ⊞
Thriving village local hosting quiz teams and a whisky club. Split-level, it has a raised dining area and a lower public bar. Bar billiards

---

is played in winter. It has a board where customers can request the guest beers they would like. The interesting menu is sometimes very exotic.
🏚 🐕 ❀ ◑ ▶ ⊟ Å ♣ P

UPPER LLANOVER
Goose & Cuckoo
Two miles from A4042 (signed from Llanover)
OS292073
☎ (01873) 880277
11.30-3, 7-11 (not Mon); 12-3, 7-10.30 Sun
Beer range varies ⊞
Delightful pub in a remote location with usually a Bullmastiff beer on and sometimes another guest. Excellent home-made food, including bread and ice-cream, is available all sessions except yoga night (Thu).
🏚 Q ◑ ♣ P

USK
Greyhound Inn
1 Chepstow Road
☎ (01291) 672074
12-3, 6-11; 12-3, 7-10.30 Sun
Hancock's HB; guest beers ⊞
Three guest beers, often unusual for the area, are normally on sale at this cosy, single-roomed pub which lies a short stroll from the town square. Popular with diners and discerning drinkers.
❀ ◑ ▶ P

Kings Head Hotel
18 Old Market Street
☎ (01291) 672963
11-11; 12-10.30 Sun
Badger Tanglefoot; Fuller's London Pride; guest beers ⊞
Real ale is available in the comfortable split-level lounge which has a huge log fire and displays fishing memorabilia. A pleasant place to relax in.
🏚 ⇔ ◑ ▶ ♣ P

Try also: **Nag's Head**, Twyn Square (Free)

Heritage Pubs
The pubs chosen as illustrations in the Guide are taken from CAMRA's National Inventory. These are pubs with unspoilt interiors that need to be preserved for future generations. The illustrations are used as examples of pubs on the inventory and may not necessarily have been chosen for inclusion in the Guide for beer quality.

INDEPENDENT BREWERIES

Cottage Spring: Upper Cwmbran

Warcop: Wentloog

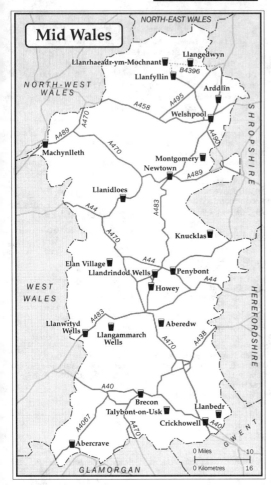

Mid Wales

NORTH-EAST WALES

Llangedwyn
Llanrhaeadr-ym-Mochnant
B4396
Llanfyllin
Arddlîn

NORTH-WEST WALES

A458
A495
Welshpool

A470
A489

Machynlleth

Montgomery
Newtown
A489

Llanidloes

A483

A44
A470

Knucklas

Elan Village
A44
Llandrindod Wells
Penybont

WEST WALES
Howey
A44

Llanwrtyd Wells
A483
Aberedw
Llangammarch Wells
A470
A438

A40
Brecon
Llanbedr
Talybont-on-Usk
Crickhowell

A4067
A470

Abercrave

GLAMORGAN

SHROPSHIRE
HEREFORDSHIRE
GWENT

0 Miles 10
0 Kilometres 16

including vegetarian and children's choices, features on the menu which is served all day until 10pm.

Old Boar's Head
14 Ship Street (by the river)
☎ (01874) 622856
11 (11.30 Mon)-2.30, 5.30-11; 11-11 Fri & Sat; 12-4.30, 7-10.30 Sun
Fuller's London Pride, ESB; Tetley Bitter; Tomos Watkin OSB H
Old riverside pub with two bars, a spacious rear one for the younger set and a smart, modern bar at the front. Photos of flooded Brecon adorn the walls. May open longer in summer when lunches are also available.

Try also: Old Cognac, High St (Bass)

CRICKHOWELL
Bear Hotel
On A40
☎ (01873) 810408
11-3, 6-11; 12-3, 7-10.30 sun
Draught Bass; Hancock's HB; Morland Old Speckled Hen; guest beer H
Ancient coaching inn now an award-winning hotel with an attractive wood-panelled bar, universally popular.

White Hart Inn
On A40, W of centre
☎ (01873) 810473
12-3, 6-11; 12-11 Sat ; 12-4, 7-10.30 Sun
Brains Bitter, Buckley's Best Bitter, Rev. James H
Small, roadside inn, formerly a toll house with the tolls on display outside. Old photographs adorn the walls in the dining room where local dishes are a speciality.

ELAN VILLAGE
Elan Valley Hotel
On B4518, approx 3 miles W of Rhayader
☎ (01597) 810448
11.30-3 (not winter) 6-11; 11-10.30 Sun
Hancock's HB; guest beers H
Built as a Victorian fishing lodge, this family-run hotel is near the magnificent Elan Valley, Wales' lakeland. Comprising two bars, a restaurant and a tea room, it provides comfort and good value in an easy-going atmosphere.

HOWEY
Drovers Arms
Off A483, 1½ miles S of

ABERCRAVE
Copper Beech
133 Heol Tawe
☎ (01639) 730269
12-11; 12-10.30 Sun
Draught Bass; Hancock's HB; Young's Special; guest beer H
Close to Brecon Beacons National Park, this pub has a long standing tradition for real ale and a very relaxed atmosphere.

ABEREDW
Seven Stars Inn
On minor road off B4567
☎ (01982) 560494
11.30-2.30, 7-11; 12-2.30, 7-10.30 Sun
Beer range varies H
Warm, friendly village pub, recently restored, set amid splendid countryside in the Wye Valley. This 1997 regional CAMRA *Pub of the Year* serves good food and stocks 13 real ales in summer (two in winter).

ARDDLÎN
Horseshoe
The Horseshoe (A483)
☎ (01938) 590318
12-3, 5.30-11; 12-10.30 Sun
Fuller's London Pride; Worthington Bitter H
Pleasant village pub with a public bar and a lounge/restaurant. Guest beers come from the Tapster's Choice range and other small independent breweries. Monthly live music staged.

BRECON
George
George Street (off The Struet)
☎ (01874) 623422
11-11; 12-10.30 Sun
Greene King Abbot; Ind Coope Burton Ale; Morland Old Speckled Hen; Tetley Bitter H
Recently refurbished family-run hotel which now features a conservatory giving an extensive view of old Brecon. A good range of local fare,

Llandrindod Wells
☎ (01597) 822508
12-2.30 (not Tue), 7-11; 12-2.30,
7-10.30 Sun
Beer range varies Ⓗ
Pleasant, two-bar village inn
on the original drover's
route, with a 13th-century
cellar. The varied home-
cooked menu is based on
local produce. The beer is
usually a house ale, but may
on occasion be replaced by
another small local brewery
product, for example Wye
Valley.
🏠 Q ⚘ 🛏 ◑ ▶ 🍴 ♣ P

KNUCKLAS
Castle Inn
Off B4355
☎ (01547) 528150
12-3, 6-11; 12-3, 6-10.30 Sun
**Draught Bass; Worthington Bitter;
guest beers** Ⓗ
Friendly, family-run pub
which doubles as the village
post office. Wood-panelled
rooms, settles and excellent
home-cooking provide a
good place to stop on the
Offa's Dyke path.
🏠 Q ⚘ 🛏 ◑ ▶ 🍴 🅰 ≈ ♣ P

LLANBEDR
Red Lion
OS241204
☎ (01873) 810754
12-2.30 (not winter Mon & Tue), 7-11;
12-11 Sat ; 12-3, 7-10.30 Sun
**Buckley's Best Bitter; guest
beers** Ⓗ
Attractive village pub next to
the church, set in the scenic
Black Mountains. Good food
includes vegetarian dishes.
Popular with hillwalkers; it
may open longer in summer.
Winter weekday lunchtime
hours may vary (often
closed), so ring first to check.
🏠 Q 🚭 ⚘ ◑ 🅰 ♣ P

LLANDRINDOD WELLS
Conservative Club
South Crescent
☎ (01597) 822126
11-2, 5.30 (4.30 Fri)-11; 11-11 Sat;
11.30-2.30, 7-10.30 Sun
**Buckley's Best Bitter; Worthington
Bitter; guest beers** Ⓗ
Comfortable and quiet club,
not as political as its name
implies. Two snooker tables,
occasional entertainment
and cooked lunches on offer.
Non-members must be
signed in.
Q ◑ 🍴 ≈ ♣

Llanerch 16th Century
Inn
Llanerch Lane (by police
station)
☎ (01597) 822086
11.30-2.30, 6-11; 11.30-11 Sat; 12-
10.30 Sun

Hancock's HB; guest beers Ⓗ
This coaching inn has
been substantially rebuilt,
but the main bar retains a
low-beamed ceiling and a
large stone hearth; cosy
lounge. It hosts occasional
quizzes and live music. No
rail service winter Sun. Boules
played in summer. No-
smoking in the lounge until
8pm.
Q 🚭 ⚘ 🛏 ◑ ▶ 🍴 ♣ P

Royal British Legion
Tremont Road (A483,
between hospital and fire
station)
☎ (01597) 822558
7 (12 Sat)-11; 12-10.30 Sun
**Ansells Bitter; Draught Bass;
Worthington Bitter; guest beers** Ⓗ
This friendly club offers a
comfortable lounge and a
games room with juke box,
snooker table, pool, darts
quoits and dominoes. Non-
members must be signed in.
South and Mid Wales
CAMRA *Club of the Year*
1999.
🚭 ▶ 🍴 ≈ ♣ ◔ P

LLANFYLLIN
Cain Valley Hotel
High Street
☎ (01691) 648366
11.30-11; 12-10.30 Sun
**Ansells Bitter; Worthington Bitter;
guest beer** Ⓗ
Long-running *Guide* entry,
with a public bar, a long back
bar and a plush wood-
panelled lounge/dining area.
Q ⚘ 🛏 ◑ ▶ 🍴 ♣ P

LLANGAMMARCH WELLS
Aberceiros Inn
SW end of village
☎ (01591) 620227
12-3 (not Mon-Wed or Fri), 6.30-11;
12-3, 7-10.30 Sun
**Hancock's HB; Worthington Bitter;
guest beer** Ⓗ
Quiet, traditional pub in an
attractive rural setting, in the
same family for 150 years.
🏠 Q ⚘ ◑ ▶ 🅰 ≈ ♣ P 🖵

LLANGEDWYN
Green Inn
On B4396
☎ (01691) 828234
11-3, 6-11; 11-11 Sat; 12-10.30 Sun
Tetley Bitter; guest beers Ⓗ
With hop bines decorating
the bar, this excellent pub
boasts three different
drinking areas. It stocks
up to four guest ales, plus a
real cider in summer. The
pub has fly fishing rights for
the nearby River Tanat.
Popular for good food,
especially at weekends; the
meals are good value.
🏠 Q 🚭 ⚘ ◑ ▶ ♣ ◔ P

LLANIDLOES
Mount Inn
China Street
☎ (01686) 412247
11-11; 11-3, 5.30-11 Sat; 12-10.30
Sun
**Draught Bass; Highgate Dark;
Worthington Bitter** Ⓗ
Excellent many-roomed inn,
including two basic bars, a
plush lounge and a games
and TV room. One bar has a
stove and settles. The listed
original stone floor was once
part of a castle. May close on
weekday afternoons if quiet.
🏠 ⚘ 🛏 ◑ ▶ 🍴 ♣ P

LLANRHAEDR-YM-
MOCHNANT
Hand Inn
On B4580
☎ (01691) 780413
11-11; 12-10.30 Sun
**Banks's Original; Green King Abbot;
Wadworth 6X** Ⓗ
Many-roomed pub
boasting a number of large
stone fireplaces, a tiled public
bar and a friendly
atmosphere.
🏠 🛏 ◑ 🍴 ♣

Three Tuns
On B4580
☎ (01691) 780263
7 (11 Sat)-11; 12-10.30 Sun
Banks's Original, Bitter Ⓗ
Unspoilt village pub with a
basic public bar, complete
with a tiled floor and
inglenook, plus a second
room with pool and darts.
🏠 ▶ 🍴 ♣

LLANWRTYD WELLS
Neuadd Arms Hotel
The Square (A483, Builth
Wells-Llandovery road)
☎ (01591) 610236
11.30-11 (may close afternoons); 12-3,
7-10.30 Sun
**Felinfoel Double Dragon; Hancock's
HB; guest beer** Ⓗ
Georgian hotel, extended in
Victorian times, hosting
regular beer festivals in Jan
(Saturnalia) and Nov (Mid-
Wales), as well as the World
Bog-Snorkelling
Championships in Aug.
🏠 Q ⚘ 🛏 ◑ ▶ 🍴 🅰 ≈ ♣ P 🖵

Stonecroft Inn
Dolecoed Road (off A483)
☎ (01591) 610332
12 (5 winter Mon-Thu)-11; 12-10.30
Sun
**Brains SA; Dunn Plowmen
Kingdom** Ⓗ
Friendly Victorian pub,
catering for locals and
visitors alike; a good
base for touring the area.
The attractive patio garden
has a barbecue area.
Families are welcome at this

385

Mid-Wales beer festival venue. Meals available at all times. No rail service winter Sun. Accommodation is in the adjoining independent youth hostel. ⋈ ⊛ ⋈ ◖ ▶ Å ⇌ ♣ P

MACHYNLLETH

Skinners Arms
Main Street (A487)
☎ (01654) 702354
11-11; 12-10.30 Sun
Burtonwood Bitter; guest beer Ⓗ
Friendly, timbered, family-run, town pub with a lively public bar and games area and a comfortable lounge/no-smoking dining area which has a superb stove in a large stone inglenook. No children under 16 allowed in the bar. The guest beer changes monthly. No food Mon. ⋈ ⊛ ◖ ▶ 🕮 ⇌ ♣

Wynnstay Arms Hotel
Maengwyn Street
☎ (01654) 702941
11-11; 12-10.30 Sun
Beer range varies Ⓗ
Small bar in a town-centre hotel serving guest beers from a wide range of breweries. The three ales always include a session bitter and two stronger beers. ⋈ ⋈ ◖ ▶ ⇌ P

MONTGOMERY

Dragon Hotel
Off B4385
☎ (01686) 668359
11-3, 6-11; 12-3, 7-10.30 Sun
Beer range varies Ⓗ
Excellent, plush bar in a 17th-century coaching inn. Guest beers come from independent breweries, including Wood's. Jazz Wed eve. Q ⋈ ◖ ▶ ♣ P

NEWTOWN

Bell Hotel
Commercial Street (B4568)
☎ (01686) 625540
12-2 (2.30 Fri), 5-11; 12-midnight Sat; 12-10.30 Sun
Six Bells Big Nev's; Tetley Bitter; guests beer Ⓗ
Edge-of-town hotel hosting live music at weekends. Popular with a wide range of customers. Six Bells beers are supplied to the hotel without fish finings, making them vegetarian. The guest beer changes weekly. Home of the Dragonfire Rocket project. ⋈ ◖ ▶ ♣ P

Cross Guns
32 Park Street (off A483)
☎ (01686) 625546

CAMRA National Pub Inventory: Black Horse, Preston, Lancashire

11-3, 7-11; 11-11 Fri & Sat; 12-10.30 Sun
Theakston Best Bitter; guest beers Ⓗ
Many-roomed, beamed pub, offering guest beers from independent breweries. A new covered courtyard, with a capacity of 200 people is a venue for regular live entertainment. Meals include Indian and Chinese dishes, plus a large barbecue for summer. May extend opening hours if enough demand. ⋈ ◖ ▶ ⇌ ♣ P

Railway Tavern
Old Kerry Road (off A483)
☎ (01686) 626151
12-2.30, 6.30-11; 11-11 Tue, Fri & Sat; 12-4, 7-10.30 Sun
Draught Bass; Worthington Bitter; guest beer Ⓗ
Small, friendly, stone-walled local, handy for the station. ⇌ ♣

Sportsman
Severn Street (off A483)
☎ (01686) 625885
11-2.30, 5.30-midnight; 11-midnight Fri & Sat; 12-3, 7-10.30 Sun
Brains SA; Tetley Bitter; guest beer Ⓗ
Friendly, town-centre local, popular with a wide range of customers. It stages Celtic music nights every Tue and a Welsh-speaking eve on Mon. A special daily £2.50 set lunch is available. The guest beer is from the Tapster's Choice range. Q ⊛ ◖ ⇌ ♣

PENYBONT

Severn Arms Hotel
At A44/A488 jct
☎ (01597) 851224
11-2.30, 6-11; 12-3, 7-10.30 Sun
Draught Bass; Brains SA; Hancock's HB; Worthington Bitter; guest beers Ⓗ
Roadside inn with an extensive garden sloping down to the River Ithon (fishing rights). A large public bar, games room, quiet secluded lounge bar and restaurant complete the picture. ⋈ Q ⊛ ⋈ ◖ ▶ 🕮 & Å ♣ P

TALYBONT-ON-USK

Star
On B4518
☎ (01874) 676635
11-3, 6-11; 11-11 Sat; 12-10.30 Sun
Beer range varies Ⓗ
Up to 12 real ales (six or eight winter) are available in this attractive, canalside pub with a large fireplace in the main bar. ⋈ ⊛ ⋈ ◖ ▶ Å ⌂

WELSHPOOL

Royal Oak Hotel
Severn Street (off A483)
☎ (01938) 552217
11-3, 5.30-11; 11-11 Fri & Sat; 12-10.30 Sun
Worthington Bitter; guest beers Ⓗ
Plush, 300-year-old coaching inn, formerly the manor house of the Earls of Powis. ⋈ Q ⋈ ◖ ▶ ⇌

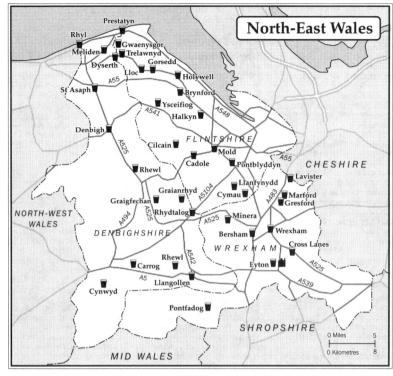

North-East Wales

Authority areas covered: Denbighshire UA, Flintshire UA, Wrexham UA

Denbighshire

CARROG

Grouse Inn
On B5436, 3/4 mile from A5
☎ (01490) 430272
12-11; 12-10.30 Sun
Lees Bitter, seasonal beers Ⓗ
Comfortable village
local a short walk from the
western terminus of the
historic Llangollen
preserved railway. It
overlooks the Dee Valley and
is very popular with visitors
in summer. Food is served all
day.
🏚 ❀ ◖ ▶ ▲ ♣ P

CYNWYD

Blue Lion
Main Street (B4401)
☎ (01490) 412106
12-3, 6-11 (12-11 summer); 11-11 Sat;
12-10.30 Sun
**Marston's Bitter; Banks's Bitter;
guest beers** (summer) Ⓗ
Friendly, traditional
village pub retaining a public
bar with a stone floor and a
small peaceful rear lounge.
Popular with visitors in
summer, it offers good value
food. Youth hostel nearby;
the pub also has one guest
room.
🏚 ⛺ ❀ ⇦ ◖ ▶ 🍴 ♣

DENBIGH

Old Vaults
40-42 High Street (signed
from A525)
☎ (01745) 815142
11-11 (1am Thu-Sat); 12-10.30 Sun
Draught Bass; guest beer Ⓗ
Small, single room with a
lively L-shaped bar decorated
with various pictures and
bric-a-brac. The upper room
is open late Thu-Sat.
◖ ▲ ♣

DYSERTH

New Inn
Waterfall Road (5 miles S of
Rhyl)
☎ (01745) 570482
12-11; 12-10.30 Sun
**Banks's Mild; Marston's Bitter,
Pedigree** Ⓗ
Popular village local
comprising three areas with a
pool table near the bar.
Handy for the local beauty
spot of Dyserth Waterfalls.
🏚 ❀ ◖ ▲ ♣ P

GRAIANRHYD

Rose & Crown
☎ (01824) 780727
4 (summer)-11; 4 (1 summer)-10.30
Sun
**Flowers IPA; Marston's Pedigree;
guest beer** Ⓗ

Welcoming pub where one
bar serves a cosy public with
an immense fire, and a
lounge. It dates back to the
early 19th century and serves
good value meals. The car
park is often used by horse-
riders; popular with walkers
and cyclists. Ring to check
availability of eve meals;
lunches served Sat and Sun.
🏚 ❀ ◖ ▶ 🍴 P

GRAIGFECHAN

Three Pigeons
On B5429, 3 miles S of
Ruthin OS147544
☎ (01824) 703178
12-3, 5.30-11; 12-3, 7-10.30 Sun
Draught Bass; guest beer Ⓗ
Spacious, rural pub in a fine
setting affording panoramic
views over the Vale of Clwyd.
A popular venue for walkers.
🏚 ❀ ◖ ▶ 🍴 ♿ ▲ ♣ P

LLANGOLLEN

Sun
49 Regent Street
☎ (01978) 860233
12-11; 12-10.30 Sun
**Plassey Bitter; Taylor Landlord;
Hydes' Anvil Mild; guest beers** Ⓗ
Welcoming pub boasting a
slate floor and oak beams
where six cask ales, cider and
a selection of foreign beers

are on offer. Good value bar food means it can get very busy Fri and Sat nights. Well worth the trip. Folk night Wed. ♨ ❀ ◖ ⅃ ৬ ▲ ₳ (steam railway) ♣ ⌣ ⛾

Wynnstay Arms
20 Bridge Street
☎ (01978) 860710
12-3, 7 (6 Fri)-11; 12-3, 7-10.30 Sun
Greene King IPA, Abbot; Ind Coope Burton Ale Ⓗ
Popular, cosy, family-run local: a small bar and two other drinking areas display a collection of horse brasses. Good value food is served in this rare local outlet for Greene King IPA. Five minutes from the steam railway.
♨ Q ➣ ❀ ⇌ ◖ ⅃ ৬ ▲
➾ (steam railway)♣ P ⅍

Try also: Bridge End (Robinsons)

MELIDEN
Melyd Arms
23 Ffordd Talargoch (A547, midway between Rhuddlan and Prestatyn)
☎ (01745) 852005
11-11; 12-10.30 Sun
Banks's Bitter; Marston's Bitter; Camerons Strongarm Ⓗ
Two-bar pub with a dining area and a pool table just off the bar area. Popular with locals and holidaymakers. Called the Miners Arms years ago due to the large local mining community (now gone).
♨ ❀ ❀ ◖ ⅃ ▲ ♣ P ⅍

PRESTATYN
Royal Victoria
Sandy Lane (near station)
☎ (01745) 854670
11.30-11; 12-3, 6.30-10.30 Sun
Burtonwood Bitter; guest beer Ⓗ
This popular town local offers a frequently changing guest beer. The pub was originally wired for electricity in 1897, 10 years before it became available. Lunches available in summer.
❀ ◖ ⅃ ▲ ➾ ♣

RHEWL (LLANGOLLEN)
Sun Inn
Off B5103 OS178449
☎ (01978) 861043
12-3, 6-11; 12-11 Sat; 12-10.30 Sun
Worthington Bitter; guest beer Ⓗ
Splendid, 14th-century drovers' inn located in the scenic Dee Valley. A small bar and side hatch serve three simply furnished rooms, frequented by walkers, fell-runners and locals. The guest ale may be absent out of season. Local CAMRA *Pub of*

the Year 1995 and '97.
♨ Q ❀ ◖ ⅃ ⊞ ▲ ♣ P

RHEWL (RUTHIN)
Drovers Arms
On A525, 2 miles N of Ruthin OS109604
☎ (01824) 703163
12-3 (not Mon), 7-11; 12-11 Sat; 12-10.30 Sun
Plassey Bitter, Fusilier; Theakston Best Bitter Ⓗ
Detached roadside village inn, providing cosy multi-roomed accommodation, and well known locally for its tasty home-cooked local produce (no food Mon). The pub was used by drovers years ago when moving cattle/sheep to market.
❀ ◖ ⅃ ▲ ♣ P ⅍

RHYDTALOG
Liver
Liver (A5104/B5430 jct)
☎ (01824) 780244
12-2, 7-11; 12-2, 7-10.30 Sun
Tetley Bitter; guest beer Ⓗ
Large, whitewashed pub on the outskirts of the Llandegla moors: two comfortable drinking and dining areas, plus a popular pool room (free of charge Mon). The patio affords good views.
♨ ❀ ◖ ⅃ ♣ P

RHYL
Splash Point
Hilton Drive (easternmost point of promenade)
☎ (01745) 353783
11.30-3, 6.30-11 (not winter Mon eve); 12-3, 7-10.30 Sun
Draught Bass; Plassey Bitter; guest beer Ⓗ
Always worth a visit, this single-storey establishment provides quality fare for drinkers and diners alike. An interesting display of brewery memorabilia complements the beers. Enjoy spectacular sea views from the front patio drinking area (weather permitting).
❀ ◖ ▲ P

Swan
13 Russell Road
☎ (01745) 336694
11-11; 12-10.30 Sun
Thwaites Mild, Bitter, Chairman's Ⓗ
Conveniently central, this civilised and homely pub is reputed to be the oldest in town. A sympathetic refurbishment has enhanced the interior and the licensee has campaigned to keep customer choice in cask beers.
❀ ◖ ⊞ ➾ ♣

Try also: Crown Bard, Rhuddlan Rd (Bass)

ST. ASAPH
Kentigern Arms
High Street
☎ (01745) 584157
12-3 (not Mon), 7-11.30; 12-3, 7-10.30 Sun
Courage Directors; John Smith's Bitter; Theakston Best Bitter, XB Ⓗ
Two-roomed, 17th-century pub whose lounge bar features wooden beams, a large open fireplace, and brasses. A no-smoking area is set aside for diners. Children welcome at lunchtime.
♨ Q ⇌ ◖ ⅃ ♣ P

Plough Inn
The Roe (400 yds from A55 roundabout)
☎ (01745) 585080
12-11; 12-10.30 Sun
Plassey Bitter; guest beers Ⓗ
This spacious stone pub, popular with drinkers and diners alike, has a restaurant and wine bar upstairs; very good facilities for wheelchair-users. The house beer, Stable Bitter, is brewed by Plassey, another Welsh guest is often also one of the three on tap.
♨ Q ❀ ◖ ⅃ ৬ ♣ P ⅍

Try also: Swan, The Roe (Free)

Flintshire
BRYNFORD
Llyn y Mawn
Brynford Hill (off B5121)
☎ (01745) 560280
5.30-11; 12-3, 6-11 Sat; 12-3, 7-10.30 Sun
Jennings Bitter; guest beers Ⓗ
Old village inn that has been tastefully extended. Twice Welsh CAMRA *Pub of the Year,* it offers six guest beers a week (two at a time), and hosts an annual beer festival in March. Booking advisable for meals (no food Mon).
♨ Q ❀ ◖ ⅃ ৬ ৳ ♣ ⌣ P ⛾

CADOLE
Colomendy Arms
Ruthin Road (off A494)
☎ (01352) 810217
7 (12 Fri & Sat)-11; 12-10.30 Sun
Beer range varies Ⓗ
Popular, two-roomed village local, stocking up to five beers. It is convenient for Loggerheads and Moel Fammau Country Parks.
♨ ❀ ▲ ♣ P

CILCAIN
White Horse
The Square (1 mile S of A541) OS177652
☎ (01352) 740142
12-3, 6.30-11; 12-11 Sat; 12-11 Sun
Banks's Bitter; guest beers Ⓗ

Whitewashed village pub near Moel Fammau Country Park where the split-level lounge is used for meals. The bar has a traditional quarry-tiled floor and a bank of old beer engines on display.
⛰ Q ❀ ◐ ◗ ⊟ ♣ P

CYMAU

Talbot

☎ (01978) 761410
12-4 (not Mon-Thu), 7-11; 12-4, 7-10.30 Sun
Hydes' Anvil Mild, Bitter; Ⓟ Jekyll's Gold Ⓗ
Popular, comfortable local where one bar serves a cosy lounge and a more bustling bar where dominoes and Sky TV are popular. This is rightly a long-standing *Guide* entry.
Q ❀ ⊟ ♣ P

EYTON

Plassey Leisure Park

The Plassey (off B5426, signed from A483)
☎ (01978) 780905
11-11 (summer only); 12-10.30 Sun
Plassey Bitter, Cwrw Tudno, Dragons Breath; guest beer Ⓗ
Diversified farm offering a golf course, caravan park, craft centre and brewery. The golf club is open all year but closes early in winter. Brewery shop sells beer to take away. Treetops Bar is open summer and the restaurant sells Plassey, too.
◐ ◗ P

GORSEDD

Druid Inn

The Village
☎ (01352) 710944
7-11; 12-3, 7-10.30 Sun
Boddingtons Bitter; Taylor Landlord; guest beers (summer) **Ⓗ**
Multi-roomed village pub, some 800 years old. Meals are served in the conservatory (Tue-Sat in summer).
⛰ ♞ ❀ ◗ ⊟ P

GWAENYSGOR

Eagle & Child

One mile N of A5151 OS075812
☎ (01745) 856391
12-3, 7-11; 12-3, 7-11 Sun
Draught Bass; Tetley Bitter; guest beers (summer weekend) **Ⓗ**
Three-roomed village pub, where shining brasses and copperware are abundant. It is popular for food all year round, its superb garden is an added draw in summer. No-smoking area only available lunchtime.
⛰ ❀ ◐ ◗ ♿ ♣ P ⚟

HALKYN

Britannia

Pentre Road (off A55, signed on main westbound expressway)
☎ (01352) 780272
11-11; 12-10.30 Sun
Lees Bitter Ⓗ
500-year-old stone pub giving good views of the Wirral and Dee estuary from the conservatory restaurant. The garden is home to various farmyard animals. A welcoming watering-hole on the main North Wales holiday route.
⛰ Q ❀ ◐ ◗ ⊟ ♿ ⛺ ♣ P

HOLYWELL

Glan yr Afon Inn

Milwr (off A5026, follow signs on A5026) OS195739
☎ (01352) 710052
12-3, 5.30-11; 12-11 Sat; 12-11 Sun
Tetley Bitter; Coach House Dick Turpin; guest beers Ⓗ
Sympathetically extended Welsh longhouse enjoying fine views over the Dee estuary. It featured in the *Guinness Book of Records* as being held in the same family for 418 years (1559-1977). A house beer is brewed by Coach House. It holds regular mini-beer festivals, and special events. Wheelchair WC. It has a children's play area.
⛰ Q ♞ ❀ 🛏 ◐ ◗ ⊟ ♿ ⛺ ♣ P

LLANFYNND

Cross Keys

☎ (01978) 760333
12-3 (not Mon-Fri), 7-11; 12-3, 7-10.30 Sun
Tetley Bitter; guest beer Ⓗ
Quiet, cosy pub where open fires make for a welcoming atmosphere. The bar is stone-floored and basic, while the lounge with its unusual raised area boasts carved settles. The guest ale is often supplied by a local independent. Parking is only accessible from direction of Ffrith.
Q ❀ ◐ ◗ ⊟ P

LLOC

Rock Inn

St Asaph Road (off A55, 1 mile from W end of A5026) OS766144
☎ (01352) 710049
11-11; 12-10.30 Sun
Burtonwood Bitter, Top Hat Ⓗ
Welcoming two-roomed pub and restaurant, run by the same family for over 20 years. Boules played. The food is very popular with locals.
⛰ ❀ ◐ ◗ ⛺ ♣ P

MOLD

Griffin

41 High Street
☎ (01352) 750697
12-11; 12-10.30 Sun
Burtonwood Bitter; guest beer Ⓗ
Friendly, lively, bare-boarded Forshaw's Alehouse. The renovation brears no resemblance to the gloomy bar it replaced, but there has been a pub on the site since 1762. Photos of old Mold decorate the walls to reflect its past. The car park is off King Street.
◐ ♣ P

Y Pentan

3 New Street
☎ (01352) 758884
11-3, 6.30-11; 11-11 Wed, Fri & Sat; 12-10.30 Sun
Banks's Original, Bitter; Marston's Pedigree; guest beer Ⓗ
The L-shaped lounge is devoted to the life and times of the Welsh language novelist Daniel Owen; the pub is named after one of his books and complements the nearby museum. Large windows look out on to a shopping street. The small sports bar is noisy.
◐ ⊟ ♣

PONTBLYDDYN

Bridge Inn

At A5104/A541 jct
☎ (01352) 770087
12-11; 12-10.30 Sun
Courage Directors; Theakston Best Bitter; guest beer Ⓗ
This half-timbered 16th-century pub boasts an impressive stone fireplace. The car park adjoins the picturesque garden on the banks of the River Alyn. Henry Morgan the 18th-century pirate was allegedly a regular here. Children welcome in the pool room and restaurant.
⛰ ♞ ❀ ◐ ◗ ♣ P

TRELAWNYD

Crown Inn

London Road (A5151, first pub on Prestatyn road, off A55)
☎ (01745) 571580
12-midnight; 12-11.30 Sun
Greenalls Mild, Bitter; Tetley Bitter; guest beer Ⓗ
Single bar village inn with adjoining rooms and a restaurant: welcoming, comfortable and cosy.
⛰ Q ♞ ❀ ◐ ◗ ⛺ ♣ P ⚟

YSCEIFIOG

Fox Inn

Signed from B5121, W of Mold OS152715

☎ (01352) 720241
5.30 (7 winter)-11, 11-11 Sat; 12-10.30 Sun

Shepherd Neame Master Brew Bitter; guest beers ⒣
17th-century rural gem in a small village. Popular with walkers, it is not the easiest place to find but well worth the effort. Several small rooms have many interesting features, such as the bench seat against the bar; the intimate dining room only seats eight.
🏚 🕸 ⓓ ▶ 🕀 🛏 ♣ ♨

Wrexham

BERSHAM
Black Lion Inn
Y Ddol (off B5097)
☎ (01978) 365588
12-11; 12-10.30 Sun
Hydes' Anvil Light, Bitter, seasonal beers ⒣
Sympathetic renovation of a parlour-style pub with a pool room. Convivial and cosy, it stands below main road level in an attractive hamlet on the Clywedog Valley Industrial Trail, next to Bersham Heritage Centre. The garden overlooks the wooded riverside.
🏚 🕸 🕀 🛏 ♣ P

CROSS LANES
Cross Lanes Hotel (Kagan's Brasserie)
Bangor Road, Marchwiel (A525)
☎ (01978) 780555
11-11; 12-10.30 Sun
Plassey Bitter ⒣
Large, stately lounge set around a central bar in a 18th-century mansion. Attached to an upmarket hotel in six acres of gardens, it is reached by a grand entrance hall containing fine panelling and a 1618 staircase, rescued from Emral Hall, Worthenbury.
🏚 🕸 🌳 ⓓ ♣ P

Kiln Inn
On B5130 (off A525, signed Cock Bank)
☎ (01978) 780429
12-3 (not Mon-Fri), 7-11 Sat; 12-3, 7-10.30 Sun
Plassey Bitter; guest beer ⒣
Former malt kiln converted to a pub circa 1800. Three small rooms, including a characterful front parlour are set around a central servery. Booking is advised for the little restaurant (no food Mon). Convivial and welcoming, this is a fine village local.
🏚 🕸 ⓓ ♣ P

GRESFORD
Griffin
Church Green
☎ (01978) 852231
1-4.30, 7-11; 1-4, 7-10.30 Sun
Greenalls Mild, Bitter ⒣
Refreshingly quiet and relaxed open-plan local. The fact that irksome background muzak and food smells are absent owes everything to the genial landlady. An attractive church and village pond are nearby.
Q 🕸 ♣ P

LAVISTER
Nags Head
Chester Road (B5445)
☎ (01244) 570486
12 (5.30 Mon & Tue)-11; 12-10.30 Sun
Draught Bass; Boddingtons Bitter; guest beers ⒣
This pub claims to be the birthplace of CAMRA in 1971 and still serves good beer in cosy surroundings. A half-glazed horseshoe-shaped bar serves a quiet, warm, lounge and a more lively bar. The eating area has recently been enlarged (eve meals served Fri and Sat).
🏚 🕸 ⓓ ▶ 🕀 ♣ P

MARFORD
Red Lion
Marford Hill
☎ (01978) 853562
5 (12 Wed-Sat)-11; 12-10.30 Sun
Burtonwood Bitter; guest beer ⒣
Restful, two-roomed local with a split-level lounge displaying prints of surrounding villages from a bygone era. The pub used to straddle the old Flintshire/Denbighshire border resulting in different drinking hours between the lounge and bar!
🕸 ⓓ 🕀 ♣ P

MINERA
Tyn-y-Capel
Church Road

(off B5426 from Coedpoeth)
☎ (01978) 757502
12-3, 7-11 (may extend in summer); 12-3, 7-10.30 Sun
Tetley Bitter; guest beer ⒣
Former drovers' pub, recently refurbished; this popular village local places a strong emphasis on food. The garden offers commanding views of the Clywedog Valley.
🕸 ⓓ ▶ P

PONTFADOG
Swan
On B4500
☎ (01691) 718273
12-3, 7-11; 12-3, 7-10.30 Sun
Brains Bitter; guest beer ⒣
Pleasant village local; the car park lies across the road next to the River Ceiriog. The bar has an imposing fireplace which separates the TV and table football from the bar; the dining room is quieter. The guest beer usually comes from a local independent. No eve meals Mon.
🏚 🕸 ⓓ ▶ ♣

WREXHAM
Albion Hotel
1 Pen-y-Bryn (400 yds from centre, down Town Hill)
☎ (01978) 364969
12-4, 7-11; 12-4, 7-10.30 Sun
Lees Bitter, seasonal beers ⒣
Lively Victorian hotel where a central bar serves various areas, including a spacious lounge. You'll find precious little cask ale for miles around so the word 'welcoming' and 'oasis' are apposite.
🛏 🕀 ⇌ (Central) ♣

Cask Marque
Pubs that carry the Cask Marque symbol indicate that the licensees have successfully passed a number of tests concerning beer quality, and display plaques to this effect in their outlets. However, these pubs have been chosen independently of Cask Marque by CAMRA. The Cask Marque symbol is added during the editing process and Cask Marque is not involved in the selection of pubs.

INDEPENDENT BREWERIES

Plassey: Eyton

Travellers Inn: Caerwys

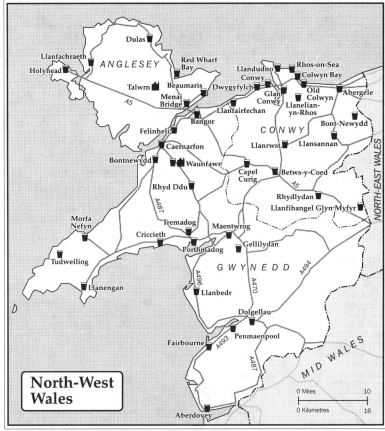

North-West Wales

Authority areas covered: Anglesey UA, Conwy UA, Gwynedd UA

Anglesey/Ynys Môn

BEAUMARIS

George & Dragon
Church Street
☎ (01248) 810491
11-11; 12-10.30 Sun
Robinson's Best Bitter Ⓗ
15th-century pub, boasting
oak beams, inglenook and
lots of brass. Ask to see the
historic wall paintings
upstairs. ☎ ◖ ♣

Olde Bull's Head Inn
Castle Street
☎ (01248) 810329
11-11; 12-10.30 Sun
**Draught Bass; Hancock's HB;
Worthington Bitter; guest beer**
(summer) Ⓗ
17th-century former
coaching inn where Dr.
Johnson and Dickens both
stayed. The oak-beamed bar
displays weaponry and china.
The restaurant enjoys an
excellent reputation for food,
and is now complemented by
a brasserie which has
wheelchair access. Limited
parking.
🏨 Q ⇔ ◖ ▮ ⊞ ♿ P ⤧

DULAS

Pilot Boat
On A5025
☎ (01248) 410205
11-11; 12-10.30 Sun
**Robinson's Best Bitter, Old
Stockport** (summer) Ⓗ
Friendly rural family
pub where the lounge
has an unusual boat-shaped
bar. Ideal for coastal and
country walks; meals are
served all day in the no-
smoking dining room.
There is also a bar/games
room.
🏨 Q ⊛ ◖ ▮ ▲ ♣ P

HOLYHEAD

79
79 Market Street
☎ (01407) 763939
11-11; 12-10.30 Sun
Beer range varies Ⓗ
Comfortable town-centre
pub of several different
drinking areas, plus a dining
area, overlooking the Irish
ferry port, which serves a
good choice of reasonably-
priced food.
◖ ▮ ⇌

LLANFACHRAETH

Holland Hotel
Cemaes Road (A5025)
☎ (01407) 740252
11-3.30, 7-11; 11-11 Sat & summer;
12-10.30 Sun
Lees GB Mild, Bitter Ⓗ
Welcoming local with
different rooms, all served
from one bar area, runner-up
in Lees recent *Pub of the Year*.
It is well sited for exploring
Anglesey and its coastal path,
and handy for the Holyhead
Irish ferries. The menu
specialises in local produce,
particularly shellfish. The
accommodation has recently
been refurbished to a high
standard.
Q ⊛ ⇔ ◖ ▮ ⊞ ♣ P

MENAI BRIDGE

Liverpool Arms
St Georges Road (between PO
and pier)
☎ (01248) 713335
11.30-3, 5.30-11; 12-3, 7-10.30 Sun
**Greenalls Bitter; Flowers Original;
guest beers** Ⓗ
Offering good food and
accommodation this 150-

year-old friendly pub, whose several rooms, nooks and crannies bear a nautical theme, is popular with locals, the sailing fraternity and students. A good base for touring Anglesey and Snowdonia.

Q ᗛ ☃ ⌂ ◖ ◗

Victoria Hotel
Telford Road
☎ (01248) 712309
11-11; 12-10.30 Sun
Draught Bass; guest beers Ⓗ
Comfortable, two-bar residential hotel, licensed for weddings. An extensive conservatory and patio area afford excellent views of the Menai Staits. It offers good food and accommodation – a new wing was added recently.

♨ ᗛ ☃ ⌂ ◖ ◗ ⊟ ♿ P

RED WHARF BAY
Ship Inn
1¹/₂ miles off A5025, near Benllech
☎ (01248) 852568
11.30-3.30, 7-11; 11-11 Sat & summer; 12-10.30 Sun
Friary Meux BB; Ind Coope Burton Ale; guest beers Ⓗ
Cosy old pub on the beach giving excellent views. Stone walls, exposed beams and log fires in winter add character. Award-winning food helps make it busy in summer and at weekends.

♨ Q ᗛ ☃ ☃ ◖ ◗ Å ♣ P ⚊

Conwy

ABERGELE
Gwindy
Market Street
☎ (01745) 833485
11-11; 12-10.30 Sun
Banks's Original; Marston's Bitter; guest beer Ⓗ
A lounge and public bar with a pool table form the core of this centrally-located, friendly popular pub. Excellent home-cooked food is served in dining area or lounge.

☃ ◖ ◗ ⊟ Å ≈ ♣

BETWS-Y-COED
Glan Aber Hotel
Holyhead Road
☎ (01690) 710325
11-11; 12-10.30 Sun
Morland Old Speckled Hen; Tetley Dark Mild, Bitter; guest beer Ⓗ
This very popular, family-run hotel is centrally located. Non-residents have the choice of three rooms catering for all tastes, in which the highly recommended meals are served. Three-star en-suite

accommodation is complemented by a more basic bunk-house annexe..

Q ᗛ ☃ ⌂ ◖ ◗ Å ≈ ♣ P

Pont-y-Pair
Holyhead Road
☎ (01690) 710407
11-11; 12-10.30 (11 summer) Sun
Greene King Abbot; Marston's Pedigree; Tetley Bitter Ⓗ
Comfortable, family-run hotel opposite the famous river bridge over the Afon Llugwy. A good selection of freshly cooked meals is served in the bar or lounge. Popular with locals and tourists, there is a pool room at the rear. Tiny car park.

♨ Q ☃ ⌂ ◖ ◗ Å ≈ ♣ P

BONT NEWYDD
Dolben Arms
OS013708
☎ (01745) 582207
7-11 (midnight supper licence), 12-10.30 Sun
Theakston XB; guest beer Ⓗ
16th-century inn and restaurant in a remote location beside the Afon Elwy at Cefn, near St. Asaph. Narrow lanes lead to this charming inn, where one bar separates into a lounge, bar, restaurant and games/family area. Sun lunch is served here.

Q ☃ ◗ ♣ P

CAPEL CURIG
Cobdens Hotel
☎ (01690) 720243
11-11; 12-10.30 Sun
Brains SA; Morland Old Speckled Hen; Tetley Bitter Ⓗ
Informal 200-year-old family-run hotel: a lounge, restaurant and climbers bar that features a natural rock face in the wall. Freshly-prepared food is important here as the pub is a member of the Campaign for Real Food. Popular all-year round; a warm welcome is assured.

♨ Q ᗛ ☃ ⌂ ◖ ◗ Å ♣ P

COLWYN BAY
Wings Social Club
Imperial Buildings, Station Square
☎ (01492) 530682
11-3, 7-11; 11-11 Sat; 12-3, 7-10.30 Sun
Lees GB Mild, Bitter Ⓗ
Ex-RAFA club, now a social club for visitors and families; CAMRA members are especially welcome – please show a membership card. The large lounge, billiards room, and snug with TV all offer great value (small charge for admission).

Q ≈ ♣

CONWY
George & Dragon
Castle Street
☎ (01492) 592305
12-11; 12-10.30 Sun
Draught Bass; M&B Mild; Morland Old Speckled Hen; Worthington Bitter; guest beer (summer) Ⓗ
A popular, but small, narrow town pub. Owned by Punch Taverns it probably offers the best choice of real ale in the ten pubs of this historic town – well worth a visit.

☃ ⌂ ◖ ◗ ≈ ♣

DWYGYFYLCHI
Dwygyfylchi Hotel
Capelulo
☎ (01492) 623395
12-3, 5.30-11; 11-11 Sat & summer; 11-10.30 Sun
Burtonwood Bitter, Top Hat Ⓗ
Traditional pub, with a lounge bar/TV area and a dining room which has a no-smoking area.

☃ ⌂ ◖ ◗ ⊟ ♣ P

GLAN CONWY
Cross Keys Inn
Llansanffraid
☎ (01492) 580292
1.30 (12 Sat)-11; 12-10.30 Sun
Marston's Pedigree Ⓗ
Small, traditional, village local, 100 yards from the station, with a bar area, a pool room, and a lounge, this small terraced pub has a good community feel about it. Outdoor seating at the front overlooks the Afon Conwy estuary.

♨ Q ☃ ≈ ♣

LLANDUDNO
London Hotel
Mostyn Street
☎ (01492) 876740
12-11; 12-10.30 Sun
Burtonwood Bitter, Top Hat, Buccaneer Ⓗ
Large, friendly, one-roomed town pub, based on a London theme, with a collection of jugs, a cased Chelsea Pensioner, and an original red telephone box. Live music is staged at weekends. A sliding partition divides the main room from the family area.

ᗛ ⌂ ◖ ≈ ♣

Olde Victoria
Church Walks
☎ (01492) 860949
11-11; 12-10.30 Sun
Banks's Original, Bitter; Camerons Strongarm; Marston's Pedigree; guest beer Ⓗ
The 'Olde Vic' is a popular and traditional Victorian pub, with a homely atmosphere. Good value food

is served in the lounge or restaurant. Children always welcome. It hosts regular quiz and folk eves.
Q ❀ ◖ ▶ ⇌ ♣

Snowdon
Tudno Street
☎ (01492) 872166
12-11; 12-10.30 Sun
Ind Coope Burton Ale; Theakston Best Bitter; guest beer H
Just off the main shopping area: a large lounge has two areas, (one with Sky TV), while the small bar contains the dartboard. Popular with locals. Outside drinking is at pavement tables.
🏰 ❀ ⊞ ⇌ ♣

LLANELIAN-YN-RHOS
White Lion Inn
☎ (01492) 515807
11-3, 6-11; 11-3, 6-10.30 Sun
Marston's Bitter, Pedigree; guest beer H
'Olde-worlde', traditional Welsh village inn with a sympathetic extension for diners. The slate-floored bar, a tiny snug and the lounge, partly date back to the 16th century. Good food and accommodation is on offer at this free house.
🏰 Q ❀ 🛏 ◖ ▶ ⊞ A P ⌿

LLANFAIRFECHAN
Llanfair Arms
Mill Road
☎ (01248) 680521
11-11; 12-10.30 Sun
Greene King IPA; guest beer H
Village Punch Taverns pub, with one main room, plus a small front lounge, and a rear pool room; a typical local.
🏰 ❀ ⇌ ♣

Try also: Village Inn, Penmaenmawr Rd (Free); **Virginia Inn,** Mill Rd (Free)

LLANFIHANGEL GLYN MYFYR
Crown Inn
☎ (01490) 420209
7 (12 Sat)-11 (closed Mon); 12-10.30 Sun
Beer range varies H
Lovely old inn beside the Afon Alwen, where a warm welcome awaits in the front bar with its open fire. It also has a pool room, and rear room where children are welcome. Fishing permits available from the pub. The guest beer(s) are often Welsh.
🏰 Q ❀ 🛏 ▶ A ♣ P

LLANRWST
New Inn
Dinbych Street
☎ (01492) 640476

11-11; 12-10.30 (11 summer) Sun
Banks's Original; Marston's Bitter, Pedigree, seasonal beers H
Popular, traditional, town pub: a single bar serves a snug, a general seating area and a rear games area. The hospitable landlord offers a warm welcome, and the regulars are friendly. The outdoor covered courtyard has picnic tables. The seasonal beers come from both Banks and Marston's.
🏰 ❀ A ⇌ ♣

Try also: Pen-y-Bont Inn, Bridge St (Free)

LLANSANNAN
Red Lion (Llew Coch)
☎ (01745) 870256
5 (12 Sat)-11; 12-10.30 Sun
Lees GB Mild, Bitter, seasonal beers H
Old village pub, popular with local farmers and visitors. An unusual layout features the original 14th-century bar area around a stove, a raised lounge and a lower bar, all relatively separate. Freshly-prepared food is available at most times. Finalist in Lees *Pub of the Year* 1999.
🏰 Q ❀ 🛏 ◖ ♣ P

OLD COLWYN
Red Lion
385 Abergele Road
☎ (01492) 515042
5 (12 Sat)-11; 12-10.30 Sun
Boddingtons Bitter; Flowers IPA; Theakston Mild; guest beers H
Popular, traditional town pub, comprising a public bar and two lounges; a proper meeting place for locals where all are welcome. CAMRA North Wales *Pub of the Year* 1999, it always has seven cask beers on, including a good number from independent breweries.
🏰 Q ❀ ⊞ ♣

RHOS-ON-SEA
Rhos Fynach Tavern
The Promenade
☎ (01492) 548185
11-11; 12-10.30 Sun
Banks's Bitter; Marston's Pedigree; guest beer H
Reputedly the oldest building in Colwyn, this pub stands on the site of an old monastery, overlooking the promenade: a large bar area with adjacent no-smoking dining area, and a cosy snug/disco area. The Monks Restaurant upstairs is open eves. 🏰 ❀ ◖ ⊞ ♿ ⇌ P

RHYDLYDAN
Giler Arms Hotel

Near A5, 2 miles E of Pentrefoelas
☎ (01690) 770612
12-11; 12-3, 6-10.30 Sun
Marston's Pedigree; Tetley Bitter; guest beer H
Friendly country hotel, a genuine free house comprising a lounge bar, pool room and a restaurant. Set in seven acres of grounds in the hidden heart of Wales, it also offers a lake for coarse fishing, a small campsite and pleasant gardens by the River Merddwr. A second guest beer is stocked in summer.
🏰 Q ❀ 🛏 ◖ ▶ ⊞ A ♣ P

Gwynedd

ABERDOVEY/ABERDYFI
Penhelig Arms Hotel
The Promenade, Terrace Road
☎ (01654) 767215
11-3.30, 6-11 (11-11 summer); 12-3.30, 6-10.30 Sun
Draught Bass; Tetley Bitter; guest beer H
Archetypal, small, friendly seaside town hotel, with ten comfortable bedrooms. Good food is served in the restaurant, as well as the rather stylish nautically-themed public bar: fish is speciality on the menu, too.
🏰 Q ❀ 🛏 ◖ ▶ A ⇌ P

BANGOR
Eryl Môr Hotel
2 Upper Garth Road (near pier)
☎ (01248) 354042
11-11; 12-10.30 Sun
Morland Old Speckled Hen; John Smith's Bitter; guest beers H
Hotel overlooking the pier and Menai Straits, offering up to two constantly changing guest beers and an extensive menu. Busy in summer and at weekends.
❀ 🛏 ◖ ▶ ⇌ P ⌿

Globe Inn
Albert Street, Upper Bangor
☎ (01248) 362095
11-11; 12-10.30 Sun
Boddingtons Bitter; Flowers IPA; guest beers H
Traditional family-run pub with a distinctive Welsh atmosphere, popular with students and locals alike. It offers a range of good value meals and snacks – all home-made, using local produce (eve meals served during university term-time). Guests usually include Flannery's and Ynys Môn beers.
◖ ▶ ⇌ ♣

Tap & Spile
Garth Road (off old A5, follow pier signs)
☎ (01248) 370835

12 (11 summer)-11; 12-10.30 Sun
Draught Bass; Fuller's London Pride; Hancock's HB H
Very popular, multi-levelled pub overlooking the pier and Menai Straits. Be prepared for a big screen TV, fruit machines and loud music.
🛏 🍴 ♣

Y Castell
Off High Street, Glanrafon (opp. Cathedral)
☎ (01248) 355866
12-11; 12-10.30 Sun
Boddingtons Bitter; Marston's Pedigree; Tetley Bitter; Wadworth 6X; guest beers H
Hogshead pub: a spacious one-roomed house offering the widest range of real ales (up to 12) in the area to a good mix of locals and students. The menu, served 12-9 (7 Fri-Sat), includes specials. Four cask ciders on tap, too.
🛏 🍴 ♿ ⊁ ☕ ⊁

Try also: Fat Cat, 161 High St (Free)

BONTNEWYDD
Newborough Arms
On A487, Porthmadog-Caernarfon road)
☎ (01286) 673126
11-11; 12-10.30 Sun
Marston's Pedigree; Tetley Dark Mild, Bitter; guest bitter H
Busy, often crowded, village pub on the main holiday route, enjoying a good reputation for food; very friendly staff. The house beer, Dragon, is brewed by Ansells.
🛏 Q 🌸 🍴 ⚐ 🅿 ⊟

CAERNARFON
Alexandra Hotel
North Road (opp. Safeway)
☎ (01286) 672871
11-11; 12-10.30 Sun
Draught Bass; Boddingtons Bitter; Flowers Original; guest beers H
Free house of original style near the town centre; this friendly local offers a variety of beers – try the Flowers.
Q 🌸 🛏 🅿

Black Boy Inn
Northgate Street (opp. castle entrance)
☎ (01286) 673023
11-11; 12-10.30 Sun
Draught Bass; guest beers H
16th-century pub within the town walls near the castle: a public bar and small lounge are both warmed by roaring fires. Good value food served. Limited parking.
🛏 Q 🌸 🍴 🅿

Try also: Y Goron Fach, Hole in the Wall St (Free)

CRICCIETH
Prince of Wales Hotel
High Street
☎ (01766) 522556
11-3, 6-11; 12-3, 7-10.30 Sun
Boddingtons Bitter; Morland Old Speckled Hen; guest beers (occasional) H
Busy local opposite the village green where a central bar serves cosy drinking areas and a split-level family area. It can get busy in summer.
🍴 🔨 ⊟

DOLGELLAU
Stag Inn
Bridge Street
☎ (01341) 422533
12-11; 12-10.30 Sun
Burtonwood Bitter H
Basic single roomed town bar, with a tiled floor one side, and a comfortable section on the other. This honest, no-frills pub is one of five of interest in the town.
🌸 🍴

FAIRBOURNE
Fairbourne Hotel
☎ (01341) 250203
11-3, 6-11; 11-11 Sat; 12-10.30 Sun
McEwan 80/-; John Smith's Bitter H
Large, 17th-century residential hotel, renowned for excellent food, friendly atmosphere, and comfortable bedrooms. An attractive, long, narrow lounge bar, with subdued lighting offers plenty of quiet corners; the front lounge/family area overlooks the estuary and is no-smoking until 9pm. Wheelchair WC.
🛏 🛏 🍴 ⚐ ♿ 🔨 🅿 ⊁

FELINHELI
Gardd Fôn
Beach Road (off main road, by the Menai Straits)
☎ (01248) 670359
11-11; 12-10.30 Sun
Burtonwood Bitter; guest beers H
Nautically-themed, 18th-century, friendly pub, busy in summer when locals are joined by visitors. The new bistro restaurant offers good food. Wonderful views over the Menai Straits can be enjoyed from the drinking area in front of the pub. Note the lovely brasses and church pews.
🛏 Q 🐕 🌸 🍴 ♣ 🅿

GELLILYDAN
Bryn Arms
Coed-y-Llwyn
☎ (01766) 590278
11-11; 12-10.30 Sun
Worthington Bitter H
Busy, modern, village local

more like a social club than a traditional pub. The public bar has a pool table, darts and TV; the lounge bar has an open stove fireplace. A true free house, it stocks beers from Bragdy Ynys Mon.
🛏 Q 🌸 🍴 ⚐ ♣ 🅿

LLANBEDR
Tŷ Mawr Hotel
☎ (01341) 241440
11-11; 12-10.30 Sun
Worthington Bitter; guest beers H
Country-style hotel, with a modern lounge bar for non-residents; popular with locals and real ale enthusiasts. A paved terrace and verandah overlook lawned gardens with outdoor seating. It stocks an interesting range of (usually Welsh) guest beers.
🛏 🌸 🛏 🍴 🔨 🅿

Try also: Victoria Hotel (Robinson's)

LLANENGAN
Sun Inn
Through Abersoch to village
☎ (01758) 712660
12-3, 6-11 (12-11 summer); 12-3, 6-10.30 (12-10.30 summer) Sun
Robinson's Hatters Mild, Best Bitter; guest beer (summer) H
17th-century, wood-panelled two-bar inn serving good value food. With safe gardens, it stands five minutes' from the beach, so is an obvious choice for families. Dogs are not allowed in the garden.
🛏 Q 🐕 🌸 🍴 ♣ 🅿

MAENTWROG
Grapes Hotel
On A496 towards Harlech
☎ (01766) 590208
11-11; 12-10.30 Sun
Beer range varies H
Comfortable, 13th-century, former coaching inn popular with locals, walkers, and tourists. Excellent value home-cooked food includes fish specials; the no-smoking dining rom doubles as a family room. Three real ales always on tap. 🛏 Q 🐕 🛏 🍴 🔨 (Ffestiniog railway narrow gauge) ♣ 🅿 ⊁

MORFA NEFYN
Cliffs Inn
Beach Road
☎ (01758) 720356
12-3, 6 (7 winter)-11; 6-11 (not winter) Sun
Brains Dark; Morland Old Speckled Hen; guest beer H
Large, friendly pub boasting a sun lounge overlooking the bay. Good value food is

CAMRA National Pub Inventory, Pot Kiln, Frilsham, Berkshire

served. Families are welcome; self catering flats available. It gets busy in summer.
Q ❀ ⇔ ◑ ⧐ ▲ P

PENMAENPOOL

George III Hotel
☎ (01341) 422525
11-11; 11-10.30 Sun
Ruddles Best Bitter; John Smith's Bitter; guest beer (summer) Ⓗ
Family-owned and -run residential hotel by the tollbridge crossing the Mawddach estuary. The cellar bar boasts a slate floor, oak beamed ceiling, and panelled benches. The hotel has a lounge and restaurant on the upper floor. Children's certificate. Wheelchair WC.
⇔ Q ❀ ⇔ ◑ ⧐ ⊞ & P

PORTHMADOG

Ship Inn
14 Lombard Street (near harbour)
☎ (01766) 512990
11-11; 12-6 (10.30 summer) Sun
Ind Coope Burton Ale; Marston's Pedigree; Morland Old Speckled Hen; Tetley Mild, Bitter; guest beers Ⓗ
Local CAMRA *Pub of the Year* 1999, full of character including interesting maritime memorabilia, not far from the Ffestiniog Railway. It stages a beer festival in March. Children welcome if dining, it offers

an excellent choice of meals and whiskies.
⇔ Q ◑ ⧐ & ▲ ⇌ ⊖ ⨦

RHYD DDU

Cwellyn Arms
On A4085, Caernarfon-Beddgelert road
☎ (01766) 890321
11-11; 12-10.30 Sun
Draught Bass; Worthington Bitter; guest beers Ⓗ
This beamed, 200-year-old pub at the foot of Snowdon, serving an extensive menu of good food, is open 365 days a year. It offers large bunkhouse accommodation in a beautiful National Park location 10 minutes walk from Cwellyn Lake; ideal for climbers and walkers. Up to six guest beers on tap.
⇔ Q ⛺ ❀ ⇔ ◑ ⧐ ▲ P

TREMADOG

Golden Fleece
The Square
☎ (01766) 512421
11.30-3, 6-11; 12-3, 6-10.30 Sun
Draught Bass; Flannery's seasonal beers Ⓗ
Old coaching inn, now a friendly local with a bistro serving good food. Children welcome. It hosts occasional live music.
⇔ Q ❀ ⇔ ◑ ⧐ & ⨦

TUDWEILIOG

Lion

On B4417
12-2, 7 (6 Fri)-11; 12-11 Sat; 12-2 (11 Easter & summer hols) Sun
Boddingtons Bitter Theakston Best Bitter; guest beer (summer) Ⓗ
Cheerful village inn with a quiet lounge and a lively public bar; families welcome. Good value food.
⛺ ❀ ⇔ ◑ ⧐ & ♣ P ⨦

WAUNFAWR

Snowdonia Parc
On A4085, Caernarfon-Beddgelert road
☎ (01286) 650409
6 (12 Sat & summer)-11; 12-10.30 Sun
Marston's Bitter, Pedigree; Snowdonia Station Bitter, Welsh Highland Bitter Ⓗ
Brew-pub located in the heart of Snowdonia with its own campsite (reduction for CAMRA members). It offers good food and home-brewed beers, plus live entertainment Sat eves. The new Welsh Highland Railway next door opens summer 2000. The garden has a children's play area.
⛺ ❀ ◑ ▲ ⇌ P ⨦

INDEPENDENT BREWERIES

Bragdy Ynys Môn: Talwrn

Snowdonia: Waunfawr

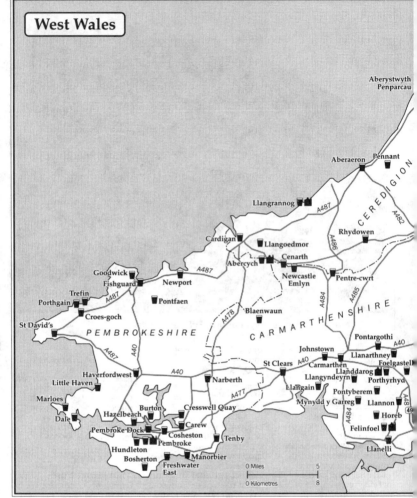

West Wales

Authority areas covered: Camarthenshire UA, Ceredigion UA, Pembrokeshire UA

Carmarthenshire

AMMANFORD

Wernolau
31 Pontamman Road (from
Ammanford-Neath road, 50
yds past Murco garage on
right)
☎ (01269) 592598
5 (5.30 winter)-11; 12-3, 7-10 Sun
**Buckley's Best Bitter; guest
beers** Ⓗ
A wide range of beers
(five guests) often rotate
here. Look hard or you will
miss the entrance to
the drive. Families
welcome; large grounds
are a bonus
♨ Q ❀ ⇌ ▶ Å

BLAENWAUN

Lamb Inn
☎ (01994) 48440

11 (5.30 winter)-11; 12-10.30 Sun
**Buckley's Rev. James; guest
beers** Ⓗ
Friendly country pub: a main
bar, including a games area,
plus a snug bar. The new
landlord has new ideas; well
worth a visit if in the area.
Å ♣ ⇔ P

CARMARTHEN

Mansel Arms
Mansel Street (near provision
market)
☎ (01267) 236385
11 (9 Wed & Sat)-11; 12-10.30 Sun
**Draught Bass; Theakston Mild;
Worthington Bitter; guest beers** Ⓗ
This busy pub near
the markets offers an
interesting choice of guest
beers, plus good food,
making it popular with
shoppers and locals.
❀ ◖ ⇌ ♣

Stag & Pheasant
34 Spilman Street
☎ (01267) 236278
11-11; 12-10.30 Sun
Worthington Bitter; guest beers Ⓗ
Town pub, enjoying a brisk
lunchtime trade; popular
with local office workers, it
was once a stable block
serving the hotel opposite.
Appetising snacks and meals
are sensibly priced.
Q ◖ ⇌

Try also: **Queens Hotel**,
Queen St (Punch)

CENARTH

Three Horseshoes
On A484
☎ (01239) 710119
11-11; 12-10.30 (closed winter
afternoons) Sun
**Ansells Mild; Buckley's Best Bitter,
Rev. James;** Ⓗ **Greene King Abbot;**

NORTH-WEST WALES
A487
Talybont
Llandre
Capel Bangor
A44
Goginan
Llanbadarn Fawr
A485
MID WALES
Tregaron
A485
Pentre-felin
Cwmann
Rhandirmwyn
A482
A483
A40
Llansawel
A40
Llandeilo
Llandybie
A483
Ammanford
GLAMORGAN

[G] **guest beer** [H]
Cosy, traditional inn with a thatched former brewhouse situated by the river. Popular with anglers, it is the HQ of the Teifi Trout Assn. Beer festivals (with entertainment) are held Bank Holidays.
🔥 Q ❀ ◐ ◑ ▲ ♣ P

CWMANN

Ram Inn
On A482, outskirts of village
☎ (01570) 422556
11-11; 12-10.30 Sun
Draught Bass; Fuller's London Pride; guest beer [H]
Popular, 16th-century pub with a large garden on the outskirts of the village; CAMRA *Best Pub in Wales* 1997.
🔥 Q ❀ ◐ ◑ ⊞ ♣ P

Try also: Cwmann Tavern (Free)

FELINFOEL

Royal Oak
33 Farmer Row (opp. brewery)
☎ (01554) 751140
11-11; 12-4, 7-10.30 Sun
Felinfoel Bitter, Double Dragon [H]
Welcoming pub, popular with older people. A dining room off the bar serves meals Wed-Sat.
Q ◐ ◑

FOELGASTELL

Smiths Arms
Off A48 ☎ (01269) 842213
11-2.30, 5-11; 12-10.30 Sun
Beer range varies [G]
Friendly pub in a quiet village. A minute or so off the main holiday route.
🔥 ❀ ◐ ◑ ♿ P

HOREB

Waunwyllt Inn
Horeb Road (off B4309 at Five Roads, 3 miles from Llanelli)
☎ (01269) 860209
12-3, 7 (6.30 Fri & Sat)-11 (12-11 summer); 12-3, 7-11 Sun
Beer range varies [H]
Families are welcome at this popular pub that lies close to the cycle path. It offers good food and en-suite accommodation.
🔥 Q ❀ 🛏 ◐ ◑ ▲ P

JOHNSTOWN

Friends Arms
St Clears Road
☎ (01267) 234073
11-11; 12-10.30 Sun
Ansells Mild; Ind Coope Burton Ale; Tetley Bitter [H]
No harsh lighting spoils this large, warm, inviting bar plus a games room.
Q ❀ ♣

LLANARTHNEY

Golden Grove
On B4300, edge of village
☎ (01558) 668551
11-11; 12-10.30 Sun
Buckley's Best Bitter, Rev. James [H]
Former coaching inn where a congenial staff supply a warm welcome and good food.
🔥 Q 🐴 ❀ 🛏 ◐ ◑ ♣ P

LLANDEILO

Castle Hotel
113 Rhosmaen Street
☎ (01558) 823446
12-11; 12-3, 7-10.30 Sun
Watkin's Whoosh, BB, Merlin's Stout, OSB, seasonal beers [H]
Many-romed pub which used to be home to the Tomos Watkin Brewery.
Q ❀ ◐ ◑ ≠

White Horse
125 Rhosmaen Street
☎ (01558) 822424
11-11; 12-10.30 Sun
Wells Bombardier; Worthington Bitter; guest beers [H]
This old coaching inn is popular with all ages. Meals served until 6pm.
🔥 ❀ ◐ ≠

LLANDYBIE

Ivy Bush
18 Church Street
☎ (01269) 850272
12-4 (not Mon or Tue), 6-11; 11-11 Fri; 12-4.30, 6.30-11 Sat; 12-2 Sun
Ind Coope Burton Ale; guest beer [H]
Recently refurbished friendly pub near the station.
≠ P

LLANELLI

Lemon Tree
2 Prospect Place (behind old brewery)
☎ (01554) 755121
12-11; 12-10.30 Sun
Buckley's Best Biter; guest beer [H]
Popular local that stages a beer festival at Easter or Whitsun. ❀

Union
Bryn Road, Seaside (off western end of bypass)
☎ (01554) 759514
11-11; 12-10.30 Sun
Buckley's IPA, Best Bitter; guest beer [H]
Friendly town pub; popular with all ages. 🔥 Q ❀ ≠ P

Try also: Thomas Arms, Felinfoel Rd (Brains)

LLANGAIN

Tafarn Pantydderwen
Old School Road (near golf course)
☎ (01267) 241560
12-3, 6-11; 12-3, 6-10.30 Sun
Flowers Original; guest beers [H]
The restaurant dominates this pub, but the landlord makes every effort to accommodate real ale drinkers by providing a range of guest beers. The excellent food is reasonably priced.
Q ❀ ◐ ◑ ▲ P

LLANGYNDEYRN

Farmers Arms
OSSN148458
☎ (01269) 842213
12-3, 6-11; 12-11 Sat; 12-10.30 Sun
Beer range varies [H]
17th-century coaching inn set in beautiful countryside, offering a variety of guest ales. 🔥 Q ❀ ♿ ♣

LLANON

Red Lion
3 Heol y Plas (Tumble-Llanelli road)
☎ (01269) 841276
5 (12 Sat)-11; 12-3, 7-10.30 Sun
Felinfoel Bitter, Double Dragon H
The Red Lion is reputed to have a secret tunnel. A good menu includes some unusual dishes. Limited parking.
🏠 Q ▶ P

LLANSAWEL

Black Lion
OS619364
☎ (01558) 685263
5 (11 Sat)-11; 12-10.30 Sun
Brains Dark; Buckley's Best Bitter; guest beer H
Village community pub that doubles as the Rugby Club HQ. It serves reasonably priced food. The guest beer is from Cottage Brewery.
◖ ▶ ♣

MYNYDD Y GARREG

Prince of Wales
Heol Minciau (between Four Roads and Kidwelly)
☎ (01554) 890522
5-11; 12-3, 7-10.30 Sun
Beer range varies H
This small pub, displaying interesting memorabilia, serves good food in a no-smoking restaurant.
🏠 Q ✿ ▶ Å P

NEWCASTLE EMLYN

Bunch of Grapes
Bridge Street
☎ (01239) 711185
11-11; 12-10.30 Sun
Courage Directors; Theakston Best Bitter; guest beer H
17th-century listed town pub featuring exposed beams, timber floors and a grapevine in the indoor garden. It hosts live music Thu eve, plus Celtic music Mon eve in summer.
🏠 ✿ ◖ ▶ Å ♣

Coopers Arms
Station Road (A484, E end of town)
☎ (01239) 710323
12-3.30, 5.30-11; 12-3, 7-10.30 Sun
Draught Bass; Bragwr Arbennig o Ceridigion Barcud Coch H
Sparkling clean pub offering an excellent choice of food, wine and bottled beers (take-away containers available). See the permanent exhibition by local artists.
Q ✿ ◖ ▶ Å ♣ P

Try also: **Ivy Bush**, Emlyn Sq. (Free)

PENTRECWRT

Plas Parke Inn
OS388387
☎ (01559) 362684
2.30-11; 2.30-11 Sun
Draught Bass; guest beer H
Lively little country pub and restaurant with a pleasant garden, convenient for both the River Teifi – popular for fishing – and the steam railway at Henllan.
🏠 ▶ Å ♣ P

PENTREFELIN (LLANDEILO)

Cottage
On A40 w of Llandeilo
☎ (01558) 822890
11-11; 12-11 Su
Flowers IPA or Watkins Woosh or OSB; Wadworth 6X H
Family-run country inn. The first three listed beers alternate. En-suite accommodation includes a four-poster bed.
🏠 ✿ 🛏 ◖ ▶ ☕ P

PONTARGOTHI

Cresselly Arms
On A40, midway between Carmarthen and Llandeilo
☎ (01267) 290221
12-3, 6.30-11; 12-3, 7-10.30 Sun
Flowers Original; Marston's Pedigree; guest beer H
Riverside pub where the garden has play equipment for younger children. Good food served. 🏠 Q ✿ ◖ ▶ P

PONTYBEREM

Pontyberem Workingman's Club
Furnace Terrace
☎ (01269) 870214
1-5, 7-11; 1-3, 7-10.30 Sun
Worthington Bitter; guest beer H
Friendly, traditional club featuring a full-sized snooker table. Q 🍴 ☕ ♣

PORTHYRHYD

Mansel Arms
Banc y Mansel (off A48, Drefach-Llanddarog road)
☎ (01267) 275305
12-3, 6-11; 12-3, 7-10.30 Sun
Beer range varies H
Friendly pub, a couple of miles off the A48, serving good food Fri and Sat eves.
🏠 Q ▶ 🍴 ♣ P

RHANDIRMWYN

Royal Oak
7 miles from Llandovery
☎ (01550) 760201
11.30-3, 6-11; 12-2, 7-10.30 Sun
Beer range varies H
Excellent pub, affording panoramic views, popular with locals and visitors alike. It is worth finding for its beer choice (up to six in summer),

good food and selection of 50 malt whiskies.
🏠 Q ✿ 🛏 ◖ ▶ Å ☕ P

ST CLEARS

Corvus
Station Road
☎ (01994) 230965
11-11; 12-10.30 Sun
Courage Best Bitter; Worthington Bitter; guest beers H
Two-bar pub at the centre of the village enjoying regular local custom. ◖ 🍴 ♣

Ceredigion

ABERAERON

Black Lion
31 Alban Square (off A487)
☎ (01545) 571382
11-11; 12-10.30 Sun
Draught Bass; Worthington Bitter; Shepherd Neame Spitfire; guest beer (summer) H
Facing the park at the centre of a charming Regency town, this bustling two-roomed pub offers a good choice of beer for the area. The guest beer, served over a long summer season, is usually from an established independent. See the collection of 1200 cigarette lighters. Limited parking.
🏠 ✿ ◖ 🍴 ♣ P

Royal Oak
30 North Road (A487)
☎ (01545) 570233
12-11 (12-3, 5.30-11 winter); 12-3, 7-10.30 Sun
Tetley Bitter; Ind Coope Burton Ale H
A plush front lounge with attractive decor leads through to a long drinking area in public bar style. Popular for lunches, the pub nonetheless retains the character of a solid town local. 🏠 Q ◖ ▶ Å

ABERYSTWYTH

Coopers Arms (Y Cŵps)
Northgate Street
☎ (01970) 624050
11-11; 12-10.30 Sun
Felinfoel Bitter, Double Dragon H
The haunt of bards and minstrels, Y Cŵps is not so much a pub as a cultural institution, hosting Irish music and set dancing monthly, plus regular jam sessions and folk music. Welsh verses and theatre posters are displayed throughout. Self-catering accommodation available in summer. 🛏 Å ☞ ♣

Flannery's
1 High Street (near market hall)
☎ (01970) 612334

WEST WALES

12-11; 12-10.30 Sun
Flannery's Spring Tide, Celtic Ale, Oatmeal Stout, Rheidol Reserve, seasonal beers H

This alehouse-style pub in the old town, formerly the Ship & Castle, continues to showcase beers from the local micro-brewery. The fine beer and good mix of custom (town, gown and tourists) saw it chosen as local CAMRA *Pub of the Year* 1999. Beer festivals sometimes held. Sun lunch served. ⚒ ≠ ♣

Rummers
Bridge Street (N end of Trefechan bridge)
☎ (01970) 625177
7-midnight (1am Thu & Fri); 7-10.30 Sun
Ind Coope Burton Ale; Tetley Bitter; guest beer H

This harbourside building has served as a warehouse, theatre, chapel and china shop, but is now well established as a welcoming hostelry, featuring candles on the tables, sawdust on the floor and jazz/folk/blues Thu-Fri eves. Guest beer is from the Tapster's Choice range. Excellent pizzas. ❀ ▶ ⚒ ≠

CAPEL BANGOR
Tynllidiart Arms
On A44
☎ (01970) 880248
11.30-3, 6-11 (may close lunchtimes winter); 12-3 (closed eve) Sun
Flannery's Spring Tide, seasonal beers; guest beers H

Well-known village pub taken over in 1999 by local micro-brewer Flannerys, who have comprehensively transformed it in their trademark alehouse style and reinstated a (very) small brewery, Bragdy Tŷ Bach, whose beers are usually available here. Eve meals Tue-Sat. ⚏ Q ⚅ ▶ ⚒

CARDIGAN
Black Lion
High Street
☎ (01239) 612532
10-11; 12-10.30 Sun
Watkin's Whoosh, BB, OSB, seasonal beers H

Historic coaching inn in a busy characterful town. It dates back to the 12th century, but the present building is 18th century, and comprises a main drinking area, small panelled snug, and a rear dining area. A welcome outpost for this ambitious brewery.
⚞ ⚰ ⚅ ⚒ ♣

Red Lion
Pwllhai (near bus terminus)
☎ (01239) 612482
11-11; 12-5.30 (may open eves

summer) Sun
Buckley's Best Bitter; Rev. James, seasonal beers H

Warm-hearted town local whose skilful 1980s refurbishment is wearing well. The large, tiled main drinking area, with darts, table skittles, and animated conversation in both Welsh and English, is joined by a lounge area and pool room. Recorded Welsh music sold; C&W performed Fri eves. No food Sun.
Q ❀ ⚅ ▶ ⚑ ⚒ ♣

GOGINAN
Druid
High Street (A44)
☎ (01970) 880650
11-11; 12-10.30 Sun
Banks's Bitter, Draught Bass; Hancock's HB; guest beer H

This welcoming and keenly run pub in an old lead-mining village is at the hub of local life. Details of guest beers and entertainment are posted on the village website (www.goginan.co.uk). The main L-shaped drinking area is complemented by a pool room, dining room and an outbuilding for gigs.
Q ❀ ⚅ ▶ ⚒ ♣ P

LLANBADARN FAWR
Black Lion
Off A44
☎ (01970) 623448
11-11; 12-10.30 Sun
Banks's Original, Bitter; P
Marston's Pedigree, seasonal beers H

Next to the village's ancient church, this old pub has seen considerable change over the years but retains its local character while also drawing students from the campus up the hill. Home-made chutney and pickles sold in season, live entertainment some Fri eves. ❀ ⚅ ⚑ ⚒ ♣ P ⚕

LLANGOEDMOR
Penllwyndu
On B4570, 3 miles E of Cardigan OS5241458
☎ (01239) 682533
3-11; 3-10.30 Sun
Buckley's Best Bitter; Ind Coope Burton Ale; guest beer H

Set at an isolated crossroads, this relaxed, old-fashioned, largely unspoilt pub reopened in 1985 after many years' closure and serves a largely local clientele. A proper old-style drinkers' pub, it is well worth seeking out. Entertainment some Sat eves. ⚞ ❀ ♣ P

LLANGRANNOG

Ship Inn
At end of B4321
☎ (01239) 654423
6-11; 12-11 Sat & summer; 12-10.30 Sun
Beer range varies H

This two-bar pub near the beach retains a good local atmosphere despite the village's tourist influx (and sometimes traffic-clogged lanes) in high summer. Just one cask beer in winter rising to a maximum of four in summer. Ceredigion bottle-conditioned beers also sold. Splendid coastal scenery and cliff walks.
⚞ Q ❀ ⚅ ▶ ⚑ ⚒ ♣ P

PENNANT
Ship Inn
300 yds S of B4577 OS513631
☎ (01545) 570355
12-3 (not Mon-Fri), 6-11 (may vary); 12-3, 7-10.30 Sun
Beer range varies H

Old-fashioned and little-changed pub, built 1754 (see the beam over the fireplace). Old photographs, Eisteddfod posters and a piano lend character to the bar; alterations/extension currently in train will hopefully not disturb the atmosphere or resident ghost.
⚞ Q ⚞ ⚒ ♣ P

PENPARCAU
Tollgate
Piercefield Lane (off A487 near A4120 roundabout)
☎ (01970) 615016
12-11 (late licence until 11.45 Fri & Sat); 12-10.30 Sun
Brain's Dark, SA, seasonal beers H

This bustling, well-run estate pub on the edge of Aberystwyth, acquired by Brains in 1999, serves a keen local clientele in its two linked, spacious rooms. A lounge has a big screen TV for major sporting events and is laid up for meals Sun lunch. Entertainment staged Fri eves. No winter eve meals Sun-Tue.
❀ ⚅ ▶ ⚑ ⚒ ♣ P ⚕

RHYDOWEN
Alltyrodyn Arms
At crossroads
☎ (01545) 590319
12-11; 12-4 (closed eve) Sun
Buckley's Best Bitter; Fuller's London Pride guest beers H

Dating back to Queen Elizabeth I, this family-run pub has no keg beers, only quality guest ales. The hub of village life, it supports local charities and groups. Ceredigion CAMRA *Pub of the Year* 1997 and '98, it also stocks Ceredigion bottle-

399

conditioned beers and sometimes a draught cider.
🏦 Q 🏠 ⇔ ( ) ▲ ♣ ⇔ P

TALYBONT

White Lion
On A487, 8 miles N of Aberystwyth
☎ (01970) 832245
11-11; 12-10.30 Sun
Banks's Original, Bitter H
Facing the village green, this friendly, attractive village inn has adapted to the modern era (family-friendly, and with a growing reputation for good food) without sacrificing its traditional character. Splendid example of the evolving pub tradition.
🏠 ⇔ ( ) ♿ ▲ ♣ P 🏛

TREGARON

Talbot Hotel
The Square
☎ (01974) 298208
11-11; 12-10.30 Sun
Boddingtons Bitter; Flannery's Celtic Ale; Marston's Pedigree H
At the heart of a small upland market town, the well-used noticeboard of this old drovers' inn shows its place at the heart of local life. Two small and cosy rooms at the front have many items of interest (read about the elephant's grave), plus a larger room at the back.
🏦 Q 🏠 ⇔ ( ) ▲ ♣ P

Pembrokeshire

ABERCYCH

Nags Head
☎ (01239) 841200
11-3, 5.30-11; 11-11 Sat; 12-10.30 Sun
Flowers Original; Nags Head Old Emrys; Worthington Bitter; guest beers H
Well-restored old smithy boasting a beamed bar, riverside garden and a micro-brewery; its Old Emrys beer is not always available.
🏦 Q 🐦 🏠 P

BOSHERSTON

St Govans Inn
☎ (01646) 661311
11-3, 7-11 (may be 11-11 summer); 12-3, 7-10.30 (may be 12-10.30 summer) Sun
Hancock's HB; Worthington Bitter; guest beers H
Village local within the National Park, popular with climbers.
Q 🏠 ( ) 🍴 ▲ ♣ P

BURTON

Jolly Sailor
Burton Ferry
☎ (01646) 600378
11.30-2.30, 6-11 (11.30-11 school

---

hols); 12-3, 7.30-10.30 Sun
Ind Coope Burton Ale; Worthington Bitter H
Riverside pub with a large garden and its own landing stage.
🏦 🏠 ( ) ▶ ⊟ ▲ P

CAREW

Carew Inn
☎ (01646) 651267
12-2.30, 4.30-11; 11-11 Sat & summer; 12-3, 7-10.30 Sun
Buckley's Rev. James; Worthington Bitter; guest beer (summer) H
Traditional pub, opposite the historic castle. It hosts regular live music.
🏦 🐦 🏠 ( ) ▲ P

COSHESTON

Cosheston Brewery
☎ (01646) 686678
12-4, 6.30-11; 12-4, 6.30-10.30 Sun
Worthington Bitter; guest beer H
Recently altered village pub; a second guest beer is sometimes stocked.
Q 🏠 ( ) ▲ ♣ P

CRESSWELL

Cresselly Arms
☎ (01646) 651210
12-3, 5-11; 7-10.30 Sun
Pembroke Two Cannons Extra; Worthington Bitter; guest beer G
Waterside pub, largely unaltered since 1900, where the beer is served from jugs. The guest beer is delivered every Mon (winter only).
🏦 Q P

CRESOGOCH

Artramont Arms
On A487
☎ (01348) 831309
7-11 (12-3, 6-11 summer); 12-3, 6-10 Fri & Sat; 12-3, 7-10.30 Sun
Brains SA; guest beer H
Friendly village local with a large bar and a dining room offering an interesting menu.
🏦 🏠 ( ) ▶ P 🍴

DALE

Griffin Inn
☎ (01646) 636227
12-3, 6-11 (12-11 summer); 12-11 Sun
Felinfoel Double Dragon; Worthington Bitter; guest beers H
Harbour pub at the end of the bay, with seats outside by the sea wall. Table skittles played.
🏦 🏠 ( ) ▶ ▲ ♣ ⇔

FISHGUARD

Royal Oak Inn
Market Square (A482)
☎ (01348) 872514
11-11; 12-10.30 Sun
Hancock's HB; guest beer H
Charming, friendly,

---

comfortable pub claiming historic connections (French forces surrendered here following the last invasion of mainland Britain in 1797). Home cooking is served at good prices from a varied menu.
🏠 ( ) ▶ ⊟ ▲ ♣

Try also: **Ship Inn**, Lower Town (Free)

FRESHWATER EAST

Freshwater Inn
☎ (01646) 672828
12-3, 6.30-11 (12-11 summer); 12-3, 7-11 Sun
Pembroke Two Cannons Extra; Theakston Old Peculier; guest beer (summer) H
Recently modernised loal affording magnificent views over the bay, serving an excellent range of food, especially local fish.
🐦 🏠 ( ) ▶ ▲ ♣ P 🍴

GOODWICK

Rose & Crown
OS947384
☎ (01348) 874449
11-11; 12-10.30 Sun
James Williams IPA; Worthington Bitter; guest beer H
Picturesque pub, close to the ferry enjoying harbour views. It has a small, but welcoming, no-smoking restaurant.
🏠 ( ) ▶ ▲ ♣ P

HAVERFORDWEST

George's
24 Market Street
☎ (01437) 766683
10.30-10.30; closed Sun
Marston's Pedigree; Wye Valley Bitter; guest beer H
Enjoy a very relaxing atmosphere, fine ales and food in this pub that has a small Celtic Arts shop at the front. Friendly staff.
Q 🏠 (⇒ 🍴

Pembroke Yeoman
Hill Street
☎ (01437) 762500
11-11; 12-3, 7-10.30 Sun
Flowers IPA; Worthington Bitter; guest beers H/G
This comfortable local attracts all ages; good food served.
🏦 ( ) ♣

Try also: **Fishguard Arms**, Old Bridge (Free)

HAZELBEACH

Ferry Inn
☎ (01646) 600770
12-3, 6-11; 12-5, 7-10.30 Sun
Worthington Bitter; guest beer H
Modernised estuary pub

offering good food in the bar and restaurant.

🛏🦽❀⚲◖🍴♿☕⚓♣ P

HUNDLETON

Speculation Inn
On B4320, just outside Hundleton
☎ (01646) 661306
12-2, 6-1l (extended in summer); 12-3 Sun

Felinfoel Bitter, Double Dragon; Worthington Bitter Ⓗ

Built in 1770 as a farmers' local, this unspoilt pub holds a children's certificate. Very inexpensive bar snacks are sold at lunchtime.

🍴🛏❀⚲♿☕⚓♣ P

LITTLE HAVEN

Swan Inn
Point Road
☎ (01437) 781256
11-3, 6-11 (12-2.30, 7-11 winter); 12-3 Sun

Worthington Bitter; guest beer Ⓗ

Quayside pub with a picturesque interior, popular for food. 🍴Q❀◖🍴☕

MANORBIER

Castle Inn
11-11; 12-10.30 Sun
Tetley Bitter; guest beers Ⓗ
Situated in a small village close to an inhabited castle and an idyllic beach.

🍴❀⚲◖🍴☕♣

MARLOES

Lobster Pot
☎ (01646) 636733
12-3, 6-11 (11-11 summer); 12-3, 6-10.30 Sun
Ansells Bitter; guest beers Ⓗ
Large modernised pub specialising in local food, particularly fish. A third guest beer is added in summer.

❀⚲◖🍴♣ P

NARBERTH

Angel Inn
High Street (one-way system)
☎ (01834) 860577
11-3, 5.30-11; 12-3, 7-10.30 Sun
Worthington Bitter; guest beers Ⓗ
Cosy, modernised, town-centre pub, popular for food; the restaurant takes last orders one hour before closing time.

🛏❀◖◖⚲◖♿☕⚓

Kirkland Arms
East Gate, St James Street
☎ (01834) 860423
11-11; 11-10.30 Sun
Felinfoel Bitter, Double Dragon; guest beer Ⓗ
Comfortable two-bar pub on the edge of a one-way system. ☕⚓ P

NEWPORT

Castle Hotel
Bridge Street (A487)
☎ (01239) 820742
11-11; 12-10.30 Sun
Wadworth 6X; Worthington Bitter; guest beer Ⓗ
Friendly popular local: an attractive bar with a real fire, and an extensive dining area.

🍴🛏❀⚲◖🍴☕ P

Llwyngwair Arms
On A487 through town
☎ (01239) 820267
11-11; 12-10.30 Sun
Worthington Bitter; James Williams IPA; guest beer Ⓗ
Unaltered pub with a dining area that serves food all day in summer (lunch and eves winter).

🍴Q◖◖🍴☕ P

PEMBROKE

Old Cross Saws Inn
109 Main Street
☎ (01646) 682475
11-11; 12-10.30 Sun
Beer range varies Ⓗ
Friendly pub, popular with Scarlet supporters, centrally located. It offers good, well-priced food plus live music Sat eve. ❀⚲◖🍴☕⚓♣

PEMBROKE DOCK

First & Last
London Road
☎ (01646) 682687
11-11; 12-10.30 Sun
Worthington Bitter; guest beer Ⓗ
Popular local offering a good variety of guest beers and well-priced bar meals. Live music staged Sat eve.

❀◖🍴☕⚓♣

Station Inn
Apley Green, Dimond Street (follow signs for Pembroke Dock) ☎ (01646) 621255
7-11; 12-3, 7-10.30 Sun
Beer range varies Ⓗ
The redundant station building at the end of the line has been brought back to life as the tap for Pembroke Brewery. It normally stocks up to four Pembroke ales, with a new beer every Tue. It hosts a beer fest in June, plus live music Sat eves.

Q◖♿🍴☕⚓♣ P

PONTFAEN

Dyffryn Arms ☆
Off B4313 OS027341
☎ (01348) 881305
Hours vary
Draught Bass or Ind Coope Burton Ale Ⓖ
1920s front room where time has stood still. The beer is still served by the jug and conversation is a must. It lies

in the Gwain Valley between the Preseli Mountains and Fishguard.

🛏Q❀🍴♣

PORTHGAIN

Sloop Inn
Near quay in village
☎ (01348) 831449
11.30-3, 6-11 (11-11 summer); 12-4, 6-10.30 Sun
Brains SA; Felinfoel Double Dragon; Worthington Bitter Ⓗ
This old fishing pub features quarrying and shipping ephemera.

🛏❀◖◖♣ P

ST DAVIDS

Farmers Arms
12-14 Goat Street OS751253
☎ (01437) 720328
11-11; 12-10.30 Sun
Flowers Original; Worthington Bitter Ⓗ
19th century stone pub maintaining many old features. Popular with fishermen and farmers, it serves good home-cooked meals. 🛏Q❀◖◖⚲🍴

TENBY

Coach & Horses
Upper Frog Street (within the town walls)
☎ (01834) 842704
12-11; 12-3, 7-10.30 Sun
Beer range varies Ⓗ
Historic town-centre pub, retaining its old character.

🛏🦽❀◖◖⚲◖♿🍴☕

Hope & Anchor
St Julian Street (off Tudor Sq)
☎ (01834) 842131
11-3, 7-11 (11-11 summer); 12-10.30 Sun
Buckley's Rev. James; Worthington Bitter; guest beer Ⓗ
Friendly local, close to the harbour. Q🍴☕

TREFIN

Ship Inn
On unclassified coast road through village OS838325
☎ (01348) 831445
12-3, 6-11; 11-10.30 Sun

INDEPENDENT BREWERIES

Ceredigion: Llangrannog

Coles: Llanddarog

Felinfoel: Felinfoel

Flannery's: Llandre

Nag's Head: Abercych

Pembroke: Pembroke

Tŷ Bach: Capel Bangor

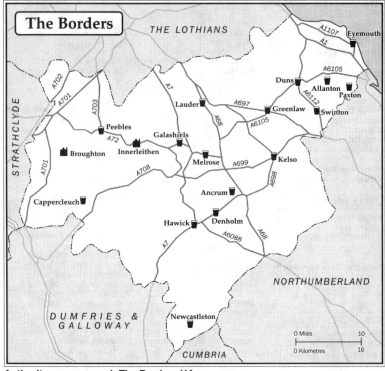

The Borders

THE LOTHIANS

Eyemouth

Duns
Allanton
Paxton

Lauder
Greenlaw
Swinton

Peebles
Galashiels

Broughton
Innerleithen
Melrose
Kelso

Cappercleuch
Ancrum

Hawick
Denholm

NORTHUMBERLAND

DUMFRIES &
GALLOWAY
Newcastleton

0 Miles 10
0 Kilometres 16

CUMBRIA

Authority area covered: The Borders UA

ALLANTON

Allanton Inn
On B6437
☎ (01890) 818260
12-2.30, 6-11 (1am Fri); 12-1am Sat;
12-midnight Sun
Beer range varies H
Old coaching inn with a
restaurant in a village
surrounded by rolling
farmland. Stone flags
surround the bar in the
comfortable, functional
interior. Good selection of
three or four real ales.
Scottish Tourist Board food
award in 1999. Children's
certificate. ♨ ❀ ⇔ ◖ ❀ P

ANCRUM

Cross Keys Inn
The Green (B6400, off A68)
☎ (01835) 830344
6-11 (midnight Thu); 5-1am Fri;
12-midnight Sat; 12.30-11 Sun
**Caledonian Deuchars IPA, 80/-;
guest beer** H
Friendly village pub with a
wonderfully unspoilt bar.
The refurbished back lounge
retains the overhead tram
lines of the former cellar.
Children's certificate.
♨ Q ☎ ❀ ⇔ ◖ ❀ P

CAPPERCLEUCH

Tibbie Shiels Inn

St Mary's Loch (off A708 at
southern end of loch)
OS241205
☎ (01750) 42231
11 (12.30 Sun)-11 (midnight Fri & Sat);
closed Mon-Wed winter afternoons;
**Belhaven 80/-; Broughton
Greenmantle** H
Cosy, remote, historic inn in
an idyllic setting between
two lochs in the isolated
Yarrow valley. A haven for
walkers, water sports
enthusiasts and those seeking
peace and solitude.
Children's certificate until
8.30. ♨ Q ❀ ⇔ ◖ ⊞ ❀ ⚲
❀ P ✕

DENHOLM

Auld Cross Keys Inn
Main Street (A698)
☎ (01450) 870305
11-2.30 (not Mon), 5-11 (midnight Thu,
1am Fri); 11-midnight Sat; 12.30-11 Sun
Beer range varies H
Picturesque, 18th-century
inn with a low ceiling and
blazing fire in the cosy bar.
To the rear is a comfortable
restaurant (no food Mon)
and lounge. Regular folk
music. Children's certificate.
♨ ❀ ◖ ⊞ ❀ P

DUNS

Whip & Saddle
Market Square

☎ (01361) 883215
11-11 (midnight Fri, 11.30 Sat); 12.30-
11.30 Sun
**Caledonian Deuchars IPA; Theakston
XB; guest beer** H
Town-centre bar, dating
from 1790. The airy interior
has wooden floors, leaded
windows and views across
the town square. The dining
room upstairs is also a family
room. Angling permits are
available. No meals Sun; eve
meals served Fri and Sat.
Q ☎ ◖ ❀

EYEMOUTH

Ship Hotel
Harbour Road
☎ (01890) 750224
11 (12 Sun)-midnight (1am Fri & Sat)
Caledonian 80/-; guest beer H
A fisherman's haunt with
more trawlers than cars
parked outside. A warm fire, a
vast selection of rums and a
wide range of maritime
memorabilia add character to
this family hotel. ♨ ☎ ❀ ⇔
◖ ⊞ ⚲ ❀ P ✕

GALASHIELS

Ladhope Inn
33 High Buckholmside (A7,
1/2 mile N of centre)
☎ (01896) 752446
11-3, 5-11; 11-11 Wed; 11-midnight
Thu-Sat; 12.30-midnight Sun

Caledonian Deuchars IPA; guest beer Ⓗ
Well-appointed, friendly local offering a vibrant Borders atmosphere. Part of a terrace row built into the hillside, dating from 1792. A single room, with an alcove area, is decorated with old local prints.
🏵 ▲ ♣

Salmon Inn
54 Bank Street
☎ (01896) 752577
11 (12.30 Sun)-11 (midnight Thu, 1am Fri & Sat)
Caledonian Deuchars IPA; Ind Coope Burton Ale; guest beer Ⓗ
Comfortable public house, popular with locals and offering a friendly welcome to visitors. The bar is decorated with old photos of Galashiels. No meals Sun; children welcome at mealtimes.
🏵 ◖ ▲ ♣

GREENLAW
Cross Keys Hotel
3 The Square
☎ (01361) 810247
11 (12.30 Sun)-midnight (1am Fri & Sat)
Beer range varies Ⓗ
Pub dating from 1867 on the main road through Greenlaw: a well-used friendly locals' bar and a small lounge (children's certificate). Note the whisky water jug collection above the wooden fronted counter.
🏚 🏵 ◖ ▶ 🍴 ▲ ♣

HAWICK
High Level
11 Green Terrace (Hope St, on SW edge of town)
☎ (01450) 377469
11-3 (not Tue); 5-midnight; 11-1am Sat; 12-30-midnight Sun
Beer range varies Ⓗ
Popular community local on a hillside above the town. The public bar has wood-panelled walls, a wooden floor, bar and gantry. Children welcome until 6pm.
Q 🍴 ▲ ♣

KELSO
Queens Head Hotel
Bridge Street
☎ (01573) 224636
11-3, 4.45-11; 11-midnight Fri; 11-1am Sat; 11.45-11 Sun
Beer range varies Ⓗ
Country town hotel with a bustling locals' bar where pool is popular. Real ale is served in the rear lounge/restaurant.
🏠 ◖ ▶ 🍴 ♣

White Swan
Abbey Row

☎ (01573) 224348
11-midnight (1am Fri & Sat); 11-midnight Sun
Caledonian Deuchars IPA; Tetley Bitter; guest beer Ⓗ
Often lively, this modernised old pub attracts a good local trade. Originally two rooms, now knocked into one and extended: the back area is for pool and a real fire warms the central part. The windows look out on to the ruins of Kelso Abbey.
🏚 🏵 ◖ ▲ ♣

LAUDER
Eagle Hotel
1 Market Place
☎ (01578) 722255
11 (12.30 Sun)-11 (midnight Thu-Sat)
Caledonian Deuchars IPA; guest beers Ⓗ
Friendly hotel in a small market town. The stone wall surrounding the fireplace and the carved wooden bar are features of the comfortable lounge. The more functional bar has an interesting mirror-backed gantry. Good food.
🏚 Q 🍴 ▶ 🍴 ▲ ♣

MELROSE
Burt's Hotel
Market Square
☎ (01896) 822285
11-2, 5 (6 Sun)-11
Draught Bass; Belhaven 80/-; beer Ⓗ
Elegant, well-appointed hotel and restaurant in the town square. The decor of the plush lounge bar reflects the hunting, fishing and shooting interests of many of the regulars. Children's certificate.
🏚 Q 🍴 ◖ ▲ P ✂

NEWCASTLETON
Liddlesdale Hotel
Douglas Square
☎ (01378) 375255
11-midnight (1am Fri & Sat); (closed 2.30-5 winter weekday afternoons); 12-11 Sun
Beer range varies Ⓗ
Small hotel, with a split-level bar, in a remote rural town. The upper level has a real fire and is where food is served. Prints of local hunting scenes and an old map decorate the walls. Children's certificate.
🏚 🍴 ◖ ▶ 🍴 ▲ ♣

PAXTON
Cross Inn
Off B6460
☎ (01289) 386267
11 (12.30 Sun)-2.30 (not Mon), 6.30-midnight
Orkney Dark Island; guest beer Ⓗ
Comfortable village pub, formerly the Hoolit's Nest.

The bar and dining room are themed on hoolits (owls) which watch the bar from every nook and cranny. Children's certificate.
🏵 ◖ 🍴 ♣ P

PEEBLES
Bridge Inn
☎ (01721) 720589
11 (12 Sun)-midnight
Caledonian Deuchars IPA; Courage Directors; Orkney Dark Island Ⓗ
The well-appointed bar is decorated with golf, fishing and rugby artefacts and a selection of jugs and bottles.
▲ ♣

Green Tree Hotel
41 Eastgate
☎ (01721) 720582
11 (12 Sun)-midnight
Caledonian 80/-; guest beer Ⓗ
Town-centre hotel which has a friendly locals' bar at the front with attractive leaded windows. To the rear is a more relaxed, comfortable lounge and a restaurant in which children are welcome. Two interesting guest beers.
🏚 🏵 🍴 ◖ 🍴 ▲ ♣ P

Neidpath Inn
27-29 Old Town
☎ (01721) 721721
11-midnight (11 Mon); 11-2.30, 5-midnight Wed; 12.30-midnight Sun
Caledonian Deuchars IPA; guest beer Ⓗ
An airy, functional public bar with a real fire contrasts with a well-appointed, comfortable lounge. The wood, glasswork and ornaments are noteworthy.
🏚 🏵 🍴 ♣

SWINTON
Wheatsheaf Hotel
Main Street
☎ (01890) 860257
11-2, 6-11 (11.30 Fri & Sat); closed Mon; 12.30-3.30, 6.30-10.30 (not winter eve) Sun
Beer range varies Ⓗ
Multi-roomed pub-cum-restaurant. A small, dimly-lit snug bar is adorned with pictures of local legend Jim Clark. Good quality food is served in the well-appointed lounge, which has pictures of country pursuits, and a wood-panelled conservatory. Children's certificate.
🏚 Q 🏵 🍴 ◖ ▶ 🍴 ♣ P

INDEPENDENT BREWERIES

Broughton: Broughton
Traquair: Innerleithen

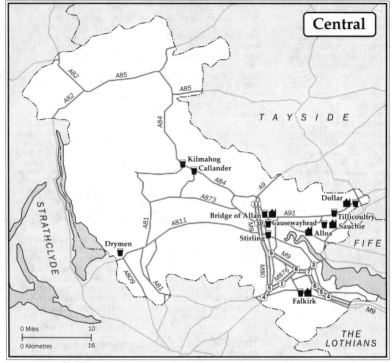

UA areas covered: Clackmannan UA, Falkirk UA, Stirling UA

BRIDGE OF ALLAN

Westerton Arms Bar
34 Henderson Street
☎ (01786) 833659
11-midnight (1am Fri & Sat);
12.30-midnight Sun

Boddingtons Bitter; Courage Directors; Theakston Best Bitter H
Lively popular, town-centre local. There is no real ale in the lounge, but it can be taken through from the bar.
◑ ▶ ≉ ♣ P

CALLANDER

Waverley Hotel
88-92 Main Street
☎ (01877) 330245
11-midnight (1am Fri & Sat); 11-midnight Sun

Caledonian 80/-; Harviestoun Bitter & Twisted; guest beers H
In an historic town at the heart of a popular tourist area, this is a very friendly, open-plan family-oriented lounge bar serving good meals. Deals are available on long weekend breaks. Normally at least one other Harviestoun beer is available.
☎ ⊨ ◑ ▶ ♣

CAUSEWAYHEAD

Birds & Bees
Easter Cornton Road (off Causewayhead Road)
☎ (01786) 473633
11-3, 5-midnight; 11-midnight Fri & Sat;
12.30-midnight Sun

Caledonian 80/-; Fuller's London Pride H
Originally a farm, retaining many original features including the animal stalls, in a spacious and charming layout. The sheep make good seats in this tourist board award-winner. Pétanque played in summer.
☀ ◑ ▶ ♣ P

DOLLAR

Castle Campbell
11 Bridge Street
☎ (01259) 742519
11-11.30 (1am Fri & Sat); 12.30-midnight Sun

Fuller's London Pride; Harviestoun Schiehallion H
Coaching inn dating back to 1822, named after the nearby NT property offering good home-cooked food and good hotel facilities. No real ale in the public bar.
▥ ☀ ⊨ ◑ ▶ ♟ P

Kings Seat
23 Bridge Street
☎ (01259) 742515
11-midnight (1am Fri & Sat); 12.30-midnight Sun

Fuller's London Pride; guest beers H
Friendly pub on the main street, ideal for the discerning real ale drinker, and serving a

wide choice of home-cooked food. There are always two Harviestoun beers available along with four other guests.
⊨ ◑ ▶ ♣

Lorne Tavern
17 Argyll Street
☎ (01259) 743423
11-midnight (1am Fri & Sat); 12.30-midnight Sun

Harviestoun Bitter & Twisted H
Friendly, traditional local, holding the oldest licence in Dollar (1850). Handy for the Ochil Hills. Meals served Wed-Sun.
☀ ⊨ ◑ ▶ ♟ ♣ P

DRYMEN

Clachan
2 The Square
☎ (01360) 660824
11 (12.30 Sun)-midnight

Caledonian Deuchars IPA H
Friendly local, dating from 1734, in a village which gets busy during the tourist season. The lounge is now a restaurant where children are allowed in for meals. ◑ ▶ ♟

Winnock
The Square
☎ (01360) 660245
12-midnight; 11-1am Fri & Sat;
12-midnight Sun

Broughton Merlin's Ale; Caledonian Deuchars IPA; Tetley Bitter; guest beer H

CAMRA National Pub Inventory: Kings Arms, Holsworthy, Devon

Pleasant hotel at the centre of a village near the eastern side of Loch Lomond. The large main bar has a restaurant leading off. It is well known for food and 'Murder Mystery' weekends.
🏨 Q ❀ ⇔ ◖ ▶ ⊟ P

FALKIRK

Eglesbrech at Behind the Wall
14 Melville Street
☎ (01324) 633338
12-11.30 (1am Thu-Sat); 12.30-midnight Sun
Beer range varies H
Local CAMRA *Pub of the Year* 1997, the alehouse is located on the upper floor of this large pub. Summer 2000 will see an expanded bar and micro-brewery with input from Bruce Williams of Heather Ales fame.
◖ ≋ (Grahamston)

Wheatsheaf Inn
16 Baxter's Wynd
☎ (01324) 623716
11-11 (12.30am Fri & Sat); 12.30-11 Sun
Belhaven 80/-; Caledonian Deuchars IPA, 80/- H
Single-storey building, over 200 years old containing some interesting mirrors from old breweries and caricatures of local people.
≋ (High/Grahamston)

KILMAHOG

Lade Inn
N of Callander at A84/A821 jct ☎ (01877) 330152
12-3, 12-11 (midnight Sat); (closed 3-5.30 Mon-Sat winter); 12.30-11 Sun
Broughton Greenmantle; Courage Directors; Orkney Red MacGregor; Isle of Skye Red Cuillin H
Nice country house in a lovely part of the country: very comfortable premises featuring a cosy lounge, good food and ceilidh every Sat eve.
🏨 Q ❀ ◖ ▶ ⊟ ᔆ P

SAUCHIE

Mansfield Arms
7 Main Street
☎ (01259) 722020
11-11.30 (11 Tue & Wed, 12.30 Fri & Sat); 12.30-11 Sun
Devon Original, Thick Black, Pride P
Typical Scottish workingman's bar, with a micro-brewery, serving its own beer on the premises. Excellent, good value bar meals available. ◖ ▶ ⊟ ᔆ ♣ P

STIRLING

Hogshead
2 Baker Street
☎ (01786) 448722
11-midnight (1am Fri & Sat); 12.30-midnight Sun
Boddingtons Bitter; Caledonian Deuchars IPA, 80/-; guest beers H
Friendly, town-centre local

and a popular stop for families and tourists. Helpful staff will pour you a sample before you buy.
◖ ▶ ≋ ᗡ

Portcullis
Castle Wynd
☎ (01786) 472290
11.30 (12 Sun)-midnight
Orkney Dark Island; guest beers H
Originally a grammar school built in 1787, now an hotel offering excellent accommodation and superb food (no meals Mon eve). The homely lounge bar is warmed by a real log fire.
🏨 ⇔ ◖ ▶ ≋ P

TILLICOULTRY

Woolpack
1 Glassford Square
☎ (01259) 750332
11-midnight (1am Fri & Sat); 12.30-11 Sun
Beer range varies H
Friendly local; this former drovers' inn is popular with locals and hillwalkers in season. ♣

INDEPENDENT BREWERIES

Bridge of Allan:
Bridge of Allan
Devon: Sauchie
Eglesbrech: Falkirk
Forth: Alloa
Harviestoun: Dollar

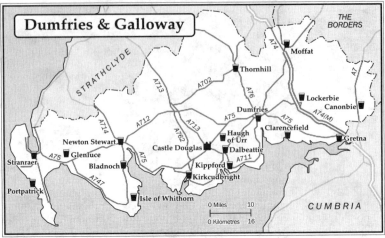

Authority area covered: Dumfries & Galloway UA

BLADNOCH

Bladnoch Inn
On A714, 6 miles S of
Newton Stewart
☎ (01988) 402200
11-11 (midnight Fri & Sat); 12.30-11
Sun
Beer range varies H
A gem, next to the newly re-
opened Bladnoch distillery. It
serves good food; children's
certificate. Parking limited.
🛏 Q ⛵ ❀ ⇌ ◖◗ Å P

CANONBIE

Riverside
☎ (0138 73) 71512
12-3, 6.30-11; 12-3 (closed eve and all
day in winter) Sun
**Caledonian Deuchars IPA; Yates
Bitter** H
Comfortable, charming pub
by the River Esk, serving
excellent food.
🛏 Q ⇌ ◖◗ P

CLARENCEFIELD

Farmers Inn
On B724, midway between
Dumfries and Annan
☎ (01387) 870675
11.30-2.30, 6-11.30 (12.30am Fri);
12-12.30am Sat; 12.30-11.30 Sun
Maclay 70/-, 80/-; guest beers H
Friendly village pub, a former
18th-century coaching inn.
🛏 Q ❀ ⇌ ◖◗ ♿ P

DALBEATTIE

Pheasant Hotel
1 Maxwell Street (A711)
☎ (01556) 610345
10.30 (12.30 Sun)-midnight
Beer range varies H
Lively, friendly, open-plan
bar with a juke box, large-
screen TV and a pool table.
Very popular with locals it
has a children's certificate.
⛵ ⇌ ◖◗ ♣

406

DUMFRIES

Douglas Arms
75 Friars Vennel
☎ (01387) 256002
11-11 (midnight Thu-Sat); 12.30-11 Sun
**Broughton Greenmantle, Oatmeal
Stout, Ghillie; Jennings Cumberland
Ale** H
Grand wee pub with a snug.
≈ ♣

New Bazaar
39 Whitesands
☎ (01387) 268776
11-11 (midnight Thu-Sat); 11-11 Sun
**Belhaven St Andrew's Ale; Sulwath
Knockendoch;** A **guest beers** H
Town-centre pub affording
views across the River Nith
towards the Camera Obscura.
Superb Victorian bar.
🛏 Q ≈ ♣

Ship Inn
97 St Michael Street
☎ (01387) 255189
11-2.30, 5-11; 12-2.30; 6.30-11 Sun
**Courage Directors; McEwan 70/-,
80/-; Morland Old Speckled Hen;
Taylor Landlord; Theakston XB;
guest beers** H
Traditional Dumfries free
house with a friendly
atmosphere and a good
selection of ales – a regular
Guide entry.
Q ≈ ♣ ✄

Tam O'Shanter
113 Queensbury Street
☎ (01387) 254055
11-11 (midnight Wed-Sat); 12.30-11
Sun
**Caledonian Deuchars IPA; guest
beers** H
Traditional characterful bar.
Good value lunchtime
snacks.
Q ≈ ♣

GLENLUCE

Kelvin House Hotel

53 Main Street (off A75)
☎ (01581) 300303
11-11 (midnight Fri & Sat); (12-3;
6-midnight winter); 12-11.30 Sun
**Orkney Red MacGregor; guest
beers** H
Small, friendly hotel near
Luce Bay in a bypassed
village. It serves ever-
changing guest ales (two in
summer), and excellent
home-cooked meals.
🛏 ⛵ ❀ ⇌ ◖◗ ⊞ Å ♣ ✄

GRETNA

Crossways Inn
Glasgow Road
☎ (01461) 337465
11-11 (midnight Fri & Sat); (11-3, 6-11
winter); 12-11 Sun
**Courage Directors; Morland Old
Speckled Hen** H
Lively pub – the first in
Scotland, a few minutes walk
from the border and handy
for the new Gretna Gateway
Centre. Real ale is served in
the lounge. ❀ ⇌ ◖◗ Å
≈ (Gretna Green) ♣ P

Solway Lodge Hotel
Annan Road
☎ (01461) 338266
11 (3 winter Mon)-11 (midnight Fri &
Sat); 12-11 (3 winter) Sun
Tetley Bitter H
Welcoming, comfortable
hotel serving good value
food. It is popular with
wedding parties in keeping
with Gretna's reputation as
Scotland's 'Love Town'.
⛵ ❀ ⇌ ◖◗ ♿ Å ≈ (Gretna
Green) P

HAUGH OF URR

Laurie Arms Hotel
On B794, 1 mile S of A75
☎ (01556) 660246
11.45-2.30, 5.30-midnight (11 Mon-
Wed winter); 11.45-5.30; 6-midnight Sun
Beer range varies H

Attractive country inn, off the beaten track; a good local giving a warm welcome in a wood-panelled bar with its fireplace of local stone. See the saucy postcards displayed in the toilets. Scottish CAMRA *Pub of the Year* 1999. Children's Certificate.
✿ ⊄ ▶ P

ISLE OF WHITHORN

Steampacket Inn
Harbour Row (A750)
☎ (01988) 500334
11(12.30 Sun)-11
Theakston XB; guest beer Ⓗ
Attractive harbourside inn, in a popular sailing centre. The unusual, stone-clad bar features a large stone fireplace. Moorings for boats within hailing distance. Children's certificate.
▨ Q ➴ ✿ ⇔ ⊄ ▶ ⊞ ♣

KIPPFORD

Anchor Hotel
Main Street
☎ (01556) 620205
11-3; 6-11 (midnight Fri); 11-midnight Sat; 11-11 (midnight Fri & Sat) summer; 11-11 Sun
Boddingtons Bitter; Theakston Best Bitter; guest beers (summer) Ⓗ
Friendly village inn set in a popular sailing centre, enjoying views over the Urr estuary. It has a wood-panelled bar, a larger lounge, a family room and a pool room. Children's certificate. Excellent food. Cottage available to rent.
▨ ➴ ✿ ⊄ ▶ A P

KIRKCUDBRIGHT

Masonic Arms
19 Castle Street
☎ (01557) 330517
11 (12.30 Sun)-midnight
Beer range varies Ⓗ
Friendly, welcoming bar, well-used by locals, featuring barrel-shaped furniture and old mirrors behind the bar.
▨ ⊞ ⅃

Selkirk Arms Hotel
High Street
☎ (01557) 330402
11 (12 Sun)-midnight
Draught Bass; Sulwath Criffel; guest beers Ⓗ
Real ale is only obvious in the comfortable lounge but it is available in the basic, lively public bar on request. Robert Burns is reputed to have written the *Selkirk Grace* here.
➴ ✿ ⇔ ⊄ ▶ ⊞ ⅃

LOCKERBIE

Somerton House Hotel
35 Carlisle Road
☎ (01576) 202583

CAMRA National Pub Inventory: carved emblem at The Black Horse Hotel, Northfield, Birmingham

11-11 (midnight Thu-Sat); 11-11 Sun
Broughton Greenmantle; Caledonian Deuchars IPA Ⓗ
Friendly, well-appointed hotel near the M74. Deservedly popular, its meals and service are excellent.
➴ ✿ ⇔ ⊄ ▶ ⅃ A P

MOFFAT

Black Bull Hotel
Church Gate
☎ (01683) 220206
11-11 (midnight Thu-Sat); 11-11 Sun
McEwan 80/-; Theakston Best Bitter; guest beers Ⓗ
Historic inn, dating from 1568; it displays Burns memorabilia in the comfortable lounge and railway artefacts in the public. The restaurant serves good, well-priced meals.
✿ ⇔ ⊄ ▶ ⊞ A ♣

NEWTON STEWART

Creebridge House Hotel
On old main road, E of river
☎ (01671) 402121
12-2.30, 6-11.30 (midnight Sat); 12.30-2.30, 7-11 Sun
Beer range varies Ⓗ
Superb country house hotel in spacious grounds, serving excellent home-cooked meals. No real ale sold Fri lunchtime. Children's certificate; bar billiards played.
➴ ✿ ⇔ ⊄ ▶ A ♣ P

PORTPATRICK

Downshire Arms Hotel
Main Street (A77, near harbour)

☎ (01776) 810300
11- midnight (1am Thu-Sat); 12-midnight Sun
Beer range varies Ⓗ
Traditional coaching inn: the public bar has a roaring fire. Excellent bar and restaurant menus feature local seafood and game. Children's certificate.
▨ ⇔ ⊄ ▶ ⊞ A ♣

STRANRAER

Ruddicot Hotel
London Road (A75)
☎ (01776) 702684
12-2.30; 5-11 (midnight Thu-Sat); 12-2.30, 6.30-11 Sun
Beer range varies Ⓗ
Small, family-run hotel near the ferry terminal and the football and rugby grounds. Note the unusual division of the bar by low screens.
Q ✿ ⇔ ⊄ A P

THORNHILL

Buccleugh & Queensberry Hotel
112 Drumlanrig Street (A76)
☎ (01848) 330215
11-midnight (1am Thu-Sat); 11-midnight Sun
Beer range varies Ⓗ
Friendly hotel in an attractive village, a popular base for fishing and shooting. It offers varied guest beers, one in winter, two in summer.
▨ Q ⇔ ⊄ ▶ ⊞ ⅃ A ♣ P ⅄

INDEPENDENT BREWERY
Sulwath: Castle Douglas

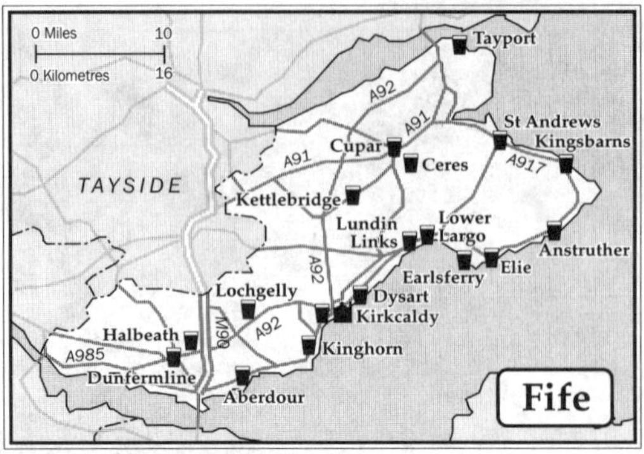

Authority area covered: Fife UA

ABERDOUR

Aberdour Hotel
38 High Street
☎ (01383) 860325
4-11; 3-11.45 Fri; 11-11.45 Sat; 12-11 Sun
Caledonian Deuchars IPA; guest beers [H]
Old coaching inn with a large bar. Lunchtime bar meals Sat & Sun; but the restaurant opens 6-9 daily.
⛰ ⚯ 🛏 ◐ ◑ ♿ ⇌ ♣ P

ANSTRUTHER

Dreel Tavern
16 High Street (A917, 1/4 mile W of centre)
☎ (01333) 310727
11-midnight; 12.30-11 Sun
Orkney Dark Island; guest beers [H]
Cosy, low-ceilinged bar in an old stone building stocking beers often from micros and smaller breweries.
⛰ Q ✿ ◐ ◑ ♣

CERES

Ceres Inn
The Cross (B939)
☎ (01334) 828305
11-3, 5-midnight ; 11-1am Thu & Fri; 11-midnight Sat & Sun
Beer range varies [H]
Small, friendly bar, full of memorabilia, in a conservation village. Ceres Highland Games are held in June behind the pub. Eve meals winter weekends.
⛰ Q ✿ ◐ ◑ ♣ P

CUPAR

Golf Tavern
11 South Road (1/4 mile from station, opp. Tesco)
☎ (01334) 654233
11 (12.30 Sun)-midnight
Beer range varies [H]
Welcoming, single-roomed pub run by a friendly bar staff. The beers are from Harviestoun.
Q ◐ ◑ ⇌

DUNFERMLINE

Coadys
16 Pilmuir Street (near bus station and golf course)
☎ (01383) 723865
11 (12.30 Sun)-11 (midnight Fri & Sat)
McEwan 80/-; Theakston Best Bitter [H]
Busy town pub with bare floorboards and a small rear lounge. ⇌

Commercial
Douglas Street
☎ (01383) 733876
11 (12.30 Sun)-11
Courage Directors; McEwan 80/-; Theakston Best Bitter, Old Peculier; guest beers [H]
Friendly town-centre pub with bare floorboards. The TV is never on. Very good value bar meals served all day. Q ◐ ◑ ⇌

Old Inn
15a Kirkgate (between Abbey and Town House)
☎ (01383) 736652
11 (12.30 Sun)-11 (midnight Fri & Sat)
Caledonian Deuchars IPA; Courage Directors; McEwan 80/-; guest beer [H]
Busy town pub featuring sports memorabilia on the walls, close to the historic town centre. ⚯ ◐ ⇌

DYSART

Royal Hotel
20 Townhead (A917, 2 miles E of Kirkcaldy centre)
☎ (01592) 654112
11 (12.30 Sun)-midnight
Beer range varies [H]
19th-century coaching inn on the main route from Kirkcaldy to St Andrews. Note the 'leather' mural behind the bar depicting old Dysart. ⚯ ✿ 🛏 ◐ ◑ ⊞ ♿ P

EARLSFERRY

Golf Tavern (19th Hole)
5 Links Road (next to Elie golf course)
☎ (01333) 330610
11-midnight (1am Fri & Sat); 12.30-1am Sun
Broughton Greenmantle; Caledonian Deuchars IPA; guest beer (summer) [H]
Quaint old public bar with etched-glass mirrors. The cosy lounge has an open fire and golfing memorabilia.
⛰ Q ⚯ ◐ ⊞ ♿ ▲ ♣

ELIE

Victoria Bar
High Street
☎ (01333) 330305
11 (12 Sun)-1am
Caledonian Deuchars IPA, 80/-; guest beer (summer) [H]
Old wooden public bar with an ornate gantry plus a lounge, games room and restaurant serving excellent food. Special nights at weekends feature Greek and Italian food.
⛰ Q ✿ 🛏 ◐ ◑ ▲ ♣ P

HALBEATH

Halbeath Park
Halbeath Retail Park (A92, off M90 jct 3)
☎ (01383) 620737
11 (12.30 Sun)-11
Boddingtons Bitter; Flowers IPA; Harviestoun Wee Stoater [H]
Comfortable, attractive 'Brewers Fayre' restaurant and bar with children's certificate.
Q ⚯ ✿ ◐ ◑ ♿ P ⚡

KETTLEBRIDGE

Kettlebridge Inn
9 Cupar Road (A92)
☎ (01337) 830232
11.30-2.30, 5-11; (4.30-midnight Fri & Sat); 12.30-11 Sun
Belhaven Sandy Hunter's Ale, 80/-, St Andrew's Ale; guest beer [H]
Welcoming country inn and restaurant on the busy A92, in this *Guide* for 16 years. No bar food Mon; restaurant closed Mon eve.
⛰ Q ◐ ◑

KINGHORN

Auld Hoose
6-8 Nethergate
☎ (01592) 891074
12 (12.30 Sun)-midnight
Broughton Greenmantle; Caledonian Deuchars IPA; guest beers [H]
Busy side-street pub, popular with locals and holidaymakers. The bar has a pool table, while the lounge is relaxing and comfortable. Handy for the station and beaches.
⛰ ⚯ ✿ ⊞ ⇌ ♣

Ship Tavern
2 Bruce Street
☎ (01592) 890655
12 (12.30 Sun)-midnight

Caledonian 80/-; Inveralmond Independence; Orkney Dark Island Ⓗ
Traditional, wood-panelled gem, boasting a fine bar counter and ornate gantry. The jug bar also remains in one of the best surviving pub interiors in the region. Meals in summer.
🏠 Q ❀ ◖ 🍴 ᕁ ≠ ♣ P

KINGSBARNS

Cambo Arms
5 Main Street
☎ (01334) 880226
11(12.30 Sun)-11 (midnight Fri & Sat)
Belhaven 80/-, St Andrew's Ale; guest beer Ⓗ
Former coaching inn in a model estate village. The welcoming bar houses trophies and memorabilia of Kingsbarns golf club, one of the oldest in the world.
🏠 Q ❀ ⇌ ◖ ▶ ♣ P

KIRKCALDY

Betty Nicols
297 High Street
☎ (01592) 642083
11-11 (midnight Sat); 11-11 Sun
Black Sheep Best Bitter; Caledonian Deuchars IPA, 80/-; Orkney Dark Island; guest beer Ⓗ
Excellent renovation of a traditional town-centre pub: a comfortable bar and a large back room.
🏠 Q ➳ ⇔

Feuars Arms ☆
28 Bogies Wynd
☎ (01592) 269056
11-3, 5-11 ;11-midnight Thu-Sun
Orkney Red MacGregor, Dark Island; guest beer Ⓗ
Superb multi-roomed Victorian interior adorned with hardwood and tiles; check out the displays in the gents' toilet! Try the welcoming but small snug off the main bar.
Q

Harbour Bar
471 High Street (coast road)
☎ (01592) 264270
11-2.30, 5-midnight; 11-midnight Thu-Sat; 12.30-midnight Sun
Belhaven 80/-; Fife Fyre; guest beers Ⓗ

Traditional, unspoilt local, home of Fyfe Brewing Company, offering four guest beers. Large murals depict the town's whaling history. Try the superb pies, made on the premises. 2000 Fife CAMRA *Pub of the Year.*
Q 🍴 ᕁ ≠

LOCHGELLY

Torleys
38 High Street (one-way section)
☎ (01592) 783727
6-11; 3-midnight Fri; 12-midnight Sat; 12.30-midnight Sun
Beer range varies Ⓗ
Old-style pub where comfortable surroundings provide a good atmosphere.
ᕁ ≠ P

LOWER LARGO

Crusoe Hotel
Main Street
☎ (01333) 320759
11 (12.30 Sun)-midnight (1am Fri)
Caledonian Deuchars IPA; guest beer (summer) Ⓗ
Seafront hotel taking its name from the book by Alexander Selkirk, native of Largo. The hotel boasts a permanent 'Selkirk' exhibition.
➳ ❀ ⇔ ◖ ▶ P

LUNDIN LINKS

Coachman's (Old Manor Hotel)
55 Leven Road (A917)
☎ (01333) 320368
11-3, 5-11, 11-11 Sat & Sun
Beer range varies Ⓗ
Small bar area in a bright, popular bistro, separate from the hotel. A single real ale is joined by a second in summer. Excellent meals.
Q ❀ ⇔ ◖ ▶ P

ST ANDREW'S

Aikmans Cellar Bar
32 Bell Street
☎ (01334) 477425
11 (12.30 Sun)-midnight
Beer range varies Ⓗ
Flagship bar below a continental-style bistro; if closed ask for real ale to be

brought upstairs. Note the rolled copper bar top from the White Star liner Oceanic (same line as the Titanic). Around 200 real ales are served each year plus a range of European bottled beers.
◖ ▶

Central Bar
77-79 Market Street
☎ (01334) 478296
11 (12.30 Sun)-midnight
Caledonian Deuchars IPA; McEwan 80/-; Morland Old Speckled Hen; Theakston Old Peculier Ⓗ
Traditional workingman's pub with a central island bar.
◖

Drouthy Neebors
209 South Street
☎ (01334) 479952
11 (12.30 Sun)-11.45 (12.45am Fri & Sat)
Belhaven 80/-, Jack Frost; guest beers Ⓗ
Well-renovated, low-ceilinged Belhaven hostelry that hosts regular social events. Meals served all day.
◖ ▶

Lafferty's
99 South Street
☎ (01334) 474543
11-12.30 (midnight Sat); 12.30-midnight Sun
Caledonian 80/-; Taylor Landlord; guest beer Ⓗ
Small, vibrant bar, with an Irish themed decor, popular with locals, students and holidaymakers. Food is served all day until 9pm.
◖ ▶

Whey Pat Tavern
1 Bridge Street
☎ (01334) 477740
11 (12.30 Sun)-11.30
Theakston XB; guest beers Ⓗ
Long established, well-run tavern where Scottish micros feature in an ever-changing range of guest ales. Lunchtime soup and sandwiches served. Q

TAYPORT

Bell Rock Tavern
4-6 Dalgliesh Street (by harbour)
☎ (01382) 552388
11 (12.30 Sun)-midnight (1am Thu & Fri)
Beer range varies Ⓗ
Busy local, bearing a strong nautical theme, overlooking the River Tay. The split-level bar stocks two ales. Children's certificate.
Q ➳ ◖ ▲ ♣

Heritage Pubs

The pubs chosen as illustrations in the Guide are taken from CAMRA's National Inventory. These are pubs with unspoilt interiors that need to be preserved for future generations. The illustrations are used as examples of pubs on the inventory and may not necessarily have been chosen for inclusion in the Guide for beer quality.

INDEPENDENT BREWERIES

Fyfe: Kirkcaldy

409

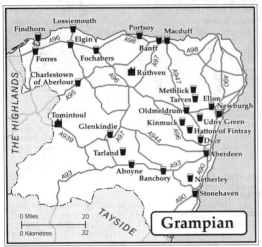

Lossiemouth
Findhorn
Portsoy
Macduff
Elgin
Banff
Forres
Fochabers
Charlestown
of Aberlour
Ruthven
Methlick
Tarves
Ellon
Oldmeldrum
Newburgh
Tomintoul
Kinmuck
Udny Green
Glenkindie
Hatton of Fintray
Dyce
Tarland
Aberdeen
Aboyne
Banchory
Netherley
Stonehaven

THE HIGHLANDS

TAYSIDE

Grampian

0 Miles 20
0 Kilometres 32

Authority areas covered: Aberdeenshire UA, City of Aberdeen UA, Moray UA

ABERDEEN

Atholl Hotel
54 Kings Gate
☎ (01224) 323505
11-2.30, 5-11 (11.30 Fri & Sat);
12-2.30, 6.30-11 Sun
Courage Directors; Taylor Landlord; guest beers Ⓗ
Traditional lounge bar in an impressive West End hotel, very popular with its predominantly middle-aged clientele it specialises in good value bar food.
⇔ Ⓒ ▶ P

Blue Lamp
121 Gallowgate (near Aberdeen College)
☎ (01224) 647472
11-midnight (lounge 1am Fri & Sat);
12.30-2.30, 6.30-11 Sun
Caledonian Deuchars IPA, 80/-; guest beers Ⓗ
Small public bar with a large, modern stone floored lounge which hosts live bands (mainly weekends). NB: for 1am drinking you must be in by midnight. The regular beers are served in the lounge only. ⊞ &

Cameron's Inn (Ma's)
6-8 Little Belmont Street
☎ (01224) 644487
11-midnight; 12.30-11 Sun
Belhaven St. Andrew's Ale; guest beers Ⓗ
Oldest inn in Aberdeen with a small public bar, unchanged for decades. The tiny listed snug makes a great contrast to the modern open-plan lounge. No food Sun.
Ⓒ ⊞ ⇌ ♣

Carriages
101 Crown Street (below Brentwood Hotel)
☎ (01224) 595440

11-2.30, 5-midnight; 6-11 Sun
Boddingtons Bitter; Caledonian Deuchars IPA; Castle Eden Ale; Courage Directors; Flowers Original; guest beers Ⓗ
Friendly, busy, city-centre bar offering an excellent and varied selection of ten ales plus bottled Belgian and German Weiss beers. Food is served in the bar and restaurant (open eves). Very limited parking.
⇔ Ⓒ ▶ ⇌ P

Globe
13 North Silver Street (off Golden Sq)
☎ (01224) 624258
11-midnight (9.30 Mon); closed Sun
Courage Directors; McEwan 80/-; guest beers Ⓗ
Recently renovated and extended, hosting live music Fri and Sat and convenient for both the theatre and Music Hall. The house beer is from Isle of Skye.
Ⓒ & ⇌

Macandrews
6 Crown Street
☎ (01224) 259971
11-midnight; 12.30-11 Sun
Beer range varies Ⓗ
Good restoration of a 'people's palace'; note the beautiful ceilings. The beer selection comes mainly from Scottish independents. No food Sun; eve snacks until 8pm. Ⓒ ⇌

Moorings
2 Trinity Quay (harbour front)
☎ (01224) 587602
11-midnight; 12.30-11 Sun
Harviestoun Bitter & Twisted; Isle of Skye Red Cuillin; guest beers Ⓗ
This one-roomed haven for heavy rock 'n' real ale fans

features guest beers predominantly from Scottish independents, always including one from Inveralmond. Live bands most weekends.
Ⓒ ⇌ ♣

No. 10 Wine Bar
10 Queen's Terrace
☎ (01224) 631928
11-midnight; 12.30-11 Sun
Caledonian Deuchars IPA, 80/-; Fuller's London Pride; guest beers Ⓗ
Cosy cellar bar with a vaulted ceiling, where all beers are served strictly without a sparkler. Good quality bar food (including breakfasts served from 9am). Very popular with the local business community.
⇔ Ⓒ ⇪ P

Old Blackfriars
52 Castle Street (on Castlegate)
☎ (01224) 581922
11-midnight; 12.30-11 Sun
Belhaven 80/-, St Andrew's Ale; Caledonian Deuchars IPA, 80/-; Inveralmond Ossian Ale; guest beers Ⓗ
This frequent local CAMRA *Pub of the Year* winner is on a split-level, notable for its excellent combination of old and new decor and imaginative use of stained glass behind the bar. Food is served all day.
Ⓒ ▶ & ⇌

Prince of Wales
7 St Nicholas Lane
☎ (01224) 640597
11-midnight; 12.30-11 Sun
Draught Bass; Caledonian 80/-; Theakston Old Peculier; guest beers Ⓗ
Unspoilt pub boasting the longest bar counter in the city, two fine gantries and a bank of eight handpumps. Good wholesome lunches; Sun breakfast served 12.30-3pm. The house beer is from Inveralmond.
Ⓒ ⇌ ♣

Under the Hammer
11 North Silver Street (off Golden Sq)
☎ (01224) 640253
5 (4 Fri, 2 Sat) midnight; 6-11 Sun
Caledonian Deuchars IPA; Inveralmond Ossian's Ale; guest beer Ⓗ
Intimate one-room cellar wine-bar pub next to the city's auction rooms. Handy for both the theatre and the music hall. ⇌

ABOYNE

Boat Inn
Charleston Road (N bank of River Dee)

☎ (013398) 86137

11-2.30, 5-11 (midnight Fri);
11-midnight Sat; 11-11 Sun

Draught Bass; guest beers ⒣

Popular riverside inn with an emphasis on food in the lounge which features a log-burning stove and a spiral staircase leading to the upper drinking area and a dining room. Children welcome.

🏠 🕷 ◑ 🍴 👶 ⅃ ♣ P

BANCHORY

Ravenswood Club (Royal British Legion)

25 Ramsay Road (off Mount St) ☎ (01330) 822347

11-3, 5-midnight; 11-midnight Sat;
12-11 Sun

Beer range varies ⒣

Extremely large club with function rooms, but beer served in one bar only. Members always make visitors welcome – bring this *Guide* with you.

🐂 🕷 ◑ 🍴 👶 ⅃ ♣ P

Scott Skinner's

North Deeside Road (A93, 1 mile E of centre)
☎ (01330) 824393

11-3, 5.30-midnight (midnight Tue-Fri); 11-midnight Sat; 11-3, 5.30-11 Sun

Beer range varies ⒣

Converted Victorian house whose Tardis-like interior includes a restaurant, games room, play area and a snug bar. Children welcome in the restaurant. It stocks a varied choice of up to three guest ales. 🏠 🐂 🕷 ◑ ⅃ ♣ P

BANFF

Castle Inn

47 Castle Street
☎ (01261) 815068

11 (12.30 Sun)-12.30am

Courage Directors; guest beer ⒣

Two-roomed pub with a pleasantly refurbished lounge and a basic public bar offering pool and darts. Popular with younger drinkers. 🍴 ⅃ ♣

CHARLESTOWN OF ABERLOUR

Mash Tun

8 Broomfield Square (follow signs to Alice Littler Park)
☎ (01340) 871771

11-11 (11.45 Thu; 12.30am Fri & Sat); (closed winter afternoons Mon-Thu); 12.30-11.45 Sun

Beer range varies ⒣

Refurbished, revitalised and renamed, now stocking a wide selection of malts, bottled beers, continental lagers, up to three real ales, and good value meals. An ideal stop when walking the Speyside Way. Children's certificate. 🕷 ◑ ⅃ P

DYCE

Tap & Spile

Aberdeen Airport Terminal, Brent Road
☎ (01224) 722331

8am-10pm; 9am-7pm Sat; 12.30-10 Sun

Boddingtons Bitter; Caledonian 80/-; Marston's Pedigree; Morland Old Speckled Hen; Tetley Bitter ⒣

Refurbished open lounge bar – a haven if your flight is delayed. 👶 ♣

ELGIN

Sunninghill Hotel

Hay Street (opp. Moray College) ☎ (01343) 547799

11-2.30; 5-11; (12.30am Fri & Sat); 12.30-2.30, 6.30-11 Sun

Ind Coope Burton Ale; guest beers ⒣

Family-run hotel in the city centre where the excellent food is just as tempting as the five beers. Children's certificate.

🕷 🍴 ◑ 👶 ⅃ ⇌ P

ELLON

Tollbooth

21-23 Station Road
☎ (01358) 721308

11-2.30, 5-11 (midnight Thu & Fri); 11-11.45 Sat; (closed lunch) 6.30-11 Sun

Draught Bass; guest beers ⒣

Converted from two semi-detached houses, with a large conservatory on the lower section of the split-level, this pub draws a predominantly mature clientele (no children allowed). Three constantly changing guest beers.
Q 🕷 👶 ♣

FINDHORN

Crown & Anchor Inn

☎ (01309) 690243

11-11 (11.45 Thu, 12.30am Fri & Sat); 12-11.45 Sun

Beer range varies ⒣

Dating from 1739 and situated on picturesque Findhorn Bay, this two-bar beamed inn serves up to four real ales and a wide variety of food. Children's certificate up to 9pm.

🏠 🕷 🍴 ◑ 👶 ♣ P

Kimberley Inn

☎ (01309) 690492

11-11 (11.45 Thu & Fri, 12.30am Sat); 12.30-11.45 Sun

Tetley Bitter; guest beers ⒣

Popular, friendly bar where the patio affords fine views over the bay. Famed for its food. Children's certificate until 8pm.

🏠 🕷 ◑ 👶 ♣ ✂

FOCHABERS

Gordon Arms Hotel

80 High Street
☎ (01343) 820508

11.30-2.30, 5-11 (12.30am Fri & Sat); 12.30-11 Sun

Caledonian Deuchars IPA; guest beers ⒣

200-year-old coaching inn at the west end of town: popular with anglers; families welcome. A good range of malt whiskies available; beer is on tap in the small public bar only, but can be brought through to the lounge or dining room.

Q 🕷 🍴 ◑ 👶 ⅃ ⇌ P

FORRES

Red Lion Hotel

12 Tollbooth Street
☎ (01309) 672716

12-11.45 (11 Tue & Wed, 12.45am Fri & Sat); 6-11 Sun

Beer range varies ⒣

A welcome return to the *Guide* for Grampian's first ever entry back in 1976. The 'Wee Beastie' is a popular town-centre howff. Beer is only sold in the lounge.

◑ 👶 ⇌ ♣

GLENKINDIE

Glenkindie Arms Hotel

OS442138
☎ (01975) 641288

11 (12.30 sun)-11 (1am Fri, midnight Sat; closed 2.30-5 winter weedays)

Beer range varies ⒣

Tiny, historic drovers' inn deep in the hills, en route to the Lecht ski area. Extensive range of food available.

🏠 🍴 ◑ P

HATTON OF FINTRAY

Northern Lights

Station Road
☎ (01224) 791261

11-1am (12.30am Sat); 12.30-11 Sun

Courage Directors; guest beers ⒣

Almost hidden down a back lane between houses in the village centre, this pub offers two guest beers and a wide selection of bar food. A quiet conservatory/lounge is used as a restaurant at lunchtime.

🏠 Q 🕷 ◑ 👶 ♣ P 🛏

KINMUCK

Boars Head Inn

Signed from B977/B993
OS 818199
☎ (01224) 791235

5-11 Mon-Thu; 4.30-1am Fri; 11-11.45 Sat; 12.30-11 Sun

Beer range varies ⒣

Traditional rural Scottish pub whose opening hours may vary; phone ahead before travelling. Q 🕷 👶 ♣ P

LOSSIEMOUTH

Clifton Bar

4 Clifton Road
☎ (01343) 812100
11-2.30, 5-11 (11.45 Wed & Thu); 11-12.30am Fri & Sat; 12.30-11 Sun
Boddingtons Bitter; Theakston Old Peculier; guest beers Ⓗ
Popular free house on the east side of town, near beach and harbour.
🏨 ❀ ⊟ ▲ ♣ P

Skerry Brae Hotel
Stotfield Road (near golf course)
☎ (01343) 812040
11-11 (11.45 Wed, 12.30am Thu-Sat); 12-11 Sun
Beer range varies Ⓗ
Popular hotel bar on the outskirts of town enjoying sea views. This extended one-room bar has a pool table, no-smoking conservatory and a large outdoor balcony. Excellent food.
🏨 ❀ ◖ ▮ ▲ ♣ P ⊬

MACDUFF

Knowes Hotel
78 Market Street
☎ (01261) 832229
12-12 (closed 2-5 midweek in winter); 12.30-11 Sun
Draught Bass; guest beer Ⓗ
Small, family-run hotel affording panoramic views of the Moray Firth. Relax in the splendour of the magnificent conservatory. Good quality bar food and a restaurant.
Q ➽ ❀ ⇌ ◖ ▲ ♣ ⊬

METHLICK

Gight House Hotel
Sunnybrae (B9170, 1/2 mile N of river)
☎ (01651) 806389
12-2.30, 5-midnight (1am Fri, 11.45 Sat); 12-11 Sun
Beer range varies Ⓗ
Attractive beamed lounge bar in a former church manse, boasting two conservatories. The home-cooked meals use local produce.The garden has amusements.
🏨 ❀ ⇌ ◖ ▮ ♣ P

Ythanview Hotel
Ellon Road
☎ (01651) 806235
11-2.30; 5-11 (1am Fri); 11-11.45 Sat; 12.30-11 Sun
Beer range varies Ⓗ
Hotel overlooking the river: a smart lounge/restaurant and a cheery public bar. Good

value home-cooked food.
🏨 Q ➽ ❀ ⇌ ◖ ▮ ⊟ ▲ ♣

NETHERLEY

Lairhillock Inn
Off B979, 3 miles S of B9077
OS 855952
☎ (01569) 730001
11-2.30, 5-11; 11-midnight Sat; 12-11 Sun
Boddingtons Bitter; Courage Directors; Flowers Original; McEwan 80/-; guest beers Ⓗ
Set in the heart of beautiful countryside, the public bar has a friendly atmosphere whilst families are welcome in the conservatory. Excellent choice of food. Look out for the 'Inn' on the roof.
🏨 Q ➽ ❀ ◖ ▮ ⊟ ▲ ♣ ⊙ P ⊬

NEWBURGH

Udny Arms Hotel
Main Street
☎ (01358) 789444
12-2.30, 5-11.30; 11-11.30 Sat; 12-11 Sun
Courage Directors; guest beers Ⓗ
Imposing, long-established stone-built hotel at the centre of an attractive coastal village, convenient for the golf course and nature reserve. The public/café bar is on the lower floor, the upstairs lounge has reduced hours Sun.
Q ❀ ⇌ ◖ ▮ ⊟ ▲ ▲ P ⊬

OLDMELDRUM

Redgarth Hotel
Kirk Brae (off A947, towards golf course)
☎ (01651) 872353
11-2.30, 5-midnight; 12-2.30, 5-11 Sun
Beer range varies Ⓗ/Ⓖ
Traditional, wood-panelled lounge bar with panoramic views. It offers an imaginative selection of seasonal guest ales and a varied menu of home-cooked food.
Q ➽ ❀ ⇌ ◖ ▮ ♣ P ⊬

PORTSOY

Shore Inn
Church Street (harbour front)
☎ (01261) 842831
11 (10 summer)-11 (midnight Thu; 12.30am Fri & Sat)
Beer range varies Ⓗ
18th-century seafaring inn nestling in the oldest harbour on the Moray Firth. It hosts an annual beer festival, during the local small boats regatta.
🏨 ❀ ◖ ▮ ▲ ♣

STONEHAVEN

Marine Hotel
9-10 Shorehead
☎ (01569) 762155

11 (12 Sun)-midnight
Caledonian Deuchars IPA; Taylor Landlord; guest beers Ⓗ
Former Scottish CAMRA *Pub of the Year* where the wood-panelled bar always stocks unusual guest beers. The picturesque harbour location makes it a must in summer. Specialises in fish dishes.
🏨 ➽ ⇌ ◖ ▮ ⊟ ▲ ♣ ⊙ ▯

Ship Inn
5 Shorehead
☎ (01569) 762617
11 (12 Sun)-midnight
Caledonian Deuchars IPA; guest beer Ⓗ
Long narrow bar, built in 1771, on the picturesque harbour. Good value meals (not served Sun eve).
Q ➽ ◖ ▮ ⊟ ▲ ▲ ♣ ⊙

TARLAND

Aberdeen Arms Hotel
The Square
☎ (01339) 881225
12-2.30, 5-11; 12-midnight Fri & Sat; 12-11 Sun
Beer range varies Ⓗ
Long, low, pine-panelled bar in a small village hotel on the main square. The small lounge has space for a few diners and those who prefer a comfy fireside armchair to enjoy their drinking.
🏨 Q ❀ ⇌ ◖ ▮ ▲ P

TARVES

Aberdeen Arms Hotel
The Square
☎ (01651) 851214
11-2.30, 5-midnight (1am Fri); 11-11.45 Sat; 12.30-11 Sun
Caledonian 80/-; Courage Directors; guest beer Ⓗ
Small, family-run hotel in the village conservation area. Note the fine mirrors in the public bar. Children's certificate until 8pm.
🏨 Q ➽ ⇌ ◖ ▮ ⊟ ▲ ♣ P ⊬

UDNY GREEN

Udny Green Hotel
Opp. village green
☎ (01651) 842337
12-3, 6 (5.30 Sun)-11 (1am Fri, 11.45 Sat); closed Mon
Beer range varies Ⓗ
Small inn with fine decor at the heart of a picturesque village in a conservation area. Children's certificate and a reduced price pensioner's menu are features. Up to two beers available.
Q ❀ ◖ ▮ ⊟ ▲ ♣ P ⊬

INDEPENDENT BREWERIES	
Borve: Ruthven	
Tomintoul: Tomintoul	

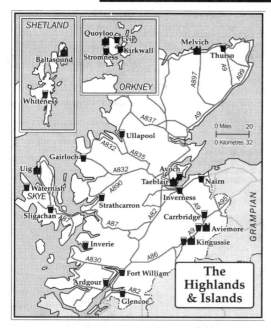

SHETLAND
Quoyloo Evie
Baltasound
Kirkwall
Stromness
Whiteness
ORKNEY
Melvich
Thurso
Ullapool
Gairloch
Uig
Waternish
SKYE
Strathcarron
Sligachan
Inverie
Ardgour
Glencoe
Avoch
Taeblair
Nairn
Inverness
Carrbridge
Aviemore
Kingussie
Fort William
GRAMPIAN

0 Miles 20
0 Kilometres 32

The
Highlands
& Islands

Authority areas covered: Highland UA, Orkney Islands UA, Shetland Islands UA, Western Islands UA

ARDGOUR

Inn at Ardgour
On A861, at the Corran ferry
☎ (01855) 841225
10am-11pm (1am Fri & Sat); 12-11 Sun
Beer range varies H
18th-century village inn
ideal for walking, wildlife
watching, sailing and
climbing. Bar meals are
served all day. The beers are
from Isle of Skye; over 100
single malts on offer.
🏨 🚭 🌑 🍴 🛡 ♣ P

AVIEMORE

Old Bridge Inn
23 Dalfaber Road (S end of
village, along ski road then
left after 300 yds)
☎ (01479) 811137
11-midnight; 12.30-11 Sun
Beer range varies H
Converted cottage,
popular with skiers
and walkers, near
Strathspey steam
railway. It specialises in
Scottish beers.
🏨 Q 🌑 🍴 🛡 ≈ P ⚊

Winkin Owl
Grampian Road
☎ (01479) 810646
11-11 (midnight Fri); 12.30-midnight Sun
**Ind Coope Burton Ale; Marston's
Pedigree; guest beers** H
Well-established local, also
popular with hillwalkers and
skiers. Good value food is
served all day.
🐚 🌑 🍴 ≈ P ⚊

AVOCH

Station Hotel
Main Street
☎ (01381) 620246
11-2.30, 5-11 (midnight Fri); 11-11.30
Sat (11-11 summer Mon-Fri); 12.30-
11.30 Sun
Beer range varies H
Busy but friendly local in a
pleasant Black Isle
village. Popular at weekends
for good value food
(served all day). Large
conservatory.
🏨 🌑 🍴 🌑 ♣ P ⚊

CARRBRIDGE

Cairn Hotel
Main Road
☎ (01479) 841212
11.30-midnight (1am Fri & Sat); 12.30
(12 summer)-11 Sun
Beer range varies H
Busy locals' bar, also popular
with visitors.
🏨 🌑 🚭 🌑 🍴 ≈ P

EVIE

Mistra
Near A966/B9057 jct.
OS365258
☎ (01856) 751216
6.30-11 (midnight Fri); 12-midnight Sat;
8-10.30 Sun
Beer range varies H
Above a shop this Howff has
spartan decor, but superb
views. The real ale is from
Orkney, also a good range of
bottled-conditioned beers.
🏨 🌑 🛡 ♣ P

FORT WILLIAM

Grog & Gruel
66 High Street
☎ (01397) 705078
11 (12 winter)-midnight (1am Thu-Sat);
5-midnight Sun
Beer range varies H
Always a fine selection of real
ales in this town centre pub.
Tex-Mex meals available.
🌑 🍴 🛡 ≈

GAIRLOCH

Old Inn
The Harbour (S end of
village)
☎ (01445) 712006
11am-midnight (11.30 Sat); 12.30-11
Sun
Beer range varies H
18th-century, family-run
traditional coaching inn,
hosting live music eves.
Good bar meals. Good walks
and fishing locally.
🐚 🌑 🚭 🌑 🍴 🍳 🛡 ♣ P

GLENCOE

Clachaig
On old road off A82, 3 miles
E of village
☎ (01855) 811252
11-11 (midnight Fri; 11.30 Sat); 12.30-
11 Sun
**Black Isle Red Kite; Heather Ale
Fraoch; Isle of Skye Red Cuillin;
Tetley Bitter; guest beers** H
Old coaching inn in a
brooding glen, surrounded
by walking and climbing
country. The bar is in a large
stone-floored room with
smaller quieter rooms off.
Can get smoky when busy.
🏨 🐚 🌑 🚭 🌑 🍴 🍳 🛡 P ⚊

INVERIE

Old Forge
Knoydart by Mallaig (by ferry
from Mallaig) OS 767001
☎ (01687) 462267
11-midnight
Beer range varies H
Accessed only by ferry or a
serious walk from
Kinlochhourn, and used
mainly by hillwalkers and
yachtsmen, the pub also
serves the local community
well. Food served all day.
🏨 Q 🌑 🌑 🛡 ♣

INVERNESS

Blackfriars
93-95 Academy Street
☎ (01463) 233881
11-11 (1am Thu & Fri, 11.45 Sat);
12.30-11 Sun
**Courage Directors; McEwan 80/-;
Marston's Pedigree; Theakston Old
Peculier; guest beers** H
Popular pub offering a good
range of guest beers in a
single large bar with small
snug alcoves. Bar meals

413

served all day.
◖◗⇌

Clachnaharry Inn
17-19 High Street,
Clachnaharry (A862, Beauly
Road, western outskirts of
town) ☎ (01463) 239806
11-11 (midnight Thu-Sat); 12.30-11.45
Sun

**Adnams Broadside; Courage
Directors; Isle of Skye Red Cuillin,
Ⓗ Blaven; Ⓖ McEwan 80/-; guest
beers** Ⓗ
Friendly, family-run, 17th-
century coaching inn
enjoying views over Beauly
Firth and the western
highlands. Good bar meals
are served all day; house
beers sold. Local CAMRA
Town Pub of the Year 1999.
🏠Q🛏🏮◖◗◱🅰

Heathmount Hotel
Kingsmills Road (uphill from
Eastgate Centre)
☎ (01463) 235877
11-11 (1am Thu & Fri, 12.30am Sat);
12.30-11 Sun

McEwan 80/-; guest beers Ⓗ
Busy lounge and public bar
featuring distinctive decor,
an imaginative, good value
menu and friendly, efficient
service. Three guest beers are
usually available (one from
the local Black Isle Brewery).
🏮🛏◖◗◱🕭⇌♣P

Phoenix
108 Academy Street
☎ (01463) 245991
11-11 (12.30am Thu & Fri, 11.30 Sat);
12.30-11 Sun

**Draught Bass; Caledonian Deuchars
IPA, 80/-; guest beers** Ⓗ
Busy, town-centre pub
boasting a rare example of an
island bar in the public. The
attractive lounge bar holds a
children's certificate. Food
served all day.
◖◗◱⇌♣

KINGUSSIE
Royal Hotel
High Street
☎ (01540) 661898
11 (12.30 Sun)-midnight (1am Thu-Sat)
Beer range varies Ⓗ
Large, extended coaching inn
now with its own brewery
(Iris Rose). Live music staged
many nights.
🏮🛏◖◗🕭🅰♣P⅍

KIRKWALL
Bothy Bar (Albert Hotel)
Mounthoolie Lane (behind
Woolworth's)
☎ (01856) 876000
11-11 (1am Thu-Sat); 12-1am Sun
**Orkney Raven, Red MacGregor, Dark
Island** Ⓗ
Public bar in a town-centre
hotel, with a country pub

feel: low, beamed ceilings
and a massive open fire.
Seafood is a speciality – try
the local scallops.
🏠🛏◖◗🅰

NAIRN
Invernairne Hotel
Thurlow Road (off Seabank
Rd; access also from West
Promenade)
☎ (01667) 452039
11-11.30 (1am Thu-Sat); 11-11.30 Sun
Beer range varies Ⓗ
Victorian seaside hotel with a
wood-panelled bar, giving a
panoramic view of Moray
Firth.
🏠Q🛏🏮🛏◖◗🕭🅰P

SLIGACHAN
Sligachan Hotel
at A850/A863 jct
☎ (01478) 650204
9am-midnight (11 Sun)
Beer range varies Ⓗ
Right by the Cuillin Hills,
benefitting from spectacular
views, this family-run, 19th-
century hotel offers good bar
meals till 9pm. An ideal base
for climbers and walkers;
families are welcome.
🏠🛏🏮🛏◖◗🕭🅰♣P

STRATHCARRON
Strathcarron Hotel
on A890 by station at head of
Loch Carron
☎ (01520) 722227
11-11, including Sun
Beer range varies Ⓗ
Typical hillwalkers' pub,
allowing full use of the hotel
facilities for campers. Meals
served all day. Spectacular
position on the Skye road.
🏠🏮🛏◖◗🅰⇌♣P

STROMNESS
Stromness Hotel
15 Victoria Street (near ferry
terminal) ☎ (01856) 850298
11 (12 Sun)-11 (1am Fri & Sat)
**Orkney Red MacGregor, Dark
Island** Ⓗ
Large first-floor lounge bar
overlooking the harbour,
packed with visiting divers in
summer and locals all year.
Families welcome. It hosts

the island's only beer festival
(Aug). 🏠🏮🛏◖◗🅰♣P

THURSO
Central Hotel
Traill Street
☎ (01847) 893129
11 (12.30 Sun)-11.45 (1am Sat)
**Morland Old Speckled Hen; guest
beers** Ⓗ
Busy, town-centre pub
serving reasonably priced
meals; a mecca for families.
Q🛏◖◗◱⇌♣

ULLAPOOL
Ferryboat Inn
Shore Street
☎ (01854) 612366
11 (12.30 Sun)-11
Beer range varies Ⓗ
Small, comfortable lounge
bar on the village waterfront
affording open views over
Loch Broom. Local CAMRA
Country Pub of the Year 1999.
🏠Q🛏🏮◖◗🅰

WATERNISH
Stein Inn
On B886, 4 1/2 miles from
Fairy Bridge, near Dunvegan
☎ (01470) 592362
12-midnight (11.30 Sat; closes 4pm
winter); 12-11 Sun
**Isle of Skye Red Cuillin; guest
beers** Ⓗ
Traditional highland inn
with fine views across Sea
Loch Bay to Rubha Maol. The
oldest inn on the Isle of Skye,
its house beer comes from
the Island's brewery. Bar
meals include local seafood.
🏠Q🏮🛏◖◗🅰♣P

WHITENESS
Westings
On A971, 10 miles NW of
Lerwick OS402464
☎ (01595) 840242
12.30-2.30, 5.30-11; 12.30-11 Sat &
Sun
Beer range varies Ⓗ
Post-war, two-bar inn set on
a hillside at the head of
Weisdale Voe, enjoying
stunning views. It has a
restaurant and a children's
certificate.
🏠🛏◖◗🕭🅰♣P

INDEPENDENT BREWERIES

Aviemore: Aviemore
Black Isle: Taeblair
Far North: Melvich
Iris Rose: Kingussie
Isle of Arran: Brodick
Isle of Skye: Uig
Orkney: Quoyloo
Valhalla: Baltasound

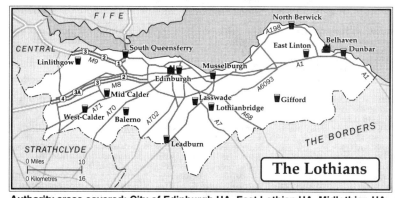

The Lothians

Authority areas covered: City of Edinburgh UA, East Lothian UA, Midlothian UA

BALERNO

Johnsburn House
64 Johnsburn Road (NW side of village)
☎ (0131) 449 3847
12.30-2.30, 5-midnight; 12-midnight Sat & Sun; closed Mon
Caledonian Deuchars IPA; guest beers H
Baronial mansion dating from 1760 and now Grade B listed. It enjoys a well deserved reputation for meals. The cosy bar (stocking four guest beers) has a convivial atmosphere and welcoming fire. Children's certificate.
🏰 Q ❀ ◖ ▮ ♣ P

DUNBAR

Volunteer Arms
17 Victoria Street (between harbour and swimming pool)
☎ (01368) 862278
11-11 (1 am Thu-Sat); 12.30-midnight Sun
Draught Bass; Belhaven 80/-; guest beer H
The history of the local lifeboats and the area adorn the walls of this oak-beamed and panelled, friendly, boisterous bar near the harbour. The bar is decorated with red bank notes and an RNLI flag proudly flies outside. Meals available April to Oct (seafood a speciality).
❀ ◖ ▮ A ≠ ♣

EAST LINTON

Bridgend Hotel
3 Bridge End
☎ (01620) 860202
12-2, 7-11(midnight Thu); 12-midnight Fri, Sat &Sun
Border Rampart; guest beer H
Village pub with a bar and comfortable lounge. The stained glass windows and rooftop statue reflect the pub's previous name, the Red Lion. Eve meals served Fri-Sun. Lined glasses used on pints only. ❀ ⇆ ◖ ▮ ▣ ♣ ▯

Drovers Inn
5 Bridge Street
☎ (01620) 860298
11.30-midnight (1am Fri-Sat); 11.30-2.30, 5-11 Mon; 12.30-1am Sun
Adnams Broadside; Caledonian 80/-; guest beers H
Formerly the Railway and overlooked by the main East Coast line viaduct, the bar has a dark, intimate, select feel. Note the marble-topped bar with brass foot rail. The good quality restaurant has a no-smoking area. Children's certificate. 🏰 ❀ ◖ ▮

EDINBURGH

Blind Beggar
97-99 Broughton Road
☎ (0131) 557 3130
11 (12 Sat)-midnight (1am Fri-Sat); 12.30-midnight Sun
Caledonian Deuchars IPA, 80/- A
Basic bar decorated with motorcyle parts and picture discs. The jukebox is turned up loud at weekends.

Bow Bar
80 West Bow
☎ (0131) 226 7667
11-11.30; 5-11 Sun
Caledonian Deuchars IPA, 80/- A
One-roomed shop dedicated to perpendicular drinking and traditional Scottish air pressure dispense. Original brewery mirrors and cigarette adverts adorn the walls. Superb range of malt whiskies and five guest beers stocked. Q ≠ (Waverley)

Cambridge Bar
20 Young Street
☎ (0131) 225 4266
11-1am (earlier if quiet); closed Sun
Caledonian Deuchars IPA, 80/-; guest beers H
On the north-west edge of the town centre, this building is classic 'New Town' dating from 1775. The wooden-floored interior has an eclectic knick-knack collection. Guest range includes a Harviestoun beer. ◖ ▮ ♣

Cloisters Bar
26 Brougham Street
☎ (0131) 221 9997
11-midnight (12.30am Fri-Sat); 12.30-midnight Sun
Caledonian Deuchars IPA, 80/-; Flying Firkin Aviator; Taylor Landlord; Thwaites Bitter; A **guest beers** H
Once a parsonage, this ale house reverberates to the sound of contented drinkers. Rare old brewery mirrors adorn the walls and the whisky selection does justice to the magnificent gantry, built with wood from a redundant church. Sunday breakfast served until 4pm.
◖ Q

Golden Rule
30 Yeaman Place
☎ (0131) 229 3413
11-11.30 (midnight Fri); 12.30-11 Sun
Draught Bass; Caledonian Deuchars IPA, 80/-; Harviestoun Bitter & Twisted, Schiehallion; guest beers H
Split-level, street-corner local in a Victorian tenement. Real ales are served in the top bar. The refurbished bottom bar is known as Rule 2. Can be smoky when busy.
≠ (Haymarket) ♣

Guildford Arms
1 West Register Street (behind Burger King at east end of Princes Street)
☎ (0131) 556 4312
11-11 (midnight Thu-Sat); 12.30-11 Sun
Draught Bass; Belhaven 60/- H **Caledonian Deuchars IPA,** P **Orkney Dark Island; guest beers** H
Busy, city-centre pub boasting ornate plaster work and ceilings, spectacular cornices and friezes, window arches and screens and an unusual wood-panelled gallery above the main bar. Six interesting guest beers include one from Harviestoun. No food Sun.
◖ ≠ (Waverley)

Hogshead
30-32 Bread Street

The Good Beer Guide 2001

☎ (0131) 211 0575
11-1am; 12.30-1am Sun
Boddingtons Bitter; Caledonian 80/-; guest beers Ⓗ/Ⓖ
Recently refurbished Whitbread alehouse, with a glass-walled cellar, converted from a Co-op. Ten ever-changing guest ales (and no nitro-keg) are offered alongside a good selection of Belgian beers and single malt whisky. Can be lively at weekends. Meals finish early Fri & Sat. Ⓓ ♿ ✄

Kay's Bar
39 Jamaica Street (mews between India and Howe St.)
☎ (0131) 225 1858
11-midnight (1am Fri & Sat); 12.30-11 Sun
Belhaven 80/-; Boddingtons Bitter; Theakston Best Bitter; guest beer Ⓗ
Convivial New Town bar decorated with whisky barrels. The back room has a well-stocked library. The lunches consist of traditional Scottish fare. ♨ Q Ⓓ ♣

Kenilworth ☆
152 Rose Street
☎ (0131) 226 4385
10-11; 9-12.45am Fri & Sat; 12.30-11 Sun
Caledonian Deuchars IPA, 80/-; Marston's Pedigree; Orkney Dark Island; guest beers Ⓗ
Classic Edinburgh pub featuring an ornate high ceiling and island bar with carved wooden gantry. The walls are tiled and there is a massive old Dryburgh mirror. The small rear lounge serves as a family room during the day. ⚲ ❀ Ⓓ

Leslie's Bar ☆
45 Ratcliffe Terrace, Newington, (2 miles S of city centre) ☎ (0131) 667 5957
11-11 (11.30 Thu; 12.30am Fri & Sat); 12.30-11.30 Sun
Draught Bass; Belhaven 80/-; Caledonian Deuchars IPA, 80/-; Taylor Landlord; guest beers Ⓗ
Superb, busy Victorian pub with one of the finest interiors in the city. A snob screen separates the saloon and snug from the public bar. Snacks available. Seek it out with a 42 or 46 bus from the city centre. ♨ Q Ⓠ ♣

Malt & Hops
45 The Shore, Leith
☎ (0131) 555 0083
12-midnight (1am Fri-Sat); 12.30-11 Sun
Tetley Bitter; Marston's Pedigree; guest beers Ⓗ
One-roomed public bar dating from 1749 and facing on to the Water of Leith. It is said to be haunted by the ghost of a previous licensee

who drowned when the cellar flooded. No food Sun. Five guest beers; children welcome until 6pm.
♨ Q ❀ Ⓓ ♣ ☺

Mathers
1 Queensferry Street
☎ (0131) 225 3549
11-midnight (1am Fri-Sat); 12.30-11 Sun
Caledonian Deuchars IPA, 80/-; Courage Directors; guest beers Ⓐ
Genuine, traditional Scottish stand-up drinking shop with a wooden floor, high ceiling and ornate plasterwork below the cornice. It boasts an excellent collection of rare brewery mirrors.
≢ (Haymarket)

McLachlan's Ale House
1 Canonmills
☎ (0131) 558 7049
11-midnight (1am Fri-Sat); 12.30-midnight Sun
Beer range varies Ⓗ
Two-roomed bar with bare floor boards, interesting cornices and plasterwork on friezes; note the fine Aitkens mirror. It caters mainly for a local clientele. Sun breakfast served 10.30-2. Ⓓ Ⓓ

Old Chain Pier
32 Trinity Crescent (foreshore between Leith and Granton) ☎ (0131) 552 1233
11-11 (midnight Thu-Sat); 12.30-11 Sun
Caledonian Deuchars IPA; Ind Coope Burton Ale; Taylor Landlord; Tetley Bitter; guest beers Ⓗ
Welcoming, cosy seafront bar on the site of the booking office of the old pier (destroyed in 1898). Decorated with sailing artefacts, it is a great place to watch ships and birds. Children allowed in the conservatory until 7pm; lunch served 12-5. ❀ Ⓓ ♣

Oxford Bar ☆
8 Young Street (near Charlotte Sq.)
☎ (0131) 539 7119
11-1am; 12.30-11 Sun
Belhaven 80/-, St Andrew's Ale; Caledonian Deuchars IPA; guest beer Ⓗ
Tiny, yet vibrant New Town drinking shop retaining aspects of its 19th-century parlour arrangement. Decorated with Burns memorabilia, this is where the 'professor' holds court in Ian Rankin's novels. Q ♣

Starbank Inn
64 Laverockbank Road (foreshore between Leith and Granton) ☎ (0131) 552 4141
11-11 (midnight Thu-Sat); 12.30-11 Sun
Belhaven Sandy Hunter's Ale, IPA, 80/-, St Andrew's Ale; Taylor Landlord; guest beers Ⓗ

Bright and airy, bare-boarded ale house divided into three areas. The decor includes rare brewery mirrors, waiters' trays and water jugs. Four interesting guest beers on tap. Q Ⓓ ♣

Winstons
20 Kirk Loan, Corstorphine (off St John's Road, A8) ☎ (0131) 539 7077
11-11.30 (midnight Thu-Sat); 12.30-11 Sun
Caledonian Deuchars IPA; Ind Coope Burton Ale; Orkney Dark Island; guest beer Ⓗ
Not far from Edinburgh Zoo, this smart, suburban lounge bar is well favoured by locals. The decor features golfing and rugby themes. Try the home-made pies (no meals Sun). Children welcome at lunchtime. Ⓓ

GIFFORD
Goblin Ha' Hotel
Main Street
☎ (01620) 810244
11-2.30, 4.30-11; 11-midnight Fri & Sat; 11-11 Sun
Caledonian Deuchars IPA; Hop Back Summer Lightning; Taylor Landlord; guest beer Ⓗ
Large village hotel with a functional public bar that has an oak-panelled counter. The lounge/cocktail bar has a comfortable seating area and a conservatory looking out over the extensive garden and play area. Good guest beer range; cider in summer. Children's certificate.
♨ ❀ ⇄ Ⓓ ♣ ☺

Tweeddale Arms Hotel
High Street
☎ (01620) 810240
11-11 (midnight Fri & Sat); 11-11 Sun
Caledonian Deuchars IPA; Greene King IPA; guest beer Ⓗ
Attractive whitewashed hotel overlooking the village green and a 300-year-old avenue of lime trees. The public bar, with its large collection of miniatures and oak counter, attracts a loyal local following. The plush lounge is popular for food. Children's certificate.
♨ Q ⇄ Ⓓ ⚲ ♣

LASSWADE
Laird & Dog Hotel
5 High Street (A768 near river bridge) ☎ (0131) 663 9219
11-11.30 (11.45 Thu, 12.30am Fri & Sat); 12.30-11.30 Sun
Beer range varies Ⓗ
Comfortable village local with an interesting bottle-shaped well. Several areas: music and pool table at one end contrasts with quieter seating areas at the other; a

416

conservatory extension is used as a restaurant, and food is also served in the bar. Children welcome until 8pm.
🏨 🍴 🍺 ♿ ♣ P

LEADBURN
Leadburn Inn
At A701/A703/A6094 jct.
☎ (01968) 672952
11-11 (11.45 Fri & Sat; midnight summer); 12.-11 (midnight summer) Sun
Caledonian Deuchars IPA, 80/-; guest beer Ⓗ
Established in 1777, this large food-oriented hostelry uses a converted railway coach as a function room. The public bar features a pot bellied stove and a picture window looking to the Pentland Hills. A conservatory links the bar to the plush lounge. Children's certificate.
🏨 Q 🍴 🍺 🍴 ♣ P

LINLITHGOW
Black Bitch
14 West Port
☎ (01506) 842147
11-11; 12.30-midnight Sun
Beer range varies Ⓗ
Traditional, friendly pub which derives its name from the town's crest. Discount for senior citizens in the bar.
Q 🍴 ≈ ♣

Four Marys
65 High Street
☎ (01506) 842171
12-11. 11-11.45 Thu-Sat; 12.30-11 Sun
Belhaven 80/-; St Andrew's Ale; Caledonian Deuchars IPA; guest beers Ⓗ
Olde-worlde country inn whose decor reflects the town's history. Forth Valley CAMRA *Pub of the Year* 2000. Beer festivals are held in May and Oct. Up to five guests all year. Home-cooked food includes local dishes. 🍺 ≈

Platform 3
1a High Street
☎ (01506) 847405
11 (12.30 Sun)-midnight
Caledonian Deuchars IPA; guest beer Ⓗ
Small, friendly, welcoming pub on the railway station approach, hosting occasional live entertainment. ≈ ♣

LOTHIANBRIDGE
Sun Inn
On A7, near Newtongrange
☎ (0131) 663 2456
11 (12.30 Sun)-midnight
Caledonian Deuchars IPA; guest beer (summer) Ⓗ
Old coaching inn close to the disused 27-span Waverley Line viaduct. The well-appointed lounge bar is

divided into drinking and eating areas and features a model railway above the bar. Set in five acres of woodland grounds; walks lead to the River Esk and Newbattle Abbey. Eve meals end at 7 (9.30 Fri-Sun).
🏨 🍴 🍺 🍴 ♣ P

MID CALDER
Torphichen Arms
36 Bank Street
☎ (01506) 880020
11-11 (midnight Thu-Sat); 12.30-midnight Sun
Caledonian Deuchars IPA, 80/-; Ind Coope Burton Ale; guest beers Ⓗ
Village local, originally an hotel, dating back to 1778. Several rooms, where the original cornices remain, now form one L-shaped bar with public and lounge areas. Bar snacks served all day; eve meals Sat and Sun (until 7pm). Children welcome until 8pm. 🍺 🍴 ♣ P

MUSSELBURGH
Levenhall Arms
10 Ravensheugh Road (B1348 near racecourse roundabout)
☎ (0131) 665 3220
11 (3 Mon-Thu winter)-11 (midnight Thu; 1am Fri & Sat); 12.30-midnight Sun
Caledonian Deuchars IPA; Ⓟ **Ind Coope Burton Ale;** Ⓗ **guest beer** Ⓟ
Busy pub, popular with locals, racegoers and visitors to the nearby golf course. The building dates from 1830 and houses a comfortable three-roomed pub. Children welcome in lounge daytime.
Q 🍴 ♿ 🍴 ≈ (Wallyford) ♣ P

Volunteer Arms (Staggs)
81 North High Street
☎ (0131) 665 9654
11-11 (11.30 Thu, midnight Fri & Sat); 11-2.30, 5-11 Tue & Wed; closed Sun
Caledonian Deuchars IPA, 80/-; guest beer Ⓗ
Run by the same family since 1858, this is a traditional, busy bar with dark wood panelling, defunct brewery mirrors and a superb gantry topped with old casks. A comfortable lounge to the rear has no real ale. Former CAMRA national *Pub of the Year*. 🍴 ♣

NORTH BERWICK
Auld Hoose
19 Forth Street
☎ (01620) 892692
11-11 (midnight Fri & Sat); 12.30-11 Sun
Beer range varies Ⓐ
Interesting, high-ceilinged, traditional Scottish drinking shop with a wooden floor around the mahogany bar.

The three-bay gantry has carved pillars and supports old whisky casks. A fine painting of the nearby Bass Rock overlooks the bar.
🏨 🍴 ≈ ♣ ♣

Nether Abbey Hotel
20 Dirleton Avenue (A198, 1/2 mile W of centre)
☎ (01620) 892802
11-11 (midnight Thu, 1am Fri & Sat); 12-11 Sun
Caledonian Deuchars IPA; Marston's Pedigree; guest beers Ⓐ
Family-run, comfortable hotel in a Victorian villa with a spacious extended bar/bistro area offering a good selection of four real ales. An ideal base for exploring the East Lothian coast. Children's certificate.
🏨 🍴 🍺 🍴 ≈ ♣ P

SOUTH QUEENSFERRY
Ferry Tap
36 High Street
☎ (0131) 331 2000
11.30-11.30 (midnight Thu, 12.30am Fri & Sat); 12.30-11.30 Sun
Caledonian Deuchars IPA, 80/-; Orkney Dark Island; guest beers Ⓗ
Well-appointed, intriguing, one-roomed, L-shaped bar with an unusual barrel-vaulted ceiling in a 300-year-old building, decorated with brewery artefacts and ephemera. 🍺 ≈ (Dalmeny)

WEST CALDER
Railway Inn
43 Main Street
☎ (01506) 871475
11.30-2.30, 5-midnight (11 Tue-Wed); 11-midnight Sat; 6.30-midnight Sun
Beer range varies Ⓗ
Well-kept bar/lounge with a large island bar and very attractive central wooden gantry. Window screens and a corniced-ceiling add to its appeal. Pool played in back room; children welcome for meals until 7pm (eve meals end at 8pm). 🍴 🍺 ♣

Join CAMRA
Join the fight to save cask beer: use the format the back of the Guide

INDEPENDENT BREWERIES
Belhaven: Belhaven
Caledonian: Edinburgh
Fisherrow: Edinburgh
Restalrig: Edinburgh

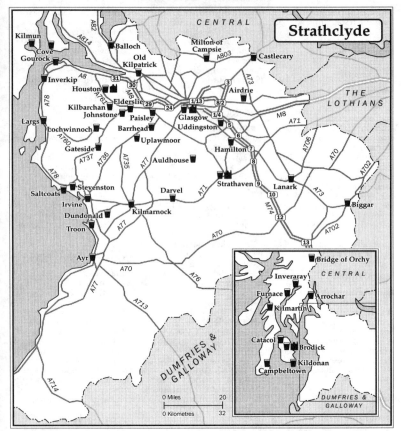

Authority areas covered: Argyll & Bute UA, City of Glasgow UA, Dunbarton & Clydebank UA, East Ayrshire UA, East Dunbartonshire UA, East Renfrewshire UA, Inverclyde UA, North Ayrshire UA, North Lanarkshire UA, Renfrewshire UA, South Ayrshire UA, South Lanarkshire UA

Note: Licensing laws permit no entry after 12pm to pubs in Gourock and Inverkip.

AIRDRIE

Cellar
79 Stirling Street
☎ (01236) 764495
11 (12.30 Sun)-midnight
Beer range varies Ⓗ
Multi-level public bar stocking two guest beers, frequently from Scottish micros. It also has a wide selection of whisky and is a past winner of the *Malt Whisky Pub of the Year* award. It has a better claim than most to be the best pub in the North Lanarkshire district.
🍺 ≠

ARROCHAR

Village Inn
On A814, 1/2 mile S of A83 jct
☎ (01301) 702279
11-midnight (1am Fri & Sat); 11-midnight Sun
Orkney Dark Island; guest beers Ⓗ
A warm, friendly, homely,

atmosphere awaits at this idyllic lochside inn. The front garden overlooks the head of Loch Long whilst offering breathtaking views of the Arrochar Alps including the Cobbler Mountain. Good food; the beer range includes Maclay's seasonal brews.
🍺 🏶 ⇌ ◖ ▶ Å P

AULDHOUSE

Auldhouse Arms
12 Langlands Road
☎ (01355) 263242
12.30-11 (midnight Thu-Sat); 12.30-11 Sun
Belhaven 80/- Ⓗ
200-year-old, totally unspoilt village pub, featuring real fires in the snugs off the bar, old paintings, plates and photographs. Well worth a visit. 🍺 Q ⇌ 🍴 ♣ P

AYR

Chestnuts Hotel
52 Racecourse Road (A719,

1 mile S of centre)
☎ (01292) 264393
11 (12 Sun)-midnight
Beer range varies Ⓗ
Recently extended lounge bar offering three changing beers, at least one of which is from a Scottish brewer. Children welcome, with a garden play area provided.
🍺 🏶 ⇌ ◖ ▶ P

Geordie's Byre
103 Main Street (over river towards Prestwick)
☎ (01292) 264925
11-11 (midnight Thu-Sat); 12.30-11 Sun
Caledonian Deuchars IPA; guest beers Ⓐ
This traditional local regularly offers four guest ales from a wide range of breweries. The small public bar can be very busy eves and Sat afternoon. The comfortable lounge (open Thu-Sat eves) displays an abundance of memorabilia.
🍴 ≠ (Newton-on-Ayr)

Old Racecourse Hotel
2 Victoria Park (A719, 1 mile
S of centre)
☎ (01292) 262873
11-midnight (12.30am Fri & Sat);
12-midnight Sun
Tetley Bitter; guest beers Ⓗ
This large, comfortable
lounge bar, which boasts an
unusual fire as a centrepiece,
regularly offers three guest
ales, one usually from a
Scottish brewery. High
quality meals and a pool/TV
room are added attractions.
🏨 Q ✿ ⇄ ◖ ▮ P

BALLOCH

Balloch Hotel
Balloch Road (near station)
☎ (01389) 752579
11-midnight (1am Fri & Sat); 11-midnight
Sun
Beer range varies Ⓗ
Ale is served in the tartan-
clad lounge/restaurant which
affords views of the southern
end of Loch Lomond. Ale can
also be ordered in the rear
bar. The outdoor area has
tables and grassy banks,
popular with swans, ducks,
walkers, tourists and locals.
✿ ⇄ ◖ ▮ ◭ ▲ ⇌ ♣ P

BARRHEAD

Waterside Inn
Glasgow Road, The Hurlet
(A736 near Hurlet)
☎ (0141) 881 2822
11-11 (midnight Fri & Sat); 12.30-11 Sun
Beer range varies Ⓗ
Comfortable bar/lounge
attached to a restaurant. Easy
chairs around a real fire make
for a relaxed atmosphere and
a traditional feel is enhanced
by the stained glass gantry
and local pictures.
🏨 ✿ ◖ ▮ ◭ ◭ P

BIGGAR

Crown Hotel
109 High Street
☎ (01899) 220116
11 (12.30 Sun)-1am
Beer range varies Ⓗ
Popular lounge bar in a small
hotel at the centre of an
attractive Borders village.
🏨 ✿ ⇄ ◖ ▮ ▲

BRIDGE OF ORCHY

Bridge of Orchy Hotel
☎ (01838) 400208
11-11 (midnight Fri & Sat); 12-11 Sun
Caledonian Deuchars IPA, 80/- Ⓗ
Hotel catering for travellers
and hillwalkers, situated on
the main road before it
climbs up to Rannoch Moor.
Bar service is in the
modernised wood-panelled
Caley Bar to one side of the
main hotel.
🏨 Q ✿ ⇄ ◖ ▮ ⇌ P

BRODICK

Brodick Bar
Alma Road (off Shore Road)
☎ (01770) 302169
11-midnight; closed Sun
Beer range varies Ⓗ
Long, white building next to
the post office: the large
bar/restaurant features a dark
wood modern decor; the
other bar room has light
wood rustic tables. Popular
with tourists and locals, it
offers a wide-ranging menu
chalked on blackboards. The
only daytime winter choice
in Brodick.
🏨 Q ◖ ▮ ◭

Duncan's Bar
Kingsley Hotel, Shore Road
(on seafront)
☎ (01770) 302531
11-2.30; 6-midnight (11-midnight
summer; closed mid-Oct – mid-March) 6-
midnight (11-midnight summer) Sun
Beer range varies Ⓗ
Large, comfortable bar at the
side of a seaside hotel,
affording excellent views
from the large front garden
across the bay to Goat Fell. It
hosts regular music sessions
in summer; the bar now
closes in winter. Always
stocks one beer from Arran
Brewery.
🏨 Q ✿ ⇄ ◖ ▮ P

Ormidale Hotel
Knowe Road (off A841, W
end of village)
☎ (01770) 302293
12-2.30 (not winter); 4.30-midnight;
12-midnight Sat & Sun
Beer range varies Ⓐ
Fine sandstone building
overlooking the sports field.
A small, friendly public bar,
plus a conservatory that gives
extra space and hosts music
in summer. The original tall
founts on a boat-shaped bar
serve local ales.
Accommodation available in
summer.
🏨 Q ✿ ⇄ ◖ ▮ ◭ P

CAMPBELTOWN

Commercial Inn
Cross Street
☎ (01586) 553703
11 (12.30 Sun)-1am
**Caledonian Deuchars IPA; guest
beers** (occasional) Ⓗ
Friendly, family-run pub,
very popular with locals and
most welcoming to visitors.
◭ ▲

CASTLECARY

Castlecary House Hotel
Main Street
☎ (01324) 840233
11-11 (11.30 Thu-Sat); 12.30-11 Sun
Beer range varies Ⓗ
Small, private hotel with

three drinking areas (most
ales are served in the Castle
Lounge). The highly
recommended restaurant
serves high teas. The village is
on the site of one of the
major forts on the Antonine
Wall.
Q ✿ ⇄ ◖ ▮ ◭ ⌣ P

CATACOL

Catacol Bay Hotel
☎ (01770) 830231
11 (12.30 Sun)-1am
**Caledonian Deuchars IPA; guest
beers** Ⓗ
Free-standing, white building
adjacent to the Twelve
Apostles, a listed terrace of
former estate houses. Great
views across the Kilbrannan
Sound to Kintyre can be
enjoyed from inside and out.
A marquee is set up for music
in summer. Sun carvery.
🏨 Q ✿ ⇄ ◖ ▮ ♣ P

COVE

Knockderry Hotel
204 Shore Road (B833)
☎ (01436) 842283
11.30-midnight; 12.30-11 Sun
Beer range varies Ⓗ
Architectural gem
boasting superb wood
panelling throughout,
situated on the picturesque
Rosneath Peninsula, offering
fine views over Loch Long.
A snooker room and a
large garden are added
attractions.
🏨 ✿ ⇄ ◖ ▮ P

DARVEL

Loudounhill Inn
On A71, 3 miles E of Darvel
☎ (01560) 320275
12-2.30 (not Wed), 5-11 (not Tue); 12-
midnight Sat; 12.30-2.30, 4.30-11 Sun
Beer range varies Ⓗ
Family-owned old
coaching inn near Loudoun
Hill, the site of an 11th-
century battle. It has a small,
cosy bar with an open fire
and a larger
lounge/restaurant with a
conservatory opening on to a
garden. Families welcome.
🏨 ✿ ⇄ ◖ ▮ ♣ P

DUNDONALD

Castle View
29 Main Street (B730)
☎ (01563) 851112
11-11 (midnight Fri & Sat); 12.30-11
Sun
Beer range varies Ⓗ
Former hotel in an historic
village whose impressive
castle dates from the 14th
century. It has a relaxing bar
area in what is otherwise
mainly a restaurant.
Q ✿ ◖ ▮ P

ELDERSLIE

Ring of Bells/Wallace Tavern
183 Main Road
☎ (01505) 322053
11-midnight (1am Fri; 12.45 Sat);
12.30-midnight Sun
Houston St Peter's Well Ⓗ
Real ale is served both the
comfy lounge (the Ring of
Bells) and the basic bar. It is
situated on the Paisley-
Johnstone bus route and, for
the more active, the
Glasgow-Irvine cycle route.
🏠 🕭 ♣ P ⚲

FURNACE

Furnace Inn
Off the main road
☎ (01499) 500200
5-midnight; 4-1am Fri; 12-1am Sat and
summer; 12.30-midnight (1am summer)
Sun
Beer range varies Ⓗ
Welcoming, stone-built pub
where the bar was once a
post office and the adjoining
dining area was formed from
the adjacent house. Only
licensed in 1987, the pub
plays an important role in
the social life of this
previously dry village. Meals
served Easter-Oct. The
accommodation is self-
catering.
🏨 ⚘ 🛏 🕭 🚹 🕭 P

GATESIDE

Gateside Inn
39 Main Road (B777, 1 mile E
of Beith)
☎ (01505) 503362
11-2.30, 5-11 (11-midnight Sat); 12.30-
11 Sun
Beer range varies Ⓐ
Cosy country inn with a
modernised timber and
stone-clad interior, in a small
village near Beith. The eating
area is to the rear, and the
main seating area is partially
screened from the bar. The
beer comes from Houston
Brewery. Eve meals served
Thu-Sun.
⚘ 🕭 P

GLASGOW

1901
1534 Pollokshaws Road,
Shawlands (Haggs Rd jct)
☎ (0141) 632 0161
12-11 (midnight Fri & Sat); 12-11 Sun
**Caledonian Deuchars IPA; Taylor
Landlord; guest beers** Ⓗ
Corner pub with large
wooden floored bar area,
offering ample seating and
standing room. It stocks four
guest ales and a small foreign
bottled beer selection
Children welcome until 9pm.
🕭 🚹 🕭 (Shawlands/Pollokshaws
W) 🍴

Allison Arms
720 Pollokshaws Road
☎ (0141) 423 1661
11-11 (midnight Fri & Sat); 12.30-11
Sun
Belhaven 80/-; Ⓟ **guest beers** Ⓗ
Friendly tenement pub on
the south side of Glasgow.
Five guest ales and a large
selection of foreign bottled
beers are usually on offer.
🚆 (Queen's Pk) ♣

Babbity Bowsters
16-18 Blackfriars Street (off
High St)
☎ (0141) 552 5055
11 (12.30 Sun)-midnight
Beer range varies Ⓐ
Conversion of an 18th-
century building attributed
to Robert Adam, the name
derives from a dance of the
time. The café-style bar is
frequented by professionals
and media folk. The excellent
food is served in the bar and
upstairs restaurant and three
or four beers are usually
available. Boules played.
🏨 Q ⚘ 🛏 🕭 🚹 🚆 (High St)
🚇 (Buchanan St) ♣ 🍴 P

Blackfriars
36 Bell Street, Merchant City
(near City Halls)
☎ (0141) 552 5924
12-midnight, including Sun
Ind Coope Burton Ale; Tetley Bitter;
Ⓗ **guest beers** Ⓗ
Bar used by locals,
commuters, students and
young people. Its pleasant
atmosphere is enhanced by
low lighting, candles and fine
brass-framed mirrors. The
beer range includes a
Houston brew, plus bottled
and draught foreign beers.
Live jazz and comedy
performed Sun eve. Food is
served 12-11.
🕭 🚹 🚆 (High St/Argyle St)
🚇 (Buchanan St) 🍴

Bon Accord
153 North Street (near
Mitchell Library)
☎ (0141) 248 4427
11-11.45; 12.30-11 Sun
**Caledonian Deuchars IPA; McEwan
80/-; Theakston Best Bitter, Old
Peculier; guest beers** Ⓗ
City pub made over in the
traditional T&J Bernard style
featuring dark wood and
chalkboards throughout the
long front bar and larger
seating area at the rear. Tours
are available of the extensive
cellar that allows the
conditioning of six or more
guest beers from
independents.
🕭 🚹 🕭 🚆 (Charing Cross)

Clockwork Beer Co.
1153-1155 Cathcart Road
(King's Park Rd jct)
☎ (0141) 649 0184

11-11 (11.30 Tue & Thu; midnight Thu-
Sat); 12.30-11 Sun
**Caledonian Deuchars IPA, 80/-;
guest beers** Ⓟ
Large, open-plan modernised
bar over two floors with its
own brewery visible on the
ground floor. It stocks four
guest ales, three Belgian and
two Czech beers, plus a wide
range of German and Belgian
bottled beers. Children's
certificate. 🛏 🕭 🚹 🕭 🚆 (Mt
Florida) 🍴 P ⚲ 🍽

Mitre Bar
12 Brunswick Street (off
Trongate)
☎ (0141) 552 3764
11-midnight; 12.30-8 Sun
Belhaven 60/-; guest beers Ⓗ
Possibly Glasgow's smallest
bar, worth finding for its
Victorian horse-shoe
bar, snob screens and gantry.
An escape from the theme
pubs and shops for visitors
and locals, it stocks a
selection of bottled and
draught continental beers.
Food is served in the bar and
upstairs lounge. 🕭 🚆 (Argyle
St) 🚇 (St. Enochs) ♣

Station Bar
55 Port Dundas Road
☎ (0141) 332 3117
11 (12.30 Sun)-midnight
**Caledonian Deuchars IPA; guest
beers** Ⓗ
Traditional street-corner
local, frequented by office
workers and professionals,
including musicians. The pub
boasts a fine McEwan's
mirror and won the *Pub and
Landlord of the Year* award for
Glasgow in 1999. A must.
🚆 (Queen St) 🚇 (Coucaddens)

Three Judges
141 Dumbarton Road (Byres
Rd jct)
☎ (0141) 337 3055
11-11 (midnight Fri ; 11.45 Sat); 12.30-
11 Sun
Maclay 80/-; guest beers Ⓗ
Traditional west-end local
which sold its 2000th beer
just in time for the
Millennium. A frequent
winner of local CAMRA
awards, it is a haven for locals
and visitors alike.
🚆 (Partick) 🚇 (Kelvin Hall)

GOUROCK

Spinnaker Hotel
121 Albert Road
☎ (01475) 633107
11-11.30 (12.30am Sat); 12.30-
midnight Sun
Beer range varies Ⓐ
Recently extended family-run
hotel on the Clyde coast.
Meals may be taken in the
dining room or on the patio
(weather permitting). Enjoy
the excellent views of the

Clyde coast towards Dunoon and beyond.

🏠 ➡ ◖▐ ⇸

HAMILTON

George

18 Campbell Street
☎ (01698) 424225
11 (12.30 Sun)-11.45
Beer range varies Ⓗ
This family-run local is a frequent winner of CAMRA's Lanarkshire *Pub of the Year* award. It runs its own twice-yearly beer festival and has three beers on tap the rest of the time.
◖ ⇸ (Central)

HOUSTON

Fox & Hounds

South Street
☎ (01505) 612448
11-midnight (1am Fri & Sat); 12.30-midnight Sun
Houston Killellan, Barochan, St Peter's Well, Formakin, seasonal beers; guest beers Ⓗ
This country pub is home to Houston Brewery. Real ale is served in all three bars and guest beers are always available in the lounge bar. It hosts regular beer festivals.
Q ◖▐ ⌸ P

INVERARY

George Hotel

Main Street East
☎ (01499) 302111
11 (12 Sun)-12.30am
Caledonian Deuchars IPA; guest beer Ⓗ
Long-established hotel, now in the fifth generation of ownership by same family. It has a lively public bar to one side, whilst a renovated lounge bar and dining areas take up much of the remaining ground floor. Very handy for a pint after visiting historic Inveraray jail.
🏠 🏠 ➡ ◖▐ ⌸ 🏔 P

INVERKIP

Inverkip Hotel

Main Street (off A78, near Kip marina)
☎ (01475) 521478
11-2.30, 5-11 including Sun
Beer range varies Ⓗ
Genuine local in a small unspoilt village on the Clyde coast. Enjoy the relaxed, cosy atmosphere in the lounge bar and adjacent alcoves. No ale is served in the public bar.
Q ➡ ⇸ P

IRVINE

Marina Inn

110 Harbour Street
☎ (01294) 274079
11.45-3, 5.45-midnight (11.45-midnight

summer); 11.45-1am Fri & Sat; 12.30-midnight Sun
Belhaven St Andrew's Ale Ⓗ
Attractive harbourside lounge bar, next to the Magnum Centre and the Scottish Maritime Museum. The emphasis is on food at lunchtime and early eve, with an extensive menu; the beer price is above average for the area. It hosts a folk session Tue eve. Children's certificate. 🏠 ◖▐ ⇸

Ship Inn

120-122 Harbour Street (by Magnum Leisure Centre)
☎ (01294) 279722
11-2.30; 5-11 (midnight Fri); 11-midnight Sat; 12.30-11 Sun
Theakston Best Bitter Ⓗ
Harbourside pub, the oldest licensed premises in town, offering high quality, good value meals. Quiet atmosphere lunchtime and early eve, but it gets livelier later on. The comfortable atmospheric interior features an unusual decorated ceiling. Children's certificate.
Q 🏠 ◖▐ ⇸

JOHNSTONE

Coanes

26 High Street
☎ (01505) 322924
11-11.30 (1am Fri, 11.45 Sat); 6.30-11.30 Sun
Caledonian Deuchars IPA, 80/-; Houston Killellan; Orkney Red Macgregor, Dark Island; guest beers Ⓗ
Town-centre local featuring a comfortable bar with fake beams and open-plan lounge where a full *à la carte* menu puts a strong emphasis on seafood. Up to five guest beers on tap.
◖▐ ⌸ ⇸

KILBARCHAN

Trust Inn

8 Low Barholm
☎ (01505) 702401
11.30-11.30 (midnight Thu-Sat, 12.30 am Fri); 12.30-11 Sun
Caledonian Deuchars IPA; Ind Coope Burton Ale; guest beers Ⓗ
Lounge bar where intimate recesses, a beamed ceiling and brasses make for a comfortable, traditional rural village local. Varied menu served (snacks only Sun). The beers come from the Tapster's Choice range.
◖▐ ⇸ (Milliken Pk)

KILDONAN

Breadalbane Hotel

On loop road through village
☎ (01770) 820284
11-midnight (1am Thu-Sat); 11-midnight Sun

Beer range varies Ⓗ
White-painted hotel on the shore at the southern end of the island. Enjoy the views to Pladda and Ailsa Craig from the front lounges. The main bar has a large stone fireplace, a corner bar and a pool table. The beers come mostly from Arran and Houston breweries.
🏠 Q 🏠 ➡ ◖▐ ♣ P

KILMARNOCK

Hunting Lodge

14-16 Glencairn Square (opp. Safeway)
☎ (01563) 522920
11-3, 5-midnight; 11-1am Fri & Sat; 12-midnight Sun
Beer range varies Ⓗ
Seven handpumps dispense an ever-changing range of beers in a large lounge bar that has distinct areas for games and dining. A venue for a local folk club (Thu) and quizzes (Mon). Children's certificate.
◖▐ ♿ ⊬

Wheatsheaf

Unit 5, Portland Gate (next to viaduct)
☎ (01563) 572483
11-midnight (1am Thu-Sat); 11-midnight Sun
Caledonian Deuchars IPA, 80/-; Courage Directors; Theakston Best Bitter; guest beers Ⓗ
Large, open-plan Wetherspoon's house with a modern theme, drawing a varied clientele. Food is served all day.
Q 🏠 ◖▐ ♿ ⇸ ⊬

KILMARTIN

Kilmartin Hotel

☎ (01546) 510250
11 (12 Sun)-1am
Beer range varies Ⓗ
Whitewashed hotel near the site of an ancient settlement. A small cosy bar leads to games and dining rooms. Note the old, long unused McGlashan handpumps on the bar with a gantry backed by brewery mirrors. A Caledonian beer is on tap regularly, plus a guest beer in summer when the home-cooked meals are available all day.
🏠 Q 🍴 🏠 ➡ ◖▐ 🏔 P ⊬

KILMUN

Coylet Inn

Loch Eck (A815, 9 miles N of Dunoon)
☎ (01369) 840426
11-2.30; 5-11; 5-midnight Fri & Sat; 12.30-2.30, 6-11 Sun
Caledonian Deuchars IPA; McEwan 80/-; guest beer Ⓗ
Attractive, inviting lochside

421

bar where you can relax around the open fire after a day's fishing, touring or walking in the hills. Boat hire available. Good bar food.
🏚 ☸ ⛴ ◖▶ 👗 P

LANARK
Horse & Jockey
56 High Street
☎ (01555) 664825
11-1am (12.45 late); 12.30-11 Sun
Beer range varies Ⓗ
Public bar, with a lounge/diner at the rear, on the main street of this historic market town. It received an award from CAMRA's Scottish Pubs Group in 1999 in recognition of a refurbishment that actually enhanced its character.
◖▶ ⇌

LARGS
Clachan
14 Bath Street (B7025, off Main Street)
☎ (01475) 672224
11-midnight (1am Thu-Sat); 12.30-11 Sun
Belhaven 80/-, IPA Ⓗ
Single-bar pub with a games room, just off the main street, near the seafront and ferry terminal. It stocks a good selection of whiskies and hosts live music Fri eve and a quiz Mon eve.
👗 ♣ ♠

LOCHWINNOCH
Brown Bull
33 Main Street (Largs Road, off A737)
☎ (01505) 843250
12-11; 11-midnight Fri; 11-11.45 Sat; 12.30-11 Sun
Houston St Peter's Well; Orkney Dark Island; guest beers Ⓗ
Extremely friendly country pub in a small village, featuring a low ceiling and pictures by local artists. The restaurant serving Scottish fare, opened in the Spring of 2000, has built up a good reputation. Close to Glasgow-Irvine cycle track, it serves regularly changing beers from the nearby Houston brewery.
🏚 Q ▶ 👗 ⇌

MILTON OF CAMPSIE
Kincaid House Hotel
Birdston Road OS650759
☎ (0141) 776 2226
12-midnight (1am Fri; 11.45 Sat); 12-midnight Sun
Taylor Landlord; guest beer Ⓗ
Notable for its impressive 'castle' frontage, the bar features beams, horse-brasses and an Alloa Brewery mirror;

the semi divided lounge has a fireplace, and there is also a conservatory. Used by locals and visitors alike it holds a Carlsberg-Tetley *Cellarmanship* award. Caravan park nearby.
🏚 ☸ ⛴ ◖▶ 👗 ▲ P

OLD KILPATRICK
Ettrick
159 Dumbarton Road
☎ (01389) 872821
11-11.45 (12.45 Fri & Sat); 12.30-11.45 Sun
Caledonian Deuchars IPA Ⓗ
Late Victorian village local with a lively public bar, handy for the Forth and Clyde canal. Smoking restrictions apply at mealtimes in the lounge, where children are admitted if dining until 7pm.
☸ ◖▶ ⇌ (Kilpatrick) P ✂

PAISLEY
Gabriels
33 Gauze Street (Silk St jct)
☎ (0141) 887 8204
11-midnight (1am Fri & Sat); 12.30-midnight Sun
Caledonian Deuchars IPA; Ind Coope Burton Ale; guest beers Ⓗ
Comfortable town-centre lounge with an oval-shaped bar and a raised dining area. Its annual Spring beer festival is now in its sixth year. No food Sun eve. Children's certificate.
◖▶ 👗 ⇌ (Gilmour St)

Hogshead
45 High Street
☎ (0141) 840 4150
11-midnight (1am Fri & Sat); 12.30-midnight Sun
Boddingtons Bitter; Ⓗ **guest beers** Ⓗ/Ⓖ
Comfortable open-plan town-centre lounge, popular with all ages during the week, and students at the weekend. Music is generally not overpowering. Meals are popular all day. Always one beer from Houston available.
◖▶ ⇌ (Gilmour St) ✂

Wee Howff
53 High Street
☎ (0141) 889 2095
11-11 (11.30 Wed & Thu; 1am Fri; midnight Sat); closed Sun
Caledonian Deuchars IPA; Ind Coope Burton Ale; guest beers Ⓗ
Small pub near the University with a warm and friendly atmosphere. The landlord was the first Burton *Master Cellarman* in Scotland.
⇌ (Gilmour St)

SALTCOATS
Salt Cot
7 Hamilton Street

☎ (01294) 465924
11-midnight (1am Thu-Sat); 12.30-midnight Sun
Caledonian Deuchars IPA, 80/-; Courage Directors; Theakston Best Bitter; guest beers Ⓗ
A very attractive conversion of a former cinema by Wetherspoon's. Although it is large, it is broken up by changes in level. Food is available all day.
Q ◖▶ 👗 ⇌ ✂ 🖥

STEVENSTON
Champion Shell Inn
5 Schoolwell Street (off A738)
☎ (01294) 463055
11-midnight (1am Thu-Sat); 12.30-midnight Sun
Beer range varies Ⓗ
Attractive bar/lounge in a listed building – the oldest inhabited building in the 'Three Towns'. Its name derives from an 18th-century competition for drinking mead from a shell. Two guest beers come from a variety of sources. Good food. ◖▶ 👗 ♣

STRATHAVEN
Weavers
1 Green Street
☎ (01357) 522648
5-midnight (1am Fri); 2-1am Sat; 7-1am Sun
Beer range varies Ⓗ
Refurbished pub at the centre of an attractive small town, once a major centre of the weaving industry. Decorated with many pictures of Hollywood stars, it gets very busy Fri and Sat eves, but is comfortable and friendly at other times. It specialises in Scottish beers.

TROON
Ardneil Hotel
51 St Meddans Street
☎ (01292) 311611
11-midnight; 12-midnight (11pm winter) Sun
Draught Bass; guest beers Ⓗ
Popular hotel next to the station and close to golf courses. The bar and restaurant are frequented by locals and visitors alike. The bar hosts a regular Wed eve quiz.
☸ ⛴ ◖▶ ⇌ ♣ P ✂

McKay's Ale House
69 Portland Street (A759)
☎ (01292) 311079
11-12.30am; 12.30-midnight Sun
Caledonian 80/-; guest beers Ⓗ
Friendly and often lively town-centre lounge bar. The three guest ales rotate on a regular basis as demonstrated by the large pumpclip collection. Occasional live music. ☸ ◖▶ ⇌

CAMRA National Pub Inventory: Black Friar, London EC4

UDDINGSTON

Rowan Tree ☆
60 Old Mill Road (next to Tunnocks bakery)
☎ (01698) 812678
11 (12.30 Sun)-midnight
Caledonian Deuchars IPA; Orkney Dark Island; guest beer Ⓗ
Vibrant community pub retaining an unspoilt wooden interior, two fireplaces and some splendid, rare brewery mirrors. A former CAMRA Scottish *Pub of the Year.*
♨ ◗ Å ⇌ ♣ P

UPLAWMOOR

Uplawmoor Hotel
66 Neilston Road (off A736, Barrhead-Irvine road)
☎ (01505) 850565
12-2.30, 5-11 (midnight Fri); 12-midnight Sun
Houston Barochan, Formakin Ⓗ
Welcoming family hotel in a village location, comprising an excellent cocktail lounge/retaurant, where the central fireplace forms a focal point, plus another lounge bar. Not

easily accessible, but well worth the effort to find.
❀ ⛵ ◗ ▸ & P

INDEPENDENT BREWERIES

Arran: Brodick
Clockwork: Strathaven
Heather: Glasgow
Houston: Houston
McLachlans: Glasgow
Miller's Thumb: Glasgow

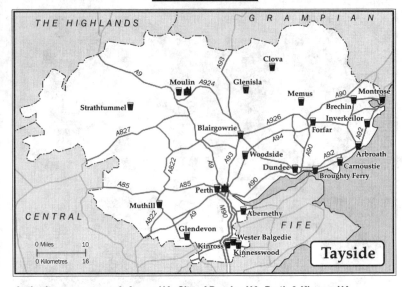

Authority areas covered: Angus UA, City of Dundee UA, Perth & Kinross UA

ABERNETHY

Cree's Inn
Main Street
☎ (01738) 850714
11-2.30, 5-11; 11-11 Sat; 12.30-11 Sun

Beer range varies Ⓗ
Formerly a listed farmhouse now a welcoming village pub, in the shadow of Abernethy Round Tower, with an oak-beamed lounge and adjacent snug area. Evening meals and accommodation should be available on publication of this *Guide*. ⚬ Q ⇔ ◖ ▶ P ✗

ARBROATH

Lochlands Bar
14-16 Lochlands Street
☎ (01241) 873286
11-11; (midnight Fri & Sat); 12.30-11 Sun

Beer range varies Ⓗ
Busy popular local, with a bar showing Sky sports channels that gets crowded on football days; quiet comfortable lounge. Beers are usually very well priced.
⊞ ≈ ♣

Old Brewhouse
Old Shorehead
☎ (01241) 879945
11-11; 12.30-11 Sun

Orkney Dark Island Ⓗ
Newly refurbished, bright, comfortable bar; all areas now serve food. It overlooks the harbour area – waves break over the building in bad weather.
❀ ◖ ▶

Viewfield Hotel
1 Viewfield Road

☎ (01241) 872446
11-midnight (1am Fri & Sat); 12.30-midnight Sun

Beer range varies Ⓗ
Small, friendly-run hotel: a long basic saloon bar with pool area and a large comfortable lounge. The juke box can be noisy at times.
⇔ ◖ ▶ ⊞ ♣ P

BLAIRGOWRIE

Ericht Ale House (Meadow Arms)
13 Wellmeadow
☎ (01250) 872469
11-11 (11.45 Fri & Sat); 12.30-11 Sun

Beer range varies Ⓗ
Traditional, town-centre pub, since 1802, full of local character. Renamed in 2000 it hosts occasional live music at weekends and stocks a range of up to six beers.
Q ⊞ 🖥

Rosemount Golf Hotel
Golf Course Road
☎ (01250) 872604
11-11 (11.45 Fri & Sat); 12-11 Sun

Beer range varies Ⓗ
Friendly traditional hotel with a comfortable lounge and restaurant area. Popular with visitors and locals alike it makes an ideal base for walking and golf.
⚬ ❀ ⇔ ◖ ▶ ﴾ P 🖥

BRECHIN

Dalhousie Bar
1 Market Street
☎ (01356) 622096
11-midnight (1am Fri & Sat); 12.30-11 Sun

Beer range varies Ⓗ
Wood-panelled, high-ceilinged bar displaying an eclectic collection of objects on walls. It is popular and gets busy with locals.
♣

BROUGHTY FERRY

Fisherman's Tavern
10-12 Fort Street (by lifeboat station)
☎ (01382) 775941
11-midnight (1am Fri & Sat); 12.30-midnight Sun

Belhaven St Andrew's Ale; Boddington's Bitter; guest beers Ⓗ
Now a hotel covering three houses, the public bar remains much the same – welcoming, busy and traditional, but there are also three other drinking areas. Deservedly popular, the sole Scottish entry in every edition of this *Guide* – wheelchair access is via the back door. ⚬ Q ☕ ⇔ ﴾ 🖥 ≈ (limited service) ♣

Old Anchor
48 Gray Street
☎ (01382) 737899
11-midnight; 12.30-11 Sun

Caledonian Deuchars IPA; guest beers Ⓗ
Open-plan lounge with one large, one small and one tiny drinking area bearing a seafaring theme. No-smoking restrictions apply lunchtime only. Two to three guest beers on tap.
☕ ◖ ▶ ≈ (limited service)

CARNOUSTIE

Station Hotel
Station Road
☎ (01241) 852447
12-2.3, 4.30-midnight; 12-1am Fri; 12-midnight Sat & Sun

Beer range varies Ⓗ
Basic wood-panelled, friendly bar featuring a theme of railways and locomotives. It is dominated by a giant TV screen which can be noisy at times. Pool room.
🏨 🚄 ⇌ ♣

CLOVA

Clova Hotel
On B955, 15 miles N of Kirriemuir
☎ (01575) 550222
11-midnight; 12.30-11 Sun
Beer range varies Ⓗ
At the end of a long drive or trek through stunning dramatic scenery waits this climbers' bar. Warm, friendly, and surprisingly busy considering its isolation, it offers varied activities during spring and summer.
🏨 ✿ 🚄 ◖ 🍴 ♣ P

DUNDEE

Drouthy Neebors
142 Perth Road
☎ (01382) 202187
11-midnight; 12.30-11 Sun
Belhaven 80/-, Caledonian Deuchars IPA Ⓗ
Scottish 'theme bar' that honours Robert Burns (hence the name). Popular with students from the nearby art college, it features lots of dark wood and Burns quotes on walls. Meals served weekdays until 6pm.
◖ ▶ ⇌ (Taybridge)

Frew's
117 Strathmartine Road
☎ (01382) 810975
11-midnight; 12.30-11 Sun
Draught Bass; McEwan 80/-; guest beer Ⓗ
Fine, traditional bar with two refurbished lounges, one bearing a sporting theme. This busy local is mobbed when United play at home – handy for both football grounds. Bar snacks available.
🍴 ♣

Hogshead
7-9 Union Street
☎ (01382) 205037
11-midnight; 12.30-11 Sun
Boddington's Bitter; Caledonian 80/-; guest beers Ⓗ
Smaller and cosier than many of the Hogshead chain, with secluded nooks. It serves good pub grub and up to five guest beers.
Q ◖ ▶ 🚄 ⇌ (Taybridge) ○

Mickey Coyle's
21-23 Old Hawkhill
☎ (01382) 225871
11--3, 5.30-midnight; 11-midnight Fri & Sat; 7-11 Sun
Broughton Greenmantle; guest beers Ⓗ

Named after a former well-known Dundee publican, this pub was once in the Guinness Book of Records as the shortest pub name – MC, recalled by a large mirror. The long, dimly-lit lounge, is popular for food (eve meals end 7.45) and gets busy during university term-time.
◖ ▶ ⇌ (Taybridge) ♣

Phoenix
103 Nethergate
☎ (01382) 200014
11 (12.30 Sun)-midnight
Caledonian Deuchars IPA; Orkney Dark Island; Taylor Landlord; guest beer (occasional) Ⓗ
Busy pub on the fringe of the city centre in the cultural quarter near the new Dundee contemporary arts centre. The reconstructed Victorian bar boasts an excellent gantry.
◖ ▶ ⇌ (Taybridge)

Speedwell Bar (Mennies) ☆
165-167 Perth Road
☎ (01382) 667783
11-midnight; 12.30-11 Sun
Beer range varies Ⓗ
This unspoilt Edwardian gem featuring etched glass windows and snob screens draws an eclectic mix of customers. The landlord also owns the Fishermans Tavern in Broughty Ferry.
Q 🚄 ♿ ⇌ (Taybridge) ♣ ⌿

Tavern
168 Perth Road
☎ (01382) 227135
11-midnight; 12.30-11 Sun
Caledonian Deuchers IPA, 80/- Ⓗ
Cosy, wood-panelled bar displaying framed pictures of old Dundee.
⇌ (Taybridge)

FORFAR

O'Hara's
41 High Street West
☎ (01307) 464350
11-2.30, 5.30-11; 11-11 Fri & Sat; closed Sun
Beer range varies Ⓗ
This beautiful, waxed wood-panelled and beamed bar is up a flight of steep stairs. Named after Scarlett O'Hara the bar and downstairs bistro bear a Burns/Scottish farming theme.
🏨 ◖ ▶

Queen Street Bar
45a Queen Street
☎ (01307) 462722
11-midnight; closed Sun
Inveralmond Lia Fail Ⓗ
Very friendly, comfortable town-centre pub, popular and busy. Dine in the restaurant off the bar area, or bar itself which also serves

very good food (eve meals available Fri and Sat). ◖ P

GLENDEVON

Tormaukin Hotel
☎ (01259) 781252
11 (12 Sun)-11
Beer range varies Ⓗ
Originally an 18th-century drovers' inn the Tormaukin provides a warm, welcoming atmosphere. It is situated in a peaceful rural setting surrounded by the Ochil Hills. The two beers are normally from Harviestoun.
🏨 Q 🚄 🚄 ◖ ▶ ▲ P

GLENISLA

Glenisla Hotel
On B591, 10 miles N of Alyth
☎ (01575) 582223
11-11 (12.30am Fri; midnight Sat); 12.30-11 Sun
Inveralmond Independence; Lia Fail; guest beer (summer) Ⓗ
Pleasant, former coaching inn, surrounded by beautiful countryside. The wood-panelled bar on two levels gives access up some steps to a delightful garden. A centre for riding, walking fishing and other pursuits.
🏨 ✿ 🚄 ◖ ▶ ♿ ▲ ♣ P

INVERKEILOR

Chance Inn
Main Street (off A92)
☎ (01241) 830308
12-2.30, 5-11; 12-11 Sat; 12.30-11 Sun
Beer range varies Ⓗ
Small, square bar in an old coaching inn, often crowded with locals, and an adjoining lounge and restaurant. Usually three beers on tap.
🚄 ◖ ▶ 🍴 ♣ P

KINNESSWOOD

Lomond Country Inn
Main Street
☎ (01592) 840253
11-11 (midnight Fri & Sat); 11-11 Sun
Beer range varies Ⓗ
Popular country inn affording a fine view over Loch Leven from the open-plan bar/restaurant.
🏨 Q 🚄 ✿ 🚄 ◖ ▶ ♿ P ⌿

KINROSS

Kirklands Hotel
High Street
☎ (01577) 863313
11-2.30, 5-11 (11.45 Sat); 12.30-11 Sun
Beer range varies Ⓗ
Traditional, small town hotel with a comfortable bar and lounge area, recently refurbished. Eve meals served 6-8.30pm.
Q 🚄 ◖ ▶ 🍴

Choosing Pubs

Pubs in the Good Beer Guide are chosen by CAMRA members and branches. There is no payment for entry, and pubs are inspected on a regular basis by personal visits, not sent a questionnaire once a year, as is the case with some pub guides. CAMRA branches monitor all the pubs in their areas, and the choice of pubs for the Guide is often the result of voting at branch meetings. However, recommendations from readers are warmly welcomed and will be passed on to the relevant CAMRA branch: please use the form at the back of the Guide.

MEMUS

Drover's Inn
5 miles N of Forfar
☎ (01307) 860322
12-2.30, 6-midnight; 12-1am Fri & Sat; 12.30-midnight Sun
Beer range varies H
Small, pine-panelled snug bar featuring dark flagstones and a black leaded range, with a long seating area off; this part was once the village post office. The building now has a restaurant and conservatory.
🏠 🕸 🕔 ▶ ⟁ 👜 P

MONTROSE

George Hotel
22 George Street
☎ (01674) 675050
11-2, 5-11; 11-11 Sat; 12-11 Sun
Beer range varies H
A hopbine-hung bar counter is the focus in this long restaurant/bar, that has comfortable seats and benches covered in wine-coloured plush. Four handpumps frequently stock local ales.
🚪 🕔 ▶ 🕸 P ⊬

Market Arms
95 High Street
☎ (01674) 673384
11-midnight; 12.30-2.30, 6.30-11 Sun
Beer range varies H
Busy, town-centre bar, totally 'vinylised' in the 1960s, apart from a beautiful stained glass panel with a roundel of a lighthouse. The friendly bar staff serve a mainly young clientele.
🕸 ♣

Sharky's
21 George Street
☎ (01674) 677375
11.30-midnight (1am Fri & Sat); 12.30-midnight Sun
Beer range varies H
Modern bar/bistro upstairs and downstairs featuring unclad stone and brick walls, unpolished floorboards and an underwater theme of sharks, boats and fishing nets. It stocks a huge range of bottled beers. Live music often performed weekends.
🕔 🕸

MOULIN

Moulin Inn
11-13 Kirkmichael Road (A924, 3/4 mile NE of Pitlochry)
☎ (01796) 472196
11-11 (11.45 Fri & Sat); 12-11 Sun
Moulin Light, Braveheart, Ale of Atholl, Old Remedial H
The oldest part of the Moulin Hotel, first opened 1695. This traditional old country inn, warmed by two log fires, provides a good choice of home-prepared local fare combined with beer from the adjoining brewhouse.
🏠 Q 🚻 🚪 🕔 ▶ 🕸 ⚓ P

MUTHILL

Village Inn
6 Willoughby Street
☎ (01764) 681451
11-11 (closed Mon Jan-March); 11-midnight Fri & Sat; 12.30-11 Sun
Beer range varies H
Friendly village local, formerly a coaching inn, with a wooden floor and real fire. The comfortable public bar bears a farming theme, the restaurant area a hunting theme. Up to four beers available in summer.
🏠 Q 🕸 🚪 🕔 ▶ P

PERTH

Greyfriars
15 South Street
☎ (01738) 633036
11-11 (11.45 Fri & Sat); 7-11 Sun
Beer range varies H
Cosy, but vibrant city-centre pub, with a friendly atmosphere within a short distance of the silvery Tay. The house beer, Friars Tipple, is brewed by Inveralmond.
🕔 🕸

Old Ship Inn
Skinnergate
☎ (01738) 624929
11-2.30, 5-11; 11-11.45 Fri & Sat; closed Sun

Caledonian Deuchars IPA; Greene King Abbot; guest beers H
Established in 1665, this is one of the oldest licensed houses in Perth. A traditional city-centre pub it has great local character and hosts regular dominoes nights.
Q 🕔 ⟁ ♣

Ring O'Bells
6 St John's Place
☎ (01738) 633493
11-11 (11.45 Fri & Sat); 12.30-11 Sun
Broughton Greenmantle; Harviestoun Bitter & Twisted, Schiehallion; guest beers H
This large, friendly, family-owned pub has a children's certificate and ramps for wheelchair access. A healthy emphasis is put on Scots micros.
🕸 🕔 ▶ ⟁ 🕸

STRATHTUMMEL

Loch Tummel Inn
On B8019, approx. 3 miles W of Queen's View
☎ (01882) 634272
11-11 (may close afternoons); 12.30-11 Sun; closed winter
Moulin Braveheart H
Old coaching inn, in an idyllic rural setting of magnificent scenery. Overlooking Loch Tummel. Closed from Oct to mid-March.
Q 🕸 🚪 🕔 P

WESTER BALGEDDIE

Balgeddie Toll Tavern
At B919/A911 jct, near Kinross
☎ (01592) 840212
11-2 (3 peak season), 5-11; 12.30-11 Sun
Ind Coope Burton Ale; guest beer H
Comfortable, rural tavern featuring wooden beams and an open fire. Originally a toll house circa 1534, it has three seating areas and a small bar.
🏠 Q 🕸 🕔 ▶ P

WOODSIDE

Woodside Inn
Main Street (A94 S of Coupar Angus)
☎ (01828) 670524
11-2, 5-11 (11.45 Fri); 11-11.45 Sat; 12.30-11 Sun
Beer range varies H
Small roadside bar and restaurant where children are welcome.
🏠 🕸 🕔 ▶ P

INDEPENDENT BREWERIES

Inveralmond: Perth
Moulin: Moulin

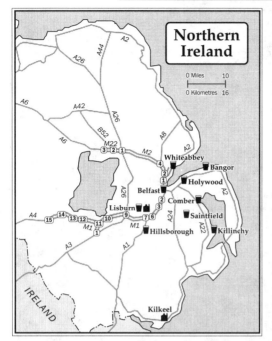

Northern Ireland

0 Miles 10

0 Kilometres 16

IRELAND

BANGOR

Esplanade

12 Ballyholme Esplanade
(opp. Ballyholme beach)
☎ (028) 902 42986
11.30-11; 12.30 Sun
Beer range varies Ⓗ
Converted three-storey
seafront house where up to
three ales are dispensed in
the bar, but will be served in
the lounge on request. The
patio affords views of Belfast
Lough. Food is served in the
bar and lounge, as well as the
upstairs dining room which
offers an *à la carte* menu.
Wheelchair WC.
🏚 Q ❀ ◖ ▶ ⊞ ⅗

BELFAST

Beaten Docket

48 Great Victoria Street (opp.
Europa Hotel)
☎ (028) 902 42986
11.30-midnight (1am Thu-Sat); 11.30-
midnight Sun
Beer range varies Ⓗ
Modern, city-centre bar
where the upstairs
entertainment/function
room has a dance floor.
There is a spacious ground-
floor bar with a small snug
and a real fire. Lunches
continue until 5 or 6pm Thu-
Sun. 🏚 ◖ ▶ ⅗ ⇌ (Gt Victoria St)

Botanic Inn

23-27 Malone Road
☎ (028) 906 60460
11-midnight (1am Wed-Sat); 11-midnight
Sun

Cains Bitter; Whitewater Glen Ale,
Belfast Special Bitter; guest beer Ⓗ
Large, recently rebuilt pub in
the university area, popular
with students and sports
fans, it is very busy eves.
🏚 ◖ ⅗

Kitchen Bar

16-18 Victoria Square (off
Cornmarket)
☎ (028) 903 24901
11.30-11; 12-7 Sun
Beer range varies Ⓗ
Traditional city-centre pub,
offering good value food and
ever-changing beers on three
handpumps. Photographs of
the demolished Empire
Theatre, which stood next
door, predominate in the
parlour bar.
🏚 ◖ ⊞ ⇌ (Central)

Rotterdam Bar

52-54 Pilot Street (from York
Gate, head towards the docks
for 300 yds)
☎ (028) 907 46021
11.30-1am; 11.30-1am Sun
Beer range varies Ⓗ
Old-fashioned bar near
Clarendon Dock. One of
Belfast's best music venues it
stages music three or four
times a week, plus outdoor
summer concerts. Children
are allowed in; great
atmosphere. No food Sun.
Sometimes real ale is not
available in the summer.
🏚 Q ❀ ◖ ⇌ (York Gate)

Try also: **McHughs**, Queens
Sq (Free)

COMBER

North Down House

Belfast Road (Castle St
roundabout)
☎ (028) 918 72242
12-midnight (1am Fri & Sat); 12.30-
midnight Sun
Beer range varies Ⓗ
Old pub (over 100 years),
with a modern outlook. A
partial refurbishment has
created a modern but cosy
lounge and an extended bar
(with pool table) run by
friendly staff. It hosts a disco
Fri; live band Sat.
⅗ ♣

HILLSBOROUGH

Hillside

21 Main Street (halfway up
the 'hill')
☎ (028) 926 82765
12-11 (1am Fri & Sat); 12-10 Sun
Beer range varies Ⓗ
Top-class bar featuring four
handpumps. Food is available
at the bar, in the refectory or
upstairs in the recommended
restaurant. The atmosphere is
warm and welcoming. The
bar manager is a real ale
enthusiast and there is a
good beer festival in July.
🏚 Q ❀ ◖ ▶ ⊞ ⅗ ⅄

Pheasant

410 Upper Ballynahinch
Road (halfway between
Lisburn and Ballynahinch)
☎ (028) 926 8056
11.30-midnight; 12.30-10.30 Sun
Beer range varies Ⓗ
Public bar and restaurant at
the heart of the Co. Down
countryside. Although it can
be difficult to find, it is well
worth the effort for its top
quality meals and beers from
Whitewater. Children
welcome.
🏚 Q ❀ ◖ ▶ ⊞ ⅗ P ⅍

Plough

3 The Square (top of the
'hill')
☎ (028) 926 82985
11.30-11; 12-10 Sun
Beer range varies Ⓗ
Popular village pub with
much wood panelling and a
variety of ornaments. Food is
served at the bar, upstairs in
Clouseau's and in a bistro at
the back. Children are not
admitted. For oyster-lovers
the Plough is heavily
involved in the annual
Oyster Festival held in
September. 🏚 Q ❀ ◖ ▶ ⊞ ⅄

HOLYWOOD

Dirty Duck

2 Kinnegar Road
☎ (028) 905 96666
11-midnight (1am Fri & Sat); 12.30-
midnight Sun

CAMRA National Pub Inventory: The Red Lion, St James, London

Beer range varies Ⓗ
Pub on the south side of
Belfast Lough, where four
handpumps offer ale from all
over the British Isles.
Excellent food, regular live
music and occasional beer
festivals are added
attractions. The family room
is open during the day.
Current Northern Ireland
CAMRA *Pub of the Year* 2000.
🏚 🍴 🏵 ◑ ▶ ≉

KILLINCHY
Daft Eddie's
Skettrick Island (Whiterock
Road, 1 mile N of Killinchy)
☎ (028) 975 41615
11.30-11 (1am Fri & Sat); 12.30-10 Sun
Whitewater Belfast Special Bitter Ⓗ
Friendly pub overlooking
Whiterock Bay and marina.
Enjoy great scenery and great
food in the bar/restaurant or
patio (book). A nautical
theme is enhanced by tile
and wood floors and a
driftwood partition. Spot the
windburnt witches and ship's
figurehead; ask about the real
'Daft Eddie'.
🏚 Q 🏵 ◑ ▶ 🍴 ♿ P

LISBURN
Taproom
Hilden Brewery, Hilden (300
yds from Hilden railway halt)
☎ (028) 926 63863
11.30-3.30 (eve by appointment);
11.30-3.30 Sun
Hilden Ale, Molly Malone's Porter Ⓗ
This is a licensed restaurant
attached to Hilden
Brewery. It stands in the
grounds of a large Georgian
house, a mile from Lisburn.
Only beers brewed on the
premises are available.
There is a brewing/Hilden
history exhibition and
tours around the brewery can
be arranged. Children
admitted.
🏚 Q 🏵 ◑ ▶ ≉ (Hilden) P

SAINTFIELD
White Horse
49 Main Street
☎ (028) 975 10417
11-11; closed Sun
Beer range varies Ⓗ
This whitewashed pub and
off-licence dominates the
main street. Five handpumps
in the main bar supply the

adjoining off-licence with
mostly Whitewater ales. It
hosts an annual beer festival
in autumn. Excellent food;
families are always welcome.
🏚 Q 🍴 ◑ ▶ ♿ ✕

WHITEABBEY
Woody's Lounge
607 Shore Road, Jordanstown
(off main road between
Belfast and Carrickfergus)
☎ (028) 908 63206
11.30-11; 1-10 Sun
Beer range varies Ⓗ
Comfortable, cosy, lounge
bar offering a friendly
welcome and good service. It
is adorned with fine prints of
the village and surrounding
area. Off-sales are available of
its good range of beers; also a
very good wine choice and
selection of malts.
Q ◑ ☗ P

INDEPENDENT
BREWERIES

Hilden: Lisburn
Whitewater: Kilkeel

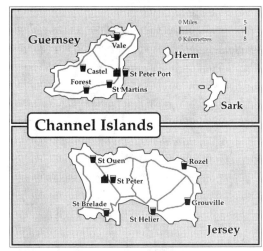

Guernsey

CASTEL

Fleur du Jardin
Kings Mills
☎ (01481) 257996
10.30-11.45; 12-3.15 Sun
Guernsey Sunbeam, seasonal beers H
Country pub with an extensive garden in an attractive setting. Fresh local produce features on the daily changed restaurant menu. The large public bar is closed during winter months.
Q ❀ ⇔ ◖ ▶ P

FOREST

Venture Inn
New Road (next door to Mallard Cinema, 2 mins from airport)
☎ (01481) 263211
10.30-midnight; closed Sun
Randalls Patois H
Traditional Guernsey hostelry with a lively and popular public bar and a recently extended lounge bar. It enjoys regular local custom but all visitors are made welcome. Well worth a visit. A mild is occasionally available. Eve meals are served Mon-Sat (Fri-Sat winter).
⚌ ◖ ▶ ⊟ P

ST MARTINS

Ambassador Hotel
Sausmarez Road
☎ (01481) 238356
12-3, 6-11.45; 12-3.30 Sun
Beer range varies H
This bar is popular with locals as well as hotel guests; situated just down from Sausmarez Manor, it was the local CAMRA *Pub of the Year* 1999. Meals can be taken in

the bar area or conservatory; the pub is closed Sun eve except for diners. The beers are supplied by Guernsey Brewery.
⇔ ◖ ▶ P

Captain's Hotel
La Fosse
☎ (01481) 238990
10-11.45; 12-3.30, 6.30-11 (closed winter) Sun
Guernsey Sunbeam H
Popular local near Moulin Huet Bay in a pretty country area, but still close to St Peter Port.
❀ ⇔ ◖ P

ST PETER PORT

Cock & Bull
Lower Hauteville
☎ (01481) 722660
11.30-2.30, 4-11.45; 11.30-11.45 Fri & Sat; closed Sun
Beer range varies H
Popular pub on a hill above the town centre, where four handpumps provide a range of beers, including Ringwood brews. Live music is staged from 9pm Tue and Thu, plus occasional other days. Snacks usually available at lunchtime (not Sat).

Drunken Duck
Le Charroterie (opp. Government Offices)
☎ (01481) 725045
11-11.30; 12-3.30 (closed eve) Sun
Badger IPA, Best Champion, Tanglefoot; guest beer H
Friendly, two-roomed pub offering a small range of tasty lunchtime snacks. Popular with all age groups, visitors are made especially welcome. It hosts occasional live music (Irish, folk). Three of the beers listed above are always on tap.
◖

Ship & Crown
North Esplanade
☎ (01481) 721368
10-11.45; 12-3.30, 6-10 Sun
Guernsey Pirates, Sunbeam, seasonal beers H
Providing picturesque views of the harbour this pub is popular with all ages. It serves good value meals in generous portions with plenty of daily specials. Three Crowns beer is Guernsey's Braye Ale rebadged.
◖

VALE

Houmet Tavern
☎ (01481) 242214
10-11.45; closed Sun
Guernsey Braye H
This pub is popular with locals and visitors for its friendly public (Anchor) bar with darts and billiards and the quiet front bar that affords superb views over the bay. Tasty meals are served promptly Mon-Sat lunch and Tue-Wed, Fri-Sat eves (7-8.45).
Q ❀ ◖ ⊟ ♣ P

Jersey

GROUVILLE

Seymour Inn
La Rue du Puits Mahaut
☎ (01534) 854558
10-11; 11-11 Sun
Guernsey Sunbeam; Tipsy Toad Jimmy's Bitter; guest beer H
Friendly local in the south-eastern corner of the island. Real ale is served in the public bar where there is a large range of games and activities; also two other lounges and a patio. Good no-nonsense food is well-priced (not served Sun). The guest beer is supplied by Tipsy Toad.
⚌ Q ❀ ◖ ▶ ⊟ ♿ ♣ P

Try also: Pembroke, Coast Rd (Randalls)

ROZEL

Rozel Bay Inn
☎ (01534) 863438
11-11, including Sun
Draught Bass; Courage Directors; guest beers H
Two-bar village pub in picturesque Rozel Bay, serving award-winning food. Live in the right parishes and the pub will send a bus to collect you!
⚌ Q ❀ ◖ ▶ ⊟ ▲ ♣ P

ST BRELADE

Old Smugglers Inn
Ouaisne Bay
☎ (01534) 741510

CAMRA National Pub Inventory: House of McDonnell, Ballycastle, Co Antrim

11-11, including Sun
Draught Bass; guest beers Ⓗ
17th-century granite pub in a beautiful setting by the beach. Jersey's only true free house, it offers a changing range of beers. A cosy bar is complemented by extensive eating areas. Local CAMRA *Good Food Pub* 1999.
🏾 Q ➳ ◑ ▲ P ✚

Try also: La Pulente, La Route de la Pulente (Randalls)

ST HELIER
Lamplighter
Mulcaster Street (near bus station)
☎ (01534) 723119
11-11, including Sun
Draught Bass; Boddingtons Bitter; Marston's Pedigree; Theakston Old Peculier; guest beer Ⓗ
The only gas-lit pub on Jersey serves the largest range of beers, plus Bulmers traditional cider. Good value no-nonsense food is also available. Local CAMRA *Pub of the Year* 1999.
◑ ♣ ✚ ☺

Original Wine Bar
Bath Street
☎ (01534) 871119
11-11; 4.30-11 Sun
Beer range varies Ⓗ
This relaxed drinking environment with pastel colours and soft furnishings

is very popular with town workers, especially women. It has an increasing real ale range and was voted local CAMRA *Best Newcomer* 1999.
◑ ♿ ✄

Prince of Wales Tavern
Hillgrove Street
☎ (01534) 737378
10-11; 11-2 Sun
Draught Bass; Marston's Pedigree; guest beers Ⓗ
Traditional market pub off a cobbled street. The pleasant garden at the back is a real sanctuary in busy St. Helier.
Q ❀ ◑

Try also: Dog & Sausage, Hilary St (Randalls)

ST MARTIN
Royal Hotel
La Grande Route de Faldouët
☎ (01534) 856289
9.30 (11 lounge)-11; 11-11 Sun
Boddingtons Bitter; guest beer Ⓗ
Spacious, popular pub next to St Martin's church. It has a large children's play area (families welcome). A quiet, comfortable lounge contrasts with the busy public bar. The upstairs restaurant is popular with locals (real ale on request; excellent food).
🏾 Q ➳ ❀ ◑ ▶ 🍴 ♿ ▲ ✚ ✄

ST OUEN
Moulin de Lecq

Grève de Lecq
☎ (01534) 482818
11-11, including Sun
Guernsey Sunbeam; Tipsy Toad Jimmy's Bitter; guest beer Ⓗ
Converted, 12th-century working watermill featuring a moving drive wheel behind the bar. The extensive outdoor area, with children's play area, is great in summer. Situated in a pleasant valley by the beach, it hosts occasional beer festivals. Local CAMRA *Best Family Pub* 1999.
🏾 Q ➳ ❀ ◑ ▶ P

ST PETER
Star & Tipsy Toad Brewery
La Route de Beaumont
☎ (01534) 485556
10-11.30; 11-11.30 Sun
Tipsy Toad Jimmy's Bitter, MMAD Toad; guest beer Ⓗ
Tipsy Toad brew-pub, this spacious, busy and popular pub caters well for drinkers, diners and families. Brewery tours are available and live music is a feature.
🏾 ➳ ❀ ◑ ▶ ♿ ♣ P

INDEPENDENT BREWERIES

Guernsey: St Peter Port
Randalls: St Peter Port
Tipsy Toad: St Peter

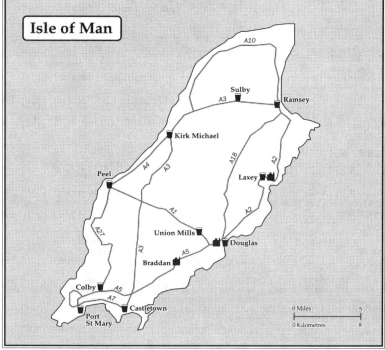

Isle of Man

A10

Sulby
A3
Ramsey

Kirk Michael

A4
A3
A18
A2

Peel
Laxey

A1
A2
A27

A3
Union Mills
Douglas
A5
Braddan
Colby
A5
A7
Castletown
Port
St Mary

0 Miles 5
0 Kilometres 8

CASTLETOWN

Castle Arms (Gluepot)
Quayside (opp. Castle
Rushen)
☎ (01624) 824673
12-11 (11.45 Fri & Sat); 12-3, 7-10.30
Sun
**Okells Mild, Bitter, seasonal
beers** Ⓗ
Comfortable, friendly local,
right on the harbourside; the
only pub to appear on a
banknote (a Manx £5 note).
🍺 🍴 ⇌ ♣

Ship
Hope Street (near harbour)
☎ (01624) 824959
12-11 (11.45 Fri & Sat); 12-3, 7-10.30
Sun
Okells Bitter Ⓗ
Back-street local; the Chart
Room bar upstairs affords
panoramic harbour views.
🏨 🍺 🏠 ⇌ P

Sidings
Victoria Road (by station)
☎ (01624) 823282
12-11 (midnight Fri & Sat); 12-3,
7-10.30 Sun
**Bushy's Bitter; Marston's Pedigree;
Theakston Mild, Best Bitter;
Wadworth 6X; guest beers** Ⓗ
Friendly pub, stocking a good
range of beers.
🏨 🍴 🍺 ⇌ P

COLBY

Colby Glen Hotel
Main Road (A7)

☎ (01624) 834853
12-11 (11.345 Fri & Sat); 12-3. 7-10.30
Sun
Okells Mild, Bitter Ⓗ
Comfortable village pub;
busy eves. It also offers a
good bar menu at lunchtime.
🏨 🍴 🍺 🏠 🍺 ⇌ P

DOUGLAS

Albert Hotel
3 Chapel Row (near bus
station)
☎ (01624) 673632
10-11 (midnight Fri & Sat); 12-3,
7-10.30 Sun
Okells Mild, Bitter Ⓗ
Well-patronised harbour free
house. Jough's is brewed
specially for the pub by Isle
of Man breweries.
🏠 ♣

Foresters Arms
St Georges Street (off Athol
St)
☎ (01624) 676509
12-11 (midnight Fri & sat); 12-3,
7-10.30 Sun
Okells Mild, Bitter Ⓗ
Excellent, basic local. A
former Castletown house –
note the windows.
🏨 🏠 ⇌ (IMR) ♣

Manor Hotel
School Road, Willaston
(housing estate in Upper
Douglas)
☎ (01624) 676957
12-11 (midnight Fri & Sat); 12-3,
7-10.30 Sun

Okell's Mild, Bitter Ⓗ
This old manor house has a
lounge appropriate to its
origins featuring extensive
wood panelling and
comfortable seating. Popular
with the nearby FE college
fraternity.
🏨 🏠 ♣ P

Old Market Inn
Chapel Row (near bus
station)
☎ (01624) 675202
10-11 (midnight Fri & Sat); 12-3,
7-10.30 Sun
Bushy's Bitter; Okell's Bitter Ⓗ
Small, busy, free house which
has defied the current
tendency to change layout
and decor according to the
latest fashion. Its traditional
features are clearly an
attraction, with the two bars
and hallway often crowded
eves and weekends.
🏨 🏠 ♣

Railway Hotel
Bridge Road (by station)
☎ (01624) 673157
12-11 (midnight Fri & Sat); 12-3,
7-10.30 Sun
Okells Mild, Bitter Ⓗ
A convenient stopping
point before or after your
steam railway journey, this
pub offers a reasonably
priced selection of
cooked meals weekdays.
Comfortable and rather basic,
large bar.
🏨 🍴 🏠 ♣

Rovers Return
11 Church Street
☎ (01624) 676459
12-11 (midnight Fri & Sat); 12-3,
7-10.30 Sun
Bushy's Mild, Bitter H
Main Bushey's outlet in
central Douglas, the Rovers
will be enjoyed by supporters
of Blackburn's footballers (see
their memorabilia in a back
room). The front room
displays photos of old
Douglas.
🏠 ♣

Saddle Inn
North Quay (off the harbour)
☎ (01624) 673161
12-11 (midnight Fri & Sat) 12-3,
7-10.30 sun
**Cains Bitter; Okells Mild, Bitter,
Spring Ram** H
Quayside local well-
supported by locals and
crews of boats moored
nearby.
⇌ ♣

Terminus Tavern
Strathallan Crescent (N end
of promenade)
☎ (01624) 624312
12-11 (midnight Fri & Sat); 12-3,
7-10.30 Sun
Okells Bitter, seasonal beers H
Convenient place for families
and transport enthusiasts to
pause whilst changing from
horse trams to electric trams.
No meals Sun; eve meal
available Thu. 🏠 Q 🐎 🕮 🌜 🕮
& ⇌ (MER)♣ P

Waterloo Hotel
77 Strand Street
☎ (01624) 670468
12-11 (midnight Fri & Sat); 12-3,
7-10.30 Sun
Okells Mild, Bitter H
Modest, two-roomed pub in
the main pedestrianised
shopping street with a
notable tiled façade.
♣

Woodbourne Hotel
Alexander Drive
☎ (01624) 676754
12-11 (11.30 Fri & Sat); winter closed,
2-4.30 weekdays; 12-3, 7-10.30 Sun
**Okells Mild, Bitter, seasonal
beers** H
Imposing brick-built edifice
in uptown Douglas. It
maintains a gents' only bar,
plus a lounge and public bar.
Q 🕮

KIRK MICHAEL
Mitre Hotel
Main Road
☎ (01624) 878244
12-11 (midnight Fri & Sat); 12-3,
7-10.30 Sun
Marston's Pedigree; Okells Bitter H
Reputed to be the oldest pub
on the island, it offers
excellent food, live music

eves, and a popular TT
vantage point.
🏠 🐎 🌜 🕮 🕮 & 🌜 ♣ P

LAXEY
Mines Tavern
Captains Hill
☎ (01624) 861484
12-11 (11.45 Fri & Sat); 12-3, 7-10.30
Sun
**Bushy's Bitter; Okells Bitter; guest
beers** H
Popular tourist pub, also
favoured by locals, displaying
tram artefacts in the bar; the
garden overlooks the tram
station.
Q 🌜 🕮 🕮 🌜 ⇌

PEEL
Royal Hotel
25 Atholl Street
☎ (01624) 842217
12-11 (midnight Fri & Sat); 12-3,
7-10.30 Sun
Okells Mild, Bitter H
Popular local, opposite the
bus station.
Q 🌜

White House
2 Tynwald Road
☎ (01624) 842252
12-11 (midnight Fri & Sat); 12-3, 7-
10.30 Sun
**Bushy's Bitter; Okells Mild, Bitter;
guest beers** H
Popular with young and old,
this pub has a good
atmosphere.
🏠 🕮 🌜 P 🕮

PORT ST MARY
Albert Hotel
Athol Street
☎ (01624) 832118
12-11 (11.45 Fri & Sat); 12-3,
7-10.30 Sun
**Draught Bass; Okells Bitter,
seasonal beers** H
Two-bar harbourside pub,
popular with local fishermen
and yachtsmen.
🏠 Q 🕮 ♣ P

Try also: Railway Station, at
level crossing (Okells)

RAMSEY
Swan Hotel

Parliament Square
☎ (01624) 814236
12-11 (midnight Fri & Sat); 12-3,
7-10.30 Sun
Okells Mild, Bitter H
Modern but pleasant pub on
the TT course.
🕮 🕮 ⊖ (MER)

Trafalgar
West Quay
☎ (01624) 814601
12-11 (midnight Fri & Sat); 12-3,
7-10.30 Sun
**Draught Bass; Bushy's Bitter; Cains
Bitter; guest beers** H
Local CAMRA *Pub of the Year*
1996 and '97; a good
drinking pub right on the
harbour, serving very good
food.
🏠 🐎 🕮 ⊖ (MCR) 🕮

SULBY
Sulby Glen Hotel
Main Road (A3, TT course)
☎ (01624) 897240
12-11 (midnight Fri & Sat); 12-3,
7-10.30 Sun
**Bushy's Bitter, seasonal beers;
Okells Bitter** H
Very popular, friendly pub
on the TT course, serving
excellent food. Local CAMRA
Pub of the Year 1998 and '99.
🏠 Q 🕮 🕮 & 🌜 ♣ P

UNION MILLS
Railway Inn
Main Road
☎ (01624) 853006
12-11 (midnight Fri & Sat); 12-3,
7-10.30 Sun
**Cains Bitter; Okells Mild, Bitter;
guest beers** H
Very popular pub on the TT
course. It has been in the
same family for 100 years
and serves an excellent pint
of mild.
🏠 Q 🌜 ♣ P

INDEPENDENT BREWERIES

Bushy's: Braddan
Okells: Douglas
Old Laxey: Laxey

Cask Marque
Pubs that carry the Cask Marque symbol indicate
that the licensees have successfully passed a
number of tests concerning beer quality, and
display plaques to this effect in their outlets.
However, these pubs have been chosen
independently of Cask Marque by CAMRA. The
Cask Marque symbol is added during the editing
process and Cask Marque is not involved in the
selection of pubs.

The Breweries

How to use The Breweries section

Breweries are listed in alphabetical order. The Independents (regional, smaller craft brewers and brew pubs) are listed first, followed by the Nationals and finally the major non-brewing Pub Groups. Within each brewery entry, beers are listed in increasing order of strength. Beers that are available for less than three months of the year are described as 'occasional' or 'seasonal' brews. Bottle-conditioned beers are also listed: these are beers that have not been pasteurised and contain live yeast, allowing them to continue to ferment and mature in the bottle as a draught real ale does in its cask.

Symbols

Ọ A brew pub: a pub that brews beer on the premises.

◆ CAMRA tasting notes, supplied by a trained CAMRA tasting panel. Beer descriptions that do not carry this symbol are based on more limited tastings or have been obtained from other sources.
Tasting notes are not provided for brew pub beers that are available in fewer than five outlets, nor for other breweries' beers that are available for less than three months of the year.

🗇 A CAMRA Beer of the Year in the past three years.

🛡 One of the 2000 CAMRA Beers of the Year, a finalist in the Champion Beer of Britain competition held during the Great British Beer Festival at Olympia in August 2000, or the Champion Winter Beer of Britain competition held earlier in the year.

☺ The brewery's beers can be acceptably served through a 'tight sparkler' attached to the nozzle of the beer pump, designed to give a thick collar of foam on the beer.

⊗ The brewery's beer should NOT be served through a tight sparkler. CAMRA is opposed to the growing tendency to serve southern-brewed beers with the aid of sparklers, which aerate the beer and tend to drive hop aroma and flavour into the head, altering the balance of the beer achieved in the brewery.

Abbreviations

OG stands for original gravity, the measure taken before fermentation of the level of 'fermentable material' (malt sugars and added sugars) in the brew. It is a rough indication of strength and is no longer used for duty purposes.

ABV stands for Alcohol by Volume, which is a more reliable measure of the percentage of alcohol in the finished beer. Many breweries now only disclose ABVs but the Guide lists OGs where available. Often the OG and the ABV of a beer are identical, ie 1035 and 3.5 per cent.
If the ABV is higher than the OG, ie OG 1035, ABV 3.8, this indicates that the beer has been 'well attenuated' with most of the malt sugars turned into alcohol. If the ABV is lower than the OG, this means residual sugars have been left in the beer for fullness of body and flavour: this is rare but can apply to some milds or strong old ales, barley wines, and winter beers.

*The Breweries Section was correct at the time of going to press and every effort has been made to ensure that all cask-conditioned and bottle-conditioned beers are included. But the dramatic changes in the brewing industry in late 1999 and 2000 mean that not all the beers listed here may be available.

The Independents
The champions of real ale

'If it wasn't for CAMRA we wouldn't be here'
Martin Roberts,
brewer, Cheriton Brewhouse, Hampshire

✳ **Indicates new entry since last edition**

ABBEY ALES

Abbey Ales Limited, The Abbey Brewery, 2
Lansdown Road, Bath Somerset, BA1 5EE
Tel (01225) 444437
Fax (01225) 443569
Web-site www.abbeyales.co.uk
E-mail am@abbeyales.co.uk
Tours by arrangement

Abbey Ales is the first new brewery in Bath
for more than 40 years and is the initiative of
experienced brewery sales and marketing
manager Alan Morgan. Bellringer was
launched at the Bath Beer Festival in 1997
and is the only beer produced on a regular
basis. It has now won two CAMRA festival
awards: the Cotswolds Festival, 1998 and
Devizes Festival, May 1999. Twelfth Night
(ABV 5%), a seasonal winter warmer, has
been introduced and a seasonal spring beer is
planned. The brewery supplies more than 80
regular accounts within a 20-mile radius of
Bath. Bellringer is available nationally
through selected wholesalers. No tied houses
at present.

Bellringer *(OG 1042, ABV 4.2%)* ◣
With a citrus and pale malt aroma, this
notably hoppy golden ale is light bodied,
clean tasting and refreshingly dry, with a balancing sweetness. Dry, bitter finish.

ABBEYDALE

Abbeydale Brewery, Unit 8, Aizlewood
Road, Sheffield, S Yorkshire S8 0YX
Tel (0114) 281 2712
Fax (0114) 281 2713

☺ Started in 1996 by Patrick Morton,
previously of Kelham Island, Abbeydale
plans to remain a craft brewery with the
emphasis on quality and interesting flavours.
100 pubs are supplied with guest beers.
Occasional/seasonal/special commission
beers: Steamhammer (OG 1046, ABV 4.7%),
White Christmas (OG 1052, ABV 5.2%),
Black Lurcher (OG 1070, ABV 7.2%),
James I (OG 1069, ABV 7.2%).

Matins *(OG 1035, ABV 3.6%)*

Abbeydale Bitter *(OG 1038, ABV 4.0%)*

Moonshine *(OG 1041, ABV 4.3%)*

Archangel *(OG 1047, ABV 4.7%)*

Dark Angel *(OG 1047, ABV 4.7%)*

Black Mass *(OG 1062, ABV 6.66%)*

Last Rites *(OG 1105, ABV 11.5%)*

ADNAMS

Adnams PLC, Sole Bay Brewery,
Southwold, Suffolk IP18 6JW
Tel (01502) 727200
Fax (01502) 727201
Web-site www.adnams.co.uk
E-mail info@adnams.co.uk
Shop 9.30-6.30 Mon-Sat
Tours by arrangement

⊗ The earliest recorded brewing on the site
of Adnams was in 1396 by Johanna de
Corby. The present brewery was taken over
by George & Ernest Adnams in 1857 and
turned into a public company in 1891. The
Adnams family was joined by the Loftus family in 1901, and Adnams still has three members of the family working within the company, with John Adnams as president, Simon
Loftus as chairman, and Jonathan Adnams as
joint managing director. Adnams remains
committed to brewing cask ale and
unthemed pubs. Real ale is available in 96 of
its 98 pubs, and it also supplies some 750
other outlets direct. New fermenting vessels
were due to be installed in 2001 to cope with
demand. Seasonal/occasional beers: Mild
(OG 1035, ABV 3.2%, February), Regatta (OG
1042, ABV 4.1%, summer), Tally Ho (OG
1075, ABV 6.8%, Christmas) ⌑, May Day
(OG 1049, ABV 5%, May). Two new beers
were announced in May 2000: Trinity and
Fisherman. Fisherman replaces both Oyster
Stout and Old. Extra was discontinued.

Bitter *(OG 1036, ABV 3.7%)* ▣▤◣
An excellent drinking beer, with the characteristic Adnams' aroma of hops, citrus fruits
and sulphur. The flavour is dry and hoppy,
with some fruit. The finish is long, dry and
hoppy.

Regatta *(OG 1043, ABV 4.3%)*
Pleasantly malty with a long finish.

Fisherman *(ABV 4.5%)*
A new dark beer using rye malt, crystal malt,
chocolate malt and oats as well as pale malt,
plus Goldings hops.

Broadside *(OG 1048, ABV 4.7%)* ◣
A mid-brown beer with a well-balanced
flavour of fruit, malt and hops on a bitter-
sweet base. The aroma is fruity, with some
underlying malt and hops. Bitter fruit finish.

435

Trinity *(ABV 5.2%)*
A new pale-coloured beer using wheat malt and a secret spice, with Styrian Goldings hops to be launched spring 2001.

ALCAZAR*
Alcazar Brewing Company, t/a Real Alcazar Ltd, 33 Church Street, Basford, Nottingham, Notts NG6 0GA
Tel (0115) 942 2002
Fax (0115) 978 2282
Tours by arrangement

⏺ The Fox & Crown pub was purchased in August 1999 by David Allen. The business, together with the old Fiddler's brewery, which was closed in November 1998, is now being operated as the Fox & Crown brew pub and the Alcazar Brewing Company: Alcazar is a Spanish word meaning fortress or palace. Following extensive refurbishment, a 12-barrel, full mash micro-brewery was installed in 1997. Brewing started in October 1999 with the first batch of the flagship brew, Brush Bitter. Beers: Vixen's Vice (ABV 5.2%), Brush Bitter (ABV 4.9%), New Dawn Millennium Ale (ABV 4.5%), Alcazar Ale (ABV 3.8%), Maple Magic Winter Ale (seasonal porter) (ABV 5%)

ALCHEMY
Alchemy Brewing Co, Unit 24c Lyon Road, Hersham, Surrey KT12 3PU
Tel/Fax (01932) 703860

Started brewing in July 1998, supplying local pubs and wholesalers, Alchemy supplies 20 outlets direct. Seasonal beer: Winter Linctus (OG 1045, ABV 4.5%, Nov-March). Beers: Halcyon Days (OG 1039, ABV 3.9%), Aurum Ale (OG 1046, ABV 4.6%).

ALES OF KENT*
The Ales of Kent Brewery Limited, Unit 30, Lordswood Industrial Estate, Revenge Road, Chatham, Kent, ME5 8UD
Tel/fax (01634) 669296
Web-site www.alesofkentbrewery.co.uk
E-mail info@alesofkentbrewery.co.uk
Tours by arrangement

A brewery developed by three biotechnologists, a 5-barrel brew plant was installed in April 1999 and first brewed in June of that year. Since then a small bottling line has been added. The plant currently produces eight cask ales (some seasonal) and two bottle-conditioned ales. Bottle-conditioned beers: Stiltman (OG 1041, ABV 4.3%), Smugglers Glory (OG 1046, ABV 4.8%). Seasonal beers: Smugglers Glory (OG 1046, ABV 4.8%, Sept-April), Brainstorm (OG 1080, ABV 8.0%, Winter).

Old Ma Weasel *(ABV 3.6%)*

Wealden Wonder *(OG 1035, ABV 3.7%)*

Smugglers Mild *(ABV 3.8%)*

Defiance *(OG 1039, ABV 4.1%)*

ALL NATIONS
⏺ All Nations, 20 Coalport Road, Madeley, Telford, Shropshire TF7 5DP
Tel (01952) 585747
Tours by arrangement

Brewing since 1789, in the same family since the 1930s and still known as 'Mrs Lewis's' after a previous legendary landlady, the All Nations was put up for sale in summer 2000.

Pale Ale *(OG 1032, ABV 3%)*

ALTRINCHAM*
Altrincham Brewing Company, Old Market Tavern, Old Market Place, Altrincham, Greater Manchester WA14 4DN
Tel (0161) 927 7062

A brewery launched early in 2000. At present most of the beer comes from an industrial unit in Lymm but there are plans to brew at the pub.

Poestje's Bollekes *(ABV 4.1%)*

ANN STREET
See Jersey.

ARCHERS
Archers Ales Ltd, Penzance Drive, Swindon, Wiltshire SN5 7JL
Tel (01793) 879929
Fax (01793) 879489
Shop 9-5 Mon-Fri, 9-12 Sat
Tours occasionally, by arrangement, at a cost.

⊗ Founded in 1979 in Swindon, the home of the Great Western Railway, Archers is in the former Weigh House, used for weighing and balancing the steam engines of a bygone age. Archers has become one of the premier regional breweries in the south. The beers have won many prizes including the Gold Medal at the Brewing Industry International Awards. The company supplies three tied houses and another 200 free trade outlets direct and via wholesalers. Occasional/seasonal beers: Marley's Ghost (OG 1071, ABV 7%, Dec-Jan). The brewery was bought by a pub group, Burns Leisure, in January 2000 and former owner Mark Wallington retired.

Village Bitter *(OG 1035, ABV 3.6%)* ⌻◆
A dry, well-balanced beer, with a full body for its gravity. Malty and fruity in the nose, then a fresh, hoppy flavour with balancing malt and a hoppy, fruity finish.

Best Bitter *(OG 1040, ABV 4%)* ◆
Slightly sweeter and rounder than Village, with a malty, fruity aroma and a pronounced bitter finish.

Black Jack Porter *(OG 1046, ABV 4.6%)* ◆
A winter beer: a black beer with intense roast malt dominant on the tongue. The aroma is fruity and there is some sweetness on the palate, but the finish is pure roast grain.

Golden Bitter *(OG 1046, ABV 4.7%)* ◆
A full-bodied, hoppy, straw-coloured brew with an underlying fruity sweetness. Very little aroma, but a strong bitter finish.

ARKELLS
Arkell's Brewery Ltd, Kingsdown, Swindon, Wiltshire SN2 6RU
Tel (01793) 823026
Fax (01793) 828864
Tours by arrangement

⊗ Established in 1843 and now one of the few remaining breweries whose shares are all held by one family. Managing director James Arkell is a great-great-grandson of founder John Arkell. Gradually expanding its tied estate, mainly along the M4 corridor, the brewery is committed to a continual programme of upgrading and refurbishment for its pubs. All 96 tied pubs serve real ale, which is also supplied direct to around 200 free trade accounts. Due to an unwelcome mutation, the 60-year-old yeast strain was changed in 2000, and all the beers have been re-tasted for this edition. Some of the malt comes from James Arkell's own farm. Fuggles and Goldings hops are used, with pale ale malt and crystal malt. There is a higher proportion of crystal malt in 3B and Kingsdown, which are 'parti-gyled', i.e. made from the same mash but then reduced with 'liquor' [water] to the required strength. Occasional/seasonal beers: Yeomanry (OG 1045, ABV 4.5%), Peter's Porter (OG 1050, ABV 4.8%), Noel Ale (OG 1055, ABV 5.5%, Christmas).

2B *(OG 1032, ABV 3.2%)*
Light brown in colour, malty but with a smack of hops and an astringent aftertaste. An ideal lunchtime beer, it has good body for its strength.

3B *(OG 1040, ABV 4%)*
A medium brown beer with a strong, sweetish malt/caramel flavour. The hops come through strongly in the aftertaste, which is lingering and dry.

Summer Ale *(OG 1040, ABV 4%)*
A pale, refreshing beer hopped with Styrian Goldings. It is served chilled. Available March–Nov.

Kingsdown Ale *(OG 1052, ABV 5%)*
A rich deep russet coloured beer, a stronger version of 3B. The malty/fruity aroma continues in the taste, which has a hint of pears. The hops come through in the aftertaste where they are complemented by caramel tones.

ARRAN*
Arran Brewery, Cladach, Brodick, Isle of Arran KA27 8DE
Tel (01770) 302353
Visitor centre

A brewery opened in May 2000 by Richard and Elizabeth Roberts. The brewing plant was bought from the Tipsy Toad Town House brew pub in St Helier, Jersey. It is a 20-barrel plant arranged on two floors, with the mash tun based above the copper and fermenters. The three cask beers are also available in carbonated bottled versions.

Arran Ale *(ABV 3.8%)*

Arran Dark *(4.3%)*

Blonde *(ABV 5%)*

ARUNDEL
Arundel Brewery Ltd, Unit 7C Ford Airfield Industrial Estate, Ford, Arundel, W Sussex BN18 0BE
Tel (01903) 733111
Fax (01903) 733381
E-mail arundelbrewery@telinco.co.uk
Web-site
web.ukonline.co.uk/arundelbrewery
Tours by arrangement

⊗ Set up in 1992, the town's first brewery in 60 years, Arundel produces beers from authentic Sussex recipes, without the use of additives. Its commitment to this tradition has led to steady growth and the brewery now supplies around 100 outlets. Under new ownership from September 1998, Arundel continues to serve and increase its range of occasional and seasonal beers including brewing Beards Best Bitter for Beards of Sussex (recently taken over by Greene King). Arundel has also taken on Welton's beers (qv). Occasional/seasonal beers: Hairy Mary (OG 1038, ABV 3.8%), Hoppycock (OG 1044, 4.4%), Footslogger (OG 1044, ABV 4.4%), Summer Daze (OG 1047, ABV 4.7%), Spooky (OG 1046, ABV 4.6%), Black Beastie (OG 1049, ABV 4.9%), Bullseye (OG 1050, ABV 5%), Old Conspirator (OG 1050, ABV 5%), Romeo's Rouser (OG 1053, ABV 5.3%), Old Scrooge (OG 1053, ABV 5.3%).

Arundel Best *(OG 1038, ABV 3.8%)* ⬦
A pale tawny beer with fruit and malt noticeable in the aroma. The flavour has a good balance of malt, fruit and hops, with a dry, hoppy finish.

Arundel Gold *(OG 1042, ABV 4.2%)* ⬦
A light golden ale with a malty, fruity flavour and a little hop in the finish.

ASB *(OG 1045, ABV 4.5%)*
A golden brown beer with roast malt and hop flavour giving way to a fruity, hoppy, bitter-sweet finish.

Stronghold *(OG 1050, ABV 5%)* ⬦
A good balance of malt, fruit and hops come through in this rich, malty beer.

Old Knucker *(OG 1055, ABV 5.5%)* ⬦
Dark brown old ale with a malt and fruit aroma. Malt dominates the taste and a bitter-sweet coffee aftertaste.
Brewed Sept–April.

For Beards:

Beards Best Bitter *(OG 1040, ABV 4%)* ⬦
Hints of fruit and hops in the aroma lead into a sweet, malty beer, with a dry, hoppy aftertaste.

For Oliver Hare Wholesale:

The Willies range: Little Willie (ABV 4%), Cold Willie (ABV 4.2%), Hard Willie (ABV 4.5%), Warm Willie (ABV 5.3%).

ASH VINE

Ash Vine Brewery,
Unit F, Vallis Trading Estate, Robins Lane,
Frome, Somerset, BA11 3DT
Tel (01373) 300041
Fax (01373) 300042
E-mail info@ashvine.co.uk
Web-site www.cherrypie.co.uk/ashvine
Tours by arrangement

⊗ The brewery originally started in
Wellington, Somerset in 1987, moved to
Trudoxhill, just outside Frome in 1989 and
moved again to Frome in 1998. The new
brewery has a 25-barrel brewhouse. 200
outlets are supplied direct and four pubs are
owned. Bottle-conditioned beers:
Penguin Porter (OG 1045, ABV 4.2%),
Longleat (OG 1047.5, ABV 4.5%),
Hop & Glory (OG 1052.5, ABV 5%).

Bitter (OG 1037.5, ABV 3.5%) ◈
A light gold bitter with a floral hop aroma. A
powerful, bitter hoppiness dominates the
taste and leads to a dry and occasionally
astringent finish. An unusual and distinctive
brew.

Challenger (OG 1044, ABV 4.1%) ◈
A mid-brown beer with a solid malt flavour
balanced by a good hoppy bitterness and
subtle citrus fruits. It can be sulphurous and
slightly metallic.

Black Bess Porter (OG 1045, ABV 4.2%) ◈
A dark copper-brown, bitter porter with roast
malt, hops and a sweet fruitiness. Roast malt
and hop nose; dry, bitter finish. Bottled as
Penguin Porter.

Decadence (OG 1047.5, ABV 4.5%)

Longleat (OG 1047.5, ABV 4.5%)

Hop & Glory (OG 1052.5, ABV 5%) ◈
A pale straw-coloured beer with a malt, fruit
and hop aroma. The taste and finish are bitter-sweet, with hops in abundance and some
citrus fruits. A complex, rich and warming
winter ale.

ASTON MANOR

Aston Manor Brewery Co Ltd,
173 Thimble Mill Lane, Aston,
Birmingham, W Midlands B7 5HS
Tel (0121) 328 4336
Fax (0121) 328 0139
Shop 10-6 Mon-Fri, 10-1 Sat

Aston Manor concentrates on packaged
beers, lagers and cider in plastic bottles. It
bought the Highgate Brewery in June 2000.

AVIEMORE

The Aviemore Brewery Co Ltd, Unit 12,
Dalfaber Ind Estate, Aviemore, PH22 1PY
Tel (01479) 812222
Fax (01479) 811465
E-mail aviemore.brewery@dial.pipex.com
Tours by arrangement

Aviemore started brewing in July 1997 and
bottling followed in November that year: two
ales and one lager are bottled. Four regular
beers and two seasonals are produced. The
company is looking for new premises as the
10-barrel plant and building are too small.
64 outlets are supplied direct. The company
also owns Tomintoul (qv). Seasonal beers:
Highland IPA (OG 1036, ABV 3.6%, April-
Sept), Strathspey Brew (OG 1042, ABV 4.2%,
Oct-April).

Ruthven Brew (OG 1039, ABV 3.8%)

Wolfes Brew (OG 1046, ABV 4.6%)

Golden Ale (OG 1046, ABV 4.5%)

Wee Murdoch (OG 1048, ABV 4.8%)

B&T

B&T Brewery Ltd, The Brewery, Shefford,
Bedfordshire SG17 5DZ
Tel (01462) 815080
Fax (01462) 850841
Tours by arrangement

⊗ Banks & Taylor, founded in 1981, was
restructured in 1994 under the name B&T
Brewery and has continued producing the
same extensive range of beers, including
monthly special brews together with contract
brewing for wholesalers and individual public houses. There are plans to consolidate rec-
iprocal trading throughout the country with
independent brewing companies. 60 outlets
are supplied direct and three pubs are owned.
Occasional/seasonal beers: Midsummer Ale
(OG 1035, ABV 3.5%), Bedfordshire Clanger
(OG 1038, ABV 3.8%), Santa Slayer (OG
1040, ABV, 4%), Born Free (OG 1040, ABV
4%, June) Barley Mow (OG 1038, ABV 3.8%,
September), In The Mood (OG 1043, ABV
4.3%, April), 18 Down (OG 1043, ABV 4.3%,
April), Turkeys Trauma (OG 1043, ABV 4.3%,
December), Bodysnatcher (OG 1043, ABV
4.4%, October), Guy Fawkes Bitter (OG 1045,
ABV 4.5%, November), Easter Extra (OG
1045, ABV 4.5%, April), Green Sand Ridge
(OG 1045, ABV 4.5%, May), Tinker (OG
1045, ABV 4.5%, April), Prince Henry (OG
1045, ABV 4.5%, November), Romeo's Ruin
(OG 1045, ABV 4.5%, February), R101 (OG
1047, ABV 4.7%, February), Aragon (OG
1047, ABV 4.7%, October), Crooked Hooker
(OG 1047, ABV 4.7%, March), Glider (OG
1048, ABV 4.8%, July), Emerald Ale (OG
1050, ABV 5%, March). Bottle-conditioned
beer: Edwin Taylor's Extra Stout (ABV 4.5%),
Dragonslayer (ABV 4.5%), Old Bat (ABV 6%),
Black Old Bat (ABV 6.5%), Shefford 2000
(ABV 6.5%).

Shefford Bitter (OG 1038, ABV 3.8%) ◈
A pleasant, predominantly hoppy session
beer with a bitter finish..

Shefford Dark Mild
(OG 1038, ABV 3.8%) ◈
A dark beer with a well-balanced taste.
Sweetish, roast malt aftertaste.

Dragonslayer *(OG 1045, ABV 4.5%)* ◆
A straw-coloured beer, dry, malty and lightly
hopped.

Edwin Taylor's Extra Stout
(OG 1045, ABV 4.5%) ◆
A pleasant, bitter beer with a strong roast
malt flavour.

Shefford Pale Ale (SPA)
(OG 1045, ABV 4.5%) ◆
A well-balanced beer with hop, fruit and malt
flavours. Dry, bitter aftertaste.

Shefford Old Strong (SOS)
(OG 1050, ABV 5%) ◆
A rich mixture of fruit, hops and malt is pre-
sent in the taste and aftertaste of this beer.
Predominantly hoppy aroma.

Shefford Old Dark (SOD)
(OG 1050, ABV 5%)
SOS with caramel added for colour. Often
sold under house names.

Black Bat *(OG 1060, ABV 6%)* ◆
A powerful, sweet, fruity and malty beer for
winter. Fruity, nutty aroma; strong roast malt
aftertaste.

2XS *(OG 1060, ABV 6%)* ◆
A reddish beer with a strong, fruity, hoppy
aroma. The taste is full-flavoured and the finish strong and sweetish.

Old Bat *(OG 1070, ABV 7%)* ◆
A powerful-tasting, sweet winter beer, with
bitterness coming through in the aftertaste.
Fruit is present in both aroma and taste.

BADGER

Hall & Woodhouse Ltd, The Brewery,
Blandford St Mary, Dorset DT11 9LS
Tel (01258) 452141
Fax (01258) 459528
9-5 Mon-Sat
Tours by arrangement

⊗ Founded in 1777 as the Ansty Brewery by
Charles Hall. Charles's son took George
Woodhouse into partnership and formed
Hall & Woodhouse. They moved to their present site at Blandford St Mary in 1899. Now a
well-established brewer trading under the
Badger trade name, it owns 204 pubs in the
south of England including the Gribble Inn
brew pub at Oving, West Sussex and supplies
700 outlets direct. In April 2000, Hall &
Woodhouse bought King & Barnes of
Horsham and closed the brewery in August.
It matched some of K&B's beers, which will
be available throughout the Badger estate as
well as the former Horsham company's 57
pubs. It will produce two of K&B's bottle-
conditioned beers, Cornucopia (ABV 6.5%)
and Faygate Dragon (ABV 4.7%). See also
Gribble Inn. Seasonal beer: New Timer (OG
1046, ABV 4.6%, winter).

Sussex *(OG 1033, ABV 3.5%)*
King & Barnes' beer matched at Blandford.

IPA *(OG 1034, ABV 3.6%)*
A light, smooth, thin-bodied bitter with a
slightly hoppy aftertaste. Always served with
a creamy head.

Badger Best *(OG 1039, ABV 4%)* ◆
A fine best bitter whose taste is strong in hop
and bitterness, with underlying malt and
fruit. Hoppy finish with a bitter edge.

Badger Champion Ale
(OG 1043, ABV 4.6%)

Old Ale (winter) *(OG 1045.5, ABV 4.5%)*
King & Barnes' beer matched at Blandford.

Tanglefoot *(OG 1047, ABV 5.1%)*

BALLARD'S

Ballard's Brewery Ltd, The Old Sawmill,
Nyewood, Petersfield, GU31 5HA
Tel (01730) 821301/821362
Fax (01730) 821742
Web-site www.real-ale-guide.co.uk
E-mail carola@ballards24.freeserve.co.uk
Shop 8.30-4.30 Mon-Fri, by appointment Sat-Sun
Tours by arrangement

⊗ Founded in 1980 at Cumbers Farm,
Trotton, Ballard's has been trading at
Nyewood (in W Sussex, despite the postal
address) since 1988 and now supplies around
70 free trade outlets. Occasional/seasonal
beers: Midhurst Mild (OG 1034, ABV 3.5%),
Golden Bine (OG 1042, ABV 4.2%, spring),
On the Hop (OG 1045, ABV 4.5%,
September), Wild (ABV 4.7%). Bottle-conditioned beers: Nyewood Gold (OG 1050, ABV
5%), Wassail (OG 1047, ABV 6%).

Trotton Bitter *(OG 1036, ABV 3.6%)* ◆
Amber, clean-tasting bitter. A roast malt
aroma leads to a fruity, slightly sweet taste
and a dry finish.

Best Bitter *(OG 1042, ABV 4.2%)* ◆
A copper-coloured beer with a malty aroma.
A good balance of fruit and malt in the
flavour gives way to a dry, hoppy aftertaste.

Nyewood Gold *(OG 1050, ABV 5%)* ⏢◆
Robust golden brown strong bitter, very
hoppy and fruity throughout, with a tasty
balanced finish.

Wassail *(OG 1060, ABV 6%)* ◆
A strong, full-bodied, fruity beer with a pre-
dominance of malt throughout, but also an
underlying hoppiness. Tawny/red in colour.

BANFIELD*

Correspondence to: Banfield Ales,
Wingfield Farm, Wing, Leighton Buzzard
LU7 0LD
Brewery located at: The Brewery, 6 Main
Street, Burrough-on-the-Hill, Leicestershire
Tel (07956) 246215
Fax (01296) 682632
E-mail Steve@banfield-ales.co.uk
Web-site www.banfield-ales.co.uk
Tours by arrangement for small parties

Banfield Ales started brewing in May 2000
using a small,4.5-barrel plant in the village of
Burrough-on-the-Hill. Brewing is done on a
spare-time basis at weekends rather than as a
full commercial venture. The range of beers
will expand if demand allows. Beer:
Burrough Hill Pale (OG 1035, ABV 3.5%).

BANK TOP

Bank Top Brewery, Unit 1, Back Lane, off
Vernon Street, Bolton, Lancashire, BL1 2LD
Tel (01204) 528865
Tours by arrangement Mon-Fri evenings

☺ John Feeney learnt about the brewing
business at Sunderland University and then

at Thomas McGuinness Brewery. In 1995 he set up Bank Top, originally as a partnership, but now on his own. His award-winning beers are supplied to 50-60 outlets locally, and he plans to move the brewery. Seasonal/occasional beers: Satanic Mills II, Judgement Day, Bank Top Porter, Knights of the Round Table, Santa's Claws (OG 1050, ABV 5%, Christmas).

Brydge Bitter *(OG 1038, ABV 3.8%)*

Fred's Cap *(OG 1040, ABV 4%)* ◀
Pale beer with a balance of malt, fruit and bitterness. Dry finish.

Gold Digger *(OG 1040, ABV 4%)* ◀
Golden coloured, with a citrus aroma, grapefruit and a touch of spiciness on the palate and a fresh, hoppy citrus finish.

Samuel Cromptons Ale
(OG 1042, ABV 4.2%) ◀
Amber beer with a fresh citrus-peel aroma. Well-balanced with hops and zesty grapefruit flavour and a hoppy, citrus finish.

Cliffhanger *(OG 1045, ABV 4.5%)* ◀
Mid-brown colour, malty/fruity aroma, followed by a malt, hops and fruit flavour and finish.

Smokestack Lightnin' *(OG 1050, ABV 5%)*

BANKS'S
The Wolverhampton & Dudley Breweries PLC, Banks's Brewery, Bath Road, Wolverhampton, W Midlands WV1 4NY
Tel (01902) 711811
Fax (01902) 329136
Tours by arrangement

☺ Wolverhampton & Dudley Breweries was formed in 1890 by the amalgamation of three local companies. Hanson's was acquired in 1943, but its Dudley brewery was closed in 1991 and its beers are now brewed at Wolverhampton. The 100 Hanson's pubs keep their own livery. In 1992, W&D bought Camerons Brewery and 51 pubs from Brent Walker. In 1999 W&D turned itself into a 'super regional' through the acquisition of Marston's of Burton-on-Trent and the Mansfield Brewery. Excluding Marston's and Mansfield outlets, the W&D estate numbers around 1,000, virtually all serving traditional ales, mostly through electric, metered dispense. Its pubs offer a 'full pint guarantee' by serving the beer in oversize glasses. There is also extensive free trade throughout the country, particularly in pubs and clubs. W&D plans to concentrate on such key brands as Banks's Original and Bitter, and

Marston's Pedigree; the future of other beers will be analysed.

Hanson's Mild *(OG 1034, ABV 3.3%)* ◀
A mid-to dark brown mild with a malty roast flavour and aftertaste.

Banks's Original *(OG 1036, ABV 3.5%)* ◀
A top-selling, amber-coloured, well-balanced, refreshing light mild.

Banks's Bitter *(OG 1038, ABV 3.8%)* ◀
A pale brown bitter with a pleasant balance of hops and malt. Hops continue from the taste through to a bitter-sweet aftertaste.

BARGE & BARREL
Barge & Barrel Brewery Co, 10-20 Park Road, Elland, HX5 9HP
Tel/Fax (01422) 375039

The brewery was set up by White Rose Inns (Pub Groups qv), which plans to supply local free trade customers. 42 pubs are owned, all are tied, and 41 serve cask-conditioned beer. Beers: Best Bitter (OG 1040, ABV 4%), Nettlethrasher (OG 1044, ABV 4.4%), Black Stump (OG 1050, ABV 5%), Leveller (OG 1057, ABV 5.7%), Myrtle's Temper (OG 1070, ABV 7%).

BARNGATES
Barngates Brewery Ltd, Barngates, Ambleside, Cumbria LA22 0NG
Tel/Fax (015394) 36575
Web-site: www.drunkenduckinn.co.uk
E-mail barngatesbrewery
@drunkenduckinn.co.uk
Barngates Brewery was set up in 1997 with a 1-barrel plant operated solely for the in-house use of the Drunken Duck Inn. In 1999, a brand new 5-barrel plant was installed and the brewery became a separate limited company. At present the brewery supplies 25-30 free trade outlets in Cumbria, with a capacity of 15 barrels a week.

Cracker Ale *(OG 1038, ABV 3.9%)*

Tag Lag *(OG 1044, ABV 4.4%)*

Chester's Strong & Ugly
(OG 1048, ABV 4.9%)

BARNSLEY
Barnsley Brewing Co Ltd, Wath Road, Elsecar, Barnsley, S Yorkshire S74 8HJ
Tel (01226) 741010
Fax (01226) 741009
Tours by arrangement

☺ Established in 1994 as the South Yorkshire Brewing Company, Barnsley changed its name in 1996 and brews with an old yeast culture from the town's long-defunct Oakwell Brewery. Demand continues to grow, with 200 outlets taking the beer. Seasonal beers: Mayflower (OG 1044, ABV 4.5%, spring), Ey Up, It's Christmas (OG 1048, ABV 4.8%).

Barnsley Bitter *(OG 1038, ABV 3.8%)* ◀
A pale brown, creamy and smooth bitter with a hoppy and fruity aroma and an even balance of hops and malt in the taste and in the long dry and bitter finish.

Oakwell *(OG 1039, ABV 4%)*

IPA *(OG 1041, ABV 4.2%)*

A beer dominated by fruit and hops, leading to a hoppy finish. Yellowish in colour; flowery aroma.

Black Heart *(OG 1044, ABV 4.6%)* ◗
A black stout with a hoppy aroma, and roasted malt flavour throughout. Chocolatey, bitter finish.

Glory *(OG 1046, ABV 4.8%)*

BARTRAMS*
Bartrams Brewery, 8 Thurston Granary, Thurston, Suffolk, IP31 3QU
E-mail captainbill@lineone.net
Tours by arrangement

Marc Bartram started the brewery in April 1999 and has built up a good trade with locals. Thirty outlets are supplied direct. He uses a 5- barrel plant purchased from Buffys Brewery, currently producing 10 barrels a week but Marc hopes to double the amount. There was a Bartrams Brewery between 1894 and 1902 run by Captain Bill Bartram and his image graces the pump clips. Occasional beers: Trial & Error (OG 1035, ABV 3.5%), Beer Elsie Bub (OG 1048, ABV 4.8%), Xmas Holly Daze (OG 1065, ABV 7%).

Marld *(OG 1034, ABV 3.4%)*
A traditional mild.

Premier Bitter *(OG 1037, ABV 3.7%)*

Red Queen *(OG 1039, ABV 3.9%)*

Bees Knees *(OG 1042, ABV 4.2%)*

Jester Quick One *(OG 1044, ABV 4.4%)* ◗
A darker than average best bitter that is more malty than hoppy, with hints of fruit in the aroma.

Captain's Stout *(OG 1048, ABV 4.8%)*

Captain Bill Bartrams Best Bitter *(OG 1048, ABV 4.8%)*

BARUM
Barum Brewery Ltd, c/o The Reform Inn, Pilton, Barnstaple, Devon EX31 1PD
Tel (01271) 329994
Fax (01271) 321590
Tours by arrangement

In 1996 the Combe Brewery in Ilfracombe was purchased and relocated to the Reform Inn in Barnstaple. Barum supplies some 60 pubs and Barnstaple Rugby Club. Seasonal beers: Gold (OG 1040, ABV 4%, summer), Barnstablasta (OG 1066, ABV 6.6%, winter).

BSE *(OG 1037, ABV 3.5%)*

Original *(OG 1044, ABV 4.4%)*

Barumburg Cask Lager *(OG 1050, ABV 5.1%)*

Challenger *(OG 1056, ABV 5.6%)*

BATEMAN
George Bateman & Son Ltd, Salem Bridge Brewery, Wainfleet, Lincolnshire PE24 4JE
Tel (01754) 880317
Fax (01754) 880939
Web-site: www.bateman.co.uk
E-mail: jaclynbateman@bateman.co.uk
Shop
Tours by arrangement

⊠ A family-owned brewery established by the present chairman's grandfather in 1874. Originally the beer was brewed for local farmers but now the range can be found in pubs throughout the country. A visitor centre was due to open in 2000. The current George, his wife Pat, daughter Jaclyn and son Stuart are all executive directors. Batemans owns 68 pubs, 63 are tied and 67 serve cask ales. Seasonal ales come in three groups, Jolly's Follies, Special Selection and Seasonal Selection. Jolly's Follies: Hair of the Dog, January (ABV 4%), Kiss Me Quick, February (ABV 4.2%), Italian Job, March (ABV 4.3%), Burlington Bertie, April (ABV 4%), Twin Towers, May (ABV 4%), Dream On, June (ABV 4.1%), Dicky Finger, July (ABV 4.1%), Summer Prom, August (ABV 4.3%), Dingo Dash, September (ABV 4%), Octopussy, October (ABV 4.2%), Cosey Tosey, November (ABV 4.3%), Champagne Charlie, December (4.4%). Special Selection: Victory Ale, Jan-Feb (ABV 5.2%), Hooker, March (ABV 4.5%), Miss Whiplash, May (ABV 4.2%), Miss Luscious, June (ABV 4.3%), Miss Voluptuous, July (ABV 4.2%), Miss Cheeky, August (ABV 4.2%), Miss Saucey, October (ABV 4.3%), Rosey Nosey, December (ABV 4.9%), Yella Belly, April-Nov (ABV 4.2%). Seasonal Selection: Winter Wellie, Jan-Feb and Nov-Dec (ABV 4.7%), Spring Breeze, March-May (ABV 4.2%), Summer Swallow, June-Aug (ABV 3.9%), Autumn Fall, Sept-Oct (4%).

Dark Mild *(OG 1033, ABV 3%)* ⬚▣◖◗
Characteristic orchard fruit and roasted nut nose with hops evident. One of the classic mild ales, although the lasting bitter finish may not be entirely true to type; nevertheless, a ruby-black gem.

XB *(OG 1037, ABV 3.7%)* ◗
A mid-brown balanced session bitter with malt most obvious in the finish. The taste is dominated by the house style apple hop, which also leads the aroma.

Valiant *(OG 1043, ABV 4.2%)* ◗
Golden-brown beer with an orchard fruit and faintly nutty aroma, and a fine underlying soft malt behind the hops.

Salem Porter *(OG 1049, ABV 4.7%)* ⬚◗
Ruby black with a brown tint to the head. The aroma is of liquorice with a subtle hint of dandelion and burdock; the initial taste is hoppy and bitter with a mellowing of all the elements in the finish.

XXXB *(OG 1050, ABV 4.8%)* ◗
A brilliant blend of malt, hops and fruit on the nose with a bitter bite over the top of a faintly banana maltiness that stays the course. A russet-tan brown classic.

BATH
Bath Ales Ltd, The Old Barn, Siston Lane, Webbs Heath, Bristol, BSW30 5LX
Tel Brewery (0117) 9615122
Office (0117) 9071797

Fax Brewery (0117) 9615122
Office (0117) 9095140
E-mail Hare@bathales.co.uk
Web-site www.bath.ales.co.uk
Tours by arrangement

⊗ Bath Ales began in 1995, formed by two for-
mer Smiles brewers and a Hardington brewer.
They started with rented kit at the Henstridge
Brewery, near Wincanton. They moved
premises and upgraded to a full steam, 15-bar-
rel plant in February 1999. Situated between
Bath and Bristol, all beer deliveries are direct to
100 plus outlets. Wholesalers are not used.
Three pubs are owned, all serving cask ale.
Bottle-conditioned beer: Gem (OG 1048,
ABV 4.8%). Seasonal/occasional beers: Spa
Extra (OG 1050, ABV 5%), Festivity (OG 1050,
ABV 5%), Rare Hare (OG 1052, ABV 5.2%).

Special Pale Ale (SPA)
(OG 1038, ABV 3.7%) ◆
Refreshing, dry, bitter beer. Aroma is of pale
and lager malts, with citrus hop. Light bodied,
full of flavour with lots of malt and good
apple/citrus, floral hops. Gold/yellow-
coloured, with a long, pale malty, bitter finish with some fruit and sweetness.

Gem Bitter *(OG 1041, ABV 4.1%)* ◆
With a malty, fruity and hoppy aroma and
taste, this medium-bodied bitter is somewhat
more dry and bitter at the end. Amber
coloured.

Barnstormer *(OG 1050, ABV 4.5%)* ◆
A smooth, well-crafted ale, mid-brown in
colour. The aroma is a combination of malts
(roast and chocolate), hops and fruit. Similar,
well balanced taste, with a complex of malt
flavours, and bitter, dry finish.

BATHAM
**Daniel Batham & Son Ltd, Delph Brewery,
Delph Road, Brierley Hill,
West Midlands DY5 2TN**
Tel (01384) 77229
Fax (01384) 482292

◉ Small brewery established in 1877 and
now in its fifth generation of family ownership. Batham's sympathetic programme of
upgrading and refurbishment in its tied
estate has been rewarded by winning
CAMRA's 1996 Joe Goodwin Award for pub
refurbishment for the Vine, one of the Black
Country's most famous pubs and the site of
the brewery. The company has nine tied
houses and supplies around 25 other outlets.
Occasional/seasonal beers: AJ's Strong Mild
Ale (OG 1048.5, ABV 5%), XXX (OG 1063.5,
ABV 6.3%, winter).

Mild Ale *(OG 1036.5, ABV 3.5%)* ◆
A fruity, dark brown mild with a malty sweetness and a roast malt finish.

Best Bitter *(OG 1043.5, ABV 4.3%)* 🍴👑◆
A pale yellow, fruity, sweetish bitter, with a
dry, hoppy finish. A good, light, refreshing
beer.

BEARDS
See Arundel and Pub Groups.

BEARTOWN
**Beartown Brewery Ltd, Unit 9, Varey Road,
Congleton, Cheshire CW12 1UW**

Tel (01260) 299964
Tours by arrangement

Congleton's links with brewing can be traced
back to 1272, when the town received charter status. Two of its most senior officers at
the time were Ale Taster and Bear Warden,
hence the name of the brewery, set up in
1994 on land that once housed a silk mill. It
became a limited company in January 1997,
after operating since 1995 as a partnership on
a part-time basis. It supplies 30 outlets direct.

Goldie Hops *(ABV 3.5%)*

Bear Ass *(OG 1038, ABV 4%)* ◆
Dark ruby-red, malty bitter with good hop
nose and fruity flavour with dry, bitter,
astringent aftertaste.

Kodiak Gold *(OG 1038, ABV 4%)* 🍴◆
Well-balanced, straw-coloured and very
drinkable with citrus fruit and hops aroma
and sharper bitter, clean, astringent aftertaste.

Bearskinful *(OG 1040, ABV 4.2%)* ◆
A tawny, malty beer, with a clean hop finish.

Polar Eclipse *(OG 1046, ABV 4.8%)* ◆
A smooth and roasty dark stout, with light
hoppy notes and a dry, bitter finish.

Black Bear *(OG 1048, ABV 5%)* ◆
Dark brown strong mild, some roast and
malt flavours, with a mellow sweetish finish.

BECKETT'S
**Beckett's Brewery Ltd, 8 Enterprise Court,
Rankine Road, Basingstoke,
Hampshire, RG24 8GE**
Tel (01256) 472986
Fax (01256) 703205
Tours by arrangement

⊗ After 16 years working for Fuller's, Richard
Swinhoe set up his own brewery in March
1997, the first in Basingstoke for 50 years.
Currently supplying 60 outlets direct, future
plans include the purchase of a brewery tap
and a range of bottle-conditioned beers. The
regular beer range is complemented by
Porterquack Ales, a series of unusual small
volume beers.

Old Town Bitter *(OG 1037, ABV 3.7%)* ◆
An intensely bitter, amber-coloured session
beer with some pale malt, fruit and butterscotch notes. Finishes uncompromisingly
bitter and dry.

Original Bitter *(OG 1040, ABV 4%)* ◆
A refreshing copper-coloured bitter with
hints of fruit and a rounded hop character.
Slightly vinous for its strength, with a suggestion of crystal malt. Long bitter finish.

Golden Grale *(OG 1045, ABV 4.5%)*

Porterquack Porter *(ABV 4.7%)* ◆
Dark brown in colour, this is a dry porter
with persistent chocolate malt in the mouth
and finish. Moderate bitterness and
deceptive strength.

Fortress Ale *(OG 1050, ABV 5%)*

BEECHAM'S
⌂ **Beecham's Bar & Brewery, Westfield
Street, St Helens, Merseyside WA10 1PZ**
Tel (01744) 623420

Fax (01744) 623400
Tours by arrangement

Beechams Brewery is a training
establishment within St Helens College of
Further Education. The brewing course has a
recognised certificate validated by the
National Open College Network. Seasonal
brews are produced.

Beechams Original Bitter
(OG 1044, ABV 4.4%)

Beechams Stout *(OG 1048, ABV 5%)* ❧
Thick, creamy, silky stout with roasty and
caramel aroma and flavours, some balancing
hop and a residual roastiness.

Crystal Wheat Beer *(OG 1048, ABV 5%)* ❧
Light, fruity wheat beer with aroma of citrus
fruits, clean, hoppy palate, and a dry finish.

BEER ENGINE
⬧ The Beer Engine, Newton St Cyres,
Exeter, Devon EX5 5AX
Tel (01392) 851282
Fax (01392) 851876
E-mail peterbrew@aol.com
Tours by arrangement.

⬛ Brew pub set up in 1983, next to the
Barnstaple branch railway line. Two other
outlets are supplied regularly and the beers
are also distributed via agencies. Seasonal
beers vary from year to year.

Rail Ale *(OG 1037, ABV 3.8%)* ❧
A straw-coloured beer with a fruity aroma
and a sweet, fruity finish.

Piston Bitter *(OG 1043, ABV 4.3%)* ❧
A mid-brown, sweet-tasting beer with a
pleasant, bitter-sweet aftertaste.

Sleeper Heavy *(OG 1052, ABV 5.3%)* ❧
A red-coloured beer with a fruity, sweet taste
and a bitter finish.

BELCHERS
See Hedgehog & Hogshead.

BELHAVEN
The Belhaven Brewing Co Limited,
Dunbar, East Lothian EH42 1RS
Tel/Fax (01368) 864488
Shop open during tours
Tours by arrangement

⬤ With a tradition of brewing going back
almost 800 years, Scotland's oldest brewery
supplies all its 69 houses, and an extensive
free trade, with cask beer. 80/- was second in
the Champion Beer of Scotland award in
1997. Belhaven has installed a 5-barrel brew
plant for experimental beers. Seasonal
beers: Festival (OG 1040, ABV 4%), Special Cargo
(OG 1045, ABV 4.5%), Rudolph's Revenge
(OG 1055, ABV 5.5%), 90/- Ale (OG 1080,
ABV 8%), Five Nations.

60/- Ale *(OG 1030, ABV 2.7%)* ⬛❧
A fine, but sadly rare, example of a Scottish
light. This bitter-sweet, reddish-brown beer is
dominated by fruit and malt with a hint of
roast and caramel, and increasing hop bitterness in the aftertaste. Belhaven's characteristic sulphuriness is evident throughout.

70/- Ale *(OG 1035, ABV 3.2%)* ❧
A malty, bitter-sweet, pale brown beer in
which hops and fruit are increasingly evident
in the aftertaste. The Belhaven sulphury nose
can be very prominent.

Sandy Hunter's Traditional Ale
(OG 1038, ABV 3.6%) ❧
A distinctive, medium-bodied beer named
after a past chairman and head brewer. An
aroma of malt, hops and characteristic sulphur greets the nose. A hint of roast combines with the malt and hops to give a bitter-
sweet taste and finish.

80/- Ale *(OG 1040, ABV 4%)* ❧
Incredibly robust, malty beer with a characteristic sulphury aroma. This classic ale has a
burst of complex flavours and a rich, bitter-
sweet finish.

Belhaven IPA *(OG 1041, ABV 4%)*

St Andrew's Ale *(OG 1046, ABV 4.9%)* ❧
A bitter-sweet beer with lots of body. The
malt, fruit and roast mingle throughout with
hints of hop and caramel.

BELVOIR
Belvoir Brewery Ltd, Woodhill,
Nottingham Lane, Old Dalby,
Leicestershire LE14 3LX
Tel/Fax (01664) 823455
Tours by arrangement

⬛ Belvoir (pronounced 'beaver') Brewery was
set up in March 1995 helped with brewing
experience gained by Colin Brown at
Theakstons and Shipstones. The brewery has
been lovingly constructed using mostly original equipment and artefacts recovered from
traditional cask ale breweries all over the
country. Time-honoured brewing methods
are used incorporating only the finest ingredients. These include traditional floor malted
Maris Otter malts, and four varieties of
Worcester whole hops (Goldings, Progress,
Challenger and Bramling Cross). A refriger-
ated cold store/cellar was added in 2000. A
bottled beer, Melton Red, was launched in
November 1999 and a bottle-conditioned,
unfiltered version is planned. 80-100 outlets
supplied direct. Occasional/seasonal beers:
Mild Ale (ABV 3.4%), Peacock's Glory (ABV
4.7%), Old Dalby (ABV 5.1%).

Whippling Golden Bitter
(OG 1036, AB V 3.6%)
Brewed for spring and summer.

Star Bitter *(OG 1039, ABV 3.9%)*
A beer designed to replicate the bitter flavour
of the old Shipstone's Bitter.

Beaver Bitter *(OG 1043, ABV 4.3%)* ❧
A light brown bitter that starts malty in both
aroma and taste, but soon develops a hoppy
bitterness. Appreciably fruity.

BEOWULF

The Beowulf Brewing Company, Waterloo
Buildings, Waterloo Road, Yardley,
Birmingham, W Midlands B25 8JR
Tel (0121) 706 4116
Fax (0121) 706 0735
Web-site www.beowulf.co.uk
E-mail cheers@beowulf.co.uk
Tours for small groups by arrangement

Entering its fourth year of production, the
Beowulf Brewing Company is well established throughout central England. It
remains Birmingham's only independent
brewery. Nearly 200 outlets serve Beowulf
beers from northern Scotland to southern
England, usually as a guest ale. There are
plans for bottled beers and further e-sales.
Seasonal beers: Wulfgar (OG 1043, ABV
4.5%, autumn/winter), Finn's Hall Porter
(OG 1048, ABV 4.7%, autumn/winter),
Dragon Smoke Stout (OG 1046, ABV 4.7%,
autumn/winter), Grendel's Winter Ale
(OG 1058, ABV 5.8%, Christmas/winter),
Tempest (OG 1038, ABV 3.9%, winter),
Blizzard (OG 1049, ABV 5%, winter),
Crackling (OG 1035, ABV 3.8%,
spring/summer), Wergild (OG 1040,
ABV 4.3% spring/summer), Offa (OG 1046,
ABV 4.8%, spring/summer), Kinsman (OG
1049, ABV 5.1%, summer/autumn), Dark
Raven (OG 1046, ABV 4.5%, occasional).

Hama *(OG 1037, ABV 3.8%)*

Noble *(OG 1038, ABV 4%)*

Wiglaf *(OG 1043, ABV 4.3%)*

Wuffa *(OG 1045, ABV 4.5%)*

Swordsman *(OG 1045, ABV 4.5%)*

Heroes Bitter *(OG 1046, ABV 4.7%)*

Mercian Shine *(OG 1048, ABV 5%)*

BERKELEY

Berkeley Brewing Co, The Brewery,
Bucketts Hill, Berkeley, Gloucestershire
GL11 9NZ
Tel (01453) 511799
Fax (01453) 811895
Tours by arrangement

This small operation was set up in an old
farm cider cellar in 1994, but did not start
brewing full-time until October 1996 when
the beer range was expanded to include seasonal ales. Forty free trade outlets are supplied. Seasonal beers: Late Starter (OG 1044,
ABV 4.5%, Oct-Nov), Early Riser (OG 1047,
ABV 4.8%, March-May), Dicky Pearce's
Winter Ale (OG 1048, ABV 4.9%, December),
Lord's Prayer (OG 1049, ABV 5%, July-Sept),
Red Hot Poker (OG 1045, ABV 4.5%, brewed
on demand).

Old Friend *(OG 1037, ABV 3.8%)*
A hoppy aroma introduces this golden,
fruity, hoppy beer, which has a gentle
hoppy, bitter finish.

Dicky Pearce *(OG 1042, ABV 4.3%)*
A copper-coloured best bitter, with a hoppy
aroma. A good balance of hop and malt in the
mouth leads to a rich, bitter-sweet aftertaste.

BERROW

Berrow Brewery, Coast Road, Berrow,
Burnham-on-Sea, Somerset TA8 2QU
Tel (01278) 751345
Off Licence 9am-9pm
Tours by arrangement

The brewery started brewing in May 1982
with 4Bs. Topsy Turvy was soon added to the
range and rapidly became a favourite. In
recent years Porter was added and 1998 saw
the introduction of two seasonal ales. Berrow
supplies 12 outlets direct. Seasonal beers:
Spring Ale, Summer Ale, Carnivale, Xmas Ale.

Berrow Brewery Best Bitter/4Bs
(OG 1038, ABV 3.9%)
A pleasant, pale brown session beer, with a
fruity aroma, a malty, fruity flavour and bitterness in the palate and finish.

Porter *(OG 1046, ABV 4.6%)*
A smooth, slightly sweet dark ruby beer with
hints of malt and a slightly bitter roast finish.
Somewhat reminiscent of a brown ale.

Topsy Turvy *(OG 1055, ABV 6%)*
A gold-coloured beer with an aroma of malt
and hops. Well-balanced malt and hops taste
and a hoppy, bitter finish with some fruit
notes.

BIG LAMP

Big Lamp Brewers, Grange Road,
Newburn, Newcastle upon Tyne NE15 8NL
Tel (0191) 2671689
Fax (0191) 2677387
Tours by arrangement

Big Lamp Brewers started in 1982 and relocated in 1996 to a 55-barrel former water
pumping station. Thirty outlets are supplied
and two pubs are owned.

Bitter *(OG 1039, ABV 3.9%)*
A good, clean tasty bitter, full of malt and
hops, with a hint of fruit and a good, hoppy
aftertaste.

Keelmans *(OG 1045, ABV 4.3%)*

Summerhill Stout *(OG 1046, ABV 4.4%)*
A tasty, rich, ruby stout with a lasting rich
roast feel and character. A malty mouthfeel
with a lingering finish.

Prince Bishop Ale *(OG 1048, ABV 4.8%)*
A rich and hoppy golden ale full of fruit.
Strong bitterness with a spicy dry finish.

Premium *(OG 1052, ABV 5.2%)*
A well-balanced, flavoursome bitter with a
big nose full of hops. The sweetness lasts into
a mellow, dry finish.

Winter Warmer *(OG 1055, ABV 5.5%)*

Old Genie *(OG 1074, ABV 7.4%)*

Blackout *(OG 1100, ABV 11%)*
A strong bitter, fortified with roast malt character and rich maltiness. Try it for its mouthfeel and lasting bitterness.

BIGFOOT

Bigfoot Traditional Ales Ltd, New Farm
Buildings, Blyton Carr, Gainsborough,
Lincolnshire DN21 3EW
Tel (01427) 811922
Fax (01427) 677901
Tours by arrangement

A brewery housed in former farm buildings, with the first commercial brew sold in February 1998. There are plans for bottled beers and, in partnership with a local pig farmer, Bigfoot sausages and hams. A visitor centre is planned. It supplies 50-60 outlets direct.

Blyton Best *(OG 1036.5, ABV 3.6%)*

Genesis *(OG 1037, ABV 3.8%)* ❧
Bitterness lingers from the initial taste into the finish; otherwise the malt and slightly fruity hop match one another in this mid-brown beer.

Gainsborough Gold
(OG 1042, ABV 4.5%) ❧
A honey malt nose leads to a hop bitterness that lingers through the aftertaste in this golden beer.

Big Foot Extra *(OG 1046, ABV 4.9%)*

BIRD IN HAND

❒ Wheal Ale Brewery Ltd, Nr Paradise Park, Trelissick Road, Hayle, Cornwall TR27 4HY
Tel/Fax (01736) 753974

Founded 1980 as Parkside Brewery, the small brewhouse is behind a large pub (Bird in Hand) converted from Victorian stables and coach house by the entrance to Paradise Park. Now brewing regularly, including some experimental beers and occasionally supplying local outlets. Beers: Miller's Ale (OG 1045, ABV 4.3%), Old Speckled Parrot (OG 1052, ABV 5.5%), Wildly Wicked (OG 1058, ABV 6.1%).

BITTER END

❒ The Bitter End Brew Pub, 15 Kirkgate, Cockermouth, Cumbria CA13 9PJ
Tel/Fax (01900) 828993

Brewpub founded in 1995.

Cockersnoot *(ABV 3.8%)*

Cuddy Luggs *(ABV 4.2%)*

Skinners Old Strong *(ABV 5.5%)*

BLACK BULL*

Black Bull (Haltwhistle) Brewery,
Black Bull, Market Square, Haltwhistle,
Northumberland NE14 0BL
Tel (01434) 320463

Bishop Ridley's Ale *(ABV 4.7%)*

BLACK DOG

Black Dog Brewery, St Hilda's Business Centre, The Ropery, Whitby, N Yorkshire Y022 4EU

Tel (01947) 821467
Fax (01947) 603301
Web-site www.synthesys.co.uk/black-dog
E-mail black_dog@lineone.net
Tours by arrangement

☺ Opened in 1997 and taking its name from the vampire who transformed himself into a black dog to land in Whitby in Bram Stoker's novel Dracula, the Black Dog Brewery is enjoying continued success. It supplies 30-40 outlets, mainly in the north of England, and three distributors on an occasional basis. New beers are introduced on a quarterly basis, some of which become regular brews. Seasonal beers: Synod (ABV 4.2%, spring), Whitby Jet (ABV 5%, winter).

Scallywag *(ABV 3.6%)*
A light, hoppy summer session beer.

Whitby Abbey Ale *(ABV 3.8%)*
A light, hoppy bitter.

First Out *(ABV 4%)*
A light, hoppy bitter.

Schooner *(ABV 4.2%)*
Medium coloured autumnal beer.

Rhatas/Black Dog Special *(ABV 4.6%)*
A dark, malty bitter.

BLACK ISLE

Black Isle Brewery, Old Allangrange,
Munlochy, Ross-shire IV8 8NZ
Tel (01463) 811871
Fax (01463) 811875

Launched in December 1998, the 5-barrel plant is based in converted farm buildings near Munlochy on the Black Isle. It supplies pubs throughout the Highlands.

Golden Eagle *(OG 1039, ABV 3.8%)* ❧
A surprisingly robust beer for its strength. A sweetish Scottish 70/- style golden amber beer bursting with malt in the nose and taste leading to a satisfying astringent bitter finish.

Red Kite *(OG 1041, ABV 4.2%)* ❧
A sweet, typically Scottish 80/- beer with an abundance of berry fruit aroma and taste. Hints of plum and mango lead to a classic bitter aftertaste.

Yellow Hammer *(OG 1042, ABV 4.3%)* ❧
A classic summer ale, this straw-coloured brew has an intense aroma of citrus fruits and hops, which is maintained through to the dry bitter finish.

Wagtail *(OG 1045, ABV 4.5%)* ❧
A glorious ruby-red beer bursting with berry fruits and roast malt, and with some coffee notes in the nose. The dark fruit flavours also prevail in the typically dry bitter finish.

BLACK SHEEP

The Black Sheep Brewery PLC, Wellgarth,
Masham, Ripon, N Yorkshire HG4 4EN
Tel (01765) 689227 (brewery)
680101 (visitor centre)
Fax (01765) 689746
E-mail visitor.centre@blacksheep.co.uk
Web-site www.blacksheep.co.uk
Shop 10-5.30 daily (Wed-Sun January-March)
Tours by arrangement daily (Wed-Sun January-March)

☺ Set up in 1992 by Paul Theakston, a member of Masham's famous brewing family, in

The Good Beer Guide 2001

the former Wellgarth Maltings, Black Sheep has enjoyed continued growth and now supplies a free trade of around 600 outlets in the Yorkshire Dales and in an 80-mile radius of Masham, but it owns no pubs. A limited number of wholesalers are also supplied. All the output is fermented in Yorkshire Square fermenters; there are six slate ones and eight stainless steel Yorkshire 'round' squares. A filtered bottled beer, Yorkshire Square Ale, is now available on draught. The Black Sheep complex includes video shows of the brewing process, a brewery shop, and a bistro open for snacks, lunches and evening meals every day (Wed-Sun only Jan to March).

Best Bitter *(OG 1039, ABV 3.8%)* ◆
A hoppy and fruity beer with strong bitter overtones, leading to a long, dry, bitter finish.

Special Ale *(OG 1046, ABV 4.4%)* ◆
A well-rounded and warming bitter beer with a good helping of hops and fruit in the taste and aroma, leading to a moderately dry, bitter aftertaste.

Yorkshire Square Ale *(ABV 5%)*
A refreshing pale beer with a long, dry, bitter finish.

Riggwelter *(OG 1056, ABV 5.9%)* ◆
A fruity bitter, with complex underlying tastes and hints of liquorice and pear drops leading to a long, dry, bitter finish.

BLANCHFIELD
Blanchfields of Fakenham, The Bull, Bridge Street, Fakenham, Norfolk NR21 9AG
Tel (01328) 862560
E-mail
Blanchfield@bullbrewery.freeserve.co.uk
Tours by arrangement

⊠ Blanchfields has been brewing since November 1997 using a custom-made 2.5 barrel plant. The company has won two gold medal awards for its beers. Six outlets supplied direct. Seasonal/occasional beers: High Hop (OG 1044, ABV 4.1%, occasional), White Bull Wheat Beer (OG 1046, ABV 4.4%, summer), Winter Warmer (OG 1055, ABV 5.9%, winter).

Black Bull Mild *(OG 1040, ABV 3.6%)* ◆
A gentle, lightly-roasted aroma leads to a muscular roast taste and a lingering finish with a growing sweet bitterness. Rich red colour.

Bull Best Bitter *(OG 1040, ABV 3.9%)* ◆
A distinctive hoppy bouquet and an over-riding hoppy bitterness provide the backbone for this quick-finishing beer.

High Hop Bitter *(ABV 4.1%)* ◆
A persistent kaleidoscope of flavour. A delicate balance of hops and bitterness is boosted by a background of sweet fruitiness.

Raging Bull Bitter *(OG 1048, ABV 4.9%)* ◆
A strong malty nose provides a good indicator for the same flavour in a solid, nutty taste. An old-fashioned beer with a rich sweetness in the finale.

Winter Warmer *(OG 1055, ABV 5.9%)* ◆
A well-rounded, rich red beer redolent of autumn fruits. Rich plum pudding flavour leads to an explosion of creamy sweet fruitiness.

BLENCOWE
Blencowe Brewing Company, c/o Exeter Arms, Barrowden, Rutland, LE15 8EQ
Tel (01572) 747247
Web-site www.exeterarms.co.uk
Tours by arrangement

The brewery was set-up in a barn within the boundaries of the pub. The 2-barrel plant was bought with the intention of supplying the pub and beer festivals only. Seasonal beers: Lover Boys (ABV 3.9%, St Valentine's), Spice Boys (ABV 6%, Easter and Xmas). Beers: Toy Boys (ABV 3.7%), Danny Boys (ABV 4.5%).

BLEWITTS
Blewitts Brewery, Sorley Tunnel Adventure Farm, Loddiswell Road, Kingsbridge, Devon TQ7 4BP
Tel (01548) 852485
Tours by arrangement

⊠ Established in 1991 as a brew pub at the Ship & Plough in Kingsbridge, owner Steve Blewitt moved the plant in 1999 to an adventure playground where visitors can watch beer being brewed. The products are still available at the Ship & Plough. Beers: Best (OG 1038, ABV 3.9%), Wages (OG 1045, ABV 4.5%), Head Off (OG 1050, ABV 5%).

BLUE ANCHOR
⌂ **Blue Anchor Inn, 50 Coinagehall Street, Helston, Cornwall TR13 8EX**
Tel (01326) 562821
Tours by arrangement

Historic thatched brew pub, possibly the oldest in Britain, originating as a monks' resting place in the 15th century. It produces powerful ales known locally as Spingo. The brewery has undergone complete refurbishment and the pub is also due for improvement, with careful attention to preserving its special character. Two outlets are supplied direct. Beers: Spingo Middle (OG 1050, ABV 5%), Spingo Best (OG 1053, ABV 5.3%), Special (OG 1066, ABV 6.6%), Easter and Christmas Special (OG 1076, ABV 7.6%).

BLUE COW
⌂ **The Blue Cow Inn and Brewery, South Witham, Nr Grantham, Lincolnshire NG33 5QB**
Tel/Fax (01572) 768432
Tours by arrangement

⊠ Opened March 1997 by Dick Thirlwell, who brews only for the pub. Beers:

Thirlwell's Cuddy (OG 1040, ABV 3.8%),
Thirlwell's Best Bitter (OG 1040, ABV 3.8%).

BLUE MOON

**The Blue Moon Brewery, 15 Market Place,
Hingham, Norfolk NR9 4AF
Tel (01953) 851115**
Originally sited at Pearces Farm, Hingham in
a converted manger. The farm has been sold
and the beers are currently brewed by Buffys
Brewery, Tivetshall until new premises are
ready. Blue Moon owns one pub and 60
outlets are supplied direct.

Easy Life *(OG 1040, ABV 3.8%)* ◆
An amber-coloured bitter with a one-sided
hoppy character. An almost overwhelming
hoppy bitterness masks a subtle fruity, sweet
background. A surprisingly clean mouthfeel
for a beer with such a dramatic flavour.

Sea of Tranquillity *(OG 1042, ABV 4.2%)* ◆
A pale-brown beer with a light malt aroma
leading to a slight malty-fruity flavour; fairly
thin for its strength but a good quaffable ale.

Dark Side *(OG 1048, ABV 4.5%)*

Hingham High *(OG 1050, ABV 5.2%)*

Milk of Amnesia *(OG 1055, ABV 5.2%)*

Liquor Mortis *(OG 1065, ABV 6.5%)*

BOAT*

⬚ Boat Brewery, Boat Inn, off Main Street,
Allerton Bywater, West Yorkshire
WF10 2BX
Tel (01977) 667788)

Aire Tonic *(ABV 3.6%)*

Plutonium *(ABV 4%)*

Super Duck *(ABV 4.3%)*

Old Knuckle Shuffler *(ABV 5%)*

BODICOTE

See Plough Inn.

BORDER

**Border Brewery Co, The Old Kiln, Brewery
Lane, Tweedmouth, Berwick upon Tweed,
Northumberland TD15 2AH
Tel (01289) 303303
Fax (01289) 302333
E-mail border@rampart.freeserve.co.uk**
Tours by arrangement

☺ The brewery opened in 1992 in an old kiln
on the site of Berwick's original defunct
Border Brewery, which was established in the
17th century. A change in ownership took
place in 1994. The brewery supplies 100 outlets. Occasional/seasonal beers: Festival Ale
(OG 1036, ABV 3.9%), Mythic Beers (OG
1040, ABV 4.3%, a new brew every 2
months), Y2K (OG 1040, ABV 4.3%),
Rudolph's Ruin (OG 1060, ABV 6.4%).

Special Bitter *(OG 1035, ABV 3.8%)*

Old Kiln Ale *(OG 1037, ABV 4%)* ◆
Good mouthfeel with balanced hops, malt
and fruit highlighting the taste. Long,
slightly sweet finish.

Farne Island Pale Ale
(OG 1037, ABV 4%) ◆
A pale brown, full-bodied, hoppy, fruity
bitter, taking its name from the
Northumberland isle. A fine nose, pleasing
taste and robust aftertaste.

Flotsam Bitter *(OG 1037, ABV 4%)*

Noggins Nog *(OG 1040, ABV 4.2%)* ◆
Dark brown robust ale. A good mix of hops
and roast malt leaves an impressive chocolate
character in the aftertaste.

Reiver's IPA *(OG 1041, ABV 4.4%)*

Rampart *(OG 1045, ABV 4.8%)*

Jetsam Bitter *(OG 1045, ABV 4.8%)*

SOB *(OG 1047, ABV 5%)* ◆
A malty ale with a resinous bitterness,
finishing with a woody dryness.

BORVE

⬚ Borve Brew House, Ruthven, Huntly,
Aberdeenshire AB54 4SG
Tel (01466) 760343
Tours by arrangement

☺ Established in 1983, Borve moved from its
original site on the Isle of Lewis five years
later to a former school on the mainland.
The school is now a pub, with the brewhouse
adjacent. Beers, cask and bottle-conditioned:
Borve Ale (OG 1040, ABV 3.9%), Tall Ships
(OG 1050, ABV 5%). Plus Extra Strong (OG
1085, ABV 10%) bottle-conditioned only.

BOSTON EXPERIENCE

⬚ The Boston Experience Ltd, 1-3 Church
Path, Woking, Surrey GU21 1EL
Tel (01483) 598586
Fax (01483) 599201
E-mail gary@boston-experience.com
Web-site www.boston-experience.com
Tours by arrangement

Opened in April 1999, the Boston Experience
offers a choice of three beers brewed to
American recipes. All the beers are chill
filtered (ie not real ale) and dispensed
directly from the cellar tanks to the bar.
Beers: Babe Ruth (ABV 3.8%), Bunker Hill
(ABV 4.3%), Boston Strangler (ABV 5.3%).

BRAGDY TY BACH*

⬚ Tynllidiart Arms, Capel Bangor,
Aberystwyth, Ceredigion
Tel (01970) 880248

Owned by Paul Kenyon, who also runs
Flannery's Brewery in Llandre (qv), Bragdy Ty
Bach (Small House Brewery) claims to be the
smallest brewery in the world. It has a brew
length of nine gallons and is based in a converted outside lavatory in the pub grounds. It
is used for trial brews. The first brew was a
ginger beer (ABV 5%) and Paul planned to
brew the world's strongest ale in the world's
smallest brewery, with an ABV of 25%, using
a Champagne yeast.

BRAGDY YNYS MON*

Cae Cwta Mawr, Talwrn,
Anglesey L177 7SD
Tel (01248) 723801
E-mail
martyn@caecwtamawr.freeserve.co.uk

Martyn Lewis started brewing in June 1999 on a 5-barrel plant acquired from Gambrinus in Liverpool.

Medra *(ABV 4%)* ◆
Attractive-looking, copper-coloured, soft, malty bitter with hints of berries in the short, dry finish.

Wennol *(ABV 4.1%)*
The name means Swallow.

Enlli *(ABV 4.4%)*
A strong mild: the name is the Welsh version of Bardsey Island.

Tarw Du *(ABV 4.5%)* ◆
The name means Black Bull. Inviting black porter-style beer that has an earthy flavour with some chocolate/coffee notes and a long, dry aftertaste.

BRAGWR ARBENNIG O GEREDIGION

2 Brynderwen, Llangrannog, Llandysul, Ceredigion SA44 6AD
Tel/Fax (01239) 654099
Tours by arrangement

The brewery planned to sell only bottle-conditioned beers but, due to demand, it is now providing the beers in cask. Most of the output is sold locally in Ceredigion, mainly through shops. The beers are also sold by mail order, wholesale from the brewery direct and are always available in the two pubs in Llangrannog, the Pentre Arms and Ship Inn. The brewhouse comprises 5-barrel ex-cellar tanks and is housed in a converted barn (Yr Hen Ysgubor) three miles from the village of Llangrannog at Wervil Grange, Pentregat. Beers: Gwrach Du (OG 1036, ABV 4%), Barcud Coch (OG 1038, ABV 4.3%), Y Ddraig Aur (OG 1044-46, ABV 5%), Yr Hen Darw Du (OG 1054-56, ABV 6.2%). All the above are available as bottle-conditioned beers in 500ml amber bottles. They are unfiltered and contain no adjuncts or additives.

BRAINS

SA Brain & Company Ltd,
The Cardiff Brewery, Crawshay Street,
Cardiff CF10 5TR
Tel (029) 2040 2060
Fax (029) 2040 3344
Web-site www.sabrain.com
Shop 9.30-5.30 Mon-Sat
Tours by arrangement

A traditional brewery that started trading under the Brain name in 1882. It was established by Samuel Arthur Brain and his uncle Joseph Benjamin Brain and is a family concern to the present day. In March 1997, the company acquired Crown Buckley and closed the Llanelli site. As it could not expand at the St Mary Street site, Brains bought the Crawshay Street brewery (formerly Hancocks) from Bass in April 1999. The company owns 202 pubs all serving cask ale, as well as having a sizeable free trade, plus interests in hotel and leisure projects in Wales and the West Country. 1,000 outlets are supplied direct. Seasonal beers: St David's Ale (OG 1041.5, ABV 4.1%), Buckley's Merlin's Oak (OG 1043.5, ABV 4.3%).

Buckley's IPA *(OG 1033.5, ABV 3.4%)*

Crown Pale Ale *(OG 1033.5, ABV 3.4%)* ◆
A thin beer, predominantly malty with a bitter-sweet finish and a background of hoppiness. A plain session beer now in its fourth brewery in 10 years.

Brains Dark *(OG 1036, ABV 3.5%)* ▤◆
A dark brown mild with a pleasant mix of roast, caramel, malt and hops, bitter-sweet with a rounded finish. A beer that benefits from good cellarmanship.

Brains Bitter *(OG 1036.5, ABV 3.7%)* ◆
A pale bitter beer, somewhat hoppy, with malt, ending in a bitter finish. Locally called 'Light'. A touch of sweetness indicates a slight change. Not the beer it once was.

Buckley's Best Bitter
(OG 1036.5, ABV 3.7%)

SA Best Bitter *(OG 1042, ABV 4.2%)* ◆
Now less distinctive, a moderately bitter beer, low aroma and noticeably sweeter, but a balance of flavours remain. The finish is now mellow. A shadow of its former self.

Rev James Original Ale
(OG 1045, ABV 4.5%)

BRAKSPEAR

WH Brakspear & Sons PLC, The Brewery,
New Street, Henley-on-Thames,
Oxfordshire RG9 2BU
Tel (01491) 570200
Fax (01491) 410254
Web-site www.brakspear.co.uk
Shop 9-6 Mon-Sat (9-7 Fri)
Tours by arrangement

⊠ Brewing took place before 1700 on the Henley site. The 19th-century brewhouse and Tun Room still incorporate the unique two-tier dropping system of fermentation. English Maris Otter malt, whole hops and Brakspear's own well water form the heart of the company's beers. 101 tied pubs are owned, all serving traditional ales. Some 100 free trade outlets are supplied direct. Seasonal beers: Resolution (ABV 4.4%, Jan-Feb), Hooray Henley (ABV 4.6%, July-Aug), Ted & Ben's Organic Beer (ABV 4.7%, March-April), Beesting (ABV 4.7%, May-June), OBJ (OG 1049, ABV 4.8%, Nov-Dec), Leaf Fall (ABV 5.1%, Sep-Oct). Bottle-conditioned beers: Vintage Ale (ABV 5.5-6.5%), Vintage Henley (OG 1055, ABV 5.5%). An organic bottled beer is planned. A new company, Honeypot Inns, has been set up in partnership with David Bruce, founder of the Firkin chain of brewpubs, to oversee the company's managed estate of seven pubs and to buy new outlets.

XXX Mild *(OG 1032, ABV 3%)* ❧
A dry, red-brown mild with a good balance of chocolate malt and roast barley. A hint of sweetness gives way to a dry, bitter finish.

Bitter *(OG 1035.5, ABV 3.4%)* 🍴❧
This copper-coloured bitter is well hopped, moderately fruity and unpretentious, with a spicy bitterness and good mouthfeel. It ends fruity, dry and pungently hoppy, and can be sulphurous at times.

XXXX Old Ale *(OG 1043.5, ABV 4.3%)* ❧
Red/brown in colour with good body. The strong, fruity aroma is well complemented by malt, hops and caramel. Its pronounced taste of malt, with discernible sweet, roast malt and caramel flavours, gives way to fruitiness. The aftertaste is of bitter-sweet chocolate, even though chocolate malt is not used.

Special *(OG 1043.5, ABV 4.3%)* 🍴❧
A honey-coloured bitter, well-balanced with fruit and a good bitter hop character. Pale malt and hops lead through to an astringent finish.

Contract beers: Bluebird (for Coniston)
(OG 1036, ABV 3.6% (also bottle-conditioned OG 1041.5, ABV 4.2%).

BRAMCOTE
See Castle Rock.

BRANDY CASK
⛫ **The Brandy Cask Pub & Brewery, Bridge Street, Pershore, Worcestershire WR10 1AJ**
Tel/Fax (01386) 552602
Tours by arrangement

⊗ Brewing started in 1995 in a refurbished bottle store in the garden of the pub. It was run as a separate business until the retirement of the brewer in September 1998. The brewery and the pub now operate under the one umbrella, the brewing being carried out by the owner/landlord. Since the change, brewing is restricted to the Brandy Cask only but a return to supplying other outlets in the future is anticipated. Occasional beer: Ale Mary (OG 1048, ABV 4.8%).

Whistling Joe *(OG 1038, ABV 3.6%)* ❧
Bitter hops dominate in this quaffable session bitter with its undertones of malt to balance sharpness.

Brandy Snapper *(OG 1042, ABV 4%)* ❧
A contrasting range of hop flavours makes way for the occasional malt notes before leaving a dry memory in the mouth.

John Baker's Original
(OG 1049, ABV 4.8%) ❧
A very palatable old ale with rich roast flavours bringing out the lurking malt and hoppiness that are always ready to pop out and surprise you.

BRANSCOMBE VALE
The Branscombe Vale Brewery, Branscombe, Seaton, Devon EX12 3DP
Tel/Fax (01297) 680511
Tours by arrangement, winter only

⊗ Brewery set up in 1992 in two cowsheds owned by the National Trust, by former dairy workers Paul Dimond and Graham Luxton, who converted the sheds and dug their own well. The NT has built an extension for the brewery to ensure future growth. It currently supplies 60 regular outlets. Seasonal beers: Anniversary Ale (OG 1044.5, ABV 4.6%, January), Hells Belles (OG 1047, ABV 4.8%, winter), Summa That (OG 1049, ABV 5%, summer), Yo Ho Ho (OG 1065, ABV 6%, Christmas).

Branoc *(OG 1037, ABV 3.8%)* ❧
A pale brown session ale. Fruit and malt aroma with a very bitter taste and finish.

BVB *(OG 1045, ABV 4.6%)* 🍷

Summa That *(OG 1049, ABV 5%)* 🍴❧
Highly drinkable, golden fruity beer with a bitter finish

BRETTVALE
See Kings Head.

BREWERY ON SEA
The Brewery on Sea Ltd, Unit 24, Winston Business Centre, Chartwell Road, Lancing, W Sussex BN15 8TU
Tel/Fax (01903) 851482

⊗ Brewery established in 1993 and increased its capacity in 1995 to around 55 barrels a week, some of which is taken by wholesalers, although up to 100 outlets are supplied direct. Beers are also brewed for East-West Ales, and the brewery often produces beers for special occasions. Seasonal beers: Mother's Dayze (ABV 4.1%, Mother's Day), Big Fat Santa (ABV 4.2%, Nov-Dec), Shamrock (ABV 4.2%, a green beer for St Patrick's Day), Shell Shock (ABV 4.3%, Easter), Leaf Thief (ABV 4.2%, autumn), Snow Belly (ABV 4.4%, Christmas), Whale Ale (ABV 4.4%, May), Valentine (ABV 4.6%, February), Up in Smoke (ABV 4.8% Guy Fawkes Night), Candyman (ABV 5%, Hallowe'en), Wild Turkey (ABV 5.2%, winter), Fireside, Bottlenose, Domino, Dragon, Gone Fishing, Sun King, Rattler, Over The Moon, Countdown 2000.

Spinnaker Bitter *(OG 1036, ABV 3.5%)* ❧
A hoppy-tasting, smooth, basic ale.

Spinnaker Mild or Lancing Special Dark
(OG 1036, ABV 3.5%)
Dark in colour and rich in flavour.

Spinnaker Golden Lite *(ABV 3.8%)*
Originally a summer brew, now brewed all year-round. Golden brown in colour and flavoursome.

Spinnaker Classic *(OG 1040, ABV 4%)* ✥
The brewery's first beer: copper-coloured,
with hints of malt in the aroma, giving way
to a fruity flavour.

Rain Dance *(ABV 4.4%)* ✥
Originally a one-off wheat beer, now a
permanent brew. Pale with a cereal aroma.

Spinnaker Buzz *(OG 1045, ABV 4.5%)* ✥
An amber-coloured beer primed with honey,
which dominates the aroma. An initial sweetness gives way to an intriguing flavour mix of
malt, honey and hops. Hoppy aftertaste.

Black Rock *(OG 1050, ABV 5.5%)*
A dark beer with a good measure of roasted
barley.

Special Crew *(OG 1050, ABV 5.5%)*
A full-bodied bitter that gains its flavour and
copper colour from a mix of pale and crystal
malts.

Spinnaker Ginger *(OG 1050, ABV 5.5%)*
Mid-light brown in colour, this beer contains
pure ginger, making it highly aromatic.

Riptide *(OG 1060, ABV 6.5%)*
A premium strong ale, fully fermented.

Tidal Wave *(OG 1065, ABV 7%)*
A dry-tasting, strong dark beer.

THE BREWERY
See Liverpool.

BREWSTER'S
Brewster's Brewing Co Ltd, Penn Lane,
Stathern, Nr Melton Mowbray,
Leicestershire LE14 4HR
Tel (01949) 861868
Fax (01949) 861901
E-mail sara@brewsters.co.uk
Web-site www.brewsters.co.uk
Tours by arrangement

Brewster is the old English term for a female
brewer and Sara Barton is a modern example.
A Master of Brewing trained at Heriot Watt
Brewing School, she then worked with
Courage before striking out alone. Brewster's
Brewery was set up in the heart of the Vale of
Belvoir in January 1998 with a 5-barrel plant.
There are plans to upgrade soon to cope with
increased demand. Beer is supplied direct to
some 200 pubs throughout central England
and further afield via wholesalers. Seasonal
beers: Claudia Wheat Beer (OG 1045, ABV
4.5%, summer), Brewster's Stocking (OG
1055, ABV 5.5%, Christmas), Frau Brau Lager
(OG 1050, ABV 5%, summer); Serendipity
range; Serendipity I (OG 1052, ABV 5.2%),
Serendipity II (OG 1043, ABV 4.3%).

Hophead *(OG 1036, ABV 3.6%)*

Marquis *(OG 1038, ABV 3.8%)*

Monty's Mild *(OG 1040, ABV 4%)*

Brewster's Bitter *(OG 1042, ABV 4.2%)*

Vale Pale Ale (VPA) *(OG 1045, ABV 4.5%)*

BRIDGE OF ALLAN
⚐ Bridge of Allan Brewery,
The Brew House, Queens Lane,
Bridge of Allan, Stirlingshire FK9 4NY
Tel (01786) 834555
Fax (01786) 833426

E-mail brewery@bridgeofallan.co.uk
Web-site www.bridgeofallan.co.uk
Shop 10-5 daily
Tours by arrangement

🌐 Bridge of Allan Brewery was formed in
1997 and is located in the leafy Victorian Spa
town of Bridge of Allan in the famous
Scottish brewing area of Forth Valley with
Stirling Castle, the Wallace Monument and
the nearby Trossocks. The 5-barrel custom-
built brewery also has a visitor centre that is
open daily from 10-5. The brewery also owns
village pubs and sells to more than 50 pubs
in Scotland with plans to distribute the beers
to England. A range of the bottled products,
Stirling Brig, Bannockburn and Sheriffmuir
are available. Seasonal beers: Summer Breeze
(OG 1046, ABV 4.4%), Wild Oats Stout (OG
1048, ABV 4.8%), Winter Warmer (OG 1050,
ABV 4.8%); other seasonals are available
throughout the year on a monthly basis.

Stirling Dark Mild *(OG 1032, ABV 3.2%)*

Stirling Bitter *(OG 1038, ABV 3.7%)*

Stirling Brig *(OG 1042, ABV 4.1%)*

Stirling IPA *(OG 1045, ABV 4.2%)*

BRIDGEWATER
⚐ Bridgewater Ales Ltd, 142 Chapel Street,
Salford, Gtr Manchester M3 6AF
Tel/Fax (0161) 831 9090
Tours by arrangement

Bridgewater Ales started brewing at the Old
Pint Pot Brewery, Salford in January 1999. Set
up by brewer Richard Bazen and ex-CAMRA
Regional Director Ken Birch, a purpose-built
brewery was completed at Chapel Street by
June 1999 and full production switched to
the new site in August. Delph Porter was
voted Beer of the Festival at Stockport in June
1999. Danny Bates has replaced Ken Birch as
head of sales and development. It was
intended to open the first tied house in 2000.
25 outlets are supplied direct. Monthly
specials are brewed.

Navigator *(OG 1039, ABV 3.8%)* 🍺✥
Amber beer with a fruity, hoppy nose.
Good malt/bitter balance and a dry, hoppy
aftertaste

Ash Blond *(OG 1042, ABV 4.2%)*
Yellow beer with a fruity aroma. Hoppy,
fruity and refreshing with a fruity finish.

Barton Ale *(OG 1043, ABV 4.3%)*

Delph Porter *(OG 1053, ABV 5.2%)*

BRISCOE'S
Briscoe's Brewery, 16 Ash Grove, Otley,
W Yorkshire LS21 3EL
Tel/Fax (01943) 466515

Brewery launched in November 1998 by
microbiologist/chemist Dr Paul Briscoe in the
cellar of his house with a 1-barrel brew
length. A new 3-barrel brewery at the rear of
the Bowling Green public house in Otley
town centre is now operational. The existing
1-barrel plant will be retained for specials and
bottled beers. The beers are full mash, most
are all malt, and no sugar is added in any of
the brews. Eleven outlets are supplied direct.
Beers: Littondale Light (OG 1039, ABV 4%),
Burnsall Classic Bitter (OG 1040, ABV 4%),

Dalebottom Dark (OG 1044, ABV 4.3%), Chevin Chaser (OG 1043, ABV 4.3%), Shane's Shamrock Stout (OG 1045, ABV 4.6%), Chevinbrau (OG 1048, ABV 5.2%).

BROADSTONE*

The Broadstone Brewing Company Ltd, PO Box 82, Waterside Brewery, Retford DN22 7ZJ
Tel (01777) 719797
Fax (01777) 719898
E-mail broadstone.brewery@virgin.net
Web-site broadstone.brewery.com
Tours by arrangement

Broadstone started brewing in September 1999 using temporary premises until completion of its permanent home at the end of 2000. The head brewer is Alan Gill, founder of Springhead Brewery 10 years ago. Further seasonal beers are planned. Seasonal beer: War Horse (OG 1055, ABV 5.8%). Beers: Broadstone Best Bitter (OG 1037.5, ABV 3.8%), Stonebridge Mild (OG 1041, ABV 4%), Charter Ale (OG 1047, ABV 4.6%), Broadstone (OG 1049.5, ABV 5%).

BROOKLANDS

See Planets.

BROUGHTON

Broughton Ales Ltd, Broughton, Biggar, The Borders ML12 6HQ
Tel (01899) 830345
Fax (01899) 830474
Shop 9-5 Mon-Fri
Tours by arrangement (eves)

☺ Founded in 1979, the company went into receivership in 1995 and was taken over by Whim Brewery owner Giles Litchfield. Half the beer is bottled (not bottle-conditioned), much of it for export. A single tied house and 200 outlets in Scotland are supplied direct from the brewery, while other customers throughout Britain are served by wholesalers. Expansion into new markets in England is going well. Seasonal/occasional beers: Broughton Special Bitter (OG 1038, ABV 3.9%), Bramling Cross (OG 1040, ABV 4.2%, summer), Northdown (OG 1042, ABV 4.5%).

IPA *(ABV 3.8%)*
Brewed for spring and summer.

Greenmantle Ale *(ABV 3.9%)* ◥
A predominantly malty aroma, a malt taste with hints of fruit and hops.

Scottish Oatmeal Stout *(ABV 4.2%)* ◥
A rare pleasure, this wonderfully dry stout has a bitter aftertaste dominated by roast malt. A distinctive malt aroma is followed by a prominent roast taste, with fruit evident throughout.

Reeket Yill *(ABV 4.8%)*

Merlin's Ale *(ABV 4.2%)* ◥
A well-hopped, fruity flavour is balanced by malt in the taste. The finish is bitter-sweet, light but dry.

80/- *(ABV 4.2%)*

The Ghillie *(ABV 4.5%)* ◥
A full-bodied ale. Hops, malt and fruit dominate the palate. The finish is dry and dominated by hop.

Black Douglas *(ABV 5.2%)*
A winter brew, dark ruby in colour.

Old Jock *(ABV 6.7%)*
Strong, sweetish and fruity in the finish. Also sold as River Tweed Festival Ale.

BROWN COW

Brown Cow Brewery, Brown Cow Road, Barlow, Selby, N Yorkshire YO8 8EH
Tel/Fax 01757 618947
Web-site www.browncowbrewery.fq.co.uk
E-mail ksimpson@uk.mdis.com

Brewing takes place in a converted outbuilding at the brewer's riverside home (the former Brown Cow Inn). The brewery is run by Susan Simpson who brews 5-7.5 barrels per week on the 2.5 barrel plant. The beers are always available at four local outlets and as guest ales to free houses in the area. 25 outlets are supplied direct. Seasonal beers: Maiden Century (OG 1039, ABV 4%, summer), Wolfhound (OG 1043, ABV 4.5%, summer), Windy Bottom (OG 1045, ABV 4.6%, autumn), Wassail Warmer (OG 1048, ABV 5%, Christmas). Beers: Brown Cow Bitter (OG 1037, ABV 3.8%), Simpsons No 4 (OG 1044, ABV 4.4%).

TOM BROWN'S

See Goldfinch.

BRUNSWICK

⚲ **The Brunswick Brewing Co, 1 Railway Terrace, Derby DE1 2RU**
Tel (01332) 290677
Fax (01332) 370226
Tours by arrangement

⊠ Purpose-built tower brewery attached to the Brunswick Inn, the first railwaymen's hostelry in the world, partly restored by the Derbyshire Historic Building Trust and bought by the present owners in 1987. Brewing began in 1991 and a viewing area allows pub-users to watch production. The beers are supplied to the inn and 13 other outlets. Numerous one-off beers are also produced. Beers: Cession Ale (OG 1037, ABV 3.7%), If (OG 1040, ABV 4%), Triple Hop (OG 1040 ABV 4%), Second Brew (OG 1042, ABV 4.2%), Railway Porter (OG 1045, ABV 4.3%), Old Accidental (OG 1050, ABV 5%).

BRYNCELYN*

Bryncelyn Brewery, Wern Fawr Public House, 47 Wern Road, Ystalyfera, Swansea SA9
Tel (01639) 843 625

The Bryncelyn (Holly Hill) Brewery received its licence and started brewing in April 1999.

The owner, Charles Harding Holly, is a big fan of Buddy Holly. Beers: Buddy Marvellous (ABV 4%), Buddys Delight (ABV 4.2%), CHH (ABV 4.5%), O Boy (ABV 4.5%), That Will Be The Sleigh (ABV 6.7%).

BUCHANAN
See Federation.

BUCKLEY
See Brains.

BUFFY'S
Buffy's Brewery, Rectory Road, Tivetshall St Mary, Norfolk NR15 2DD
Tel/Fax (01379) 676523
E-mail buffy@users.breworld.net
Tours by arrangement

⊗ Established in 1993, the brewing capacity is now 45 barrels per week and Buffy's will be able to carry out one more expansion pro-gramme before looking for bigger premises. Duncan Walker, formerly of Scotts of Lowestoft, is the new head brewer who is bringing not only his expertise but making some refinements to the range. More sea-sonal ales may be introduced if the demand is strong enough. 200 outlets are supplied direct. Seasonal beer: Hollybeery (ABV and recipe changes each year).

Norwich Terrier *(OG 1036, ABV 3.6%)* ◆
Clean honey blossom aroma gives an indica-tion of the light refreshing hoppiness of the intitial taste of this amber beer. A fruity bit-terness augments the flavour. The finish is long as the bitter edge develops intensity.

Bitter *(OG 1039, ABV 3.9%)* ◆
A good balance of hops and bitterness is softened by a sweet malty background. The bitterness carries through to a clean, lingering finish.

Mild *(OG 1042, ABV 4.2%)* ◆
Reddish colour and a glorious blackberry bouquet. This transforms to a sweet malty flavour underpinned by a big roast base. The finish is still dominated by a roasted warm sweetness but ends quickly.

Polly's Folly *(OG 1043, ABV 4.3%)* ◆
A booming fruit nose introduces a gooseberry fruitiness to the sweet malty flavour of this copper-coloured best bitter. The fruitiness continues to the end of a long sweet finish.

Hopleaf *(OG 1044.5, ABV 4.5%)* ◆
Hops and caramel in the nose introduce a gentle mix of flavour from which fruit and hops emerge in their own right. Hops con-tinue to influence the finish as the fruitiness subsides into a sweetish light background.

India Pale Ale *(OG 1046, ABV 4.6%)* ◆
Full-bodied pale ale with a crisp, rounded flavour. Bitterness comes through in the long aftertaste.

Polly's Extra Folly *(OG 1049, ABV 4.9%)* ◆
A well-balanced ale with a fruity aroma and light citrus notes; similar to Polly's Folly but with more fruit and a tawny colour.

Ale *(OG 1055, ABV 5.5%)* ◆
A tawny, old fashioned Christmas pudding beer. Rich, plummy aroma and a sweet fruity

flavour laced with malt. The finish develops through to a smooth malty flavour abetted by sweet bitterness.

Festival 9X *(OG 1088, ABV 9%)*

BULLMASTIFF
Bullmastiff Brewery, 14 Bessemer Close, Leckwith, Cardiff CF11 8DL
Tel (029) 2066 5292

Small craft brewery run by two brothers. The name derives from their love of the Bullmastiff breed. They have won many awards for the beers but have no ambitions for expansion or owning any pubs, preferring to concentrate on quality control. 30 outlets are supplied direct. Seasonal beers: Summer Moult (OG 1044, ABV 4.3%), Spring Fever (OG 1044, ABV 4.3%), Southpaw (OG 1049, ABV 4.7%, autumn).

Gold Brew *(OG 1040, ABV 3.8%)* ◆
Champion Beer of Wales 1999. A refreshing, hoppy aroma and taste dominate a fine blend of malt and fruit with a lasting, hoppy bitterness.

Best Bitter *(OG 1042, ABV 4%)* ◆
A well-balanced beer with a hoppy, bitter and fruity finish. A fine example of a best bitter.

Cardiff Dark *(OG 1045, ABV 4.2%)*

Jack The Lad *(OG 1043, ABV 4.1%)* ◆
A tasty amber beer with a strong hop presence throughout. Malt and fruit add depth to the flavour, which ends in a long, bitter finish.

Thoroughbred *(OG 1047, ABV 4.5%)* ◆
A tasty, premium bitter with hops strong in the aroma and flavour balanced by fruit and malt with a bitter finish.

Brindle *(OG 1051, ABV 5%)* ◆
A full-bodied, flavoursome beer. Fruit and hops combine with bitterness to give a satis-fying finish.

Son of a Bitch *(OG 1064, ABV 6%)* ◆
A powerful amber beer with a complex mix of hops, malt and fruit with balancing bitter-ness. Slightly lighter of late but still warming, tasty and drinkable.

Mogadog *(OG 1095, ABV 10%)*

BUNCES
See Stonehenge.

BURTON BRIDGE
Burton Bridge Brewery, Bridge Street, Burton upon Trent, Staffordshire DE14 1SY
Tel (01283) 510573
Fax (01283) 515594
Tours by arrangement

◉ Brewery established in 1982 by Bruce Wilkinson and Geoff Mumford, two refugees from Allied Breweries who finished up at Ind Coope of Romford. Burton Bridge now has three pubs in the town including an enlarged Brewery Tap. It supplies 300 outlets direct. Bottle-conditioned beers are bottled at the brewery and include commemorative beers: Burton Porter (OG 1045, ABV 4.5%), Bramble Stout (OG 1050, ABV 5%), Empire Pale Ale (OG 1075, ABV 7.5%), Tickle Brain (OG 1080, ABV 8%).

Summer Ale *(OG 1038, ABV 3.8%)*
Only available during British Summer Time. A beer with a strong hop aroma and a dry, bitter finish.

XL Bitter *(OG 1040, ABV 4%)* ◆
A golden, malty bitter, with a faint, hoppy and fruity aroma. An excellent mix of flavours follows, with fruitiness dominating.

Bridge Bitter *(OG 1042, ABV 4.2%)* ◆
Amber-coloured and malty. Clean tasting with little aroma but superb, bitter, hoppy aftertaste.

Burton Porter *(OG 1045, ABV 4.5%)* ◆
Dark ruby-red, with a faint aroma. The taste combines moderate liquorice flavour with hops and fruit; slightly sweet. Dry, astringent aftertaste.

Gold Medal Ales *(OG 1045, ABV 4.5%)*
A changing monthly beer.

Spring Ale *(OG 1047, ABV 4.7%)*
Available March-April.

Staffordshire Knot Brown
(OG 1048, ABV 4.8%)
An autumn beer.

Brew *(OG 1050, ABV 5%)*

Hearty Ale *(OG 1050, ABV 5%)*
Available Nov-Jan.

Top Dog Stout *(OG l050, ABV 5%)* ◆
A winter brew with a strong roast malt and fruit mix, developing into a potent malt and roast malt aftertaste.

Festival Ale *(OG 1055, ABV 5.5%)* ◆
A full-bodied, copper-coloured, strong but sweet beer. The aroma is hoppy, malty and slightly fruity. Malt and hops in the flavour give way to a fruity finish. Tremendous mouthfeel.

Old Expensive *(OG 1065, ABV 6.5%)* ▮
A barley wine of deep red hue, malty aroma but strong caramel taste leading to a hoppy, fruity bitter finish. Tasty and satisfying, tremendous mouthfeel. Available Oct-March.

For Feelgood Bar and Catering Services:

Stairway to Heaven *(OG 1050, ABV 5%)*

For Lakeland Brewing Co:

Amazon *(OG 1045, ABV 4.5%)*

BURTONWOOD

Thomas Hardy Burtonwood Ltd, Bold Lane, Burtonwood, Warrington, Cheshire WA5 4PJ
Tel (01925) 220022 Fax (01925) 229033
Tours by arrangement (charge)

☺ Family-run brewery that in 1998 merged its brewing operation with Thomas Hardy of Dorchester (qv) to form Thomas Hardy Burtonwood Ltd. The stand-alone brewing company supplies Eldridge Pope pubs in Dorset and surrounding counties and Burtonwood pubs in the North-west as well as doing contract brews. Burtonwood is now a separate pub-owning company (qv). A brewing operation is still conducted at Burtonwood, which produces the following beers for Burtonwood pubs: occasional: Black Parrot (OG 1040, ABV 3.9%), James Forshaw's Bitter (OG 1039, ABV 4%), Buccaneer OG 1052, ABV 5.2%).

Bitter *(OG 1037, ABV 3.7%)* ◆
A well-balanced, refreshing, malty bitter, with good hoppiness. Fairly dry aftertaste.

Top Hat *(OG 1046, ABV 4.8%)* ◆
Soft, nutty, malty and a little sweet. Fairly thin for its gravity. Seasonal only now.

BUSHY'S

The Mount Murray Brewing Co Ltd, Mount Murray, Castletown Road, Braddan, Isle of Man IM4 1JE
Tel (01624) 661244
Fax (01624) 611101
Tours by arrangement

☺ Set up in 1986 as a brew pub, Bushy's moved to its present site in 1990, when demand outgrew capacity. It owns four tied houses and the beers, all brewed to the stipulations of the Manx Brewers' Act of 1874, are also supplied to 20 other outlets. Occasional/seasonal beers: Summer Ale (OG 1036, ABV 3.6%, July), Celtibration Ale (OG 1040, ABV 4%), Piston Brew (OG 1045, ABV 4.5%, for the TT races in May-June), Old Bushy Tail (OG 1045, ABV 4.5%), Old Shunter (OG 1045, ABV 4.5%, Aug-Sept), Lovely Jubbely Christmas Ale (OG 1052, ABV 5.2%).

Ruby (1874) Mild *(OG 1035, ABV 3.4%)*

Export Bitter *(OG 1038, ABV 3.8%)* ◆
An aroma full of pale malt and hops introduces you to a beautifully hoppy, bitter beer. Despite the predominant hop character, malt is also evident. Fresh and clean-tasting.

Manannan's Cloak *(OG 1038, ABV 3.8%)*

BUTCOMBE

Butcombe Brewery Ltd, Butcombe, Bristol BS40 7XQ
Tel (01275) 472240
Fax (01275) 474734
Tours by arrangement (trade only)

✖ One of the most successful of the newer breweries, set up in 1978 by a former Courage Western director, Simon Whitmore. During 1992-93, the brewery virtually doubled in size (for the third time) and, after 18 years of brewing just a single beer, a second ale went into production in 1996 after further plant development. Butcombe has recently acquired a further two pubs, bringing its estate up to six houses (although none is tied) and it also supplies 350 other outlets within a 50-mile radius of the brewery.

Bitter *(OG 1039, ABV 4%)* ◈
A malty and notably bitter beer, with subtle citrus fruit qualities. It has a hoppy, malty, citrus and very slightly sulphur aroma and a long, dry, bitter finish with light fruit notes. Amber coloured.

Gold *(OG 1047, ABV 4.7%)* ◈
Yellow gold in colour, medium bodied and well balanced, with good pale malt, hops and bitterness. Quite fruity, slightly sweet, with an abiding dryness. Belies its strength.

BUTTERKNOWLE

See Castle Eden.

BUTTS

Butts Brewery Ltd, Northfield Farm, Great Shefford, Hungerford, Berkshire RG17 7BY
Tel (01488) 648133
Fax (01189) 321840
Tours by arrangement

▧ Brewery set up in converted farm buildings in 1994 with plant acquired from Butcombe. Butts now supplies 80 outlets, mainly in Berkshire, but also in Oxfordshire, Hampshire and Wiltshire. Occasional beer: Golden Brown (OG 1050, ABV 5%).

Jester *(OG 1035, ABV 3.5%)* ◈
This amber-coloured beer is fruity and slightly buttery, with an excellent hop aroma supported by pale malt. Aroma and bittering hops balance in the mouth, leading to a dry, hoppy finish.

Bitter *(OG 1040, ABV 4%)* ◈
A traditional southern-style bitter, pale brown in colour with a good bitter hop character and some fruity tendencies.

Blackguard *(OG 1045, ABV 4.5%)* ◈
A rich, fruity red-brown porter with hints of crystal and chocolate malt in the mouth. A blackcurrant aroma and taste are well-balanced with bitterness and malt characters, followed by a dry, bitter and roast finish.

Barbus Barbus *(OG 1046, ABV 4.6%)* ▨◈
The pale malt in this amber beer is tempered with a hint of crystal malt, well balanced by hops and fruit, leading to a long, complex and bitter-sweet finish. Very drinkable.

CAINS

The Robert Cain Brewery Ltd, Stanhope Street, Liverpool, Merseyside L8 5XJ
Tel (0151) 709 8734
Fax (0151) 708 8395
E-mail LLB@Cains.dk
Web-site www.breworld.com/cains
Tours by arrangement Mon-Thu evenings

◉ The Robert Cain Brewery was first established on this site in 1850, but was bought by Higsons in the 1920s, then by Boddingtons in 1985. Whitbread took control of the Boddington's breweries in 1990 and closed the site. Re-opened as Robert Cain Brewery, now a division of Brewery Group Denmark A/S. There are plans to increase the beer portfolio dramatically over next three years. Cain's has nine tied houses and 313 outlets are supplied direct. Occasional/seasonal beers: Dragon Heart (ABV 5%, Feb/March), Dr Duncans Elixir (ABV 4.5%, April/May), Sundowner (ABV 4.5%, June/July), Triple

Hop (ABV 4.5%, Aug/Sept), Cains Red (ABV 4.5%, Oct/Nov), Blackout Winter Warmer (ABV 5%, Dec/Jan).

Dark Mild *(OG 1033.5, ABV 3.2%)* ▣◈
A smooth, dry and roasty dark mild, with some chocolate and coffee notes.

Dr Duncans IPA *(OG 1036, ABV 3.5%)*

Traditional Bitter *(OG 1038.5, ABV 4%)* ◈
A darkish, full-bodied and fruity bitter, with a good hoppy nose and a dry aftertaste.

Formidable Ale *(OG 1048, ABV 5%)* ◈
A bitter and hoppy beer with a good dry aftertaste. Sharp, clean and dry.

CALEDONIAN

Caledonian Brewing Company Ltd, 42 Slateford Road, Edinburgh EH11 1PH
Tel (0131) 337 1286 Fax (0131) 313 2370
E-mail charlotte.tindall
@caledonian-brewery.co.uk
Web-site www.caledonian-brewery.co.uk
Shop
Tours by arrangement

◎ Established in 1869, the brewery was bought by Vaux in 1919 and saved from closure by a management buy-out in 1987. Caledonian still brews in three direct-fired open coppers and remains committed to investing in its brewery and brands. Over 400 outlets are supplied direct. There are 12 seasonal beers a year plus one-offs. Caledonian Brewery does not own any licensed outlets. Occasional beer: Merman XXX (OG 1050, ABV 4.8%). Bottle-conditioned beer: Tempus Fugit (ABV 5%) ▣

Murrays Summer Ale
(OG 1036, ABV 3.6%) ◈
A clean-tasting, thirst-quenching, golden session beer, with hop and fruit evident throughout. A bitter beer, balanced by malt in the taste and aftertaste.

Deuchars IPA *(OG 1038, ABV 3.8%)* ▨▣◈
At its best, an extremely tasty and refreshing amber-coloured session beer. Hops and fruit are very evident and are balanced by malt throughout. The lingering aftertaste is delightfully bitter and hoppy.

80/- Ale *(OG 1042, ABV 4.1%)* ▣◈
A predominantly malty, copper-coloured beer, well balanced by hop and fruit; a complex Scottish heavy with the hop characteristics of a best bitter. Less complex than it once was.

Golden Promise *(OG 1048, ABV 5%)*
An organic beer, pale in colour, with pronounced hop character. Floral and fruity on the nose.

Lorimers IPA *(ABV 5.2%)*

CAMBRINUS*

Cambrinus Craft Brewery, Home Farm, Knowsley Park, Knowsley L34 4AQ
Tel (0151) 546 2226
Tours by arrangement

Cambrinus has had a helter-skelter history: it opened in July 1997, closed in January 1999 and re-opened in October 1999. There are plans to expand the beer range. Approximately 30 outlets are supplied direct. Seasonal beers: Lamp Oil (OG 1045, ABV 4.5%, late autumn), Boot Strap (OG 1045, ABV 4.5%, early spring), Epoch (OG 1050, ABV 5%, Millennium but continues to be brewed), Celebrance (OG 1060, ABV 6.5%, Christmas). Beers: Herald (OG 1036, ABV 3.7%), Yardstick (OG 1040, ABV 4%), Deliverance (OG 1040, ABV 4.2%).

CAMERONS

Camerons Brewery Company, Lion Brewery, Hartlepool TS24 7QS
Tel (01429) 266666
Fax (01429) 868195
Tours by arrangement

☺ This major brewer of real ale, established in 1865, went through a period of neglect for some 17 years when it was owned by Ellerman Shipping Lines and then the Brent Walker property group. In 1992, Camerons was bought by Wolverhampton & Dudley Breweries in a deal that included the brewery, 51 pubs and the brands. With solid investment and a successful re-launch of the beers, Camerons is going from strength to strength. Lined oversized glasses are used in all its pubs. The company has 172 tied houses, most of which take real ale, and the beers are also widely available in the free trade.

Bitter *(OG 1036, ABV 3.6%)* ◥
A light bitter, but well-balanced, with hops and malt.

Strongarm *(OG 1042, ABV 4%)* ◥
A well-rounded, ruby-red ale with a distinctive, tight creamy head; initially fruity, but with a good balance of malt, hops and moderate bitterness.

CANNON ROYALL

☐ The Cannon Royall Brewery, The Fruiterer's Arms, Uphampton, Ombersley, Worcestershire WR9 0JW
Tel (01905) 621161 Fax (01562) 743262
Tours by arrangement (occasional)

☒ The first brew was in July 1993 in a converted cider house behind the Fruiterer's Arms pub. It has increased capacity from five barrels to more than 16 a week. The brewery has a tied house, the Fox and Monkwood Green. Cannon Royall supplies a number of outlets in the West Midlands and Worcestershire.

Fruiterer's Mild *(OG 1037, ABV 3.7%)* ◥
This dark mild has a rich mixture of roast and fruit flavours. The complex blend of flavours makes this a really delicious drink.

Flintlock/Plonker *(OG 1038, ABV 3.8%)* ◥
A tangy session bitter, well hopped and satisfying.

Arrowhead *(OG 1039, ABV 3.9%)* ◥
A sharp-tasting session bitter with lots of hoppy notes and a clean aftertaste.

Buckshot *(OG 1045, ABV 4.5%)* ◥
The balance of hop and malt flavours with a hint of fruitiness are just right in this premium bitter.

Armageddon *(ABV 5.8%)* ◥
A lingering aftertaste is testament to this dry, very bitter premium ale with a drinkability that belies its strength. One to sup with respect.

Millward's Millennium *(ABV 5.8%)* ◥
A dark winter warmer that is brimful of sweet and fruity flavours with a hint of roast flavours leaving a complex yet satisfying aftertaste.

CAPTAIN COOK*

☐ The Captain Cook Brewery Ltd, White Swan, 1 West End, Stokesley, Middlesbrough TS9 5BL
Tel (01642) 710263
Fax (01642) 714245
E-mail Joonanbri@aol.com
Tours by arrangement

The Captain Cook Brewery, with a 4-barrel plant, began brewing in March 1999. It was officially opened by a regular of the White Swan, Mr James Cook, on his 79th birthday. Ale is brewed exclusively for pub and there are no plans to supply other pubs. However a supply of bottled beer is planned. Beers: Sunset (OG 1040, ABV 4%), Slipway (OG 1042, ABV 4.2%), Porter (OG 1044, ABV 4.4%), Windjammer (OG 1045, ABV 4.5%).

CASTLE EDEN

Castle Eden Brewery Ltd, Castle Eden, Hartlepool, Co Durham TS27 4SX
Tel (01429) 836007
Fax (01429) 839292
E-mail dpkneda-group.co.uk
Tours by arrangement

An independent brewery once more thanks to a management buy-out from Whitbread in late 1998. Originally attached to a 17th-century coaching inn, the old Nimmo's Brewery, established in 1826, was bought by Whitbread in 1963 and suffered the indignity of becoming 'Whitbread East Pennines'. Nevertheless, it was always semi-detached from Whitbread head office and produced some of the best cask ales within the group. It has an important contract to brew for Whitbread (though this may change under Whitbread's new owners), while on the cask front it has revived the Nimmos name. Approximately 300 outlets are supplied direct. Forty-five tied houses are owned with 30 serving cask-conditioned beer. Seasonal beers: Winter Knights, Spring Knights, Summer Knights, Autumn Knights.

Castle Eden Bitter *(OG 1039, ABV 3.9%)*

Castle Eden Ale *(OG 1042, ABV 4.2%)* ☐◥
Amber, fruity premium ale, usually dry-hopped. Bitter flavours with a lingering aftertaste. Slight maltiness develops as cask empties.

Nimmo's XXXX *(OG 1044, ABV 4.4%)* ◥
A smooth golden, fruity bitter. Full-bodied but not as bitter as might be expected. Lingering and satisfying aftertaste.

Castle Eden Porter *(OG 1046, ABV 4.6%)*

Castle Eden also brews two of the cask ales formerly produced by the now-closed Butterknowle Brewery:

Castle Eden Banner Bitter
(OG 1040, ABV 4%)

Castle Eden Conciliation Ale
(OG 1042, ABV 4.2%)

CASTLE ROCK

Castle Rock Brewery Ltd, Queens Bridge
Road, The Meadows, Nottingham NG2 1NB
Tel/Fax (0115) 985 1615
E-mail Castlerock@Tynemill.co.uk
Shop
Tours by arrangement

Castle Rock Brewery is Nottingham's only
full-mash brewery. It began life as the
Bramcote Brewing Company in 1996. A reputation for quality beers soon grew, and
became apparent to the East Midlands pub
chain, Tynemill. This interest coincided with
the local council's decision that Bramcote
Brewing Company was outgrowing its
premises and, if it were to get bigger, it
should move on. An ideal partnership
between Tynemill and Bramcote Brewing
Company created the Castle Rock Brewery at
today's site close to Nottingham's historic
castle rock. Since the alliance in 1998, Castle
Rock products have become constant in the
local free trade with little going to market
through wholesalers. Following the success
of the World Cup cricket special brew Middle
Wicket, Castle Rock has created a Rugby
World Cup brew named Rolling Ruck.
Seasonal beers: Daze Collection (ABV 3.8%,
summer, autumn, winter and Christmas).

Nottingham Pale Ale *(ABV 3.6%)*

Hemlock *(ABV 4%)*

Snowhite *(ABV 4.2%)*

Bendigo *(ABV 4.5%)*

Salsa *(ABV 4.5%)*

Elsie Mo *(ABV 4.7%)*

Trentsman *(ABV 4.8%)*

Black Jack Stout *(ABV 4.9%)*

Stairway *(ABV 5.2%)*

CAYTHORPE

Caythorpe Brewery, 3 Gonalston Lane,
Hoveringham, Nottingham NG14 7JH
Tel/Fax (0115) 966 4376

Tours by arrangement

Set up in 1997 by an ex-Home Brewery
employee, the beers are brewed at the Black
Horse in Caythorpe. It supplies some 50 local
outlets. Occasional beers (brewed on a
rota/seasonal basis): Light Horse (ABV 3.7%),
Leading Light (ABV 3.8%), Landlady (ABV
4.2%, in honour of the Black Horse's owner),
Dark Horse (ABV 4.3%), Too Grand (ABV
4.8%), Crazy Horse (ABV 5%).

Dover Beck Bitter *(OG 1037, ABV 4%)*

Old Nottingham Extra Pale Ale
(OG 1038.6, ABV 4.2%)

Birthday Bitter *(OG 1039.2, ABV 4.5%)*

CHALK HILL

Chalk Hill Brewery, Rosary Road,
Norwich, Norfolk NR1 4DA
Tel (01603) 477078
Tours by arrangement

⊠ Run by former Reindeer brewpub owner
Bill Thomas and his partners, Chalk Hill
began production with a 15-barrel plant in
1993. It is looking forward to a bright future
since taking on award-winning David Winter
(ex-Woodforde's) as head brewer, and is
developing plans for expansion and new
brews. Chalk Hill supplies its own two pubs
and 20 local free trade outlets. The beers are
also available nationwide via beer agencies.
Occasional beer: IPA (OG 1055, ABV 5.3%).

Brewery Tap *(OG 1036, ABV 3.6%)* ◆
Pleasant session drink. A gentle blend of
hoppy bitterness leads to a light refreshing
finish.

CHB *(OG 1042, ABV 4.2%)* ◆
Solid malty aroma gives this copper-coloured
beer a good start. The well-matched fruity
sweetness complements the malty base. As
the beer progresses, a bitter-sweet treacly
hoppiness becomes dominant.

Dreadnought *(OG 1050, ABV 4.9%)* ◆
A traditionally robust strong ale. Reminiscent
of a rich fruit cake, the fruity overtones are
counter-balanced by a mellow bitterness.

Flintknapper's Mild *(OG 1050, ABV 5%)* ◆
A throwback to the milds of history.
Although a roasted barley flavour dominates
throughout, a surprisingly bitter edge and a
defined vinous quality in this dark red ale.
This shows why milds were once so popular.

IPA *(OG 1055, ABV 5.3%)* ◆
Mid-brown in colour, stronger than most
IPAs, with hints of fruit in the aroma leading
to a rounded fruit and floral balance; hop
character comes through in the aftertaste.

Old Tackle *(OG 1056, ABV 5.6%)* ◆
The malted 'Ovaltiney' taste matches the
flowery aroma. An inherent sweetness and a
chewy feel to a reddish brown beer that
needs to be savoured slowly.

CHERITON

▯ The Cheriton Brewhouse, Cheriton,
Alresford, Hampshire SO24 0QQ
Tel (01962) 771166
Fax (01962) 771595
E-mail bestbeer1@aol.com
Tours by arrangement

⊠ Purpose-built brewery, opened in 1993 by the proprietors of the Flower Pots Inn (next door). The brewery is now working close to its weekly capacity of 50 barrels to supply 30-40 outlets as well as a second tied house. Occasional/seasonal beers: Village Elder (ABV 3.8%, spring-early summer), Beltane (OG 1045, ABV 4.5%, spring), Flower Power (OG 1052, ABV 5.2%), Turkey's Delight (ABV 5.9%, Christmas).

Pots Ale (OG 1036.5, ABV 3.8%) 🍷
Pale brown, with a hoppy nose. A well-balanced bitter and hoppy taste leads through to the aftertaste.

Cheriton Best Bitter
(OG 1043, ABV 4.2%) 🍺🍷
A malty and fruity taste continues into the aftertaste. A dark brown beer with a malty and fruity nose.

Diggers Gold (OG 1046, ABV 4.6%) 🍺🍷
A golden beer with a citric, hoppy aroma; bitter and hoppy in all respects. A dry finish.

CHILTERN
The Chiltern Brewery, Nash Lee Road, Terrick, Aylesbury, Buckinghamshire HP17 0TQ
Tel (01296) 613647
Fax (01296) 612419
Shop 9-5 Mon-Sat
Tours by arrangement (individual tour most Saturdays at noon)

⊠ Established by Richard and Lesley Jenkinson in 1980, the first brew, Chiltern Ale, was followed in 1982 by Beechwood Bitter. Three Hundred Old Ale joined the ranks in 1988 to celebrate the eighth anniversary, with Bodgers Barley Wine in 1990 for the 10th and John Hampden's Ale in 1995 for the 15th anniversary. A brewery shop opened in 1989, followed by a small museum in 1994. Buckinghamshire County Celebration Ale has been replaced with Lord Leicester Ale. Bottle-conditioned beer: Bodgers Barley Wine (OG 1080, ABV 8.5%).

Chiltern Ale (OG 1038, ABV 3.7%) 🍷
A refreshing session bitter, amber in colour, with a predominantly malty character. The aroma is of pale malt with a hint of grape, with some sweetness in the mouth and a short finish.

Beechwood Bitter (OG 1043, ABV 4.3%) 🍷
A pale brown, refreshing beer with a rich butter-toffee aroma, lots of pale malt and fruit in the mouth and a finish that is more sweet and fruity than bitter.

Three Hundred Old Ale
(OG 1049/50, ABV 4.9%) 🍷
A strong old ale with some crystal malt and

roast character plus hints of liquorice. Deceptively strong.

CHURCH END
Church End Brewery Ltd, The Griffin Inn, Church Road, Shustoke, Warwickshire B46 2LB
Tel (01675) 481567
Fax (01675) 481254
Tours by arrangement

A small brewery in a 350-year-old stable workshop with a 4-barrel capacity opened in 1994. It produces unusual beers (banana, lemon, spices and herbs) made at different times of the year. It is on the look-out for a tied pub to combat the threat of pub companies squeezing out guest beers. Church End supplies 50-100 outlets. Occasional beers: Mild Quaker (ABV 3.4%), Anchor Bitter (ABV 4%), Hooker Ale or Rusty Dudley (ABV 4.5%), Pews Porter (ABV 4.5%), Silent Night (ABV 4.5%, Christmas), Willie Brew'd (ABV 4.5%, Burns Night), Stout Coffin (ABV 4.6%), Shustoke Surpryes (ABV 4.8%), Cracker or Four King Ale (ABV 5%, Christmas), Father Brown (ABV 6%), Rest in Peace (ABV 7%).

Cuthberts (OG 1038, ABV 3.8%) 🍷
A refreshing, hoppy beer, with hints of malt, fruit and caramel taste. Lingering bitter aftertaste.

Gravediggers (OG 1038, ABV 3.8%) 🍷
A premium mild. Black and red in colour, with a complex mix of chocolate and roast flavours, it is almost a light porter. Available in spring and summer.

Wheat-a-Bix (OG 1042, ABV 4.2%) 🍷
A wheat beer; clear, malty and pale, combining German hops and English wheat.

What the Fox's Hat
(OG 1043, ABV 4.2%) 🍷
A beer with a malty aroma and a hoppy and malty taste with some caramel flavour.

Pooh Beer (OG 1044, ABV 4.3%) 🍷
A bright golden beer brewed with honey. Sweet, yet hoppy; moreish.

Vicar's Ruin (OG 1044, ABV 4.4%) 🍷
A straw-coloured best bitter with an initially hoppy, bitter flavour, softening to a delicate malt finish.

Old Pal (OG 1055, ABV 5%) 🍷
A strong, copper-coloured ale, full of rich, malty flavours. Three different types of hops are used; dry finish.

CITY OF CAMBRIDGE
City of Cambridge Brewery Ltd, 19 Cheddars Lane, Cambridge CB5 8LD
Tel (01223) 353939
Tours by arrangement

⊠ Opened in May 1997 as a 5-barrel brew plant, it planned to double capacity in 1999. 70 outlets are supplied direct. Bottle-conditioned beer: Hobson's Choice (ABV 4.1%).

Jet Black (OG 1037, ABV 3.7%)
A rare example of the dark bitter class of beer, bursting with hop aroma.

Boathouse Bitter (OG 1038, ABV 3.8%) 🍷
Copper-brown and full-bodied session bitter starting with impressive citrus and floral hop; grassy, fruity notes and cooked vegetables are

The Good Beer Guide 2001

present with finally a fading, gentle bitterness.

Hobson's Choice *(OG 1041, ABV 4.1%)* 🏠🍺
A highly drinkable, golden brew with a pronounced hop aroma and taste, and a fruity, bitter balance in the mouth, finishing gently dry. Vegetable notes occur when young.

Atomsplitter *(OG 1047, ABV 4.7%)* 🍺
Robust copper-coloured strong bitter with hop aroma and taste and distinct vegetably sulphur edge.

Parkers Porter *(ABV 5.3%)*

Bramling Traditional *(OG 1055, ABV 5.5%)*

CLARK'S

HB Clark Co (Successors) Ltd, Westgate Brewery, Westgate, Wakefield, W Yorkshire WF2 9SW
Tel (01924) 373328
Fax (01924) 372306
Shop (cash and carry) 8-5 Mon-Fri; 8-1pm Sat-Sun
Tours by arrangement

⊛ Founded in 1905, Clark's ceased brewing during the keg revolution of the 1960s and 1970s. Resumed cask ale production in 1982. Supplied by direct delivery to 150 outlets and in addition to wholesalers and distributors throughout England and Scotland. Clark's has six tied houses with five serving cask-conditioned beer. Monthly and occasional beers are also available.

Traditional *(ABV 3.8%)* 🍺
A copper-coloured, well-balanced, smooth beer, with a malty and hoppy aroma, leading to a hoppy, fruity taste and a good, clean, strong malt flavour. Bitterness and dryness linger in the taste and aftertaste.

Festival Ale *(ABV 4.2%)* 🍺
A light, fruity, pleasantly hopped premium bitter with a good fruity, hoppy nose. Moderate bitterness follows, with a dry, fruity finish. Gold in colour.

City Gent *(ABV 4.2%)*

Burglar Bill *(ABV 4.4%)* 🍺
A good, hoppy, fruity aroma precedes an enjoyable, strongly hoppy and fruity taste, with moderate bitterness and good malt character. A lingering, dry, hoppy finish follows. Dark brown in colour.

Black Cap *(ABV 4.4%)*

Rams Revenge *(ABV 4.6%)*

Golden Hornet *(ABV 5%)*

Hammerhead *(ABV 5.7%)*

Winter Warmer *(ABV 6%)*

CLEARWATER

Clearwater Brewery, 2 Devon Units, Hatchmoor Industrial Estate, Torrington, Devon EX38 7HP
Tel (01805) 625242
Tours by arrangement

Brian Broughton, formerly of Barum, took over the closed St Giles in the Wood Brewery in January 1999 and has continued with many improvements since. 70 outlets are supplied direct. Beers: Cavalier (ABV 4%), Beggars Tipple (ABV 4.2%), Ramblers Tipple (ABV 4.5%), Oliver's Nectar (ABV 5.2%).

CLOCKWORK

🏠 RH & JG Graham t/a Graham Enterprises, The Clockwork Beer Co, 1153/55 Cathcart Road, Glasgow G42 9HB
Tel/Fax 0141 6490184
Tours by arrangement

A husband and wife partnership bought a Glasgow pub in 1977, gutted it and rebuilt it to include a micro-brewery in the middle of the bar. They started brewing in December 1997. Beers (which use primarily American Hops): Amber IPA (OG 1038, ABV 3.8%), Red Alt Beer (OG 1045, ABV 5%), Original Lager (OG 1048, ABV 4.8%), Hazy Daze Fruit Beer range (OG 1050, ABV 5%): Seriously Ginger is permanent, with others produced as the fruit is available (eg kiwi, raspberry and banana). A Monthly Special (OG 1042, ABV 4.1/4.2%) is also brewed using European hops.

COACH HOUSE

The Coach House Brewing Company Ltd, Wharf Street, Howley, Warrington, Cheshire WA1 2DQ
Tel (01925) 232800
Fax (01925) 232700

⊛ Brewery founded in 1991 by four ex-Greenall Whitley employees. In 1995 Coach House increased its brewing capacity to cope with growing demand and it now delivers to outlets throughout England, Wales and Scotland, either direct or via wholesalers. The brewery also produces specially commissioned beers and brews three beers for non-brewing company John Joule of Stone, tel: (01785) 814909. Seasonal beers: Wizards Wonder Halloween Bitter (OG 1042, ABV 4.2%, October), Cracker Barrel Bitter (OG 1046, ABV 4.6%, November), Dewi Sant Heritage Ale (OG 1047, ABV 4.7%, March), Regal Birthday Ale (OG 1047, ABV 4.7%, April), St Patrick's Leprechaun Ale (OG 1047, ABV 4.7%, March), St George's Heritage Ale (OG 1049, ABV 4.9%, April), Bootleg Valentines Ale (OG 1050, ABV 5%, February), Combine Harvester (OG 1052, ABV 5.1%, late summer), Burns Auld Sleekit (OG 1055, ABV 5.5%, January), Anniversary Ale (OG 1060, ABV 6%), Cheshire Cat (OG 1060, ABV 6%), Three Kings Christmas Ale (OG 1060, ABV 6%).

Coachman's Best Bitter *(OG 1037, ABV 3.7%)* 🍺
A well-hopped, malty bitter, moderately fruity with a hint of sweetness and a peppery nose.

Honeypot Bitter *(OG 1038, ABV 3.8%)*

Ostlers Summer Pale Ale *(OG 1038, ABV 4%)* 🍺
Light, refreshing and bitter, with a hint of pepper and a dry finish.

Gunpowder Strong Mild *(OG 1039, ABV 3.8%)* 🍺
Dark brown, lightly hopped, malty mild with faint roast undertones. Easy drinking but not as characterful as it once was.

Dick Turpin *(OG 1042, ABV 4.2%)* 🍺
Malty, hoppy pale brown beer with some initial sweetish flavours leading to a short, bitter aftertaste. Also sold under other names as a pub house beer.

Squires Gold Spring Ale

(OG 1042, ABV 4.2%) 🌟
A golden spring beer. New Zealand hops give intense bitterness followed by a strong chocolate flavour from amber malt. Uncompromising and characterful.

Flintlock Best Bitter *(ABV 4.4%)*
A very pale, light beer.

Innkeeper's Special Reserve
(OG 1045, ABV 4.5%) 🌟
A darkish, full-flavoured bitter. Quite fruity, with a strong, bitter aftertaste.

Gingernut Premium *(OG 1050, ABV 5%)*

Posthorn Premium Ale
(OG 1050, ABV 5%) 🌟
Well-hopped and fruity, with bitterness and malt also prominent. Hoppy aroma and fruity aftertaste.

Taverners Autumn Ale
(OG 1050, ABV 5%) 🌟
A fruity, bitter, golden ale with a slightly dry aftertaste. A warming, autumnal ale.

Blunderbus Old Porter
(OG 1055, ABV 5.5%) 🌟
A superb winter beer. The intense roast flavour is backed by coffee, chocolate and liquorice, and hints of spice and smoke. Well-hopped with massive mouthfeel. An intense, chewy pint that is surprisingly refreshing and moreish.

For Joule:

Old Knotty *(OG 1037, ABV 3.7%)*

Old Priory *(OG 1044, ABV 4.4%)*

Victory Brew *(OG 1050, ABV 5%)*

COCK
🍺 The Cock Tavern, Harborough Road, Kingsthorpe, Northamptonshire NN2 7AZ
Tel (01604) 715221

Brew pub opened in 1995 as the Hop House Brewery, after the refurbishment and renaming of the Cock Hotel. In 1996 its parent company, Labatt Retail, sold out to Enterprise Inns, which then sold the pub on to McManus Taverns, a local pub chain. Only one beer is produced, which is also sold in some other McManus pubs. At the Cock itself, the beer is kept under blanket pressure.

Bitter *(ABV 4%)*

COLES*
🍺 Coles Family Brewery, White Hart Inn, Llanddarog, Nr Carmarthen SA32 8NT
Tel/Fax (01267) 275395

Coles Family Brewery was started by Cain, one of the sons, in March 1999. Cwrw Blasus, meaning 'tasty beer, was the first brew made and has continued to be the main ale for the brewery. Each cask is brewed individually, giving a more traditional flavour than a large brewery's commercial flavour. From time to time different brews are experimented with such Spiced Cwrw Nadolig, Porter, Stout, Mild, and Golden. There are plans to make a traditional lager. Beers: Best Mild (OG 1037, ABV 3.8%), Twrogs Golden Summer Ale (OG 1040, ABV 4.2%), Cwrw Blasus (OG 1042, ABV 4.5%), Spiced Cwrw Nadolig (OG 1042, ABV 4.5%), Stout (OG 1045, ABV 4.5%), Porter (OG 1050, ABV 5%).

CONCERTINA
🍺 The Concertina Brewery, 9A Dolcliffe Road, Mexborough, S Yorkshire S64 9AZ
Tel (01709) 580841
Tours by arrangement

A brewery in the cellar of a club, once famous for its concertina band, it started brewing in 1992. The plant is continuously upgraded and produces eight barrels a week and supplies 25 outlets.

Club Bitter *(ABV 3.9%)* 🌟
A fruity session bitter with a good bitter flavour.

Old Dark Attic *(OG 1038, ABV 3.9%)*
A dark brown beer with a fairly sweet, fruity taste.

Best Bitter *(OG 1038.5, ABV 3.9%)* 🌟
This mid-brown bitter has lots of hops on the nose, a hoppy taste and a dry finish, plus gentle fruitiness throughout.

One-eyed Jack *(OG 1039, ABV 4%)*
Fairly pale in colour, with plenty of hop bitterness. Brewed with the same malt and hops combination as Bengal Tiger, but more of a session beer. Also known as Mexborough Bitter.

Bengal Tiger *(OG 1043, ABV 4.6%)* 🍴🌟
Light amber ale with an aromatic hoppy nose followed by a wonderful combination of fruit and bitterness. A very smooth finish.

Dictators *(OG 1044, ABV 4.7%)*

Ariel Square Four *(OG 1046, ABV 5.2%)*

CONISTON
🍺 Coniston Brewing Co Ltd, Coppermines Road, Coniston, Cumbria LA21 8HL
Tel (015394) 41133
Fax (015394) 41177
E-mail i.s.bradley@btinternet.com
Tours by arrangement
Shop 11-11

CONISTON
BREWING Co.

☺ A 10-barrel brewery set up in 1995 behind the Black Bull coaching inn, it achieved national fame when it won the Champion Beer of Britain competition in 1998 for Bluebird Bitter. It is now brewing 30 barrels a week and supplies 20 local outlets direct. Brakspear brews and bottles Bluebird for Coniston in bottle-conditioned form at ABV 4.2%. Seasonal beer: Blacksmith's Ale (OG 1047.5, ABV 5%, Dec-Feb).

Bluebird Bitter *(OG 1036, ABV 3.6%)* 🍴🌟
A fruity hoppiness with a hint of geranium in the aroma; full, grainy maltiness with a fruity, complex hoppiness. Beautifully balanced, consistent and satisfying.

Opium (*OG 1040, ABV 4%*) ♦
Copper-coloured with distinctly fruity,
hoppy aromas; a well-balanced flavour with
malt, hops and fruit, and more bitter and
astringent in the aftertaste.

Old Man Ale (*OG 1042.5, ABV 4.4%*) ♦
Delicious fruity, winey beer with complex,
well-balanced richness.

CORVEDALE*

⛫ Corvedale Brewery, Sun Inn, Corfton,
Craven Arms, Shropshire SY7 9DF
Tel (01584) 861503 (brewery)
/239 (Sun Inn)
Tours by arrangement

Norman Pearce decided to start brewing
because of his interest in real ale and the
availability of a suitable building. Beer:
Norman's Pride (OG 1043, ABV 4.3%).

COTLEIGH

Cotleigh Brewery, Ford Road,
Wiveliscombe, Somerset TA4 2RE
Tel (01984) 624086
Fax (01984) 624365
E-mail cotleigh@cloveruk.net
Tours by arrangement

⊗ Situated in the historic brewing town of
Wiveliscombe, Cotleigh Brewery is one of the
oldest and most successful small breweries in
the West Country. The brewery, which
started trading in 1979, is housed in specially
converted premises with a modern brew
plant capable of producing 140 barrels a
week. 150 pubs, mostly in Devon and
Somerset, are supplied direct from the brewery and the beers are also widely available
across the country via selected wholesalers.
Two beers are produced exclusively for the
Kent wholesalers East-West Ales Ltd, tel:
(01892) 834040. Occasional beers: Old
Buzzard (see below) and a number of other
beers are produced on a monthly guest beer
rota: Swift (OG 1030, ABV 3.2%), Nutcracker
Mild (OG 1036, ABV 3.6%), Kiwi Pale Ale
(OG 1039, ABV 3.9%), Harvest Ale (OG 1040,
ABV 4%), Blue Jay Bitter (OG 1042, ABV
4.2%), Hobby Ale (OG 1042, ABV 4.2%),
Goshawk (OG 1043, ABV 4.3%), Kookaburra
Bitter (OG 1044, ABV 4.4%), Peregrine Porter
(OG 1045, ABV 4.4%), Golden Eagle (OG
1045, ABV 4.5%), Merlin Ale (OG 1049, ABV
4.8%), Old Buzzard (OG 1048, ABV 4.8%,
winter), Osprey (OG 1050, ABV 5%),
Monmouth Rebellion (OG 1050, ABV 5%),
Snowy Ale (OG 1050, ABV 5%), Hawkshead
(OG 1055, ABV 5.5%), Red Nose Reinbeer
(OG 1050, ABV 5%, Christmas).

Harrier SPA (*OG 1035, ABV 3.6%*) ♦
A winter brew. A straw-coloured beer with a
hoppy aroma and taste, followed with a
hoppy, bitter finish. Plenty of flavour for a
light beer.

Tawny Bitter (*OG 1038, ABV 3.8%*) ♦
A mid-brown-coloured beer with a hoppy
aroma, a hoppy but well-balanced flavour,
and a hoppy, bitter finish.

Barn Owl Bitter (*OG 1045, ABV 4.5%*) ▣♦
A dark amber beer with a malty aroma backed
by hops; smooth, full-bodied taste with hops
dominating, followed by malt. The finish is
hoppy balanced with a little malt.

Old Buzzard (*OG 1048, ABV 4.8%*) ♦
A rich dark ruby beer with a roast malt nose, a
rich, chewy malt palate with a hint of bitterness. Long finish with hops and roast malt.

For East-West Ales:

Aldercote Ale (*OG 1042, ABV 4.2%*)

Aldercote Extra (*OG 1046, ABV 4.7%*)

COTTAGE

Cottage Brewing Co Ltd,
The Old Cheese Dairy, Hornblotton Road,
Lovington, Somerset BA7 7PS
Tel (01963) 240551 Fax (01963) 240383
Tours by arrangement

⊗ Brewery founded in West Lydford in 1993
and upgraded to a 10-barrel plant in 1994.
Owned by a former airline captain, the com-
pany got off to a flying start with Norman's
Conquest taking the Champion Beer of
Britain title at the 1995 Great British Beer
Festival. Other awards followed and, on the
strength of this success, the brewery moved
to larger premises in 1996, doubling the
brewing capacity at the same time. In 1997
Golden Arrow won the silver medal for Best
Bitter at GBBF. In January 1999 Norman's
Conquest won the Gold Medal for strong
beers at the Great British Winter Beer
Festival. The beers are served in 500 outlets
nationally, with occasional local deliveries
made by the company's steam lorry. The
names mostly follow a railway theme and
during 1999 the brewery introduced its
Millennium Ales series. Seasonal beers:
Goldrush (OG 1049, ABV 5%), Golden Arrow
(OG 1044, ABV 5.4%), Santa's Steaming Ale
(OG 1055, ABV 5.5%, Christmas). Occasional
beer: Broadgauge Bitter (ABV 3.9%).

Southern Bitter (*OG 1037, ABV 3.7%*) ♦
Gold coloured beer with malt and fruity hops
on the nose. Malt and hops in the mouth
with a long fruity, bitter finish.

Wheeltappers Ale (*OG 1039, ABV 4%*)

Champflower (*OG 1043, ABV 4.2%*) ♦
Amber beer with fruity hop aroma, full hop
taste and powerful bitter finish.

Golden Arrow (*OG 1044, ABV 4.5%*) ♦
Golden beer with powerful floral hoppy
aroma, a fruity, full-bodied taste with a dry,
bitter finish.

Somerset & Dorset Ale (S&D)
(*OG 1044, ABV 4.4%*) ♦
A well-hopped, malty brew, with a deep red
colour.

Our Ken (*OG 1044, ABV 4.5%*)

(GWR) Great Western (*OG 1053, ABV 5.4%*)
A stronger and darker version of S&D, with a
full-bodied maltiness.

Norman's Conquest
(*OG 1066, ABV 7%*) ▣♦
A dark strong ale, with plenty of fruit in the
aroma and taste; rounded vinous, hoppy
finish.

COTTAGE SPRING*

Cottage Spring Brewery, Gorse Cottage,
Graig Road, Upper Cwmbran, Cwmbran,
Torfaen NP44 5AS
Tel (0780) 346 6346

Cottage Spring Brewery is a craft brewery situated on the slopes of Mynydd Maen in Upper Cwmbran in Gwent's Eastern Valley. With an output of up to 40 barrels a week, the brewery takes its name from the cottage where it was built and the local spring that supplies the water used for brewing liquor. The brewer produces four regular cask beers that are all produced using traditional methods and ingredients. Ten outlets are supplied direct. Beers: Drayman's Bitter (OG 1036, ABV 3.5%), Drayman's Gold (OG 1038, ABV 3.8%), Crow Valley Bitter (OG 1042, ABV 4.2%), The Full Malty (OG 1050, ABV 5.2%).

COUNTRY LIFE

◻ Country Life Brewery, Pig on the Hill, Pusehill, Westward Ho!, Devon EX39 5AH
Tel (01237) 477615
Fax (01237) 425979
E-mail simon@countrylife.freeserve.co.uk
Shop open during pub hours
Tours by arrangement

The 2.5-barrel plant was bought from the Lundy Island brewery in the Bristol Channel and set up by Simon Lacey at the Pig on the Hill pub. Due to popular demand for Old Appledore, a 5-barrel fermenter has been acquired. The brewing process can be seen from the pub through large viewing screens. 15 plus outlets are supplied direct. Beers: Old Appledore (OG 1036, ABV 3.7%), Wallop (OG 1043, ABV 4.4%), Golden Pig (OG 1047, ABV 4.7%), Country Bumpkin (OG 1057, ABV 5.7%).

COX & HOLBROOK

Cox & Holbrook, Hillcroft House, High Road, Great Finborough, Stowmarket, Suffolk IP14 3AQ
Tel/Fax (01449) 770682
Tours by arrangement

David Cox, an accountant by profession, bought his 5-barrel plant in early 1997. It's possibly one of the most travelled microbreweries, having started life as Mackintosh Croft Head Brewery, soon to become Sutherland's of Edinburgh before journeying south to its present home. The emphasis is on dark ales, stouts and porters. The short-term plan is to concentrate on free trade outlets and to expand the range of products in bottle and cask. Six outlets are supplied direct. Beers: Crown Mild (OG 1034, ABV 3.4%), Shelley Dark (OG 1036, ABV 3.6%), Old Mill Bitter (OG 1036, ABV 3.8%), Albion Pale Ale (OG 1043, ABV 4.5%), Stowmarket Porter (OG 1045, ABV 4.5%), Iron Oak Single Stout (OG 1045, ABV 4.5%), Prentice Strong Dark Ale (OG 1053, ABV 5.3%). Bottle-conditioned beers: Albion, Storm Watch, East

Anglian Pale, Stowmarket Porter, Iron Oak, all OGs and ABVs as above.

Buoys Bitter *(ABV 3.3%)* ◆
A pale, malty beer with a fruity aroma and aftertaste.

East Anglian Pale Ale
(OG 1050, ABV 5%) ◆
A very drinkable pale beer with a hoppy taste and fruit to follow.

Storm Watch *(OG 1050, ABV 5%)* ◆
An amber, fruity beer with a bitter aftertaste. Does not taste as strong as it really is: beware.

COX'S YARD

◻ Cox's Yard (Charles Wells Ltd), Bridgefoot, Stratford-on-Avon, Warwickshire CV37 6YY
Tel (01789) 404600
Fax (01789) 404633
E-mail Info@Cox'sYard.co.uk
Web-site www.CoxsYard.co.uk
Shop 9-5
Tours by arrangement

The brewery, part of a development by large Bedford regional Charles Wells, is housed in the engine shed of the sawmill in an old timber yard that now comprises the Jester pub, a restaurant, gift shop and the Stratford Tales attraction, in addition to the micro-brewery. The site was opened in August 1998 and the first brew left the brewery, which uses equipment from the Ancient Druids at Cambridge, in October 1998. The brewery can be seen through large glass windows from the pub. Talks on the brewery are given regularly by the brewer. Approximately 47 outlets are supplied direct. Occasional beers: Old Timber (OG 1050, ABV 5%), Cox's Millennium Mash (OG 1052, ABV 5.2%) and other regular seasonal brews. Beer: Jester Ale (OG 1038, ABV 3.8%).

CRANBORNE

The Cranborne Brewery, Sheaf of Arrows, 4 The Square, Cranborne, Dorset BH21 5PR
Tel (01725) 517456
Tours by arrangement

⊠ The brewery, set up in a stable block behind the Sheaf of Arrows pub, went into production at Easter 1996, initially to serve just that pub. It now supplies a further two outlets direct and there are plans for the beers to be distributed further afield. Beers: Quarrel (OG 1038, ABV 3.8%), Quiver (OG 1038, ABV 3.8%), Porter (ABV 4%), Summer Ale (ABV 4%), Seasonal Ale (ABV 6%).

CREWKERNE

◻ Crewkerne Brewery, c/o Crown Inn, 34 South Street, Crewkerne, Somerset TA18 8DB
Tel (01460) 72464
Tours by arrangement

Brewery established in December 1997, it brews two beers, one of which won CAMRA's Best Somerset Beer 1998. Ten outlets are currently supplied.

Crew Brew *(OG 1040, ABV 4%)*

Mainsail *(OG 1045, ABV 4.5%)*

Jack Tar *(OG 1052, ABV 5%)*

CROPTON

♥ Cropton Brewery, Woolcroft,
Cropton, nr Pickering,
N Yorkshire YO18 8HH
Tel (01751) 417330
Fax (01751) 417310
Shop 10-4 Summer
Tours by arrangement

☺ Brewing returned to Cropton in 1984 when
the cellars of the pub were converted to
accommodate a micro-brewery. The plant
was extended in 1988, but by 1994 it had outgrown the cellar and a purpose-built brewery
was installed in the grounds of Woolcroft
Farm behind the pub. Cropton's seven additive-free beers are supplied to 70-100 independent outlets direct and nationwide through
wholesalers. All the beers are available bottle-
conditioned and can be purchased from the
visitor centre attached to the brewery's own
pub, the New Inn. Special brews: Rudolph's
Revenge (ABV 4.6%), TGIAOB (ABV 4.5%).

King Billy *(OG 1039, ABV 3.6%)* ◆
A refreshing, straw-coloured bitter, quite
hoppy, with a strong, but pleasant, bitter finish that leaves a clean, dry taste on the palate.

Two Pints *(OG 1040, ABV 4%)* ◆
A good, full-bodied bitter. Malt flavours initially dominate, with a touch of caramel, but
the balancing hoppiness and residual sweetness come through.

Scoresby Stout *(OG 1044, ABV 4.2%)* ◆
A classic of the style. A jet-black stout whose
roast malt and chocolate flavours contrast
with a satisfying bitter finish.

Honey Gold Bitter *(ABV 4.2%)*

Uncle Sam's *(OG 1044, ABV 4.4%)*
A clean-tasting and refreshing premium pale
ale. The overriding characteristic is the fruity
bouquet yielded by authentic American
ingredients.

Backwoods Bitter *(OG 1049, ABV 4.7%)* ◆
A malty premium bitter, tawny-coloured and
full-bodied. A long and satisfying, sweet finish contains an abundance of fruit flavours.

Monkmans Slaughter
(OG 1060, ABV 6%) 🍺◆
Rich-tasting and warming; fruit and roast
malt in the aroma and taste, with dark
chocolate, caramel and autumn fruit notes.
Subtle bitterness continues into the
aftertaste.

CROUCH VALE

Crouch Vale Brewery Limited, 12 Redhills
Road, South Woodham Ferrers,
Chelmsford, Essex CM3 5UP
Tel (01245) 322744
Fax (01245) 329082
E-mail cvb@cwcom.net
Tours by arrangement

⊗ Founded in 1981, Crouch Vale has grown
steadily to become one of the longest established micro-breweries in the eastern counties. In addition to its brewing operation, the
company is a major wholesaler of guest cask-
conditioned beers and a supplier to regional
beer festivals. A bottle beer is planned. 200
outlets are supplied direct. Two tied houses
are owned, both serving cask-conditioned
beer. Occasional/seasonal beers: Blackwater

Mild (ABV 3.7%), The Golden Duck (ABV
3.8%), Feering Ferret (ABV 4%), Snowdrop
(ABV 4.1%), Topsail (ABV 4.3%), Yardarm
(ABV 4.3%), The Conkeror (ABV 4.3%),
Santa's Session (ABV 4.3%), Fireball (ABV
4.5%), Kursaal Flyer (ABV 4.5%), Essex
Skipper (ABV 4.6%), Santa's Revenge (ABV
5.2%), Fine Pale Ale (ABV 5.9%), Willie
Warmer (ABV 6.4%). Bishop's Bitter (ABV
3.7%) is brewed under contract.

Woodham IPA *(OG 1036, ABV 3.6%)* ◆
A pale brown, good session bitter with a fruity
aroma and well-balanced malt and hops.

Best Dark Ale *(OG 1036, ABV 3.6%)*

Best Bitter *(OG 1040, ABV 4%)* ◆
Mid-brown session beer with hops and malt
on the nose. Grainy and hoppy with a short
finish.

Millennium Gold *(OG 1042, ABV 4.2%)* ◆
A golden, easy drinking premium ale,
notably bitter at the end but with a balance
of malt, hops and fruit in the mouth after a
light, malty aroma.

Strong Anglian Special or SAS
(OG 1048, ABV 4.8%) ◆
Tawny, full-bodied strong bitter with an initially hoppy aroma and taste balanced by
malt with a bitter aftertaste.

Essex Porter *(OG 1049, ABV 4.9%)*

CROWN BUCKLEY
See Brains.

CROWN INN
♥ Munslow, nr Craven Arms,
Shropshire SY7 9ET
Tel (01584) 841205
Fax (01584) 841255
E-mail v.clandlord@tinyworld.uk
Tours during business hours

Pub-brewery established in 1994 with a
2-barrel plant, it has taken over the Dog at
Worfield and is now brewing for both pubs.
One other local outlet is supplied. Ironmaster
(OG 1041, ABV 4.2%) is brewed solely for the
Golden Ball in Ironbridge. Seasonal beer:
Butcher's Baubles (OG 1054, ABV 5.8%,
Christmas). Beers: Butcher's Best
(OG 1038, ABV 3.8%).

CUCKMERE HAVEN
The Cuckmere Haven Brewery,
c/o The Golden Galleon, Exceat Bridge,
Cuckmere Haven, East Sussex BN25 4AB

Tel (01323) 892247 or 899261
Fax (01323) 892555
E-mail galleon@mistral.co.uk
Tours by arrangement

⊠ Brewing began in May 1994, using yeast supplied by Harveys of Lewes. There are plans to move the brewery into a new extension to the pub and to expand to a 5-barrel mash tun and five fermenters. As a result of the height of the building, the brewhouse will be designed as a mini tower brewery with a shop. Seasonal/occasional beers: Swallows Return (OG 1039, ABV 4%, spring), Saxon King Stout (OG 1041, ABV 4.2%), Dark Velvet (OG 1046, ABV 4.7%, autumn).

Best Bitter *(OG 1040, ABV 4.1%)* ◆
Malty overtones in the aroma are joined by a hoppy bitterness in the flavour.

Guvnor *(OG 1046, ABV 4.7%)*

Golden Peace *(OG 1054, ABV 5.5%)*
An amber-coloured, strong beer.

DALESIDE

Daleside Brewery Ltd, Unit 1 Camwal Road, Starbeck, Harrogate, N Yorkshire HG1 4PT
Tel (01423) 880022
Fax (01423) 541717
Web-site www.dalesidebrewery.co.uk
E-mail daleside@rapidial.co.uk
Tours by arrangement

☺ Formerly Big End Brewery, founded in 1985, the company moved to new premises and changed its name in 1992. After years of gradual expansion, capacity was increased in June 2000 when plant was bought from Vaux. The beers are available nationwide. Occasional beers: Christmas Classic (ABV 4.5%), Auld Lang Syne (ABV 4.1%), Ripon Jewel (ABV 5.8%)

Nightjar *(OG 1038, ABV 3.7%)* ◆
A fruity, amber-coloured, medium-hopped beer with some sweetness. Leads to a sharp, slightly subdued, long, bitter finish.

Old Legover *(OG 1042, ABV 4.1%)* ◆
A well-balanced, mid-brown, refreshing beer that leads to an equally well-balanced, fruity and bitter aftertaste.

Old Lubrication *(OG 1042, ABV 4.1%)* ◆
Plenty of malt, fruit and hops with a hint of sweetness leading to a moderate-to-strong bitter aftertaste in this complex dark ale.

Greengrass Old Rogue Ale
(OG 1046, ABV 4.5%) ◆
A well-balanced, robust, tawny bitter with strong hop and fruit overtones, with a long, dry finish.

Crack Shot *(OG 1047, ABV 4.5%)*
Strong mid-brown ale with reddish tint. Well balanced and full bodied.

Monkey Wrench *(OG 1056, ABV 5.3%)* ⬚◆
A powerful strong ale, mid-brown to ruby in hue. Aromas of fruit, hops, malt and roast malt give way to well-balanced fruit, malt and hoppiness on the tongue, with some sweetness throughout. A very flavoursome beer.

Morocco Ale *(ABV 5.5%)* ⬚◆
A powerful, dark brew with malt and fruit in the taste. A spicy beer in which ginger predominates and can at times overpower.

Brewed to an Elizabethan recipe found at Levens Hall in Cumbria and 'modernised' in the 17th century when spice was added. The beer is becoming increasingly more widely available.

For AVS Wholesalers of Gravesend:

Shrimpers *(ABV 4.1%)*
Mid-brown, well-rounded and well balanced best bitter.

DARK HORSE

Dark Horse Brewery Ltd, Adams Yard, Maidenhead Street, Hertford, Hertfordshire SG14 1DR
Tel (01992) 509800
E-mail enquiries@darkhorsebrewery.co.uk
Web-site darkhorsebrewery.co.uk

⊠ The brewery started in 1994 in the cellar of the White Horse pub and has been taken over by new owners, although founder Ian Harvey retains an interest. New brews are currently being developed, while most of the existing range will continue. 11 outlets are supplied direct.

Ale *(OG 1038, ABV 3.6%)*
A tasty bitter, with a hint of roast grain.

Moonrunner *(OG 1040, ABV 3.8%)*

Sunrunner *(OG 1042, ABV 4.1%)*
A well-balanced, full-flavoured bitter, with fruit notes and a strong, bitter finish.

Fallen Angel *(OG 1042, ABV 4.2%)* ⬚

Black Widow *(OG 1047, ABV 4.5%)*

St Elmo's Fire *(OG 1046, ABV 4.6%)*

Death Wish *(OG 1053, ABV 5%)*

DARK STAR

Dark Star Brewing Co Ltd (incorporating Skinner's of Brighton), Evening Star, 55 Surrey Street, Brighton, E Sussex BN1 3PB
Tel (01273) 701758 or 328931
Tours by arrangement

⊠ A brewery set up by Peter Skinner and Peter Halliday in 1994 in the cellar of their pub, the Evening Star. In 1995 they formed Dark Star Brewing Co with Rob Jones (formerly of Pitfield Brewery), adding Rob's Dark Star beers alongside the Skinner's range. Both company names are used on the beers, but are not connected to Skinner's Cornish Ales (qv). There have been many different brews and styles to supplement the regular beers. The beers are supplied to Peter Skinner's two pubs (the other being the Gardener's Arms in Lewes), and to 10 outlets. Seasonal beers: Cliffe Hanger Porter (OG 1053, ABV 5.5%, winter) and Critical Mass (OG 1070, ABV 7%, Christmas). Beers: Roast Mild (OG 1036, ABV 3.5%), Pale Ale (OG 1038, ABV 3.7%), Golden Gate (OG 1043, ABV 4.3%), Meltdown Ginger Beer (OG 1060, ABV 6%).

Dark Star *(OG 1050, ABV 5%)* ◆
Dark full-bodied ale with a roast malt aroma and a dry, bitter stout-like finish.

Zingibier *(OG 1045, ABV 4.5%)* ⬚

DARKTRIBE

DarkTribe Brewery, 25 Doncaster Road, Gunness, Scunthorpe,

N Lincolnshire DN15 8TG
Tel (01724) 782324
E-mail dixie@darktribe.greatxscape.net

⊗ This small brewery was built during the summer of 1996 in a workshop at the bottom of the garden by Dave 'Dixie' Dean, and is still run as a part-time business. The beers generally follow a marine theme, recalling Dixie's days as a marine engineer in the Merchant Navy and his enthusiasm for sailing. Plans include buying a pub and giving up the day job. Three outlets are supplied direct. Occasional/seasonal beers: Gunness Stout (OG 1040, ABV 4.1%), Jolly Roger (OG 1043, ABV 4.5%), Sixteen Bells (OG 1057, ABV 6.5%, Christmas/New Year), Dixie's Midnight Runner (OG 1057, ABV 6.5%), Dark Destroyer (OG 1083, ABV 9.7%).

Dixie's Mild *(OG 1036, ABV 3.6%)*

Full Ahead *(OG 1037, ABV 3.8%)* ❧
A malty smoothness backed by a slightly fruity hop give a good bitterness to this amber-brown bitter.

Futtocks *(OG 1040, ABV 4.2%)*

Dr Griffin's Mermaid *(OG 1043, ABV 4.5%)*

Galleon *(OG 1044, ABV 4.7%)* ⌸❧
A tasty, golden, smooth, full-bodied ale with fruity hops and consistent malt. The thirst-quenching bitterness lingers into a well-balanced finish.

Aegir Ale *(OG 1044, ABV 4.7%)*

Twin Screw *(OG 1047, ABV 5.1%)* ❧
A fruity, rose-hip tasting beer, red in colour. Good malt presence with a dry, hoppy bitterness coming through in the finish.

Brewed for Duffield Brewing Company:

Thorold Special *(OG 1037, ABV 3.8%)*

Duffields *(OG 1040, ABV 4.2%)*

DARWIN

Darwin Brewery Ltd, 5 Castle Close, Crook, Co Durham DL15 8LU
Tel (01833) 763200
Fax (0191) 515 2531
E-mail brewlab@sunderland.ac.uk
Web-site www.darwinbrewery.co.uk
Tours by arrangement (including tasting at local venue)

☺ The Darwin Brewery first brewed beers in 1994 and expanded with the acquisition of the Hodge's Brewery in Crook, County Durham. Hodge's Brewery beers are still brewed in the plant, which also produces dedicated Darwin Brewery beers as well as specialist trial beers from Brewlab at the University of Sunderland. The brewery produces a range of high-quality beers with the strong individual character of the North-east region and specialises in historical recreations of past beers such as Flag Porter, a beer produced with a yeast rescued from a shipwreck in the English Channel. Future plans are to develop retail sales and commission further historical research for lost beers. 80 outlets are supplied direct. Occasional beers: Prof's Pint, Siddeley's Purge, Wheatfield Ale.

Darwin's Bitter *(OG 1038, ABV 3.8%)*

Evolution Ale *(OG 1042, ABV 4%)*
A dark amber, full-bodied bitter with a malty flavour and a clean, bitter aftertaste.

Hodge's Original *(OG 1040, ABV 4%)* ❧
Smooth, with a soft, bitter taste and generally light character. Ending with a stronger, slightly fruity and bitter aftertaste.

Durham Light Ale *(OG 1042, ABV 4%)*

Richmond Ale *(OG 1048, ABV 4.5%)*

Saints Sinner *(OG 1052, ABV 5%)*
A rich, smooth-tasting, ruby-red ale with a fruity aroma and hop character in the taste.

Killer Beer *(OG 1054, ABV 6%)*
A strong beer made with honey.

Extinction Ale *(OG 1086, ABV 8.3%)*

DAVIS'ES
See Grainstore.

DEEPING
Deeping Ales, 12 Peacock Square, Blenheim Way, Market Deeping, Peterborough PE6 8LW
Tel (01778) 348600
Fax (01778) 348750
Tours by arrangement

⊗ Formed in 1996, the brewery was bought by Kent businessman Jonathon Hughes with the original recipes and brewer. Half the output goes to the Tonbridge area of Kent, the rest to Peterborough. There are plans to expand the range of beers.

Amber *(OG 1037, ABV 3.7%)*

Red *(OG 1040, ABV 4.1%)*
Ruby-coloured flagship ale.

Glory *(OG 1043, ABV 4.3%)*

St George *(OG 1045, ABV 4.5%)*

Special *(OG 1048, ABV 4.8%)*
A stronger version of Red.

Snow *(OG 1050, ABV 5%)*

Gunpowder *(OG 1051, ABV 5.2%)*
After its success as a bonfire brew it is now a permanent beer.

DENT
Dent Brewery, Hollins, Cowgill, Dent, Cumbria LA10 5TQ
Tel (01539) 625326
Fax (01539) 625033
Web-site martin@dentbrew.u-net.com
Tours by arrangement (minimum six people)

☺ Brewery set up in a converted barn in the Yorkshire Dales in 1990, originally to supply just three local pubs. It now has two tied houses and supplies 50 free trade outlets direct. Its own distribution company, Flying Firkin, (01282) 865923, delivers all over northern England and is making some inroads into the south. All Dent's beers are brewed using the brewery's own spring water.

Bitter *(OG 1036, ABV 3.7%)* ❧
A faintly fragrant, malty nose leads to a sweetish, malty, bitter flavour with a little fruit. Light in body with a short, dry, bitter finish.

Rambrau *(OG 1039, ABV 4.2%)*
A cask-conditioned lager.

Ramsbottom Strong Ale
(OG 1044, ABV 4.5%) ❧
This complex, mid-brown beer has a warming, dry, bitter finish to follow its unusual combination of roast, bitter, fruity and sweet flavours.

T'Owd Tup *(OG 1058, ABV 6%)* ⌑❧
A rich, fully-flavoured, strong stout with a coffee aroma. The dominant roast character is balanced by a warming sweetness and a raisiny, fruit-cake taste that linger on into the finish.

For Flying Firkin:

Aviator *(OG 1038, ABV 4%)* ⌑❧
This medium-bodied amber ale is characterised throughout by strong citrus and hoppy flavours that develop into an enjoyable bitter finish.

Kamikaze *(OG 1048, ABV 5%)* ⌑❧
Hops and fruit dominate this full-bodied, golden, strong bitter, with a pleasant, dry bitterness growing in the aftertaste. Look also for citrus and honey in the nose, and a spicy finish.

DERWENT

Derwent Brewery,
Units 2a/2b Station Road Industrial Estate,
Silloth, Cumbria CA5 4AG
Tel (016973) 31522
Fax (016973) 31523
Tours by arrangement

☺ Set up in 1997 in Cockermouth by Hans Kruger and Frank Smith, both ex-Jennings, together with Mike Askey, as the Bitter End Brewing Co. In December 1996 it moved to Silloth as Derwent Brewery. It supplies beers throughout the north of England and organises the Silloth Beer Festival in August.

Bitter *(OG 1036, ABV 3.6%)* ❧
Very malty amber beer with a distinct roast flavour and a very dry aftertaste.

Mutineers Ale *(OG 1041, ABV 4.1%)* ❧
Aromas of roast and fruit. A sweet, light brown bitter with some roast in the middle and a rising bitter finish.

Hansi's Oktober Fest *(OG 1042, ABV 4.2%)*

Dozy Brewer *(OG 1042, ABV 4.4%)*

Bill Monks *(OG 1045, ABV 4.5%)* ❧
A mid-brown ale with a faintly flowery and fruity aroma. Fruity in the mouth and then a quickly arriving intense bitterness.

O Cocker *(OG 1050, ABV 5%)*
A pale brown beer with some initial fruit and

malt, turning quickly into a lingering bitterness.

DERWENT ROSE

⌑ Derwent Rose Brewery, Grey Horse, 115 Sherburn Terrace, Consett, Co Durham DH8 6NE
Tel (01207) 502585
E-mail paul@thegreyhorse.co.uk
Web-site www.thegreyhorse.co.uk

County Durham's newest micro-brewery is based in Consett's oldest surviving pub (152 years old in 2000). It produced its first brew in a former stable block behind the pub in 1997. Other occasional and celebratory beers are produced. Beers: 3 Giants (ABV 3.2%), Mutton Clog (ABV 3.8%), Paddy's Delight (ABV 3.8%), Steel Town (ABV 3.8%), Target Ale (ABV 4%), Conroy's Stout (ABV 4.1%), Red Dust (ABV 4.2%), Swordmaker (ABV 4.5%), Angel Ale (ABV 5%), Coast 2 Coast (ABV 5%), Derwent Deep (ABV 5%), Devil's Dip (ABV 9%).

DEVON

⌑ Devon Ales Ltd, 7 Main Street, Sauchie, Alloa, FK10 3JR
Tel (01259) 722020
Fax (01259) 716636
E-mail john.gibson@btinternet.com
Tours by arrangement

☺ The brewery opened in 1994. A cask-conditioned lager is planned. Two pubs are owned and four outlets are supplied direct. Beers: Original (OG 1038, ABV 3.9%), Thick Black (OG 1044, ABV 4.4%), Pride (OG 1048, ABV 4.8%).

DONNINGTON

Donnington Brewery, Stow-on-the-Wold, Gloucestershire GL54 1EP
Tel (01451) 830603

⊠ Thomas Arkell bought a 13th-century watermill in idyllic countryside in 1827, and he began brewing on the site in 1865. It is owned and run by a direct family descendant, Claude Arkell, and the millwheel is still used to drive small pumps and machinery. Donnington supplies its own 15 tied houses and a number of free trade outlets.

XXX *(OG 1035, ABV 3.3%)* ❧
Thin in aroma but very flavoursome. More subtle than others in its class, it has some hops and traces of chocolate and liquorice in the taste and a notably malty finish.

BB *(OG 1035, ABV 3.3%)* ❧
A pleasant amber bitter with a slight hop aroma, a good balance of malt and hops in the mouth and a bitter aftertaste.

SBA *(OG 1045, ABV 4.2%)* ❧
Malt dominates over bitterness in the subtle flavour of this premium bitter, which has a hint of fruit and a dry malty finish.

DRIFTWOOD*

⌑ Driftwood Spars Hotel, Trevaunance Cove, St Agnes, Cornwall TR5 0RT
Tel (01872) 552428/553323
Fax (01872) 553701
Tours by arrangement

Gordon and Jill Treleaven started brewing in 2000 in this famous Cornish pub and hotel that dates from the 17th century. The brewery is based in the former Flying Dutchman fish and chips shop across the road from the hotel. The 1-barrel plant was bought from the Royal Inn, Horsebridge, in Devon. Pale malt comes from Tuckers of Newton Abbot and the hops are Fuggles and Goldings. Beer: Cuckoo Ale (OG 1047, ABV 4.7%).

DRUNKEN DUCK
See Barngates Brewery

DRUMMONDS*
Drummonds Brewery, Unit 1, 443 London Road, Sheffield, South Yorkshire S2 4HJ
Tel (0114) 255 4024

A brewery launched in February 1999 but up for sale in summer 2000.

DUFFIELD
⌽ The Duffield Brewing Co, Thorold Arms, High Street, Harmston, Lincoln LN5 9SN
Tel (01522) 720358
Web-site
www.thethorold@aledrinkers.co.uk
E-mail thethorold@aledrinkers.co.uk

Founded in November 1996 in the cellar of the Thorold Arms, it currently brews just nine gallons of beer at a time to serve the free house. Beers: Bitter (OG 1038, ABV 3.6%), Mulley's Irish Stout (OG 1044, ABV 4.6%), Extra Special Bitter (OG 1057, ABV 4.8%). Thorold Bitter (ABV 3.8%) and Duffield Special Bitter (ABV 4.2%), (also bottle-conditioned) are brewed for Duffield by DarkTribe.

DUNN PLOWMAN
Dunn Plowman, The Brewhouse, Bridge Street, Kington, Herefordshire HR5 3DL
Tel (01544) 231993 07715 711863 (m)
Fax (01544) 231985
E-mail dunnplowman.brewery@talk21.com

Brewery established in 1987 as a brew pub, it moved to Leominster in 1992 and then to its present site in 1994. The brewery supplies the Queens Head, its brewery tap, and 12 other outlets within a 30-mile radius. It is run by husband and wife team Steve and Gaye Dunn. Seasonal beer: Crooked Furrow (ABV 6.5%, in cask Nov-Jan, all year in bottles). Beers: Brewhouse Bitter (ABV 3.8%), Early Riser (ABV 4%), Kingdom (ABV 4.5%).

DURHAM
The Durham Brewery, Unit 5A, Bowburn North Industrial Estate, Bowburn, Co Durham DH6 5PF
Tel (0191) 3771991
Fax (0191) 3770768
Web-site www.durham-brewery.co.uk
E-mail gibbs@durham-brewery.co.uk
Shop
Tours by arrangement

Brewery established in 1994 and upgraded to a 10-barrel plant. 100 outlets are supplied direct. Seasonal beers: Sunstroke (ABV 3.6%, April-Oct), Sanctuary (ABV 6%, Oct-May).

Magus (OG 1038, ABV 3.8%) ◆
Golden, refreshing dry bitter. An excellent session and summer ale with a medium fruity/dry aftertaste.

Green Goddess (ABV 3.8%)

White Gold (OG 1040, ABV 4%)

Black Velvet (ABV 4%)

White Velvet (OG 1042, ABV 4.2%) ◆
Smooth, golden bitter with a tangy hop and fruit taste. Aftertaste lingers with a pleasant fruitiness.

Celtic (OG 1043, ABV 4.2%) ◆
A mid-brown ale with a slight malty and fruity aroma. The aftertaste is predominantly dry and well-balanced.

Black Bishop (ABV 4.5%)

Black Friar (ABV 4.5%)

Canny Lad (OG 1045, ABV 4.5%)

Invincible (ABV 4.5%)

White Sapphire (ABV 4.5%)

White Bishop (OG 1046, ABV 4.8%) ⌷◆
Excellent golden strong ale. Bags of hoppiness in aroma and taste, with a complex of flavours in the aftertaste.

Pagan (OG 1047, ABV 4.8%) ◆
There's a decent balance of malt and hops in this premium ale. Slight sweetness in the mouth and a faint bitter aftertaste are preceded by a hint of fruit in the aroma.

Cuthberts Ale (OG 1048, ABV 5%)

EARL SOHAM
⌽ Earl Soham Brewery, The Victoria, Earl Soham, Suffolk IP13 7RL
Tel (01728) 685934 (Brewery)
(01728) 685758 (The Victoria)
Temp E-mail
malc@walker173.freeserve.co.uk

⊠ Brewing for 16 years, the plant is based behind the Victoria pub in an attractive village setting. With two tied houses to supply, including the refurbished Station at Framlingham, and a thriving free trade business, plans are well advanced to expand and move the brewery to larger premises within Earl Soham. Seasonal beer: Jolabrugg (OG 1055, ABV 5%, Christmas).

Gannet Mild (OG 1034, ABV 3.3%)
An unusual, full-tasting mild with a bitter

finish and roast flavours that compete with underlying maltiness.

Victoria Bitter *(OG 1037, ABV 3.6%)*
A characterful, well-hopped, malty beer with a tangy, hoppy aftertaste.

Sir Roger's Porter *(OG 1042, ABV 4.1%)*
Full-flavoured dark brown malty beer with bitter overtones, and a fruity aftertaste.

Albert Ale *(OG 1045, ABV 4.4%)*
Hops dominate every aspect of this beer, but especially the finish. A fruity, astringent beer.

Pullman Porter *(OG 1050, ABV 5%)*
A porter featuring roast malts, with a hint of chocolate in the flavour and aroma, and a clean, dry finish.

EAST-WEST ALES
See Brewery on Sea and Cotleigh.

EASTWOOD'S
See Barge & Barrel.

ECCLESHALL
Eccleshall Brewery, Castle Street, Eccleshall, Stafford ST21 6DF
Tel (01785) 850300
Fax (01785) 851452
Tours by arrangement

⊠ Brewery opened in out buildings behind the George Hotel in 1995. Originally a 10-barrel plant, production increased in 1997 to approximately 25-30 barrels a week. Two pubs are owned, both serving cask-conditioned beer. 50 outlets are supplied direct.

Slaters Bitter *(OG 1036, ABV 3.6%)* 🗗
Malt and hops combine with a fruity flavour in this light amber beer.

Slaters Original *(OG 1040, ABV 4%)*
A distinctive, creamy amber beer.

Top Totty *(OG 1040, ABV 4%)*
A summer beer.

Slaters Premium *(OG 1043, ABV 4.4%)*
Strong, but light and creamy, dry bitter, darker than the other brews.

Slaters Supreme *(OG 1044, ABV 4.7%)*
A well-hopped, dry bitter added to the range in 1997.

ELDRIDGE POPE
See Thomas Hardy and Pub Groups.

ELGOOD'S
Elgood & Sons Ltd, North Brink Brewery, Wisbech, Cambridgeshire PE13 1LN
Tel (01945) 583160
Fax (01945) 587711
Shop 10-5 Wed-Sun (May-Sep)
Tours by arrangement

⊠ A 200-year-old Georgian riverside brewery where a visitor centre and gardens are open from 1 May to 31 Oct. Elgood's is committed to producing a range of quality real ales including the award-winning Black Dog Mild, Champion Beer of East Anglia 1999. 43 pubs are owned, all are tied, all but one serving cask-conditioned beer. 100 plus outlets are supplied direct. Seasonal beers: Old Black

Shuck (OG 1045.8, ABV 4.5%, winter), Barleymead (OG 1048.8, ABV 4.8%, September), Reinbeer (OG 1059.8, ABV 5.9%, December), Wenceslas Winter Warmer (OG 1075.8, ABV 7.5%, December), North Brink Porter (OG 1055.8, ABV 5%).

Black Dog Mild
(OG 1036.8, ABV 3.6%) 🍺🗗🌢
Black dry mild with an abiding chocolatey character, subtle raisin fruit and a long bitter finish.

Cambridge Bitter
(OG 1038.5, ABV 3.8%) 🌢
Impressive tawny-red session bitter with a light fruity aroma, well-defined hop and an underlying malty flavour. Bitterness builds into a long finish.

Pageant Ale *(OG 1043.8, ABV 4.3%)*

Golden Newt *(OG 1044.5, ABV 4.6%)* 🌢
Fragrant hops and orange fruit aromas introduce this golden bitter. Citrus, resiny hop fills the mouth, and the finish is delightfully bitter, with hops and fruit persisting.

Greyhound Strong Bitter
(OG 1052.8, ABV 5.2%) 🌢
Full-bodied, tawny brew, with a mouth-filling blend of malty sweetness and fruit. Starts with berry fruits on the nose and ends surprisingly bitter.

MARTIN ELMS
See Nethergate.

ENVILLE
Enville Ales, Enville Brewery, Cox Green, Enville, Stourbridge, W Midlands DY7 5LG
Tel (01384) 873728
Fax (01384) 873770
E-mail INFO@envilleales.com
Web-site www.envilleales.com

⊛ Brewery on a picturesque Victorian farm complex. Using the same water source as the original village brewery (closed in 1919), the beers also incorporate more than three tons of honey annually (produced on the farm), using recipes passed down from the proprietor's great-great aunt. Enville's owner, H Constantine-Cort, had originally intended to go into full-time beekeeping with brewing as a sideline, but the position is now reversed; the brewery grows its own barley, too. Seasonal beer: Phoenix IPA (OG 1048-50, ABV 4.8%, April-Sept).

Chainmaker Mild *(OG 1036-38, ABV 3.6%)*

Bitter *(OG 1036-38, ABV 3.8%)* 🌢
A straw-coloured, hoppy and bitter beer that leaves a malty, moreish aftertaste.

Simpkiss Bitter *(OG 1036-38, ABV 3.8%)* 🌢
A medium-bodied, golden bitter. The refreshing, hoppy taste lingers.

Nailmaker Mild *(OG 1040-42, ABV 4%)*

Enville White *(OG 1040-42, ABV 4.2%)* 🌢
A clean, well-balanced, golden, sweet bitter, light in flavour. An appealing beer.

Czechmate Saaz *(OG 1041-43, ABV 4.2%)*

Enville Ale *(OG 1044-45, ABV 4.5%)*
A pale gold, medium-bodied bitter. Light hops and sweet fruit in the taste; a hint of honey in the aroma and aftertaste.

Enville Porter *(OG 1044-1045, ABV 4.5%)*

Ginger Beer *(OG 1044-46, ABV 4.6%)*

Gothic *(OG 1050-52, ABV 5.2%)* ◆
Malt, hops and caramel combine with a strong roast malt taste in this dark, stout-like beer. Well-balanced, with lurking hints of honey. Available October-March.

EVENING STAR
See Dark Star.

EVERARDS
Everards Brewery Ltd, Castle Acres,
Narborough, Leicester LE9 5BY
Tel (0116) 201 4100
Fax (0116) 281 4199
E-mail: mail@everards.co.uk
Tours by arrangement (CAMRA branches)

⊠ An independent, family-owned brewery run by the great, great grandson of the founder. Based at Narborough on the outskirts of Leicester, Everards celebrated its 150th anniversary in 1999. A developing estate of 154 high quality pubs is based largely in Leicestershire and surrounding counties. Nearly all the pubs serve a full range of cask-conditioned ales and many serve guest ales. Everards ales are all brewed to individual recipes using only the finest English hops and barley. The principal ales are all dry-hopped and conditioned for a week prior to dispatch from the brewery. Tiger Best Bitter is the most widely distributed ale and can now be found all over Britain. Daytime weekday tours can be arranged for CAMRA branches. 500 outlets are supplied direct. Seasonal beers: Perfick (ABV 4.5%, spring), Equinox (ABV 4.8%, autumn).

Beacon Bitter *(OG 1036, ABV 3.8%)* ◆
The sulphurous aroma of this copper-coloured session beer presages a malty-hop bitterness that continues into a long bitter-sweet finish. Sulphur present throughout – a typical Burton snatch.

Tiger Best *(OG 1041, ABV 4.2%)* 🗍◆
Mid-brown in colour, this somewhat unexciting brew has a sulphurous malty nose and a well-balanced palate that continues into a long, bitter-sweet finish.

Original *(OG 1050, ABV 5.2%)* ◆
Beautifully full-bodied, the sulphurous hop-malt aroma of this red-brown strong beer is followed by a malty bitterness that continues into a late finish. Very smooth and wall-balanced.

EVESHAM
⛆ SM Murphy Associates Ltd,
The Evesham Brewery, Rear of the Green Dragon, 170 Oat Street, Evesham,
Worcestershire WR11 4PJ
Tel/Fax (01386) 443462
Tours by arrangement

⊛ Brewery set up in 1992 in the old bottle store at the Green Dragon Inn in Evesham. The owner and licensee, Steve Murphy, currently supplies another four outlets direct. The brewery has become a tourist attraction, drawing thousands of visitors each year. 'Asum' in the beer names is the local pronunciation of Evesham. Seasonal beer: Santa's

Nightmare (OG 1060, ABV 6%).

Asum Ale *(OG 1038, ABV 3.8%)* ◆
The smell of hops leads to a delicate balance of malts and fruity flavour before you come to the potent finish this beer possesses.

Asum Gold *(OG 1050, ABV 5.2%)* ◆
A well-balanced premium ale that has all the range of tastes from malt to a fruity hoppiness that make it a very satisfying drink.

EXE VALLEY
Exe Valley Brewery, Silverton, Nr Exeter,
Devonshire EX5 4HF
Tel (01392) 860406
Fax (01392) 861001
Brewery tours not available except to pre-arranged groups – charge made.

⊠ Established in a redundant barn in 1984 as Barron's Brewery by former publican Richard Barron, the company expanded in 1991 when Richard was joined by former brewers' agent Guy Sheppard and the name was changed to Exe Valley. Beers are brewed traditionally from own spring water, using Devon malt and English hops. Approximately 50 outlets are supplied direct. Occasional/seasonal beer: Devon Summer (OG 1038, ABV 3.9%, June-Aug), Barron's Dark (OG 1039, 4.1%, occasional), Spring Beer (OG 1042, ABV 4.3%, March-May), Autumn Glory (OG 1044, ABV 4.5%, Sept-Nov), Devon Dawn (OG 1043, ABV 4.5%, New Year), Curate's Choice (OG 1047, ABV 4.8%, occasional), Winter Glow (OG 1056, ABV 6%, Dec-Feb).

Bitter *(OG 1036, ABV 3.7%)* ◆
Fruity aroma and taste with a hint of caramel through the aroma, taste and finish.

Barron's Hopsit *(OG 1040, ABV 4.1%)* ◆
Straw-coloured beer with strong hop aroma, hop and fruit flavour and a bitter hop finish.

Dob's Best Bitter *(OG 1040, ABV 4.1%)* 🗍◆
Malt and fruit aroma with a pleasant fruity taste and bitter finish.

Devon Glory *(OG 1046, ABV 4.7%)*
Mid-brown, fruity-tasting pint with a sweet, fruity finish.

Mr Shepperd's Crook
(OG 1046, ABV 4.7%) ◆
Smooth, full-bodied, mid-brown beer with a malty-fruit nose and a sweetish palate leading to a bitter, dry finish.

Exeter Old Bitter *(OG 1046, ABV 4.8%)* ◆
A well-balanced beer with a malt/fruit aroma
and taste, and a complex, sweet, fruity finish.

EXMOOR

**Exmoor Ales Limited,
Golden Hill Brewery,
Wiveliscombe,
Somerset TA4 2NY
Tel (01984) 623798
Fax (01984) 624572
Web-site www.exmoorales.co.uk**
Tours by arrangement

⊗ Somerset's largest brewery was founded in
1980 in the old Hancock's plant, which had
been closed since 1959. It quickly won
national acclaim, as its Exmoor Ale took the
Best Bitter award at CAMRA's Great British
Beer Festival that year, the first of many
prizes. The brewery has enjoyed many years
of continuous expansion and steadily
increasing demand. Around 250 pubs in the
South-west are supplied directly, and others
nationwide via wholesalers and pub chains.
Bottled beer (not bottle conditioned):
Exmoor Gold (ABV 5%) available from brewery or certain supermarkets nationally.
Seasonal/occasional beers: Hound Dog (OG
1041, ABV 4%, March-May), Wild Cat (OG
1044, ABV 4.4%, Sept-Nov), Exmas (OG
1050, ABV 5%, Nov-Dec).

Ale *(OG 1039, ABV 3.8%)* ◆
A pale brown beer with a malty aroma, a
malty, dry taste and a bitter and malty finish.

Fox *(OG 1043, ABV 4.2%)*

Gold *(OG 1045, ABV 4.5%)* ◆
Yellow/golden in colour, with a malty aroma
and flavour, and a slight sweetness and
hoppiness. Sweet, malty finish.

Hart *(OG 1049, ABV 4.8%)* ◆
Mid-brown beer with a hoppy aroma, rich
malty, full-bodied palate, following through
to a sharp, hoppy finish.

Stag *(OG 1050, ABV 5.2%)* ◆
A pale brown beer, with a malty taste and
aroma, and a bitter finish.

Beast *(OG 1066, ABV 6.6%)* ■↺◆
Full-bodied, fruity black beer with roasted
malt palate and a roast/fruity finish.
Available Oct-April.

FALSTAFF*

**Falstaff Brewery, 24 Society Place,
Normanton,
Derby DE23 6UH
Tel (01332) 299914
Fax (01332) 381819
Web-site thefalstaff.co.uk**
Tours by arrangement

The Falstaff Brewery was founded at the end
of the last century by the father and son partnership of Peter and Adrian Parkes, who
already owned the Falstaff Tavern, Silverhill
Road, Derby. The 3.5-barrel micro-brewery is
based in an adjoining property and is run as
a separate business, using the pub as its premier outlet and showcase.
Beers: Summer Ale (ABV 3.7%), Hit & Miss
(ABV 4.5%), Falstaff Festival (ABV 4.8%),
Falstaff Folly (ABV 5.6%), Oh! Mr Porter
(ABV 3.8%).

FAR NORTH

⊽ **Far North Brewery, Melvich Hotel,
Melvich by Thurso, Sutherland KW14 7YJ
Tel (01641) 531206
Fax (01641) 531347
E-mail melvichtl@aol.com
Web-site
www.smoothhound.co.uk/hotels/melvich
.html**

Peter Martin was born in Scotland but lived
in London for 18 years. He moved to
Sutherland in spring 1996, a real ale desert.
He is currently brewing one cask at a time for
the weekly consumption of guests working at
the nuclear site at Dounreay. He plans to
install a 4-barrel plant to increase production. If visiting, phone in advance as beer is
not always available. Beers: Real Mackay
(OG 1042, ABV 4.1%), Old Mackay (OG
1068, ABV 6.5%, winter).

FARMERS ARMS

**Lower Apperley, Gloucestershire
GL19 4DR
Tel (01452) 780307**

⊗ The brewery was started in August 1993
making just two beers under the name of
Mayhems Brewery. In October 1997 the
brewery was taken over by Wadworth. The
Farmers Arms now brews every week and
Wadworth supplies six of its tied pubs with
Oddas Light.

Oddas Light *(OG 1038, ABV 3.8%)* ◆
A hoppy, refreshing, golden bitter with a
clean, bitter taste and a lingering hint of malt
followed by a bitter aftertaste.

Mayhem's Sundowner
(OG 1044, ABV 4.5%) ◆
Malt predominates in this smooth, easy-
drinking bitter with a slight bitter-sweet
aftertaste.

FARMERS BOY
See Verulam Brewery.

FAT GOD'S
See Queen's Head.

FEATHERSTONE

**Featherstone Brewery, Unit 3, King Street
Buildings, King Street, Enderby,
Leicestershire LE9 5NT
Tel (0116) 275 0952
Mobile 0966 137762**

⊗ Small brewery that specialises in supplying
custom-brewed beers to pubs for sale under

house names. Personalised beers are brewed to order, minimum volume four barrels.

Howes Howler *(OG 1035, ABV 3.6%)*

Best Bitter *(OG 1041, ABV 4.2%)*

Vulcan Bitter *(OG 1048, ABV 5.1%)*

FEDERATION

Federation Brewery Ltd, Lancaster Road, Dunston, Tyne and Wear NE11 9JR
Tel (0191) 460 9023
Fax (0191) 460 1297
Production (0191) 460 8853
Tours by arrangement

☺ Clubs brewery that produces only bright beers. The Buchanans range of cask beers is now produced under licence by Robinsons of Stockport.

Buchanan's Best Bitter
(OG 1035.5, ABV 3.6%)

Buchanan's Original
(OG 1044.5, ABV 4.4%)

FELINFOEL

Felinfoel Brewery Co Ltd, Farmers Row, Felinfoel, Llanelli, Carmarthenshire SA14 8LB
Tel (01554) 773357
Fax (01554) 752452
E-mail enquiries@felinfoel-brewery.com
Web-site www.felinfoel-brewery.com
Shop Mon-Fri 9-4, Sat 10-12

☺ Founded in the 1830s by David John, although the present Grade II listed buildings were built in 1878. The company is still family owned and now the oldest brewery in Wales. It was the first brewery in Europe to can beer. Supplies cask ale to most of its 83 houses and to roughly 50 free trade outlets.

Dragon Bitter Ale *(OG 1034, ABV 3.4%)*

Best Bitter *(OG 1038, ABV 3.8%)* ◆
A well-balanced session bitter, light on aroma with some sweetness in the mouth and building in the finish.

Double Dragon Ale *(OG 1042, ABV 4.2%)* ◆
A sharp, crisp, malty bitter with an apple aroma that builds on the palate along with bitterness and a hint of sulphur leading to a pleasant crisp apple finish.

FENLAND

The Fenland Brewery, Unit 4, Prospect Way, Chatteris, Cambs PE16 6TZ
Tel (01354) 695852 (office)
696776 (Brewery)
Fax (01354) 695852
E-mail fenland@users.breworld.net
Tours by arrangement

▨ Research chemist Dr Rob Thomas and his wife Liz set up the brewery in 1997, opening the first brewery in the town for 65 years. Several awards followed, allowing the brewery to establish itself firmly in Cambridgeshire. Plans are now underway to expand direct deliveries into Norfolk and Lincolnshire. 50 outlets are supplied direct. Occasional/seasonal beers: Tall Tale Pale Ale (ABV 3.6%, summer), Paranoia (ABV 4.2%, autumn), Smokestack Lightning (ABV 4.2%, spring), FractAle (ABV 4.5%, spring),

Sparkling Wit (ABV 4.5%, September), Straw Bear Ale (ABV 4.5%, January), Winter Warmer (ABV 5.5%, November), Rudolph's Rocket Fuel (ABV 5.5%, December).

FBB (Fenland Brewery Bitter) *(ABV 4%)* ◆
Balanced copper-amber bitter, full-bodied with malt and butterscotch, a pronounced hop flavour in the mouth and a long dry finish.

Doctor's Orders *(ABV 5%)*

Rudolph's Rocket Fuel *(ABV 5.5%)* ◆
Strong, pungent ginger spice dominates the aroma and taste of this warming, winter brew. There is also fruit, cinnamon and a hint of roast malt in the mouth, but a surprisingly restrained, bitter-sweet finish.

FERNANDES

Fernandes Brewery, The Old Malt House, 5 Avison Yard, Kirkgate, Wakefield, W Yorkshire WF1 1UA
Tel (01924) 291709 (Brewery) 369547 (Office)
Shop (and off-licence) 10-6
Tours by arrangement

☺ The brewery opened in 1997 and is housed in a 19th-century malthouse. It incorporates a home-brew shop and specialist beer off-licence. A real ale bar called Fernandes Brewery Tap opened in June 1999 and it was recently awarded Pub of the Season and went on to achieve CAMRA Pub of the Year for 1999 from the Wakefield Branch.

Maltshovel Mild *(ABV 3.8%)*

Copper Beater *(ABV 3.8%)*

Brewery Tap Bitter *(ABV 4.1%)*

Wakefield Pride *(ABV 4.5%)*

Old Globe Premium *(ABV 5.1%)*

Double Six *(ABV 6%)*

Sam Wellers Extra Stout *(ABV 6%)*

The Empress of India *(ABV 6%)*

Moodies Mild *(ABV 6%)*

Six Ringers *(ABV 6%)*

FIDDLERS

Fiddlers Ales Ltd, The Brewhouse, Fox & Crown, Church Street, Old Basford, Nottinghamshire NG6 0GA
Tel/Fax (0115) 942 2002
Tours by arrangement

Using new plant originally destined for the United States, the brewery was installed in autumn 1996 and went into service in December. Initially brewing solely for the Fox & Crown, Fiddlers now supplies around 20 local outlets. Occasional/seasonal beers: Summer Ale (OG 1040, ABV 4.2%), Old Basford Pale Ale (OG 1052, ABV 5.2%), Ruby Ale (OG 1055, ABV 5.5%), Old Fashioned Porter (OG 1065, ABV 6.6%).

Mild *(OG 1034, ABV 3.4%)*

Best Bitter *(OG 1037, ABV 3.7%)*

Finest *(OG 1045, ABV 4.5%)*

FILO

⬓ First In Last Out Brewery, 14-15 High Street, Old Town, Hastings,

E Sussex TN34 3EY
Tel (01424) 425079
Tours by arrangement

The FILO Brewery (previously named St
Clements Brewery) has been running since
1985, brewing the same two ales, Crofters
and Cardinal. The pub brewery is still run by
the owner, Mike Bigg. A new brewhouse was
planned to be installed in 2000. Beers:
Crofters (OG 1040, ABV 3.8-4.2%) and
Cardinal (OG 1045, ABV 4.2-4.5%).

FISHERROW*

Fisherrow Brewery Limited, Unit 12,
Duddingston Yards, Duddingston Park
South, Edinburgh EH15 3NX
Tel (0131) 621 5501
Fax (0131) 621 9552
E-mail sales@fisherrow.co.uk
Web-site www.fisherrow.co.uk
Tours by arrangement

The brewery was launched in July 1999 on a
council-owned industrial unit and the plant
is made from converted dairy equipment.
The owners made history by putting pictures
of the construction on the brewery web site
each evening so progress could be monitored. The first brew was in October 1999
and progress has been good. Future plans
include taking on the next door unit. 100
outlets supplied direct. Two strengths are
given for Porter as there are plans to brew the
stronger version as a special. Seasonal/occa-
sional beers: Autumn Ale (ABV 4.2%), Porter
(ABV 4% or 8%), Bears Ale (ABV 3.8%), Mick
the Tick's 12,000th Tick (ABV 5.8%).
Beers: India Pale Ale (ABV 3.8%), Golden
Heavy (ABV 4%), Burgh Bitter (ABV 4.2%),
Nut Brown Ale (ABV 4.8%), Export Pale Ale
(ABV 5.2%).

FLAGSHIP

The Flagship Brewery, Unit 2 Building 64,
The Historic Dockyard, Chatham, Kent
ME4 4TE
Tel (01634) 832828
Tours by arrangement

⊠ The brewery was established in 1995 by
home-brewing enthusiast Andrew Purcell in
partnership with his father-in-law. It became
a limited company in February 2000. It is
located in a uniquely preserved Georgian
dockyard, now promoted as the South-east's
premier tourist attraction, the World Naval
Base. Production has steadily increased with

at least 60 regular outlets served direct and
further outlets supplied by wholesalers and
other breweries. From June 1999 it has operated another 5-barrel brewing plant at the
brew pub, the Tap 'n' Tin, 24 Railway Street,
Chatham. Occasional/seasonal beers: Victory
Mild (OG 1036, ABV 3.5%), Spring Pride (OG
1041, ABV 4%), BST British Summer Time
(OG 1042, ABV 4.4%), Frigging Yuletide (OG
1054, ABV 5.5%), Old Sea Dog Stout (OG
1055, ABV 5.5%), Nelson's Blood (OG 1056,
ABV 6%).

Capstan (OG 1038, ABV 3.8%)
A medium-dry beer with a balanced malt and
hop flavour and hints of honey.

Destroyer (OG 1039, ABV 4%)

Ensign (OG 1042, ABV 4.2%)
A fruity ale, with a good balance of malt and
hops.

Spanker (OG 1042, ABV 4.2%)
A version of Ensign.

Friggin in the Riggin (OG 1045, ABV 4.7%)
A premium bitter with a smooth malt flavour
and a bitter-sweet aftertaste.

Crow's Nest (OG 1048, ABV 4.8%)
A straw-coloured, sweet and fruity ale with a
hoppy aroma.

Friggin Millennium (OG 1048, ABV 5%)

Futtock Ale (OG 1050, ABV 5.2%)
A fruity, ruby-coloured ale, with a roast malt
aftertaste.

FLANNERY'S

Flannery's Brewery Ltd, Tyn Parc Farm,
Llandre, Bow Street, Aberystwyth,
Ceredigion SY24 5BU
Tel/Fax (01970) 820332
Tours by arrangement

Formed in May 1997, brewing took place in a
2-barrel plant in the old kitchen of the Ship
& Castle pub, now re-named Flannery's. It's
authentically Irish as the landlady hails from
Kilkenny. In late 1998, Flannery's purchased
Dyffryn Clwyd Brewery, Denbigh, and
moved the 10-barrel plant to Llandre, four
miles north of Aberystwyth. The small plant
was brewing to capacity; the new 10-barrel
kit will enable planned expansion to
progress. 40 outlets are supplied direct.
Seasonal beers: Brewer's Gold (OG 1041, Jan-
Feb), Ddraig Goch/Red Dragon (OG 1049,
March-April), Brewer's Bounty (OG 1045,
July-Aug), Harvest Moon (OG 1045, Sept-
Oct), Brewer's Bluff (OG 1044, May-June), No
Idea (OG 1055, Nov-Dec).

Spring Tide (OG 1039)

Celtic Ale (OG 1042) ◈
Tawny best bitter; the hops and malt balance
gives a gentle bitterness that builds to a long-
lasting finish.

Oatmeal Stout (OG 1044) ▉◈
Champion Beer of Wales 1998. An aroma
and palate of roast malt with a hint of
liquorice, roasted barley and chocolate malt.

Rheidol Reserve (OG 1048)

Under the Dyffryn Clwyd label:

Dr Johnson's Draught (OG 1039)

Cwrw Arbennig Porthmon/Drover's

Special Ale *(OG 1042)* ✎
Reddish-brown, malty best bitter with a light hoppy taste. Some vanilla fruitiness in initial aroma and taste.

Pedwar Bawd/Four Thumbs *(OG 1048)*

FLOWER POTS INN
See Cheriton.

FORGE
Forge Brewery Limited, Two Sawyers, Pett, Hastings, E Sussex TN35 4HB
Tel (0845) 6061616
01892 782745
E-mail clive@paramount-action.demon.co.uk
Web-site www.Forgebrewery.co.uk
Tours by arrangement

Forge Brewery acquired the Pett Brewing Company in November 1998, retaining the brewers and beers of the former company. The original brewery was established in 1995. The brewery has since expanded both the product range and customer base and is now serving more than 150 customers. The brewery has recently acquired its first pub, the Two Sawyers, where the brewery is based, and the range of Forge beers and guest beers are sold. Occasional/seasonal beers: Ewe Could Be So Lucky (ABV 6%), Santa Forge (ABV 6%), Heavy Petting (ABV 6%).

Forge Bitter *(ABV 3.2%)*

Forge Anvil *(ABV 3.5%)*

Forge Cuddle *(ABV 3.8%)*

Brothers Best *(ABV 3.9%)*
A hoppy, amber-coloured, session beer.

Forge Smithy *(ABV 4%)*

Black Pett *(ABV 4.6%)*

Pett Progress *(ABV 4.6%)*
Hoppy aroma, full body and a slightly bitter aftertaste.

Summer Eclipse *(ABV 4.6%)*

Forge Original *(ABV 5%)*

FORTH*
Forth Brewery Co Ltd, Eglinton, Kelliebank, Alloa FK10 1NU
Tel (01259) 725511
Fax (01259) 725522

E-mail
duncankellock@forthbrewery.freeserve.co.uk

A new brewing company set up by former Maclay head brewer Duncan Kellock and partners when Maclay stopped brewing in 1999. As well as Forth's two cask beers, it produces the full range for Maclay's 35 pubs. Forth's beers are distributed by Belhaven, Caledonian, Beer Seller, Flying Firkin and Maclay.

Steamboat Ale *(ABV 4%)*

Puffer Ale *(ABV 4.1%)*

For Maclay:

70/- *(OG 1037, ABV 3.6%)*

80/- *(OG 1041, ABV 4%)*

Kane's Amber Ale *(OG 1041, ABV 4%)*

Wallace IPA *(OG 1046, ABV 4.5%)*

For Heather Ale:

Heather Ale *(OG 1042, ABV 4%)*

FOUR RIVERS
Four Rivers Brewing Co Ltd, Unit 10 Hawick Crescent Industrial Estate, Newcastle-upon-Tyne, Tyne & Wear NE6 1AS
Tel/Fax (0191) 276 5302
Tours by arrangement

☹ The company went into receivership in summer 2000 and its future is in doubt. In late 1996 Trevor Smith, the founder of Newcastle upon Tyne's Hadrian Brewery, set up Four Rivers with Mike Wallbank, formerly of the Tap & Spile pub chain. They began brewing two cask-conditioned ales as well as special seasonal brews. In May 1997, Four Rivers bought the Hadrian Brewery and the right to brew its famous beers again. Four Rivers now brews its own range alongside Hadrian Ales in the same small brewery by the River Tyne. 40 outlets are supplied direct. Seasonal beers: Rowan Ale (OG 1042, ABV 4.2%), Hadrian Emperor (OG 1050, ABV 5%).

Moondance *(OG 1038, ABV 3.8%)* ✎
Dry, bitter ale. Hints of malt lead to a hoppy taste with a long aftertaste. The beer can lack body and sometimes appears bland.

Gladiator Bitter *(OG 1039, ABV 4%)*

Legion Ale *(OG 1042, ABV 4.2%)* ✎
A full-flavoured, tawny-coloured beer full of hops and fruit. Long, bitter finish.

Centurion Best Bitter
(OG 1045, ABV 4.5%) ✎
Smooth, well-balanced ale with the full flavour of hops. Very drinkable, ending quite dry.

FOX & HOUNDS (STRATHCLYDE)
See Houston.

FOXFIELD BREWERY
Foxfield Brewery, Prince of Wales, Foxfield, Broughton in Furness, Cumbria LA20 6BX
Tel (01229)716238
See Prince of Wales and Tigertops.

FRANKLIN'S

Franklin's Brewery, Bilton Lane, Bilton, Harrogate, N Yorkshire HG1 4DH
Tel (01423) 322345

⊛ Brewery set up in 1980 and now run by Leeds CAMRA founder-member Tommy Thomas, supplying guest beers to 10 pubs in North Yorkshire, plus beer festivals. Occasional beers: Summer Blotto (OG 1052, ABV 4.7%), Winter Blotto (OG 1047, ABV 4.7%).

Bitter *(OG 1038, ABV 3.8%)* ◆
A tremendous hop aroma precedes a flowery hop flavour, combined with malt. Long, hoppy, bitter finish. A fine, unusual amber bitter.

My Better Half *(OG 1060, ABV 5%)*

DT's *(OG 1045, ABV 4.5%)*

FRANKTON BAGBY

The Old Stables Brewery, Green Lane, Church Lawford, Rugby, Warwickshire CV23 9EF
Tel (02476) 540770
Tours by arrangement

Frankton Bagby is an independent brewery established in 1999 by three local families. The 5-barrel plant is housed in a small 18th-century stable block that has been carefully renovated by Warwickshire craftsmen. A specialist micro-brewery engineer undertook the design and installation of the equipment for the brewhouse. Frankton Bagby is passionately committed to brewing a range of top quality beers and has already achieved considerable success in the area. More than 90 outlets are supplied direct. Occasional/seasonal beers: Little Beauty (OG 1034, ABV 3.4%, occasional), Midsummer Madness (OG 1038, ABV 3.8%, summer) First Born (OG 1042, ABV 4.2%, occasional), Toastmaster (OG 1050, ABV 5%, winter), Christmas Pud (OG 1070, ABV 7%, Christmas). Beers: Ribtickler (OG 1038, ABV 3.8%), Squires Brew (OG 1042, ABV 4.2%), Rugby Special (OG 1045, ABV 4.5%), Old Retainer (OG 1050, ABV 5%).

FREEDOM

Freedom Brewing Company Ltd, The Coachworks, 80 Parsons Green Lane, Fulham, London SW6 4HU
Tel (0171) 731 7372
Fax (0171) 731 1218
Tours by arrangement

⊗ The brewery opened in 1995 as the first dedicated lager micro-brewer in Britain. Aiming to put the taste back into the style, it brews an unpasteurised premium lager following the edicts of the German Beer Purity Law, the Reinheitsgebot. The beer is available in more than 300 London bars. An organic version of its Pilsner is produced for the Duke of Cambridge in Islington. Freedom also owns the Soho Brewery, a pub-restaurant in Covent Garden, re-badged as the Freedom Brewing Company: 41 Earlham Street, London WC2, (020) 7240 0606. Beers: Freedom Pilsner Lager (ABV 5%) brewed in Fulham; Freedom Pale Ale (ABV 4.5%), Honey (ABV 4.5%), Soho Red (ABV 4.7%), and Freedom Wheat (ABV 5%) in Covent Garden. The beers are stored and served by gas pressure.

FREEMINER

Freeminer Brewery Ltd, The Laurels, Sling, Coleford, Gloucestershire GL16 8JJ
Tel (01594) 810408
Fax (01594) 810640
Tours by arrangement

⊗ Freeminer Brewery was established in 1992. Located in the Royal Forest of Dean, it takes many of its beer names from the ancient rights of the local tradition of mining, using both mine names and mining terms. Freeminer was one of the first small breweries to move into the renewed market for bottle-conditioned beer, winning awards over several years for single hop varietal ales. Its efforts have been recognised by listings with three major supermarket chains, and export orders both in Europe and the United States. Even though it has a rural location, the brewery makes great efforts through a network of national distributors to ensure that its beers can be enjoyed nationwide. Occasional beers: Gold Standard (OG 1050, ABV 5%), Hopewell Special (OG 1050, ABV 5%). Bottle-conditioned beers: Bitter (OG 1038, ABV 4%), Speculation Ale (OG 1047, ABV 4.8%), Shakemantle Ginger Ale (OG 1050, ABV 5%), Slaughter Porter (OG 1050, ABV 5%), Trafalgar IPA (OG 1060, ABV 6%), Deep Shaft Stout (OG 1060, ABV 6.2%).

Bitter *(OG 1038, ABV 4%)* ◆
A light, hoppy session bitter with an intense hop aroma and a dry, hoppy finish.

Strip and At It *(OG 1038, ABV 4%)* ◆
A pale summer bitter with a refreshing, hoppy taste and a smooth, hoppy finish with a hint of bitterness.

Iron Brew *(OG 1044, ABV 4.2%)* ◆
A ruby red bitter with a rich malt character with some hoppiness.

Speculation Ale *(OG 1047, ABV 4.8%)* ◆
An aromatic, chestnut-brown, full-bodied beer with a smooth, well-balanced mix of malt and hops and a predominantly hoppy aftertaste.

Celestial Steam Gale
(OG 1050, ABV 5%) ◆
A pale, full-bodied ale. Bitterness is immediately present, with some hoppiness in the mouth and finish.

Gold Standard *(OG 1050, ABV 5%)*
A new addition to the range made with First Gold hop variety.

Shakemantle Ginger Ale
(OG 1050, ABV 5%) ◆
A refreshing ginger ale brewed for summer. Unfined, with a high wheat content, it is like a European-style wheat beer. Ginger dominates throughout, mingled with a light hoppiness. Champion Beer of Britain Speciality Beer 1998.

Slaughter Porter *(OG 1050, ABV 5%)* ◆
A dark, full-bodied ale, mainly produced for spring and autumn. The roast malt flavour is followed by a hoppy finish.

Deep Shaft Stout *(OG 1060, ABV 6.2%)* ◆
A black, complex stout. A roast malt and bit-

ter chocolate flavour is followed by a hoppy finish.

Trafalgar IPA *(OG 1060, ABV 6%)* ◆
Pale, heavily hopped traditional IPA with a pronounced bitterness; hoppy nose, malt and hops on the palate and a dry, hoppy finish.

FROG ISLAND

Frog Island Brewery, The Maltings, Westbridge, St James' Road, Northampton NN5 5HS
Tel (01604) 587772
Fax (01604) 750754
E-mail beer@frogislandbrewery.co.uk
Tours by arrangement

⊠ Started in 1994 by home-brewer Bruce Littler and business partner Graham Cherry in a malthouse built by the long-defunct brewery, Thomas Manning & Co, Frog Island expanded from a 5-barrel plant to 10 barrels in 1998. It specialises in personalised beer bottles, available by mail order. 40 free trade outlets are supplied. Seasonal beers: Fuggled Frog (OG 1035, ABV 3.5%, May), Head in the Clouds (OG 1045, ABV 4.5%, August). Bottle-conditioned beers: Fire Bellied Toad (OG 1050, ABV 5%), Croak & Stagger (OG 1054, ABV 5.6%).

Best Bitter *(OG 1040, ABV 3.8%)* ◆
A complex beer, with malt, roast malt and fruit, plus a hint of sulphur, before a powerful kick of hop bitterness and astringency in the aftertaste. Pale brown in colour, and light on the tongue.

Shoemaker *(OG 1043, ABV 4.2%)* ◆
The Cascade hop citrus notes on the tongue are preceded by a huge malty aroma with passion fruit and roast characteristics. The malty aftertaste fades into a dry, nuttiness. Rich, pale brown and complex.

Fire Bellied Toad *(OG 1044, ABV 4.4%)*

Natterjack *(OG 1048, ABV 4.8%)* ◆
Deceptively robust, golden and smooth. Fruit and hop aromas fight for dominance before the grainy astringency and floral palate give way to a long, strong, dry aftertaste with a hint of lingering malt.

Croak & Stagger *(OG 1056, ABV 5.8%)* ◆
The initial honey/fruit aroma is quickly overpowered by roast malt then bitter chocolate and pale malt sweetness on the tongue. Gentle, bitter-sweet finish. A winter brew.

FROMES HILL

♀ The Wheatsheaf Inn & Fromes Hill Brewery, Wheatsheaf Inn, Fromes Hill, nr Ledbury, Herefordshire HR8 1HT
Tel/Fax (01531) 640888
Tours by arrangement

⊠ Brewery founded in 1993, supplying the Wheatsheaf and four other outlets with beers produced with local hops. Beers: Buckswood Dingle (OG 1038, ABV 3.6%), Overture (OG 1042, ABV 4.2%).

FROME VALLEY BREWERY

Frome Valley Brewery, Mayfields, Bishop's Frome, Herefordshire WR5 5AS
Tel (01531) 640321

Brewery founded in May 1997 and

established in a former 18th-century hop kiln in the depth of the Frome Valley. It supplies the local pubs and also supplies bottled beers to local craft shops. All the beers are made with spring water.

Frome Valley Premium Bitter
(OG 1038, ABV 3.8%)
A traditional beer, good bitterness, with a light aroma. Local hops and spring water used.

Tawny Ale *(OG 1041, ABV 4.2%)*

Pale Ale *(OG 1041, ABV 4.2%)*

Blackmoor Stout *(OG 1042, ABV 4.3%)*

Naughty Noughty *(OG 1061, ABV 6.4%)*

FRUITERER'S ARMS

See Cannon Royall.

FULLER'S

Fuller, Smith and Turner PLC, Griffin Brewery, Chiswick Lane South, Chiswick, London W4 2QB
Tel (020) 8996 2000 Fax (020) 8995 0230
Web-site www.fullers.co.uk
Shop 10-6 Mon-Sat 12-4 Sun
Tours by arrangement

⊠ Fuller, Smith & Turner's Griffin Brewery in Chiswick is London's oldest brewery. A brewery has stood on this same Chiswick site for more than 350 years. Messrs Fuller, Smith & Turner formed their partnership in 1845 and direct descendants of the founding families are still involved in the running of the company. In spite of technical advances, traditional brewing methods have been maintained. Fuller's beers have a unique record. In the 23 years that CAMRA has held the Champion Beer of Britain competition, Fuller's has won the Beer of the Year award five times. The beers have been Best in Class no less than nine times and ESB has been voted Best Strong Ale an unprecedented seven times. All but one of Fuller's 217 pubs serves cask ales. Fuller's also supplies 973 other outlets. Fuller's Organic Honey Dew (cask and bottle), is the world's first honey-flavoured organic ale and a new winter ale, Jack Frost, is made with the addition of blackberries. Occasional/seasonal beers: Summer Ale (OG 1038.5, ABV 3.9%), Organic Honey Dew (OG 1042.8, ABV 4.3%, spring), Red Fox (OG 1042.8, ABV 4.3%, autumn), Jack Frost (OG 1044.8, ABV 4.5%, winter). Bottle-conditioned beers: 1845 Celebration Ale (OG 1063.8, ABV 6.3%) ⬚, Vintage Ale (OG 1089, ABV 8.5%).

Chiswick Bitter *(OG 1034.5, ABV 3.5%)* ▦◆
A distinctively hoppy, refreshing beer, with underlying maltiness and a lasting bitter finish. Champion Beer of Britain 1989.

Summer Ale *(OG 1038.5, ABV 3.9%)* ◆
A refreshing, golden, hoppy bitter with balancing malt flavour. Available June-Sept.

London Pride *(OG 1040.5, ABV 4.1%)* ▦⬚◆
An award-winning beer with a good, malty base and a rich balance of well-developed hop flavours.

ESB *(OG 1054.8, ABV 5.5%)* ▦⬚◆
A strong pale brown ale of great character. The immediate full-bodied maltiness gives way to a rich hoppiness in the finish.

FYFE

⚑ Fyfe Brewing Company, 469 High Street, Kirkcaldy, Fife KY1 2SN
Tel/Fax (01592) 646211
Tours by arrangement

☻ Established in 1995 behind the Harbour Bar, it was Fife's first brew pub in the 20th century. Most of the output is taken by the pub, the remainder being sold direct to 20 local outlets and to the free trade via wholesalers. Seasonal beer: Cauld Turkey (OG 1060, ABV 6%, winter).

Rope of Sand *(OG 1037, ABV 3.7%)* ◆
A quenching bitter. Malt and fruit throughout, with a hoppy, bitter aftertaste.

Auld Alliance *(OG 1040, ABV 4%)* ◆
A very bitter beer with a lingering, dry, hoppy finish. Malt and hop, with fruit, are present throughout, fading in the finish.

Lion Slayer *(OG 1042, ABV 4.2%)*

Fyfe Fyre *(OG 1048, ABV 4.8%)*

GALE'S

George Gale & Co Ltd, The Hampshire Brewery, Horndean, Hampshire PO8 0DA
Tel (023) 9257 1212
Fax (023) 9259 8641
E-mail Gales@mcmail.com
Web-site www.Gales.co.uk
Shop 10-5 Mon-Fri 10-2 Sat
Tours by arrangement

☒ In 1847 Richard Gale, a local trader, bought the Ship & Bell inn and its small brewery, and by 1853 his youngest son, George, had taken over running the brewery. He expanded the business by buying local inns and the farm buildings adjacent to the inn, which he developed into a substantial brewery. In 1869 the brewery was destroyed by fire, but by the end of the year had been rebuilt and much of the present building results from that time. In 1896 George Gale sold his major share in the brewery to the Bowyer family, who still control the company today. All 117 tied houses serve cask ale. Gale's also supplies 650 free trade outlets direct. Seasonal/occasional beers: Trafalgar Ale (OG 1042, ABV 4.2%, Battle of Trafalgar, October), Hampshire Glory (OG 1043, ABV 4.3%, June), Happy Hog (OG 1044, ABV 4.4%, February), Easter Frolic (OG 1043, ABV 4.4%, April), Harvest Ale (OG 1045, ABV 4.5%, September), Christmas Ale (OG 1050, ABV 5%, December). Bottle-conditioned beers: HSB (OG 1050, ABV 4.8%), Festival Mild (OG 1052, ABV 4.8%), Christmas Ale (OG 1080, ABV 8%), Trafalgar Ale (OG 1090, ABV 9%), Prize Old Ale (OG 1094, ABV 9%) ⬡.

Butser Bitter *(OG 1034, ABV 3.4%)* ◆
A mid-brown chestnut beer. A slightly malty and fruity aroma preludes a sweet taste, with some fruit and malt. The aftertaste is sweet and fruity with a little bitterness.

GB *(OG 1040, ABV 4%)* ◆
A medium-bodied, deep golden brown brew that is initially malty sweet, has a fruity middle period with a hint of burnt orange and a dry hop flower tasting bitter finish. Several of the characteristics are ruined if served through a sparkler.

Winter Brew *(OG 1044, ABV 4.2%)* ◆
A rich winter ale, containing Prize Old Ale. Almost black in colour, it has a roast malt aroma with fruit and caramel, all of which are echoed in the taste and finish. Available Nov-March.

HSB *(OG 1050, ABV 4.8%)* 🍺◆
A mid-brown beer with a fruity aroma. The full-bodied, sweet and fruity taste, with some maltiness, follows through to the aftertaste. For those with a sweet tooth.

Festival Mild *(OG 1052, ABV 4.8%)* 🍺⬡◆
Black in colour, with a red tinge. The aroma is fruity. A sweet, fruity and malty taste, with some caramel, carries through to the aftertaste, but with more bitterness.

GLENTWORTH

Glentworth Brewery,
Glentworth House, Crossfield Lane,
Skellow, Doncaster,
S Yorkshire DN6 8PL
Tel (01302) 725555
Fax (01302) 724133

☻ Started in 1996 in buildings behind a former dairy, with a 5-barrel plant and maximum of two brews a week. More than 120 outlets are supplied direct within a 50-mile radius. Beers: Light Year (OG 1039, ABV 3.9%) ⬡, Donny Rover (OG 1041, ABV 4.1%), Amber Gambler (OG 1042, ABV 4.3%), Lightmaker (OG 1043, ABV 4.5%). Seasonals include Amber Gambler (OG 1042, ABV 4.3%), Lightmaker (OG 1043, ABV 4.5%), Whispers (OG 1045, ABV 4.5%), Full Monty (OG 1048, ABV 5%) .

GOACHER'S

P&DJ Goacher, Unit 8, Tovil Green Business Park, Maidstone, Kent ME15 6TA
Tel (01622) 682112
Tours by arrangement

☒ Kent's oldest small independent brewer, set up in 1983 by Phil and Debbie Goacher, producing all-malt ales with only local Kentish hops for two tied houses and around 30 free trade outlets in the mid-Kent area. Special, a mix of Light and Dark ales, is also available to pubs for sale under house names.

Real Mild Ale *(OG 1033, ABV 3.4%)* 🗂
A full-flavoured malty ale with a background bitterness.

Fine Light Ale *(OG 1036, ABV 3.7%)* 🗂🍺
A pale, golden brown bitter with a strong, floral, hoppy aroma and aftertaste. A hoppy and moderately malty session beer.

Best Dark Ale *(OG 1040, ABV 4.1%)* 🍺
An intensely bitter beer, balanced by a moderate maltiness, with a complex aftertaste. Now back to its original darker colour.

Crown Imperial Stout *(OG 1044, ABV 4.5%)*
Brewed to celebrate Goachers' 15th year – an occasional brew.

Gold Star Ale *(OG 1050, ABV 5.1%)*
A pale ale (now brewed all year).

Maidstone Porter *(OG 1050, ABV 5.1%)*
A dark ruby winter beer with a roast malt flavour.

Old 1066 Ale *(OG 1066, ABV 6.7%)*
A black, potent old ale, produced in winter only.

GODDARDS

Goddards Brewery Ltd, Barnsley Farm, Bullen Road, Ryde, Isle of Wight PO33 1QF
Tel (01983) 611011
Fax (01983) 611012
E-mail goddardsbrewery.ltd.uk

⊗ Housed in a picturesque, converted 18th-century barn on a farm near Ryde, the brewery went into production in 1993. Sales of its award-winning beers have been rising steadily – 1999 set a new record – and brewery capacity quadrupled in 1997, although this is partly to allow for kegging and production of a Liberty lager. A cold sterile filtered (ie not pasteurised) version of Fuggle-Dee-Dum is now brewed and shipped in bulk for packaging by Hampshire Bottling Ltd. Around 40 outlets are supplied and Goddards has acquired its first pub, the Wishing Well at Pondwell, Ryde, and plans to add a further four or five pubs to provide a small pub estate. Occasional/seasonal beer: Ale of Wight (OG 1038, ABV 4%, spring), Duck's Folly (OG 1050, ABV 5.2%, early autumn), Inspiration (OG 1050, ABV 5.2%), Winter Warmer (OG 1052, ABV 5.2%, winter).

Special Bitter *(OG 1038.5, ABV 4%)* 🗂🍺
A refreshing, straw-coloured, easy-drinking bitter with a wonderfully flowery hop aroma that carries right through to a satisfying aftertaste.

Fuggle-Dee-Dum *(OG 1048.5, ABV 4.8%)* 🍺
Tawny full-flavoured, rich malty ale with a pleasing consistency of malty sweetness complemented by a hoppy bitterness that produces that essential bite that makes you want more.

Iron Horse *(OG 1049, ABV 4.8%)* 🍺
Superb roast old ale/porter style beer with complex roast malty-fruity bitterness consistent through the tasting experience – and what an experience. Available late autumn.

Inspiration Ale *(OG 1050, ABV 5.2%)* 🍺
Straw-coloured pale strong ale with a predominantly bitter fruity flavour balanced by a sweet undertone.

Winter Warmer *(OG 1052, ABV 5.2%)* 🍺

Good example of the seasonal winter ale style but with a refreshing bitterness that cleans the palate of the sweetness inherent in this style of beer.

GOFF'S

Goff's Brewery Ltd, 9 Isbourne Way, Winchcombe, Gloucestershire GL54 5NS
Tel (01242) 603383
Fax (01242) 603959
Tours by arrangement

⊗ A family concern that started brewing in 1994, using plant purchased from Nethergate Brewery. Goff's now supplies 200 outlets.

Knight Rider *(OG 1036, ABV 3.6%)*

Jouster *(OG 1040, ABV 4%)* 🗂🍺
A drinkable, tawny-coloured ale, with a light hoppiness in the aroma. It has a good balance of malt and bitterness in the mouth, underscored by fruitiness, with a clean, hoppy aftertaste.

Fallen Knight *(OG 1044, ABV 4.4%)* 🍺
A tawny-coloured premium bitter, dry hopped for a delicate floral aroma. A good balance of malt and fruit in the mouth with a bitter-sweet finish. Autumn ale now brewed all year round.

White Knight *(OG 1046, ABV 4.7%)* 🍺
A well-hopped bitter with a light colour and full-bodied taste. Bitterness predominates in the mouth and leads to a dry, hoppy aftertaste. Deceptively drinkable for its strength.

Black Knight *(OG 1053, ABV 5.3%)* 🍺
A dark, ruby-red tinted beer with a strong chocolate malt aroma. It has a smooth, dry, malty taste, with a subtle hoppiness, leading to a dry finish. A classic winter porter.

GOLDFINCH

Goldfinch Brewery, 47 High East Street, Dorchester, Dorset DT1 ZHU
Tel (01305) 264020

⊗ Brewery established in 1987 at rear of Tom Brown's public house in Dorchester. Originally a 1-barrel plant, it has been increased to four barrels. The brewery supplies two pubs and 10 other free trade outlets direct, plus others via wholesalers. Occasional beer: Mayor J Porter (OG 1044, ABV 4.5%, November/February).

Tom Brown's Best Bitter
(OG 1039, ABV 4%) 🍺
Clean, refreshing session beer. Moderate fruit and hops in the aroma and taste, balanced well with a little caramel sweetness.

Midnight Sun Special Pale Ale
(OG 1045, ABV 4.5%) 🍺
A well-balanced golden bitter, light in body with hops, fruit and bitterness in moderation.

Flashman's Clout Strong Ale
(OG 1048, ABV 4.8%) 🍺
A tawny/mid-brown beer with an attractive, honeyed aroma, and a bitter-sweet taste with malt and some hops. Hoppiness continues through to give a bitter edge to the aftertaste.

Midnight Blinder *(OG 1050, ABV 5%)* 🍺
A reddish brown, full-bodied strong bitter. Dark malts dominate the bitter-sweet flavour, continuing into the hoppy aftertaste.

DOROTHY GOODBODY

See Wye Valley.

GOOSE EYE

Goose Eye Brewery, Ingrow Bridge, South Street, Keighley, W Yorkshire BD22 5AX
Tel (01535) 605807 (0468) 200265 (m)
Fax (01535) 605735
Tours by arrangement

⊛ Re-established in 1991, Goose Eye supplies 50-60 regular outlets, mainly in West and North Yorkshire and Lancashire. Its beers are also available through national wholesalers and pub chains. It now produces an ever expanding and diverse range of occasional beers, sometimes brewed to order, and is diversifying into wholesaling and bottled beers (filtered but not pasteurised). No-Eye Deer is often rebadged under house names. Occasional/seasonal beers: Spellbound (OG 1040, ABV 4%, Halloween), Summer Jack's (OG 1042, ABV 4.2%, summer), Wandy Wabbit (OG 1042, ABV 4.2%, Easter), Cockeyed Goose (OG 1062, ABV 6.2%, Christmas), Christmas Goose (OG 1052, ABV 5.2%).

Barmpot *(OG 1038, ABV 3.8%)*

No-Eyed Deer *(OG 1038, ABV 3.8%)* ◆
A faint fruity aroma, hoppy fruit flavours and some malt characterise this refreshing, gold-coloured beer. The bitter finish is quite short.

Bronte *(OG 1040, ABV 4%)* ◆
A pale brown beer with a weak aroma. Malt and bitterness dominate the taste with some background fruit and hops. The lingering aftertaste is dry and bitter.

Wharfedale *(OG 1045, ABV 4.5%)*
A copper-coloured best bitter, becoming increasingly hard to find.

Pommies Revenge *(OG 1052, ABV 5.2%)*
A light-coloured, full-bodied and fruity, strong bitter.

GRAINSTORE

Davis'es Brewing Company Ltd,
The Grainstore Brewery, Station Approach, Oakham, Rutland LE15 6RE
Tel (01572) 770065
Fax (01572) 770068
E-mail hopsdavis@aol.com
Tours by arrangement

⊠ Now flying the banner for Rutland-brewed beers, the Grainstore, the smallest county's largest brewery, has been brewing since 1995. The brewery's curious name comes from the fact that it was founded by Tony Davis and Mike Davies. After 30 years in the industry, latterly with Ruddles, Tony decided to set up his own business after finding a derelict Victorian railway grainstore building. The brewing is designed traditionally, relying on whole hops and Maris Otter barley malt. 60 outlets are supplied direct. Seasonal beers: Springtime (OG 1045, ABV 4.5%, March-May), Gold (OG 1045, ABV 4.5%, May-Oct), Harvest IPA (OG 1045, ABV 4.5%, Sept-Oct), Three Kings (OG 1045, ABV 4.5%, Nov-Dec), Winter Nip (OG 1070, ABV 7.3%, Nov-Dec).

Cooking *(OG 1036, ABV 3.6%)* ◆
A smooth, copper-coloured beer, full-bodied for its gravity. Malt and hops on the nose; malt and fruit to the taste, with a malty aftertaste.

Triple B *(OG 1042, ABV 4.2%)* ◆
Initially, hops dominate over malt in both the aroma and taste, but fruit is there, too. All three linger in varying degrees in the sweetish aftertaste of this tawny brew.

Steaming Billy Bitter *(OG 1043, ABV 4.3%)*

Springtime *(OG 1045, ABV 4.5%)*
A new seasonal offering.

Ten Fifty *(OG 1050, ABV 5%)* ◆
This full-bodied, tawny beer is hoppy and fruity right into the aftertaste. A little malt on the nose and in the initial taste, with an underlying sweetness and an increasing bitterness.

GREEN DRAGON

See Evesham.

GREEN DRAGON

Q **Green Dragon Free House & Brewery, Broad Street, Bungay, Suffolk NR35 1EE**
Tel/Fax (01986) 892681
Tours by arrangement

⊠ The Green Dragon was purchased from Brent Walker in 1991 and the buildings at the rear converted to a brewery. In 1994 the plant was expanded and moved into a converted barn across the car park. The 100 per cent increase in capacity allowed the production of a larger range of ales, including seasonal and occasional brews, but the beers are only available at the pub itself and a couple of other outlets. Beers: Milden (ABV 3.4%), Chaucer Ale (OG 1037, ABV 3.8%), Bridge Street Bitter (OG 1046, ABV 4.5%), Green Dragon Lager (ABV 4.5-5%), Dragon (OG 1055, ABV 5.5%), Wynter Warmer (ABV 7%).

GREEN JACK

Green Jack Brewing Co Ltd, Unit 2 Harbour Road Industrial Estate, Oulton Broad, Lowestoft, Suffolk NR32 3LZ
Tel (01502) 587905
Fax (01502) 582621
Tours by arrangement

⊠ Brewery that started in 1993 on the old Forbes Brewery site with a capacity of 900 barrels a year but Green Jack hopes to increase to 1,200 barrels to meet pub demand

and also for bottling. Two fermenting tanks and a mash tun have been purchased to allow for expansion. The brewery supplies around 30 outlets direct, as well as its own three pubs. Wholesalers also take the beers. Bottle-conditioned beer: Ripper (OG 1076, ABV 8.7%). Occasional/seasonal beers: Mild (OG 1034, ABV 3%), Honey Bunny (OG 1041, ABV 4%, spring), Summer Dream (OG 1041, ABV 4%, summer), Old Thunderbox (OG 1041, ABV 4%, winter), Norfolk Wolf Porter (OG 1050, ABV 5.2%), Lurcher (OG 1052, ABV 5.4%), Gobsmacked (OG 1067, ABV 7.5%).

Green Jack *(OG 1037, ABV 3.5%)* ✦
A hoppy, pale brown light bitter with an underlying malty sweetness and a long, dry aftertaste.

Canary *(OG 1039, ABV 3.8%)* ✦
Golden yellow, fruity pale ale with a clean, hoppy-fruity palate ending dry and hoppy.

Grass Hopper *(OG 1043, ABV 4.2%)* ✦
Copper-coloured hoppy bitter with balancing malt throughout and a developing fruitiness.

Orange Wheat *(OG 1043, ABV 4.2%)*

Golden Sickle *(OG 1047, ABV 4.8%)* ✦
Amber, full-bodied bitter beer with a smooth, gentle balance of hops and malt, and lasting bitterness.

Gone Fishing *(OG 1049, ABV 5%)*

Norfolk Wolf Porter
(OG 1050, ABV 5.2%) ✦
Dark and full-bodied with a malty aroma, then a dry roast malt taste with a bold hop balance, ending with a restrained, dryish finish

Lurcher *(OG 1052, ABV 5.4%)*
A sharp-tasting, fruity, strong bitter.

Gobsmacked *(OG 1067, ABV 7.5%)*

Ripper *(OG 1076, ABV 8.5%)*

GREENE KING

Greene King PLC, Westgate Brewery, Bury St Edmunds, Suffolk IP33 1QT
Tel (01284) 763222
Fax (01284) 706502
Web-site www.greeneking.co.uk
Tours by arrangement (01284 714382)

⊠ Founded in 1799, Greene King celebrated its 200th birthday in 1999 and transformed itself into a 'super regional' with the acquisition of Morland and Ruddles brands. It closed the Morland Brewery in Abingdon. Greene King now owns 1,620 pubs in East Anglia, the Thames Valley and South-east England, 98 per cent of them serving cask beer. 3,000 free trade outlets are supplied direct. Seasonal beers: Black Baron (ABV 4.3%, Sept-Oct), The Sorcerer (ABV 4.5%, March-April 1999). Bottle-conditioned beer: Hen's Tooth (ABV 6.5%). Strong Suffolk Vintage Ale (ABV 6%), while not bottle conditioned, is a classic beer blended in the 18th-century tradition with a strong ale stored in wooden vats for two years and a lower-strength pale beer.

Martha Greene *(OG 1032, ABV 3.1%)*
A light bitter brewed only for Greene King managed pubs.

XX Dark Mild *(OG 1036, ABV 3%)* ✦
Smooth and sweet, with a bitter aftertaste.

The beer is enjoying greater promotion and has increased sales.

IPA *(OG 1036, ABV 3.6%)* ✦
A bland session bitter with some hops on the nose and a slightly astringent aftertaste.

Ruddles Best *(OG 1035-39, ABV 3.7%)*

Triumph Ale *(OG 1044, ABV 4.3%)* ✦
A pale, hoppy beer. It has very little aroma but it has a character all its own. Well worth a try.

Ruddles County *(OG 1046-50, ABV 4.7%)*

Abbot Ale *(OG 1048, ABV 5%)* ✦
A full-bodied, very distinctive beer with a bitter-sweet aftertaste.

Old Speckled Hen *(OG 1048-52, ABV 5.2%)*
Beer acquired from Morland.

GREEN TYE

Green Tye Brewery, Green Tye, Much Hadham, Hertfordshire SG10 6JP
Tel/Fax (01279) 841041
E-mail enquiries@gtbrewery.co.uk
Web-site www.gtbrewery.co.uk
Tours by arrangement

A brewery set up in a purpose-built building in October 1999, behind the Prince of Wales pub (a separate business) by William Compton and Gary Whelan. It currently produces eight barrels a week, supplying direct to seven outlets in Hertfordshire and Essex. A dark mild and seasonal beers are planned. Beer: Shot in the Dark (OG 1036, ABV 3.6%), IPA (OG 1036, ABV 3.7%), Snowdrop (OG 1040, ABV 3.9%), Wheelbarrow (OG 1044, ABV 4.3%).

For Chequers Inn, Wareside, Herts:

Treacleminer's Ale *(OG 1044, ABV 4.3%)*.

GRIBBLE INN

♫ The Gribble Brewery, Gribble Inn, Oving, nr Chichester, W Sussex PO20 6BP
Tel/Fax (01243) 786893
E-mail elderflower@msn.co.uk
Tours by arrangement

⊠ A micro-brewery owned by Hall & Woodhouse (Badger qv) on the site of the Gribble Inn, which has expanded its portfolio of beers and ales and now supplies in excess of 30 outlets along the south coast from London to Taunton and Exeter.

King & Barnes Mild Ale
(OG 1032, ABV 3.5%)
Matched beer from the former Horsham brewery.

Ewe Brew *(OG 1040, ABV 3.8%)*
Winter.

Fursty Ferret *(OG 1045, ABV 4%)*

Ale *(OG 1047, ABV 4.1%)*

Oving Bitter *(OG 1048, ABV 4.5%)*

Reg's Tipple *(OG 1050, ABV 5%)*

Porterhouse *(OG 1050, ABV 5.1%)*

Plucking Pheasant *(OG 1048, ABV 5.2%)*

Black Adder II *(OG 1060, ABV 5.8%)*

Pig's Ear *(OG 1060, ABV 5.8%)*
Autumn.

Wobbler *(OG 1075, ABV 7.2%)*
A winter brew.

GRIFFIN INN
See Church End.

GRIMSDALES*
GBC(Kent)Ltd, t/a Grimsdales Brewery Co,
Unit 2 Pound Lane, Kingsnorth, Ashford,
Kent TN23 3EJ
Tel (01233) 630900
Fax (01233) 633990

Not currently brewing, beer contract-brewed
at present by Pilgrim Brewery, Reigate. One
pub is owned serving cask-conditioned beer.
100 outlets are supplied direct. Seasonal beer:
Clerics Consolation (ABV 4.5%). Beers: Mr
Grimsdales Bitter (ABV 3.6%), AKB (ABV
3.6%), Becketts Best Bitter (ABV 4%),
Lightning Strike (ABV 4.9%), Apocalypse
(ABV 5%), Grumpys Gripewater (ABV 5%).

GUERNSEY
The Guernsey Brewery Co (1920) Ltd,
South Esplanade, St Peter Port,
Guernsey, Channel Isles GY1 1BJ
Tel (01481) 720143
Fax (01481) 710658
Web-site www.hbgroup.com/bucktrouts/

⊠ One of two breweries on the island, serving
its stronger than average real ales in 13 of its
33 pubs. Originally opened as the London
Brewery in 1856, it became a Guernsey registered company in 1920 on the introduction
of income tax on the mainland. It was
acquired in 1978 by Bucktrout, a Guernsey
wine and spirit company with several pubs
on the island. In 1988 Bucktrout merged with
Ann Street, now Jersey Brewery; Guernsey
cask ale is available in selected Jersey Brewery
houses. 11 outlets are supplied direct.

Braye Mild *(OG 1037, ABV 3.8%)* ◆
Copper-red in colour, with a complex aroma
of malt, hops, fruit and toffee. The rich,
mellow flavour combines malt, fruit, hops
and butterscotch, while the finish has malt
and hops. Full-flavoured, surprisingly dry
and hoppy.

Pirates Ale *(OG 1042, ABV 4%)*

Sunbeam Bitter *(OG 1045, ABV 4.2%)* ◆
Golden in colour, with a fine malt aroma.
Malt and fruit are strong on the palate and
the beer is quite dry for its strength. Excellent
dry malt and hop finish.

Millennium Ale *(OG 1050, ABV 4.6%)*

HADRIAN
See Four Rivers.

HAGGARDS*
Haggards Brewery Limited, c/o 577 King's
Road, London SW6 2EH
Tel 0207 384 2246
E-mail andrewhaggard@haggardsbrewery
.fsnet.co.uk
Web-site haggardsbrewery.com
Tours by arrangement

The brewery was set up in December 1998 to
supply beer to the Imperial pub on King's
Road in London. The brewery is owned and
run by two brothers, both of whom used to
work in the City of London but gave up their
jobs to run the pub and establish the brewery. During the next year it is planned to distribute the beer more widely. The brewery
has a capacity of five barrels and was
designed and commissioned by Rob Jones of
the Dark Star Brewery in Brighton. Haggards
supplies pubs other than the Imperial only
on request. Only one beer is brewed, which is
sold under the name of Haggards Imperial
Best Bitter at the pub; when sold to the free
trade it's called Haggards Horny Ale.

Haggards Imperial Best Bitter
(OG 1043, ABV 4.2%) ◆
Tawny beer that is fruity and sweet with little
hop character.

HALE & HEARTY
▯ Hale & Hearty Brewery, 104 Upper Hale
Road, Farnham, Surrey GU9 0PB
Tel/Fax (01252) 735278

⊠ Hale & Hearty was established in November
1996. The seasonal ales are mostly second-
fermented with fruit. The Rockin' Robin won
Best Strong Ale at the Woking Beer Festival in
1997. One pub is owned. Seasonal beers:
Elderflower Spring Ale (ABV 4.5%), Rockin'
Robin (ABV 5.3%), Plum Pudding (ABV
5.3%), Rudolph's Ruin. Beers: Upper Ale
(ABV 3.8%), Wicket Bitter (ABV 4.3%).

HALL & WOODHOUSE
See Badger

HAMBLETON
Nick Stafford Hambleton Ales, Holme-on-
Swale, Thirsk, N Yorkshire YO7 4JE
Tel (01845) 567460 Fax (01845) 567741
E-mail sales@hambletonales.co.uk
Web-site www.hambletonales.co.uk
Shop 9-4
Tours by arrangement

☺ Established in 1991 by Nick Stafford on
the banks of the River Swale in the heart of
the Vale of York, the brewery produces 50
barrels a week. The bottling line caters for
micro and large brewers, handling more than
20 brands. New brewing equipment was
installed in March 2000 increasing capacity
to 100 barrels a week. A mail-order service for
all bottle brands is available from the brewery or its web-site. 100 outlets are supplied
direct. Hambleton brews beers under
contract for the Village Brewer wholesale
company: (01325) 374887.

Bitter *(OG 1036.5, ABV 3.6%)* ◆
Rich, hoppy aroma rides through this light
and drinkable beer. Taste is bitter with citrus
and marmalade aroma and solid body. Ends
dry with a spicy mouthfeel.

Goldfield *(OG 1040, ABV 4.2%)* ◆
A light amber bitter with good hop character
and increasing dryness. A fine blend of malts
gives a smooth overall impression.

Stallion *(OG 1040, ABV 4.2%)* ◆
A premium bitter, moderately hoppy
throughout and richly balanced in malt and
fruit, developing a sound and robust bitterness, with earthy hop drying the aftertaste.

Stud *(OG 1042, ABV 4.3%)* ◆
A strongly bitter beer, with rich hop and fruit. It ends dry and spicy.

Nightmare *(OG 1050, ABV 5%)* ◼◆
Fully deserving its acclaim, this impressively flavoured beer satisfies all parts of the palate. Strong roast malts dominate, but hoppiness rears out of this complex blend.

For Village Brewer:

White Boar *(OG 1037.5, ABV 3.7%)* ◆
A light, flowery and fruity ale; crisp, clean and refreshing, with a dry-hopped, powerful but not aggressive, bitter finish.

Bull *(OG 1039, ABV 4%)* ◆
A fairly thin, but well-hopped bitter, with a distinct dryness in the aftertaste.

Old Ruby *(OG 1048, ABV 4.8%)* ◆
A full-bodied, smooth, rich-tasting dark ale. A complex balance of malt, fruit character and creamy caramel sweetness offsets the bitterness. A classic old ale.

HAMPSHIRE
Hampshire Brewery Ltd, 6-8 Romsey Industrial Estate, Greatbridge Road, Romsey, Hampshire SO51 0HR
Tel (01794) 830000
Fax (01794) 830999
E-mail online@Hampshire-brewery.co.uk
Shop 9-5.30 Mon-Fri 9-12 Sat
Tours by arrangement

▩ Set up in 1992, the brewery outgrew its capacity in Andover and has now completed its expansion with a move to a larger site in Romsey. Pride of Romsey was launched to celebrate the move and has already won several awards in both cask and bottle-conditioned form. In May 1999 the brewery started to brew Strong's Best Bitter to the old Romsey brewery's original recipe exclusively for Whitbread local tenancies. One-off and seasonal beers are brewed twice a month. The in-house bottling plant produces bottle-conditioned beers: King Alfred's (OG 1038, ABV 3.8%), Pendragon (OG 1048, ABV 4.8%), Pride of Romsey (OG 1050, ABV 5%) ⬚, 1066 (OG 1062, ABV 6%).

King Alfred's *(OG 1038, ABV 3.8%)* ◆
A mid-brown beer, featuring a malty and hoppy aroma. A malty taste leads to a hoppy, malty and bitter finish.

Strong's Best Bitter *(OG 1038, ABV 3.8%)*

Ironside *(OG 1042, ABV 4.2%)* ◆
A beer with little aroma, but some malt. The taste has solid fruit with lasting hops and malt. The aftertaste is more bitter and malty. Pale brown in colour.

Lionheart *(OG 1045, ABV 4.5%)*
A smooth, golden best bitter.

Pendragon *(OG 1048, ABV 4.8%)*
A full-bodied and fruity premium ale.

Pride of Romsey *(OG 1050, ABV 5%)*
Champion Beer of Hampshire 2000.

1066 *(OG 1062, ABV 6%)*

HANBY
Hanby Ales Ltd, New Brewery, Aston Park, Soulton Road, Wem, Shropshire SY4 5SD
Tel/Fax (01939) 232432
E-mail hanby@dial.pipex.com
Tours by arrangement

▩ Hanby was set up in 1990 by three partners. The 12-barrel plant is being upgraded to 20-barrels due to demand. A bottling plant is planned in the next three years. Hanby supplies some 200-300 pubs direct and others via wholesalers. Bottle-conditioned beer: Hanby Premium (ABV 4.6%). Occasional/seasonal beers: Cherry Bomb (OG 1060, ABV 6%), Joy Bringer (OG 1060, ABV 6%).

Black Magic Mild *(OG 1033, ABV 3.3%)* ◆
A dark, reddish-brown mild, which is dry and bitter with a roast malt taste.

Drawwell Bitter *(OG 1039, ABV 3.9%)* ◆
A hoppy beer with excellent bitterness, both in taste and aftertaste. Beautiful amber colour.

All Seasons Bitter *(OG 1042, ABV 4.2%)*

Rainbow Chaser *(OG 1043, ABV 4.3%)*
A pale beer brewed with Pioneer hops.

Wem Special *(OG 1044, ABV 4.4%)*
A pale, smooth, hoppy bitter.

Cascade *(OG 1045, ABV 4.5%)*

Premium Bitter *(OG 1046, ABV 4.6%)* ◆
Formerly Treacleminer, a pale brown beer that is sweeter and fruitier than the beers above. Slight malt and hop taste.

Old Wemian Ale *(OG 1049, ABV 4.9%)*
Golden-brown colour with an aroma of malt and hops and a soft, malty palate.

Taverners Ale *(OG 1053, ABV 5.3%)*

HAND IN HAND
See Kemptown.

HANSON'S
See Banks's.

THOMAS HARDY
Thomas Hardy Burtonwood Brewery, Weymouth Avenue, Dorchester, Dorset DT1 1QT
Tel (01305) 250255
Fax (01305) 258381
Tours by arrangement

▩ Founded by the Eldridge family as the Green Dragon Brewery in 1837, it now operates as the Thomas Hardy Brewery following a management buy out in March 1997, leaving Eldridge Pope to concentrate on pub ownership (see Pub Groups). In 1998 it set up a joint venture with Burtonwood Brewery (qv). Thomas Hardy brews Eldridge Pope's beers under contract, and also brews and packages for other breweries. There are no plans to continue brewing the classic bottle-conditioned beer Thomas Hardy's Ale (OG 1125, ABV 12%).

For Eldridge Pope:

Pope's Traditional (*OG 1038, ABV 3.8%*) ◄
Formerly Eldridge Pope Best Bitter. A mixture of malt and hop with a hint of fruit.

Hardy Country (*OG 1040, ABV 4.2%*) ◄
A dry, hoppy beer with faint undertones of malt and fruit. The taste is smooth despite a bitter edge that continues into the finish.

Royal Oak (*OG 1048, ABV 5%*) ◄
A full-bodied beer with a distinctive banana aroma and a mainly sweet, fruity taste. This is balanced by malt and some hops and there is a fruity finish to this smooth, well-rounded brew.

For Morrells' pubs:

Oxford Bitter (*OG 1038, ABV 3.7%*)

Varsity (*OG 1041, ABV 4.3%*)

Graduate (*OG 1051, ABV 5.2%*)

For Refresh, a beer marketing company set up to sell the Usher's beer range:

Best Bitter (*ABV 3.8%*)

Founders Ale (*ABV 4.5%*)

Spring Fever, Summer Madness, Autumn Frenzy and Winter Storm (*all ABV 4%*)

HARDYS & HANSONS

Hardys & Hansons PLC, Kimberley Brewery, Nottingham NG16 2NS
Tel (0115) 938 3611 Fax (0115) 945 9055
Tours by arrangement

☺ Established in 1832 and 1847 respectively, Hardys & Hansons were two competitive breweries until a merger in 1931 produced the present company. The brewery is today controlled by descendants of the original families. The majority of its 246 tied houses take its award-winning real ales, mostly drawn by metered dispense into oversized glasses, although Kimberley Classic, and increasingly the Bitter, are served by hand-pull. Around 100 other outlets are also supplied direct. A range of seasonal ales, with a rotation or new beer every month under the Cellarman's Cask banner, has extended Hardys & Hansons' geographical availability and reputation. Occasional/seasonal beers: Frolicking Farmer (ABV 4.2%), Peddler's Pride (ABV 4.3%), Guzzling Goose (ABV 4.4%), Rocking Rudolph (ABV 5%), Guinea Gold (ABV 4.5%), Vintage 1832 (ABV 4.6%), Original Gravity (ABV 4.1%).

Kimberley Best Mild
(*OG 1035, ABV 3.1%*) ◄
A deep ruby mild dominated by chocolate malt. The fruitiness and caramel sweetness are well balanced in the taste, with a faintly hoppy finish.

Kimberley Best Bitter
(*OG 1039, ABV 3.9%*) ◄
A beer with a flowery, hoppy and fruity nose, although malt is never far away. Fruity hop is evident in the taste and there is a consistent bitterness.

Kimberley Classic (*OG 1047, ABV 4.8%*) ◄
A brown beer with an amber hue. Bitter throughout, it has a fruity hop nose, with malt behind the hops in the taste and aftertaste. It is not always easy to find (occasionally alternating with seasonals).

HART

🖵 Hart Brewery, Cartford Hotel, Cartford Lane, Little Eccleston, Lancashire PR3 0YP
Tel (01995) 671686
Fax (01772) 797069
Tours by arrangement

☺ Brewery founded in 1994 in a small private garage, it moved to premises at the rear of the Cartford Hotel in 1995. With a 10-barrel plant, Hart now supplies direct to 170 outlets nationwide. A monthly beer is available alongside the regular range. Seasonal beers: Liberator (OG 1037, ABV 3.7%, September), Fylde Ale (OG 1040, ABV 4%, April), Criminale Porter (OG 1041, ABV 4%, October), Mayson Premier (OG 1042, ABV 4%, August), High Octane Gold Beach (OG 1043, ABV 4.2%, May), Excalibur (OG 1045, ABV 4.5%, June), Hart of Steel (OG 1045, ABV 4.5%, July), No Balls (OG 1045, ABV 4.5%, Christmas), Arena (OG 1050, ABV 4.8%), Andrew's Cobblestone Stout (OG 1050, ABV 5%, February), Old Ram (OG 1050, ABV 5%, March), Amadeus (OG 1055, ABV 5.5%, November), Merrie Hart Stout (OG 1055, ABV 5.5%, January).

Cleo's Asp (*OG 1037, ABV 3.7%*) ◄
A smooth golden brew with a light, fruity aroma, a slow burst of fruit and hop flavours and a restrained, dry, hoppy finish.

Beth's Arrival (*OG 1040, ABV 4%*)

Ambassador (*OG 1041, ABV 4.2%*)
This ruby-red beer is a little drier than others in the range. Brewed with crystal and chocolate malts and Kent Fuggles hops.

Squirrels Hoard (*OG 1042, ABV 4%*)
Brewed for the Cartford Hotel and CAMRA festivals. Pale and crystal malts produce a wonderfully nutty flavour.

Off Your Trolley (*OG 1045, ABV 4.5%*)

Nemesis (*OG 1046, ABV 4.5%*)
A light amber-coloured beer with a refreshing flavour.

Road to Rome (*OG 1050, ABV 5%*)
Originally brewed for CAMRA's 25th anniversary, now a permanent addition to the range. A rich, ruby-red beer with a full malt flavour and a sweet aftertaste.

HARTLEYS
See Robinsons.

HARVEYS

Harvey & Son (Lewes) Ltd, The Bridge Wharf Brewery, 6 Cliffe High Street, Lewes, E Sussex BN7 2AH
Tel (01273) 480209
Fax (01273) 483706
Shop 9.30-4.45 Mon-Sat
Tours by arrangement (two-year waiting list)

☒ Established in 1790, this independent family brewery operates from the Bridge Wharf Brewery on the banks of the River Ouse in Lewes. The brewery was re-built in 1881 and is a classic Victorian 'tower' site, with the brewing process flowing by gravity from floor to floor. A major development in 1985 doubled the brewhouse capacity and subsequent additional fermenting capacity has seen production rise to in excess of 34,000

The Good Beer Guide 2001

barrels a year. Still a family-run company, Harveys supplies real ale to all its 44 pubs and 600 free trade outlets in Sussex and Kent. Seasonal beers: Family Ale (OG 1020, ABV 2.2%, June), Knots of May Light Mild (OG 1030, ABV 3%, May), Sussex XXXX Old Ale (OG 1043, ABV 4.3%, October-May), Kiss (OG 1048, ABV 4.8%, February), Southdown Harvest Ale (OG 1050, ABV 5%, September), 1859 Porter (OG 1053, ABV 4.8%, March), Tom Paine (OG 1055, ABV 5.5%, July), Bonfire Boy (OG 1066, ABV 5.8%, November), Christmas Ale (OG 1090, ABV 8.1%, December). Bottle-conditioned beer: 1859 Porter (OG 1053, ABV 4.8%).

Sussex XX Mild Ale
(OG 1030, ABV 3%) 🎱❦
A dark copper-brown colour. Roast malt dominates the aroma and palate leading to a sweet, caramel finish.

Sussex Pale Ale *(OG 1033, ABV 3.5%)* ❦
An agreeable, light bitter with malt and hops dominating the aroma, while a hoppy bitterness develops throughout the taste, to dominate the finish.

Sussex Best Bitter
(OG 1040, ABV 4%) 🍺❦
Full-bodied brown bitter. A hoppy aroma leads to a good malt and hop balance and a dry aftertaste.

Sussex XXXX Old Ale
(OG 1043, ABV 4.3%) 🍺🎱❦
Brewed Oct-May: a rich, dark beer with a good malty nose, with undertones of roast malt, hops and fruit. The flavour is a complex blend of roast malt, grain, fruit and hops with some caramel. Malty caramel finish with roast malt.

Armada Ale *(OG 1045, ABV 4.5%)* 🎱❦
Hoppy amber best bitter. Well-balanced fruit and hops dominate throughout with a fruity palate.

HARVIESTOUN
Harviestoun Brewery Ltd, Devon Road, Dollar, Clackmannanshire FK14 7LX
Tel (01259) 742141
Fax (01259) 743141
e-mail harviestoun@talk21.com

⊛ Hand-built in a 200-year-old stone byre by two home-brew enthusiasts in 1985, this small brewery operates from a former dairy at the foot of the Ochil Hills, near Stirling. A new custom-built brewing plant was installed in 1991 and Harviestoun now serves 70 outlets in central Scotland as well as wholesalers' customers throughout Britain. A bottling line was installed in 1999; Harviestoun plans to bottle a range of beers and for other breweries as well. Occasional beers: Spring Fever (OG 1038, ABV 3.8%, March), Fresher's Bitter (OG 1039, ABV 3.9%, October), Cutlass Sharp (OG 1038, ABV 4%, August), Lochinvar (OG 1040, ABV 4%, April), American Red (OG 1040, ABV 4.1%, September), Belgian White (OG 1043, ABV 4.3%, July), Mayfest Wheat Beer (OG 1044, ABV 4.4%, May), Old Engine Oil (OG 1045, ABV 4.4%, November), Black Lager (OG 1044, ABV 4.5%, February), Good King Legless (OG 1044, ABV 4%, April), Burn's Ale (OG 1047, ABV 4.6%, January), Auld Lang Syne (OG 1047, ABV 4.7%,

December), Natural Blonde (ABV 4%), Gremlin (ABV 4.3%), Hitchhiker Bitter (ABV 4%), Sandpiper (ABV 3.9%, June), Storm Force (ABV 4.2%, February), Liberation (ABV 4.5%, January).

Wee Stoater *(OG 1034, ABV 3.6%)*

Brooker's Bitter & Twisted
(OG 1038, ABV 3.8%) 🍺❦
Aggressively hoppy beer with fruit throughout. A bitter-sweet taste with a long, dry, bitter finish. A refreshing golden session beer that was Champion Beer of Scotland 1999.

Turnpike *(ABV 4.1%)*

Ptarmigan *(OG 1045, ABV 4.5%)* ❦
A well-balanced, bitter-sweet beer in which hops and malt dominate. The blend of malt, hops and fruit produces a clean, hoppy aftertaste.

Schiehallion *(OG 1048, ABV 4.8%)* 🍺🎱❦
A Scottish cask lager, brewed using a lager yeast and Hersbrucker hops. A hoppy aroma, with fruit and malt, leads to a malty, bitter taste with floral hoppiness and a bitter finish.

HEATHER
Heather Ale Ltd, Craigmill Brewery, Craigmill, Strathaven, Lanarkshire, Scotland ML10 6PB
Tel (01357) 529529
Fax (01357) 522256
E-mail fraoch@heatherale.co.uk
Web-site www.heatherale.co.uk
Shop 12-6 Mon-Sat
Tours by arrangement

Bruce Williams started brewing Fraoch (Gaelic for heather and pronounced 'Frook') in 1992 at the now closed West Highland Brewery in Argyll. Production moved to Maclay's brewery in Alloa the following year and from there in 1999 to a combination of their own brewery at an old mill in Strathaven and the new Forth Brewery in Alloa. All cask products are made in Strathaven while the bottled products are brewed and bottled at Forth. Heather Ale is made with flowering heather, while Pictish is a stronger version for the dark winter months. The Strathaven Brewery is also producing a couple of hopped ales, the first of which Paley Aley is distinctively hopped. 30 outlets are supplied direct. Seasonal beers: Grozet Gooseberry Wheat Ale (OG 1052,

ABV 5.3%, Sept-Feb), Pictish Heather Ale (OG 1052, ABV 5.3%, Dec-April), Ebulum Elderberry Black Ale (OG 1065, ABV 6.5%, Oct-Jan).

Paley Aley *(OG 1039, ABV 3.9%)*

Fraoch Heather Ale
(OG 1042, ABV 4.1%) ▣🏠❧
A beer with a floral, peaty aroma, a spicy, herbal, woody flavour and a dry finish.

HEDGEHOG & HOGSHEAD
▣ Belchers Brewery, 100 Goldstone Villas, Hove, E Sussex BN3 3RX
Tel (01273) 324660

▣ Brew pub chain established with two outlets (Hove and Southampton) in 1990 by David Bruce of Firkin fame, who sold them in 1994 to Grosvenor Inns who then sold them to Sirenia, now part of the Ambishus pub group (qv). Only the Hove pub currently brews. Beers: BiBi or Best Bitter (OG 1042, ABV 4.2%), Bootleg Bitter (OG 1052, ABV 5.2%).

HENSTRIDGE
Henstridge Brewery, Gibbs Marsh, Bow Bridge Works, Henstridge Trading Estate, Henstridge, Somerset BA8 0TH
Tel (01963) 363150
Fax (01963) 363864

▣ After 15 years of making just about everything used in the brewing trade, David Vickery decided it was time to try making some beer himself and in 1994 Henstridge Brewery was born. It still brews just one beer for local outlets and pubs further afield via an agent. See Bath Brewery.

Vickery's Bill *(OG 1040, ABV 4%)*

HESKET NEWMARKET
Hesket Newmarket Brewery Ltd, Old Crown, 1 mile SE of Caldbeck, Cumbria OS341386
Tel/Fax (016974) 78066
E-mail brewery@hesket.ndo.co.uk
Web-site www.bdksol.demon.co.uk/hesket
Tours by arrangement, tel: (016974) 78288

☺ Brewery set up in 1988 in a barn behind the Old Crown pub in an attractive North Lakes village. Its beers are named after local fells, with the notable exception of Doris's 90th Birthday Ale (Doris died in 1995, aged 96). Around 20 pubs take the beers regularly and many more on an occasional basis. The brewery also produces house beers for local pubs. Early in 1999 brewer Jim Fearnley and his wife Liz announced they wished to retire and villagers raised the funds to run the brewery as a co-operative. On 17 December 1999 Jim and Liz finally sold the brewery to Hesket Newmarket Brewery Ltd. Occasional/seasonal beers: Show Ale (OG 1040, ABV 3.9%), Anniversary Ale (OG 1043, ABV 3.8%), Medieval Ale (OG 1045, ABV 4.3%), Kern Knott's Cracking Stout (OG 1057, ABV 5%), Ayala's Angel (OG 1080, ABV 7%, Christmas).

Great Cockup Porter *(OG 1035, ABV 2.8%)*
A refreshing, chocolate-tasting beer.

Blencathra Bitter *(OG 1035, ABV 3.1%)* ❧
A malty, tawny ale, mild and mellow for a bitter, with a dominant caramel flavour.

Skiddaw Special Bitter
(OG 1035, ABV 3.7%) ❧
An amber session beer, malty throughout, thin with a dryish finish.

Pigs Might Fly *(OG 1043, ABV 4.3%)* ❧
Roast, chocolate and malt dominate this full-tasting, well-balanced tasty ale.

Doris's 90th Birthday Ale
(OG 1045, ABV 4.3%) ❧
Golden brown with a caramel and barley sugar aroma. Full tasting and satisfying, drying in the aftertaste to a more balanced finish.

Catbells Pale Ale *(OG 1052, ABV 5.1%)* ❧
A powerful golden ale with a well-balanced malty bitterness, ending with a bitter and decidedly dry aftertaste.

Old Carrock Strong Ale
(OG 1064, ABV 5.6%)
A dark red, powerful ale.

HEXHAMSHIRE
Hexhamsbire Brewery, c/o Dipton Mill, Dipton Mill Road, Hexham, Northumberland NE46 1YA
Tel (01434) 606577

▣ A family brewery set up in a redundant farm building in 1992. No adjuncts are used in the beers, which are produced for its single tied house, the Dipton Mill Inn and 10-20 other outlets. Seasonal beer: Old Humbug (OG 1055, ABV 5.5%).

Devil's Elbow *(OG 1036, ABV 3.6%)*

Shire Bitter *(OG 1037, ABV 3.8%)* ❧
A bitter beer with a malty overtone.

Devil's Water *(OG 1041, ABV 4.1%)* ❧
A beer of mixed character and unexpected range of flavours. Malt dominates and bitterness gradually declines, giving a strong sweet finish.

Whapweasel *(OG 1048, ABV 4.8%)*
This malty bitter has a lasting hoppiness and a smooth mouthfeel.

HIGH FORCE
▣ High Force Hotel and Brewery, Forest-in-Teesdale, Barnard Castle, Co Durham DL12 0XH
Tel (01833) 622222
Shop 11-11
Tours by arrangement

☺ Founded in 1995, High Force Brewery claims to be the highest in Britain at 1,060 feet, next to England's highest waterfall, High Force. The brewery has won the Best Beer in Festival award at several venues in England, and for the second year running Cauldron Snout Beer was voted North-east Beer of the Year. Bottle-conditioned beers on sale in the hotel bar are Cauldron Snout and Forest XB. Brewing courses for beginners also available on request. 12 outlets are supplied direct.

Teesdale Bitter *(OG 1040, ABV 3.8%)* ❧
A well-balanced session ale with lingering fruit character and spicy aftertaste.

Forest XB *(OG 1044, ABV 4.2%)* ❧

A smooth malty flavoured beer, with a solid bitterness and almond undertones to a spicy finish.

Cauldron Snout (OG 1056, ABV 5.6%) 📛◆
A dark and creamy ale with a smooth roasted taste and a rich, solid body. Deceptively drinkable.

HIGH PEAK
See Lloyds.

HIGHGATE
Highgate & Walsall Brewing Company Ltd, Sandymount Road, Walsall, W Midlands WS1 3AP.
A subsidiary of Aston Manor of Birmingham
Tel (01922) 644453
Fax (01922) 644453
Tours by arrangement

☺ Highgate, which celebrated its centenary in 1998, was an independent brewery until 1938 when it was taken over by Mitchells & Butlers and subsequently became the smallest brewery in the Bass group. It had been under threat of closure for some years until a management buy out brought it back into the independent sector in 1995. Some of the original equipment in the traditional Victorian tower brewery is still in use. Highgate now has 10 tied houses and is aiming for an estate of 50. All the tied houses supply real ale and Highgate has an expanding free trade, with more than 200 outlets in the Midlands supplied direct and further afield via wholesalers. The company also has a contract to supply Bass. It was bought by Aston Manor in June 2000. Seasonal/occasional beers: Old Ale (OG 1053.7, ABV 5.1%, Nov-Jan), Black Pig (OG 1044.7, ABV 4.4%).

Dark Mild (OG 1036.7, ABV 3.4%) 📛◆
A dark brown Black Country mild with a good balance of malt and hops, and traces of roast flavour following a malty aroma.

Fox's Nob (OG 1039.7, ABV 3.6%)

Bitter (OG 1039.7, ABV 3.7%)

Saddlers Celebrated Best Bitter (OG 1044.7, ABV 4.3%) ◆
A fruity, pale yellow bitter with a strong hop flavour and a light, refreshing bitter aftertaste.

Breacais (OG 1044.7, ABV 4.6%)
A beer made with whisky malt.

Old Ale (OG 1053.7, ABV 5.1%) ◆
A winter beer (Nov-Jan): a dark brown/ruby-coloured old ale, full-flavoured, fruity and malty, with a complex aftertaste with hints of malt, roast, hops and fruit.

For Bass:

M&B Mild (OG 1034.7, ABV 3.2%)

HIGHWOOD
Highwood Brewery Ltd, Melton Highwood, Barnetby, N Lincolnshire DN38 6AA
Tel (01652) 680020
Fax (01652) 680010
E-mail tomwood@users.breworld.net
Web-site www.tom-wood.com
Tours by arrangement

☒ Highwood started brewing in a converted Victorian granary in 1995 and now uses malt made from barley grown on the family farm. 100 outlets are supplied direct.

Tom Wood Dark Mild (OG 1035, ABV 3.5%)

Tom Wood Best Bitter (OG 1035, ABV 3.5%) 📛◆
A good citric passion fruit hop on the nose and taste, which dominates the background malt. A lingering hoppy and bitter finish makes this amber bitter very drinkable.

Tom Wood Shepherd's Delight (OG 1040, ABV 4%) ◆
Malt is the dominant taste in this amber brew, although the fruity hop bitterness complements it all the way.

Tom Wood Lincolnshire Legend (OG 1041, ABV 4.2%) ◆
An orange fruity hop is balanced by malt on the nose and taste, where there is also a good bitter bite lingering into the aftertaste of this copper chestnut beer.

Tom Wood Harvest Bitter (OG 1041.5, ABV 4.3%) ◆
A well-balanced amber beer where the hops and bitterness just about outdo the malt.

Tom Wood Old Timber (OG 1043, ABV 4.5%) ◆
Hoppy on the nose, but featuring well-balanced malt and hops otherwise. A slight, lingering roast/coffee flavour develops, but this is generally a bitter, darkish brown beer.

Tom Wood Bomber County (OG 1046, ABV 4.8%) ◆
An earthy malt aroma but with a complex underlying mix of coffee, hops, caramel and apple fruit. The beer starts bitter and intensifies but all its mahogany characteristics stay on until the end.

HILDEN
Hilden Brewing Company, Hilden House, Hilden, Lisburn, Co Antrim BT27 4TY
Tel (028 92) 663863
Fax (028 92) 603511
E-mail hilden.brewery@uk.gateway.net
Shop 11.30-5
Tours 11.30 + 2.30 Tue-Sat

☺ Hilden was established in 1981 by Ann and Seamus Scullion in stables alongside a Georgian country house. It supplies Hilden Ale to a handful of pubs in Northern Ireland, with the full range exported to some pubs in England. The beers are available in a visitor centre at Hilden House. Bottle-conditioned beer: Original (OG 1047, ABV 4.6%).

Hilden Ale (OG 1038, ABV 4%) ◆
An amber-coloured beer with an aroma of malt, hops and fruit. The balanced taste is slightly slanted towards hops, and hops are also prominent in the full, malty finish. Bitter and refreshing.

Molly Malone's Porter (OG 1048, ABV 4.6%)
Dark ruby-red porter with complex flavours of hop bitterness and chocolate malt.

Scullion's Irish (OG 1048, ABV 4.6%)
Initially smooth on the palate, it finishes with a clean, hoppy aftertaste. Won Supreme Champion award at Irish Independent Brewers' Festival in Dublin, March 2000.

HOBSONS

Hobsons Brewery & Co Ltd, Newhouse
Farm, Tenbury Road, Cleobury Mortimer, nr
Kidderminster, Worcestershire DY14 8RD
Tel/Fax (01299) 270837
Shop 8-5 weekdays
Tours by arrangement

☒ Established in 1993, Hobsons moved to its
current premises in 1996. Production has
grown to 50 barrels a week. 92 outlets are
supplied direct.

Best Bitter *(OG 1038.5, ABV 3.8%)* ◆
A pale brown to amber, medium-bodied beer
with strong hop character throughout. It is
consequently bitter, but with malt
discernible in the taste.

Town Crier *(OG 1045, ABV 4.5%)*
A straw-coloured bitter.

Old Henry *(OG 1052, ABV 5.2%)*

HODGE'S BREWERY

See Darwin.

HOGS BACK

Hogs Back Brewery, Manor Farm, The
Street, Tongham, Surrey GU10 1DE
Tel (01252) 783000
Fax (01252) 782328
Web-site www.hogsback.co.uk
Shop 9-6 Mon, Tue and Sat; 9-8.30 Wed-
Fri; 10-4.30 Sun
Tours by arrangement 6.30 Wed-Fri; 11am and 2.30
Sat; 2.30 Sun

☒ This purpose-built brewery was set up in a
restored, 18th-century farm building in 1992
and the popularity of its ales – particularly
the award-winning TEA – has resulted in a
major plant change to double the production
capacity. From small beginnings, with just a
single beer, Hogs Back now brews nearly 20
beer types on a regular or occasional basis.
The brewery has undergone another major
expansion programme, installing a fully-fit-
ted new conditioning/racking room and new
cask cellar. New fermentation vessels were
commissioned for late 1999 and the company has acquired a 500-year-old barn to
house a new brewery shop and off-licence. A
new bottling and labelling system has been
installed to met the demand for bottled
beers. There are plans to bottle Hop Garden
Gold and OTT. The brewery still has a ghost,
known to walk the brewery gallery, and
believed to be a former local vicar.
Occasional/seasonal beers: Dark Mild
(OG 1036, ABV 3.4%), That's All Fawkes
(OG 1038, ABV 3.6%), APB or A Pinta Bitter
(OG 1037, ABV 3.5%), Summer Capers
(OG 1042, ABV 4%), Easter Teaser (OG 1044,
ABV 4.2%), Friday 13th (OG 1044, ABV
4.2%), Blackwater Porter (OG 1046, ABV
4.4%), BSA or Burma Star Ale (OG 1048, ABV
4.5%), St Georges Ale (OG 1048, ABV 4.6%,
St Georges Day), Autumn Seer (OG 1050,
ABV 4.8%, autumn), Tattoo (OG 1049, ABV
4.8%), Arena (OG 1050, ABV 4.8%), YES or
Your Every Success (OG 1050, ABV 5%),
Fuggles Nouveau (OG 1052 ABV 5%),
Goldings Nouveau (OG 1052, ABV 5%),
Utopia (OG 1058, ABV 5.4%), OTT or Old
Tongham Tasty (OG 1066, ABV 6%),
Brewster's Bundle (OG 1076, ABV 7.6%),

Santa's Wobble (OG 1077, ABV 7.5%,
Christmas), A over T or Aromas over
Tongham (OG 1091, ABV 9%), Wheat Your
Whistle (4.8%, for the summer). Bottle-con-
ditioned beers: TEA (OG 1044, ABV 4.2%),
BSA (OG 1048, ABV 4.5%), Vintage Ale (OG
1070, ABV 6%), Brewster's Bundle (OG 1076,
ABV 7.4%), Wobble in a Bottle (OG 1077,
ABV 7.5%), A over T (OG 1091, ABV 9%).

Hair of the Hog *(OG 1038, ABV 3.5%)* ◆
An honest, refreshing pale brown session
beer with a good bitter hop character
balanced with pale malt and fruit. A dry,
bitter finish.

Legend *(OG 1038, ABV 4%)* ◆
Complex and drinkable, this golden coloured
beer contains both wheat and lager malts,
and has a dry, malty and bitter taste that
lingers. Available September.

TEA or Traditional English Ale
(OG 1044, ABV 4.2%) ▼◆
The brewery's flagship beer is pale brown,
with a hoppy and slightly fruity aroma, supported by malt in the taste. A well-crafted,
bitter-sweet beer with a long dry finish.

Advent Ale *(OG 1046, ABV 4.6%)* ◆
Dark red-brown in colour, this easy-to-drink
winter ale tastes of dark malts and roast barley, with liquorice hints in the finish.
Available Christmas.

Hop Garden Gold *(OG 1048, ABV 4.6%)* ◆
A malty, pale golden beer with hints of
banana and pineapple, with a good balance
of aroma and bittering hops and a long dry
finish.

Rip Snorter *(OG 1052, ABV 5%)* ◆
A strong, malty and fruity, reddish-brown
bitter with a slight hop flavour.

HOLDEN'S

Holden's Brewery Limited (Hopden
Brewery), George Street, Woodsetton,
Dudley, W Midlands DY1 4LN
Tel (01902) 880051
Fax (01902) 665473
E-mail Hbrewery@aol.com
Web-site www.holdensbrewery.co.uk
Shop 11-10 Mon-Sat; 12-3, 7-10 Sun
Tours by arrangement

⊚ Family brewery going back four generations, Holden's began life as a brew pub
when Edwin and Lucy Holden took over the
Park Inn (now the brewery tap) in the 1920s,

which has recently been refurbished to its former Victorian heritage. With 21 pubs the tied estate is continuing to grow. Some 45 other outlets are also supplied with Holden's cask ales. Occasional/seasonal beers: Black Country Stout (OG 1035, ABV 3.6%), Old XL Ale (OG 1072, ABV 7.2%, Christmas).

Black Country Mild
(OG 1037, ABV 3.7%) ❧
A good, red/brown mild; a refreshing, light blend of roast malt, hops and fruit, dominated by malt throughout.

Black Country Bitter
(OG 1039, ABV 3.9%) ❧
A medium-bodied, golden ale; a light, well-balanced bitter with a subtle, dry, hoppy finish.

XB *(OG 1041, ABV 4.2%)* ❧
Named after founder Lucy Blanche Holden, this is a sweeter, slightly fuller version of the Bitter. Sold in different outlets under different names.

Special Bitter *(OG 1051, ABV 5.1%)* ❧
A sweet, malty, full-bodied amber ale with hops to balance in the taste and in the good, bitter-sweet finish.

HOLT

Joseph Holt Group PLC, Derby Brewery, Empire Street, Cheetham, Manchester M3 1JD
Tel (0161) 834 3285
Fax (0161) 834 6458
Tours Saturday only 10-11.15am, £10 per person donation to Holt Radium Institute at the Christie Hospital. Groups of 12-15 only. Tours may be restricted in 2001 to March to May only.

⊕ This family brewery was established in 1849 by Joseph Holt and celebrated 150 years in brewing in 1999. In recent years new equipment for the brewing process has been installed to comply with demand for the ever-expanding estate of pubs. Bitter is often delivered in 54-gallon hogsheads and the brewery hopes that one day there will be a demand for Mild in hogsheads. 127 pubs are owned, all serving cask-conditioned beer. Holts became a limited company in 1951 and was quoted on the Stock Exchange but in March 2000 the company applied to re-purchase all the shares and to become de-listed. This will make the company even more secure from takeovers, being family run and truly independent once more.

Mild *(OG 1032, ABV 3.3%)* ❧
An exceptionally dark beer with a complex aroma and taste. Roast malt is prominent, but so are hops and fruit. Strong in bitterness for a mild, with a long-lasting, satisfying aftertaste.

Bitter *(OG 1040, ABV 4%)* ⬚❧
A tawny beer with a good hop aroma. Although balanced by malt and fruit, the

uncompromising bitterness can be a shock to the unwary.

HOME COUNTY

Home County Brewers, The Old Brewery, Station Road, Wickwar, Gloucestershire GL12 8NB
Tel/Fax (01454) 294045
Shop working hours, 6.30 Fri
Tours by arrangement

Set up in November 1997 close to the Wickwar Brewery in south Gloucestershire, with a 5-barrel brew length. There are plans to expand the premises. 24 outlets are supplied direct.

Golden Brown *(OG 1035, ABV 3.5%)* ❧
Golden brown, clean tasting, light malt ale with a very subtle aroma. Slightly dry and moderately bitter. Dry, malty finish. A gentle bitter.

Wichen *(OG 1042, ABV 4.2%)* ❧
Pale brown, this has a malty and fruity aroma with a little hop. Medium bodied, with a good, malty taste throughout, some hops and complex fruit, and a slightly dry, bitter finish.

Old Tradition *(OG 1048, ABV 4.8%)* ❧
Brown, mid to full-bodied beer that is malty throughout but has balancing fruit and hops. Bitter-sweet. Predominantly malty aroma. Mellow.

Country Pride *(OG 1050, ABV 5%)* ❧
Mid-bodied for its gravity, it has a malt/fruit aroma with subtle chocolate hints. Mid-brown in colour, bitter-sweet tasting with a slightly dry, malt aftertaste.

HOOK NORTON

The Hook Norton Brewery Co Ltd, Brewery Lane, Hook Norton, Banbury, Oxon OX15 5NY
Tel (01608) 737210
Fax (01608) 730294
Shop in visitor centre with a small museum 8.30-4.30 Mon-Fri
Tours by arrangement

⊗ The Hook Norton Brewery can trace its origins back to 1849 when John Harris set up in business as a maltster. He soon started brewing himself and in 1872 built a small three-storey brewery. In 1896 major building work started with new stables and offices, followed by the six-storey tower brewery still in use today. Much of the original brewing equipment is still in use, including a 25hp steam engine that provides nearly all the motive power. Hook Norton owns 39 pubs and supplies approximately 250 free trade accounts. All Hook Norton draught beers are cask conditioned and dry hopped. All the beers use water drawn from wells beneath the brewery, Maris Otter malt and English Challenger, Fuggles and Goldings hops. Seasonal beers: Haymaker (OG 1052, ABV 5%, July-Aug), Twelve Days (OG 1058, ABV 5.5%, Dec-Jan).

Best Mild *(OG 1032, ABV 3%)* ❧
A dark, red/brown mild with a malty aroma and a malty, sweetish taste, tinged with a faint hoppy balance. Malty in the aftertaste.

Best Bitter *(OG 1035, ABV 3.4%)* ⬚❧
A fruity and hoppy aroma introduces this complex, well-crafted amber bitter. Moderate

maltiness underpins the hops, leading to a long, bitter-sweet finish.

Generation *(OG 1041, ABV 4%)* ✦
A pale brown best bitter, predominantly hoppy but balanced with moderate malt and banana fruit. The fruit and malt decline to a relatively short, hoppy finish.

Old Hooky *(OG 1048, ABV 4.6%)* ✦
A well-balanced and full-bodied pale copper beer that is fruity with pale and crystal malt and hops on the aroma and taste. The hoppy character gives way to a sweet and fruity finish.

Double Stout *(OG 1050, ABV 4.8%)* ✦
This dry, dark red-brown stout has masses of roast malt flavour but not too much depth of character. The finish is dry and powdery.

HOP BACK
Hop Back Brewery PLC,
Units 20-24 Batten Road Industrial Estate,
Downton, Salisbury,
Wiltshire SP5 3HU
Tel (01725) 510986
Fax (01725) 513116
E-mail sales@hopback.co.uk
Web-site www.hopback.co.uk

⊠ Started by John Gilbert in 1985 at the Wyndham Arms in Salisbury, the brewery has expanded steadily ever since. It went public via a Business Expansion Scheme support plan in 1993 and has enjoyed rapid continued expansion. Summer Lightning is the winner of many awards. The brewery has six tied houses, including the Hop Leaf in Reading (see Reading Lion Brewery) and Hop Back also sells directly to 80 other outlets. Seasonal beers: Cob Nut Brown (ABV 3.8%), Flint Knapper (ABV 3.8%), Cuckoo Pint (ABV 4%), Jack O'Lantern (ABV 4.2%), Fawkes Finale (ABV 4.6%), Winter Lightning (ABV 5.5%). Bottle-conditioned beers: Thunderstorm (OG 1048, ABV 5%), Summer Lightning (OG 1049, ABV 5%) 🗗, Taiphoon (ABV 4.2%), Crop Circle (ABV 4.2%).

GFB/Gilbert's First Brew
(OG 1034, ABV 3.5%) ✦
A golden beer, with the sort of light, clean quality that makes it an ideal session ale. A hoppy aroma and taste lead to a good, dry finish. Refreshing.

Best Bitter *(OG 1040, ABV 4%)*

Crop Circle *(OG 1041, ABV 4.2%)*

Entire Stout *(OG 1043, ABV 4.5%)* 🗗✦
A rich, dark stout with a strong roasted malt flavour and a long, sweet and malty aftertaste. A beer suitable for vegans. Also produced with ginger.

Thunderstorm *(OG 1048, ABV 5%)* ✦
A softly bitter, easy-drinking wheat beer.

Summer Lightning
(OG 1049, ABV 5%) ▮🗗✦
A pleasurable pale bitter with a good, fresh, hoppy aroma and a malty, hoppy flavour. Finely balanced, it has an intense bitterness leading to a long, dry finish. Though strong, it tastes like a session ale.

HOP HOUSE
See Cock.

HOP LEAF
See Reading Lion.

HORSEBRIDGE
See Royal Inn.

HOSKINS
Tom Hoskins Brewery PLC, Tom Hoskins Brewery, Beaumanor Road,
Leicester LE4 5QE

Hoskins was bought by Archers of Swindon in June 2000. The site may become a brewery museum. The main brands, Bitter, Tom's Gold and Churchill's Pride, may be brewed at Swindon. Hoskins owned 19 pubs.

HOSKINS & OLDFIELD
Hoskins & Oldfield Brewery Ltd, North Mills, Frog Island, Leicester LE3 5DH
Tel (0116) 251 0532
E-mail HOB@neptunegroup.demon.co.uk
Web-site
www.neptunegroup.demon.co.uk/HOB

The brewery set up by two members of Leicester's famous brewing family, Philip and Stephen Hoskins, in 1984, after the sale of the old Hoskins Brewery. Opened their first tied house in 1999, The Ale Waggon in Leicester City Centre. The company supplies more than 15 outlets directly, and others nationwide via wholesalers. Occasional/seasonal beers: Midnight Express (ABV 5%), Tom Kelly's Christmas Pudding Porter (OG 1052, ABV 5%, Christmas), Reckless Raspberry (OG 1055, ABV 5.5%, a wheat beer with raspberries), Petulant Peach (OG 1055, ABV 5.5%), Pioneer Gold (ABV 4.8%).

HOB Best Mild *(OG 1036, ABV 3.5%)* ✦
An almost black coloured beer, with malt and hops in the taste. A former champion mild of Britain.

Brigadier Bitter *(OG 1036, ABV 3.6%)*
An ordinary bitter.

HOB Bitter *(OG 1041, ABV 4%)* ✦
A copper-coloured best bitter with a hoppy-malty nose and dominated by hop bitterness throughout.

Little Matty *(OG 1041, ABV 4%)*
A complex brown/red beer.

White Dolphin *(OG 1041, ABV4%)*
A fruity wheat beer.

IPA *(OG 1042, ABV 4.2%)*
A well-hopped pale ale.

Tom Kelly's Stout *(OG 1043, ABV 4.2%)*
A dark, dry stout.

Supreme *(OG 1045, ABV 4.4%)*
A very light gold best bitter.

Grandad Tom's Porter
(OG 1050, ABV 4.8%)
Brewed using honey and oats.

EXS Bitter *(OG 1051, ABV 5%)*
A malty, full-bodied premium bitter.

O4 Ale *(OG 1052, ABV 5.2%)*
A red/brown coloured, full-flavoured ale.

Ginger Tom *(OG 1053, ABV 5.2%)*
A ginger beer.

Old Navigation Ale *(OG 1071, ABV 7%)* 🍺
A strong ruby/black beer.

Christmas Noggin *(OG 1100, ABV 10%)*
A potent barley wine. Despite its name, available all year.

HOUSTON

⌂ Houston Brewing Company, South Street, Houston, Renfrewshire PA6 7EN
Tel (01505) 612620 (brewery)
614528 (office)
Fax (01505) 614133
E-mail caroline@houston-brewing.co.uk
Web-site www.houston-brewing.co.uk
Shop open during pub opening
Tours by arrangement

Family-owned brewery attached to the Fox and Hounds pub. It started brewing in 1997. 150 outlets are now supplied direct. Seasonal beers: Jock Frost (OG 1045, ABV 4.5%, winter), Texas (OG 1045, ABV 4.5%, spring).

Killellan *(OG 1037, ABV 3.7%)*

Barochan *(OG 1041, ABV 4.1%)*

St Peter's Well *(OG 1042, ABV 4.2%)* 🍺🌾
A golden beer with hoppy aroma. A well-balanced taste with malt, fruit and hop leading to an increasingly hoppy, bitter-sweet finish.

Formakin *(OG 1043, ABV 4.3%)*

HUDDERSFIELD

The Huddersfield Brewing Company,
c/o Unit J, Shaw Park, Silver Street East,
Aspley, Huddersfield,
W Yorkshire HD5 9AF
Tel (01484) 300028/534120
Fax (01484) 542709
Tours by arrangement

The brewery was launched in November 1997 by Robert Johnson of Kitchen Brewery (qv). Operating from the same address, it produces a completely different range of beers. One penny from each pint sold goes to local charities. 200 outlets are supplied direct.

Town Bitter *(ABV 3.8%)*
Dark tan in colour with a malty character ending with a good bitterness.

Huddersfield Pride *(ABV 4.4%)*
Dark-straw in colour with a rich, malty flavour, medium bitterness, with a well-hopped nose finishing with a deep fruity aftertaste.

Wilson's Wobble Maker *(ABV 5%)*
Golden-coloured with a smooth, malty manner from the German malt, a dry-hopped nose and a fruity flavour.

SARAH HUGHES

⌂ Sarah Hughes Brewery, Beacon Hotel, 129 Bilston Street, Sedgley, W Midlands DY3 1JE
Tel (01902) 883380
Tours by prior arrangement

◉ Opened originally in the 1860s behind the Beacon Hotel, Sarah Hughes bought the brewery in 1921 and started to brew the beer now called Dark Ruby. After lying idle for 30 years, the brewery was re-opened in 1987 by John Hughes, who continued the tradition and recipe of his grandmother. More seasonal and occasional beers are planned. One pub is owned and more than 100 outlets are supplied direct. Beers are now exported to the United States. Seasonal beer: Snow Flake (OG 1078, ABV 8%). Bottle-conditioned beer: Dark Ruby (OG 1058, ABV 6%).

Pale Amber *(OG 1038, ABV 4%)*
A well-balanced beer, initially slightly sweet but with hops close behind.

Surprise *(OG 1048, ABV 5%)* 🌾
A bitter-sweet, medium-bodied, hoppy ale with some malt.

Dark Ruby *(OG 1058, ABV 6%)* 🍺🗂🌾
A dark ruby strong ale with a good balance of fruit and hops, leading to a pleasant, lingering hops and malt finish.

HULL

The Hull Brewery Company Limited,
144-148 English Street, Hull,
E Yorkshire HU3 2BT
Tel (01482) 586364
Fax (01482) 586365
E-mail Ellwood@brewcrew.co.uk

◉ The name of the closed Hull Brewery was resurrected after a 15-year absence when a new brewery opened in 1989. It was forced into liquidation in 1994 and the assets taken over by local businessman Dieter Ellwood, who formed a new company. It acquired its first tied house in 1995 from Bass, and bought a second from Bass in 2000. It now supplies around 100 other pubs. A bottling plant was added in 1997.

Mild *(OG 1033, ABV 3.3%)* 🌾
Roasted malt dominates this very good example of a dark mild. Dark red/black in colour, it has a good balance of fruit and hop flavours with a smooth finish.

Ellwood's Best Bitter
(OG 1038, ABV 3.8%) 🌾
A golden, straw-coloured session bitter, smooth and rounded, with subtle hints of hops and malt and a refreshing aftertaste.

Bitter *(OG 1039, ABV 3.8%)* 🌾
A refreshing copper bitter, with a predominantly hoppy aroma. The initial bitter aftertaste leads to a pleasant, lingering maltiness. Complex.

Northern Pride *(OG 1042, ABV 4.2%)*
A distinctive, full-bodied beer, with a malty aroma.

The Governor *(OG 1046, ABV 4.3%)*

A full-bodied, amber-coloured premium ale; a deceptively powerful brew with a malty taste and a distinctive hop aroma.

HUMPTY DUMPTY

Humpty Dumpty Brewery, Stables Brewhouse, 17 The Havaker, Reedham, Norfolk NR13 3HG
Tel (01493) 701818
Fax 700340 (call first)
E-mail mick@humptydumptybrewery
.freeserve.co.uk
Tours by arrangement

Humpty Dumpty Brewery was opened in 1998 by Mick Cottrell. Situated behind the Railway Tavern, Humpty Dumpty remains an independent brewery selling to 150 pubs around the country. The nicknames of the beers come from old locomotives or railway themes. Seasonals: Lemon Ale (ABV 3.8%), Christmas Chuckle (ABV 4.1%). Gobbler bottle- conditioned ale is available in 500ml bottles.

Nord Atlantic (ABV 3.7%) ◆
A copper-brown bitter with little aroma. A sweet malty taste develops toffee overtones. A long, bitter-sweet finish for a beer that has a surprising lightness of body.

Little Sharpie (ABV 3.8%) ◆
A delicate hoppy aroma is a forerunner to a sweet hoppy lagerish flavour. A clean golden yellow bitter with a finish in which bitterness grows.

Un Petit Deux Petit (ABV 4.1%) ◆
A cosmopolitan beer with a bit of everything. Amber coloured with a soft sweetness taking the edge off a malty bitter base. Bitterness dominates a thin, drifting finish.

Claud Hamilton (ABV 4.3%) ◆
With its dark brown colouration, this old style oyster stout is a stirring mix of roast fruity sweetness. The bitter-sweet finish draws out a hint of caramel toffee.

Butt Jumper (ABV 4.8%) ◆
Heavyweight beer with a deep fruity sweetness of sultanas. A bitter hoppiness develops but the sweetness remains and dominates to the end. Tawny in colour and flavour.

Railway Sleeper (ABV 5%) ◆
A sweet plummy fruitiness blankets an underlying malty bitterness. Full and rich in flavour, the aftertaste develops an increasing malt bias that does not fade.

HYDES

Hydes' Brewery Ltd, 46 Moss Lane West, Manchester M15 5PH
Tel (0161) 226 1317
Fax (0161) 227 9593
E-mail paul.jefferies@btinternet.com
Web-site www.hydesbrewery.co.uk
Tours by arrangement

☺ A family-controlled brewing company marrying traditional and state of the art techniques, it was first established at the Crown Brewery, Audenshaw, Manchester in 1863 and on its present site, the former Greatorex Brothers Brewery, since the turn of the 19th century. It supplies cask ale to all its 66 tied houses and directly to more than 70 free trade outlets. 1999 saw the rebranding of the company and products, with the introduc-

tion of a flagship premium ale, Jekyll's Gold, to the cask portfolio. A successful programme of seasonal cask ales is now well established with a new beer appearing every two months. Seasonal beers: Harry Vederchi (ABV 4.8%, Jan-Feb), Clever Endeavour (ABV 4.5%, March-April), Hair Raid (ABV 4.2%, May-June), Your Bard (ABV 4%, June-July), Henry's Hampton (ABV 4.4%, Sept-Oct), Rocket Fuel (ABV 5%, Nov-Dec).

Traditional Mild (OG 1033.5, ABV 3.5%) ◆
A mid-brown beer with malt and citrus fruit on the aroma and taste. Quite sweet in the mouth but drier in the aftertaste.

Light Mild (OG 1033.5, ABV 3.5%) ◆
A lightly-hopped, amber-coloured session beer with a refreshing lemon fruitiness and a brief but dry finish.

Dark Mild (OG 1033.5, ABV 3.5%)

Traditional Bitter (OG 1036.5, ABV 3.8%) ◆
A good-flavoured bitter, with a malty and fruity nose, malt and hop in the taste, with a fruity background, and good bitterness through into the aftertaste.

Jekyll's Gold Premium Ale
(OG 1042, ABV 4.3%) ◆
Pale gold in colour, fruity nose with a touch of sulphur. A well-balanced beer with hops, fruit and malt all in evidence, and a dry, hoppy finish.

ICENI

Iceni Brewery, 3 Foulden Road, Ickburgh, Norfolk IP26 5BJ
Tel (01842) 878922
Fax (01842) 879216
Tours by arrangement

⊗ Iceni Brewery started in January 1995 and for four years grew slowly, mainly supplying guest beers. From mid-1998 the beer range has been produced in bottle-conditioned form. In January 1999 Iceni Brewery produced LAD Lager in cask and bottle-conditioned versions. Last year Iceni joined with nine other East Anglia Breweries to form the East Anglia Brewery Trail. 33 outlets are supplied direct. Special beers are brewed for festivals.

Fine Soft Day (OG 1038, ABV 4%)

Celtic Queen (OG 1038, ABV 4%)
A light summer ale, packed with flavour.

Boadicea Chariot Ale (OG 1038, ABV 3.8%)
A well-balanced session bitter.

Deirdre of the Sorrows
(OG 1042, ABV 4.4%)
A gold-coloured ale with a distinctively pleasant taste that lingers.

Roisin Dubh (OG 1042, ABV 4.4%)
The name means 'Dark Rose': a sweet, smooth dark ale.

Gold (OG 1045, ABV 5%)
A strong ale, sun gold in colour. Crisp taste; smooth and deceptive for its strength.

LAD Lager (OG 1048, ABV 5%)

Raspberry Wheat (OG 1048, ABV 5%)

INVERALMOND

**The Inveralmond Brewery Ltd;
1 Inveralmond Way, Perth PH1 3UQ**

Tel/Fax (01738) 449448
E-mail info@inveralmond-brewery.co.uk
Web-site www.inveralmond-brewery.co.uk
Shop 9-5

⊛ Established in April 1997, the Inveralmond Brewery was the first brewery in Perth for more than 30 years. Set up by Heriot-Watt trained, ex-Ruddles, Courage and S&N brewer Fergus Clark, the brewery supplies more than 150 outlets direct, with wholesalers supplying pubs nationwide. Ossian's Ale and Lia Fail are now also available in bottle.

Independence *(OG 1040, ABV 3.8%)*
An amber-red, sweetish beer with a hint of spiciness in the aroma.

Ossian's Ale *(OG 1042, ABV 4.1%)* ▢◆
Well-balanced, easily drinkable beer in 80/-style. A full-bodied amber ale dominated by fruit and hop with a bitter-sweet taste. The finish is predominantly fruity.

Thrappledouser *(OG 1043, ABV 4.3%)*

Lia Fail *(OG 1048, ABV 4.7%)*
The name is the Gaelic title of the Stone of Destiny; a malty, full-bodied brew with chocolate notes and a balanced finish.

IRIS ROSE
⚲ Iris Rose Brewery, The Royal Hotel, High Street, Kingussie PH21 1HX
Tel (01540) 661898
Fax (01540) 661061
Tours by arrangement

The brewery opened in August 1997 originally just to brew for its own three hotels. Demand for the beers has led them to brew 10 barrels a week in summer and three to four barrels a week in winter, supplying a further six outlets and beer festivals. All the beers are also available bottle-conditioned. Beers: Summer Ale (OG 1035, ABV 3.5%), Carls Best Bitter (OG 1036, ABV 3.7%), Roseburn Bitter (OG 1038, ABV 3.8%), Liquorice Kingussie (OG 1038, ABV 3.9%), Craig Bheag (OG 1042, ABV 4.3%), Cynack Glory (OG 1042, ABV 4.4%), Ginger Ale (OG 1042, ABV 4.4%), Strathspey Heavy (OG 1045, ABV 4.6%), Black Five (OG 1049, ABV 5%), Harpole IPA (OG 1050, ABV 5.1%), Zoe's Old Grumpy (OG 1075, ABV 8.2%).

ISLE OF MAN
See Okells.

ISLE OF SKYE
The Isle of Skye Brewing Company (Leann an Eilein), The Pier, Uig, Isle of Skye IV51 9XY
Tel (01470) 542477
Fax (01470) 542488
E-mail info@skyebrewery.co.uk
Web-site skyebrewery.co.uk
Shop 10-6 Mon-Sat 12-5 Sun Apr-Oct
Tours by arrangement

⊛ Established in 1995, Isle of Skye's trade continues to expand steadily, both directly and via wholesalers, to cover most of mainland Britain. The island itself now has 11 hotels serving cask ale from the brewery and

many others stock the bottled range. The company serves 60 outlets direct.

Young Pretender *(OG 1039, ABV 4%)* ◆
Golden amber ale with hop and fruit on the nose. The bitter taste is dominated by fruit and hop, the latter lingering into the dry, bitter finish.

Red Cuillin *(OG 1041, ABV 4.2%)* ◆
A burst of fruit with malt and hop notes introduce this tawny reddish beer. These characteristics continue into the wonderful bitter-sweet taste. A very dry and bitter finish.

Hebridean Gold *(OG 1041.5, ABV 4.3%)* ▢◆
A superb golden coloured beer that is brewed using oats. Hops and fruit dominate the bitter taste and increasingly dry, citrus finish.

Black Cuillin *(OG 1044, ABV 4.5%)*

Blaven (originally Avalanche)
(OG 1047, ABV 5%) ◆
An amber-coloured, bitter-sweet beer dominated by fruit and hop throughout. There is also malt in the taste and increasing bitterness in the long, dry finish.

ITCHEN VALLEY
Itchen Valley Brewery Limited, Shelf House, New Farm Road, Alresford, Hampshire SO24 9QE
Tel (01962) 735111
Fax (01962) 735678
Web-site www.itchenvalley.com
Shop 9-3.30 Mon-Fri
Tours by arrangement

⊗ The brewery, founded in 1997, had a fine first year culminating in winning a bronze at the Great British Beer Festival in 1998, barely a year after starting brewing. The brewery now has more than 100 regular account customers taking the full range of beer in casks and the brewery is expanding to meet demand. In late 1999 the brewery installed bottling plant and all its beers are now available in 500ml bottles from supermarkets, off-licenses, direct from the brewery and online from the brewery web-site. The web-site features an online tour and real tours are undertaken each month at the brewery. Seasonal beers: Easter Bunnies (OG 1043, ABV 3.9%, Easter), Red Roses (OG 1041, ABV 4%, Valentines week), Father Christmas (OG 1057, ABV 5.5%, Christmas).

Godfathers *(OG 1042, ABV 3.8%)* 🛢
A pale brown beer with a hoppy aroma. A malty and bitter taste leads through to the finish.

Fagin's *(OG 1041, ABV 4.1%)*

Wykehams *Glory (OG 1045, ABV 4.3%)*

Judge Jeffreys *(OG 1048, ABV 4.5%)*

Wat Tyler *(OG 1057, ABV 5.5%)*

JENNINGS
Jennings Bros PLC, Castle Brewery, Cockermouth, Cumbria CA13 9NE
Tel (01900) 823214
Fax (01900) 827462
Shop 9-5 Mon-Sun summer
Tours by arrangement 11-2 spring/summer

⊚ Founded in 1828, Jennings moved to its present site by the Derwent and at the foot of Cockermouth Castle in 1874, where it still uses its own well water. Although there is no longer any family involvement, many of the company's shares are owned by local people. Around 200 free trade outlets are supplied direct with many more via a network of wholesalers throughout the country. A £1 million investment programme was launched in 1999 to upgrade the brewery and increase output. Real ale is available in most of Jenning's 111 tied houses. The company is committed to an integrated pub and brewery business. Seasonal beers: Cross Buttock Ale (ABV 4.5%, autumn), La'al Cockle Warmer (ABV 6.5%,winter).

Dark Mild *(OG 1031, ABV 3.1%)* ◆
Roast dominates the nose with a bitter-sweetness in the mouth and a rising astringent bitterness.

Bitter *(OG 1035, ABV 3.5%)* ◆
A tawny brown malty ale with a chocolate malt roast character. Distinct and rising bitterness.

Cumberland Ale *(OG 1040, ABV 4%)* ◆
A creamy amber-gold malty ale with hop resin and fruity notes; rising bitterness balances well.

Cocker Hoop *(OG 1047, ABV 4.8%)* 🛢◆
A rich, creamy, copper-coloured beer with raisiny maltiness balanced with a resiny hoppiness, with a developing bitterness towards the end.

Sneck Lifter *(OG 1055, ABV 5.1%)* ◆
A strong, warming, dark red and tawny ale with a complex treacle-like sweetness remaining with some dryness in the aftertaste.

JERSEY
Ann Street Brewery Co Ltd t/a Jersey Brewery, 57 Ann Street, St Helier, Jersey JE1 1BZ
Tel (01534) 31561
Fax (01534) 67033
Tours by arrangement

Jersey, better known as Ann Street, has phased out cask ale after a brief flirtation in 1997 and 1998. It has 50 tied houses, of which 12 take real ale, including beers from its sister company, Guernsey Brewery. Jersey Brewery also has an interest in the Tipsy Toad brew pub (qv).

JOHN O'GAUNT
John O'Gaunt Brewing Co Ltd, Unit 45 Rural Industries, John O'Gaunt, Melton Mowbray, Leicestershire LE14 2RE
Tel/Fax (01664) 454777
Tours by arrangement

⊗ The brewery was set up by Celia Atton next to the Stag and Hounds pub at nearby Borough on the Hill and moved in 1998 to share the equipment of the Parish Brewery (qv). The first beer, Robin a Tiptoe, was named after a local landmark. Some 20 local outlets are supplied but brewing is low-key as most effort goes into running the inn.

Robin a Tiptoe *(OG 1043, ABV 3.9%)*

Cropped Oak *(OG 1047, ABV 4.4%)*

Coat O' Red *(OG 1052, ABV 5%)*

JOLLYBOAT
The Jollyboat Brewery, 4 Buttgarden Street, Bideford, Devon EX39 2AU
Tel (01237) 424343
Tours by arrangement

⊗ Receivers were called in in summer 2000 and the future of the brewery is in doubt. Bottle-conditioned beer: Privateer (OG 1048, ABV 4.8%).

Buccaneers *(OG 1037, ABV 3.8%)*
A pale brown summer bitter with a pleasant presence of hops and bitterness from the nose through to the aftertaste.

Mainbrace Bitter *(OG 1042, ABV 4.2%)* ◆
Pale brown brew with a rich fruity aroma and a bitter taste and aftertaste.

Plunder *(OG 1048, ABV 4.8%)* 🛢◆
A good balance of malt, hops and fruit are present on the aroma and palate of this red/brown-coloured beer with a bitter finish.

Contraband *(OG 1055, ABV 5.8%)*
A porter available November-March.

JOULE
See Coach House.

JUDGES
Judges Real Ale Brewery Ltd, 34 Ludgate Hill, Birmingham B3 1EH
Tel (07836) 380700

Judges was set up in 1992 and moved to bigger premises. It was bought in 1999 by chartered surveyor Richard Lewis after it had closed for a short period and moved to Birmingham in 2000. Seasonal beer: Santa's Surprise (5%).

M'Lud Bitter *(ABV 3.3%)*

Barrister's Bitter *(ABV 3.5%)*

Verdict *(ABV 4%)*

Coombe Ale *(ABV 4.2%)*

Grey Wig *(ABV 4.2%)*

Magistrate's Delight *(ABV 4.6%)*

Old Gavel Bender *(ABV 5%)*

Solicitor's Ruin *(ABV 5.6%)*

JUWARDS
Juwards Brewery, Unit 14G,
c/o Fox Brothers & Co Ltd, Wellington,
Somerset TA21 OAW
Tel (01823) 667909

⊗ Brewery founded in 1994 in old woollen mill to produce 10 to 12 barrels a week maximum, using plant with a 6-barrel brew length. Trading started by going far and wide but is gradually becoming more localised as the brewery becomes established: 14 outlets are supplied direct. A 10-barrel plant was bought in 1999 to increase production.

Bitter (OG 1038.5, ABV 3.8%) ◆
Amber-coloured bitter, hoppy aroma, well-balanced malt and hops on the palate with hints of honey. Hoppy, bitter finish, again with honey notes.

Golden (OG 1042.5, ABV 4.2%)
Occasional beer.

Winter Brew (OG 1044, ABV 4.3%)
A seasonal porter.

Premium (OG 1046.5, ABV 4.6%) ◆
Full bodied, mid-brown beer. Fruit and hops in the nose. Malt and fruit taste with fruity, hoppy finish.

KELHAM ISLAND
Kelham Island Brewery Ltd, Alma Street,
Sheffield, S Yorkshire S3 8SA
Tel (0114) 249 4804
Fax (0114) 249 4803
Shop 9-5
Tours by arrangement

☺ Kelham Island Brewery was formed in 1990 in the back yard of the Fat Cat pub. In 1999 the brewery moved 100 yards up the street to new, purpose-built premises capable of taking the company well into the 21st century. The old brewery site now houses a visitor centre and pre-arranged tours are welcome. 150 outlets are supplied direct. Seasonal beers: Wheat Bier (ABV 5%, summer), Bete Noire (ABV 5.5%, winter), Grande Pale (ABV 6.6%, winter).

Fat Cat Pale Ale (ABV 3.6%)

Bitter (OG 1037.5, ABV 3.8%) ◆◆
A clean, characterful, crisp, pale brown beer. The nose and palate are dominated by refreshing hoppiness and fruitiness, which, with a good bitter dryness, last in the aftertaste.

Sheffield Best Bitter (ABV 4%) ◆
A malty nose leading to a dry, fruity flavour with a distinct bitter aftertaste. A refreshing beer.

Golden Eagle (OG 1042.5, ABV 4.2%) ◆
An excellent hoppy, fruity best bitter. The aroma is strong in hops with a slight fruitiness that gets stronger in the taste and in the finish, which is moderately bitter.

Easy Rider (OG 1044.5, ABV 4.5%) ◆
A pale, straw-coloured beer with a sweetish flavour and delicate hints of citrus fruits. A beer with hints of flavours rather than full bodied.

Wheat Bier (OG 1051, ABV 5%)
A summer beer.

Pale Rider (OG 1051.5, ABV 5.2%) ◆
A full-bodied, straw-pale ale, with a good fruity aroma and a strong fruit and hop taste. Its well-balanced sweetness and bitterness continue in the finish.

Bete Noire (OG 1056, ABV 5.5%) ◆
A dark ruby winter beer with little aroma. Malt and caramel, along with some fruitiness and dryness, are in the taste, which also has plum notes and chocolate, and develops into a dry, but sweet, aftertaste.

Grande Pale (OG 1066, ABV 6.6%)
A strong, full-bodied pale ale with a mellow hop aroma. A winter brew.

KELTEK
Keltek Brewery, Unit 3A, Restormel
Industrial Estate, Liddicoat Road,
Lostwithiel, Cornwall PL22 0HG
Tel/Fax (01208) 871199
Tours by arrangement

⊗ Keltek Brewery moved to Lostwithiel in January 1999 and started brewing again in March of that year. Monthly specials and house beers for pubs are brewed. A range of bottle-conditioned beers was due to be available from April 2000. One pub is owned, the Globe in Lostwithiel. 50 outlets in Cornwall and North Devon are supplied direct. Seasonal/occasional beers: Revenge (OG 1070, ABV 7%, Sept-March), Cross (OG 1038, ABV 3.8%), Knight (OG 1044, ABV 4.4%).

Dark Mild (OG 1038, ABV 3.8%)

Golden Lance (OG 1038, ABV 3.8%)

Magik (OG 1042, ABV 4.2%)

King (OG 1051, ABV 5.1%)

KEMPTOWN
⚲ Kemptown Brewery Co Ltd, 33 Upper St
James's Street, Brighton, E Sussex BN2 1JN
Tel (01273) 699595
Tours by arrangement

⊗ Brewery established in 1989 and built in the tower tradition behind the Hand in Hand, which is possibly the smallest pub in England with its own brewery. It takes its name and logo from the former Charrington's Kemptown Brewery 500 yards away, which closed in 1964. Six free trade outlets are supplied. Seasonal/occasional beers: Tippers Tipple (ABV 4.5%), Trailblazer (ABV 4.5%), Celebrated Staggering Ale (ABV 5%), Crewsaver, Dragons Blood.

Brighton Bitter (OG 1036, ABV 3.6%) ◆
A refreshing, dry beer, with malt and hops in the flavour and a dry, hoppy finish.

Bitter (OG 1041, ABV 4%) ◆
Amber-gold, clean-tasting bitter. A malty aroma and a hoppy start in the mouth give way to intense bitterness.

Ye Old Trout Ale (OG 1045, ABV 4.5%)

SID/Staggering in the Dark
(OG 1052, ABV 5.2%) ◆
A dark, almost black, beer with a vinous nose and a complex flavour, with roast and bitterness giving way to a dry finish.

Old Grumpy (OG 1062, ABV 6.2%)

KENT GARDEN
Kent Garden Brewery, Unit 13,

Davington Mill, Bysingwood Road,
Faversham, Kent ME13 7UB
Tel (01795) 532211
Tours by arrangement

Brewing equipment came from the
Steampacket Brewery in Knottingley,
West Yorkshire. Bottle-conditioned beers are
planned. Beers: Corn Rose (ABV 3.6%), Happy
Major (ABV 4%), Blue Rocket (ABV 4.5%).

KING & BARNES

**King & Barnes Ltd, The Horsham Brewery,
18 Bishopric, Horsham,
W Sussex RH12 1QP**

Tragically, this much-loved family-owned
brewery, dating back 200 years and on the
present site since 1850, closed in August 2000.
When a takeover bid was made by Shepherd
Neame (which promised to keep the brewery
open) the K&B management looked for an
alternative buyer, which arrived in the shape
of Hall & Woodhouse of Blandford in Dorset,
brewers of Badger beers (qv). H&W closed the
brewery and said it would match some of the
Horsham ales: see Badger and Gribble Inn.
Worthington White Shield has returned to
Burton-on-Trent: see Museum Brewing Co,
Interbrew/Bass section of National and
International section.

KING & SMART*

**King & Smart Lincolnshire Brewery,
Building No 30, Binbrook Technical
Estate, Market Rasen, Lincolnshire
Tel (01522) 512919**

Martin and Carl Smart are two keen home
brewers who wanted to go the extra mile and
brew cask beer. They joined forces with Peter
Smart to buy a 20-barrel brew plant that has
been in operation since mid-1999.

Forever Amber *(ABV 3.8%)*

Lincoln Ale *(ABV 4%)*

Ruby Tuesday *(ABV 4%)*

Brookenby Dark *(4.4%)*

KINGS HEAD

(formerly Brettvale Brewing Co Ltd)
**Kings Head Brewing Co, Kings Head,
132 High Street, Bildeston, Ipswich,
Suffolk IP7 7ED
Tel/Fax (01449) 741434
E-mail kingshead_brewery@fsmail.com**

⊠ The brewery was set up with a 5-barrel
plant in old stables behind the Kings Head.
The owners intend to increase output this
year to supply more outlets. Bottled beer may
be produced in the future. Five to six outlets
are supplied direct. Occasional beer: Y2K (OG
1044/46, ABV 4.5%). Beers: Best Bitter (OG
1036, ABV 3.8%), Blondie (OG 1038/40, ABV
4%), First Gold (OG 1042/44, ABV 4.3%),
Billy (OG 1047/49, ABV 4.8%), Dark Vader
(OG 1055, ABV 5.4%).

KITCHEN

**The Kitchen Brewery Ltd, Unit J,
Shaw Park, Silver Street, Aspley,
Huddersfield, W Yorkshire HD5 9AF
Tel (01484) 300028**

Fax (01484) 542709
Tours by arrangement

☻ Brewery founded in 1996 by CAMRA
member Robert Johnson in the pickling shed
at the Shaw Park Industrial Complex, with a
5-barrel plant that uses steam as a heat
source. It also houses the new Huddersfield
Brewing Company (qv). The beers, whose
names are derived from Robert's first career as
a chef, are on sale in local pubs and in pubs
in Northamptonshire, Robert's home county.
The beer range varies every two months with
the addition of new special brews. 400 outlets are supplied direct. Bottle-conditioned
beer: Tormented Turnip (ABV 4.5%).
Seasonal/occasional beers: Tubby Tangerine
(ABV 4%), Waitress (ABV 4.2%), Syllabub (ABV
4.2%), Goblin Waitress (ABV 4.3%), Carrot
Cruncher (ABV 4.4%), Porter (ABV 4.7%),
Potage (ABV 4.7%), Raisin Stout (ABV 4.8%),
Chef's Cut (ABV 5%), Plum Duff (ABV 5.2%).

LAKELAND

**Lakeland Brewing Company, 1 Sepulchre
Lane, Kendal, Cumbria LA9 4NJ
Tel/Fax (01539) 734528**

☻ In spite of the name, Lakeland doesn't
brew: all the beers are contract-brewed, the
bottle-conditioned ones by Burton Bridge
(qv). The beers are named after novels by
Swallows and Amazons children's writer
Arthur Ransome, most of whose books were
set in the Lake District. 15 outlets are
supplied direct. Bottle-conditioned beers:
Amazon (OG 1047, ABV 4.5%), Great
Northern (ABV 1050, ABV 5%), Winter
Holiday (OG 1050, ABV 5%). Seasonal/occa-
sional beers: Lakeland Terrier (OG 1038, ABV
3.8%), Damson Beer (OG 1045, ABV 4.4%),
Winter Holiday (OG 1050, ABV 5%). Beers:
Kendal Bitter (OG 1040, ABV 4%), Amazon
(OG 1047, ABV 4.5%), Great Northern
(OG 1050, ABV 5%).

LANGTON*

☗ Langton Brewery, Bell Inn, Main Street,
East Langton, Leicestershire LE16 7TW
Tel (01858) 545 278
Fax (01858) 545 748

Langton is run by two partners, Alistair
Chapman and Derek Hewitt, publican and
customer respectively of the Bell Inn. Hewitt

is a retired banker who brought his business experience to underscore Chapman's knowledge of the pub trade. They installed an existing 20-barrel brewing plant in outbuildings of the 17th-century Bell. They now brew 90 gallons a time of Caudle Bitter (named after the range of local hills) and Bowler, which marks the Bell Inn's long association with Langton Cricket Club, whose ground is opposite the inn. Both beers are available for take-away in nine-gallon casks or 10-litre polypins.

Caudle Bitter *(ABV 3.9%)*

Bowler *(ABV 4.8%)*

LARKINS

Larkins Brewery Ltd, Larkins Farm, Chiddingstone, Edenbridge, Kent TN8 7BB
Tel (01892) 870328
Fax (01892) 871141
Tours by arrangement November-February

⊗ Larkins Brewery was founded in 1986 by the Dockerty family, farmers and hop growers, who bought the Royal Tunbridge Wells Brewery. The company moved to Larkins Farm in October 1989. Only hops grown in Kent are used; some are grown and picked on the farm. Larkins owns one pub and 60 outlets are supplied direct with additive-free beers.

Traditional Ale *(OG 1035, ABV 3.4%)*
A tawny-coloured beer.

Chiddingstone Bitter *(OG 1040, ABV 4%)*
A malty and slightly fruity, bitter ale, with a malty finish. Copper-red in colour.

Best Bitter *(OG 1045, ABV 4.4%)* ✍
Full-bodied, slightly fruity and unusually bitter for its gravity.

Porter *(OG 1055, ABV 5.2%)* ✍
Each taste and smell of this potent black winter beer reveals another facet of its character. An explosion of roasted malt, bitter and fruity flavours leaves a bitter-sweet aftertaste.

LEADMILL*

**The Leadmill Brewery Co,
118 Nottingham Road, Selston,
Nottingham,
Notts NG16 6BX**
Tel 01773 819280/07971 189915 (m)

Leadmill was established in February 1999, originally using an 18- gallon home-brewing plant. A 2-barrel plant was installed in August of that year, enabling five brews to be made each week. There are plans to look for new premises and to upgrade to a 10-barrel plant. Beer is currently brewed in a converted pig sty behind a 200-year-old cottage. Approximately 40 outlets are supplied direct. Seasonal beer: Wild Weasel (OG 1038, ABV 3.9%). Beers: Arc-light (OG 1041, ABV 4.2%), Rolling Thunder (OG 1044, ABV 4.5%), Linebacker (OG 1045, ABV 4.6%), Agent Orange (OG 1047, ABV 4.9%), Niagara (OG 1049, ABV 5%), Apocalypse Now (OG 1050, ABV 5.2%).

LEANN AN EILEIN

See Isle of Skye.

LEATHERBRITCHES

⬡ **Leatherbritches Brewery, Bentley Brook Inn, Fenny Bentley, Ashbourne, Derbyshire DE6 1LF**
Tel (01335) 350278
Fax (01335) 350422

⊛ Leatherbritches Brewery is housed behind the Bentley Brook Inn, just north of Ashbourne, a pub owned by the parents of brewery founder Bill Allingham. Launched in 1994, it soon outgrew its initial capacity of five barrels a week and has been expanded. Around 35 other local outlets take the beer, as do the three pubs owned by the Steamin' Billy company. Bottle-conditioned beers: Stout (ABV 4%), plus ales for special occasions. Seasonal beers: Ginger Spice (OG 1040, ABV 4% summer), Raspberry Belter (OG 1040, ABV 4%, summer festival), Takin' The Pith (wheat beer) (OG 1043, ABV 4.3% summer), Plum Porter (OG 1050, ABV 5%, autumn), Festival Mild (OG 1053, ABV 5.3%, May festival), Robert Catesby (OG 1053, ABV 5.3%, November), Tarebrane (OG 1058, ABV 6%, winter).

Goldings *(OG 1036, ABV 3.6%)*

Belt 'n' Braces *(OG 1038, ABV 3.8%)*
A light-coloured, hoppy session beer; a dry finish.

Belter *(OG 1040, ABV 4%)*

Stout *(OG 1040, ABV 4%)*
A beer with a dominant chocolate flavour, smooth and fruity, with a long, satisfying finish.

Ashbourne Ale *(OG 1045, ABV 4.5%)*

Steamin' Billy Bitter *(OG 1045, ABV 4.5%)*
A dry-hopped version of Ashbourne Ale.

Hairy Helmet *(OG 1047, ABV 4.7%)*

Bespoke *(OG 1050, ABV 5%)*
A rich, well-balanced, fruity, full-bodied premium bitter.

LEES

JW Lees & Co (Brewers) Ltd, Greengate Brewery, Middleton Junction, Manchester M24 2AX
Tel (0161) 643 2487
Fax (0161) 655 3731
Tours by arrangement

⊛ Family-owned brewery founded in 1828 by John Willie Lees and now employing sixth-generation family members. In 1995 Lees took on its first full-time cooper for almost 30 years (half its cask beer is still delivered in traditional oak casks). A new range of seasonal beers is being developed. All the brewery's 175 pubs (most in north Manchester) serve real ale, which is also supplied to 150 other outlets direct. Seasonal beers: Archer Stout (March-April), Fudger Ale May-June), Scorcher (July-August), Sloeberry Ale (Sept/Oct), MM Nov/Dec).

GB Mild *(OG 1032, ABV 3.5%)* ✍
Malty and fruity in aroma. The same flavours are found in the taste, but do not dominate in a beer with a rounded and smooth character. Dry, malty aftertaste.

JW Lees Bitter *(OG 1037, ABV 4%)* ✍
A pale beer with a malty, fruity aroma and a

distinctive, malty, dry and slightly metallic taste. Clean, dry Lees finish.

Moonraker *(OG 1073, ABV 7.5%)* ▨▢◆
A reddish-brown beer with a strong, malty, fruity aroma. The flavour is rich and sweet, with roast malt, and the finish is fruity yet dry. Available only in a handful of outlets.

LEITH HILL

⬙ The Plough Inn & Leith Hill Brewery, Coldharbour Lane, Coldharbour, Nr Dorking, Surrey RH5 6HD
Tel (01306) 711793
Fax (01306) 710055
Tours by arrangement

⊗ Leith Hill started in the summer of 1996 to supply the Plough Inn. The home-made equipment has a 1-barrel brew length. The owners plan to buy a 2.5-barrel brew plant to halve brewing time and improve consistency. Seasonal ales. Beers: Crooked Furrow (OG 1040, ABV 4%), Tallywhacker (OG 1056, ABV 5.6%).

LEYDEN*

⬙ Leyden Brewery, Lord Raglan, Nangrehves, Bury, Lancs BL9 6SP
Tel 0161 764 6680
Tours by arrangement

Brewery constructed by Brian Farnworth that started production in October 1999. There are plans for new regular and seasonal brews. One pub is owned. Beers: Nanny Flyer (OG 1042, ABV 3.8%), Raglan Sleeve (OG 1046, ABV 4.6%).

LICHFIELD

Lichfield Brewery, John Thompson Inn, Ingleby, Derbyshire DE7 1HW
Tel (01332) 863033 Fax (01283) 712438
Tours by arrangement

Lichfield Brewery began brewing in 1992 and in June 1998, wishing to increase its capacity further, it began sharing premises with Lloyds Country Beers at the John Thompson Inn, a move which is proving mutually beneficial. The brewery continues to develop both its trading area and its beer range, with agencies or direct delivery. One-off brews supplement the regular and seasonal range, using an ever-wider selection of hops and malt blends. 200 outlets are supplied. Seasonal/occasional beers: Steeplechase (OG 1037, ABV 3.7%, summer), Bellringer (OG 1037, ABV 3.7%), Sheriff's Ride (OG 1042, ABV 4.2%, autumn), Resurrection (OG 1043, ABV 4.3%, spring), Happy New Beer (OG 1047, ABV 4.7%, New Year), Cavalier (OG 1047, ABV 4.7%), Xpired (OG 1048, ABV 4.8%), Mincespired (OG 1058, ABV 5.8%, Christmas).

Inspired *(OG 1040, ABV 4%)* ◆
Dark brown, malty beer with hops and some fruit aroma and bitter finish.

Resurrection Ale *(OG 1043, ABV 4.3%)*
Formerly a spring beer, now in the permanent range.

Steeplejack *(OG 1045, ABV 4.5%)* ◆
Pale brown, with a distinct aroma of malt and hops, tingles the palate and leaves a pleasant, dry finish.

Musketeer *(OG 1046, ABV 4.6%)*

Gargoyle *(OG 105, ABV 5%)*
Full bodied, fruity yet bitter strong ale.

LIDSTONES

Lidstones Brewery, Coltsfoot Green, Wickhambrook, Nr Newmarket, Suffolk CB8 8UW
Tel 01440 820232
E-mail lidstones_brewery@talk21.com
Tours by arrangement

Trading since April 1998, Peter Fairhall continues to develop recipes for a wide range of quality real ales using the best ingredients. In June 1999 his sister Jane joined as sales administrator. They have taken over their first pub, the Kingston Arms, Cambridge, where they plan to install a small brewery. Beers: Rowley Mild (ABV 3.2%), Thirstquencher (ABV 3.6%), Hoppy Top (ABV 3.9%), Lucky Punter (ABV 4.1%), Suffolk Draught (ABV 4.3%), Prime Meridian (ABV 4.5%), Bookies Revenge (ABV 4.6%), Colquhoun's Dark Mischief Stout (ABV 5%), Storm Brew (ABV 5.3%), Lidstones Old Ale (ABV 6.%).

LINFIT

⬙ Linfit Brewery, 139 Lane Top, Linthwaite, Huddersfield, W Yorkshire HD7 5SG
Tel (01484) 842370
Tours by arrangement

⊛ Nineteenth-century brew pub (CAMRA National Pub of the Year 1997) that recommenced brewing in 1982, producing an impressive range of ales for sale here and in the free trade as far away as Manchester (27 regular outlets). New plant installed in 1994 has almost doubled its capacity. Occasional/seasonal beers: Smoke House Ale (OG 1050, ABV 5.3%), Springbok Bier (OG 1055, ABV 5.7%), Xmas Ale (OG 1077, ABV 8.6%).

Mild *(OG 1032, ABV 3%)* ◆
Roast malt dominates this straightforward dark mild, which has some hops in the aroma and a slightly dry flavour. Malty finish.

Bitter *(OG 1035, ABV 3.7%)* ◆
A refreshing session beer. A dry-hopped aroma leads to a clean-tasting, hoppy bitterness, then a long, bitter finish with a hint of malt.

Cascade *(OG 1038, ABV 4%)*

Gold Medal *(OG 1040, ABV 4.2%)*

Ginger Beer *(OG 1040, ABV 4.2%)*

Special *(OG 1041, ABV 4.3%)* ❧
Dry-hopping provides the aroma for this rich and mellow bitter, which has a very soft profile and character: it fills the mouth with texture rather than taste. Clean, rounded finish.

Janet Street Porter *(OG 1043, ABV 4.5%)*
A smooth, dry porter with a bitter, roasted malt character.

Autumn Gold *(OG 1045, ABV 4.7%)* ❧
Straw-coloured best bitter with hop and fruit aromas, then the bitter-sweetness of autumn fruit in the taste and the finish.

English Guineas Stout
(OG 1050, ABV 5.3%) ❧
A fruity, roast aroma preludes a smooth, roasted malt, chocolatey flavour which is bitter but not too dry. Excellent appearance; good, bitter finish.

Old Eli *(OG 1050, ABV 5.3%)*
A well-balanced premium bitter with a dry-hopped aroma and a fruity, bitter finish.

Leadboiler *(OG 1060, ABV 6.6%)* ❧
Powerful malt, hop and fruit in good balance on the tongue, with a well-rounded bitter sweet finish.

Enoch's Hammer *(OG 1075, ABV 8%)* ❧
A straw-coloured beer with malt, hop and fruit aromas. Mouth-filling, smooth malt, hop and fruit flavours with a long, hoppy bitter finish. Dangerously drinkable.

LIVERPOOL
The Liverpool Brewing Company,
The Brewery, 21-23 Berry Street,
Liverpool L1 9DF
Tel (0151) 709 5055
Tours by arrangement

⊛ Brew pub with a 5-barrel plant set up in 1990 to brew solely for the Black Horse & Rainbow pub, renamed The Brewery in 1996. Seasonal beers are available and bottle-conditioned beers are planned. Six pubs are owned with four serving cask-conditioned beer. Six outlets are supplied direct.

Young Stallion *(OG 1038, ABV 3.6%)*

Red *(OG 1040, ABV 3.8%)*

Blondie *(OG 1044, ABV 4.1%)*

First Gold *(OG 1044, ABV 4.2%)*

Rocket *(OG 1045, ABV 4.3%)*

Celebration *(OG 1050, ABV 4.8%)*

LLOYDS
Lloyds Country Beers Ltd, John Thompson Brewery, Ingleby, Derbyshire DE73 1HW
Tel (01332) 863426
Tours by arrangement

⊗ Lloyds is the separate business set up to sell the beers brewed at the John Thompson Inn (qv) to the free trade. Despite problems in establishing a brand image in the guest beer market, and faced with a fluctuating demand, it still supplies around 150 outlets, mainly in the Midlands. Its single-hop brews, produced on a monthly basis, have been well received. It is also brewing the beers of the High Peak Brewery until suitable premises are found for that company.

Derby Bitter or JTS XXX

(OG 1042, ABV 4.1%)
Full and fruity.

IPA (Ingleby Pale Ale)
(OG 1045, ABV 4.5%)
A new summer beer.

Scratching Dog *(OG 1045, ABV 4.5%)*

Vixen Velvet *(OG 1045, ABV 4.5%)*
A winter porter.

VIP (Very Important Pint)
(OG 1048, ABV 4.7%)
A heavier, darker version of the bitter.

For High Peak:

Peak Pale *(ABV 3.8%)*

Bagman's Bitter *(OG 1045, ABV 4.5%)*

Cracken *(ABV 5.5%, Christmas)*

LONDON BEER COMPANY
See Pitfield.

LUGTON
⌂ Lugton Inn & Brewery, Lugton,
Ayrshire KA3 4DZ
In receivership summer 2000.

McGUINNESS
Thomas McGuinness Brewing Co,
Cask & Feather, 1 Oldham Road, Rochdale,
Lancashire OL16 1UA
Tel/Fax (01706) 711476
Tours by arrangement

Formed in November 1991, the brewery averages 15-20 barrels a week. It supplies real ale to its own pub and several other outlets direct. Seasonal beer: Dark (ABV 4.6%).

Feather Plucker Mild *(ABV 3.4%)* ❧
A dark brown beer, with roast malt dominant in the aroma and taste, with hints of chocolate. Satisfying bitter and roast finish.

Best Bitter *(ABV 3.8%)* ❧
Gold in colour with a hoppy aroma: a clean, refreshing beer with hop and fruit tastes and a hint of sweetness. Bitter aftertaste.

Special Reserve Bitter or SRB
(ABV 4%) ❧
A tawny beer, sweet and malty, with underlying fruit and bitterness, and a bitter-sweet aftertaste.

Junction Bitter *(ABV 4.2%)* ❧
Mid-brown in colour, with a malty aroma. Maltiness is predominant throughout, with some hops and fruit in the taste and bitterness coming through in the finish.

Tommy Todd's Porter *(ABV 5%)* ⬚❧
A winter warmer, with a fruit and roast aroma, leading to a balance of malt and roast malt flavours, with some fruit. Not too sweet for its gravity.

MACLACHLANS*
⌂ MacLachlans Brew Bar,
57 West Regent Street, Glasgow G2 2AE
Tel (0141) 332 0595
Fax (0141) 332 3007
E-mail maclachlansbrewbar.com
Web-site www.maclachlansbrewbar.com
Tours by arrangement

In the early 1900s there were nearly 100 brew bars within 200 metres of Glasgow Cross (traditionally all pubs were brew bars). Today, MacLachlans is the only city-centre bar to feature its own in-house brewery. MacLachlans uses only fresh organic, GM-fee and Scottish ingredients in brewing and food production, except for hops which are imported from mainland Europe. Amid a decor of Pictish imagery with contemporary design, four giant mirrored brewing tanks are situated above the bar on a solid steel platform. The tanks hold 1,500 pints each of the house beer, stored under CO_2 pressure. Just added to the range is a strong black beer made with roasted Scots porridge oats called Cu Chulainn, named after a famous Pictish warrior. Beers: IPA (ABV 3.8%), Kolsch (ABV 4.1%).

MACLAY
See Forth Brewery

McMULLEN
McMullen & Sons Ltd, 26 Old Cross, Hertford, Hertfordshire SG14 1RD
Tel (01992) 584911
Fax (01992) 500729
Tours by arrangement

⊗ Hertfordshire's oldest independent brewery, founded in 1827 by Peter McMullen. The Victorian tower brewery, which houses the original oak and copper-lined fermenters still in use today, was built on the site of three wells. Cask ale is served in all McMullen's 135 pubs in Hertfordshire, Essex and London (although all managed houses use cask breathers on all beers), and also supplied directly to 60 free trade outlets. Seasonal beers are brewed for a limited period under the banner of McMullen Special Reserve at OG 1050, ABV 5%. The award-winning Stronghart winter ale has not been brewed since 1997.

Original AK *(OG 1034, ABV 3.7%)* ◄
A pleasant mix of malt and hops leads to a distinctive, dry aftertaste that isn't always as pronounced as it used to be.

Country Best Bitter
(OG 1042, ABV 4.3%) ◄
A full-bodied beer with a well-balanced mix of malt, hops and fruit throughout.

Gladstone *(OG 1042, ABV 4.3%)* ◄
Amber-coloured beer. A mix of malt, hops and fruit in the aroma and taste lead to a dryish finish.

MALLARD
Mallard Brewery, 15 Hartington Avenue, Carlton, Nottingham NG4 3NR
Tel/Fax (0115) 952 1289
E-mail Philip.Mallard@tesco.net
Tours by arrangement (small groups)

⊗ Phil Mallard started brewing in 1973 as a home brewer with Boots beer kits and by 1988 had graduated to a full mash and whole hop brew. In 1994, with the encouragement of his wife, Gill, they decided to try commercial brewing from a shed at the back of their house. He built and installed a 2-barrel plant and started brewing in August 1995. The brewery is a mere nine square metres and

contains a hot liquor tank, mash tun, copper, and three fermenters. The major launch of the brewery was at the Nottingham Beer Festival in October 1995. Since then production has risen from one barrel a week to between six and eight barrels a week, which is the plant's maximum. Phil has no plans at present to expand and now supplies around 40 outlets, of which seven are on a regular weekly basis. He has also launched a small-scale bottling enterprise and plans to produce bottled beers as limited editions supplied direct from the brewery by mail order. Seasonal beer: Owd Duck (OG 1048, ABV 4.8%, Oct-May), DA (OG 1058, ABV 5.8%, Nov-March), Quismas Quacker (OG 1061, ABV 6%, Nov-Dec). Bottle-conditioned beers: Owd Duck (OG 1048, ABV 4.8%), Friar Duck (OG 1047, ABV 5%), DA (OG 1058, ABV 5.8%), Quismas Quacker (OG 1061, ABV 6%).

Waddlers Mild *(OG 1039, ABV 3.7%)*
A dark ruby mild with a fruity chocolate flavour in the mouth and a fruity finish.

Duck & Dive *(OG 1037, ABV 3.7%)*
A light single-hopped beer made from the new dwarf hop, First Gold. A bitter beer with a hoppy nose, good bitterness on the palate and a dry finish.

Best Bitter *(OG 1038, ABV 4%)* ◄
Golden brown, fruity and hoppy to the nose, with malt more apparent in the taste than anywhere else. The fruity hop carries through to a bitter, dry finish.

Duckling *(OG 1039, ABV 4.2%)*
A crisp refreshing bitter with a hint of honey and citrus flavour. Dry hopped.

Spittin' Feathers *(OG 1043, ABV 4.4%)*

Drake *(OG 1044, ABV 4.5%)*
A full-bodied premium bitter, with malt and hops on the palate and a fruity finish.

Duck Down Stout *(OG 1045, ABV 4.6%)*

Owd Duck *(OG 1048, ABV 4.8%)* ◄
Intensely roasty, this ruby/brown drink has moderate undertones of fruit and faint hops throughout.

Friar Duck *(OG 1047, ABV 5%)*
A pale full malt beer, hoppy with a hint of blackcurrant flavour.

DA *(OG 1058, ABV 5.8%)*
A dark, sweetish winter ale.

Quismas Quacker *(OG 1060, ABV 6%)*

MALTON
Malton Brewery Company Ltd, rear of Suddaby's Crown Hotel, 12 Wheelgate, Malton, N Yorkshire YO17 7HP
Tel (01653) 697580
Fax (01653) 691812
E-mail neil@suddabys.demon.co.uk
Tours by arrangement

⊛ The Malton Brewery Company was founded in the stable block at the rear of the Crown Hotel in Wheelgate, Malton in 1984 by the late Bob Suddaby, licensee of the hotel, Colin Sykes, an industrial chemist, and Geoff Woollons, a retired head brewer. The brewery is now run by the Suddaby family with Neil, also licensee of the hotel, in charge with Alan Brayshaw as chief brewer. Special accommodation packages linked to a day in the brewery are planned for CAMRA members. Thirty outlets are supplied direct. Occasional and seasonal beer: Double Heart (OG 1038, ABV 4%), Carousel Bitter (OG 1046, ABV 5%, winter special).

Malton Pale Ale (*OG 1034, ABV 3.3%*)

Double Chance (*OG 1038, ABV 3.8%*) ◗
A clean-tasting, amber bitter in which hops predominate. Little malt character, but hop and fruit flavours lead to a smooth, bitter finish.

Golden Chance (*OG 1039, ABV 4.3%*)
A full-bodied dark amber bitter with hops and gentle fruitiness, with a lingering dry finish.

Pickwick's Porter (*OG 1042, ABV 4.2%*) ◗
A dry, nutty porter with an abundance of malt and roast aromas and flavours. The grainy malts combine with autumnal fruit flavours into a dry finish.

Crown Bitter (*OG 1044, ABV 4,5%*) ◗
A strong, malty pale ale, well-balanced by hop aromas and fruit flavours.

Dog Breath (*OG 1049, ABV 4.9%*)
A blend of Owd Bob and Double Chance.

Owd Bob (*OG 1055, ABV 6%*) ◗
A deep ruddy-brown coloured ale with a rich, warming feel. Powerful malt, roast, hops and fruit attack the nose and palate. The sweet finish, with malt and roast malt flavours, is balanced by a late trace of bitterness.

MALVERN HILLS
Malvern Hills Brewery Ltd, 15 West Malvern Road, Great Malvern WR14 4ND
Tel (01684) 560165
Fax (01684) 577336
E-mail MHB.ales@tesco.net
Web-site homepages.tesco.net/~MHB.ales

A 9-barrel capacity brewery opened in a former explosive store in a disused quarry in North Malvern. Local free trade and whole-salers are being supplied. A spring beer and a bottled beer are planned. Seasonal beer: Worcestershire Whym (OG 1042, ABV 4.2%).

Malvern Hills Bitter
(*OG 1039, ABV 3.9%*) ◗
Bitterness throughout with a sweet fruitiness staking a claim on the tongue and leaving a vivid memory in the mouth.

Black Pear (*OG 1044, ABV 4.4%*) ◗
A complex array of flavours including an acidic fruitiness as well as a cereal maltiness make this an absorbing drink.

Dr Gully's Winter Ale
(*OG 1052, ABV 5.2%*) ◗
Rich, velvety malt flavours prevail in this classic winter warmer, leaving a warm satisfying aftertaste.

MAN IN THE MOON
The Man in the Moon Brewery, Unit L1, Elms Park Farm, Bitteswell, nr Lutterworth, Leicestershire LE17 4RA
Tel (0116) 2750275
Tours by arrangement

⊗ The brewery opened in 1996 and has since moved to a new site, redeveloped its product range and enjoyed rapid expansion. It cur-

rently supplies 12 free trade outlets direct, and it has plans to buy a couple of pubs of its own.

Harvest Moon (*OG 1038, ABV 3.7%*)

Eclipse (*OG 1041, ABV 4.1%*)

Ivory Stout (*OG 1040, ABV 4.1%*)

Werewolf (*OG 1050, ABV 5%*)

MANSFIELD
Mansfield Brewery PLC, Littleworth, Mansfield, Nottinghamshire NG18 1AB.
A subsidiary of Wolverhampton & Dudley Breweries.
Tel (01623) 625691
Fax (01623) 658620
Shop
Tours by arrangement

☺ Founded in 1855, Mansfield is now one of the major regional brewers with a tied estate of some 500 houses, three-quarters of which sell real ale, and substantial club and free trade accounts. It made a welcome return to cask ale production in 1982 after a break of 10 years. The purchase of Hull's North Country Brewery in 1985 and subsequent sizeable pub acquisitions have helped to bring Mansfield's award-winning ales, all fermented in traditional Yorkshire Squares, to a wider audience. The business was bought by Wolverhampton & Dudley Breweries in 2000 and there were immediate question marks over the future of the brewery when W&D managing director David Thompson announced in May 2000 that he was looking at plans to rationalise his plants. Club and free trade outlets are supplied. Occasional seasonal brews with a sporting theme are produced. W&D has made it clear it will concentrate on core brands and in April 2000 it stopped production of Old Baily, seen as a direct competitor to Marston's Pedigree. The future of Riding Bitter is also in doubt.

Mansfield Cask Dark Mild (formerly Riding Mild) (*OG 1035, ABV 3.5%*) ◗
Chocolate malt on the nose leads to black-currant fruit on the taste, with hops finishing. The chocolate malt character continues throughout this ruby-black beer.

Riding Bitter (*OG 1035, ABV 3.6%*) ◗
A beer first aimed at Mansfield's Yorkshire market. Mid-brown and moderately bitter, it is dominated by an aromatic, fruity hop, but with malt always present.

Mansfield Bitter (*OG 1038, ABV 3.9%*) ◗
This mid-brown bitter is well balanced in taste but has hops to the fore on the nose and malt lingering in the aftertaste, although some bitterness is discernible.

For Scottish Courage:

Matthew Brown Lion Bitter
(*OG 1034, ABV 3.5%*)

Wilson's Original Bitter
(*OG 1035, ABV 3.5%*)

MARBLE
⚑ The Marble Brewery, 73 Rochdale Road, Manchester M4 4HY
Tel (0161) 832 5914
Tel/Fax (0161) 819 2694
Tours by arrangement with the brewer, Mark Dade

Launched in December 1998 in the Marble Arch Inn in North Manchester, the 5-barrel plant brews twice a week and supplies The Bar in Chorlton, Manchester and the Marble Beerhouse in Charlton, Manchester. The brewery won first and second prize for Liberty IPA and McKenna's Revenge Porter in the Speciality Beers Category at the 1998 Huddersfield CAMRA Beer Festival. Now supplying N/4 Bitter as the official beer in the Northern Quarter of Manchester (available in real ale outlets in the area). It also supplies other real ale pubs as well as beer festivals. Seasonal beers: Spooky Marble (OG 1038, ABV 3.8%, Halloween), The Ginger Marble (OG 1045, ABV 4.5%, occasional), Summer Marbles (OG 1047, ABV 4.7%), Dobber (OG 1060, ABV 6.5&, winter), Wee Star (OG 1080, ABV 9%, Christmas).

Chorlton Bitter *(OG 1038, ABV 3.8%)*

N/4 Bitter *(OG 1038, ABV 3.8%)*

Marble Bitter *(OG 1040, ABV 4%)*

Liberty IPA *(OG 1046, ABV 4.6%)*

Totally Marbled *(OG 1050, ABV 5%)*

McKenna's Revenge Porter
(OG 1050, ABV 5%)

MARCHES

Marches Ales, Unit 6, Western Close, Southern Avenue Industrial Estate, Leominster, Herefordshire HR6 0QD
Tel (01568) 610063
Shop
Tours by arrangement

⊠ Set up in 1995 in purpose-built premises, a new fermentation room was installed in 1998 and several new beers were introduced, including single varietal hop beers with such hop varieties as First Gold. All other beers take their names from local history. Some beers are now bottled. Eighty outlets are supplied direct. Bottle-conditioned beers: Gold (ABV 4%), Corn Spirit (ABV 4.4%), Priory Ale (ABV 4.5%).

BHB *(OG 1038, ABV 3.8%)*

Lempster Ore *(OG 1036, ABV 3.8%)*

Forever Autumn *(OG 1040, ABV 4.2%)* ◀
Hop fruitiness predominates in a complex array of flavours, to give a rich aftertaste.

Gold *(OG 1045, ABV 4.5%)*

Lord Protector *(OG 1046, ABV 4.7%)*

Priory Ale *(OG 1048, ABV 4.8%)*
Available Oct-March.

Jenny Pipes Blonde Biere
(OG 1050, ABV 5.2%)

MARSTON MOOR

Marston Moor Brewery, Crown House, Kirk Hammerton, York, YO26 8DD
Tel/Fax (01423) 330341

☺ Small but expanding brewery, set up in 1983 and moved to the rear of its first tied house, the Crown, in 1988. The pub was closed in 1993. The company currently produces 750 barrels a year and supplies around 200 free trade outlets. It also installs brewing plant and acts as a consultant to micro-brewers, both here and abroad; to date

it has helped set up 30 breweries in Britain. Seasonal beer: Porter (OG 1040-42, ABV 4.2%, winter).

Cromwell Bitter *(OG 1036-38, ABV 3.6%)* ◀
A golden beer with hops and fruit in strong evidence on the nose. Bitterness as well as fruit and hops dominate the taste and long aftertaste.

Prince Rupert Mild *(OG 1039-40, ABV 4%)*

Pilsener *(OG 1039-40, ABV 4%)*

Brewers Pride *(OG 1040-42, ABV 4.2%)* ◀
A light but somewhat thin, fruity beer, with a hoppy, bitter aftertaste.

Merriemaker *(OG 1044-46, ABV 4.5%)*

Brewers Droop *(OG 1048-50, ABV 5%)*
A pale, robust ale with hops and fruit notes in prominence. A long, bitter aftertaste.

Trooper *(OG 1048-50, ABV 5%)*

MARSTON'S

Marston, Thompson & Evershed PLC, The Brewery, Shobnall Road, Burton upon Trent, Staffordshire DE14 2BW.
A subsidiary of Wolverhampton & Dudley Breweries.
Tel (01283) 531131
Fax (01283) 510378
Shop 10-3 Mon-Fri 9.30-12 Sat
Tours by arrangement, ring (01283) 507391

☺ After a long and bitter struggle, Marston's was bought by the expanding and acquisitive Wolverhampton & Dudley Group in 1999. Marston's is the only brewery still using the Burton Union system of fermentation for Pedigree Bitter, with yeast propagated in the unions used for all other brews. Marston's reinforced its commitment to this method in 1992 with a £1 million investment in a new union room. Real ale is available throughout the company's estate, which stretches from Yorkshire to Hampshire. W&D planned to stop production of Marston's Bitter but changed its mind following a revolt by drinkers and licensees in such areas as North Wales and Greater Manchester, where the beer outsells Pedigree. The Head Brewer's Choice scheme (noted as HBC in Good Beer Guide pub entries) offers a range of new brews to selected outlets for two weeks at a time but now alternates with Banks's Special Brews. Marston's also enjoys a large free trade, thanks to trading agreements with

The Good Beer Guide 2001

many regional and national brewers. Bottle-conditioned beer: Oyster Stout (OG 1045, ABV 4.5%).

Bitter *(OG 1038, ABV 4%)* ◆
An amber/tawny session beer that can often be sulphury in aroma and taste. At its best, a splendid, subtle balance of malt, hops and fruit follows a faintly hoppy aroma and develops into a balanced, dry aftertaste.

Pedigree *(OG 1043, ABV 4.5%)* ◆
Sulphurous aroma giving way to hops. Tastes hoppy and fruity and leaves a bitter after-taste. The classic Burton pale ale.

Owd Rodger *(OG 1080, ABV 7.6%)* ⬚◆
Strong, dark red, fruity barley wine. Sweet start with a liquorice character develops into fruit and hops and finishes with a spicy, dry, lingering aftertaste. Now only brewed by special arrangement.

For Carlsberg-Tetley:

Ind Coope Burton Ale
(OG 1047 ABV 4.8%) ◆
A full-bodied beer, hops, fruit and malt present throughout, with a lingering complex aftertaste.

For Tesco (bottle conditioned):

Tesco Select Ales IPA *(OG 1048, ABV 5%)*

Tesco Select Ales Porter
(OG 1048, ABV 5%)

For Wetherspoons:

Sundance *(OG 1048, ABV 5%)*
An IPA-style beer.

MASH & AIR

⌂ Mash and Air, 40 Charlton Street, Manchester M1 3HW
Tel (0161) 661 6161
Fax (0161) 661 6060

Brew-restaurant founded in 1997 in converted mill, specialising in tutored beer-tasting lunches, with beers brewed to accompany various meals. Tours (with a meal) on Saturdays. All beers are conditioned and stored in cellar tanks using a CO2 system. Beers: Peach (ABV 5%), Mash (ABV 5.1%), Mash Wheat (ABV 5%), Blackcurrant Porter (ABV 5.3%), India Pale Ale (ABV 5.3%), Scotch (ABV 6%).

MASH 2

⌂ Mash 2 Ltd, 19/21 Great Portland Street, London W1N 5DB
Tel (0171) 637 5555 Fax (0171) 637 7333

Brew-restaurant, part of the same group that owns Mash & Air in Manchester. The in-house brewery produces international beer styles on a rotation basis, including a Blackcurrant Porter, Scotch, IPA, Peach, Extra Stout and Pils. The beers are stored in cellar tanks using a CO2 system. Regular beer: Mash Wheat (OG 1048, ABV 5.2%).

MAULDONS

⊠ Mauldons Brewery, 7 Addison Road, Chilton Industrial Estate, Sudbury, Suffolk CO10 2YW
Tel/Fax (01787) 311055
Tours by arrangement

Company set up in 1982 by former Watney's brewer Peter Mauldon, whose family had its own local brewery in the late 18th century. Its extensive beer list changes frequently and is supplied to 150 free trade outlets in East Anglia, as well as pubs further afield via wholesalers. Peter Mauldon retired in 2000 and sold the company to Steve Sims, former sales manager with Adnams, and his wife, Alison. Seasonal beers: May Bee (OG 1037, ABV 3.7%, May), Broomstick Bitter (OG 1040, ABV 4%, Hallowe'en), Mother's Ruin (OG 1040, ABV 4%, Mothering Sunday), George's Best (OG 1045, ABV 4.4%, St George's Day), Love Potion No. 9 (OG 1045, ABV 4.5%, St Valentine's Day), Bah Humbug (OG 1049, ABV 4.9%, Christmas), Mr McTavish (OG 1050, ABV 5%, January), Gunpowder Blast (OG 1063, ABV 6%, Guy Fawkes Night), Christmas Reserve (OG 1066, ABV 6.6%), Midsummer Gold (OG 1040, ABV 4%), Mid Autumn Gold (OG 1041, ABV 4.2%), Midwinter Gold (OG 1045, ABV 4.5%).

May Bee *(OG 1037, ABV 3.7%)*
Softer than Moletrap, with added honey. Available in May.

Moletrap Bitter *(OG 1037, ABV 3.8%)* ◆
Previously Best Bitter, a well-balanced session beer with a crisp, hoppy bitterness balancing sweet malt.

Original Porter *(OG 1040, ABV 3.8%)* ◆
A black beer with malt and roast malt flavours dominating. Some hop in the finish.

Dickens *(ABV 4%)*
A new beer introduced by the new owners in 2000.

Eatanswill Old XXXX
(OG 1042, ABV 4%) ◆
Taking its name from the title given to Sudbury by Dickens in Pickwick Papers, this is a winter ale of deep red and brown hue, with well-balanced fruit and malt plus a slight sweetness on the palate, ending in a pleasant roast bitterness.

Squires Bitter *(OG 1044, ABV 4.2%)* ◆
A best bitter with a good, malty aroma and a reasonably balanced flavour, which leans towards malt. Hops come through late and crisply into the aftertaste.

Black Satin *(OG 1045, ABV 4.5%)*

Suffolk Pride *(OG 1050, ABV 4.8%)* ◆
Formerly Suffolk Punch, a full-bodied, strong bitter. The malt and fruit in the aroma are reflected in the taste and there is some hop character in the finish. Deep tawny/red in colour.

Black Adder *(OG 1053, ABV 5.3%)* ◆
A dark stout. Roast malt is strong in the aroma and taste, but malt, hop and bitterness provide an excellent balance and a lingering finish. Champion Beer of Britain 1991.

White Adder *(OG 1053, ABV 5.3%)* ◆
A pale brown, almost golden, strong ale. A warming, fruity flavour dominates and lingers into a dry, hoppy finish.

Suffolk Comfort *(OG 1065, ABV 6.6%)*
A clean, hoppy nose leads to a predominantly malty flavour in this full-bodied beer. Dry, hoppy aftertaste.

MAYHEM
See Farmers Arms.

MAYPOLE
The Maypole Brewery, North Laithes Farm, Wellow Road, Eakring, Newark, Nottinghamshire NG22 0AN
Tel (01623) 871690

⊗ Brewery established in March 1995 in an 18th-century converted farm building. Its name comes from the permanent giant maypole that is a feature of neighbouring Wellow. One beer, Lion's Pride (OG 1038, ABV 3.9%) is brewed just for the Olde Red Lion opposite the maypole. It currently supplies around 40 outlets on an occasional basis. Maypole also brews one-off beers for festivals and other events. Seasonal/occasional beers: Mayfair (OG 1037, ABV 3.8%, spring/summer), Old Homewrecker (OG 1047, ABV 4.7%, winter), Donner and Blitzed (OG 1048, ABV 5.1%, Christmas), Brew 2K (OG 1044, ABV 4.5%, to order).

Lion's Pride *(OG 1038, ABV 3.9%)*

Celebration *(OG 1040, ABV 4%)* ◆
A ruddy-brown bitter in which malt dominates. Some fruity hop in the nose and taste, with an initial sweetness that dries into a bitter finish where the fruit and hops meet the malt.

Centenary Ale *(OG 1041, ABV 4.2%)*
A light-coloured bitter with a fruity nose and a dry aftertaste. There are hints of vanilla in this crisp, refreshing, full-bodied beer.

Flanagan's Stout *(OG 1043, ABV 4.4%)*
Brewed initially for St Patrick's Day: a full-bodied, rich stout. An initial burnt malt dryness gives way to a smooth, mellow, lingering aftertaste with hints of liquorice, dark chocolate and coffee.

Mayday *(OG 1045, ABV 4.5%)* ◆
A tawny best bitter, with malt and a hint of dates on the nose. The taste is predominantly fruit and malt again, which becomes more bitter and hoppy in the finish.

Mae West *(OG 1044, ABV 4.6%)*
A blonde, Belgian-style summer beer. Citrus flavours predominate in the nose and taste. A deceptively drinkable beer for its strength.

Poleaxed *(OG 1046, ABV 4.8%)*
A tawny, smooth beer. Damsons come out in the nose and taste and give way to a slightly burnt aftertaste. A full-bodied, warming beer.

MEANTIME*
Meantime Brewing Co,
2 Penhall Road, Greenwich,
London SE7 8RX
Tel (020) 8293 1111
E-mail sales@mean-time.co.uk
Web-site mean-time.co.uk

New specialist brewery run by Alistair Hook, formerly of Freedom and Mash. He brews bespoke classic beer styles for customers with their own labels and concentrates on cold-fermented lagers and warm-fermented Bavarian-style wheat beers. He also produces bottle-conditioned beers for own-label sales. He plans his own range of classic lagers, such as a Vienna Red.

MELBOURN
Melbourn Brothers, All Saints Brewery, All Saints Street, Stamford, Lincolnshire PE9 2PA
Tel (01780) 752186

The brewery dates back to 1825 and ceased operating in 1974. It re-opened in 1978 and closed in 1993. It began brewing again on a trial basis in 1997 and then full time in 1999 between October and March. It is owned by Samuel Smith of Tadcaster (qv). Bottled beers: Strawberry (ABV 3.4%), Apricot (ABV 3.4%).

MIGHTY OAK
Mighty Oak Brewing Company Ltd, 9 Prospect Way, Hutton Industrial Estate, Brentwood, Essex CM13 1XA
Tel (01277) 263007
Fax (01277) 228670
E-mail Moakbrew@aol.com
Tours by arrangement

⊗ The Mighty Oak Brewing Company came into being following the closure of Ind Coope's Romford Brewery, when brewing engineer John Boyce was made redundant. Established in 1996, Mighty Oak has increased capacity twice and is currently growing at the rate of 33 per cent a year. It now brews 30 barrels a week and is actively looking for new premises in the area. It is brewery policy to sell direct and less than three per cent of production goes to wholesalers. The brewery has some 200 customers in Essex, Suffolk, Herts, Kent, Wiltshire, Somerset and Gloucestershire. Occasional beers: Brass Monkey (OG 1041.2, ABV 4.1%, Jan-March), Oscar Wilde Mild (ABV 3.7%, Jan, April-May, Aug-Sept, Nov), Ale Dancer (OG 1042.5, ABV 4.2%, April-June), Saffron Gold (OG 1043.3, ABV 4.3%, July-Sept), Bingle Jells (OG 1052, ABV 5.2%, Nov-Dec), Sleigh Rider (OG 1038.5, ABV 3.8%, Nov-Dec), Yellow Snow (OG 1038.5, ABV 3.8%, Nov-Dec), Essex Hop-Pot (ABV 3.7%), Twenty-Thirst Century (ABV 5.5%).

Barrackwood IPA
(OG 1035.7, ABV 3.6%) ◆

Amber-coloured beer with a predominantly malty taste and a pleasantly refreshing bitter finish.

Ruby Tuesday *(OG 1040.2, ABV 3.9%)*

Burntwood Bitter
(OG 1040.9, ABV 4%) ■⛏◆
Full-flavoured tawny best bitter with malt and balancing hops, and a dryish finish.

Simply The Best *(OG 1043.9, ABV 4.4%)* ◆
A tawny, full-bodied best bitter with a light balance of malt and hops and a bitter-sweet finish.

Essex County Ale *(OG 1045.4, ABV 4.6%)*

Mighty Oak *(OG 1047, ABV 4.8%)*

MILK STREET*
The Milk Street Brewery, The Griffin,
Milk Street, Frome BA11 3DB
Tel (01373) 467766
Tours by arrangement

The brewery was commissioned in September 1999 and capacity is 20 barrels a week. Three beers are currently brewed with seasonal beers produced every two months. The brewery was designed by Rik Lyall using his experience gained as head brewer for Bunce's, Hopback and Cotleigh breweries. 22 outlets are supplied direct. Beers: Alchemy (OG 1040, ABV 4%), Nick's (OG 1045, ABV 4.4%), Beer (OG 1050, ABV 5%).

MILLERS THUMB
⛏ Millers Thumb Brewing Co,
t/a The Canal, 300 Bearsden Road,
Glasgow Gl3 1EP
Tel (0141) 954 5333
Fax (0141) 954 5533
Shop open as bar
Tours by arrangement

American-style brew restaurant; the beers are filtered and carbonated. Seasonal beer: Blitzen Brun (OG 1055, ABV 5.1%). Beers: Lighthouse Ale (OG 1034, ABV 3.2%), Black Canyon (OG 1048, ABV 3.9%), Red Rooster (OG 1048, ABV 4.1%), Thumb Blonde (OG 1048, ABV 4.5%), Independence Ale (OG 1052, ABV 5.1%), Woodcutters IPA (OG 1054, ABV 5.3%).

MILTON*
Milton Brewery, Cambridge Ltd,
Unit 111, Norman Industrial Estate,
Cambridge Road, Milton,
Cambridge CB4 6AT
Tel (01223) 226198
Fax (01223) 226199
E-mail enquiries@miltonbrewery.co.uk
Web-site www.miltonbrewery.co.uk
Tours by arrangement

Founded in summer 1999, the Milton Brewery revives a brewing history absent in Milton for 75 years. With a 15-barrel brew length, the brewery supplies an increasing number (60-70) of free trade outlets in the Cambridge area and beyond. The beer names have a strong classical theme.

Minotaur *(OG 1035, ABV 3.3%)* ◆
Rich and very full-bodied for its strength, a malty chocolateyness predominates, but vanilla and liquorice flavours also surface.

Jupiter *(OG 1037, ABV 3.5%)* ◆
Golden session beer whose delicately hoppy flavour leads to a satisfying bitter finish.

Neptune *(OG 1039, ABV 3.8%)* ◆
Delicious hop aromas introduce this well-balanced, nutty and refreshing copper-coloured ale. Good hoppy finish.

Pegasus *(OG 1043, ABV 4.1%)* ◆
Hops dominate the first impressions of this majestic ale, but the long, fruity/toffee finish shows that this is anything but a one-dimensional brew.

Cyclops *(OG 1055, ABV 5.3%)*
Brewed with three different malts and four varieties of hops, this full-bodied and complex ale rewards serious investigation.

Mammon *(OG 1070, ABV 7%)*
Rich, dark and warming winter ale.

MOLE'S
Mole's Brewery (Cascade Drinks Ltd),
5 Merlin Way, Bowerhill,
Melksham,
Wiltshire SN12 6TJ
Tel (01225) 704734/708842
Fax (01225) 790770
E-mail cascade@cableinet.co.uk
Web-site molesbrewery.com
Shop 9-5
Tours by arrangement

⊠ In 1982 Moles Brewery was built on the site of Cascade Drinks, a drinks manufacturer and wholesaler, to brew cask conditioned beer for local consumption, using Wiltshire grown and malted Maris Otter barley and choice Kent hops of the Fuggle and Golding varieties. In 1997 the brewery was expanded with a new brewhouse and 25-barrel brewing equipment. Moles Brewery now produces a selection of beers to suit all palates locally, nationally and internationally. Thirteen pubs are owned, 12 serving cask-conditioned beer. It currently supplies more than 100 free trade outlets direct. Bottle-conditioned beer: Brew 97 (OG 1050, ABV 5%). Seasonal beers: Barleymole (OG 1042, ABV 4.2%, summer), Molennium (OG 1045, ABV 4.5%), Moel Moel (OG 1060, ABV 6%, winter).

Tap Bitter *(OG 1035, ABV 3.5%)*
A top quality session bitter with a smooth, malty flavour and clean bitter finish. Pale brown in colour.

Best Bitter *(OG 1040, ABV 4%)*
Well-balanced golden colour bitter, clean, dry and malty with some bitterness and delicate floral hop flavour.

Molegrip *(OG 1043, ABV 4.3%)*
A rich red-ruby autumn seasonal beer, hoppy, malty and fruity with a long, dry finish.

Landlords Choice *(OG 1045, ABV 4.5%)*
Dark-coloured strong, smooth, hoppy bitter with a rich fruity palate and malty finish.

Barleymole *(OG 1042, ABV 4.2%)*
A straw-coloured, well-hopped bitter with a delightful floral hop aroma and clean, full-flavoured malty finish brewed for the summer season.

Holy Moley *(OG 1047, ABV 4.7%)*
A deep honey-coloured spring-time seasonal beer with ample upfront maltiness balanced by a satisfying bitter finish.

Brew 97 *(OG 1050, ABV 5%)*
A mid-brown, full-bodied beer with a gentle malt and hop aroma. The rich flavour is malty, with fruit, hop and traces of vanilla. A wonderfully warming, malty ale.

MOOR

Moor Beer Company, Whitley Farm, Ashcott, Bridgwater, Somerset TA7 9QW
Tel/Fax (01458) 210050
E-mail arthurframpton@virgin.net
Web-site www.moorbeer.com
Tours by arrangement

⊗ Based in a redundant workshop, Arthur and Annette Frampton started brewing on their former dairy farm in February 1996. Their 10-barrel plant and its brews are now well established in the West Country with wholesalers taking their beer farther afield. Monthly specials are produced and 40 outlets are supplied direct. Bottle-conditioned beer: Old Freddy Walker (OG 1074, ABV 7.3%).

Withy Cutter *(OG 1041, ABV 3.8%)* ◆
A lightly malty, pale brown beer with a moderate bitter finish.

Merlin's Magic *(OG 1044, ABV 4.3%)* ◆
Dark amber-coloured, complex, full-bodied beer, with fruity notes.

Peat Porter *(OG 1045, ABV 4.5%)* ◆
Dark brown/black beer with an initially fruity taste leading to roast malt taste with a little bitterness. A slightly sweet malty finish.

Chandos Gold *(OG 1052, ABV 5%)* ◆
Straw-coloured beer with spicy hop aroma, malt with hints of vanilla on the palate, long fruit and hop finish.

Old Freddy Walker *(OG 1074, ABV 7.3%)* ◆
Rich, dark strong ale with a fruity complex taste, leaving a fruitcake finish.

MOORHOUSES

Moorhouses Brewery (Burnley) Ltd,
4 Moorhouse Street, Burnley,
Lancashire BB11 5EN
Tel (01282) 422864/416004
Fax (01282) 838493
Tours by arrangement

☺ Brewers of famous hop bitters from 1865, Moorhouses switched to cask beer production in 1978. A succession of owners failed to develop the company until it was taken over in 1985 by Bill Parkinson, since when it has grown substantially. A modern brewhouse was installed in 1988 and more fermenting vessels were added in 1991 to keep up with demand. The company owns six pubs, all serving cask-conditioned beer and supplies real ale to around 200 free trade outlets.

Black Cat *(OG 1036, ABV 3.4%)* ▧▯◆
An excellent dark, fruity ale. Smooth and well-balanced with fruity, chocolate and coffee flavours to complement the bitter roast character that lingers on in the aftertaste.

Premier Bitter *(OG 1036, ABV 3.7%)* ◆
A clean and satisfying hoppy, bitter aftertaste rounds off this consistent, well-balanced brew. Look for a floral hop aroma and generous fruity, hoppy, bitter flavours.

Pride of Pendle *(OG 1040, ABV 4.1%)*

Pendle Witches Brew
(OG 1050, ABV 5.1%) ◆
Fruit, hops and malt combine on the nose and follow through into the taste, balanced by some sweetness. The finish is bitter and dry.

MORDUE

Mordue Brewery, Unit 21A,
West Chirton North Industrial Estate,
Shiremoor, Tyne & Wear NE29 8SF
Tel/Fax (0191) 2961879
E-mail beerquestions@ibm.net
Web-site www.morduebrewery.com
Tours by arrangement

☺ Founded by brother Garry and Matthew Fawson, Mordue won the Champion Beer of Britain award in 1997 with Workie Ticket. A new brewery is now fully operational, with a 20-barrel brew length and a weekly capacity of 120 barrels. 150 outlets are supplied direct while southern distribution is handled by Batemans. The Fawsons have discovered that the original Mordue family, who ran a brewery on Wallsend village green in the 19th century, is directly related to George Stephenson, inventor of the Rocket, the first commercial steam locomotive. Seasonal beers: Summer Tyne (ABV 3.6%), Autumn Tyne (ABV 4%), 2000/AD (ABV 4.5%), Wallsend Brown Ale (ABV 4.6%), Black Midden Stout (ABV 4.6%), Winter Tyne (ABV 4.7%). Both Radgie Gadgie and Workie

Ticket are now available in bottle.

Five Bridges *(ABV 3.8%)* ◆
An amber, fruity beer with a good hint of hops. The bitterness carries on in the aftertaste. A good session beer.

Geordie Pride *(ABV 4.2%)* ◆
A well-balanced, hoppy bitter with a long, bitter finish. This amber beer has and a hoppy, fruity aroma and a long, bitter finish.

Workie Ticket *(ABV 4.5%)* ▯◆
A complex, tasty beer with malt and hops throughout. A long, satisfying bitter finish. Champion Beer of Britain 1997.

Radgie Gadgie *(ABV 4.8%)* ▯◆
A strong, easy-drinking, tawny northern ale, with balanced hops, fruit and malt and a long, lingering finish. Deceptively drinkable. Winner of the Strong Bitter class in Champion Beer of Britain competition 1998.

MORLAND

Closed by Greene King in January 2000. Some of the brands have been transferred to Greene King's Bury St Edmunds site (qv).

MOULIN

⚑ RTR Catering Ltd, Moulin Hotel & Brewery, Kirkmichael Road, Pitlochry Perthshire PH16 5EW
Tel (01796) 472196
Fax (01796) 474098
Shop 12-3 daily
Tours by arrangement

⊛ Opened in August 1995 during celebrations for the hotel's 300th anniversary, Moulin supplies three outlets. Bottle-conditioned beer: Ale of Atholl (OG 1043, ABV 4.5%).

Light *(OG 1035, ABV 3.7%)* ◆
Thirst-quenching, straw-coloured session beer, with a light, hoppy, fruity balance ending with a gentle, hoppy sweetness.

Braveheart *(OG 1039, ABV 4%)* ◆
An amber bitter, with a delicate balance of malt and fruit and a Scottish-style sweetness.

Ale of Atholl *(OG 1043, ABV 4.5%)* ◆
A reddish, quaffable, malty ale, with a solid body and a mellow finish.

Old Remedial *(OG 1050.5, ABV 5.2%)* ◆
A distinctive and satisfying dark brown old ale, with roast malt to the fore and tannin in a robust taste

NAGS HEAD
⬗ Nags Head Inn, Abercych, Boncath, Pembrokeshire SA37 0HJ
Tel (01239) 841200

Pub-brewery producing just one brew on an occasional basis largely for its own consumption. Two outlets are supplied direct. Beer: Old Emrys (OG 1038-40, ABV 3.8-4%).

NENE VALLEY
See Leyland.

NETHERGATE
Nethergate Brewery Co Ltd, 11-13 High Street, Clare, Suffolk CO10 8NY
Tel (01787) 277244
Fax (01787) 277123
Tours by arrangement (trade and CAMRA groups)

⊠ Small brewer of award-winning beers, set up in 1986, which continues to use traditional methods and no additives. The Umbel beers are infused with coriander seeds, recalling an ancient brewing style. 200 free trade outlets are now supplied, mainly in East Anglia; the number is expected to grow to 250 by the end of the year. Old Growler is now bottle-conditioned. Seasonal/occasional beers: Swift Spring Ale (OG 1041, ABV 4.1%, spring), Swallow Ale (OG 1042, ABV 4.2%, summer), Autumn Ale (OG 1043, ABV 4.3%, autumn), Golden Gate (OG 1045, ABV 4.5%, summer), Domesday Ale (ABV 4.5%, one-off), Christmas Ale (OG 1048, ABV 4.8%, Nov-Dec).

Priory Mild *(OG 1036, ABV 3.5%)*

IPA *(OG 1036, ABV 3.5%)* ◆
An apple crisp, refreshing session beer, hoppy throughout, without fully masking the malt. Lingering, bitter aftertaste.

Umbel Ale *(OG 1039, ABV 3.8%)* ▮⬖⬗◆
Wort is percolated through coriander seeds to give a wonderful, warming, spicy fruit tang to both the taste and aroma. The hops are strong enough to make themselves known and a strong, bitter malt finish hits late.

Suffolk County Best Bitter (formerly Nethergate Bitter) *(OG 1039, ABV 4%)* ◆
A dark bitter in which delightful malt and hop aromas give way to a well-balanced palate. Rich malts and powerful bitterness dominate the flavour, ending in a strong, bitter finish.

Augustinian Ale *(OG 1048, ABV 4.8%)*
A new pale beer using pale and crystal malts with Kent Challenger and Slovenian Styrian Goldings hops.

Old Growler *(OG 1050, ABV 5%)* ⬗◆
A complex and satisfying porter, smooth and distinctive. Sweetness, roast malt and fruit feature in the palate, with bitter chocolate lingering. The finish is powerfully hoppy.

Umbel Magna *(OG 1050, ABV 5%)* ⬗◆
The addition of coriander to the Old Growler wort completes the original 1750s recipe for this distinctive dark beer. The powerful spiciness only adds to this porter's appeal.

NEWBY WYKE
Newby Wyke Brewery, 13 Calder Close, Grantham, Lincolnshire NG31 7QT
Tel/Fax (01476) 402167
Tours by arrangement

The brewery, named after a Hull trawler skippered by brewer Rob March's grandfather, was set up in a converted garage at his home in Grantham. Forty outlets are supplied direct. Brewing started in November 1998 with a 2.5 barrel plant. Brewing capacity has increased from five barrels to 7.5 barrels a week. Two beers are produced on a regular basis: Stamford Gold (OG 1042, ABV 4.4%) for the Green Man, Stamford, and Lord Willoughby (named after another Hull trawler) (OG 1045, ABV 4.8%) for the Willoughby Arms, Little Bytham. Seasonal beers: Summer Session Bitter (OG 1038, ABV 3.8%), Kingston Amber Wheat Beer (OG 1048, ABV 5.2%), Distant Grounds IPA (OG 1048, ABV 5.2%), Black Squall Porter (OG 1044, ABV 4.6%), Homeward Bound (OG 1056, ABV 6%, winter). Beers: Sidewinder (OG 1038, ABV 3.8%), Skipper Eddie's Ale (SEA) (OG 1039, ABV 4%), Slingshot (OG 1041, ABV 4.2%), Slipway (OG 1041, ABV 4.2%), Newby Wyke Bitter (OG 1042, ABV 4.4%), Benvolio (OG 1045, ABV 4.8%) and White Squall (OG 1045, ABV 4.8%).

NORTH DOWNS
See Weltons.

NORTH COTSWOLD*

North Cotswold Brewery, Ditchford Farm, Moreton-in-Marsh, Glos GL55 9RD
Tel (01608) 663947

Brewing was started in February 1999 by brothers David and Roger Tilbrook on a 2.5-barrel plant, from the closed Viking Brewery. A new 10-barrel plant was installed in March 2000. The brewery is in Warwickshire, despite the Gloucestershire postal address, on the estate of Lord Willoughby De Broke. Two mainstream beers are produced with other seasonal planned and 20 outlets are supplied direct. Beers: Genesis (OG 1038, ABV 4%), Four Shires (OG 1040, ABV 4.2%).

NORTH YORKSHIRE

North Yorkshire Brewing Company, Pinchinthorpe Hall, Pinchinthorpe, Guisborough, N Yorkshire TS14 8HG
Tel/Fax (01287) 630200
Tours by arrangement

☺ Brewery founded in 1989 that moved in 1998 to Pinchinthorpe Hall, a moated, listed medieval ancient monument near Guisborough that has its own spring water. The site also includes a hotel, restaurant and bistro. More than 100 free trade outlets are currently supplied. Seasonal beers: Love Muscle (ABV 4%, February), Honey Bunny (ABV 4.2%, April), Rocket Fuel (ABV 5%, November), Xmas Herbert (ABV 4.4%, December).

Prior's Ale *(OG 1036, ABV 3.6%)* ♦
Light, refreshing and surprisingly full-flavoured for a pale, low gravity beer, with a complex, bitter-sweet mixture of malt, hops and fruit carrying through into the aftertaste.

Best Bitter *(OG 1036, ABV 3.6%)*

Archbishop Lee's Ruby Ale
(OG 1040, ABV 4%)
A full-bodied beer with a malty aroma and a balanced malt and hops taste, with vanilla notes.

Bord Best *(OG 1040, ABV 4%)*

Cereal Killer *(OG 1045, ABV 4.5%)*

Fools Gold *(OG 1046, ABV 4.6%)*

Golden Ale *(OG 1046, ABV 4.6%)* ♦
A well-hopped, lightly malted, golden pre-mium bitter, using Styrian and Goldings hops.

Flying Herbert *(OG 1047, ABV 4.7%)*

Lord Lee's *(OG 1047, ABV 4.7%)* ♦
A refreshing, red/brown beer with a hoppy aroma. The flavour is a pleasant balance of roast malt and sweetness that predominates over hops. The malty, bitter finish develops slowly.

NORTHUMBERLAND

The Northumberland Brewery Ltd, at Earth Balance, West Sleekburn Farm, Bomarsund, Bedlington, Northumberland NE22 7AD
Tel/Fax (01670) 822112
Bar 11-3
Tours by arrangement

☺ The brewery went into production on an industrial estate in 1996, but the ecology-conscious owners moved after a year to a purpose-built, solar-powered brewery on the 220-acre, environmentally sustainable Earth Balance community site, where there is a brewery tap. The beers are not yet organic as the raw materials are not available but the owners plan to grow and malt their own organic barley. There is an extensive free trade for the beers.

Castles Bitter *(OG 1038, ABV 3.8%)*
A session bitter.

County Ale *(OG 1039, ABV 4%)*
A smooth, hoppy bitter.

Balance Ale *(OG 1042, ABV 4.2%)*

Secret Kingdom *(OG 1042, ABV 4.3%)*
A dark, malty beer.

Best Bitter *(OG 1046, ABV 4.5%)*
A full-bodied bitter.

Sheepdog *(OG 1047, ABV 4.7%)*

Bomar Bitter *(OG 1049, ABV 5%)*
A strong, light-coloured premium bitter.

O'HANLON'S

O'Hanlon's Brewing Company Ltd, Great Barton Farm, Clyst St Lawrence, Devon EX5 2NY
(01491) 826 466 (temporary number)

☒ Brewery set up in 1996 initially to supply John O'Hanlon's own pub in Clerkenwell, but has expanded to serve around 80 other outlets direct, with others using the beers via wholesalers. In the summer of 2000, O'Hanlon's sold its pub and announced it planned to move the brewery to Devon later in the year. Seasonal beers: Maltsters Weiss (OG 1038, ABV 4%, spring/summer), Rye Beer (OG 1042, ABV 4.3%, autumn), Christmas Ale (OG 1043, ABV 4,3%, December).

Fire Fly *(OG 1035, ABV 3.6%)* ♦
Malty and fruity light bitter. Hints of orange in the taste.

Blakeley's Best *(OG 1040, ABV 4.2%)* ♦
Premium ale with complex flavours. Hoppy nose and finish are balanced by a fruity malt taste.

Dry Stout *(OG 1041, ABV 4.2%)* ♦
Dark brown with a hint of red. Roast malt dominates from start to finish with bitterness also present in the taste.

Myrica Ale *(OG 1039, ABV 4.2%)* ♦
The use of honey and bog myrtle for flavour produces a sweet, malty yellow beer with no noticeable bitterness.

Wheat *(ABV 4%)*

Port Stout *(OG 1041, ABV 4.4%)*
A black beer with a roast malt aroma that remains in the taste but gives way to hoppy bitterness in the aftertaste.

Red Ale *(OG 1044, ABV 4.5%)* ◆
A typical Irish red ale. Well balanced but fruity with a good, dry, hoppy finish.

OAKHAM

Oakham Ales, 80 Westgate, Peterborough, Cambridgeshire PE1 2AA
Tel (01733) 358300
Fax (01733) 310022
Tours by arrangement (no charge to CAMRA visits)

⊗ Established in 1993 in industrial units on a Rutland trading estate, Oakham found a new owner in 1995. A move to Peterborough in November 1998 has proved successful, with brewing taking place in the Brewery Tap, a converted former unemployment office. Business has expanded and new plant, increasing the brew length to 35 barrels, makes this one of the largest brew pubs in Europe. Oakham also supplies two other associated pubs, plus 40-50 free houses. Seasonal/occasional beers: Chaos (OG 1044, ABV 4.4%, March-April), Five Leaves Left (OG 1045, ABV 4.5%, autumn), Mompesson's Gold (OG 1050, ABV 5%, summer), Four Horsemen (OG 1051, ABV 5.1%, winter), Old Tosspot (OG 1052, ABV 5.2%, winter), Black Hole Porter (OG 1055, ABV 5.5%, winter), Cold Turkey (OG 1063, ABV 6.3%, winter).

Jeffrey Hudson Bitter or JHB
(OG 1038, ABV 3.8%) ▇◨◆
Impressive straw-coloured quaffing bitter with bold floral, grassy hop, grapefruit and kiwi fruit and a little sweetness followed by a long, dry aftertaste.

White Dwarf Wheat Beer
(OG 1043, ABV 4.3%) ▇◆
Full-bodied yellow-golden beer with a well-defined citrus hop, rounded off with a gentle underlying malty sweetness in the mouth but ending bone-dry with hops holding up well.

Bishops Farewell *(OG 1046, ABV 4.6%)* ◆
A well-rounded, full-bodied strong bitter, yellow in colour with a strong hoppy aroma joined by floral fruity flavours in the mouth

with a grainy background and a dry, fruity finish.

Old Tosspot *(OG 1052, ABV 5.2%)* ◆
Powerful and complex tawny ale with spicy hop, an array of fruity flavours and a distinctive smooth malty background, ending dry and bitter.

OAKHILL

Oakhill Brewery, The Old Maltings, High Street, Oakhill, Bath, Somerset BA3 5BX
Tel (01749) 840134
Fax (01749) 840531
Tours by arrangement Tue evening, £3.50 per person, max 25 people

⊗ Situated high in the Mendip Hills in Somerset, this brewery was set up by a farmer in 1984 in an old fermentation room of the original Oakhill Brewery (established in 1767 and burnt down in 1924). By the mid-1990s the brewery had outgrown its original premises and moved in 1997 to the old maltings building in Oakhill that had been newly renovated, with a brewing capacity of more than 300 barrels a week. It now supplies five tied houses and some 200 free trade outlets direct.

Bitter *(OG 1037, ABV 3.5%)*

Best Bitter *(OG 1040, ABV 4%)* ◆
A clean-tasting, tangy bitter, with a good hop content and citrus fruit and malt balance. Dry finish; light hop aroma. Very quenching.

Black Magic Stout *(OG 1045, ABV 4.5%)* ◆
A black/brown bitter stout with roast malt and a touch of fruit on the nose. Smooth roast malt and bitterness in the taste, with mellow coffee and chocolate.

Mendip Gold *(OG 1045, ABV 4.5%)*

Yeoman 1767 Strong Ale
(OG 1050, ABV 5%) ◆
A strong, pale brown, full-bodied bitter, with a floral hop palate and notable fruitiness. Dry, bitter, lasting finish.

Mendip Twister *(OG 1069, ABV 6.3%)*

OAKWELL

Oakwell Brewery, Pontefract Road, Barnsley, S Yorkshire
Tel (01226) 296161
Fax (01226) 771457

The brewery closed in 1970 shortly after being taken over by John Smiths of Tadcaster. Brewing re-commenced in January 1997 with plans for expansion on the original site. It supplies some 30 outlets direct. Beers: Barnsley Bitter (OG 1036, ABV 3.8%), Old Tom (OG 1036, ABV 3.8%)

OKELLS

Okell & Son Ltd, Kewaigue, Douglas, Isle of Man IM2 1QG
Tel (01624) 661120
Fax (01624) 624253
E-mail okells@heronandbrearley.com
Tours by arrangement

⊛ Founded in 1874 by Dr Okell and formerly trading as Isle of Man breweries, this is the main brewery on the island, having taken over and closed the rival Castletown Brewery in 1986. The brewery moved in 1994 to a new, purpose-built plant at Kewaigue. All beers are produced under the Manx Brewers' Act 1874 (permitted ingredients: water, malt, sugar and hops only). All of the company's 55 pubs sell real ale and more than 70 free trade outlets are also supplied direct. Occasional beers: Castletown Bitter (ABV 4%), Manx Cat (ABV 4%), Wheel Ale (ABV 4.2%), Spring Ram (ABV 4.2%), Poleaxed (ABV 4.2%), Autumn Dawn (ABV 4.2%), Chequered Flag (ABV 4.2%), Summer Storm (ABV 4.2%), Hoptunaa (ABV 4.2%), Olde Skipper (ABV 4.5%), St Nick (ABV 4.5%), Falcon Strong Ale (ABV 5%).

Mild *(OG 1034, ABV 3.4%)* ◆
A genuine, well-brewed mild ale, with a fine aroma of hops and crystal malt. Reddish-brown in colour, this beer has a full malt flavour with surprising bitter hop notes and a hint of blackcurrants and oranges. Full, malty finish.

Bitter *(OG 1035, ABV 3.7%)* ◆
A golden beer, malty and superbly hoppy in aroma, with a hint of honey. Rich and malty on the tongue, it has a wonderful, dry, malt and hop finish. A complex but rewarding beer.

Spring Ram *(OG 1040, ABV 4.2%)*

Poleaxed *(OG 1040, ABV 4.2%)*

Autumn Dawn *(OG 1040, ABV 4.2%)*

Heart-Throb *(OG 1042, ABV 4.5%)*

OLD BARN
Old Barn Bewery, The Industrial Estate, Tow Law, County Durham
Tel/Fax (01388) 819991

Established in August 1998, with the first brew supplied to the Durham Beer Festival, it now supplies Fitzgerald's pub chain, occasionally the Durham Beer Company, and 30-plus free houses in a 20-mile radius of Tow Low. It also supplies pubs with their own personalised and named beer. Beers: Antistress (ABV 3.6%), Sheepdog (ABV 4.4%), Collywobble (ABV 4.7%); the last two available as bottle-conditioned ales.

Sheepdog *(ABV 4.4%)* ◆
A good example of a sweet North-eastern beer, with a full fruity taste and a bitter aftertaste.

OLD BEAR
◘ Old Bear Brewery, 6 Keighley Road, Cross Hills, Keighley, W Yorkshire BD20 7RN
Tel (01535) 632115
Tours by arrangement.

⊗ Brewery founded in 1993 by former Goose Eye Brewery owner Bryan Eastell, next to the pub in which he is a partner, producing beers brewed with local spring water. Five other free trade outlets are also supplied including a brewery-owned pub in Colne, Lancashire. Occasional beers: Ursa Minor (OG 1044, ABV 4.6%), Ursa Major (OG 1056, ABV 5.8%), Old Grizzly (ABV variable).

Bitter *(OG 1038, ABV 3.9%)* ◆
A refreshing and easy-to-drink bitter. The balance of malt and hops gives way to a short, dry, bitter aftertaste.

OLD CANNON*
◘ Old Cannon Brewery Ltd, 86 Cannon Street, Bury St Edmunds, Suffolk IP33 1JR
Tel (01284) 768769
Fax (01284) 701137
E-mail rej@btinternet.com

Pub built in 1845 along with its own brewery. Brewing ceased in 1917 and the pub (St Edmunds Head) was closed by Greene King in 1995. It re-opened in December 1999 complete with unique state-of-the-art brewery housed in the bar area. Brewing started in January 2000. Further beers are planned as are bottled products. One pub owned serving cask-conditioned beer.

Best Bitter *(OG 1040, ABV 3.8%)* ◆
A fruity, hoppy bitter that is very refreshing and full of flavour.

Powder Monkey *(OG 1047, ABV 4.7%)*

Gunner's Daughter
(OG 1052, ABV 5.5%) ◆
A well-balanced, dark bitter, not overly hoppy but with a hoppy aftertaste and a sweet, fruity taste.

OLD CHIMNEYS
Old Chimneys Brewery,
The Street, Market Weston, Diss,
Norfolk IP22 2NZ
Tel (01359) 221411
Tours by arrangement

⊠ Tiny craft brewery opened in 1995 by former Greene King/Broughton brewer Alan Thomson, producing beers mostly named after local endangered species. Despite the postal address, the brewery is in Suffolk. An annual bottle-conditioned beer limited to 1,000 bottles each year is produced, beginning with Twa Thusend Gear Ealu (Two Thousand Year Ale in Old English) (OG 1108, ABV 9.5%), for the Millennium. A move to larger premises in the same village is planned. Old Chimneys currently supplies 40 outlets direct. Occasional/seasonal beers: Bittern Bitter (OG 1039, ABV 4.1%, summer), Great Raft Bitter (OG 1042, ABV 4.2%, winter), Polecat Porter (OG 1042, ABV 4.2%), Black Rat Stout (OG 1044, ABV 4.4%), Nightingale (OG 1046, ABV 4.5%, spring), Golden Pheasant (OG 1045, ABV 4.7%, summer), Natterjack Premium Ale (OG 1050, ABV 5% winter), Winter Cloving (OG 1078, ABV 7.5%, winter).

Military Mild *(OG 1035, ABV 3.3%)* ◆◆
A moreish dark mild, with good body for its gravity. Light roast bitterness features, with a crisp, dry, malt and hop aftertaste.

Swallowtail IPA *(OG 1038, ABV 3.7%)* ◆
A session bitter, with hop dominating over a toffee, nutty flavour.

OLD FORGE
See under Forge.

OLD LAXEY
◘ Old Laxey Brewing Co Ltd, c/o Shore Hotel, Old Laxey, Isle of Man IM4 7DA
Tel (01624) 862451
Tours by arrangement

⊛ The brewery started producing beer three years ago behind the Shore Hotel in a former stable. It has a 5-barrel plant that can be seen through a viewing window in the brewery bar. Twelve outlets are supplied direct.

Bosun Bitter *(OG 1038, ABV 3.8%)*

OLD LUXTERS
Old Luxters Vineyard Winery & Brewery, Hambleden, Henley-on-Thames, Oxfordshire RG9 6JW
Tel (01491) 638330
Fax (01491) 638645
Shop 9-5 Mon-Fri, 11-5 Sat-Sun
Tours by arrangement

⊗ Buckinghamshire brewery (despite the postal address) set up in 1990 in a 17th-century barn by David Ealand, owner of Chiltern Valley Wines. Apart from the brewery and vineyard, the site also houses an art gallery and a cellar shop. The brewery supplies a few local free trade outlets and pubs further afield via wholesalers. Occasional brews are produced to order for other independent breweries, and these are often also supplied bottle conditioned. Bottle-conditioned beers: Barn Ale (OG 1052, ABV 5.4%), Dark Roast Ale (OG 1048, ABV 5%), Gold (OG 1048, ABV 5%).

Barn Ale Bitter *(OG 1038, ABV 4%)*
A fruity, aromatic, fairly hoppy, bitter beer.

Barn Ale Special *(OG 1042.5, ABV 4.5%)* ✎
The original Barn Ale: predominantly malty, fruity and hoppy in taste and nose, and tawny/amber in colour. Fairly strong in flavour: the initial, sharp, malty and fruity taste leaves a dry, bitter-sweet, fruity after-taste. It can be slightly sulphurous.

Dark Roast Ale *(OG 1048, ABV 5%)*

OLD MILL
Old Mill Brewery Ltd, Mill Street, Snaith, Goole, E Yorkshire DN14 9HU
Tel (01405) 861813
Fax (01405) 862789
Tours by arrangement

⊛ Small brewery opened in 1983 in a 200-year-old former malt kiln and corn mill. A new brewhouse was installed in 1991 to increase the brew-length to 60 barrels and the brewery is building up its tied estate (now 17 houses). The innovation of selling beer in plastic, non-returnable handicasks has meant that the beer can now be found nationwide. Around 200 free trade outlets are supplied direct from the brewery. A bottling plant was installed in 1997. 16 seasonal beers are brewed.

Traditional Mild *(OG 1035, ABV 3.4%)* ✎
A satisfying roast malt flavour dominates this easy-drinking, quality dark mild.

Nellie Dene *(OG 1035, ABV 3.5%)* ✎
A well-hopped, straw-coloured beer with hops throughout, slightly fruity in the middle and a refreshing bitter finish. Lots of flavour for its strength.

Traditional Bitter *(OG 1038, ABV 3.9%)* ✎
The Old Mill character has returned to this beer, though bitterness remains at a premium. It has a malty nose and initial flavour, with hops hiding until the lingering finish.

Old Curiosity *(OG 1044, ABV 4.5%)* ✎
Slightly sweet and malty to start with, with malt flavours all the way through. A good, well-roasted, balanced beer.

Bullion *(OG 1045, ABV 4.7%)* ✎
The malty and hoppy aroma is followed by a neat mix of hop and fruit tastes within an enveloping maltiness. Dark brown/amber in colour.

Blackjack *(OG 1050, ABV 5%)*

OLD PINT POT
⚲ Old Pint Pot Brewery, Adelphi Street, Salford, Greater Manchester M3 6EM
Tel (O161) 839 1514

⊛ Brewing began in summer 1996 at this Salford pub, which is part of the locally-based Honeycomb Leisure group. The one beer has no constant name or strength, but it is a full mash brew and is cask conditioned. It is sold here and in one other pub.

OLDERSHAW
Oldershaw Brewery, 12 Harrowby Hall Estate, Grantham, Lincolnshire NG31 9HB
Tel/Fax (01476) 572135 (07801) 512735 (m)
Tours by arrangement

⊗ Experienced home-brewer Gary Oldershaw and his wife Diane set up the brewery at their home in January 1997. Grantham's first brewery for 30 years, Oldershaw now supplies 60 local free houses. They still concentrate on supplying outlets direct and are enjoying steady growth. A third fermenting vessel was added in 1999 to increase capacity to 15 barrels a week. They are now experimenting with bottle-conditioned beers. Oldershaw brews regular specials, usually with a single hop variety. Occasional/seasonal beers: Sunnydaze (OG 1040, ABV 4%, a summer wheat beer), Topers Tipple (OG 1044, ABV 4.5%, winter), Yuletide (OG 1051, ABV 5.2%, December).

Harrowby Bitter *(OG 1036, ABV 3.6%)* ✎
Bitter and hoppy session beer, light brown in colour. Faint fruit and malt support the slow-dying hop character.

High Dyke *(OG 1039, ABV 3.9%)*

Newton's Drop *(OG 1041, ABV 4.1%)* ✎
Balanced malt and hops but with a strong bitter, lingering taste in this mid-brown beer.

Veteran Ale *(OG 1041, ABV 4.1%)*

Ermine Ale *(OG 1042, ABV 4.2%)* ◆
Golden brown with a fruity hop the dominant feature on nose and taste giving a bitterness that lasts; malt plays a supporting role.

Caskade *(OG 1042, ABV 4.2%)*

Grantham Stout *(OG 1043, ABV 4.3%)*

Regal Blonde *(OG 1044, ABV 4.4%)* ◆
Straw coloured lager-style beer with a good malt/hop balance throughout; strong bitterness on the taste lingers.

Old Boy *(OG 1047, ABV 4.8%)* ◆
A full-bodied amber ale, fruity and bitter with a hop/fruit aroma. The malt that backs that taste dies in the long finish.

ORCHARD*

Delacloud Ltd, Orchard Brewery Bar,
15 Market Hill, Barnsley S70 2PX
Tel (01226) 288906
Tours by arrangement

The Orchard Brewery Bar opened in December 1999. Seven pubs are now owned, three serving cask-conditioned ales. Beers: Orchard Bitter (ABV 3.9%), Nortons Bitter (ABV 3.9%), Tykes Bitter (ABV 4.6%).

ORCHARD

Orchard Brewery, Little Acres, Silversides Lane, Scoreby Brook, Brigg, Lincolnshire
Tel (01652) 657174
Tours by arrangement

The brewery is a two-barrel unit.

Splash Back Mild *(ABV 3.4%)*

Pond Water Bitter *(ABV 4%)*

ORGANIC*

The Organic Brewhouse, Unit 1,
Higher Bochym Rural Workshops,
Curry Cross Lane, nr Mullen, Helston,
Cornwall TR12 7AZ
Tel (01326) 241555
Tours by arrangement

A brewery established early in 2000 on the Lizard peninsular overlooking Goonhilly Downs. It is dedicated to brewing organic real ales, using its own source of natural mineral water. Designed as a 'tower brewery', with the brewing process flowing from level to level, it supplies a number of outlets in the South-west. Additional ales are planned as the availability of organic ingredients increases.

Lizard Point *(OG 1042, ABV 4%)*

ORKNEY

Orkney Brewery Ltd, Quoyloo, Stromness,
Orkney KW16 3LT
Tel (01856) 841802
Fax (01856) 841754
E-mail beer@orkneybrewery.co.uk
Web-site www.orkneybrewery.co.uk
Tours by arrangement sometimes

⊛ Set up in 1988 in an old school building by former licensee Roger White. Cask ales now represent 90 per cent of sales. The brewery was completely modernised in 1995 with new buildings replacing a single cramped room. The beers are available nationwide via

wholesalers. Occasional beers: Northern Light (OG 1038, ABV 3.8%), White Christmas (OG 1051, ABV 5%, December).

Raven Ale *(OG 1038, ABV 3.8%)* ◆
A pale brown beer in which fruit predominates. Roast is evident in the aroma and taste, and hop in the taste and aftertaste. Initially sweet, but with a satisfying dry, bitter aftertaste.

Dragonhead Stout *(OG 1040, ABV 4%)* ◆
A strong, dark malt aroma flows into a dry malt and roast flavour with hints of caramel and fruit. The roast malt continues to dominate the aftertaste and blends with chocolate to develop a strong, dry finish. Hard to find.

Red MacGregor *(OG 1040, ABV 4%)* ◆
Smooth tasting, full-bodied, tawny red ale with a powerful smack of malt to start and a long, bitter and malty finish.

Dark Island *(OG 1045, ABV 4.6%)* ◆
Dark, beautifully balanced and full of roast malt and fruit, and a hint of caramel. A sweetish taste leads to a long-lasting, roasted, slightly bitter finish. Full-bodied and deceptively drinkable. If beer was whisky, this would be it.

Skullsplitter *(OG 1080, ABV 8.5%)* ▥▤

OSSETT

Ossett Brewing Company t/a Ossett
Brewery, Brewers Pride, Healey Road,
Ossett, W Yorkshire
Tel (01924) 261333
Tours by arrangement

Small brewery opened at the back of the Brewers Pride pub and run by former publican Bob Hunter and Bob Lawson, a brewer with more than 30 years' experience with Tetley in Leeds and Kelham Island in Sheffield. Occasional beers: Silver Fox (ABV 4.1%), Two Bobs (OG 1043.5, ABV 4.3%), Silver Link (ABV 4.6%), Warrior Bitter (OG 1049.5, ABV 4.8%) and Quick Silver (ABV 5%). Seasonal Beers: Summa Bobs (OG 1042.5, ABV 4.2%, summer), Ace of Spades Porter (OG 1045.5, ABV 4.5%, winter). Beers: Special Bitter (OG 1039.5, ABV 3.9%), Silver King (OG 1041.5, ABV 4.3%), Dazzler (OG 1044.5, ABV 4.5%), Excelsior (OG 1051.5, ABV 5.2%).

OTTER

Otter Brewery Ltd, Mathayes, Luppitt,
Honiton, Devon EX14 4SA
Tel (01404) 891285
Fax (01404) 891124
Tours by arrangement weekday evenings

⊠ Named after its position at the headsprings of the River Otter, the brewery began operation in 1990 under David McCaig, formerly of Whitbread. Steady growth over the following eight years has meant the need for a plant that can produce 30 barrels, with a capacity of 135 barrels a week. No further expansion is planned. The brewery also bottles its own beers. All beers are brewed with local spring water and its own yeast culture. 130 outlets supplied direct. Seasonal beer: Otter Claus (ABV 5%, Christmas).

Bitter *(OG 1036, ABV 3.6%)* ▣◆
Well-balanced amber session bitter with a

fruity nose and bitter taste and aftertaste.

Bright *(OG 1039, ABV 4.3%)* ✍
Fruit and hop aroma in a straw-coloured bitter with a strong bitter finish.

Ale *(OG 1043, ABV 4.5%)* ✍
A mid-brown best bitter. Fruity aroma and taste with a slightly sweet and fruity finish.

Head *(OG 1054, ABV 5.8%)*
Fruity aroma and taste with a pleasant bitter finish. Dark brown and full bodied.

OUTLAW
See Rooster's.

PACIFIC ORIENTAL
◊ Pacific Oriental, 1 Bishopsgate,
London EC2N 3AB
Tel (0171) 929 6868
Fax (0171) 929 7227
E-mail peter.f@orgplc.co.uk

Pacific Oriental is a state of the art boutique brewery based in the heart of the City of London. Brewing commenced in August 1998 and permanent brews are a Pilsner lager and a bitter with at least one other beer always on offer. These include a wheat beer, a golden ale and a red beer. The copper brewhouse is on full display at the front of the restaurant. The beers are filtered and served by mixed gas dispense. Beers: Gold (OG 1040, ABV 4%), Orchard (OG 1044, ABV 4.4%), Bishops (OG 1045, ABV 4.5%), Dragon (OG 1044, ABV 4.6%), Pils (OG 1048, ABV 5%) and Weiss (OG 1048, ABV 5%).

PACKHORSE
Packhorse Brewing Co Ltd, 5 Somers Road,
Southsea, Portsmouth,
Hampshire PO5 4PR
Tel (023) 9275 0450

Packhorse Brewery was resurrected in Portsmouth from the former Ashford Brewery. It produces infusion mash, 100 per cent malt ales as opposed to the decoction lagers of the Ashford days. Seasonal beer: Rudolph's Revenge (OG 1072, ABV 7.9%). Beer: Best Bitter (OG 1037, ABV 3.8%).

PALMERS
JC & RH Palmer Ltd, Old Brewery,
Bridport, Dorset DT6 4JA
Tel (01308) 422396
Fax (01308) 421149
E-mail enquiries@palmersbrewery.com
Web-site www.palmersbrewery.com
Shop 9-6 Mon-Thu, 9-8 Fri-Sat
Tours by arrangement ring 01308 427500

⊗ Britain's only thatched brewery, founded in 1794, situated by the sea in an idyllic location in West Dorset. The company is run by brothers John and Cleeves Palmer, great-grandsons of Robert Henry and John Cleeves Palmer, who bought the company in 1896. Its tenanted estate of 60 pubs all offer real ale. Three pubs were refurbished in 2000 and the Sea Trout was purchased in Staverton, Devon. A further 100 free trade outlets are supplied direct, and Palmer's beers reach a wider audience throughout the south via wholesalers. Dorset Gold was added to the

portfolio. Occasional beer: Tally Ho! (OG 1055, ABV 5.5%).

Bridport Bitter *(OG 1030, ABV 3.2%)* ✍
A light beer with a hoppy aroma, a bitter, hoppy taste with some malt, and a bitter aftertaste.

Dorset Gold *(OG 1036, ABV 3.7%)* ✍
Darker than might be expected, almost copper, with a light body that can become cloying. Hop and fruit dominate from the aroma right through to the dry, bitter finish.

IPA *(OG 1040, ABV 4.2%)* ✍
A deep copper beer that is hoppy and bitter throughout. Fruit and malt undertones give some balance in the aroma and taste, and there is a lingering bitter aftertaste.

200 *(OG 1052, ABV 5%)* ✍
Full-bodied, caramel sweetness and fruity aroma are balanced with a dry finish, not excessively bitter. A deep-copper ale, originally brewed to mark the brewery's 200th anniversary.

PARADISE
See Bird in Hand.

PARISH
◊ The Parish Brewery, Courtyard of The
Old Brewery Inn, High Street,
Somerby, Leicestershire LE14 2PZ
Tel (01664) 454781/454801
Fax (01664) 454777
Tours by arrangement

⊗ Parish started life at Burrough on the Hill in 1982 and moved to its present location after expanding to a 20-barrel plant in 1992. The Parish Brewery was one of the first brew pubs to start up in the Midlands and is famous for brewing the strongest beer in the world, with an ABV of 23%, as listed in the Guinness Book of Records. It currently supplies 20 local outlets.

Mild *(OG 1038, ABV 3.6-8%)*

Parish Special Bitter or PSB
(OG 1040, ABV 3.8-4%)

Farm Gold *(OG 1039, ABV 3.9%)*

Somerby Premium *(OG 1040, ABV 4%)*

Poachers Ale *(OG 1060, ABV 6%)*

Baz's Bonce Blower
(OG 1100, ABV 10-11%)

PARKER
See Cannon.

PASSAGEWAY
Passageway Brewing Company, Unit G8,
Queens Dock Commercial Centre, Norfolk
Street, Liverpool, Merseyside L1 0BG
Tel (0151) 708 0730
Fax (0151) 709 0925
Tours by arrangement

☺ Adventurous brewery established in 1994
that experiments with continental beer
styles. Yeast from a Belgian monastic brewery
is used, and some water from St Arnold's well
in Belgium is added to the copper during
each brew of St Arnold (named after
Belgium's patron saint of brewers). 50 outlets
are supplied direct.

Docker's Hook *(OG 1038, ABV 3.6%)* ◆
A mid-brown, full-bodied ale. Banana fruitiness dominates the palate and aftertaste.

Redemption *(OG 1040, ABV 4%)* ◆
A dry, tart and clean beer brewed with rye.

Genuine Blonde Wheat Beer
(OG 1042, ABV 4.2%)
Naturally cloudy wheat beer with complex
fruit and hoppy flavours and a distinctive
aroma. Available in fined and unfined
versions.

St Arnold *(OG 1050, ABV 5%)* ◆
Deep ruby in colour, this is a bitter and fruity
beer, yet not sweet. Hop, roast malt, chocolate and liquorice flavours also fight for
attention in the taste and dry aftertaste. A
complex, heavy beer, reminiscent of a
Belgian brown ale.

Dubbel *(OG 1060, ABV 6%)*

Tripel *(OG 1065, ABV 7%)*

Advent *(OG 1065, ABV 7%)*

PAYN*
Payn Breweries Ltd, Unit 1 Eco Site,
St Mary's Road, Ramsey, Cambs PE17 1SL
Tel (01487) 710800
Fax (01487) 710900
E-mail Sales@payn.co.uk
Web-site www.payn.co.uk
Tours by arrangement

Payn Breweries bought Leyland Breweries
when the company got into financial trou-
ble. The new brewery was built in Ramsey in
June 1999, using most of the original equip-
ment and has a current capacity of 50 barrels
a week. 100 plus outlets are supplied direct.
Occasional beers are produced on a monthly
basis. Beers: Bullseye (OG 1038, ABV 3.8%),
Fenland Gold (OG 1042, ABV 4.2%), Ramsey
Pride (OG 1050, ABV 5%), Strong Old Noll
(OG 1081, ABV 8%), Ramsey Ruin
(OG 1320, ABV 13%).

PEMBROKE
Pembroke Brewery Co, Eaton House, 108
Main Street, Pembroke,
Pembrokeshire SA71 4HN
Tel (01646) 682517
Fax (01646) 682008
Tours by arrangement

⊗ Brewery started in April 1994 in former
stables to rear of the owner's house. A
5-barrel plant provides flexibility in
producing numerous specials as well as the
regular beers. A tied house, the Station Inn, is
in nearby Pembroke Dock. The pub serves a
new test brew each week and stages an
annual beer festival. 10-15 outlets are
supplied direct. Seasonal beers: Sound
Whistle (OG 1038, ABV 3.8%, summer),
Signal Failure (OG 1060, ABV 6%, winter).

The Darklin Mild *(OG 1035, ABV 3.5%)*

Two Cannons Extra *(OG 1036, ABV 3.6%)*

Dimond Lager *(OG 1041, ABV 4.1%)* ◆
A straw-coloured lager-style beer with a light
hoppy aroma with sweetness balancing the
bitterness to give a robust finish.

Main Street Bitter *(OG 1041, ABV 4.1%)*

Golden Hill Ale *(OG 1045, ABV 4.5%)*

Old Nobbie Stout *(OG 1045, ABV 4.5%)* ◆
A drinkable stout with aroma of roast and
caramel coming through on the palate. The
slight bitterness gives way to sweetness in the
finish.

Off the Rails *(OG 1051, ABV 5.1%)*

PETT
See Old Forge.

PHOENIX
Oak Brewing Co. Ltd t/a Phoenix Brewery,
The Phoenix Brewery, Green Lane,
Heywood, Greater Manchester OL10 2EP
Tel (01706) 627009
Tours by arrangement

☺ Company established as Oak Brewery in
1982 at Ellesmere Port. It moved in 1991 to
Heywood and changed its name in 1996 to
Phoenix (after the original name of the brew-
ery it occupies). Now supplies more than 150
free trade outlets mostly in the North-west
and West Yorkshire. Seasonal beers: Monkey
Town Mild (ABV 3.9%, May), Black Shadow
(ABV 4%, May), Arizona (ABV 4.1%, June-
Oct), Monkey Business (ABV 4.1%, April),
Rip-Rap (ABV 4.1%, Bonfire Night),
Whirlwind (ABV 4.1%, October), Jovian
(ABV 4.2%, February), One for the Wode
(ABV 4.3%), Shamrock (ABV 4.3%, St
Patrick's Day), Snowbound (ABV 4.3%, Nov-
Feb), Spinning Jenny (ABV 4.3%, October), St
George's Flag (ABV 4.3%, St George's Day),
March Hare (ABV 4.4%, March), May Fly
(ABV 4.4%, May), Christmas Kiss (ABV 4.5%,
Nov-Dec), Midsummer Madness (ABV 4.5%,
June-Aug), Tennis Elbow (ABV 4.5%, July),
Uncle Fester (ABV 4.5%, Halloween),
Firecracker (ABV 4.7%, Bonfire Night),
Massacre (ABV 4.7%, Valentines Day),
Resurrection (ABV 4.7%, Easter), Spooky
Brew (ABV 4.7%, Halloween), Sticky Wicket
(ABV 4.7%, June-Sept), Struggling Monkey
(ABV 4.7%, June) Porter (ABV 5%, Nov-Jan),
Humbug (ABV 7%, Oct-Jan).

Bantam *(ABV 3.5%)* ◆
Light brown beer with a fruity aroma.
Balance of malt, citrus fruit and hop in taste.
Hoppy, bitter finish.

Best Bitter *(ABV 3.9%)*

Hopwood Bitter *(ABV 4.3%)* ◆

Amber beer with a hoppy, fruity nose and palate. Dry, hoppy finish.

Old Oak *(ABV 4.5%)* ◆
A well-balanced, brown beer with a multitude of mellow fruit flavours. Malt and hops balance the strong fruitiness in the aroma and taste and the finish is malty, fruity and dry.

Thirsty Moon *(ABV 4.6%)* ◆
Fruity, malty aroma to this amber beer. Malt, fruit and bitter taste and a dry, hoppy finish.

Bonneville *(ABV 4.8%)*
A malty beer with a short hop finish.

Double Dagger *(ABV 5%)* ◆
A pale brown, malty brew, more pleasantly dry and light than its gravity would suggest. Moderately fruity throughout; a hoppy bitterness in the mouth balances the strong graininess.

Wobbly Bob *(ABV 6%)* ◆
A red/brown beer with a malty, fruity aroma. Strongly malty and fruity in flavour and quite hoppy, with the sweetness yielding to a dryness in the aftertaste.

PICKS

♦ Picks Brewery, Red Lion Hotel, Willows Lane, Green Haworth, Accrington, Lancashire BB5 3SJ
Tel (01254) 233194
Tours by arrangement

The brewery is sited in the cellar of the pub. The brewing equipment was made by owner Steven Pickles from stainless steel: there's a hot liquor tank and copper combined, a mash tun and three fermenting tanks. Steven has started supplying the free trade, with just a few local outlets. Six regular beers are produced and he plans to produce a real lager for the summer. Beers: Moorgate Mild (OG 1035, ABV 3.5%), Pale Ale (OG 1036, ABV 3.7%), Bedlam Bitter (OG 1038, ABV 3.9%), Lions Main (OG 1041, ABV 4,2%), Picks Porter (OG 1042, ABV 4.5%), Lions Pride (OG 1045, ABV 4.9%).

PICTISH*

Pictish Brewing Company, Unit 9, Canalside Industrial Estate, Woodbine Street East, Rochdale, Lancs OL16 5LB
Tel/Fax (01706) 522 227
Tours by arrangement

Brewery established in March 2000 by Richard Sutton, formerly senior brewer for the north with the Firkin Brewery until Punch Taverns took over the former Allied Domecq estate and closed the Firkin breweries in 1999. The brewery supplies free trade outlets in the North-west direct and plans to introduce a range of monthly specials in the near future. Beers: Brewers Gold (OG 1038, ABV 3.8%), Celtic Warrior (OG 1042, ABV 4.2%), Pictish Porter (OG 1045, ABV 4.4%).

PILGRIM

Pilgrim Ales, The Old Brewery, West Street, Reigate, Surrey RH2 9BL
Tel (01737) 222651
Fax (01737) 225785

⊠ Set up in 1982, and moved to Reigate in 1985, Pilgrim has gradually increased its capacity and its beers have won both local and national awards, although sales are mostly concentrated in the Surrey area (around 60 outlets). Occasional/seasonal beers: Autumnal (OG 1045, ABV 4.5%, Sept-Oct), Excalibur (OG 1045, ABV 4.5%, March-May), The Great Crusader (OG 1063, ABV 6.5%, June-Aug), Pudding (OG 1075, ABV 7.3%, Nov-Jan). Bottle-conditioned beers: Progress (ABV 4.3%), Springbock (ABV 5.2%), Pudding (ABV 6.8%).

Surrey Bitter *(OG 1037, ABV 3.7%)* ◆
A clean, well-balanced session bitter. Hop flavour comes through in the finish.

Porter *(OG 1040, ABV 4%)* ◆
This porter, with a rich mouthfeel, has a good balance of dark malts, with berry fruit flavours declining to a short finish.

Progress *(OG 1040, ABV 4%)* ◆
Reddish-brown in colour, with a predominantly malty flavour and aroma, although hops are also evident in the taste.

Saracen *(OG 1047, ABV 4.5%)* ◆
Roast malt dominates the aroma of this black stout, but hops balance the roast malt flavour, leading to a bitter finish.

Crusader *(OG 1047, ABV 4.9%)* ◆
A light, golden beer with a good marriage of malt and hops from aroma through to finish.

Talisman *(OG 1049, ABV 5%)* ◆
A strong ale with a mid-brown colour, a fruity, malt flavour and a faint hoppiness.

Springbock *(OG 1050, ABV 5.2%)*
A Bavarian-style wheat beer.

PITFIELD

Pitfield Brewery (The Beer Shop), 14 Pitfield Street, London N1 6EY
Tel (0207) 739 3701
Shop 11-7 Mon-Fri, 10-4 Sat
Tours by arrangement

⊠ The Beer Shop was founded in 1980 to supply real ale and international bottled beers. A 5-barrel brewery was installed to produce Pitfield Bitter. Dark Star was introduced in 1985 and in 1987 won the title of Best New Beer and was runner-up in the Champion Beer of Britain competition. The following year, it won the overall Champion Beer of Britain title; the beer has now been renamed Black Eagle. In the summer of 1996 The Beer Shop moved into larger premises, with the brewery in one building and shop next door. The Beer Shop now stocks more than 500 different beers from around the world and a large range of home brewing and wine making supplies. In 200, the brewery started to use only organic malt in all its brews which are suitable for vegans. Six outlets are supplied direct.

Original *(OG 1037, ABV 3.7%)* ◆
Hoppy bitter with a balancing fruity maltiness. Quite sweet in the taste but a good hoppy finish.

East Kent Goldings *(OG 1042, ABV 4.2%)*

Eco Warrior *(OG 1045, ABV 4.5%)*
Brewed with organic ingredients, including New Zealand Hallertau hops.

Hoxton Heavy *(OG 1048, ABV 4.8%)*

Black Eagle *(OG 1050, ABV 5%)* ◆

Dark brown old ale with a roast malt flavour but underlying hops. Quite sweet.

PLANETS

HG Wells Planets Brewery,
Crown Square, Woking,
Surrey GU21 1HR
Tel (01483) 727100
Fax (01483) 712701

❌ Brewery opened in 1996 in a leisure complex, supplying its full mash beers only to the house bars initially, although now selling to the free trade under the name of Brooklands Brewery. At the leisure complex the beers are kept under a blanket of gas in cellar tanks. Beers: Bobbies Bitter (OG 1042, ABV 4.2%), HG's Ale (OG 1052, ABV 5%).

PLASSEY

Plassey Brewery, The Plassey, Eyton,
Wrexham LL13 0SP
Tel (01978) 780922
Fax (01978) 781195
Shop 1.30-5 Wed-Sun winter;
1.30-5 Tue-Sun summer
Tours by arrangement

Brewery founded in 1985 on the 250-acre Plassey Estate, which also incorporates a touring caravan park, craft centres, a golf course, three licensed outlets for Plassey's ales, and a brewery shop. 30 free trade outlets also take the beers. Seasonal beer: Ruddy Rudolph (OG 1046, ABV 4.5%, Christmas). Bottle-conditioned beer: Royal Welch Fusilier (OG 1046, ABV 4.5%).

Bitter *(OG 1041, ABV 4%)* ❧
Full-bodied and distinctive best bitter. Good balance of hops and fruit flavours with a lasting dry bitter aftertaste.

Royal Welch Fusilier *(OG 1046, ABV 4.5%)*

Welsh Stout *(OG 1046, ABV 4.6%)* ❧
A dry, roasty stout, sweetish; a long, dry finish.

Cwrw Tudno *(OG 1048, ABV 5%)* ▊❧
A mellow sweetish premium beer with classic Plassey flavours of fruit and hops.

Dragon's Breath *(OG 1060, ABV 6%)* ❧
A fruity, strong bitter, smooth and quite sweet, though not cloying, with an intense, fruity aroma. A dangerously drinkable winter warmer.

PLOUGH INN

◊ Bodicote Brewery, The Plough, 9 High Street, Bodicote, Banbury, Oxon OX15 4BZ
Tel (01295) 262327 (brewery)
Web-site www.banbury-cross.co.uk/
Tours by arrangement

❌ Brewery founded in 1982 at the Plough, 9 High Street (hence the beer name), which has been in the same hands since 1957. Two other outlets are also supplied with its full mash beers. Two popular week-long beer festivals are held each year in February and August. Seasonal beers: Three Goslings (OG 1041, ABV 3.9%, May-Oct), Old English Porter (OG 1047, ABV 4.4%, Oct-May). Beers: Bodicote Bitter (OG 1035, ABV 3.3%), No. 9 (OG 1044, ABV 4.3%), Triple X (OG 1060, ABV 6.3%).

POOLE

The Brewhouse Brewery,
68 High Street, Poole,
Dorset BH15 IDA
Tel (01202) 682345
Tours by arrangement, limited to CAMRA members due to space restrictions.

Brewery established in 1980 by David Rawlins who opened the Brewhouse pub in 1983. The brewery now has a capacity to brew about 1,000 barrels a year, and serves more than 15 outlets direct with a widespread free trade through wholesalers. Poole Brewery is also used to brew one-off beers and has close links to the Hogshead and JD Wetherspoon chain of pubs. Seasonal beer: Pie-eyed Pudding (ABV 4.5%).

Best Bitter *(OG 1038, ABV 3.8%)*
The brewery's original session bitter: amber-coloured and well balanced.

Holes Bay Hog *(OG 1044, ABV 4.5%)*
Light amber in colour, this beer is brewed from pale malt and malted wheat, and has a distinctive, dry-hopped character and a refreshing aftertaste.

Bosun Bitter *(OG 1045, ABV 4.6%)*
The brewery's top-selling beer. A rich, amber-coloured beer with a smooth, crisp, powerful malty flavour and a pronounced hoppy aftertaste.

For Hogshead

Hedgehog *(ABV 5.2%)*

PORTER

Porter Brewing Co Ltd,
Rossendale Brewery, The Griffin Inn,
Hud Rake,
Haslingden,
Lancashire BB4 5AF
Tel/Fax (01706) 214021
Tours by arrangement

❌ The Griffin Inn opened in 1994 and now has five tied houses. All the pubs serve real ale and a few other local outlets also take the beer. Occasional/seasonal beers: Timmy's Ginger Beer (OG 1042, ABV 4.2%), Stout (OG 1056, ABV 5.5%, Sept-Oct), Sleighed (OG 1064, ABV 6.5%, Dec-Jan), Celebration Ale (OG 1068, ABV 7.1%, July-Aug).

Dark Mild *(OG 1033, ABV 3.3%)*
A true dark mild, with a slight maltiness and a good hint of roast in the finish.

Bitter *(OG 1037, ABV 3.8%)*
A dark beer for a standard bitter, with a good, sharp, northern bitterness that lingers through to the back of the throat, and a dry finish.

Rossendale Ale *(OG 1041, ABV 4.2%)*
An initial slight malty sweetness leads through to a deep, fruity taste and a lingering fruity finish.

Porter *(OG 1050, ABV 5%)*
A rich beer with a slightly sweet, malty start, counter-balanced with sharp bitterness and a noticeable roast barley dominance.

Sunshine *(OG 1050, ABV 5.3%)*
An intensely hoppy and bitter golden ale, full-bodied with some malt, a robust mouthfeel and a lingering bitterness.

POTTON

The Potton Brewery Company, 10
Shannon Place, Potton, Sandy,
Bedfordshire
Tel (01767) 261042
Web-site www.potton-brewery.co.uk
Tours by arrangement

Run by Clive Towner and Robert Hearson,
both ex-managers of Greene King at
Biggleswade, they resurrected the Potton
Brewery Company name after it disappeared
as a result of a takeover in 1922. 100 outlets
are supplied direct. Beers: Potton No l
(OG 1037, ABV 2.2%), Shannon IPA
(OG 1035, ABV 3.6%), Phoenix (OG 1040,
ABV 3.8%), Butlers Ale (OG 1042, ABV 4.3%),
Shambles (OG 1042, ABV 4.3%), Village Bike
(OG 1042, ABV 4.3%), Pride of Potton
(OG 1057, ABV 6%).

POWELL

See Wood.

PRINCE OF WALES

⟡ Prince of Wales, Foxfield, Broughton in
Furness, Cumbria LA20 6BX
Tel (01229) 716238

⊛ A 3-barrel plant run by Stuart and Lynda
Johnson, CAMRA enthusiasts, in the old stables attached to the Prince of Wales inn. New
beers are frequently produced. The brewery
supplies a few outlets direct. Beers: Mild (OG
1032, ABV 3%), Sands (OG 1038, ABV 3.6%),
White Coombe (OG 1052, ABV 5%),
Kinghorn Wheat Beer (OG 1052, ABV 5%).

PRINCETOWN

Princetown Breweries Ltd., The Brewery,
Tavistock Road, Princetown,
Devon PL20 6QF
Tel (01822) 890789
Fax (01822) 890719
Tours by arrangement

⊠ Brewery established in 1994 by a former
Gibbs Mew and Hop Back brewer. The capacity was increased to 60 barrels a week in 1998.
It supplies four pubs owned by a sister company and 16 other local outlets. Bottle-conditioned beer: Jail Ale (OG 1046.5, ABV 4.8%).

Dartmoor IPA *(OG 1039.5, ABV 4%)* ❧
Flowery hop aroma and taste with a bitter
aftertaste to this full-bodied, amber-coloured
beer.

Jail Ale *(OG 1047.5, ABV 4.8%)* ❧
Hops and fruit predominate in the flavour of
this mid-brown beer, which has a slightly
sweet aftertaste.

QUAY

The Quay Brewery (t/a Lapin Noir),
Brewers Quay, Hope Square, Weymouth,
Dorset DT4 8TR
Tel (01305) 777515
Shop 10-5.30 daily
Tours by arrangement

⊠ Brewery set up in summer 1996 in the old
Devenish and Groves brewery buildings, 10
years after the closure of Devenish. Although
Greenalls owns the complex, the brewery is
independent and is open to visitors as part of
the Timewalk attraction. A Victorian Tastings
Bar and shop opened in Easter 1997. Two
additional 5-barrel fermenters were added in
1998. There are plans to reopen the Groves
Victorian fermenting room. Quay has quickly
developed local trade, with 50 outlets taking
the beers. Both Summer Knight and Silent
Knight are wheat beers. Occasional beer:
Groves Oatmeal Stout (OG 1048, ABV 4.7%).

Weymouth Harbour Master *(OG 1036,
ABV 3.6%)* ❧
Well-balanced, nut-brown session beer, sweet-
ish, but not cloying, thanks to the dry finish.
May be badged by pubs as a house beer.

Summer Knight *(OG 1038, ABV 3.8%)*

Weymouth SPA *(OG 1036-40, ABV 4%)* ❧
While having the malt and caramel taste and
dryness of the house style, a bitter finish
marks this golden beer out in the brewery's
range.

Weymouth JD 1742
(OG 1038-42, ABV 4.2%) ❧
Clean-tasting easy-drinking bitter. Well
balanced with lingering bitterness after
moderate sweetness.

Bombshell Bitter
(OG 1042-46, ABV 4.5%) ❧
Cleaner tasting than might be expected from
the deep copper colour and fruity aroma.
Caramel sweetness dominates the taste.

Old Rot *(OG 1048-50, ABV 5%)* ❧
Warming finish despite a rather light caramel
and malt taste. Hint of sulphur and yeasti-
ness throughout.

Silent Knight *(OG 1055-60, ABV 5.9%)*

QUEEN'S HEAD

⟡ Fat God's Brewery, Queen's Head, Iron
Cross, Evesham, Worcestershire WR11 5SH
Tel (01386) 871012
Fax (01386) 871362
E-mail fatgod@globalnet.co.uk
Web-site www.fatgodsbrewery.co.uk

⊠ The pub has been operated by Andy and
Kym Miller since 1986 (bought from
Whitbread in 1992) and the brewery was
installed in 1997. Full mash beers are available direct from the brewery within a 50-mile
radius. Seasonal beers: Merry Millers Rusty
Dusty (OG 1040, ABV 4%), Merry Millers

Summer Sensation (OG 1042, ABV 4.3%), Merry Millers Spring Celebration (OG 1044, ABV 4.5%), Merry Millers Winter Wobbler (OG 1047, ABV 4.9%, November-February).

Fat God's Bitter *(OG 1036, ABV 3.6%)* ✦
Balanced between maltiness and hoppiness, this mainly hoppy beer leaves a clean, dry aftertaste.

Morris Dancer *(OG 1039, ABV 3.9%)*

Porter of the Vale *(OG 1041, ABV 4.1%)*

Thunder and Lightning
(OG 1042, ABV 4.3%) ✦
Malt is the main taste in this premium bitter. Hops are there in the mouth, but the final impression is one of malt.

RAILWAY TAVERN
⛴ The Famous Railway Tavern Brewing Co, 58 Station Road, Brightlingsea, Essex CO7 0DT
Tel (01206) 302581

Beers: Crab & Winkle (OG 1040, ABV 3.7%), Bladderwrack (OG 1050, ABV 5%).

RAINBOW
⛴ Rainbow Inn & Brewery, 73 Birmingham Road, Allesley Village, Coventry, W Midlands CV5 9GT
Tel (01203) 402888
Fax (01203) 407415
Tours by arrangement

⊗ Started brewing in October 1994 with a 2-barrel plant, upgraded to 4-barrels in May 1996. Seasonal beer: Santas Spice (OG 1050, 5%, Christmas), 20 Shilling, and a German-style wheat beer. Beers: Piddlebrook (OG 1037, ABV 3.8%), Firecracker (OG 1050, ABV 5%).

RANDALLS
RW Randall Ltd, St Julian's Avenue, St Peter Port, Guernsey, CI, GY1 3JG
Tel (01481) 720134
Shop 10-5 Mon-Sat
Tours by arrangement

⊗ The smaller of Guernsey's two breweries, it was purchased by PH Randall from Joseph Gullick in 1868. Successive generations have continued to run the business, except during the period of the German occupation, when it ceased brewing until after the war. Randalls owns 22 pubs (18 of which are tied) but only three serve real ale. Do not confuse with Randalls Vautier of Jersey, which no longer brews. Occasional beer: Stout (ABV 7%). Bottle-conditioned beers: Mild (ABV 3.4%), Bitter (ABV 5%).

Patois Ale *(OG 1046, ABV 5%)* ✦
Amber in colour, with a hoppy aroma. Bitter and hoppy both in the palate and finish.

RAT & RATCHET
⛴ The Rat & Ratchet Brewery, 40 Chapel Hill, Huddersfield, W Yorkshire HD1 3EB
Tel (01484) 516734
Tours by arrangement

⊛ An alehouse where beer has been brewed since 1994 to supply just the pub and occa-sional beer festivals. The beer range varies, the aim being to have at least one Rat beer available most of the time.

RAVEN
See Winfields.

RCH
RCH Brewery, West Hewish, Weston-super-Mare, Somerset BS24 6RR
Tel (01934) 834447
Fax (01934) 834167
Shop
Tours by arrangement

⊗ A brewery originally installed by previous owners in the early 1980s behind the Royal Clarence Hotel at Burnham-on-Sea, but since 1993 brewing has taken place on a commer-cial basis in a former cider mill at West Hewish. A new 30-barrel plant was installed in 2000. RCH now supplies 100 outlets direct and the award-winning beers are available nationwide through its own wholesaling company, which also distributes beers from other small independent breweries. Bottle-conditioned beers: Pitchfork (ABV 4.3%), Old Slug Porter (ABV 4.5%), Firebox (ABV 6%).

Hewish IPA *(ABV 3.6%)* ✦
A pale brown/amber coloured, light hoppy bitter with some malt and fruit. Slightly less fruit in the finish. Floral, citrus hop aroma.

PG Steam *(ABV 3.9%)* ⬚✦
Very floral hop aroma with some fruit. Amber/gold in colour, it is medium-bodied, hoppy and bitter, with some malt, fruit and subtle sweetness. Finish is similar. Complex, multi-layered red ale.

Pitchfork *(ABV 4.3%)* ⬚⬚✦
Yellow/gold bitter with a floral, citric hop aroma with pale malt. Hops predominate in a full-bodied similar taste, which is slightly sweet. Finish is just as good, if longer.

Old Slug Porter *(ABV 4.5%)* ⬚⬚✦
Dark brown in colour with a good aroma of chocolate, coffee, roast malt and hops. Taste is similar, fullish-bodied with dark fruits. Complex, rich stout.

East Street Cream *(ABV 5%)* ⬚✦
Malty with chocolate hints, this hoppy, fruity, bitter-sweet ale has flavours that all vie for dominance. Pale-brown in colour, it is a creamy, well-crafted ale.

Firebox *(ABV 6%)* ✦
Full-bodied, smooth and full flavoured. Nice combination of malt, floral citrus hop and fruit bitter-sweet flavours. Mid-brown.

READING LION

⬦ Reading Lion Brewery, The Hop Leaf,
163-165 Southampton Street, Reading,
Berkshire RG1 2QZ
Tel (0118) 931 4700
Tours by arrangement

⊠ Brewery opened by Hop Back Brewery in
1995 at the Hop Leaf pub, a former
Inntrepreneur house, Reading's first real ale
brewery since Courage closed the old
Simonds site in the late 1970s. The 5-barrel
plant came from the Wyndham Arms in
Salisbury and beers are stored in both casks
and cellar tanks (no blanket pressure). The
beers are brewed on an occasional basis,
mainly for the pub, with occasional brews for
other Hop Back pubs and the free trade.
Beers: Hop Leaf Bitter (ABV 4.2%) and Rye &
Coriander (ABV 4.2%).

REBELLION

Rebellion Beer Company, Bencombe Farm,
Marlow Bottom, Buckinghamshire
SL7 3LT
Tel/Fax (01628) 476594
E-mail tim@rebellionbeer.freeserve.co.uk
Shop 8-6 Mon-Fri, 9-4 Sat
Tours by arrangement (CAMRA branches only)

⊠ Opened in 1993, Rebellion fills the gap left
in Marlow by Whitbread, which shut down
Wethereds in 1988. Rebellion moved to a
new site in Marlow and increased brewing
capacity from 50 to 200 barrels a week, having purchased the development brewery
from Courage at Reading. The new brewery
will now allow Rebellion to grow and produce a much wider range of beer styles. 160
outlets are supplied direct. Beers (including a
range of seasonal brews) are also produced
for Scanlon's Brewery, (01895) 256270,
which ceased production in summer 1997.
Seasonal beers: Overdraft (OG 1043, ABV
4.3%, spring), Blonde Bombshell (OG 1043,
4.3%, summer), Roasted Nuts (OG 1046, ABV
4.6%, winter), Old Codger (OG 1052, ABV
5%, winter).

IPA *(OG 1039, ABV 3.7%)* ◥
Copper-coloured bitter, sweet and malty,
with resinous and red apple flavours.
Caramel and fruit decline to leave a dry, bitter and malty finish.

Smuggler *(OG 1042, ABV 4.1%)* ◥
A red-brown beer, well-bodied and bitter
with an uncompromisingly dry, bitter finish.

Blonde Bombshell *(OG 1043, ABV 4.3%)*
A summer brew, brewed using only pale and
lager malts, giving the beer a light, golden
colour.

Mutiny *(OG 1046, ABV 4.5%)* ◥
Tawny in colour, this full-bodied best bitter is
predominantly fruity and moderately bitter
with crystal malt continuing to a dry finish.

Red Oktober *(OG 1047, ABV 4.7%)*
An autumn beer in the style of a German alt-
bier. Brewed using crystal and rye malts and
continental hops, it has a deep reddish hue.

Zebedee *(OG 1048, ABV 4.7%)*
The spring offering: light in colour, crisp and
refreshing with a delicate floral aroma.

Old Codger *(OG 1052, ABV 5%)*
A heart-warming winter ale with a full,

dark-roasted malt character. The hops give
contrast, but do not overpower the richness
of the malt,

For Scanlon's:

Spike *(OG 1046, ABV 4,5%)*

RECTORY

Rectory Ales Ltd, Streat Hill Farm
Outbuilding, Streat Hill, Streat, Hassocks,
Sussex BN6 8RP
Tel/Fax (01273) 890570
Tours by arrangement

⊠ Rectory was founded in 1996 by the Rector
of Plumpton, the Rev Godfrey Broster, to
generate funds for the maintenance of the
three churches in his parish. 107 parishioners
are shareholders. The brewing capacity has
been increased to 25 barrels a week. Some
seasonal beers are also produced. 30 outlets
are supplied direct. Seasonal beer: Christmas
Cheer (ABV 3.8%, December).

Parson's Porter *(ABV 3.8%)*

Rector's Pleasure *(ABV 3.8%)*

Rector's Light Relief *(ABV 3.8%)*

Rector's Revenge *(ABV 5.4%)* ◥
Copper-brown strong bitter with a complex
aroma, becoming more hoppy in the mouth
with a dry, bitter finish.

RED LION HOTEL
See Picks.

REDRUTH

Redruth Brewery (1742) Ltd, Redruth,
Cornwall TR15 1RB
Tel (01209) 212244 Fax (01209) 313793
Shop noon-6pm Mon-Sat
Tours by arrangement

Since May 1995, Redruth Brewery has been
owned by the Hong Kong-based Dramfield
Group. Cask-conditioned beer was estab-
lished in 1998 after a break of nearly 10
years. More than 200 outlets are supplied in
the South-west. Seasonal beers: Rudolph the
Redruth Brain Beer (OG 1056, ABV 5.5%,
Christmas). Beers: Crofty Cornish Bitter
(OG 1037, ABV 3.6%), Cornish Original
(OG 1042, ABV 4.1%), Cornish Rebellion
(OG 1049, ABV 4.8%), Miners Mild
(OG 1037, ABV 3.6%).

RED SHOOT

⬦ Red Shoot Brewery, Toms Lane,
Linwood, Ringwood, Hampshire SP6 3RB
Tel (01425) 475792

The brewery was commissioned at Easter
1998 with Forest Gold as the first brew.
Tom's Tipple was introduced in November
1998 as a winter brew and is now a permanent brand. Red Shoot would like to expand
but the size of plant (2.5 barrels) makes this
difficult. Beers: Forest Gold (ABV 3.8%),
Tom's Tipple (ABV 4.8%).

REEPHAM

Reepham Brewery, Unit 1, Collers Way,
Reepham, Norwich, Norfolk NR10 4SW
Tel (01603) 871091

⊗ A family-owned micro-brewery started by a chemical engineer and an architect (father and son) in 1983. The purpose-built brewing equipment was supplied by Peter Austin and installed in a new industrial unit in Reepham. Awards include Champion Beer twice at Norfolk Festival with Velvet Sweet (Milk) Stout and runner-up in class at GBBF. Recent developments include a new beer, St Agnes. Brews the Fat Cat's house beers in Norwich. Some 20 outlets are supplied direct. Bottle-conditioned beers: Rapier Pale Ale (OG 1042, ABV 4.3%), Velvet (OG 1045, ABV 4.5%), St Agnes (1046, ABV 4.6%).

LA Bitter *(ABV 2%)*

Granary Bitter *(OG 1038, ABV 3.8%)* ⌂❧
A gold-coloured beer with a light hoppy aroma followed by a malty sweetish flavour with some smoke notes. A well-balanced beer with a long, moderately hoppy aftertaste.

Rapier Pale Ale *(OG 1042, ABV 4.3%)* ▧❧
A crisp, hoppy aroma leads to a clean hoppy taste underpinned by a bitter base and smoky maltiness. A superb balance of bitterness and hops in a long-drawn out finish.

Norfolk Wheaten *(OG 1045, ABV 4.5%)*

Velvet Sweet Stout
(OG 1045, ABV 4.5%) ❧
A smooth, slightly sweet stout in the vein of traditional milk stouts. A smooth roast barley beginning introduces a flowing maltiness. A fruity edge comes to the fore as the flavours mature.

St Agnes *(OG 1046, ABV 4.6%)*

Bittern *(OG 1050, ABV 5%)*

Brewhouse *(OG 1055, ABV 5.5%)*
A strong winter ale.

RESTALRIG

Restalrig Village Brewery Ltd, Unit 5b Loaning Road, Restalrig, Edinburgh
Tel (0131) 468 6969
Fax (0131) 468 7071
Tours by arrangement

☺ A brewery set up in June 1997 in an old woollen mill with a plant capable of producing 100 barrels a week. The plant was purchased from the Minera/City Arms brew pub near Wrexham, with additional storage tanks from Buckleys. Future plans include bottled beers. 100 outlets are supplied direct.

Leith IPA *(OG 1038, ABV 3.8%)*

Youngs IPA *(OG 1038, ABV 3.8%)*

Youngs Golden Heavy *(OG 1040, ABV 4%)*

Otter of Leith *(OG 1042, ABV 4.2%)*

Restalrig 80/- *(OG 1044, ABV 4,4%)*

RIDLEYS

TD Ridley & Sons Ltd, Hartford End Brewery, Chelmsford, Essex CM3 1JZ
Tel (01371) 820316
Fax (01371) 821216
E-mail techcentre@ridley.co.uk
Web-site www.ridleys.co.uk
Tours by arrangement

⊗ Ridleys was established by Thomas Dixon Ridley in 1842 and is still family run. It is cur-

rently expanding and improving its estate of 67 tenanted pubs. As well as its main beers, Ridleys is establishing a range of event beers. It also supplies 350 other outlets. Event beers: Millenium Ale (ABV 4%, Nov-Jan), Valentine (ABV 3.9%, February), Mild Manners (ABV 3.8%, May), Snow Joke (ABV 4.5%, January), Hoppy Easter (ABV 4.3%, April), Fisherman's Whopper (ABV 4.3%, June), Santa's Secret (ABV 4.8%, December), Big Tackle (ABV 4.1%, March), Five Rings (4.1%, August). Seasonal beers: Witchfinder Porter (OG 1047, ABV 4.3%, winter), Spectacular (OG 1047, ABV 4.6%, summer), Winter Winner (OG 1050, 4.8%, Christmas).

IPA *(OG 1034, ABV 3.5%)* ❧
Tawny session bitter with a gentle balance of malt and hops. Character can vary, but often has caramel overtones.

Mild *(OG 1034, ABV 3.5%)* ❧
A dark mild, with a light aroma of roast malt and subdued hop. Quite bitter for a mild, with roast malt and fruit in the taste and a balanced, dry finish with hops and roast malt.

ESX Best *(OG 1043, ABV 4.3%)* ❧
Mid-brown best bitter with balanced malt and hops, bitter-sweet with caramel and a complex aftertaste.

Witchfinder Porter *(OG 1045, ABV 4.3%)* ❧
Dark brown caramel-dominated winter beer with roast malt after a malty fruity aroma.

Rumpus *(OG 1049, ABV 4.5%)* ❧
Faint hops, sweet taste with a light fruity, malty balance and a short aftertaste with some lingering malt.

Spectacular *(OG 1048, ABV 4.6%)* ❧
A pale, straw-coloured beer with a flowery nose. It has a delicate malty flavour and a rather bitter aftertaste.

RINGWOOD

Ringwood Brewery Ltd, Christchurch Road, Ringwood, Hampshire BH24 3AP
Tel (01425) 471177
Fax (01425) 480273
E-mail info@ringwoodbrewery.co.uk
Web-site www.ringwoodbrewery.co.uk
Shop 9.30-5 Mon-Fri 9.30-12 Sat
Tours by arrangement, also individual visits every Thursday at 3pm between May and September but book in advance

⊗ Ringwood, which celebrated 21 years of brewing in 1999, was set up in 1978 by legendary micro-brewery builder Peter Austin, and moved in 1986 to attractive 18th-century buildings, formerly part of the old Tunks brewery. A new brewhouse was commissioned at the end of 1994, and a new fermenting room completed in 1995. The 21st anniversary was marked by commissioning a new copper and steam boiler. 450 outlets are supplied direct. Four pubs are owned, all serving cask-conditioned beer. Ringwood's impressive success, under managing director David Welsh, has moved the brewery out of the ranks of micro-brewers and is now a small regional. Bottle-conditioned beer: Fortyniner (OG 1049, ABV 4.9%). Seasonal beers: Boon Doggle (OG 1039, ABV 3.9%, May-Sept), XXXX Porter (OG 1048, ABV 4.7%, Oct-March).

Best Bitter *(OG 1038, ABV 3.8%)* ◆
A well-balanced golden brown beer. A malty and hoppy aroma leads through to a malty taste with some sweetness. Malty and bitter finish, with some fruit present.

True Glory *(OG 1043, ABV 4.3%)* ◆
A malty aroma leads to a hoppy taste with malt and fruit, followed by a malty, hoppy and fruity aftertaste. Copper-coloured.

XXXX Porter *(OG 1048, ABV 4.7%)* 🍺◆
An aroma of roasted malt leads to a rich, roasted malt taste with coffee and fruit. The aftertaste is malty and bitter. Almost black in colour with a slight ruby-red tinge. Available Oct-March.

Fortyniner *(OG 1049, ABV 4.9%)* ◆
Pale brown in colour. A malty and fruity aroma leads to a well-balanced taste of malt and hops. Fruity finish.

Old Thumper *(OG 1056, ABV 5.6%)* ◆
A mid-brown beer. A fruity aroma preludes a sweet, malty taste with some fruit. Surprisingly bitter aftertaste, with malt and fruit.

RIVERHEAD

⬦ Riverhead Brewery Ltd, 2 Peel Street,
Marsden, Huddersfield,
W Yorkshire HD7 6BR
Tel (01484) 841270
Tours by arrangement

◎ The Riverhead Brewery Tap is a brew pub that opened in October 1995 after its conversion from an old grocery store. It serves its own seven brews plus the occasional specials mainly related to local activities ie Jazz Biter (for Marsden Jazz Festival), and Ruffled Feathers Bitter (Marsden Cuckoo Day). The brewery also supplies 10 local outlets occasionally.

Sparth Mild *(OG 1038, ABV 3.6%)* 🍺◆
A light-bodied, dry, mild, with a dark ruby colour. Fruity aroma with roasted flavour and a dry finish.

Butterley Bitter *(OG 1038, ABV 3.8%)* ◆
A dry, amber-coloured hoppy session beer.

Deer Hill Porter *(OG 1040, ABV 4%)*

Jazz Bitter *(OG 1040, ABV 4%)*

Ruffled Feathers *(OG 1042, ABV 4.2%)*

Cupwith Light Bitter *(OG 1042, ABV 4.2%)*
Fruity and hoppy golden best bitter, with a dry, bitter finish.

Black Moss Stout *(OG 1043, ABV 4.3%)* ◆
Roast malt and fruit aromas from a lightly-hopped dry stout with a chocolatey finish.

March Haigh Special Bitter
(OG 1046, ABV 4.6%)

Redbrook Premium Bitter
(OG 1055, ABV 5.5%) ◆
A rich and malty strong beer, with malt and fruit aroma and sweet, fruity aftertaste.

St Swellands *(OG 1074, ABV 7.4%)*

ROBINSON'S

Frederic Robinson Ltd, Unicorn Brewery,
Stockport, Cheshire SK1 1JJ
Tel (0161) 480 6571   Fax (0161) 476 6011
Shop 9-5 Mon-Sat
Tours by arrangement
◎ Major family brewery founded in 1838 in the Unicorn Inn. The company moved to the present site in 1865. Robinson's bought Hartleys of Ulverston in 1982 and closed the brewery in 1991; only Hartleys XB is still brewed. The company supplies real ale to all its 400 tied houses in the North-west and North Wales and to free trade outlets.

Hatters Mild *(OG 1032, ABV 3.3%)* ◆
A light mild with a fruit and malt aroma, it has a refreshing, dry, malty flavour and aftertaste. A darkened version is available in a handful of outlets and badged Dark Mild.

Old Stockport Bitter
(OG 1034, ABV 3.5%) ◆
A beer with a refreshing taste of malt, hops and citrus fruit, a characteristic fruity aroma, and a short, dry finish.

Hartleys XB *(OG 1040, ABV 4%)* ◆
An overly sweet and malty bitter with a bitter citrus peel fruitiness and a hint of liquorice in the finish.

Best Bitter *(OG 1040, ABV 4.2%)* ◆
Amber beer with an aroma of citrus fruit, spices and earthy hop. Hoppy, bitter and quite fruity to taste with a short bitter finish.

Frederics *(OG 1049, ABV 5%)* 🍺◆
A gold-coloured beer with an aroma of orange and a hint of spice. Citrus fruit and hops on the taste with a dry hoppy finish.

Old Tom *(OG 1079, ABV 8.5%)* 🍺🍾◆
A full-bodied, dark beer, it has malt, fruit and chocolate in the aroma. A delightfully complex range of flavours including dark chocolate, full maltiness, treacle toffee and fruits lead to a long, bitter-sweet aftertaste.

For Federation (qv):

Buchanan's Best Bitter
(OG 1035, ABV 3.6%)

Buchanan's Original
(OG 1044.5, ABV 4.4%)

ROCKINGHAM

Rockingham Ales,
c/o 25 Wansford Road, Elton,
Cambridgeshire PE8 6RZ
Tel (01832) 280722

Part-time micro-brewery established in 1997 and operating from a converted farm building near Blatherwyke, Northamptonshire (business address as above). Supplies half a dozen local outlets with beers brewed on a rota basis, supplemented with specials brewed to order. Seasonal beers: Fineshade (OG 1038, ABV 3.8%, autumn), Sanity Clause (OG 1042, ABV 4.1%, Christmas), Old Herbaceous (OG 1046, ABV 4.5%, winter).

Blatherwyke Bitter *(OG 1038, ABV 3.8%)*

Forest Gold *(OG 1040, ABV 3.9%)*

Hop Devil *(OG 1039, ABV 3.9%)*

A1 Amber Ale *(OG 1041, ABV 4%)*

Fruits of the Forest *(OG 1042, ABV 4.1%)*

ROOSTER'S

Rooster's Brewing Co Ltd,
20 Claro Business Centre,
Claro Road, Harrogate,
N Yorkshire HG1 4BA
Tel/Fax (01423) 561861
E-mail seanf@roosters.co.uk
Web-site www.roosters.co.uk

⊛ Rooster's Brewery was opened in October 1993 by Sean and Alison Franklin. They now make a total of 40 barrels a week. Under the Rooster's label they make seven regular beers while a subsidiary label, Outlaw Brewing Co, produces beers that may become regular Rooster brands. They change materials or process or both to make a new beer every two months. Sean Franklin is a devotee of hops and uses many varieties, including North American, in his brews. 70-80 outlets are supplied direct. Seasonal beers: Nectar (OG 1050, ABV 5%), Silver Lining (OG 1041-43, ABV 4.3%), Oyster Stout (OG 1041-43, ABV 4.3%).

Special *(OG 1038, ABV 3.9%)* 🍺❧
A yellow-coloured beer with an intense fruity/floral aroma, which is carried through the taste where it is joined by a well-balanced bitter character.

Scorcher *(OG 1042, ABV 4.3%)* ❧
Golden, aromatic and fruity, with balancing bitterness. The fruitiness is carried through into the aftertaste, where the bitterness tends to increase. A well-balanced beer.

Yankee *(OG 1042, ABV 4.3%)* ❧
A straw-coloured beer with a delicate, fruity aroma leading to a well-balanced taste of malt and hops with a slight evidence of sweetness, followed by a refreshing, fruity/bitter finish.

Cream *(OG 1046, ABV 4.7%)* ❧
A pale-coloured beer with a complex, floral bouquet leading to a well-balanced refreshing taste. Fruit lasts throughout and into the aftertaste.

Rooster's *(OG 1046, ABV 4.7%)* ❧
A light amber beer with a slightly hoppy nose. Strong malt flavours, with a slight toffee character, precede an unexpected hoppy finish.

Outlaw beers: Mayflower (ABV 3.7%), Zulu Porter (ABV 4.7%), Silver Lining (ABV 4.7%), Desperado (ABV 4.3%), Silver Bullet (ABV 4.7%), Stars and Stripes (ABV 4.7%)

ROSSENDALE
See Porter.

ROTHER VALLEY

Rother Valley Brewing Company,
Station Road, Northiam,
E Sussex TN31 6QT
Tel (01797) 253535
Fax (01797) 253550
Tours by arrangement

⊗ Rother Valley was established in Northiam in 1993 on a hop farm overlooking the river that mark the boundary between Kent and Sussex. It brews only with hops grown next to the brewery. Special beers are brewed to order and 55 outlets are supplied direct. Occasional/seasonal beers: Lighterman (OG 1036, ABV 3.5%, April-Sept), Wheat Beer (OG 1039, ABV 3.8%, occasional), Blues (OG 1050, ABV 5%, Oct-March), Hoppy Dolly Daze (ABV varies, Christmas).

Lighterman *(OG 1036, ABV 3.5%)*

Wheat Beer *(OG 1039, ABV 3.8%)*

Level Best *(OG 1040, ABV 4%)* ❧
Full-bodied tawny session bitter with a malt and fruit aroma, malty taste and a dry, hoppy finish.

Spirit Level *(OG 1047, ABV 4.6%)* ❧
Tawny best bitter. Initial hoppy fruitiness leads to a well-balanced sweet mixture of flavours with a dry aftertaste.

ROYAL CLARENCE
See RCH.

RUDDLES
See Greene King; brewery closed.

RUDGATE

Rudgate Brewery Ltd, 2 Centre Park,
Marston Business Park, Rudgate,
Tockwith, York, N Yorkshire YO26 7QF
Tel/Fax (01423) 358382
Tours by arrangement

☻ Brewery founded in 1992, located in an
old armoury building on a disused airfield. It
supplies 150 outlets with beers fermented in
open square vessels. A range of seasonal beers
is produced including wheat beers, a stout
and Stranges Xmas Special.

Viking *(OG 1038, ABV 3.8%)* ❦
An initially warming and malty, full-bodied
beer, with hops and fruit lingering into the
aftertaste.

Battleaxe *(OG 1042, ABV 4.2%)* ❦
A well-hopped bitter with slightly sweet
initial taste and light bitterness. Complex
fruit character gives a memorable aftertaste.

Ruby Mild *(OG 1044, ABV 4.4%)*
Nutty rich ruby ale, stronger than usual for a
mild.

RYBURN

♉ Ryburn Brewery, c/o Ram's Head,
Wakefield Road, Sowerby Bridge, Halifax,
W Yorkshire HX6 2AZ
Tel (01422) 835413/63355876

☻ Founded in 1989 in a former dye works,
this brewery is now in its fourth home
beneath its single tied house. Efforts are
being concentrated on supplying the pub,
with limited free trade sales.

Best Mild *(OG 1033, ABV 3.3%)* ❦
More akin to a thin, sweet stout than a dark
mild, this dark brown beer has a 'rum and
raisin' aroma, a slightly fruity, burnt taste
and a short, dry finish.

Best Bitter *(OG 1038, ABV 3.6%)* ❦
A thin beer, initially sweet with some bitterness in the aftertaste.

Light *(OG 1042, ABV 4.4%)*

Rydale Bitter *(OG 1044, ABV 4.2%)* ❦
A lightly hopped, sweet bitter with a growing
dry, bitter finish.

Luddite *(OG 1048, ABV 5%)* ❦
This sweetish, black stout is dominated
throughout by a roast maltiness. The finish is
dry and quite bitter.

Stabbers *(OG 1052, ABV 5.2%)* ❦
A fruity sweetness competes with bitterness
and malt and leads to a dry aftertaste in this
golden amber, strong bitter. There is some
background sulphur throughout.

Coiners *(OG 1060, ABV 6%)* ❦
Fruit, a syrupy sweetness and some
background bitterness characterise this
strong bitter and develop into a short but
increasingly dry finish.

SADDLEWORTH

♉ Saddleworth Brewery, Church Inn,
Church Lane, Uppermill, Saddleworth,
Greater Manchester OL3 6LW
Tel (01457) 820902
Fax (01457) 820831

☻ The brewery is in an old brewhouse, which
until three years ago, had not brewed for
more than 130 years. The copper is still fired
by direct flame to give a fuller flavour to the
beer. New developments in 1999 saw the
introduction of a new fermentation room,
barrelling room and cold room. The brew
house has an additional copper and mash
tun. Brewery trips are planned. Beers:
Saddleworth More (ABV 3.8%), Hop Smacker
(ABV 4.1%), Bert Corner (ABV 4.1%), Ayrtons
Ale (ABV 4.1%), Shaft Bender (ABV 5.4%),
Christmas Carol (ABV 7.4%, Christmas).

ST AUSTELL

St Austell Brewery Co Ltd, 63 Trevarthian
Road, St Austell, Cornwall
Tel (01726) 74444
Fax (01726) 68965
E-mail StaBrewery@Compuserve.com
Web-site www.StAustellBrewery.Co.UK
Shop 9.30 to 4.30 Mon to Fri
Visitor Centre and tours tel (01726) 66022

☒ Founded by Walter Hicks, St Austell
Brewery has been brewing in the town since
1851, the present brewery dating from the
early 1890s. The company remains in family
hands and brews real ale for sale in all of its
150 tied houses, as well as an increasing
presence in the free trade throughout Devon
and Cornwall. St Austell Brewery also act as a
regional distributor for Carlsberg-Tetley for
whom it brews Dartmoor Best Bitter, recreat-
ing a beer from the closed Ferguson's Brewery
at Plympton. St Austell Brewery is fiercely
independent and committed to the future of
brewing quality ales. An attractive visitor
centre offers guided tours and souvenirs from
the brewery. The brewery hosts its own Celtic
Beer Festival late in the year. Bottle-conditioned beer: Clouded Yellow (ABV 5%).

Bosun's Bitter *(OG 1032, ABV 3.1%)* ❦
A refreshing session beer, sweetish in aroma
and bitter-sweet in flavour. Lingering, hoppy
finish.

XXXX Mild *(OG 1037, ABV 3.6%)* ⊡❦
Little aroma, but a strong, malty character. A
caramel-sweetish flavour is followed by a
good, lingering aftertaste that is sweet but
with a fruity dryness.

Tinners Ale *(OG 1038, ABV 3.7%)* ❦
A deservedly popular, golden beer with an
appetising malt aroma and a good balance of
malt and hops in the flavour. Lasting finish.

Daylight Robbery *(OG 1043, ABV 4.2%)*

Trelawny's Pride *(OG 1044, ABV 4.4%)* ❦
A beer that if served through a swan neck
and sparkler is robbed of aroma and taste.

Hicks Special Draught or HSD
(OG 1051, ABV 5%) ❦
An aromatic, fruity, hoppy bitter that is initially sweet and has an aftertaste of pronounced bitterness, but whose flavour is
fully rounded. A good premium beer.

For Carlsberg-Tetley:

Dartmoor Best Bitter
(OG 1037.5, ABV 3.9%)

ST GEORGE'S

St George's Brewing Co Ltd, Old
Bakehouse, Bush Lane, Callow End,

Worcester WR2 4TF
Tel/Fax (01905) 831316
Tours by arrangement

St George's Brewery is situated half way between Worcester and Malvern in an old bakehouse and started trading in October 1998. It was founded by Martin Soden and his father, George. Only the finest English ingredients are used. A little Malvern water is used in every brew. There are plans to produce bottle-conditioned beers in small quantities. 30-40 outlets are supplied direct. Seasonal beers: Autumn Gold (OG 1040, ABV 3.9%), Fire (OG 1050, ABV 4.9%).

Summertime Ale *(ABV 3.7%)* ◆
Well-hopped and sweet, this light beer has lots of fruity undertones with a full-flavoured aftertaste.

St George's Pride *(OG 1039, ABV 3.8%)* ◆
A subtle blend of flavours give it a slight hint of sweet fruitiness.

War Drum *(ABV 4%)* ◆
Fruity hoppiness battles with a malty background to dominate in this brew. Finally a truce is declared, leaving no losers.

Jackpot *(ABV 4.4%)* ◆
A potent malt and fruit nose leads into a strongly hopped bitter, although there is no strong aftertaste.

St George's Gold *(ABV 4.5%)*
There are lots of flavours to enjoy in this premium bitter. With a sharp, hoppy taste dominating, a refreshing drink is created with a dry, clean aftertaste.

ST GILES IN THE WOOD
See Clearwater.

ST PETER'S
St Peter's Brewery Co Ltd, St Peter South Elmham, Bungay, Suffolk NR35 1NQ
Tel (01986) 782322
Fax (01986) 782505
E-mail beers@stpetersbrewery.co.uk
Web-site www.stpetersbrewery.co.uk
Shop 9-6
Tours by arrangement

⊠ St Peter's Brewery was opened in 1996 in former dairy buildings behind the ancient St Peter's Hall in 1996. It now produces an extensive range of beers in cask and bottle (not bottle-conditioned) including fruit beers and a spiced ale. Thirty-three outlets are supplied direct and three tied pubs all serve cask-conditioned beer.

Best Bitter *(ABV 3.7%)*

Mild *(ABV 3.8%)*

Extra *(ABV 4.3%)*

Organic Ale *(ABV 4.5%)*

Golden Ale *(ABV 4.7%)*

Wheat Beer *(ABV 4.7%)*

Elderberry Fruit Beer *(ABV 4.7%)*

Grapefruit Fruit Beer *(ABV 4.7%)*

Spiced Ale *(ABV 4.7%)*

Suffolk Gold *(ABV 4.9%)*

Old Style Porter *(ABV 5.1%)*

Honey Porter *(ABV 5.1%)*

Strong Ale *(ABV 5.1%)*

Winter Ale *(ABV 6.5%)*

Spiced Ale *(ABV 6.5%)*

Summer Ale *(ABV 6.5%)*

Cream Stout *(ABV 6.5%)*

SALOPIAN
Salopian Brewing Co Ltd, 67 Mytton Oak Road, Shrewsbury, Shropshire SY3 8UQ
Tel (01743) 248414
Fax (01743) 358866
Shop 9-5 weekdays
Tours by arrangement

⊗ The brewery was started in 1995 in an old dairy on the outskirts of Shrewsbury. Partners Wilf Nelson and brewer Martin Barry are developing cask sales locally and nationally through wholesalers, and the plant is gradually being increased in size. Bottle-conditioned beers are brewed at Brakspear, and the company is attempting to develop sales through additional national outlets. Fifty-five outlets are supplied direct. Bottle-conditioned beers: Minsterley Ale (OG 1044.5, ABV 4.5%), Gingersnap (OG 1048, ABV 4.7%), Goodall's Gold (OG 1048, ABV 4.7%), Jigsaw (OG 1049, ABV 4.8%), Puzzle (OG 1049, ABV 4.8%), Entire Butt (OG 1049, ABV 4.8%), Answer (OG 1049, ABV 4.8%), Cerise de Salop (OG 1048, ABV 4.8%), Firefly (OG 1051, ABV 5%).

Shropshire Gold *(OG 1040/41, ABV 3.8%)*

Choir Porter *(OG 1046, ABV 4.5%)*

Minsterley Ale *(OG 1045, ABV 4.5%)*
A premium bitter using three kinds of hops.

Gingersnap Dark Wheat
(OG 1046, ABV 4.5%)

Golden Thread *(OG 1050, ABV 5%)*

Puzzle White Wheat *(OG 1049, ABV 4.8%)*

Jigsaw Black Wheat *(OG 1050, ABV 4.8%)*

Ironbridge Stout *(OG 1050, ABV 5%)* 🍶
A red-coloured, malty strong ale.

SCANLON'S
Scanlon's Fine Ales, Rainbow Industrial Estate, Trout Road, Yiewsley, Middlesex UB7 7XT
Tel (01895) 256270

Scanlon's sells eight beers on a regular basis produced for the company at the following breweries:

Vale Brewery, Haddenham, Bucks:

Frays Mild *(OG 1036, ABV 3.6%)*

Colne Valley Bitter *(OG 1042, ABV 4.1%)*

Ealing Porter *(OG 1045, ABV 4.4%)*

Lord Ashford's Special Reserve
(OG 1052, ABV 5%)
A stout produced Dec-Jan.

O'Hanlon's Brewery:

Middlesex Gold *(OG 1039, ABV 3.8%)*

Elthorne White *(OG 1043, ABV 4.2%)*
A wheat beer produced March-Oct.

Brunel Premier Ale *(OG 1050, ABV 4.8%)*

Rebellion, Marlow, Bucks:

Spike *(OG 1046, ABV 4.5%)*

SCATTOR ROCK

Scattor Rock Brewery Ltd,
Unit 5 Gidley's Meadow, Christow, Exeter,
Devon EX6 7QB
Tel/Fax (01647) 252120
Tours by arrangement

Brewery set up in 1998 and situated within the boundaries of the Dartmoor National Park and named after a well-known local landmark. 60 plus outlets are supplied direct on a permanent or regular basis. Occasional beers: Scotch Ale (ABV 4.5%), Night Porter (ABV 5.2%), Quarryman Stout (ABV 4.4%), Brain Dead (ABV 7%) plus various monthly specials. Bottle-conditioned beers: Scatty Bitter (OG 1040, ABV 3.8%), Teign Valley Tipple (OG 1042, ABV 4%), Golden Valley (OG 1046, ABV 4.6%), Scatter Brain (OG 1049, ABV 4.8%), Devonian (OG 1051, ABV 5%).

Scatty Bitter *(OG 1040, ABV 3.8%)*

Teign Valley Tipple *(OG 1041, ABV 4%)*

Skylark *(OG 1043, ABV 4.2%)*

Golden Valley *(OG 1047, ABV 4.6%)*

Scatter Brain *(OG 1049, ABV 4.8%)*

Devonian *(OG 1051, ABV 5%)*

SELBY

Selby (Middlebrough) Brewery Ltd, 131
Millgate, Selby, N Yorkshire YO8 3LL
Tel (01757) 702826
Shop 10-2 and 6-10 Mon-Sat

☺ Old family brewery that resumed brewing in 1972 after a gap of 18 years but which is now mostly involved in wholesaling. Its beers, which are brewed on an occasional basis, are available, while stocks last (only in bulk) at the shop and not at the company's single pub. They are also sold as guest beers in the local free trade. Beers: No. 1 (OG 1040, ABV 4%), No. 3 (OG 1040, ABV 4%), Old Tom (OG 1065, ABV 6.5%).

SHARDLOW

Shardlow Brewing Company Ltd, The Old Brewery Stables, British Waterways Yard, Cavendish Bridge, Leicestershire LE72 2HL
Tel/Fax (01332) 799188
E-mail brewery@fsbusiness.co.uk
Tours by arrangement

⊗ The brewery opened in 1993 in the old kiln house of the original Cavendish Bridge Brewery (closed in the 1920s), and moved in December 1996 to new premises, at the same site on the River Trent, opposite Shardlow Marina. The new brewery is situated on two floors of former stables that retain some

original features. Shardlow supplies 40 free trade outlets. Occasional beers: Narrowboat (ABV 4.3%).

Chancellors Revenge *(ABV 3.6%)*

Best Bitter *(ABV 3.9%)*

Kiln House *(ABV 4.1%)*

Goldenhop *(ABV 4.1%)*

Old Stable Brew *(ABV 4.4%)*

Cavendish Gold *(ABV 4.5%)*

Reverend Eaton's Ale *(ABV 4.5%)*
A medium strong beer with a sweet aftertaste.

Mayfly *(ABV 4.8%)*

Platinum Blonde *(ABV 5%)*

Whistle Stop *(OG 1050, ABV 5%)*

SHARP'S

Sharp's Brewery, Pityme Industrial Estate,
Rock, Wadebridge, Cornwall PL27 6NU
Tel (01208) 862121
Fax (01208) 863727
Tours by arrangement

⊗ Founded in 1994, the brewery has enjoyed rapid expansion. It supplies the free trade in Devon and Cornwall, and the beers are also widely available throughout the Home Counties via wholesalers.

Cornish Coaster *(OG 1037, ABV 3.6%)* ✎
A smooth, easy-drinking beer, golden in colour, with a fresh hop aroma and dry malt and hops in the mouth. The finish starts malty but becomes dry and hoppy.

Doom Bar Bitter *(OG 1040, ABV 4%)* ✎
A rich, golden brown beer with a hint of barley. Dry malt and hops in the mouth. The malty finish becomes dry and hoppy. Fresh hop aroma.

Eden Ale *(OG 1043, ABV 4.4%)*

Sharp's Own *(OG 1043, ABV 4.4%)* ✎
A deep golden brown beer with a delicate hops and malt aroma, and dry malt and hops in the mouth. Like the other beers, its finish starts malty but turns dry and hoppy.

Will's Resolve *(OG 1046, ABV 4.6%)*

Special *(OG 1052, ABV 5.2%)* ✎
Deep golden brown with a fresh hop aroma. Dry malt and hops in the mouth; the finish is malty but becomes dry and hoppy.

SHEPHERD NEAME

Shepherd Neame Ltd, 17 Court Street,
Faversham, Kent ME13 7AX
Tel (01795) 532206
Fax (01795) 538907
E-mail company@shepherd-neame.co.uk
Web-site www.shepherd-neame.co.uk
Shop 9-5 Mon-Fri
Tours by arrangement

⊗ Kent's major independent brewery is believed to be the oldest continuous brewer in the country since 1698, but records show brewing commenced on the site as far back as the 12th century. The same water source is still used today, steam engines are employed and the mash is produced in two teak tuns that date from 1910. A visitors' reception hall is housed in a restored medieval hall (tours by arrangement). The company has 390 tied houses in the South-east, nearly all selling cask ale, but tenants are encouraged to keep beers under blanket pressure if the cask is likely to be on sale for more than three days. More than 500 other outlets are also supplied direct. In 2000 Shepherd Neame made a takeover bid for King & Barnes of Horsham in order to secure additional brewing capacity. K&B was sold instead to Hall & Woodhouse, who closed the brewery. Shepherd Neame is still seeking additional brewing capacity, either by building on a greenfield site or buying another brewery. Seasonal beers: Early Bird Spring Hop Ale (OG 1038.5, ABV 4.3%, spring), Late Red Autumn Hop Ale (OG 1042, ABV 4.5%, autumn) ⬚, Original Porter (OG 1044, ABV 4.8%, winter), Goldings Summer Hop Ale (OG 1042, ABV 4.7%, summer).

Master Brew Bitter
(OG 1032.5, ABV 3.7%) ❧
A distinctive bitter, mid-brown in colour, with a hoppy aroma. Well-balanced, with a nicely aggressive bitter taste from its hops, it leaves a hoppy/bitter finish, tinged with sweetness.

Best Bitter *(OG 1036, ABV 4.1%)* ❧
Mid-brown, with less marked characteristics than the bitter. However, the nose is very well-balanced and the taste enjoys a malty, bitter smokiness. Malty, well-rounded finish. It also appears under the name Canterbury Jack.

Spitfire Premium Ale *(OG 1039, ABV 4.5%)*
A commemorative Battle of Britain brew for the RAF Benevolent Fund's appeal, now a permanent feature.

Bishops Finger *(OG 1045.5, ABV 5%)*
A cask-conditioned version of a famous bottled beer, introduced in cask in 1989.

SHIP & PLOUGH
See Blewitts.

SHOES
Shoes Brewery, Three Horse Shoes Inn, Norton Canon, Hereford HR4 7BH
Tel/Fax (01544) 318375

Landlord Frank Goodwin had long been a home brewer, but decided in 1994 to brew on a commercial basis for his pub. The beers are brewed from malt extract, stored in casks and dispensed under a blanket of mixed gas.

Beers: Norton Ale (OG 1038, ABV 3.6%), Canon Bitter (OG 1040, ABV 4.1%). Limited edition only: Farriers 2000 (ABV 13.4%, unfiltered, bottle-conditioned).

SHRALEY BROOK*
Shraley Brook Brewing Company, Studio 3, Townhouse Farm, Alsager Road, Audley, Stoke-on-Trent, Staffs ST7 8JQ
Tel/Fax (01782) 723792
Tours by arrangement

Previously known as the Rising Sun Brewery, brewing was revived after a gap of two years using new recipes devised by three regulars of the pub. Naming of the beers has followed an English Civil War theme. Fifteen outlets are supplied direct. Beers: Charles' First Brew (OG 1043, ABV 4.2%), Executioner (OG 1049, ABV 4.9%, occasional), Golden Sovereign (OG 1053, ABV 5.2%, occasional).

SHUGBOROUGH
See Titanic.

SIX BELLS
Six Bells Brewery, Church Street, Bishop's Castle, Shropshire SY9 5AA
Tel (01588) 638930
Tours by arrangement

⊠ Brewing commenced in January 1997 with plant made from dairy equipment with a 5-barrel brew length. The brewery was upgraded in 1999 to expand to 20-barrel capacity and a bottling line. Six Bells has six regular outlets while a further 35 pubs take the beers as guest ales.

Big Nev's *(OG 1037, ABV 3.8%)*
A pale, fairly hoppy bitter.

Marathon Ale *(OG 1040, ABV 4%)*
Dark and malty.

Cloud Nine *(OG 1043, ABV 4.2%)*
Pale, well hopped with a citrus finish. Available Spring to October.

Spring Forward *(OG 1047, ABV 4.6%)*
Originally a spring beer but now permanent: dry, hoppy and amber in colour.

Brew 101 *(OG 1048, ABV 4.8%)*

Old Recumbent *(OG 1053, ABV 5.2%)*
Well hopped winter ale available October to Spring.

SKINNER'S
Skinner's Brewery, Riverside View, Newham, Truro, Cornwall TR1 2SU
Tel (01872) 271885
Fax (01872) 271886
Shop
Tours by arrangement

⊠ A brewery founded in July 1997 by Steve and Sarah Skinner, formerly of the Tipsy Toad Brewery in Jersey, which they founded. The beer names are based on Cornish folklore characters. The brewery has won many awards in its short life, including Supreme Champion at the SIBA Maltings Festival, Newton Abbot, in 1998, with Cornish Knocker. This was followed in 1999 with a repeat performance with Betty Stogs. Also in 1999 Who Put the Lights Out? won a gold

The Good Beer Guide 2001

medal in the National Beauty of Hops competition. Skinner's owns one pub, the Skinners Ale House in Newquay. Occasional beer: Jingle Knockers (ABV 5.5%), Christmas).

Coast Liner *(ABV 3.4%)*
A crisp, light brown, hoppy session bitter.

Spriggan Ale *(OG 1038, ABV 3.8%)* ◆
A light golden hoppy bitter. Well balanced with a smooth bitter finish.

Betty Stogs Bitter *(ABV 4%)* ◆
A pale amber, mid-strength bitter with hoppy overtones.

Cornish Knocker Ale
(OG 1044.5, ABV 4.5%) ◆
A strong, clean tasting golden ale. Distinctive flowery aroma with a lasting finish.

Figgy's Brew *(ABV 4.5%)* ◆
A classic dark premium strength bitter. Full flavoured with a smooth finish.

Who Put the Lights Out? *(ABV 5%)*
Strong single hop amber ale first brewed to mark the solar eclipse in 1999.

SKINNER'S OF BRIGHTON
See Dark Star.

SLATERS
See Eccleshall.

SMILES
Smiles Brewing Co Ltd, Colston Yard, Colston Street, Bristol BS1 5BD
Tel (0117) 929 7350
Fax (0117) 925 8235
Web-site www.smiles.co.uk
Shop 8.30-7pm
Tours by arrangement

⊗ Smiles Brewing Co, founded in 1977, is a traditional tower brewery. The mainstream brands are complemented by monthly specials. The tied estate has increased to 17 houses, all selling cask ale. The brewery also supplies more than 250 other outlets. The brewery has an e-store on the web-site where fresh beer and memorabilia can be purchased. Monthly beers: Bristol Porter (ABV 4.7%, January), Old Tosser (ABV 4.3, February), March Hare (ABV 4%, March), April Fuel (ABV 4.8%, April), May Fly (ABV 4.5%, May), Zummer Vat Ale (ABV 4%, June), Maiden Leg Over (ABV 3.5%, July), Glorious 12th (ABV 3.8%, August), Wurz Ale Gone (ABV 4.1%, September), Old Russ Ale (ABV 4.4%, October), Roman Cand Ale (ABV 5.5%, November), Holly Hops (ABV 5%, December). Other beers – 'as the mood take us' – can be found on the web-site.

Golden *(OG 1038, ABV 3.8%)* ▉◆
A refreshing, yellow-gold ale with a nicely-balanced malt, hop and fruit aroma that continues in a bitter-sweet light-bodied taste. More dry and bitter in the finish.

Best *(OG 1041, ABV 4.1%)*
Pale brown, well-balanced, mid-bodied, bitter-sweet ale with malt, hops and fruit lasting throughout.

Heritage *(OG 1053, ABV 5.2%)* ◆
A complex, red-brown, medium to full-bodied fruity ale, with an aroma of malt, chocolate and hops. Lasting, bitter-sweet finish.

For Scottish Courage:

BA *(OG 1034, ABV 3.3%)* ◆
Gentle aroma of pale malt and spicy hops, which is reflected in the taste. Finish is drier and more bitter. A light traditional session ale, amber/light.

SAMUEL SMITH
Samuel Smith Old Brewery (Tadcaster), High Street, Tadcaster, N Yorkshire LS24 9SB
Tel (01937) 832225
Fax (01937) 834673
Tours by arrangement

⊛ Dating from 1758, Samuel Smiths is Yorkshire's oldest brewery. Although related to the nearby much larger John Smith's (now owned by Scottish Courage), who originally owned the old brewery, Samuel Smith's is a radically different company, still family-owned, fiercely independent and with a great belief in tradition. The beer is brewed from well water without the use of adjuncts (brewing sugar has been phased out) and fermented in traditional Yorkshire Squares. All real ale is supplied in wooden casks made and repaired by the brewery's own cooper. Cask ale is sold in the large majority of the 200-plus tied houses, although sadly cask has been replaced by nitro-keg in a number of outlets, especially in London, and there is now only one cask brand. While not bottle conditioned, Sam Smith's range of bottled beers, including Taddy Porter, Imperial Stout, and Best Organic Ale, are of outstanding quality.

Old Brewery Bitter (OBB)
(OG 1040, ABV 4%) ◆
Malt dominates the aroma, with an initial burst of malt, hops and fruit in the taste, which is sustained in the aftertaste.

SNOWDONIA
Snowdonia Parc Brewery, Snowdonia Park Hotel, Waunfawr, Caernarfon, Gwynedd LLS5
Tel (01286) 650409
Fax (01286) 650733
Tours by arrangement

Snowdonia started brewing in spring 1998 in a 2-barrel brew length brewhouse. The pub is the station master's house for the Welsh Highland Railway: Waunfawr stop was due to open in the summer of 2000. Seasonal beer: Haf (ABV 5%). Beers: Station Bitter (ABV 3.8%), Tywyll (meaning Dark) (ABV 5%), Experimental Ale (ABV 5%), Haf (meaning summer) (ABV 5%).

SPINNING DOG*
⌂ Spinning Dog Brewery, the Victory, St Owen's Street, Hereford HR1 2QD
Tel (01432) 342125/274998
Fax (01432) 342125
E-mail jfkenyon@aol.com
Tours by arrangement

⊗ The brewery opened in January 2000 following the purchase of the Victory pub from Wye Valley Brewery. There were plans for a second beer around ABV 4%. The brewery is

HEREFORD
OG. 1036°

a 4-barrel brew length with an 8-barrel weekly capacity. Small quantities of beer are available for take-home sales. Beers: Chase Your Tail (OG 1036, ABV 3.6%), Get Your King (OG 1040, ABV 4%).

SP SPORTING ALES

SP Sporting Ales Ltd, Cantilever Lodge, Stoke Prior, Leominster, Herefordshire HR6 0LG
Tel/Fax (01568) 760226

⊠ Small brewery that opened in April 1996 and is now supplying more than 65 outlets. Its main beer, Dove's Delight, is sold under various names.

Winners *(ABV 3.5%)*

Dove's Delight *(OG 1040, ABV 4%)*

SPRINGHEAD

Springhead Brewery, Unit 3, Sutton Workshops, Old Great North Road, Sutton-on-Trent, Newark, Nottinghamshire NG23 6QS
Tel (01636) 821000
Fax (01636) 821150
E-mail springhead@compuserve.com
Web-site www.springhead.co.uk

⊠ Springhead started out as the country's smallest brewery but moved to larger premises in 1994. In 1997 brewing was temporarily halted but the brewer succeeded in attracting new backers and re-launched the company in 1998. Brewery tours available lunchtime or evenings by arrangement in the new visitor centre. Most of the beer names are associated with the English Civil War.

Hersbrucker Weizenbier *(OG 1035, ABV 3.6%)*
A wheat beer with a gentle aroma, light, refreshing with a dry finish. Available March-Sept.

Surrender *(OG 1035, ABV 3.6%)*
A burnished, copper-coloured bitter with a stunning combination of malt and hops. Long dry finish. Wonderfully refreshing.

Bitter *(OG 1040, ABV 4%)*
A clean-tasting, easy-drinking hoppy beer. Also available bottle conditioned.

Puritans Porter *(OG 1040, ABV 4%)*
A porter, dark but not heavy. Smooth with a lingering finish of roasted barley.

Roundhead's Gold *(OG 1042, ABV 4.2%)*
Golden light, made with wild flower honey. Refreshing but not too sweet with the glorious aroma of Saaz hops. Also available bottle conditioned.

Rupert's Ruin *(ABV 4.2%)*

Goodrich Castle *(OG 1044, ABV 4.4%)*
Brewed following a 17th-century recipe using rosemary. Pale ale, light on the palate with a bitter finish and a delicate flavour.

The Leveller *(OG 1046, ABV 4.8%)*
Dark, smoky, intense flavour with a toffee finish. Brewed in the style of Belgian Trappist ales. Also available bottle conditioned.

Gardener's Tap *(ABV 5%)*

Roaring Meg *(OG 1052, ABV 5.5%)*
Smooth and sweet with a dry finish and citrus honey aroma. Also available bottle-conditioned.

Cromwell's Hat *(OG 1060, ABV 6%)*
Silky and robust with a hint of juniper and cinnamon. Available Oct- March. Also available bottle conditioned.

STANWAY

Stanway Brewery, Stanway, Cheltenham, Gloucestershire GL54 5PQ
Tel (01386) 584320

⊠ Small brewery founded in 1993 with a 5-barrel plant, which confines its sales to the Cotswolds area (around 25 outlets). Seasonal beer: Lords-a-Leaping (OG 1045, ABV 4.5%, Christmas).

Stanney Bitter *(OG 1042, ABV 4.5%)* ◆
A light, refreshing, amber-coloured beer, dominated by hops in the aroma, with a bitter taste and a hoppy, bitter finish.

STEAMIN' BILLY
See Leatherbritches.

STOCKS
See Hull and Pub Groups, Century Inns.

STONEHENGE

Stonehenge Ale, The Old Mill, Mill Road, Netheravon, Salisbury, Wiltshire SP4 9QB
Tel (01980) 670 631
Fax (01980) 671 187
E-mail stonehenge_ales@bigfoot.com
Web-site site www.stonehengeales.sagenet.co.uk
Shop 9-5 Mon-Fri, 11-1 Sat
Tours by arrangement

⊠ A tower brewery, originally named Bunce's Brewery after late founder Tony Bunce, housed in a listed building on the River Avon, established in 1984 and sold to Danish master brewer Stig Anker Andersen in 1993. Its cask-conditioned beers are delivered to around 60 free trade outlets within a radius of 50 miles, and a number of wholesalers are also supplied. Seasonal beers: Sign of Spring (OG 1044, ABV 4.6%, March-April), Second to None (OG 1044, ABV 4.6%, May-July), Stig Swig (OG 1050, ABV 5%, Aug-Oct), Rudolph (OG 1050, ABV 5%, Nov-Jan).

Benchmark *(OG 1035, ABV 3.5%)* ◆

A pleasant, bitter ale of remarkable character. The taste is malty, the aroma subtle and the long finish is dry on the palate.

Pigswill *(OG 1040, ABV 4%)*
A beer first brewed for the Two Pigs pub at Corsham, now more widely available.

Best Bitter *(OG 1042, ABV 4.1%)*
A complex malty and bitter beer with noticeable fruit and a long, bitter aftertaste.

Heel Stone *(OG 1042, ABV 4.3%)*
Crisp, refreshing amber bitter with a blackcurrant aroma and a dry, lingering and bitter aftertaste.

Great Dane (cask-conditioned lager) *(OG 1044, ABV 4.6%)*

Danish Dynamite *(OG 1050, ABV 5%)*
A light golden, slightly fruity, dry strong ale with hop and bitter balance.

Old Smoky *(OG 1050, ABV 5%)* ✥
A delightful, warming, dark bitter ale, with a roasted malt taste and a hint of liquorice surrounding a developing bitter flavour.

STORM*
The Storm Brewing Co, Cheshire Bakeries, Hulley Road, Macclesfield, Cheshire SK10 2LP
Tel (01625) 432978/615856
Tours by arrangement

Storm started brewing in October 1998 under the guidance of Brian Rider of Wickwar Brewery. Two partners, Hugh Thompson and Dave Stebbings, brew five barrels a week on a part-time basis at present. Storm currently supplies approximately 30 outlets in the Macclesfield area. There were plans in 2000 to add a third fermenter and a new brew, Storm Damage.

Beaufort's Ale *(OG 1036, ABV 3.8%)*

Ale Force *(OG 1038, ABV 4.2%)* ✥
Amber, smooth-tasting, complex beer that balances malt, hop and fruit on the taste, leading to a roasty, slightly sweet aftertaste.

Windgather *(OG 1043, ABV 4.5%)*
Pale brown, refreshing, clean-tasting best bitter, complex with a rich aftertaste.

Storm Damage *(ABV 4.7%)*

STRAWBERRY BANK
Strawberry Bank Brewery, Masons Arms, Cartmel Fell, Grange-over-Sands, Cumbria LA11 6NW
Tel (0153 95) 68486
Fax (0153 95) 68780
Tours by arrangement

⊛ Strawberry Bank is based at the rear of the Masons Arms pub which has both freemasons and Arthur Ransome connections: masons used meet here in secret when they were illegal, while the famous children's writer lived up the lane next to the pub. The only regular beer is the superb Damson fruit beer using Lyth Valley damsons. Beers: Ned's Tipple (OG 1040, ABV 4%), Blackbeck (OG 1045, ABV 4.5%), Damson Ale (OG 1060, ABV 6%), Rulbuts (OG 1060, ABV 6%).

SULWATH
Sulwath Brewers Ltd, The Brewery, King Street, Castle Douglas DG7 1DT Office: Strathmore, 14 Babbington Gardens, Hardthorn, Dumfries DG2 9JB
Tel/Fax (01387) 255849
E-mail allen@scottdavis98.freeserve.co.uk
Shop
Tours by arrangement

⊛ A small, privately-owned company that started brewing in 1995. It sells cask ales direct to the licensed trade and currently has 53 outlets for draught, with a further 25 supermarkets and licensed shops for bottled Criffel & Knockendoch. Sulwath moved from its original site at Southerness to larger premises at Castle Douglas in 2000 to cope with increased business and incorporate a small bottling plant on site. A visitor centre was due to open in the summer of 2000. Occasional beer: John Paul Jones (OG 1038, ABV 4%).

Cuil Hill *(OG 1039, ABV 3.6%)*

Criffel *(OG 1043, ABV 4.6%)*

Knockendoch *(OG 1047, ABV 5%)*

SUMMERSKILLS
Summerskills Brewery, 15 Pomphlett Farm Industrial Estate, Broxton Drive, Billacombe, Plymouth, Devon PL9 7BG
Tel/Fax (01752) 481283

⊗ Originally established in a vineyard in 1983 at Bigbury on Sea, Summerskills moved to its present two years later. National distribution via carefully vetted wholesalers ensures nationwide coverage for the company's prize-winning beers. Occasional/seasonal beers: Menacing Dennis (OG 1044, ABV 4.5%), Turkey's Delight (OG 1050, ABV 5.1%, Christmas).

Cellar Vee *(OG 1037, ABV 3.7%)*

Best Bitter *(OG 1042, ABV 4.3%)* ✥
A mid-brown beer, with plenty of malt and hops through the aroma, taste and finish. A good session beer.

Tamar *(OG 1042, ABV 4.3%)* ✥
A tawny-coloured bitter with a fruity aroma and a hop taste and finish.

Whistle Belly Vengeance *(OG 1046, ABV 4.7%)* ✥

A red/brown beer with a beautiful malt and fruit taste and a pleasant, malty aftertaste.

Indiana's Bones *(OG 1055, ABV 5.6%)* ◆
A mid-brown beer with a good balance of fruit and malt in the aroma and taste, and a sweet, malty finish.

SUNSET*
☐ Sunset Cider & Wine Ltd,
The Leggers Inn, Stable Buildings,
Savile Wharf, Mill Street East, Dewsbury,
West Yorkshire WF12 9BD
Tel (01924) 502846
Tours by arrangement

An old converted hay loft in a canal basin, the brewery is situated under the pub and brews twice a week. Beers: Canal No 5 (OG 1038, OG 3.8%), Marriots Mild (OG 1040, ABV 4%), Peat Cutter (OG 1040, ABV 4%), Canal No 7 (OG 1042, ABV 4.2%), Pharoes Curse (OG 1046, ABV 4.6%), Canal No 7+ (OG 1050, ABV 5%), Canal No 9 (OG 1062, ABV 6%).

SUTTON
Sutton Brewing Co, 31 Commercial Road,
Coxside, Plymouth, Devon PL4 0LE
Tel/Fax (01752) 205010
Tours by arrangement

⊗ The brewery was built alongside the Thistle Park Tavern, near Plymouth's Sutton Harbour, in 1993. It went into production the following year to supply the pub and one other outlet. It now sells to more than 80 outlets in and around Plymouth, and a bigger plant and additional fermenters have been installed to cope with demand. Occasional/seasonal beers: Hopnosis (OG 1045, ABV 4.5%, spring), Weetablitz (OG 1045, ABV 4.5%, spring/summer), Eddystone (OG 1050, ABV 5%), Old Pedantic (OG 1051, ABV 5%, autumn), Bodmin Beast (OG 1056, ABV 5.5%), Plymouth Porter (OG 1060, ABV 6%, winter), Sleigh'd (OG 1056-60, ABV 6%, Christmas).

Plymouth/Dartmoor Pride
(OG 1040, ABV 3.8%)

XSB *(OG 1045, ABV 4.2%)* ◆
Amber nectar with a fruity nose and a bitter finish.

Wild Blonde *(ABV 1044, ABV 4.4%)*

Sutton Comfort *(OG 1047, ABV 4.5%)* ◆
Hoppy tasting mid-brown beer with a bitter hop finish underscored by malt and fruit.

Pandamonium *(OG 1050, ABV 4.8%)*
A dark brown beer with a distinct roast malt aroma, taste and finish.

Knickadroppa Glory *(OG 1054, ABV 5.5%)*

SWALE
Swale Brewery, Unit 1 D2 Trading Estate,
Castle Road, Sittingbourne,
Kent ME10 3RH
Tel (01795) 426871
Fax (01795) 410808
E-mail john.davidson
@swale-brewery.co.uk
Web-site www.swale-brewery.co.uk
Shop 11-4 Mon-Fri 11-2 Sat
Tours by arrangement

⊗ Swale Brewery was opened in 1995 in Milton Regis, expanded and moved to new premises on the east side of Sittingbourne in 1997. Cask ales are brewed on a regular basis and are changed four times a year. Four bottle-conditioned beers are brewed all year. Further expansion was carried out in 1999 giving the brewery a capacity of 80 barrels a week. 100 outlets are supplied direct. Bottle-conditioned beers: Whitstable Oyster Stout (OG 1045, ABV 4.5%), Indian Summer (OG 1050, ABV 5%), Kentish Gold (OG 1050, ABV 5%), Old Dick (OG 1051, ABV 5.2%).

Kentish Pride *(OG 1040, ABV 3.8%)*
A clean-tasting, light brown-coloured ale, dry-hopped with East Kent Goldings.

Copper Oast *(OG 1041, ABV 4%)*

Indian Summer *(OG 1043, ABV 4.2%)*
Won Champion Beer of Kent in 1997, originally a seasonal beer for autumn, now brewed all year round.

Cocklewarmer *(of 1050, ABV 5%)*

SWALED ALE
Swaled Ale Brewery, c/o West View,
Gunnerside, Richmond,
N Yorkshire DL11 6LD
Tel (01748) 886441
Tours by arrangement

⊗ Established in May 1995 by real ale drinker Fred Bristow, who was frustrated by the lack of local beer choice. The brewery was set up as an indulgence rather than a business to produce hand-crafted beers of a quality seldom achieved by bigger brewers handicapped by economic and commercial constraints. The two main outlets are the Kings Head, Gunnerside (the brewery tap) and the Punch Bowl Inn, Low Row, Swaledale. Beers appear regularly as guests and at CAMRA festivals. Swaled Ale beers are named after local lead mines.
Seasonal beers: Hoppy Christmas (OG 1044-46, ABV 4.5%), Winter Warmer (OG 1056-57, ABV 5.5%), Beldi Weiss Wheat Beer (OG 1056-57, ABV 5.5%, summer-autumn). Beers: Priscilla Pale (OG 1037-38, ABV 3.8%), Old Gang Bitter (OG 1044-46, ABV 4.4%), Surrender Ale (OG 1045-47, ABV 4.7%).

SWANSEA
☐ Swansea Brewing Company, Joiners,
50 Bishopston Road, Bishopston,
Swansea, SA3 3EJ Office: 74 Hawthorne
Avenue, Uplands, Swansea SA2 0LY
Tel Brewery (01792) 232658 Office 290197

☺ Opened April 1996, this is the first commercial brewery in the Swansea area for almost 30 years. It doubled its capacity within the first year and now produces five regular beers and occasional experimental ones. Three regular outlets are supplied direct plus various free trade outlets in the south Wales area. Occasional beers: St Teilo's Tipple (OG 1048, ABV 5.5%, Christmas), Barland Strong (OG 1052, ABV 6%), Railway Sleeper (OG 1060, ABV 7%).

Mumbles Light *(OG 1034, ABV 3.9%)*

Deep Slade Dark *(OG 1035, ABV 4%)*

Bishopswood Bitter
(OG 1038, ABV 4.3%) ⬚◆

A pale brown bitter with a delicate aroma of malt and an undertone of hops. A balanced bitter taste with a hint of caramel and sulphur leading on to a long, dry finish with some fruitiness.

Three Cliffs Gold *(OG 1042, ABV 4.7%)*

Original Wood *(OG 1048, ABV 5.2%)*

TALLY HO

◻ Tally Ho, 14 Market Street, Hatherleigh,
Devon EX20 3JN
Tel (01837) 810306
Fax (01837) 811079
Tours by arrangement

⊠ The Tally Ho hotel has revived the 200-year-old tradition of brewing on the same site. Its beers are produced from a full mash, with no additives, and, as well as sales at the pub itself, beer agencies now take the beers. Bottle-conditioned beer: Midnight Madness (ABV 5.5%). Beers: Market Ale (ABV 3.7%), Tarka's Tipple (ABV 4%), Nutters (ABV 4.6%), Midnight Madness (ABV 5%), Thurgia (ABV 6%).

TAP 'N' TIN*

◻ The Tap 'n' Tin Brew Pub, 24 Railway Street, Chatham, Kent ME4 4JT
Tel (01634) 847926
Tours by arrangement

The brewery was established in June 1999 in conjunction with the conversion of a former storage warehouse to a brew pub. Much of the décor of the pub has been created using tin sheeting from which the 'tin' part of the name has been derived. All of the wood used for the conversion is recycled. The brewing operations are carried out by the Flagship Brewery (qv), and production distributed to the brewery's regular outlets and to other outlets via wholesalers and other breweries. Beers: Caulkers Bitter (OG 1038, ABV 3.7%), Floggin (OG 1041, ABV 4.1%), Captins Tackle (OG 1041, ABV 4.2%), Yardarm (OG 1042, ABV 4.3%).

TAYLOR

Timothy Taylor & Co Ltd, Knowle Spring Brewery, Belina Street, Keighley, W Yorkshire BD21 1AW
Tel (01535) 603139
Fax (01535) 691167
Web-site www.timothy-taylor.co.uk

◉ Independent family-owned company established in 1858 and which moved to the site of the Knowle Spring in 1863. Its prize-winning ales, which use Pennines spring water, are served in all 23 of the brewery's pubs as well as 400 other outlets. A new boiler and cask washer were installed in 1999 and new fermenters were installed in July 2000 to increase production.

Golden Best *(OG 1033, ABV 3.5%)* ⬛◆
A clean-tasting and refreshing amber-coloured mild with a light hoppy taste, a hoppy, bitter finish and background malt and fruit throughout. A good session beer.

Dark Mild *(OG 1034, ABV 3.5%)* ◆
The malt of the underlying Golden Best combines with a caramel sweetness in this dark brown beer with a bitter aftertaste.

Porter *(OG 1041, ABV 3.8%)* ◆
Sweetness and caramel can dominate this beer if it is served too young. However, when mature, the sweetness is balanced by fruity flavours and bitterness in the finish.

Best Bitter *(OG 1037, ABV 4%)* ⬛◆
Hops and a citrus fruitiness combine well against some background malt in this drinkable bitter. Bitterness increases down the glass and lingers in the aftertaste.

Landlord *(OG 1042, ABV 4.3%)* ⬛◆
An increasingly dry, bitter finish complements the pungent hoppiness and complex fruitiness of this full-flavoured and well-balanced beer. Champion Beer of Britain 1999.

Ram Tam *(OG 1043, ABV 4.3%)* ◆
A dark brown winter beer with red hints. Caramel dominates the aroma and leads to sweetish toffee and chocolate flavours in the taste, well-balanced by the hoppy fruitiness of the underlying Landlord. Increasingly dry and bitter finish.

TEIGNWORTHY

Teignworthy Brewery, The Maltings, Teign Road, Newton Abbot, **Devon TQ12 4AA**
Tel (01626) 332066
Fax (01626) 330153
Shop 10-5 weekdays at Tuckers Maltings

⊠ Brewery established in 1994 by John and Rachel Lawton, now brewing 25 barrels a week for 50 outlets in Devon and Somerset. Beers are bottled on site. The brewing is based in the historic Tuckers Maltings; there are tours of the maltings and brewery every 45 minutes between Easter and the end of October. Tucker's shop stocks the full range of Teignworthy bottle-conditioned beers, and also has a mail order service. Seasonal beers: Christmas Cracker (OG 1060, ABV 6%, winter). Bottle-conditioned beers: as cask beers.

Reel Ale *(OG 1039.5, ABV 4%)* ◆
Clean, sharp-tasting bitter with lasting hoppiness; predominantly malty aroma.

Spring Tide *(OG 1043.5, ABV 4.3%)* ◆
An excellent, full and well-rounded mid-brown beer with a dry, bitter taste and aftertaste.

Beachcomber *(OG 1045.5, ABV 4.5%)* ◆
A pale brown beer with a light refreshing fruit and hop nose, grapefruit taste and a dry, hoppy finish.

Maltster's Ale *(OG 1049.5, ABV 5%)* ◆
Available Oct-April: a mid-brown full-flavoured beer with a hint of chocolate turning to vanilla. Strong malt aftertaste.

TEME VALLEY

⚲ Teme Valley Brewery, Talbot Inn,
Knightwick, Worcestershire WR6 5PH
Tel (01886) 821235 Fax (01886) 821060
Tours by arrangement

The brewery is based at the Talbot at
Knightwick in Worcestershire, owned and
run by the Clift family for 17 years. It is the
only inn that brews its own beer from its
own hops – though hop farmer Philip Clift
announced in June 2000 that he planned to
sell his farm and hop fields; he hoped that
new buyers would continue to grow hops,
currently Fuggles, Goldings and Bramling
Cross. A brewery was installed in the early
part of 1997 and now brews a range of beers
using the local hops and Maris Otter malt.
Hop Nouvelle is made with green hops taken
straight from the Worcestershire fields and
used undried to bring out their fresh aromatic flavour. Seasonal beer: Hop Nouvelle
(OG 1041, ABV 4.1%, Oct-Nov).

T'Other *(OG 1035, ABV 3.5%)* ✦
A subtle aroma of hops is followed by a fuller
taste that brings out the more understated
malts in this light bitter.

This *(OG 1037, ABV 3.7%)* ✦
A rich array of aromas is well-matched with
fruity/hoppy flavours that then lead to a delicate aftertaste.

That *(OG 1041, ABV 4.1%)* ✦
There are plenty of malty notes on the nose,
which then give way to a hoppiness balanced
with a roast background.

Wot Wassail *(OG 1058, ABV 6%)* ✦
A model stout with all the rich, chocolate
smack that defines this sharp, dry, flavoursome drink.

THREE B'S*

Three B's Brewery, Unit 19, Hamilton
Street, Blackburn, Lancs BB2 4AJ
Tel (01254) 208154
Tours by arrangement

Robert Bell designed and began building the
2-barrel brewery in October 1997. In October
1998 he obtained premises in Hamilton
Street, Blackburn to set up the brewery and
complete the project. The first beers went on
sale in January 1999; two bitters 3.8% and
4.3%. a mild at 3.6% and a strong pale ale at
5.2%. In May 1999 a 4.6% bitter was introduced. A 4.8% porter style beer replaced the
mild in October 1999. 20 outlets are supplied
direct. Beers: Bobbin's Bitter (OG 1039, ABV
3.8%), Tackler's Tipple (OG 1045, ABV 4.3%),
Pinch Noggin' (OG 1048, ABV 4.6%),
Knocker Up (OG 1050, ABV 4.8%), Shuttle
Ale (OG 1055, ABV 5.2%).

THREE HORSESHOES
See Shoes.

THREE TUNS
⚲ The Three Tuns Brewing Co Ltd,
The Three Tuns Inn,
Salop Street,
Bishop's Castle, Shropshire SY9 5BW
Tel (01588) 638797
Fax (01588) 638081
E-mail tunsinn.freeserve.co.uk
Web-site www.thethreetunsinn.co.uk
Tours by arrangement

⊗ The Three Tuns is a superb Victorian
miniature tower brewery producing
traditional ales and bottle-conditioned beers.
It's thought that brewing has taken place on
the site since 1642. Much of the original
19th-century equipment is still used, along
with the 17th-century timber-framed malt
store next to the brewery. A new brewer,
Malcolm Lane, is busily developing new
beers for cask and bottle. Three Tuns' beers
are used in the acclaimed dishes in the pub's
restaurant. Seven outlets are supplied direct
and beers are available via the web-site.
Occasional beers: Cleric's Cure (OG 1048,
ABV 5%), Bellringer (OG 1058, ABV 6.3%),
Old Scrooge (OG 1063, ABV 6.5%, winter).
Bottle-conditioned beer: Clerics' Cure (OG
1048, ABV 5%), Bellringer (OG 1058, ABV
6.3%), Old Scrooge (OG 1063, ABV 6.5%).

Sextons Bitter *(OG 1036, ABV 3.7%)*

XXX Bitter *(OG 1041, ABV 4.3%)*

Offa's Ale *(OG 1046, ABV 4.9%)*

THWAITES

Daniel Thwaites Brewery PLC,
PO Box 50, Star Brewery,
Blackburn,
Lancashire BB1 5BU
Tel (01254) 686868
Fax (01254) 681439
E-mail Info@Thwaites.co.uk
Web-site www.Thwaites.co.uk
Tours by arrangement

⊛ One of the oldest family-run Lancashire
firms, founded by excise officer Daniel
Thwaites in 1807 and still brewing at the
Star Brewery. It owns 390 tenanted pubs and
65 managed ones, with some 850 free trade
accounts. Investment in technology has
produced a modern brewhouse but
Thwaites' commitment to cask ales is undiminished. A brewery shop is due to open as
part of the visitor centre. Seasonal beers:
Bloomin' Ale (OG 1037, ABV 4%, spring),
Morning Glory (OG 1037, ABV 3.8%, summer), Golden Charmer (OG 1043, ABV 4.5%,
autumn), Winter Warmer (OG 1052, ABV
5.5%, winter).

Best Mild *(OG 1033, ABV 3.3%)* ✦
A rich, dark mild presenting a smooth, malty
flavour and a pleasant, slightly bitter finish.

Best Bitter *(OG 1036, ABV 3.6%)* ✦
A clean-tasting, refreshing session bitter,
combining bitterness and biscuity flavours
and with a lingering bitter finish.

Chairman's *(OG 1039, ABV 4.2%)*

Daniel's Hammer *(OG 1047, ABV 5%)*

TIGERTOPS

Tigertops Brewery, 22 Oakes Street,
Flanshaw, Wakefield,
W Yorkshire WF2 9LN
Tel (01924) 378538/ (01229) 716238
Tours by arrangement

⊚ Tigertops was established in 1995 by
Stewart Johnson, a former chairman of the
Wakefield branch of CAMRA, and his wife,
Linda. The Johnsons also now own the
Foxfield Brewery in Cumbria. Many of the
beers are made with Belgian and German
malts.

Dark Wheat Mild
(OG 1036, ABV 3.6%)

Axeman's Block
(OG 1036, ABV 3.6%)

Sessions *(OG 1038, ABV 3.8%)*

Dark Rye *(OG 1038, ABV 4%)*

Weiss Bier *(OG 1044, ABV 4.6%)*

Axeman Light *(OG 1046, ABV 5%)*

Martz Bier *(OG 1050, ABV 5.2%)*

Wheat Bock *(OG 1058, ABV 6.4%)*

TINDALL

Tindall Ales Brewery, Thwaite Road,
Ditchingham, Bungay, Suffolk NR35 2EA
Tel/Fax (01508) 518392
Tours by arrangement

The brewery is a family-run business established in October 1998 and is situated on the
edge of the medieval Tindall Wood. Twenty
outlets are supplied direct. All the beers are
available in bottle-conditioned form.

Summer Loving *(ABV 3.6%)*

Best Bitter *(ABV 3.7%)* ◆
The malty nose opens into a light but malty
taste. This pale brown bitter has a bitter-
sweet citrus background that persists into a
long, bitter finish.

Mild *(ABV 3.7%)* ◆
A dark red mild with a gentle roasted malt
nose. Roast is the dominant flavour throughout, masking a thin malty bitterness. The finish is light and quick with the bitterness now
matching the predominate roastiness.

Resurrection *(ABV 3.8%)*

Alltime *(ABV 4%)* ◆
A malt-based best bitter. This amber coloured
bitter has a malty nose as a lead into a malty
freshness that complements the sweet, fruity
overtones. A long ending develops a filling
hop and caramel feel.

Autumn Brew *(ABV 4%)* ◆
Classic old ale. Dark brown in colour and
rich in flavour. A plummy malt backbone
continues to the end and gives a smooth velvety feel. Caramel notes intrude, bringing in
a burnt edge to a superb, complex ale.

Christmas Cheers *(ABV 4%)*

Extra *(ABV 4.5%)* ◆
Deep malty bouquet. Initial taste heavy with
malt and citric bitterness. Residual hoppiness
is softened as the finish continues its malty
dominance. This bitter is tawny in colour
with a well-balanced clean feel.

TIPSY TOAD

⌂ The Tipsy Toad Brewery, St Peter's
Village, Jersey JE3 7AA
Tel (01534) 485556
Fax (01534) 485559
Tours by arrangement

⊠ A brew pub launched by Steve Skinner
(now brewing in Cornwall) in 1992 and
taken over by Jersey Brewery in December
1997. Under new head brewer Patrick Dean,
the Tipsy Toad is hoping to expand sales
throughout the Channel Islands, with the
Jersey Brewery distributing the beers through
its tied estate. Seasonal beers: Festive Toad
(OG 1077, ABV 8%).

Tipsy Toad Ale *(OG 1038, ABV 3.8%)*

Jimmy's Bitter *(OG 1042, ABV 4.2%)*

Horny Toad *(OG 1050, ABV 5%)*

Dixie's Wheat Beer *(OG 1041, ABV 4%)*

Naomh Pádraig's Porter
(OG 1045, ABV 4.4%)

TIRRIL*

⌂ Tirril Brewery, the Queen's Head Inn,
Tirril, Penrith, Cumbria CA10 2JF
Tel (01768) 863219
Fax (01768) 863243
E-mail brewery@queensheadinn.co.uk
Web-site www.queensheadinn.co.uk
Tours by arrangement (maximum four people at a time)

J Siddle's Tirril Brewery was closed in
September 1899, although not on the site of
the pub. Following the conversion of an old
toilet block, a 2.5-barrel plant was squeezed
in, with a copper mash tun in the ladies and
fermenters in the gents. Pub and brewery
stage an annual beer and sausage festival
every summer. Beers: John Bewsher's Best
Bitter (OG 1037.5, ABV 3.8%), Thomas Slee's
Academy Ale (OG 1040.5, ABV 4.2%).

TISBURY

Tisbury Brewery Ltd, Oakley Business
Park, Dinton, Salisbury, Wilts SP3 5EU
Tel (01722) 716622
Fax (01722) 716644
E-mail mail tis.brew@virgin.net
Tours by arrangement

⊠ Housed in the old village workhouse, converted by maltster Archibald Beckett in 1868
but rebuilt after a fire in 1885, the brewery
ceased production in 1914. It re-opened as
Tisbury Brewery in 1980 but this foundered,
leaving the premises to be taken over by
Wiltshire Brewery, which brewed here until
closing the site in 1992. The new Tisbury
Brewery took over the building and began
production in April 1995, but in the summer
of 2000 moved to a new site near Salisbury. It
now provides beer for more than 200 outlets,
using the slogan 'The small brewery with the
big taste'. Plans are underway to treble production capacity. Bottle-conditioned beers:
Stonehenge (ABV 4.2%), Fanfare, Ale Fresco,
Real Nut Ale. Seasonal beers, all OG 1045,
ABV 4.5%: Old Mulled Ale (Nov-Jan), Fanfare
(March-May), Ale Fresco (June-Aug), Real Nut
Ale (Sept-Oct).

Stonehenge *(ABV 3.8%)* ◆
A golden/amber-coloured beer with a malty

nose. The malty taste has hints of fruit and hop. Full-bodied for its strength.

2000 & Thirst *(ABV 4.2%)*
Available until 2001.

Archibald Beckett *(ABV 4.3%)* ◆
A malty, full-bodied, dark amber bitter with some caramel on the nose. Strong hop flavours come through in the taste.

Nadderjack *(ABV 4.3%)*
A golden, full-bodied, well-balanced bitter with a spicy hop finish.

TITANIC
The Titanic Brewery, Harvey Works, Lingard Street, Burslem, Stoke-on-Trent, Staffordshire ST6 1ED
Tel (01782) 823447
Fax (01782) 812349
Tours by arrangement

☺ Named in honour of the Titanic's Captain Smith, who hailed from Stoke, the brewery was founded in 1985 and moved to larger premises in 1991, installing new brewing plant in 1995. In 1996 Titanic began brewing for demonstration purposes on the log-fired Victorian micro-brewery in the Staffordshire County Museum at Shugborough Hall. The company now supplies more than 200 free trade outlets, as well as two pubs of its own. Seasonal beer: Christmas Ale (OG 1080, ABV 7.8%). Shugborough Brewery: Coachman's Tipple (ABV 4.7%, Jan-Feb), Butler's Revenge (ABV 4.9%, March-April), Milady's Fancy (ABV 4.6%, May-June), Farmer's Half (ABV 4.8%, July-Aug), Gardener's Retreat (ABV 4.7%, Sept-Oct), Lordship's Own (ABV 5%, Nov-Dec). Shugborough brews are also available in bottle-conditioned form in the same periods.

Mild *(ABV 3.5%)*

Best Bitter *(OG 1036, ABV 3.5%)* ◆
A crisp, clean, refreshing bitter with a good balance of fruit, malt and hops. Bitter finish.

Lifeboat Ale *(OG 1040, ABV 4%)* ◆
A fruity and malty, dark red/brown beer, with a fruity finish.

Premium *(OG 1042, ABV 4.1%)* ◆
An impressive, well-balanced pale brown bitter with hops and fruit in the aroma, which develop into a full flavour and a dry, hoppy finish.

Stout *(OG 1046, ABV 4.5%)* ◆
A dark combination of malt and roast with some hops. Strongly flavoured and well-balanced.

White Star *(OG 1050, ABV 4.8%)* ◆
A bitter-sweet amber ale with a fruity taste and a long fruit aftertaste.

Captain Smith's *(OG 1054, ABV 5.2%)* ◆
A full bodied, dark red/brown beer, hoppy and bitter with malt and roast malt flavours, and a long, bitter-sweet finish.

Wreckage *(ABV 7.2%)*

TOLLY COBBOLD
Tollemache & Cobbold Brewery Ltd, Cliff Road, Ipswich, Suffolk IP3 0AZ
Tel (01473) 231723
Fax (01473) 280045
E-mail tolly.cobbold@btconnect.com
Web-site site www.tollycobbold.co.uk
Shop for brewery tours only
Tours by arrangement

▨ Tolly Cobbold is one of the oldest brewing companies in the country, founded by Thomas Cobbold in 1723. After years of uncertainty under a succession of owners (Ellerman Shipping Lines, the Barclay Brothers and Brent Walker) the company has been independent for more than 10 years and has a small but growing pub estate of seven outlets and operates as a major wholesaler and contract distributor, supplying more than 700 product lines to the licensed trade in East Anglia. A new brewery was built in 1995 and the old Victorian tower brewery is used for fully-guided brewery tours for the public. The site has now become a major tourist attraction. 200 outlets are supplied direct. Seasonal beers: Cobnut Special (OG 1044.5, ABV 4.2%, September), Sunshine (OG 1044.5, ABV 4.5%, June-July), Tolly Shooter (OG 1049.5, ABV 5%, March-April), Old Strong Winter Ale (OG 1050.5, ABV 5%, Nov-Feb).

Mild *(OG 1032.5, ABV 3.2%)* ◆
A tasty mild with fruit, malt and roast malt characters, and a pleasing aftertaste. It tends to lose complexity when forced through a sparkler.

Bitter *(OG 1035.5, ABV 3.5%)* ◆
A light, mid-brown-coloured malty beer lacking bitterness.

Original Best Bitter
(OG 1038.5, ABV 3.8%) ◆
A slightly stronger bitter with assertive hop character throughout. The finish is bitter, but with a good balancing maltiness. Disappointingly hard to find.

IPA *(OG 1040, ABV 4.2%)*
A best bitter, full of citrus fruit flavours and flowery hoppiness.

Old Strong Winter Ale
(OG 1050, ABV 5%) ◆
Available Nov-Feb. A dark winter ale with plenty of roast character throughout. Lingering and complex aftertaste.

Tollyshooter *(OG 1050, ABV 5%)* ◆
A reddish premium bitter with a full, fruity flavour and a long, bitter-sweet aftertaste. Good hop character, too. Named after the Sir John Harvey-Jones TV series, Troubleshooter, in which Tolly featured.

TOMINTOUL

Tomintoul Brewery Co Ltd, Mill of
Auchriachan, Tomintoul, Ballindalloch,
Banffshire AB37 9EQ
Tel (01807) 580333
Fax (01807) 580358

⊛ Brewery opened in November 1993 in an
old watermill, in an area renowned for malt
whisky and salmon. Around 80 outlets are
currently supplied and wholesalers take the
beer into England and Northern Ireland. The
company was bought by Aviemore (qv) in
2000, which handles sales and distribution.
Seasonal ales: Scottish Bard (OG 1044, ABV
4.4%),Grand Slam (OG 1047, ABV 4.7%),
Caillie (OG 1040, ABV 4%), Trade Winds IPA
(OG 1049, ABV 4.5%), Black Gold (OG
1048.5, ABV 4.4%), Witches' Cauldron (OG
1049, ABV 4.9%), Saint's Ale (OG 1043, ABV
4.5%), Santa's Sledgehammer (OG 1058, ABV
6.3%). Stag is now available bottled, but not
bottle-conditioned.

Laird's Ale *(OG 1038, ABV 3.8%)* ◆
A well-balanced brew with some hops in the
lingering fruity finish.

Stag *(OG 1039.5, ABV 4.1%)* ◆
A powerful, malty nose with less hop character on the palate than in the early brews. This
tawny brew has a lingering, malty, gently bitter aftertaste.

Nessie's Monster Mash
(OG 1044, ABV 4.4%) ◆
A mahogany-coloured, full malty brew with
a creamy mouthfeel leading to a satisfying,
fruity finish.

Culloden *(OG 1046, ABV 4.6%)* ◆
Not as hoppy as the other Tomintoul beers,
but packed full of maltiness on the palate
and with a creamy, roast finish. A smooth,
full-bodied mid-brown brew.

Wild Cat *(OG 1049.5, ABV 5.1%)* ▯◆
A deep amber brew in the old ale style but
with a good balance of hops on the palate
and an intense, hoppy, fruity finish. Goes
well with stovies and oatcakes in front of a
real open fire in winter.

TOWNES

▯ Townes Brewery, Speedwell Inn,
Lowgates, Staveley, Chesterfield,
Derbyshire S43 3TT
Tel (01246) 472252
Tours by arrangement

⊠ Townes Brewery started in May 1994 in an
old bakery on the outskirts of Chesterfield
using a 5-barrel plant; it was the first brewery
in the town for more than 40 years. After a
period of steady progress, the Speedwell Inn
at Staveley was bought and the plant was
moved to the rear of the pub. The first brew
at Staveley was in November 1997 and, after
a period of renovation, the pub opened a
year later. It was the first brew pub in North
Derbyshire in the 20th century. It sells the
full range of Townes Beers. Small-scale
bottling is being considered. Twenty plus
outlets are supplied direct. Seasonal beers:
GMT (OG 1042, ABV 4.2%, winter), IPA
(OG 1045, ABV 4.5%, summer).

Sunshine *(OG 1036, ABV 3.6%)*
A light-coloured session beer with a full finish.

Golden Bud *(OG 1038, ABV 3.8%)*

Best Lockoford Bitter *(OG 1040, ABV 4%)*

GMT *(OG 1042, ABV 4.2%)*
A pale, spicy ale with a malty base and a
hoppy finish. Available winter only.

Staveleyan *(OG 1048, ABV 4.8%)*

TRAQUAIR

Traquair House Brewery Ltd, Traquair
Estate, Innerleithen, Peeblesshire,
Scotland EH44 6PP
Tel (01896) 831370
Fax (01896) 830639
E-mail enquiries@traquair.co.uk
Web-site www.traquair.co.uk
Shop and Brewery Museum 10.30-5.30 daily April-Oct
Tours by arrangement April-Sept

⊛ The 18th-century brewhouse is based in
one of the wings of Traquair House (more
than 1,000 years old) and was rediscovered
by the 20th Laird, the late Peter Maxwell
Stuart, in 1965. He began brewing again
using all the original equipment (which
remained intact, despite having lain idle for
more than 100 years). The brewery has been
run by Peter's daughter, Catherine Maxwell
Stuart, since his death in 1990. All the beers
are oak-fermented and 60 per cent of
production is exported (mostly bottled
Traquair House Ale and Jacobite Ale). Some
five outlets take the cask beer.

Bear Ale *(OG 1050, ABV 5%)* ◆
A powerful malt and fruit aroma precedes a
deep, rich taste bursting with fruit. This
lingers while subtly changing into a long-
lasting dry, bitter finish.

House Ale *(ABV 7.2%)*

Jacobite Ale *(ABV 8%)*

TRAVELLERS INN

▯ The Travellers Inn Brewing Company,
Tremerchion Road, Pen-y-Cefn, Caerwys,
Flintshire, North Wales CH7 5BL
Tel (01352) 720251

Pub-brewery that is not at present in production. The one beer is brewed for the pub by
Coach House.

Roy Morgan's Original Ale *(OG 1042)*

TRIMDON

Trimdon Cask Ales, Unit 2c, Trimdon
Grange Industrial Estate, Trimdon Grange,
Co Durham TS29 6PA
Tel (01429) 880967
Fax (01429) 882276

Small brewery that was launched in 1999. All
their beers have something to do with coal
seams or mines in general. Beers: Tilley Bitter
(ABV 4.3%), Busty Bitter (ABV 4.3%), Harvey
Bitter (ABV 4.9%), Pitprop Bitter (ABV 6.2%).

TRING

The Tring Brewery Company Ltd,
81-82 Akeman Street, Tring,
Hertfordshire HP23 6AF
Tel (01442) 890721
Fax (01442) 890740
Tours by arrangement

⊗ Established in 1992, this 32-barrel brewery brought brewing back to Tring after an absence of 50 years. The brewery supplies 30-60 outlets. Occasional beers are produced. Seasonal beer: Death or Glory Ale (OG 1070, ABV 7.2%, brewed October 25 to commemorate the Charge of the Light Brigade in 1854 and sold Dec-Jan). Bottle-conditioned beer: Death or Glory Ale (OG 1070, ABV 7.2%).

Finest Summer Ale *(OG 1037, ABV 3.7%)*
Available May-Sept; a refreshing summer ale with a proportion of wheat malt in the mash.

The Ridgeway Bitter
(OG 1039, ABV 4%) ✦
A beer with a pleasant mix of flowery hops, malt and fruit flavours before a dryish aftertaste.

Old Icknield Ale *(OG 1049, ABV 5%)*
A beer with a distinct, hoppy flavour and a dry, bitter aftertaste.

TRIPLE FFF

Triple fff Brewing Company, Unit 3, Old Magpie Works, Four Marks, Alton, Hampshire GU34 2DN
Tel/Fax (01420) 561422

Established in October 1997, and now working under the sole proprietorship of Graham Trott, Triple fff has made steady progress. An expansion from five to 10-barrel capacity is planned for the near future. Winner of 14 awards, the brewery supplies around 100 outlets and also uses wholesalers to distribute to all parts outside its own delivery area. Seasonal beer: Witches Promise (ABV 6%, also available in bottle).

Billericay Dickie *(ABV 3.8%)* ✦
Pale brown, moderately fruity and bitter, this beer has a slightly floral character imparted by the aroma hops used. Hints of crystal malt, peat and butterscotch add to the complexity of this bitter.

Pressed Rat & Warthog *(ABV 3.8%)* ▮▯✦
A dry, roasty dark brown mild with good body and a suggestion of blackcurrant. Moderately bitter, with a short dry and fruity finish.

After Glow *(ABV 4%)* ▮✦
A superbly hoppy, award-winning bitter. Straw-coloured, with honey and citrus fruit on the nose, the beer is well balanced, with a good body and an aromatic hoppy and fruity finish.

Moondance *(ABV 4.2%)* ✦
An amber-coloured best bitter, wonderfully hopped, with a huge hop aroma, balanced by bittering hops and malt. Bitterness increases in the finish as the fruit declines.

Stairway to Heaven *(ABV 4.6%)* ▯✦
An aroma of pale and crystal malts introduces this pale brown beer with a flavour of summer fruits. Well balanced, with a dry and fruity finish.

Dazed and Confused *(ABV 4.6%)* ✦
A strongish beer, pale yellow in colour, with pale and lager malts plus a suggestion of elder flower. Refreshing and only moderately bitter.

Comfortably Numb *(ABV 5%)*

Little Red Rooster *(ABV 5%)*

TRUEMAN'S

Sam Trueman's Brewery, Henley House, School Lane, Medmenham, Marlow, Buckinghamshire SL7 2HJ
Tel (01491) 576100
Fax (01491) 571764
E-mail Brewery@henleyhouse.co.uk
Web-site www.crownandanchor.co.uk

☺ Sam Trueman's beer was available through wholesalers throughout the country but, as a result of wholesalers not paying bills, the owners bought the Crown & Anchor in Marlow, where Best (cask) and Lager (unfiltered but pressurised) are always available, plus one of the other three brews, and three guest ales. Sam Truemans' beers are not sold anywhere else. Bottle-conditioned beer: Percy's Downfall (OG 1082, ABV 8.2%).

Best *(OG 1036, ABV 3.5%)*

Tipple *(OG 1041, ABV 4.2%)*

Bees Knees *(OG 1043, ABV 4.3%)*

Gold *(OG 1050, ABV 5%)*

Percy's Downfall *(OG 1084, ABV 8.2%)*
Available Christmas.

ULEY

Uley Brewery Ltd, The Old Brewery, Uley, Gloucestershire GL11 5TB
Tel (01453) 860120
E-mail uley.beer@cwccom.net
Tours by arrangement

⊗ Brewing at Uley began in 1833 at Price's Brewery and after a long gap the premises were restored and Uley Brewery opened in 1985. It serves 40-50 free trade outlets in the Cotswolds area. Seasonal beer: Pigor Mortis (OG 1062, ABV 6%, Nov-Dec).

Hogshead PA *(OG 1036, ABV 3.5%)* ✦
A pale-coloured, hoppy session bitter with a good hop aroma and a full flavour for its strength, ending in a bitter-sweet aftertaste.

Uley Bitter *(OG 1040, ABV 4%)* ✦
A copper-coloured beer with hops and fruit in the aroma and a malty, fruity taste, underscored by a hoppy bitterness. The finish is dry, with a balance of hops and malt.

Old Ric *(OG 1045, ABV 4.5%)* ✦
A full-flavoured, hoppy bitter with some fruitiness and a smooth, balanced finish. Distinctively copper-coloured.

Old Spot Prize Ale *(OG 1050, ABV 5%)* ✦
A distinctive full-bodied, red/brown ale with a fruity aroma, a malty, fruity taste, with a hoppy bitterness, and a strong, balanced aftertaste.

Pig's Ear Strong Beer
(OG 1050, ABV 5%) ✦

A pale-coloured beer, deceptively strong. Notably bitter in flavour, with a hoppy, fruity aroma and a bitter finish.

USHERS

Ushers Brewery Ltd, 68 Fore Street, Trowbridge, Wiltshire BA14 8HQ
Tel (01225) 763171
Fax (01225) 774289
Tour groups by arrangement

This famous West Country brewery, founded in 1824 by Thomas Usher, became part of the Watney Group (later Grand Met) in 1960. In 1991 Ushers regained its independence but in 1999 it merged with the Alehouse Company of Southampton, which renamed itself InnSpired Inns. In 2000 InnSpired closed the brewery to concentrate on a 1,000-strong estate of pubs. Some of the Usher's beers were transferred to the Thomas Hardy Brewery in Dorchester and will be supplied to InnSpired and other companies by Refresh UK, which operates at the Trowbridge address. See Pub Groups.

VALE

Vale Brewery Company, Thame Road, Haddenham, Buckinghamshire HP17 8BY
Tel (01844) 290008
Fax (01844) 292505
E-mail valebrewery@yahoo.com.uk
Tours by arrangement

⊠ After many years working for large regional breweries and allied industries, brothers Mark and Phil Stevens opened a small, purpose-built brewery in Haddenham. This revived brewing in a village where the last brewery closed at the end of World War II. The plant was expanded in November 1996 and now has a capacity of 40 barrels. All beer is traditionally brewed without adjuncts, chemicals, or preservatives. Around 200 local outlets take the beers. Seasonal beers: Hadda's Spring Gold (ABV 4.6%), Hadda's Summer Glory (ABV 4%), Hadda's Autumn Ale (ABV 4.5%), Hadda's Winter Solstice (ABV 4.1%), Good King Senseless (ABV 5.2%).

Black Swan Dark Mild *(ABV 3.3%)*

Notley Ale *(ABV 3.3%)* ◥
A refreshing copper-coloured session bitter with some malt in the aroma and taste, and an uncompromisingly dry finish.

Wychert Ale *(ABV 3.9%)*
A full-flavoured beer with nutty overtones.

Black Beauty Porter *(ABV 4.3%)*

Edgar's Golden Ale *(ABV 4.3%)* ◥
A golden, hoppy best bitter with some sweetness and a dry, bitter-sweet finish. An unpretentious and well-crafted beer.

VALHALLA*

Valhalla Brewery, Shetland Refreshments Ltd, Baltasound, Unst, Shetland ZE2 9DX
Tel/Fax (01957) 711658
Tours by arrangement

Valhalla Brewery opened in December 1997 on the island of Unst in the Shetland Isles, making it the most northerly brewery in Great Britain. It is run by husband and wife

team Sonny and Sylvia Priest plus some part-timers. The latest acquisition was a bottling plant installed in August 1999, which has greatly increased sales. As space is now limited, especially for tours, it is hoped to add a large store and visitor centre. Beers: Auld Rock (ABV 4.5%, cask and bottle), White Wife (ABV 3.8% cask, 4.5% bottle).

White Wife *(ABV 3.8%)* ◥
Predominantly malty aroma with hop and fruit, which remain on the palate. The after-taste is increasingly bitter.

VENTNOR

Ventnor Brewery Ltd, 119 High Street, Ventnor, Isle of Wight PO38 1LY
Tel (01983) 856161
Fax (01983) 856404
Web-site www.ventnorbrewery.co.uk
Shop 9-5
Tours by arrangement

⊠ Based on the Isle of Wight, Ventnor Brewery has been brewing the finest ales since the early 1840s. Using traditional recipes of malt, hops and the unique ingredient of St Boniface natural spring water, Ventnor Brewery continues the tradition of brewing high quality, hand-crafted cask and bottled ales for the island and beyond. Sixty outlets are supplied direct. All the beers are available in bottle, all but SunFire are available bottle conditioned. Seasonal ales are also available.

Golden *(OG 1040, ABV 4%)* ◥
Well-balanced, easy-drinking bitter with an interesting slight honey/yeasty aftertaste.

SunFire *(OG 1044, ABV 4.3%)* ◥
A generously and distinctively bittered amber beer that could be toned down if pulled through a sparkler.

Oyster Stout *(OG 1046, ABV 4.5%)* ◥
A thin stout/dark mild with real oysters in the brew.

Kangaroo *(OG 1048, ABV 4.8%)* ◥
Tawny sweetish, malty strong beer.

Wight Spirit *(OG 1050, ABV 5%)* ◥
Interesting pale, hoppy, strong bitter with a surprising reversal of flavours from taste to aftertaste.

Sandrock *(OG 1057, ABV 5.6%)* ◥
Unique and excellent novelty beer brewed with smoked malt, produced for the Scotch whisky market, lending a smooth peaty malt flavour not dissimilar to a good malt whisky.

VENTONWYN

Ventonwyn Brewing Company, Unit 2B, Grampound Road, Nr Truro, Cornwall TR2 4TB
Tel (01726) 884367
Tours by arrangement

Ventonwyn was founded by James Vincent, formerly of Vincent's Brewery in Grampound, which ceased brewing in January 1998 due to extensive fire in an old mill. The new brewery is named after a local tin mine and all the beers are named after defunct Cornish mines. There are plans to bottle beers. A new beer is brewed once a

month for the guest beer trade. Thirty outlets are supplied direct. Beers: Old Pendeen (OG 1040, ABV 4%), Levant Golden (OG 1040, ABV 4%).

VERULAM

Verulam Brewery, 134 London Road, St Albans, Hertfordshire AL1 1PQ
Tel (01727) 766702
Tours by arrangement

⊗ Brewery housed behind the Farmers Boy pub run by Viv and Tina Davies. A cask-conditioned lager, VB Lager, is also brewed and there are monthly specials.

Special *(OG 1037, ABV 3.8%)* ◆
Well-balanced session beer with a dryish aftertaste.

IPA *(OG 1039, ABV 4%)* ◆
Impressive straw-coloured, very hoppy and bitter beer.

Farmers Joy *(OG 1043, ABV 4.5%)* ◆
A malty beer with overtones of sweetness.

VILLAGE

See Hambleton.

WADWORTH

Wadworth & Co Ltd, Northgate Brewery, Devizes, Wiltshire SN10 1JW
Tel (01380) 723361
Fax (01380) 724342
E-mail sales@wadworth.co.uk
Web-site www.wadworth.co.uk
Shop Mon-Sat 9-7.30
Tours by arrangement (June via Devizes Festival and September Brewery Month)

⊗ Market town brewery set up in 1885 by Henry Wadworth and one of the few remaining breweries to sell beer locally in oak casks; the brewery still employs a cooper. Though solidly traditional, with its own dray horses, it continues to invest in the future and to expand, producing up to 2,000 barrels a week to supply a wide-ranging free trade in the South of England, as well as its own 250 pubs. All but two of the tied houses serve real ale and 6X remains one of the South's most famous beers, with national distribution through Whitbread, though this relationship may change under Whitbreadís new owner. Wadworth also owns two brew pubs: the Farmers Arms (qv) and the Red Shoot (qv). Seasonal/occasional beers: Summersault (ABV 1038, ABV 4%), Old Timer (OG 1055, ABV 5.8%, Dec-Jan), Valentines (OG 1043, ABV 4.5%, February), Easter Ale (OG 1043, ABV 4.5%), Hophouse Mount Hood Mild (OG 1034, ABV 3.4%, May), Malt & Hops (OG 1043, ABV 4.5%, September).

Henry's Original IPA
(OG 1035, ABV 3.6%) ◆
A golden brown-coloured beer with a gentle, malty and slightly hoppy aroma, a good balance of flavours, with maltiness gradually dominating, and then a long-lasting aftertaste to match, eventually becoming biscuity. A good session beer.

6X *(OG 1040, ABV 4.3%)* ◆
Copper-coloured ale with a malty and fruity nose and some balancing hop character. The flavour is similar, with some bitterness and a lingering malty, but bitter finish. Full-bodied and distinctive.

Summersault *(OG 1038, ABV 4%)* ◆
A pale, fragrantly hoppy, refreshing beer made with Saaz lager hops.

Farmers Glory *(OG 1046, ABV 4.5%)* ◆
This dark beer can be delightfully hoppy and fruity, but varies in flavour and conditioning. The aroma is of malt and it should have a dryish, hoppy aftertaste.

For Farmers Arms (Mayhem Brewery):

Odda's Light/Sundowner

For Red Shoot:

Everest Gold/Tom's Tipple

WARCOP

Warcop Country Ales, 9 Nellive Park, St Brides, Wentloog, Gwent NP1 9SE
Tel/Fax (01633) 680058

Brewery based in a converted milking parlour. Beers: Pit Shaft (ABV 3.4%), Arc Light (ABV 3.5%), Pitside (ABV 3.7%), Pit Prop (ABV 3.8%), Hilston Premier (ABV 4%), Casnewydd (ABV 4%), Black and Amber (ABV 4%), Steelers (ABV 4.2%), Furnace (ABV 4.5%), Dockers (ABV 5%), Black and Amber Special (ABV 5%), Black and Amber Extra (ABV 6%), Red Hot Furnace (ABV 9%).

WARDEN

See Merivales.

WARWICKSHIRE

The Warwickshire Beer Co Ltd, Cubbington Brewery, Queen Street, Cubbington, Nr Leamington Spa, Warwickshire CV32 7NA
Tel (01926) 450747
Fax (01926) 887357
Shop 8-12 Sat (weekdays ring first)
Tours by arrangement

A 6-barrel plant opened in a former village bakery by Phil Page, it was commissioned by Warwick District Council to produce a commemorative bottled beer to celebrate the redevelopment of Warwick market place. The brewery intends to expand a range of bottled beers and there are plans to buy a pub. Sixty outlets are supplied direct. Seasonal beer: St Patrick's Ale (OG 1044, ABV 4.4%). Regular beers: Best (OG 1039, ABV 3.9%), Ffiagra (OG 1042, ABV 4.2%), Castle Ale (OG 1046, ABV 4.6%), Golden Wonder (OG 1049, ABV 4.9%), Ragged Staff (OG 1055, ABV 5.5%), Blackjack (OG 1060, ABV 6%).

TOMOS WATKIN

Tomos Watkin Ltd, Phoenix Brewery, Unit 3, Century Park, Valley Way, Swansea Enterprise Park, Swansea SA6 8RP
Tel (01792) 775333
Fax (01792) 775779
E-mail enquiries@tomoswatkin.com
Web-site www.tomaswatkin.com
Shop 9-5
Tours by arrangement

☺ An aggressively expanding brewery that was established by Simon Buckley, formerly of Buckley's and Ushers, adopting the name of a Llandovery company that ceased production in 1928. Brewing commenced in December 1995 and Tomos Watkin now supplies 300-400 outlets. In July 2000, the brewery moved from Llandeilo to Swansea to a bigger, custom-built brewhouse. There are plans to expand the tied house estate to 20 pubs. The beer range is liable to change. The web-site, developed by Swansea University, is interactive and callers will be able to view the brewing process. Seasonal beers: Cwrw Haf (OG 1042, ABV 4.2%, summer), Dewi Sant (OG 1042, ABV 4.2%, Easter).

Whoosh (OG 1037, ABV 3.7%)

BB (OG 1040, ABV 4%) ◥
An amber-coloured beer with a short-lived hoppy and malty aroma. Hops, malt and a hint of fruit in the mouth lead to a building bitterness that overpowers sweetness in the aftertaste.

Cwrw Cayo (OG 1040, ABV 4%)

Merlin's Stout (OG 1042, ABV 4.2%)

OG (OG 1042, ABV 4.2%)

OSB (OG 1045, ABV 4.5%) ⬛◥
A delicate aroma of fruit and hops with

bitterness building and a hint of fruit, leading to a mellow finish.

Cwrw Santa (OG 1047, ABV 4.6%)

Canon's Choice (OG 1047, ABV 4.7%)

WAWNE*

Wawne Brewery, 14 Green Lane, Wawne, East Yorkshire HU7 5XT.
Tel (01482) 835400

Set up in April 1999 by home-brew enthusiast Mike Gadie in his garage. He delivers locally himself and through Clark's Kitchen and Small Beer. Waghen is the old name for Wawne.

Monks Mild (OG 1033, ABV 3.2%) ◥
This dark mild assaults the drinker with rich, roasted malt flavours. Strong roasted coffee mixes with a good balance of fruit and hops. Tasty throughout, it has a dry, bitter finish. A gem.

St Peters (OG 1037, ABV 3.8%) ◥
Fresh and fruity, this golden/copper coloured beer mixes both bitterness and sweetness well. The hop flavours come through to give a dry and bitter aftertaste.

Waghen (OG 1040, ABV 4.1%) ◥
An easily drinkable premium beer, amber in colour with a crisp mix of floral hops and fruitiness. Full flavoured with a hint of caramel.

WEATHEROAK

Coach and Horses Inn, Weatheroak Hill, Alvechurch, West Midlands B48 7EA
Tel (0498) 773894 (m) (0121) 445 4411 (eves)
E-mail
weatheroakales@withybed.fsnet.co.uk
Tours by arrangement

The brewery was set up in 1997 in an out-house of the Coach & Horses Inn by Dave and Pat Smith by agreement with pub own-ers Phil and Sheila Meads. The first brew was produced in January 1998. A real ale off-licence has been opened in nearby Alvechurch. There are plans to bottle beer in the near future. Wetheroak supplies 40 out-lets direct.

Light Oak (ABV 3.6%) ◥
Very dry throughout, this light bitter has lots of floral hoppiness to enjoy.

Weatheroak (ABV 4.1%) ◥
A distinctly sharp drink that is dry through-out with a malty undertone.

Celebration (ABV 4.2%) ◥
There is an evident fruity flavour to enjoy all the way to the finish in this premium bitter.

Redwood (ABV 4.7%) ◥
Richly malted flavours contrast well with a dry bitterness before closing with an arid aftertaste.

Triple Tipple (ABV 5.1%)
A hefty premium bitter with a fine combina-tion of malt and hops.

WEETWOOD

Weetwood Ales Ltd, Weetwood Grange, Weetwood, Tarporley, Cheshire CW6 0NQ
Tel (01829) 752377

☺ Brewery set up at an equestrian centre in 1993. In 1998, the 5-barrel plant was replaced by a 10-barrel kit. Around 100 regular customers are now supplied.

Best Bitter *(OG 1038.5, ABV 3.8%)* ◆
A clean, dry and malty bitter with little aroma. Bitterness dominates the finish.

Eastgate Ale *(OG 1044.5, ABV 4.2%)* ◆
Well-balanced, pale refreshing beer with malty, fruity taste and short, dry finish.

Old Dog Bitter *(OG 1045, ABV 4.5%)* ◆
A fuller-bodied version of the bitter: fruitier, with a hint of sweetness.

Oasthouse Gold *(OG 1050, ABV 5%)* ◆
Sweet, golden beer with some light malt and hop flavours. Typical Weetwood sharp aftertaste. It is deceptively drinkable for a beer of this strength.

WELLS

Charles Wells Ltd, Eagle Brewery, Havelock Street, Bedford MK40 4LU
Tel (01234) 272766
Fax (01234) 279000
E-mail postmaster@charleswells.co.uk
Tours by arrangement

☒ The largest independent family-owned brewery in the country established in 1876 and still run by descendants of the founder. The brewery has been on this site since 1976 and 290 of its 300 pubs serve cask ale, though about 50 per cent use cask breathers. Wells also supplies around 600 other outlets direct. A bottling line was added in 1996. Its export market of 23 countries earned it a Queen's Award for Export in 1997. In February 2000 Charles Wells bought the John Bull Pub Company in Europe from Allied Domecq, giving it a dedicated estate of 28 franchised outlets from central to eastern Europe. The company runs 40 other retail outlets in Europe, mainly in Italy and Spain.
Seasonal ales: Josephine Grimbley (OG 1041, ABV 4.1%).

Eagle IPA *(OG 1035, ABV 3.6%)* ◆
A refreshing, copper-amber session bitter with a well-defined citrus hop aroma and taste, and a nutty, malty background ending dry.

Bombardier Premium Bitter
(OG 1042, ABV 4.3%) ◆
Gentle citrus hop is balanced by traces of malt in the mouth, and this pale brown best bitter ends with a lasting dryness. Sulphur often dominates the aroma, particularly with younger casks.

Fargo *(OG 1050, ABV 5%)* ◆
A winter beer to search for. Hops, fruit and sulphur are prominent on the nose, followed by a bitter, citrus fruit flavour with a little malt to add a slight sweetness. Hops and fruit in the long, dry finish.

WELTONS

Weltons North Downs Brewery Ltd, Unit 24 Vincent Works, Vincent Lane, Dorking, Surrey RH4 3HQ
Tel (01306) 888655

☒ The brewery was conceived, designed and built by Ray Welton, a former beer wholesaler, and installed in a renovated milking parlour on Rugge Farm in Capel near Dorking in 1995. In 1997 the brewery moved to a factory unit in Dorking. 140 outlets are regularly supplied direct. The complete range of beers was taken on by Arundel (qv) in 2000: the range is liable to change.
Occasional beers: Easter Special (ABV 4.1%, March), May Gold (ABV 4.1%, May, a wheat beer), Tam O'Shanter (ABV 4.1%, January), Burning Wicket (ABV 4.4%, July), Coronation Ale (ABV 4.4%, May and June), Winter Old (ABV 4.5% December), Passion Ale (ABV 4.5%, February), Midsummer Passion (ABV 4.5%, June), St George's Special (ABV 4.6%, April), Bloody Bosworth Bitter Battle (ABV 4.6%, August), Guy Fawkes Revenge (ABV 4.6%, November), Wenceslegless (ABV 4.8%, December), IPA (ABV 4.9%), Abinger Hammer (ABV 5.2%, March and May), Wellingtoffs Cannon (ABV 5.4%), Dr French's Old Remedy (ABV 5.5%, November), Nelson's Cannon (ABV 5.6%, October).

Dorking Pride *(ABV 2.8%)* ◆
A remarkable resurrection of the loved and lost 'boy's bitter' style, this amber beer has an excellent hop flavour for its strength, good balance and a long, dry and bitter finish. Overall, this bitter has a far better flavour than many stronger beers.

Best Bitter *(OG 1038, ABV 3.8%)* ◆
Copper in colour, this beer tastes of a blend of pale and crystal malts with surprising roast undertones. Moderately bitter and dry finish.

Old Cocky *(OG 1043, ABV 4.3%)* ◆
An amber-coloured best bitter with a hoppy aroma, hints of crystal malt plus pale malt and a satisfyingly dry, hoppy finish.

Busy Lizzie *(ABV 4.6%)* ◆
This gingery beer is amber in colour with a suggestion of butterscotch and a dry, bitter and slightly fruity finish.

Summer Special *(OG 1048, ABV 4.8%)* ◆
A complex light golden beer, with deep malt fruitiness on the tongue, followed by hops and a deep aroma.

Tower Power *(OG 1050, ABV 5%)* ◆
A predominantly fruity copper-hued ale with a whisky malt character. Resinous in the mouth, hints of apple lead to a malty and bitter finish.

Old Harry *(OG 1051, ABV 5.2%)*
Easy drinking, golden copper-coloured beer with both malt and hop flavours. Available Oct-Jan.

WENTWORTH*

Wentworth Brewery Ltd, The Powerhouse, The Gun Park, Wentworth, Rotherham, S Yorkshire S62 7TF
Tel (01226) 747070
Fax (01226) 747050
E-mail paul@the-commercial.freeserve.co.uk
Tours by arrangement

Wentworth was built during the summer of 1999, using equipment from two defunct Sheffield breweries, Stones and Wards. Brewing started in August 1999 and the first brew, WPA, won Best Beer of the Festival and a festival organised by the Sheffield branch of CAMRA). Wentworth has a 10-barrel plant

The Good Beer Guide 2001

with scope, room and intention to increase to a 25-barrel brew length. The owners plan to create a small tied estate, beginning with the purchase of a brewery tap. Approximately 40 outlets are supplied direct. Occasional beer: Gunpark Dark (OG 1034, ABV 3.4%).

Venture *(ABV 3.6%)* ◆
A session bitter with a rather bitter taste that dominates the aftertaste.

WPA *(ABV 4%)* ◆
An extremely well-hopped IPA-style beer that leads to some astringency. A very bitter beer.

Best Bitter *(ABV 4.1%)* ◆
A hoppy bitter beer with hints of citrus fruits. A bitter taste dominates the aftertaste.

Oatmeal Stout *(ABV 4.8%)* ◆
Bucketfuls of roast and chocolate malts with coffee overtones lead to a bitter aftertaste.

Gryphon *(ABV 5.1%)* ◆
A golden, clean-tasting, full-bodied strong bitter with a bitter-sweet taste and aftertaste.

Rampant Gryphon *(ABV 6.2%)* ◆
A strong, well-balanced golden ale with hints of fruit and sweetness but which retains a hoppy character.

WEST BERKSHIRE
The West Berkshire Brewery Co Ltd, The Old Bakery, Yattendon, Thatcham, Berkshire RG18 0UE
Tel/Fax (01635) 202968 office and Brewhouse 1; 202638 Brewhouse 2
Tours strictly by arrangement only

⊠ A brewery established in 1995 by Dave and Helen Maggs in converted farm buildings in the grounds of the Pot Kiln pub, although the businesses are separate. Production started on a 5-barrel plant, but in 1999 a 25-barrel plant was added at a second site in Yattendon. The original plant remains at the Pot Kiln and will continue to brew the house beer, special brews, and will feed a new bottling plant. Alongside the new plant is the Yattendon Craft Gallery that sells the brewery's T-shirts, sweat shirts and mugs. More than 30 outlets take the beers regularly and they appear as guest ales in other pubs. Brick Kiln Bitter (OG 1041, ABV 4%) is only available at the Pot Kiln. Bottle-conditioned beer: The Last Order (OG 1057, ABV 6.4%)

Skiff *(OG 1036, ABV 3.6%)* ◆
A pale brown session bitter with a good balance of malts and a pleasant hop aroma bouquet.

Mr Chubb's Lunchtime Bitter *(OG 1037, ABV 3.7%)*

Maggs Magnificent Mild *(OG 1039, ABV 3.8%)* ◆
An easy-to-drink southern mild with a good balance of malt and hops for the style. This dark red-brown beer has a short, dry finish.

Good Old Boy *(OG 1041, ABV 4%)* ◆
A well-balanced, fruity and hoppy beer with some sweetness in the finish.

Good Ordinary Bitter *(OG 1042, ABV 4%)* ◆
A complex, fruity best bitter, copper in colour. Pale and crystal malts accompany a hint of chocolate and a vine fruit aroma.

Dr Hexter's Wedding *(OG 1042, ABV 4.1%)*
There are hints of grapefruit in this pale coloured beer, with strong hop aromas and a long, bitter finish.

Graft Bitter *(OG 1045, ABV 4.3%)* ◆
A well-balanced beer, with fruit aromas, a malty character and a bitter finish.

Dr Hexter's Healer *(OG 1050, ABV 5%)* ◆
A full-bodied, vinous and sweet, end-of-the-evening beer that tastes stronger than it is. Tawny in colour, fruity and warming, with masses of malt and roast character.

Gold Star *(OG 1052, ABV 5.2%)* ◆
A pale brown beer, fruity and deceptively strong, with well-balanced fruit, malt and hops.

WEST YORKSHIRE*
West Yorkshire Brewery, Victoria Buildings, Burnley Road, Luddendenfoot, Halifax HX2 6AA
Tel (01422) 885930
Tours by arrangement

Formerly the Black Horse Brewery, it was acquired by Jim King of the Drinks Link wholesale company. Brewing re-started in July 1999 and brewer David Sanders, formerly of the Feast & Firkin, Leeds, joined in December 1999. Beers: Baht'At (OG 1038, ABV 3.8%), Yorkshireman (OG 1041, 4.1%), Fear Nowt (OG 1045, ABV 4.5%). One-off beers are also produced.

WHEAL ALE
See Bird in Hand.

WHEATSHEAF INN
See Fromes Hill.

WHIM
Whim Ales, Whim Farm, Hartington, Nr Buxton, Derbyshire SK17 0AX
Tel (01298) 84991
Fax (01298) 84702

⊠ Brewery opened in 1993 in outbuildings at Whim Farm by Giles Litchfield who bought Broughton Brewery (qv) in 1995. There are plans for the two breweries to distribute each other's beers in their localities. Whim's beers are available in 50-70 outlets and the brewery's tied house, the Wilkes Head in Leek, Staffs. Some one-off brews are produced. Occasional/seasonal beers: Snow White (OG 1043, ABV 4.5%, a wheat beer); Special Ale (OG 1047, ABV 4.7%), Old Izaak (OG 1050, ABV 5%, winter), Bass's Wreck (ABV 5.5%), Black Christmas (OG 1065, ABV 6.5%, winter).

Arbor Light *(OG 1035, ABV 3.6%)*
Light-coloured bitter, sharp and clean with lots of hop character and a delicate light aroma.

538

Magic Mushroom Mild
(OG 1037, ABV 3.8%)
Ruby-black in colour, well balanced with a complex mix of flavours and a sweet finish.

Hartington Bitter *(OG 1038, ABV 4%)*
A light, golden-coloured, well-hopped session beer. A dry finish with a spicy, floral aroma.

Hartington IPA *(OG 1045, ABV 4.5%)*
Pale and light-coloured, smooth on the palate allowing malt to predominate. Slightly sweet finish combined with distinctive light hop bitterness. Well rounded.

WHITE

White Brewing Company, The 1066 Country Brewery, Pebsham Farm Industrial Estate, Pebsham Lane, Bexhill, E Sussex TN40 2RZ
Tel (01424) 731066

⊗ Brewery founded in May 1995 by husband-and-wife team David and Lesley White to serve local free trade outlets and some wholesalers, brewing five to 10 barrels a week. Visits by appointment only.

1066 Country Bitter *(OG 1040, ABV 4%)*
Amber-gold in colour, a light, sweetish beer with good malt and hop balance, and a bitter, refreshing finish.

WHITEWATER

Whitewater Brewing Co, 40 Tullyframe Road, Kilkeel, Co Down N Ireland BT34 4RZ
Tel/Fax (016967) 69449
Tours by arrangement

☺ Brewery founded in May 1996 on a farm outside Kilkeel with a 5-barrel brew length and 40-barrel conditioning capacity. It now supplies around 15 outlets in Northern Ireland, and other outlets throughout the British Isles via wholesalers, with beers that have already won beer festival prizes, including first at Belfast in 1996 and 1997. Seasonal/occasional beers: Cascade (OG 1040, ABV 4%), Solstice Pale (OG 1040, ABV 4%, summer), Mayflower (OG 1042, ABV 4.1%, summer), Bee's Endeavour (OG 1048, ABV 4.8%, summer), Knight Porter (OG 1050, ABV 5%, autumn/winter).

Best Bitter *(ABV 3.7%)*

Mountain Ale *(ABV 4.2%)*

Belfast Special Bitter *(OG 1046, ABV 4.5%)*

For Mill Ale: Glen Ale *(ABV 4.2%)*

WICKED HATHERN*

Wicked Hathern Brewery Ltd, 46 Derby Road, Hathern, Loughborough, Leics LE12 5LD.
Tel/fax (01509) 842 585
E-mail Brewery@Hathern.com
Tours by arrangement: small charge.

A 2.5-barrel brewery that opened in January 2000. Hathern is a Saxon word for hawthorn. Beers: Hawthorn Gold (OG 1035, ABV 3.5%), WHB (OG 1038, ABV 3.8%), Soar Head (OG 1048, ABV 4.8%). For other pubs: Sam's Enchanted Evening (OG 1048, ABV 4.8%).

WICKWAR

Wickwar Brewing Co, Arnolds Cooperage, The Old Cider Mill, Station Road, Wickwar, Gloucestershire GL12 8NB
Tel/Fax (01454) 294168
Shop 7.30-4.30 Mon-Fri
Tours by arrangement

⊗ Brewery launched on the 'Glorious First of May 1990' (Guest Beer Order day) by two Courage tenants with the aim of providing guest ales for their three tenancies. The business proved so successful that they dropped the pubs to concentrate on directly supplying their other regular outlets (now totalling around 150). The brewery operates from the cooper's shop of the old Arnold, Perret & Co brewery. Bottle-conditioned beers: Old Arnold (ABV 4.8%), Station Porter (ABV 6.1%).

Coopers' WPA *(OG 1036.5, ABV 3.5%)* ❧
Well-balanced, light, refreshing brew with hops, citrus fruit, apple/pear flavour and notable malt character. Yellow/gold in colour, it has a bitter, dry finish.

Brand Oak Bitter (BOB)
(OG 1039, ABV 4%) ❧
A distinctive blend of hops, malt and apple/pear and citrus fruits. The slightly sweet taste turns into a fine, dry bitterness with a similar malty lasting finish. Amber coloured.

Dogs Hair *(ABV 4%)*

Olde Merryford Ale
(OG 1048, ABV 4.8%) ❧
An amber/pale brown, full-flavoured, well-balanced ale, with malt, hops and cherry fruit throughout. Slightly sweet, with a long-lasting, malty, dry fruity and increasingly bitter finish.

Station Porter *(OG 1059, ABV 6.1%)* ▯❧
Rich, smooth, dark brown ale. Roast malt/coffee/chocolate/dark fruit aroma reflected in the complex and spicy, bitter-sweet taste. Long, smooth, warming, roast finish. Available Oct-Dec.

WILLY'S

▯ **Willy's Brewery Ltd, 17 High Cliff Road, Cleethorpes, Lincolnshire DN35 8RQ**
Tel (01472) 602145
Fax (01472) 603578
Tours by arrangement

☺ Brewery opened in 1989 to provide beer for two outlets in Grimsby and Cleethorpes. It has a 5-barrel plant with maximum capacity of 15 barrels a week. The brewery can be viewed at any time from pub or street.

Original Bitter *(OG 1038, ABV 3.8%)* ❧
A light brown 'sea air' beer with a fruity, tangy hop on the nose and taste, giving a strong bitterness tempered by the underlying malt.

Burcom Bitter *(OG 1044, ABV 4.2%)* ❧
A dark ruby colour, sometimes known as Mariner's Gold, although the beer is dark ruby in colour. It is a smooth and creamy brew with a sweet chocolate-bar maltiness, giving way to an increasingly bitter finish.

Last Resort *(OG 1044, ABV 4.3%)*

Weiss Buoy *(OG 1045, ABV 4.5%)*
A cloudy wheat beer.

Coxswains Special Bitter
(OG 1050, ABV 4.9%)

Old Groyne *(OG 1060, ABV 6.2%)* ✦
An initial sweet banana fruitiness blends with malt to give a vanilla quality to the taste and slightly bitter aftertaste. A copper-coloured beer reminiscent of a Belgian ale.

WINCHESTER*
Winchester Ale Houses Ltd, Head Office, 4A London Road, Horndean, Hants PO8 0BZ
Tel (020) 9259 2233
Tours by arrangement

Winchester Ales was started by Geoff Hartridge in November 1998 with the opening of the Blacksmiths Arms in Chichester. This was followed with the Hole in the Wall in Southsea. The Winchester Arms and Clarence Tavern opened in February and March 1999 respectively and brewing at both sites followed shortly, supplying all four pubs. Finally the White Horse in Wallington, Fareham, opened in September 1999. Seasonal/occasional beers: Anvil Bitter (OG 1036, ABV 3.6%), Coriander (OG 1040, ABV 4%), Maple Syrup Bitter (OG 1043, ABV 4.2%), Old Chapel Porter (OG 1044, ABV 4.4%, winter), Invincible Stout (OG 1046, ABV 4.5%, winter), Dragon Fire (OG 1049, ABV 5%, St Georges Day), Winchester Weiss (OG 1049, ABV 5%), True Blue (OG 1053, ABV 5.4%). Beers: Old Chapel Bitter (OG 1038, ABV 3.8%), Buckland Best Bitter (OG 1042, ABV 4.1%), Hole Hearted (Golden Ale) (OG 1048, ABV 4.7%), Blakes Gosport Bitter (OG 1053, ABV 5.2%).

WINFIELDS
⚑ **Winfields Brewery, The Raven, Bedford Street, Portsmouth, Hampshire PO5 4BT**
Tel (023) 9282 9079

⊗ Small pub brewery set up in 1995, just serving the pub itself and only brewing occasionally. Beers: Mild (ABV 3.5%), Bitter (ABV 3.7%), Stout (ABV 3.8%), Winter Brew (ABV 4.5%).

WOLF
The Wolf Brewery Ltd, 10 Maurice Gaymer Road, Attleborough, Norfolk NR17 2QZ
Tel (01953) 457775 Fax (01953) 457776
E-mail sales@wolfale.demon.co.uk
Web-site www.wolfale@demon.co.uk
Tours by arrangement

⊗ Brewery founded by the former owner of the Reindeer Brewery in 1996, using a 20-barrel plant housed on the site of the old Gaymer's cider orchard. 200 outlets are supplied direct.

Golden Jackal *(OG 1039, ABV 3.7%)* ✦
A singularly hoppy golden bitter with strong bitter overtones. This moves on to a quick dry finish that emphasises the bitterness.

Wolf In Sheeps Clothing
(OG 1039, ABV 3.7%) ✦
A strong malty aroma introduces a complex mix of malt, hops and bitterness. Caramel notes merge with a roasty, nutty finish to complement the consistent fruity bitterness.

Wolf Bitter *(OG 1041, ABV 3.9%)* ✦

Consistent bitterness supports an honest hoppiness. A growing peachy fruitiness is apparent the longer the finish progresses. A session beer with a difference.

Coyote Bitter *(OG 1044, ABV 4.3%)* ⬚✦
Something for everyone in this wide-ranging amber/golden beer. The rounded fruitiness matches the hoppy notes without overpowering the bitter-sweet background. A well-rounded but quick finish with subtle sweetness.

Newshound 2000 *(ABV 4.5%)* ✦
Amber malt provides rich colour, a distinct nose and a solid malty base. Old English Herald hops add balance and a refreshing bitterness. Slow-burning finish with a hint of caramel.

Woild Moild *(OG 1048, ABV 4.8%)* ✦
Old-fashioned beer with dominant roast malt backbone. The residual blackcurrant fruitiness sweetens the bitterness in the well-balanced finish. A flavoursome, well-balanced, dark brown beer.

Granny Wouldn't Like It
(OG 1049, ABV 4.8%) ▦⬚✦
Unusual caramel base binds all the flavours of beer in a symphony of taste. Malt, hops, fruit sweetness and bitterness all flow in balanced proportions.

Timber Wolf *(OG 1060, ABV 5.8%)* ✦
Strong elderberry notes give a rich, warm flavour base. Other flavours masked by the initial fruity sharpness. A soft bitterness can be found in the aftertaste as the richness loses its initial intensity.

WOLVERHAMPTON & DUDLEY
See Banks's, Camerons, Mansfield and Marston's.

WOOD
The Wood Brewery Ltd, Wistanstow, Craven Arms, Shropshire SY7 8DG
Tel (01588) 672523 Fax (01588) 673939
Tours by arrangement

⊗ The brewery was started in 1980 in buildings next to the Plough Inn. Several expansions of the premises have taken place and the Sam Powell Brewery and its beers were acquired in 1991. Production averages 60 barrels a week and future plans include increased fermentation capacity, more storage and a brewery visitor centre. 200 outlets are supplied direct. One pub is owned at present. Seasonal/occasional beers: Ironmasters (OG 1037, ABV 3.6%), Summer That! (OG 1039, ABV 3.9%), Hell For Leather (OG 1039, ABV 4%), Woodcutter (OG 1042, ABV 4.2%), Saturnalia (OG 1041, ABV 4.2%), Breast Stroke (OG 1043, ABV 4.3%), Governor's IPA (OG 1044, ABV 4.5%), Wheatear (OG 1044, ABV 4.5%), Holy Cow (OG 1046, ABV 4.5%), Natural Selection (OG 1048, ABV 4.6%), Get Knotted (OG 1047, ABV 4.7%), Hopping Mad (OG 1047, ABV 4.7%), Remembrance Ale (OG 1049, ABV 4.8%), Anniversary Ale (OG 1050, ABV 5%), Bonfire Brew (OG 1054, ABV 5.4%), Old Fireside (OG 1056, ABV 5.5%), Christmas Cracker (OG 1061, ABV 6%). Bottle-conditioned beers: Armada (OG 1040, ABV 4%), Hopping Mad (OG 1047,

ABV 4.7%), Shropshire Lad (OG 1051, ABV 5%), Christmas Cracker (OG 1061, ABV 6%).

Wallop *(OG 1034, ABV 3.4%)*

Sam Powell Best Bitter
(OG 1034, ABV 3.4%)

Sam Powell Original Bitter
(OG 1037, ABV 3.7%)

Parish Bitter *(OG 1040, ABV 4%)* ◆
A blend of malt and hops with a bitter after-taste. Pale brown in colour.

Special Bitter *(OG 1042, ABV 4.2%)* ◆
A tawny brown bitter with malt, hops and some fruitiness.

Shropshire Lad *(OG 1045, ABV 4.5%)*

Sam Powell Old Sam *(OG 1046, ABV 4.6%)*

Wonderful *(OG 1048, ABV 4.8%)* ◆
A mid-brown, fruity beer, with a roast and malt taste.

WOODBURY
Woodbury Brewery, Home Farm Cottage, Great Witley, Worcs WR6 6JJ
Tel (01299) 896219
Tours by arrangement

Brewery set up in 1997 in a stable block by Peter Kent as a part-time venture. The output from this 5-barrel plant is sold through free trade outlets in Worcestershire, Herefordshire and Shropshire.

White Goose *(OG 1039, ABV 3.8%)* ◆
Richly flavoured with sharp, pungent hops, this is one for bitter drinkers to enjoy.

Old House Bitter *(OG 1044, ABV 4.3%)*

Monumental Bitter *(OG 1051, ABV 5%)*

WOODFORDE'S
Woodforde's Norfolk Ales (t/a Woodforde's Ltd), Broadland Brewery, Woodbastwick, Norwich, Norfolk NR13 6SW
Tel (01603) 720353
Fax (01603) 721806
E-mail info@woodfordes.co.uk
Web-site www.woodfordes.co.uk
Shop 10.30-3.30 Mon-Fri 11.30-3.30 Sat-Sun May-Sept; closed Oct-April
Tours by arrangement

⊠ Founded in 1981 in Drayton near Norwich, Woodforde's moved to a converted farm complex, with greatly increased production capacity, in the picturesque Broadland village of Woodbastwick in 1989. It brews an extensive range of beers and runs three tied houses with some 250 other outlets supplied on a regular basis. Bottle-conditioned beers: Wherry Best Bitter (OG 1038, ABV 3.8%),

Great Eastern Ale (OG 1043, ABV 4.3%), Nelson's Revenge (OG 1045, ABV 4.5%), Norfolk Nog (OG 1049, ABV 4.6%), Baldric (OG 1052, ABV 5.6%), Norkie (OG 1050, ABV 5%), Headcracker (OG 1069, ABV 7%), Norfolk Nips (OG 1085, ABV 8.5%). With the exception of Norfolk Nips, these are only sold at the Woodforde's Visitor Centre.

Mardler's Mild *(OG 1035, ABV 3.5%)* ◆
Smooth and gentle, this dark red beer has no overwhelming flavours. An insistent roast maltiness provides a counter to the bitter-sweet fruitiness and a short but light finish.

Ketts Rebellion *(OG 1036, ABV 3.6%)* ◆
Brewed to celebrate the 450th anniversary of Kett's Rebellion, this moderately bitter session beer retains a hoppiness to the finish. Sweet caramel notes fade in the finish.

Wherry Best Bitter
(OG 1038, ABV 3.8%) ▮▯◆
Amber in colour with golden syrupy flavour that binds a well-balanced classic creamy bitter. A fine blend of hops, bitterness and fruit gives a light but complex feel. A long, consistent finish with little flavour loss.

Great Eastern Ale *(OG 1043, ABV 4.3%)* ◆
Brewed in 1994 for the 150th anniversary of the Great Eastern Railway, using pale and lager malts. These bring an initial light maltiness that complements the fruity bitterness of English hops. Inherent sweetness soon ends.

Nelson's Revenge *(OG 1045, ABV 4.5%)* ◆
A full-bodied pale amber beer with the rich flavour of Dundee cake. Sultana fruitiness is balanced by a hoppy bitterness to give a full but light feel. The finish continues to develop into a warm, mellow glow.

Norkie *(OG 1050, ABV 5%)* ◆
Named after the Norfolk farmworkers who travelled to Burton to work in the breweries there, and aimed at the lager drink. Light on the tongue with a sweet, fruity flavour but little underlying hoppiness. Malty finish is short but defined.

Norfolk Nog *(OG 1049, ABV 4.6%)* ▯◆
A traditional Norfolk recipe, this reddish beer has an initial explosion of roast malt bitterness. This settles down as a malty sweetness makes its presence felt. Maintains a dominant roast dryness to the end.

Headcracker *(OG 1069, ABV 7%)* ▮▯◆
Pale copper colouring and a mellow nose are pleasantly deceptive. A full-bodied plummy flavour with a palatably bitter edge. Continues to a mature maple finish to the end of the glass.

WOODHAMPTON
Woodhampton Brewing Co, Woodhampton Farm, Aymestrey, Leominster, Herefordshire HR6 9TA
Tel (01568) 770503
Tours by arrangement

⊠ Woodhampton opened in May 1997 in the heart of the Herefordshire countryside using its own spring water supply. It is currently a 5-barrel plant supplying around 30 pubs in the locality.

Red Kite *(OG 1036, ABV 3.6%)*

Jack Snipe *(OG 1041, ABV 4.1%)*

Kingfisher Ale *(OG 1044, ABV 4.4%)*

Wagtail *(OG 1048, ABV 5%)*

WOODY WOODWARD'S

See Fox & Hounds, Shropshire.

WORFIELD

**Worfield Brewing Co Ltd, Unit 1A
The Bullring, Station Lane, Off Hollybush
Road, Bridgnorth, Shropshire WV16 4AR
Tel (01746) 769606**
Tours by arrangement

Set up in 1994 at the Davenport Arms, the
plant of the Red Cross Brewery was purchased and the brewery relocated in 1998. It
has relocated again to the above address,
which is on the same water supply as the previous premises. Future plans include moving
yet again to converted farm buildings to
enable expansion and possibly bottling.
The brewery sells beer wholesale to 23 free
trade outlets. There are occasional special
brews such as Hermitage Old Ale
(OG 1092, ABV 8.8%).

JLK Pale Ale *(OG 1037, ABV 3.8%)*

Hopstone Bitter *(OG 1040, ABV 4%)*

Nailers OBJ *(OG 1041, ABV 4.2%)*

Shropshire Pride *(OG 1046, ABV 4.5%)*

Burcote Premium Pale
(OG 1050, ABV 4.9%)

Reynolds Redneck *(OG 1057, ABV 5.5%)*

WORLDHAM

**Worldham Brewery, Smiths Farm, East
Worldham, Alton, Hampshire GU34 3AT
Tel (0420) 83383
Fax (0420) 83600**
Tours by arrangement

Located in the Hampshire hop-growing area
in an old oast house.

Old Dray *(OG 1042-44, ABV 4.4%)*

Barbarian *(OG 1050-52, ABV 5.2%)*

WYCHWOOD

**The Wychwood Brewery Co Ltd,
Eagle Maltings, The Crofts, Witney,
Oxon, OX8 7AZ
Tel (01993) 702574
Fax (01993) 772553
E-mail intray@wychwood.co.uk
Web-site www.wychwood.co.uk**
Shop 9-5 Mon-Fri
Tours only for CAMRA branch visits

⊠ Set up as Glenny Brewery in 1983, in the
old maltings of the extinct Clinch's brewery,
Wychwood moved to a new site in 1987 and
was radically revamped during 1992, when
nine pubs were acquired (leased from Allied
Domecq or Inntrepreneur) by its sister company Hobgoblinns Ltd. The company now
runs 30 managed pubs (10 free of the tie, the
rest tied) in towns across the South and
South-west, all re-styled in the bare boards
and breweriana idiom, most renamed
Hobgoblin and all taking real ale. Wychwood
also supplies about 70 other outlets. As a con-
sequence of the extra demand, the brewery

moved back to the old Clinch's site in 1994.
It is now brewing more than 500 barrels a
week. Seasonal beer: Black Wych (February),
Fiddlers (ABV 4%, May), Dogs Bollocks
(November), plus a seasonal brew for every
month.

Shires XXX *(OG 1036, ABV 3.7%)* ✦
A copper-coloured session beer with a fruity
and malty aroma and admirable hop character. Good body for its strength. Fruit declines
to a dry finish.

Fiddler's Elbow *(ABV 4%)* ✦
A spicy amber beer, complex, with a spicy hop
aroma and a suggestion of cinnamon. Easy to
drink, with a crisp and refreshing finish.

Special *(OG 1042, ABV 4.2%)* ✦
Tawny best bitter with a characteristic apple
aroma and taste balanced by some malt and
hops. A dry and bitter finish.

The Dog's Bollocks
(OG 1052, ABV 5.2%) ✦
A strong golden beer reminiscent of hot cross
buns. Fruity, malty and sweet with butterscotch notes. Brewed only in November.

Hobgoblin *(ABV 4.5%)* ✦
Powerful, full-bodied, copper-red, well-balanced brew. Strong in roasted malt, with a
moderate, hoppy bitterness and a slight
fruity character. (Sept-March).

Black Wych *(ABV 5%)* ✦
A complex, dark red-brown stout with lots of
roast barley and hints of blackcurrant, leading to a dry and moderately hoppy finish.

WYE VALLEY

**Wye Valley Brewery Ltd, 69 St Owen
Street, Hereford HR1 2JQ
Tel 01432 342546 Fax 01432 266553**

⊠ The Wye Valley Brewery was launched in
1985 at the Nags Head in Canon Pyon,
Herefordshire. It moved to the rear of the
Barrels pub at the above address in 1986. A
22-barrel plant was installed in 1992 and a
considerable expansion to the brewery was
also undertaken. The beers are distributed
locally weekly and to many parts of the
country on a monthly basis by the brewery's
own transport.

Bitter *(OG 1036, ABV 3.5%)* ✦
A beer whose aroma gives little hint of the
bitter hoppiness that follows right through
to the aftertaste.

Dorothy Goodbody Traditional Bitter
(OG 1038, ABV 3.8%) ✦

Hereford Pale Ale *(OG 1040, ABV 4%)* ✦
A pale, hoppy, malty brew with a hint of
sweetness before a dry finish.

Dorothy Goodbody Springtime Ale
(OG 1040, ABV 4%)

Dorothy Goodbody Summertime Ale
(OG 1042, ABV 4.2%)

Dorothy Goodbody Autumn Delight
(OG 1044, ABV 4.4%)

Butty Bach *(OG 1046, ABV 4.5%)*

Dorothy Goodbody Wholesome Stout
(OG 1046, ABV 4.6%) ▆✦
A smooth and satisfying stout with a bitter
edge to its roast flavours. The finish combines
roast grain and malt.

Independent Breweries W/Y

Dorothy Goodbody Winter Tipple
(OG 1047, ABV 4.7%)

Travellers Best *(OG 1050, ABV 5%)*

Dorothy Goodbody Christmas Ale
(OG 1060, ABV 6%)

WYRE PIDDLE
Wyre Piddle Brewery,
Craycombe Farm, Fladbury,
Nr Evesham, Worcestershire
WR10 2QS
Tel/Fax (01386) 860473

⌧ Brewery established by a former publican
and master builder in a converted stable in
1992. The brewery owns five pubs and
around 200 pubs in the south Midlands take
the beers. The brewery relocated and
upgraded its equipment in 1997. For the
Green Dragon, Malvern: Dragon's Downfall
(ABV 3.9%), Dragon's Revenge (ABV 4%). For
Severn Valley Railway: Royal Piddle (ABV
4.2%). Bottle-conditioned beer: Piddle in the
Hole (ABV 4.6%).

Piddle in the Hole
(OG 1039, ABV 3.9%) ◕
Copper coloured and quite dry with lots of
hops and fruitiness throughout.

Piddle in the Wind *(ABV 4.5%)* ◕
This drink has a superb mix of flavours. A
nice hoppy nose through to a lasting aftertaste makes it a good, all-round beer.

Piddle in the Snow *(ABV 5.2%)* ◕
A dry, strong taste all the way through draws
your attention to the balance between malt
and hops in the brew. A glorious way to end
an evening's drinking.

YATES
Yates Brewery, Ghyll Farm,
Westnewton, Carlisle,
Cumbria CA5 3NX
Tel/fax (016973) 21081
E-mail
graeme@yatesbrewery.freeserve.co.uk
Tours by arrangement

☺ Established in 1986 in range of outbuildings at Ghyll Farm, Westnewton, the brewery was bought in 1998 by Graeme and
Caroline Baxter, who had previously owned
High Force Brewery in Teesdale. More beers
have been added to the range and direct distribution now includes Tyneside and
Wearside in addition to the traditional
stronghold of the Lake District. Fifty outlets
are supplied direct. Occasional beers:
Collabortion (OG 1035, ABV 3.5%), Best
Cellar (OG 1052, ABV 5.8%).

Bitter *(OG 1035, ABV 3.7%)* ◕
Caramel and hop flower aromas with
refreshing, intense hoppiness and fresh
maltiness, followed by a bitter and malty
end. Caramel/butterscotch flavours
throughout.

No 3 *(OG 1040, ABV 4.2%)*

XB *(OG 1043, ABV 4.5%)*

Premium *(OG 1048, ABV 5.2%)* ◕
Yellow beer with malty caramel tastes balanced by the rising bitterness to give a well-
balanced beer with consistent appeal.

YORK
The York Brewery Company Ltd, 12 Toft
Green, Micklegate, York, YO1 6JT
Tel (01904) 621162 Fax (01904) 621126
Web-site www.yorkbrew.demon.co.uk
E-mail aw@yorkbrew.demon.co.uk
Shop 11-8 daily
Tours daily

☺ York started production in 1996, the first
brewery in the city for 40 years. A visitor centre, gift shop and bar were added in 1999. It
is designed as a show brewery, with a gallery
above the 20-barrel brew plant giving visitors
a view of the fermenting and conditioning
rooms. There are plans to open its own pub
in York city centre. More than 400 pubs take
the beer. Occasional/seasonal beers: Mildly
Mad (ABV 3.3%), 100 Not Out (ABV 3.9%),
Last Drop Bitter (ABV 4.5%), Bug Bitter
(ABV 4.6%), Stocking Filler (ABV 4.8%).

Stonewall *(ABV 3.7%)* ◕
A light amber bitter with little maltiness but
strong hop and fruit aromas and flavours.
Clean-tasting, its hoppiness leads to a dry,
bitter finish.

Brideshead Bitter *(ABV 4%)* ◕
Hoppy and fresh-tasting with some fruit and
a citrus note. A good session ale with a
slightly dry finish.

Yorkshire Terrier *(ABV 4.2%)* ◕◕
Refreshing and distinctive, well-balanced
fruit and hops in the aroma and taste, with a
background of malt. Hoppy bitterness
remains assertive in the aftertaste of this
amber-gold brew.

Centurion's Ghost Ale *(ABV 5%)* ◕
Dark ruby in colour, full-tasting with mellow
roast malt character balanced by bitterness
that lingers into the aftertaste. Hops and fruit
in the mouth.

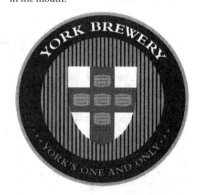

YOUNG'S
Young & Co's Brewery PLC,
The Ram Brewery, High Street,
Wandsworth, London SW18 4JD
Tel (020) 8875 7000 Fax (020) 8875 7100
Web-site www.youngs.co.uk/
Shop 10-6, Mon-Sat
Daily tours of the brewery and stables.
Tel: (020) 8875 7005

⌧ Beer has been brewed continuously here
since 1581, making it the oldest site in
Britain for beer production. The present

brewery was founded in 1675 and bought by Charles Young & Anthony Bainbridge in 1831; the business was continued by the Young family and, although it is a public company, it remains very much a family affair. Young's was the only London brewer to eschew the keg revolution in the 1970s. The company brews award-winning beers in the traditional manner and also produces up to four seasonal beers. Even its keg lagers are brewed to the German Purity Law. More than 1,000 free-trade outlets are supplied throughout Britain, concentrated in London and the South-east. Young's growing tied estate stands at more than 180 pubs. The brewery has outlawed pouring back spilt or unsold beer in its tied houses and recommends the use of cask breathers only if its smallest casks cannot be consumed within three days. Bottle-conditioned beer: Special London Ale (ABV 6.4%) ⬚.

Bitter *(OG 1036, ABV 3.7%)* ⬚◈
Initial maltiness is soon overcome by a bitter hoppiness that lingers. Malt predominates on the nose of this golden brown beer.

Triple A *(OG 1040, ABV 4%)*
A new pale summer beer aimed at younger drinkers.

Special *(OG 1046, ABV 4.6%)* ◈
Malty and fruity with good balancing hop character. Bitter-sweet in the finish.

Waggle Dance *(OG 1049, ABV 5%)* ⬚
Beer brewed with honey. The brand was bought from the Vaux/Swallow Group in the summer of 1999 and is available cask-conditioned and in bottle.

Winter Warmer *(OG 1055, ABV 5%)* ⬚◈
A dark reddish-brown ale with a roast malt aroma and flavour, leading to a sweet, fruity finish. Caramel is also present throughout. Available Oct-March.

R.I.P.

The following breweries closed since the 2000 edition.

Aldchlappie, Kirkmichael, Perthshire

Backdykes, Thornton, Fife

Baynards, Rudgwick, W Sussex

Bevvied Bull, Burton-on-Trent

Blackawton, Devon (though new owners are hoping to revive it)

Brecknock, Ystradgynlais, Swansea

Easingwold, N Yorkshire

Fox & Hounds, Stottesdon

Hoskins, Leicester

Kent, Deal

King & Barnes, Horsham

Ledbury, Herefordshire

Mitchells, Lancaster

Morland, Abingdon

Scott's, Lowestoft

Steam Packet, Knottingley

Stony Rock, Stoke-on-Trent

Tudor, Reading

Ushers, Trowbridge

Worth, Keighley

IN RECEIVERSHIP:

Four Rivers, Newcastle-on-Tyne

Jollyboat, Bideford

Lugton, Ayrshire

New Breweries

The following new breweries were reported as the Guide was being completed. Some of them may not yet be in full production.

Bluebell
⬚ Bluebell Brewery, Bluebell Inn, Cransegate South, Whaplode St Catherines, Spalding, Lincolnshire PE12 6SN
Tel (01406) 540300

Clarence
Clarence Tavern & Old Chapel Brewery, 1 Clarence Road, Gosport, Hants PO12 1BB
Tel (01705) 529726 (pub)
⬚ Pub owned by InnSpired (Pub Groups qv) but which continues to brew.

Donoghue
⬚ Donoghue Brewing Co, Black Horse Inn, Mill Lane, Grainthorpe, Louth, Lincolnshire LN11 7HU
Tel (01472) 388229

Freedom
Freedom Brewery, Ganton House, 14-16 Ganton Street, London W1V 1LB
Tel (020) 7287 4982
⬚ A new outlet for the Freedom group (qv).

Goldthorn
Goldthorn Brewery Co, Sunbeam Street, Wolverhampton WV2 4NG

London Bridge
London Bridge Brewery, Borough Market, London SE1.
The former Bishop's Brewery, owned by Andy Bishop, planning to brew again.

Old Cottage
Old Cottage Beer Company, Heritage Site, Anglesey Road, Burton-on-Trent, Staffs DE13 1PF
Tel (07780) 900006

Sarah's Hophouse
⬚ Sarah Hophouse, Railway Inn, 131 High Street, Golborne, Warrington WA3 3TG
Tel (01942) 728202

White Hart
⬚ White Hart Inn, Llanddarog, Carmarthenshire SA32 1NT
Tel (01267) 275395

The National
(...and then there was one)

SCOTTISH COURAGE
**Scottish and Newcastle PLC,
Fountain House, 160 Dundee Street,
Edinburgh EH11 1DQ
Tel (0131) 656 5000
Fax (0131) 656 5217**

Scottish Courage is the biggest brewing group owned by a British-based company with close to 30 per cent of the market, though Interbrew UK, owners of Bass and Whitbread, has a 32 per cent share. ScotCo has formed a partnership with Danone of France, with an option to buy Brasseries Kronenbourg during the next three years. Scottish & Newcastle was formed in 1960 as the result of a merger between Scottish Brewers (Younger and McEwan) and Newcastle Breweries. In 1995 it bought Courage from its Australian owners, Foster's. Since 1991 Courage had been a brewing group without pubs, following a swap of pubs and breweries with Grand Metropolitan in a bid to avoid the Government's Beer Orders. Since the merger that formed Scottish Courage, the group has rationalised by closing its breweries in Nottingham, Halifax and, in the autumn of 1999, the historic Courage [George's] Brewery in Bristol, a dedicated cask ale plant. George's Bitter Ale is now brewed under contract by Smiles, with the remaining beers transferred to John Smith's in Tadcaster.

FOUNTAIN
**Fountain Brewery, 159 Fountainbridge,
Edinburgh EH3 9YY
Tel (0131) 229 9377
Fax (0131) 228 9522**

The once legendary home of McEwan's and Younger's cask ales has now axed all its real ales save for one.

McEwan 80/- *(OG 1042, ABV 4.2%)*
A thin-bodied beer with a cloying metallic aftertaste; bland and sweet with some maltiness. The ABV has been decreased from 4.5% but with no decrease in price for the consumer.

JOHN SMITH'S
**Scottish Courage Brewing Ltd,
John Smith's Brewery, Tadcaster,
N Yorkshire LS24 9SA
Tel (01937) 832091
Fax (01937) 833766**
Tours by arrangement

The brewery was built in 1879 by a relative of Samuel Smith (qv). John Smith's became part of the Courage group in 1970. Major expansion has taken place since the formation of Scottish Courage, with 11 new fermenting vessels installed.

Webster's Green Label Best
(OG 1032, ABV 3.2%)

Webster's Yorkshire Bitter
(OG 1035, ABV 3.5%)

John Smith's Cask Bitter
(OG 1036, ABV 3.8%) ◆
A copper-coloured beer, well-balanced but with no dominating features. It has a short hoppy finish.

Courage Best Bitter *(OG 1038, ABV 4%)*

John Smith's Magnet
(OG 1040, ABV 4%) ◆
An almost ruby-coloured beer with a complex aroma of hops, malt and citrus fruit. Malt dominates the taste and aftertaste.

Courage Directors *(OG 1045, ABV 4.8%)*

McCOWANS*
**McCowans Brewhouse
(Scottish & Newcastle Breweries PLC),
Unit 1 Fountainpark, Dundee Street,
Edinburgh EH11 1AJ
Tel (0131) 228 8198
Fax (0131) 228 8201**
Tours by arrangement

Ö Opened in December 1999, the brewery equipment was imported from the United States. It is unusual for a brew pub as the mash mixer doubles as a copper whirlpool and there is a separate lauter tun where the sugary extract or wort is run off from the spent grains. The brewery is named after William McCowan, the first chemist employed by William Younger. The brews are the brewery's own recipes, but occasionally traditional Youngers brews will be produced: Youngers No 3 has been brewed. Fifteen-20 outlets are supplied direct. Occasional/seasonal beers: Lager (OG 1042, ABV 4.7%), 6 Nations Ale (OG 1050, ABV 5.2%), Millennium Ale (OG 1057, ABV 5.5%). Beers: IPA (OG 1038, ABV 3.7%), 80/- (OG 1044, ABV 4.5%).

THEAKSTON
**T&R Theakston Ltd, Wellgarth, Masham,
Ripon, N Yorkshire HG4 4YD
Tel (01765) 680000
Fax (01765) 689414**
Shop April-Oct, open every day; Nov-Dec limited opening. Brewery tours: tel 01765 689057

Founded in 1827 and based on the present site since 1875, Theakston became part of S&N in 1987. More than £1 million has been invested in the brewery and in developing a museum of brewing but most of Theakston's production now takes place in Newcastle (see below). The same pump clips are used for both Masham and Newcastle beers so the consumer is not told where the beers are sourced; any drinkers fortunate enough to look into pub cellars can identify Masham-racked beers as they are sometimes delivered in wooden casks: the brewery still employs coopers.

545

Mild Ale *(OG 1035, ABV 3.6%)* ◆
A rich and smooth mild ale with a creamy body and a rounded liquorice taste. Dark ruby/amber in colour, with a mix of malt and fruit on the nose, and a dry, hoppy aftertaste.

Best Bitter *(OG 1036, 3.6%)* ◆
A dry and metallic bitter with light hop character when fresh. Older samples lose character and end watery and pale.

Black Bull Bitter *(OG 1037, ABV 3.9%)* ◆
Dry and hoppy bitter with moderate fruit and bitterness initially but ends dry with a spicy astringency.

XB *(OG 1044, ABV 4.6%)* ◆
A sweet-tasting bitter with background fruit and spicy hop. Some caramel character gives this ale a malty dominance.

Old Peculier *(OG 1057, ABV 5.7%)* ▢◆
A strong fruity character dominates in this malty roasted ale. Dark malts and liquorice blend into a rainbow of flavour, balancing a smooth sweetness in young casks but tasting dry when older.

TYNE

Tyne Brewery, Gallowgate, Newcastle upon Tyne, Tyne & Wear NE99 1RA
Tel (0191) 232 5091
Fax (0191) 261 2301

Home of Newcastle Breweries formed in 1890 from the amalgamation of five local companies. It brewed little cask ale in recent years until it took on the bulk of Theakston's production. See above for Theakston tasting notes.

Theakston Mild Ale *(OG 1035, ABV 3.6%)*

Theakston Best Bitter *(OG 1036, ABV 3.6%)*

Home Bitter *(OG 1038, ABV 3.8%)*
Brewed for pubs in the Nottinghamshire area.

Theakston Cool Cask *(OG 1042, ABV 4.2%)*

Launched in May 2000, distribution was restricted to the North of England but a national roll-out was planned for the autumn. The beer is served through special cellar and dispense equipment designed to deliver it at a temperature of 10 degrees C.

Theakston XB *(OG 1044, ABV 4.6%)*

Theakston Old Peculier *(OG 1057, ABV 5.7%)*

ORANGE

Orange Brewery, 37-39 Pimlico Road, London SW1W 8NE
Tel/Fax (020) 7730 5984

⬡ Pub-brewery opened in 1983 and refurbished in 1995. The full-mash brews are stored in cellar tanks under a blanket of CO2. Seasonal beers: Chelsea Blossom (OG 1037, ABV 3.7% March-June), SW19 (OG 1039, ABV 3.9%, to coincide with Wimbledon), Pimlico Porter (OG 1046, ABV 4.6% Nov-March), Donner & Blitzed (OG 1049, ABV 5%, December), Sloane Danger (OG 1057, ABV 6%, Nov-March), Spiritual Reunion (OG 1057, ABV 5.9% Nov-March). Beers: SW1 (OG 1041, ABV), SW2 (OG 1050, ABV 5%), Victoria Lager (OG 1048, ABV 5%) and SW1 (smooth) (OG 1041, ABV 4%).

YORKSHIRE GREY

2-6 Theobalds Road, London WC1X 8PN
Tel (020) 7405 8287
Fax (020) 7831 2359

⬡ Pub-brewery near London's legal heartland in the Inns of Court, High Holborn and the old Fleet Street. The brewery was extensively refurbished in 1995 and the beers have been full mash brews since 1996 though they are kept under a blanket of CO2 in cellar tanks. There are numerous seasonal and one-off brews. Beers: Chelsea Blossom (OG 1036, ABV 3.8%), Barristers Best (OG 1038, ABV 3.8%), QC Best (OG 1045, ABV 4.5%), Supreme Pale Ale (OG 1050, ABV 5%), Holborn Strangler (OG 1059, ABV 6%).

The Internationals

CARLSBERG-TETLEY

Carlsberg-Tetley Brewing Ltd,
Bridge Street,
Northampton NN1 1PZ
Tel (01604) 668866

A wholly-owned subsidiary of Carlsberg of
Copenhagen, Denmark. Carlsberg is an
international giant best known for its pale
lagers, though in Denmark it brews a large
range of beers, including brown lagers and a
porter-stout, all made by cold fermentation.
In Britain its lagers are brewed at a dedicated
plant in Northampton.

Carlsberg-Tetley Brewing Ltd,
PO Box 142, The Brewery, Leeds, W
Yorkshire LS1 1QG
Tel (0113) 259 4594
Fax (0113) 259 4000

The historic Joshua Tetley Brewery where
brewing has taken place since 1792 and
under the Tetley name since 1822. An
additional 19 Yorkshire square fermenting
vessels were commissioned in 1996. It is the
biggest dedicated cask ale brewery in Britain.
The Tetley Wharf Brewery Centre has closed.

Tetley Dark Mild
(OG 1031, ABV 3.2%) ✒
A reddish, mid-brown beer with a light malt
and caramel aroma. A well-balanced taste of
malt and caramel follows, with good
bitterness and a satisfying finish.

Tetley Mild *(OG 1034, ABV 3.3%)* ✒
A mid-brown beer with a light malt and
caramel aroma. A well-balanced taste of malt
and caramel follows, with good bitterness
and a dry, satisfying finish.

Ansells Mild *(OG 1035, ABV 3.4%)*

Ansells Bitter *(OG 1035, ABV 3.7%)*

Benskins Bitter *(OG 1035, ABV 3.7%)*

Friary Meux Bitter *(OG 1035, ABV 3.7%)*

Tetley Bitter *(OG 1035.5, ABV 3.7%)* ✒
A variable amber-coloured light, dry bitter
with a slight malt and hop aroma, leading to
a moderate bitterness with a hint of fruit,
ending with a dry and bitter finish.

For 'Greenalls'
aka Inn Partnership/Nomura

Greenalls Mild *(OG 1034, ABV 3.3%)*

Greenalls Bitter *(OG 1036.5, ABV 3.8%)*

Ind Coope Burton Ale: see Marston's.

GUINNESS

Guinness Brewing GB,
Park Royal Brewery, London NW10 7RR
Tel (020) 8965 7700
Fax (020) 8963 5120

An Anglo-Irish giant that has world-wide
brewing operations and distribution. In
London is brews draught keg and pasteurised
bottled stouts only.

INTERBREW

Interbrew UK, a wholly-owned subsidiary
of Interbrew of Leuven/Louvain, Belgium.
Porter Tun House, Capability Green,
Luton, Beds LU1 3LS
Tel (01582) 391166
Fax (01582) 397397

Interbrew, the result of a merger in Belgium
between Stella Artois and Piedboeuf, is an
international giant, owning Labatt of Canada
and Moretti of Italy. It is a major player in
the European market with such lager brands
as Stella Artois and Jupiler. It has some
interest in ale brewing with the cask- and
bottle-conditioned 'white' beer, Hoegaarden,
and the 'abbey beer' Leffe. It has a ruthless
track record of closing plants and disposing
of brands. In the summer of 2000 it bought
both Whitbread's and Bass's brewing
operations. The number of plants and brands
below are liable to be pruned, as are the
names of the companies.

BASS

Bass Brewers Ltd, 137 High Street, Burton-
on-Trent, Staffordshire DE14 1J7
Tel (01283) 511000
Fax (01283) 513326

Founded in 1777, Bass was once a proud ale
brewer but before its sale had concentrated
on nitro-keg, lager and alcopops. In 1999
Bass sold its Cardiff brewery to Brains and
closed its Sheffield brewery. The Burton site
includes the former neighbouring Ind Coope
plant.

BIRMINGHAM

Bass Mitchells & Butlers, Cape Hill
Brewery, PO Box 27, Smethwick,
Birmingham, West Midlands B16 0PQ
Tel (0121) 558 1481

M&B Brew XI *(OG 1039.5, ABV 3.8%)*
A sweet, malty beer with a hoppy, bitter
aftertaste.

M&B Mild
is brewed under contract by the Highgate
Brewery, Walsall (qv).

BURTON

Bass B Brewery, 137 Station Street,
Burton-on-Trent, Staffordshire DE14 1JZ
Tel (01283) 511000

Draught Bass *(OG 1043.3, ABV 4.4%)*
Once the Rolls-Royce of cask beer, it is now
just a Ford Fiesta. Cost-cutting (the beer is no
longer dry-hopped in cask) and indifferent
quality control mean the beer is all too often
overly malty and cloying.

Bass C Brewery, Burton-on-Trent (formerly
Carlsberg-Tetley's Ind Coope Brewery):
address and telephone number as above

Worthington Dark Mild
(OG 1034.5, ABV 3%)

Stones Bitter *(OG 1037, ABV 3.7%)*

Hancock's HB *(1038, ABV 3.6%)*

Worthington Bitter *(OG 1038, ABV 3.6%)*

MUSEUM BREWING CO

The Bass Museum, Horninglow Street,
Burton-on-Trent,
Staffordshire DE14 1YQ
Tel (01283) 511000 ext 3507
Fax (01283) 513509
E-mail
Brewery@museum.brewers.bass.com
Shop (in Bass Museum) 9.30-4.30
Tours by arrangement

The Museum Brewing Co, based within the
Bass Museum, is part of the Bass Group but
has a large degree of independence. Its position is likely to be reviewed by Interbrew. It
began brewing in 1994 and has a licence to
recreate some of the older Bass beers that
have been discontinued. The brewery dates
from 1920 with some equipment going back
to 1840. It has a maximum capacity of 60
barrels a week. It produces mainly cask-conditioned beers but five per cent of its output
is bottle conditioned. As well as historic
beers, the brewery produces seasonal brands
and creates ales for CAMRA festivals. Historic
Beers: Offilers Bitter (OG 1037, ABV 4%),
Nob Mild (OG 1037, ABV 3.9%), Massey's
Bitter (OG 1038, ABV 4.1%), Joules Bitter
(OG 1038, ABV 4.1%), P2 Imperial Stout (OG
1078, ABV 8%), Bass No 1 Barley Wine (OG
1105, ABV 10.5%). Other beers: Victoria Ale
(OG 1033, ABV 3.9%), Five Hides (OG 1037,
ABV 4%), Centennial (OG 1041, ABV 4.3%),
Masterpiece (OG 1048, ABV 5.4%).

Worthington White Shield
(OG 1050.5, ABV 5.6%)

**Worthington White Shield was named
Champion Bottle-conditioned Beer of
Britain at the 2000 Great British Beer
Festival. It was brewed by King and
Barnes but the beer has now returned
to Burton-on-Trent.**

WHITBREAD

Porter Tun House, Capability Green,
Luton, Bedfordshire LU1 3LS
Tel (01582) 391166
Fax (01582) 397397

At the heart of British brewing since the
early 18th century and the celebrated commercial producer of first porter and then
pale ale, Whitbread seemed to regain its
belief in ale in the early and mid-1990s with
a range of new cask ales produced for its Ale
House and Hogshead outlets. But the mar-

keting department and accountants forced
the company to concentrate on big volume
brands, Stella Artois in particular. Before its
collapse and sale to Interbrew, it was brewing more nitro-keg Boddingtons Bitter than
the cask version.

BODDINGTONS

Strangeways Brewery, PO Box 23,
Strangeways,
Manchester M60 3WB
Tel (0161) 828 2000
Fax (0161) 828 2213
Tours by arrangement

Established in 1778 and bought by
Whitbread in the 1980s when the
Boddington company, which had already
taken over and closed Oldham Brewery,
decided to leave brewing and become a pub
retailer. Whitbread closed the Cheltenham
Brewery in 1999 and transferred production
of its cask beers to Manchester. It has also
phased out Boddingtons Mild and Oldham
Mild.

Boddingtons Bitter
(OG 1034.5, ABV 3.8%) ◆
A golden, straw-coloured beer in which the
grainy malt, hop and bitter character can be
spoiled by a cloying sweetness.

Flowers IPA *(OG 1036, ABV 3.6%)*

Trophy Bitter *(OG 1036, ABV 3.8%)*

Whitbread Best Bitter
(OG 1036, ABV 3.6%)

Flowers Original *(OG 1044, ABV 4.4%)*

FELLOWS, MORTON & CLAYTON

Fellows, Morton & Clayton Brewhouse
Company, 54 Canal Street,
Nottingham NG1 7EH
Tel (0115) 950 6795
Fax (0115) 953 9838

♫ Pub that began brewing in 1980 and still
uses malt extract. Beers: Fellows Bitter
(OG 1042, ABV 3.8%), Post Haste (OG 1051,
ABV 4.4%), Christmas Cracker (OG 1063,
ABV 6%).

FROG & PARROT

Frog & Parrot Brewhouse, Division Street,
Sheffield, S Yorkshire S1 4GF
Tel (0114) 272 1280

♫ Brew pub launched in 1982. The beers are
brewed from malt extract and stored in casks
and are occasionally available in a few other
pubs. Brewing is suspended during long students' vacations. Occasional/one-off brews.
Beer: Roger & Out (OG 1125, ABV 12.5%).

LASS O' GOWRIE

Lass O'Gowrie Brewhouse, 36 Charles
Street, Manchester M1 7DB
Tel (0161) 273 6932
Tours by arrangement

♫ Victorian pub that was revamped and
reopened as a malt extract brew pub in 1983
and is now part of the Hogshead division.
The brewery in the cellar is visible from the
bar and the beer is now stored in casks.
Occasional/one-off brews. Beers: Lass
O'Gowrie (OG 1035, ABV 3.8%), Lass
O'Gowrie (OG 1042, ABV 4.7%).

Pub Groups

Pub groups developed rapidly in the 1990s in the wake of the government's Beer Orders that required national brewers to give their tenants the right to buy guest beers free of the tie. Rather than improve pubgoers' choice, the brewers preferred to sell off most or all of their tenanted estates. As pub groups are not owned by brewers, they do not have to offer guest beers, and many focus on heavily-discounted national brands. As a result of the sale of Bass's and Whitbread's breweries, pub chains that state below that they take beers from those companies may revise their suppliers.

AMBISHUS

Ambishus Pub Company PLC, Hill House, 118 High Street, Uxbridge, Middlesex UB8 1JT
Tel (01895) 272345
Fax (01895) 272555

Ambishus is a rapidly-expanding managed pub operator. Since flotation in 1998, the company has doubled in size, successfully consolidating five groups of pubs acquired from JD Wetherspoon, Regent Inns, Slug & Lettuce (qv) and Smith & Jones. The estate currently numbers 61 pubs, predominantly based within the M25. Its main regular cask beers come from Courage, Fuller's and Greene King.

AVEBURY TAVERNS

Avebury Taverns Ltd, Sterling House, 20 Station Road, Gerrards Cross, Buckinghamshire SL9 8EL
Tel (01753) 482600

Avebury is a dedicated tenanted pub group, one of the top 10 independent pub companies in the country. Established in 1997, there was a management buy-out in August 1999 and successful refinancing through securitisation in 2000. Avebury operates more than 700 pubs throughout England and Wales trading as free houses, and offers a range of tenancy agreements. Supply contracts are held with all major brewers, and some regional and local brewers, offering tenants a choice of more than 50 cask-conditioned ales.

ASCOT ESTATES

See Mayfair Taverns.

BASS

Bass Leisure Retail, Cape Hill, PO Box 27, Birmingham, West Midlands B16 0PQ
Tel (0121) 558 1481
Fax (0121) 558 2515

Following the sale of its brewing interests to Interbrew, Bass is now a leisure and retail company, and is one of the world's leading hoteliers through ownership of Holiday Inns. Bass Leisure Retail runs 3,000 pubs, bars and restaurants and employs more than 5,000 people. Its brands include Vintage Inns, traditional British pubs, Ember Inns, local pubs, and Goose, traditional pubs offering food and drink. All these outlets offer cask ales: Ember Inns always have one cask ale available and could have as many as four if the volume is sustainable. Vintage Inns will always stock Draught Bass and one other, again if the volume is sustainable. Goose pubs have the highest sales of cask ale. The company acquired 550 pubs from Allied Domecq in late 1999, the majority of which stock Tetley Bitter and now Draught Bass. This acquisition has given Bass some historic gems such as the Philharmonic in Liverpool, the Bear in Oxford, and several in London, including the Black Friar. Bass Leisure Retail offers a selection of cask beers: as well as Draught Bass, Worthington Bitter, Stones, Hancocks, M&B Mild and Brew XI, a number of guest ales are also available, including Adnams, Highgate Bitter, Fuller's London Pride and Morland Old Speckled Hen.

BEARDS

Beards of Sussex Ltd, West End, Herstmonceux, E Sussex BN27 4NN
Tel (01323) 832777
Fax (01323) 832833

Former brewing company, founded in 1797, that opted out of production in 1959. After contracting out its beers to Harveys from 1960 to 1986, Beards abandoned brewing altogether and became a cask ale wholesaler as well as pub company. In July 1998 Beards was bought by Greene King, adding 43 pubs to its estate.

BURTONWOOD

Burtonwood Brewery PLC, Bold Lane, Burtonwood, Warrington, Cheshire WA5 4PJ
Tel (01925) 225131

Brewing at the Burtonwood, Cheshire, site is operated by Thomas Hardy Burtonwood, a joint venture formed in October 1998 between Burtonwood Brewery and Thomas Hardy Brewery of Dorchester. Burtonwood operates almost 500 pubs, the majority of which are traditional tenancies. Burtonwood's cask ales and a monthly changing cask from an independent brewer are made available to all Burtonwood tenancies. Approximately half of the Burtonwood estate stocks cask ale.

CAFE INNS

Cafe Inns PLC, 3 St Thomas's Road, Chorley, Lancashire PR7 1HP
Tel (01257) 262424
Fax (01257) 260497

Established in 1987, the company now runs 85 outlets (73 tenanted, 12 managed) in the North-west. The figure includes one restaurant and two coffee shops. The pubs sell beers from Bass and Scottish Courage.

CATMERE

**Catmere Ltd, Station Road, Scunthorpe,
North Lincolnshire DN15 6PY
Tel (01724) 861703
Fax (01724) 861708**

Catmere owns 10 pubs, nine managed, one
tenanted, mostly in the free trade, but it
plans to expand to 12 sites. Its guest ales are
supplied by Bass, Courage, Mansfield, W&D
and the Beer Seller. One of its outlets, the
Honest Lawyer, at Scunthorpe, offers
regional and micro-brewery cask ales,
changing on a daily basis.

CENTURY INNS

Formed in 1991 by Cameron's employees
who bought 195 pubs from Bass, Century
was one of the earliest of the new pub
groups. It was bought by Enterprise Inns (qv)
early in 1999.

CM GROUPS

See Commer Inns.

TOM COBLEIGH

**Tom Cobleigh, Spencer House,
Cliftonville Road, Northampton NN1 5BU
Tel (01604) 745000**

Established in 1992 with just two pubs, the
estate has grown to 90 across England and
Scotland. The company was taken over by
the Rank Group in 1996. Licensees choose
beers from a head office range of national
and regional ales, with Scottish Courage as
the main supplier. A list of rotating guest
beers is also offered. The tenanted estate of
pubs was acquired in 1994 from Whitbread,
though these are signed as belonging to the
Nice Pub Company.

COMMER INNS

**Commer Group Ltd, Commer House,
Station Road, Tadcaster,
N Yorkshire LS24 9JF
Tel (01937) 833311
Fax (01937) 834236
Web-site www.commer.co.uk
E-mail commer@commer.co.uk**

Freehold-owned estate with 75 pubs run as
tenancies from the north Midlands up to the
North-east. Supplies come from Bass,
Carlsberg-Tetley, Scottish Courage and
Whitbread. All casks ales on suppliers' lists
are available to tenants. Commer
Management (managed division) has
15 pubs.

CONQUEST INNS

**Conquest Inns Ltd, 1st floor,
172 Bullsmoor Lane, Enfield,
Middlesex EN1 4SE
Tel (01992) 717718
Fax (01992) 717788**

Conquest Inns is a subsidiary of the Jersey
Brewing Company and operates an estate,
mainly tenanted, of 50 pubs. Most of the
pubs are in the South-east, but the company
plans to expand at the rate of 20 pubs a year.
Beers come from Bass and Scottish Courage,
and the company has no definitive policy on
cask ale, leaving the choice to tenants.

CROWDED HOUSE

**Crowded House Pub Company,
31 High Street North,
Dunstable,
Bedfordshire LU6 1HX
Tel (01582) 471363**

Formed with the purchase of 40 former
Beefeater pub/restaurants from Whitbread
for £36 million in May 1998, it plans to
return the pubs to their original, pre-
Beefeater names and shy away from any
kind of theming or branding. It has supply
agreements with Scottish Courage and
Whitbread.

JT DAVIES

**JT Davies & Sons Ltd,
7 Aberdeen Road, Croydon,
Surrey CR0 1EQ
Tel (020) 8681 3222
Fax (020) 8760 0390**

Wine merchants now controlling 35
tenancies and eight managed houses in the
South-east, its main suppliers are Bass and
Scottish Courage, with some beers from
Fuller's and Harveys.

DAVY

**The Davy Group, 59-63 Bermondsey Street,
London SE1 3XF
Tel (020) 7407 9670
Fax (020) 7407 5844**

Wine merchants and shippers since 1870,
Davy's has been opening wine
bars/restaurants in the London area since
1965, taking previously unlicensed
properties and creating a Dickensian,
sawdust, nooks-and-crannies type of
establishment. Its Davy's Old Wallop (ABV
4.8%) is a re-badged brew of undeclared
origin (though Courage Directors fits the
bill). This is usually served in pewter
tankards or copper jugs. The company
currently runs around 50 outlets, including a
few pubs.

DEVONSHIRE

**The Devonshire Group,
Devonshire House, Surrey Road, Nelson,
Lancashire BB9 7TZ
Tel (01282) 690033**

Set up in 1991 as the national brewers sold
off tenanted pubs, Devonshire now has 34
managed houses and plans to expand to 60
by 2002. It was named Independent Pub
Chain of the Year in 1997 by Publican
newspaper.

DISCOVERY INNS

See Enterprise Inns.

ELDRIDGE POPE
Eldridge, Pope & Co PLC, Weymouth Avenue, Dorchester, Dorset ST1 1QT
Tel (01305) 251251
Fax (01305) 258300

Founded as the Green Dragon Brewery in 1837, Eldridge Pope finally divorced itself from brewing in 1996 when it split into two wings, the brewing side becoming known as Thomas Hardy Brewery (see Independents). The company now runs 200 pubs, 124 managed, the rest tenanted. It takes Eldridge Pope beers from Thomas Hardy and has supply agreements with Carlsberg-Tetley and Scottish Courage.

ENTERPRISE INNS
Enterprise Inns PLC, Cranmore Avenue, Shirley, Solihull, W Midlands B90 4LE
Tel (0121) 733 7700
Fax (0121) 733 6447

Formed in 1991 with an initial acquisition of 372 pubs from Bass, the company has grown rapidly and its current estate of some 2,600 pubs incorporates pubs purchased through the acquisitions of John Labatt Retail, Discovery Inns, Gibbs Mew, Mayfair Taverns, Century Inns (Tap & Spile) and most recently Swallow Inns and Restaurants. Enterprise believes that the leased and tenanted approach to operating pubs provides licensees with the opportunity to run their own pubs without the cost associated with buying it. A good range of cask beers from all the major brewers, as well as many of the regionals, is available through the Enterprise central distribution network.

FAMOUS
Famous Pub Company PLC, 510 Hertford Road, Enfield, Greater London EN3 5SS
Tel (020) 8805 4055
Fax (020) 8805 0115

Expanding pub company established with the purchase of 37 pubs from Whitbread in February 1996. The company currently owns 45 tenanted pubs in London and the Home Counties. Famous is supplied by Whitbread. Some tenants are allowed a guest beer.

FITZGERALD
Sir John Fitzgerald Ltd, Cafe Royal Buildings, 8 Nelson Street, Newcastle upon Tyne, Tyne & Wear NE1 5AW
Tel (0191) 232 0664
Fax (0194) 261 4509

Long-established, family-owned property and pubs company. Its pubs convey a free house image, most offering a good choice of cask beers, including guest ales from smaller craft breweries. The 31 pubs are mainly in the North-east but there are new outlets in Edinburgh, Harrogate and London.

GIBBS MEW
Anchor House, Netherhampton Road, Salisbury, Wiltshire SP2 8RA
Tel (01722) 411911
Fax (01722) 411486

Established in 1898, the company closed its Anchor House brewery in 1997 to concentrate on its estate. It was bought by Enterprise Inns in February 1998. The company owns 330 pubs, around 300 tied; most are in the South of England and around 200 serve cask-conditioned beer.

GRAND PUB COMPANY
See Unique.

GRAY
Gray & Sons (Chelmsford) Ltd, Rignals Lane, Galleywood, Chelmsford, Essex CM2 8RE
Tel (01245) 475181
Fax (01245) 475182

Former Chelmsford brewery that ceased production in 1974 and now supplies its 49 tied houses in Essex with a choice of cask beers from Greene King and Shepherd Neame. The tenants are also free to choose from a bi-monthly guest list that features at least 10 different ales.

GREENALLS
Once-famous Warrington brewery that got out of brewing and has now even given up on pub owning, too, selling its estate to Inn Partnership, a subsidiary of Nomura.

HEAVITREE
Heavitree Brewery PLC, Trood Lane, Matford, Exeter, Devon EX2 8YP
Tel (01392) 217733
Fax (01392) 229939

A West Country brewery, established in 1790, which gave up production in 1970 to concentrate on running pubs. The current estate, which is mainly confined to Devon, stands at 116: 11 managed, and the rest tenanted or leased. The pubs are tied to beers from the Whitbread Cask Collection, with some products from Bass and Thomas Hardy.

HONEYCOMBE
Honeycombe Leisure, Muldoons, 50 Water Lane, Ashton, Preston, Lancs PR2 2NL
Tel (01772) 723764

This 25 year-old company owns 44 managed houses. Beers are supplied by the nationals plus Burton Bridge, Eccleshall, Moorhouses, Phoenix and Timothy Taylor and most micro-brewers in the North-west. Honeycombe also has its own micro-brewery based in Salford.

INN BUSINESS
Inn Business Group PLC, The Firs, Whitchurch, nr Aylesbury, Bucks HP22 4TH
Tel (01296) 640000
Fax (01296) 640070

Inn Business runs some 500 traditional pubs in southern England, the Midlands and the North-east, following the acquisition of Mart Taverns and Sycamore Taverns in 1996. The pubs are predominantly tenanted, but also include traditional food and alehouse managed outlets. Beers come from Bass, Carlsberg-Tetley, Scottish Courage and Whitbread, and include the guest beers they supply. The Hooden Horse branded pubs offer spicy food and real ales.

INN PARTNERSHIP

PO Box 2, Greenalls Avenue, Warrington, Cheshire WA4 6RH
Tel (01925) 651234
Fax (01925) 402560

Company owned by Nomura and bought from Greenalls in December 1998 with 1,000 franchised pubs and 240 tenancies.

INNSPIRED

InnSpired Pubs PLC, Directors House, 68 Fore Street, Trowbridge, Wiltshire BA14 8JF
Tel (01225) 763171
Fax (01225) 774289

InnSpired represents the remains of Ushers of Trowbridge, a famous West Country brewery founded in 1824. Ushers became part of Grand Metropolitan in 1960. When the brewery passed into Courage's control, a management buy-out restored its independence in 1991. In 1999 Ushers merged with the Alehouse Company of Southampton. With the involvement of the Alchemy group, it was always likely that the new owners would opt to concentrate on real estate and retailing. Brewing ceased early in 2000. InnSpired has a large estate of close to 1,000 pubs. 'Usher's' cask beers are brewed for InnSpired by Thomas Hardy of Dorchester; other brands, such as Manns Brown Ale and the Lowenbrau range of lagers, are brewed by Burtonwood. A separate company, Refresh UK, which operates from the same Trowbridge offices, has been set up to retail the Usher's brands. InnSpired says it will take beers from other suppliers for its estate and the range of 'Usher's' brands may contract.

INNTREPRENEUR

Inntrepreneur Pub Company Ltd, Suite 2, Pegasus House, Haddenham Aerodrome Industrial Estate, Haddenham, Bucks HP17 8LJ
Tel (01844) 293500
Fax (01844) 293520

Inntrepreneur, with a 4,000-strong pub estate, was the pub-owning company formed by Courage (Foster's) and Grand Metropolitan as part of a pubs-for-breweries swap in 1991. It was bought by Nomura in 1997 and most of its pubs have been transferred to Nomura's Unique Pub Company (qv). Inntrepreneur now has an estate of 100 tenancies and around 600 leased outlets and their future is uncertain under Nomura ownership.

MACLAY

Maclay Group PLC, Thistle Brewery, Alloa FK10 1ED
Tel (01259) 723387
Fax (01259) 216511

Maclay, founded in 1830, stopped brewing in September 1999. It owns 35 pubs and its full range of cask ales is brewed under licence by a new brewing company, Forth (qv).

MAYFAIR TAVERNS

Mayfair Taverns Ltd, The Old Malt House, St John's Road, Banbury, Oxfordshire OX16 8HX
Tel (01295) 275012
Fax (01295) 278677

Company established with a management buy-out from Ascot Estates and the purchase of 251 Ascot pubs in April 1996: Ascot's remaining pubs are being gradually disposed of as the company winds down. Mayfair's pubs are spread throughout most of the country, as far north as Bradford and Manchester, and are either three-year tenancies or are leased on 20-year contracts. Beers are supplied entirely by Scottish Courage and Carlsberg-Tetley.

MERCURY TAVERNS

Mercury Taverns PLC, Mercury House, Amber Business Village, Amington, Tamworth, Staffordshire B77 4RP
Tel (01827) 310000
Fax (01827) 310530

The company runs 160 pubs (31 managed, the rest tenanted), scattered from Cumbria and the North-east to South Wales and into London and the South-east. Marston's and Wolverhampton & Dudley jointly acquired two-thirds of the company in 1996, supplying their beers to the pubs, but they have since sold their shares in the company. Part of the group is the Irish-themed Dublin Pub Company. Mercury was bought by Pubmaster in June 1998 for £35 million.

MILL HOUSE

Mill House Inns, Century House, Westcott Venture Park, Westcott, Bucks HP18 0XB
Tel (01296) 652600
Fax (01296) 652626

Mill House has 54 managed pubs nationwide, ranging from town bars to country pubs and family pub-diners. Its main supply agreement is with Bass.

NICE PUB COMPANY

See Tom Cobleigh.

OLD ENGLISH INNS

Old English Inns PLC, Castle House, 21/23 Station Road, New Barnet, Herts EN5 1PA
Tel (020) 8275 3333
Fax (020) 8275 3334
E-mail central.reservations @oldenglishinns.co.uk
Web-site www.oldenglish.co.uk

A seven year-old company running 102 coaching inns and 53 pub/restaurants. All the pubs and inns are managed and extend across England from Cheshire to Lincolnshire southwards. All have restaurants and more than two thirds offer accommodation. All sell cask ale, the main range being supplied by Scottish Courage with guest ales supplied by regional brewers.

PARAMOUNT

Paramount PLC, Suite H3, Steam Mill Business Centre, Steam Mill Street, Chester CH3 5AN
Tel (01244) 321171
Fax (01244) 317665

Founded in 1987, Paramount now owns 163 pubs; 52 are under the Real Inns banner and the estate is made up entirely of tenancies. Distribution is centrally controlled, with beers from Burtonwood, Bass, Whitbread and Scottish Courage. 106 pubs take cask ale permanently, and three ale houses with a wide range of beers are also operated. Twelve houses take a different independent guest ale each week.

PHOENIX

Phoenix Inns Ltd, Pegasus House, Haddenham Aerodrome Industrial Estate, Haddenham, Bucks HP17 8LJ
Tel (01844) 293500

Operating from the same offices as Inntrepreneur, Phoenix is owned by Nomura and currently runs 500 tenancies.

PUB ESTATE

The Pub Estate Company Ltd, 3-5 Ashfield Road, Chorley, Lancashire PR7 1LH
Tel (01257) 238800
Fax (01257) 233918

Company established with the purchase of 230 pubs from Scottish & Newcastle, it currently has 335 pubs (28 managed, the rest tenanted or leased) based in the north of England and Scotland. The pubs offer beers from Bass, Carlsberg-Tetley, Scottish Courage and Whitbread, but some licensees have guest beer rights. The company's aim is to convert all pubs to three-year leases that would offer no guest beer entitlement and would mean all pubs being served by a favoured supplier, probably Scottish Courage.

PUBMASTER

Pubmaster Ltd, Greenbank, Hartlepool TS24 7QS
Tel (01429) 266699
Fax (01429) 278457
Web site www.pubmaster.co.uk

Company formed in 1991 to take over the pub estate of Brent Walker. Following a management buy-out in 1996, Pubmaster has continued to grow, with recent acquisitions from Mercury Taverns, Devonshire Pub Company and Swallow. It is currently operating more than 2000 pubs in conjunction with its tenants. Pubmaster stocks beers from Bass, Carlsberg-Tetley, Whitbread and some independents.

PUNCH GROUP

Punch Retail Ltd
107 Station Road, Burton-on-Trent, Staffs DE14 1BZ
Tel (01283) 54530

Managed side of the business, based in the former offices of Allied Domecq. It operates 1,060 pubs. Beers include Tetley Bitter.

Punch Pub Company
Lincoln House, Wellington Crescent, Fradley Park, Lichfield, Staffs WS13 8RZ
Tel (01543) 443500

Leased and tenanted side of the business, it operates 4,160 pubs, restaurants, café bars and night clubs. Beers include Tetley Bitter and Worthington Bitter.
Punch was formed by a team led by Hugh Osmond, the founder of Pizza Express, with the purchase of the Bass leased estate in April 1998. In the summer of 1999 Punch, with the backing of Bass, bought Allied Domecq's pub estate. It sold 550 former managed houses to Bass and now owns some 5,000 pubs itself. Punch claims its lessees are free to take guest beers but supplying brewers are closely monitored and have to offer substantial discounts to be accepted. A number of small brewers have lost their trade with Punch as a result of being unable to offer acceptable discounts. In the summer of 2000 Punch said it was offering new terms to some of its lessees that would enable them to choose from a list of 300 drinks brands – but only two of those brands are cask ales, Tetley and Worthington. The group is refusing to stock any Scottish Courage beers following a dispute over discounts.

RANDALLS VAUTIER

Randalls Vautier Ltd, PO Box 43, Clare Street, St Helier, Jersey JE4 8NZ
Tel (01534) 887788
Fax (01534) 888350

Brewery that ceased production in 1992, it now runs 30 pubs on Jersey selling beers from Bass, Scottish Courage, Marston's and Whitbread. Not to be confused with Randalls of Guernsey (see Independents).

REGENT INNS

Regent Inns PLC, 77 Muswell Hill, London N10 3PJ
Tel (020) 8375 3000
Fax (020) 8375 3001

Founded in 1980, Regent owns 115 managed pubs in London and the Home Counties, and is growing by 20 pubs a year. Expansion into the Midlands and the north is taking place. Most of the pubs are unbranded and are allowed to retain their own identities and are not tied to any supplier. Most pubs feature a wide range of national, local and seasonal cask ales chosen by managers. The company has contracts with Bass, Scottish Courage and Whitbread, plus half a dozen regional breweries, but licensees can also take beer from the Beer Seller wholesaler. Branded pubs include Walkabout Inns and Jongleurs.

RYAN

Ryan Elizabeth Holdings PLC,
Ryan Precinct, 33 Fore Street, Ipswich,
Suffolk IP4 1JL
Tel (01473) 217458
Fax (01473) 258237

The company's 54 pubs in East Anglia, many bought from national brewers, are mostly leased to individual operators on 35-year contracts, although eight are managed. The pubs are generally free of the tie but some have a tie to Bass. A subsidiary company, Elizabeth Hotels, operates independent bars/pubs in its hotels with a local community focus, offering four to five real ales and live entertainment. The main beer supplier is Bass but Adnams, Greene King, Tolly Cobbold and Nethergate also supply beers.

SCORPIO INNS

Scorpio Inns Ltd, Commerce House,
Abbey Road, Torquay,
Devon TQ2 5PJ
Tel (01803) 296111
Fax (01803) 296202

Pub group formed in 1991, it now runs 111 pubs (nearly all tenanted). These stock beers from Bass and Whitbread, and are located in South Wales, the Bristol and Hereford areas, and along the M4 corridor to Swindon.

SFI GROUP

SFI Group PLC, SFI House,
165 Church Street East, Woking,
Surrey GU21 1HJ
Tel (01483) 227900
Fax (01483) 227903

Established in 1986, the SFI Group, formerly Surrey Free Inns, runs around 100 pubs and café bars in England, Scotland and Wales. The number is set to increase, with further acquisitions planned. Beers come from national brewers and a range of smaller regional brewers. Cask ale is a feature of the Litten Trees outlets. Not all the pubs are branded: around 20, such as the Ostrich Inn, at Colnbrook, near Heathrow, have kept their own identity.

SLUG & LETTUCE

The Old Schoolhouse,
London Road, Shenley,
Hertfordshire WD7 9DX
Tel (01923) 855837
Fax (01923) 857992

Formerly Grosvenor, this group runs 48 pubs in the South-east, all under the Slug & Lettuce name. All other pubs have been sold to Ambishus (qv). The group has a supply deal with Scottish Courage.

SWALLOW

In July 1999 Vaux Breweries ceased to exist. Swallow closed its Sunderland and Sheffield plants, sold 659 tenanted and three managed pubs to Pubmaster (qv) and then sold its remaining pubs to Whitbread. In July 2000 the group was the subject of a bid from SFI (qv).

SYCAMORE INNS

See Inn Business

TRENT TAVERNS

Trent Taverns Ltd, PO Box 1061,
Gringley on the Hill, Doncaster,
S Yorkshire DN10 4ED
Tel (01777) 817408
Fax (01777) 817247

Company set up by a former S&N employee, its 84 tenanted pubs in the Midlands and the South are mostly leased from Whitbread, with some freehold acquisitions. They sell beers from the Scottish Courage and Whitbread lists, including regional brewers' cask ales factored through them.

TUDOR INNS & TAVERNS

Tudor Inns and Taverns Ltd, 2nd Floor,
141 Week Street, Maidstone,
Kent ME14 1RE
Tel (01622) 661782
Fax (01622) 661717

Formerly Inn Kent Leisure, the group has an estate of 33 pubs in Kent, Sussex, Bucks, Surrey and Gloucestershire. Cask beers come from Scottish Courage, Shepherd Neame and Whitbread.

TYNEMILL

Tynemill Ltd, 2nd Floor, Victoria Hotel,
Dovecote Lane, Beeston,
Nottingham NG9 1JG
Tel (0115) 925 3333
Fax (0115) 922 6741

Founded by former CAMRA chairman Chris Holmes, Tynemill has been established in the East Midlands for more than 20 years, and now owns 17 pubs. It has a 'pubs for everyone' philosophy, avoiding trends and gimmicks, and concentrating on quality cask ales and food in good surroundings, including public bars where space permits. It plans to expand along similar lines. Regional and micro-brewers make up the bulk of the products. Bass and Whitbread currently supply draught lagers.

UNIQUE

Unique Pub Company Ltd, Mill House,
Aylesbury Road, Thame, Oxon OX9 3AT
Tel (01844) 262000
Fax (01844) 261332

Formed in December 1998 by Nomura Principal Finance Group, Unique owns 700 tenanted and 2,000 leasehold pubs, the best of the Inntrepreneur and Phoenix estates. Through its wholly-owned supply company SupplyLine Services, Unique pubs can access more than 200 drinks brands from national and a range of regional brewers including Smiles, Lees, Shepherd Neame and Young's. In 2000, Unique announced the launch of a pilot scheme with SIBA, the Society of Independent Brewers, to give Unique licensees in the north greater access to a wider range of cask ales from independent brewers.

WETHERSPOON

JD Wetherspoon PLC, Wetherspoon House, Central Park, Reeds Crescent, Watford, Hertfordshire WD1 1QH
Tel (01923) 477 777
Fax (01923) 219810
Web-site www.jdwetherspoon.co.uk

Wetherspoon is a vigorous and independent pub retailer that currently owns more than 410 managed pubs, with rapid plans for expansion. No music is played in any of the pubs, all offer no-smoking areas, and food is served all day. Two standard beers from Scottish Courage are available to managers: Theakston Best Bitter and Courage Directors. Each pub also has one regional ale from the likes of Cains, Fuller's, Shepherd Neame and Wolverhampton & Dudley, with at least two guest beers. There is at least one beer festival a year, either in the spring or autumn. A policy, introduced in 1997, of offering beer in oversized lined glasses was abandoned a year later.

WHARFEDALE

Wharfedale Taverns Ltd, Highcliffe Court, Greenfold Lane, Wetherby, W Yorkshire LS22 6RG Tel (01937) 580805
Fax (01937) 580806
E-mail
wharfedale_taverns@compuserve.com

A company set up in 1993 by former Tetley employees to lease 90 pubs from that company, it currently owns 17 pubs, mainly in Yorkshire. It also runs 40 to 50 other houses with agreements from national brewers and larger pub companies. Fifty-five houses are managed and seven are tenanted. It planned to acquire a further five freehold properties during 1999/2000 and to take on more long-term leases. It is developing its Wharfedale Traditional Taverns concept: four houses are under this banner and all future acquisitions will fit into the concept. The main beers come from Carlsberg-Tetley; guest beers are from C-T's Tapster's Choice.

WHITBREAD

Whitbread Pub Company, The Brewery, Chiswell Street, London EC1Y 4SD
Tel (020) 7606 4455
Fax (020) 7615 1000

With the Whitbread Beer Company sold in 2000 to Interbrew, this once-mighty company, at the heart of British brewing since the 18th century, is now a retailer. It is divided into Whitbread Pub Partnerships, totalling 1,717 leased outlets, and Whitbread Taverns, totalling 1,639 managed outlets, including Brewers Fayre, Kiln and Kettle, Hogshead, Peppers, Pitchers, Wayside Inns, Family Inns, and Real Pub Co. Whitbread Restaurants division includes Beefeater, TGI Friday's, Pelican and Pizza Hut UK. The

Whitbread Hotel Company owns 3,421 Marriott Hotels, 1,528 Marriott Country Clubs, 5,069 Swallow Hotels acquired from the Swallow Group, 2,229 managed Travel Inns and 1,0186 franchised Travel Inns. It also owns David Lloyd Leisure (tennis, golf and fitness clubs), and First Quench, a drinks company that includes Wine Rack, Bottoms Up, Thresher, and Victoria Wines.

WHITE ROSE

White Rose Inns PLC, Chantrell House, 1 Chantrell Court, The Calls, Leeds, W Yorkshire LS2 7HA
Tel (0113) 2461332
Fax (0113) 2461350

The group has 44 houses in total – four managed houses and 40 tenancies in Yorkshire with supplies from Carlsberg-Tetley, Bass, Black Sheep and its own micro-brewery, the Barge & Barrel Brewery Company, based at the Barge & Barrel at Elland.

WILLIAMS

James Williams (Narberth), 7 Spring Gardens, Narberth, Pembrokeshire SA67 7BP
Tel (01834) 862200
Fax (01834) 862202

A privately-owned concern, founded in 1830 and operating 54 pubs in west and mid Wales. Tenants are mainly supplied by Bass, Brains Crown Buckley, Carlsberg-Tetley and Whitbread. A house ale, James Williams IPA, brewed by Brains, is also available. Over the past year regional brands have also been taken, including beers from Adnams, Banks, Bateman, Everards, Jennings, Felinfoel and Shepherd Neame. The company has a regular, extensive guest cask-conditioned beer policy.

WIZARD INNS

City Gate, 17 Victoria Street, St Albans AL1 3JJ
Tel (01727) 792200
Fax (01727) 792210

Former CAMRA national chairman Chris Hutt, also the ex-boss of Midsummer Inns and Unicorn Inns, purchased 30-40 former Phoenix Inns pubs to set up this new company. Nomura, the Japanese bank that owns Unique Pub company, has a £9.5 million stake. Wizard Inns operates traditional, unbranded pubs. All the pubs are managed and serve a selection of real ales.

YATES'S

Yates's Wine Lodges Ltd, Peter Yates House, Manchester Road, Bolton, Greater Manchester BL3 2PY
Tel (01204) 373737
Fax (01204) 388383

Company founded in Oldham in 1884 by wine merchant Peter Yates, it now runs 95 managed pubs in locations from Scotland to London. Beers are mainly from Bass, Scottish Courage and Whitbread, with some regional ales also featured. Boddingtons Bitter is sold at one price nationwide.

Other notable pub chains
Operated by, or divisions of, brewing companies or pub groups

All Bar One (Bass)

Artist's Fare (ex-Morland, now Greene King)

Barras & Co (Scottish Courage)

Bar Central (Grosvenor Inns)

Beefeater (Whitbread)

Bert's Bars (Alloa)

BieRRex (Century Inns)

Bill Bentley's Wine Bars (Young's)

Bootsy Brogan's (Glendola Leisure)

Brewer's Fayre (Whitbread)

Café Rouge (Whitbread)

Countryside Hotels (Greene King)

Dave & Busters (Bass)

Dublin Pub Company (Mercury Taverns)

Edwards (Bass)

Festival Ale Houses (Carlsberg-Tetley)

Firkin (Bass & Punch)

Fork & Pitcher (Bass)

Forshaw's (Burtonwood)

Harvester (Bass)

Harvey Floorbangers (Regent Inns)

High Street Taverns (Grosvenor Inns)

Hobgoblinns (Wychwood)

Hogshead (Whitbread)

Hooden Horse (Inn Business)

Hungry Horse (Greene King)

It's a Scream (Bass)

JJ Moon's (Wetherspoon)

Jongleurs (Regent Inns)

King's Fayre (Greene King)

Lacon Inns (Adnams)

Landlord's Table (Mansfield)

Milestone Restaurants and Taverns (Wolverhampton & Dudley)

Mr Q's (Bass)

Newt & Cucumber (ex-Morland, now Greene King)

O'Neills (Bass)

Pickled Newt (Greene King)

Pitcher & Piano (W&D/Marston's)

Pizza Hut (Whitbread)

PJ Pepper (Whitbread)

Rat & Carrot (Greene King)

Scruffy Murphy's (Bass/Punch)

Shamus O'Donnell's (Enterprise Inns)

Spoofers (Regent Inns)

T&J Bernard's (Scottish Courage)

Tap & Spile (Enterprise Inns: four have been leased to Castle Eden Brewery)

TGI Friday's (Whitbread)

Toby Restaurants (Bass)

Tut 'n' Shive (Whitbread)

Vantage Inns (Burtonwood)

Vintage Inns (Bass)

Walkabout Inns (Regent Inns)

Wayside Inns (Whitbread)

Wig & Pen (ex-Morland, now Greene King)

Wirral Taverns (Enterprise Inns)

What's Brewing CAMRA

NEWSPAPER OF THE CAMPAIGN FOR REAL ALE   MAY 2000

Top regionals invest millions in expanding real ale market
Indies lead fightback

by Ted Bruning

BRITAIN'S independent brewers are blasting back in a powerful bid to re-establish real ale as the tap tipple in the nation's pubs.

For while the smooth-b-sorted nationals are letting cask beer die of neglect, the zionals realise that disc, characterful cask their lifeblood.

nal giants Wolver- & Dudley and

holidays in Southwold – to do the voice-overs.

The campaign, called Adnams Characters and based on real Adnams drinkers, started its first burst on Anglia TV on 17 April.

Also on TV is London brewer Fuller's, which has put £1.5 million behind its ne Whatever You Do, pp

the affluent Thames Valley.

Meanwhile Cardiff brewer Brains has mounted a £5 million expansion drive into the region as part of its plan to double its estate to 400. They range from Bar Essential in Bristol to the Old Station in Hallatrow, Somerset.

Brakspear of Henley-on-Thr   icking the od a pro

Keep in touch with all the changes in breweries and pub groups by joining CAMRA and receiving What's Brewing every month.

The Beers Index
Your quick guide to real ales of the UK.
Over 2,000 beers are highlighted

Beldi Weiss Wheat Beer Swaled Ale *527*
Belfast Special Bitter Whitewater *539*
Belgian White Harviestoun *482*
Bellringer Abbey *435*; Lichfield *495*;
Three Tuns *529*
Belt 'n' Braces Leatherbritches *494*
Beltane Cheriton *457*
Belter Leatherbritches *494*
Benchmark Stonehenge *525*
Bendigo Castle Rock *456*
Bengal Tiger Concertina *459*
Benskins Bitter Carlsberg-Tetley *547*
Benvolio Newby Wyke *504*
Bert Corner Saddleworth *520*
Bespoke Leatherbritches *494*
Best Cellar Yates *543*
Best Lockoford Bitter Townes *532*
Bete Noire Kelham Island *492*
Beth's Arrival Hart *481*
Betty Stogs Bitter Skinner's *524*
BHB Marches *499*
BiBi Hedgehog & Hogshead *483*
Big Fat Santa Brewery on Sea *449*
Big Nev's Six Bells *523*
Big Tackle Ridleys *517*
Bill Monks Derwent *465*
Billericay Dickie Triple fff *533*
Billy Kings Head *493*
Bingle Jells Mighty Oak *501*
Birthday Bitter Caythorpe *456*
Bishop Ridley's Ale Black Bull *445*
Bishop's Bitter Crouch Vale *462*
Bishops Farewell Oakham *506*
Bishops Finger Shepherd Neame *523*
Bishops Pacific Oriental *510*
Bishopswood Bitter Swansea *527*
Bittern Reepham *517*
Bittern Bitter Old Chimneys *507*
Black Adder Mauldons *500*
Black Adder II Gribble Inn *478*
Black and Amber Warcop *535*
Black and Amber Extra Warcop *535*
Black and Amber Special Warcop *535*
Black Baron Greene King *478*
Black Bat B&T *439*
Black Bear Beartown *442*
Black Beastie Arundel *437*
Black Beauty Porter Vale *534*
Black Bess Porter Ash Vine *438*
Black Bishop Durham *466*
Black Bull Bitter Theakston
(Scottish Courage) *546*
Black Bull Mild Blanchfield *446*
Black Canyon Millers Thumb *502*
Black Cap Clark's *458*
Black Cat Moorhouses *503*
Black Christmas Whim *538*
Black Country Bitter Holden's *486*
Black Country Mild Holden's *486*
Black Country Stout Holden's *486*
Black Cuillin Isle of Skye *490*
Black Dog Mild Elgood's *467*
Black Dog Special Black Dog *445*
Black Douglas Broughton *451*
Black Eagle Pitfield *512*
Black Five Iris Rose *490*
Black Friar Durham *466*
Black Gold Tomintoul *532*
Black Heart Barnsley *441*
Black Hole Porter Oakham *506*
Black Jack Porter Archers *436*
Black Jack Stout Castle Rock *456*
Black Knight Goff's *476*
Black Lager Harviestoun *482*
Black Lurcher Abbeydale *435*
Black Magic Mild Hanby *480*
Black Magic Stout Oakhill *506*
Black Mass Abbeydale *435*
Black Midden Stout Mordue *503*
Black Old Bat B&T *438*
Black Parrot Burtonwood *453*
Black Pear Malvern Hills *498*
Black Pett Forge *472*
Black Pig Highgate *484*
Black Rat Stout Old Chimneys *507*
Black Rock Brewery on Sea *450*
Black Satin Mauldons *500*
Black Shadow Phoenix *511*
Black Squall Porter Newby Wyke *504*
Black Stump Barge & Barrel *440*
Black Swan Dark Mild Vale *534*

Black Velvet Durham *466*
Black Widow Dark Horse *463*
Black Wych Wychwood *542*
Blackbeck Strawberry Bank *526*
Blackcurrant Porter Mash and Air *500*
Blackcurrant Porter Mash 2 *500*
Blackguard Butts *454*
Blackjack Old Mill *508*; Warwickshire *536*
Blackmoor Stout Frome Valley *474*
Blackout Big Lamp *444*
Blackout Winter Warmer Cains *454*
Blacksmith's Ale Coniston *459*
Blackwater Mild Crouch Vale *462*
Blackwater Porter Hogs Back *485*
Bladderwrack Railway Tavern *515*
Blakeley's Best O'Hanlon's *505*
Blakes Gosport Bitter Winchester *540*
Blatherwyke Bitter Rockingham *519*
Blaven Isle of Skye *490*
Blencathra Bitter Hesket Newmarket *483*
Blitzen Brun Millers Thumb *502*
Blizzard Beowulf *444*
Blonde Arran *437*
Blonde Bombshell Rebellion *516*
Blondie Kings Head *493*; Liverpool *496*
Bloody Bosworth Bitter Battle Weltons *537*
Bloomin' Ale Thwaites *529*
Blue Jay Bitter Cotleigh *460*
Blue Rocket Kent Garden *493*
Bluebird Coniston (Brakspear) *449*
Bluebird Coniston *459*
Blues Rother Valley *519*
Blunderbus Old Porter Coach House *459*
Blyton Best Bigfoot *445*
Boadicea Chariot Ale Iceni *489*
Boathouse Bitter City of Cambridge *457*
BOB Wickwar *539*
Bobbies Bitter Planets *513*
Bobbin's Bitter Three B's *529*
Boddingtons Bitter Interbrew *548*
Bodgers Barley Wine Chiltern *457*
Bodicote Bitter Plough Inn *513*
Bodmin Beast Sutton *527*
Bodysnatcher B&T *438*
Bomar Bitter Northumberland *505*
Bombardier Premium Bitter Wells *537*
Bombshell Bitter Quay *514*
Bonfire Boy Harveys *482*
Bonfire Brew Wood *540*
Bonneville Phoenix *512*
Bookies Revenge Lidstones *495*
Boon Doggle Ringwood *518*
Boot Strap Cambrinus *455*
Bootleg Bitter Hedgehog & Hogshead *483*
Bootleg Valentines Ale Coach House *458*
Bord Best North Yorkshire *505*
Born Free B&T *438*
Boston Strangler Boston Experience *447*
Bosun Bitter Old Laxey *508*; Poole *513*
Bosun's Bitter St Austell *520*
Bottlenose Brewery on Sea *449*
Bowler Langton *494*
Brain Dead Scattor Rock *522*
Brainstorm Ales of Kent *436*
Bramble Stout Burton Bridge *452*
Bramling Cross Broughton *451*
Bramling Traditional City of Cambridge *458*
Brand Oak Bitter Wickwar *539*
Brandy Snapper Brandy Cask *449*
Branoc Branscombe Vale *449*
Brass Monkey Mighty Oak *501*
Braveheart Moulin *504*
Braye Mild Guernsey *479*
Breacais Highgate *484*
Breast Stroke Wood *540*
Brew Burton Bridge *453*
Brew 2K Maypole *501*
Brew 97 Mole's *502*
Brew 101 Six Bells *523*
Brewer's Bluff Flannery's *471*
Brewer's Bounty Flannery's *471*
Brewer's Gold Flannery's *471*
Brewers Droop Marston Moor *499*
Brewers Gold Pictish *512*
Brewers Pride Marston Moor *499*
Brewery Tap Chalk Hill *456*
Brewery Tap Bitter Fernandes *470*
Brewhouse Reepham *517*
Brewhouse Bitter Dunn Plowman *466*
Brewster's Bundle Hogs Back *485*
Brewster's Stocking Brewster's *450*
Brick Kiln Bitter West Berkshire *538*

Brideshead Bitter York *543*
Bridge Bitter Burton Bridge *453*
Bridge Street Bitter Green Dragon *477*
Bridport Bitter Palmers *510*
Brigadier Bitter Hoskins & Oldfield *487*
Bright Otter *510*
Brighton Bitter Kemptown *492*
Brindle Bullmastiff *452*
Bristol Porter Smiles *524*
Broadgauge Bitter Cottage *460*
Broadside Adnams *435*
Bronte Goose Eye *477*
Brookenby Dark King & Smart *493*
Brooker's Bitter & Twisted Harviestoun *482*
Broomstick Bitter Mauldons *500*
Brothers Best Forge *472*
Brunel Premier Ale Scanlon's (O'Hanlon's) *522*
Brush Bitter Alcazar *436*
Brydge Bitter Bank Top *440*
BSA Hogs Back *485*
BSE Barum *441*
BST British Summer Time Flagship *471*
Buccaneer Burtonwood *453*
Buccaneers Jollyboat *491*
Buchanan's Best Bitter Federation (Robinson's) *470*
Buchanan's Original Federation (Robinson's) *470*
Buckland Best Bitter Winchester *540*
Buckley's Best Bitter Brains *448*
Buckley's IPA Brains *448*
Buckley's Merlin's Oak Brains *448*
Buckshot Cannon Royall *455*
Buckswood Dingle Fromes Hill *474*
Buddy Marvellous Bryncelyn *452*
Buddys Delight Bryncelyn *452*
Bug Bitter York *543*
Bull Village Brewer (Hambleton) *480*
Bull Best Bitter Blanchfield *446*
Bullion Old Mill *508*
Bullseye Arundel *437*; Payn *511*
Bunker Hill Boston Experience *447*
Buoys Bitter Cox & Holbrook *461*
Burcom Bitter Willy's *539*
Burcote Premium Pale Worfield *542*
Burgh Bitter Fisherrow *471*
Burglar Bill Clark's *458*
Burlington Bertie Batemans *441*
Burma Star Ale Hogs Back *485*
Burn's Ale Harviestoun *482*
Burning Wicket Weltons *537*
Burns Auld Sleekit Coach House *458*
Burnsall Classic Bitter Briscoe's *450*
Burntwood Bitter Mighty Oak *502*
Burrough Hill Pale Banfield *439*
Burton Porter Burton Bridge *452, 453*
Busty Bitter Trimdon *532*
Busy Lizzie Weltons *537*
Butcher's Baubles Crown Inn *462*
Butcher's Best Crown Inn *462*
Butler's Revenge Shugborough (Titanic) *531*
Butlers Ale Potton *514*
Butser Bitter Gale's *475*
Butt Jumper Humpty Dumpty *489*
Butterley Bitter Riverhead *518*
Butty Bach Wye Valley *542*
BVB Branscombe Vale *449*

C

Caillie Tomintoul *532*
Cambridge Bitter Elgood's *467*
Canal No 5 Sunset *527*
Canal No 7 Sunset *527*
Canal No 7+ Sunset *527*
Canal No 9 Sunset *527*
Canary Green Jack *478*
Candyman Brewery on Sea *449*
Canny Lad Durham *466*
Canon Bitter Shoes *523*
Canon's Choice Tomos Watkin *536*
Capstan Flagship *471*
Captain Bill Bartrams Best Bitter Bartrams *441*
Captain Smith's Titanic *531*
Captain's Stout Bartrams *441*
Captins Tackle Tap 'n' Tin *528*
Cardiff Dark Bullmastiff *452*
Cardinal FILO *471*
Carls Best Bitter Iris Rose *490*
Carnivale Berrow *444*
Carousel Bitter Malton *498*
Carrot Cruncher Kitchen *493*
Cascade Hanby *480*; Linfit *495*; Whitewater *539*

Caskade Oldershaw *509*
Casnewydd Warcop *535*
Castle Ale Warwickshire *536*
Castles Bitter Northumberland *505*
Castletown Bitter Okells *507*
Catbells Pale Ale Hesket Newmarket *483*
Caudle Bitter Langton *494*
Cauld Turkey Fyfe *475*
Cauldron Snout High Force *484*
Caulkers Bitter Tap 'n' Tin *528*
Cavalier Clearwater *458*; Lichfield *495*
Cavendish Gold Shardlow *522*
Celebrance Cambrinus *455*
Celebrated Staggering Ale Kemptown *492*
Celebration Liverpool *496*; Maypole *501*; Weatheroak *536*
Celebration Ale Porter *513*
Celestial Steam Gale Freeminer *473*
Cellar Vee Summerskills *526*
Celtibration Ale Bushy's *453*
Celtic Durham *466*
Celtic Ale Flannery's *471*
Celtic Queen Iceni *489*
Celtic Warrior Pictish *512*
Centenary Ale Maypole *501*
Centennial Museum (Interbrew) *548*
Centurion Best Bitter Hadrian (Four Rivers) *472*
Centurion's Ghost Ale York *543*
Cereal Killer North Yorkshire *505*
Cerise de Salop Salopian *521*
Cession Ale Brunswick *451*
Chainmaker Mild Enville *467*
Chairman's Thwaites *529*
Challenger Ash Vine *438*; Barum *441*
Champagne Charlie Batemans *441*
Champflower Cottage *460*
Champion Ale Badger *439*
Chancellors Revenge Shardlow *522*
Chandos Gold Moor *503*
Chaos Oakham *506*
Charles' First Brew Shraley Brook *523*
Charter Ale Broadstone *451*
Chase Your Tail Spinning Dog *525*
Chaucer Ale Green Dragon *477*
CHB Chalk Hill *456*
Chef's Cut Kitchen *493*
Chelsea Blossom Orange (Scottish Courage) *546*
  Yorkshire Grey (Scottish Courage) *546*
Chequered Flag Okells *507*
Cherry Bomb Hanby *480*
Cheshire Cat Coach House *458*
Chester's Strong & Ugly Barngates *440*
Chevin Chaser Briscoe's *451*
Chevinbrau Briscoe's *451*
CHH Bryncelyn *452*
Chiddingstone Bitter Larkins *494*
Chiswick Bitter Fuller's *474*
Choir Porter Salopian *521*
Chorlton Bitter Marble *499*
Christmas Carol Saddleworth *520*
Christmas Cheer Rectory *516*
Christmas Cheers Tindall *530*
Christmas Chuckle Humpty Dumpty *489*
Christmas Classic Daleside *463*
Christmas Cracker Fellows, Morton & Clayton (Interbrew) *548*; Teignworthy *528*; Wood *540*
Christmas Goose Goose Eye *477*
Christmas Kiss Phoenix *511*
Christmas Noggin Hoskins & Oldfield *488*
Christmas Pud Frankton Bagby *473*
Christmas Reserve Mauldons *500*
Churchill's Pride Hoskins *487*
City Gent Clark's *458*
Claud Hamilton Humpty Dumpty *489*
Claudia Wheat Beer Brewster's *450*
Cleo's Asp Hart *481*
Cleric's Cure Three Tuns *529*
Clerics Consolation Grimsdales (Pilgrim) *479*
Clever Endeavour Hydes *489*
Cliffe Hanger Porter Dark Star *463*
Cliffhanger Bank Top *440*
Cloud Nine Six Bells *523*
Clouded Yellow St Austell *520*
Club Bitter Concertina *459*
Coachman's Best Bitter Coach House *458*
Coachman's Tipple Shugborough (Titanic) *531*
Coast Liner Skinner's *524*
Coast 2 Coast Derwent Rose *465*
Coat O' Red John O'Gaunt *491*
Cob Nut Brown Hop Back *487*
Cobnut Special Tolly Cobbold *531*
Cocker Hoop Jennings *491*

Ind Coope Burton Ale Carlsberg-Tetley
(Marston's) *500*
Independence Inveralmond *490*
Independence Ale Millers Thumb *502*
Indian Summer Swale *527*
Indiana's Bones Summerskills *527*
Ingleby Pale Ale Lloyds *496*
Innkeeper's Special Reserve Coach House *459*
Inspiration Ale Goddards *476*
Inspired Lichfield *495*
Invincible Durham *466*
Invincible Stout Winchester *540*
Iris Rose Inveralmond *490*
Iron Brew Freeminer *473*
Iron Horse Goddards *476*
Iron Oak Single Stout Cox & Holbrook *461*
Ironbridge Stout Salopian *521*
Ironmaster Crown Inn *462*
Ironmasters Wood *540*
Ironside Hampshire *480*
Italian Job Batemans *441*
Ivory Stout Man in the Moon *498*

J

Jack Frost Fuller's *474*
Jack O'Lantern Hop Back *487*
Jack Snipe Woodhampton *541*
Jack Tar Crewkerne *461*
Jack The Lad Bullmastiff *452*
Jackpot St George's *521*
Jacobite Ale Traquair *532*
Jail Ale Princetown *514*
James Forshaw's Bitter Burtonwood *453*
James I Abbeydale *435*
Janet Street Porter Linfit *496*
Jazz Bitter Riverhead *518*
Jeffrey Hudson Bitter Oakham *506*
Jekyll's Gold Premium Ale Hydes *489*
Jenny Pipes Blonde Biere Marches *499*
Jester Butts *454*
Jester Ale Cox's Yard *461*
Jester Quick One Bartrams *441*
Jet Black City of Cambridge *457*
Jetsam Bitter Border *447*
JHB Oakham *506*
Jigsaw Salopian *521*
Jimmy's Bitter Tipsy Toad *530*
Jingle Knockers Skinner's *524*
JLK Pale Ale Worfield *542*
Jock Frost Houston *488*
John Baker's Original Brandy Cask *449*
John Bewsher's Best Bitter Tirril *530*
John Paul Jones Sulwath *526*
John Smith's Cask Bitter Scottish Courage *545*
John Smith's Magnet Scottish Courage *545*
Jolabrugg Earl Soham *466*
Jolly Roger DarkTribe *464*
Josephine Grimbley Wells *537*
Joules Bitter Museum (Interbrew) *548*
Jouster Goff's *476*
Jovian Phoenix *511*
Joy Bringer Hanby *480*
JTS XXX Lloyds *496*
Judge Jeffreys Itchen Valley *491*
Judgement Day Bank Top *440*
Junction Bitter McGuinness *496*
Jupiter Milton *502*
JW Lees Bitter Lees *494*

K

Kamikaze Flying Firkin (Dent) *465*
Kane's Amber Ale Maclay (Forth) *472*
Kangaroo Ventnor *534*
Keelmans Big Lamp *444*
Kendal Bitter Lakeland *493*
Kentish Gold Swale *527*
Kentish Pride Swale *527*
Kern Knott's Cracking Stout
Hesket Newmarket *483*
Ketts Rebellion Woodforde's *541*
Killellan Houston *488*
Killer Beer Darwin *464*
Kiln House Shardlow *522*
Kimberley Best Bitter Hardys & Hansons *481*
Kimberley Best Mild Hardys & Hansons *481*
Kimberley Classic Hardys & Hansons *481*
King Keltek *492*
King & Barnes Mild Ale Gribble Inn *478*
King Alfred's Hampshire *480*
King Billy Cropton *462*

Kingdom Dunn Plowman *466*
Kingfisher Ale Woodhampton *542*
Kinghorn Wheat Beer Prince of Wales *514*
Kingsdown Ale Arkell's *437*
Kingston Amber Wheat Beer Newby Wyke *504*
Kinsman Beowulf *444*
Kiss Harveys *482*
Kiss Me Quick Batemans *441*
Kiwi Pale Ale Cotleigh *460*
Knickadroppa Glory Sutton *527*
Knight Keltek *492*
Knight Porter Whitewater *539*
Knight Rider Goff's *476*
Knights of the Round Table Bank Top *440*
Knockendoch Sulwath *526*
Knocker Up Three B's *529*
Knots of May Light Mild Harveys *482*
Kodiak Gold Beartown *442*
Kolsch MacLachlans *497*
Kookaburra Bitter Cotleigh *460*
Kursaal Flyer Crouch Vale *462*

L

LA Bitter Reepham *517*
La'al Cockle Warmer Jennings *491*
LAD Lager Iceni *489*
Laird's Ale Tomintoul *532*
Lakeland Terrier Lakeland *493*
Lamp Oil Cambrinus *455*
Lancing Special Dark Brewery on Sea *449*
Landlady Caythorpe *456*
Landlord Taylor *528*
Landlords Choice Mole's *502*
Lass O'Gowrie Interbrew *548*
Last Drop Bitter York *543*
The Last Order West Berkshire *538*
Last Resort Willy's *539*
Last Rites Abbeydale *435*
Late Red Autumn Hop Ale Shepherd Neame *523*
Late Starter Berkeley *444*
Leadboiler Linfit *496*
Leading Light Caythorpe *456*
Leaf Fall Brakspear *448*
Leaf Thief Brewery on Sea *449*
Legend Hogs Back *485*
Legion Ale Hadrian (Four Rivers) *472*
Leith IPA Restalrig *517*
Lemon Ale Humpty Dumpty *489*
Lempster Ore Marches *499*
Levant Golden Ventonwyn *535*
Level Best Rother Valley *519*
Leveller Barge & Barrel *440*
The Leveller Springhead *525*
Lia Fail Inveralmond *490*
Liberation Harviestoun *482*
Liberator Hart *481*
Liberty IPA Marble *499*
Lifeboat Ale Titanic *531*
Light Horse Caythorpe *456*
Light Oak Weatheroak *536*
Light Year Glentworth *475*
Lighterman Rother Valley *519*
Lighthouse Ale Millers Thumb *502*
Lightmaker Glentworth *475*
Lightning Strike Grimsdales (Pilgrim) *479*
Lincoln Ale King & Smart *493*
Linebacker Leadmill *494*
Lion Slayer Fyfe *475*
Lion's Pride Maypole *501*
Lionheart Hampshire *480*
Lions Main Picks *512*
Lions Pride Picks *512*
Liquor Mortis Blue Moon *447*
Liquorice Kingussie Iris Rose *490*
Little Beauty Frankton Bagby *473*
Little Matty Hoskins & Oldfield *487*
Little Red Rooster Triple fff *533*
Little Sharpie Humpty Dumpty *489*
Little Willie Oliver Hare (Arundel) *437*
Littondale Light Briscoe's *450*
Lizard Point Organic *509*
Lochinvar Harviestoun *482*
London Pride Fuller's *474*
Longleat Ash Vine *438*
Lord Ashford's Special Reserve Scanlon's
(Vale) *521*
Lord Lee's North Yorkshire *505*
Lord Leicester Ale Chiltern *457*
Lord Protector Marches *499*
Lord Willoughby Newby Wyke *504*
Lord's Prayer Berkeley *444*

Natural Blonde Harviestoun 482
Natural Selection Wood 540
Naughty Noughty Frome Valley 474
Navigator Bridgewater 450
Nector Rooster's 519
Ned's Tipple Strawberry Bank 526
Nellie Dene Old Mill 508
Nelson's Blood Flagship 471
Nelson's Cannon Weltons 537
Nelson's Revenge Woodforde's 541
Nemesis Hart 481
Neptune Milton 502
Nessie's Monster Mash Tomintoul 532
Nettlethrasher Barge & Barrel 440
New Dawn Millennium Ale Alcazar 436
New Timer Badger 439
Newshound 2000 Wolf 540
Newton's Drop Oldershaw 508
Niagara Leadmill 494
Nick's Milk Street 502
Night Porter Scattor Rock 522
Nightingale Old Chimneys 507
Nightjar Daleside 463
Nightmare Hambleton 480
Nimmo's XXXX Castle Eden 455
No Balls Hart 481
No Idea Flannery's 471
No-Eyed Deer Goose Eye 477
Nob Mild Museum (Interbrew) 548
Noble Beowulf 444
Noel Ale Arkell's 437
Noggins Nog Border 447
Nord Atlantic Humpty Dumpty 489
Norfolk Nips Woodforde's 541
Norfolk Nog Woodforde's 541
Norfolk Wheaten Reepham 517
Norfolk Wolf Porter Green Jack 478
Norkie Woodforde's 541
Norman's Conquest Cottage 460
Norman's Pride Corvedale 460
North Brink Porter Elgood's 467
Northdown Broughton 451
Northern Light Orkney 509
Northern Pride Hull 488
Norton Ale Shoes 523
Nortons Bitter Orchard 509
Norwich Terrier Buffy's 452
Notley Ale Vale 534
Nottingham Pale Ale Castle Rock 456
No I Potton 514
No. 1 Selby 522
No. 3 Selby 522
No 3 Yates 543
No. 9 Plough Inn 513
Nut Brown Ale Fisherrow 471
Nutcracker Mild Cotleigh 460
Nutters Tally Ho 528
Nyewood Gold Ballard's 439

O

O Boy Bryncelyn 452
O Cocker Derwent 465
O4 Ale Hoskins & Oldfield 487
Oakwell Barnsley 440
Oasthouse Gold Weetwood 537
Oatmeal Stout Flannery's 471; Wentworth 538
OBB Samuel Smith 524
OBJ Brakspear 448
Octopussy Batemans 441
Odda's Light Mayhem (Wadworth) 535
Oddas Light Farmers Arms 469
Off the Rails Pembroke 511
Off Your Trolley Hart 481
Offa Beowulf 444
Offa's Ale Three Tuns 529
Offilers Bitter Museum (Interbrew) 548
OG Tomos Watkin 536
Oh! Mr Porter Falstaff 469
Old Accidental Brunswick 451
Old Appledore Country Life 461
Old Arnold Wickwar 539
Old Basford Pale Ale Fiddlers 470
Old Bat B&T 438
Old Black Shuck Elgood's 467
Old Boy Oldershaw 509
Old Brewery Bitter Samuel Smith 524
Old Bushy Tail Bushy's 453
Old Buzzard Cotleigh 460
Old Carrock Strong Ale Hesket Newmarket 483
Old Chapel Bitter Winchester 540
Old Chapel Porter Winchester 540

Old Cocky Weltons 537
Old Codger Rebellion 516
Old Conspirator Arundel 437
Old Curiosity Old Mill 508
Old Dalby Belvoir 443
Old Dark Attic Concertina 459
Old Dick Swale 527
Old Dog Bitter Weetwood 537
Old Dray Worldham 542
Old Eli Linfit 496
Old Emrys Nags Head 504
Old Engine Oil Harviestoun 482
Old English Porter Plough Inn 513
Old Expensive Burton Bridge 453
Old Fashioned Porter Fiddlers 470
Old Fireside Wood 540
Old Freddy Walker Moor 503
Old Friend Berkeley 444
Old Gang Bitter Swaled Ale 527
Old Gavel Bender Judges 491
Old Genie Big Lamp 444
Old Globe Premium Fernandes 470
Old Grizzly Old Bear 507
Old Growler Nethergate 504
Old Groyne Willy's 540
Old Grumpy Kemptown 492
Old Harry Weltons 537
Old Henry Hobsons 485
Old Herbaceous Rockingham 519
Old Homewrecker Maypole 501
Old Hooky Hook Norton 487
Old House Bitter Woodbury 541
Old Humbug Hexhamshire 483
Old Icknield Ale Tring 533
Old Izaak Whim 538
Old Jock Broughton 451
Old Kiln Ale Border 447
Old Kiln Hardys & Hansons 481
Old Knotty Joule (Coach House) 459
Old Knucker Arundel 437
Old Knuckle Shuffler Boat 447
Old Legover Daleside 463
Old Lubrication Daleside 463
Old Ma Weasel Ales of Kent 436
Old Mackay Far North 469
Old Man Ale Coniston 460
Old Mill Bitter Cox & Holbrook 461
Old Mulled Ale Tisbury 530
Old Navigation Ale Hoskins & Oldfield 488
Old Nobbie Stout Pembroke 511
Old Nottingham Extra Pale Caythorpe Ale 456
Old Oak Phoenix 512
Old Pal Church End 457
Old Peculier Theakston (Scottish Courage) 546
Old Pedantic Sutton 527
Old Pendeen Ventonwyn 535
Old Priory Joule (Coach House) 459
Old Ram Hart 481
Old Recumbent Six Bells 523
Old Remedial Moulin 504
Old Retainer Frankton Bagby 473
Old Ric Uley 533
Old Rot Quay 514
Old Ruby Village Brewer (Hambleton) 480
Old Russ Ale Smiles 524
Old Scrooge Arundel 437; Three Tuns 529
Old Sea Dog Stout Flagship 471
Old Shunter Bushy's 453
Old Slug Porter RCH 515
Old Smoky Stonehenge 526
Old Speckled Hen Greene King 478
Old Speckled Parrot Bird in Hand 445
Old Spot Prize Ale Uley 533
Old Stable Brew Shardlow 522
Old Stockport Bitter Robinson's 518
Old Strong Winter Ale Tolly Cobbold 531
Old Style Porter St Peter's 521
Old Tackle Chalk Hill 456
Old 1066 Ale Goacher's 476
Old Thumper Ringwood 518
Old Thunderbox Green Jack 478
Old Timber Cox's Yard 461
Old Timer Wadworth 535
Old Tom Oakwell 506; Robinson's 518; Selby 522
Old Tongham Tasty Hogs Back 485
Old Tosser Smiles 524
Old Tosspot Oakham 506
Old Town Bitter Beckett's 442
Old Tradition Home County 486
Ye Old Trout Ale Kemptown 492
Old Wemian Ale Hanby 480
Old XL Ale Holden's 486

Railway Sleeper Humpty Dumpty *489*;
  Swansea *527*
Rain Dance Brewery on Sea *450*
Rainbow Chaser Hanby *480*
Raisin Stout Kitchen *493*
Ram Tam Taylor *528*
Ramblers Tipple Clearwater *458*
Rambrau Dent *465*
Rampant Gryphon Wentworth *538*
Rampart Border *447*
Rams Revenge Clark's *458*
Ramsbottom Strong Ale Dent *465*
Ramsey Pride Payn *511*
Ramsey Ruin Payn *511*
Rapier Pale Ale Reepham *517*
Rare Hare Bath *442*
Raspberry Belter Leatherbritches *494*
Raspberry Wheat Iceni *489*
Rattler Brewery on Sea *449*
Raven Ale Orkney *509*
Real Mackay Far North *469*
Real Nut Ale Tisbury *530*
Reckless Raspberry Hoskins & Oldfield *487*
Rector's Light Relief Rectory *516*
Rector's Pleasure Rectory *516*
Rector's Revenge Rectory *516*
Red Cains *454*; Deeping *464*; Liverpool *496*
Red Ale O'Hanlon's *506*
Red Alt Beer Clockwork *458*
Red Cuillin Isle of Skye *490*
Red Dragon Flannery's *471*
Red Dust Derwent Rose *465*
Red Fox Fuller's *474*
Red Hot Furnace Warcop *535*
Red Hot Poker Berkeley *444*
Red Kite Black Isle *445*; Woodhampton *541*
Red MacGregor Orkney *509*
Red Nose Reinbeer Cotleigh *460*
Red Oktober Rebellion *516*
Red Queen Bartrams *441*
Red Rooster Millers Thumb *502*
Red Roses Itchen Valley *490*
Redbrook Premium Bitter Riverhead *518*
Redemption Passageway *511*
Redwood Weatheroak *536*
Reeket Yill Broughton *451*
Reel Ale Teignworthy *528*
Reg's Tipple Gribble Inn *478*
Regal Birthday Ale Coach House *458*
Regal Blonde Oldershaw *509*
Regatta Adnams *435*
Reinbeer Elgood's *467*
Reiver's IPA Border *447*
Remembrance Ale Wood *540*
Resolution Brakspear *447*
Rest in Peace Church End *457*
Resurrection Lichfield *495*; Phoenix *511*;
  Tindall *530*
Resurrection Ale Lichfield *495*
Rev James Original Ale Brains *448*
Revenge Keltek *492*
Reverend Eaton's Ale Shardlow *522*
Reynolds Redneck Worfield *542*
Rhatas Black Dog *445*
Rheidol Reserve Flannery's *471*
Ribtickler Frankton Bagby *473*
Richmond Ale Darwin *464*
The Ridgeway Bitter Tring *533*
Riding Bitter Mansfield *498*
Riding Mild Mansfield *498*
Riggwelter Black Sheep *446*
Rip Snorter Hogs Back *485*
Rip-Rap Phoenix *511*
Ripon Jewel Daleside *463*
Ripper Green Jack *478*
Riptide Brewery on Sea *450*
Road to Rome Hart *481*
Roaring Meg Springhead *525*
Roast Mild Dark Star *463*
Roasted Nuts Rebellion *516*
Robert Catesby Leatherbritches *494*
Robin a Tiptoe John O'Gaunt *491*
Rocket Liverpool *496*
Rocket Fuel Hydes *489*; North Yorkshire *505*
Rockin' Robin Hale & Hearty *479*
Rocking Rudolph Hardys & Hansons *481*
Roger & Out Frog & Parrot (Interbrew) *548*
Roisin Dubh Iceni *489*
Rolling Ruck Castle Rock *456*
Rolling Thunder Leadmill *494*
Roman Cand Ale Smiles *524*
Romeo's Rouser Arundel *437*

Romeo's Ruin B&T *438*
Rooster's Rooster's *519*
Rope of Sand Fyfe *475*
Roseburn Bitter Iris Rose *490*
Rosey Nosey Batemans *441*
Rossendale Ale Porter *513*
Roundhead's Gold Springhead *525*
Rowan Ale Four Rivers *472*
Rowley Mild Lidstones *495*
Roy Morgan's Original Ale Travellers Inn
  (Coach House) *532*
Royal Oak Eldridge Pope (Thomas Hardy) *481*
Royal Piddle Wyre Piddle *543*
Royal Welch Fusilier Plassey *513*
Ruby Ale Fiddlers *470*
Ruby (1874) Mild Bushy's *453*
Ruby Mild Rudgate *520*
Ruby Tuesday King & Smart *493*; Mighty Oak *502*
Ruddles Best Greene King *478*
Ruddles County Greene King *478*
Ruddy Rudolph Plassey *513*
Rudolph Stonehenge *525*
Rudolph the Redruth Brain Beer Redruth *516*
Rudolph's Revenge Belhaven *443*; Cropton *462*;
  Packhorse *510*
Rudolph's Rocket Fuel Fenland *470*
Rudolph's Ruin Border *447*; Hale & Hearty *479*
Ruffled Feathers Bitter Riverhead *518*
Rugby Special Frankton Bagby *473*
Rulbuts Strawberry Bank *526*
Rumpus Ridleys *517*
Rupert's Ruin Springhead *525*
Rusty Dudley Church End *457*
Ruthven Brew Aviemore *438*
Rydale Bitter Ryburn *520*
Rye & Coriander Reading Lion *516*
Rye Beer O'Hanlon's *505*

S

SA Best Bitter Brains *448*
Saddlers Celebrated Best Bitter Highgate *484*
Saffron Ale Mighty Oak *501*
Saint's Ale Tomintoul *532*
Saints Sinner Darwin *464*
Salem Porter Batemans *441*
Salsa Castle Rock *456*
Sam Powell Best Bitter Wood *541*
Sam Powell Old Sam Wood *541*
Sam Powell Original Bitter Wood *541*
Sam Wellers Extra Stout Fernandes *470*
Sam's Enchanted Evening Wicked Hathern *539*
Samuel Cromptons Ale Bank Top *440*
Sanctuary Durham *466*
Sandpiper Harviestoun *482*
Sandrock Ventnor *534*
Sands Prince of Wales *514*
Sandy Hunter's Traditional Ale Belhaven *443*
Sanity Clause Rockingham *519*
Santa Forge Forge *472*
Santa Slayer B&T *438*
Santa's Claws Bank Top *440*
Santa's Nightmare Evesham *468*
Santa's Revenge Crouch Vale *462*
Santa's Secret Ridleys *517*
Santa's Session Crouch Vale *462*
Santa's Sledgehammer Tomintoul *532*
Santa's Steaming Ale Cottage *460*
Santa's Surprise Judges *491*
Santa's Wobble Hogs Back *485*
Santas Spice Rainbow *515*
Saracen Pilgrim *512*
SAS Crouch Vale *462*
Satanic Mills II Bank Top *440*
Saturnalia Wood *540*
Saxon King Stout Cuckmere Haven *463*
SBA Donnington *465*
Scallywag Black Dog *445*
Scatter Brain Scattor Rock *522*
Scatty Bitter Scattor Rock *522*
Schiehallion Harviestoun *482*
Schooner Black Dog *445*
Scorcher Lees *494*; Rooster's *519*
Scoresby Stout Cropton *462*
Scotch Ale Scattor Rock *522*
Scotch Mash 2 *500*
Scotch Mash and Air *500*
Scottish Bard Tomintoul *532*
Scottish Oatmeal Stout Broughton *451*
Scratching Dog Lloyds *496*
Scullion's Irish Hilden *484*
SEA Newby Wyke *504*

Stamford Gold Newby Wyke 504
Stanney Bitter Stanway 525
Star Bitter Belvoir 443
Stars and Stripes Outlaw (Rooster's) 519
Station Bitter Snowdonia 524
Station Porter Wickwar 539
Staveleyan Townes 532
Steamboat Ale Forth 472
Steamhammer Abbeydale 435
Steamin' Billy Bitter Leatherbritches 494
Steaming Billy Bitter Grainstore 477
Steel Town Derwent Rose 465
Steelers Warcop 535
Steeplechase Lichfield 495
Steeplejack Lichfield 495
Sticky Wicket Phoenix 511
Stig Swig Stonehenge 525
Stiltman Ales of Kent 436
Stirling Bitter Bridge of Allan 450
Stirling Brig Bridge of Allan 450
Stirling Dark Mild Bridge of Allan 450
Stirling IPA Bridge of Allan 450
Stocking Filler York 543
Stonebridge Mild Broadstone 451
Stonehenge Tisbury 530
Stones Bitter Interbrew 547
Stonewall York 543
Storm Brew Lidstones 495
Storm Force Harviestoun 482
Storm Watch Cox & Holbrook 461
Stout Coffin Church End 457
Stowmarket Porter Cox & Holbrook 461
Stranges Xmas Special Rudgate 520
Strathspey Brew Aviemore 438
Strathspey Heavy Iris Rose 490
Straw Bear Ale Fenland 470
Strawberry Melbourn 501
Strip and At It Freeminer 473
Strong Anglian Special Crouch Vale 462
Strong Old Noll Tarn 511
Strong's Best Bitter Hampshire 480
Strongarm Camerons 455
Stronghold Arundel 437
Struggling Monkey Phoenix 511
Stud Hambleton 480
Suffolk Comfort Mauldons 501
Suffolk County Best Bitter Nethergate 504
Suffolk Draught Lidstones 495
Suffolk Gold St Peter's 521
Suffolk Pride Mauldons 500
Summa Bobs Ossett 509
Summa That Branscombe Vale 449
Summer Blotto Franklin's 473
Summer Breeze Bridge of Allan 450
Summer Capers Hogs Back 485
Summer Daze Arundel 437
Summer Dream Green Jack 478
Summer Eclipse Forge 472
Summer Jack's Goose Eye 477
Summer Knight Quay 514
Summer Knights Castle Eden 455
Summer Lightning Hop Back 487
Summer Loving Tindall 530
Summer Madness Ushers (Thomas Hardy) 481
Summer Marbles Marble 499
Summer Moult Bullmastiff 452
Summer Prom Batemans 441
Summer Session Bitter Newby Wyke 504
Summer Special Weltons 537
Summer Storm Okells 507
Summer Swallow Batemans 441
Summer That! Wood 540
Summer Tyne Mordue 503
Summerhill Stout Big Lamp 444
Summersault Wadworth 535
Summertime Ale St George's 521
Sun King Brewery on Sea 449
Sunbeam Bitter Guernsey 479
Sundance Wetherspoon's (Marston's) 500
Sundowner Cains 454
Sundowner Mayhem (Wadworth) 535
SunFire Ventnor 534
Sunnydaze Oldershaw 508
Sunrunner Dark Horse 463
Sunset Captain Cook 455
Sunshine Porter 513; Tolly Cobbold 531;
  Townes 532
Sunstroke Durham 466
Super Duck Boat 447
Supreme Hoskins & Oldfield 487
Supreme Pale Ale Yorkshire Grey
  (Scottish Courage) 546

Surprise Sarah Hughes 488
Surrender Springhead 525
Surrender Ale Swaled Ale 527
Surrey Bitter Pilgrim 512
Sussex Badger 439
Sussex Best Bitter Harveys 482
Sussex Pale Ale Harveys 482
Sussex XX Mild Ale Harveys 482
Sussex XXXX Old Ale Harveys 482
SW1 Orange (Scottish Courage) 546
SW2 Orange (Scottish Courage) 546
SW19 Orange (Scottish Courage) 546
Swallow Ale Nethergate 504
Swallows Return Cuckmere Haven 463
Swallowtail IPA Old Chimneys 507
Swift Cotleigh 460
Swift Spring Ale Nethergate 504
Swordmaker Derwent Rose 465
Swordsman Beowulf 444
Syllabub Kitchen 493
Synod Black Dog 445

T

T'Other Teme Valley 529
T'Owd Tup Dent 465
Tackler's Tipple Three B's 529
Tag Lag Barngates 440
Taiphoon Hop Back 487
Takin' The Pith Leatherbritches 494
Talisman Pilgrim 512
Tall Ships Borve 447
Tall Tale Pale Ale Fenland 470
Tally Ho Adnams 435
Tally Ho! Palmers 510
Tallywhacker Leith Hill 495
Tam O'Shanter Weltons 537
Tamar Summerskills 526
Tanglefoot Badger 439
Tap Bitter Mole's 502
Tarebrane Leatherbritches 494
Target Ale Derwent Rose 465
Tarka's Tipple Tally Ho 528
Tarw Du Bragdy Ynys Mon 448
Tattoo Hogs Back 485
Taverners Ale Hanby 480
Taverners Autumn Ale Coach House 459
Tawny Ale Frome Valley 474
Tawny Bitter Cotleigh 460
TEA Hogs Back 485
Ted & Ben's Organic Beer Brakspear 448
Teesdale Bitter High Force 483
Teign Valley Tipple Scattor Rock 522
Tempest Beowulf 444
Tempus Fugit Caledonian 454
Ten Fifty Grainstore 477
1066 Hampshire 480
1066 Country Bitter White 539
Tennis Elbow Phoenix 511
Tesco Select Ales IPA Marston's 500
Tesco Select Ales Porter Marston's 500
Texas Houston 488
TGIAOB Cropton 462
That Teme Valley 529
That Will Be The Sleigh Bryncelyn 452
That's All Fawkes Hogs Back 485
Thick Black Devon 465
Thirlwell's Best Bitter Blue Cow 447
Thirlwell's Cuddy Blue Cow 447
Thirstquencher Lidstones 495
Thirsty Moon Phoenix 512
This Teme Valley 529
Thomas Hardy's Ale Eldridge Pope (Thomas
Hardy) 480
Thomas Slee's Academy Ale Tirril 530
Thorold Bitter Duffield 466
Thorold Special Duffield (DarkTribe) 464
Thoroughbred Bullmastiff 452
Thrappledouser Inveralmond 490
3B Arkell's 437
Three Cliffs Gold Swansea 528
3 Giants Derwent Rose 465
Three Goslings Plough Inn 513
Three Hundred Old Ale Chiltern 457
Three Kings Grainstore 477
Three Kings Christmas Ale Coach House 458
Thumb Blonde Millers Thumb 502
Thunder and Lightning Queen's Head 515
Thunderstorm Hop Back 487
Thurgia Tally Ho 528
Tickle Brain Burton Bridge 452
Tidal Wave Brewery on Sea 450

The Good Beer Guide 2001

Wheat-a-Bix Church End *457*
Wheatear Wood *540*
Wheatfield Ale Darwin *464*
Wheel Ale Okells *507*
Wheelbarrow Green Tye *478*
Wheeltappers Ale Cottage *460*
Wherry Best Bitter Woodforde's *541*
Whippling Golden Bitter Belvoir *443*
Whirlwind Phoenix *511*
Whispers Glentworth *475*
Whistle Belly Vengeance Summerskills *526*
Whistle Stop Shardlow *522*
Whistling Joe Brandy Cask *449*
Whitbread Best Bitter Interbrew *548*
Whitby Abbey Ale Black Dog *445*
Whitby Jet Black Dog *445*
White Adder Mauldons *500*
White Bishop Durham *466*
White Boar Village Brewer (Hambleton) *480*
White Bull Wheat Beer Blanchfield *446*
White Christmas Abbeydale *435*; Orkney *509*
White Coombe Prince of Wales *514*
White Dolphin Hoskins & Oldfield *487*
White Dwarf Wheat Beer Oakham *506*
White Enville *467*
White Gold Durham *466*
White Goose Woodbury *541*
White Knight Goff's *476*
White Sapphire Durham *466*
White Squall Newby Wyke *504*
White Star Titanic *531*
White Velvet Durham *466*
White Wife Valhalla *534*
Whitstable Oyster Stout Swale *527*
Who Put the Lights Out? Skinner's *524*
Whoosh Tomos Watkin *536*
Wichen Home County *486*
Wicket Bitter Hale & Hearty *479*
Wight Spirit Ventnor *534*
Wiglaf Beowulf *444*
Wild Ballard's *439*
Wild Blonde Sutton *527*
Wild Cat Exmoor *469*; Tomintoul *532*
Wild Oats Stout Bridge of Allan *450*
Wild Turkey Brewery on Sea *449*
Wild Weasel Leadmill *494*
Wildly Wicked Bird in Hand *445*
Will's Resolve Sharp's *522*
Willie Brew'd Church End *457*
Willie Warmer Crouch Vale *462*
Wilson's Original Bitter Scottish Courage (Mansfield) *498*
Wilson's Wobble Maker Huddersfield *488*
Winchester Weiss Winchester *540*
Windgather Storm *526*
Windjammer Captain Cook *455*
Windy Bottom Brown Cow *451*
Winners SP Sporting Ales *525*
Winter Blotto Franklin's *473*
Winter Brew Gale's *475*; Juwards *492*; Winfields *540*
Winter Cloving Old Chimneys *507*
Winter Glow Exe Valley *468*
Winter Holiday Lakeland *493*
Winter Knights Castle Eden *455*
Winter Lightning Hop Back *487*
Winter Linctus Alchemy *436*
Winter Nip Grainstore *477*
Winter Old Weltons *537*
Winter Storm Ushers (Thomas Hardy) *481*
Winter Tyne Mordue *503*
Winter Warmer Big Lamp *444*; Blanchfield *446*; Bridge of Allan *450*; Clark's *458*; Fenland *470*; Goddards *476*; Swaled Ale *527*; Thwaites *529*; Young's *544*
Winter Wellie Batemans *441*
Winter Winner Ridleys *517*
Witches Promise Triple fff *533*
Witches' Cauldron Tomintoul *532*
Witchfinder Porter Ridleys *517*
Withy Cutter Moor *503*
Wizards Wonder Halloween Bitter Coach House *458*
Wobble in a Bottle Hogs Back *485*
Wobbler Gribble Inn *479*
Wobbly Bob Phoenix *512*
Woild Moild Wolf *540*
Wolf In Sheeps Clothing Wolf *540*
Wolfes Brew Aviemore *438*
Wolfhound Brown Cow *451*
Wonderful Wood *541*
Woodcutter Wood *540*

Woodcutters IPA Millers Thumb *502*
Woodham IPA Crouch Vale *462*
Worcestershire Whym Malvern Hills *498*
Workie Ticket Mordue *503*
Worthington Bitter Interbrew *548*
Worthington Dark Mild Interbrew 547
Worthington White Shield Museum (Interbrew) *548*
Wot Wassail Teme Valley *529*
WPA Wentworth *538*
Wreckage Titanic *531*
Wuffa Beowulf *444*
Wulfgar Beowulf *444*
Wurz Ale Gone Smiles *524*
Wychert Ale Vale *534*
Wykehams Glory Itchen Valley *491*
Wynter Warmer Green Dragon *477*

X

XB Batemans *441*; Holden's *486*; Theakston (Scottish Courage) *546*; Yates *543*
XL Bitter Burton Bridge *453*
Xmas Herbert North Yorkshire *505*
Xmas Holly Daze Bartrams *441*
Xpired Lichfield *495*
XSB Sutton *527*
XX Dark Mild Greene King *478*
XXX Batham *442*; Donnington *465*
XXX Bitter Three Tuns *529*
XXX Mild Brakspear *449*
XXXB Batemans *441*
XXXX Mild St Austell *520*
XXXX Old Ale Brakspear *449*
XXXX Porter Ringwood *518*

Y

Y Ddraig Aur Bragwr Arbennig O Geredigion *448*
Y2K Border *447*; Kings Head *493*
Yankee Rooster's *519*
Yardarm Crouch Vale *462*; Tap 'n' Tin *528*
Yardstick Cambrinus *455*
Yella Belly Batemans *441*
Yellow Hammer Black Isle *445*
Yellow Snow Mighty Oak *501*
Yeoman 1767 Strong Ale Oakhill *506*
Yeomanry Arkell's *437*
YES Hogs Back *485*
Yo Ho Ho Branscombe Vale *449*
Yorkshire Square Ale Black Sheep *446*
Yorkshire Terrier York *543*
Yorkshireman West Yorkshire *538*
Young Pretender Isle of Skye *490*
Young Stallion Liverpool *496*
Youngs Golden Heavy Restalrig *517*
Youngs IPA Restalrig *517*
Your Bard Hydes *489*
Your Every Success Hogs Back *485*
Yr Hen Darw Du Bragwr Arbennig O Geredigion *448*
Yuletide Oldershaw *508*

Z

Zebedee Rebellion *516*
Zingibier Dark Star *463*
Zoe's Old Grumpy Iris Rose *490*
Zulu Porter Outlaw (Rooster's) *519*
Zummer Vat Ale Smiles *524*

Readers' recommendations

Suggestions for pubs to be included or excluded

All pubs are surveyed by local branches of the Campaign for Real Ale. If you would like to comment on a pub already featured, or any you think should be featured, please fill in the form below (or copy it), and send it to the address indicated. Your views will be passed on to the branch concerned. Please mark your envelope with the county where the pub is, which will help us to sort the suggestion efficiently.

Pub name:

Address:

Reason for recommendation/criticism:

Pub name:

Address:

Reason for recommendation/criticism:

Pub name:

Address:

Reason for recommendation/criticism:

Your name and address:

Please send to: [Name of county] Section, Good Beer Guide, 230 Hatfield Road, St Albans, Hertfordshire AL1 4LW

CAMRA Books and Gifts

CAMRA Books (non-members' prices)	Price	Quantity	Total
Good Beer Guide 2001	£11.99		
Good Beer Guide 2000 SOLD OUT			
Good Beer Guide 1999	£3.00		
Good Beer Guide 1998	£3.00		
Good Beer Guide 1997	£3.00		
Brew Classic European Beers at Home	£8.99		
Guide to Cellarmanship	£4.99		
CAMRA Beer & Pubs Quiz Book	£1.00		
Called to the Bar (The first 21 years of CAMRA)	£9.99		
Kegbuster Remembers by Bill Tidy	£3.99		
Brewery Breaks	£1.99		
Guide to Home Brewing (3rd Edition)	£8.99		
Brew British Real Ales at Home	£8.99		
Good Beer to Northern France	£7.99		
Good Bottled Beer Guide by Jeff Evans	£9.99		
CAMRA Guide to Good Pub Food (5th Edition)	£9.99		
Room at the Inn by Jill Adam (2nd Edition)	£8.99		
A Century of British Brewers	£8.95		
Guide to Belgium, Holland and Luxembourg by Tim Webb	£9.99		
The Hop Guide	£2.50		
Great Beers of Belgium by Michael Jackson	£14.99		
Beers of France (Hardback)	£11.95		
Country Ales and Breweries (Hardback)	£15.99		
Britain's 500 Best Pubs by Roger Protz (Hardback)	£16.99		
Historic Inns of England by Ted Bruning (Hardback)	£14.99		
Pubs of the River Thames by Mark Turner (Hardback)	£14.99		
Pubs for Families	£7.99		
	TOTAL		

● Prices include postage and packing to the UK
● Add £1.50 per book in European Union (£3 for GBG)
● Add £2.50 per book elsewhere (£6 for GBG)

Credit Card Orders can be placed by calling 01727 867201 or our Action Line 0845 60 30 20 8. Any queries, please phone 01727 867201.

● **Please allow up to 21 days for delivery**
● **Please allow up to 35 days for delivery overseas**

LOCAL GUIDE	Price	Qty.		Price	Qty.
Abercolwyn (1998)	£1.75		Leeds (1997)	£1.50	
Amsterdam (1997)	£2.99		South-East London (1995)	£4.95	
Avon (1996)	£3.99		South-West London (1997)	£4.95	
Bedfordshire (1995)	£2.95		Malvern Hills (1996)	£1.20	
Boston (1998)	£3.95		Redditch – Needles,		
Cheshire (1998)	£4.95		Nails & Salt (1997)	£2.00	
Cornwall (1998)	£3.99		Sheffield (1996)	£2.00	
Craven Dales (1999)	£1.70		Shrewsbury (1996)	£1.20	
North-East Essex			Stockport – Viaducts		
& Suffolk Borders	£3.00		& Vaults II (1996)	£3.95	
Gloucestershire (1996)	£4.50		Suffolk (1997)	£4.95	
Hardy Country			Surrey (1997)	£4.95	
– West Dorset (1996)	£2.50		Swindon (1998)	£2.00	
Isle of Wight (1998)	£3.50		Worcester (1995)	£1.50	
			TOTAL		

● Please add 50p per local guide for postage to the UK
● Add £1.50 per local guide for postage to the European Union
● Add £2.50 per local guide for postage elsewhere.
● **Please allow up to 21 days for delivery**

574

CAMRA Gifts	Price	Quantity	Total
Traditional CAMRA Mirror	£22.50		
Wooden Key Fob	£1.95		
CAMRA Lapel Badge (Red Square)	£2.50		
CAMRA Bar Towel (Black)	£1.50		
CAMRA Tea Towel	£3.50		
CAMRA Ballpoint Pen (6 For £3) Mail Order Price	£0.70		
PVC Bottle Opener (Yellow)	£1.00		
Fridge Magnet	£1.50		
Leather Bookmark (Blue, Green or Red)	£1.00		
PVC Good Beer Guide Cover	£2.95		
"Full Pint" Wristwatch	£14.95		
Pewter CAMRA Earrings (pierced)	£8.95		
Pewter CAMRA Pendant	£4.95		
Pewter CAMRA Neck Thong	£4.95		
CAMRA Tray	£3.95		
Golf Umbrella (incl p&p with mailing tube)	£16.95		
Exhibition Bag	£12.50		

CAMRA Clothing	Price	Quantity	Total
CAMRA Tie *Navy Blue*	£7.95		
Mild Logo Silk Tie *Navy Blue*	£14.95		
CAMRA Logo T-Shirt *White* (L/XL/XXL)	£4.95		
Save British Breweries T-Shirt *White* (M/L)	£4.95		
Fault Finders T-Shirt *Cream* (M/XXL)	£7.50		
Cider & Perry T-Shirt *White* (L/XL/XXL)	£11.95		
CAMRA Embroidered Sweatshirt *Grey* (M to XXL)	£13.95		
CAMRA Rugby Shirt *Red/Grey Quarters* (L only)	£15.00		
CAMRA Padded Jacket *Navy Blue* (L/XL)	£37.50		
Baseball Caps *Black*	£9.95		
CAMRA Socks 'Mine's A Full Pint' *Grey*	£3.50		
Children's 'Dad & Me' T-Shirt *White* (Please state age)	£4.50		
CAMRA Polo Shirt *Royal Blue* (M to XXXL)	£16.50		
CAMRA summer jacket (XL only)	£37.50		
Fleece-lined jacket *Navy Blue* (L/XL/XXL)	£29.95		
TOTAL			

- Prices include postage and packing to the UK
- Please add £1.50 per item In European Union
- Please add £2.50 per item elsewhere

- **Please allow up to 21 days for delivery**
- **Please allow up to 35 days for delivery overseas**

Please send to:
CAMRA, 230 Hatfield Road,
St Albans,
Hertfordshire AL1 4LW

(cheques made payable to CAMRA must accompany all orders). To place a credit card order, phone (01727) 867201 and ask for the Products Secretary.

NAME

ADDRESS

Postcode

An offer for CAMRA members
GOOD BEER GUIDE
Annual Subscription

Being a CAMRA member brings many benefits, not least the big discount on the Good Beer Guide. *Now you can take advantage of an even bigger discount on the* Guide *by taking out an annual subscription.*

Simply fill in the form below and the Direct Debit form opposite (photocopies will do if you don't want to spoil your book), and send them to CAMRA at the usual St Albans address.

You will then receive the *Good Beer Guide* automatically every year. It will be posted to you before the official publication date and before any other postal sales are processed.

You won't have to bother with filling in cheques every year and you will receive the book at a lower price than other CAMRA members (the 2001 edition, for instance, was sold to annual subscribers at only £7).

So sign up now and be sure of receiving your copy early every year.

Note: This offer is open only to CAMRA members and is only available through using a Direct Debit instruction to a UK bank (use the form opposite, or copy it if you do not want to spoil your book). The offer is limited to one copy per member per year. Additional copies can be ordered separately at the CAMRA member's usual price. This offer applies to the 2002 *Guide* onwards.

Name

CAMRA Membership No.

Address and Post code

I wish to purchase the *Good Beer Guide* annually by Direct Debit and I have completed the Direct Debit instructions to my bank which are enclosed.

Signature   Date

Instruction to your bank or building society to pay by Direct Debit

Please fill in and send to the Campaign for Real Ale Limited, 230 Hatfield Road, St Albans, Herts AL1 4LW

Direct Debit
This Guarantee should be detached and retained by the payer.

The Direct Debit Guarantee
● This Guarantee is offered by all banks and building societies that take part in the Direct Debit Scheme. The efficiency and security of the scheme is monitored and protected by your own bank or building society.
● If the amounts to be paid or the payment dates change, CAMRA will notify you within ten working days in advance of your account being debited or as otherwise agreed.
● If an error is made by CAMRA or your bank or building society, you are guaranteed a full and immediate refund from our branch of the amount paid. You can cancel a Direct Debit at any time by writing to your bank or building society. Please also send a copy of your letter to CAMRA.

Originator's identification number

9 2 6 1 2 9

For CAMRA official use only
This is not part of the instruction to your bank or building society

Membership number

Name

Postcode

Instruction to your bank or building society
Please pay CAMRA Direct Debits from the account detailed on this instruction subject to the safeguards assured by the Direct Debit Guarantee. I understand this instruction may remain with CAMRA and, if so, will be passed electronically to my bank/building society.

Signature(s)

Date

Postcode

Name and full postal address of your bank or building society

To the manager   Bank or building society

Address

Postcode

Name(s) of Account Holder(s)

Bank or building society account number

Branch sort code

Reference number

Banks and building societies may not accept Direct Debit instructions for some types of account

577

Join CAMRA
Free for three months!

- Has a pub near you been closed or ruined?
- Has your local brewery been taken over or its beers lost their flavour?
- Are you concerned about the price of a pint?

If you can answer 'yes' to any or all of these questions you are sure to benefit from becoming a member of CAMRA.

The Campaign for Real Ale is a voluntary organisation consisting of over 57,000 ordinary drinkers, run by an unpaid, elected National Executive and backed by a small core of professional executives. It speaks for drinkers everywhere in fighting to save pubs and breweries from closure, and in attempting to improve quality and to ensure pub standards are raised.

- As a member you can have your say about the issues which affect you. You can stand for election to office, attend the annual conference to speak and vote, and help organise local campaigns.
- You can help select pubs for the *Good Beer Guide*, help out at beer festivals and enjoy some excellent social activities.
- You can receive big discounts on the *Good Beer Guide* and other CAMRA books and products, free or reduced price admission to CAMRA beer festivals, plus the *What's Brewing* newspaper, delivered to your door each month. All new members receive the Members' Handbook as soon as they are registered.
- All this is available at the bargain price of just £14 per year (£17 per year for two people living at the same address).
- What's more you can even join for three months at no cost and see if you think it's worthwhile being a member.
- Fill in the application form below (or a photocopy of it) and the Direct Debit form on the previous page. If after three months you decide not to continue just write to CAMRA, cancel your membership and you will owe nothing.
Note: If you do not wish to take up the trial offer, but wish to join CAMRA anyway, fill in the application form and return it to us with a cheque for your first year's subscription. To pay by credit card, contact the Membership Secretary on (01727) 867201.
- Full annual membership £14
- Joint annual membership (two people at the same address) £17
- Life membership £168 (single)/£204 (joint)
- Under-26 membership £8 single/£11 joint.
Concessionary rates available on request.

Please delete as appropriate:
- ❏ I/We wish to take advantage of the trial membership, and have completed the instructions overleaf.
- ❏ I/We wish to become members of CAMRA
- ❏ I/We agree to abide by the memorandum and articles of association of the company.
- ❏ I/We enclose a cheque/PO for £   (payable to CAMRA)

NAME(S)

Address and Post Code

Date of birth

Signature(s)

To: CAMRA, 230 Hatfield Road, St Albans, Hertfordshire AL1 4LW